New Zealand

Charles Rawlings-Way
Brett Atkinson, Sarah Bennett, Peter Dragicevich,
Scott Kennedy

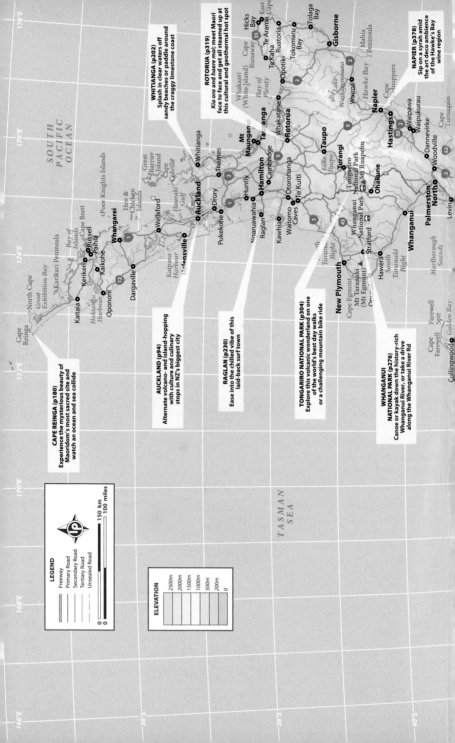

CAPE REINGA (p180)
Experience the mysterious beauty of Maoridom's most sacred site and watch an ocean and sea collide

WHITIANGA (p202)
Splash in clear waters off sandy beaches or paddle around the craggy limestone coast

ROTORUA (p319)
Kia ora and *haere mai*: meet Maori face to face and get all steamed up at this cultural and geothermal hot spot

NAPIER (p378)
Sip on syrah amid the art deco ambience of the Hawke's Bay wine region

AUCKLAND (p94)
Alternate volcano- and island-hopping with culture and culinary stops in NZ's biggest city

RAGLAN (p230)
Ease into the chilled vibe of this laid-back surf town

TONGARIRO NATIONAL PARK (p304)
Explore this volcanic wonderland on one of the world's best day walks or a challenging mountain bike ride

WHANGANUI NATIONAL PARK (p276)
Canoe or kayak down the history-rich Whanganui River, or take a drive along the Whanganui River Rd

SOUTH PACIFIC OCEAN

TASMAN SEA

LEGEND
Freeway
Primary Road
Secondary Road
Tertiary Road
Unsealed Road

0   150 km
0   100 miles

ELEVATION
2500m
2000m
1500m
1000m
500m
200m
0

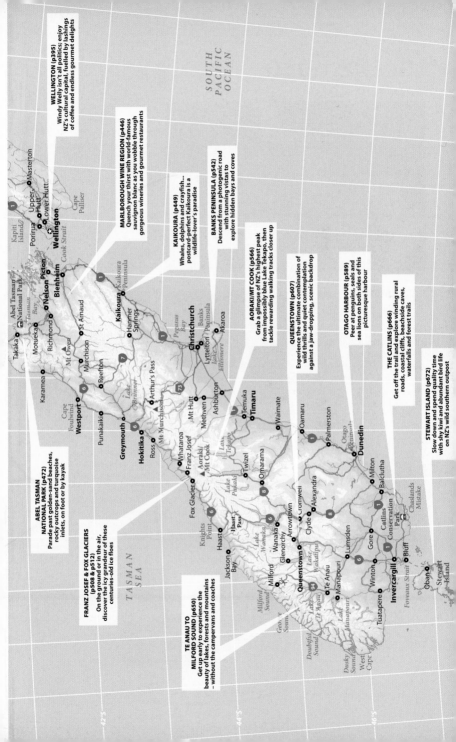

WELLINGTON (p395)
Windy Welly isn't all politics; enjoy NZ's cultural capital, fuelled by lashings of coffee and endless gourmet delights

MARLBOROUGH WINE REGION (p446)
Quench your thirst with world-famous sauvignon blanc as you wobble through gorgeous wineries and gourmet restaurants

KAIKOURA (p449)
Whales, dolphins and crayfish... postcard-perfect Kaikoura is a wildlife-lover's paradise

BANKS PENINSULA (p542)
Descend from a photogenic road with stunning vistas to explore hidden bays and coves

AORAKI/MT COOK (p566)
Grab a glimpse of NZ's highest peak from impossibly blue Lake Tekapo, then tackle rewarding walking tracks closer up

QUEENSTOWN (p607)
Experience the ultimate combination of wild thrills and quiet contemplation against a jaw-dropping, scenic backdrop

OTAGO HARBOUR (p589)
Peer at penguins, seals and sea lions on both sides of this picturesque harbour

THE CATLINS (p672)
Get off the trail and explore winding rural roads, coastal cliffs, beachside caves, waterfalls and forest trails

STEWART ISLAND (p672)
Slow down and spend quality time with kiwi and abundant bird life on NZ's wild southern outpost

TE ANAU TO MILFORD SOUND (p650)
Get up early to experience the beauty of lakes, forests and mountains – without the campervans and coaches

FRANZ JOSEF & FOX GLACIERS (p508 & p512)
On the ground or in the air, discover the icy grandeur of these centuries-old ice floes

ABEL TASMAN NATIONAL PARK (p472)
Parade past golden-sand beaches, rocky outcrops and turquoise inlets, on foot or by kayak

SOUTH PACIFIC OCEAN

TASMAN SEA

On the Road

CHARLES RAWLINGS-WAY
Coordinating Author
New Zealand is so flush with swoon-worthy vistas, empty swathes of coastline and rampant, snowcapped mountain ranges that the locals are often often blasé about the smaller stuff. This isn't to say that it's any less beautiful, it's just less big! Wairere Falls (p351), a picture-perfect little waterfall tumbling down a cliff behind Whakatane's main street, goes almost unheralded.

SCOTT KENNEDY You can't come to Queenstown (p607), the Adventure Capital of the World, and not scare yourself – *right*? In a town where all things *fear* and *beer* intermingle, I found myself hanging over the edge of a cliff wondering what the hell I was doing. No turning back, all there was to do was lean back and enjoy the ride.

BRETT ATKINSON I didn't spy any whales during my time in the Catlins, but this wind-up cetacean at the Lost Gypsy Gallery (p668) was definitely the next best thing. It's bigger than most of Blair Sommerville's other kinetic sculptures, and loads of fun. Later, I did increase my marine mammal tally, and spied a sea lion chilling on the beach near nearby Nugget Point.

SARAH BENNETT Tipped off by members of the local mountain-bike club, I needed little encouragement to check out the new Canaan Downs loop track (p476). Despite a few tricky bits and the odd sheep hazard, I managed to stay in the saddle most of the time. I also got a little air – woo hoo!

PETER DRAGICEVICH Matakana (p148), north of Auckland, may be well and truly gentrified (would you believe that these hard-nosed giantesses adorn the new public toilets), but if you're a lover of wine, food and beaches – and I'm guilty on all counts – it's a great stop. Just beware the terminal *hongi* (traditional Maori greeting).

For full author biographies see p725.

New Zealand Highlights

New Zealand is spectacular, sure, but what is it about this small nation that makes it a must-visit destination?

We asked a passionate bunch of Kiwis to tell us what part of Aotearoa they love the most. From the Far North to the Deep South, from bustling cities to lonely beaches – in the following pages we present their personal choices of the very best of NZ.

After you've browsed their selection, you're going to want to get out there and find your own favourite NZ spot. You might find it between these pages, or you might find it on your own. Either way, you'll discover an intriguing land of diverse highlights, and you'll understand why Lonely Planet keeps coming back year after year.

MICAH WRIGHT

GOLDEN BAY, MARLBOROUGH

Golden Bay (p475) has all the elements of wonder for me: beautiful, rugged terrain, an amazing array of artists and world-class food. It's my annual trip there, however, that really gets the wildlife excited. You haven't lived until you've been chased by a wild seal. That's what happened to me the last time I visited Wharariki Beach with its wild windswept dunes and giant rock formations. It really is the land of the lost. You must traverse farmland, hills and bush to get there, but it's well worth it for the stunning ocean views. After this adventure I recommend a hearty meal of wild-boar pie at the Naked Possum Café. While you're there be sure to buy some possum-fur nipple warmers. Then, to complete the day, you should aim for the Mussel Inn for their wonderful Captain Cooker Manuka Honey Beer, but be sure to stop on the way for a cold dip in any one of the refreshing rivers. Could be a bit nippy…but hey, you've got your warmers!

Rhys Darby, Actor & Stand-up Comic

OLIVER STREWE

WAITOMO CAVES, WAIKATO

The best way to experience the Waitomo glowworm caves (p242) is via black-water rafting. It's an exhilarating experience and involves getting dressed up in a wetsuit (laughing at how funny everyone looks is half the fun), choosing an inflatable inner tube to sit in (another hilarious experience) and travelling through the limestone caves with two guides, your wits, and the glowworms. It is a real hands-on experience and requires some agility and the guts to jump backwards down some small waterfalls as you make your way through the tunnels. You finish off the trip quietly drifting through the caves in your tube, looking at the glowworms with your head lamp turned off.

Dr Farah Rangikoepa Palmer, Former Captain of the Black Ferns (NZ's Women's Rugby Team)

KIERAN SCOTT

WAIHEKE ISLAND, AUCKLAND REGION

Thirty years ago, Waiheke Island (p131) was home to an eclectic mix of outlaws who could not (or chose not to) live in 'normal' society: hippies and hermits, alternative healers and writers, potters and pot growers, and everything in between. Sometime in the late eighties, Waiheke was 'discovered', and it's quite a different place now. But even with all the changes – fine dining, vineyards and luxury holiday homes – Waiheke Island's identity and spirit are still undeniable. The beautiful weather remains the same, as do the phenomenal vistas, the lush bush and native birds, the chooks in your neighbours' backyards, the feeling that everything deserves to move a little slower (we call it 'Waiheke time'), the smell of honeysuckle, the crystal waters, the best fish and chips ever, the house I was born in and, probably, still a few pot growers. Waiheke was, and remains, like nowhere else on the planet.

Zoë Bell, Stuntwoman & Actor

WHANGANUI RIVER

Whanganui has a good black-sand surfing beach out at Castlecliff where I'm from, and a famous 'upside-down' river (as Dad calls it) where all the silt floats on the top – muddy coloured, but still gorgeous. The river (p276) is truly breathtaking and also happens to be the longest navigable river in the country. Join a guided canoe or boat trip down the river, over rapids that are challenging but not deathly, through spectacular broody lush bush and visit historical places like Jerusalem – where one of our more famous poets James K Baxter lived for a while.

Peter Gordon, Chef, Food Writer & Restaurateur

DISCOVER WANGANUI

EAST CAPE (P361)

Where the black Raukumara Ranges
Lie out east of everywhere,
The land's been stripped by sun
and rain,
Until its bones are bare.
In this land of snarl-lipped razor
backs
Of possums, deer and rats,
They talk a lot of working dogs
And the man from Footrot Flats.

**The Ballad of Footrot Flats, by
Murray Ball**

OLIVER STREWE

CHRISTCHURCH, CANTERBURY

I have been lucky enough to visit over 100 countries, but as the saying goes, there's just no place like home, and for me that's Christchurch (p519). My parents run a B&B just outside the city, and over the years I've sent dozens of people from all over the world to stay with them. My Dad is an agricultural scientist, and a walking encyclopaedia when it comes to the region's fauna and flora.

I love that within a few hours of Christchurch you can get close to Humpback whales, explore the spectacular mountains that starred in the *Lord of the Rings* trilogy, race crystal-clear braided rivers in a jet boat, sample world-class wines, and even surf and ski on the same day.

Downtown Christchurch has an old-school English charm with punters making their way down the River Avon, trams cruising through city streets and families sharing a picnic in the breathtaking Hagley Park.

Phil Keoghan, TV Presenter/Producer & Author

WWW.CHRISTCHURCHNZ.COM

ROB SUISTED / NATURESPIC.COM

COLAC BAY, SOUTHLAND

Where two different strands of my ancestry found themselves: an American whaler captain, rumoured to be part-Tahitian, and a Kai Tahu/Kati Mamoe woman had a son who was my great-grandfather. There's not a lot in Colac Bay (p659) except beach and surf and the local *marae*. Oh, and there's Surfer Dude riding his wave at a slant angle. Classic baches and rock-fishing…a bit of fossicking along the low-tide line, and perhaps a trip to Cozy Nook? But the quintessential attraction of Colac Bay is the sound of those seas, that surf homing in: I have spent days, listening, wandering, listening, pondering, going to sleep with sea-song in my ears. It's a really choice place to blob out for a day or three or more. Be warned that the winds can be exceedingly strong, and bear Antarctic cold-ness with them – but there is also frequent calm and sun…

Keri Hulme, Poet & Author

PAUL KENNEDY

THE FAR NORTH

I love the north of the north island (p175), the beaten, bloody and beautiful landscape and *wairua*. The small towns and cities up north, where I grew up, reach out all along the moody west coast. As kids, my brother and I would sneak in to Ngawha Springs and have our mud baths in the morning – smelling of rotten eggs for the rest of the day. In Opononi we'd go crab hunting on the rocks with Uncle Rata, then take the car ferry from Rawene home. At Pawarenga – a dusty old Maori town – we'd go horse riding with the cuzzies, learn Maori with my Grandpa, eat *karahu* and oysters, and, as we grew up, drink with the aunties and uncles. We'd drive to Kaitaia to buy all our food for the next week, and hang at the local pubs. Then further north for the Mangonui fish n' chip shop, the best *kai* in Aotearoa. When we were tired, we'd drive to Ahipara and sleep on the beach.

Anika Moa, Singer/Songwriter

LOUISE HYA

REES VALLEY, QUEENSTOWN REGION

As many times a year as I can, I travel to a holiday hut up the Rees Valley (p628), at the top end of Lake Wakatipu. I love the lake, the majesty of the surrounding mountains, the good weather in the basin, the walks, the rivers, the end-of-the-world feeling and the laconic people who live nearby. Everyone who has visited me up here is infected by the ready magic of the landscape and the sensation of worldly troubles dissolving. Lake Sylvan is one of many good bush walks in the area – a fairly short walk for this scale of landscape, but the intimacy of being inside the bush immediately gives you a sense of delight. Recently the lake has been high and is phenomenal to swim in.

Jane Campion, Film-maker & Screenwriter

BEACHES

MICHAEL GEBIC

I have always been drawn to the coast, but if I said French Pass, I'd have to mention Te Hapua. And if I mentioned Te Hapua, I would have to add Drunken Bay, Rangitoto Island. Which would mean I'd need to mention Mana Island...so here's a poem about three people on any one, and all, of these shorelines.

It's called *To do with horizons*

Why a man, a woman and child
stand on a beach
throw stones out to sea?

It's a flint-stoned beach –
they are well armed –
this could go on for weeks.

The enemy? must be
the sea
and all the sea

Does to a man,
a woman and a child –
to do with horizons.

Any wonder they throw stones?
Sam Hunt, Poet

HANMER SPRINGS, CANTERBURY

Hanmer Springs (p548) is a peaceful getaway 130km northwest of Christchurch, an easy 1½-hour drive through picturesque scenery including vineyards, rivers, mountains and small country townships.

When you arrive in the small alpine village you're greeted by the hot mineral springs for which Hanmer is noted, which are well used by visitors. Other attractions in and around the village include a golf course, forest walks, horse riding, jetboating, water rafting, bungee, cycling, a small ski field, pitch-and-putt activities, and shops. There is also plenty of motel and apartment accommodation within easy walking distance of restaurants and bars. For me, it is a place to relax and enjoy a hassle-free environment.

Sir Richard Hadlee, Former NZ Cricketer

ROBERT BIRD / ALAMY

TOURISM AUCKLAND

HILLARY TRAIL (P142), AUCKLAND REGION

My family grew up loving Auckland's wild west coast, where the Tasman Sea pounds the black-sand beaches and black-back gulls ride the westerlies. Our family has walked and explored and lived out here for nearly a century and this is also where we came to grieve after my mother and sister were killed in 1975, where the invigorating salty air and the marvellous wild vistas to the Tasman Sea worked like a balm for our broken hearts. My father would come here to dream up and then prepare for new expeditionary challenges. It seemed the right sort of environment for someone like him: not a passive coastline, but active and exciting, with huge cliffs, crashing waves, thick bush and a tantalising far-away horizon.

Peter Hillary, Mountaineer & Explorer

WELLINGTON

Wellington (p395) is a beautiful city, with a striking waterfront surrounded by bush-clad hills, and sightseeing and photo opportunities are plentiful. Downtown, it's easy to get around on foot and there are plenty of cafes and restaurants to stop at for a break. It's also a very family-friendly city: Wellington Zoo is a special place to take the family to check out the brave one-legged kiwi, while just a short bus ride away, Te Papa, the national museum, mixes history and modern technology under the one roof. Wellingtonians are always really friendly and welcoming and ready to help visitors to their city.

Tana Umaga, Former All Black Captain

PAUL KENNEDY

ABEL TASMAN NATIONAL PARK, MARLBOROUGH

Abel Tasman National Park (p472), at the very top of the South Island, is a place of breathtaking beauty. Whether you opt for long or short coastal track walks, or sea-kayaking around the bays, you'll be left spellbound by the native flora and fauna and mesmerised by the spectacular ocean views and famous golden beaches. If you're feeling a little lazy you could take the sea shuttle from Kaiteriteri Beach to Awaroa Bay, passing by Split Apple Rock and a seal colony on the way, and stay at Awaroa Lodge for a couple of nights. It's tucked away in the wilderness and is only accessible by foot or boat, giving you a nice bit of luxury either side of a one day hike (be sure to put in an order for a yummy packed lunch!).

Hayley Westenra, Singer, Songwriter & Unicef Ambassador

DAVID WALL

Contents

Regional Map Contents

Northland p152

Auckland Region p94

Coromandel Region p192

Waikato & the King Country p222

Bay of Plenty p319

Taranaki p252

Central Plateau p288

The East Coast p360

Whanganui & Palmerston North p269

Wellington Region p395

Marlborough & Nelson p430

The West Coast p483

Christchurch & Canterbury p518

Queenstown & Wanaka p607

Fiordland & Southland p643

Otago p573

Stewart Island p673

Destination New Zealand

You probably know all about the scenic side of New Zealand – the NZ of tourist ads, *Lord of the Rings* and nature documentaries. You may also know about its reputation as an action-adventure destination. This is, after all, a nation that is so dedicated to doing odd things with bits of rubber and plastic that it invented bungy jumping, black-water rafting and zorbing. Some of you may even know about NZ's anti-nuclear stand, its passion for rugby, its fondness for sheep. Maybe you've tucked into some NZ lamb, spread NZ butter on your toast or downed a particularly zingy bottle of Marlborough sauvignon blanc.

Despite the country's growing profile on the international stage, there's one dimension of a trip to NZ that you probably haven't counted on: the extent to which the average Kiwi will genuinely want you to have a really, really good time. The more cynical might call it insecurity, but whatever the motivation, it's in the interactions with everyday, eager-to-please Kiwis that lasting memories are made. In the words of an enduring Maori proverb: *He aha te mea nui o te ao? He tangata! He tangata! He tangata!* (What is the most important thing in the world? It is people! It is people! It is people!).

Which is not to say that everyone wanders around with Prozac grins, hugging trees. A short drive on Auckland's motorways will quickly dispel that notion. New Zealanders, like the rest of the world, are still struggling to shrug off the gloom of the global economic crisis, which pushed the economy into recession and sent unemployment soaring.

What a difference a couple of years makes! In the last edition of this book we wrote of the strength of the economy, low unemployment, high export returns from the farming sector and large budget surpluses. Back then the severe-seeming but highly respected Helen Clark was prime minister. In 2008, just as the US was trading in George Bush for Barack Obama, NZ displayed its typically contrary attitude to world trends by shifting from a centre-left government to a centre-right one. Clark was ousted after nine years in power and went on to accept the third-highest job at the UN – Head of the UN Development Programme.

Enter John Key. NZ's new prime minister is surfing a wave of popularity due in large part to his image as a thoroughly likeable Kiwi bloke. He's the guy pictured, beer in hand, hosting a barbecue for NZ's future king, Prince William. He's the goofy guy slipping down the stairs and breaking his arm at a Chinese New Year celebration. His laid-back manner says as much about the NZ way of life as the former PM's penchant for wilderness hikes and mountain climbing.

But enough politics: most Kiwis are more interested in the rugby. In 2011, NZ will play host to the Rugby World Cup (RWC) and chances are, whether you travel before, during or after the tournament, you'll be thoroughly sick of hearing about rugby by the end of your stay.

Rugby plays a special part in the nation's consciousness, partly because it was one of the first things in which NZ truly excelled. The All Blacks are the most successful rugby team in history (with a 74% winning record), but they've only snagged the Cup once. After yet another dazzling failure in France in 2007, the All Blacks are determined to redeem themselves on home soil. The fragile national psyche took a beating then, with distraught Kiwis turning to each other, saying, 'We suck at the only thing we're good at!'

Actually, that's not quite true. NZ is the current world champion in rugby league (yes, it is a different game) and women's rugby, and the runner-up in netball. And by the time you read this, the national soccer (football) team will have played in its second-ever FIFA World Cup. Who knows, it may even have won its first-ever Cup match.

But all of those achievements will pale into insignificance if NZ dips out of the RWC in the finals rounds for the *fifth* consecutive time. If you're travelling in spring 2011, come armed with enough tissues to console a nation, but expect mass hysteria in the event of a victory.

Counterbalancing the hard-man rugby image, the country's other icon is soft, fluffy…and delicious. If NZ built its national pride on rugby, it built its economy on sheep. In 1982, sheep numbers peaked at 70.3 million, or 22 sheep per person. Since then the removal of government subsidies and the lure of the profitable dairy industry have seen flocks fall drastically, leaving each New Zealander with less than eight sheep to keep them company.

Not only are cows not as cuddly as sheep, they have a much bigger carbon hoofprint. Farming them requires more intensive methods, including more fertiliser, feed and water. On top of that, the methane produced by the nation's seven-million-strong herd makes up a large proportion of NZ's harmful greenhouse gas emissions – leading the former government to consider a 'fart tax'.

For now, however, farts are free and whatever the economic or rugby prognosis, you can be guaranteed of a warm welcome by the majority of people you encounter in NZ. Kiwis love sharing their spectacular country with visitors and in turn seeing it anew through foreign eyes. They never tire of being reminded of the rugged beauty of their beaches, mountains, fiords, glaciers, native forests and thermal regions. And once you experience these natural highlights, you won't tire of reminding them.

'the average Kiwi will genuinely want you to have a really, really good time'

Getting Started

By world standards, New Zealand is an easy, accessible place to visit. Amiable locals, a moderate climate, good personal security, brilliant roads, well-organised activities and the fantastic i-SITE visitor information centre network (see p697) make travelling here a breeze! There's also a network of around 30 Department of Conservation (DOC) visitor centres around NZ – a handy resource for planning activities in parks, and for natural and cultural features. There are eating and accommodation options for all budgets, from a felafel and a dorm bunk to a crayfish dinner and a spa suite.

If you're scuttling between cities pursuing urban virtues, you won't need to do much forward planning, but if you're tramping into the wilderness or devising a cycling epic, do some research on equipment, accommodation, track and hut passes, and weather, and book what you need to well in advance.

WHEN TO GO

The warmer high-season months (November to April) are ripe for outdoor exploration. Summer (December to February) is also when Kiwis crank up the food and wine festivals, concerts and sports events. December in the far north can be rainy, however. If you're a snow bunny, visit when the powder is thickest – June to August is skiing high season. Remember, though, that in winter, warm-weather beach towns might be half asleep.

See Climate Charts (p687) for more information.

If you want a *real* holiday, staying and eating in your venues of choice, avoid school holidays (particularly late December to early February) and public holidays (p691). In the less touristed 'shoulder' period from late February to April, the weather is at its best (less chance of rain), the kids are back at school, and the ocean is still warm(ish) – a much better time to travel.

NZ is smack-bang in the middle of the Roaring Forties; these prevailing west-to-east winds buffet the country year-round, ranging from gentle breezes to tempestuous gales. On both islands it's drier in the east than in the west, where mountain ranges snare moisture-laden winds from the Tasman Sea. It's usually a few degrees cooler on the South Island than the North Island. Wherever you are, remember that NZ has a maritime climate – the weather changes rapidly. Anyone tramping at any time of year needs to be well prepared for all weather conditions. The **New Zealand Mountain Safety Council** (☎ 04-385 7162; www.mountainsafety.org.nz) has the information you need – available from DOC visitor centres nationwide.

DON'T LEAVE HOME WITHOUT...

- Double-checking the visa situation (see p698)
- A travel-insurance policy covering you for high-risk activities (see p691)
- Insect repellent to keep the sandflies at bay (see p688)
- The ability to get excited over a game of rugby (p44)
- Your driver's licence – the best way to see NZ's nooks and crannies is at your own speed (p709)
- A bottomless appetite for Kiwi food and wine (p60)
- A mobile phone (p697) for booking restaurants and accommodation on the hop
- An open ear and a notepad to jot down the NZ bands you're going to download when you get home (see www.amplifier.co.nz)

COSTS & MONEY

In recent years burgeoning tourism in NZ has seen prices rise with demand. However, if you're visiting from Europe or North America, it's still a fairly economical destination, unless you're throwing yourself out of a plane or jetboating every day. Activities like these generally top expense lists – think carefully about what you'll spend your money on.

Gastronomes will find food to be surprisingly pricey – cooked breakfasts at snazzy cafes average around $16, while main courses at top-end restaurants cost $30 and beyond. Food in remote areas also costs more, without necessarily being of better quality.

If you do some sightseeing, eat out once or twice a day and stay in cheap motels or B&Bs, budget on at least $150 per day (per person, travelling as a pair), not including car hire or activities. Packing kids into your suitcases obviously means greater expense, but museums, cinemas, and tour and activity organisers usually offer discounts for youngsters, and there are plenty of open-air attractions available for free!

At the low-cost end, if you camp or stay in hostels, cook your own meals, repress the urge to drink beer, tackle attractions independently and travel on a bus pass, you could probably eke out an existence on $80 per day. But if you want to enjoy the occasional restaurant meal and glass of wine, then $100 per day is more realistic.

HOW MUCH?

Cup of decent coffee $4

Movie ticket $14

Dorm bed $25-35

Motel room $100-160

Magnificent scenery $0

TRAVELLING RESPONSIBLY

Since our inception in 1973, Lonely Planet has encouraged readers to tread lightly, travel responsibly and enjoy the magic that independent travel affords. International travel is growing at a jaw-dropping rate, and we still firmly believe in the benefits it can bring – but, as always, we encourage you to consider the impact your visit will have on both the global environment and the local economies, cultures and ecosystems.

It's not hard to make your NZ trip ecosavvy. For starters, check out our GreenDex (p745), which lists ecofriendly operators. Volunteer some of your time to a local environmental program. Consider carbon-offsetting your flights. If you're taking a tour, ask about the company's environmental policies: are they NZ-owned? Sensitive to indigenous culture? How do they dispose of rubbish? Support NZ businesses rather than multinational chains and eat at local restaurants and buy from farmers markets that sell locally sourced produce. Instead of car hire, consider car-pooling to travel from town to town; check hostel noticeboards to find a ride. Stay at hotels and hostels that actively engage in recycling and waste reduction. If you're tramping into the forests or along the coast, carry out your rubbish, travel in small groups, camp on durable surfaces, and don't wash in or near water sources.

DIY NZ

At Lonely Planet we love travel (no kidding...), and we reckon part of the adventure is to fly by the seat of your pants. We're dedicated to bringing you comprehensive in-depth destination coverage, but we also encourage you to ditch your guidebook. Really! Go AWOL for a day or a week and explore NZ beyond the pages of a book.

Low population density = empty spaces – it's easy to get off the beaten track. Buy a detailed road map, pick a little town down a little road and go for it – you can't really lose when the scenery is so great. Scan the bulletin boards at local cafes for performances that night or swap a yarn or two with locals at a country pub. Kiwis are famously friendly – ask them about their favourite places to eat, hang out or blow off steam.

After your trip, drop us a line and tell us what you discovered: www.lonelyplanet.com/contact.

TOP 10

MANDATORY MOVIES

Spending an evening or three watching classic NZ movies makes a great intro to the country's much-publicised scenery, and will help you get under the national skin. Captured on celluloid, wry humour and an often-bleak mysticism await. See p47 for reviews of these and other locally produced films.

1 *Once Were Warriors* (1994) Director: Lee Tamahori

2 *The Lord of the Rings* trilogy (2001–03) Director: Peter Jackson

3 *Whale Rider* (2002) Director: Niki Caro

4 *Rain* (2001) Director: Christine Jeffs

5 *The Piano* (1993) Director: Jane Campion

6 *In My Father's Den* (2004) Director: Brad McGann

7 *Kaikohe Demolition* (2004) Director: Florian Harbicht

8 *Boy* (2010) Director: Taika Waititi

9 *Out of the Blue* (2006) Director: Robert Sarkies

10 *Sione's Wedding* (2006) Director: Chris Graham

BRILLIANT BOOKS

Escapist plots, multilayered fiction, reinvented realities and character-driven social commentary: Kiwi literature presents an opportunity to learn much about the country, drawing on NZ's unsettled history, burgeoning cultural awareness and the physical power of the landscape. See p47 for more on NZ literature.

1 *The Bone People* (1988) Keri Hulme

2 *Mister Pip* (2007) Lloyd Jones

3 *The Carpathians* (1988) Janet Frame

4 *Potiki* (1986) Patricia Grace

5 *Bulibasha: King of the Gypsies* (1994) Witi Ihimaera

6 *Live Bodies* (1998) Maurice Gee

7 *The 10pm Question* (2009) Kate de Goldi

8 *The Vintner's Luck* (2000) Elizabeth Knox

9 *Opportunity* (2007) Charlotte Grimshaw

10 *Hibiscus Coast* (2005) Paula Morris

FESTIVAL FRENZY

Kiwis love to party, and many travellers plan their journeys around food, wine and arts fiestas. Following are some of our favourite excuses to get festive. For nationwide events and further suggestions, see the Directory (p689) and the Festivals & Events sections in destination chapters.

1 **World Buskers Festival** (www.worldbuskers festival.com) Christchurch, January (p531)

2 **Parihaka** (www.parihaka.com) Taranaki, January (see boxed text, p266)

3 **Rippon Festival** (www.ripponfestival.co.nz) Wanaka, February (p636)

4 **Fringe NZ** (www.fringe.org.nz) Wellington, February/March (p406)

5 **Pasifika Festival** (www.aucklandcity.govt.nz/ whatson/events/pasifika) Auckland, March (p113)

6 **New Zealand Gold Guitar Awards** (www. goldguitars.co.nz) Gore, June (p666)

7 **Queenstown Winter Festival** (www.winter festival.co.nz) Queenstown, June/July (p618)

8 **Nelson Arts Festival** (www.nelsonartsfestival. co.nz) Nelson, October (p460)

9 **Seafest** (www.seafest.co.nz) Kaikoura, October (p452)

10 **Opotiki Rodeo** (www.rodeonz.co.nz) Opotiki, December (p357)

For more tips online:

Department of Conservation (DOC; www.doc.govt.nz/getting-involved) Conservation events and programs that visitors can engage with.

Leave No Trace (www.lnt.org) Low-impact camping and tramping tips.

Lonely Planet (www.lonelyplanet.com/responsibletravel) Tips on sustainable travel.

Organic Explorer (www.organicexplorer.co.nz) Comprehensive guide to ecofriendly places to eat, stay and explore throughout NZ.

TRAVEL LITERATURE

Given NZ's starring role on the world tourism stage, the current bloom in dedicated NZ travel literature isn't surprising.

Bob Moore, a Wellington-based Englishman, traversed every kilometre of State Hwy 1 (NZ's national drag) then wrote *The 1 Thing: A Small Epic Journey Down New Zealand's Mother Road* (2006). Lyttelton-based Joe Bennett, another Englishman-in-NZ, wrote *A Land of Two Halves* (2004), a tale of hitchhiking around the country.

If you're into cycling, pick up *Long Cloud Ride* by Josie Dew (2007). Dew – a roaming Brit cyclist – chronicles her nine-month, 10,000km NZ journey. Through wind and rain, she gets close to the Kiwi psyche.

Liberal-minded travellers who don't mind the odd tree-hug will love *Slipping into Paradise: Why I Live in New Zealand* by Jeffrey Moussaieff Masson (2004), a gushing sonnet to NZ from a relative newcomer to the country.

How to Watch a Game of Rugby by Spiro Zavos (2004) is a brilliant insight into the national preoccupation by a respected sports journalist, and will ensure you don't ask stupid questions when you're watching the All Blacks at the pub. In the same series, astronomer Richard Hall helps you find the Southern Cross in *How to Gaze at the Southern Stars* (2005).

They're not technically travel lit, but fans of Kiwi films will enjoy Hamish McDouall's *100 Essential New Zealand Films* (2009), and history buffs will be engrossed by the comprehensive *Penguin History of New Zealand* (2003) by Michael King.

INTERNET RESOURCES

100% Pure New Zealand (www.newzealand.com) NZ's official tourism site, with comprehensive visitor info.

Department of Conservation (DOC; www.doc.govt.nz) Indispensable DOC parks, recreation and conservation info across NZ.

Destination New Zealand (www.destination-nz.com) Travel guide with excellent website listings.

DineOut (www.dineout.co.nz) Restaurant reviews and info across the nation.

Living Landscapes (www.livinglandscapes.co.nz) Maori tourism operators across NZ.

Lonely Planet (www.lonelyplanet.com) Get started with NZ summaries and travellers trading info on the Thorn Tree.

Muzic.net (www.muzic.net.nz) Gigs, reviews, bios, charts — Wellington rock to Dunedin dub.

New Zealand Tourism Online (www.tourism.net.nz) Commercial site with 10,000-plus listings and plenty of useful info.

Stuff (www.stuff.co.nz, www.stuff.co.nz/blogs) NZ news (sourced from Fairfax New Zealand publications) and an array of blogs.

Te Ara (www.teara.govt.nz) An online encyclopaedia of NZ.

Itineraries
SHORT BREAKS

AUCKLAND ENCOUNTER   Four to Seven Days / Auckland to Auckland
Bounce around Auckland's stellar bars and restaurants, museums, islands and beaches – multicultural NZ at its most engaging.

Check out the Maori gallery at the **Auckland Museum** (p98), then cross the Domain to **K Rd** (p119) for lunch. Take our architectural **walking tour** (p111), stopping at **Auckland Art Gallery** (p103) and the impossible-to-miss **Sky Tower** (p103). **Ponsonby** (p120) awaits for dinner and drinks.

Ferry over to **Rangitoto Island** (p129), then to **Devonport** (p121) for a meal. Check out **Cheltenham Beach** (p105), then dine at the **Engine Room** (p121). Explore the **Waitakere Ranges Regional Park** (p141), **Karekare** (p142) and **Piha** (p142), then hit the **Kingsland** (p120) restaurants. Have breakfast in **Mt Eden** (p120), climb **Maungawhau** (p99) then ferry-hop to **Waiheke Island** (p131) for some wineries and beaches.

Not far from Auckland, you can snorkel at **Goat Island Marine Reserve** (p150), explore the legendary **Bay of Islands** (p161), ocean-gaze at **Cape Reinga** (p180), ogle the giant trees at **Waipoua Kauri Forest** (p187), explore the **Waitomo Caves** (p242), surf at **Raglan** (p230) or beach yourself at **Whitianga** (p202).

Some say Auckland is just Sydney for beginners. We think not. Sydney doesn't have access to two oceans, nor does it have the amazing melange of Polynesian culture on offer in the 'City of Sails'. Enjoy the big smoke, then explore some local highlights with this 450–900km itinerary.

CHRISTCHURCH EXPLORER

Four to Seven Days /
Christchurch to Christchurch

Winging in to Christchurch with a week or so up your sleeve, there'll be plenty to keep you entertained, both urban and wild.

Hit the city running with a kick-ass coffee at a **High St cafe** (p535), then a juddery circuit on the city's **tramway** (p525) to assess the lay of the land. Jump off at the **Arts Centre** (p525) and have a sticky-beak around the galleries in the area. Other essentials to check off your list include the **Canterbury Museum** (p525) and the **Christchurch Art Gallery** (p525), and don't miss an evening session in the kooky bars in **Lyttelton** (p542) and restaurants in **Sumner** (p534).

The Avon River cuts a lazy, inoffensive ribbon through town – check the flow in the **Botanic Gardens** (p524) or push off into the stream on a **punt** (p527). Close down the day with some boozy wanderings around **Poplar St** and **SOL Sq** (p536).

Swarm into the **shops** on High St (p538), before chilling your bones at the **International Antarctic Centre** (p526), or paddling a Maori canoe and tucking into a traditional Maori feast at **Willowbank Wildlife Reserve** (p527).

Enough city already? Take a trip out of town for a ride on the **gondola** (p527), then cruise out to the formerly volcanic **Banks Peninsula** – explore Francophile **Akaroa** (p542) with its wildlife-rich harbour, and the peninsula's photogenic outer bays.

Spend a few nights on the rambling road: head a couple of hours north for some whale-watching and crayfishing in **Kaikoura** (p449), wander west to **Lake Tekapo** (p561) and the snowy heights of **Aoraki/Mt Cook** (p566), or south to check out the zany boulders at **Moeraki** (p604); don't miss dinner at **Fleur's Place** (p604).

Christchurch has that unusual mix of urban civility and wild abandon just beyond the doorstep. Spend a few days pinballing between downtown bars, shops, museums and galleries, then hit the road (Jack) and chase down some mountains, whales, lakes and forests on this 650–750km trail.

KIWI CLASSICS

12 Days / Auckland to Auckland

With just 12 days, you're gonna have to move fast to squeeze in all the good bits, north and south!

The City of Sails, **Auckland** (p94) is a South Pacific melting pot – spend a few days here shopping, eating, drinking and savouring NZ at its most cosmopolitan and worldly. Truck north to the **Bay of Islands** (p161) for a dose of aquatic adventure, then scoot back to check out the forests and beaches on the **Coromandel Peninsula** (p191). Further south in **Rotorua** (p319), get a nose full of egg-gas, giggle at volcanic mud-bubbles and experience some Maori culture. Get your skates on and cruise down to **Napier** (p378), NZ's archetypal art-deco sun-city. While you're here, don't miss the bottled offerings of the **Hawke's Bay Wine Country** (p388). Down in **Wellington** (p395), the coffee's hot, the beer's cold and wind from the politicians generates its own low-pressure system.

Swan over to the South Island for a few days to experience the best the south has to offer. Start with a tour through the **Marlborough Wine Region** (p446), then jump on a boat/plane/helicopter for a close encounter with a massive marine mammal in **Kaikoura** (p449). Refined, manicured **Christchurch** (p519) is next, followed by the coast road south to the wildlife-rich **Otago Peninsula** (p585), which juts abstractly away from the Victorian facades of student-filled **Dunedin** (p574). Try to catch some live music while you're in town!

Head inland via SH8 to bungy-obsessed **Queenstown** (p607). If you have time, you'll never forget an encounter with **Franz Josef Glacier** (p508) and **Fox Glacier** (p512) on the West Coast. Play aeroplane hopscotch from **Hokitika** (p500) to Christchurch and back to Auckland.

Classy cities, geothermal eruptions, fantastic wine, Maori culture, glaciers, extreme activities, isolated beaches and forests: these are a few of NZ's favourite things, and what you'll want to see if you're a first-time, short-trip visitor. Sample the best of both islands on this 3000km trip.

TRAVEL FURTHER

ICONS & BEYOND   Four to Six Weeks / Auckland to Christchurch

Virgin visitors to the country will want to check out NZ's tourist icons, and maybe throw in some active wilderness experiences for good measure.

Cruise the sail-filled harbours of hip inner-city **Auckland** (p94), then take SH1 north to the glorious, winterless **Bay of Islands** (p161): surfboards, kayaks, scuba gear – take your pick. South of Auckland, hold your nose through the sulphurous sweats of **Rotorua** (p319), then hook further south for idyllic **Taupo** (p289) and go tramping around the triple-peaked wilderness of **Tongariro National Park** (p304). Take SH43 west to New Plymouth and an eyeful of photogenic **Mt Taranaki** (p251), then shuffle southeast to Whanganui, detouring along gorgeous **Whanganui River Road** (p276). Stay up late in caffeinated **Wellington** (p395) and watch the nocturnal freak show pass onwards to oblivion.

Across Cook Strait, head west for some kayaking in **Abel Tasman National Park** (p472), or disappear into the **Marlborough Sounds** (p436) for a day.

Heading further west, track down the rain-swept West Coast with its iconic **glaciers** (p508 & p512), all the way to long-lost **Jackson Bay** (p516), then head over Haast Pass to adrenaline-addicted **Queenstown** (p607). Mix and match highways to Te Anau for the beguiling side-road to **Milford Sound** (p617), then backtrack to SH6 and head north, swapping over to SH8 for an eyeful of cloud-piercing **Aoraki/Mt Cook** (p566), before veering east back to cathedral-centred **Christchurch** (p519). Take an afternoon to explore the amazing **Banks Peninsula** (p542), south of town.

Check some big-ticket attractions off your list, with kayaking, tramping and wildlife-watching breaking up the road trip. Take your time on this well-travelled 3300km route – switch into holiday mode, embrace nature and savour the flavours of dual-island travel.

OFF THE BEATEN TRAIL   Four to Six Weeks / Auckland to Christchurch

Journey to the ends of NZ and experience places far removed from urban clash and humdrum.

Beat a hasty retreat from hypertensive **Auckland** (p94) to tiny **Tutukaka** (p159) and visit the fish-rich waters and underwater labyrinths of the **Poor Knights Islands** (p159). Beyond the Bay of Islands is rugged Aupouri Peninsula, the tip of which is **Cape Reinga** (p180), shrouded in solitude and Maori lore.

Venture back south through Rotorua to the lush leaf-scapes of **Te Urewera National Park** (p374) and the craggy ranges of **East Cape** (p361). Follow SH2 south into the sheepy **Wairarapa** (p422) before soaring over the otherworldly, cloud-wrapped Rimutaka Range and along wiggly Akatarawa Rd to the deserted beaches of the **Kapiti Coast** (p419). If you have time, float offshore to mystical **Kapiti Island** (p421). Chug across Cook Strait to Picton, then lose your way in the waterways of the **Marlborough Sounds** (p436).

Detour west past artsy Nelson to ecofriendly, chilled-out **Golden Bay** (p475; more paintbrushes than people) and enormous **Kahurangi National Park** (p480). Travel southwest, where a memorable road north of Westport trundles up to the caverns of **Oparara Basin** (p489). Southbound, divert to the inland extremities of **Arthur's Pass National Park** (p552), and don't miss a voyage on desolate **Doubtful Sound** (p656). Ferry yourself to end-of-the-world **Stewart Island** (p672), then kick back in the overgrown **Catlins** (p666) for a couple of days.

Detour north on SH8 through Central Otago, passing tiny towns en route to mountain-biking **Alexandra** (p592) and hang-glider-hung **Omarama** (p602). Trek back to the east coast via the **Waitaki Valley** (p602) on SH83, then hop south to mellow **Oamaru** (p597) before a big-city reality check back in **Christchurch** (p519).

It's hard to find paths-less-travelled in NZ these days, but this epic 5400km route from NZ's northernmost fingernail to its detached southern toe takes in plenty of vacant landscapes. If your timing's good, you may feel like you've carved off a slice of heaven all for yourself.

TAILORED TRIPS

PLANES, TRAINS & AUTOMOBILES

With camera-conducive panoramas out every NZ window, getting from A to B is half the fun.

For a bird's-eye view of NZ, take a glider trip over **Omarama** (p602), a scenic flight above **Milford Sound** (p617), a chopper ride over **Aoraki/Mt Cook** (p569) and the **West Coast glaciers** (p508 & p512), or a knee-trembling hang-glide above **Nelson** (p459) or **Queenstown** (p614).

Trainspotting romantics should try the **Taieri Gorge Railway** (p585), the **Overlander** (p127) from Auckland to Wellington via the Raurimu Spiral and Tongariro National Park, or the **TranzAlpine** (p499) epic from Christchurch to Greymouth over snowbound Arthur's Pass.

The best stretches of Kiwi tarmac include State Highway 6 (**SH6**) down the West Coast (especially around Punakaiki and from Haast to Queenstown); **SH73** from Christchurch to Greymouth across Arthur's Pass; lonesome **SH35** around East Cape; the rainy **Whanganui River Road** (p280); bleak **SH2** from Wellington to Featherston over the Rimutaka Range; and **SH60** over Takaka Hill west of Motueka.

Bobbing around in a boat, the **Wellington–Picton ferry** (p416) is a perfect Marlborough Sounds snapshot. Take a kayak trip around **Abel Tasman National Park** (p474), **Doubtful Sound** (p657) or **Okarito Lagoon** (p506), a safari up the **Haast River** (p515), a jetboat thrill-ride in **Queenstown** (p612) or paddleboat cruise on the **Whanganui River** (p273).

FOODIE NZ

Forget porridge and meat-and-two-veg: contemporary Kiwi cuisine is a gourmet delight, highlighted by fab food festivals, boutique wineries, locally sourced produce and traditional Maori fare.

Look for these foodie fiestas: **Harvest Hawke's Bay** (p387), **Gisborne Food & Wine Festival** (p370), **Whitianga Scallop Festival** (p203), **Hokitika Wild Foods Festival** (p502), **Kawhia Kai Festival** (p240), **Bluff Oyster & Southland Seafood Festival** (p665), **Seafest** (p452) in Kaikoura, the **Marlborough Wine Festival** (p444) and **Toast Martinborough** (p424).

For local produce, hit the organic green-grocers or **Hawke's Bay Farmers Market** (p390), **Lyttelton Farmers Market** (p542) near Christchurch, **Dunedin Farmers Market** (p582) or the **Nelson Market** (p458).

For a *hangi* (Maori feast), try Tikitiki's **Eastender Backpackers** (p364), or **Mitai Maori Village** and **Tamaki Maori Village** (p323) in Rotorua.

History James Belich

New Zealand's history is not long, but it is fast. In less than a thousand years these islands have produced two new peoples: the Polynesian Maori and European New Zealanders. The latter are often known by their Maori name, 'Pakeha' (though not all like the term). NZ shares some of its history with the rest of Polynesia, and with other European settler societies, but has unique features as well. It is the similarities that make the differences so interesting, and vice versa.

MAKING MAORI

Despite persistent myths (see the boxed text, p30), there is no doubt that the first settlers of NZ were the Polynesian forebears of today's Maori. Beyond that, there are a lot of question marks. Exactly where in east Polynesia did they come from – the Cook Islands, Tahiti, the Marquesas? When did they arrive? Did the first settlers come in one group or several? Some evidence, such as the diverse DNA of the Polynesian rats that accompanied the first settlers, suggests multiple founding voyages. On the other hand, only rats and dogs brought by the founders have survived, not the more valuable pigs and chickens. The survival of these cherished animals would have had high priority, and their failure to be successfully introduced suggests fewer voyages. See Kawhia (p240) and the boxed text on p354 for the tales of just two of the great migratory canoes that made the voyage.

NZ seems small compared to Australia, but it is bigger than Britain, and very much bigger than other Polynesian islands. Its regions vary wildly in environment and climate. Prime sites for first settlement were warm coastal gardens for the food plants brought from Polynesia (kumara or sweet potato, gourd, yam and taro); sources of workable stone for knives and adzes; and areas with abundant big game. NZ has no native land mammals apart from a few species of bat, but 'big game' is no exaggeration: the islands were home to a dozen species of moa (a large flightless bird), the largest of which weighed up to 240kg, about twice the size of an ostrich. There were also other species of flightless bird and large sea mammals such as fur seals, all unaccustomed to being hunted. For people from small Pacific islands, this was like hitting the jackpot. The first settlers spread far and fast, from the top of the North Island to the bottom of the South Island within the first 100 years. High-protein diets are likely to have boosted population growth.

By about 1400, however, with big-game supply dwindling, Maori economics turned from big game to small game – forest birds and rats – and from hunting to gardening and fishing. A good living could still be made, but it required detailed local knowledge, steady effort and complex communal

One of NZ's foremost modern historians, James Belich has written a number of books on NZ history and hosted the TV documentary series *NZ Wars*.

For more about Maui and other mythological figures, Maori tribal structure and performing arts, see Maori Culture, p53.

Similarities in language between Maori and Tahitian indicate close contact in historical times. Maori is about as similar to Tahitian as Spanish is to French, despite the 4294km separating these island groups.

TIMELINE

AD 1000–1200	1642	1769
Possible date of the arrival of Maori in NZ. Solid archaeological evidence points to about AD 1200, but much earlier dates have been suggested for the first human impact on the environment.	First European contact: Abel Tasman arrives on an expedition from the Dutch East Indies (Indonesia) to find the 'Great South Land'. The party leaves without landing after a sea skirmish with Maori, but its legacy remains in the country's name.	European contact recommences with visits by James Cook and Jean de Surville. Despite some violence, both managed to communicate with Maori, and this time NZ's link with the outside world proved permanent.

THE MORIORI & THEIR MYTH

One of NZ's most persistent legends is that Maori found mainland NZ already occupied by a more peaceful and racially distinct Melanesian people, known as the Moriori, whom they exterminated. This myth has been regularly debunked by scholars since the 1920s, but somehow hangs on.

To complicate matters, there were real 'Moriori', and Maori did treat them badly. The real Moriori were the people of the Chatham Islands, a windswept group about 900km east of the mainland. They were, however, fully Polynesian, and descended from Maori – 'Moriori' was their version of the same word. Mainland Maori arrived in the Chathams in 1835, as a spin-off of the Musket Wars, killing some Moriori and enslaving the rest. But they did not exterminate them. The mainland Moriori remain a myth.

---

organisation, hence the rise of the Maori tribes. Competition for resources increased, conflict did likewise, and this led to the building of increasingly sophisticated fortifications, known as *pa*. Vestiges of *pa* earthworks can still be seen around the country, on the hilltops of Auckland for example.

The Maori had no metals and no written language (and no alcoholic drinks or drugs). But their culture and spiritual life was rich and distinctive. Below Ranginui (sky father) and Papatuanuku (earth mother) were various gods of land, forest and sea, joined by deified ancestors over time. The mischievous demigod Maui was particularly important. In legend, he vanquished the sun and fished up the North Island before meeting his death between the thighs of the goddess Hine-nui-te-po in an attempt to conquer the human mortality embodied in her. Maori traditional performance art, the group singing and dancing known as *kapa haka,* has real power, even for modern audiences. Visual art, notably woodcarving, is something special – 'like nothing but itself', in the words of 18th-century explorer-scientist Joseph Banks.

ENTER EUROPE

NZ became an official British colony in 1840, but the first authenticated contact between Maori and the outside world took place almost two centuries earlier in 1642, in Golden Bay at the top of the South Island. Two Dutch ships sailed from Indonesia, to search for southern land and anything valuable it might contain. The commander, Abel Tasman, was instructed to pretend to any natives he might meet 'that you are by no means eager for precious metals, so as to leave them ignorant of the value of the same'.

When Tasman's ships anchored in the bay, local Maori came out in their canoes to make the traditional challenge: friends or foes? Misunderstanding this, the Dutch challenged back, by blowing trumpets. When a boat was lowered to take a party between the two ships, it was attacked. Four crewmen were killed. Tasman sailed away and did not come back; nor did any other European for 127 years. But the Dutch did leave a name: 'Nieuw Zeeland' or 'New Sealand'.

Abel Tasman named NZ Statenland, assuming it was connected to Staten Island near Argentina. It was subsequently named after the province of Zeeland in Tasman's Holland.

1790s	1818–36	1840
Whaling ships and sealing gangs arrive in the country. Relations are established with Maori, with Europeans depending on the contact for essentials such as food, water and protection.	Intertribal Maori 'Musket Wars' take place: tribes acquire muskets and win bloody victories against tribes without them. The war tapers off in 1836, probably as a result of the equal distribution of weapons.	On 6 February, the Treaty of Waitangi is signed by 40 chiefs in a sovereignty settlement presented by William Hobson. Copies of the treaty are circulated countrywide to collect signatures. NZ becomes a nominal British colony.

Contact between Maori and Europeans was renewed in 1769, when English and French explorers arrived, under James Cook (see the boxed text, p32) and Jean de Surville. Relations were more sympathetic, and exploration continued, motivated by science, profit and great power rivalry. Cook made two more visits between 1773 and 1777, and there were further French expeditions.

Unofficial visits, by whaling ships in the north and sealing gangs in the south, began in the 1790s. The first mission station was founded in 1814, in the Bay of Islands, and was followed by dozens of others: Anglican, Methodist and Catholic. Trade in flax and timber generated small European-Maori settlements by the 1820s. Surprisingly, the most numerous category of European visitor was probably American. New England whaling ships favoured the Bay of Islands for rest and recreation; 271 called there between 1833 and 1839 alone. To whalers, 'rest and recreation' meant sex and drink. Their favourite haunt, the little town of Kororareka (now Russell) was known to the missionaries as 'the hellhole of the Pacific'. New England visitors today might well have distant relatives among the local Maori.

One or two dozen bloody clashes dot the history of Maori-European contact before 1840 but, given the number of visits, inter-racial conflict was modest. Europeans needed Maori protection, food and labour, and Maori came to need European articles, especially muskets. Whaling stations and mission stations were linked to local Maori groups by intermarriage, which helped keep the peace. Most warfare was between Maori and Maori: the terrible intertribal 'Musket Wars' of 1818–36. Because Northland had the majority of early contact with Europe, its Ngapuhi tribe acquired muskets first. Under their great general Hongi Hika, Ngapuhi then raided south, winning bloody victories against tribes without muskets. Once they acquired muskets, these tribes saw off Ngapuhi, but also raided further south in their turn. The domino effect continued to the far south of the South Island in 1836. The missionaries claimed that the Musket Wars then tapered off through their influence, but the restoration of the balance of power through the equal distribution of muskets was probably more important.

Europe brought such things as pigs (at last) and potatoes, which benefited Maori, while muskets and diseases had the opposite effect. The negative effects have been exaggerated, however. Europeans expected peoples like the Maori to simply fade away at contact, and some early estimates of Maori population were overly high – up to one million. Current estimates are between 85,000 and 110,000 for 1769. The Musket Wars killed perhaps 20,000, and new diseases did considerable damage too (although NZ had the natural quarantine of distance: infected Europeans usually recovered or died during the long voyage, and smallpox, for example, which devastated native Americans, did not make it here). By 1840, the Maori had been reduced to about 70,000, a decline of at least 20%. Maori bent under the weight of European contact, but they certainly did not break.

Rumours of late survivals of the giant moa bird abound, but none have been authenticated. So if you see a moa in your travels, photograph it – you have just made the greatest zoological discovery of the last 100 years.

Scottish influence can still be felt in NZ, particularly in the south of the South Island. NZ has more Scottish pipe bands per capita than Scotland itself.

For a thorough overview of NZ history from Gondwanaland to today, visit http://history-nz.org.

1844	1853–56	1860–61
Young Ngapuhi chief, Hone Heke, challenges British sovereignty, first by cutting down the British flag at Russell, and then by sacking the town itself. The ensuing Northland War continues till 1846.	Provincial and central elected governments established. In 1853 the first elections are held for the New Zealand parliament; votes are restricted to adult, male, British subjects, and Maori votes are limited due to property-right rules.	First Taranaki war. Starting with the controversial swindling of Maori land by the government at Waitara, the war involves many military participants from the Waikato tribes (despite being traditional enemies of the Taranaki Maori).

CAPTAIN JAMES COOK *Tony Horwitz*

If aliens ever visit earth, they may wonder what to make of the countless obelisks, faded plaques and graffiti-covered statues of a stiff, wigged figure gazing out to sea from Alaska to Australia, from NZ to North Yorkshire, from Siberia to the South Pacific. James Cook (1728–79) explored more of the earth's surface than anyone in history, and it's impossible to travel the Pacific without encountering the captain's image and his controversial legacy in the lands he opened to the West.

For a man who travelled so widely, and rose to such fame, Cook came from an extremely pinched and provincial background. The son of a day labourer in rural Yorkshire, he was born in a mud cottage, had little schooling, and seemed destined for farm work – and for his family's grave plot in a village churchyard. Instead, Cook went to sea as a teenager, worked his way up from coal-ship servant to naval officer, and attracted notice for his exceptional charts of Canada. But Cook remained a little-known second lieutenant until, in 1768, the Royal Navy chose him to command a daring voyage to the South Seas.

In a converted coal ship called *Endeavour*, Cook sailed to Tahiti, and then became the first European to land at NZ and the east coast of Australia. Though the ship almost sank after striking the Great Barrier Reef, and 40% of the crew died from disease and accidents, the *Endeavour* limped home in 1771. On a return voyage (1772–75), Cook became the first navigator to pierce the Antarctic Circle and circled the globe near its southernmost latitude, demolishing the ancient myth that a vast, populous and fertile continent surrounded the South Pole. Cook also crisscrossed the Pacific from Easter Island to Melanesia, charting dozens of islands between. Though Maori killed and cooked 10 sailors, the captain remained strikingly sympathetic to islanders. 'Notwithstanding they are cannibals,' he wrote, 'they are naturally of a good disposition'.

On Cook's final voyage (1776–79), in search of a northwest passage between the Atlantic and Pacific, he became the first European to visit Hawaii, and coasted America from Oregon to Alaska. Forced back by Arctic pack ice, Cook returned to Hawaii, where he was killed during a skirmish with islanders who had initially greeted him as a Polynesian god. In a single decade of discovery, Cook had filled in the map of the Pacific and, as one French navigator put it, 'left his successors with little to do but admire his exploits'.

But Cook's travels also spurred colonisation of the Pacific, and within a few decades of his death, missionaries, whalers, traders and settlers began transforming (and often devastating) island cultures. As a result, many indigenous people now revile Cook as an imperialist villain who introduced disease, dispossession and other ills to the Pacific (hence the frequent vandalising of Cook monuments). However, as islanders revive traditional crafts and practices, from tattooing to *tapa*, they have turned to the art and writing of Cook and his men as a resource for cultural renewal. For good and ill, a Yorkshire farm boy remains the single most significant figure in the shaping of the modern Pacific.

Tony Horwitz is a Pulitzer-winning reporter and nonfiction author. In researching Blue Latitudes (or Into the Blue), Tony travelled the Pacific – 'boldly going where Captain Cook has gone before'.

1861	**1868–72**	**1882**
Gold discovered in Otago by Gabriel Read, an Australian prospector. As a result, the population of Otago climbs from less than 13,000 to over 30,000 in six months.	East Coast war. Te Kooti, having led an escape from his prison on the Chatham Islands, leads a holy guerrilla war in the Urewera region. He finally retreats to establish the Ringatu Church.	First refrigerated cargo to Britain. Exports to Britain had been dominated by the wool trade, but this development allows diversification into meat and dairy, and establishes NZ's early lead in the industry.

MAKING PAKEHA

By 1840, Maori tribes described local Europeans as 'their Pakeha', and valued the profit and prestige they brought. Maori wanted more of both, and concluded that accepting nominal British authority was the way to get them. At the same time, the British government was overcoming its reluctance to undertake potentially expensive intervention in NZ. It too was influenced by profit and prestige, but also by humanitarian considerations. It believed, wrongly but sincerely, that Maori could not handle the increasing scale of unofficial European contact. In 1840, the two peoples struck a deal, symbolised by the treaty first signed at Waitangi on 6 February that year. The Treaty of Waitangi now has a standing not dissimilar to that of the Constitution in the US, but is even more contested. The original problem was a discrepancy between British and Maori understandings of it. The English version promised Maori full equality as British subjects in return for complete rights of government. The Maori version also promised that Maori would retain their chieftainship, which implied local rights of government. The problem was not great at first, because the Maori version applied outside the small European settlements. But as those settlements grew, conflict brewed.

In 1840, there were only about 2000 Europeans in NZ, with the shanty town of Kororareka (now Russell) as the capital and biggest settlement. By 1850, six new settlements had been formed with 22,000 settlers between them. About half of these had arrived under the auspices of the New Zealand Company and its associates. The company was the brainchild of Edward Gibbon Wakefield, who also influenced the settlement of South Australia. Wakefield hoped to short-circuit the barbarous frontier phase of settlement with 'instant civilisation', but his success was limited. From the 1850s, his settlers, who included a high proportion of upper-middle-class gentlefolk, were swamped by succeeding waves of immigrants that continued to wash in until the 1880s. These people were part of the great British and Irish diaspora that also populated Australia and much of North America, but the NZ mix was distinctive. Lowland Scots settlers were more prominent in NZ than elsewhere, for example, with the possible exception of parts of Canada. NZ's Irish, even the Catholics, tended to come from the north of Ireland. NZ's English tended to come from the counties close to London. Small groups of Germans, Scandinavians and Chinese made their way in, though the last faced increasing racial prejudice from the 1880s, when the Pakeha population reached half a million.

Much of the mass immigration from the 1850s to the 1870s was assisted by the provincial and central governments, which also mounted large-scale public works schemes, especially in the 1870s under Julius Vogel. In 1876, Vogel abolished the provinces on the grounds that they were hampering his development efforts. The last imperial governor with substantial power was the talented but Machiavellian George Grey, who ended his second

The Waitangi Treaty Grounds (p168), where the Treaty of Waitangi was first signed in 1840, is now a tourist attraction for Kiwis and non-Kiwis alike. Each year on 6 February, Waitangi hosts treaty commemorations and protests.

'I believe we were all glad to leave New Zealand. It is not a pleasant place. Amongst the natives there is absent that charming simplicity... and the greater part of the English are the very refuse of society.' Charles Darwin, referring to Kororareka (Russell), in 1860.

1890–1912	1893	1914–18
The Liberal government is in power over an economy recovering from depression. Their major leader is Richard John Seddon, 'King Dick, as I am usually known'.	Votes for women granted, following a campaign led by Kate Sheppard, who had been petitioning the government for years. NZ becomes the first country in the world to grant the vote to women.	NZ's contribution to WWI is quite staggering for a country of just over one million people: about 100,000 NZ men serve overseas, and close on 60,000 became casualties, mostly on the Western Front in France.

Maurice Shadbolt's *Season of the Jew* (1987) is a semifictionalised story of bloody campaigns led by warrior Te Kooti against the British in Poverty Bay in the 1860s. Te Kooti and his followers compared themselves to the Israelites who were cast out of Egypt.

governorship in 1868. Thereafter, the governors (governors-general from 1917) were largely just nominal heads of state; the head of government, the premier or prime minister, had more power. The central government, originally weaker than the provincial governments, the imperial governor and the Maori tribes, eventually exceeded the power of all three.

The Maori tribes did not go down without a fight, however. Indeed, their resistance was one of the most formidable ever mounted against European expansion, comparable to that of the Sioux and Seminole in the US. The first clash took place in 1843 in the Wairau Valley, now a wine-growing district. A posse of settlers set out to enforce the myth of British control, but encountered the reality of Maori control. Twenty-two settlers were killed, including Wakefield's brother, Arthur, along with about six Maori. In 1845, more serious fighting broke out in the Bay of Islands, when Hone Heke sacked a British settlement. Heke and his ally Kawiti baffled three British punitive expeditions, using a modern variant of the traditional *pa* fortification. Vestiges of these innovative earthworks can still be seen at Ruapekapeka (south of Kawakawa). Governor Grey claimed victory in the north, but few were convinced at the time. Grey had more success in the south, where he arrested the formidable Ngati Toa chief Te Rauparaha, who until then wielded great influence on both sides of Cook Strait. Pakeha were able to swamp the few Maori living in the South Island, but the fighting of the 1840s confirmed that the North Island at that time comprised a European fringe around an independent Maori heartland.

In the 1850s, settler population and aspirations grew, and fighting broke out again in 1860. The wars burned on sporadically until 1872 over much of the North Island. In the early years, a Maori nationalist organisation, the King Movement (see the boxed text, p225), was the backbone of resistance. In later years, some remarkable prophet-generals, notably Titokowaru and Te Kooti (see the boxed text, p368), took over. Most wars were small-scale, but the Waikato War of 1863–64 was not. This conflict, fought at the same time as the American Civil War, involved armoured steamships, ultramodern heavy artillery, telegraph and 10 proud British regular regiments. Despite the odds, the Maori won several battles, such as that at Gate Pa, near Tauranga, in 1864. But in the end they were ground down by European numbers and resources. Maori political, though not cultural, independence ebbed away in the last decades of the 19th century. It finally expired when police invaded its last sanctuary, the Urewera Mountains, in 1916.

'Kaore e mau te rongo – ake, ake!' (Peace never shall be made – never, never!) War chief Rewi Maniapoto in response to government troops at the battle of Orakau, 1864

WELFARE & WARFARE

From the 1850s to the 1880s, despite conflict with Maori, the Pakeha economy boomed on the back of wool exports, gold rushes and massive overseas borrowing for development. The crash came in the 1880s, when NZ experienced its Long Depression. In 1890, the Liberals came to power, and stayed there until 1912, helped by a recovering economy. The Liberals were NZ's first

1935–49	1939–45	1974
First Labour government in power, under Michael Savage. This government creates NZ's pioneering version of the welfare state, and also takes some independent initiatives in foreign policy.	NZ troops back Britain and the Allied war effort during WWII, while a hundred thousand or so Americans arrive from 1942 to protect NZ from the Japanese.	Pacific Island migrants who have outstayed visas (dubbed 'overstayers') subjected to Dawn Raids (crackdowns by immigration police) under Robert Muldoon and the National government. These raids continue till the early 1980s.

organised political party, and the first of several governments to give NZ a reputation as 'the world's social laboratory'. NZ became the first country in the world to give women the vote in 1893, and introduced old-age pensions in 1898. The Liberals also introduced a long-lasting system of industrial arbitration, but this was not enough to prevent bitter industrial unrest in 1912–13. This happened under the conservative 'Reform' government, which had replaced the Liberals in 1912. Reform remained in power until 1928, and later transformed itself into the National Party. Renewed depression struck in 1929, and the NZ experience of it was as grim as any. The derelict little farmhouses still seen in rural areas often date from this era.

In 1935, a second reforming government took office: the First Labour government, led by Michael Joseph Savage, easily NZ's favourite Australian. For a time, the Labour government was considered the most socialist government outside Soviet Russia. But, when the chips were down in Europe in 1939, Labour had little hesitation in backing Britain.

NZ had also backed Britain in the Boer War (1899–1902) and WWI (1914–18), with dramatic losses in WWI in particular. You can count the cost

> To find out more about the New Zealand Wars, visit www.newzealand wars.co.nz.

LAND WARS *Errol Hunt*

Five separate major conflicts made up what are now collectively known as the New Zealand Wars (also referred to as the Land Wars or Maori Wars). Starting in Northland and moving throughout the North Island, the wars had many complex causes, but *whenua* (land) was the one common factor. In all five wars, Maori fought both for and against the government, on whose side stood the Imperial British Army, Australians and NZ's own Armed Constabulary. Land confiscations imposed on the Maori as punishment for involvement in these wars are still the source of conflict today, with the government struggling to finance compensation for what are now acknowledged to have been illegal seizures.

Northland war (1844–46) 'Hone Heke's War' began with the famous chopping of the flagpole at Kororareka (now Russell, p165) and 'ended' at Ruapekapeka (south of Kawakawa). In many ways, this was almost a civil war between rival Ngapuhi factions, with the government taking one side against the other.

First Taranaki war (1860–61) Starting in Waitara, the first Taranaki war inflamed the passions of Maori across the North Island.

Waikato war (1863–64) The largest of the five wars. Predominantly involving Kingitanga (see the boxed text, p225), the Waikato war was caused in part by what the government saw as a challenge to sovereignty. However, it was land, again, that was the real reason for friction. Following defeats such as Rangiriri (p224), the Waikato people were pushed entirely from their own lands, south into what became known as the King Country.

Second Taranaki war (1865–69) Caused by Maori resistance to land confiscations stemming from the first Taranaki war, this was perhaps the war in which the Maori came closest to victory, under the brilliant, one-eyed prophet-general Titokowaru. However, once he lost the respect of his warriors (probably through an indiscretion with the wife of one of his warriors), the war too was lost.

East Coast war (1868–72) Te Kooti's holy guerrilla war; see the boxed text, p368.

---

in almost any little NZ town. A central square or park will contain a memorial lined with names – more for WWI than WWII. Even in WWII, however, NZ did its share of fighting: a hundred thousand or so New Zealanders fought in Europe and the Middle East. NZ, a peaceful-seeming country, has spent much of its history at war. In the 19th century it fought at home; in the 20th, overseas.

'God's own country, but the devil's own mess.' Prime Minister Richard (King Dick) Seddon, speaking on the source of NZ's self-proclaimed nickname 'Godzone'.

BETTER BRITONS?

British visitors have long found NZ hauntingly familiar. This is not simply a matter of the British and Irish origin of most Pakeha. It also stems from the tightening of NZ links with Britain from 1882, when refrigerated cargoes of food were first shipped to London. By the 1930s, giant ships carried frozen meat, cheese and butter, as well as wool, on regular voyages taking about five weeks one way. The NZ economy adapted to the feeding of London, and cultural links were also enhanced. NZ children studied British history and literature, not their own. NZ's leading scientists and writers, such as Ernest Rutherford and Katherine Mansfield (see the boxed text, p404), gravitated to Britain. This tight relationship has been described as 'recolonial', but it is a mistake to see NZ as an exploited colony. Average living standards in NZ were normally better than in Britain, as were the welfare and lower-level education systems. New Zealanders had access to British markets and culture, and they contributed their share to the latter as equals. The list of 'British' writers, academics, scientists, military leaders, publishers and the like who were actually New Zealanders is long. Indeed, New Zealanders, especially in war and sport, sometimes saw themselves as a superior version of the British – the Better Britons of the south. The NZ-London relationship was rather like that of the American Midwest and New York.

'Recolonial' NZ prided itself, with some justice, on its affluence, equality and social harmony. But it was also conformist, even puritanical. Until the 1950s, it was technically illegal for farmers to allow their cattle to mate in fields fronting public roads, for moral reasons. The 1953 American movie, *The Wild One*, was banned until 1977. Sunday newspapers were illegal until 1969, and full Sunday trading was not allowed until 1989. Licensed restaurants hardly existed in 1960, nor did supermarkets or TV. Notoriously, from 1917 to 1967, pubs were obliged to shut at 6pm. Yet the puritanical society of Better Britons was never the whole story. Opposition to Sunday trading stemmed, not so much from belief in the sanctity of the Sabbath, but from the belief that workers should have weekends too. Six o'clock closing was a standing joke in rural areas, notably the marvellously idiosyncratic region of South Island's west coast. There was always something of a Kiwi counterculture, even before imported countercultures took root from the 1960s.

Wellington-born Nancy Wake (codenamed 'The White Mouse') led a guerrilla attack against the Nazis with a 7000-strong army. She had the multiple honours of being the Gestapo's most-wanted person and being the most decorated Allied servicewoman of WWII.

There were also developments in cultural nationalism, beginning in the 1930s but really flowering from the 1970s. Writers, artists and film-makers were by no means the only people who 'came out' in that era.

1985	1987	1992
Rainbow Warrior sunk in Auckland Harbour by French government agents to prevent the Greenpeace protest ship from making its intended voyage to Moruroa, where the French government is conducting a nuclear-testing program.	The international stock market crash known as 'Black Monday' hits the NZ economy particularly hard, following optimistic financial investment in the free-market atmosphere. The economy takes years to recover.	Government begins reparations for land confiscated in the Land Wars, and confirms Maori fishing rights in the 'Sealord deal'. Major settlements of historical confiscation follow including, in 1995, reparations for the Waikato land confiscations.

COMING IN, COMING OUT

The 'recolonial' system was shaken several times after 1935, but managed to survive until 1973, when Mother England ran off and joined the Franco-German commune now known as the EU. NZ was beginning to develop alternative markets to Britain, and alternative exports to wool, meat and dairy products. Wide-bodied jet aircraft were allowing the world and NZ to visit each other on an increasing scale. NZ had only 36,000 tourists in 1960, compared with more than two million a year now. Women were beginning to penetrate first the upper reaches of the workforce and then the political sphere. Gay people came out of the closet, despite vigorous efforts by moral conservatives to push them back in. University-educated youths were becoming more numerous and more assertive.

The Ministry for Culture & Heritage's history website (www.nzhistory.net.nz) is an excellent source of info on NZ history.

From 1945, Maori experienced both a population explosion and massive urbanisation. In 1936, Maori were 17% urban and 83% rural. Fifty years later, these proportions had reversed. The immigration gates, which until 1960 were pretty much labelled 'whites only', widened, first to allow in Pacific Islanders for their labour, and then to allow in (East) Asians for their money. These transitions would have generated major socioeconomic change whatever happened in politics. But most New Zealanders associate the country's recent 'Big Shift' with the politics of 1984.

The Six o'clock Swill referred to the frantic after-work drinking at pubs when men tried to drink as much as possible from 5.05pm until strict closing time at 6pm.

In 1984, NZ's third great reforming government was elected – the Fourth Labour government, led nominally by David Lange and in fact by Roger Douglas, the Minister of Finance. This government adopted an antinuclear foreign policy, delighting the left, and a more-market economic policy, delighting the right. NZ's numerous economic controls were dismantled with breakneck speed. Middle NZ was uneasy about the antinuclear policy, which threatened NZ's ANZUS alliance with Australia and the US. But in 1985, French spies sank the antinuclear protest ship *Rainbow Warrior* (see the boxed text, p177) in Auckland Harbour, killing one crewman. The lukewarm American condemnation of the French act brought middle NZ in behind the antinuclear policy, which became associated with national independence. Other New Zealanders were uneasy about the more-market economic policy, but failed to come up with a convincing alternative. Revelling in their new freedom, NZ investors engaged in a frenzy of speculation, and suffered even more than the rest of the world from the economic crash of 1987.

NZ's staunch antinuclear stance earned it the nickname 'The Mouse that Roared'.

The early 21st century is an interesting time for NZ. Like NZ food and wine, film and literature are flowering as never before, and the new ethnic mix is creating something very special in popular music. There are continuities, however – the pub, the sportsground, the quarter-acre section, the bush, the beach and the bach – and they too are part of the reason people like to come here. Realising that NZ has a great culture, and an intriguing history, as well as a great natural environment, will double the bang for your buck.

1996	2004	2008
NZ changes from a two-party 'first past the post' (FPP) electoral system to Mixed Member Proportional (MMP) representation, allowing minority parties such as the Greens to take a representative role in government.	Maori TV begins broadcasting – for the first time, a channel committed to NZ content and the revitalisation of Maori language and culture hits the small screen.	An election replaces nine-year Labour prime minister Helen Clark with a National (conservative) government under John Key.

The Culture

THE NATIONAL PSYCHE

New Zealand is like that little guy at school when they're picking rugby teams – quietly waiting to be noticed, desperately wanting to be liked. Then, when he does get the nod, his sheer determination to prove himself propels him to score a completely unexpected try. When his team-mates come to congratulate him he stares at the ground and mumbles, 'It was nothing, ay'.

While a proud little nation, Kiwis traditionally don't have time for show-offs. Jingoistic flag-waving is generally frowned upon. People who make an impression on the international stage are respected and admired, but flashy tall poppies have traditionally had their heads lopped off. This is perhaps a legacy of NZ's early egalitarian ideals – the ones that sought to avoid the worst injustices of the 'mother country' (Britain) by breaking up large land holdings and enthusiastically adopting a 'cradle to grave' welfare state. 'Just because someone's got a bigger car than me, or bigger guns, doesn't make them better' is the general Kiwi attitude.

NZ has rarely let its size get in the way of making a point on the international stage. A founding member of the League of Nations (the precursor to the UN), it ruffled feathers between the world wars by failing to blindly follow Britain's position. It was in the 1980s, however, that things got really interesting.

Modern Kiwi culture pivots on that decade. Firstly, the unquestioned primacy of rugby union as a source of social cohesion (which rivalled the country's commitment to the two world wars as a foundation of nation-building) was stripped away when tens of thousands of New Zealanders took to the streets to protest a tour by the South African rugby side in 1981. They held that the politics of apartheid not only had a place in sport, they trumped it. The country was starkly divided; there were riots in paradise. The scar is still strong enough that most New Zealanders over 35 will recognise the simple phrase 'The Tour' as referring to those events.

The tour protests both harnessed and nourished a political and cultural renaissance among Maori which had already been rolling for a decade. Three years later, that renaissance found its mark when a reforming Labour government gave statutory teeth to the Waitangi Tribunal, an agency that has since guided a process of land return, compensation for past wrongs and interpretation of the Treaty of Waitangi – the 1840 pact between Maori and the Crown – as a living document.

At the same time antinuclear protests that had been rumbling for years gained momentum, with mass blockades of visiting US naval ships. In 1984 Prime Minister David Lange barred nuclear-powered or armed ships from entering NZ waters. The mouse had roared. As a result the US threw NZ out of ANZUS, the country's main strategic military alliance, which also included Australia, declaring NZ 'a friend but not an ally'.

The following year an event happened that would completely change the way NZ related to the world when French government agents launched an attack in Auckland Harbour, sinking Greenpeace's antinuclear flagship *Rainbow Warrior* and killing one of its crew. Being bombed by a country that NZ had fought two world wars with and the muted or nonexistent condemnation by other allies left an indelible mark. It strengthened NZ's resolve to follow its own conscience in foreign policy and in 1987 the NZ Nuclear Free Zone, Disarmament & Arms Control Act became law.

For many, Sir Edmund Hillary, the first person to climb Mt Everest, was the consummate New Zealander: humble, practical and concerned for social justice. A public outpouring of grief followed his death in 2008.

Ironically, the person responsible for the nuclear age was a New Zealander. In 1917 Ernest Rutherford was the first to split the nucleus of an atom. His face appears on the $100 note.

From the Boer to the Vietnam War, NZ had blithely trotted off at the behest of the UK or US. Not anymore, as is demonstrated by its lack of involvement in the invasion of Iraq. That's not to say that the country shirks its international obligations. NZ troops continue to be deployed in peacekeeping capacities throughout the world and are currently active in Afghanistan.

If that wasn't enough upheaval for one decade, 1986 saw another bitter battle split the community – this time over the decriminalisation of homosexuality. The debate was particularly rancorous, but the law that previously incarcerated consenting gay adults was repealed – paving the way for the generally accepting society that NZ is today. Just 13 years later Georgina Beyer, an openly transsexual former prostitute, would win a once safe rural seat off a conservative incumbent – an unthinkable achievement in most of the world.

'...a sordid act of international state-backed terrorism...' – Prime Minister David Lange, describing the bombing of the *Rainbow Warrior* (1986)

Yet while the 1980s saw the country jump to the left on social issues, simultaneously economic reforms were carried out that were an extreme step to the right (to paraphrase one-time Hamiltonian Richard O'Brien's song *The Time Warp*). The bloated public sector was slashed, any state assets that weren't bolted to the floor were sold off, regulation was removed from many sectors, trade barriers dismantled and the power of the unions greatly diminished.

If there is broad agreement that the economy had to be restructured, the reforms carried a heavy price. The old social guarantees are not as sure. New Zealanders work long hours for lower wages than their Australian cousins would ever tolerate. Compared with other Organisation for Economic Co-operation and Development (OECD) nations, family incomes are low, child poverty rates are high and the gap between rich and poor is widening.

Yet there is a dynamism about NZ that was rare in the 'golden weather' years before the reforms. NZ farmers take on the world without the massive subsidies of yore, and Wellington's inner city – once virtually closed after dark by oppressive licensing laws – now thrives with great bars and restaurants.

As with the economic reforms, the 'Treaty process' of redress and reconciliation with Maori makes some New Zealanders uneasy, more in their uncertainty about its extent than that it has happened at all. A court decision suggesting that some Maori might have unforeseen rights to stretches of the country's seabed and foreshore (not the beaches themselves, but the area from the high tide outwards) hit a raw nerve among some. The assumption had long been that access to the beach was a NZ birthright, although its basis in law proved to be shaky. The conservative National Party, then ailing in opposition, tapped into public unease over this new and unexpected dimension to the Treaty process, claiming the country was moving towards 'separatism' – and shot up in the opinion polls. The Labour government, spooked by the public response, passed a law that confirmed the seabed and foreshore in Crown (public) ownership but offered Maori groups the chance to explore their 'customary rights' to places they had traditionally used.

Many Maori, feeling they had been denied due process, were angry, and a *hikoi* (march) of 15,000 protested at parliament, amid speculation that political allegiances were being re-drawn. The speculation was well founded: the momentum generated by the *hikoi* led directly to the formation of the Maori Party, which now holds five of the seven electorates reserved for Maori (unseating a Labour MP in each). The Maori Party currently has a 'confidence and supply' agreement with the National-led government and, at the time of research, it seems likely that they will win some concessions on the foreshore and seabed issue from their former foes.

For the younger generation, for whom the 1980s are prehistory, political apathy is the norm. Perhaps it's because a decade of progressive government has given them little to kick against – unlike those politicised by the anti–Iraq War movements in the UK, US and Australia. Ironically, as NZ has finally achieved its own interesting, independent cultural sensibility, the country's youth seem more obsessed by US culture than ever.

This is particularly true within the hip-hop scene where a farcical identification with American gangsta culture has developed into a worrying youth gang problem. Even more ridiculous is the epidemic of boy racers, pulling burnouts and street-racing in souped-up V8s.

Despite all the change, key elements of the NZ identity are an unbroken thread, and fortune is still a matter of economics rather than class. If you are well served in a restaurant or shop, it will be out of politeness or pride in the job, rather than servility.

In country areas and on bush walks don't be surprised if you're given a cheery greeting from passers-by, especially in the South Island. In a legacy of the British past, politeness is generally regarded as one of the highest virtues. A 'please' and 'thank you' will get you a long way. The three great exceptions to this rule are: a) on the road, where genteel Dr Jekylls become raging Mr Hydes, especially if you have the misfortune of needing to change lanes; b) if you don't speak English very well; and c) if you are Australian.

The latter two traits are the product of insularity and a smallness of world view that tends to disappear among Kiwis who have travelled (and luckily many do). The NZ/Australian rivalry is taken much more seriously on this side of the Tasman Sea. Although it's very unlikely that Kiwis will be rude outright, visiting Aussies must get pretty sick of the constant ribbing, much of it surprisingly ill-humoured. It's a sad truth that while most Australians would cheer on a NZ sports team if they were playing anyone other than their own, the opposite is true in NZ.

You might on your travels hear the phrase 'number-eight wire' and wonder what on earth it means. It's a catchphrase New Zealanders still repeat to themselves to encapsulate a national myth: that NZ's isolation and its pioneer stock created a culture in which ingenuity allowed problems to be solved and tools to be built from scratch. A NZ farmer, it was said, could solve pretty much any problem with a piece of number-eight wire (the gauge used for fencing on farms).

It's actually largely true – NZ farms are full of NZ inventions. One reason big offshore film and TV producers bring their projects here – apart from the low wages and huge variety of locations – is that they like the can-do attitude and ability to work to a goal of NZ technical crews. Many more New Zealanders have worked as managers, roadies or chefs for famous recording artists (everyone from Led Zeppelin and U2 to Madonna) than have enjoyed the spotlight themselves. Which just goes to show that New Zealanders operate best at the intersection of practicality and creativity, with an endearing (and sometimes infuriating) humility to boot.

LIFESTYLE

Living on an island has its perks, especially in summer. By the middle of the week your average Kiwi office worker is keeping a nervous watch on the weather, praying that the rain will hold off for the weekend so that they can head to the beach, maybe start working on the garden or at least get the kids out of the house for a few hours. Of course, the more gung-ho are already making the most of the long summer evenings – there's Carmen the teacher taking the kayak out fishing after school; and Steven the quantity surveyor with the surfboard in the car, itching to hit the breaks during the last few hours of daylight.

In 2009 NZ topped the Global Peace Index earning the distinction of being rated the world's most peaceful country.

NZ is defined as a state in the Australian constitution. At the time of Australia's federation into one country it was hoped that NZ would join. On this side of the Tasman that idea proved as unpopular then as it does now.

Kiwi inventions include the disposable syringe, nonshortable electric fence, Navman GPS and the child-proof top for pill bottles.

For all the stereotypes of the active healthy Kiwi, other clichés are just as real. Susan's working late at the office. Again. (New Zealanders have among the longest working hours in the developed world.) She'll probably grab some fast food on her way home and, yes, she does want fries with that. (A quarter of NZ adults are obese.) Then there's Dean, hanging around on the street with his other teenage mates, trying to look staunch while sweating into his hoodie. The fact is, there is no one NZ lifestyle.

Most Kiwis (except perhaps the farmers) would probably wish it rained a little less and they got paid a little more, but it sometimes takes a few years travelling on their 'Big OE' (Overseas Experience – a traditional right of passage) before they realise how good they've got it. In a 2009 study of the quality of life in the world's major cities, Auckland was rated fourth-equal and Wellington 12th.

For most of its history, NZ's small population and plentiful land has seen its people live in stand-alone houses on large, green sections. And while that's still the norm, for a number of reasons it has started to change.

In Auckland, concern about suburban sprawl and poor public transport, and the gentrification of once-poor inner-city suburbs, has seen a boom in

> No matter where you are in NZ, you're never more than 128km from the sea.

'SO, WHAT DO YOU THINK OF NEW ZEALAND?' *Russell Brown*

That, by tradition, is the question that visitors, especially important ones, are asked within an hour of disembarking in NZ. Sometimes they might be granted an entire day's research before being asked to pronounce, but asked they are. The question – composed equally of great pride and creeping doubt – is symbolic of the national consciousness.

When George Bernard Shaw visited for four weeks in 1934, he was deluged with what-do-you-think-of questions from newspaper reporters the length of the country. Although he never saw fit to write a word about NZ, his answers to those newspaper questions were collected and reprinted as *What I Saw in New Zealand: the Newspaper Utterances of George Bernard Shaw in New Zealand*. Yes, people really were that keen for vindication.

Other visitors were willing to pronounce in print, including the British Liberal MP, David Goldblatt, who came to NZ to convalesce from a heart attack in 1955, became fascinated with the place and wrote an intriguing and prescient little book called *Democracy At Ease: a New Zealand Profile*.

Goldblatt found New Zealanders a blithe people; kind, prosperous, fond of machines, frequently devoid of theory. In 'a land in which the practice of neighbourliness is most strongly developed' no one went wanting, yet few seemed to aspire. He admired the country's education system and its newspapers, despaired of its tariffs and barriers and wondered at laws that amounted to 'the complete control of the individual by the government'.

He was far from the first visitor to muse about NZ's contradictions – the American academic Leslie Lipson, who weathered the WWII years at Wellington's Victoria University, admired NZ's 'passion for social justice' but fretted about its 'restraint on talent' and 'lack of cultural achievement'.

For the *bon vivant* Goldblatt, the attitude towards food and drink was all too telling. Apart from one visit to a clandestine European-style restaurant in Auckland, where the bottles were hidden under tables, he found only 'the plain fare and even plainer fetch and carry of the normal feeding machine of this country' and shops catering 'in the same pedestrian fashion for a people never fastidious – the same again is the order of the day'.

Thus, a people with access to some of the best fresh ingredients on earth tended to boil everything to death. A nation strewn almost its entire length with excellent microclimates for viticulture produced only fortified plonk. Material comfort was valued, but was a plain thing indeed.

It took New Zealanders a quarter of a century more to shuck 'the same dull sandwiches', and embrace a national awareness – and, as Goldblatt correctly anticipated, it took 'hazards and misfortunes' to spur the 'divine discontent' for change.

But when it did happen, it *really* happened.

Russell Brown is a journalist and manager of the popular Public Address blog site (www.publicaddress.net).

terraced housing and apartments, either in the central city or on its fringes. As immigration-fuelled population growth continues to put pressure on space and prices, more Auckland citizens are learning to do without the birthright of owning their own home – let alone one with a backyard.

'How do you feel about your life as a whole?' In 2009, 86% responded 'satisfied' or 'very satisfied' to a Statistics NZ poll.

Wellington's inner-city boom is slightly different. As the public service has shrunk and large companies have moved their head offices away, old office buildings and warehouses have been converted for apartment living.

At the same time, a parallel trend has seen a rush to the coastlines, and to beautiful areas such as Nelson, at the top of the South Island, where property values have rocketed and orchards have been ploughed under to make way for more housing. In the process, an icon of the Kiwi lifestyle, the bach (pronounced 'batch') – a rough beach house, often passed down through families – has begun to disappear. Many New Zealanders feel this as a loss, especially when the land goes to foreign buyers, and the fear that coastal land is getting beyond the reach of ordinary families is a significant political issue.

The growth in economic inequality in recent decades is a serious problem. In a few poor urban areas such as South Auckland, two or three families may share a single house, with attendant public health problems. A partial return to the public housing policies that created a chunk of the country's current housing stock aims to address this problem.

According to a 2009 survey, the happiest women in the country live in the Bay of Plenty, while the happiest men live in Nelson/Marlborough. Wellingtonians were the least happy.

Family trends, meanwhile, are similar to those in other Western countries: New Zealanders are marrying later (the median age for marriage has increased from just over 20 to over 30 years of age in the last 20 years) or not marrying at all. For those under 25 years of age, de facto unions are now more common than formal marriage, and about a third of all people between the ages of 15 and 44 who are living in partnerships are not legally married. About 21,000 couples still get married every year, and half that many get divorced.

The law extends matrimonial property principles to unmarried couples, including same-sex couples. Despite the obligatory outrage from conservatives, civil unions were introduced in 2005 – creating a new category of union similar to but separate from marriage – with the support of the majority of the population.

ECONOMY

NZ may be a long way away from just about everywhere but it is not immune to the vagaries of the global economy. In the quarter to June 2009 it just edged out of its worst recession in 30 years, following six quarters of negative growth. At the time of research it was uncertain as to whether the recovery would hold.

NZ escaped the worst of the global financial crisis due in part to the strength of its banking sector, which was never exposed to the subprime mortgage crisis that triggered the problem. NZ's Gross Domestic Product (GDP) currently stands at around $128 billion per annum. Unemployment has risen to 6.5% – a nine-year high.

The median annual income is $24,400, and wealth is far less evenly spread than it was 25 years ago – 18% earn more than double that, while 43% survive on less than $20,000. The wealthiest region is Wellington, where one in 20 adults reaps more than $100,000 per annum.

NZ now has the sixth worst gap between rich and poor in the developed world, according to a 2009 UN report.

With regards to wealth, NZ sits 22nd among the 30 OECD countries on a measure of GDP per head in terms of 'purchasing power parity', indicating that its people are nearly a quarter less affluent than those of Australia, or roughly as wealthy as the average South Korean.

Back in the heady post-WWII days, NZ was towards the top of the list, buoyed by strong demand for wool, meat and dairy products. Things changed for the worse in 1973 when the country's preferential arrangements with

Britain ceased after the UK joined the European Economic Community (later the European Union). NZ was forced to find new markets, and now it exports mainly to Australia, the US, Japan and China. The main commodities exported (in order of value) are dairy products, meat, wood, fish and machinery. The country imports a great deal more than it exports (especially consumer and other manufactured goods) leading to a problematic balance of payments.

POPULATION & MULTICULTURALISM

There are an estimated 4.4 million resident New Zealanders, and almost one in three of them live in the largest city, Auckland, where growth has been fuelled both by a long-term drift north and more recent waves of immigration. The general drift to the cities means that urban areas now account for about 86% of the population.

The Maori population was somewhere between 100,000 and 200,000 at the time of first European contact 200 years ago. Disease and warfare subsequently brought the population near to collapse, but a high birth rate now sees about 15% of New Zealanders (565,000 people) identify as Maori, and that proportion is likely to grow.

The implication of the Treaty of Waitangi is one of partnership between Maori and the Crown (representing the New Zealanders who are 'Pakeha', or of British heritage), together forging a bicultural nation. After decades of attempted cultural assimilation it's now accepted in most quarters that the indigenous culture has a special and separate status within the country's ethnic mix. For example, Maori is an official language and there is a separate electoral role granting Maori guaranteed parliamentary seats.

NZ's population would hit 11 million if it were to take in all the people that wanted to settle there, according to Gallup, who rated it third in its 2009 Potential Net Migration Index.

Yet room has had to be found for the many New Zealanders of neither British nor Maori heritage. In each new wave of immigration there has been an unfortunate tendency to demonise before gradually accepting and celebrating what the new cultures have to offer. This happened with the Chinese in the mid-19th century, Croatians at the beginning of the 20th, Pacific Islanders in the 1970s and most recently the Chinese again in the 1990s. That said, NZ society is more integrated and accepting than most. People of all races are represented in all levels of society and race isn't an obstacle to achievement.

Auckland has been the prime destination for ethnic Chinese since immigration rules were relaxed in 1987. While many Asian immigrants have chosen to cluster in Auckland's eastern suburbs, visitors are often surprised by the 'Asianisation' of its central city, where thousands of East Asian students reside, either studying at Auckland University, learning English, or both.

Occasional incidents involving Asians – including some high-profile Asian-on-Asian crimes – have added to disquiet about Asian immigration in some parts of society. But opinion polls indicate that most Aucklanders tend to value the contribution of new migrants. Today, 13% of Aucklanders are of Asian extraction and it's estimated that numbers will reach 400,000 within seven years.

People born in other countries make up 23% of NZ residents. Of these, the main regions of origin are the UK and Ireland (29%), the Pacific Islands (15%), Northeast Asia (15%) and Australia (7%).

About 20% of Auckland Chinese were born in NZ, but considerable attention has been focused on the so-called '1.5 generation': young Chinese born overseas but socialised (and sometimes educated) in NZ. The traditionally quiescent culture of Chinese New Zealanders has been challenged in recent years, and a dynamic group of young ethnic Asians is emerging into leadership roles not only within their own community, but in wider NZ society.

Auckland is easily the most multicultural centre in NZ, with only slightly over half of the population of European descent (as opposed to around 80% in most of the South Island). It is effectively the capital of the South Pacific, with nearly 177,000 people of Pacific Island heritage living there. Pacific Islanders make up about 7% of the nation's population but 14% of Auckland's.

In percentage terms, Auckland is the seventh largest city for people of Chinese origin outside of China.

NZ never had an official 'white' immigration policy as Australia did, but for decades it tended to regard itself as an outpost of Britain. Now it is other influences – NZ's role in the Pacific, its burgeoning economic links to Asia, its offering of sanctuary to refugees – that will continue to shape what it is to be a New Zealander.

SPORT

The arena where Kiwis have most sated their desperation for recognition on the world stage is sport. For most of the 20th century, NZ's All Blacks dominated international rugby union, with one squad even dubbed 'The Invincibles'. Taking over this pastime of the British upper class did wonders for national identity and the game is now interwoven with NZ's history and culture. So when the All Blacks dip out of the Rugby World Cup at semifinal stage (as they have done no fewer than four times in recent tournaments), there is national mourning. Few seem to take solace in (or barely notice) the success of the NZ women's team, the Black Ferns, who have won the last three Women's Rugby World Cups. Below top international level, the Super 14 competition (with teams from Australia and South Africa) offers the world's best rugby, although local purists still prefer the National Provincial Championship (NPC).

For all rugby's influence on the culture, don't go to a game expecting to be caught up in an orgy of noise and cheering. Rugby crowds at Auckland's Eden Park (p124) are as restrained as their teams are cavalier, but they get noisier as you head south. Fans at Canterbury's excellent AMI Stadium (p538) are reputed to be the most one-eyed in the land.

In contrast, a home game for the NZ Warriors rugby league team at Auckland's Mt Smart Stadium (p124) is a thrilling spectacle, especially when the Polynesian drummers kick in. The Warriors are the only NZ team in the Australian NRL (National Rugby League) competition. Rugby League has traditionally been considered the working-class sport and support is strongest from Auckland's Maori, Polynesian and other immigrant communities.

RUGBY WORLD CUP 2011

On September 9, 2011 a burly bunch of men in black jerseys will start slapping their meaty thighs, rolling their eyes back in their heads, poking out their tongues and hurtling a blood-thirsty chant at their opposition. Such is NZ's rugby tradition. An overwhelming majority of the crowd packed into Auckland's Eden Park for the match against Tonga that marks the start of the 7th Rugby World Cup will be hoping and praying that the same ritual will be repeated here on October 23 at the final.

In the interim, 20 teams (divided into four pools of five) will be competing in games held all over the country, from Whangarei in the north to Invercargill in the south. The quarter finals are scheduled for the weekend of October 8 and 9 (in Wellington and Christchurch), with the semifinals in Auckland the following weekend. Expect accommodation to be scarce at these times.

Tickets go on sale to the public in late 2010, with a ballot for tickets for the finals held in early 2011 (see www.rugbyworldcup.com for details). Prices range from as little as $30 (children $15), for pool games featuring the minnows, up to $450 for top seats at All Blacks pool matches. Quarter finals tickets start at $190 and finals from $390.

If you can't nab (or can't afford) a ticket, the main centres are planning public events with big screens to follow the proceedings, particularly Auckland which is considering turning Princes Wharf into 'party central' for the duration. Whether you find yourself cheering on Namibia at a match or you watch all the action from a small-town pub, it's guaranteed to be a fascinating time to visit.

NZ are the current rugby league world champions, taking the trophy from Australia (in Australia) in 2008. Defeating the neighbours in their favourite game brought a smile to the faces of even the strongest supporters of the rival rugby code.

By the time this book is published the All Whites, NZ's national soccer (football) squad will have competed in the 2010 FIFA World Cup, qualifying for the second time in history. Nobody expects them to do as well as the rugby league boys but getting there is a huge achievement for such a rugby-mad nation. Scoring a few goals or (gasp!) winning a game would be the icing on the cake.

Netball is the leading sport for women and the one in which the national team, the Silver Ferns, perpetually vies for world supremacy with the Australians – one or other of the countries has taken the world championship at every contest (except for a tie in 1979). The rivalry has intensified since 2008 when both countries disbanded their national club leagues to start a new trans-Tasman competition featuring five teams from each country.

Cricket is the established summer team sport, and the State Shield (one-day) and State Championship provincial competitions take place alongside international matches involving the national side, the Black Caps, through the summer months. Wellington's Basin Reserve is the last sole-use test cricket venue in the main centres (and only a few minutes' walk from the bars and restaurants of Courtenay Pl) while New Plymouth's Pukekura Park (p255) is simply one of the prettiest cricket grounds in the world.

Other sports in which NZ pushes above its weight include sailing, rowing, canoeing, equestrian and triathlon. The most Olympic medals NZ has won have been in athletics, particularly in track and field events.

New Zealanders not only watch sport, they play it. Many workplaces have social teams or groups of mates get together for a friendly match. The most popular sports for men to participate in are (in order) golf, cricket, tennis, touch football and rugby union. For women it's netball, tennis, golf, touch football and skiing. Other popular active pursuits include kayaking, mountain biking, walking and running.

The first referee in the world to use a whistle to halt a game was William Atack of Christchurch. He thought of this now seemingly obvious and ubiquitous refereeing tool in 1884.

MEDIA

Almost all NZ cities have their own morning newspapers, sometimes coexisting with the Auckland-based *New Zealand Herald* (www.nzherald.co.nz).

The magazine market is more varied, and dominated by independent publishers. The *Listener* (like the *Herald,* owned by Australian company APN) is published weekly and offers TV and radio listings. Auckland's own magazine, *Metro,* is a good-looking guide to the style of the city. *Cuisine* is a sleek, popular and authoritative guide to food and wine.

Free-to-air TV is dominated by the two publicly owned TV New Zealand channels (TV One and TV2), versus the Australian-owned TV3 and its sibling music channel C4. Maori TV is a great source of locally produced programming as well as screening some interesting foreign documentaries and films. Much of it is broadcast in Maori, although subtitles are often added.

Radio Sport carries one of the sounds of the NZ summer: cricket commentaries. The public broadcaster, Radio New Zealand, is based in Wellington: its flagship, National Radio, offers strong news and feature programming and is available nationwide. The network of student stations, the bNet, offers an engaging and adventurous alternative (they're also the best place to hear about local gigs), and the most sophisticated of the stations, Auckland's 95bFM, is influential in its advocacy of new alternative music.

There is also a nationwide network of *iwi* (tribal) stations, some of which, including Waikato's Radio Tainui, offer welcome respite from the commercial

networks – others, such as Auckland's Mai FM, take on the commercial
broadcasters at their own game. Also worth noting are the national Pacific
Island station Niu FM and the dance station George FM, which started from
a bedroom in Auckland's Grey Lynn and can now be heard in 16 towns.

For interesting analysis of the issues of the day and the buzz on the streets
check out the excellent *Public Address* blog site (www.publicaddress.net).
Wellington is well serviced by the *Wellingtonista* (www.wellingtonista.com),
which serves up 'random stuff about NZ's capital city'.

RELIGION

Although the national anthem, 'God Defend New Zealand', is an appeal to
the Almighty, and parliament begins every day with prayers, New Zealanders
are not a particularly pious people – far less so, according to polls, than
Australians. A New Zealander is more likely to be spiritually fulfilled in the
outdoors than in church. The land and sea were spiritual constants in pre-
European Maori culture and they are scarcely less so today.

NZ is predominantly a Christian country (56%), although over a third
of the population claim no religious affiliation at all. The number of people
identifying as Christian has been falling – by 5% between the 2001 and 2006
censuses – although religion remains strong in the Pacific Island community,
where 80% are members of that faith.

Reflecting its English heritage, NZ is nominally Anglican; where religion
has a place in public affairs it will be of that flavour. Yet the Catholic Church
is gaining ground, increasing its numbers by 5% in recent years. Catholicism
now has 508,000 adherents to Anglicanism's 555,000.

Maori spirituality has been fused with Christianity since colonisation in
movements such as Ratana and Ringatu, but is increasingly expressed in
its own right.

Immigrants have brought their faiths with them, but religions such as
Islam, Hinduism, Sikhism, Judaism and Buddhism in total account for less
than 4% of the population.

WOMEN IN NEW ZEALAND

NZ is justifiably proud of being the first country in the world to give women
the vote (in 1893). Kate Sheppard, the hero of the women's suffrage movement, even features on the $10 bill.

Despite that early achievement, the real role for women in public life was
modest for many years. That can hardly be said now. The country has had
two female prime ministers and for a time in 2000 every key constitutional
position was held by a woman, including the attorney general, chief justice,
governor general and head of state – although New Zealanders can't take
credit for choosing Betty Windsor for that role. At the same time a Maori
queen headed the Kingitanga (see the boxed text, p225) and a woman led
NZ's biggest listed corporation.

Glamorous Rotorua-born
Jean Batten, known
as Hine-o-te-Rangi
(Daughter of the Skies),
was a famous pilot and
the most famous New
Zealander of the 1930s.
During a glittering career,
she broke several records
for long-distance solo
flights.

Yet, even with the presence of a Ministry of Women's Affairs, some
benefits have been slow to come to ordinary NZ women: paid parental
leave was only instituted in 2002, for example. As in most other countries,
women's wages tend to be lower than men's, although the gap is closing.
Women are nearly twice as likely to work more than one job and there
are three times more men in the top earnings decile (over $67,000 per
annum) than women.

When NZ women complain that there aren't enough decent men to
go around, they've got a point: there are 104 women for every 100 men.
The man shortage is particularly acute for straight women in their 30s, an
age at which Kiwi blokes are more likely to be living overseas than their

countrywomen. If they do snag a keeper, chances are he'll be older – the median age for brides is 30, while its 33 for bridegrooms.

On the plus side, women live longer: the average life expectancy for women is 82, as opposed to 78 for men.

NZ has shamefully high rates of domestic and child abuse. A 2007 study suggested that as many as a quarter of NZ women had suffered some form of sexual abuse by the time they were 15. The figures were higher for rural women.

ARTS
Literature

A nationalist movement arose in literature in the 1930s, challenging the notion of NZ being an annex of the 'mother country' and striving for an independent identity. Some writers who appeared then – especially the poets Allen Curnow, Denis Glover, ARD Fairburn and RAK Mason – became commanding figures in the definition of a new culture, and were still around in the 1950s to be part of what prominent historian Keith Sinclair (himself a poet) called the time 'when the NZ intellect and imagination came alive'.

Katherine Mansfield's work began a NZ tradition in short fiction, and for years the standard was carried by novelist Janet Frame, whose dramatic life was depicted in Jane Campion's film of her autobiography, *An Angel at My Table*. Her novel *The Carpathians* (1989) won the Commonwealth Writers' Prize. A new era of international recognition began in 1985 when Keri Hulme's haunting *The Bone People* won the Booker Prize (the world is still waiting for the follow-up, *Bait*).

It wasn't until 2007 that another Kiwi looked likely to snag the Booker. Lloyd Jones' *Mister Pip* was pipped at the post, but the nomination rocketed his book up literature charts the world over.

Less recognised internationally, Maurice 'gee-I've-won-a-lot-of-awards' Gee has gained the nation's annual top fiction gong for *Blindsight* (2005), *Live Bodies* (1998), *Going West* (1992), *The Burning Boy* (1990), *Plumb* (1978) and *A Glorious Morning Comrade* (1975). His much-loved children's novel *Under The Mountain* (1979) was made into a seminal NZ TV series in 1981 and then a major motion picture in 2009. In 2004 the adaptation of another of his novels, *In My Father's Den* (1972), won major awards at international film festivals and is one of the country's highest grossing films. His latest novel is *Access Road* (2009).

Some of the most interesting and enjoyable NZ fiction voices belong to Maori writers. Witi Ihimaera's novels give a wonderful insight into small-town Maori life on the East Coast – especially *Bulibasha* (1994) and *The Whale Rider* (1987), which was made into an acclaimed film – while *Nights In The Gardens Of Spain* (1996) casts a similar light on Auckland's gay scene. His most recent novel is *The Trowenna Sea* (2009). Patricia Grace's work is similarly filled with exquisitely told stories of rural *marae*-centred life: try *Mutuwhenua* (1978), *Potiki* (1986) or *Tu* (2004).

Also worth checking out are Elizabeth Knox (*The Vintner's Luck*, 1998; *The Angel's Cut*, 2009), Charlotte Grimshaw (*Opportunity*, 2007) and Emily Perkins (*Novel About My Wife*, 2008).

Cinema & TV

If you first got interested in NZ by watching it on the silver screen, you're in good company. Peter Jackson's NZ-made *Lord of the Rings* (*LOTR*) trilogy was the best thing to happen to NZ tourism since Captain Cook.

Yet NZ cinema is hardly ever easy-going. In his BBC-funded documentary, *Cinema of Unease*, NZ actor Sam Neill described the country's film industry

In 1989 when Penny Jamieson was consecrated as the Bishop of Dunedin she became the world's second ever female Anglican bishop and the first to lead a diocese in her own right.

Witi Ihimaera wrote his novel *The Whale Rider* in a three-week burst in 1987, inspired by his daughters' complaints that he took them to movies with only male heroes.

NEW ZEALAND'S LORD OF THE REELS *Errol Hunt*

Peter Jackson was already a hero to NZ's small film industry before he directed his career-defining *Lord of the Rings* (*LOTR*) trilogy. From his very first film, *Bad Taste* (vomit-eating aliens and exploding sheep; 1987), it was obvious that he was a unique talent. It was followed by *Meet the Feebles* (muppets on acid; 1989) and an even gorier zombie movie, *Braindead* ('I kick ass for the Lord'; 1992). Two slightly-less-bloodstained films – *Heavenly Creatures* (1994) and *The Frighteners* (1996) – preceded the *LOTR* films, while *King Kong* (2005) and *The Lovely Bones* (2009) have followed in the tiny hobbits' giant footsteps.

The effect of the three *LOTR* films on NZ was unparalleled: the country embraced Jackson and his trilogy with a passion. Wellington was renamed Middle-earth for the week of the first film's release in late 2001, a Minister for the *LOTR* was named in the NZ government and Jackson was made a Companion of the New Zealand Order of Merit for his services in the film industry. The frenzy only increased for the second and third films, especially when the world premiere (*world* premiere!) of *The Return of the King* was held in Wellington in December 2003, and of course went on to win a record 11 Oscars.

For rainy-weekend viewing, hit the Jackson DVD back-catalogue and look for the man himself. He stars as both the chainsaw-wielding Derek and Robert the Alien in *Bad Taste*, and has cameos as the undertaker's assistant in *Braindead*, a hobo outside a cinema in *Heavenly Creatures* and a clumsy, chain-wearing biker in *The Frighteners*. In the *LOTR* films, Jackson appears as a belching hobbit outside a pub in *The Fellowship of the Ring*, a stone-throwing Helms Deep defender in *The Two Towers* and a captain of the Corsairs in *The Return of the King*. In *King Kong*, a slimmed-down Jackson plays a biplane machine gunner, while in *The Lovely Bones* he's a customer in the camera store.

as 'uniquely strange and dark', producing bleak, haunted work. One need only watch Lee Tamahore's harrowing *Once Were Warriors* (1994) to see what he means.

Other than 2003's winner *Return of the King, The Piano* is the only NZ movie to be nominated for a Best Picture Oscar. Jane Campion was the first Kiwi nominated as Best Director and Peter Jackson the first to win it.

The *Listener*'s film critic, Philip Matthews, makes a slightly more upbeat observation: 'Between (Niki Caro's) *Whale Rider*, (Christine Jeffs') *Rain* and *Lord of the Rings*, you can extract the qualities that our best films possess. Beyond slick technical accomplishment, all share a kind of land-mysticism, an innately supernatural sensibility'.

You could add to this list Jane Campion's *The Piano* (1993), Brad McGann's *In My Father's Den* (2004), James Napier-Roberston's *I'm Not Harry Jenson* (2009) and Jackson's *Heavenly Creatures* (1994) – all of which use magically lush scenery to couch disturbing violence. It's a land-mysticism constantly bordering on the creepy.

Even when Kiwis do humour it's as resolutely black as their rugby jerseys. Check out Jackson's early splatter-fests (see the boxed text, above), Taika Cohen's oddball loser-palooza *Eagle vs Shark* (2007) and Jonathan King's sickly hilarious *Black Sheep* (2006) – 'get ready for the violence of the lambs'. Exporting NZ comedy hasn't been easy, yet the HBO-produced TV musical parody *Flight of the Conchords* – featuring a mumbling, bumbling Kiwi folk-singing duo trying to get a break in New York – has found surprising international success, particularly in the supposed irony-free zone that is the US.

The only Kiwi actors to have won an Oscar are Anna Paquin (for *The Piano*) and Russell Crowe (for *Gladiator*). Paquin was born in Canada but moved to NZ when she was four, while Crowe moved from NZ to Australia at the same age.

New Zealanders have gone from never seeing themselves in international cinema to having whole cloned armies of Temuera Morrisons invading the universe in *Star Wars*. Familiar faces such as Cliff Curtis and Karl Urban seem to constantly pop up playing Mexican or Russian gangsters in action movies. Many of them got their start in long-running soap opera *Shortland St* (7pm weekdays, TV2).

Other local shows worth catching are *Outrageous Fortune*, a rough-edged comedy-drama set in West Auckland, and *bro'Town*, a better-drawn

Polynesian version of *South Park*. It's the Polynesian giggle-factor that seems likeliest to break down the bleak house of NZ cinema. The *bro'Town* boys (who also do stand-up comedy as the Naked Samoans) hit the big screen with the feel-good-through-and-through *Sione's Wedding* in 2006 – with the second-biggest local takings of any NZ film.

While another *LOTR*-style blockbuster has proved illusive, the NZ film industry has quietly continued producing well-crafted, affecting movies such as *Dean Spanley* (2008), *The Strength Of Water* (2009), *The Topp Twins: Untouchable Girls* (people's choice documentary winner at the Toronto and Melbourne film festivals, 2009) and *The Lovely Bones* (2009).

Music   Gareth Shute

New Zealand music began with the early forms of *waiata* (singing) developed by Maori following their arrival in the country. The main musical instruments were wind instruments made of bone or wood, the most well-known of which is the *nguru* (commonly known as the 'nose flute'), while percussion was provided by chest- and thigh-slapping. These days, the liveliest place to see Maori music being performed is at Kapa Haka competitions (see p689), in which groups compete with their own routines of traditional song and dance. In a similar vein is the Pasifika Festival (p113) in Auckland, which has sections that represent each of the Pacific Islands. It is a great place to see both traditional and modern forms of Polynesian music, whether that means modern hip-hop beats or throbbing Cook Island drums, or island-style guitar, ukulele, and slide guitar.

European music first arrived in New Zealand with immigrants from Europe, and steadily developed local variants over the early 1900s. In the 1950s Douglas Lilburn became one of the first internationally recognised NZ classical composers. More recently the country has produced a number of world-renowned musicians in this field, including opera singer Dame Kiri Te Kanawa, million-selling pop diva Hayley Westenra, composer John Psathas (who composed music for the 2004 Olympic Games) and composer/percussionist Gareth Farr (who also performs in drag under the name, Lilith). Each of the main universities in New Zealand runs its own music school and these often have free concerts which visitors can attend. More large scale performances are held at various venues within the Edge conglomerate of venues in Auckland (p124), the Town Hall/Michael Fowler Centre in Wellington (p414), and the Town Hall in Christchurch (p537).

New Zealand also has a strong rock music scene, its most acclaimed exports being the revered indie label Flying Nun and the music of the Finn Brothers (p50). In 1981 Flying Nun was started by Christchurch record store owner, Roger Shepherd. Many of the early groups came from Dunedin, where local

Gareth Shute is the author of four books, including *Hip Hop Music In Aotearoa* and *NZ Rock 1987–2007*. He is also a musician and has toured the UK, Europe, and Australia as a member of The Ruby Suns and The Brunettes. He now plays in The Conjurors and The Cosbys.

A wide range of cultural events are listed on www.nzlive.com – this is a good place to find out about Kapa Haka performances.

MIDDLE-EARTH TOURISM

If you are one of those travellers inspired to come down under by the scenery of the *LOTR* movies, you won't be disappointed. Jackson's decision to film in NZ wasn't mere patriotism. Nowhere else on earth will you find such wildly varied, unspoiled landscapes.

You will doubtless recognise some places from the films. For example, Hobbiton (near Matamata; p238), Mt Doom (instantly recognisable as towering Ngauruhoe; p307) or the Misty Mountains (the South Island's Southern Alps). The visitor information centres in Wellington, Twizel or Queenstown should be able to direct you to local *LOTR* sites of interest. If you're serious about finding the exact spots where scenes were filmed, buy a copy of Ian Brodie's nerdtastic *The Lord of the Rings: Location Guidebook*, which includes instructions, and even GPS coordinates, for finding all the important scenes.

Concerts and classical music recitals can be found at www.event finder.co.nz. For more specific information on the NZ classical music scene, see: www.sounz .org.nz.

musicians took the do-it-yourself attitude of punk but used it to produce a lo-fi indie-pop which received rave reviews from the likes of *NME* in the UK and *Rolling Stone* magazine in the US. *Billboard* even claimed in 1989: 'There doesn't seem to be anything on Flying Nun Records that is less than excellent.' Many of the musicians from the Flying Nun scene still perform live to this day, including David Kilgour (from The Clean), Martin Phillipps (from The Chills), and Shayne Carter (from the Straitjacket Fits, now fronting Dimmer). Chick's Hotel (p584) in Port Chalmers (near Dunedin) and the Dux De Lux (p536) in Christchurch (and during the winter, its sister bar in Queenstown – see p623) continue to be home to a flourishing indie-rock scene. Also recommended is Wunderbar (p542) in Lyttelton (near Christchurch) which is a rustic venue with a fantastic hillside view of the harbour below.

Flying Nun was recently bought back by its original owner, Roger Shepherd, and continues to release exciting new acts such as The Mint Chicks. Other young indie labels have also sprung up in the meantime including Lil Chief Records and Arch Hill Recordings. For more adventurous listeners, Bruce Russell continues to play in influential underground group The Dead C, and releases music through his Corpus Hermeticum label.

Since the new millennium, the NZ music scene has developed a new vitality after the government convinced commercial radio stations in the country to adopt a voluntary quota of 20% local music. This has enabled the more commercially orientated musicians to have solid careers. Rock groups such as Shihad, The Feelers, and Op-shop have thrived in this environment, as have a set of soulful female solo artists (who all happen to have Maori heritage): Bic Runga, Anika Moa, and Brooke Fraser (daughter of All Black, Bernie Fraser).

One of the most complete listings of NZ bands that have existed over the last couple of decades is available at www .muzic.net.nz. A thriving community of bloggers also discuss local music at www.nzmusic.com.

However, the genres of music that have been adopted most enthusiastically by Maori and Polynesian New Zealanders have been reggae (in the 1970s) and hip hop (in 1980s), which has led to distinct local variants of these musical styles. In Wellington, a thriving jazz scene took on a reggae influence to create a host of groups that blend dub, roots, and funky jazz – most notably Fat Freddy's Drop. Most of the venues for this music can be found

THE BROTHERS FINN

There are certain tunes that all Kiwis can sing along to, given a beer and the opportunity. The music of Tim and Neil Finn makes up a good proportion of these, and many of their songs have gone on to be international hits.

Tim Finn first came to prominence in late-70s group, Split Enz. When their original guitarist quit, Neil flew over to join the band in the UK despite being only 15 at the time. Split Enz amassed a solid following in Australia, New Zealand, and Canada before disbanding in 1985. Neil then formed Crowded House with two Australian musicians (Paul Hester and Nick Seymour) and one of their early singles, 'Don't Dream It's Over' went on to hit number two on the US charts. Tim later did a brief spell in the band, during which the brothers wrote 'Weather With You' – a song which reached number seven on the UK charts, pushing their album *Woodface* to gold sales. The original line-up of Crowded House played their final show in 1996, in front of 100,000 people on the steps of the Sydney Opera House (though Finn and Seymour reformed the group briefly in 2007 and continue to tour and record occasionally). Tim and Neil have both released a number of solo albums, as well as combining for the occasional album as the Finn Brothers.

More recently, Tim's solo career was reinvigorated when one of his songs was picked up for the movie *The Chronicles of Narnia: The Lion, the Witch & the Wardrobe*. Neil has also remained busy, organising a set of shows/releases under the name Seven Worlds Collide, which is a collaboration with well-known overseas musicians, including Jeff Tweedy (Wilco), Johnny Marr (The Smiths), and members of Radiohead. Both Tim and Neil were born in the small town of Te Awamutu and the local museum has a collection that documents their work (p233).

ICONIC NEW ZEALAND SONGS

Listed below are 20 songs that any self-respecting Kiwi is bound to know. If you'd like a local soundtrack for your NZ visit, then you might consider downloading the following 20 songs (legally of course) to your MP3 player either via i-Tunes or through www.amplifier.co.nz, which specialises in NZ music downloads. Alternatively, you may wish to search out the collection, *The Great New Zealand Songbook,* or the series of *Nature's Best* compilations.

Bic Runga (1997) Sway	**Hello Sailor** (1977) Blue Lady
Che Fu and DLT (1996) Chains	**John Rowles** (1970) Cheryl Moana Marie
The Chills (1991) Heavenly Pop Hit	**Kiri Te Kanawa** (this version, 1999) Pokarekare Ana
Chris Knox (1990) Not Given Lightly	**Ladyhawke** (2009) Magic
The Clean (1981) Tally Ho	**Savage** (2008) Swing
Crowded House (1986) Don't Dream it's Over	**Scribe** (2003) Not Many
David Dobbyn with Herbs (1986) Slice of Heaven	**Shihad** (1997) Home Again
Dragon (1978) April Sun in Cuba	**Split Enz** (1982) Six Months in a Leaky Boat
The Exponents (1991) Why Does Love Do This to Me?	**Straitjacket Fits** (1987) She Speeds
Fourmyula (1969) Nature	**The Swingers** (1981) Counting the Beat

along Courtenay Place or between the shops on Cuba Mall (see p413). The national public holiday, Waitangi Day, on February 6th also happens to fall on the birthday of Bob Marley and yearly reggae concerts are held on this day in Auckland and Wellington.

The local hip-hop scene has its heart in the suburbs of South Auckland, which have a high concentration of Maori and Pacific Island residents. This area is home to one of New Zealand's foremost hip-hop labels, Dawn Raid, which takes its name from the infamous early-morning house raids of the 1970s that police performed on Pacific Islanders who outstayed their visas. Dawn Raid's most successful artist is Savage, who sold a million copies of his single 'Swing' after it was featured in the movie, *Knocked Up*. Within New Zealand, the most well-known hip-hop acts are Scribe, Che Fu, and Smashproof (who broke the record for the longest running single at number one). Hip-hop shows in Auckland are held at a wide range of venues, though popular favourites are 4:20 and Rising Sun (p124) and funk-fuelled club, Khuja Lounge (p124).

Early in the new millennium, New Zealand became known as a home for garage rock after the international rise of two local acts: the Datsuns and the D4. In Auckland the main venues for rock music are the Kings Arms (p123) and Cassette Number Nine (p124), though two joint venues in St Kevins Arcade (off Karangahape Rd) are also popular – the Wine Cellar/Whammy Bar (p123). Wellington is also rife with live music venues from Mighty Mighty (p412), to the San Francisco Bath House (p414), to Bodega (p414).

Dance music had its strongest following in Christchurch in the 1990s, when it gave rise to the popular dub/electronica outfit, Salmonella Dub. Drum 'n' bass remains popular locally and has spawned internationally successful acts such as Concord Dawn and Shapeshifter.

In summer, many of the beachfront towns throughout the country are visited by touring bands (winery shows are also popular). One venue of note in this respect is the Leigh Sawmill Café (p149) in Leigh (85km from Auckland), which also offers accommodation and is located near the popular scuba-diving/snorkelling spot at Goat Island.

A number of festivals also take place over the summer months, including the local leg of the Big Day Out (p112), new year's celebration Rhythm & Vines (p370), and the Christian-rock festival, Parachute (www.parachutemusic.com),

An up-to-date list of gigs in the main centres is listed at www.groove guide.co.nz. For those interested in indie rock, a great source of information is www.cheese ontoast.co.nz, which lists gigs and has interviews/photographs of bands (both local and international).

The TV show, *Popstars*, originated in New Zealand though the resulting group, True Bliss, was short-lived. The series concept was then picked up in Australia, the UK, and the US, before inspiring the *Idol* series.

How Bizarre was a massive hit in Europe, the UK, the US, and Australia during 1996. The song was by OMC – an acronym for 'Otara Millionaire's Club', which made light of OMC's poverty-stricken home suburb of Otara.

in January (held near Wellington). Also recommended is the underground festival held early each year by A Low Hum (www.alowhum.com). Lovers of world music may enjoy the local version of Womad (p257), which is held in New Plymouth and features both local and overseas acts that draw from traditional music forms.

Visual Arts

The NZ 'can do' attitude extends to the visual arts. If you're visiting a local's home don't be surprised to find one of the owner's paintings on the wall or one of their mate's sculptures in the back garden, pieced together out of bits of shell, driftwood and a length of the magical 'number-eight wire'.

This is symptomatic of a flourishing local art and crafts scene cultivated by lively tertiary courses churning out traditional carvers and weavers, jewellery makers, multimedia boffins, and moulders of metal and glass. The larger cities have excellent dealer galleries representing interesting local artists working across all mediums.

Not all the best galleries are in Auckland or Wellington. The energetic Govett-Brewster Art Gallery (p254) – home to the legacy of sculptor and film-maker Len Lye – is worth a visit to New Plymouth in itself, and Gore's Eastern Southland Gallery (p666) has an important and growing collection of works by Ralph Hotere, Rita Angus and others.

Traditional Maori art has a distinctive visual style with well-developed motifs that have been embraced by NZ artists of every race. In the painting medium, these include the cool modernism of the work of Gordon Walters and the more controversial pop-art approach of Dick Frizzell's *Tiki* series. Likewise, Pacific Island themes are common, particularly in Auckland. An example is the work of Niuean-born Auckland-raised John Pule, who is also a poet and novelist.

It should not be surprising that in a nation so defined by its natural environment, landscape painting constituted the first post-European body of art. John Gully and Petrus van der Velden were among those to arrive and paint memorable (if sometimes overdramatised) depictions of the land.

A little later, Charles Frederick Goldie painted a series of compelling, realist portraits of Maori, who were feared to be a dying race. Debate over the political propriety of Goldie's work raged for years, but its value is widely accepted now: not least because Maori themselves generally acknowledge and value them as ancestral representations.

Rita Angus' 1936 work *Cass* was voted the country's greatest painting in a 2006 poll. It hangs at the Christchurch Art Gallery.

From the 1930s NZ art took a more modern direction and produced some of the country's most celebrated artists including Rita Angus, Toss Woollaston and Colin McCahon. McCahon is widely regarded to have been the country's most important artist. His paintings might seem inscrutable, even forbidding, but, even where McCahon lurched into Catholic mysticism or quoted screeds from the Bible, his spirituality was rooted in geography. His bleak, brooding landscapes evoke the sheer power of NZ's terrain. The influence of his dramatic, simple canvasses can be seen in the work of celebrated current artists, such as Ralph Hotere and Shane Cotton.

Maori Culture John Huria

'Maori' once just meant 'common' or 'everyday', but now it means…let's just begin this chapter by saying that there is a lot of 'then' and a lot of 'now' in the Maori world. Sometimes the cultural present follows on from the past quite seamlessly; sometimes things have changed hugely; sometimes we just want to look to the future.

Maori today are a diverse people. Some are engaged with traditional cultural networks and pursuits; others are occupied with adapting tradition and placing it into a dialogue with globalising culture. The Maori concept of *whanaungatanga* – family relationships – is important to the culture. And families spread out from the *whanau* (extended family) to the *hapu* (subtribe) and *iwi* (tribe) and even, in a sense, beyond the human world and into the natural and spiritual worlds.

Maori are New Zealand's *tangata whenua* (people of the land), and the Maori relationship with the land has developed over hundreds of years of occupation. Once a predominantly rural people, many Maori now live in urban centres, away from their traditional home base. But it's still common practice in formal settings to introduce oneself by referring to home: an ancestral mountain, river, sea or lake, or an ancestor. There's no place like home, but it's good to be away as well.

If you're looking for a Maori experience in NZ you'll find it – in performance, in conversation, in an art gallery, on a tour…

MAORI THEN

Some three millennia ago people began moving eastwards into the Pacific, sailing against the prevailing winds and currents (hard to go out, easier to return safely). Some stopped at Tonga and Samoa, and others settled the small central East Polynesian tropical islands.

The Maori colonisation of Aotearoa began from an original homeland known to Maori as Hawaiki. Skilled navigators and sailors travelled across the Pacific, using many navigational tools – currents, winds, stars, birds and wave patterns – to guide their large, double-hulled ocean-going craft to a new land. The first of many was the great navigator Kupe who arrived, the story goes, chasing an octopus named Muturangi. But the distinction of giving NZ its well-known Maori name – Aotearoa – goes to his wife, Kuramarotini, who cried out, '*He ao, he ao tea, he ao tea roa!*' (A cloud, a white cloud, a long white cloud!).

Kupe and his crew journeyed around the land, and many places around Cook Strait (between the North and South Islands) and the Hokianga in Northland still bear the names that they gave them and the marks of his passage. Kupe returned to Hawaiki, leaving from (and naming) Northland's Hokianga. He gave other seafarers valuable navigational information. And then the great *waka* (ocean-going craft) began to arrive.

The *waka* that the first setters arrived on, and their landing places, are immortalised in tribal histories. Well-known *waka* include *Takitimu, Kurahaupo, Te Arawa, Mataatua, Tainui, Aotea* and *Tokomaru*. There are many others. Maori trace their genealogies back to those who arrived on the *waka* (and further back as well).

What would it have been like making the transition from small tropical islands to a much larger, cooler land mass? Goodbye breadfruit, coconuts, paper mulberry; hello moa, fernroot, flax – and immense space (relatively speaking). NZ has over 15,000km of coastline. Rarotonga, by way of contrast,

John Huria (Ngai Tahu, Muaupoko) has an editorial, research and writing background with a focus on Maori writing and culture. He was senior editor for Maori publishing company Huia (NZ) and now runs an editorial and publishing services company, Ahi Text Solutions Ltd (www.ahitextsolutions.co.nz).

Kupe's passage is marked around NZ: he left his sails (Nga Ra o Kupe) near Cape Palliser as triangular landforms; he named the two islands in Wellington Harbour Matiu and Makoro after his daughters; his blood stains the red rocks of Wellington's south coast.

Arriving for the first time in NZ, two crew members of *Tainui* saw the red flowers of the pohutu-kawa tree, and they cast away their prized red feather ornaments, thinking that there were plenty to be had on shore.

has a little over 30. There was land, lots of it, and a flora and fauna that had developed more or less separately from the rest of the world for 80 million years. There was an untouched, massive fishery. There were great seaside mammalian convenience stores – seals and sea lions – as well as a fabulous array of birds.

The early settlers went on the move, pulled by love, by trade opportunities and greater resources; pushed by disputes and threats to security. When they settled, Maori established *mana whenua* (regional authority), whether by military campaigns, or by the peaceful methods of intermarriage and diplomacy. Looking over tribal history it's possible to see the many alliances, absorptions and extinctions that went on.

Histories were carried by the voice, in stories, songs and chants. Great stress was placed on accurate learning – after all, in an oral culture where people are the libraries, the past is always a generation or two away from oblivion.

Maori lived in *kainga*, small villages, which often had associated gardens. Housing was quite cosy by modern standards – often it was hard to stand upright while inside. From time to time people would leave their home base and go to harvest seasonal foods. When peaceful life was interrupted by conflict, the people would withdraw to *pa*, fortified dwelling places.

And then Europeans began to arrive (see p30).

> Maori legends are all around you as you tour NZ: Maui's *waka* became today's Southern Alps; a *taniwha* formed Lake Waikaremoana in its death throes; and a rejected Mt Taranaki walked into exile from the central North Island mountain group, carving the Whanganui River.

MAORI TODAY

Today's culture is marked by new developments in the arts, business, sport and politics. Many historical grievances still stand, but some *iwi* (Ngai Tahu and Tainui, for example) have settled historical grievances and are major forces in the NZ economy. Maori have also addressed the decline in Maori language use by establishing *kohanga reo, kura kaupapa Maori* and *wananga* (Maori-medium preschools, schools and universities). There is now a generation of people who speak Maori as a first language. There is a network of Maori radio stations, and Maori TV is attracting a committed viewership. A recently

---

HOW THE WORLD BEGAN

In the Maori story of creation, first there was the void, then the night, then Rangi-nui and Papa-tu-a-nuku (sky father and earth mother) came into being, embracing with their children nurtured between them. But nurturing became something else. Their children were stifled in the darkness of their embrace. Unable to stretch out to their full dimensions and struggling to see clearly in the darkness, their children tried to separate them. Tawhiri-matea, the god of winds, raged against them; Tu-mata-uenga, the god of war, assaulted them. Each god child in turn tried to separate them, but still Rangi and Papa pressed against each other. And then Tane-mahuta, god of the great forests and of humanity, placed his feet against his father and his back against his mother and slowly, inexorably, began to move them apart. Then came the world of light, of demigods and humanity.

In this world of light Maui, the demigod ancestor, was cast out to sea at birth and was found floating in his mother's topknot. He was a shape-shifter, becoming a pigeon or a dog or an eel if it suited his purposes. He stole fire from the gods. Using his grandmother's jawbone, he bashed the sun so that it could only limp slowly across the sky, so that people would have enough time during the day to get things done (if only he would do it again!). Using the South Island as a canoe, he used the jawbone as a hook to fish up Te Ika a Maui (the fish of Maui) – the North Island. And, finally, he met his end trying to defeat death itself. The goddess of death, Hine Nui Te Po, had obsidian teeth in her vagina (obsidian is a volcanic glass that takes a razor edge when chipped). Maui attempted to reverse birth (and hence defeat death) by crawling into her birth canal to reach her heart as she slept. A small bird – a fantail – laughed at the absurd sight. Hine Nui Te Po awoke, and crushed Maui between her thighs. Death one, humanity nil.

revived Maori event is becoming more and more prominent – Matariki, or Maori New Year. The constellation Matariki is also known as the Pleiades. It begins to rise above the horizon in late May or early June and its appearance traditionally signals a time for learning, planning and preparing as well as singing, dancing and celebrating. Watch out for talks and lectures, concerts, dinners, and even formal balls.

RELIGION

Christian churches and denominations are important in the Maori world: televangelists, mainstream churches for regular and occasional worship, and two major Maori churches (Ringatu and Ratana) – we've got it all.

You can check out a map that shows *iwi* distribution and a good list of *iwi* websites on Wikipedia (www.wikipedia.org).

But in the (non-Judaeo Christian) beginning there were the *atua Maori*, the Maori gods, and for many Maori the gods are a vital and relevant force still. It is common to greet the earth mother and sky father when speaking formally at a *marae*. The gods are represented in art and carving, sung of in *waiata* (songs), invoked through *karakia* (prayer and incantation) when a meeting house is opened, when a *waka* is launched, even (more simply) when a meal is served. They are spoken of on the *marae* and in wider Maori contexts. The traditional Maori creation story is well known and widely celebrated (see the boxed text, opposite).

THE ARTS

There are many collections of Maori *taonga* (treasures) around the country. Some of the largest and most comprehensive are at Wellington's Te Papa Museum (p403) and the Auckland Museum (p98). Canterbury Museum (p525) in Christchurch also has a good collection, and Hokitika's West Coast Historical Museum (p500) has an exhibition showing the story of *pounamu* (nephrite jade, or greenstone).

Depending on area, the *powhiri* has gender roles: women *karanga* (call), men *whaikorero* (orate); women lead the way on to the *marae*, men sit on the *paepae* (the speakers' bench at the front). In a modern context, the debate around these roles continues.

You can stay up to date with what is happening in the Maori arts by reading *Mana* magazine (available from most newsagents), listening to *iwi* stations (www.irirangi.net) or weekly podcasts from Radio New Zealand (www.radionz.co.nz/genre/maori,pacific). Maori TV also has regular features on the Maori arts – check out www.maoritelevision.com.

Maori TV went to air in 2004, an emotional time for many Maori who could at last see their culture, their concerns and their language in a mass medium. Over 90% of content is NZ made, and programs are in both Maori and English: they're subtitled and accessible to everyone. If you want to really get a feel for the rhythm and metre of spoken Maori from the comfort of your own chair, switch to Te Reo, a Maori-language-only channel.

Ta Moko

Ta moko is the Maori art of tattoo, traditionally worn by men on their faces, thighs and buttocks, and by women on their chins and lips. *Moko* were permanent grooves tapped into the skin using pigment (made from burnt caterpillar or kauri gum soot), and bone chisels: fine, sharp combs for broad work, and straight blades for detailed work. Museums in the major centres – Auckland, Wellington and Christchurch – all display traditional implements for *ta moko*.

See Ngahuia Te Awekotuku's *Mau Moko: The World of Maori Tattoo* (2007) for the big picture, with powerful, beautiful images and an incisive commentary.

The modern tattooist's gun is common now, but bone chisels are coming back into use for Maori who want to reconnect with tradition. Since the general renaissance in Maori culture in the 1960s, many artists have taken up *ta moko* and now many Maori wear *moko* with quiet pride and humility.

Can visitors get involved, or even get some work done? The term *kirituhi* (skin inscriptions) has arisen to describe Maori motif-inspired modern tattoos that non-Maori can wear. If you'd like to experience *ta moko*, or even get *kirituhi*, your first stop is www.tamoko.org.nz. This website has articles, galleries and links to artists within NZ.

Carving

Traditional Maori carving, with its intricate detailing and curved lines, can transport the viewer. It's quite amazing to consider that it was done with stone tools, themselves painstakingly made, until the advent of iron (nails suddenly became very popular).

Some major traditional forms are *waka* (canoes), *pataka* (storage buildings), and *wharenui* (meeting houses). You can see sublime examples of traditional carving at Te Papa (p403) in Wellington, and at the following:

Auckland Museum (p98) Maori Court.

Hell's Gate (p336) Carver in action every day; near Rotorua

Otago Museum (p575) Nice old *waka* and *whare runanga* (meeting house) carvings, Dunedin.

Parihaka (p266) Historic site on Surf Highway 45, Taranaki.

Putiki Church (p271) Interior covered in carvings and *tukutuku* (wall panels), Whanganui.

Taupo Museum & Art Gallery (p291) Carved meeting house.

Te Manawa (p281) Museum with a Maori focus, Palmerston North.

Waikato Museum (p225) Beautifully carved *waka taua* (war canoe), Hamilton.

Wairakei Terraces Taupo (p299) Carved meeting house.

Waitangi Treaty Grounds (p168) *Whare runanga* and *waka taua*.

Whakarewarewa Thermal Village (p322) The 'living village' – carving, other arts, meeting house and performance, Rotorua.

Whanganui Regional Museum (p271) Wonderful carved *waka*, Whanganui.

The apex of carving today is the *whare whakairo* (carved meeting house). A commissioning group relates its history and ancestral stories to a carver, who then draws (sometimes quite loosely) on traditional motifs to interpret or embody the stories and ancestors in wood or composite fibreboard.

Rongomaraeroa Marae, by artist Cliff Whiting, at Te Papa in Wellington is a colourful example of a contemporary re-imagining of a traditional art form. The biggest change in carving (as with most traditional arts) has been in the use of new mediums and tools. Rangi Kipa uses a synthetic polymer called Corian to make his *hei tiki*, the same stuff that is used to make kitchen benchtops. You can check out his gallery at www.rangikipa.com.

Weaving

For information on Maori arts today, check out Toi Maori www.maoriart.org.nz.

Weaving was an essential art that provided clothing, nets and cordage, footwear for rough country travel, mats to cover earthen floors, and *kete* (bags) to carry stuff in. Many woven items are beautiful as well as practical. Some were major works – *korowai* (cloaks) could take years to finish. Woven predominantly with flax and bird feathers, they are worn now on ceremonial occasions, a stunning sight.

Working with natural materials for the greater good of the people involved getting things right by maintaining the supply of raw material and ensuring that it worked as it was meant to. Protocols were necessary, and women were dedicated to weaving under the aegis of the gods. Today, tradition is greatly respected, but not all traditions are necessarily followed.

CONNECTION WITH THE LAND

The best way to learn about the relationship between the land and the *tangata whenua* is to get out there and start talking with Maori. See the Maori New Zealand boxed texts in individual chapters for recommendations on Maori experiences in each area.

Flax was (and still is) the preferred medium for weaving. To get a strong fibre from flax leaves, weavers scraped away the leaves' flesh with a mussel shell, then pounded until it was soft, dyed it, then dried it. But contemporary weavers are using everything in their work: raffia, copper wire, rubber – even polar fleece and garden hoses!

The best place to experience weaving is to contact one of the many weavers running workshops. By learning the art, you'll appreciate the examples of weaving in museums even more. And if you want your own? Woven *kete* and backpacks have become fashion accessories and are on sale in most cities. Weaving is also found in dealer art galleries around the country.

Haka

Experiencing *haka* can get the adrenaline flowing, as it did for one Pakeha observer in 1929 who thought of dark Satanic mills: 'They looked like fiends from hell wound up by machinery'. *Haka* can be awe-inspiring; it can also be uplifting. The *haka* is not only a war dance – it is used to welcome visitors, honour achievement, express identity or to put forth very strong opinions.

Haka involves chanted words, vigorous body movements, and *pukana* (when performers distort their faces, eyes bulging with the whites showing, perhaps with tongue extended).

The well-known *haka* 'Ka Mate', performed by the All Blacks before rugby test matches, is credited to the cunning fighting chief Te Rauparaha. It celebrates his escape from death. Chased by enemies, he hid himself in a food pit. After they had left, a friendly chief named Te Whareangi (the 'hairy man' referred to in the *haka*), let him out; he climbed out into the sunshine and performed 'Ka Mate'.

You can experience *haka* at various cultural performances including at Mitai Maori Village (p323), Tamaki Maori Village (p323), Te Puia (p321) and Whakarewarewa Thermal Village (p322) in Rotorua; Katoro Waka Heritage Tours (p527) and Ko Tane (p526) in Christchurch; Maori Tours (p452) in Kaikoura; and Myths & Legends Eco-tours (p436) in Picton.

But the best displays of *haka* are at the national Te Matatini National Kapa Haka Festival (www.tematatini.org.nz), when NZ's top groups compete. It is held every two years, with the next festival in February 2011 in Gisborne.

Contemporary Visual Art

A distinctive feature of Maori visual art is the tension between traditional Maori ideas and modern artistic mediums and trends. Shane Cotton produced a series of works that conversed with 19th-century painted meeting houses, which themselves departed from Maori carved houses. Kelcy Taratoa uses toys, superheroes and pop urban imagery alongside weaving and carving design.

Of course not all Maori artists use Maori motifs. Ralph Hotere is a major NZ artist who 'happens to be Maori' (his words), and his career-long exploration of black speaks more to modernism than the traditional *marae* context.

Contemporary Maori art is by no means only about painting. Many other artists use installations as the preferred medium – look out for work by Jacqueline Fraser and Peter Robinson.

There are some great permanent exhibitions of Maori visual arts in the major centres. Both the Auckland and Christchurch Art Galleries hold strong collections, as does Wellington's Te Papa.

Contemporary Theatre

The 1970s saw the emergence of many Maori playwrights and plays, and theatre is a strong area of the Maori arts today. Maori theatre drew heavily on

Before you go touring NZ, pick up a Manaaki Card. This little beauty of a card will get you discounts at most Maori-operated tourist attractions. It also doubles as a phone card. See www.manaaki.co.nz.

See Hirini Moko Mead's *Tikanga Maori*, Pat and Hiwi Tauroa's *Visiting a Marae*, and Anne Salmond's *Hui* for detailed information on Maori customs.

the traditions of the *marae*. Instead of dimming the lights and immediately beginning the performance, many Maori theatre groups began with a stylised *powhiri* (see above), had space for audience members to respond to the play, and ended with a *karakia* (blessing or prayer) or a farewell.

Taki Rua is an independent producer of Maori work for both children and adults and has been in existence for over 25 years. As well as staging its shows in the major centres, it also tours most of its work – check out its website (www.takirua.co.nz) for the current offerings. Maori drama is also often showcased at the professional theatres in the main centres as well as the biennial New Zealand International Festival. Hone Kouka and Briar

VISITING MARAE

As you travel around NZ, you will see many *marae* complexes. Often *marae* are owned by a descent group. They are also owned by urban Maori groups, schools, universities and church groups, and they should only be visited by arrangement with the owners. Some *marae* that may be visited include: Huria Marae (p340) in Tauranga; Koriniti Marae on the Whanganui River Rd (p280); Pipitea Marae in Wellington (p399); and Te Papa Museum Marae in Wellington (p403).

Marae complexes include a *wharenui* (meeting house), which often embodies an ancestor. Its ridge is the backbone, the rafters are ribs, and it shelters the descendants. There is a clear space in front of the *wharenui* (ie the *marae atea*). Sometimes there are other buildings: a *wharekai* (dining hall); a toilet and shower block; perhaps even classrooms, play equipment and the like.

Hui (gatherings) are held at *marae*. Issues are discussed, classes conducted, milestones celebrated and the dead farewelled. Te reo Maori (the Maori language) is prominent, sometimes exclusively so.

Visitors sleep in the meeting house if a *hui* goes on for longer than a day. Mattresses are placed on the floor, someone may bring a guitar, and stories and jokes always go down well as the evening stretches out…

The Powhiri

If you visit a *marae* as part of an organised group, you'll be welcomed in a *powhiri*. The more common ones are outlined here.

There may be a *wero* (challenge). Using *taiaha* (quarter-staff) moves a warrior will approach the visitors and place a baton on the ground for a visitor to pick up.

There is a *karanga* (ceremonial call). A woman from the host group calls to the visitors and a woman from the visitors responds. Their long, high, falling calls begin to overlap and interweave and the visiting group walks on to the *marae atea*. It is then time for *whaikorero* (speechmaking). The hosts welcome the visitors, the visitors respond. Speeches are capped off by a *waiata* (song), and the visitors' speaker places *koha* (gift, usually an envelope of cash) on the *marae*. The hosts then invite the visitors to *hariru* (shake hands) and *hongi* (see below). Visitors and hosts are now united and will share light refreshments or a meal.

The Hongi

Press forehead and nose together firmly, shake hands, and perhaps offer a greeting such as 'Kia ora' or 'Tena koe'. Some prefer one press (for two or three seconds, or longer), others prefer two shorter (press, release, press). Men and women sometimes kiss on one cheek. Some people mistakenly think the *hongi* is a pressing of noses only (awkward to aim!) or the rubbing of noses (even more awkward).

Tapu

Tapu (spiritual restrictions) and *mana* (power and prestige) are taken seriously in the Maori world. Sit on chairs or seating provided (never on tables), and walk around people, not over them. The *powhiri* is *tapu*, and mixing food and *tapu* is right up there on the offence-o-meter. Do eat and drink when invited to do so by your hosts. You needn't worry about starvation: an important Maori value is *manaakitanga* (kindness).

Grace-Smith (both have published playscripts available) have toured their works around NZ and to festivals in the UK.

Contemporary Dance

Contemporary Maori dance often takes its inspiration from *kapa haka* and traditional Maori imagery. The exploration of pre-European life also provides inspiration. For example a Maori choreographer, Moss Patterson, used *kokowai* (a body-adorning paste made from reddish clay and shark oil) as the basis of his most recent piece of the same name.

NZ's leading specifically Maori dance company is the Atamira Dance Collective (www.atamiradance.co.nz). They have been producing critically acclaimed, beautiful and challenging work since 2000. If that sounds too earnest, another choreographer to watch out for is Mika Torotoro, who happily blends *kapa haka,* drag, opera, ballet and disco into his work. You can check out clips of his work at www.mika.co.nz.

Music plays an important role in traditional and contemporary Maori culture: see p49 for more details.

Maori Film-making

Although there had already been successful Maori documentaries (*Patu!* and the *Tangata Whenua* series are brilliant, and available from some urban video stores), it wasn't until 1987 that NZ had its first fiction feature-length movie by a Maori director with Barry Barclay's *Ngati.* Mereta Mita was the first Maori woman to direct a fiction feature with *Mauri* (1988). Both Mita and Barclay had highly political aims and ways of working, which involved a lengthy pre-production phase, during which they would consult with and seek direction from their *kaumatua* (elders). Films with significant Maori participation or control include the harrowing *Once Were Warriors* and the uplifting *Whale Rider.* Oscar-shortlisted Taika Waititi, of Te Whanau-a-Apanui descent, wrote and directed *Eagle vs Shark.*

The New Zealand Film Archive (www.filmarchive.org.nz) is a great place to experience Maori film, with most showings being either free or relatively inexpensive. It has offices in Auckland (p125) and Wellington (p400).

The first NZ hip-hop song to become a hit was Dalvanius Prime's 'Poi E', which was sung entirely in Maori by the Patea Maori Club. It was the highest-selling single of 1984 in NZ, outselling all international artists.

Maori Writing

There are many novels and collections of short stories by Maori writers, and personal taste will govern your choices. How about approaching Maori writing regionally? Read Patricia Grace (*Potiki, Cousins, Dogside Story, Tu*) around Wellington, and maybe Witi Ihimaera (*Pounamu, Pounamu, The Matriarch, Bulibasha, The Whale Rider*) on the North Island's East Coast. Keri Hulme (*The Bone People, Stonefish*) and the South Island go together like a mass of whitebait bound in a frying pan by a single egg (ie very well). Read Alan Duff (*Once Were Warriors*) anywhere, but only if you want to be saddened, even shocked. Definitely take James George (*Hummingbird, Ocean Roads*) with you to Auckland's West Coast beaches and Northland's Ninety Mile Beach. Paula Morris (*Queen of Beauty, Hibiscus Coast, Trendy but Casual*) and Kelly Ana Morey (*Bloom, Grace is Gone*) – hmm, Auckland and beyond? If poetry appeals you can't go past the giant of Maori poetry in English, the late, lamented Hone Tuwhare (*Deep River Talk: Collected Poems*). Famously sounding like he's at church and in the pub at the same time, you *can* take him anywhere.

Food & Drink Lauraine Jacobs

Lauraine Jacobs is an award-winning food writer, and food editor of *Cuisine* magazine. Passionate about NZ's wine and food, she travels the country extensively seeking out the best culinary experiences and new and exciting wines and food products.

New Zealand's international reputation as a clean, green producer of food products is well earned: its temperate climate, fertile soil and balance of sunshine and rainfall allows farmers to grow an abundance of produce for local and export markets; and there is an emphasis throughout the country on fresh, natural production.

With good advice on where to eat, and regional and seasonal specialities and the local wines to match them with, travelling in NZ can be a culinary adventure not to be missed.

FROM THE HANGI TO INTERNATIONAL-FUSION CUISINE

Before European settlement, Maori people ate a diet predominantly made up of fish, bird and root vegetables such as kumara (sweet potatoes brought from Polynesia and cultivated in NZ). They often cooked their food in an underground pit known as a *hangi*.

The first European settlers (most of whom were British) introduced beef, sheep and pigs to the country, and for more than a century thereafter the Kiwi diet was a stolid fare similar to the prewar food served up throughout the UK. There was lots of bread and potatoes, and plain cooking – with roasting and boiling as the predominant culinary techniques. Bland meat (mutton and beef) with three vegetables was served up throughout the nation each night for dinner.

For an authoritative guide to food and wine, visit www.cuisine.co.nz.

For some, that style of cooking continues today, often supplemented by the international fast-food brands found throughout the country. However, over the past 30 years there has been a massive shift towards a more varied, internationally inspired diet. NZ has embraced Asia and the Pacific Islands, and immigration from those regions has brought new flavours and cooking styles to NZ kitchens. At the same time, young New Zealanders have set off on overseas experiences and returned home with a keen appetite for lighter, fresher fare and a fusion of the culinary delights experienced in the Mediterranean and the East, or the 'new' British cuisine they have learnt about working in kitchens and pubs in the UK. The main style of cuisine now found in NZ cafes and restaurants is best described as Pacific Rim fusion, incorporating elements and ingredients from the countries of Southeast Asia, India and the Pacific.

Some farmers have also moved to diversify from traditional pastoral farming and ventured into vines, olives and kiwifruit. Wine and kiwifruit

---

ORGANIC NEW ZEALAND

No one is more aware of the importance of sustainability of the land than the farmers of NZ. With the country's economy, past and future, dependent on agricultural and pastoral industries, maintaining clean, unpolluted soil, water and air is a constant consideration.

Organic production and awareness is growing rapidly – many New Zealanders embrace the idea of organic food, convinced of the health benefits, and actively seek certified organic produce – and organic stores can be found in every major city throughout the country. In farmers markets and supermarkets organically grown and produced food will be proudly displayed and labelled as such.

However, in a country that produces more food than it could possibly consume, many food products are still imported. To really taste the goodness of NZ it is necessary to check that the meat, poultry, vegetables and fruit on menus and in stores has been grown in NZ.

POLYNESIAN SPECIALITIES

Some foods are highly prized by the Maori and Pacific Island population, but won't be found on many menus.

Mutton bird is not for everyone, as it is very fatty and has a fishy taste, but is a must for travellers who venture to Stewart Island. Equally fatty is *palusami*, traditionally a favourite with Pacific Islanders. Taro leaves or spinach are slow-cooked with coconut and corned beef to make this rich tasty meal.

Puha (prickly sow thistle) is a popular feature of Maori cooking, found growing wild in backyards and farms across the country. These leafy greens are boiled up with pork, mussels or mutton bones.

Kina and paua (abalone) are two types of shellfish to seek out. Kina is a sea urchin found among rocks on the coastline, with roe that is eaten raw from within the spiny shell. Paua has dark black meat and can be grilled or minced for fritters; it's very expensive and has a meaty savoury flavour.

Recently chefs have become interested in a range of local herbs and spices, which they add to meat and fish dishes. Peppery horopito (a bush pepper), scented kawakawa (bush basil) and kelp salt (from the seaweed plant) can be found on menus and in packets in speciality food stores.

---

particularly – industries hardly dreamed of 35 years ago – have grown from boutique operations to huge export earners.

STAPLES & SPECIALITIES
Meat

One of the joys of NZ fare is grass-fed meat. Cattle, sheep and venison munch on lush pastures year-round, enjoying the freedom of the outdoors and producing meat that's lean, tasty and sustainably grown.

Lamb is a must for any meat-eating visitor, whether it's taken as marinated chops sizzling on the barbecue, a roast leg with traditional mint sauce enjoyed around the farm table or a stylish dish in a top restaurant. The perfect accompaniments are roasted potatoes, chunks of kumara and fresh green vegies.

New Zealanders also love their steak, and restaurants often list at least one fine-grained beef dish. Following hard on the heels of the sauvignon-blanc phenomenon, local red wines have garnered international attention, and both pinot noir and syrah varietals make a fine accompaniment to any red-meat meal.

Seafood

With more than 19,000km of pristine coastline and the largest fishing grounds of any country on earth, seafood is also a must-try on any culinary tour of NZ. Shellfish abound in coastal waters; the highly rated Bluff oysters are first choice with locals. It's rare, however, to find an oyster freshly shucked to order in NZ. Fish shops, supermarkets and markets sell fresh oysters, sometimes in the shell, but most often already shucked and packed in sea water in small plastic containers.

Seafood specialities include Greenshell mussels (which are tasty and often far larger than those served in other parts of the world), cockles, clams and scallops. Crayfish (a rock lobster) is rich and sweet, but expensive. Whitebait are much prized tiny threadlike fish that are most commonly served in fritters, and can be tracked down on the west coasts of both islands during the months of September through December. Getting takeaway fish and chips, a popular meal that is good value and in plentiful supply throughout NZ, is a common Friday-night family ritual.

Apart from large-scale salmon, oyster and mussel farming, NZ's aquaculture industry is still in its infancy. Keen fishermen will find plenty of places to catch their own rainbow or brown trout in the many lakes and rivers of

The Wildfoods Festival is held in Hokitika in March, with gastronomically challenging treats such as deep-fried huhu grubs (a fat, nutritious larvae) or fish eyes and marinated duck tongues.

Bluff oysters are a wild species unique to NZ dredged from the deep waters near Bluff from mid-April until the strictly administered quota catch is filled.

TOP EATING EXPERIENCES

Just as the climate changes from south to north, so do the local speciality foods of each region. In more upmarket restaurants, menus often reflect pride in the regional produce. Chefs carefully seek the very best, and celebrate fresh locally grown fruit, vegetables, olive oils and meat and locally caught fish, and often credit their suppliers on their menus. Cafes also occasionally pay homage to local producers.

Some specialities to look for on menus in the far north and the Auckland region are avocados, nuts, citrus fruits and Asian vegetables, as the subtropical climate allows them to flourish. North Island fish differ from the catch of more southern fishermen: fresh snapper, hapuku, tarakihi and flounder are common in the north; in the colder south there's more emphasis on groper, sole, brill, blue cod and turbot.

High-quality local lamb and beef can be found in Hawke's Bay, Taranaki, Wairarapa, Canterbury and Southland, and cervena venison (a low-fat, healthy red meat) is mostly raised in these regions, too.

A variety of fruits thrive in most of NZ's grape-growing districts, and travellers will also find some great local food matches with the speciality wines of each region. Farmers market stall holders will willingly point travellers in the direction of restaurants and cafes that champion and use local produce.

Our authors' favourite NZ eating experiences:

■ Mt Maunganui's shiny new food haven, **Providores Urban Food Store** (p347), maintains a beachy, raffish charm while delivering a serious dose of culinary quality. Surf videos flickered across the walls as I tried to choose between buttery fresh-baked pastries, home-smoked meats and cheeses, sticky organic jams and killer coffee (…or all of the above). Further east around the Bay of Plenty, lonesome Maketu has seen better days, but it's worth a detour if only to visit legendary **Maketu Pies** (p350). I snaffled a mint-and-lamb special from the factory-shop pie warmer and wolfed it down on the foreshore, pastry flakes flying on the salty breeze. *Charles Rawlings-Way*

■ It's not often that you get to sample every single item on a menu, but a friend's Hen's Party lunch at **Clooney** (p119) gave me just that opportunity (I was the bridesman – it was a very modern wedding). Every single dish was a winner – interesting, deftly executed and delicious. One wit quipped, 'Great, the strippers have arrived', just as two well-known middle-

NZ, and will be the only visitors to enjoy these treats as trout cannot be sold lawfully.

Fresh Produce

Fresh local produce can be found everywhere from farmers markets to local supermarkets, specialty food stores and road-side stalls. In the North, look for citrus fruit at farm stands around Kerikeri, avocados and kiwifruit near Tauranga and apples and stone fruit in Hawke's Bay. In the South, there are fruit and vegetable stalls throughout Nelson and Marlborough; freshly dug potatoes can be bought directly from farmers near Oamaru; and some excellent dried fruit can be sampled at several stops around Cromwell in Central Otago.

Sweets & Desserts

Visitors should also look for uniquely NZ foods such as pavlova (an indulgent cream-and-fruit-topped meringue cake) and hokey pokey ice cream (a vanilla ice cream filled with nuggets of crunchy golden toffee). Those with a sweet tooth will fall in love with the range of varietal honeys with the aromas of the specific vegetation of the region in which they are made – especially Manuka honey, which has extraordinary healthful and healing properties.

The furry-skinned kiwifruit with an emerald green, vitamin C–rich interior has become the champion of pastry chefs worldwide. Its sister, known as Gold, has a smoother skin and pale yellow interior that's even higher in vitamin C.

aged conservative politicians sat down at the next table. It's that kind of place. **Mangonui Fish Shop** (p179) is a very different kind of place. A stingray swam past while I was polishing off my fish and chips. Magic! *Peter Dragicevich*

■ It's official: Stewart Island's **Kai Kart** (p679) is NZ's southernmost eatery, and I reckon you could travel the length of the country without finding better fish and chips. The wee caravan turns out incredibly fresh blue cod and delicious battered mussels or oysters. Order up large, wrap up warm, and eat alfresco with the southern ocean winds whipping up in your face. Don't forget to grab a bottle of satay sauce to go with the mussels. In the Catlins, I may have been slightly underwhelmed by NZ's own, more subtle version of Niagara Falls, but the nearby **Niagara Falls Café** (p670) left me with no feelings of disappointment. Housed in a restored 19th-century schoolhouse, the cafe and art gallery is definitely worth a stop. My first visit was for South Island's best coffee and cheesecake, and I returned a few days later with my wife and enjoyed wonderful parmesan-baked blue cod. Beers from the Invercargill Brewery, and Central Otago wines, are also pretty compelling reasons to drop by. *Brett Atkinson*

■ Nowhere on my travels did I find the Kiwi home-baking tradition in finer fettle than at the **Wakamarinian Café** (p442) in Havelock. To quote the owner of the Havelock Garden Motel, 'If you don't love the raspberry-and-white-chocolate shortcake, there must be something wrong with you'. Too true! But there's more to life than pastry. There's paua ravioli, signature dish of **Logan-Brown** (p411). Housed in a grand 1920s banking chamber on groovy Cuba St, this is Wellington's – and NZ's – best. *Sarah Bennett*

■ Eating in Queenstown is an under-rated pleasure. If you're in the mood for some quick eats you can't go past **Fergburger** (p622). This perennial favourite has become an essential Queenstown experience. Ferg's so sewn into the collective dining fabric that it has become a must for all Queenie visitors – backpacker or billionaire. Rightfully so – the burgers are *that* good. Those wanting to eat indoors, or at least without thumping drum 'n' bass, should look no further then around the corner at **Solero Vino** (p621). This fine-dining French restaurant is the bee's knees for the cultured culinary crowd. Delicate flavours, amazing wine and awesome service – *bon appetit*! *Scott Kennedy*

The Dairy

Owner-operated stores, known locally as the 'dairy', are ubiquitous in small towns and city suburbs. All manner of food items, from ice creams rolled to order, bread and milk to newspapers and almost every staple need are stocked.

DRINKS

After work, around the barbecue, at the beach and in cafes up and down the country, beer, wine and cocktails are part of the social culture.

The zingy Marlborough sauvignon blanc – with fresh, fruity, almost herbal aromas that leap out of the glass – holds a unique position in the wine world, and is sought after all over the globe. Walk into any restaurant, and almost every table will be graced with a bottle or two of opened wine to accompany the meal. All supermarkets sell local wines, often at bargain prices, but the very best NZ wines are mainly sold in specialist wine stores or found on the wine lists of the better restaurants.

Beer, too, has long been part of the Kiwi culture, and boutique hand-crafted beers abound. Nelson – the region where hops, an essential ingredient in beer, are grown – has become a treasure trove of boutique beers and visitors can call in to several operations to pick up 'a dozen' or two to take to the beach.

For years only recognised for high-quality cheddar cheese, many small producers are now making artisan cheeses from cow's, sheep and goat's milk. All NZ cheese is made (by law) from pasteurised milk.

WINE TOURING

Visitors to NZ who have a real passion for food and wine can follow a wine trail right through the country from north to south, rather than following traditional tourist routes. Tour options include cycling or guided tours in minivans, organised by wine experts. Where good wines are created, there's usually good local food too.

Within each wine region there are numerous wineries that welcome visits at the cellar door, and many have good restaurants with food matched to the wines grown and produced on the estate.

As most international visitors arrive through the airport of Auckland, a great place to start is with a day visit to Matakana (p148) for its pinot gris, or to Waiheke Island (p131), a 45-minute ferry ride from Auckland's downtown, to taste the island's intense red wines and local chardonnays.

To take in the major wine-making areas, first head south from Auckland to Hawke's Bay (p373) for chardonnays and syrahs. This is a vast area so careful planning of a trail is essential to avoid endless criss-crossing. Next it's off through extensive sheep country to the Wairarapa to try the renowned pinot noirs of Martinborough (p423). From there an exhilarating drive over the Rimutaka hills will get you to Wellington, from where you can cross Cook Strait to Marlborough by ferry or air.

Marlborough's sauvignon blancs have made their mark internationally and firmly established NZ's credibility in the world of wine. (A side trip to experience the aromatic white wines of Nelson is also suggested.)

The wine tourist can then hit the trail through Waipara and North Canterbury (p547) for rieslings and pinot noirs, and finish in the scenic Central Otago region (p589) where wine tourism is a popular addition to the area's famous adventure tourism. The pinot noirs of Otago exhibit all the characteristics of the wild thyme- and heather-clad hills throughout the region.

Another speciality drink to look for is the internationally acclaimed 42Below vodka, a great example of Kiwi ingenuity. Innovator Geoff Ross produced uniquely NZ flavoured vodkas (kiwifruit, Manuka honey, feijoa and more), presented them in elegant bottles and then sold his company to Bacardi for many millions. He's been retained by Bacardi to oversee and guard the standards.

Coffee drinking has also become an important part of NZ culture, coinciding with the rise and rise of the cafe. To find the best coffee, follow the tried and tested rule of joining the crowd at the busiest spot in town.

CELEBRATIONS

During the harvest period in late summer (February to April) wine and food is celebrated in many of the wine regions with local festivals. Wine flows freely, there's no shortage of food stalls with local specialities, and it's all terrific fun, especially as the day lengthens and the wine kicks in.

Some visitors may be fortunate enough to attend a Maori *hangi,* a feature of almost any gathering, occasion or funeral at the *marae* (Maori meeting house). A pit is dug, a fire lit and stones placed in it. When the set-up is finally deemed hot enough, chicken, lamb, pork, kumara, potatoes, corn, pumpkin and other vegetables are covered with sacks and placed over the hot stones. The pit is covered with earth and the food steamed for an hour or two before being lifted out and carried to the table. The flavour of the food, which is usually not seasoned with spices or herbs, is earthy and tender. A great deal of associated drinking, chatter and comradeship are very much part of a *hangi.*

As NZ has evolved into a more multicultural society, many different ethnic groups have introduced their own celebrations. Pasifika, a festival celebrating Polynesian culture, takes place in Auckland over a weekend in February. It's two days of eating Island foods such as Pacific fruits and vegetables, sticky coconut buns, suckling pig, baked spinach or taro leaves with coconut and much more. Island sports, singing and cultural dancing take place.

Smoking is banned in the workplace and any public place where food or drink is served, and it is considered very bad manners to smoke indoors or without requesting permission.

The Diwali celebration of the Indian community has also become part of the Auckland calendar and many tiny food stalls are set up near the harbour in October for a weekend celebration. Spicy aromas waft through the air, and the vast array of savoury snacks and jewel-like sweets are irresistible.

In rural areas, agricultural and pastoral associations host annual showcases of farming practices and animal displays at local showgrounds. These fun days are full of competitions and events; food tends to be hearty, but hardly gourmet, including basic pies, hamburgers, barbecued sausages and hot dogs.

WHERE TO EAT & DRINK

The main cities are remarkably well served with a range of eating choices, from restaurants where the food is stylish and imaginative to small places where the ambience is simple, but the food authentic and prepared with love. Cafes are found everywhere, particularly in towns along the main touring routes, and usually serve hearty country fare. Many cafes open at 7am but close around 4pm or 5pm and don't serve dinner. For pub and restaurant opening hours see p686.

B&Bs in the more remote regions will often cook dinner, but usually only by request well ahead of arrival. Country-style pubs can be found in most places, and although very few offer a 'gastro' experience, they serve up a basic menu to accompany a frothy cold beer.

Farmers markets are generally held on Saturday or Sunday mornings, and all are great places to explore local food culture, meet local food producers and taste some terrific fresh food. Most have a mobile coffee stand, and usually there will be an entrepreneur serving a 'breakfast roll' bun stuffed with fried eggs and bacon.

> Check out what Auckland and Wellington restaurants have to offer at www.menus.co.nz or www.dineout.co.nz.

> The restaurant industry is NZ's largest private-sector employer, with nearly 4% of the total workforce.

TOP 10 MICROBREWERIES

New Zealanders sure can brew up a storm! Here are our picks for the best Kiwi microbreweries you're likely to find:

Brew Moon Brewery (p547) The roadside Brew Moon Brewery in Amberley lures visitors in with three different beers on tap and an excellent cafe. Try the chocolatey Brew Moon Dark Side Stout. Amberley is just before the Waipara Valley wine region in North Canterbury.

Croucher Brewing Co (p332; www.croucherbrewing.co.nz) Croucher's crafty pale ale and pilsner rule the roost at Rotorua's boozy Underground Bar.

Emerson's Brewery (p582; www.emersons.co.nz) Dunedin is full of students, and students like beer – and how blessed they are to drink Emerson's! Wheat beers, pilsners, porters, and bitter ales heavy on the malt and spice.

Founders Brewery (p458; www.biobrew.co.nz) NZ's first certified organic brewery is in Nelson. Take a behind-the-scenes tour and sip the immaculate product.

Hallertau (p144; www.hallertau.co.nz) Auckland beer boffins are big fans of this microbrewery, where sexy packaging and barrel-aged beers collide (its 'Porter Noir' does time in old pinot barrels!). The pale ale is hoppy heaven.

Moa Beer (p449; www.moabeer.co.nz) Winemaker's son Josh Scott produces a range of excellent bottle-fermented beers at his tasting room–bar in the thick of Marlborough's vineyards.

Renaissance Brewing Co (p449; www.renaissancebrewing.co.nz) Seriously good ales with the medals to prove it. A fantastic use for a former ice-cream factory in Blenheim.

Three Boys Brewery (www.threeboysbrewery.co.nz) Three Boys IPA is available at discerning bars and restaurants in Christchurch. Packed with hops, it's an authentic version of the Indian Pale Ales originally crafted to last the long sea journey to colonial India.

Wanaka Beerworks (p633; www.wanakabeerworks.co.nz) Look for this brewery's beers in restaurants around Queenstown and Wanaka. The Brewski pilsner is packed with floral, hoppy flavours and is an excellent rendition of a Czech-style lager.

White Cliffs Organic Brewery (p261; www.organicbeer.co.nz) White Cliffs enjoys a reputation far beyond Taranaki, particularly for Mike's Mild – an amber ale with notes of fruit and roasted nuts: a real connoisseur's drop.

TO MARKET, TO MARKET

Farmers markets are a relatively new introduction to the shopping options in NZ. In the past five years there has been extraordinary growth and from one market in 2001 (at Whangarei, in the north), the number has steadily increased each year to more than 50 throughout the country.

Most are held on weekend mornings and are happy local affairs where visitors will meet local producers and find fresh produce. It's a great way to find out just what food is the speciality of the region. Mobile coffee carts are usually present, and tastings are often offered by enterprising and innovative stall holders selling value-added food products.

Always take a bag to carry purchases in as many of the sustainable-minded markets ban the use of plastic bags. Arrive as early as possible – the best produce always sells out very quickly.

Look at www.farmersmarkets.org.nz to find dates and times of farmers markets throughout NZ.

VEGETARIANS & VEGANS

Vegetarians need not worry that they will not find suitable food around NZ. There isn't a great range of vegetarian restaurants, but almost all restaurants and cafes offer vegetarian choices on their menus (although sometimes only one or two). Many cafes also provide gluten-free and vegan options. Always check that the stocks and sauces are vegetarian, as chefs who have not traditionally cooked for those with strict vegetarian diets tend to think of vegetarian cooking as simply omitting the main serving of meat or fish from a meal.

It always pays to mention any dietary requirement when making a reservation at a restaurant or B&B, and it's essential in this meat-loving country to mention it to the host when invited to a private home.

Environment
Vaughan Yarwood

THE LAND

New Zealand is a young country – its present shape is less than 10,000 years old. Having broken away from the supercontinent of Gondwanaland (which included Africa, Australia, Antarctica and South America) in a stately geological dance some 130 million years ago, it endured aeons of uplift and erosion, buckling and tearing, and the slow fall and rise of the sea as ice ages came and went. Straddling the boundary of two great colliding slabs of the earth's crust – the Pacific plate and the Indian/Australian plate – to this day NZ remains the plaything of nature's strongest forces.

> Vaughan Yarwood is a historian and travel writer who is widely published in NZ and internationally. His most recent book is *The History Makers: Adventures in New Zealand Biography.*

The result is one of the most varied and spectacular series of landscapes in the world, ranging from snow-dusted mountains and drowned glacial valleys to rainforests, dunelands and an otherworldly volcanic plateau. It is a diversity of landforms you would expect to find across an entire continent rather than a small archipelago in the South Pacific.

Evidence of NZ's tumultuous past is everywhere. The South Island's mountainous spine – the 650km-long ranges of the Southern Alps – is a product of the clash of the two plates; the result of a process of rapid lifting that, if anything, is accelerating. Despite NZ's highest peak, Aoraki/Mt Cook (p566), losing 10m from its summit overnight in a 1991 landslide, the Alps are on an express elevator that, without erosion and landslides, would see them 10 times their present height within a few million years.

On the North Island, the most impressive changes have been wrought by volcanoes. Auckland is built on an isthmus peppered by scoria cones, on many of which you can still see the earthworks of *pa* (fortified villages) built by early Maori. The city's biggest and most recent volcano, 600-year-old Rangitoto Island (p129), is just a short ferry ride from the downtown wharves. Some 300km further south, the classically shaped cone of snowcapped Mt Taranaki/Egmont (p261) overlooks tranquil dairy pastures.

But the real volcanic heartland runs through the centre of the North Island, from the restless bulk of Mt Ruapehu in Tongariro National Park (p304) northeast through the Rotorua lake district (p324) out to NZ's most

---

RESPONSIBLE TRAVEL

Toitu te whenua – care for the land. Help protect the environment by following these guidelines:

■ Treat NZ's forests and native wildlife with respect. Damaging or taking plants is illegal in most parts of the country.

■ Remove rubbish. Litter is unsightly and can encourage vermin and disease. Rather than burying or burning, carry out what you carry in.

■ In areas without toilet facilities bury toilet waste in a shallow hole away from tracks, huts, campsites and waterways.

■ Keep streams and lakes pure by cleaning away from water sources. Drain waste water into the soil to filter out soaps and detergent. If you suspect contamination, boil water for three minutes, filter, or chemically treat it before use.

■ Where possible use portable fuel stoves. Keep open fires small, use only dead wood and make sure the fire is out by dousing it with water and checking the ashes before leaving.

■ Keep to tracks where possible. Get permission before crossing private land and move carefully around livestock.

ENVIRONMENTAL ISSUES IN AOTEAROA NEW ZEALAND *Nandor Tanczos*

Most people think of Aotearoa New Zealand as clean and green, a place that respects the environment. We have the NZ Forest Accord to protect native forests, national parks and reserves now cover a third of the country, marine reserves continue to pop up around the coast, and our antinuclear legislation seems unassailable. A closer look, however, reveals a dirtier picture.

New Zealand has one of the highest per capita rates of greenhouse-gas emissions in the world. We are one of the most inefficient users of energy in the developed world. Public transport is negligible in most places and ecological values play little part in urban planning or building design. Add to that the ongoing battle being fought in many communities over the disposal of sewage and toxic waste into waterways, a conflict often spearheaded by *tangata whenua* (local Maori people), and the 'clean and green' label begins to look seriously compromised.

Our biggest polluting sector is pastoral farming, responsible for half of our greenhouse-gas emissions. The importation of European sheep and cattle-grazing systems has left many hillsides with marginal productivity, bare of trees and prone to erosion. Grazing threatens many waterways, with stock causing damage to stream and lake margins and run-off causing nutrient overload leading to eutrophication and algal blooms. Dairy farming, the worst culprit due to its intensity, is expanding into areas often poorly suited to this kind of land use, relying on a massive increase in the use of irrigation. Over-allocation of water has become a problem in many areas as a result. Regional councils and farming groups are fencing and planting stream banks to protect water quality, but their efforts are outstripped by the sheer growth in dairying.

The election of the centre-right National Government in 2008 has led to the unravelling of a number of important environmental protections. They have gutted the already inadequate Emissions Trading Scheme. The world-leading Resource Management Act has been significantly weakened, and the Government is proposing to open up Department of Conservation and other

---

active volcano, White Island (p355), in the Bay of Plenty. Called the Taupo Volcanic Zone, this great 250km-long rift valley – part of a volcano chain known as the 'Pacific Ring of Fire' – has been the seat of massive eruptions that have left their mark on the country physically and culturally.

Most spectacular were the eruptions from the volcano that created Lake Taupo (p289). Considered the world's most productive volcano in terms of the amount of material ejected, Taupo last erupted 1800 years ago in a display that was the most violent anywhere on the planet within the past 5000 years.

You can experience the aftermath of volcanic destruction on a smaller scale at Te Wairoa (the Buried Village; p337), near Rotorua on the shores of Lake Tarawera. Here, partly excavated and open to the public, lie the remains of a 19th-century Maori village overwhelmed when nearby Mt Tarawera erupted without warning. The famous Pink and White Terraces (one of several claimants to the popular title 'eighth wonder of the world') were destroyed overnight by the same upheaval.

The GreenDex (p745) at the end of this book lists ecofriendly places to explore, stay or dine throughout NZ. Discover more about ecotourism across the country with Leonie Johnsen's *Organic Explorer New Zealand* (www.organicexplorer. co.nz).

But when nature sweeps the board clean with one hand she often rebuilds with the other: Waimangu Valley (p337), born of all that geothermal violence, is the place to go to experience the hot earth up close and personal amid geysers, silica pans, bubbling mud pools, and the world's biggest hot spring. Or you can wander around Rotorua's Whakarewarewa Thermal Village (p322), where descendants of Maori displaced by the eruption live in the middle of steaming vents and prepare food for visitors in boiling pools.

A second by-product of movement along the tectonic plate boundary is seismic activity – earthquakes. Not for nothing has NZ been called 'the Shaky Isles'. Most quakes only rattle the glassware, but one was indirectly responsible for creating an internationally celebrated tourist attraction…

In 1931, an earthquake measuring 7.9 on the Richter scale levelled the Hawke's Bay city of Napier (p378) causing huge damage and loss of life.

protected land for mining. Local communities in places like the Coromandel Peninsula are now gearing up for a rerun of the fierce environmental battles of the 1970s and '80s, which ended with the Coromandel being declared off limits to mining.

Despite these things, New Zealand has some advantages. A relatively high proportion of our energy comes from renewable hydro-generation. Farm animals, except for pigs and chickens, are almost all grass fed and free range. We are starting to get serious about waste minimisation and resource recovery. But our biggest saving grace is our small population. As a result, Aotearoa is a place well worth visiting. This is a beautiful land with enormous geographical and ecological diversity. Our forests are unique and magnificent, and the bird species that evolved in response to an almost total lack of mammalian life are spectacular, although now reduced in numbers due to introduced predators such as rats, stoats and hedgehogs.

The responsibility of New Zealanders is to make change for ecological sustainability, not just at a personal level, but at an institutional and infrastructural level. The responsibility of visitors to Aotearoa New Zealand is to respect our unique biodiversity, and to query and question: every time you ask where the recycling centre is; every time you express surprise at the levels of energy use, car use and water use; every time you request organic food at a cafe or restaurant; you affect the person you talk to.

Aotearoa New Zealand has the potential to be a world leader in ecological wisdom. We have a strong tradition to draw from – the careful relationship of reciprocity that Maori developed with the natural world over the course of many, many generations. We live at the edge of the Pacific, on the Rim of Fire, a remnant of the ancient forests of Gondwanaland. We welcome conscious travellers.

Nandor Tanczos is an activist, researcher and educator based in Ngaruawahia. He was a Member of Parliament for the Green Party until 2008.

Napier was rebuilt almost entirely in the then-fashionable art-deco architectural style, and walking its streets today you can relive its brash exuberance in what has become a mecca for lovers of art deco (p378).

Travellers to the South Island can also see some evidence of volcanism – if the remains of the old volcanoes of Banks Peninsula (p542) weren't there to repel the sea, the vast Canterbury Plains, built from alpine sediment washed down the rivers from the Alps, would have eroded away long ago.

But in the south it is the Southern Alps themselves that dominate, dictating settlement patterns, throwing down engineering challenges and offering outstanding recreational opportunities. The island's mountainous backbone also helps shape the weather, as it stands in the path of the prevailing westerly winds which roll in, moisture-laden, from the Tasman Sea. As a result bush-clad lower slopes of the western Southern Alps are among the wettest places on earth, with an annual precipitation of some 15,000mm. Having lost its moisture, the wind then blows dry across the eastern plains towards the Pacific coast.

The North Island has a more even rainfall and is spared the temperature extremes of the South – which can plunge when a wind blows in from Antarctica. The important thing to remember, especially if you are tramping at high altitude, is that NZ has a maritime climate. This means weather can change with lightning speed, catching out the unprepared.

NZ is one of the most spectacular places in the world to see geysers. Rotorua's short-lived Waimangu geyser, formed after the Mt Tarawera eruption, was once the world's largest, often gushing to a dizzying height of 400m.

WILDLIFE

NZ may be relatively young, geologically speaking, but its plants and animals go back a long way. The tuatara, for instance, an ancient reptile unique to these islands, is a Gondwanaland survivor closely related to the dinosaurs, while many of the distinctive flightless birds (ratites) have distant African and South American cousins.

Due to its long isolation, the country is a veritable warehouse of unique and varied plants, most of which are found nowhere else. And with separation of the landmass occurring before mammals appeared on the scene, birds and insects have evolved in spectacular ways to fill the gaps.

The now extinct flightless moa, the largest of which grew to 3.5m tall and weighed over 200kg, browsed open grasslands much as cattle do today (skeletons can be seen at Auckland Museum, p98), while the smaller kiwi still ekes out a nocturnal living rummaging among forest leaf litter for insects and worms much as small mammals do elsewhere. One of the country's most ferocious-looking insects, the mouse-sized giant weta, meanwhile, has taken on a scavenging role elsewhere filled by rodents.

As one of the last places on earth to be colonised by humans, NZ was for millennia a safe laboratory for such risky evolutionary strategies, but with the arrival first of Maori and soon after of Europeans, things went downhill fast.

Many endemic creatures, including moa and the huia, an exquisite songbird, were driven to extinction, and the vast forests were cleared for their timber and to make way for agriculture. Destruction of habitat and the introduction of exotic animals and plants have taken a terrible environmental toll and New Zealanders are now fighting a rearguard battle to save what remains.

Birds & Animals

The first Polynesian settlers found little in the way of land mammals – just two species of bat – but forests, plains and coasts are alive with birds. Largely lacking the bright plumage found elsewhere, NZ's birds – like its endemic plants – have an understated beauty which does not shout for attention.

Among the most musical is the bellbird, common in both native and exotic forests everywhere except Northland, though like many birds it is more likely to be heard than seen. Its call is a series of liquid bell notes, most often sounded at dawn or dusk.

B Heather and H Robertson's *Field Guide to the Birds of New Zealand* is a comprehensive guide for birdwatchers and a model of helpfulness for anyone even casually interested in the country's remarkable bird life.

The tui, another nectar eater and the country's most beautiful songbird, is a great mimic, with an inventive repertoire that includes clicks, grunts and chuckles. Notable for the white throat feathers which stand out against its dark plumage, the tui often feeds on flax flowers in suburban gardens but is most at home in densely tangled forest ('bush' to New Zealanders).

Fantails are commonly encountered on forest trails, swooping and jinking to catch insects stirred up by passing hikers, while pukeko, elegant swamp-hens with blue plumage and bright red beaks, are readily seen along wetland margins and even on the sides of roads nearby – be warned, they have little road sense.

If you spend any time in the South Island high country, you are likely to come up against the fearless and inquisitive kea – an uncharacteristically drab green parrot with bright red underwings. Kea are common in the car parks of the Fox and Franz Josef Glaciers (p512 and p508), where they hang out for food scraps or tear rubber from car windscreens.

Then there is the takahe, a rare flightless bird thought extinct until a small colony was discovered in 1948, and the equally flightless kiwi, NZ's national emblem and the nickname for New Zealanders themselves.

The kiwi has a round body covered in coarse feathers, strong legs and a long, distinctive bill with nostrils at the tip for sniffing out food. It is not easy to find them in the wild, but they can be seen in simulated environments at excellent nocturnal houses. One of the best is the Otorohanga Kiwi House (p241), which also has other birds, including native falcons, moreporks (owls) and weka.

To get a feel for what the bush used to be like, take a trip to Tiritiri Matangi Island (p135). This regenerating island is an open sanctuary and one of the country's most successful exercises in community-assisted conservation.

BIRDWATCHING

The flightless kiwi is the species most sought after by birdwatchers. Sightings of the Stewart Island subspecies are common at all times of the year. Elsewhere, wild sightings of this increasingly rare nocturnal species are difficult, apart from in enclosures. Other birds that twitchers like to sight are the royal albatross, white heron, Fiordland crested penguin, yellow-eyed penguin, Australasian gannet and wrybill.

On the Coromandel Peninsula, the Firth of Thames (particularly Miranda) is a haven for migrating birds, while the Wharekawa Wildlife Refuge at Opoutere Beach is a breeding ground of the endangered NZ dotterel. There's also a very accessible Australasian gannet colony at Muriwai, west of Auckland, and one in Hawke's Bay. There are popular trips to observe pelagic birds out of Kaikoura, and royal albatross viewing on the Otago Peninsula.

Two good guides are the newly revised *Field Guide to the Birds of New Zealand*, by Barrie Heather and Hugh Robertson, and *Birds of New Zealand: Locality Guide* by Stuart Chambers.

MARINE MAMMAL–WATCHING

Kaikoura, on the northeast coast of the South Island, is NZ's nexus of marine mammal-watching. The main attraction here is whale-watching, but this is dependent on weather conditions, so don't expect to just be able to rock up and head straight out on a boat for a dream encounter. The sperm whale, the largest toothed whale, is pretty much a year-round resident, and depending on the season you may also see migrating humpback whales, pilot whales, blue whales and southern right whales. Other mammals – including fur seals and dusky dolphins – are seen year-round.

Kaikoura is also an outstanding place to swim with dolphins. Pods of up to 500 playful dusky dolphins can be seen on any given day. Dolphin swimming is common elsewhere in NZ, with the animals gathering off the North Island near Whakatane, Paihia, Tauranga, and in the Hauraki Gulf, and off

---

KIWI SPOTTING

The kiwi is a threatened species, and with the additional difficulty of them being nocturnal, it's only on Stewart Island (p672) that you might easily see one in the wild. They can, however, be observed in many artificially dark 'kiwi houses':

- Auckland Zoo (p99)
- Otorohanga Kiwi House Native Bird Park (p241)
- National Aquarium of New Zealand, Napier (p380)
- Nga Manu Nature Reserve, Waikanae (p422)
- Pukaha Mt Bruce National Wildlife Centre, near Masterton (p427)
- Wellington Zoo (p403)
- Southern Encounter Aquarium & Kiwi House, Christchurch (p524)
- Orana Wildlife Park, Christchurch (p526)
- Willowbank Wildlife Reserve, Christchurch (p527)
- Kiwi Birdlife Park, Queenstown (p609)

Akaroa on the South Island's Banks Peninsula. Seal swimming is possible in Kaikoura and in the Abel Tasman National Park.

Swimming with sharks is also possible, though with a protective cage as a chaperone; you can do it in Tutukaka and Gisborne.

Trees

No visitor to NZ (particularly Australians!) will go for long without hearing about the damage done to the bush by that bad-mannered Australian import, the brush-tailed possum. The long list of mammal pests introduced to NZ accidentally or for a variety of misguided reasons includes deer, rabbits, stoats, pigs and goats. But the most destructive by far is the possum, 70 million of which now chew through millions of tonnes of foliage a year despite the best efforts of the Department of Conservation (DOC) to control them.

Among favoured possum food are NZ's most colourful trees: the kowhai, a small-leaved tree growing to 11m, that in spring has drooping clusters of bright yellow flowers (NZ's national flower); the pohutukawa, a beautiful coastal tree of the northern North Island which bursts into vivid red flower in December, earning the nickname 'Christmas tree'; and a similar crimson-flowered tree, the rata. Rata species are found on both islands; the northern rata starts life as a climber on a host tree (that it eventually chokes).

The few remaining pockets of mature centuries-old kauri are stately emblems of former days. Their vast hammered trunks and towering, epiphyte-festooned limbs, which dwarf every other tree in the forest, are reminders of why they were sought after in colonial days for spars and building timber. The best place to see the remaining giants is Northland's Waipoua Kauri Forest (p187), home to three-quarters of the country's surviving kauri.

Now the pressure has been taken off kauri and other timber trees, including the distinctive rimu (red pine) and the long-lived totara (favoured for Maori war canoes), by one of the country's most successful imports – *Pinus radiata*. Pine was found to thrive in NZ, growing to maturity in just 35 years, and plantation forests are now widespread through the central North Island – the southern hemisphere's biggest, Kaingaroa Forest, lies southeast of Rotorua.

You won't get far into the bush without coming across one of its most prominent features – tree ferns. NZ is a land of ferns (more than 80 species) and most easily recognised are the mamaku (black tree fern) – which grows to 20m and can be seen in damp gullies throughout the country – and the 10m-high ponga (silver tree fern) with its distinctive white underside. The silver fern is equally at home as part of corporate logos and on the clothing of many of the country's top sportspeople.

Lifestyles of New Zealand Forest Plants, by J Dawson and R Lucas, is a beautifully photographed foray into the world of NZ's forests. Far from being drab and colourless, these lush treasure houses are home to ancient species dating from the time of the dinosaurs. This guidebook will have you reaching for your boots.

NATIONAL PARKS

A third of the country – more than five million hectares – is protected in environmentally important parks and reserves that embrace almost every conceivable landscape: from mangrove-fringed inlets in the north to the snow-topped volcanoes of the Central Plateau, and from the forested fastness

---

TOWERING KAURI

When Chaucer was born this was a sturdy young tree. When Shakespeare was born it was 300 years old. It predates most of the great cathedrals of Europe. Its trunk is sky-rocket straight and sky-rocket bulky, limbless for half its height. Ferns sprout from its crevices. Its crown is an asymmetric mess, like an inverted root system. I lean against it, give it a slap. It's like slapping a building. This is a tree out of Tolkien. It's a kauri.

Joe Bennett (A Land of Two Halves) referring to the McKinney kauri in Northland.

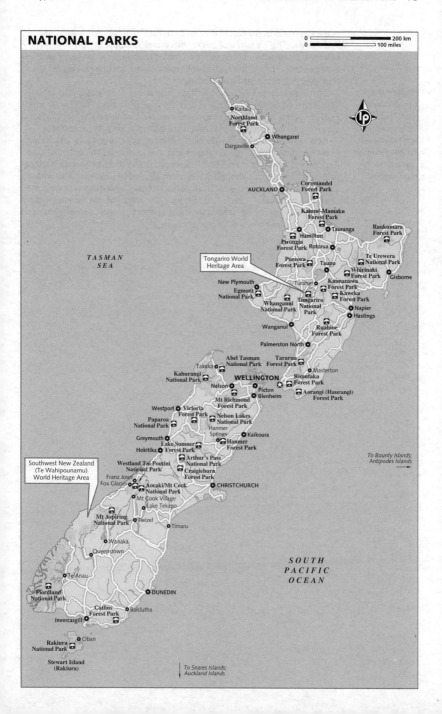

of the Ureweras in the east to the Southern Alps' majestic mountains, glaciers and fiords. The 14 national parks, three maritime parks and two marine reserves, along with numerous forest parks, offer huge scope for wilderness experiences, ranging from climbing, snow skiing and mountain biking to tramping, kayaking and trout fishing.

The Department of Conservation website (www.doc.govt.nz) has useful information on the country's national parks, tracks and walkways. It also lists backcountry huts and campsites.

Three places are World Heritage areas: NZ's Subantarctic Islands, Tongariro National Park (p304) and Te Wahipounamu (p651), an amalgam of several national parks in southwest NZ that boast the world's finest surviving Gondwanaland plants and animals in their natural habitats.

Access to the country's wild places is relatively straightforward, though huts on walking tracks require passes and may need to be booked in advance. In practical terms, there is little difference for travellers between a national park and a forest park, though dogs are not allowed in national parks without a permit. Camping is possible in all parks, but may be restricted to dedicated camping grounds – check first. Permits are required for hunting (game birds), and licences are needed for inland fishing (trout, salmon); both can be bought online at www.fishandgame.org.nz.

Active New Zealand

New Zealand's astounding natural assets encourage even the laziest lounge lizards to drag themselves outside. Many travellers come here for the sole purpose of getting active, but the great outdoors aren't just the domain of thrill-seeking tourists. Outdoor culture is ingrained in Kiwi life: from family camping holidays to elite mountaineering, wandering into the wilderness and experiencing NZ's unpeopled majesty is the national habit.

It will come as no surprise then that outdoor activities across the nation are accessible and supremely well organised. Commercial operators can hook you up with whatever kind of experience floats your boat – from bungy jumping off a canyon to sea kayaking around a national park – but the beauty of NZ is that you can do a lot of stuff under your own steam, without tagging along on a tour. This is still a wild frontier – don't miss the chance to engage with nature one on one, a million miles from home, just you and the great void.

Adrenaline-pumping activities obviously have an element of risk – particularly white-water rafting, kayaking and anything that involves falling from a great height – but the perception of danger is part of the thrill. Despite some recent mishaps, chances of an accident remain negligible, but make sure you have travel insurance that fully covers you for any planned activities – for more info see p691.

See p685 for tips on less active sports like aerial sightseeing, fishing, sailing and golf; and p71 for the low-down on bird- and marine-mammal-watching.

TRAMPING

Tramping (aka bushwalking, hiking or trekking) is the perfect vehicle for a close encounter with NZ's natural beauty. There are thousands of kilometres of tracks – some well marked, some barely a line on a map – plus an excellent network of huts enabling trampers to avoid lugging tents and (in some cases) cooking gear. Before plodding off into the forest, get up-to-date information from the appropriate authority – usually the **Department of Conservation** (DOC; www.doc.govt.nz), or regional i-SITE visitor information centres.

Tracks beneath the highest numbers of feet are the Routeburn, Milford, Tongariro Northern Circuit (and the one-day Tongariro Alpine Crossing), Kepler, Lake Waikaremoana, Queen Charlotte and Abel Tasman Coast. If you've got your heart set on a summer walk along the Milford, Routeburn or any other Great Walk, check out the booking requirements and get in early. If you want to avoid the crowds, go in the shoulder season. DOC staff can help plan tramps on lesser-known tracks; see the DOC website for details.

If you're planning your first walk, check out www.tramper.co.nz – a fantastic website with track descriptions and track ratings.

When to Go

Tramping high season is during the school summer holidays, from two weeks before Christmas until the end of January – avoid it if you can. The best weather is from January to March, though most nonalpine tracks can be walked enjoyably at any time from about October through to April. Winter

---

VOLUNTOURISM

NZ presents a swathe of active, outdoorsy opportunities for travellers to get some dirt under their fingernails and participate in conservation programs. Programs can include anything from tree-planting and weed removal to track construction, habitat conservation and fencing. Ask about local opportunities at any regional i-SITE visitor information centre, or check out www.conservationvolunteers.org.nz and www.doc.govt.nz/getting-involved, both of which allow you to browse for opportunities by region. See also WWOOFing (p683).

(June to August) is not the time to be out in the wild, especially at altitude – some paths close in winter because of avalanche danger and lower levels of facilities and services.

What to Bring

For a primo tramp, the primary considerations are your feet and shoulders. Make sure your footwear is tough as old boots, and that your pack isn't too heavy. Adequate wet-weather gear is essential, especially on the South Island's waterlogged West Coast. If you're camping or staying in huts without stoves (eg on the Abel Tasman Coast Track or Lake Waikaremoana Track), bring a camping stove. And don't forget your scroggin – a mixture of dried fruit and nuts (and sometimes chocolate) for munching en route.

If you don't want to be itching and scratching for weeks, bring some insect repellent on your tramp to keep the sandflies at bay (see p688).

Books

DOC publishes detailed books on the flora and fauna, geology and history of NZ's national parks, plus leaflets (50c to $2) detailing hundreds of walking tracks across NZ.

Lonely Planet's *Tramping in New Zealand* describes around 50 walks of various lengths and degrees of difficulty. Mark Pickering and Rodney Smith's *101 Great Tramps* has suggestions for two- to six-day tramps around the country. The companion guide, *202 Great Walks: the Best Day Walks in New Zealand*, by Mark Pickering, is handy for shorter, family-friendly excursions. *Accessible Walks*, by Anna and Andrew Jameson, is an excellent guide for elderly, disabled and family trampers, with detailed access information on 100-plus South Island walks.

New trampers should check out *Don't Forget Your Scroggin* by Sarah Bennett and Lee Slater – all about being safe and happy on the track. The *Birdseye Tramping Guides* from Craig Potton Publishing have fab topographical maps, and there are countless books covering tramps and short urban walks around NZ – scan the bookshops.

Maps

The topographical maps produced by **Land Information New Zealand** (LINZ; www.linz.govt.nz) are a safe bet. Bookshops don't often have a good selection of these, but LINZ has map-sales offices in major cities and towns, and DOC offices often sell LINZ maps for local tracks. Outdoor stores also stock them (see the boxed text, p82). LINZ' map series includes park maps (national, state and forest parks), dedicated walking-track maps, and highly detailed 'Topomaps' (you may need two or three of these for one track).

Track Classification

Tracks are classified according to various features, including level of difficulty. In this chapter we loosely refer to the level of difficulty as easy, medium, hard or difficult. The widely used track classification system is as follows:

Short Walk Well formed; allows for wheelchair access or constructed to 'shoe' standard (ie walking boots not required). Suitable for people of all ages and fitness levels.

Walking Track Easy and well-formed longer walks; constructed to 'shoe' standard. Suitable for people of most ages and fitness levels.

Easy Tramping Track or Great Walk Well formed; major water crossings have bridges and track junctions have signs. Light walking boots required.

Tramping Track Requires skill and experience; constructed to 'boot' standard. Suitable for people of average physical fitness. Water crossings may not have bridges.

Route Requires a high degree of skill, experience and navigation skills. Well-equipped trampers only.

Track Safety

Thousands of people tramp across NZ without incident, but every year a few folks meet their Maker in the mountains. Some trails are only for the experienced, fit and well-equipped – don't attempt these if you don't fit the bill. NZ's climatic changeability subjects high-altitude walks to snow and ice, even in summer, so always check weather and track conditions before setting off. Consult a DOC visitor centre and leave your intentions with a responsible person before starting longer walks. See also www.mountainsafety.org.nz.

The Great Walks

NZ's nine official 'Great Walks' (one of which is actually a river trip!) are the country's most popular tracks. Natural beauty abounds, but prepare yourself for crowds, especially over summer when folks from around the globe pull on their boots.

All nine Great Walks are described in this guidebook and in Lonely Planet's *Tramping in New Zealand,* and are detailed in pamphlets provided by DOC visitor centres. You will also find a park map handy.

To tramp these tracks you'll need to buy a Great Walk Pass before setting out, sold at DOC visitor centres near each walk. These track-specific passes cover you for hut accommodation (from $12 to $45 per person per night, depending on the track and the season) and/or camping (free to $15 per person per night). You can camp only at designated camping grounds; note there's no camping on the Milford Track. In the off-peak season (May to September), Backcountry Hut Passes ($90, valid for 12 months) and pay-as-you-go hut tickets can be used instead of a Great Walk Pass in many huts (see p79). Kids under 18 stay in huts and camp for free on Great Walks.

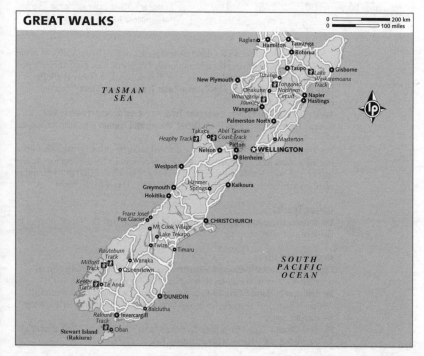

GREAT WALKS

NEW ZEALAND'S NINE 'GREAT WALKS'

Walk	Distance	Duration	Difficulty	Description
Abel Tasman Coast Track (p472)	51km	3–5 days	Easy to medium	NZ's most popular walk (or sea kayak); beaches and bays in Abel Tasman National Park (South Island)
Heaphy Track (p480)	82km	4–6 days	Medium to hard	Forests, beaches and karst landscapes in Kahurangi National Park (South Island)
Kepler Track (p646)	60km	3–4 days	Easy to Medium	Lakes, rivers, gorges, glacial valleys and beech forest in Fiordland National Park (South Island)
Lake Waikaremoana Track (p375)	46km	3–4 days	Easy to medium	Lake views, bush-clad slopes and swimming in Te Urewera National Park (North Island)
Milford Track (p651)	54km	4 days	Easy	Rainforest, crystal-clear streams and 630m-high Sutherland Falls in Fiordland National Park (South Island)
Rakiura Track (p676)	36km	3 days	Medium	Bird life (kiwi!), beaches and lush bush on remote Stewart Island (off the South Island)
Routeburn Track (p630)	32km	3 days	Medium	Eye-popping alpine scenery around Mt Aspiring and Fiordland National Parks (South Island)
Tongariro Northern Circuit (p307)	41km	3–4 days	Medium to hard	Through the active volcanic landscape of Tongariro National Park (North Island); see also Tongariro Alpine Crossing (p308)
Whanganui Journey (p278)	145km	5 days	Easy	Canoe or kayak down the Whanganui River in Whanganui National Park (North Island)

DOC has introduced a booking system for six of the Great Walks, to avoid overcrowding and protect the environment. Trampers must book their chosen hut or campsite and specify dates when they purchase a Great Walk Pass.
Lake Waikaremoana Track, Abel Tasman Coast Track, Heaphy Track – bookings required year-round
Kepler Track, Milford Track, Routeburn Track – bookings required October to April
Rakiura Track, Tongariro Northern Circuit, Whanganui Journey – bookings not required

Bookings can be made online (www.doc.govt.nz), by email (greatwalksbooking@doc.govt.nz), by phone, by fax or in person at DOC offices close to the tracks. For full details see the DOC website. There's no charge to do a day walk on any track, but you have to pay if you're staying overnight.

Other Tracks

Of course, there are a lot more walks in NZ than just the Great ones! Try these on for size:

NORTH ISLAND

Cape Reinga Coastal Walkway A 50km, three-day, easy beach tramp (camping only) in Northland. A 132km six- to eight-day route is also possible. See www.doc.govt.nz.
Mt Holdsworth–Jumbo Circuit A medium-to-hard, three-day tramp in Holdsworth Forest Park, out of Masterton. The walk passes through forest and over the top of alpine Mt Holdsworth. See www.doc.govt.nz.
Pouakai Circuit A 25km, two- to three-day loop passing lowland rainforest, cliffs and subalpine forest at the foot of Mt Taranaki in Egmont National Park. See p262.

Tongariro Alpine Crossing A brilliant, 18km, one-day, medium tramp through Tongariro National Park. See p308.

SOUTH ISLAND

Arthur's Pass There are many walks in Arthur's Pass National Park; most are difficult. See p552.

Banks Peninsula Track A 35km, two-day (medium) or four-day (easy) walk over the hills and along the coast of Banks Peninsula, crossing private and public land near Akaroa. See p544.

Greenstone and Caples Tracks Two harder tracks on conservation land, just outside Fiordland National Park. They both meet up with the Routeburn Track – a great way to start or finish this popular walk. See p630.

Hump Ridge Track An excellent, three-day, 53km circuit beginning and ending at Bluecliffs Beach on Te Waewae Bay, 20km from Tuatapere. See p658.

Inland Pack Track A 27km medium tramp in Paparoa National Park, following river valleys through the karst landscape near Punakaiki on the West Coast. See p492.

Kaikoura Coast Track An easy, three-day, 40km walk over private and public land along the spectacular coastline 50km south of Kaikoura. See p452.

Matukituki Valley Walks Good medium-to-hard walks in the Matukituki Valley, in Mt Aspiring National Park near Wanaka. See p633.

North-West Circuit A hard, muddy, eight- to 12-day walk on Stewart Island. See p676.

Queen Charlotte Track A three- to five-day medium walk in the Marlborough Sounds, affording great water views. Top-notch accommodation and water transport available. See p438.

Rees-Dart Track A 70km, four- to five-day hard tramping track in Mt Aspiring National Park, through river valleys and traversing an alpine pass. See p631.

St James Walkway This 65km, three- to five-day medium tramping track in Lake Sumner Forest Park/Lewis Pass Reserve passes through sumptuous subalpine scenery. See p551.

Wangapeka and Leslie-Karamea Tracks The Wangapeka is a four- to five-day medium tramping track along river valleys and overpasses. The Leslie-Karamea is a 90km to 100km, five- to seven-day tramp for experienced walkers only, negotiating river valleys, gorges and passes. The two tracks traverse the South Island's northwest, between Golden Bay and Karamea. See p481.

Guided Walks

Experienced, independent hikers are usually prepared to do some track research, book hut tickets, buy and cook their own food, and lug their tents across the mountains of NZ – but guided walks offer an alternative. If you're new to tramping or just want a more comfortable experience, quite a few companies can escort you through the wilds, usually staying in comfortable huts with meals cooked and equipment carried for you.

Places on the North Island where you can sign up for a guided walk include Lake Waikaremoana (p377) and Tongariro National Park (p304). On the South Island try Kaikoura (p452), the Milford Track (p652), Heaphy Track (p477) or Hollyford Track (p651). Prices for a four-night guided walk start at around $1500, and rise towards $2000 for deluxe guided experiences.

Due to open in late 2010, Te Araroa (www.teararoa.org.nz) is ambitious: a 3000km walking trail from Cape Reinga in NZ's north to Bluff in the south, linking existing trails and adding new sections. Stay tuned...

Backcountry Hut & Camping Fees

DOC has a huge network of backcountry huts (more than 950) in NZ's national and forest parks. There are 'Great Walk' category huts (with mattress-equipped bunks or sleeping platforms, water supply, toilets, heating, and often solar lighting, cooking facilities and a warden); 'Serviced Huts' (mattress-equipped bunks or sleeping platforms, water supply, heating, toilets and sometimes cooking facilities); 'Standard Huts' (no cooking equipment or heating); and 'Basic Huts' (just a shed!). Details about the services in every hut can be found on the DOC website. Backcountry hut fees per adult per night range from free to $45, with tickets bought in advance at DOC visitor centres. Children under 10 can use huts free of charge; 11- to 17-year-olds are charged half-price. If you do a lot of tramping, DOC sells an annual

Backcountry Hut Pass (adult/child $90/45), applicable to most huts except those identified in the DOC Backcountry Huts brochure – which includes many Great Walk huts in summer (for which you'll need a Great Walk Pass – see p77). Backcountry hut tickets and passes can be used to procure a bunk or campsite on some Great Walks in low season (May to September).

Depending on the hut category, a night's stay may use one or two tickets. When you arrive at a hut, date your tickets and put them in the box provided. Accommodation is on a first-come, first-served basis.

DOC also manages 250 vehicle-accessible 'Conservation Campsites'. The most basic of these ('basic' sites) are free; 'standard' and 'serviced' grounds cost between $3 and $14 per adult per night. Serviced grounds have full facilities (flush toilets, tap water, showers and picnic tables); they may also

---

RESPONSIBLE TRAMPING

To help preserve the ecology and beauty of NZ, have a scan through the following tramping tips. If you went straight from the cradle into a pair of hiking boots, some of these will seem ridiculously obvious; others you mightn't have considered. Online, www.lnt.org is a great resource for low-impact hiking, and the DOC site www.camping.org.nz has plenty more responsible camping tips. When in doubt, ask DOC or i-SITE staff.

The ridiculously obvious:

- If you can, time your tramp to avoid peak season: less people = less stress on the environment and fewer snorers in the huts.
- Carry out *all* your rubbish (including unglamorous items like condoms, tampons and toilet paper). Burying rubbish disturbs soil and vegetation, encourages erosion, and animals will probably dig up what you bury anyway.
- Don't use detergents, shampoo or toothpaste in or near watercourses, even if the products are biodegradable.
- Don't depend on open fires for cooking. Instead, use lightweight kerosene, alcohol or Shellite (white gas) stoves; avoid cookers powered by disposable butane gas canisters.
- Where there's a toilet, use it. Where there isn't one, dig a hole and bury your by-product (at least 15cm deep, 100m from any watercourse). Cover it up with soil and a rock. In snow, dig down until you're into the dirt.
- If a track passes through a muddy patch, just plough straight on through – skirting around the outside increases the size of the bog.
- Always seek permission to camp on private land.

You mightn't have considered:

- Wash your dishes 50m from watercourses; use a scourer, sand or snow instead of detergent.
- If you *really* need to scrub your bod, use biodegradable soap and a bucket, at least 50m from any watercourse. Spread the waste water around widely to help the soil filter it.
- If open fires are allowed, use only dead, fallen wood in existing fireplaces (collecting firewood around campsites strips the forest bare in quick time). Don't surround fires with rocks, and leave any extra wood for the next happy camper.
- Keep food-storage bags out of reach of scavengers by tying them to rafters or trees.
- Feeding wildlife can lead to unbalanced populations, diseases and animals becoming dependent on handouts. Keep your dried apricots to yourself.
- If you're bunking down in local accommodation near trailheads, consider environmentally savvy places; for some great sustainable accommodation choices see p745

have barbecues, a kitchen and a laundry. Standard grounds have toilets and water supply and perhaps barbecues and picnic tables.

Getting There & Away

Getting to and from trailheads can be a problem, except for popular trails serviced by public and dedicated trampers' transport. Having a vehicle only helps with getting to one end of the track (you still have to collect your car afterwards). If the track starts or ends down a dead-end road, hitching will be difficult.

Of course, tracks that are easily accessed by public transport (eg Abel Tasman) are also the most crowded. An alternative is to arrange private transport, either with a friend or by chartering a vehicle to drop you at one end then pick you up at the other. If you intend to leave a vehicle at a trailhead and return for it later, don't leave anything valuable inside – theft from cars in isolated areas is a significant problem.

EXTREME ADVENTURE

Bungy jumping was made famous by Kiwi AJ Hackett's 1986 plunge from the Eiffel Tower, after which he teamed up with champion NZ skier Henry van Asch to turn the endeavour into a profitable enterprise. The fact that a pant-wetting, illogical activity like bungy jumping is now an everyday pursuit in NZ says much about how 'extreme sports' have evolved here. Bungy, skydiving, jetboating, paragliding and kiteboarding are all well established, but keep an eye out for weird-and-wonderful activities like zorbing (rolling down a hill inside a transparent plastic ball), quad-biking, cave rafting, river sledging (white-water body boarding) and blokarting (windsurfing on wheels). Auckland's Sky Jump (p109) and Sky Screamer (p109) and Queenstown's Shotover Canyon Swing (p611) and Ledge Sky Swing (p611) are variations on the extreme theme – all against the laws of nature, and all great fun!

The 109m-high Shotover Canyon Swing in Queenstown is touted as the world's highest rope swing.

Bungy Jumping

Bungy jumping (hurtling earthwards from bridges with nothing between you and eternity but a gigantic rubber band strapped to your ankles) has plenty of daredevil panache.

Queenstown is a spider's web of bungy cords, including a 43m jump off the Kawarau Bridge (which also has a bungy theatre and museum), a 47m leap from a ledge at the top of the gondola, and the big daddy, the 134m Nevis Bungy. Other South Island bungy jumps include Waiau River (near Hanmer Springs) and Mt Hutt ski field. On the North Island, try Taupo, Auckland, Rotorua and Mokai Bridge over the Rangitikei River.

Skydiving

Ejecting yourself from a plane at high altitude is big business in NZ. There are plenty of professional operators, and at most drop zones the views on the way up (not to mention the way down) are sublime.

Some operators and clubs offer static-line jumps and Accelerated Free Fall courses, but for most first-timers a tandem skydive is the way to go. After bonding with a fully qualified instructor, you get to experience up to 45 seconds of high-speed free fall before the chute opens. The thrill is worth every dollar (specifically as much as $250/330/430 for a 9000/12,000/15,000ft jump). You'll pay extra for a video/DVD/photograph of your exploits.

Try tandem skydiving in Auckland, Matamata, Tauranga, the Bay of Islands, Taupo and Rotorua on the North Island; or in Nelson, Motueka,

The rather literally named New Zealand Parachute Federation (www.nzpf.org) is the governing body for skydiving in NZ. Check the website for info and operator listings.

TOP GEAR

Around the country, here are the best places to fix a fractured tent pole or buy a warmer sleeping bag:

- Auckland: **Kathmandu** (Map p100; ☎ 09-377 7560; www.kathmandu.co.nz; 200 Victoria St; ⓨ 9am-5.30pm Mon-Thu, 9am-7pm Fri, 9am-5pm Sat, 10am-4.30pm Sun)
- Christchurch: **Snowgum** (Map p522; ☎ 03-365 4336; www.snowgum.co.nz; 637 Colombo St; ⓨ 9am-5.30pm)
- Dunedin: **Bivouac Outdoor** (Map p576; ☎ 03-477 3679; www.bivouac.co.nz; 171 George St; ⓨ 9am-5.30pm Mon-Thu, 9am-6pm Fri, 9am-4pm Sat, 10am-4pm Sun)
- Hamilton: **Bivouac Outdoor** (Map p226; ☎ 07-839 4206; www.bivouac.co.nz; 611 Victoria St; ⓨ 9.30am-5.30pm Mon-Fri, 10am-4pm Sat, 10am-3pm Sun)
- Kaikoura: **R&R Sport** (Map p450; ☎ 03-319 5028; www.rrsport.co.nz; 14 West End; ⓨ 9am-7pm Mon-Sat, to 5.30pm in winter, 10am-4pm Sun)
- Napier: **Kathmandu** (Map p379; ☎ 06-835 5859; www.kathmandu.co.nz; 8 Dickens St; ⓨ 9am-5.30pm Mon-Thu, 9am-6pm Fri, 9am-4pm Sat, 10am-4pm Sun)
- Nelson: **R&R Sport** (Map p458; ☎ 03-548 4999; www.rrsport.co.nz; cnr Rutherford & Bridge Sts; ⓨ 9am-5.30pm Mon-Thu, 9am-7pm Fri, 9.30am-4pm Sat, 10am-3pm Sun)
- New Plymouth: **Kiwi Outdoors** (Map p254; ☎ 06-758 4152; www.kiwioutdoorsstores.co.nz; 18 Ariki St; ⓨ 8.30am-5pm Mon-Fri, 9am-2.30pm Sat, 10am-2pm Sun)
- Palmerston North: **Bivouac Outdoor** (Map p282; ☎ 06-359 2162; www.bivouac.co.nz; 400 Ferguson St; ⓨ 9am-5.30pm Mon-Thu, 9am-6pm Fri, 9am-4pm Sat, 10am-4pm Sun)

Christchurch, Fox Glacier, Methven, Wanaka, Queenstown, Te Anau and Kaikoura on the South Island.

Jetboating

The jetboat is a local invention, dreamed up by CWF Hamilton in 1957. An inboard engine sucks water into a tube in the bottom of the boat, and an impeller driven by the engine blows it out of a nozzle at the stern in a high-speed stream. The boat is steered simply by directing the jet stream. Jetboats make short work of shallow and white water because there are no propellers to damage, there's better clearance under the boat and the jet can be reversed instantly for quick braking. The jet's instant response enables these craft to execute passenger-drenching 360-degree spins almost within the length of the boat.

On the South Island, the Shotover and Kawarau Rivers near Queenstown and the Buller River near Westport are renowned jetboating waterways. The Dart River is less travelled but also good, and the Waiatoto River near Haast is a superb wilderness experience, as is the Wilkin River in Mt Aspiring National Park. Try also the Kawarau River (out of Cromwell), the Waiau River (out of Te Anau) and the Wairahurahiri River (out of Tuatapere).

On the North Island, the Whanganui, Motu, Rangitaiki and Waikato Rivers are excellent for jetboating, and there are sprint jets at the Agrodome in Rotorua. Jetboating around the Bay of Islands in Northland is also de rigueur, particularly the trip to the Hole in the Rock.

Paragliding & Kiteboarding

Paragliding is perhaps the easiest way for humans to achieve assisted flight. The sport involves taking to the skies in what is basically a parachute that's been modified so it glides through the air. After a half-day of instruction you should be able to do limited solo flights, and before you know it you could be soaring through the sky, 300m high. The **New Zealand Hang Gliding and**

- Queenstown: **Outside Sports** (Map p612; ☎ 03-441 0074; www.outsidesports.co.nz; 36 Shotover St; ☺ 8am-8pm)
- Rotorua: **Outdoorsman Headquarters** (Map p335; ☎ 07-345 9333; www.outdoorsman.co.nz; 6 Tarawera Rd; ☺ 9am-5.30pm)
- Taupo: **Outdoor Attitude** (Map p298; ☎ 06-378 6628; www.outdoorattitude.co.nz; 37 Tuwharetoa St; ☺ 9am-5pm Mon-Fri, 9am-4pm Sat, 10am-3pm Sun)
- Tauranga: **Bivouac Outdoor** (Map p339; ☎ 07-579 5127; www.bivouac.co.nz; 131 Willow St; ☺ 9am-5pm Mon-Fri, 9am-4pm Sat, 10am-3pm Sun)
- Te Anau: **Outside Sports** (Map p645; ☎ 03-249 8195; www.sportsworldteanau.co.nz; 38 Town Centre; ☺ 9am-9pm)
- Wanaka: **Outside Sports** (Map p634; ☎ 03-443 7966; www.good-sports.co.nz; 17-23 Dunmore St; ☺ 9am-5.30pm)
- Wellington: **Bivouac Outdoor** (Map p400; ☎ 04-473 2587; www.bivouac.co.nz; 39 Mercer St; ☺ 9am-5.30pm Mon-Thu, 9am-7pm Fri, 10am-5pm Sat, 11am-5pm Sun)
- Whanganui: **Kathmandu** (Map p272; ☎ 06-348 2262; www.kathmandu.co.nz; 128 Victoria Ave; ☺ 9am-5pm Mon-Fri, 10am-4pm Sat)
- Whangarei: **Kathmandu** (Map p156; ☎ 09-438 7193; www.kathmandu.co.nz; 22 James St; ☺ 9am-5.30pm Mon-Fri, 9am-4pm Sat, 10am-3pm Sun)

Paragliding Association (www.nzhgpa.org.nz) rules the roost. One of the best places to learn the skills is Wanaka Paragliding (p635).

Tandem flights, where you are strapped to an experienced paraglider, are offered all over the country. Popular tandem experiences include those in Queenstown, in Nelson, and from Te Mata Peak in Hawke's Bay.

Kiteboarding (aka kitesurfing), where a mini parachute drags you across the ocean on a mini surfboard, is pretty 'extreme', and can be attempted at Paihia, Tauranga, Mt Maunganui, Raglan, Wellington and Nelson. You can tee up lessons at most of these places, too. Karikari Peninsula near Cape Reinga on NZ's northern tip is a kiteboarding mecca.

SKIING & SNOWBOARDING

Global warming is triggering a worldwide melt, but NZ remains an essential southern-hemisphere destination for snow bunnies, with downhill, cross-country and ski mountaineering all passionately pursued. Heliskiing, where choppers lift skiers to the top of long, isolated stretches of virgin snow, also has its fans. The NZ ski season is generally June to October, though it varies considerably from one ski area to another, and can run as late as November.

Unlike Europe, America or even Australia, NZ's commercial ski areas aren't generally set up as 'resorts' with chalets, lodges or hotels. Rather, accommodation and après-ski carousing are often in surrounding towns that connect with the slopes via daily shuttles.

The variety of locations and conditions makes it difficult to rate the ski fields in any particular order. Some people like to be near Queenstown's party scene or the classic volcanic scenery of Mt Ruapehu; others prefer the high slopes and quality runs of Mt Hutt, uncrowded Rainbow or less-stressed club skiing areas. Club areas are publicly accessible and usually less crowded and cheaper than commercial ski fields, even though nonmembers pay a slightly higher fee. Many club areas have lodges you can stay at, subject to availability – winter holidays and weekends will be fully booked, but midweek you'll be OK.

Visitor information centres in NZ, and the New Zealand Tourism Board (NZTB) internationally, have brochures on the various ski areas and packages, and can make bookings. Lift passes can cost anywhere from $35 to $90 a day (roughly half for children and two-thirds for students). Lesson-and-lift packages are available at most areas. Ski-equipment rental (skis, boots and poles) starts at around $40 a day; snowboard-and-boots hire starts at around $45. Prices decrease for multiday hire. Try to rent equipment close to where you'll be skiing, so you can exchange gear if there's a problem with the fit.

North Island

TONGARIRO NATIONAL PARK

The North Island is dominated by volcanic-cone skiing. Rumbling Mt Ruapehu in Tongariro National Park is the premier ski zone.

On either side of Mt Ruapehu (a near neighbour of Mt Ngaruhoe, aka Mt Doom from *Lord of the Rings*), the twin resorts **Whakapapa** and **Turoa** (☎ Whakapapa 07-892 3738, snow-phone 08-322 2182, Turoa 06-385 8456, snow-phone 08-322 2180; www.mtruapehu.com; daily lift pass adult/child $83/48) comprise NZ's largest ski area. Lift passes are valid at both resorts. Whakapapa, 6km above Whakapapa Village in Tongariro National Park, has 30 groomed runs. There are plenty of snowboarding possibilities, cross-country, downhill and ski touring, a terrain park and the highest lift access in the country. You can drive yourself up to the slopes or take a shuttle minibus from Whakapapa Village, National Park township, Taupo or Turangi. Smaller Turoa has a beginners'

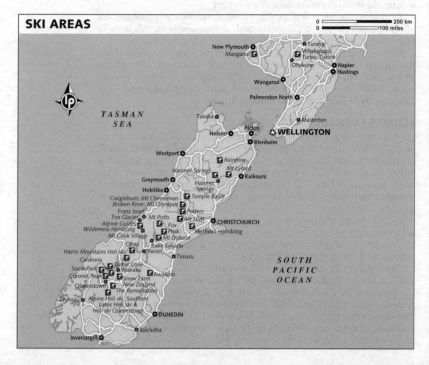

SKI AREAS

lift, snowboarding, downhill and cross-country skiing. There's no road toll or parking fee and daily ski-area transport is available from Ohakune 16km away, which has the liveliest post-ski scene in the north.

Club-operated **Tukino** (☎ 0800 885 466, 06-387 6294, snow-phone 08-822 5000; www.tukino. co.nz; daily lift pass adult/child $45/25) is on the eastern side of Mt Ruapehu, 50km from Turangi. It's quite remote, 14km down a gravel road from the sealed Desert Rd (SH1), and you need a 4WD vehicle to get in (or make a prior arrangement to use club transport). Because access is so limited the area is uncrowded, but most runs are beginner or intermediate.

See Tongariro National Park (p304) for more information.

For a range of snowboarding and skiing tours in the North Island, go to www.newzealandsnowtours.com.

TARANAKI

Manganui (☎ 027 280 0860, snow-phone 06-759 1119; www.skitaranaki.co.nz; daily lift pass adult/ child $40/25) offers volcano-slope, club-run skiing on the eastern slopes of spectacular Mt Taranaki in the Egmont National Park, 22km from Stratford. You can ski off the summit; when conditions permit, it's a sweaty two-hour climb to the crater, but the exhilarating 1300m descent compensates.

For local information, see Mt Taranaki (p261).

South Island
QUEENSTOWN & WANAKA

NZ's best-known (and top-rated) skiing is on the South Island, most of it revolving around the resort towns of Queenstown and Wanaka.

The Queenstown region's oldest ski field is **Coronet Peak** (☎ 0800 365 696, 03-442 4620, snow-phone 03-442 1970; www.nzski.com; daily lift pass adult/child $93/51). A multi-million dollar snow-making system and treeless slopes provide excellent skiing for all levels. The consistent gradient and the many undulations make this a snowboarder's paradise. Night skiing usually happens on Friday and Saturday, from late June to late September. Shuttles run from Queenstown, 18km away.

Visually remarkable, the **Remarkables** (☎ 03-442 4615, snow-phone 03-442 4615; www. nzski.com; daily lift pass adult/child $87/48) is also near Queenstown (28km away) – shuttle buses run during the season. It has an equal smattering of beginner, intermediate and advanced runs, with chairlifts and beginners' tows, and is a family-friendly field (kids under 10 ski free). Look for the sweeping run called Homeward Bound.

The highest and largest of the southern lakes ski areas, **Treble Cone** (☎ 03-443 7443, snow-phone 03-443 7444; www.treblecone.com; daily lift pass adult/child $89/39) is in a spectacular location 26km from Wanaka, with steep slopes suitable for intermediate to advanced skiers. Treble Cone also has numerous half-pipes and a terrain park for snowboarding.

Around 34km from Wanaka, **Cardrona** (☎ 03-443 7341, snow-phone 03-443 7007; www.cardrona.com; daily lift pass adult/child $85/42) has several high-capacity chairlifts, beginners' tows and extreme terrain for snowboarders. Buses run from Wanaka during the ski season, and also from Queenstown. Cardrona has acquired a reputation for the services it offers skiers with disabilities, and it was the first resort on the South Island to have an on-field crèche. In summer, the mountain bikers take over.

NZ's only commercial Nordic (cross-country) ski area, **Snow Farm New Zealand** (☎ 03-443 7542; www.snowfarmnz.com; daily trail pass adult/child $35/15) is 35km from Wanaka on the Pisa Range, high above Lake Wanaka. There are 50km of groomed trails and thousands of hectares of open rolling country for classic ski touring. Huts with facilities are dotted along the top of the Pisa Range.

Snow Park (☎ 03-443 9991; www.snowparknz.com; daily lift pass adult/child $75/40) is NZ's only dedicated freestyle ski and board area, with a plethora of pipes, terrain parks, boxes, rails, hits and snow-making facilities. There's backpacker-style accommodation, a restaurant and a bar here, too. It's 34km from Wanaka; 58km from Queenstown.

For info on local facilities, see Queenstown (p607) and Wanaka (p632).

SOUTH CANTERBURY

The commercial ski area **Ohau** (☎ 03-438 9885; www.ohau.co.nz; daily lift pass adult/child $68/26) lines the flanks of Mt Sutton, 42km from Twizel. Expect a high percentage of intermediate and advanced runs, excellent terrain for snowboarding and cross-country skiing, and a ski lodge to sleep in. See Lake Ohau & Ohau Forests (p566) for more accommodation information.

The 3km-wide basin at **Mt Dobson** (☎ 03-685 8039, snow-phone 0900 39 888; www.dobson.co.nz; daily lift pass adult/child $65/25), a commercial ski area 26km from Fairlie, caters for learners and has a large intermediate area, a terrain park and famously dry powder. On a clear day you can see Aoraki/Mt Cook and the Pacific Ocean from the Mt Dobson summit. **Fox Peak** (☎ 03-696 4808, snow-phone 03-688 0044; www.foxpeak.co.nz; daily lift pass adult/child $45/15) is a club ski area 29km from Fairlie in the Two Thumb Range. Fox Peak has four rope tows; there's good cross-country skiing from the summit. There's also dorm-style accommodation at Fox Lodge, 3km below the ski area. For info on nearby facilities, see Fairlie (p561).

Round Hill (☎ 021 680 694, snow-phone 03-680 6977; www.roundhill.co.nz; daily lift pass adult/child $65/32) is a small field with wide, gentle slopes perfect for beginners and intermediates, about 32km from Lake Tekapo village. See Lake Tekapo (p561) for details on local accommodation.

CENTRAL CANTERBURY

Mt Hutt (☎ 03-302 8811, snow-phone 03-308 5074; www.nzski.com; daily lift pass adult/child $87/48) is one of the highest ski areas in the southern hemisphere, as well as one of NZ's best. It's close to Methven and can be reached by bus from Christchurch (118km to the west). Ski shuttles run to/from both towns. The ski area's access road is a rough, unpaved ride – drivers should be extremely cautious when the weather is lousy. Mt Hutt has beginner, intermediate and advanced slopes, with a six-seater chairlift, various other lifts and heliskiing to slopes further afield. The wide-open faces are good for snowboard learners. For info on where to stay and eat in the area, see Methven (p554).

Exclusive Mt Potts is **HeliPark New Zealand** (☎ 0800 435 472, 03-303 9060; www.mtpotts.co.nz, www.helipark.co.nz; access incl 1st run $225, per subsequent run $85) – one of NZ's snow-white gems, sitting above the headwaters of the Rangitata River, 75km from Methven. It offers a helicopter-accessed skiing experience. Accommodation and meals are available at a lodge 8km from the ski area – dinner, bed and breakfast (DB&B) costs from $109. For info on the nearby town of Mt Somers, see p556.

The closest commercial ski area to Christchurch is **Porters** (☎ 03-318 4002, snow-phone 03-383 8888; www.skiporters.co.nz; daily lift pass adult/child $75/40), 96km away on the Arthur's Pass road. Its Big Mama, at 620m, is one of the steepest runs in NZ, but there are wider, gentler slopes, too. There's a half-pipe for snowboarders, good cross-country runs along the ridge, and lodge accommodation (DB&B $83). For accommodation in the area, see Craigieburn Forest Park (p551).

Temple Basin (☎ 03-377 7788, snow-phone 03-383 8888; www.templebasin.co.nz; daily lift pass adult/child $60/35) is a club field 4km from the Arthur's Pass township. It's a 50-minute walk uphill from the car park to the ski-area lodges. There's floodlit skiing at night and excellent backcountry runs for snowboarders. For info on local facilities, see Arthur's Pass (p552).

Websites such as www.snow.co.nz, www.chillout.co.nz and www.nzski.com provide ski reports, employment opportunities, webcams and virtual tours across NZ.

Craigieburn Valley (☎ 03-318 8711, snow-phone 03-383 8888; www.craigieburn.co.nz; daily lift pass adult/child $65/35), centred on Hamilton Peak, is 40km from Arthur's Pass. It's one of NZ's most challenging club areas, with intermediate and advanced runs (no beginners). Not far away is **Broken River** (☎ 03-318 8713, snow-phone 03-383 8888; www.brokenriver.co.nz; daily lift pass adult/child $60/35), another club field, with a 15- to 20-minute walk from the car park and a real sense of isolation. See Craigieburn Forest Park (p551) and Arthur's Pass (p552) for details of local places to stay and eat.

Another cool club area in the Craigieburn Range is family-friendly **Mt Cheeseman** (☎ 03-344 3247, snow-phone 03-383 8888; www.mtcheeseman.co.nz; daily lift pass adult/child $60/30), 112km from Christchurch (the closest club to the city). Based on Mt Cockayne, it's a wide, sheltered basin with drive-to-the-snow road access. Also in Craigieburn (difficult to find, but worth the search) is **Mt Olympus** (☎ 03-318 5840, snow-phone 03-383 8888; www.mtolympus.co.nz; daily lift pass adult/child $60/30), 58km from Methven and 12km from Lake Ida. This club area has four tows that lead to intermediate and advanced runs, and there are solid cross-country trails to other areas. Access is sometimes 4WD-only, depending on conditions. Lodge accommodation is available. See Craigieburn Forest Park (p551) and Arthur's Pass (p552) for details of local places to stay and eat near Mt Cheeseman and Mt Olympus.

NORTHERN SOUTH ISLAND

There are two ski areas near Hanmer Springs. Accommodation is on-field, or you can stay in the township (p548). **Hanmer Springs** (☎ 027 434 1806, snow-phone 03-383 8888; www.skihanmer.co.nz; daily lift pass adult/child $55/25) is based on Mt St Patrick, 17km from Hanmer Springs township, with mostly intermediate and advanced runs. There are natural and groomed pipe-rides for snowboarders too. **Mt Lyford** (☎ 03-315 6178, snow-phone 03-366 1220; www.mtlyford.co.nz; daily lift pass adult/child $60/30) is 60km from both Hanmer Springs and Kaikoura, and 4km from Mt Lyford village. It's a 'resort' in the true sense, with accommodation and plenty of food options available. There's a good mix of runs, suiting beginner, intermediate and advanced skiers and boarders, and a terrain park.

The sunny Nelson region also has a ski area, just 100km away (a similar distance from Blenheim). **Rainbow** (☎ 03-521 1861, snow-phone 0832 226 05; www.skirainbow.co.nz; daily lift pass adult/child $62/30) borders the Nelson Lakes National Park, with varied terrain, minimal crowds and good cross-country skiing. Chains are often required. St Arnaud (p464) is the closest town (32km).

OTAGO

Awakino (☎ 03-313 7229; www.skiawakino.com; daily lift pass adult/child $35/25) in North Otago is a small player on the scene, but worth a visit for intermediate skiers. Oamaru (p597) is 45km away on the coast; Omarama (p602) is 66km inland. Weekend lodge-and-ski packages are good value.

Heliskiing

NZ's remote heights are tailor-made for heliskiing. From July to October, operators cover a wide off-piste (off the beaten slopes) area along the Southern Alps. The cost ranges from around $750 to $1200 for three to eight runs. HeliPark New Zealand (opposite) at Mt Potts is a dedicated heliski park. Heliskiing is also available at Coronet Peak, Treble Cone, Cardrona, Mt Hutt, Mt Lyford, Ohau and Hanmer Springs. Alternatively you can contact an independent operator:

Alpine Heli-Ski (☎ 03-441 2300; www.alpineheliski.com; Queenstown)
Backcountry Helicopters NZ (☎ 0800 583 945, 03-443 9032; www.heliskinz.com; Wanaka)
Harris Mountains Heli-ski (☎ 03-442 6722; www.heliski.co.nz; Queenstown & Wanaka)

The *NZ Ski & Snowboard Guide*, published annually by Brown Bear, is a brilliant reference for powder-hounds, detailing NZ's 26 ski areas. Check it out at www.brownbear.co.nz/ski

Heli Ski Queenstown (☎ 0800 123 4354, 03-442 7733; www.flynz.co.nz; Queenstown)
Methven Heliski (☎ 03-302 8108; www.methvenheli.co.nz; Methven)
Southern Lakes Heliski (☎ 03-442 6222; www.southernlakesheliski.co.nz; Queenstown)
Wilderness Heliski (☎ 03-435 1834; www.wildernessheli.co.nz; Aoraki/Mt Cook)

MOUNTAIN BIKING

NZ is laced with quality mountain-biking opportunities. Mountain bikes can be hired in major towns or adventure-sports centres like Queenstown, Wanaka, Nelson, Picton, Taupo and Rotorua, which also have repair shops.

Various companies will take you up to the tops of mountains and volcanoes (eg Mt Ruapehu, Christchurch's Port Hills, Cardrona and the Remarkables) so you can hurtle down without the grunt-work of getting to the top first. Rotorua's Redwood Grove offers famously good mountain biking, as do the 42 Traverse near Tongariro National Park township (close to Tongariro National Park), the Alexandra goldfield trails in Central Otago, and Twizel near Mt Cook. Other North Island options include Woodhill Forest, Waihi, Te Aroha, Te Mata Peak and Makara Peak in Wellington; down south try Waitati Valley and Hayward Point near Dunedin, Canaan Downs near Abel Tasman National Park, Mt Hutt, Methven and the Banks Peninsula.

Some traditional tramping tracks are open to mountain bikes, but DOC has restricted access in many cases due to track damage and the inconvenience to walkers, especially at busy times. Never cycle on walking tracks in national parks unless it's permissible (check with DOC), or risk heavy fines and the unfathomable ire of hikers. The Queen Charlotte Track is a good one to bike, but part of it is closed in summer.

Classic New Zealand Mountain Bike Rides details short and long rides all over NZ (see www.kennett.co.nz). *New Zealand Mountain Biker* (www.nzmtbr.co.nz) mag comes out every two months.

CYCLE TOURING

On any given stretch of highway, especially during summer, you'll come across plenty of pannier-laden cyclists with one eye on the scenery and the other looking out for potholes. Not that potholes are really an issue – the roads here are generally solid. Most towns offer touring-bike hire, at either backpacker hostels or specialist bike shops. Bike service and repair shops can be found in big towns; see the regional chapters in this book.

Some excellent cycle-touring books are available, including Lonely Planet's *Cycling New Zealand,* and the *Pedallers' Paradise* booklets by Nigel Rushton (see www.paradise-press.co.nz). Anyone planning a cycling tour (particularly of the South Island) should check out the self-guided tour options at www.cyclehire.co.nz.

Almost every town-to-town and over-the-mountain NZ road attracts cyclists. If you're not after altitude, the Central Otago Rail Trail (p592) between Middlemarch and Clyde is a winner. The Little River Rail Trail (p528) in Canterbury (en route to Banks Peninsula) is also fabulous. For an off-the-beaten-highway option, try the Southern Scenic Route (p658) from Invercargill round Tuatapere to Te Anau.

The proposed $50-million **New Zealand Cycle Trail** (www.tourism.govt.nz/our-work/new-zealand-cycle-trail-project) – a national bike path from Kaitaia to Bluff – is still in the developmental stages, with some stages already open: watch this space…

Online, www.cycletour.co.nz has loads of two-wheeled info.

SEA KAYAKING

Highly rated sea kayaking areas in NZ's north include the Hauraki Gulf (particularly off Waiheke and Great Barrier Islands), the Bay of Islands and Coromandel Peninsula; in the south, try the Marlborough Sounds (Picton) and along the coast of Abel Tasman National Park, where kayaking is almost as popular as tramping. Fiordland is also a hot spot, with a heap of tour operators in Te Anau, Milford, Doubtful Sound and Manapouri arranging spectacular trips on local lakes and fiords. Also try the Otago Peninsula, Stewart Island and Kaikoura down south; or Waitemata Harbour, Hahei, Raglan and East Cape up north. The **Kiwi Association of Sea Kayakers** (KASK; www. kask.org.nz) is the main NZ organisation.

CANOEING

Canoeing is so popular on the North Island's Whanganui River that it's been designated one of NZ's 'Great Walks'! You can also dip your paddle into northern lakes like Lake Taupo and Lake Rotorua, as well as freshwater lakes on the South Island.

Many backpacker hostels close to canoe-friendly waters have Canadian canoes and kayaks for hire or free use, and loads of commercial guided trips (for those without equipment or experience) are offered on rivers and lakes throughout the country. Many trips have an eco element such as birdwatching – a prime example is the beautiful Okarito Lagoon on the West Coast of the South Island.

WHITE-WATER RAFTING & KAYAKING

There are almost as many white-water rafting possibilities as there are rivers in the country, and there's no shortage of companies to get you into the rapids. **Whitewater NZ** (www.rivers.org.nz) covers all things white-water.

Popular South Island rafting rivers include the Shotover and Kawarau Rivers near Queenstown, while the Rangitata River (south of Christchurch) is considered one of the country's best. The northern end of the island also has great rafting options, including the Buller River near Murchison and Karamea River near Westport. Other West Coast possibilities include the Arnold and Waiho Rivers.

On the North Island there are plenty of raft-worthy rivers too: try the Rangitaiki, Wairoa, Motu, Mokau, Mohaka, Waitomo, Tongariro and Rangitikei. There are also the Kaituna Cascades near Rotorua, the highlight of which is the 7m drop at Okere Falls.

Rivers are graded from I to VI, with VI meaning 'unraftable'. The grading of the Shotover Canyon varies from III to V+, depending on the time of year. The Kawarau River is rated IV; the Rangitata River has everything from I to V. On the rougher stretches there's usually a minimum age limit of 12 or 13 years. Safety equipment is supplied by operators. The **New Zealand Rafting Association** (NZRA; www.nz-rafting.co.nz) has an online river guide, and lists registered operators.

From September to April, the **New Zealand Kayak School** (☎ 03-352 5786; www. nzkayakschool.com) in Murchison offers intensive multiday courses in white-water kayaking from introductory to advanced levels (from $395).

HORSE RIDING

Horse riding is commonplace in NZ. Unlike some other parts of the world where beginners get led by the nose around a paddock, here you can really get out into the countryside on a farm, forest or beach. Rides range from one-hour jaunts (from around $50) to week-long, fully catered treks.

On the North Island, Taupo has options for wilderness horse trekking and for rides in the hills overlooking thermal regions. The Coromandel Peninsula, Waitomo, Pakiri, Ninety Mile Beach, Rotorua, the Bay of Plenty and East Cape are top places for an equine encounter.

On the South Island, all-day horseback adventures happen around Kaikoura, Nelson, Mt Cook, Lake Tekapo, Hanmer Springs, Queenstown,

For wannabe paddlers, the Sea Kayak Operators Association of New Zealand (www.skoanz.org. nz) website has a map of NZ paddling destinations and links to operators working in each area.

Check the Whitewater NZ (www.rivers.org. nz) website for rainfall and river-flow updates around the country.

NZ's premier kayaking magazine is *New Zealand Kayak*, published every two months – look for it in newsagencies.

Glenorchy, Methven, Mt Hutt, Cardrona, Te Anau and Dunedin. Treks are also offered alongside Paparoa National Park on the West Coast.

For equine info online, see the **Auckland SPCA Horse Welfare Auxiliary Inc** (www.horsetalk.co.nz) website. For trek-operator listings see www.truenz.co.nz/horse-trekking or www.newzealand.com.

ROCK CLIMBING

On the North Island, popular rock-climbing areas include the Mt Eden Quarry in Auckland; Whanganui Bay, Kinloch, Kawakawa Bay and Motuoapa near Lake Taupo; Mangatepopo Valley and Whakapapa Gorge on the Central Plateau; Humphries Castle and Warwick Castle on Mt Taranaki; and Piarere near Cambridge. Wharepapa, about 20km southeast of Te Awamutu, is regarded as one of the best places in the country for climbing.

On the South Island, the Port Hills area above Christchurch has countless climbs, and 100km away on the road to Arthur's Pass is Castle Hill, with great friction climbs and bouldering. West of Nelson, the marble and limestone mountains of Golden Bay and Takaka Hill provide prime climbing. Other options are Long Beach (north of Dunedin), and Mihiwaka and Lovers Leap on the Otago Peninsula.

> The website www.climb.co.nz has the low-down on the hottest rock-climbing spots around NZ, plus access and instruction info.

MOUNTAINEERING

NZ has a proud mountaineering history – this was, after all, the home of Sir Edmund Hillary (1919-2008), who, along with Tenzing Norgay, was the first to summit Mt Everest. When he came back down, Hillary famously uttered to friend George Lowe, 'Well, George, we knocked the bastard off!'.

The Southern Alps are studded with impressive peaks and challenging climbs. The Aoraki/Mt Cook region is outstanding; others extend along the spine of the South Island from Tapuaenuku (in the Kaikoura Ranges) and the Nelson Lakes peaks in the north to the rugged southern mountains of Fiordland. Another area with climbs for all levels is Mt Aspiring National Park. To the south in the Forbes Mountains is Mt Earnslaw, flanked by the Rees and Dart Rivers.

> Covering 17 legendary NZ mountains, Hugh Logan's *Classic Peaks of New Zealand* is a classic mountaineering read.

The Christchurch-based **New Zealand Alpine Club** (NZAC; ☎ 03-377 7595; www.alpineclub.org.nz) proffers professional information, and produces the annual *NZAC Alpine Journal* and the quarterly *The Climber* magazine. Professional outfits for training, guiding and advice can be found at Wanaka, Aoraki/Mt Cook, Lake Tekapo, and Fox and Franz Josef Glaciers.

SCUBA DIVING

NZ is prime scuba territory, with warm waters up north, brilliant sea-life and plenty of interesting dive sites for beginners and experts.

On (or rather, off) the North Island, get wet at the Bay of Islands Maritime and Historic Park, Hauraki Gulf Maritime Park, the Bay of Plenty, Great Barrier Island, Goat Island Marine Reserve, the Alderman Islands, Te Tapuwae o Rongokako Marine Reserve near Gisborne, and Sugar Loaf Islands Marine Park near New Plymouth. The Poor Knights Islands, off the east coast of the North Island, are reputed to have the best diving in NZ – the late, great Jacques Cousteau rated them among the top 10 diving spots in the world. Nearby is the diveable wreck of the Greenpeace flagship *Rainbow Warrior*.

Down south, the Marlborough Sounds Maritime Park has some interesting dives, including the *Mikhail Lermontov*, the largest diveable cruise-ship wreck in the world. Fiordland is highly unusual in that the region's extremely heavy rainfall and mountain runoff leaves a layer of peaty, brown freshwater sitting on top of some of the saltwater fiords, notably Dusky Sound, Milford Sound

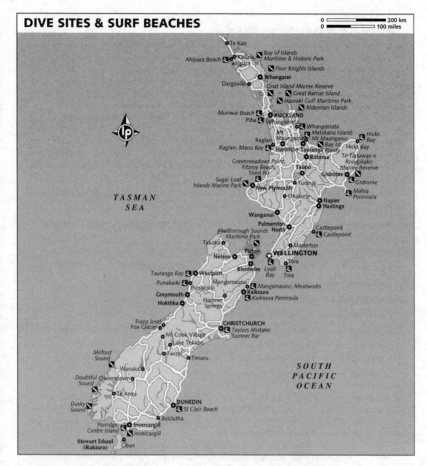

DIVE SITES & SURF BEACHES

and Doubtful Sound. The freshwater filters out light and discourages the growth of seaweed, so divers can experience amazingly clear pseudo-deep-water conditions not far below the surface. Invercargill, with its Antarctic waters, also has a diving club.

Expect to pay anywhere from $170 for a short, introductory, pool-based scuba course; and from $495 for a four-day, PADI-approved, ocean dive course. One-off organised boat- and land-based dives start at around $165.

For more on NZ's explorable depths contact the **New Zealand Underwater Association** (☎ 09-623 3252; www.nzunderwater.org.nz) in Auckland. The **Dive New Zealand** (www.divenewzealand.com) website is a treasure-trove of underwater information, with the low-down on dive and wreck sites, plus listings of operators, clubs and shops.

CAVING

Caving (aka spelunking) opportunities abound in NZ's honeycombed karst (limestone) regions. You'll find active local clubs and organised tours around Auckland, Waitomo, Whangarei, Westport and Karamea. Golden Bay also

SURFING IN NEW ZEALAND *Josh Kronfeld*

As a surfer I feel particularly guilty in letting the reader in on a local secret – NZ has a sensational mix of quality waves perfect for beginners and experienced surfers. As long as you're willing to travel off the beaten track, you can score some great, uncrowded waves. The islands of NZ are hit with swells from all points of the compass throughout the year. So, with a little weather knowledge and a little effort, numerous options present themselves. Point breaks, reefs, rocky shelves and hollow sandy beach breaks can all be found – take your pick!

Surfing has become increasingly popular in NZ and today there are surf schools up and running at most premier surf beaches. It's worth doing a bit of research before you arrive: **Surfing New Zealand** (www.surfingnz.co.nz) recommends a number of surf schools on its website. If you're on a surf holiday in NZ, consider purchasing a copy of the *New Zealand Surfing Guide,* by Mike Bhana.

Surf.co.nz (www.surf.co.nz) provides information on many great surf spots, but most NZ beaches hold good rideable breaks. Some of the ones I particularly enjoy:

- **Waikato** Raglan, NZ's most famous surf break and usually the first stop for overseas surfies
- **Coromandel** Whangamata
- **Bay of Plenty** Mt Maunganui, now with a 250m artificial reef that creates huge waves, and Matakana Island
- **Taranaki** Fitzroy Beach, Stent Rd and Greenmeadows Point all lie along the 'Surf Highway'
- **East Coast** Hicks Bay, Gisborne city beaches and Mahia Peninsula
- **Wellington Region** Beaches such as Lyall Bay, Castlepoint and Tora
- **Marlborough & Nelson** Kaikoura Peninsula, Mangamaunu and Meatworks
- **Canterbury** Taylors Mistake and Sumner Bar
- **Otago** Dunedin is a good base for surfing on the South Island, with access to a number of superb breaks, such as St Clair Beach
- **West Coast** Punakaiki and Tauranga Bay
- **Southland** Porridge and Centre Island

NZ water temperatures and climate vary greatly from north to south. For comfort while surfing, wear a wet suit. In summer on the North Island you can get away with a spring suit and boardies; on the South Island, a 2-3mm steamer. In winter on the North Island use a 2-3mm steamer, and on the South Island a 3-5mm with all the extras.

Josh is a keen surfer originally hailing from the Hawke's Bay region. While representing the All Blacks (1995-2000) he successfully juggled surfing, pop music and an international rugby career.

has some mammoth caves. One of the most awesome caving experiences is the 100m abseil into the Lost World *tomo* (cave) near Waitomo. Local underground organisations include the **Wellington Caving Group** (www.caving. wellington.net.nz) and the **Auckland Speleo Group** (www.asg.org.nz). For more info see the **New Zealand Speleological Society** (www.caves.org.nz) website.

Auckland Region

Paris may be the city of love, but Auckland is the city of many lovers, according to its Maori name, Tamaki Makaurau. In fact, her lovers so desired this beautiful place that they fought over her for centuries.

It's hard to imagine a more geographically blessed city. Its two magnificent harbours frame a narrow isthmus punctuated by volcanic cones and surrounded by fertile farmland. From any of its numerous vantage points you'll be astounded at how close the Tasman Sea and Pacific Ocean come to kissing and forming a new island.

As a result, water's never far away – whether it's the ruggedly beautiful west-coast surf beaches or the glistening Hauraki Gulf with its myriad islands. The 135,000 pleasure crafts filling Auckland's marinas have lent the city its most durable nickname: the 'City of Sails'.

Within an hour's drive from the high-rise heart of the city are dense tracts of rainforest, thermal springs, deserted beaches, wineries and wildlife reserves. Yet big-city comforts have spread to all corners of the Auckland Region: a decent coffee or chardonnay is usually close at hand.

Yet the rest of the country loves to hate it, tut-tutting about its traffic snarls and the supposed self-obsession of the quarter of the country's population that call it home. With its many riches, Auckland can justifiably respond to its detractors, 'Don't hate me because I'm beautiful'.

HIGHLIGHTS

- Going with the flows, exploring Auckland's fascinating **volcanic field** (p98)
- Getting back to nature on the island sanctuaries of the beautiful **Hauraki Gulf** (p129)
- Being awed by the Maori *taonga* (treasures) of the **Auckland Museum** (p98)
- Going west to the mystical and treacherous black sands of **Karekare** (p142) and **Piha** (p142)
- Swimming with the fish at **Goat Island Marine Reserve** (p150)
- Schlepping around world-class wineries and beaches on **Waiheke Island** (p131)
- Buzzing around the cafes and bars of **Kingsland** (p120) and **Ponsonby** (p120)
- Soaking up the Polynesian vibe at the **Pasifika Festival** (p113), held in March at Western Springs Park

- Telephone code: 09
- www.aucklandnz.com
- www.arc.govt.nz

AUCKLAND REGION

MAORI NZ: AUCKLAND REGION

Evidence of Maori occupation is literally carved into Auckland's volcanic cones (p98). The dominant *iwi* (tribe) of the isthmus was Ngati Whatua, but these days there are Maori from almost all NZ's *iwi* living here, sometimes collectively known as Ngati Akarana, or the Auckland Tribe.

For an initial taste of Maori culture, start at Auckland Museum (p98), where there's a wonderful Maori collection, a massive war canoe and a culture show. For a more personalised experience, take either Mohio's Urban Maori tour (p112) or Ngati Whatua's Tamaki Hikoi (p112).

Climate

Auckland has a mild climate, with the occasional frost in winter and high humidity in summer. Summer months have an average of eight days of rain, but the weather is famously fickle, with 'four seasons in one day' possible at any time of the year.

AUCKLAND

pop 1.2 million

Auckland's a city of volcanoes, with the ridges of lava flows forming its main thoroughfares and its many cones providing islands of green within the sea of suburbs. As well as being by far the largest, it's the most multicultural of

NZ's cities. A sizable Asian community rubs shoulders with the biggest Polynesian population of any city in the world.

The traditional Kiwi aspiration for a free-standing house on a quarter-acre section has resulted in a vast, sprawling city. The CBD was long ago abandoned to commerce, and inner-city apartment living has only just started to catch on. While geography has been kind, city planning has been less so. Unbridled and ill-conceived development has left the centre of the city with some architectural embarrassments. To get under Auckland's skin you're best to head for the rows of Victorian and Edwardian villas in its hip inner-city suburbs.

HISTORY

Maori occupation in the Auckland area dates back around 800 years. Initial settlements were concentrated on the coastal regions of the Hauraki Gulf islands, but gradually the fertile isthmus beckoned and land was cleared for growing food.

Over hundreds of years Tamaki's many different tribes wrestled for control of the area, building *pa* (fortified villages) on the numerous volcanic cones. The Ngati Whatua *iwi* (tribe) from the Kaipara Harbour took the upper hand in 1741, occupying the major *pa* sites. During the Musket Wars of the 1820s they were decimated by the northern tribe Ngapuhi, leaving the land all but abandoned.

At the time of the signing of the Treaty of Waitangi in 1840, Governor Hobson had his base at Okiato, near Russell in the Bay of Islands. When Ngati Whatua chief Te Kawau offered 3000 acres of land for sale on the northern edge of the Waitemata Harbour, Hobson decided to create a new capital, naming it after one of his patrons, George Eden (Earl of Auckland).

Beginning with just a few tents on a beach, the settlement quickly grew, and soon the port was kept busy exporting the region's produce, including kauri timber. However, it lost its capital status to Wellington after just 25 years.

Since the beginning of the 20th century Auckland has been NZ's fastest-growing city and its main industrial centre. Political deals may be done in Wellington, but Auckland is the big smoke in the land of the long white cloud.

AUCKLAND REGION FACTS

Eat Multiculturally, at one of the city's numerous food halls (p118)

Drink Waiheke Island rosé on a hot summer's day

Read *Under The Mountain* (1979) – Maurice Gee's teenage tale of slimy things lurking under Auckland's volcanos

Listen to *One Tree Hill* (1987) – U2's elegy to their Kiwi roadie is no less poignant now the tree's gone (see p99)

Watch *Sione's Wedding* (2006), Chris Graham's comedy set in Grey Lynn and central Auckland

Swim at Onetangi (p131)

Festival Pasifika (p113)

Tackiest tourist attraction Sheepworld's fluorescent flock of sheep – New Rave goes too far (p148)

Go green Encounter endangered birds among the regenerated forest of Tiritiri Matangi Island (p135)

ORIENTATION

The Auckland isthmus runs roughly west–east, with Waitemata Harbour lying to the north (feeding into the Hauraki Gulf) and Manukau Harbour to the south (feeding into the Tasman Sea). The Harbour Bridge links the city to the North Shore, with the CBD to its east.

The commercial heart of the city is Queen St, which runs from the waterfront up to Newton's Karangahape Rd (K Rd), a lively, bohemian, sometimes gritty strip of inexpensive restaurants and boisterous bars.

In the early days, the area immediately east of the city tended to be upmarket and Anglican, while the west was more Catholic and working-class. While they're all rather pricey neighbourhoods nowadays, Parnell and Remuera retain vestiges of old-money snobbery while Ponsonby and Grey Lynn are slightly more alternative. Mt Eden sits somewhere between the two, both physically and sociologically.

The airport is 23km south of the city centre.

Maps

Auckland Map Centre (Map p100; ☎ 09-309 7725; www.aucklandmapcentre.co.nz; 209 Queen St; ◷ 9am-5pm Mon-Fri, 10am-4pm Sat)

INFORMATION
Bookshops

Unity Books (Map p100; ☎ 09-307 0731; 19 High St; ◷ 8.30am-7pm Mon-Thu, 8.30am-9pm Fri, 9am-6pm

AUCKLAND REGION

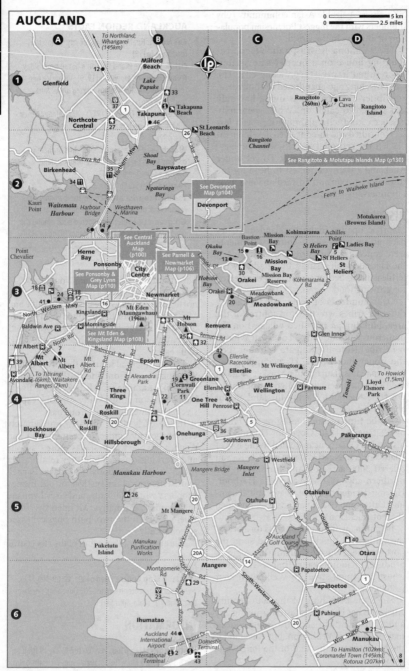

AUCKLAND

0 — 5 km
0 — 2.5 miles

See Rangitoto & Motutapu Islands Map (p130)

See Devonport Map (p104)

See Central Auckland Map (p100)

See Parnell & Newmarket Map (p106)

See Ponsonby & Grey Lynn Map (p110)

See Mt Eden & Kingsland Map (p108)

To Northland; Whangarei (145km)

Ferry to Waiheke Island

Sat, 11am-6pm Sun) Excellent independent bookshop with knowledgeable staff.

Whitcoulls (Map p100; ☎ 09-984 5400; 210 Queen St; ☿ 8am-7pm Mon-Thu, 8am-9pm Fri, 9am-6pm Sat, 10am-6pm Sun) Local chain with good travel and fiction sections.

Women's Bookshop (Map p110; ☎ 09-376 4399; 105 Ponsonby Rd; ☿ 10am-6pm Mon-Fri, 10am-5pm Sat & Sun) A community resource as well as a good independent bookshop.

Emergency

Ambulance, fire service & police (☎ 111)
Auckland Central police station (Map p100; ☎ 09-302 6400; cnr Vincent & Cook Sts)

Internet Access

Expect to pay around $3 an hour at internet cafes; a few are open 24 hours. Parnell has a free wi-fi zone, which you should be able to access from most cafes along the strip.

Internet Resources

Auckland NZ (www.aucklandnz.com) Official tourist site.
Auckland Regional Council (ARC; www.arc.govt.nz) Information about regional parks and events.
Dine Out (www.dineout.co.nz) Locals' comments on restaurants.
MAXX Regional Transport (www.maxx.co.nz) Public transport timetables and route planner.

Medical Services

Auckland City Hospital (Map p100; ☎ 09-379 0000; Park Rd, Grafton; ☿ 24hr) The city's main hospital; has an accident and emergency (A&E) section.

Auckland Metro Doctors & Travelcare (Map p100; ☎ 09-373 4621; 17 Emily Place, Auckland Central; ☿ 9am-5.30pm Mon-Fri, 10am-2pm Sat) Specialises in health care for travellers, such as vaccinations and travel consultations.
Starship Children's Hospital (Map p100; ☎ 09-367 0000; Park Rd, Grafton; ☿ 24hr) Has its own A&E department.

Media

Metro Glossy monthly magazine covering Auckland issues in depth.
New Zealand Herald (www.nzherald.co.nz) The country's biggest daily newspaper.

Money

There are plenty of moneychangers, banks and ATMs, especially on Queen St. For weekend banking visit the **ASB** (Map p100; cnr Queen & Customs Sts; ☿ 9am-4.30pm Mon-Fri, 9am-4.30pm Sat, 10am-4pm Sun) in Westfield Downtown.

Post

Wellesley St post office (Map p100; 24 Wellesley St) The place to pick up poste restante mail (ID is required).

Tourist Information

Auckland Domestic Airport i-SITE (Map p96; ☎ 09-256 8480; ☿ 6am-10pm) In the Air New Zealand section of the domestic airport.
Auckland International Airport i-SITE (Map p96; ☎ 09-275 6467; ☿ 24hr) Located on your left as you exit the customs hall. You can make free calls to Auckland accommodation providers from here.

AUCKLAND IN...

Two Days

Book ahead for tomorrow night's dinner. Breakfast in **Ponsonby** (p120) and take the Link Bus to **Auckland Museum** (below) for the Maori gallery and culture show. Wander through the Domain towards **K Rd** (p119), where you can grab lunch. Follow the walking tour on p111, stopping along the way for at least a quick whiz around the NZ section of the **Auckland Art Gallery** (p103). End with a relaxing drink or meal at the **Viaduct Harbour** (p107).

On day two, grab breakfast in the city before catching the 9.15am ferry to **Rangitoto** (p129). This will give you time to explore the volcanic island before it starts to bake. Catch the 12.45pm ferry to **Devonport** (p104) for lunch. If you've still got energy, check out **North Head** (p105) and then cool off at **Cheltenham Beach** (p105), if the weather and tide permit. Stay on the North Shore for a memorable dinner at the **Engine Room** (p121) or **Eight.Two** (p121).

Four Days

On the third day, head west. Grab breakfast in **Titirangi** (p141) before exploring the **Waitakere Ranges Regional Park** (p141), **Karekare** (p142) and **Piha** (p142). If you don't have a car, book in a day trip with **Mohio Tours** (p112). On the way back, stop in at **Elevation** (p142) for a glass of wine and breathtaking views of the city. Freshen up for a night eating and drinking your way around **Kingsland** (p120).

On day four, breakfast in **Mt Eden** (p120) and then climb **Maungawhau** (opposite). Catch the train back to Britomart for the 11am ferry to **Waiheke Island** (p131). Have lunch and dinner at a winery, and spend the afternoon at the beach (or more wineries if the weather's bad). Don't miss the last ferry back.

Auckland i-SITE (Map p100; ☎ 09-363 7182; www.aucklandnz.com; Sky Tower Atrium, cnr Victoria & Federal Sts; ☺ 8am-8pm)

Automobile Association (AA; Map p100; ☎ 09-966 8919; www.aa.co.nz; 99 Albert St; ☺ 9am-5pm Mon-Fri) Maps and accommodation directories.

Cornwall Park Information Centre (Map p96; ☎ 09-630 8485; www.cornwallpark.co.nz; Huia Lodge; ☺ 10am-4pm)

Devonport i-SITE (Map p104; ☎ 09-446 0677; www.tourismnorthshore.org.nz; 3 Victoria Rd; ☺ 8.30am-5pm) Internet access and information.

DOC information centre (Map p100; ☎ 09-379 6476; www.doc.govt.nz; 137 Quay St; ☺ 9am-5pm Mon-Fri, 10am-3pm Sat)

New Zealand i-SITE (Map p100; ☎ 09-307 0612; 137 Quay St; ☺ 9am-5.30pm May-Oct, 8am-7pm Nov-Apr)

Takapuna i-SITE (Map p96; ☎ 09-486 8670; 49 Hurstmere Rd; ☺ 8.30am-5pm Mon-Fri, 10am-3pm Sat & Sun)

SIGHTS
Auckland Volcanic Field

Some cities think they're tough by living in the shadow of a volcano. Auckland's built on 50 of them and, no, they're not all extinct. The last one to erupt was Rangitoto (p129) about 600 years ago and no one can predict when the next eruption will occur. Auckland's quite literally a hot spot – with a reservoir of magma 100km below waiting to bubble to the surface. But relax: this has only happened 19 times in the last 20,000 years.

Some of Auckland's volcanoes are cones, some are filled with water and some have been completely quarried away. Moves are afoot to register the field as a World Heritage site and protect what remains. Most of the surviving cones show evidence of terracing from when they formed a formidable series of Maori *pa*.

Apart from those mentioned separately in this section, these sites are also worth a visit:
Mt Wellington (Maungarei; Map p96)
Mt Albert (Owairaka; Map p96)
Mt Roskill (Map p96)
Lake Pupuke (Map p96)
Mt Mangere (Map p96)
Mt Hobson (Map p96)

Auckland Museum & Domain

Covering about 80 hectares, the green swathe of the **Auckland Domain** (Map p106) contains sports fields, interesting sculpture, formal gardens, wild corners and the **Wintergarden** (Map p106; admission free; ☺ 9am-5.30pm Mon-Sat, 9am-7.30pm Sun Nov-Mar, 9am-4.30pm Apr-Oct), with its fernery, tropical house, cool house, cute cat statue and neighbouring cafe. The mound in the centre of the park is all that remains of **Pukekaroa** (Map p106), one of Auckland's volcanoes. At its humble peak, a totara surrounded by a palisade honours the first Maori king (see the boxed text, p225).

Dominating it all is the magnificent **Auckland Museum** (Map p106; ☎ 09-309 0443; www. aucklandmuseum.com; adult/child $5/free; ☒ 10am-5pm), an imposing Greek temple with an impressive modern dome. Its comprehensive display of Pacific Island and Maori artefacts on the ground floor deserves to be on your 'must see' list. Highlights include a 25m war canoe and an extant carved meeting house from the Thames area (see p194) that you can enter (remove your shoes first).

Bookings are required for the **museum highlights guided tour** (☎ 09-306 7048; adult/child $10/5; ☒ 10.30am & 2pm). **Maori gallery tours** (same prices) take place at 11.30am and 2pm. Daily **Maori cultural performances** (adult/child $25/13; ☒ 11am, noon & 1.30pm) provide a good (and good-humoured) introduction to things Maori.

Admirers of the male form should check out the Domain's **Grafton Gate** (Map p100; Park Rd), a wonderful art-deco sandstone construction topped with a larger-than-life bronze nude.

Walking here from the city will take about 30 minutes, or you can catch the Link Bus (p128) to the neighbouring hospital.

One Tree Hill (Maungakiekie)

This volcanic cone (Map p96) was the isthmus' key *pa* and the greatest fortress in the country. It's easy to see why: a drive or walk to the top (182m) offers amazing 360-degree views. At the summit is the grave of John Logan Campbell, who gifted the land to the city in 1901, requesting that a memorial (the imposing obelisk and statue above the grave) be built to the Maori people. Nearby is the stump of the last 'one tree' (see the boxed text, below).

Allow a few hours to explore the craters and surrounding **Cornwall Park** (Map p96), with its impressive mature trees and historic cottage. The information centre (opposite) has fascinating interactive displays illustrating what the *pa* would have looked like when 5000 people lived here.

Near the excellent **children's playground**, the **Stardome Observatory** (Map p96; ☎ 09-624 1246; www. stardome.org.nz; adult/child $16/8) offers regular stargazing and planetarium shows that aren't dependent on Auckland's fickle weather (usually 8pm Wednesday to Saturday; phone ahead).

To get here from the city, take bus 328 from Customs St to Manukau Rd (adult/child $4.30/2.40, 21 minutes). By car, take the Greenlane exit of the Southern Motorway and turn right into Green Lane West.

Mt Eden (Maungawhau)

The view from Mt Eden (Map p108), Auckland's highest cone (196m), is superb. The symmetrical crater (50m deep) is known as Te Ipu Kai a Mataaho (the Food Bowl of Mataaho, the god of things hidden in the ground) and is highly *tapu* (sacred); don't enter it, but feel free to explore the remainder of the mountain. The remains of *pa* terraces and storage pits are clearly visible.

On its eastern slopes, **Eden Gardens** (Map p108; ☎ 09-638 8395; 24 Omana Ave, Epsom; adult/child $6/free; ☒ 9am-4pm) is a horticultural showpiece noted for camellias, rhododendrons and azaleas.

Western Springs

Auckland Zoo (Map p96; ☎ 09-360 3800; www.auckland zoo.co.nz; Motions Rd; adult/child $19/9; ☒ 9.30am-5.30pm) is an excellent modern zoo with spacious, natural compounds. The infrared lighting of the nocturnal house offers a rare chance to see

---

ONE TREE TO RULE THEM ALL

Looking at One Tree Hill, your first thought will probably be 'Where's the bloody tree?'. Good question. Up until 2000 a Monterey pine stood at the top of the hill. This was a replacement for a sacred totara that was chopped down by British settlers in 1852. Maori activists first attacked the foreign usurper in 1994, finishing the job in 2000. It's unlikely that another tree will be planted until local land claims have moved closer to resolution, but you can bet your boots that this time around it'll be a native.

Auckland's most beloved landmark achieved international recognition in 1987 when U2 released the song 'One Tree Hill' on their acclaimed *The Joshua Tree* album. It was only released as a single in NZ, where it went to number one.

AUCKLAND REGION

CENTRAL AUCKLAND

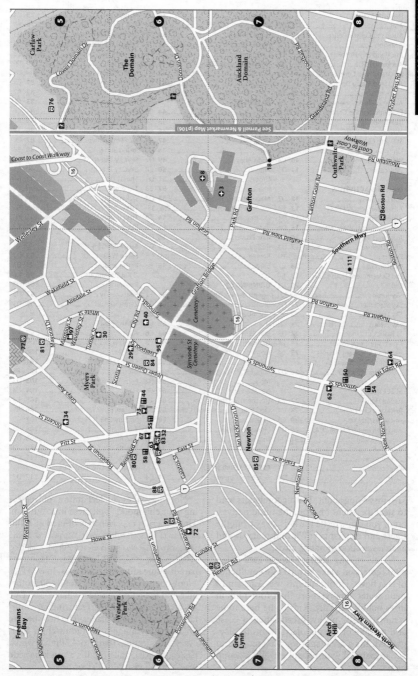

kiwi fossicking about. The big foreigners tend to steal the attention from the timid natives, but if you can wrestle the kids away from the tigers and elephants you'll find tuataras and a large selection of native birds.

Neighbouring **Western Springs Park** (Map p96) centres on a lake formed by a confluence of lava flows. Until 1902 this was Auckland's main water supply; more than four-million litres bubble up daily. Kids come here to be traumatised by pushy, bread-fattened geese and partake of the popular adventure playground. It's a great spot for a picnic and to get acquainted with playful pukeko (swamp hens).

Nothing makes you feel quite as old as seeing your childhood appliances in a museum. That sobering experience is offered at **MOTAT** (Museum of Transport & Technology; Map p96; ☎ 09-815 5800; www.motat.org.nz; 805 Great North Rd; adult/child $14/7; ◷ 10am-5pm), a 19-hectare trainspotter's paradise spreading over two sites. In MOTAT 1 look out for Helen Clark's Honda 50 motorbike and the cutesy pioneer village. MOTAT 2 is an aircraft graveyard, featuring rare military and commercial planes. The two sites are linked by a vintage tram (adult/child $2/1, every 30 minutes, 10am to 4.30pm), which passes the park and zoo. It's a fun kids' ride whether you visit MOTAT or not.

From the city, catch any bus (adult/child $3.20/1.80, 16 minutes) heading west via Great North Rd. By car, take the Western Springs exit from the North Western Motorway.

Auckland Art Gallery

The **Auckland Art Gallery** (Map p100; ☎ 09-379 1349; www.aucklandartgallery.com; admission free; 10am-5pm) spreads over two neighbouring buildings. The **Main Gallery** (cnr Wellesley & Kitchener Sts), built in French chateau style, isn't terribly big, but it houses important works by Pieter Bruegel the Younger and Guido Reni in the European collection, and an extensive collection of NZ art. It's worth calling in for the intimate 19th-century portraits of tattooed Maori subjects by Charles Goldie and Gottfried Lindauer alone. The **New Gallery** (cnr Wellesley & Lorne Sts) concentrates on contemporary art and temporary exhibitions (with varying admission charges). Ten commercial galleries can be found in the immediate vicinity.

If you're reading this before April 2011, the Main Gallery is closed for a major renovation. You'll find the highlights of the permanent collection housed in the New Gallery.

Sky Tower

The impossible-to-miss **Sky Tower** (Map p100; ☎ 09-363 6000; www.skycityauckland.co.nz; cnr Federal & Victoria Sts; adult/child $25/8; 8.30am-10.30pm Sun-Thu, 8.30am-11.30pm Fri & Sat) looks like a giant hypodermic giving a fix to the heavens. Spectacular lighting renders it even more space-age at night. The colours change for special events and shooting fireworks make it even more phallic on New Year's Eve.

The tower is the best part of the SkyCity complex, a tacky 24-hour casino with restaurants, cafes, bars and a hotel. At 328m it is the tallest structure in the southern hemisphere. A lift takes you up to the observation decks in 40 stomach-lurching seconds; look down through the glass floor panels if you're after an extra kick. It costs $3 extra to catch the skyway lift to the ultimate viewing level. Late afternoon is a good time to go up: you can sip a beverage in the Sky Lounge as the sun sets. See p109 for crazy stuff you can do while you're up here.

Kelly Tarlton's Antarctic Encounter & Underwater World

Housed in old stormwater and sewage holding tanks is this unique **aquarium** (Map p96; ☎ 09-531 5065; www.kellytarltons.co.nz; 23 Tamaki Dr, Orakei; adult/child $32/16; 9.30am-5.30pm). A transparent tunnel runs along the centre of the tank, through which you travel on a conveyor belt, with the fish, including sharks and stingrays, swimming around you. You can step off at any time to take a closer look.

The big attraction, however, is the permanent winter wonderland known as Antarctic Encounter. It includes a walk through a replica of Scott's 1911 Antarctic hut, and a ride aboard a heated Snow Cat through a frozen environment where a colony of king and gentoo penguins lives at sub-zero temperatures. Displays include an Antarctic scientific base of the future and exhibits on the history of Antarctica. Needless to say, this whole experience is a fantastic adventure for adults travelling with children.

Less fantastic are the entry queues at busy times of the year. Book online for a shorter wait.

Buses numbered 745 to 769 head here from Britomart. There's also a free shark-shaped shuttle bus that departs 172 Quay St (opposite the ferry terminal) on the hour between 9am and 4pm (except 2pm) and SkyCity's atrium 10 minutes later (departing Kelly Tarlton's 40 minutes later).

Tamaki Drive

This scenic, pohutukawa-lined road heads east from the city, hugging the waterfront. In summer it's a jogging/cycling/rollerblading blur offering plenty of eye candy.

Just past Kelly Tarlton's, Hapimana St heads up to Bastion Point (see the boxed text, p105) and the **Michael Joseph Savage Memorial** (Map p96). Savage (1872–1940) was the country's first Labour prime minister and widely considered one of its best. His socialist reforms left him adored by the populace, as this elaborate cliff-top garden mausoleum demonstrates. Follow the lawn to a WWII gun embankment – one of many that line the harbour.

Below the headland is **Mission Bay**, a popular beach with an iconic fountain, historic mission house, restaurants and bars. Safe swimming beaches **Kohimarama** and **St Heliers** follow. Further east along Cliff Rd, the **Achilles Point lookout** (Map p96) offers panoramic views. At its base is **Ladies Bay**, where nudists put up with mud and shells for the sake of seclusion.

Buses 745 to 769 from Britomart follow this route.

Albert Park & Auckland University

Hugging the hill on the city's eastern flank, **Albert Park** (Map p100) is a charming Victorian formal garden overrun by students during term time, the more radical of whom periodically deface the statues of Governor Grey and Queen Victoria. Auckland University campus stretches over several streets and incorporates a row of stately **Victorian merchant houses** (Map p100; Princes St) and **Old Government House** (Map p100; Waterloo Quadrant). The latter was the colony's seat of power from 1856 until 1865, when Wellington became the capital.

The **University Clock Tower** (Map p100; 22 Princes St) is Auckland's architectural triumph. The stately 'ivory' tower (1926) tips its hat towards art nouveau (the incorporation of NZ flora and fauna into the decoration) and the Chicago School (the way it's rooted into the earth). It's usually open, so wander inside.

At the centre of the campus is a wall of the **Albert Barracks** (1847; Map p100), a fortification that enclosed nine hectares, including Albert Park, during the New Zealand Wars.

Devonport

Located at the bottom of the North Shore, Devonport makes a pleasant day trip by ferry from the city. Quaint without being sickeningly twee, it retains a village atmosphere,

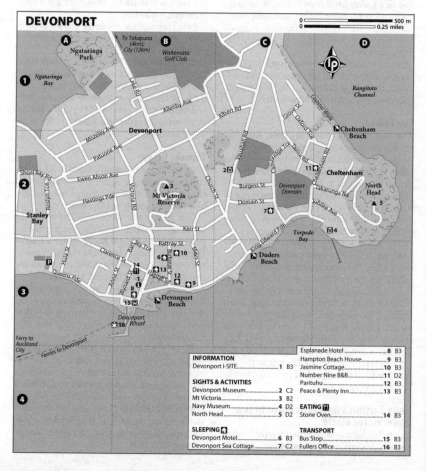

DEVONPORT

0 _____ 500 m
0 _____ 0.25 miles

To Takapuna (4km);
City (12km)

Ngataringa Park

Waitemata Golf Club

Ngataringa Bay

Rangitoto Channel

Coastal Walk

Lake Rd

Allenby Ave

Albert Rd

Cheltenham Beach

Mozeley Ave

Devonport

Patuone Ave

Grove St

Oxford Tce

Cambridge Tce

Tainui Rd

Cheltenham

Shoal Bay Rd

Ewen Alison Ave

Burgess St

Devonport Domain

Takarunga Rd

North Head

Roslyn Tce

Hastings Pde

Victoria Rd

Church St

Domain St

Jubilee Ave

Stanley Bay

Mt Victoria Reserve

Kerr St

Torpedo Bay

Cameron St

Rattray St

May St

King Edward Pde

Duders Beach

Clarence St

Queens Pde

Flagstaff Tce

Anne St

Wynyard St

Devonport Beach

Devonport Wharf

Ferry to Auckland City

Ferries to Devonport

INFORMATION		
Devonport i-SITE	1	B3

SIGHTS & ACTIVITIES		
Devonport Museum	2	C2
Mt Victoria	3	B2
Navy Museum	4	D2
North Head	5	D2

SLEEPING		
Devonport Motel	6	B3
Devonport Sea Cottage	7	C2
Esplanade Hotel	8	B3
Hampton Beach House	9	B3
Jasmine Cottage	10	B3
Number Nine B&B	11	D2
Parituhu	12	B3
Peace & Plenty Inn	13	B3

EATING		
Stone Oven	14	B3

TRANSPORT		
Bus Stop	15	B3
Fullers Office	16	B3

WHAT BECAME OF NGATI WHATUA?

By the end of the 1840s Maori were already a minority in the Auckland area, and eventually the Ngati Whatua o Orakei *hapu* (subtribe) was reduced to a small block of land in the vicinity of Okahu Bay and Bastion Point. In 1886 Bastion Point was confiscated by the government for military use, and then in 1908 more land was taken to build a sewage pipe that pumped raw effluent into the water in front of the *hapu*'s last remaining village at Okahu Bay. All but the cemetery was confiscated in 1951, with the people dragged out of their homes and the village destroyed to 'clean up' the area before the royal visit of Queen Elizabeth II.

When the government decided to sell the prime real estate on Bastion Point in 1977, the *hapu* staged a peaceful occupation that lasted for 507 days before they were once again dragged into custody. It was a seminal moment in the Maori protest movement. During the next decade the government apologised and returned the land where the *marae* now stands. At the time of research, further negotiations between the government and *hapu* were progressing, with several of the volcanic cones likely to be part of the final settlement. The former railway land on which the Vector Arena now sits has already been returned.

---

with many well-preserved Victorian and Edwardian buildings and loads of cafes. If your interests are less genteel, there are two volcanic cones and easy access to the first of the North Shore's beaches.

The navy is based here, its history on display at the **Navy Museum** (Map p104; ☎ 09-445 5186; www.navymuseum.mil.nz; King Edward Pde; admission by donation; ☉ 10am-4.30pm). Its civilian neighbours have theirs preserved in the **Devonport Museum** (Map p104; ☎ 09-445 2661; www.devonportmuseum.org. nz; 33a Vauxhall Rd; admission free; ☉ 2-4pm Sat & Sun).

Mt Victoria (Takarunga; Map p104; Victoria Rd) and **North Head** (Maungauika; Map p104; Takarunga Rd; ☉ 6am-10pm) were Maori *pa* and are both still fortresses of sorts, with the navy maintaining a presence. Both have gun embankments and North Head is riddled with tunnels. Started at the end of the 19th century in response to the Russian threat, they were extended during WWI and WWII. The gates are locked at night, but that's never stopped teenagers from jumping the fence and terrifying themselves in the tunnels. Devonport Museum stands on the remains of a third cone that was largely quarried away.

For a self-guided tour of historic buildings, pick up the *Old Devonport Walk* pamphlet from the i-SITE (p98).

Ferries to Devonport (adult/child $10/5 return, 12 minutes) depart from the Auckland Ferry Building every 30 minutes (hourly after 7pm) from 6.15am to 11pm (until 1am Friday and Saturday), and from 7.15am to 10pm on Sundays and public holidays. Some Waiheke Island and Rangitoto ferries also stop here.

North Shore Beaches

A succession of fine swimming beaches stretches from North Head to Long Bay. The gulf islands provide a picturesque backdrop and shelter them from strong surf, making them safe for supervised children. Aim for high tide unless you fancy a lengthy walk to waist-deep water. **Cheltenham Beach** (Map p104) is a short walk from Devonport. **Takapuna Beach** (Map p96), closest to the Harbour Bridge, is Auckland's answer to Bondi and the most built up. Nearby **St Leonards Beach** (Map p96), popular with gay men, requires clambering over rocks at high tide.

Parnell & Newmarket

Parnell likes to think of itself as a village, although the only tractors to be seen are the SUVs driven by the affluent suburb's soccer mums. Inexplicably, it has an excellent selection of budget accommodation, although it's doubtful that backpackers will be frequenting the pricey eateries of the main strip. Neighbouring Newmarket is a busy shopping precinct, known for its boutiques.

This is one of Auckland's oldest areas and has retained several heritage buildings. **Highwic** (Map p106; ☎ 09-524 5729; www.historic.org. nz; 40 Gillies Ave; adult/child $7.50/free; ☉ 10.30am-noon & 1-4.30pm Wed-Sun) is a marvellous example of a Carpenter Gothic house (1862), sitting amid lush, landscaped grounds. **Ewelme Cottage** (Map p106; ☎ 09-379 0202; www.historic.org.nz; 14 Ayr St; adult/ child $7.50/free; ☉ 10.30am-noon & 1-4.30pm Fri-Sun) is a storybook affair that was built for a clergyman in 1864 and has been left in startlingly good condition.

PARNELL & NEWMARKET

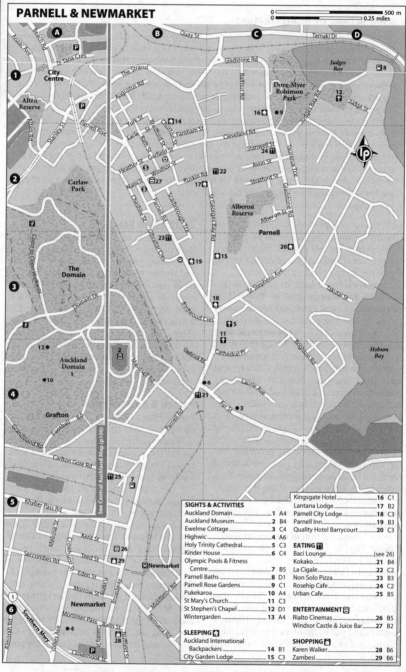

Close to Ewelme Cottage is the simply restored **Kinder House** (Map p106; ☎ 09-379 4008; 2 Ayr St; adult/child $4/2; ☑ 11am-3pm Tue-Sun), built of volcanic stone (1857). Designed by Frederick Thatcher, it displays the subtle but skilful watercolours and memorabilia of the Reverend Dr John Kinder (1819–1903), who was the headmaster of the Church of England Grammar School. Enthusiastic and informative guided tours are provided.

Holy Trinity Cathedral (Map p106; ☎ 09-303 9500; www.holy-trinity.org.nz; Parnell Rd; ☑ 10am-3pm Mon-Sat, 11am-3pm Sun) is worth visiting for its modern stained-glass windows. Its blue-coloured rose window, designed by English artist Carl Edwards, is particularly striking above the simple kauri altar. Next door is **St Mary's** (Map p106), a wonderful wooden Gothic Revival church (1886), with a burnished wooden interior and lovely stained-glass windows.

The **Parnell Rose Gardens** (Map p106; Gladstone Rd) are blooming excellent from November to March. A pleasant stroll leads to peaceful **Judges Bay** and tiny **St Stephen's Chapel** (Map p106; Judge St), built for the signing of the constitution of NZ's Anglican Church (1857).

Civic Theatre

Opening its doors in 1929, the mighty **Civic** (Map p100; ☎ 09-357 3355; www.civictheatre.co.nz; cnr Queen & Wellesley Sts) is one of seven 'atmospheric theatres' remaining in the world and a fine survivor from cinema's Golden Age. The auditorium has lavish Moorish decoration and a starlit southern-hemisphere sky in the ceiling, complete with cloud projections. The foyer is an Indian indulgence, with elephants and monkeys hanging from every conceivable fixture. Buddhas were planned to decorate the street frontage but were considered too risqué at the time – they chose neoclassical naked boys instead!

If at all possible, try to attend a performance here. It's mainly used for touring musicals, big premieres and Film Festival screenings (see p113).

Viaduct Harbour

Once a busy commercial port, the Viaduct Harbour was given a major makeover leading up to the 1999/2000 and 2003 America's Cup tournaments. It's now a fancy dining and boozing precinct for the boat-shoes brigade, and guaranteed to have at least a slight buzz any night of the week. Historical plaques, in-teresting sculpture and the chance to gawk at millionaires' yachts make it a pleasant place for a stroll.

The well-presented **Voyager – New Zealand Maritime Museum** (Map p100; ☎ 09-373 0800; www.nzmaritime.org; cnr Quay & Hobson Sts; adult/child $16/8; ☑ 9am-5pm) traces NZ's seafaring history from Maori voyaging canoes to the America's Cup. Recreations include a tilting 19th-century steerage-class cabin and a fab 1950s-era bach (holiday home). Its newest showcase, *Blue Water Black Magic*, is a tribute to Sir Peter Blake, the Whitbread-Round-The-World and America's Cup-winning yachtsman who was murdered in 2001 while on an environmental monitoring trip on the Amazon. Check the website for details of semiregular historic steamboat and sailing-ship cruises.

St Patrick's Cathedral

Auckland's Catholic **cathedral** (Map p100; ☎ 09-303 4509; www.stpatricks.org.nz; 43 Wyndham St; ☑ 7am-7pm) is one of its loveliest buildings. Polished wood and Belgian stained glass lend warmth to the interior of this majestic Gothic Revival church (1907). There's a historical display in the old confessional on the left-hand side.

Alberton

A classic colonial mansion (1863), **Alberton** (Map p96; ☎ 09-846 7367; www.historic.org.nz; 100 Mt Albert Rd; adult/child $8/free; ☑ 10.30am-4pm Wed-Sun) offers tours and was used as a location for some scenes in *The Piano*. Bring a picnic lunch and enjoy the grounds.

Auckland Botanical Gardens

The 64-hectare **Auckland Botanical Gardens** (Map p96; ☎ 09-267 1457; Hill Rd, Manurewa; admission free; ☑ 8am-6pm) has dozens of themed gardens, threatened plants, and a hell of a lot of brides and grooms. By car, take the Southern Motorway, exit at Manurewa and follow the signs. Otherwise take the train to Manurewa ($5.70, 40 minutes) and then walk along Hill Rd (1.5km) or catch bus 466 ($1.60, 15 minutes).

ACTIVITIES

Trading on the country's action-packed reputation, Auckland has sprouted its own set of insanely frightening activities. Look around for backpacker reductions or special offers before booking anything.

MT EDEN & KINGSLAND

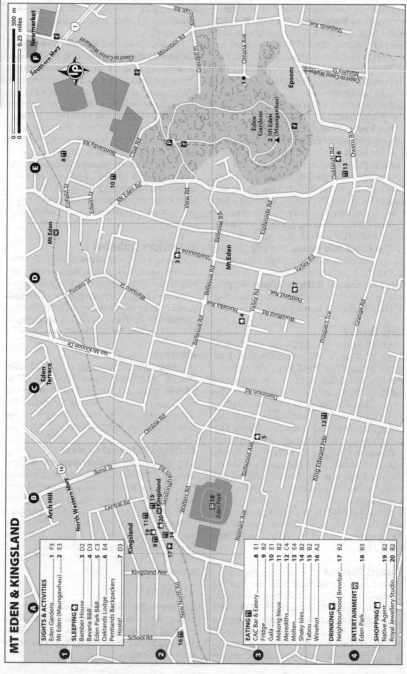

SIGHTS & ACTIVITIES
Eden Gardens	1 F3
Mt Eden (Maungawhau)	2 E3

SLEEPING
Bamber House	3 D2
Bavaria B&B	4 D3
Eden Park B&B	5 C3
Oaklands Lodge	6 E4
Pentlands Backpackers Hostel	7 D3

EATING
CAC Bar & Eatery	8 E1
Fridge	9 B2
Gala	10 E1
Mekong Neua	11 B2
Meredits	12 C4
Molten	13 E4
Shaky Isles	14 B2
Tabou	15 B2
Winehot	16 A2

DRINKING
Neighbourhood Brewbar	17 B2

ENTERTAINMENT
Eden Park	18 B3

SHOPPING
Native Agent	19 B2
Royal Jewellery Studio	20 B2

Spiderman Activities

The wise men of bungy, **AJ Hackett Bungy & Bridge Climb** (Map p96; ☎ 09-361 2000; www.ajhackett.com/nz; Westhaven Reserve, Curran St) offer the chance to climb up or jump off the Auckland Harbour Bridge. Both the 40m bungy leap and the 1½-hour guided tour along the arch (with a harness attached to a static line) cost $120.

Not to be outdone, the Sky Tower (p103) offers an ever-expanding selection of pant-wetting activities. If you thought the observation deck was for pussies, **Sky Walk** (Map p100; ☎ 0800 759 925; www.skywalk.co.nz; adult/child $135/100; ◷ 10am-5.30pm) involves circling the 192m-high, 1.2m-wide outside halo of the tower without rails or a balcony – but with a safety harness (they're not completely crazy). **Sky Jump** (Map p100; ☎ 0800 759 586; www.skyjump.co.nz; adult/child $195/145; ◷ 10am-5.30pm) is an 11-second, 85km/h base wire jump from the observation deck. It's more like a parachute jump than a bungy and it's a rush and a half. You can combine both in the Look 'n Leap package ($260).

Sky Screamer (Map p100; ☎ 09-377 1328; www.reversebungy.com; cnr Albert & Victoria Sts; ride $40; ◷ 10.30am-10pm Sun-Thu, 10am-2am Fri & Sat) involves being strapped into a seat and reverse-bungied 60m up in the air. Should you hurl, rest assured – you can get a video of it.

Cruises

Getting out on the water is an intrinsic part of the Auckland experience. If you can't afford a cruise or yacht, take a ferry instead; details are listed in each destination section.

Fullers (Map p100; ☎ 09-367 9111; www.fullers.co.nz; Ferry Bldg, 99 Quay St) operates ferry services (Birkenhead, Northcote Point, Devonport, Rangitoto, Waiheke Island, Great Barrier Island) and daily harbour cruises (adult/child $35/18, 1½ hours, 10.30am and 1.30pm), which include a stop on Rangitoto, a complimentary cuppa and a free return ticket to Devonport.

360 Discovery (Map p100; ☎ 09-307 8005; www.360discovery.co.nz; Pier 4 kiosk, Quay St) also runs ferries (Gulf Harbour, Motuihe, Tiritiri Matangi, Coromandel Town) along with the Harbour Discovery cruise (adult/child $29/15, 1½ hours), departing at 10am, noon and 2.30pm, which stops at Devonport, Rangitoto, Motuihe and Orakei Wharf (for Kelly Tarlton's Antarctic Encounter).

Sailing

Hey, this is the 'City of Sails' and nothing gets you closer to the heart and soul of Auckland than sailing on the gulf.

Sail NZ (Map p100; ☎ 0800 397 567; www.sailnewzealand.co.nz; Viaduct Harbour) heads out on genuine America's Cup yachts (adult/child $150/110, two hours). This experienced and highly regarded outfit also offers daily Whale and Dolphin Safaris (adult/child $150/100); dolphins are spotted 90% of the time and whales 75%. Its *Pride of Auckland* fleet of glamorous large yachts offers tours ranging from the 90-minute Coffee Cruise (adult/child $70/37) to the full-day Sailing Adventure (adult/child $135/110).

Gulfwind Sailing Academy (Map p96; ☎ 09-521 1564; www.gulfwind.co.nz; Westhaven Marina) provides cruises (half-/full-day $395/795 for up to six people), as well as personalised tuition and flexible small-group sailing courses; a two-day RYA Start Yachting course costs $545.

Penny Whiting Sailing School (Map p96; ☎ 09-376 1322; www.pennywhiting.com; Westhaven Marina) runs courses that consist of five three-hour practical sailing lessons ($650).

Tramping

Visitors centres, DOC offices and public libraries have pamphlets on walks in and around Auckland. The city council's *Auckland City's Walkways* pamphlet has a good selection of urban walks, including the **Coast to Coast Walkway** (Map p96; 16km, four hours). Heading clear across the country, from Waitemata Harbour to Manukau Harbour, the walk encompasses Albert Park, the University, the Domain, Mt Eden (Maungawhau) and One Tree Hill (Maungakiekie), keeping as much as possible to reserves rather than city streets. Starting from the Viaduct Basin and heading south, it's marked by yellow markers and milestones; heading north from Onehunga there are blue markers. To get back to the city, take bus 328, 334, 348 or 354 from Onehunga Mall ($5.40, 50 minutes).

Hang Gliding & Skydiving

Active Sky Hang Gliding (☎ 021 170 3646; www.activeskyhanggliding.co.nz) lets you fly like a kahu (native hawk – NZ doesn't have eagles) in a tandem flight ($175) off the cliffs at Kariotahi beach, southwest of Auckland.

NZ Skydive (☎ 09-373 5778; www.nzskydive.co.nz) offers an exhilarating tandem skydive from

12,000ft (including a 7000ft free fall) for $299; capture your excitement/terror on DVD for $165. It all takes place at Mercer airfield, 55km south of Auckland.

Swimming

When the weather conspires to keep you off the beaches, Auckland offers excellent alternatives:

Olympic Pools & Fitness Centre (Map p106; ☎ 09-522 4414; www.theolympic.co.nz; 77 Broadway; adult/child $7/4.50; ☼ 5.45am-10pm Mon-Fri, 7am-8pm Sat & Sun) Pools, gym, sauna, steam room and crèche.

Parnell Baths (Map p106; ☎ 09-373 3561; www.parnellbaths.co.nz; Judges Bay Rd; adult/child $5.70/3.90; ☼ 6am-8pm Mon-Fri, 8am-8pm Sat & Sun Nov-Apr)

Outdoor saltwater pools with an awesome 1950s mural and popular sunbathing areas.

Other Activities

Fergs Kayaks (Map p96; ☎ 09-529 2230; www.fergskayaks.co.nz; 12 Tamaki Dr, Okahu Bay; ☼ 9am-6pm Mon-Fri, 8am-6pm Sat & Sun) hires out kayaks ($15 to $40 per hour or $50 to $120 per day), bikes (per hour/day $20/120) and inline skates (per hour/day $15/30). Day and night guided kayak trips are available to Devonport (8km, three hours, $95) or Rangitoto Island (13km, six hours, $120).

NZ Surf Tours (☎ 09-828 0426; www.newzealandsurftours.com) runs day-long surfing courses ($120) that include transport, equipment and two lessons. A five-day small-group course ($799,

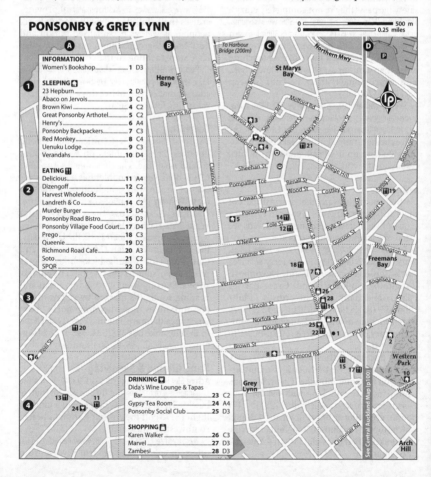

PONSONBY & GREY LYNN

0   500 m
0   0.25 miles

INFORMATION	
Women's Bookshop	1 D3

SLEEPING	
23 Hepburn	2 D3
Abaco on Jervois	3 C1
Brown Kiwi	4 C2
Great Ponsonby Arthotel	5 C2
Henry's	6 A4
Ponsonby Backpackers	7 C3
Red Monkey	8 C4
Uenuku Lodge	9 C3
Verandahs	10 D4

EATING	
Delicious	11 A4
Dizengoff	12 C2
Harvest Wholefoods	13 A4
Landreth & Co	14 C2
Murder Burger	15 D4
Ponsonby Road Bistro	16 D3
Ponsonby Village Food Court	17 D4
Prego	18 C3
Queenie	19 D2
Richmond Road Cafe	20 A3
Soto	21 C2
SPQR	22 D3

DRINKING	
Dida's Wine Lounge & Tapas Bar	23 C2
Gypsy Tea Room	24 A4
Ponsonby Social Club	25 D3

SHOPPING	
Karen Walker	26 C3
Marvel	27 D3
Zambesi	28 D3

To Harbour Bridge (200m)

Herne Bay

St Marys Bay

Northern Mwy

Ponsonby

Grey Lynn

Freemans Bay

Western Park

Arch Hill

See Central Auckland Map (p100)

October to May) heads to Ahipara (p182) and includes accommodation, transport and food.

Both the **Dive Centre** (Map p96; ☎ 09-444 7698; www.divecentre.co.nz; 97 Wairau Rd, Takapuna; PADI Open Water $499) and **Orakei Scuba Centre** (Map p96; ☎ 09-524 2117; www.orakeidive.co.nz; 234 Orakei Rd, Remuera; PADI Open Water $399-599) have dive shops and run courses.

Balloon Expeditions (☎ 09-416 8590; www.balloon expeditions.co.nz; flight $320) and **Balloon Safaris** (☎ 09-415 8289; www.balloonsafaris.co.nz; flight $330) offers early-morning hot-air balloon flights that take about four hours (one hour in the air), with breakfast and a bottle of bubbles.

Rainbow's End Adventure Park (Map p96; ☎ 09-262 2030; www.rainbowsend.co.nz; 2 Clist Cres, Manukau; superpass adult/child $45/35; ☺ 10am-5pm) has enough rides (including a corkscrew roller coaster and the 'Power Surge'), shows and interactive entertainment to keep the kids happy all day, plus plenty of sugary snacks to fuel it all. Superpasses allow unlimited rides.

WALKING TOUR

Auckland's CBD can seem grim and generic, so this walk aims to show you some interesting hidden nooks and architectural treats.

Start among the funky second-hand boutiques of **St Kevin's Arcade (1)** and take the stairs down to Myers Park. Look out for the reproduction of **Michelangelo's Moses (2)** to the right at the bottom of the stairs. Continue through the park, taking the stairs on the right just before the overpass to head up to street level.

Heading down Queen St, you'll pass the **Auckland Town Hall (3**; p124) and **Aotea Square (4)**, the civic heart of the city. On the next corner is the wonderful **Civic Theatre (5**; p107). Turn right on Wellesley St and then left onto Lorne St. Immediately to your right is the **New Gallery (6**; p103) and a pretty little square with tiling celebrating the suffragettes who won NZ women the vote before anywhere else in the world. Head up the stairs and cross the road to the **Main Gallery (7**; p103).

Take the stairs up into **Albert Park (8**; p104) and cross through to the **University Clock Tower (9**; p104). Head onto campus, taking the path to the right of the building, and you'll come out on a grassy quadrant and the remains of the **Albert Barracks (10**; p104). Cut through the centre of the university, following the signs to **Old Government House (11**; p104).

Head back to Princes St, where there's an interesting row of Victorian merchants'

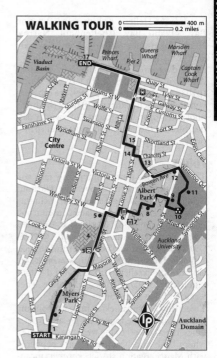

WALKING TOUR

WALK FACTS

Start St Kevin's Arcade, Karangahape Rd
Finish Viaduct Harbour
Distance 4km
Duration Around two hours

houses and, on the corner, the **former synagogue (12)**. Take Bowen Ave and cut through the park to the **Chancery precinct (13)**, an upmarket area of designer stores and cafes. A small square leads to **High St (14)**, Auckland's main fashion strip. Take a left onto **Vulcan Lane (15)**, lined with historic pubs. Turn right onto Queen St and follow it down to the **Britomart Train Station (16)**, housed in the grand former Central Post Office. You're now standing on reclaimed land – the original shoreline was at Fort St.

Turn left on Quay St and head to **Viaduct Harbour (17**; p107), where you can explore along the waterline or just grab a beverage.

AUCKLAND FOR CHILDREN

Auckland has plenty to keep kids entertained, whatever the weather. All of the east coast beaches (St Heliers, Kohimarama, Mission Bay, Okahu Bay, Cheltenham, Narrow Neck, Takapuna, Milford, Long Bay) are safe for supervised kids, while Rainbow's End Adventure Park (p111), Kelly Tarlton's Antarctic Encounter & Underwater World (p103) and Auckland Zoo (p99) are other favourites. Parnell Baths (p110) has a children's pool and is open year-round. On a wintry day, head to the thermal pools at Parakai (p145) or Waiwera (p147).

TOURS

Three-hour bus tours will typically take you around the city centre, over the Harbour Bridge and out along Tamaki Dr, including stops at Mt Eden, the Auckland Museum and Parnell, for about $67. **Gray Line** (☎ 09-307 7880; www.graylinetours.co.nz) and **Great Sights** (☎ 09-583 5790; www.greatsights.co.nz) both offer this service.

Mohio Tours (☎ 09-551 3177; www.mohiotours. com) runs an excellent Urban Maori day tour (adult/child $195/100) for small groups. They leave Mt Eden to the buses, and head to One Tree Hill (Maungakiekie) instead, pointing out features of the mountain *pa* site. After a quick lunch it's off to the west-coast beaches, where bush and beach walks are peppered with Maori creation stories, *karakia* (incantations) and explanations of the traditional uses of plants. More personalised tours can be tailored to your interests, such as visits with local artists.

Another recommended Maori-led tour is Ngati Whatua's **Tamaki Hikoi** (☎ 0800 282 552; www.tamakihikoi.co.nz; adult/child $80/40), which includes transfers up Mt Eden (Maungawhau) and a three-hour guided walk pointing out features of significance, from the mountain down to the harbour.

The hop-on, hop-off **Explorer Bus** (☎ 0800 439 756; www.explorerbus.co.nz; adult/child $35/15) departs from the Ferry Building every hour from 10am to 3pm (more frequently in summer), heading to 14 tourist sites around the central city.

Other options:

Auckland Adventures (☎ 09-379 4545; www.auck landadventures.co.nz; afternoon/day tours $85/120) The afternoon tour (12.45pm to 5pm) includes Muriwai gannet colony, an orchard, wineries and Mt Eden; day tours (9am to 5pm) can include a hike or mountain-biking experience.

Auckland Ghost Tours (☎ 09-630 5721; www. aucklandghosttours.com; adult/child $50/25) Stories about Auckland's scary side – and we don't just mean the

architecture – shared on a two-hour walking tour of the central city.

Bush & Beach (☎ 0800 423 224; www.bushandbeach. co.nz; 5hr/7hr walks $135/205) Guided walks in the Waitakere Ranges, black-sand beaches and the central city.

Fine Wine Tours (☎ 09-529 5227; www.insidertouring. co.nz) Tours the West Auckland wineries, including lunch: four-hour tour ($149), with cheese ($169); six-hour tour including Muriwai Beach and a microbrewery ($269); food and wine tour with stops at city providores ($199).

Great Taste Tours (☎ 09-424 1741; www.greattaste tours.co.nz; tours $115-245) Food, wine and art tours in either Matakana or Kumeu.

Hiking NZ (☎ 0800 697 232; www.hikingnewzealand. com) Runs 'hiking safaris' leaving from Auckland: Volcanic Plateau ($745, five days); Far North ($795, six days); and Volcanoes & Rainforest ($1550, 10 days).

Ports of Auckland Tours (☎ 0800 360 3472; www.360discovery.co.nz; ⊗ tours Tue fortnightly) Free hour-long boat tours around the ports; bookings essential.

TIME Unlimited (☎ 09-446 6677; www.newzealand tours.travel) To Integrate Maori Experiences (TIME) is the motto. A hefty set of cultural, fishing, kayaking, trekking and sightseeing tours are outlined on its website, including excellent kayak-fishing excursions (day/overnight $290/590).

Wine Trail Tours (☎ 09-630 1540; www.winetrail tours.co.nz) Small-group tours around West Auckland wineries and the Waitakere Ranges (half-/full-day $105/215; further afield to Matakana ($235); or a combo of the two ($235).

FESTIVALS & EVENTS

Check www.aucklandnz.com for full details of what's on in the city.

January

ASB Classic (www.asbclassic.co.nz) Watch some leading women tennis players warm up for the Aussie Open; held early January at the ASB Tennis Centre.

Heineken Open (www.heinekenopen.co.nz) The men's equivalent; held mid-January.

Big Day Out (www.bigdayout.com) Australasia's biggest music festival, attracting big-name alternative bands and lots of Kiwi up-and-comers to Mt Smart Stadium in mid-January.

Auckland Anniversary Day Regatta (www.regatta. org.nz) The 'City of Sails' lives up to its name; Monday of last weekend in January.

Music In Parks A series of free gigs and movies in parks around the city; runs until March.

February

Waitangi Day Festival Maori culture, food and a free concert, held at Okahu Bay on February 6.

Devonport Food & Wine Festival (www.devonport winefestival.co.nz) Sip and sup with the smart set at this two-day festival in mid-February.

Big Gay Out (www.biggayout.co.nz) The big event on the gay and lesbian calendar; 12,000 people descend on Coyle Park, Pt Chevalier for a free festival.

Mission Bay Jazz & Blues Streetfest (www.jazz andbluesstreetfest.com) New Orleans comes to the Bay as jazz and blues bands line both sides of the street as the sun sets; held late February.

Lantern Festival (www.asianz.org.nz) Three days of Asian food and culture in Albert Park to welcome the lunar New Year.

Starlight Symphony The Auckland Philharmonic entertains picnickers in the Domain; late February.

March

Auckland Cup Week (www.aucklandcupweek.co.nz) Try to spot the winner at the biggest horse race of the year; at Ellerslie Racecourse, early March.

Auckland Festival (www.aucklandfestival.co.nz) Held in odd-numbered years, this is Auckland's biggest celebration of the arts.

Pasifika Festival Western Springs Park hosts this excellent (and giant) Polynesian party with music, dancing and food; held in early to mid-March.

Polyfest (www.asbpolyfest.co.nz) Auckland secondary schools' Maori and Pacific Islands cultural festival – the biggest Pacific Islander (PI) cultural festival in the world.

Royal Easter Show (www.royaleastershow.co.nz) Fun for all the family, with an agricultural flavour.

April/May

NZ International Comedy Festival (www.comedy festival.co.nz) Three-week laughfest with local and international comedians; held mid-April to early May.

NZ Boat Show (www.boatshow.co.nz) One of the world's best yachting nations shows off its wares – find something to float your boat; held mid-May.

Auckland Art Fair (www.aucklandartfair.co.nz) Held in May in odd-numbered years at the Viaduct Harbour.

Out Takes (www.outtakes.org.nz) Gay and lesbian film festival, running from late May to early June.

July

New Zealand International Film Festival (www. nzff.telecom.co.nz) Auckland goes crazy for art-house films from mid- to late July.

September

Air New Zealand Fashion Week (www.nzfashion week.com) Is any country better qualified to show what you can do with merino wool and a sense of imagination? Find the next Karen Walker or Kate Sylvester here. Held in mid- to late September.

Heritage Festival Two weeks of fabulous (mainly free) tours of Auckland's neighbourhoods and historic buildings.

October

Diwali Festival Of Lights (www.asianz.org.nz/diwali) Auckland's Indian community light up the Viaduct with an explosion of colour, music and dance; held in mid-October.

November

Queen of the Whole Universe (www.queenwhole universe.com) A fundraising drag-fest (queens not cars) held at the Aotea Centre in mid-November.

December

Christmas in the Park (www.christmasinthepark.co.nz) A party so big it has to be held in the Auckland Domain.

SLEEPING

Our accommodation listings for Auckland fall into the following categories:

- Budget – doubles under $100
- Midrange – cheapest doubles from $100 to $200
- Top End – doubles more than $200

Budget

Invariably the backpackers who leave with a bad impression of Auckland have stayed in crummy, noisy hostels in the city centre. Not all of the cheap city accommodation is bad – the ones we've listed are all perfectly acceptable – but you're better off grabbing a bed in the surrounding suburbs. Parnell is relatively pricey but it has some excellent hostels. Mt Eden and Ponsonby have some good options, but the otherwise backpacker-friendly suburbs of Kingsland and Grey Lynn are poorly served.

CENTRAL AUCKLAND

Nomads Auckland (Map p100; ☎ 09-300 9999; www.no madsauckland.com; 16 Fort St; dm $22-30, r $80-90; 💻 🛜) Bustling is an understatement for this large backpackers with a cafe, bar, nightclub, reading room, travel agency, female-only floor and a roof deck with sauna and spa. All of the dorms have lockers and the private rooms have TVs but not necessarily windows.

Frienz.com (Map p100; ☎ 09-307 6437; www.frienz.com; 27-31 Victoria St; dm $23-28, d $72; 💻 🛜) Raising the bar for this part of town, Frienz has actually put an effort into its decor (crazy wallpaper and bright colours) and into organising regular social events (free barbecue nights, poker tournaments etc). Add to that free internet

AUCKLAND REGION

access, fridges in the private rooms and a terrific rooftop terrace and you get the inner city's best hostel.

City Groove (Map p100; ☎ 09-303 4768; www.city groove.co.nz; 6 Constitution Hill; dm $24-26, tw/d $60/65; P ⌨) Nestled in a forgotten strip of inner-city houses edging a steep park near the university, this homely hostel has only seven rooms and a great backyard.

Base Auckland (Map p100; ☎ 09-358 4877; www. stayatbase.com; 229 Queen St; dm $27-29, d $74-92, q $130; ⌨ 🛜) With more than 500 beds and a network of sightseeing and job-seeking contacts, this is the place where many young visitors get their bearings. If you don't like a hive of activity (or stained carpets and ceiling panels), then you'll need to go elsewhere, as this place hums with questions about where the cheapest places to eat can be found, who's got work where, whether bungy jumping's worth it and where the cute guys/girls are. There's a bar to aid this last search.

City Lodge (Map p100; ☎ 09-379 6183; www.citylodge. co.nz; 150 Vincent St; s/tr $68/118, d $88-98; P ⌨ 🛜) City Lodge is a very well-run, purpose-built tower for the budget market. The bright, tiny rooms and stamp-sized bathrooms may be plain, but they make a perfectly comfortable, clean and secure resting place. There's a fantastic industrial-style kitchen, cleaned daily by housekeepers, and a comfy, modern lounge and TV room.

Aspen House (Map p100; ☎ 09-379 6633; www.aspen house.co.nz; 62 Emily Pl; s $69, d $89-129, tr $99-149, q $219; P ⌨ 🛜) Located on a sweet, steep street a stone's throw from one of Auckland's most intriguing little parks, the Aspen is split into a renovated wing (high ceilings, en suites) and an older wing (lumpy beds, two toilets between 12 rooms). It's worth paying more for the former. The excellent communal spaces, friendly staff and tucked-away location make this the best of the inner-city hostels.

Hotel Formule 1 (Map p100; ☎ 09-308 9140; www. formule1.co.nz; 20 Wyndham St; r $75; ⌨) You'll feel like a giant in the minirooms with teensy TVs, stereos, ironing boards and kitchenettes, but they're clean and stocked with everything you need. The building itself is spectacularly skinny.

NEWTON

Auckland City YHA (Map p100; ☎ 09-309 2802; www.yha. co.nz; 18 Liverpool St; dm $24-41, s/d/tr $69/82/94; ⌨ 🛜) Struggle up one of the city's steepest streets to this big, impersonal tower block near the K Rd party strip. The rooms are clean and well kept, and some have views and terraces.

Auckland International YHA (Map p100; ☎ 09-302 8200; www.yha.co.nz; 5 Turner St; dm $26-31, d $88-124, tr $118; P ⌨) Clean and brightly painted, this 170-bed YHA has a friendly vibe, good security, a games room and lots of lockers. In short, it's your typical, well-run YHA.

BK Hostel (Map p100; ☎ 09-307 0052; www.bkhostel. co.nz; 3 Mercury Lane; s $40-45, d $50-58, tr $81; ⌨ 🛜) Prices are cheaper for windowless rooms, but if you're planning to be partying in the neighbourhood's all-night clubs, that might be an advantage. The hostel is housed in a cool 1910 building with high ceilings and decent security.

PARNELL

Auckland International Backpackers (Map p106; ☎ 09-358 4584; www.aucklandinternationalbp.com; 2 Churton St; dm $23-25, s $48, d $62-72; ⌨) Eat in the sunroom, in the large dining room or out in the small garden at this backstreet backpackers. Linen and towels cost extra for dorm dwellers.

Lantana Lodge (Map p106; ☎ 09-373 4546; www.lantana lodge.co.nz; 60 St Georges Bay Rd; dm/s/d/tr $26/65/70/90; P ⌨) There are only eight rooms available in this cosy villa, on a quiet street with an instantly welcoming, social vibe. It's not flash by any means, but it's clean enough to be homely.

City Garden Lodge (Map p106; ☎ 09-302 0880; www. citygardenlodge.co.nz; 25 St Georges Bay Rd; dm $28-30, s/d $52/68, tw $58-68; P ⌨ 🛜) Housed within a character-filled, two-storey house built for Tongan royalty, this friendly and well-run backpackers has a lovely garden and high-ceilinged rooms with solid period features. If you need privacy a cute double room will do the trick, and if you need to unwind, indulge in some yoga on the front lawn.

Quality Hotel Barrycourt (Map p106; ☎ 09-303 3789; www.barrycourt.co.nz; 20 Gladstone Rd; r $95-165, units $120-199; ⌨ 🛜) A mixed bag of more than 100 motel rooms and units are available in this large, well-maintained complex with friendly multilingual staff. The older south wing is spacious but dated, while the north wing has some fantastic harbour views. Simple, cheaper rooms with kitchenette in the south wing are a good deal.

Parnell Inn (Map p106; ☎ 09-358 0642; www.parnell inn.co.nz; 320 Parnell Rd; d $99-120, tw $130, tr $145-155, q $170; P ⌨ 🛜) You'll get a chipper welcome at this revamped, good-looking motel, with new-look furniture and local photography on the walls. Smaller studios are on your right as you walk down the hall from reception; larger, sunnier rooms are on your left. Rooms 3 and 4 have great harbour views.

MT EDEN
Oaklands Lodge (Map p108; ☎ 09-638 6545; www. oaklands.co.nz; 5a Oaklands Rd; dm $23-25, s $43, d $60-66; 🖳 🛜) Situated in one of Mt Eden's loveliest quiet suburban streets, this bright, well-kept hostel is close to Mt Eden village and city buses. The communal facilities are in good knick.

Bamber House (Map p108; ☎ 09-623 4267; www. hostelbackpacker.com; 22 View Rd; dm $25-28, d $66-86; 🖳 🛜) The original house here is a mansion of sorts, with some nicely maintained period trimmings. The new prefab cabins have less character but come with en suites. There's plenty of space for its 60-odd guests to stretch out on the lawns and there's a playground for the kids. All in all, an excellent choice.

Pentlands Backpackers Hostel (Map p108; ☎ 09-638 7031; www.pentlands.co.nz; 22 Pentland Ave; dm $26-28, s $42, d $64; 🖳 🛜) Down a peaceful tree-lined cul-de-sac, Pentlands offers a homely environment, small dorms, a sunny deck and quiet tables on the lawn.

PONSONBY & HERNE BAY
Uenuku Lodge (Map p110; ☎ 09-378 8990; www.uenuku lodge.co.nz; 217 Ponsonby Rd; dm $24-28, s $49, d $58-78, tr/q $93/112; 🅿 🖳 🛜) This gay-friendly hostel is well located and some of the rooms afford city views. There's a decent lounge, a large kitchen, good security and an attractive outdoor area.

Ponsonby Backpackers (Map p110; ☎ 09-360 1311; www.ponsonby-backpackers.co.nz; 2 Franklin Rd; dm $25-27, s/d $42/60; 🖳 🛜) The interiors don't live up to the imposing exterior of this turreted wooden villa, commanding a corner site on tree-lined Franklin Rd. Yet it's kept reasonably clean and the staff are charming.

Brown Kiwi (Map p110; ☎ 09-378 0191; www.brown kiwi.co.nz; 7 Prosford St; dm $26-28, d/tr $68/84; 🅿 🖳 🛜) As unassuming as its namesake, this two-storey hostel is tucked away in a busy-by-day commercial strip, a stone's throw from all the good shopping and grazing opportunities. Dorms have four or eight beds, and the triple rooms are set in the small, verdant garden courtyard.

ourpick Verandahs (Map p110; ☎ 09-360 4180; www.verandahs.co.nz; 6 Hopetoun St; dm $26-28, s $53, d $70-88, tr $90; 🖳 🛜) Ponsonby Rd, K Rd and the city are an easy walk from this grand hostel, housed in two neighbouring villas overlooking the mature trees of Western Park. The bunkless dorms sleep a maximum of five people.

Red Monkey (Map p110; ☎ 09-360 7977; www. theredmonkey.co.nz; 49 Richmond Rd; weekly s/d/apt $185/230/260; 🖳) If you're planning to stay for a week or longer, make this renovated villa your home away from home. There are lamps, bedside tables and built-in wardrobes in all the smartly decorated rooms, including three in the quiet back garden. It's well worth booking ahead.

Abaco on Jervois (Map p110; ☎ 09-360 6850; www. abaco.co.nz; 57 Jervois Rd; r $75-269; 🅿) The upstairs rooms at this motel have been transformed into a stylish, neutral-toned escape. Furnishings are modern and comfortable, with plenty of fluffy white towels for spa lovers, and slick stainless-steel kitchenettes (which include dish drawers and proper ovens). Downstairs the darker, unrenovated rooms are a good deal, especially if you're planning on spending all your time at the cafes across the road.

NORTH SHORE
Takapuna Beach Holiday Park (Map p96; ☎ 09-489 7909; www.takapunabeachholidaypark.co.nz; 22 The Promenade, Takapuna; campsites $32, cabins $65, caravans $65-80, units $115; 🖳 🛜) Superbly positioned looking onto one of Auckland's most popular beaches, this little park is a smart proposition. The clean, new cabins have decks.

Auckland North Shore Motels & Holiday Park (Map p96; ☎ 09-418 2578; www.nsmotels.co.nz; 52 Northcote Rd, Takapuna; sites per 2 people $35, dm $38, units $48-145; 🅿 🖳 🛜 🖳) An indoor pool, spa and 24-hour check-in are all available at this oddly located holiday park and motel complex near the motorway, 4km north of the Harbour Bridge. Despite the position it's surprisingly peaceful.

OTHER AREAS
Ambury Regional Park campsite (Map p96; ☎ 09-366 2000; www.arc.govt.nz; Ambury Rd, Mangere; sites per adult/child $10/5) A slice of country in the middle of suburbia, this regional park is also a working farm. Facilities are limited (a vault toilet, warm showers and not much shade) but it's handy to the airport, right on the water and dirt cheap.

Duke's Midway Lodge (Map p96; ☎ 09-625 4399; www.dukes.co.nz; 4 Vagus Pl, Royal Oak; d $95-110, tr/q $125/165; 🛜 📺) Duke's brings a touch of Las Vegas to suburban Auckland's Vagus Pl, thanks to its rather eye-catching swimming pool which takes the shape of a guitar. In every other respect, Duke's is a well-priced run-of-the-mill motor lodge. Rooms are comfortable, with OK beds, cable TV and decent bathrooms, while the quiet location (off busy Pah Rd, midway to the airport) means you'll sleep soundly.

Midrange

Most motels (of which there are plenty) and B&Bs fall into this category. There are few options in the city centre, where accommodation swings from hostels to luxury hotels. Devonport has masses of beautiful Edwardian B&Bs within a relaxing ferry ride of the CBD.

CENTRAL AUCKLAND & NEWTON

Quadrant (Map p100; ☎ 09-984 6000; www.thequadrant.com; 10 Waterloo Quadrant; apt $123-400; 📺 🖥 🛜) Slick, central and full of all the whiz-bang gadgets, this apartment-style complex in the nicest part of the city is an excellent option. The only catch is that the apartments are tiny and the bathrooms beyond small.

Elliott Hotel (Map p100; ☎ 09-308 9334; www.theelliotthotel.com; cnr Elliott & Wellesley Sts; apt $139-209; 🖥 🛜) Housed in one of the city's grandest historic buildings (1880s), this apartment-style hotel is much plusher than the price implies. Rooms may not be huge but the high ceilings will let your spirits rise.

Langham (Map p100; ☎ 09-379 5132; www.auckland.langhamhotels.co.nz; 83 Symonds St; r $190-370, ste $470-2420; 📺 🖥 🛜 📺) The Langham may be five-star, but the glamour of the giant chandelier in the reception dissipates somewhat once you reach the low-ceilinged guest floors. Perhaps that's why you can often nab a special and take advantage of the faultless service and heavenly beds at a midrange price.

Other options:

Auckland City Hotel (Map p100; ☎ 09-925 0777; www.achhobson.co.nz; 157 Hobson St; r $120-130, ste $270; 📺 🖥 🛜) The heritage frontage opens onto a modern block with smart, spacious apartments at very reasonable prices.

CityLife (Map p100; ☎ 09-379 9222; www.heritagehotels.co.nz/citylife-auckland; Durham St; r $165-483, ste $185-1890; 📺 🖥 🛜 📺) A worthy tower-block hotel offering hundreds of rooms over dozens of floors.

PARNELL & NEWMARKET

Parnell City Lodge (Map p106; ☎ 09-377 1463; www.parnellcitylodge.co.nz; 2 St Stephens Ave; apt $105-170; 📺) Old and newer sections are available in this motel, where every unit is different, some have a bit of character and all have a kitchenette. It's on a busy intersection though, so traffic noise might be a nuisance if you're a light sleeper.

Off Broadway Motel (Map p96; ☎ 09-529 3550; www.offbroadway.co.nz; 11 Alpers Ave; units $139-255; 🛜) The Off Broadway is a dandy little performer in Auckland's accommodation scene and deserves a few stage-door Johnnies singing its praises. The three small studios are a little dark but the larger studios are a great deal as they have a balcony and bathtub. Executive suites have separate bedrooms and represent very good value.

Kingsgate Hotel (Map p106; ☎ 0800 782 548, 09-377 3619; www.millenniumhotels.co.nz; 92 Gladstone Rd; r $140-199, tr $155-229; 🖥 🛜 📺) Opposite the Parnell Rose Gardens, this large hotel has generic rooms clustered in landscaped 'Tudor' or 'Colonial' blocks (although they look the same to us), together with a restaurant, pool, spa and plenty of parking. It's popular with tour groups.

MT EDEN

Bavaria B&B (Map p108; ☎ 09-638 9641; www.bavariabandbhotel.co.nz; 83 Valley Rd; s $105-115, d $149-165; 🖥 🛜) This clean, long-running B&B in a spacious villa has been freshened up with new carpets and a coat of paint. The rooms are big and airy, and there's a decent TV lounge, dining room and deck where guests can mix and mingle.

Eden Park B&B (Map p108; ☎ 09-630 5721; www.bedandbreakfastnz.com; 22 Bellwood Ave; s $135-155, d $200-225; 🖥 🛜) If you know any rugby fans who require chandeliers in their bathrooms, send them here. The hallowed turf of Auckland's legendary rugby ground is only a block away and while the rooms aren't overly large for the prices, they mirror the Edwardian elegance of this fine wooden villa.

PONSONBY & GREY LYNN

23 Hepburn (Map p110; ☎ 09-376 0622; www.23hepburn.co.nz; 23 Hepburn St; r $185-205; 📺 🛜) The three boutique rooms are a symphony in muted whites and creams, inducing the pleasant sensation of waking up inside an extremely chic pavlova. You can sleep in as long as you like as the continental breakfast is self-service –

left in your in-room fridge the previous evening.

our pick Henry's (Map p110; ☎ 09-360 2700; www.henrysonpeel.co.nz; 33 Peel St; r/apt $200/240; ☜ ☺) These beautiful wooden villas are what Auckland's inner suburbs are all about. Henry's has been stylishly renovated, adding en suites to the downstairs rooms and a self-contained harbour-view apartment above.

NORTH SHORE
Parituhu (Map p104; ☎ 09-445 6559; www.parituhu.co.nz; 3 King Edward Pde, Devonport; r $100-150) This gay-friendly accommodation consists of just one double bedroom with a private bathroom in the owners' waterfront bungalow. It's a homely, relaxing and welcoming place.

Jasmine Cottage (Map p104; ☎ 09-445 8825; www.photoalbum.co.nz/jasmine; 20 Buchanan St, Devonport; r $120) Scrupulously maintained and cute as a button, this little courtyard garden hut behind the owner's house has its own kitchenette.

Devonport Sea Cottage (Map p104; ☎ 09-445 7117; www.homestaysnz.co.nz/listings/46; 3a Cambridge Tce, Devonport; r $130) Head up the path to your own self-contained cottage, which holds everything you'll need for a relaxing stay near the sea (including a set of French doors opening onto a garden). Excellent weekly rates are on offer in winter.

Devonport Motel (Map p104; ☎ 09-445 1010; www.devonportmotel.co.nz; 11 Buchanan St, Devonport; r $130) This minimotel has just two simple units in the back garden, but they're modern, clean, self-contained and in a nice quiet location that's still close to Devonport's action (such as it may be).

Number Nine B&B (Map p104; ☎ 09-445 3059; tainui@xtra.co.nz; 9 Tainui Rd, Devonport; r $170) You'll get a warm welcome from Christine and Pari at this cosy home that has two attractive rooms for guests, one with a claw-foot tub. If you fancy a game of golf at the nearby club, you can borrow clubs here and have a round organised.

Emerald Inn (Map p96; ☎ 09-488 3500; www.emerald-inn.co.nz; 16 The Promenade, Takapuna; units $171-297, villa/cottage $450/675; ☐ ☜ ☺) No, it's not an Irish pub. This leafy complex has lush gardens, smart furnishings and the beach at the end of the road. The luxury self-contained holiday homes have views to Rangitoto.

OTHER AREAS
Nautical Nook (Map p96; ☎ 09-521 2544; www.nauticalnook.com; 23b Watene Cres, Orakei; s/d $97/157) If you're

a sailing buff you'll find a kindred spirit in Keith, who runs this cosy homestay with his wife Trish. The lounge and terrace have views over the harbour, and Okahu Bay is close at hand.

Jet Park (Map p96; ☎ 09-275 4100; www.jetpark.co.nz; 63 Westney Rd, Mangere; r $135-165, ste $240-275; ☐ ☺) Friendly Jet Park has a decent vibe, even though many of its rooms follow the 'could be anywhere' design ethos that seems to be compulsory if you want to sleep near an airport. There are arrival/departure screens in the lobby and free airport shuttles. Kick back by the pool, which resembles something from an episode of *Hawaii 5-0*.

Omahu Lodge (Map p96; ☎ 09-524 5648; www.omahulodge.co.nz; 33 Omahu Rd, Remuera; s $160-200, d $195-240, ste $295; ☜ ☺) Art and family photos cover the walls at this cheerful, deluxe B&B. The three en-suite rooms in the main house all have neighbourhood views, but the spacious suite opens straight onto the enticing solar-heated pool. Free gifts of wine, beer and snacks are a nice touch.

Top End
Auckland has plenty of luxury hotels, with many of the big chains taking up inner-city real estate.

CENTRAL AUCKLAND
our pick Hotel de Brett (Map p100; ☎ 09-925 9000; www.hoteldebrett.com; 2 High St; r $290-590; ☐ ☜) Supremely hip, this lavishly refurbished historic hotel has been zooshed up with supercool stripey carpets and clever designer touches in every nook of the extremely comfortable rooms. Prices include breakfast, free broadband and a pre-dinner drink.

Westin (Map p100; ☎ 09-909 9000; www.westin.com/auckland; 21 Viaduct Harbour Ave; r $435-710; ☐ ☐ ☺) Auckland's Westin has outdone itself with simple, exquisite design, Maori art and sumptuous furnishings (we love the 250-thread-count sheets and goose-down pillows). There's water everywhere you look – in the form of the harbour or tinkling water features – which is very restful, as long as it doesn't induce a constant need to pee.

PONSONBY
Great Ponsonby Arthotel (Map p110; ☎ 09-376 5989; www.greatpons.co.nz; 30 Ponsonby Tce; r $235-400; ☐ ☐) Not as slick as the others in this bracket but this deceptively spacious Victorian villa has

gregarious hosts, impressive sustainability practices, great breakfasts and it's located a stone's throw from cool Ponsonby Rd in a quiet cul-de-sac. Studio apartments open onto an attractive rear courtyard.

NORTH SHORE
Esplanade Hotel (Map p104; ☎ 09-445 1291; www.esplanadehotel.co.nz; 1 Victoria Rd, Devonport; r $200-375, ste $350-750) This beautiful boutique hotel takes pride of place on the corner in a 1903 heritage building. It features lovingly tended period details such as supremely high ceilings, and has much more style than many of the luxury hotels in the city centre. It's perfectly located and achingly romantic, with sumptuous rooms that steadfastly refuse to fall into cookie-cutter territory when it comes to decor.

Hampton Beach House (Map p104; ☎ 09-445 1358; www.hamptonbeachhouse.co.nz; 4 King Edward Pde, Devonport; r $205-280; 🖳 🛜) One of a fine strip of waterside mansions, this upmarket, gay-friendly, Edwardian B&B has rooms with views and others opening onto the rear garden. It's all very tastefully done; expect quality linen and gourmet breakfasts.

Peace & Plenty Inn (Map p104; ☎ 09-445 2925; www.peaceandplenty.co.nz; 6 Flagstaff Tce, Devonport; s $195-265, d $265-350; 🅿 🖳) This perfectly located, wonderful five-star period house is stocked with antique furnishings and a thousand conversation pieces – the charming Judith can tell you the provenance of each and every one of them. The romantic, luxurious rooms have en suite, TV, flowers, free sherry/port and local chocolates. A delight, and truly exceptional.

REMUERA
Aachen House (Map p96; ☎ 09-520 2329; www.aachenhouse.co.nz; 39 Market Rd; r $390-590; 🛜) An exceptional boutique B&B, Aachen House is a grand old dame that's still looking mighty fine. The attention to painstaking detail is impressive: fresh flowers, hair turbans, shell-shaped soap and complementary port. Come breakfast time, the chef cooks up a gourmet storm.

EATING
Because of its size and ethnic diversity, Auckland tops the country when it comes to dining options and quality. Lively eateries have sprung up to cater to the numerous Asian students, offering inexpensive Japanese,

Chinese and Korean staples. If you're on a budget, you'll fall in love with the city's food halls.

Aucklanders love a good coffee, so you never have to walk too far to find a decent cafe. Suburbs such as Ponsonby, Grey Lynn, Kingsland, Mt Eden, Parnell and Devonport are teeming with them. Some double as wine bars or have gourmet aspirations, while others are content to fill their counters with fresh, reasonably priced snacks.

Ponsonby attracts a hip, young crowd who come to drink and dine before heading out to party. The upmarket Princes Wharf and Viaduct Basin waterfront area is where some of the buzziest and busiest restaurants have sprung up. This area is popular with suits and tourists, and can be especially heaving on Friday and Saturday evenings. Two petite enclaves that have recently established themselves as foodie favourites are Kingsland and the West Lynn shops on Richmond Rd, Grey Lynn.

Central Auckland
MacGregor Brothers (Map p100; ☎ 09-309 9924; 17 Wellesley St; snacks $5-7; 🕑 6.30am-3pm Mon-Fri) The wonderful internal features of this petite art-deco shopfront have survived, making this a great spot for a quality coffee and cake served on fine china.

Reslau (Map p100; ☎ 09-309 5039; 39 Elliott St; snacks $5-10; 🕑 7am-8.30pm Mon-Sat) Spilling into the laneway, this tiny cafe-wine bar literally has a trolley-load of delicious snacks and light meals.

Ima (Map p100; ☎ 09-300 7252; 57 Fort St; breakfast $5-18, lunch $13-22, dinner $18-32; 🕑 breakfast & lunch Mon-Sat, dinner Wed-Sat) Named after the Hebrew word for mother, the menu is a harmonious blend of Israeli, Palestinian, Yemenite and Lebanese dishes. Excellent coffee, too.

Raw Power (Map p100; ☎ 09-303 3724; Level 1, 10 Vulcan Lane; mains $7-17; 🕑 7am-4pm Mon-Fri, 11am-4pm Sat; 🅥) Vegetable-shaped salt-and-pepper shakers, superbright walls and the freshest ingredients entice punters to this upstairs eatery, popular with visiting vegetarian/vegan rock royalty. Grab a window seat if you can.

Euro (Map p100; ☎ 09-309 9866; Shed 22, Princes Wharf; mains $23-80; 🕑 lunch & dinner) Euro is a thoroughly slick package of imaginative Mod-NZ cuisine, good-looking wait staff and sexy surrounds. The harbour views aren't the greatest, but the dishes are always pretty as a picture.

O'Connell St Bistro (Map p100; ☎ 09-377 1884; 3 O'Connell St; lunch $28-32, dinner $29-45; ☺ lunch Tue-Fri, dinner Mon-Sat) Delightful O'Connell St is a grown-up treat, with elegant decor and truly wonderful food and wine, satisfying lunchtime powerbrokers and dinnertime daters. The menu leans heavily on the duck, salmon and lamb side of things.

ourpick Grove (Map p100; ☎ 09-368 4129; St Patrick's Sq, Wyndham St; mains $32-48; ☺ lunch Mon-Fri, dinner Mon-Sat) Romantic fine dining at its best: the room is cosy and moodily lit, the menu encourages sensual experimentation and the service is effortless. If you can't find anything to break the ice from the extensive wine list, give it up mate – it's never going to happen.

Clooney (Map p100; ☎ 09-358 1702; 33 Sale St; mains $36-44; ☺ lunch Fri, dinner Mon-Sat) Like the Hollywood actor of the same name, Clooney is suave, stylish and extremely sophisticated. While the taste combinations are complex (venison with cocoa *millefeuille,* preserved cherries, black pudding and licorice jus, for example) the outcomes are faultless.

For quick eats, head to **Revive** (Map p100; ☎ 09-307 1586; 16 Fort St; mains $8-14; ☺ 11am-8pm Mon-Thu, 11am-3pm Fri; Ⓥ), a vegetarian heaven that has an enticing salad bar and extremely economical daily meal deals. Fast food that's healthy? Healthy food that's cheap and tasty? How can this be?

For authentic Asian fare, you can't beat the large, no-frills **Food Alley** (Map p100; ☎ 09-373 4917; 9 Albert St; mains $9-17; ☺ 10.30am-10pm) food court, where nearly every meal comes in under $12. Choose between Chinese, Indian, Thai, Vietnamese, Turkish, Malaysian, Korean, Japanese and Indonesian.

Newton

K Rd is known for its late-night clubs, but cafes and plenty of inexpensive ethnic restaurants are mixed in with the fashion boutiques, tattooists and adult shops.

Rasoi (Map p100; ☎ 09-377 7780; 211 K Rd; mains $6-17; ☺ lunch & dinner Mon-Sat; Ⓥ) Lip-smackingly good (and delightfully cheap) vegetarian thali and South Indian food can be found here, together with lassi and Indian sweets.

Alleluya (Map p100; ☎ 09-377 8424; St Kevin's Arcade, K Rd; mains $10-19; ☺ breakfast & lunch) Alleluya is a very cool little cafe-cum-bar in the city's hippest arcade. It has moreish cakes and lots of vegetarian options.

Satya (Map p100; ☎ 09-377 0007; 271 K Rd; mains $11-26; ☺ lunch Mon-Sat, dinner daily; Ⓥ) Hugely popular, this humble-looking and humbly priced eatery has the best *dahi puri* (an entrée of chickpea, potato and yoghurt on a pappadam) and masala dosa (a crepe filled with potato-and-onion curry) in town.

O'Sarracino (Map p100; ☎ 09-309 3740; 3 Mt Eden Rd; mains $16-38; ☺ dinner Tue-Sat) A delicious reminder that Neapolitan cuisine offers so much more than pizza, this excellent restaurant serves generous antipasti, light and simple pasta, and delectable seafood *secondi.* The somewhat grand surroundings were once the chapel of a funeral parlour.

French Cafe (Map p100; ☎ 09-377 1911; 210 Symonds St; mains $40; ☺ lunch Fri, dinner Tue-Sat) The legendary French Cafe has been rated as one of Auckland's top restaurants for around 20 years now and it still continues to excel. The cuisine is (unsurprisingly) French, but chef Simon Wright manages to sneak in some Pacific Rim touches. Book well ahead if you want to snag a table.

Parnell

Kokako (Map p106; ☎ 09-366 4464; 492 Parnell Rd; mains $8-17; ☺ breakfast & lunch; Ⓥ) Kokako offers vegetarian, fair trade and organic delights in a smart cafe atmosphere that won't unduly strain the bank balance – a feat nearly as rare as the native bird it's named after. There's a good selection of counter food as well as delicious cooked breakfasts.

Rosehip Cafe (Map p106; ☎ 09-369 1182; 82 Gladstone Rd; mains $13-25; ☺ 7am-4pm) The name fits: it's near the Rose Gardens and it's pretty hip. It's a tad pricey but the food's delicious, particularly the buttermilk pancakes and the Vietnamese-style squid.

Non Solo Pizza (Map p106; ☎ 09-379 5358; 259 Parnell Rd; mains $23-39; ☺ lunch & dinner) Like the name says, there's not only pizza on offer here – delicious though that is. NSP has a bewilderingly large menu of classic Italian antipasto, pasta and grills and a cool street-facing bar with a chandelier made of Peroni bottles. *Bellissimo.*

Newmarket

Urban Cafe (Map p106; ☎ 09-966 6977; 139 Carlton Gore Rd; mains $7-18; ☺ breakfast & lunch) Its urbanity highlighted by an industrial aesthetic, this chic cafe serves spicy Baghdad baked eggs (with lentils and Turkish bread), daily pasta dishes and enticing sweet stuff.

Baci Lounge (Map p106; ☎ 09-529 4360; Level 1, Rialto Centre, Broadway; mains $9; ☽ 9.30am-10.30pm) Round padded booths are nestled among the shelves at this very appealing bookshop-cafe. Devour delicious counter food (salads, paninis, fancy pies, gluten-free slices) and literary greats all at the same time.

Mt Eden

CAC Bar & Eatery (Map p108; ☎ 09-630 5790; 26 Normanby Rd; tapas $8-19; ☽ lunch & dinner) The terrible name references the Colonial Ammunition Company, who was responsible for erecting the very sturdy bluestone walls of this stylishly renovated warehouse. Cannonballs have since given way to risotto balls and the only danger is from taste explosions emanating from the tapas menu – particularly from the 12-hour lamb.

Gala (Map p108; ☎ 09-623 1572; Zone 23, Edwin St; mains $9-20; ☽ breakfast & lunch) Mixing modern architecture and antique silver tea services, this bright cafe brings sophistication to the prison precinct. The whiteboard menu is crammed with interesting options: try My Mother-in-law's North Indian Eggs for a fragrant version of eggs on toast.

Molten (Map p108; ☎ 09-638 7236; 422 Mt Eden Rd; mains $29-35; ☽ lunch Tue-Sat, dinner Mon-Sat) Under the volcano's shadow, Molten oozes neighbourhood charm. The consistently excellent seasonal menu fuses Pacific Rim tastes into a delicious whole.

Merediths (Map p108; ☎ 09-623 3140; 385 Dominion Rd; mains $38, degustation $100; ☽ lunch Thu & Fri, dinner Tue-Sat) Dining at Merediths is the culinary equivalent of black-water rafting – tastes surprise you at every turn, you never know what's coming next and you're left with a sense of breathless exhilaration. You'll need to book well in advance to secure a table for the weekend degustation-only sittings; this is one of NZ's best restaurants.

Kingsland

Fridge (Map p108; ☎ 09-845 5321; 507 New North Rd; mains $8-18; ☽ breakfast & lunch; Ⓥ) Serves excellent coffee, gourmet pies, healthy salads and wraps, and drool-inducing cakes.

Shaky Isles (Map p108; ☎ 09-815 3591; 492 New North Rd; mains $8-19; ☽ breakfast & lunch; 🛜) Kingsland's coolest cafe has cute cartoons on the wall and free wi-fi. They do excellent breakfasts and super-food salads, but it's hard to go past 'good stuff in a bun', the good stuff

being mushrooms, avocado, feta, pesto and mayonnaise.

Mekong Neua (Map p108; ☎ 09-846 0323; 483 New North Rd; mains $17-24; ☽ dinner; Ⓥ) Plundering the cuisine of Northeast Thailand and Laos, this welcoming restaurant will fill your head with delicious fragrances and dreams of rice paddies.

Winehot (Map p108; ☎ 09-815 9463; 605 New North Rd; mains $19-26; ☽ dinner Tue-Sat) Behind an unlikely-looking doorway, this tiny black-painted and chandelier-festooned hideaway serves up hearty French cuisine and an extensive wine list.

Tabou (Map p108; ☎ 09-846 3474; 462 New North Rd; mains $28-32; ☽ lunch Tue-Fri, dinner Tue-Sun) Elegant and refined but informal and friendly, Tabou is the French restaurant you wish was in your neighbourhood. It doubles as a bar later in the evening.

Ponsonby

Auckland's busiest restaurant-cafe-bar strip is so damn cool it has its own website (www.ponsonbyroad.co.nz).

Dizengoff (Map p110; ☎ 09-360 0108; 256 Ponsonby Rd; mains $5-18; ☽ 7am-5pm) This superstylish shoebox crams in a mixed crowd of corporate and fashion types, gay guys, Jewish families, Ponsonby denizens and visitors. Mouth-watering scrambled eggs, tempting counter food, heart-starting coffee, plus a great stack of reading material if you tire of eavesdropping and people-watching.

Queenie (Map p110; ☎ 09-378 8977; 24 Spring St, Freemans Bay; breakfast $7-17, lunch $12-21; ☽ breakfast & lunch Mon-Sat) Kiwiana reigns supreme at this eccentric corner cafe with one wall devoted to a 1950s paint-by-numbers Maori maiden mural. The food is a step up from standard cafe fare, with a short, adventurous menu justifying the prices.

Landreth & Co (Map p110; ☎ 09-360 7440; 272 Ponsonby Rd; mains $12-23; ☽ 7am-4pm) A popular brunch spot with an old-Ponsonby feel and a sunny rear courtyard. For something a bit different, try the kedgeree (kippers, rice and egg).

Prego (Map p110; ☎ 09-376 3095; 226 Ponsonby Rd; mains $22-35; ☽ noon-midnight) This friendly and stylish Italian restaurant covers all the bases, with a fireplace in winter and a courtyard in summer. And on the subject of bases, the pizza is pretty damn fine, as are the inventive Italian mains.

Ponsonby Road Bistro (Map p110; ☎ 09-360 1611; 165 Ponsonby Rd; mains $26-34; ⌚ lunch Mon-Fri, dinner Mon-Sat) Portions are massive at this modern, upmarket restaurant with an Italian/French sensibility and first-rate service. Pick at a charcuterie platter over a glass of wine on the street tables.

SPQR (Map p110; ☎ 09-360 1710; 150 Ponsonby Rd; mains $26-40; ⌚ lunch & dinner) This ivy-covered Ponsonby Rd hot spot is well known for good Roman-style, thin, crusty pizzas and excellent Italian-influenced mains. The surrounds are a stylish blend of the industrial and the chic, the lights *low* (bring your reading glasses!), the buzz constant and the staff smooth and camp all at the same time.

Soto (Map p110; ☎ 09-360 0021; 13 St Marys Rd; mains $29-31; ⌚ lunch Tue-Fri, dinner Tue-Sat) Auckland has a surfeit of excellent Japanese restaurants but this is the best. The staff glide by in kimonos leaving a trail of exquisitely presented dishes in their wake – including sushi, sashimi and *zensai* (Japanese tapas).

For quick eats, try **Murder Burger** (Map p110; ☎ 09-550 5500; 128a Ponsonby Rd; burgers $8-17; ⌚ lunch & dinner), where there is no gilding the lily: the staff wear Meat Is Murder T-shirts, the logo features a diabolically carnivorous-looking kitty and the burgers are full of free-range, organic dead stuff: eye fillet, Angus sirloin, chicken, wild boar, venison, ostrich and fish.

The city's best food hall is **Ponsonby Village Food Court** (Map p110; 106 Ponsonby Rd; mains $8-18; ⌚ 10am-10pm; V). Choose between Italian, Japanese, Malaysian, Chinese, Turkish, Thai, Lao, Indian, Mexican and the best Vietnamese in the central city.

Grey Lynn

Richmond Road Cafe (Map p110; ☎ 09-360 5559; 318 Richmond Rd; mains $13-29; ⌚ 7am-4pm) Auckland's current 'it' cafe, and with good reason. The service is impeccable and the menu is full of well-priced and interesting cafe fare. If it doesn't have a cardamom-cream or lavender-syrup twist it's too boring for this place. Try the spiced banana and rum porridge with fresh coconut.

Delicious (Map p110; ☎ 09-360 7590; 472 Richmond Rd; mains $26-29; ⌚ lunch Wed-Fri, dinner Tue-Sat) The name doesn't lie. Foodies flock to this neighbourhood eatery for simple but first-rate pasta at reasonable prices. They don't take bookings so expect to wait – it's always busy.

North Shore

Stone Oven (Map p104; ☎ 09-445 3185; 5 Clarence St, Devonport; mains $5-19; ⌚ 6.30am-4.30pm; ☐) On weekends you'll want to get in early or get ready to queue for the breads, pastries, cakes and baked goods. Perfect for scoffing *in situ*, or away from the madding crowd.

Takapuna Beach Cafe (Map p96; ☎ 09-484 0002; The Promenade, Takapuna; mains $13-25; ⌚ 7am-6pm) With a menu that reads like a travel magazine (Moroccan eggs, Tunisian eggplant, French-style terrine, chorizo, pancetta…) and absolute beach views, it's no wonder this modern cafe is constantly buzzing. If you can't snaffle a table you can always grab an award-winning ice cream or snack from the attached shop.

Engine Room (Map p96; ☎ 09-480 9502; 115 Queen St, Northcote; meals $31-34; ⌚ dinner Tue-Sat) A strong contender for Auckland's best restaurant, this informal eatery serves up lighter-than-air goat's cheese soufflés, inventive whiteboard mains and oh-my-God chocolate truffles. It's worth booking ahead and catching the ferry.

Eight.Two (Map p96; ☎ 09-419 9082; 82 Hinemoa St, Birkenhead; mains $35-37; ⌚ dinner Tue-Sat) Hollowed out of an old villa, this dazzlingly white dining room offers a similarly modern menu and a great wine list. Catch the Birkenhead ferry from the city for a memorable night out.

Self-catering

You'll find large supermarkets (Countdown, Foodtown, New World, Pak N Save, Woolworths) in most neighbourhoods. As well as the places listed here, self-caterers should consider the Otara Market and Avondale Sunday Market for cheap, fresh vegetables; see p126.

No self-respecting city with a position like this should be without a fish market. **Auckland Fish Market** (Map p100; ☎ 09-379 1490; www.aucklandfishmarket.co.nz; cnr Jellicoe & Daldy Sts; ⌚ 7am-6.30pm) not only has a boisterous early-morning auction, but also a market, eateries and a seafood-cooking school.

City Farmers Market (Map p100; ☎ 09-232 7933; www.cityfarmersmarket.co.nz; cnr Gore & Galway Sts; ⌚ 8.30am-12.30pm Sat) stocks fresh seasonal produce and fancy treats.

ourpick La Cigale (Map p106; ☎ 09-366 9361; 69 St Georges Bay Rd; ⌚ market 8am-1pm Sat, 9am-2pm Sun) caters to Francophiles and homesick Gauls, stocking all manner of French produce (wine, cheese, tinned snails etc), and the in-house cafe (mains $7.50 to $17.50) serves delicious

PASIFIKA

There are nearly 180,000 Pacific Islanders (PI) living in Auckland, making it the world's principal Polynesian city. Samoans are by far the largest group, followed by Cook Islanders, Tongans, Niueans, Fijians, Tokelauans and Tuvaluans. The biggest PI communities can be found in South Auckland and pockets of West and Central Auckland.

Like the Maori renaissance of recent decades, Pasifika has become a hot commodity for Auckland hipsters. You'll find PI motifs everywhere: in art, architecture, fashion, homewares and especially in music. Movies *Sione's Wedding* and *No. 2* have put PI Auckland on the big screen, while *bro'Town* is NZ's answer to *South Park*. Ironically, as Pakeha Aucklanders look to the Pacific, PI teenagers turn to Black America for inspiration. Hip-hop culture is massive in Auckland, with home-grown rap at an all-time high.

The annual Pasifika Festival (p113) is one of the city's best events. Thousands descend on Western Springs Park to load up on island food, hang out in the sun and catch cultural performances. If you miss it, you can get a taste of the Pacific vibe at the Otara and Avondale markets (p126) or at any hip-hop night in the city's clubs. Check out Pauanesia (p126) for interesting gifts and art.

delicatessen platters ($18). Yet it's during the weekend farmers markets that this *cigale* (cicada) really chirps. Lose yourself among stalls laden with produce, home-made jam, honey and all manner of tasty snacks.

Auckland's legendary organics store **Harvest Wholefoods** (Map p110; ☎ 09-376 3107; 405 Richmond Rd; ☺ 9am-7pm Mon-Fri, 9am-5pm Sat, 10am-5pm Sun; Ⓥ), stocks planet-friendly fresh produce, grocery items and cosmetics. It's a meat-free zone, but there's an organic butchery across the road.

DRINKING

Auckland's nightlife tends to be quiet during the week and positively funereal on Sunday, but wakes up late on Friday and Saturday, when most pubs and bars are open until 1am or later. If in doubt head to Ponsonby, K Rd or the bottom end of the city.

Central Auckland

Agents & Merchants/Racket (Map p100; ☎ 09-309 5852; 46-50 Customs St) Tucked into their own covered laneway with an outdoor fireplace and sofas, this duo conjures an old-world yet thoroughly modern atmosphere. A&M serves excellent tapas and wine while Racket kicks off a little later with DJs on duty.

Bluestone Room (Map p100; ☎ 09-302 0930; 9 Durham Lane; ☺ 11am-late Mon-Fri, 4pm-late Sat) There's no shortage of character in this 1861 stone building, secreted down a dingy alley in the old part of town (a glassed-over well in the floor dates to 1841). The Rolling Stones played here in the '60s and live blues and rock are still a feature on the weekends.

Chambers Bar (Map p100; ☎ 09-309 8151; 6 O'Connell St; ☺ 4pm-late Tue-Sat) Sneak down the stairs to a glamorous world of sparkling chandeliers, leather couches and artful cocktails.

Hotel de Brett (Map p100; ☎ 09-925 9000; 2 High St; ☺ noon-late) Grab a cocktail in the chic art-deco Housebar or nab a spot by the fire in the Atrium, an interesting covered space fashioned from the alleyway between the old buildings.

Lenin Bar (Map p100; ☎ 09-377 0040; Princes Wharf; ☺ 3pm-late) This Russian-themed affair boasts numerous vodkas and DJs from Thursday to Saturday. A window looks into Minus 5° Bar, giving you a glimpse of the icy world without the chills (or prices).

Minus 5° Bar (Map p100; ☎ 09-377 6702; Princes Wharf; before/after 6pm $25/30; ☺ noon-1am Sun-Wed, noon-2am Thu-Sat) Everything from the seats to your glass is made of ice. Put on special clothing (including gloves and shoes) and sip a complimentary vodka-based cocktail. You can only stay inside the shimmering ice world for 30 minutes, making it a quick way to blow your cold hard cash.

Mo's (Map p100; ☎ 09-366 6066; cnr Wolfe & Federal Sts; ☺ 4pm-3am Mon-Fri, 8pm-3am Sat) There's something about this tiny corner bar that makes you want to invent problems just so the bar-person can solve them with soothing words and an expertly poured martini.

Northern Steamship Co. (Map p100; ☎ 09-374 3952; 122 Quay St) Standard lamps hang upside-down from the ceiling while the bar mural dreams of NZ summer holidays in this cool big pub by the train station.

Occidental Belgian Beer Cafe (Map p100; ☎ 09-300 6226; 6 Vulcan Lane; ◷ 7am-late Mon-Fri, 9am-late Sat & Sun) Belgian beer, Belgian food (plenty of *moules* and *frites* – mussels and chips) and live music are on offer at this historic (1870) pub.

Pasha (Map p100; ☎ 09-355 0077; Princes Wharf; ◷ 4pm-late) Awesome cocktails and Moorish exoticism combine in this impressive Viaduct bar.

Shakespeare (Map p100; ☎ 09-373 5396; 61 Albert St; ◷ 24hr) An old-fashioned corner pub with a sunny terrace and an in-house microbrewery.

Newton
Galbraith's Alehouse (Map p100; ☎ 09-379 3557; 2 Mt Eden Rd; ◷ noon-11pm Mon-Sat, noon-10pm Sun) Brewing up real ales and lagers on-site, this English-style pub offers bliss on tap. The backdoor beer garden trumps the brightly lit bar.

Wine Cellar (Map p100; ☎ 09-337 8293; St Kevin's Arcade, K Rd; ◷ 5pm-midnight Mon-Thu, 5pm-2am Fri & Sat) Secreted down some stairs in an arcade, this is the kind of bar that Buffy the Vampire Slayer would have hung out in on Auckland-based assignments. It's dark, grungy and very cool, with regular live music in the neighbouring Whammy Bar.

Kingsland
Neighbourhood Brewbar (Map p108; ☎ 09-529 9178; 498 New North Rd; ◷ 11am-late Mon-Fri, noon-late Sat & Sun) With picture windows overlooking Eden Park and a front terrace that's already pick-up central after dark, this upmarket pub is guaranteed to be the place-to-be during the Rugby World Cup.

Ponsonby & Grey Lynn
Along Ponsonby Rd, the line between cafe, restaurant, bar and club gets blurred. A lot of food places also have live music or become clubs later on.

Gypsy Tea Room (Map p110; ☎ 09-361 6970; 455 Richmond Rd; ◷ 4-11.30pm Sun-Thu, 3pm-2am Fri & Sat) No one comes here for tea. This cute wine/cocktail bar has dishevelled charm in bucketloads.

Dida's Wine Lounge & Tapas Bar (Map p110; ☎ 09-376 2813; 54 Jervois Rd; ◷ 11am-late) Great food and an even better wine list attract a grown-up crowd. Easy, cougar.

Ponsonby Social Club (Map p110; ☎ 09-361 2320; 152 Ponsonby Rd; ◷ 5pm-late) Half-and-half alleyway and bar, the back end of this long, narrow

space heaves on the weekends when the DJs crank out classic funk and hip-hop.

ENTERTAINMENT
The *NZ Herald* has an in-depth run-down of the coming week's happenings in its *Time Out* magazine on Thursday and again in its Saturday edition. If you're planning a big night along K Rd, then visit www.kroad.co.nz for a detailed list of bars and clubs.

Tickets for most major events can be bought from:

Ticketek (☎ 09-307 5000; www.ticketek.co.nz) Outlets include Aotea Centre and SkyCity Atrium.

Ticketmaster (☎ 09-970 9700; www.ticketmaster. co.nz) Outlets at Real Groovy (p126), Vector Arena (p124) and Britomart station.

Live Music
Dogs Bollix (Map p100; ☎ 09-376 4600; www.dogsbollix .co.nz; cnr K & Newton Rds) This Irish pub is a live-music venue from Tuesday to Sunday but doesn't only play Irish music. Spot local musos here when they're off-duty.

Thirsty Dog (Map p100; ☎ 09-377 9190; www.thirsty dog.co.nz; 469 K Rd; ◷ 11am-late) This Dog's both thirsty and noisy, with a decent sound system and a regular roster of local bands.

Kings Arms Tavern (Map p100; ☎ 09-373 3240; www.kingsarms.co.nz; 59 France St; ◷ 11am-late) One of Auckland's leading small venues for live (and local) rock bands, which play most nights. A rite of passage if you want to get into the local scene.

AN AUCKLAND PLAYLIST

Download these Auckland songs to your MP3 player for cruising the city's streets:

- *Chains* – Che Fu and DLT
- *Kare Kare* – Crowded House
- *Hopetoun Bridge* – Dave Dobbyn
- *Andy* – The Front Lawn
- *Auckland CBD Part Two* – Lawrence Arabia
- *Dominion Rd* – The Mutton Birds
- *A Brief Reflection* – Nesian Mystik
- *We Are the OMC* – Otara Millionaires Club
- *Haul Away* – Split Enz
- *One Tree Hill* – U2

Windsor Castle & Juice Bar (Map p106; ☎ 09-356 3650; www.thewindsor.co.nz; 144 Parnell Rd) Established in 1847, this once grungy boozer was at the heart of Auckland's pub-rock scene of the 1970s and '80s. In 2009 it reopened its doors, completely zooshed up, but committed to re-establishing itself as the city's pre-eminent live rock pub.

For big international and major local bands, the main venues in Auckland include the following:

Mt Smart Stadium & Supertop (Map p96; ☎ 09-571 1603; www.mtsmartstadium.co.nz; Maurice Rd, Penrose)

North Shore Events Centre (Map p96; ☎ 09-443 8199; www.nseventscenter.zes.zeald.com; Argus Pl, Glenfield)

Vector Arena (Map p100; ☎ 09-358 1250; www.vectorarena.co.nz; Mahuhu Cres, City)

Western Springs Stadium (Map p96; ☎ 09-849 3807; Great North Rd, Western Springs)

Nightclubs

The Viaduct and K Rd are the main places to find late-night clubs, but there are also a few around Fort St and Ponsonby Rd. Some clubs have a cover charge, depending on the night and the event.

Cassette Number Nine (Map p100; ☎ 09-366 0196; www.cassettenine.com; 9 Vulcan Lane; entry Fri & Sat $10; ☺ 5pm-late) Auckland's most out-there hipsters gravitate to this eccentric bar/club where swishy nouvelle New Romantic clones rub shoulders with girls in very short dresses and the music ranges from live indie to international DJ sets.

Ink & Coherent (Map p100; ☎ 09-358 5103; www.inkcoherent.co.nz; 268 & 262 K Rd; entry free-$45) Neighbouring clubs for serious dance aficionados, sometimes hosting big name DJs.

Rising Sun & 4:20 (Map p100; ☎ 09-358 5643; www.420.co.nz; 373 K Rd) Downstairs is a straight-out nightclub hosting different nights (particularly hip-hop, but also electro, crunk, reggaetron etc), while upstairs is a large room with a view and another small dance floor.

Khuja Lounge (Map p100; ☎ 09-377 3711; 536 Queen St; ☺ 8pm-3am Wed-Sat) Above the Westpac building, this laid-back venue offers DJs and jazz/soul/hip-hop bands.

Boogie Wonderland (Map p100; ☎ 09-361 6093; www.boogiewonderland.co.nz; cnr Galway & Queen Sts; ☺ 9pm-late Thu-Sat) As trashy and fun as it sounds, the disco never ended in this basement club that's popular with women of a certain age.

Sport

Eden Park (Map p108; ☎ 09-815 5551; www.edenpark.co.nz; Reimers Ave, Kingsland) This is the stadium for top rugby (winter) and cricket (summer) matches, and at the time of research it was well in the throes of its Rugby World Cup 2011 makeover. The All Blacks, the Black Caps and the Auckland Blues all play here. To get there, take the train from Britomart to Kingsland station.

Mt Smart Stadium Hosts soccer, rugby league (Warriors) and *really* big-name concerts (see left).

ASB Tennis Centre (Map p100; ☎ 09-373 3623; 72 Stanley St) In January the women's ASB Classic is followed by the men's Heineken Open. Some famous tennis names show up to battle it out at this venue.

Theatre, Classical Music & Comedy

Aotea Sq and the buildings that surround it comprise Auckland's main arts and entertainment complex, branded the **Edge** (☎ 09-357 3355; www.the-edge.co.nz), comprising the Town Hall, Civic Theatre and Aotea Centre.

Auckland Town Hall (Map p100; 305 Queen St) This elegant Edwardian venue (1911) hosts concert performances by the likes of the NZ Symphony Orchestra (www.nzso.co.nz) and Auckland Philharmonia (www.apo.co.nz).

Aotea Centre (Map p100; 50 Mayoral Dr) Auckland's main venue for theatre, dance, ballet and opera, with two main stages: the cavernous ASB Auditorium and the tiny Herald Theatre. Auckland Theatre Company (www.atc.co.nz), Silo Theatre (www.silotheatre.co.nz) and NZ Opera (www.nzopera.com) all regularly perform here.

Civic Theatre (Map p100; cnr Queen & Wellesley Sts) This restored grand dame of a theatre (p107) is used by major touring productions, including opera, musicals and live theatre, as well as by the Auckland International Film Festival (p113).

Classic Comedy Club (Map p100; ☎ 09-373 4321; www.comedy.co.nz; 321 Queen St; tickets $5-27) Auckland's top venue for comedy, with performances most nights. There are late shows on Friday and Saturday.

Other theatres:

Maidment Theatre (Map p100; ☎ 09-308 2383; www.maidment.auckland.ac.nz; Auckland University, 8 Alfred St)

SkyCity Theatre (Map p100; ☎ 09-363 6000; www.skycity.co.nz; cnr Victoria & Federal Sts)

GAY & LESBIAN AUCKLAND

One of Auckland's nicknames is the Queen City, so it's fitting that it has the country's biggest gay population. While the bright lights attract gays and lesbians from all over the country, the even brighter lights of Sydney eventually steal many of the 30- to 40-somethings, leaving a gap in the demographic. There are a handful of gay venues, but they're not as buzzy as you might expect.

To find out what's going on, grab a copy of the fortnightly newspaper *Express* (available from gay venues) or log on to www.gaynz.com. The big events on the calendar are the Big Gay Out (p113), Out Takes film festival (p113) and Queen of the Whole Universe (p113).

Venues change with alarming regularity, but these ones, along with straight-friendly SPQR (p121), are the stayers:

■ **Family** (Map p100; ☎ 09-309 0213; www.familybar.co.nz; 270 K Rd) Trashy, brash and young, but this bar can be a lot of fun.

■ **Naval & Family** (Map p100; ☎ 09-373 3409; cnr K Rd & Pitt St) Family's sister bar, directly across the road, has more of a pub feel.

■ **Urge** (Map p100; ☎ 09-307 2155; www.urgebar.co.nz; 490 K Rd; ☼ 9pm-late Thu-Sat) Older and hairier than Family, this is the country's longest-running gay bar, with DJs Friday and Saturday nights, raunchy parties and lots of cruising.

■ **Dot's** (Map p100; ☎ 09-379 7335; www.dotsbar.com; 223 Symonds St; ☼ 3pm-late Tue-Sun) Camp as they come, with drag shows every Friday and Saturday.

■ **Centurian** (Map p100; ☎ 09-377 5571; 18 Beresford St; admission before/after 3pm $21/26; ☼ noon-2am Sun-Thu, 11am-6am Fri & Sat) Gay men's sauna.

Cinemas

Most cinemas offer cheaper rates on weekdays before 5pm; Tuesday is usually bargain day.

SkyCity Queen St (Map p100; ☎ 09-979 2401; www.skycitycinemas.co.nz; Level 3, 291 Queen St; adult $10-15.50, child $8-9.50) Part of SkyCity Metro, a modernistic mall that includes Borders bookshop, bars and a food court.

Academy Cinemas (Map p100; ☎ 09-373 2761; www.academycinemas.co.nz; 44 Lorne St; adult/concession $15/11) In the basement of the Central City Library is the Academy, which shows independent foreign and art-house films.

Rialto Cinemas (Map p106; ☎ 09-529 2218; www.rialto.co.nz; 167 Broadway, Newmarket; adult $10-16, child $8-10) Screens art-house and international, plus some mainstream fare.

NZ Film Archives (Map p100; ☎ 09-379 0688; www.filmarchive.org.nz; 300 K Rd; ☼ 11am-5pm Mon-Fri, 11am-4pm Sat) A wonderful resource of more than 1000 Kiwi feature films and documentaries dating from 1905, which you can watch for free on a TV screen. See p21 for some recommended Kiwi feature films.

SHOPPING

Followers of fashion should head to High St, Chancery Lane, Newmarket, Ponsonby Rd and K Rd. An official All Black rugby shirt costs around $180. The central city area (especially Queen St) has lots of stores selling outdoor clothes and equipment.

Clothing & Accessories

Karen Walker City (Map p100; ☎ 09-309 6299; 15 O'Connell St); Newmarket (Map p106; ☎ 09-522 4286; 6 Balm St); Ponsonby (Map p110; ☎ 09-361 6723; 171 Ponsonby Rd) Join Madonna and Björk in wearing Walker's cool (but pricey) threads.

Marvel (Map p110; ☎ 09-376 4204; 143 Ponsonby Rd) Smart, tailored shirts and trousers in interesting fabrics and quirky partywear are the mainstays of this excellent local menswear designer.

Royal Jewellery Studio (Map p108; ☎ 09-846 0200; 486 New North Rd) Displaying interesting work by local artisans, including some beautiful Maori designs, this is a great place to pick up authentic *pounamu* (greenstone) jewellery.

Zambesi City (Map p100; ☎ 09-303 1701; cnr Vulcan Lane & O'Connell St); Newmarket (Map p106; ☎ 09-523 1000; 38 Osborne St); Ponsonby (Map p110; ☎ 09-360 7391; 169 Ponsonby Rd) Hands-down, the most interesting and influential fashion label to come out of the country, and much sought after by local and international celebs.

Gifts & Souvenirs

Pauanesia (Map p100; ☎ 09-366 7782; 35 High St) A colourful treasure-trove of Polynesian craft and gifts.

Native Agent (Map p108; ☎ 09-845 3289; 507b New North Rd) There's a strong Maori bent to the jewellery, clothing and knick-knacks on offer here, and it's all NZ-made.

O'Kai Oceanikart (Map p100; ☎ 09-379 9051; 65 K Rd) Pan-Pacific art, from well-known artists like Fatu Feu'u to exciting up-and-comers.

Markets

Otara Market (Map p96; ☎ 09-274 0830; Newbury St; ☻ 6am-noon Sat) Held in the car park between the Manukau Polytech and the Otara town centre, this market has a real Polynesian atmosphere, and you can buy South Pacific food, music and fashions. Take bus 497 from Britomart ($5.40, 50 minutes).

Avondale Sunday Market (Map p96; ☎ 09-818 4931; Avondale Racecourse, Ash St; ☻ 6am-noon Sun) A similar vibe to the Otara Market; take the train to Avondale station.

Music

Real Groovy (Map p100; ☎ 09-302 3940; 438 Queen St) A music-lovers' nirvana, this huge store has masses of new, second-hand and rare releases, as well as concert tickets, giant posters, DVDs, books, magazines and clothing.

GETTING THERE & AWAY

Air

Auckland International Airport (Map p96; ☎ 09-275 0789; www.auckland-airport.co.nz) is 21km south of the city centre. It has an international terminal and a domestic terminal, each with a tourist information centre. A free shuttle service operates every 20 minutes (6am to 10.30pm) between the terminals and there's also a signposted footpath (about a 1km walk).

At the international terminal there's a free phone for accommodation bookings. Both terminals have left-luggage facilities, ATMs and car-rental desks, although you get better rates from companies in town.

Auckland is the major gateway to NZ, and a hub for domestic flights. See p702 for information on international flights.

Domestic airlines operating to and from Auckland and the destinations they serve:

Air New Zealand (Map p100; ☎ 09-336 2400; www.airnewzealand.co.nz; cnr Customs & Queen Sts) Kaitaia,

---

> **PLANE DELAYED? TIME FOR A TIPPLE!**
>
> Clearly the roar of jets doesn't bother grapes, as NZ's most awarded winery is just 4km from the airport. The parklike grounds of **Villa Maria Estate** (Map p96; ☎ 09-255 0666; 118 Montgomerie Rd; ☻ 9am-6pm Mon-Fri, 10am-5pm Sat & Sun) are a green oasis in the encircling industrial zone. Short tours ($5) take place at 11am and 3pm. There's a charge for tastings ($5), but lingering over wine and antipasto on the terrace sure beats hanging around the departure lounge.

Kerikeri, Whangarei, Hamilton, Tauranga, Whakatane, Gisborne, Rotorua, Taupo, New Plymouth, Napier, Whanganui, Palmerston North, Masterton, Wellington, Nelson, Blenheim, Christchurch, Queenstown and Dunedin.

Fly My Sky (☎ 09-256 7025; www.flymysky.co.nz) Great Barrier Island.

Great Barrier Airlines (☎ 09-275 9120; www.greatbarrierairlines.co.nz) Great Barrier Island.

Jetstar (☎ 0800 800 995; www.jetstar.com) Wellington, Christchurch and Queenstown.

Bus

The main long-distance bus company in Auckland, as for the rest of NZ, is **InterCity** (☎ 09-583 5780; www.intercity.co.nz) and its travel and sightseeing arm **Newmans Coach Lines** (www.newmanscoach.co.nz). Its buses go to almost all bigger towns and the main tourist areas. Services leave from the **SkyCity Coach Terminal** (Map p100; ☎ 09-913 6220; 102 Hobson St).

Naked Bus (www.nakedbus.com) buses travel along SH1 as far as Paihia (four hours) and Wellington (12 hours), as well as heading to Waitomo Caves (3¾ hours) Whitianga (3¾ hours), Tauranga (3½ hours), Gisborne (nine hours) and Napier (12 hours). Fares start from $1. **Dalroy Express** (☎ 0508 465 622; www.dalroytours.co.nz) operates a daily service between Auckland and New Plymouth ($59, 5½ hours). **Main Coachline** (☎ 09-278 8070; www.maincoachline.co.nz) runs six buses per week between Auckland and Dargaville ($48, three hours). All of these buses stop on Quay St, opposite the Ferry Building (Map p100).

Go Kiwi (☎ 07-866 0336; www.go-kiwi.co.nz) has daily door-to-door shuttle services to/from Auckland, Thames and Whitianga along with seasonal services to Tauranga and Rotorua.

Car

HIRING A CAR

Auckland has countless car-hire operators and is the best city in which to hire (or buy) a vehicle for touring NZ or the city itself. Some good deals can be had for long-term hire, but be warned that cheapest is not necessarily the best.

A swag of car-rental companies can be found conveniently grouped together along Beach Rd and Stanley St close to the city centre. The major companies (Avis, Budget, Hertz and Thrifty) are reliable, offer full insurance and have offices at the airport and all over the country. They are more expensive, but rates are often negotiable for longer hires or off-season.

If you are prepared to take limited insurance and risk losing an excess of around $750, then the cheaper operators offer some pretty good deals. Prices vary with the season, the age of the car and length of hire. Ignore prices quoted in brochures and shop around by phone. Always read the hire agreement thoroughly before you sign.

Some of the more reputable car-hire companies (which may also hire out sleeper vans and campervans):

A2B (Map p100; ☎ 0800 222 929, 09-377 0824; www. a2b-car-rental.co.nz; 11 Stanley St) Cheap older cars with no visible hire-car branding, making them less of a thief-magnet.

Britz (Map p96; ☎ 0800 831 900, 09-275 9090; www. britz.co.nz; 36 Richard Pearse Dr, Mangere)

Budget (Map p100; ☎ 0800 283 438, 09-529 7788; www.budget.co.nz; 163 Beach Rd)

Escape (Map p100; ☎ 0800 216 171, 021 288 8372; www.escaperentals.co.nz; 7 Gore St) Eccentrically painted campervans.

Explore More (Map p96; ☎ 0800 447 363, 09-255 0620; www.exploremore.co.nz; 36 Richard Pearse Dr, Mangere)

Go Rentals (Map p96; ☎ 0508 246 684, 09-525 7321; www.gorentals.co.nz; 688 Great South Rd, Penrose)

Hertz (Map p100; ☎ 0800 654 321, 09-367 6350; www. hertz.co.nz; 154 Victoria St)

Jucy (Map p100; ☎ 0800 399 736, 09-374 4360; www. jucy.co.nz; 2-16 The Strand)

Maui (Map p96; ☎ 0800 651 080, 09-255 3910; www. maui.co.nz; 36 Richard Pearse Dr, Mangere)

Omega (Map p100; ☎ 0800 525 210, 09-377 5573; www.omegarentals.com; 75 Beach Rd)

Thrifty (Map p100; ☎ 0800 737 070, 09-309 0111; www.thrifty.co.nz; 150 Khyber Pass Rd)

BUYING A CAR

For stays of two months or more, many people look at buying a car. You can buy through dealers on the buy-back scheme, at car fairs or auctions, or through ads at backpacker hostels. Before buying a car you must check that it is mechanically sound, has not been stolen, and does not have money owing on it to a finance company or bank.

Buy-backs, where the dealer agrees to buy back your car for an agreed price (often 50% of what you pay), are not a good deal, but offer a safety net if you have trouble selling the car.

A popular way to buy a car is at the car fairs where people bring their own cars to sell them. Arrive between 8.30am and 9.30am for the best choice; car fairs are over by about noon. For a credit check quote chassis and licence-plate numbers. Mechanical inspection services, credit agencies and Auto Check details are on hand at the following car fairs:

Auckland Car Fair (Map p96; ☎ 09-529 2233; www. carfair.co.nz; Ellerslie Racecourse, Green Lane East; ☾ 9am-noon Sun) It's the largest car fair and it costs $30 to display your vehicle.

City Car Fair (Map p100; ☎ 09-837 7817; cnr Halsey & Gaunt Sts; ☾ 9am-1pm Sat) It costs $20 to display your car.

Motorcycle

NZ Motorcycle Rentals (Map p96; ☎ 09-486 2472; www. nzbike.com; 72 Barrys Point Rd, Takapuna) offers motorbike hire for $105 to $400 a day (insurance excess is $1500 and upwards). Guided tours are also available.

Train

Overlander (☎ 0800 872 467; www.tranzscenic.co.nz) trains arrive at and depart from **Britomart station** (Map p100; Queen St), the largest underground diesel train station in the world. They depart from Auckland at 7.25am (daily late September to April, Friday to Sunday otherwise) and arrive in Wellington at 7.25pm (the return train from Wellington departs and arrives at the same time). Useful stops include Hamilton (2½ hours), Otorohanga (three hours), Te Kuiti (3¼ hours), Taumarunui (4½ hours), National Park (5½ hours), Ohakune (6½ hours), Palmerston North (9½ hours) and Paraparaumu (11 hours). A standard fare to Wellington is $118, but a limited number of *Go Anywhere* discounted seats are available for each journey at $49, $69 and $89 (first-in, first-served).

GETTING AROUND

To/From the Airport

The **Airbus Express** (☎ 09-366 6400; www.airbus. co.nz; one way/return adult $16/23, backpacker $14/21, child $6/12) runs every 15 minutes from 7am to 7.30pm and every 30 minutes from 7.30pm to 7am, between the terminals and the city. Stops include Mt Eden Rd (as requested), Symonds St, Queen St and the Ferry Terminal. Reservations are not required and you buy a ticket from the driver. The trip takes less than an hour each way (longer during rush hour).

The convenient door-to-door **Super Shuttle** (☎ 0800 748 885; www.supershuttle.co.nz) will charge about $25 for one person heading between the airport and a city hotel. You'll save money per head if there's a group of you. The price increases if you want to go to an outlying suburb.

A taxi between the airport and the city costs around $70.

Bicycle

Adventure Cycles (Map p96; ☎ 09-940 2453; www.adventure -auckland.co.nz/adventurecycles; 9 Premier Ave, Western Springs; hire per day $20-40, per week $90-150, per month $200-300; ⏰ 7.30am-7pm Thu-Mon) hires out road, mountain and long-term touring bikes, runs a buy-back scheme and does repairs.

Maxx Regional Transport (☎ 09-366 6400; www. maxx.co.nz) publishes free cycle maps, available from public buildings such as stations, libraries and i-SITEs. Bikes can be taken on ferries (free) and trains ($1), but only folding bikes are allowed on buses.

Boat

Fullers and 360 Discovery both run ferries from Quay St in the city. See p109 for destinations.

Car & Motorcycle

Auckland's motorways jam up badly at peak times, particularly the Northern and Southern. It's best to avoid them between 7am and 9am, and from 5pm to 7pm. Things also get tight around 3pm during term time, which is the end of the school day.

Expect to pay for parking in central Auckland during the day, from Monday to Saturday. Most parking meters (from $1 an hour) are pay-and-display; follow the instructions, collect your ticket and display it inside your windscreen. You usually don't have to pay between 6pm and 8am or on Sunday – check the meters and parking signs carefully.

Prices can be steep at parking buildings. Better value are the council-run open-air parks near the train station, Beach Rd ($7 per day) and on Ngaoho Pl, off The Strand ($5 per day).

Public Transport

Due to rampant privatisation during the 1980s, Auckland's public transport system is run by a hodgepodge of different operators, none of which seem to co-operate. As a result there are few integrated public transport passes. The Auckland Regional Council is trying to sort out the mess and runs the excellent **Maxx** (☎ 09-366 6400; www.maxx.co.nz) information service, covering buses, trains and ferries. The website has an excellent trip-planning feature.

BUS

Bus routes spread their tentacles throughout the city. Many services terminate around Britomart station (Map p100). Bus stops often have electronic displays, giving an estimate of waiting times. Be warned: they lie.

Single-ride fares in the inner city are 50c for an adult and 30c for a child (you pay the driver when you board), but if you're travelling further afield there are fare stages from $1.60/1 (adult/child) to $9.70/5.80. A one-day pass (which includes the North Shore ferries) costs $11, while a weekly pass costs $45 ($40 from an agent) – there's no reduction for children.

The environmentally friendly Link Bus ($1.60, every 10 to 15 minutes, 6am to 11.30pm) is a very handy service that travels clockwise and anticlockwise around a loop that includes Queen St, SkyCity, Victoria Park Market, Ponsonby Rd, K Rd, Newmarket, Parnell and Britomart station.

The red City Circuit bus (every 10 minutes, 8am to 6pm) provides free transport around the inner city from Britomart station, up Queen St, past Albert Park to Auckland University, across to the Sky Tower and back to Britomart.

TRAIN

Auckland's train service is excellent but a bit limited. Trains are generally clean, cheap and (usually) on time – although any hiccup on the lines can bring down the entire network. You will need to refer to a timetable, as they aren't particularly frequent.

Impressive Britomart station (Map p100) has food retailers, foreign-exchange facilities and a ticket office. Downstairs are plush toilets and left-luggage lockers.

There are just three train routes: one runs west to Waitakere, while two run south to Pukekohe. Services are at least hourly and run from around 6am to 8pm (later on the weekends). A $13 Discovery Pass allows a day's travel on most bus, train and North Shore ferry services. Otherwise, pay the conductor on the train (one stage $1.40); they'll come to you. All trains have wheelchair ramps.

Taxi

Auckland's many taxis usually operate from ranks, but they also cruise popular areas. **Auckland Co-op Taxis** (☎ 09-300 3000) is one of the biggest companies. Flagfall is $3, then it's $2.40 to $2.60 per kilometre. There's a surcharge for transport to and from the airport and cruise ships.

HAURAKI GULF ISLANDS

The Hauraki Gulf, stretching between Auckland and the Coromandel Peninsula, is dotted with *motu* (islands) and gives the Bay of Islands some rather stiff competition in the beauty stakes. Some are only minutes from the city and make excellent day trips: wine-soaked Waiheke and volcanic Rangitoto really shouldn't be missed. Great Barrier requires more effort (and cash) to get to, but provides an idyllic escape from modern life.

There are 47 islands in the Hauraki Gulf Maritime Park, administered by DOC. Some are good-sized islands, others are no more than rocks jutting out of the sea. They're loosely put into two categories: recreation and conservation. The recreation islands can easily be visited and their harbours are dotted with yachts in summer. The conservation islands, however, have restricted access. Permits are required to visit some, while others are closed refuges for the preservation of rare plants and animals, especially birds.

The gulf is a busy highway for marine mammals. Sei, minke and Bryde's whales are regularly seen in its outer reaches, along with orcas and bottlenose dolphins. You might even spy a passing humpback.

Information

The DOC information centre (p98) and the New Zealand i-SITE (p98), both on the Auckland waterfront, are good sources of information, maps and walking pamphlets.

Getting There & Around

Most island ferries leave from the Auckland waterfront, but some depart from Devonport, Half Moon Bay (East Auckland), Gulf Harbour (Whangaparaoa Peninsula) and Sandspit (near Warkworth). If you miss the last ferry, **Auckland Water Taxis** (☎ 0800 890 007; www.watertaxis.co.nz) operates a 24-hour water-taxi service (Auckland to Waiheke has a minimum charge of $210; to Rangitoto, $100). See also p109 for cruises and p109 for sailing trips.

RANGITOTO & MOTUTAPU
pop 75

Sloping elegantly from the waters of the gulf, 260m **Rangitoto** (www.rangitoto.org), the largest and youngest of Auckland's volcanic cones, provides a picturesque backdrop to all of the city's activities. As recently as 600 years ago it erupted from the sea and was probably active for several years before settling down. Maori living on Motutapu (Sacred Island), to which Rangitoto is now joined by a causeway, certainly witnessed the eruptions, as footprints have been found embedded in ash and oral history details several generations living here before the eruption.

The island makes for a great day trip. Its harsh scoria slopes hold a surprising amount of flora and there are excellent walks, but you'll need sturdy shoes and plenty of water. Although it looks steep, up close it's more like an egg sizzling in a pan. The walk to the summit only takes an hour and is rewarded with sublime views. At the top a loop walk goes around the crater's rim. A walk to lava caves branches off the summit walk and takes 30 minutes return. There's an information board with walk maps at the wharf.

Motutapu (www.motutapu.org.nz), in contrast to Rangitoto, is mainly covered in grassland, which is grazed by sheep and cattle. Archaeologically, this is a very significant island, with the traces of centuries of continuous human habitation etched into its landscape.

A **DOC campsite** (☎ 09-372 7348; www.doc.govt.nz; Home Bay; adult/child $5/2.50) has basic facilities, with only a water tap and flush toilet provided.

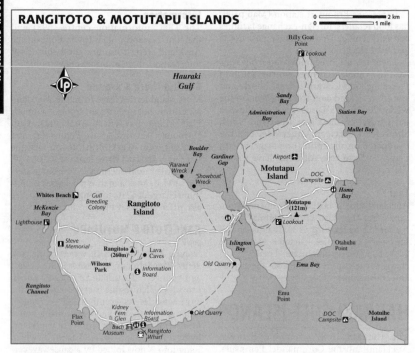

RANGITOTO & MOTUTAPU ISLANDS

Bring cooking equipment, as open fires are forbidden. It's a three-hour walk from Rangitoto wharf; Fullers run a weekend-only service to Home Bay in the summer months.

Fullers (☎ 09-367 9111; www.fullers.co.nz; adult/child return $25/13) has 20-minute ferry services to Rangitoto from Auckland's Ferry Building (three daily on weekdays, four on weekends) and Devonport (two daily). Fullers also offers the **Volcanic Explorer** (adult/child $55/28), a guided tour around the island in a canopied 'road train', to a 900m boardwalk leading to the summit. Prices include the ferry.

Reubens (☎ 0800 111 616; www.reubens.co.nz; return $64) operates a shuttle service to Islington Bay on Wednesday, Friday, Saturday and Sunday (also Mondays from November to March).

MOTUIHE ISLAND

Between Waiheke and Rangitoto Islands, 176-hectare Motuihe Island has a lovely white-sand beach and a fascinating history. There are three *pa* sites, last occupied by the Ngati Paoa tribe. The island was sold in 1840 (for a heifer, blankets, frocks, garden tools, pots and pans) and from 1872 to 1941 served as a quarantine station. During WWI the dashing swashbuckler Count von Luckner launched a daring escape from the island (where he was interned with other German and Austrian nationals), making it 1000km to the Kermadec Islands before being recaptured.

Motuihe has been rendered pest-free and is now subject to a vigorous reforestation project by enthusiastic volunteers. As a result, endangered birds have started to return, including the loquacious tieke (saddleback). Contact the **Motuihe Trust** (☎ 0800 668 844; www.motuihe.org.nz) if you want to get involved.

Apart from the trust's headquarters, the only accommodation on the island is a basic **DOC campsite** (Map p130; ☎ 09-379 6476; www.doc.govt. nz; adult/child $5/2.50); only toilets and water are provided. There are no shops or permanent residents.

360 Discovery (☎ 0800 888 006; www.360discovery. co.nz; adult/child return $24/15) runs three daily ferries to/from Auckland. On the weekends you can choose between heritage- and restoration-themed guided tours ($7.50, summer only). **Reubens** (☎ 0800 111 616; www.reubens.co.nz; adult/child return $34/17) operates a shuttle service four to five days a week.

WAIHEKE ISLAND
pop 7700

Waiheke is 93 sq km of island bliss only a 35-minute ferry ride from the CBD. Once they could hardly give land away here; nowadays multimillionaires rub shoulders with the old-time hippies and bohemian artists who gave the island its green repute. Auckland office workers fantasise about swapping the daily motorway crawl for a watery commute and a warm, dry microclimate.

On Waiheke's city side, emerald waters lap at rocky bays, while its ocean flank has some of the region's best sandy beaches. While beaches are the big drawcard, wine is a close second. There are 17 boutique wineries to visit, many with swanky restaurants and breathtaking city views. On top of that, the island boasts dozens of galleries and craft stores.

Waiheke has been inhabited since at least the 14th century, most recently by Ngati Paoa, and there are more than 40 *pa* sites scattered around the island. Europeans arrived with the missionary Samuel Marsden in the early 1800s and the island was soon stripped of its kauri forest.

Orientation & Information

Nearly 2km from Matiatia wharf is Oneroa, the main village, with a sandy beach. The eastern half of the island (locals call it the bottom end) is lightly populated and well worth exploring. There are petrol stations in Oneroa and Onetangi, ATMs in Oneroa and a supermarket in Ostend.

The **Waiheke Island i-SITE** (☎ 09-372 1234; 2 Korora Rd; www.waihekenz.com; 9am-5pm) and library (with free internet access) are in the Artworks complex. They also have a (usually unstaffed) counter in the ferry terminal at Matiatia Wharf.

Sights & Activities
ART & CULTURE

The **Artworks complex** (☎ 09-379 2020; 2 Korora Rd) houses a **community theatre** (☎ 09-372 2941; www.artworkstheatre.org.nz), an art-house **cinema** (☎ 09-372 4240; www.wicc.co.nz) and an attention-grabbing **art gallery** (☎ 09-372 9907; www.waihekeart gallery.org.nz; admission free; 10am-4pm). Also part of the complex is **Whittaker's Musical Museum** (☎ 09-372 5573; www.musical-museum.org; admission by donation; 1-4pm), a collection of antique concert instruments.

The **Waiheke Island Historic Village** (☎ 09-372 2970; www.waihekemuseum.org.nz; 165 Onetangi Rd; admission by donation; noon-4pm Wed, Sat & Sun) displays Islander artefacts in six restored buildings.

Connells Bay (☎ 09-372 8957; www.connellsbay.co.nz; Cowes Bay Rd; adult/child $30/15; by appointment, late Oct to late Apr) is a pricey but excellent private sculpture park featuring a stellar roster of NZ artists. Admission is by way of guided tour.

Another jealousy-inducing private property open to visitors is **Te Whau Garden** (☎ 09-372 6748; www.tewhaugarden.co.nz; 31 Vintage Lane; admission $10; 9am-5pm), giving you the opportunity to wander steep pathways through rainforest, wetlands and gardens scattered with sculpture.

The *Waiheke Art Map* brochure, free from the i-SITE, lists 37 galleries and craft stores.

BEACHES

Waiheke's two best beaches are **Onetangi**, a long stretch of white sand at the centre of the island, and **Palm Beach**, a pretty little horseshoe

---

BATTLE OF THE BACHES

During the 1920s a dinky set of simple baches started to sprout on Rangitoto on land leased from the council, forming a thriving community of holiday-makers. In the 1930s prison labour was used to construct roads, public toilets, tennis courts and a swimming pool out of the scoria. It was back-breaking work, but the men weren't locked up and by all accounts enjoyed island life. The threat of fire was, and is, a constant danger for the bach-holders – the baking scoria keeping the leaf litter tinder-dry.

During the 1970s and '80s the bach community itself came under threat – a significant number of houses were removed when their leases expired, with the plan to remove them all. Following a public outcry, the remaining communities were listed as Historic Areas by the Historic Places Trust in 1997. Just left of the wharf, a 1929 bach has been fully restored and opened as a **Bach Museum** (admission by donation; 9.30am-3.30pm Sat & Sun summer only).

WAIHEKE ISLAND

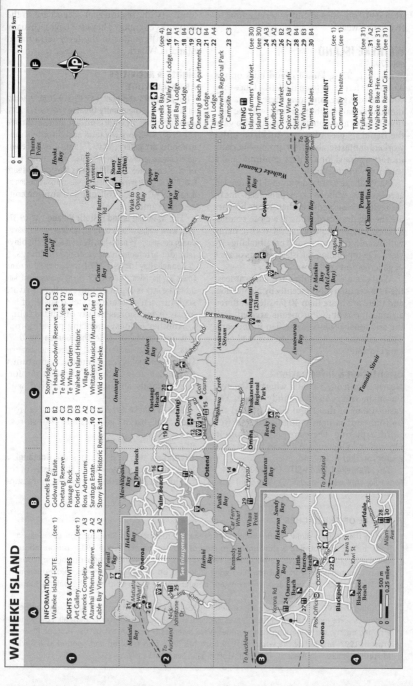

INFORMATION

Waiheke Island i-SITE.................................(see 1)	

SIGHTS & ACTIVITIES

Art Gallery.................................(see 1)	
Artworks Complex.................................**1** A3	
Atawhai Whenua Reserve.................................**2** A2	
Cable Bay Vineyards.................................**3** A2	
Connells Bay.................................**4** B2	
Goldwater Estate.................................**5** B2	
Onetangi Reserve.................................**6** C2	
Passage Rock.................................**7** D3	
Poderi Crisci.................................**8** D3	
Ross Adventures.................................**9** A2	
Saratoga Estate.................................**10** C2	
Stony Batter Historic Reserve.................................**11** E1	
Stonyridge.................................**12** C2	
Te Haahi-Goodwin Reserve.................................**13** D3	
Te Motu.................................(see 12)	
Te Whau Garden.................................**14** B3	
Waiheke Island Historic Village.................................**15** C2	
Whittakers Musical Museum.................................(see 1)	
Wild on Waiheke.................................(see 12)	

SLEEPING

Connells Bay.................................(see 4)	
Crescent Valley Eco Lodge.................................**16** B2	
Fossil Bay Lodge.................................**17** A1	
Hekerua Lodge.................................**18** B4	
Kina.................................**19** C2	
Onetangi Beach Apartments.................................**20** C2	
Punga Lodge.................................**21** B4	
Tawa Lodge.................................**22** A4	
Whakanewha Regional Park Campsite.................................**23** C3	

EATING

Island Farmers' Market.................................(see 30)	
Island Thyme.................................(see 30)	
Lure.................................**24** A3	
Mudbrick.................................**25** A2	
Ostend Market.................................**26** B2	
Spice Wine Bar Cafe.................................**27** A3	
Stefano's.................................**28** B4	
Te Whau.................................**29** B3	
Thymes Tables.................................**30** B4	

ENTERTAINMENT

Cinema.................................(see 1)	
Community Theatre.................................(see 1)	

TRANSPORT

Fullers.................................**31** A2	
Waiheke Auto Rentals.................................(see 31)	
Waiheke Bike Hire.................................(see 31)	
Waiheke Rental Cars.................................(see 31)	

bay between Oneroa and Onetangi. Both have nudist sections; head west just past some rocks in both cases. **Oneroa** and neighbouring **Little Oneroa** are also excellent.

WINERIES

Waiheke's hot, dry microclimate has proved excellent for Bordeaux reds, syrah and some superb rosés. Because of an emphasis on quality rather than quantity, the premium wine produced here is relatively expensive. It's also NZ's only wine region where all the wineries charge for tastings (from $3 to $10; sometimes free if you make a purchase). Some are spectacularly located and worth a visit for that reason alone. Over summer many extend their hours, some even sprouting temporary restaurants.

Goldwater Estate (☎ 09-372 7493; www.goldwater wine.com; 18 Causeway Rd; ☺ noon-4pm Wed-Sun Mar-Nov, daily Dec-Feb) Waiheke's wine pioneers, Goldwater has been producing wine from these 21 acres for over 30 years.

Passage Rock (☎ 09-372 7257; www.passagerock wines.co.nz; 438 Orapiu Rd; ☺ noon-4pm) Excellent pizza among the vines.

Poderi Crisci (☎ 09-372 2148; www.podericrisci.co.nz; 205 Awaawaroa Rd; ☺ 11am-4.30pm Thu-Sun) Recently purchased by the Italian-born patriarch behind Non Solo Pizza (p119), we expect great things from the soon-to-come cafe. Italian varietals (Montepulciano, Nebbiolo) and olives have been planted alongside the existing pinot grigio and merlot.

Saratoga Estate (☎ 09-372 6450; www.saratoga estate.com; 72 Onetangi Rd; ☺ 11am-4pm) With a cafe and microbrewery on-site.

Stonyridge (☎ 09-372 8822; www.stonyridge.co.nz; 80 Onetangi Rd; ☺ 11.30am-5pm) Famous organic reds, an atmospheric cafe, tours ($10, 35 minutes, 11.30am Saturday and Sunday) and the occasional dance party.

Te Motu (☎ 09-372 6884; www.temotu.co.nz; 76 Onetangi Rd; ☺ 11am-4pm Wed-Sun) Shares the same driveway as Stonyridge and also has a restaurant.

Wild On Waiheke (☎ 09-372 3434; www.wildon waiheke.co.nz; 82 Onetangi Rd; ☺ 11am-4pm Thu-Sun, daily in summer) If you like to shoot stuff after a few drinks, this winery and microbrewery offers tastings, archery, clay shooting, *pétanque* and a giant chess board.

See also Te Whau (p135), Cable Bay (p135) and Mudbrick (p135). Pick up the *Waiheke Island of Wine* map for a complete list.

TRAMPING

The *Explore Waiheke Island's Walkways* pamphlet has detailed maps and descriptions of eight excellent coastal hikes that take from one to three hours. Some head to the Royal Forest & Bird Protection Society's three reserves: **Onetangi** (Waiheke Rd), **Te Haahi-Goodwin** (Orapiu Rd) and **Atawhai Whenua** (Ocean View Rd). Other tracks traverse the **Whakanewha Regional Park**, a haven for rare coastal birds.

At the bottom end of the island, the **Stony Batter Historic Reserve** (www.fortstonybatter.org.nz; Stony Batter Rd; admission/tour $8/15; ☺ 10am-3.30pm) has WWII tunnels and gun emplacements that were built in 1941 to defend Auckland's harbour. The walk leads through private farmland, and derives its name from the boulder-strewn fields. Bring a torch.

KAYAKING

It's the fervently held opinion of Ross of **Ross Adventures** (☎ 09-372 5550; www.kayakwaiheke.co.nz; Matiatia beach; 2hr/4hr/day trips $55/85/145, per hr hire from $25) that Waiheke offers kayaking every bit as good as the legendary Abel Tasman National Park. He should know – Ross has been offering guided kayak trips for over 20 years. Experienced sea kayakers can comfortably circumnavigate the island in four days, exploring hidden coves and sand spits inaccessible by land.

Tours

Ananda Tours (☎ 09-372 7530; www.ananda.co.nz) Offers a food and wine tour ($95) and a Wine Connoisseur's Tour ($190). Small-group, informal tours can be customised, including visits to artists' studios.

Fullers (☎ 09-367 9111; www.fullers.co.nz; Matiatia Wharf) Runs a Wine On Waiheke Tour (adult $115, 4¾ hours, departs Auckland 1pm) that visits three of the island's top wineries and includes a platter of nibbles. Taste Of Waiheke (adult $112, 5½ hours, departs Auckland 11am) also includes three wineries plus an olive grove and light lunch. There's also a 1½-hour Explorer Tour of the island (adult/child $48/24, departs Auckland 10am, 11am and noon). All prices include the ferry and an all-day bus pass.

Waiheke Executive Transport (☎ 0800 372 200; www.waiheketransport.co.nz) Short tours (from $15), wine tours (half-day/day/premium $55/71/95), arts and crafts tours ($71) and walking tours (from $25).

Waiheke Island Adventures (☎ 09-372 6127; www. waihekeislandadventures.com) Scenic tours ($25), vineyard tours ($25), or Stony Batter tours ($35) in a 15-seater bus. Art and beach tours also available.

Festivals & Events

Sculpture on the Gulf (www.sculptureonthegulf.co.nz) A wacky 2km cliff-top sculpture walk, held every second January (odd-numbered years).

Waiheke Food & Wine Festival (www.whatson waiheke.co.nz; admission $60) Sometimes shifts but currently on Waitangi Day (6 February).

Sleeping

Waiheke is so popular in the summer holidays that many locals rent out their houses for exorbitant rates and bugger off elsewhere. You'll need to book ahead and even then there are very few bargains. Prices drop considerably in winter, especially midweek.

BUDGET

Whakanewha Regional Park campsite (☎ 09-366 2000; www.arc.govt.nz; Gordons Rd; sites per adult/child $10/5) A pretty but basic campsite with toilets, cold showers, gas barbecues and drinking water. Phone ahead for the code to unlock the gate.

Hekerua Lodge (☎ 09-372 8990; www.hekerualodge. co.nz; 11 Hekerua Rd, Oneroa; sites per person $17, dm $36, s/tr $53/108, d $80-110, cabin $270; 🖳 🗩) This secluded hostel is surrounded by native bush and has a barbecue, stone-tiled pool, sunny deck, casual lounge area and its own walking track. It's far from luxurious, but it has a laid-back feel, no doubt assisted by the serene images of Buddha and the Tibetan prayer flags flapping about.

Fossil Bay Lodge (☎ 09-372 8371; www.fossil bay.webs.com; 58 Korora Rd, Oneroa; sites per person $18, s $35-45, d $67; 🛜) Three cutesy cabins open onto a courtyard facing the main building, which houses the toilets, a large communal kitchen and living area and, on the other side, a Steiner kindergarten. Apart from the occasional squawking duck (or toddler), it's a peaceful place.

Kina (☎ 09-372 8971; www.kinabackpackers.co.nz; 419 Seaview Rd, Onetangi; dm/s/tw $24/45/56, d $65-75; 🛜) This scuffed but well-positioned hostel has a large garden overlooking Onetangi Beach. The dorms are a little cell-like but have only two bunk beds, and linen is provided. Mountain bikes can be hired.

MIDRANGE & TOP END

our pick Tawa Lodge (☎ 09-372 9434; www.pungalodge. co.nz; 15 Tawa St, Oneroa; r $110, apt $165-200) Between the self-contained cottage at the front and the apartment at the rear are three reasonably priced loft rooms sharing a small kitchen and bathroom. On a hot day there's a wonderfully languid vibe as guests spill out onto the deck.

Punga Lodge (☎ 09-372 6675; www.pungalodge. co.nz; 223 Ocean View Rd, Oneroa; r $140-160, apt $135-200; 🖳) Both the colourful en-suite rooms

in the house and the self-contained garden units have access to decks looking onto a lush tropical garden. There's a spa, and prices include home-made breakfast, afternoon tea and wharf transfers.

Crescent Valley Eco Lodge (☎ 09-372 4321; www. waihekeecolodge.co.nz; 50 Crescent Rd East, Ostend; r $145) Surrounded by bush and peaceful gardens this little ecoretreat has only two tidy rooms, affable hosts and a spa pool under the stars. Bathrooms are private but not en suite.

Onetangi Beach Apartments (☎ 09-372 0003; www.onetangi.co.nz; 27 The Strand, Onetangi; apt $185-400; 🛜) Three different blocks of townhouses are clumped together, all offering smart, modern, perfectly located, well-managed accommodation, along with a spa and sauna. Best (and priciest) are the Strand Apartments, with large decks overlooking the sea.

Connells Bay (☎ 09-372 8957; www.connellsbay. co.nz; Cowes Bay Rd; cottage $350-450) Fancy your own private art-filled retreat that combines the best of the country and the seaside and is luxurious without being glitzy? Descend to this extraordinary property via a perilously steep driveway to the sculpture garden (p131). The century-old weatherboard two-bedroom cottage is comfortable and chic, with kauri floors, a smart kitchen, veranda, garden and absolute water frontage.

Eating

Priding itself on the finer things in life, Waiheke has some excellent eateries, and if you're lucky the views will be enough to distract from the hole being bored into your hip pocket. The island's isolation is an excuse for overcharging yet simultaneously limits the capacity to find good staff. Consequently you may find yourself paying exorbitantly for meals served by clueless local teenagers.

Spice Wine Bar Cafe (☎ 09-372 7659; 153 Ocean View Rd, Oneroa; mains $7-14; 🕑 breakfast & lunch) A snappy little place with tables on the street, excellent coffee and delectable lemon tarts.

Lure (☎ 09-372 9035; 29 Waikare Rd, Oneroa; mains $8-18; 🕑 breakfast & lunch) Enjoy beach views, great coffee, enticing counter food and a short focused menu. The chicken Caesar salad is superb.

Stefano's (☎ 09-372 5309; 18 Hamilton Rd, Surfdale; mains $16-27; 🕑 5.30-9.30pm Wed-Mon) Stefano's is the best-smelling joint on Waiheke, serving pasta staples and wonderful pizzas in the presence of a dodgy mural. It also does takeaways.

Thymes Tables (☎ 09-372 3400; 8 Miami Ave, Surfdale; mains $31; ☽ dinner Tue-Sat) Fussy eaters should look elsewhere as this excellent French-style eatery offers only one or two dishes per evening, which change daily. The food is as elegant as the white-walled dining room, and the island's best deli is downstairs.

Te Whau (☎ 09-372 7191; 218 Te Whau Dr; mains $33-40; ☽ lunch Wed-Mon, dinner Sat) Perched on the end of Te Whau peninsula, this winery restaurant has exceptional views, food and service, and one of the finest wine lists you'll see in the country (1982 Chateau Mouton Rothschild, $3000). Try its impressive Bordeaux blends, merlot and rosé for $3 per taste (11am to 5pm).

Cable Bay Vineyards (☎ 09-372 5889; www.cablebayvineyards.co.nz; 12 Nick Johnstone Dr; mains $36-49; ☽ lunch & dinner) Impressive ubermodern architecture, sculpture and beautiful views set the scene for this acclaimed restaurant. The food is sublime but the service isn't always. If the budget won't stretch to a meal, stop in for a wine tasting ($5) or a drink on the terrace.

Mudbrick (☎ 09-372 9050; 126 Church Bay Rd; mains $38-42; ☽ lunch & dinner) Auckland and the gulf are at their glistening best when viewed from Mudbrick's picturesque veranda. The adventurous menu is crammed with quality ingredients, well put together. This venue also offers tours and wine tasting ($5 to $10, 11am to 5pm).

For fresh local produce head to the bustling **Ostend market** (Ostend Hall, Belgium St; ☽ 8am-1pm Sat) or the **Island Farmers Market** (8 Belgium St; ☽ 11am-2pm Sun). For prepackaged gourmet meals, deli goodies, tempting pastries and excellent coffee, clock in on Island Thyme (see Thymes Tables, above). There's a supermarket in Ostend.

Drinking
Apart from the wineries, you'll find some swanky bars in Oneroa, local pubs in Surfdale and Ostend, and nice spots for an afternoon drink on the waterfront in Onetangi.

Getting There & Away
Fullers (☎ 09-367 9111; www.fullers.co.nz; adult/child return $32/16; ☽ 5.20am-11.45pm Mon-Fri, 6.25am-11.45pm Sat, 7am-9.30pm Sun) has frequent ferries from Auckland to Matiatia Wharf (on the hour from 9am to 5pm), some via Devonport.

Sealink (☎ 09-300 5900; www.sealink.co.nz; adult/child/car/motorcycle return $30/17/130/48; ☽ 4.30am-6.30pm Mon-Thu, 4.30am-8pm Fri, 6am-6.30pm Sat, 8am-6.30pm Sun) runs car ferries to Kennedy Point, mainly from Half Moon Bay (East Auckland) but some leave from the city. The ferry runs at least every two hours and takes 45 minutes; bookings are essential.

You can pick up the **360 Discovery** (☎ 0800 888 006; www.360discovery.co.nz) tourist ferry at Orapiu on its journey between Auckland and Coromandel Town (see p200).

Getting Around
BUS
The island has regular bus services, starting from Matiatia Wharf and heading through Oneroa (adult/child $1.40/80c, 3 minutes) on their way to all the main settlements, as far west as Onetangi (adult/child $4/2.20, 30 minutes). Enquire through **MAXX** (☎ 09-366 6400; www.maxx.co.nz). A day pass (adult/child $8/5) is available from the Fullers counter at Matiatia Wharf.

CAR & BICYCLE
The island has 12km-, 25km- and 70km-loop bicycle routes, but prepare for a lot of hills. Mountain bikes (half-/full day $20/30) can be hired at **Waiheke Bike Hire** (☎ 09-372 7937; Matiatia Wharf; ☽ 9am-5pm), or you can cheat on the inclines with electric bikes. The i-SITE also rents mountain bikes (half-/full day $20/30) and scooters (day/overnight $50/60).

Waiheke Auto Rentals (☎ 09-372 8998; www.waihekerentals.co.nz; Matiatia Wharf; car/scooter/motorbike/4WD from $50/55/75/80) and **Waiheke Rental Cars** (☎ 09-372 8635; www.waihekerentalcars.co.nz; Matiatia Wharf; car/4WD from $50/80) offer rentals, but you must be over 21 and pay 65c a kilometre for cars or 4WDs. The insurance excess (deposit) is $1000.

TAXI
Try **Waiheke Taxi Co-op** (☎ 09-372 8038), **Waiheke Taxis** (☎ 09-372 3000) or **Waiheke Independent Taxis** (☎ 0800 300 372).

TIRITIRI MATANGI ISLAND
This magical, 220-hectare, predator-free **island** (www.tiritirimatangi.co.nz) is home to the tuatara (NZ's pint-sized dinosaur) and lots of endangered native birds, including the very rare and colourful takahe. Other birds that can be seen here include the bell bird,

OTHER ISLANDS

Little Barrier Island, located 25km northeast of Kawau Island, is NZ's ark: a predator-free refuge for endangered birds, reptiles and plants. Access to the island is highly restricted, and a DOC permit is required for landing on this closely guarded sanctuary. The steep volcanic cliffs help keep out intruders.

Motuora Island, halfway between Kawau and Tiritiri Matangi, has 80 predator-free hectares and is used as a kiwi 'crèche'. There's a wharf on the west coast of the island, but you'll need your own boat to get here. The **DOC campsite** (☎ 027 492 8586; www.doc.govt. nz; adult/child $6/3) requires bookings and provides toilets, cold showers and water. It also rents a **bach** ($55) that sleeps five; bring your own linen and food.

stitch bird, saddleback, whitehead, kakariki, kokako, little spotted kiwi, brown teal, NZ robin, fernbird and penguins; 78 different species have been sighted in total. The saddleback was once close to extinction with just 150 left, but now there are more than 600 on Tiritiri alone. To experience the dawn chorus in full flight, stay overnight at the **DOC bunkhouse** (☎ 09-425 7812; www.doc.govt.nz; adult/child $24/18); book well ahead.

Ngati Paoa were the last tribe to live here. The land was sold to the Crown in 1841, deforested and farmed until the 1970s. Since 1984 hundreds of volunteers have planted 250,000 native trees and the forest cover has regenerated. An 1864 lighthouse stands on the eastern end of the island.

From Wednesday to Sunday, **360 Discovery** (☎ 0800 888 006; www.360discovery.co.nz; return Auckland/ Gulf Harbour $66/39) has ferries to the island, leaving Auckland at 9am and Gulf Harbour (on the Whangaparaoa Peninsula) at 9.50am (check-in 30 minutes prior). They arrive back in Gulf Harbour at 4pm and Auckland at 4.50pm. A guided walk on the island is a good deal at $5/2.50 per adult/child.

KAWAU ISLAND
pop 300

Kawau Island lies 50km north of Auckland off the Mahurangi Peninsula. There are no proper roads through the island, the residents relying totally on boats. The main attraction is **Mansion House** (☎ 09-422 8882; adult/child $4/2; ☿ noon-2pm Mon-Fri, noon-3.30pm Sat & Sun), an impressive wooden manor extended from an 1845 structure by Governor George Grey, who purchased the island in 1862. It houses a fine collection of Victoriana, including some of Grey's effects, and is surrounded by the original exotic gardens. A set of short walks (10 minutes to two hours) are signposted from Mansion House, leading to beaches, the old copper mine and a lookout; download DOC's *Kawau Island Historic Reserve map* (www. doc.govt.nz).

Kawau Lodge (☎ 09-422 8831; www.kawaulodge. co.nz; North Cove; s $160, d $195-220) is an ecoconscious boutique hotel with its own jetty, wrap-around decks and views. Meals ($10 to $60) can be arranged, as can excursions on the 42ft yacht or power catamaran.

In the north of the island, on Kawau's only sandy beach, the upmarket **Beach House Resort** (☎ 09-422 8850; www.kawauresort.co.nz; Vivian Bay; ste $320-440) has rooms facing the beach, facing a large paved courtyard or in a cottage set back in the bush. All meals are included in the rate, as is equipment for fishing, snorkelling, kayaking and sailing.

If you haven't packed a picnic, the idyllically situated **Mansion House Cafe Restaurant** (☎ 09-422 8903; lunch $12-18, dinner $18-28; ☿ hours vary) will be a welcome relief, serving all-day breakfasts, sandwiches and hearty evening meals. It's also your only option for stocking up on bread, milk, ice and pre-ordered newspapers.

Reubens (☎ 0508 282 552; www.aucklandescape. co.nz) is based at Sandspit (p149) and operates daily cruises to Kawau (adult/child return $47/25; departs 10.30pm daily and 2.30pm weekends and summer holidays; returns 2.30pm and 5pm). The Super Cruise (adult/ child $65/28, barbecue lunch $22/10) departs Sandspit at 10.30am and circles the island, delivering the post to 75 different wharves. It also runs a water-taxi service (minimum charge $125).

GREAT BARRIER ISLAND
pop 900

Great Barrier (Aotea) is the largest island in the gulf (285 sq km) and NZ's fourth-largest behind North, South and Stewart Islands. It's rugged and scenic, resembling the Coromandel Peninsula to which it was once joined. Named by Captain James Cook,

Great Barrier Island later became a whaling, mining and logging centre, but all these industries have had their day. Most of the island is publicly owned and managed by DOC.

Great Barrier has unspoilt beaches, hot springs, old kauri dams, a forest sanctuary and a network of tramping tracks. Because there are no possums on the island, the native bush is lush. The west coast has safe sandy beaches, while the east coast beaches are good for surfing. Mountain biking, swimming, fishing, diving, boating, kayaking and just relaxing are other popular activities.

Although only 88km from Auckland, Great Barrier seems a world – and a good many years – away. The island has no supermarket, no electricity supply (only private generators) and no main drainage (only septic tanks); many roads are unsealed; and petrol costs are high. Mobile-phone reception is very limited and there are no banks, ATMs or street lights. It's a wild, untamed and very special place with its own rules, and is a definite breath of fresh air.

From around mid-December to mid-January is the peak season, so make sure you book transport, accommodation and activities well in advance.

Orientation

Tryphena is the main settlement, 4km from the ferry wharf at Shoal Bay. Strung out along several kilometres of coastal road, it consists of a few dozen houses, a primary school and a handful of shops and accommodation places. From the wharf it's 3km to Mulberry Grove, and then another 1km over the headland to Pa Beach and the Stonewall Store.

The airport is at Claris, a small settlement with a general store, bottle shop, laundrette, vehicle-repair garage, pharmacy, adventure centre and cafe, 10km north of Tryphena. Whangaparapara is an old timber town and the site of the island's 19th-century whaling activities. Port Fitzroy is the other main harbour on the west coast, a one-hour drive from Tryphena. Only these four main settlements have petrol and diesel available.

Information

The free *This Is Great Barrier Island* (www.greatbarriernz.com) pamphlet has a handy map and is full of useful information, as is the *Great Barrier Island Visitor Information Guide* booklet (www.thebarrier.co.nz). There's an information kiosk at the GBI Rent-A-Car office in Claris (p141). Claris Texas Cafe (p140) has internet access and you'll find post offices in Tryphena and Claris.

Aotea Health Centre (☎ 09-429 0356; Hector Sanderson Rd, Claris; ☼ 9am-4pm Mon-Fri)

DOC office (☎ 09-429 0044; www.doc.govt.nz; Port Fitzroy; ☼ 8am-4.30pm Mon-Fri) Call in for brochures, maps, weather information and to sign the intentions book for longer walks.

Visitor information centre (☎ 09-429 0848; Port Fitzroy; ☼ 9.30am-3pm Mon-Sat)

Activities
SWIMMING & SURFING

Beaches on the west coast are safe, but care needs to be taken on the surf-pounded eastern beaches. **Medlands Beach**, with its wide sweep of white sand, is one of the best beaches on the island and is easily accessible from Tryphena. Remote **Whangapoua** in the northeast requires more effort to get to, while **Kaitoke**, **Awana Bay** and **Harataonga** on the east coast are also worth a visit.

Okiwi Bar has an excellent right-hand break, while Awana has both left- and right-hand breaks. Tryphena's bay, lined with pohutu-kawa, has sheltered beaches.

OTHER WATER SPORTS

There's pinnacle diving, shipwreck diving, lots of fish and more than 33m visibility at some times of the year.

Hooked on Barrier (☎ 09-429 0740; info@greatbarrier lodge.co.nz; 89 Hector-Sanderson Rd, Claris) sells and hires out diving, snorkelling, fishing, surfing and kayak (both from $35 per hour) gear. You can dive from a beach or charter a boat through **Tryphena Charters** (☎ 09-429 0596).

Aotea Sea Kayaks (☎ 09-429 0664; www.greatbarrier kayaks.co.nz; Mulberry Grove, Tryphena) runs harbour ($50, two hours), sunset ($60, two hours), snorkelling ($90, four hours) and phosphorescent night paddles ($90). Kayaks (per day $40 to $60) and snorkelling equipment (per day $25) can be hired, as well as sea kayaks kitted out with lines and tackle for fishing (per day $80).

MOUNTAIN BIKING

With rugged scenery and little traffic on the roads, mountain biking is a popular activity here. There's a designated 20km mountain bike trail through the forest from Whangaparapara Rd towards Port Fitzroy.

AUCKLAND REGION

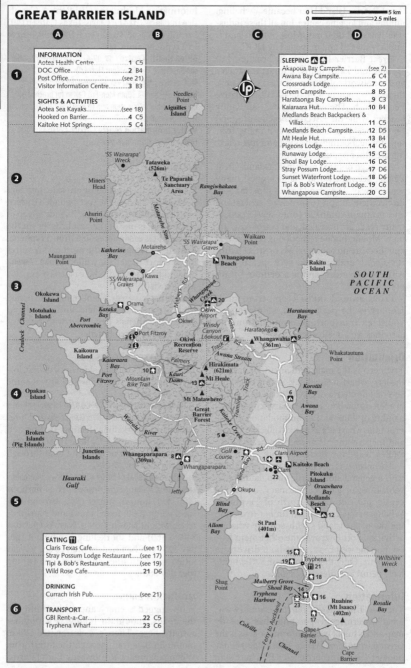

GREAT BARRIER ISLAND

0 .... 5 km
0 .... 2.5 miles

INFORMATION
Aotea Health Centre........................1 C5
DOC Office......................................2 B4
Post Office..............................(see 21)
Visitor Information Centre...............3 B3

SIGHTS & ACTIVITIES
Aotea Sea Kayaks........................(see 18)
Hooked on Barrier.........................4 C5
Kaitoke Hot Springs.......................5 C4

SLEEPING
Akapoua Bay Campsite..................(see 2)
Awana Bay Campsite.......................6 C4
Crossroads Lodge...........................7 C5
Green Campsite..............................8 B5
Harataonga Bay Campsite...............9 C3
Kaiaraara Hut...............................10 B4
Medlands Beach Backpackers &
  Villas...11 C5
Medlands Beach Campsite.............12 D5
Mt Heale Hut...............................13 B4
Pigeons Lodge...............................14 C6
Runaway Lodge.............................15 C5
Shoal Bay Lodge...........................16 D6
Stray Possum Lodge......................17 D6
Sunset Waterfront Lodge...............18 D6
Tipi & Bob's Waterfront Lodge......19 C6
Whangapoua Campsite..................20 C3

EATING
Claris Texas Cafe..........................(see 1)
Stray Possum Lodge Restaurant.....(see 17)
Tipi & Bob's Restaurant................(see 19)
Wild Rose Cafe..............................21 D6

DRINKING
Currach Irish Pub..........................(see 21)

TRANSPORT
GBI Rent-a-Car.............................22 C5
Tryphena Wharf............................23 C6

'SS Wairarapa'
Wreck
Tataweka
(526m)
Needles
Point
Aiguilles
Island

Te Paparahi
Sanctuary
Area
Rangiwhakaea
Bay

Miners
Head

Motairehe Stm

Ahuriri
Point

Katherine
Bay
Maunganui
Point
Motairehe
'SS Wairarapa'
Graves
Whangapoua
Beach
Waikaro
Point

Okokewa
Island
'SS Wairarapa'
Graves
Kawa
Rakitu
Island

Motuhaku
Island
Karaka
Bay
Orama
Okiwi
Whangapoua
Creek
Okiwi
Airport
Windy
Canyon
Lookout
Harataonga
Bay

SOUTH
PACIFIC
OCEAN

Cradock Channel

Port
Abercrombie
Port Fitzroy
Okiwi
Recreation
Reserve
Harataonga
Whangawahia
(361m)

Kaikoura
Island
Kaiaraara
Bay
Palmers
Kauri
Dams
Hirakimata
(621m)
Mt Heale
Awana Stream
Whakatautuna
Point

Opakau
Island
Port
Fitzroy
Mountain
Bike Trail
Mt Matawhero
Great
Barrier
Forest
Korotiti
Bay
Awana
Bay

Wairahi River
Kaitoke Creek
Tramline Track

Broken
Islands
(Pig Islands)
Junction
Islands
Whangaparapara
(309m)
Whangaparapara
Golf
Course
Claris Airport
Kaitoke Beach
Claris

Hauraki
Gulf
Jetty
Okupu
Blind Rd
Pitokuku
Island
Oruawharo
Bay
Medlands
Beach

Blind
Bay
Allom
Bay
St Paul
(401m)
Wiltshire
Wreck

Shag
Point
Tryphena
Mulberry Grove
Shoal Bay
Tryphena
Harbour
Ruahine
(Mt Isaacs)
(402m)
Rosalie
Bay

Colville
Ferry to Auckland
Cape
Barrier Rd
Cape
Barrier

Channel

Cycling on other DOC walking tracks is prohibited.

You can hire a bike from GBI-Rent-A-Car (p141) for $30 per day.

WALKING

Many people come here for the walks, but be aware that trails are not always well sign-posted, although they are regularly upgraded. Be properly equipped with water and food, and be prepared for bad weather. The best tramping trails are in the Great Barrier Forest north of Whangaparapara, where there has been a great deal of reforestation.

The most spectacular short walk is from Windy Canyon to Hirakimata (Mt Hobson). **Windy Canyon**, which is only a 15-minute walk from the main Port Fitzroy–Harataonga (Aotea) road, has spectacular rock outcrops and affords great views of the island. From Windy Canyon, an excellent trail continues for another 1½ hours through scrubby forest to **Hirakimata** (621m), the highest point on the island, with views across to the Coromandel and Auckland on a fine day. Near the top of the mountain are lush forests and a few mature kauri trees that survived the logging days. From Hirakimata it's two hours through forest to the hut closest to Port Fitzroy and then 45 minutes to Port Fitzroy itself.

Another very popular walk is the **Kaitoke Hot Springs Track**. The natural hot pools in a bush stream can be reached from Whangaparapara Rd (45 minutes).

A more challenging tramp is the **Tramline Track** (five hours), which starts on Aotea Rd and follows old logging tramlines to Whangaparapara Harbour. The track is hilly and in some parts the clay becomes slippery after rain. Of a similar length but flatter is the 11km **Harataonga Coastal Walk** (five hours) which heads from Harataonga Bay to Whangapoua.

Many other trails traverse the forest, taking between 30 minutes and five hours. Pick up a copy of DOC's fold-out *Great Barrier Island* hiking brochure ($2), which has a detailed map and short descriptions of 23 hikes. It's available from the DOC office and the various accommodation places.

There is a good trampers' bus service that will drop you at the start of a trail and pick you up at the other end; see Getting Around, p141 for details.

Sleeping

There are half a dozen campsites and backpacker hostels, and more than 50 lodges, cottages and B&Bs spread around the island. Some places cater for a range of visitors, from backpackers and campers to luxury-seeking honeymooners, and also run restaurants and bars that are open to nonguests. Prices are generally quite steep for what's offered but drop in the off-season; summer prices are quoted here. **Island Accommodation** (☎ 09-429 0995; www.islandaccommodation.co.nz) offers a booking service, which is particularly handy for finding self-contained cottages for longer stays.

BUDGET

DOC campsites (www.doc.govt.nz; adult/child $9/4.50) There are campsites at Harataonga Bay, Medlands Beach, Akapoua Bay, Whangapoua, The Green (Whangaparapara) and Awana Bay. All have basic facilities, including water, cold showers (none at The Green), chemical toilets and a food preparation area. You need to bring your own gas cooking stove as open fires are prohibited. Book in advance online as the sites are not staffed.

Kaiaraara & Mt Heale Huts (www.doc.govt.nz; adult/child $15/5) These DOC huts in the Great Barrier Forest sleep between 24 and 28 people in bunk-rooms. Facilities include cold water, chemical toilets and a kitchen with a wood stove. Bring your own sleeping bag and cooking equipment. Book online.

Stray Possum Lodge (☎ 09-4290109; www.straypossum .co.nz; 64 Cape Barrier Rd; sites per person $12, dm/d/tr/q $23/70/85/100, chalets $135-195) Nestled in the bush south of Tryphena is this popular place with its own bar and restaurant (see p140). A stray possum wouldn't stand a chance against the two resident German shepherds, which are a little unnerving as a welcome party. The chalets are self-contained and sleep up to six. In the dorms you'll be charged $5 extra for linen.

Runaway Lodge (☎ 09-429 0628; www.runaway lodge.co.nz; 41 Medlands Rd, Tryphena; dm $25, d $90-130, tr $125-150, q $145-170) A well-tended sunny garden surrounds this small, tidy block of mezzanine units, perched on the hill just above Tryphena. One has been set up as a six-sleeper dorm (linen $10 extra) but even this has an en suite and cooking facilities.

Medlands Beach Backpackers & Villas (☎ 09-429 0320; www.medlandsbeach.com; 9 Mason Rd; dm/d $25/70, villas $120-200) Buddhas meditate in the garden of this chilled-out house on the hill, overlooking beautiful Medlands Beach. The backpackers area is simple but tidy and there's a little double cabin for romantic budgeteers at a slight remove from the rest. The self-contained villas sleep up to six.

Crossroads Lodge (☎ 09-429 0889; www.xroadslodge. com; 1 Blind Bay Rd, Claris; dm/s/d $30/45/70; 🖳) This comfy, low-key backpackers is 2km from the airfield and close to the forest walks and hot springs. Mountain bikes can be hired, and golf clubs can be borrowed to play on the nearby nine-hole golf course.

MIDRANGE & TOP END
Shoal Bay Lodge (☎ 09-429 0890; www.shoalbaylodge. co.nz; 145 Shoal Bay Rd, Tryphena; apt $110-240) Hidden among the trees these comfy self-contained apartments offer sea views, bird song, solar power, environmentally friendly cleaning products and cruelty-free toiletries. Best is the three-bedroom lodge with its sunset-guzzling deck.

our pick Pigeons Lodge (☎ 09-429 0437; www.pigeons lodge.co.nz; 179 Shoal Bay Rd; apt/d $145/175) Above the beach, south of Tryphena, this lovely lodge has a 2.5-acre bush setting, friendly management and good breakfasts (free for B&B guests, $15 for apartment dwellers).

Tipi & Bob's Waterfront Lodge (☎ 09-429 0550; www.waterfrontlodge.co.nz; Puriri Bay Rd, Tryphena; units $195-320) West of Tryphena, these smart but pricey motel-style units have some wonderful sea views. The complex includes a restaurant and bar (see right).

Sunset Waterfront Lodge (☎ 09-429 0051; www. sunsetlodge.co.nz; Mulberry Grove, Tryphena; apt $189-234) Gaze across the lawn to the sea from the attractive studio units, or fight over who's going to get the pointy room in the two-bedroom A-frame villas. There's a small shop and cafe next door.

Eating & Drinking
In summer, most places are open daily but for the rest of the year the hours are sporadic. There's a monthly guide as to what's open when posted on www.thebarrier.co.nz but it still pays to call ahead for an evening meal.

Wild Rose Cafe (☎ 09-429 0905; Blackwell Dr, Tryphena; mains $5-18; 🕑 9am-3pm) Wild Rose does the best impersonation of an Auckland cafe on the island, albeit with the addition of local crowd-pleasers such as toasted sandwiches and burgers. It uses free-range, organic and local produce whenever possible.

Claris Texas Cafe (☎ 09-429 0811; 129 Hector-Sanderson Rd, Claris; mains $7.50-15; 🕑 8am-4pm; 🖳 🛜) While it doesn't live up to the promise of its quirky name, this is the best gap-filler in the centre of the island, serving pretty good nachos, salads and pies.

Currach Irish Pub (☎ 09-429 0211; Blackwell Dr, Tryphena; mains $14-28; 🕑 from 4pm) This lively and child-friendly pub has a changing menu of seafood, steak and burgers, and is the island's social centre. Rub shoulders with local musos on Thursday jam nights.

Stray Possum Lodge Restaurant (☎ 09-429 0109; 64 Cape Barrier Rd; mains $14-30; 🕑 dinner) Offers pizzas and a varied menu in a convivial atmosphere (especially in summer), and is fully licensed. Ring ahead as opening hours aren't set in stone.

Tipi & Bob's Restaurant (☎ 09-429 0550; www. waterfrontlodge.co.nz; Puriri Bay Rd, Tryphena; mains $26-30; 🕑 breakfast & dinner) Serving simple but satisfying meals in large portions, this popular haunt has an inviting deck overlooking the harbour. There's a cheaper bistro menu in the bar.

Self-caterers will find small stores in Tryphena, Claris, Whangaparapara and Port Fitzroy.

Getting There & Away
AIR
Great Barrier Airlines (☎ 09-275 9120; www.greatbarrier airlines.co.nz; one-way standard/advance $109/89) flies from Auckland Domestic Airport (at least three daily), North Shore Aerodrome (Map p94; south of Orewa, at least two daily) and Whangarei (one-way $129; twice weekly). All flights take about 30 minutes and stop at both Claris and Okiwa. The fly/boat deal ($169) is a cheaper return option, with one leg by ferry to/from Auckland.

Fly My Sky (☎ 09-256 7025; www.flymysky.co.nz; one-way standard/advance $109/89, fly/boat deal adult/child $169/110) flies at least three times a day from Auckland. Cheaper flights are available if you travel to the island on a Sunday or leave on a Friday ($66).

BOAT
Sealink (☎ 09-300 5900; www.sealink.co.nz; return adult/child/car/motorcycle $120/80/350/95) is the main provider, running car ferries from three to six days a week from Wynyard Wharf in Auckland to Tryphena's Shoal Bay (4½ hours).

Fullers (☎ 09-367 9111; www.fullers.co.nz; adult/child one way $69/39) runs faster services (2½ hours) from Auckland's Ferry Building to Tryphena's Shoal Bay (some continue to Port Fitzroy) from mid-December to the end of January, as well as on the Labour Day and Easter long weekends. Look out for early bird specials.

Getting Around

Most roads are narrow and windy but even small hire cars can handle the unsealed sections.

Great Barrier Travel (☎ 0800 426 832; www.great barriertravel.co.nz) runs shuttles all around the island and an excellent trampers' service, which can drop you off at any of the main trailheads and pick you up at the other end. Call for specific prices (Tryphena to Claris is $15, for example) or purchase a multi-use pass (day/weekend/three-day $50/75/99). The associated **Aotea Car Rentals** (☎ 0800 426 832; www.aoteacarrentals.co.nz) hires out cars (from $55), 4WDs (from $75) and vans (from $99). Rentals clients get to use the trampers' shuttles for free.

GBI Rent-A-Car (☎ 09-429 0062; www.greatbarrier island.co.nz; 67 Hector-Sanderson Rd, Claris) has a somewhat battered fleet of cars starting at $55 and 4WDs from $85. It also operates shuttles; from Claris to Tryphena ($20), Medlands ($15), Whangaparapara ($30) and Port Fitzroy ($30, minimum four passengers).

Many of the accommodation places will pick you up from the airport or wharf if notified in advance.

WEST OF AUCKLAND

West Auckland epitomises rugged: wild black-sand beaches, bush-shrouded ranges, and mullet-haired and black-T-shirt-wearing 'Westies'. The latter is just one of several stereotypes of the area's denizens. Others include the back-to-nature hippie, the eccentric bohemian artist and the dope-smoking surfer dude, all attracted to a simple life at the edge of the bush.

Add to the mix Croatian immigrants, earning the fertile fields at the base of the Waitakere Ranges the nickname 'Daly Valley' after the Dalmatian coast where many hailed from. These pioneering families planted grapes and made wine, unwittingly founding one of NZ's major industries.

TITIRANGI
pop 3200

This little village marks the end of Auckland's suburban sprawl and is a good place to spot all of the stereotypes mentioned above over a caffe latte, fine wine or cold beer. Once home to NZ's greatest modern painter, Colin McCahon, there remains an artsy feel to the place. Titirangi means 'Fringe of Heaven' – an apt name for the gateway to the Waitakere Ranges, or indeed a hair salon. This is the last stop for petrol and ATMs on your way west.

Lopdell House Gallery (☎ 09-817 8087; www.lopdell. org.nz; 418 Titirangi Rd; admission free; ⏰ 10am-4.30pm) is an excellent modern art gallery housed in the former Hotel Titirangi (1930) at the edge of the village.

It's a mark of the esteem in which Colin McCahon is held that the house he lived and painted in during the 1950s has been opened to the public as a minimuseum, **McCahon House** (www.mccahonhouse.org.nz; 67 Otitori Bay Rd, French Bay; admission $5; ⏰ 10am-2pm Wed, Sat & Sun). The swish pad next door is home to the artist lucky enough to win the McCahon Arts Residency. Look for the signposts pointing down Park Rd, just before you reach Titirangi village.

Surrounded by native bush, the Frank Lloyd Wright-inspired **Fringe of Heaven** (☎ 09-817 8682; www.fringeofheaven.com; 4 Otitori Bay Rd; d $185-220, tr $225-260; **P**) offers glorious views over Manukau Harbour, an outdoor bath, glowworms in the garden and a songbird choir – all within 20 minutes of the city centre. The 'bed' and 'breakfast' parts of the equation are pretty special too.

Great for Westie watching, the popular licensed **Hardware Café** (☎ 09-817 5059; 404 Titirangi Rd; mains $5-31; ⏰ 8am-5pm Mon & Tue, 8am-10pm Wed-Sun) serves delicious and reasonably priced cooked breakfasts and lunches along with a tempting array of counter food. More substantial evening meals start from $22.

WAITAKERE RANGES

This 16,000-hectare wilderness was covered in kauri until the mid-19th century, when logging claimed most of the giant trees. A few stands of ancient kauri and other mature natives survive amid the dense bush of the regenerating rainforest, which is now protected inside the **Waitakere Ranges Regional Park**. Bordered to the west by the wildly beautiful beaches on the Tasman Sea, the park's rugged terrain makes an excellent day trip from Auckland.

Scenic Drive winds its way 28km from Titirangi to Swanson, passing waterfalls and lookouts. The **Arataki visitors centre** (☎ 09-817 0077; www.arc.govt.nz; Scenic Dr; ◷ 9am-5pm daily Sep-Apr, 10am-4pm Mon-Fri, 9am-5pm Sat & Sun May-Aug) is 6km west of Titirangi and is a brilliant starting point for exploring the ranges. As well as providing information on the 250km of trails in the area, this impressive, child-friendly centre, with its Maori carvings (some prodigiously well-hung) and spectacular views, is an attraction in its own right. The giant carving that greets visitors at the entrance depicts the ancestors of the Kawerau *iwi*. You can also book here for several basic **campsites** (☎ 09-366 2000; adult/child $5/3) within the park – toilets are provided but there's nothing much else.

A 1.6km nature trail opposite the centre leads visitors past labelled native species, including mature kauri. This is also the starting point for the 70km **Hillary Trail**, opened in 2010 to honour NZ's most famous son, Everest-conqueror Sir Edmund Hillary. It can be tackled in stages or in its four-day entirety, staying at campsites along the way. Walkers head to the coast at Huia then tick off all the iconic Westie beaches: Whatipu, Karekare, Piha and, Sir Ed's favourite, remote Anawhata. From here you can continue up the coast through Bethells Beach to Muriwai or head through bush to the Cascades Kauri area to end at Swanson train station.

Other noted walks in the park, all taking in impressive waterfalls, include the Kitekite Track (1.8km, 45 minutes one way), the Fairy Falls Track (5.7km, three-hour loop) and the Auckland City Walk (1.5km, one-hour loop).

AWOL Canyoning (☎ 09-834 0501; www.awol adventures.co.nz; half-/full day $135/165) offers plenty of slippery, slidey, wet fun in Piha Canyon. Pick-up from Auckland (if required), lunch and snacks are included in the price. Night trips ($155) provide plenty of glowworm action. **Canyonz** (☎ 0800 422 696; www.canyonz.co.nz; trips $175) runs canyoning trips from Auckland to the Blue Canyon, which has a series of 18 waterfalls ranging from 2m to 25m in height.

There are a couple of miniature train rides through the ranges; both must be booked in advance. The **Rain Forest Express** (☎ 09-302 8028; www.watercare.co.nz; 280 Scenic Dr; 2½hr trip adult/child $25/12) departs from Jacobsons' Depot and follows an old logging track through several

tunnels deep into the bush. You'll need to book well ahead; check the website for the schedule. Less regular are the 3½-hour brunch or twilight trips (adult/child $28/14), the latter offering glimpses of glowworms and cave weta. On the other side of the park the **Waitakere Tramline Society** (☎ 09-818 4946; www.waitakeretram line.org.nz; adult/child $10/5) runs four scenic trips every Sunday that pass through a glowworm tunnel en route to the Waitakere Falls and Dam. Trips start from the end of Christian Rd, which runs south of Swanson station.

In a city not short on great views, **Elevation** (☎ 09-814 1919; 473 Scenic Dr; mains $16-29; ◷ lunch & dinner Wed-Sun) has the best of them. Perched on a slope 350m above Auckland, this restaurant even looks down on the Sky Tower. Apart from being the only half-decent eatery between Titirangi and Piha, it has excellent pizzas.

KAREKARE

Few stretches of sand have more personality than Karekare. Those prone to metaphysical musings inevitably settle on descriptions such as 'spiritual' and 'brooding'. Perhaps history has left its imprint: in 1825 it was the site of a ruthless massacre of the local Kawerau *iwi* by Ngapuhi invaders. Wild and gorgeously undeveloped, this famous beach has been the setting for onscreen moments both high- and lowbrow, from Oscar-winner *The Piano* to *Xena, Warrior Princess*.

From the car park the quickest route to the black-sand beach involves wading through an ankle-deep stream. Karekare rates as one of the most dangerous beaches in the country, with strong surf and ever-present rips, so don't even think about swimming unless the beach is being patrolled by lifeguards (usually only in summer). Pearl Jam singer Eddie Vedder nearly drowned here while visiting Neil Finn's Karekare pad.

Follow the road over the bridge and uphill along Lone Kauri Rd for 100m. A short track begins on the left, leading to the impressive **Karekare Falls**. This leafy picnic spot is the start of several walking tracks.

Karekare has no shops of any description and no public transport. To get here take Scenic Dr and Piha Rd until you reach the well-signposted turn-off to Karekare Rd.

PIHA

If you notice an Auckland surfer dude with a faraway look, chances are they're daydreaming about Piha…or just stoned. This beautifully rugged, iron-sand beach has long been a favourite for refugees from the city's stresses – whether for day trips, weekend teenage parties or holidays.

Although Piha is popular, it's also incredibly dangerous, with wild surf and strong undercurrents; so much so that it's spawned its own popular reality TV show, *Piha Rescue*. If you don't want to inadvertently star in it, always swim between the flags, where lifeguards can provide help if you get into trouble.

Piha may be bigger and more populated than Karekare, but there's still no supermarket, liquor shop, bank or petrol station, although there is a small general store that doubles as a cafe, takeaway shop and post office.

There's no public transport, but **NZ Surf'n'Snow Tours** (☎ 09-828 0426; www.newzealand surftours.com) provides shuttles when the surf's up ($25 one way).

Sights & Activities

The view of the coast as you drive down Piha Rd is spectacular. Perched on its haunches near the centre of the beach is **Lion Rock** (101m), whose 'mane' glows golden in the evening light. It's actually the eroded core of an ancient volcano and a Maori *pa* site. A path at the south end of the beach takes you to some great lookouts. At low tide you can walk south along the beach and watch the surf shooting through a ravine in another large rock known as the **Camel**. A little further along, the waves crash through the **Gap** and form a safe swimming hole. A small colony of blue penguins nests at the beach's north end.

Surfboards (three hours/day $25/35), wet suits ($8/15) and boogie boards ($15/25) can be hired from Piha Surf Shop & Crafts (right). Private surfing lessons can also be arranged.

Sleeping & Eating

Piha Domain Motor Camp (☎ 09-812 8815; pihacamp@ xtra.co.nz; 21 Seaview Rd; sites per adult/child $10/6, cabins s/d/tr $50/60/85) Smack-bang on the beach, this well-kept campsite doesn't have a lot of shelter from the elements but it's cheap as chips. The cabins are tiny but clean.

Piha Surf Accommodation (☎ 09-812 8723; www. pihasurf.co.nz; 122 Seaview Rd; caravans & cabins per person $24-40) Each basic but charmingly tatty caravan has its own linen, TV, fridge, cooker, long-

drop toilet and shares a very simple shower. The private cabins have the same rudimentary bathroom arrangement but are a more comfortable option.

our pick **Piha Beachstay** (☎ 09-812 8381; www. pihabeachstay.co.nz; 38 Glenesk Rd; dm/s $30/70, d $80-140; 🖳 🛜) Attractive and ecofriendly, just like the surf lifesaver who runs it, this wood-and-glass lodge has extremely smart facilities. It's 1km from the beach but there's a little stream at the bottom of the property and bushwalks nearby. In winter an open fire warms the wonderful large communal lounge.

Black Sands Lodge (☎ 021 969 924; www.pihabeach. co.nz/Black-Sands-Lodge.htm; Beach Valley Rd; cabin $130, apt $210-260; 🖳 🛜) With said sands only steps away, these two modern apartments with private decks match their prime location with attractive touches such as stereos, DVD players, good firm beds with natty bed linen and polished floorboards. The cabin is kitted out in a 1950s Kiwiana bach style and shares a bathroom with the main house. Bikes and wi-fi are free for guests, and in-room massage and lavish catered dinners can be arranged on request. It's gay-friendly too.

Piha Cafe (☎ 09-812 8808; www.thepihacafe.co.nz; 20 Seaview Rd; mains $10-24; 🕑 7.30am-5pm, extended in summer) Amid a storm (in a teacup) of controversy, this attractive ecofriendly cafe (solar energy, worm farm, own bore water) opened for business in 2010. Fears that hordes of cafe-society types would destroy Piha's sand-between-toes crustiness have dissipated and now at least you can enjoy a decent meal and coffee between surfs.

Piha Store (☎ 09-812 8844; Seaview Rd; 🕑 8am-5.30pm Mon-Fri, 8am-6pm Sat & Sun) has groceries, ice cream and home baking.

Shopping

West Coast Gallery (☎ 09-812 8029; www.westcoast gallery.co.nz; Seaview Rd; 🕑 10am-5pm Thu-Sun) The work of more than 180 local artists is sold from this small not-for-profit gallery next to the Piha fire station.

Piha Surf Shop & Crafts (☎ 09-812 8723; www.piha surf.co.nz; 122 Seaview Rd; 🕑 8am-5pm) A family-run venture, with well-known surfboard designer Mike Jolly selling his wares downstairs and wife Pam selling crafts and coffee upstairs.

TE HENGA (BETHELLS BEACH)

Breathtaking Bethells Beach is reached by taking Te Henga Rd at the northern end of Scenic

Dr. It's another raw, black-sand beach with surf, windswept dunes and bush walks, such as the popular one over giant sand dunes to Lake Wainamu (starting near the bridge on the approach to the beach).

Bethells Beach Cottages (☎ 09-810 9581; www. bethellsbeach.com; 267 Bethells Rd; cottages $335-620) has two charming, self-contained cottages and an apartment, all in a hillside setting with sea and sunset views. Meals can be arranged which generate as much admiration as the accommodation.

KUMEU & AROUND

West Auckland's main wine-producing area still has some vineyards that are owned by the original Croatian families who kick-started NZ's wine industry. Unlike on Waiheke Island, most cellars here offer free tastings. It's only about 30km from central Auckland; take the Northwestern Motorway (SH16) and follow the signs. For internet access, try **Kumeu Library** (298 Main Rd).

Still owned by the Brajkovich family, **Kumeu River** (Map p94; ☎ 09-412 8415; 550 SH16, Kumeu; ☯ 9am-5pm Mon-Fri, 11am-5pm Sat) produces wonderful chardonnay and pinot gris. Another Croat-Kiwi family vineyard, **Soljans Estate** (Map p94; ☎ 09-412 2680; 366 SH16, Kumeu; ☯ 9am-5.30pm) also boasts a wonderful **cafe** (mains $16-33; ☯ 11am-3.30pm Mon-Fri, 9am-3.30pm Sat & Sun) offering exceptionally tasty brunch dishes, Dalmatian-style squid and Vintner's platters crammed with Mediterranean treats. At **Coopers Creek** (Map p94; ☎ 09-412 8560; 601 SH16, Huapai; ☯ 9am-5.30pm Mon-Fri, 10.30am-5.30pm Sat & Sun) you can buy a bottle, spread out a picnic in the attractive gardens and, from January to Easter, enjoy Sunday afternoon jazz sessions.

If you'd rather hit the hops, **Hallertau** (☎ 09-412 5555; www.hallertau.co.nz; 1171 Coatesville-Riverhead Hwy; lunch $11-22, dinner $24-33; ☯ 11am-late) offers tasting paddles of five of its microbrews ($12), served on the vine-covered terrace edging its bar and restaurant.

Architecturally impressive, **Bees Online** (☎ 09-411 7953; 791 SH16, Waimauku; mains $14-27; ☯ 11am-4pm Mon-Fri, 9am-5pm Sat & Sun) allows you to watch the busy bees at work from safely behind glass, and then taste the results in the store. The wonderful cafe showcases not only honey but also native bush ingredients. Mum and dad might even get a coffee in peace while the kids play spot-the-queen in the hive.

Buses 54, 55, 66 and 67 head here from Lower Albert St in Central Auckland.

MURIWAI BEACH

Yet another rugged black-sand surf beach, stretching 60km, Muriwai Beach's main claim to fame is the **Takapu Refuge gannet colony**, spread over the southern headland and outlying rock stacks. Viewing platforms get you close enough to watch (and smell) these fascinating seabirds. Every August hundreds of adult birds return to this spot to hook up with their regular partners and get busy – expect lots of outrageously cute neck-rubbing, bill-touching and general snuggling. The net result is a single chick per season; December and January are the best times to see the little fellas testing their wings before embarking on an impressive odyssey (see the boxed text, below).

Nearby, a couple of short tracks will take you through beautiful native bush to a lookout that offers views along the length of the beach. Wild surf and treacherous rips mean that swimming is safe only when the beach is patrolled (swim between the flags). Apart from surfing, Muriwai Beach is a popular spot for hang gliding, parapunting, kiteboarding and horse riding. There are also tennis courts, a golf course and a cafe that doubles as a take-away chippie.

Muriwai Beach Motor Camp (☎ 09-411 9262; www. muriwaimotorcamp.co.nz; Muriwai Beach; sites per adult/child $12/5) is a sheltered campsite under the shade of pines right by the beach, with a communal kitchen and coin-operated laundry.

KIWIS OR GANNETS?

After honing their flying skills, young gannets get the ultimate chance to test them – a 2000km journey to Australia. They usually hang out there for several years before returning home, never to attempt the journey again. Once back in the homeland they spend a few years waiting for a piece of waterfront property to become available in the colony, before settling down with a regular partner to nest – returning to the same patch of dirt every year.

In that regard, perhaps the gannet's a more fitting symbol for many young Aucklanders than the kiwi.

HELENSVILLE
pop 2500

A smattering of historical buildings, antique shops and cafes makes village-like Helensville a good whistle-stop for those taking SH16 north. The **visitor information centre** (☎ 09-420 8060; www.helensville.co.nz; 87 Commercial Rd; ☉ 10am-4.30pm) has details on the area, including free brochures detailing the *Helensville Heritage Trail* and *Helensville Riverside Walkway*. **Helensville Library** (Commercial Rd) has free internet access.

Aquatic Park Parakai Springs (Map p94; ☎ 09-420 8998; www.parakaisprings.co.nz; 150 Parkhurst Rd; adult/child $16/8; ☉ 10am-9pm), 2km northwest of Helensville, has large hot-spring swimming pools, private spas ($6 per hour) and a couple of hydroslides. Aucklanders bring their bored children here on wet wintry days as a cheaper alternative to Waiwera (p147). If you stay at the **camping ground** (sites per adult/child $10/8), next door, you can enter the hot pools for half price.

Woodhill Mountain Bike Park (☎ 027-278 0949; www.bikepark.co.nz; adult/child $6/4, bike hire per hr $25-30; ☉ 10am-5pm Mon, Tue, Thu & Fri, 10am-10pm Wed, 8am-5pm Sat & Sun) has many challenging tracks (including jumps and beams) around Woodhill Forest, 14km south of Helensville. Its neighbour is **Tree Adventures** (☎ 0800 827 926; www.tree adventures.co.nz; price per 1/4/8/9 courses $15/37/42/62; ☉ 9.30am-5.30pm), a set of nine high-ropes courses consisting of swinging logs, nets, balance beams, Tarzan swings and a flying fox. Also heading through the forest is **4 Track Adventures** (☎ 09-420 8104; www.4trackadventures. co.nz; 1/2/3hr tours $155/215/255), this time on quad bikes. A beach ride is included on the two- and three-hour tours. Pick-up from Auckland is $50 per person.

Extreme 4WD Adventures (☎ 0800 493 238; www.extreme4wd.co.nz; 606 Peak Rd; 1-2 people $180) offers the chance to charge around a special two-hour adventure trail in a 4WD.

Malolo House B&B (☎ 09-420 7262; www.helensville.co.nz/malolo.htm; 110 Commercial Rd; dm $30-35, d $65-120) is a wonderful kauri villa that served for a time as the town's hospital. Beautifully refurbished, it offers a range of restful accommodation, including two luxury en-suite doubles, cheaper ones with shared bathrooms and a small dorm. There's also a spa and a guest lounge with views.

Buses 66 and 67 head from near Britomart (Lower Albert St) to Parakai and Helensville ($9.70, 1½ hours).

NORTH OF AUCKLAND

The Auckland region sprawls 90km north of the CBD to just past the point where SH16 and SH1 converge at Wellsford. Beaches, regional parks, tramping trails, quaint villages, wine, kayaking and snorkelling are the main drawcards.

LONG BAY REGIONAL PARK

The northernmost of Auckland's East Coast Bays, Long Bay is a popular family picnic and swimming spot, attracting over a million visitors a year. A three-hour-return coastal walk heads north from the sandy beach to the Okura River, taking in secluded Grannys Bay and Pohutukawa Bay (which attracts nude bathers).

Regular buses head to Long Bay (adult/child $6.50/3.80, one hour) from Albert St in the city. The $11 day pass is the best option; enquire through **Maxx** (☎ 09-366 6400; www.maxx.co.nz). If you're driving, leave the Northern Motorway at the Oteha Valley Rd exit, heading towards Browns Bay, and follow the signs.

SHAKESPEAR REGIONAL PARK

Shooting out eastward just before Orewa, the Whangaparaoa Peninsula is a heavily developed spit of land with a sizable South African expat community. At its tip is the gorgeous 376-hectare **Shakespear Regional Park**. Sheep, cows, peacocks and pukeko ramble over the grassy headland, while pohutukawa-lined **Te Haruhi Bay** provides great views of the gulf islands and the city. Walking tracks take between 40 minutes and two hours, exploring native forest, WWII gun embankments, Maori sites and lookouts. If you can't bear to leave, there's an idyllic beachfront **campsite** (☎ 09-366 2000; www.arc.govt.nz; adult/child $10/5) with flush toilets and cold showers.

It's possible to get here via a torturous bus trip (about two hours; routes 896, 898 and 899) from Auckland's Britomart station; enquire via **Maxx** (☎ 09-366 6400; www.maxx.co.nz). The one-way fare is $9.70, so it's best to buy an $11 day pass. An alternative is to take the **360 Discovery** (☎ 09-424 5510; www.360discovery.co.nz) ferry service to Gulf Harbour (adult/child $13.40/8), a Noddy-town development of matching townhouses, a marina, country club and golf course. Enquire at the ferry office about picking up a bus or taxi from here. Alternatively, walk or cycle the remaining 3km to the park. The ferry is a good option for cyclists wanting to skip the boring road trip out of Auckland; carry-on bikes are free.

OREWA
pop 7300

Locals have fears that Orewa is turning into NZ's equivalent of Queensland's Gold Coast, but until they start exporting retirees and replacing them with bikini-clad parking wardens that's unlikely to happen. It is, however, very built-up and high-rise apartment towers have begun to sprout.

Information

Hibiscus Coast i-SITE (☎ 09-426 0076; 214a Hibiscus Coast Hwy (HCH)); 🕙 9am-5pm Mon-Fri, 10am-4pm Sat & Sun) Information and internet access.

Post office (Hillary Sq)

Sights & Activities

The 3km-long sheltered and sandy beach is patrolled by lifeguards in the peak season.

The **Alice Eaves Scenic Reserve** (Old North Rd), to the north of the town, is 10 hectares of native bush with labelled trees, a *pa* site, a lookout and easy short walks. The 8km **Millennium Walkway** starts from South Bridge, looping through this and other parks before returning along the beach; follow the blue route markers.

Snowplanet (☎ 09-427 0044; www.snowplanet.co.nz; 91 Small Rd, Silverdale; day pass adult/child from $54/42; 🕙 10am-10pm) is a winter wonderland that allows every day to be a snowy one, with indoor skiing, tobogganing and snowboarding. It's just off SH1, 8km south of Orewa.

Sleeping

Orewa Beach Top 10 Holiday Park (☎ 0800 673 921; www.orewabeachtop10.co.nz; 265 HCH; sites per adult/child $21/9, cabins $52-89, flats $98-114; 💻) Taking up a large chunk of the beach's south end, this well-kept park has excellent facilities. The prefab 'tourist flats' even have art on the walls and bedside lamps. Road noise can be a problem.

Marco Polo Backpackers Lodge (☎ 09-426 8455; www.marcopolo.co.nz; 2d Hammond Ave, Hatfields Beach; sites per person $19, dm $26-28, s/d $48/66) The lush garden lends a tropical vibe to this hillside complex, a few kilometres north of Orewa. The rooms are simple and there's no TV to spoil the peace.

Pillows Travellers Lodge (☎ 09-426 6338; www.pillows.co.nz; 412 HCH; dm $20, r $49-65) Eleven rooms open onto a pleasant garden at this well-located backpackers. There are separate male and female dorms, a spa pool, a relaxing lounge, free tea and coffee, a piano and TVs in the private rooms.

Orewa Motor Lodge (☎ 09-426 4027; www.orewamotorlodge.co.nz; 290 HCH; units $135-185; 🛜) One of a string of motels that line Orewa's main road, this complex has scrupulously clean wooden units that are prettied up with hanging flower baskets. There's also a spa pool.

Waves (☎ 09-427 0888; www.waves.co.nz; cnr HCH & Kohu St; units $176-293) Like a motel only much flasher, this complex offers spacious, self-contained, modern units with double glazing, wall-mounted CD players and smart furnishings. The downstairs units have gardens and most have spa baths. Best of all, it's only a few metres from the beach.

Eating

Plantation (☎ 09-426 5083; 226 Hibiscus Coast Hwy; mains $4-21; 🕙 7.30am-8pm) Any Auckland kid who's ever headed north has pestered their parents to stop here for an ice cream. It also has pies, takeaway food, cooked meals and a nice selection of counter food.

Asahi (☎ 09-426 0065; 6 Bakehouse Lane; mains $12-22; 🕙 9am-3pm Mon, 9am-9pm Tue-Sat) Asahi is a handy little option for a Japanese fix. The *bento* boxes ($21.50) are recommended.

There's also a big branch of the **New World** (11 Moana Ave; 🕙 7am-10pm) supermarket chain for snacks and self-catering.

Getting There & Away

Direct buses run between Orewa and Albert St in the city (adult/child $9.70/5.80, 75 minutes), as well as Shakespear Regional Park (adult/child $3.20/1.80, 40 minutes) and Waiwera (adult/child $1.60/1, 10 minutes). **Maxx** (☎ 09-366 6400; www.maxx.co.nz) handles all bus enquiries.

WAIWERA

This pleasant river-mouth village has a great beach, but it's the *wai wera* (hot waters) that people come here for. Warm mineral water bubbles up from 1500m below the surface to fill the 19 pools of the **Waiwera Infinity Thermal Spa Resort** (☎ 09-427 8800; www.waiwera.co.nz; 21 Main Rd; adult/child $25/15; 🕑 9am-9pm Sun-Thu, 9am-10pm Fri & Sat). There's a movie pool, 10 big slides, barbecues, private tubs ($40) and a health spa. If you can't face driving afterwards, luxuriously appointed modern houses have been built nearby (doubles $215 to $245); enquire about indulgence packages.

For those with simpler needs, the **Holiday Park** (☎ 09-426 5270; www.waiweraholidaypark.co.nz; 37 Waiwera Pl; sites per adult/child $18/9, cabins $65; 🖵) has a great possie, right by the water, and friendly management.

Squeezed between the Waiwera and Puhoi Rivers, the exquisite 134-hectare **Wenderholm Regional Park** has a diverse ecology, abundant bird life, beaches and walks (30 minutes to 2½ hours). **Couldrey House** (☎ 09-528 3713; adult/child $3/free; 🕑 1-4pm Sat & Sun, daily Boxing Day-Easter), the original homestead (1860s), is now a museum. A **campsite** (☎ 09-366 2000; adult/child $10/5) provides tap water and long-drop toilets only.

Bus 895 from Auckland's Albert St heads to Waiwera (adult/child $9.70/5.80, one hour) via Orewa; enquire through **Maxx** (☎ 09-366 6400; www.maxx.co.nz).

PUHOI
pop 450

Forget dingy cafes and earnest poets – this quaint village is a slice of the real Bohemia. In 1863 around 200 immigrants from the present-day Czech Republic settled in what was then dense bush. The **Bohemian Museum** (www.puhoihistoricalsociety.org.nz; Puhoi Rd; adult/child $3/free; 🕑 1-4pm Sat & Sun, daily Christmas-Easter) tells their story of hardship and perseverance. Next door is the village's pretty **Catholic Church** (1881), with an interesting tabernacle painting, stained glass and statues.

Puhoi River Canoe Hire (☎ 09-422 0891; www. puhoirivercanoes.co.nz; 84 Puhoi Rd) hires kayaks and Canadian canoes, either by the hour (single/double kayak $20/40) or for an excellent 8km downstream journey from the village to Wenderholm Regional Park (single/double kayak $40/80, including return transport). Bookings are essential.

In the 1879 **Puhoi Hotel** (☎ 09-422 0812; cnr Saleyards & Puhoi Rds; 🕑 10am-10pm) there's character and then some, with bar walls completely covered in old photos, animal heads and vintage household goods.

Puhoi Cottage Tea Rooms (☎ 09-422 0604; 50 Ahuroa Rd; 🕑 9.30am-5pm Thu-Tue), 500m beyond the village, is well known for its Devonshire teas ($10). Just 3km further on is the **Art of Cheese Cafe** (☎ 09-422 0670; 275 Ahuroa Rd; platters $19-22; 🕑 9am-5pm), where the people understand that any balanced diet consists of about 90% cheese. Watch cheese being made, buy a big hunk of yellow happiness or dine on very good platters in the licensed cafe. There's also a kids' menu and playground.

Puhoi is a kilometre west of SH1; the turn-off is 2km past the Johnstone Hills tunnel.

MAHURANGI & SCANDRETT REGIONAL PARKS

Straddling the head of Mahurangi Harbour, this boaties' paradise has three distinct 'fingers': Mahurangi West, accessed from a turn-off 3km north of Puhoi; Scott Point on the eastern side, with road access 16km southeast of Warkworth; and isolated Mahurangi East, which can only be reached by boat. The park incorporates areas of coastal forest, *pa* sites and a historic homestead and cemetery. Its sheltered beaches offer prime sandy spots for a dip or picnic and there are loop walks ranging from 1½ to 2½ hours. **Accommodation** (☎ 09-366 2000; www.arc.govt.nz; sites per person $5-10, baches $100-120) is available in four basic campsites and four baches sleeping six to eight.

On the way to Mahurangi West you'll pass **Zealandia Sculpture Garden** (☎ 09-422 0099; www.zealandiasculpturegarden.co.nz; 138 Mahurangi West Rd; admission $10; 🕑 10am-4pm Sat & Sun Nov-Dec & Feb-Mar, 10am-4pm daily Jan), where the work of Terry Stringer is showcased within impressive architecture and grounds. There are guided tours at 11am and 2pm.

On the ocean side of the Mahurangi Peninsula, **Scandrett Regional Park** has a sandy beach, walking tracks, patches of regenerating forest, another historic homestead, more *pa* sites and great views towards Kawau Island. Three **ARC baches** (☎ 09-366 2000; www.arc.govt.nz; baches $120) are available for rent.

WARKWORTH
pop 3300

River-hugging Warkworth makes for a pleasant pit stop, its dinky main street retaining a village atmosphere. Grab a free *Heritage Trail* brochure from the **Warkworth i-SITE** (☎ 09-425 9081; www.warkworthnz.com; 1 Baxter St; ⏰ 8.30am-5pm Mon-Fri, 9am-4.30pm Sat, 9am-3pm Sun; 💻 🖥) if you've got some time to kill.

Just south of town, the 8.5-hectare **Parry Kauri Park** has short walks and a couple of giant kauri trees, including the 800-year-old McKinney kauri (girth 7.6m). Also at the park, the small **Warkworth & District Museum** (☎ 09-425 7093; www.wwmuseum.orcon.net.nz; Tudor Collins Dr; adult/child $6/1; ⏰ 9am-3.30pm) features pioneer-era exhibits.

About 5km south of Warkworth, the **Honey Centre** (Map p94; ☎ 09-425 8003; www.honeycentre.co.nz; cnr SH1 & Perry Rd; ⏰ 8.30am-5pm) has a cafe, free honey tasting and glass-fronted hives. The shop sells all sorts of bee-related products, from candles to mead.

Nearby, **Ransom Wines** (Map p94; ☎ 09-425 8862; www.ransomwines.co.nz; Valerie Close; tasting free with purchase, otherwise $5 donation to Tawharanui Open Sanctuary; ⏰ 10am-5pm Tue-Sun) produces great food wines and showcases them with matching tapas ($16 for five) and tasting platters ($18).

Sheepworld (Map p94; ☎ 09-425 7444; www.sheepworldfarm.co.nz; SH1; adult/child $14/7, incl sheep & dog show $24/8; ⏰ 9am-5pm), 4km north of Warkworth, offers farm experiences for city slickers (kids' pony rides, lamb feeding) and the ubiquitous sheep and dog show (showtimes 11am and 2pm). The **Black Sheep Café** (mains $8-16) serves home-baked goods and coffee. In late September Sheepworld hosts the eccentric two-week **Warkworth Scarecrow Festival**.

Two kilometres further north, a walkway leads from SH1 through the regenerating **Dome Forest** to the Dome summit (336m). On a fine day you can see the Sky Tower from a lookout near the top. The summit walk takes about 1½ hours return, or you can continue for a gruelling seven-hour one-way tramp through the **Totora Peak Scenic Reserve**, exiting on Govan Wilson Rd.

Bridge House Lodge & Shark Bar (☎ 09-425 8351; www.bridgehouse.co.nz; 16 Elizabeth St; tw $75, d $85-100, tr $125) has a riverside location and a mixed bag of rooms – some newer and nicer than others but all clean enough. The refurbished bar (open 11am to 1am) is downright swanky, dishing up fancy pub grub including chorizo burgers and pizzas (mains $15 to $30).

InterCity (☎ 09-583 5780; www.intercity.co.nz) and associated daily buses stop here heading to/from Auckland ($27, one hour), Orewa ($18, 24 minutes), Whangarei ($31, two hours), Paihia ($42, three hours) and Kerikeri ($44, 3½ hours). **Naked Bus** (☎ 0900 625 33 per min $1.80; www.nakedbus.com) heads to Auckland and as far north as Paihia, with limited advance fares starting from $1.

MATAKANA & AROUND

Matakana suffers from reverse alcoholism – the more wine gets poured into it, the more genteel it becomes. A few years ago it was a nondescript rural village with a handful of heritage buildings and an old-fashioned country pub. Now the locals watch bemused as Auckland's chattering classes idle away the hours in stylish wine bars and cafes. The most striking symbol of the transition is the fantastical **Matakana Cinemas** (☎ 09-422 9833; www.matakanacinemas.co.nz; 2 Matakana Valley Rd; adult/child $15/8) complex, its domed roof reminiscent of an Ottoman bathhouse. The humble **Farmers Market** (⏰ 8am-1pm Sat) is held in its shadow – or should that be Farmers Upmarket?

The reason for this epicurean ecstasy is the success of the area's boutique wineries. They're developing a name for pinot gris, merlot, syrah and a host of obscure varietals. Local vineyards are detailed in the free *Matakana Coast Wine Country* (www.matakanacoast.com) and *Matakana Wine Trail* (www.matakanawine.com) brochures. Both are available from the **Matakana Information Centre** (☎ 09-422 7433; www.matakanavillage.co.nz; ⏰ 10am-1pm) in the foyer of the cinema. In the same building, the **Vintry** (☎ 09-423 0251; tastings from $8.50; ⏰ 10am-10pm) is a wine bar that serves as a one-stop cellar door for all the producers.

Vineyards open for regular tastings include:
Ascension Wine Estate (☎ 09-422 9601; www.ascensionwine.co.nz; 480 Matakana Rd; tasting $3-5, refundable with purchase; ⏰ 11am-4pm Mon-Fri, 10am-5pm Sat & Sun) Has an acclaimed restaurant (mains $17 to $34).

Hyperion Wines (☎ 09-422 9375; www.hyperion-wines.co.nz; 188 Tongue Farm Rd; ❤ 10am-5pm Sat & Sun)
Omaha Bay Vineyard (☎ 09-423 0022; www.omahabay.co.nz; 189 Takatu Rd; tastings $5, refundable on purchase; ❤ 11am-5pm Wed-Sun);

Brick Bay Wines is the home of the **Brick Bay Sculpture Trail** (☎ 09-425 4690; www.brickbaysculpture.co.nz; Arabella Lane; adult/child $10/8; ❤ 10am-5pm), an hour-long artistic ramble through the wonderfully sculpted grounds. Tastings and snacks are available at the chic cafe.

Morris & James (☎ 09-422 7116; www.morrisandjames.co.nz; 48 Tongue Farm Rd; ❤ 8am-4.30pm Mon-Fri, 9am-5pm Sat & Sun) has creative, colourful ceramics for sale and a lovely courtyard cafe. There are free weekday tours at 11.30am.

The nearest swimming beach is **Omaha**, 7km east, with a long stretch of white sand, good surf and holiday homes. Shortly after the Omaha turn-off, the partly unsealed Takatu Rd leads to the 588-hectare **Tawharanui Regional Park** at the end of the peninsula. This special place is an open sanctuary for native birds, protected by a pest-proof fence, while the northern coast is a marine park (bring a snorkel). There are plenty of walking tracks (1½ to four hours) but the main attraction is Anchor Bay, one of the region's finest white-sand beaches. **Camping** (☎ 09-366 2000; www.arc.govt.nz; sites per adult/child $10/5) is allowed at a basic site near the beach and the ARC also has a six-person bach for hire ($120).

Sleeping
Sandspit Holiday Park (☎ 09-425 8610; www.sandspitholidaypark.co.nz; 1334 Sandspit Rd, Sandspit; sites per adult/child $15/8, cabins $50-160; 🖥 ☎) A campsite masquerading as a pioneer village, this wonderful place incorporates historic buildings and faux shopfronts into its facilities. The self-contained waterside cottages are excellent. It's right by the water at Sandspit, 8km from Matakana village.

Matakana House Motel (☎ 09-422 7497; www.matakanahouse.co.nz; 975 Matakana Rd; apt $110-360) Right in the middle of the village but far enough back from the pub to avoid the noise, this motel is more like a set of terraced townhouses. Ranging from studios to two-bedroom apartments, they're a smart proposition.

Eating & Drinking
Brookview Teahouse (☎ 09-423 0390; 1335 Leigh Rd; Devonshire tea $12; ❤ 10am-4pm Wed-Mon) Devoted to

the pursuit of the perfect cuppa, this delightful bungalow surrounded by boxed gardens serves traditional morning and afternoon teas (scones, lamingtons and club sandwiches), and light lunches.

Tapiano (☎ 09-423 0383; mains $29-36; ❤ lunch Fri-Sun, dinner Tue-Sun) Snagging the stream frontage of the cinema complex (opposite), Matakana's flashest restaurant's menu meanders around the Mediterranean – from hearty French classics to tagines and tapas ($9 to $15) – along with tempting brunch standards ($10 to $17) during the day.

Matakana House (☎ 09-422 9770; 11 Matakana Valley Rd; ❤ 3pm-late Mon-Fri, noon-late Sat & Sun) A real local pub, this 1903 wooden hotel has taxidermied animals everywhere, a beer garden out front and occasional live music and DJs. It's an affectation-free zone.

Getting There & Away
Matakana village is a 10km drive northeast of Warkworth along Matakana Rd; there's no public transport. Ferries for Kawau Island (see p136) leave from Sandspit, 8km east of Warkworth along Sandspit Rd.

LEIGH
pop 390
Appealing little Leigh (www.leighbythesea.co.nz) has a picturesque harbour dotted with fishing boats, and a decent swimming beach at Matheson Bay. Its two main drawcards are its proximity to Goat Island (p150) and the legendary Leigh Sawmill live-music venue.

Goat Island Dive (☎ 0800 348 369, 09-422 6925; www.goatislanddive.co.nz; 142a Pakiri Rd; ❤ 9am-5pm) has a shop in Leigh and a boat that can take you diving anywhere in the Hauraki Gulf, including wreck dives, at any time of year. Snorkel, fin and mask hire is $18. Gear for a two-tank dive costs $100, dive trips are $80 to $140, and a shore dive with instruction is $250. PADI courses ($500), including Advanced and Rescue, are offered.

Leigh Sawmill Café, Micro Brewery & Accommodation (☎ 09-422 6019; www.sawmillcafe.co.nz; 142 Pakiri Rd; brunch $9-26, dinner $25-31; ❤ 10am-late daily late Dec–mid-Feb, 5-9pm Thu & 10am-1am Fri-Sun mid-Feb–late Dec) is a spunky little venue that's a regular stop on the summer rock circuit, sometimes attracting surprisingly big names. The pizzas are thin and crunchy like they should be, and best enjoyed in the garden on a lazy summer's evening. If you imbibe too much at the on-site

microbrewery (🕙 1-5pm Fri-Sun), there's accommodation inside an old sawmill shed, including backpacker rooms ($25, $40 with linen) and massive doubles with en suites ($125). Alternatively, you can hire the Cosy Sawmill Family Cottage (from $300, sleeps 10).

Leigh Rd heads northeast from Matakana village; there's no public transport.

GOAT ISLAND MARINE RESERVE

Quick, grab the highlighter for this one. Only 3km from Leigh, this 547-hectare area was established in 1975 as the country's first marine reserve. In a scant 30 years the sea has reverted to a giant aquarium, giving an impression of what it was like before humans arrived. You only need step knee-deep into the water to see snapper (the big fish with blue dots and fins), blue maomao and stripy parore swimming around. You can snorkel or scuba dive from the beach, and there are dive areas all round Goat Island, just offshore. You can see colourful sponges, forests of brown seaweed, boarfish, crayfish, stingrays and, if you're very lucky, orcas and bottle-nosed dolphins. Visibility is claimed to be at least 10m, 75% of the time.

Excellent interpretive panels explain the area's Maori significance (it was the landing place of one of the ancestral canoes) and provide pictures of the species you're likely to encounter.

A **glass-bottomed boat** (☎ 09-422 6334; www. glassbottomboat.co.nz; adult/child $25/13) provides a great all-year on-the-hour trip around Goat Island to see the underwater life. Trips last 45 minutes and run from the beach. When the sea is too rough the boat doesn't operate; ring to check.

Beach Hire (☎ 09-422 6663) rents kayaks and snorkelling gear either from the beach or from a neighbouring house. Snorkelling gear ($14),

wetsuits ($16 to $18) and underwater cameras ($35) can be hired at **Seafriends** (☎ 09-422 6212; www.seafriends.org.nz; 7 Goat Island Rd; 🕙 9am-7pm), 1km before Goat Island beach. You can hire a mask with a lens if you are short-sighted or a buoyant wetsuit if you are a poor swimmer. Seafriends also runs a saltwater aquarium, marine education centre and cafe.

If one day's snorkelling isn't enough, **Goat Island Camping** (☎ 09-422 6185; www.goatislandcamping.co.nz; Goat Island Rd; sites per adult/child $18/8, caravans & cabins $60-100, units $150-190) occupies view-greedy farmland above the beach. Pitch a tent, snaffle a hippy caravan or splash out on the self-contained unit with spa. It's just a shame that the bathroom facilities are so limited.

PAKIRI

Stunning Pakiri Beach, 12km past Goat Island (4km of the road is unsealed), is an unspoilt expanse of white sand and rolling surf. In 2005 the Auckland Regional Council purchased a 52-hectare chunk from champion boxer David Tua, creating Auckland's 25th regional park. No doubt the ARC will in time develop walking tracks and campsites to its usual high standards, preserving this magical location for future generations.

Pakiri Beach Holiday Park (☎ 09-422 6199; www. pakiriholidaypark.co.nz; 261 Pakiri River Rd; sites per adult/ child $15/8, dm $25-30, cabins $80-170, units $130-310) has a shop and good units in a secure beachfront setting.

Just 6km on from Pakiri is **Pakiri Horse Riding** (☎ 09-422 6275; www.horseride-nz.co.nz; Rahuikiri Rd), which has more than 80 horses for superb bush-and-beach rides ranging from one hour ($55) to all day ($250) or longer 'safaris'. **Accommodation** (dm/cabin/4-bedroom house $30/150/500) is provided in basic but spectacularly situated beachside cabins or a comfortable house secluded among the dunes.

Northland & the Bay of Islands

For many New Zealanders, the phrase 'up north' conjures up sepia-toned images of family fun in the sun, pohutukawa in bloom and dolphins frolicking in pretty bays. It's uttered in almost hallowed tones, as if describing a mythical place. From school playgrounds to work cafeterias, owning a bach (holiday house) 'up north' is a passport to popularity.

Beaches are the main drawcard and they're present in profusion. Take your pick from surfy or sheltered, massive or minuscule, fashionable or forgotten, and from sand that's golden, grey, pink or blindingly white. There are beaches suited to all sorts of aquatic pursuits imaginable, including splashing about in the nuddy. Visitors from more crowded countries are flummoxed to wander onto beaches without a scrap of development or another human being in sight.

Northland's reserves shelter the most spectacular remnants of the ancient kauri forests that once blanketed the top of the country. The remaining giant trees are an awe-inspiring sight and one of the nation's treasures.

It's not just natural attractions that are on offer: history hangs heavily here as well. The country was colonised from the top down by successive migrations from Polynesia and a strong Maori presence remains to this day, adding an extra dimension to any visit. The Bay of Islands was also the site of the first permanent European settlement, as well as the signing of the Declaration of the Independence of New Zealand (NZ) by local chiefs in 1835 and the Treaty of Waitangi five years later. Northland is unquestionably the birthplace of the nation.

HIGHLIGHTS

- Leaving footprints in the sand anywhere along **Bream Bay** (p154)
- Watching oceans collide while souls depart at **Cape Reinga** (p180)
- Paying homage to the ancient giants of the **Waipoua Kauri Forest** (p187)
- Diving at one of the world's top spots, the **Poor Knights Islands** (p159)
- Claiming your own island paradise among the many in the **Bay of Islands** (p161)
- Surfing the sand dunes at **Ninety Mile Beach** (p180) or Hokianga's **North Head** (p186)
- Delving into history and culture at the **Waitangi Treaty Grounds** (p168)

★ Cape Reinga

★ Ninety Mile Beach

★ Bay of Islands
Waitangi ★

North Head ★   Waipoua ★ Kauri Forest   ★ Poor Knights Islands

★ Bream Bay

- Telephone code: 09 | - www.northlandnz.com | - www.kauricoast.co.nz

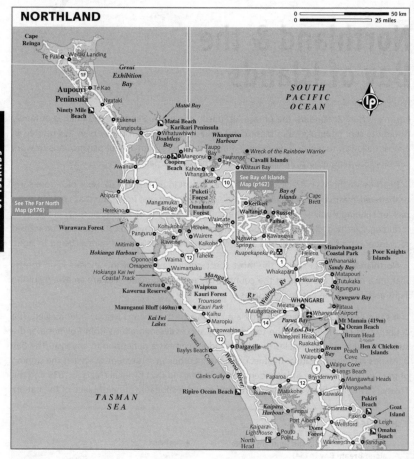

Climate

The 'winterless north' averages seven rainy days per month in summer but 16 in winter. Temperatures are often a degree or two warmer than Auckland, especially on the east coast.

Getting There & Around

There are two main routes heading north: SH1 on the east coast, and SH12, which branches off at Brynderwyn and follows the west coast to the Hokianga before rejoining SH1 near Kaikohe. This chapter roughly follows an anticlockwise loop, starting with the east coast, but you should choose your direction based on your interests and the prevailing weather.

Whangarei, Kerikeri and Kaitaia all have domestic airports, connecting through Auckland to international flights. Northland has no passenger train service, but **InterCity** (☎ 09-583 5780; www.intercity.co.nz) and associated buses ply SH1 from Auckland to Kaitaia. **Naked Bus** (☎ 0900 625 33, per min $1.80; www.nakedbus. com; advance fares from $1) covers the same route but only as far as Paihia. Other areas are poorly served, with only **Main Coachline** (☎ 09-278 8070; www.maincoachline.co.nz) heading from Auckland along SH12 as far as Dargaville (six services per week).

Only tourist buses head to Cape Reinga, the Hokianga and Waipoua Kauri Forest. The **Magic Travellers Network** (☎ 09-358 5600; www. magicbus.co.nz) has a useful service from Paihia

NORTHLAND & THE BAY OF ISLANDS

NORTHLAND & THE BAY OF ISLANDS FACTS

Eat Kumara, Dargaville's knobbly purple claim to fame (p189)

Drink Orange juice, Kerikeri's signature squeeze (p172)

Read *The House of Strife* (1993), Maurice Shadbolt's novel set during the Northland War

Listen to *Treaty* (1998) by Moana & the Moahunters

Watch *The Strength of Water* (2009), small-town Hokianga life on the big screen

Swim at Mermaid Pool, Matapouri (p159)

Festival Waitangi Day (p168)

Tackiest tourist attraction Ancient Kauri Kingdom (p181)

Go green Sing to the trees with Footprints Waipoua (p186)

to Auckland (in that direction only) via the Hokianga and Kauri Coast on SH12. The fixed fare ($69, four buses weekly) allows you to stop anywhere along the route, as often as you like.

See the end of each town section for detailed bus options. For details on backpacker discounts, passes and hop-on, hop-off tourist services, see p706.

WHANGAREI DISTRICT

To truly experience this area you have to be prepared to get wet. Beach after clear-watered beach offers munificent opportunities for swimming, surfing, splashing about or just wading in the shallows. Consequently the hot spots heave with Kiwi holidaymakers at peak times, but even then it's possible to find isolated stretches of sand where your footprints are the only ones.

If you're reading this and you're a diving fanatic, drop everything and head to Tutukaka immediately. The neighbouring Poor Knights Islands are considered one of the world's top diving spots.

MANGAWHAI
pop 1200

Magical Mangawhai – that's what the official road sign says, and such signs don't tend to lie. Leave SH1 at Kaiwaka and drive 13km east (there's no bus) to snug Mangawhai village at the base of a horseshoe harbour. But it's at Mangawhai Heads, 5km further on, that the enchantment really takes hold.

A narrow spit of powdery white sand stretches for kilometres to form the south head, sheltering a seabird sanctuary. Across the water sits an uncomplicated holiday town with a surf beach at its northern tip. Life-savers patrol on weekends in summer and daily during school holidays, but despite the rollers it's not especially dangerous. The **Mangawhai Cliffs Walkway** (three hours return) starts here, affording extensive views of sea and land.

Various Maori tribes inhabited the area before the 1660s, when Ngati Whatua became dominant. In 1807 Ngati Whatua defeated Ngapuhi from the north in a major battle, letting the survivors escape. One of them was Hongi Hika, who in 1825 returned, armed with muskets obtained from Europeans. The ensuing bloodbath all but annihilated Ngati Whatua and the district became *tapu* (sacred, taboo). British squatters moved in and were rewarded with land titles by the government in the 1850s. Ceremonies were only performed to lift the *tapu* in the 1990s.

MAORI NZ: NORTHLAND & THE BAY OF ISLANDS

The Northland region, known to Maori as Te Tai Tokerau, has a long and proud Maori history and today has one of the country's highest percentages of Maori people. Along with the East Coast, it's a place where you might hear Maori being spoken. In mythology the region is known as the tail of the fish of Maui.

Maori sites of particular significance include the Waitangi Treaty Grounds (p168), Cape Reinga (p180) and Tane Mahuta (p187).

Maori cultural experiences are offered by Footprints Waipoua (p186), Sandtrails Hokianga (p185), Terenga Paraoa (p157), Waka Tai-a-Mai (p170) and Culture North (p170). Many businesses catering to travellers are owned or run by Maori individuals or *hapu* (subtribal) groups. **Tai Tokerau Tourism** (www.taitokerau.co.nz) lists dozens of them on its website, and many of them are reviewed in this chapter.

Mangawhai Heads has a part-time **information centre** (☎ 09-431 5090; www.mangawhai.co.nz; Molesworth Dr; ☼ 2-5pm Fri, 11am-5pm Sat, 10am-1pm Sun) next to full-time information panels.

In Mangawhai village, the **Mangawhai District Museum** (Moir St; adult/child $2/1; ☼ 10.30am-1pm Sat) has a tiny display of settler and Maori artefacts. Combine it with a trip to the **farmers market** (☼ 9am-1pm Sat), next door in the library hall, and stock up on local organic produce including wine and olive oil.

Smashed Pipi Cafe, Bar, Restaurant & Gallery (☎ 09-431 4848; www.smashedpipi.co.nz; 40 Moir St; mains $9-18; ☼ breakfast & lunch daily, dinner Thu-Sat) is a funky combination, with occasional live music in the bar, vibrant ceramics and glassware in the gallery (open 9am to 5.30pm), and counter food and a blackboard menu in the cafe.

Rural France comes to the village in the form of **Bennetts** (☎ 09-431 5072; www.bennettsof mangawhai.com; 52 Moir St; mains $30-32; ☼ shop 9am-4.30pm, cafe breakfast & lunch Tue-Sun, dinner Fri & Sat), a chocolaterie and cafe where you can sit by the fountain in the courtyard listening to Edith Piaf while pigging out on *macarons*, gateaux and delectable truffles.

Mangawhai Heads is where you'll want to stay. **Coastal Cow Backpackers** (☎ 09-431 5444; www.mangawhaibackpackers.com; 299 Molesworth Dr; dm/d/tr/q $23/56/76/96) is a homely hostel with cow-themed decorative touches. The rooms are clean and simple.

The boutique **Mangawhai Lodge B&B** (☎ 09-431 5311; www.seaviewlodge.co.nz; 4 Heather St; s $150-185, d $175-230; 🖳 🛜) has a commanding position and great views. The comfortable, smartly furnished rooms have access to the picture-perfect wraparound veranda.

Milestone Cottages (☎ 09-431 4018; www.milestone cottages.co.nz; 27 Moir Pt Rd; cottages $200-320; 🐾) conjure a Pasifika paradise with its lush tropical gardens and self-contained cottages (sleeping up to five). Free videos, kayaks, croquet and *pétanque* are available.

Sail Rock Cafe (☎ 09-431 4051; 12a Wood St; mains $12-28; ☼ 9.30am-late) takes justified pride in its salt-and-pepper squid, a dish that provokes an almost-religious experience in many a diner. At the tail end of a day's surfing this is the place to chat about the break that got away over an ice-cold beer.

On the last Sunday of the month it's the Heads' turn for the **farmers market** (Wood St; ☼ 9am-1pm).

WAIPU & BREAM BAY
pop 1980

Generations of Kiwi kids have giggled over the name 'Waipu'; the makers of Imodium missed a golden opportunity by failing to adopt it as their product's brand name for the NZ market. Be that as it may, Waipu and neighbouring **Waipu Cove** are bonny wee places.

The original 934 British settlers came from Scotland via Nova Scotia (Canada) between 1853 and 1860. These dour Scots at least had the good sense to eschew frigid Otago, where so many of their kindred settled, for sunnier northern climes. Their story comes to life through holograms, a short film and interactive displays at the **Waipu Museum** (☎ 09-432 0746; 36 The Centre; adult/child $8/3; ☼ 9.30am-4.30pm; 🖳). Only 10% of current residents are direct descendants, but there's a big get-together on 1 January every year, when the **Highland Games** (☎ 09-432 1514; www.waipugames.co.nz; adult/child $15/5), established in 1871, take place in Caledonian Park.

Bream Bay has miles of blissfully deserted beach, blighted only slightly by a giant oil refinery at the north end. At **Uretiti**, a stretch of beach near a **Department of Conservation (DOC) campsite** (SH1; sites per adult/child $7/3.50) is unofficially considered 'clothing optional'. Over New Year the crowd is evenly split between Kiwi families, hardcore European nudists and gay guys.

Information

Tourist information and internet access are available at the museum.

Sleeping

Camp Waipu Cove (☎ 09-432 0410; www.campwaipu cove.com; Cove Rd; sites per s/d/tr $20/30/45, cabins $50-105) Taking up a fair chunk of beach, this is a large and comfortable camping ground with spotless facilities.

Stonehouse (☎ 09-432 0432; www.stonehousewaipu. co.nz; 641 Cove Rd; dm/s/d/tr/q $20/110/120/150/180) On the main road between Waipu Cove and Waipu is this unique Cornish-style house built of huge stone slabs. Guests are accommodated in separate units and can use a kayak or rowing boat to cross the saltwater lagoon and get to the ocean beach. The backpackers' loft is a cutesy attic, but you'll have to brave an outhouse toilet.

Waipu Wanderers Backpackers (☎ 09-432 0532; www.wanderers@xtra.co.nz; 25 St Marys Rd; dm/s/d $30/45/60;

🔊) There are only three rooms at this bright and friendly backpackers in Waipu township – a real home away from home – with free fruit in season.

Dragon Tree Lodge (☎ 09-946 0899; www.dragontree. co.nz; 239 Massey Rd; r $180-230; 🖳 🔊) Sometime between our last edition and this one, this hilltop retreat changed from a women's only B&B run by a charming lesbian couple to a men's only B&B run by a charming gay couple – which no doubt caused confusion to many of our readers. It offers a rural ambience, stylish furnishings and superb views over Bream Bay from the rooms and the outdoor spa.

Eating

Waipu Cafe/Deli (☎ 09-432 0990; 29 The Centre; mains $10-20; 🕑 9am-4pm) Self-caterers and coffee hounds should check out this cute little deli with 'serious fudge brownies'.

Pizza Barn (☎ 09-432 1011; 2 Cove Rd; mains $11-24; 🕑 11.30am-late Wed-Sun Apr-Nov, daily Dec-Mar) In Waipu even the pizza place has a tartan logo. It also has popular platters, light fare and hunger-assuaging pizzas that go well with cold beer as this cool place morphs into a bar.

Beach House (☎ 09-432 0877; 891 Cove Rd; mains $20-35; 🕑 lunch Sun, dinner Wed-Sun) With a reputation as one of Northland's best, this little restaurant offers hearty meals in a distinctive courtyard enclosed by *ponga* (tree fern) logs.

Getting There & Away

Waipu Cove can be reached by a particularly scenic route heading from Mangawhai Heads through Langs Beach. Otherwise turn off SH1, which skirts Waipu, 38km south of Whangarei.

InterCity (☎ 09-583 5780; www.intercity.co.nz) and associated daily buses stop here on the way from Auckland ($36, 2½ hours) to Whangarei ($22, 30 minutes), Paihia ($32, two hours) and Kerikeri ($33, 2½ hours) via Warkworth ($23, 1¼ hours).

Naked Bus (☎ 0900 625 33, per min $1.80; www. nakedbus.com; advance fares from $1) heads daily to Auckland (two hours), Warkworth (one hour), Whangarei (40 minutes) and Paihia (two hours).

WHANGAREI

pop 45,800

On the pretty-to-ugly continuum Whangarei sits somewhere in the middle. But beauty is never far away and there are plenty of attrac-

tive natural and artistic things to keep you distracted in Northland's gateway. You may be pleasantly surprised by the interesting choice of eateries and the general 'going off'-ness of the bars on a Saturday night. The city centre has an inordinate number of hairdressers and parking lots – although the standard of coiffure or car isn't noticeably different from the Kiwi average.

Information

Automobile Association (AA; ☎ 09-438 4848; 17 James St; 🕑 8.30am-5pm Mon-Fri)
DOC office (☎ 09-470 3300; www.doc.govt.nz; 149 Bank St; 🕑 8.30am-4pm Mon-Fri)
Post office (16-20 Rathbone St) Offers poste restante.
Quay Info (Town Basin; 🕑 9am-5pm) Housed in Clapham's Clocks; internet access.
Whangarei i-SITE (☎ 09-438 1079; www.whangarei nz.com; 92 Otaika Rd/SH1; 🕑 8.30am-5pm Mon-Fri, 9am-4.30pm Sat & Sun) Information, cafe, toilets and internet access ($6 per hour).

Sights & Activities

The budget traveller's answer to Waitomo, **Abbey Caves** (Abbey Caves Rd; admission free) is an undeveloped network of three caverns full of glowworms and limestone formations, 4km east of town. Grab a torch, strong shoes and a mate (you wouldn't want to be stuck down here alone if things go pear-shaped) and prepare to get wet. The surrounding reserve is a forest of crazily shaped rock extrusions. If you're staying at neighbouring Little Earth Lodge (p157), you can borrow helmets and hire head torches.

The 26m-high **Whangarei Falls** (Otuihau; Ngunguru Rd) are the Paris Hilton of NZ waterfalls – not the most impressive but reputedly the most photographed. Short walks provide views of the water cascading over the edge of an old basalt lava flow. The falls can be reached on the Tikipunga bus ($3, Monday to Saturday only), leaving from Rose St in the city.

The free *Whangarei Walks* brochure, available from the i-SITE, has maps and detailed descriptions of some excellent local tracks. The **Hatea River Walk** follows the river from the Town Basin to the falls (three hours return). Along the way you'll pass the **AH Reed Memorial Kauri Park** (Whareora Rd), where you can take a 35-minute detour that includes a cleverly designed boardwalk high up in the treetops.

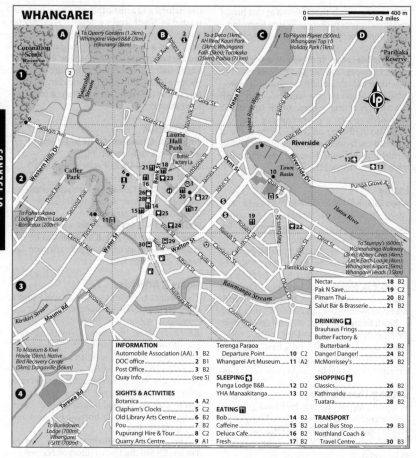

WHANGAREI

0 ———— 400 m
0 ———— 0.2 miles

INFORMATION		
Automobile Association (AA) .	**1**	B2
DOC office	**2**	B1
Post Office	**3**	B2
Quay Info	(see 5)	

SIGHTS & ACTIVITIES		
Botanica	**4**	A2
Clapham's Clocks	**5**	C2
Old Library Arts Centre	**6**	B2
Pou	**7**	B2
Pupurangi Hire & Tour	**8**	C2
Quarry Arts Centre	**9**	A1

Terenga Paraoa		
Departure Point	**10**	C2
Whangarei Art Museum	**11**	A2

SLEEPING		
Punga Lodge B&B	**12**	D2
YHA Manaakitanga	**13**	D2

EATING		
Bob	**14**	B2
Caffeine	**15**	B2
Deluca Cafe	**16**	B2
Fresh	**17**	B2

Nectar	**18**	B2
Pak N Save	**19**	C2
Pimarn Thai	**20**	B2
Salut Bar & Brasserie	**21**	B2

DRINKING		
Brauhaus Frings	**22**	C2
Butter Factory & Butterbank	**23**	B2
Danger! Danger!	**24**	B2
McMorrissey's	**25**	B2

SHOPPING		
Classics	**26**	B2
Kathmandu	**27**	B2
Tuatara	**28**	B2

TRANSPORT		
Local Bus Stop	**29**	B3
Northland Coach & Travel Centre	**30**	B3

Longer tracks head through **Parihaka Reserve**, encompassing the remnants of a volcanic cone (241m) and a major *pa* (fortified village) site. The city is spread out for inspection from the lookout at the top, which is equally accessible by car. Southeast of Whangarei, the **Waimahanga Walkway** in Onerahi is an easy 1½-hour tramp through mangroves, along an old railway embankment.

Other tracks head through **Coronation Scenic Reserve**, an expanse of bush just west of the centre that includes two *pa* sites and abandoned quarries that have been converted into inspiring community projects. Green-fingered volunteers have transformed **Quarry Gardens** (☎ 09-437 7210; www.whangareiquarrygardens.org.nz; Russell Rd; admission by donation; ☼ 8am-5pm) into a

blissful park with a lake, waterfalls, pungent floral aromas, wild bits, orderly bits and lots of positive energy. On the other side of the reserve, the **Quarry Arts Centre** (☎ 09-438 1215; www.quarryarts.org; 21 Selwyn Ave; admission free; ☼ 9.30am-4.30pm) is an eccentric village of artists' studios and co-operative galleries.

The **Old Library Arts Centre** (☎ 09-430 6432; www.apt.org.nz; 7 Rust Ave; ☼ 10am-4pm Tue-Fri, 9am-noon Sat) exhibits local artists in a wonderful art-deco building. Between this and the library is **Pou**, an intriguing sculpture consisting of 10 large poles carved with Maori, Polynesian, Celtic and Korean motifs. Grab an interpretive pamphlet from the library. The newest addition is a brightly painted Croatian gumdigger with a gum-seeking stake in one hand and his heart on fire for his woman back home – portrayed upside down and balanced on his head (see the boxed text, p182).

The **Whangarei Art Museum** (☎ 09-430 4240; www. whangareiartmuseum.co.nz; admission by donation; 🕑 10am-4pm Tue-Fri, noon-4pm Sat & Sun) is an interesting little gallery with changing displays in cute **Cafler Park**, which spans Waiarohia Stream.

Nearby, **Botanica** (☎ 09-430 4200; First Ave; admission free; 🕑 10am-4pm) displays native ferns, tropical plants and cacti, although the 'restful' music might have you murderously agitated.

Clapham's Clocks (☎ 09-438 3993; Town Basin; adult/child $8/4; 🕑 9am-5pm) is far more interesting than it sounds. This collection of 1400 ticking, gonging and cuckoo-ing timepieces constitutes the National Clock Museum.

West of Whangarei, 5km down the road to Dargaville at Maunu, is the **Museum & Kiwi House** (☎ 09-438 9630; www.whangareimuseum.co.nz; SH14; adult/child $10/5; 🕑 10am-4pm). The complex includes a veritable village of 19th-century buildings and an impressive collection of Maori artefacts. It also offers a rare chance to see a North Island brown kiwi, although he's a bit shy and doesn't always feel the need to face his adoring public. Beside the museum is the **Native Bird Recovery Centre** (☎ 09-438 1457; www.whangareinativebirdrecovery.org.nz; admission by donation; 🕑 10.30am-4.30pm Tue-Thu, noon-4.30pm Mon & Fri), which nurses sick and injured birds back to health. Say hi to Woof Woof, the talking tui.

Skydive Ballistic Blondes (☎ 0800 695 867; www.sky diveballisticblondes.co.nz; 12,000ft tandem $380) is not only the oddest-named skydiving outfit in the country, but also the only one licensed to land on the beach (Ruakaka, Ocean Beach or Paihia).

Tours

Pupurangi Hire & Tour (☎ 09-438 8117; www.hire ntour.co.nz; Jetty 1, Riverside Dr) Offers hour-long waterfall abseils in the Kauri Park ($35), hour-long bike tours of the town ($35), six-person *waka* (canoe) trips on the river ($35) or 2½-hour combos of the above ($85). It also hires kayaks (per hour $15), *waka* ($20), aquacycles ($15), bikes ($15) and rollerblades ($10).

Terenga Paraoa (☎ 09-430 3083; www.tours.maori. nz; departs Town Basin; adult/child $50/30; 🕑 9.30am & 1pm) Guided 2½-hour Maori cultural tour taking in Parihaka Pa, Whangarei Falls and the Kauri Park.

Sleeping
BUDGET
our pick **Little Earth Lodge** (☎ 09-430 6562; www. littleearthlodge.co.nz; 85 Abbey Caves Rd; sites per person/

dm/s/d/tr $15/28/54/64/84; 🖳 🛜) One of the very best hostels, Little Earth might spoil you for all the rest. Set on a farm 4km from town and right next to Abbey Caves (p155), the place is brimming with art and Balinese furnishings. Forget dorm rooms crammed with nasty spongy bunks: settle down in a proper cosy bed with nice linen and a maximum of two roommates. Resident critters include miniature horses Tom and Jerry, and the lovable pooch Muttley.

Whangarei Top 10 Holiday Park (☎ 09-437 6856; www.whangareitop10.co.nz; 24 Mair St; sites per person $17, units $50-121; 🖳 🛜) This holiday park has friendly owners, a better-than-average set of units and supershiny stainless-steel surfaces.

Bunkdown Lodge (☎ 09-438 8886; www.bunkdown lodge.co.nz; 23 Otaika Rd; dm $25-26, s/tw/d $53/53/55; 🖳) There's a homely atmosphere to this lovely old villa, which is a short walk from the town centre. Two large lounges well equipped with board games encourage socialising.

YHA Manaakitanga (☎ 09-438 8954; www.yha.co.nz; 52 Punga Grove Ave; dm/r $25/63; 🖳 🛜) This small, easy-going hostel has only a handful of rooms on a quiet hillside overlooking the river. It has a covered deck and barbecue area, and a short walk leads through the bush to glowworms.

Punga Lodge B&B (☎ /fax 09-438 3879; 9 Punga Grove Ave; s/d $55/75) Just down from the YHA, this well-kept B&B is a regular suburban home, but the guest rooms have a sense of privacy and space. Request the one with the balcony and views.

MIDRANGE & TOP END
Whangarei Views B&B (☎ 09-437 6238; www. whangareiviews.co.nz; 5 Kensington Heights Rise; s/d/tr/q $99/160/200/240; 🛜) The name clearly articulates its prime proposition: views over the city and then some. Modern and peaceful, it has a self-contained two-bedroom flat downstairs and a B&B room in the main part of the house.

Pilgrim Planet (☎ 09-459 1099; www.pilgrimplanet. co.nz; 63 Hatea Dr; r $110-130; 🖳 🛜) Upmarket rooms open onto a shared kitchen and lounge, giving this smart place the sociability of a hostel but without the German teenagers living off rice and canned corn (not that there's anything wrong with that!).

Pohutukawa Lodge (☎ 09-430 8634; www.pohutukawa lodge.co.nz; 362 Western Hills Dr; units $115-150; 🖳 🛜) Just west of town, this straightforward, nicely furnished motel has 14 units with well-kept facilities and ample parking.

Lodge Bordeaux (☎ 09-438 0404; www.lodgebord eaux.co.nz; 361 Western Hills Dr; units $190-300; 🖳 🖭) Sitting somewhere between a superschmick motel and an apartment hotel, Lodge Bordeaux has tasteful units with stellar kitchens and bathrooms, private balconies and excellent wines available.

Eating

Bob (☎ 09-438 0881; 29 Bank St; breakfast $6-16, lunch $15-17; 🕑 breakfast & lunch) Hey Bob, nice coffee. How would you describe yourself? Deli? Cafe? All that fancy produce spices up the standards – like the kransky sausages in the big breakfast. Nice one, Bob.

Caffeine (☎ 09-438 6925; 4 Water St; meals $6-17; 🕑 7am-2.30pm Mon-Fri, 7am-1.30pm Sat & Sun) There's no prize for guessing what the regular junkies are here for. Nice brekkies and cafe snacks too.

Deluca Cafe (☎ 09-438 7154; 6 Rust Ave; mains $7-19; 🕑 breakfast & lunch Mon-Sat) Sink into one of the moulded white-plastic chairs at this stylish yet relatively reasonably priced cafe and order something delectable from the cabinet.

Nectar (☎ 09-438 8084; 88 Bank St; mains $9-24; 🕑 breakfast & lunch Mon-Sat, dinner Tue-Sat) Oozing boho cool, Nectar has strong fair-trade coffee, hip staff, chilled-out grooves and urban views from the back of a fabulous old building. Breakfast couldn't be sweeter than the passionfruit muesli sundae.

Fresh (☎ 09-438 2921; 12 James St; mains $10-20; 🕑 8am-4pm Mon-Fri, 8am-2pm Sat) Fresh as a daisy with white walls and supersized flower photography, this chic cafe serves up great coffee and interesting breakfasts.

Pimarn Thai (☎ 09-430 0718; 12 Rathbone St; mains $16-22; 🕑 lunch & dinner Mon-Sat; 🔽) As gaudy as every good Thai restaurant should be – there's plenty of gold and glass bling on the walls and around the necks of the serving staff. The lengthy menu features all Thailand's blockbuster dishes, including a tasty *pad thai*.

Salut Bar & Brasserie (☎ 09-430 8080; 69 Bank St; lunch $20, dinner $26-32; 🕑 lunch & dinner) A grand setting for a boozy lunch. Grab one of the booths scooped out of dark chocolate leather and settle in for delicious fresh dishes such as the tuna carpaccio salad.

ourpick à Deco (☎ 09-459 4957; 70 Kamo Rd, Kensington; mains $34-36; 🕑 lunch Wed-Fri, dinner Tue-Sat) Northland's best restaurant, with an inventive menu that prominently features

local produce: Northland scallops, Tutukaka tuna, Waimate mushrooms, Kaipara flounder, Dargaville kumara (sweet potato) and the native flavours of horopito and manuka. Art-deco fans will adore the setting – a wonderfully curvaceous marine-style villa with original fixtures.

For quick eats or self-catering, consider the following:

Stumpy's (☎ 09-438 1775; 121 Riverside Dr; meals $4-18; 🕑 10am-7pm Mon-Thu, 10am-8pm Fri-Sun) A legendary chippie with a seafood basket ($12) that could leave you stumped.

Pak N Save (☎ 09-438 1488; Carruth St; 🕑 8am-9pm Mon-Fri, 8am-8pm Sat & Sun) The big, budget supermarket.

Drinking & Entertainment

Brauhaus Frings (☎ 09-438 4664; 104 Dent St; 🕑 10am-late) This popular microbrewery has a range of great chemical-free beers, a terrace, board games and live music on Wednesday and Friday nights.

McMorrissey's (☎ 09-430 8081; 7 Vine St; 🕑 noon-late) A better-than-average Irish pub with cosy old-world decor and live music (trad Irish, rock and jam sessions).

ourpick Butter Factory & Butterbank (☎ 09-430 0044; 8 Butter Factory Lane & 84 Bank St; 🕑 4pm-late Wed-Sat) Tucked away in a back lane, Butter Factory is an atmospheric wine bar with stone walls, exposed beams and so-cool-it-hurts staff. As the hours dissolve, DJs kick in and the crowd spills outside. It's proved so popular that it's taken over the old bank upstairs and converted it into a nearly-as-cool tapas and cocktail bar.

Danger! Danger! (☎ 09-459 7461; 37 Vine St; 🕑 10.30am-very late) Be very afraid: you may find yourself screaming along as the covers band belts out 'Living on a Prayer' to the packed-out scrum of booze hags and hogs at this popular and populist wood-clad barn.

Shopping

Kathmandu (☎ 09-438 7193; 22 James St; 🕑 9am-5.30pm Mon-Fri, 9am-4pm Sat, 10am-3pm Sun) A branch of the excellent outdoor and travel supplies chain, selling everything from tents to plug adapters.

Classics (☎ 09-430 8867; 41 Bank St) Interesting eclectica, from Rubik's cubes to literature.

Tuatara (☎ 09-430 0121; 29 Bank St) A primo spot for funky Maori and Pasifika design, art and craft.

Getting There & Around

AIR

Whangarei Airport (WRE; ☎ 09-436 0047; www.whangarei airport.co.nz; Handforth St) is at Onerahi, 6km east of the centre. Taxis into town cost around $25. A city bus stops 400m away on Church St ($3, 19 buses on weekdays, six on Saturday).

Air New Zealand (☎ 0800 737 000; www.airnz.co.nz) Flies to Auckland (35 minutes, seven to nine daily) and Wellington (1½ hours, weekdays).

Great Barrier Airlines (☎ 09-275 9120; www. greatbarrierairlines.co.nz) Flies to Great Barrier Island (30 minutes, one-way $129, twice weekly).

Salt Air Xpress (☎ 09-402 8338; www.saltair.co.nz) Flies to Kerikeri and Auckland's North Shore ($139, 30 minutes), every day except Saturday.

BUS

Buses stop outside the **Northland Coach & Travel Centre** (☎ 09-438 3206; 3 Bank St; ☿ 8am-5pm Mon-Fri, 8.30am-2.30pm Sat & Sun). There's a left-luggage service here.

InterCity (☎ 09-583 5780; www.intercity.co.nz) and associated daily buses head to Auckland ($40, three hours), Orewa ($34, 2¼ hours), Waipu ($22, 30 minutes), Paihia ($27, 80 minutes) and Kerikeri ($24, 1¾ hours).

Naked Bus (☎ 0900 625 33, per min $1.80; www. nakedbus.com; advance fares from $1) heads daily to Auckland (2¼ hours), Warkworth (90 minutes), Waipu (40 minutes) and Paihia (1¼ hours).

A private operator runs a **Whangarei-to-Dargaville Shuttle** (☎ 021 380 187; fare $10) on weekdays.

Local buses leave from across the square on Rose St. Useful routes head to Whangarei Falls and the airport. In summer there are special services to Ocean Beach and Waipu Cove.

TAXI

A1 Cabs (☎ 0800 438 3377)
Kiwi Carlton Cabs (☎ 09-470 2299)

WHANGAREI HEADS

Whangarei Heads Rd winds 35km along the northern reaches of the harbour to its entrance, passing mangroves and picturesque pohutukawa-lined bays. Holiday homes, B&Bs and galleries are dotted around the water-hugging small settlements. There are great views from the top of **Mt Manaia** (419m), a sheer rock outcrop above McLeod Bay, but prepare for a lung- and leg-busting 1½-hour climb.

Bream Head caps off the finger of land. A five-hour one-way walking track from Urquharts Bay to Ocean Beach passes through the Bream Head Scenic Reserve and lovely Smugglers Bay and Peach Cove. DOC's *Whangarei District Walks* brochure gives options that break this into smaller legs.

Magnificent **Ocean Beach** stretches for miles on the other side of the peninsula. There's decent surfing to be had and lifeguards patrol the beach in summer. A detour from Parua Bay takes you to glorious **Pataua**, a small settlement that lies on a shallow inlet linked to a surf beach by a footbridge.

At McLeod Bay, take the long leafy drive down to **Breakaway Retreat** (☎ 09-434 0711; www. breakawayretreat.co.nz; 1856 Whangarei Heads Rd; house $290-380), a semidetached two-bedroom house where the lawn terminates at a secluded slice of beachfront paradise. There are warmly wooden interiors, a spa bath and free kayaks.

A magical spot on a summer's day, **Parua Bay Tavern** (☎ 09-436 5856; 1034 Whangarei Heads Rd; ☿ 11.30am-late) is a friendly pub set on a thumb-shaped peninsula, with a sole pohutukawa blazing red against the green water. Grab a seat on the deck, a cold beverage and a decent pub meal.

Whangarei's regular buses don't venture beyond Onerahi, but in summer there are special services to Ocean Beach.

TUTUKAKA COAST & THE POOR KNIGHTS ISLANDS

If Goat Island Marine Reserve (p150) whetted your appetite, diving at the Poor Knights is the feast followed by a wafer-thin mint that might cause your stomach to explode. Apart from the natural underwater scenery (see the boxed text, p160), two decommissioned navy ships have been sunk nearby for divers to explore.

Following the road northeast of Whangarei for 26km, you'll first come to the sweet village of **Ngunguru** near the mouth of a broad river. **Tutukaka** is a kilometre further on, its marina bustling with yachts, dive crews and game-fishing boats.

From Tutukaka the road heads slightly inland, popping out 10km later at the golden sands of **Matapouri**. At the beach's north end a sign points through the long grass to **Mermaid Pool**, a deep natural rock pool with crystal-clear water flushed out by the tide. It's an effort to reach but well worth it; follow the track through an unlikely looking hole in the rock, turn right and clamber along the rocks for about 10 minutes.

Continuing north from Matapouri, the wide expanse of **Sandy Bay**, one of Northland's premier surf beaches, comes into view. Longboarding competitions are held here in summer. The road then loops back to join SH1 at Hikurangi. A branch leading off from this road doubles back north to the coast at **Whananaki**, where there are more glorious beaches and the Otamure Bay **DOC campsite** (sites per adult/child $7/3.50).

Activities

Dive trips leave from Tutukaka and cater for first-timers and experts.

Dive! Tutukaka (☎ 0800 288 882; www.diving.co.nz; Marina Rd; ☺ 7am-7pm) is deservedly the main operator, winning an array of tourism, business and environmental awards. It offers a variety of dive courses and excursions, including a five-day PADI open-water course ($695). Perhaps the jewel in its crown is the much-raved-about Perfect Day Ocean Cruise ($129), which includes a commentary, lunch and snacks, snorkelling from a platform in the middle of the marine reserve, kayaking through caves and arches, and sightings of dolphins and rare seabirds (usually), and occasionally whales, orcas and fur seals. Cruises depart at 11am, returning at 4.15pm.

Yukon Dive (☎ 09-434 4506; www.yukon.co.nz; full day $125) is a small operator that takes groups of four to eight.

If you've got the bushy bushy blond hairdo and baggy boardies but need credibility to pull off the look, **Tutukaka Surf Co** (☎ 09-434 4135; www.tutukakasurf.co.nz; Marina Dr, Tutukaka; 2hr lesson $75) runs regular surf lessons at 9am most days in summer and on the weekends otherwise,

operating from whichever beach has the best beginner breaks that day. If you've already got the skills, you can hire or buy a board here.

Sleeping

Tutukaka Holiday Park (☎ 09-434 3938; www.tutukaka -holidaypark.co.nz; Matapouri Rd, Tutukaka; sites per adult/child $15/7, dm $25, cabins $70-180) Look for the giant marlin at the gate of this well-kept complex, not far from the marina. Facilities are clean and bright, and communal areas are in good condition.

Bellmain House (☎ 09-434 3898; www.bellmainhouse. co.nz; 2049 Ngunguru Rd, Ngunguru; s $70, d $115-120, cottage $140-180; 🖳) Share this homely house with the welcoming hosts or nab the self-contained cottage in the garden (sleeps four).

Lupton Lodge (☎ 09-437 2989; www.luptonlodge. co.nz; 555 Ngunguru Rd, Glenbervie; s $125-160, d $160-200, tr $225; 🏊) The rooms are spacious, luxurious and full of character in this historic homestead (1896), peacefully positioned in farmland halfway between Whangarei and Ngunguru. Wander the orchard, splash around the pool or shoot some snooker in the guest lounge.

Eating & Drinking

Schnappa Rock (☎ 09-434 3774; breakfast/lunch $6-20, dinner $26-33; ☺ breakfast, lunch & dinner) Filled with expectant divers in the morning and those capping off their Perfect Days in the evening, this cafe-restaurant-bar is often buzzing – not least because of the excellent coffee. Top NZ bands play on summer weekends.

Whangarei Deep Sea Anglers Club (☎ 09-434 3249; mains $9-23; ☺ 4-8pm Tue-Thu & Sun, 4-10pm Fri & Sat) This venue plays host to the nicely named Moocha's, where standard eats (burgers, fish and chips, ham steaks) and a good children's

---

MARINE RICHES AT THE POOR KNIGHTS

Established in 1981, this marine reserve is rated as one of the world's top-10 diving spots. The islands are bathed in a subtropical current from the Coral Sea, so varieties of tropical and subtropical fish not seen in other NZ waters are observed here. The waters are clear, with no sediment or pollution problems. The 40m to 60m underwater cliffs drop steeply to the sandy bottom and are a labyrinth of archways, caves, tunnels and fissures that attract a wide variety of sponges and colourful underwater vegetation. Manta rays are common.

The two main volcanic islands, Tawhiti Rahi and Aorangi, were home to the Ngai Wai tribe, but since a raiding-party massacre in the early 1800s the islands have been *tapu* (forbidden). Even today the public is banned from the islands, in order to protect their pristine environment. Not only do tuatara and Butler's shearwater breed here, but there are unique species of flora, such as the Poor Knights red lily.

menu mingle with mounted fish and garrulous locals.

Marina Pizzeria (☎ 09-434 3166; pizzas $13-24; ☺ lunch & dinner Thu-Sun) Everything is homemade at this excellent takeaway and restaurant – the bread, the pasta, the pizza and the ice cream.

Getting There & Away

In summer there are buses from Whangarei (enquire at the i-SITE, p155). **Tutukaka Shuttles** (☎ 021-901 408) depart Whangarei at 7.10am and 3pm, and Tutukaka at 8.15am and 4.30pm ($15). Dive! Tutukaka has free daily shuttles from Whangarei for its customers.

RUSSELL RD

The quickest route to Russell takes SH1 to Opua and then crosses by ferry. The old Russell Rd is a snaking scenic route that adds about half an hour to the trip.

The turn-off is easy to miss, 6km north of Hikurangi at Whakapara. It's worth a stop after 14km at the **Gallery & Cafe** (☎ 09-433 9616; mains $9-17; ☺ 10am-5pm) high above Helena Bay for excellent organic fair-trade coffee, scrummy cake, amazing views and a gander at some interesting Kiwiana art and craft. Is there anything that corrugated iron can't do?

At **Helena Bay** an unsealed detour leads 8km to **Mimiwhangata Coastal Park**, a gorgeous part of the coastline with sand dunes, pohutukawa trees, jutting headlands and picturesque beaches. **DOC** (☎ 09-433 6554; www.doc. govt.nz) manages a range of accommodation in the reserve, including a well-appointed lodge ($500 to $2000 per week) and a simpler but comfortable cottage and beach house (both $350 to $1500 per week); each sleeps seven to eight people. Basic camping (per adult/child $8/4) is available at secluded Waikahoa Bay.

Back on Russell Rd, you'll find the **Farm** (☎ 09-433 6894; www.thefarm.co.nz; 3632 Russell Rd, Tutaematai; sites per person/dm/s $12/20/30, d $60-80), a chilled-out backpackers rambling through various buildings, including an old woolshed fitted out with a mirror ball. Best of all, you can arrange a horse trek or motorbike ride through the 1000-acre working farm. The dorms are basic but the cabins and en-suite rooms are much more comfortable.

At an intersection shortly after the Farm, Russell Rd branches off to the left for an unsealed, winding section traversing the **Ngaiotonga Scenic Reserve**. Unless you're planning to explore the forest (there are two short

walks: the 20-minute **Kauri Grove Nature Walk** and the 10-minute **Twin Bole Kauri Walk**) you're better off veering right onto the sealed Rawhiti Rd. After 2.6km, a side road leads to the **Whangaruru North Head Scenic Reserve**, which has beaches, another **DOC campsite** (☎ 09-433 6160; sites per adult/child $7/3.50), walks and fine coastal scenery.

If you want to head directly to Russell, continue along Rawhiti Rd for another 7km before veering left onto Manawaora Rd, which skirts a succession of idyllic tiny bays before reconnecting with Russell Rd. At Jacks Bay, **Russell B&B** (☎ 09-403 7887; www.russellbedandbreak fast.co.nz; 24 Kingfisher Rd; d $125-135, bach $130) has a quiet bush location overlooking the water. Choose between a room in the house and a self-contained bach (sleeping three). From here it's a further 16km to Russell.

Otherwise take a detour to isolated **Rawhiti**, a small Ngapuhi settlement where life still revolves around the *marae*. Rawhiti is the starting point for the tramp to **Cape Brett** (www.capebrett walks.co.nz), a tiring eight-hour, 16.3km walk to the top of the peninsula where overnight stays are possible in DOC's **Cape Brett Hut** (sites per adult/child $12/6). An access fee is charged for crossing private land (full track adult/child $30/15, day walkers adult/child $10/5), which you can pay at the Russell Booking & Information Centre (p166). Another option is to take a water taxi (p172) to Cape Brett lighthouse from Russell, Paihia or Rawhiti and walk back.

A shorter one-hour walk leads through Maori land and the **Whangamumu Scenic Reserve** to Whangamumu Harbour. There are more than 40 ancient Maori sites on the peninsula and the remains of an unusual whaling station. A net fastened between the mainland and Net Rock was used to ensnare or slow down whales so the harpooners could get an easy shot in.

BAY OF ISLANDS

Undeniably pretty, the Bay of Islands ranks as one of NZ's top tourist drawcards. The footage that made you want to come to NZ in the first place no doubt featured lingering shots of lazy, sun-filled days on a yacht floating atop these turquoise waters punctuated by around 150 undeveloped islands. The reality is that NZ has many beautiful spots and this bay, while wonderful, could be a teensy bit overhyped.

What sets it apart from the rest is its fascinating history and substantial tourist infrastructure. Paihia has one of the best selections of budget accommodation of anywhere in the country. After that the budget goes out the window as a bewildering array of boat trips clamour to wrestle money out of your wallet. There's no point coming here if you don't head out on the water, so be prepared to fork out.

The Bay of Islands is a place of enormous historical significance. Maori knew it as Pewhairangi and settled here early in their migrations. As the site of NZ's first permanent English settlement (at Russell), it is the birthplace of European colonisation. It was here that the Treaty of Waitangi was drawn up and first signed in 1840; the treaty remains the linchpin of race relations in NZ today (see p33).

Activities
SCUBA DIVING
The Bay of Islands offers some fine subtropical diving, made even better by the sinking of the 113m navy frigate HMNZS *Canterbury* in

Deep Water Cove near Cape Brett. Local operators also head to the wreck of the *Rainbow Warrior* off the Cavalli Islands, about an hour from Paihia by boat.

Dive HQ (Map p169; ☎ 09-402 7551; www.divenz.com; Williams Rd, Paihia; reef & wreck $215) offers combined reef and wreck trips to either the *Canterbury* or the *Rainbow Warrior*. Various PADI courses are available and gear can be hired.

Dive North (☎ 09-402 5369; www.divenorth.co.nz; reef & wreck $235) heads to the *Rainbow Warrior* and other sites, and offers lunch and free pick-ups from Paihia.

SEA KAYAKING
There are plenty of opportunities for kayaking around the bay, either on a guided tour or by renting and going it alone.

Coastal Kayakers (Map p169; ☎ 09-402 8105; www.coastalkayakers.co.nz; Te Karuwha Pde, Paihia) Runs guided tours (half-/full-/two-day tours $60/80/130; minimum two people. Kayaks can also be rented (half-/full day $30/40).

Island Kayaks (Map p169; ☎ 09-402 6078; www.baybeachhire.co.nz; Marsden Rd, Paihia; half-/full-day tour $55/90) Operates from Bay Beach Hire.

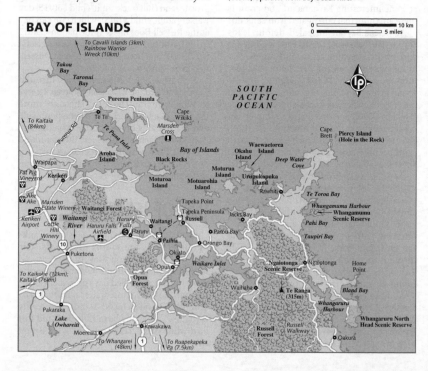

BAY OF ISLANDS

SKYDIVING

NZ Skydive (☎ 0800 427 593; www.nzskydive.com)
Operates from Haruru Falls or Kerikeri Airfields, offering 12,000ft tandem skydives ($299).

Skydive Zone (☎ 09-407 7057; www.skydivezoneboi. co.nz) From Kerikeri Airfield; 12,000/15,000ft tandem $290/355.

OTHER ACTIVITIES

Bay Beach Hire (Map p169; ☎ 09-402 6078; www. baybeachhire.co.nz; Marsden Rd, Paihia; ⊙ 9am-5.30pm) Hires kayaks (from $10 per hour), small sailing catamarans ($50 first hour, $25 per additional), small motor boats ($65 first hour, $25 per additional), mountain bikes ($20 per day), boogie boards ($25 per day), fishing rods ($10 per day), wet suits and snorkelling gear ($15 per day).

Flying Kiwi Parasail (☎ 0800 359 691; www.parasail -nz.co.nz) One-hour parasailing trips ($79 to $89), leaving from Paihia's wharf hourly during summer.

Salt Air (☎ 09-402 8338; www.saltair.co.nz) Has scenic flights including a five-hour flight-and-4WD tour to Cape Reinga and Ninety Mile Beach ($395). Helicopter flights out to the Hole in the Rock cost $215.

Tours

Where do you start? First by praying for good weather, as torrential rain or choppy seas could literally put a dampener on some options. The information centre at Paihia is extremely helpful and can book tours. Some of the hostels can arrange cheap deals and several of the main operators offer backpacker specials.

BOAT TRIPS

You can't leave the Bay of Islands without taking some sort of cruise and there are plenty of vessels keen to get you on board, including sailing boats, jetboats and large launches.

Boats leave from either Paihia or Russell, calling into the other town as their first stop.

Fullers (☎ 0800 653 339; www.dolphincruises.co.nz) runs full-day (adult/child $99/50) and half-day ($89/45) tours, taking in the Hole in the Rock off Cape Brett (passing through it if conditions are right) and stopping on an island. The full day 'Cream Trip' follows the old supply and mail route around the islands and includes dolphin swimming and boom netting (where you can get close to the critters while being dragged through the water in a net).

Overnight Cruises

The cheapest way to spend a night on the water is aboard the **MV Souvenir** (☎ 0800 773 569; dm/4-person cabin $125/400), an unglamorous but sturdy 40-ton boat that stops at various DOC reserves before finding a remote anchorage. You'll need to bring your own lunch for the first day and any booze or snacks.

You just need to roll up to the **Rock** (☎ 0800 762 527; www.rocktheboat.co.nz; 22hr cruise $178), a former vehicle ferry that's now a floating hostel, with four-bed dorms, twin and double rooms, and (of course) a bar. A private room costs an extra $20 per person. The cruise departs at 5pm and includes a barbecue and seafood dinner with live music, then a full day spent island-hopping, fishing, kayaking, snorkelling and swimming.

A more glamorous option is Fullers' launch **Ipipiri** (☎ 0800 653 339; www.overnightcruise.co.nz; s/d $642/732), where the accommodation is by way of en-suite state rooms, all meals are included, and if you get sick of lazing around the bar on the sundeck, you can partake in kayaking, snorkelling or island walks.

DETOUR: TOILET, TRAIN & GLOWING GRUBS

Kawakawa is just an ordinary Kiwi town, located on SH1 south of Paihia, but the public toilets (60 Gillies St) were designed by Austrian-born artist and ecoarchitect Friedensreich Hundertwasser. He lived near Kawakawa in an isolated house without electricity from 1973 until his death in 2000. The most photographed toilets in NZ are typical Hundertwasser – lots of wavy lines decorated with ceramic mosaics and brightly coloured bottles, and with grass and plants on the roof. Other examples of his work can be seen in Vienna and Osaka.

Kawakawa's other claim to fame is the railway line running through the centre of the main street, on which you can take a 40-minute spin on the **Gabriel the steam engine** (☎ 021 171 2697; www.bayofislandsvintagerailway.org.nz; adult/child $10/3; ⊙ 11am, noon, 1pm, 2pm Fri-Sun).

South of town, a signpost from SH1 points to **Kawiti Glowworm Caves** (☎ 09-404 0583; adult/child $15/7.50; ⊙ 8.30am-4.30pm). Explore the insect-illuminated caverns with a 30-minute subterranean tour.

Ecocruz (☎ 0800 432 627; www.ecocruz.co.nz; cruises dm/d $595/1350) is a highly recommended three-day/two-night sailing cruise aboard the 72ft ocean-going yacht *Manawanui,* with an emphasis on the marine environment. Prices include accommodation, food, fishing, kayaking and snorkelling.

Sailing

The best way to explore the bay is under sail. In most cases you can either help crew the boat (no experience required), or just spend the afternoon island-hopping, sunbathing, swimming, snorkelling, kayaking and fishing. Recommended boats offering day trips:

Carino (☎ 09-402 8040; www.sailingdolphins.co.nz; adult/child $99/60) A 50ft catamaran offering swimming with dolphins and a barbecue lunch ($6).

Gungha II (☎ 0800 478 900; www.bayofislands sailing.co.nz; trips $85) A beautiful 65ft ocean yacht with a friendly crew offering freshly made sandwiches.

On the Edge (☎ 09-402 8234; www.explorenz.co.nz; adult/child $120/79) NZ's fastest commercial catamaran, capable of speeds over 30 knots. It also has a licensed bar.

Phantom (☎ 0800 224 421; www.yachtphantom.com; adult/child $99/50) A fast 50ft racing sloop, known for its wonderful food (10 people maximum, BYO allowed).

R Tucker Thompson (☎ 09-402 8430; www.tucker. co.nz; adult/child $120/60) A majestic tall ship with daily tours that include a barbecue lunch. Run by a charitable trust with an education focus, it partners with the Historic Places Trust and DOC for special sailings.

She's a Lady (☎ 0800 724 584; www.bay-of-islands. com; trips $90) Try your hand at snorkelling or paddling about in a see-through-bottomed kayak.

If you're interested in learning to sail, **Great Escape Yacht Charters** (☎ 09-402 7143; www.great escape.co.nz; yacht hire per day $160-390) offers sailing lessons, including a two-day course ($345), which can be combined with an additional three-day yacht hire ($590).

Dolphin Swimming

These trips operate all year and you get to cruise around the islands as well as watch or swim with dolphins. They have a high success rate and operators generally offer a free trip if dolphins are not sighted. Dolphin swims are subject to weather and sea conditions, with restrictions if the dolphins have young. As well as encountering bottlenose and common dolphins, you may see orcas, other whales and penguins. With all operators a portion of the cost goes towards marine research, via DOC.

Dolphin Discoveries (☎ 09-402 8234; www.ex plorenz.co.nz; adult/child $89/45) was the first to offer dolphin-swimming trips in the bay. The price includes a four-hour trip, with an additional $30 payable if you choose to swim.

As well as the Cream Trip, Fullers offers a three-hour dolphin-swimming cruise (adult/child $89/45, $30 extra for swim). The only yacht to be licensed for dolphin swims is *Carino.*

Jetboating

Fasten your seatbelt for a high-speed Hole in the Rock trip on board a jetboat – good fun and handy if you're short on time. **Mack Attack** (☎ 0800 622 528; www.mackattack.co.nz; adult/child $85/40) and Fuller's **Excitor** (☎ 09-402 7421; www.awesomenz. com; adult/child $89/45) have daily 1½-hour trips.

CAPE REINGA TOURS

It's cheaper and quicker to do trips to Cape Reinga from Ahipara, Kaitaia or Doubtless Bay (see p181). But if you're short on time, several long day trips (10 to 12 hours) leave from the Bay of Islands. They all drive one way along Ninety Mile Beach, stopping to sandboard on the dunes and at Ancient Kauri Kingdom.

Fullers (☎ 0800 653 339; www.dolphincruises.co.nz) runs regular bus tours and backpacker-oriented versions, both stopping at Puketi Forest. Its standard, child-friendly version (adult/child $115/58) includes an optional barbecue lunch at Houhora ($23). Otherwise there's **Awesome NZ** (☎ 0800 653 339; www.awe somenz.com; tour $99), with louder music, more time sandboarding and stops to chuck a Frisbee around at Taputaputa Beach and devour fish and chips at Mangonui.

Dune Rider (☎ 09-402 8234; www.explorenz.co.nz; adult/child $139/109) tours also sample Mangonui's feted fish and chips and includes a stop at Gumdiggers Park.

HOKIANGA & WAIPOUA FOREST TOURS

Transport options to these west-coast destinations are limited, so a day trip makes sense if you don't have your own car or if you're time starved. **Crossings Hokianga** (☎ 0800 653 339; www. dolphincruises.co.nz; adult/child $93/47) leaves Paihia at 8.30am and heads to the forest for a one-hour tour with a Footprints Waipoua guide (p186). Then it's back to Opononi, where there's a choice of a crayfish lunch ($65) or a picnic ($17). Rawene and Kohukohu follow, heading back to Paihia by 4pm. The tours run according to demand, but you can enquire about stopping off overnight and picking up the rest of the tour at a later date.

Festivals & Events

Tall Ship Race Held in Russell on the first Saturday of January.

Waitangi Day Various ceremonial events at Waitangi on 6 February.

Country Rock Festival (www.country-rock.co.nz) Second weekend in May.

Russell Birdman Where a bunch of lunatics with flying contraptions jump off the wharf into the frigid (July) waters to the amusement of all.

Jazz & Blues Festival (www.jazz-blues.co.nz) Second weekend in August.

Weekend Coastal Classic (www.coastalclassic.co.nz) NZ's largest yacht race, from Auckland to the Bay of Islands, held on Labour Weekend in October.

RUSSELL
pop 820

Although it was once known prosaically as 'the hellhole of the Pacific', those coming to Russell for debauchery will be sadly

disappointed: they've missed the orgies on the beach by 170 years. Instead they'll find a sweetly historic town that is a bastion of cafes, gift shops and B&Bs.

Before it was known as a hellhole, or even as Russell, it was Kororareka (Sweet Penguin), a fortified Ngapuhi village. In the early 19th century the tribe permitted it to become Aotearoa's first European settlement. It quickly became a magnet for rough elements such as fleeing convicts, whalers and drunken sailors. By the 1830s dozens of whaling ships at a time were anchored in the harbour. Charles Darwin described it in 1835 as full of 'the refuse of society'.

In 1830 the settlement was the scene of the so-called Girls' War, when two pairs of Maori women were vying for the attention of a whaling captain called Brind. A chance meeting between the rivals on the beach led to verbal abuse and fighting. This minor conflict quickly escalated as family members rallied around to avenge the insult and harm done to their respective relatives. Hundreds were killed and injured over a two-week period before missionaries managed to broker a peace agreement.

NORTHLAND & THE BAY OF ISLANDS

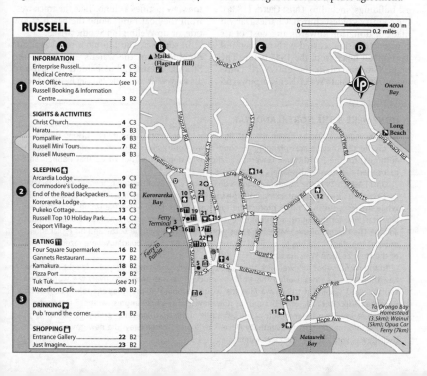

RUSSELL

0 — 400 m
0 — 0.2 miles

INFORMATION
Enterprise Russell...........................1 C3
Medical Centre................................2 B2
Post Office.................................(see 1)
Russell Booking & Information
Centre...3 B2

SIGHTS & ACTIVITIES
Christ Church..................................4 C3
Haratu..5 B3
Pompallier......................................6 B3
Russell Mini Tours..........................7 B2
Russell Museum..............................8 B3

SLEEPING
Arcadia Lodge.................................9 C3
Commodore's Lodge.....................10 B2
End of the Road Backpackers.......11 C3
Kororareka Lodge..........................12 D2
Pukeko Cottage.............................13 C3
Russell Top 10 Holiday Park.........14 C2
Seaport Village.............................15 C2

EATING
Four Square Supermarket.............16 B2
Gannets Restaurant......................17 B2
Kamakura......................................18 B2
Pizza Port......................................19 B2
Tuk Tuk.....................................(see 21)
Waterfront Cafe............................20 B2

DRINKING
Pub 'round the corner...................21 B2

SHOPPING
Entrance Gallery............................22 B2
Just Imagine..................................23 B2

After the signing of the Treaty of Waitangi in 1840, Okiato (where the car ferry now leaves from) was the residence of the governor and the temporary capital. The capital was officially moved to Auckland in 1841 and Okiato, which was by then known as Russell, was eventually abandoned. The name Russell ultimately passed to Kororareka – a marginally better choice than Bruce or Barry.

Information

Enterprise Russell (Traders Mall; 🛜) Internet access.
Medical Centre (☎ 09-403 7690; Church St)
Post office (Traders Mall)
Russell Booking & Information Centre (☎ 09-403 8020; www.russellinfo.co.nz; ⏱ 8.30am-4.30pm Apr-Sep, 8am-7pm Oct-Mar) On the pier.

Sights & Activities

The small but modern **Russell Museum** (☎ 09-403 7701; www.russellmuseum.org.nz; 2 York St; adult/child $7.50/2; ⏱ 10am-4pm) has a well-presented Maori section, a large 1:5-scale model of Captain Cook's *Endeavour* and a 10-minute video on the town's history.

Russell lays claim to some of NZ's oldest buildings, including **Christ Church** (1836), the country's oldest church. Charles Darwin made a donation towards the cost of its construction. It's scarred with musket and cannonball holes from the 1845 battle. The biggest memorial in the graveyard commemorates Tamati Waka Nene, a powerful

Ngapuhi chief from the Hokianga who sided against Hone Heke in the Northland War.

Pompallier (☎ 09-403 9015; www.pompallier.co.nz; The Strand; tours adult/child $7.50/free; ⏱ 10am-4pm) is a rammed-earth building constructed in 1842 to house the Roman Catholic mission's printing press, which printed a staggering 40,000 books in Maori. In the 1870s it was converted into a private home but it has been restored to its original state, complete with tannery and printing workshop. On the excellent guided tour you get to play with the tools and learn how to 'skive off' and become a 'dab hand'. It's the last remaining building of the Catholic mission in the Western Pacific.

Run by the local *marae* society, the recently opened **Haratu** (☎ 09-403 7212; cnr The Strand & Pitt St; ⏱ 10am-5pm) brings authentic Maori art and craft to the Russell waterfront, most of which is available for purchase. There are also audiovisual displays and information boards.

Overlooking Russell is **Maiki** (Flagstaff Hill; Flagstaff Rd), where Hone Heke chopped down the flagpole four times. You can drive up but the view justifies a climb. Take the track west from the boat ramp along the beach at low tide, or up Wellington St otherwise.

In summer, you can often rent kayaks or dinghies from the water's edge along the Strand. About 1.5km behind Russell and an easy walk or cycle is **Long Beach** (Oneroa

---

HONE HEKE & THE NORTHLAND WAR

Just five years after he had been the first signatory to the treaty, Ngapuhi chief Hone Heke was so disaffected that he was planning to chop down Kororareka's flagstaff, a symbol of British authority, for the fourth time. Governor FitzRoy was determined not to let that happen and garrisoned the town with soldiers and marines.

On 11 March 1845 the Ngapuhi staged a diversionary siege of the town. It was a great tactical success, with Chief Kawiti attacking from the south and another party attacking from Long Beach. While the troops rushed off to protect the township, Hone Heke felled the Union Jack on Maiki (Flagstaff Hill) for the fourth and final time. The British were forced to evacuate to ships lying at anchor. The captain of the HMS *Hazard* was wounded severely in the battle and his replacement ordered the ships' cannons to be fired on the town; most of the buildings were razed. The first of the New Zealand Wars had begun.

In the months that followed, British troops (united with Hokianga Ngapuhi) fought Heke and Kawiti in several battles. During this time the modern *pa* was born, effectively the world's first sophisticated system of trench warfare. It's worth stopping at the **Ruapekapeka Pa Historic Reserve** (Ruapekapeka Rd), off SH1 south of Kawakawa, to see how impressive these fortifications were. Here you can wander the site of the last battle of the Northland War, brought to life through detailed information boards. Eventually Heke, Kawiti and George Grey (the new governor) made their peace, with no side the clear winner.

Bay Beach). Turn left (facing the sea) to visit Donkey Bay, a small cove that is an unofficial nudist beach.

Tours

Russell Mini Tours (☎ 09-403 7866; cnr The Strand & Cass St; adult/child $25/10; ⏰ 11am, noon, 1pm & 2pm May-Sep, plus 10am, 3pm & 4pm Oct-Apr) Minibus tour with commentary.

See p163 for other tours around the bay.

Sleeping

Being a tourist trap, Russell has few decent midrange options. There are several tiny budget lodges, but you'll need to book ahead at busy times. If budget's not a consideration, Russell does luxury very well.

BUDGET

Pukeko Cottage (☎ 09-403 8498; www.pukekocottage backpackers.co.nz; 14 Brind Rd; s/d $25/50) More like staying at a mate's place than a hostel, this homely house has just two bedrooms for rent and a caravan in the back garden. It's certainly not dirty, but the cleanliness is bloke-standard. Barry, the artist owner, is always up for a chat.

End of the Road Backpackers (☎ 09-403 8827; 13 Brind Rd; dm/d $30/60; Ⓟ) Another tiddler, this basic bach sleeps only four people in two bedrooms (a double and a twin). It's a quiet spot with views over the marina.

our pick Wainui (☎ 09-403 8278; stocken@xtra.co.nz; 92d Te Wahapu Rd; dm/d/tr $30/60/90) Hard to find but well worth the effort, this modern bush retreat with direct beach access has only two rooms sharing a pleasant communal space. It's 5km from Russell on the way to the car ferry. Take Te Wahapu Rd and then turn right into Waiaruhe Way.

Seaport Village (☎ 09-403 7833; www.seaport village.co.nz; 10 Chapel St; dm $30, d $130-195, apt $150-390) This central 'village' spans all price brackets, with comfortable B&B rooms with polished wooden floors and self-contained multiroom apartments. The two linked dorms have proper mattresses, an en suite and a kitchen – and they're just over the fence from the local pub.

Russell Top 10 Holiday Park (☎ 09-403 7826; www. russelltop10.co.nz; 1 James St; sites per 2 people $39, units $80-230; 🖳) This leafy park has a small store, good facilities, wonderful hydrangeas, tidy cabins and nice units. Showers are clean, but metered.

MIDRANGE & TOP END

Kororareka Lodge (☎ 09-403 8494; www.kororareka.com; 22 Oneroa Rd; r $125-148) A solid option, sitting on the hill between the township and the beach. The front rooms have views, while the cheaper ones at the back only have small windows and share bathrooms. A communal lounge and deck compensate.

Commodore's Lodge (☎ 09-403 7899; www.commo doreslodgemotel.co.nz; 28 The Strand; units $150-650; 🐾) Being the envy of every passer-by makes up for the lack of privacy in the front apartments facing the waterfront promenade. Spacious, nicely presented units are the order of the day here, along with a really nice pool and free kayaks, dinghies and bikes.

Arcadia Lodge (☎ 09-403 7756; www.arcadialodge. co.nz; 10 Florance Ave; d $190-295) The stylish, characterful rooms of this 1890 hillside house are decked out with interesting antiques and fine linen, while the breakfast is probably the best you'll eat in town – it's not only organic, it's delicious. Enjoy the homemade muesli and Kerikeri orange juice while taking in a tranquil bay view.

Orongo Bay Homestead (☎ 09-403 7527; www. thehomestead.co.nz; Aucks Rd; s/d $400/650; 🛜) This wooden homestead (c 1860) was NZ's first American consulate, located a discreet 4km from Russell's rabble. It now contains four stylishly plush rooms, two in the house and two in the converted barn facing a chocolate-box lake. When one of the charming hosts is an acclaimed food critic, you can be assured that the breakfast will be memorable (dinners by arrangement).

Eating & Drinking

For a country so hooked on cafe culture and a town so touristy, it's disappointing that Russell doesn't have more on offer.

Pizza Port (☎ 09-403 8869; Cass St; pizza $11-20; ⏰ 5-9pm Mon-Wed, noon-9pm Thu-Sun) There are a couple of tables, but you're better off grabbing one of the gourmet wood-fired pizzas and battling the seagulls at the beach.

Waterfront Cafe (☎ 09-403 7589; 23d The Strand; mains $12-18; ⏰ breakfast & lunch) It's a sausage-roll-and-custard-square kind of place, but it's Russell's best weekday breakfast option.

Tuk Tuk (☎ 09-403 7111; 19 York St; mains $15-24; ⏰ 10am-11pm; Ⓥ) Thai fabrics adorn the tables and Thai favourites fill the menu. In clement weather grab a table out front and watch Russell's little world go by.

Gannets Restaurant (☎ 09-403 7990; cnr York & Chapel Sts; mains $15-31; ☷ dinner Tue-Sat) This funky eatery has an emphasis on seafood that would put a smile on any gannet's beak.

our pick Kamakura (☎ 09-403 7771; 29 The Strand; lunch $15-30, dinner $29-33; ☷ breakfast Sat & Sun, lunch & dinner daily) The flashest option in Russell by a long way, this restaurant has a breezy beach-house feel. The Pacific Rim menu gainfully plunders Asian and French styles to produce beautifully presented, delicious meals. In summer it hosts a monthly artisan market (www.artisanmarket.co.nz).

Pub 'round the corner (☎ 09-403 7831; 19 York St; ☷ noon-10pm Sun & Mon, noon-midnight Tue-Sat) A cool, cosy tavern with a beer garden and pool tables, in the same complex as Tuk Tuk.

There's a **Four Square supermarket** (The Strand) on the waterfront.

Shopping

Entrance Gallery (☎ 09-403 7716; 13 York St) A genuinely local gallery, where Russell's artists have been selling their wares for over 22 years.

Just Imagine… (☎ 09-403 8360; 25 York St) Full of gorgeous glassware and paintings, this gallery also offers art junkies a caffeine fix.

Getting There & Away

The quickest way to reach Russell by car is via the car ferry (car and driver $10, motorcycle and rider $5, passenger adult/child $1/50c), which runs every 10 minutes from Opua (5km from Paihia) to Okiato (8km from Russell), between 6.50am and 10pm. Buy your tickets on board. If you're travelling from the south, a scenic alternative is Russell Rd (p161).

On foot, the quickest and easiest way to reach Russell is on the regular passenger ferry (adult/child one way $6/3, return $10/5) from Paihia. It runs from 7am to 7pm (until 10pm October to May), generally every 20 minutes but hourly in the evenings. Buy your tickets on board or at the i-SITE in Paihia.

PAIHIA & WAITANGI

pop 1800 & 800

The birthplace of NZ (as opposed to Aotearoa), Waitangi inhabits a special, somewhat complex place in the national psyche – aptly demonstrated by the mixture of celebration, commemoration, protest and apathy that accompanies the nation's birthday (Waitangi Day, 6 February).

It was here that the long-neglected and much-contested Treaty of Waitangi was first signed between Maori chiefs and the British Crown, establishing British sovereignty or something a bit like it, depending on whether you're reading the English or Maori version of the document. If you're interested in coming to grips with NZ's history and race relations, this is the place to start.

Joined to Waitangi by a bridge, Paihia would be a fairly nondescript coastal town if it wasn't the main entry point to the Bay of Islands.

Information

Bay of Islands i-SITE (☎ 09-402 7345; www.visit northland.co.nz; Marsden Rd; ☷ 8am-5pm Mar–mid-Dec, 8am-8pm mid-Dec–Feb; ☐ ☎) Information and internet access ($4 per hour).

Maritime Building (Marsden Rd) Tour operators and internet access ($4 per hour); buses stop outside.

Medical services (☎ 09-402 8407; Selwyn Rd; ☷ 8.30am-5pm Mon-Fri)

Post office (2 Williams Rd) Offers poste restante service.

Sights & Activities

WAITANGI TREATY GROUNDS

A visit to the **Waitangi Treaty Grounds** (☎ 09-402 7437; www.waitangi.net.nz; 1 Tau Henare Dr; adult/child $20/10; ☷ 9am-5pm mid-Apr–Oct, 9am-7pm Nov–mid-Apr) is a must for every itinerary. It's full of cultural icons – the colonial-style Treaty House with its manicured garden and lawns, the surrounding bush full of native birds, the spiritual *whare* and the warlike *waka*, the three flags (UK, NZ and Maori) and the hillside views of a still-beautiful land.

The **Treaty House** has special significance in NZ's history. Built in 1832 as the four-room home of British resident James Busby, eight years later it was the setting for the signing of the Treaty of Waitangi. The house, with its gardens and lawn running down to the bay, was restored in 1989 and is preserved as a memorial and museum. Inside are photographs and displays, including a facsimile copy of the treaty.

Just across the lawn, the magnificently detailed **whare runanga** (meeting house) was completed in 1940 to mark the centenary of the treaty. The fine carvings represent the major Maori tribes.

Near the cove is the 35m **waka taua** (war canoe) *Ngatokimatawhaorua*. It too was built for the centenary, and a photographic exhibit

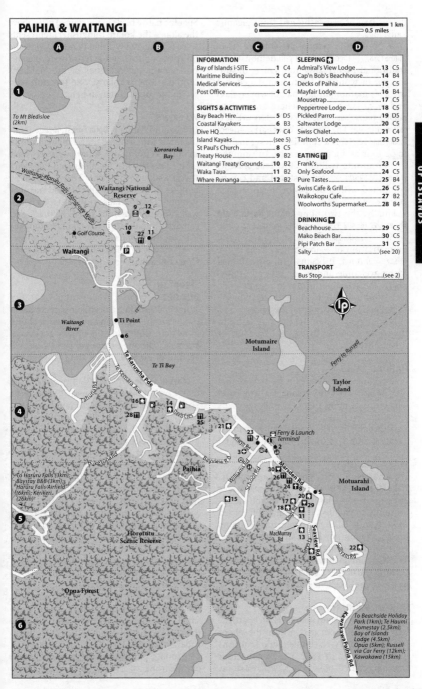

PAIHIA & WAITANGI

0 — 1 km
0 — 0.5 miles

INFORMATION
Bay of Islands i-SITE **1** C4
Maritime Building **2** C4
Medical Services **3** C4
Post Office **4** C4

SIGHTS & ACTIVITIES
Bay Beach Hire **5** D5
Coastal Kayakers **6** B3
Dive HQ **7** C4
Island Kayaks ....(see 5)
St Paul's Church **8** C5
Treaty House **9** B2
Waitangi Treaty Grounds **10** B2
Waka Taua **11** B2
Whare Runanga **12** B2

SLEEPING
Admiral's View Lodge **13** C5
Cap'n Bob's Beachhouse **14** B4
Decks of Paihia **15** C5
Mayfair Lodge **16** B4
Mousetrap **17** C5
Peppertree Lodge **18** C5
Pickled Parrot **19** D5
Saltwater Lodge **20** C5
Swiss Chalet **21** C4
Tarlton's Lodge **22** D5

EATING
Frank's **23** C4
Only Seafood **24** C5
Pure Tastes **25** B4
Swiss Cafe & Grill **26** C5
Waikokopu Cafe **27** B2
Woolworths Supermarket **28** B4

DRINKING
Beachhouse **29** C5
Mako Beach Bar **30** C5
Pipi Patch Bar **31** C5
Salty ....(see 20)

TRANSPORT
Bus Stop ....(see 2)

details how it was fashioned from gigantic kauri logs.

A 30-minute **cultural performance** (adult/child $15/8; ☺ check website or call) demonstrates traditional Maori song and dance, including *poi* (a women's formation dance that involves manipulating a ball of woven flax) and *haka* (war dance). There are various **guided tours** (adult/child $15/8; ☺ check website or call) available. The **Ultimate Waitangi Experience** (adult/child $25/14) is a combined ticket including a tour and a performance. In summer, the 45-minute twilight show **Land of Plenty** (adult/child $25/8; ☺ 6pm) is staged and can be combined with a drinks or meal package at the cafe.

Finally, the two-hour **Culture North Night Show** (☎ 09-402 5990; www.culturenorth.co.nz; admission $60; ☺ 7.30pm Mon-Sat Oct-Apr) is a wonderful dramatisation of Maori history held in the *whare runanga*. It begins with a traditional Maori welcome and heads into an atmospheric theatrical performance accompanied by a sound-and-light show. Free transfers from Paihia are included in the price.

NZ citizens are entitled to free entry to the treaty grounds; bring your passport or drivers' license.

HARURU FALLS

A few kilometres upstream from Waitangi are the attractive horseshoe Haruru Falls, which are lit up at night. A walkway leads along the Waitangi River and on a boardwalk through the mangroves from here to the Treaty Grounds (6km, 2½ hours one-way).

WAKA JOURNEY

For a hands-on experience of Maori culture, **Waka Tai-a-Mai** (☎ 09-405 9990; www.taiamaitours.co.nz; 2hr trip $75; ☺ 10am & 1pm Oct-Apr) gives you the opportunity to paddle a traditional 50ft carved *waka* (canoe). Leaving from the Waitangi bridge, the journey heads up to the Haruru Falls before visiting a replica Maori village. The Ngapuhi hosts wear traditional garb and perform the proper *karakia* (incantations), as well as some excellent storytelling.

ST PAUL'S CHURCH

Paihia's **St Paul's Church** (Marsden Rd) isn't particularly old (1925), but it stands on the site of NZ's first church – a simple raupo (bulrush) hut constructed in 1823. It's an altogether charming church, built from Kawakawa stone.

Spot the native birds in the stained glass above the altar – the kotare (kingfisher) represents Jesus (the king plus 'fisher of men'), while the tui (parson bird) and kereru (wood pigeon) portray the personalities of the Williams brothers (one scholarly, one forceful) who set up the mission station here.

WALKING

Just behind Paihia is **Opua Forest**, a regenerating forest with walking trails ranging from 10 minutes to five hours. A few large trees have escaped axe and fire, including some big kauri. If you walk up from School Rd for about 30 minutes, you'll find a couple of good lookouts. Pamphlets with details on all the Opua Forest walks are available from the i-SITE (free). You can drive into the forest by taking Oromahoe Rd west from Opua.

An easy 5km track follows the coast from Opua to Paihia.

Sleeping
BUDGET

What makes Paihia a desirable base for backpackers is the high standard and great choice of hostels. Kings Rd is the main 'backpackers' row', although there are gems scattered around elsewhere. All of the following are excellent.

Mayfair Lodge (☎ 09-402 7471; www.mayfairlodge. co.nz; 7 Puketona Rd; sites per person $15, dm/s/tw/d/q $25/55/62/65/108; ▣) Set apart from the rest but handy for the supermarket, Mayfair has colourful fish on the walls and resin toilet seats inset with shellfish.

Pickled Parrot (☎ 09-402 6222; www.pickledparrot. co.nz; Greys Lane; sites per person $18, dm $25-27, s/d $58/64; ▣ ☜) Surrounded by tropical plants, this friendly, well-maintained backpackers' stalwart has cute cabins, free bikes, free breakfast, a good vibe and, of course, a pet parrot.

Beachside Holiday Park (☎ 09-402 7678; www. beachsideholiday.co.nz; 1290 SH11; sites per person $20, units $70-230; ▣) Wake up at the water's edge at this sheltered camping ground, south of the township. The angular lemon cabins have 1970s charm, and there are kayaks for hire.

Mousetrap (☎ 09-402 8182; www.mousetrap.co.nz; 11 Kings Rd; dm $23-26, r $62; ▣) There are plenty of small chill-out areas in this friendly nautical-themed (which is much better than being rodent-themed) hostel. It has a variety of nice rooms, plus bikes, barbecues and boules out the front.

Peppertree Lodge (☎ 09-402 6122; www.peppertree. co.nz; 15 Kings Rd; dm $25-28, r $68-78; 💻 🤶) Simple, tidy rooms with high ceilings are on offer, plus there's a stash of bikes, racquets, kayaks and two barbecues for guests' use, making this a sociable choice.

Cap'n Bob's Beachhouse (☎ 09-402 8668; www. capnbobs.co.nz; 44 Davis Cres; dm/s $26/50, d $62-88; 💻) This small backpackers is a home-away-from-home, with hard-working owners, sea views from the veranda and more than a touch of charm. It's popular, so book ahead.

Saltwater Lodge (☎ 09-402 7075; www.saltwater lodge.co.nz; 14 Kings Rd; dm $27-33, d/tr/q $115/135/155; 💻 🤶) Even the dorms at this excellent, large, purpose-built backpackers have attached bathrooms, bedding and lockers. Cow-print and red-leather couches make for a cool communal lounge. There are large balconies, a bar and free bicycles, movies and racquets.

MIDRANGE & TOP END
Admiral's View Lodge (☎ 09-402 6236; www.admi ralsviewlodge.co.nz; 2 MacMurray Rd; apt $110-270; 💻) This hillside lodge offers natty units with balconies just begging for a relaxed sunset gin and tonic. Some have spa baths and bay views.

Baystay B&B (☎ 09-402 7511; www.baystay.co.nz; 93a Yorke Rd, Haruru Falls; r $115-145; 💻 🤶) Probably the only accommodation in NZ to have a Johnny Mnemonic pinball machine in the lounge room, this isn't your average B&B. Enjoy valley views from the spa pool of this slick, gay-friendly establishment.

Te Haumi Homestay (☎ 09-402 6818; joshlefi@xtra. co.nz; 41b Te Haumi Dr; s/d $125/140) A proper homestay, at Te Haumi you'll join the hospitable hosts for breakfast in the morning and wine and nibbles in the evening – yet once you're in your comfy downstairs room you'll have all the privacy you'll need. The house backs on to a nature reserve and has bay views. Listen for kiwi at night.

ourpick Tarlton's Lodge (☎ 09-402 6711; www. tarltonslodge.co.nz; 11 Sullivans Rd; r incl breakfast $150-240) Striking architecture combines with up-to-the-minute decor in this hilltop B&B with expansive bay views. Of the three luxurious suites in the main building, two have their own outdoor spa. The mid-priced rooms are in an older building across the lane but they share the same aesthetic, pleasing panoramas and breakfast.

Swiss Chalet (☎ 09-402 7615; www.swisschalet.co.nz; 3 Bayview Rd; units $165-460) This motel has a spa, barbecue, Sky TV and a wide range of good clean rooms with balconies. There's a slight (Swiss) cheese factor but you can't accuse it of looking anonymous.

Decks of Paihia (☎ 09-402 6146; www.decksofpaihia. com; 69 School Rd; d $195-245; 💻 🤶) Architecturally impressive, this place offers light, modern bedrooms, granite bathrooms and a big deck with bay views. The elegant pool, set between house and bush, is irresistible.

Bay of Islands Lodge (☎ 09-402 6075; www.bayof islandslodge.co.nz; SH11, Port Opua; d $580; 🤶) This luxurious, private retreat affords glorious views and has a chic little pool with an infinity lip. A wheelchair-accessible room is available.

Eating
ourpick Waikokopu Cafe (☎ 09-402 6275; Waitangi Treaty Grounds; mains $14-20; 🕙 9am-5pm) The setting is a cracking start – by a pond, backed by bush and overlooking the Treaty Grounds. The locale is matched by Kiwi icons on the menu – the ever popular 'fush and chips' and the Rainbow Warrior, 'French toast sunk in maple syrup, bacon and banana'.

Frank's (☎ 09-402 7590; 68 Marsden Rd; mains $14-22; 🕙 breakfast, lunch & dinner) While it moonlights as a cafe and a bar, it's as a pizza parlour that Frank's really shines. Share a large pizza for a well-priced carbo load.

Swiss Cafe & Grill (☎ 09-402 6701; 48 Marsden Rd; mains $17-29; 🕙 dinner) Unpretentious but excellent, this waterfront restaurant has a wide-ranging and eclectic menu, which includes pizza, nicely prepared fish dishes and Swiss comfort food such as schnitzel and home-made strudel.

Only Seafood (☎ 09-402 6066; 40 Marsden Rd; mains $29-33; 🕙 dinner) A superb place for local seafood, with dishes ranging from the simple (catch-of-the-day with lemon and parsley) to all manner of creamy, spicy concoctions. The fat Pacific oysters served with soy, wasabi and pickled ginger are sublime.

Pure Tastes (☎ 09-402 0003; 116 Marsden Rd; breakfast $16-19, mains $31-34; 🕙 breakfast, lunch & dinner) Occupying a small canvas-and-glass corner of the Paihia Beach Resort, this first-rate restaurant serves interesting, beautifully presented Pacific fusion food using mainly Northland ingredients.

Self-caterers can buy supplies at **Woolworths supermarket** (6 Puketona Rd; 🕙 7am-10pm).

Drinking & Entertainment

God bless backpackers: they certainly keep the bars buzzing. There are plenty of places along Kings Rd and in the town centre to explore, so don't feel hemmed in by our list.

Pipi Patch Bar (☎ 09-402 7111; 18 Kings Rd; ☾ 4pm-late) The party hostel has the party bar: a funky spot with large video screens and a decent terrace. You'll be shuffled inside at midnight to keep the neighbours happy – although most of them are backpackers who'll be here anyway.

Salty (☎ 09-402 6080; 14 Kings Rd; ☾ 4.30pm-1am) Attached to Saltwater Lodge, this bar serves OK pizzas and has karaoke, games and quizzes.

Beachhouse (☎ 09-402 7479; 16 Kings Rd; ☾ 8am-midnight) There's live music Thursday through Sunday nights at this lively place, decorated with leis and a trippy surfie/Pasifika-fantasy mural.

Mako Beach Bar (☎ 09-402 8952; 50 Marsden Rd; ☾ noon-late) If you get sick of hanging around with other travellers, head to this locals' hangout where you might catch some live music on the weekends.

Getting There & Around

All buses serving Paihia stop at the Maritime Building by the wharf. **InterCity** (☎ 09-583 5780; www.intercity.co.nz) and associated buses head daily to Auckland ($25, four hours), Whangarei ($23, 70 minutes), Kerikeri ($17, 25 minutes), Mangonui ($30, 80 minutes) and Kaitaia ($37, two hours). **Naked Bus** (☎ 0900 625 33 per min $1.80; www.nakedbus.com; advance fares from $1) departs at 7.20am for Whangarei (95 minutes) and Auckland (four hours), carrying on to Rotorua (8½ hours), Taupo (10 hours) and Napier (12 hours).

Various daily tours head to Cape Reinga (see p164), while the Crossings Hokianga tour is based on demand. Another Opononi option is to purchase the Paihia-Auckland leg of the **Magic Travellers Network** (☎ 09-358 5600; www.magicbus.co.nz) hop-on, hop-off service. The fare ($69, four buses weekly) includes unlimited stops and pick-ups anywhere along the route, including the Waipoua Forest and Dargaville.

Ferries depart regularly for Russell. If you've more money to spend and less time to wait, **Ocean Blue Water Taxis** (☎ 021 273 1655; fishcatcher@xtra.co.nz) and **Paihia Island Shuttle** (☎ 0800 387 892; www.islandshuttle.co.nz) will take you anywhere.

For bikes, visit **Bay Beach Hire** (☎ 09-402 6078; www.baybeachhire.co.nz; Marsden Rd; ☾ 9am-5.30pm).

URUPUKAPUKA ISLAND

The largest of the bay islands, Urupukapuka is the only one with a regular ferry service and a choice of accommodation. The **Urupukapuka Island Archaeological Walk** takes five hours and visits Ngare Raumati *pa* sites dating back to the 16th century – a DOC pamphlet is available. Ngare Raumati were defeated by Ngapuhi in 1829.

There are **DOC campsites** (sites per adult/child $8/4) at Cable, Sunset and Urupukapuka Bays. They have water supplies, cold showers (except Sunset Bay) and composting toilets; bring food, a stove and fuel. Idyllically positioned **Zane Grey Resort** (☎ 09-402 5207; www.zanegrey.co.nz; Otehei Bay; dm/d/cottage $30/85/125) has a restaurant and bar and hires kayaks.

Explore NZ (☎ 09-402 8234; www.explorenz.co.nz) runs a ferry service departing from Paihia ($40 return).

KERIKERI

pop 5900

Kerikeri means 'dig dig', and a lot of digging goes on in the surrounding fertile farmland. Famous for its oranges, Kerikeri also produces plenty of kiwifruit (don't call them kiwis unless you want to offend Kiwis), vegetables and, increasingly, wine. If you're looking for some back-breaking, poorly paid work that Kiwis (the people, as opposed to kiwifruit) aren't keen to do, your working holiday starts here.

Information

Post office (6 Hobson Ave) Has poste restante service.

Procter Library (☎ 09-407 0773; www.kerikeri.co.nz; Cobham Rd; ☾ 8am-5pm Mon-Fri, 9am-2pm Sat, 9am-1pm Sun; ☏) The library has tourist information and free internet access.

Sights & Activities

KERIKERI BASIN

A snapshot of early Maori and Pakeha interaction is offered by a cluster of historic sites centred on this picturesque river basin. In 1819 the powerful Ngapuhi chief Hongi Hika allowed Rev Samuel Marsden to start a mission under the shadow of his **Kororipo Pa**.

The **Mission House** is the country's oldest wooden building (1822) and contains some original fittings and chattels. Its neighbour,

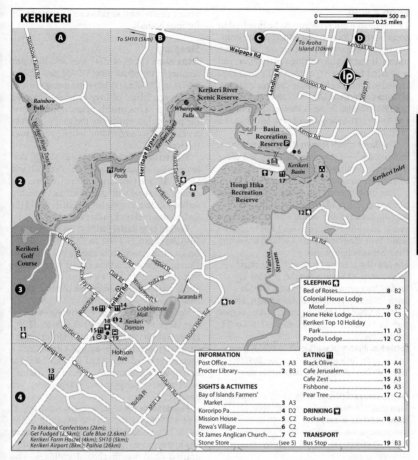

KERIKERI

0	500 m
0	0.25 miles

To SH10 (5km)
To Aroha Island (10km)
Kendall Rd
Waipapa Rd
Mission Rd
Landing Rd
Salwyn Pl
Rainbow Falls Rd
Rainbow Falls
Kerikeri River Track
Kerikeri River Scenic Reserve
Wharepoke Falls
Kemp Rd
Basin Recreation Reserve ●6
Kerikeri Basin
Fairy Pools
Heritage Bypass
Kerikeri River Track
Peacock Gardens
Kerikeri Gr
Kerikeri Inlet
Hongi Hika Recreation Reserve
Pa Rd
Wairoa Stream
Kerikeri Golf Course
Golf View Rd
Fairway Dr
King Rd
Support St
Stella Rd
Jacaranda Pl
Hone Heke Rd
Clark Rd
Windsworth La
Homestead Pl
Kerikeri Rd
Cobblestone Mall
Kerikeri Domain
Butler Rd
Aranga Rd
Cannon Dr
Hobson Ave
Norfolk Pl
Mill La
Cobham Rd

To Makana Confections (2km);
Get Fudged (2.5km); Cafe Blue (2.6km)
Kerikeri Farm Hostel (4km); SH10 (5km);
Kerikeri Airport (8km); Paihia (26km)

INFORMATION
Post Office	1 A3
Procter Library	2 B3

SIGHTS & ACTIVITIES
Bay of Islands Farmers' Market	3 A3
Kororipo Pa	4 D2
Mission House	5 C2
Rewa's Village	6 C2
St James Anglican Church	7 C2
Stone Store	(see 5)

SLEEPING
Bed of Roses	8 B2
Colonial House Lodge Motel	9 B2
Hone Heke Lodge	10 C3
Kerikeri Top 10 Holiday Park	11 A3
Pagoda Lodge	12 C2

EATING
Black Olive	13 A4
Cafe Jerusalem	14 B3
Cafe Zest	15 A3
Fishbone	16 A3
Pear Tree	17 C2

DRINKING
Rocksalt	18 A3

TRANSPORT
Bus Stop	19 B3

the **Stone Store** (☎ 09-407 9236; 246 Kerikeri Rd; ☺ 10am-5pm Nov-Apr, 10am-4pm May-Oct), is the oldest stone building in NZ (1836). It sells interesting gifts as well as the type of goods that used to be sold in the store – although these days you'll have a hard time bartering pigs for muskets. Tours ($10) of the Mission House depart from here and include entry to the displays on the 1st floor of the store.

Just up the hill is a marked historical walk, which leads to the *pa* site. Huge war parties led by Hika once departed from here, terrorising much of the North Island and slaughtering thousands during the Musket Wars (see p30). The role of missionaries in arming Ngapuhi remains controversial. The walk emerges near the cute wooden **St James Anglican Church** (1878).

There's an ongoing campaign to have the area including the store, house and neighbouring *pa* recognised as a Unesco World Heritage Site.

If you had a hard time imagining the *pa* in its original state, take the footbridge across the river to **Rewa's Village** (☎ 09-407 6454; Landing Rd; adult/child $5/1; ☺ 9.30am-4.30pm), a fascinating mock-up of a traditional Maori fishing village.

Starting from the neighbouring scenic reserve the 4km-long Kerikeri Walkway leads to the 27m **Rainbow Falls**, passing by the Wharepoke Falls and the Fairy Pools. Alternatively, you can reach the Rainbow Falls from Rainbow Falls Rd, in which case it's only a 10-minute walk.

FOOD & WINE

Everyone in Kerikeri seems to be involved in some cottage industry or other, as the bombardment of craft shops on the way into town attests. If you're a recovering sugar junkie, you may need to drive into town with your eyes closed to avoid the boutique chocolate factory **Makana Confections** (☎ 09-407 6800; www.makana. co.nz; 504 Kerikeri Rd; ⏰ 9am-5.30pm) and **Get Fudged** (☎ 09-407 1111; www.getfudged.co.nz; 560 Kerikeri Rd; ⏰ 8.30am-5pm).

The **Bay of Islands Farmers Market** (www.boifm.org. nz; Hobson Ave; ⏰ 8.30am-noon Sun) is a good place to sample a range of what the region has to offer, from sausages to *limoncello*.

The little-known red grape chambourcin has proved particularly suited to the region's subtropical humidity, along with pinotage and syrah, so while Northland isn't known for its wine, four vineyards near Kerikeri are doing their best to change this:

Ake Ake (Map p162; ☎ 09-407 8230; www.akeake vineyard.co.nz; 165 Waimate North Rd; ⏰ 10am-6pm Tue-Sun) Has a swanky restaurant (lunch $14 to $26, dinner $26 to $31; open lunch Tuesday to Sunday, dinner Tuesday to Saturday), a *pétanque* court, and offers vineyard tours ($5, 11.30am Saturday and Sunday) and tastings ($3, free if dining).

Cottle Hill Winery (Map p162; ☎ 09-407 5203; www. cottlehill.co.nz; Cottle Hill Dr; ⏰ 10am-5pm Nov-Mar, 10am-5pm Wed-Sun Apr-Oct) Tastings $5; free with purchase.

Fat Pig Vineyard (Map p162; ☎ 09-407 3113; www. fatpig.co.nz; 177 Puketotara Rd; ⏰ 11am-6pm)

Marsden Estate Winery (Map p162; ☎ 09-407 9398; www.marsdenestate.co.nz; Wiroa Rd; ⏰ 10am-5pm Sep-Jun, 10am-4pm Tue-Sun Jul & Aug) Offers meals and platters on its deck.

Total Tours (☎ 0800 264 868; www.totaltours.co.nz) has full-day food, wine and craft tours ($99), half-day wine tours ($75) and evening *Wine & Dine* tours ($120), departing from Paihia's Maritime Building.

AROHA ISLAND

Aroha Island Ecological Centre (☎ 09-407 5243; www. arohaisland.co.nz; Rangitane Rd; admission free; ⏰ 9.30am-5.30pm Thu-Tue) is located on a tiny 5-hectare island (Map p162), 10km northeast of Kerikeri, reached via a permanent causeway through mangroves. The island provides a haven for the North Island brown kiwi and other native birds, as well as an excellent picnic spot for their nonfeathered admirers. There's a visitor centre, and kayaks can be rented ($25 for four hours).

Sleeping

Aroha Island (☎ 09-407 5243; www.arohaisland.co.nz; Rangitane Rd; sites per adult/child $15/7.50, dm/s $20/65, d $90-120, tr $110-140, q $130-160) Kip among the kiwi on the eco island of love (*aroha*). There's a wide range of reasonably priced options, from the peaceful campsites by the shelly beach to an extremely comfortable lodge gazing over the water.

Kerikeri Top 10 Holiday Park (☎ 09-407 9326; www. kerikeritop10.co.nz; Aranga Rd; sites per adult/child $15/11, units $78-245; 🖳 🛜) This large, attractive, riverside camping ground with good facilities is within walking distance of the town centre. Avoid the joyless attached backpackers.

Kerikeri Farm Hostel (☎ 09-407 6989; http://kkfarm hostel.blogspot.com; 1574 SH10; dm/s/d $25/43/58; 🖳 🛜) Less a farm, more an orange grove, this spot 4km out of town features a quiet rural cottage that sleeps only 12. It's a homely place, with a sole chandelier adding a bit of bling to the cosy lounge.

Hone Heke Lodge (☎ 09-407 8170; www.honeheke. co.nz; 65 Hone Heke Rd; dm $25, s $43-63, d $58-80; 🖳 🛜) Hone Heke has a row of single-storey rooms with their own fridges, a small kitchen and a sociable covered courtyard. Weekly rates are available and recreation areas (TV lounge, pool tables, ping pong, barbecues) are good.

Pagoda Lodge (☎ 09-407 8617; www.pagoda.co.nz; 81 Pa Rd; d $85-160, tr $130-270, q $190-390) Built in the 1930s by an oddball Scotsman with an Asian fetish, this lodge features pagoda-shaped roofs grafted onto weatherboard cottages. The property descends to the river and is dotted with Buddhas and two- to three-'room' tents with proper beds ($65 to $140). The Jade House – built to hold a collection that now resides in the British Museum – is a smartly decorated studio cottage.

Colonial House Lodge Motel (☎ 09-407 9106; www. colonialhousemotel.co.nz; 178 Kerikeri Rd; units $100-195; 🛜 🖵) The Colonial has restful rooms opening onto a tropical garden. It may be getting on a bit, but it has freshened itself up with wi-fi and DVD players.

Bed of Roses (☎ 09-407 4666; www.bedofroses.co.nz; 165 Kerikeri Rd; d $225-325; 🖳) Much more comfortable than an actual bed of roses, this stylish B&B is furnished with French antiques, luxe linens and comfy beds. The interesting building has an art-deco ambience and awe-some views.

Eating & Drinking

Fishbone (☎ 09-407 6065; 88 Kerikeri Rd; mains $6-17; ❂ breakfast & lunch) Stylish Fishbone does a great coffee and serves imaginative food; Dr Seuss fans should try the green (pesto) eggs and ham.

Cafe Zest (☎ 09-407 7164; 73 Kerikeri Rd; mains $7-17; ❂ breakfast & lunch) Bathed in Kerikeri's orange glow, cute little Zest serves up a tempting array of counter food with plenty of vegetarian options.

Cafe Blue (☎ 09-407 5150; 582 Kerikeri Rd; mains $9-18; ❂ 9am-3pm) It may be on the main road into town but this garden cafe is a peaceful oasis, serving sandwiches, salads, renowned Cornish pasties and sub-$20 grills.

Black Olive (☎ 09-407 9693; 308 Kerikeri Rd; mains $11-32; ❂ dinner Tue-Sun) Call in for popular pasta and pizza takeaways, or grab a seat in the restaurant or garden.

Pear Tree (☎ 09-407 8479; 215 Kerikeri Rd; mains $15-30; ❂ lunch & dinner) Lovely views of the basin from this homestead are this restaurant's big drawcard, ably matched by the food.

Cafe Jerusalem (☎ 09-407 1001; Cobblestone Mall, Kerikeri Rd; mains $16-19; ❂ 11am-late) Northland's best falafels, served with a smile and a social vibe.

Rocksalt (☎ 09-407 1050; Kerikeri Rd; ❂ 11am-9pm Mon-Tue, 11am-11pm Wed-Thu, 11am-2am Fri & Sat) The most popular nightspot in town, this smart bar has a beer garden and an orange-neon radiance.

See Food & Wine, opposite, for some self-catering options.

Getting There & Away

AIR

Bay of Islands (Kerikeri) Airport (Map p162; ☎ 09-407 7147; www.bayofislandsairport.co.nz; 218 Wiroa Rd) is 8km southwest of town. **Air New Zealand** (☎ 0800 737 000; www.airnz.co.nz) operates three to five flights daily (except Sunday) from Auckland (40 minutes); see its website for prices and discounts. **Salt Air Xpress** (☎ 09-402 8338; www.saltair.co.nz) flies to Whangarei and Auckland's North Shore ($169, 30 minutes), every day except Saturday.

BUS

InterCity (☎ 09-583 5780; www.intercity.co.nz) and partner buses leave from a stop on Cobham

Rd, opposite the library. Daily services head to Auckland ($55, five hours), Whangarei ($24, 1¾ hours), Paihia ($17, 25 minutes), Mangonui ($24, 54 minutes) and Kaitaia ($33, 1½ hours).

THE FAR NORTH

If it sounds remote, that's because it is. The far-flung Far North is always playing second fiddle to the Bay of Islands for attention and funding, yet the subtropical tip of the North Island has more breathtaking coastline per square kilometre than anywhere but the offshore islands. Parts of the Far North are noticeably economically depressed and in places could best be described as gritty. While the 'winterless north' may be a popular misnomer, summers here are long and leisurely. Here's your chance to get off the beaten track, although that often means unsealed roads.

MATAURI & TAURANGA BAYS

It's a short detour from SH10, but the loop route leading inland to these awesome beaches is a world away from the glitzy face presented for tourists in the Bay of Islands.

Matauri Bay is a long sandy surf beach, 18km off SH10, with the 17 Cavalli Islands scattered offshore. **Matauri Bay Holiday Park** (☎ 09-405 0525; www.matauribay.co.nz; sites per adult/child $18/8, cabins $100-130) takes up the north end of the beach and has a shop (which sells booze) and petrol station. On top of the headland above the park is a monument to the *Rainbow Warrior* (see the boxed text, p177); the Greenpeace ship's underwater resting place among the Cavalli Islands is a popular dive site (see p162).

DOC maintains a 12-person **hut** (☎ 09-407 0300; www.doc.govt.nz; sites per adult/child $12/6) on Motukawanui Island, but you'll need a boat or kayak to reach it and you'll need to book ahead. Only water, mattresses and a composting toilet are provided; bring everything else.

Back on the main road the route heads west, passing through pleasant Te Ngaere village and a succession of little bays before the turn-off to Tauranga Bay, a smaller beach where the sand is a peachy pink colour. **Tauranga Bay Holiday Park** (☎ 09-405 0436; www.taurangabay.co.nz; sites per person $15, cabins $60-160; ▣ ☎) has well-maintained accommodation on the picturesque beachfront, but it lacks trees and bears the brunt of the weather. A minimum $50

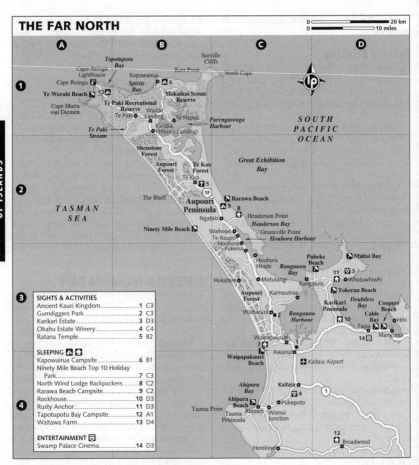

THE FAR NORTH

charge per night for campsites and a seven-night minimum stay apply in January.

Down a private road leading from Tauranga Bay, **Northland Sea Kayaking** (☎ 09-405 0381; www.northlandseakayaking.co.nz; half-/full day tours $65/85) leads kayak explorations of this magical coastline of coves, sea caves and islands. Accommodation is available in conjunction with tours for $20 extra per person.

There's no public transport to these parts or to neighbouring Whangaroa.

WHANGAROA HARBOUR

Just around the headland from Tauranga Bay is the narrow entrance to Whangaroa Harbour. The small fishing village of Whangaroa is 6km from SH10 and calls itself the 'Marlin Capital of NZ', meaning it's a popular place to dislocate your shoulder while trying to land a Lee Marvin–sized monster. **Boyd Gallery** (☎ 09-405 0230; Whangaroa Rd; 8am-7pm) is the general store but also acts as a tourist information office.

There are plenty of charter boats for **game-fishing** (December to April). Prices start at around $1200 a day. If you're planning to hook a marlin, insist on it being released once caught – striped marlin is one of NZ's least-sustainable species (see the boxed text, p178).

The 15m yacht **Sea Eagle** (☎ 09-405 1963; www.seaeaglecharters.com; per person $110, minimum 2) makes day trips to the Cavalli Islands, where there are excellent beaches, diving spots, snorkelling opportunities and walks. Longer charters can also be arranged.

An excellent 20-minute hike starts from the car park at the end of Old Hospital Rd and goes up **St Paul's Rock** (213m), which dominates the village. At the top you have to use a wire cable to pull yourself up, but the views make it worth the effort.

The **Wairakau Stream Track** north to Pekapeka Bay begins near the church hall on Campbell Rd in Totara North on the other side of the bay. The two-hour hike passes through farmland, hills and shoreline before arriving at DOC's **Lane Cove Cottage** (☎ 09-407 8474; sole occupancy $160), which has 16 beds and composting toilets. Bring everything else and book ahead. **Duke's Nose Track** (45 minutes each way) starts behind the cottage and leads up Kairara Rocks; look for the Duke of Wellington's aquiline profile in the rock face.

On the other side of the harbour's north head is **Taupo Bay**, a surf beach that attracts a loyal Kiwi contingent in summer. It's reached by an 11km, partly unsealed road signposted from SH10.

Sleeping & Eating

Sunseeker Lodge (☎ 09-405 0496; www.sunseekerlodge. co.nz; Old Hospital Rd; sites per person $15, dm/s $25/50, d $50-86, units $150-250; 🖳) Up the hill in Whangaroa, this friendly lodge has a sublime spa with a jaw-dropping view, hires out kayaks and motor boats, and will pick you up from Kaeo on SH10.

our pick **Kahoe Farms Hostel** (☎ 09-405 1804; www.kahoefarms.co.nz; dm/s $25/53, d $68-88) On SH10, 10km north of the turn-off to Whangaroa, this hostel has a deservedly great reputation – for its comfortable accommodation, for its bucolic setting, for its home-cooked Italian food, but mostly for its welcoming young owners. The backpackers' villa is great but there's an even more atmospheric cottage slightly up the hill with excellent value en-suite rooms. There are bushwalks on the property to old kauri dams and swimming holes, and you can hire a kayak to tackle the harbour.

Marlin (☎ 09-405 0347; Whangaroa Rd; mains $12-25; 🕙 lunch & dinner) A friendly local pub with good honest tucker served from the attached cafe.

THE BOMBING OF THE RAINBOW WARRIOR

On the morning of 10 July 1985, New Zealanders awoke to news reporting that a terrorist attack had killed a man in Auckland Harbour. The Greenpeace flagship *Rainbow Warrior* had been sunk at its anchorage at Marsden Wharf, where it was preparing to sail to Moruroa Atoll near Tahiti to protest against French nuclear testing.

It took some time to find out exactly what had happened, but a tip-off from a Neighbourhood Watch group lead to the arrest of two French foreign intelligence service (DGSE) agents, posing as tourists. The agents had detonated two mines on the boat in staggered explosions – the first designed to cause the crew to evacuate and the second to sink her. However, after the initial evacuation, some of the crew returned to the vessel to investigate and document the attack. Greenpeace photographer Fernando Pereira was drowned below decks following the second explosion.

The arrested agents pleaded guilty to manslaughter and were sentenced to 10 years' imprisonment. In response, the French government threatened to embargo NZ goods from entering the European Economic Community – which would have crippled NZ's economy. A deal was struck whereby France paid $13 million to NZ and apologised, in return for the agents being delivered into French custody on a South Pacific atoll for three years. France eventually paid over $8 million to Greenpeace in reparation – and the bombers were quietly freed before their sentence was served.

Initially French President Mitterrand denied any government involvement in the attack, but following an inquiry he eventually sacked his Defence Minister and the head of the DGSE, Admiral Pierre Lacoste. On the 20th anniversary of the attack, Le Monde newspaper published a report from Lacoste dating from 1986 declaring that the president had personally authorised the operation.

The bombing left a lasting impact on NZ, and French nuclear testing at Moruroa ceased for good in 1996. The wreck of the *Rainbow Warrior* was re-sunk near Northland's Cavalli Islands, where it can be explored by divers. The masts were bought by the Dargaville Museum and overlook the town. The memory of Fernando Pereira endures in a peaceful bird hide in Thames. A memorial to the boat sits atop a Maori *pa* site at Matauri Bay, north of the Bay of Islands.

DOUBTLESS BAY

pop 6030

The bay gets its unusual name from an entry in Cook's logbook, where he wrote that the body of water was 'doubtless a bay'. No kidding, Cap'n. It's a bloody big bay at that, with a string of pretty swimming beaches heading towards the Karikari Peninsula.

The main centre, **Mangonui** (meaning 'Big Shark'), retains a fishing-port feel, despite cafes and gift shops now infesting its well-labelled line of historical waterfront buildings. They were constructed in the days when Mangonui was a centre of the whaling industry (1792–1850) and exported flax, kauri wood and gum.

The popular holiday settlements of **Coopers Beach**, **Cable Bay** and **Taipa** are restful pockets of beachside gentrification.

Information

Doubtless Bay visitor information centre (☎ 09-406 2046; www.doubtlessbay.co.nz; 118 Waterfront Rd, Mangonui; ✆ 10am-4pm Mon-Sat; ▢)
Post office (Beach Rd, Mangonui)

Sights & Activities

Grab the free **Heritage Trail** brochure from the information centre for a 3km self-guided walk taking in 22 historic sites. Other walks lead to attractive **Mill Bay**, west of Mangonui, and **Rangikapiti Pa Historic Reserve**, with ancient Maori terracing and a spectacular view of Doubtless Bay – particularly at sunrise and sunset. A walkway runs from Mill Bay to the top of the *pa*, but you can drive nearly to the top if you're not feeling energetic.

You can sample and purchase the best of the region's wines at the **Far North Wine Centre** (☎ 09-406 2485; www.farnorthwinecentre.co.nz; 60 Waterfront Dr, Mangonui; ✆ 11am-4pm Wed-Mon) and then pick up some Pasifika knick-knacks at nearby **Flax Bush** (☎ 09-406 1510; www.flaxbush.co.nz; 50 Waterfront Dr).

At Hihi, 15km northeast of Mangonui, is **Butler Point**, where you can take a guided tour around the small **Whaling Museum** (☎ 09-406 0006; www.butlerpoint.co.nz; Marchant Rd; adult/child $12/2; ✆ by appointment), housed in a Victorian homestead (1843) with lovely gardens. Its first owner, Captain Butler, left Dorset when he was 14 and at 24 was captain of a whaling ship. He settled here in 1839, had 13 children and became a trader, farmer, magistrate and Member of Parliament.

FISH FOR THE FUTURE

While NZ's fisheries are more tightly controlled than most, conservation groups are quick to point out that most fishing is still unsustainable at present levels. The **Royal Forest & Bird Protection Society** (☎ 0800 200 064; www.forestandbird.org.nz) publishes an annual *Best Fish Guide*, which is downloadable from its website. The following are the best and worst choices if you're hankering for a seafood chow-down.

- **Ten best** Kina, anchovy, pilchard, sprats, skipjack tuna, garfish, yellow-eyed mullet, cockles, kahawai, blue cod

- **Ten worst** Orange roughy, bluefin tuna, oreos (deepwater dory), shark (lemonfish/rig), snapper, bluenose, jack mackerel, squid, skate, striped marlin

---

Sleeping

There's plenty of accommodation around the bay but most is horribly overpriced in summer – the following recommendations being noble exceptions. Outside the peak months things settle down considerably.

our pick **Puketiti Lodge** (☎ 09-406 0369; www.puketiti lodge.co.nz; 10 Puketiti Dr; dm/s/d/tr $40/90/130/150; ▢) If this is what they mean by flashpacking, bring it on. For $40 you get a comfy bunk in a spacious six-person dorm opening on to a large deck with awesome views, a locker big enough for the burliest backpack and, most surprisingly, breakfast. The private en-suite rooms are much more luxurious than the price implies. Turn inland at Midgley Rd, 6km south of Mangonui village, just after the Hihi turn-off.

Rosie's B&B (☎ 09-406 1443; www.rosiesbandb.co.nz; 136 SH10; r $80) Informal Rosie's offers two unremarkable but reasonably priced en-suite rooms in a Coopers Beach house. Try for the upstairs one; it's small but has a balcony with sea views.

Doubtless Bay Lodge (☎ 09-406 1661; www.doubt lessbaylodge.co.nz; 33 Cable Bay Block Rd; s/d $80/120) A 10-minute walk from Coopers Beach, this hillside lodge offers motel-style privacy coupled with B&B-style friendliness and food. Rooms have cable TV and facilities for making a nice cuppa. It was on the market when we visited, so we hope the new owners maintain the high standards.

Old Oak (☎ 09-406 1250; www.theoldoak.co.nz; 66 Waterfront Dr, Mangonui; s $125, d $175-225, ste $295) When we visited, the paint was still drying on this atmospheric 1861 kauri inn, which was in the throes of being completely reborn as an elegant boutique hotel. The Old Oak oozes character, not least because the building is reputedly haunted.

Mangonui Waterfront Motel (☎ 09-406 0347; www.mangonuiwaterfront.co.nz; Waterfront Dr; apt $155-245) Sleeping two to eight people, these historic apartments on the Mangonui waterfront have loads of character, each one different but all with balconies, a sense of space and its own barbecue. Try to book 100-year-old Tahi.

Eating

There are a few cafes, takeaways and stores scattered around the other beaches, but Mangonui has the best eating options – and they're actually pretty great.

Mangonui Fish Shop (☎ 09-406 0478; Waterfront Dr; mains $5-25; ☷ 10am-8pm) You can eat outdoors over the water in this licensed and deservedly famous fish-and-chip shop, which also sells smoked fish and seafood salads. Grab a crayfish salad and a cold beer, and all will be right with the world.

Waterfront Cafe & Bar (☎ 09-406 0850; Waterfront Dr; brunch $7-21, dinner $14-29; ☷ 8.30am-late) The best cafe in the Far North, Waterfront has an inventive menu, water views, friendly service and old-world charm. For breakfast try the market fish on spinach with citrus hollandaise.

our pick **Thai Chef** (☎ 09-406 1220; 80 Waterfront Dr; mains $18-26; ☷ dinner Tue-Sun) While we're on the superlatives, this is quite simply the best Thai restaurant we've found in the upper North Island, Auckland included. Dishes have names such as *3 Alcoholics* and *Bananas with Hairy Legs*. The *Sexy Little Duck* is irresistible.

There's also a **Four Square supermarket** (Waterfront Rd) next to the post office.

Entertainment

Swamp Palace Cinema (☎ 09-408 7040; Oruru Rd) This tiny cinema is quite the experience, often offering a verbal prelude to the screenings. It's 7km inland from Taipa.

Getting There & Away

InterCity (☎ 09-583 5780; www.intercity.co.nz) buses stop at the BP service station on Waterfront Dr in Mangonui, travelling to Kaitaia ($21, 40 minutes) and Kerikeri ($24, 54 minutes). The same services stop outside the wholesalers in Coopers Beach, opposite the shop in Cable Bay and outside the Shell station in Taipa. **Busabout Kaitaia** (☎ 09-408 1092; www.cbec.co.nz) has services to Kaitaia ($5, one hour).

KARIKARI PENINSULA

The oddly shaped Karikari Peninsula bends into a near-perfect right angle. The result is beaches facing north, south, east and west in close proximity; if the wind's annoying you or you want to catch some surf, a sunrise or a sunset, just swap beaches. Despite its natural assets, the peninsula's blissfully undeveloped, with farmers well outnumbering tourist operators. There's no public transport and you won't find a lot of shops or eateries either.

Sights & Activities

Tokerau Beach is the long, lovely stretch forming the western edge of Doubtless Bay. Neighbouring **Whatuwhiwhi** is smaller and more built-up, facing back across the bay. **Maitai Bay**, with its tiny twin coves, is the loveliest of them all, at the lonely end of the peninsula down an unsealed road. It's a great spot for swimming – sheltered enough for the kids but with enough swell to body surf.

Rangiputa faces west at the elbow of the peninsula; the pure white sand and crystal-clear sheltered waters come straight from a Pacific Island daydream. A turn-off on the road to Rangiputa takes you to remote **Puheke Beach**, a long, windswept stretch of snow-white sand dunes forming Karikari's northern edge.

This unique setup makes Karikari Peninsula one of the world's premium spots for kiteboarding, or at least that's the opinion of the experienced crew at **Airzone Kitesurfing School** (☎ 09-408 7129; www.kitesurfnz.com; 1-/2-day course $175/325). You can chase the wind around the peninsula; learners get to hone their skills on flat water before heading to the surf.

An ominous sign of creeping gentrification is the luxury golf club and winery on the way to Maitai Bay. Impressive **Karikari Estate** (Map p176; ☎ 09-408 7222; www.karikariestate.co.nz; Maitai Bay Rd; tastings $12; ☷ 11am-5pm) produces acclaimed red wines and has a cafe attached (mains $14 to $25).

Sleeping & Eating

DOC campsite (☎ 09-408 6014; www.doc.govt.nz; Maitai Bay; sites per adult/child $8/4) A large camping ground with chemical toilets and cold showers.

Rusty Anchor (Map p176; ☎ 0800 787 892; www. rustyanchor.co.nz; 1 Tokerau Beach Rd; sites per person $10, dm $25, d/tr/q $65/85/105; 🖳) A one-stop backpackers' haven, with an information centre, a bar, takeaways and a laundromat as part of the complex.

Rockhouse (Map p176; ☎ 09-406 7151; rochousian@clear.net.nz; Inland Rd; s/d/tr $30/50/75) Fred Flintstone meets Hundertwasser at this guest house, just 1km off SH10, which has unusual but comfortable en-suite accommodation.

Whatuwhiwhi Top 10 Holiday Park (☎ 09-408 7202; www.whatuwhiwhitop10.co.nz; 17 Whatuwhiwhi Rd; sites per 2 people $40, units $96-375; 🖳) This camping ground has good facilities, kayaks for hire and a great location – sheltered by hills and overlooking the beach.

White Sands Apartments (☎ 09-408 7080; www. whitesands.co.nz; Rangiputa Beach; units $125-185) Seventies style imbues these comfortable wooden units. There's a shop downstairs and within a few steps your feet will find the white sand.

CAPE REINGA & NINETY MILE BEACH

Maori consider Cape Reinga (Te Rerenga-Wairua) the jumping-off point for souls as they depart on the journey to their spiritual homeland. That makes the Aupouri Peninsula a giant diving board, and it certainly resembles one – long and thin, it reaches 108km to form NZ's northern extremity. On its west coast Ninety Mile Beach (Ninety Kilometre Beach would be more accurate) is a continuous stretch lined with high sand dunes, flanked by the Aupouri Forest.

Sights

Standing at windswept **Cape Reinga lighthouse** and looking out over the ocean gives a real end-of-the-world feeling. This is where the waters of the Tasman Sea and Pacific Ocean meet, breaking together into waves up to 10m high in stormy weather. Little tufts of cloud often cling to the ridges, giving sudden spooky chills even on hot days. Visible on a promontory slightly to the east is a spiritually significant 800-year-old **pohutukawa tree**; souls are believed to slide down its roots. Out of respect to the most sacred site in Maoridom,

don't go near the tree and refrain from eating or drinking anywhere in the area.

Contrary to expectation, Cape Reinga isn't actually the northernmost point of the country; that honour belongs to Surville Cliffs further to the east. A walk along Te Werahi Beach to **Cape Maria van Diemen** (five hours loop) takes you to the westernmost point. This is one of many sections of the three- to four-day, 53km **Cape Reinga Coastal Walkway** (from Kapowairua to Te Paki Stream) that can be tackled individually. Beautiful **Tapotupotu Bay** is a two-hour walk east of Cape Reinga, via Sandy Bay and the cliffs. From Tapotupotu Bay it's an eight-hour walk to the eastern end of **Kapowairua** (Spirits Bay). Both bays are also accessible by road.

A large chunk of the land around Cape Reinga is part of the **Te Paki Recreation Reserve** managed by DOC. It's public land with free access; leave the gates as you found them and don't disturb the animals. There are 7 sq km of giant sand dunes on either side of the mouth of Te Paki Stream. Clamber up to take flying leaps off the dunes or toboggan down them.

On the east coast, **Great Exhibition Bay** has dazzling snow-white silica dunes. There's no public road access, but some tours pay a *koha* (donation) to cross Maori farmland or approach the sand by kayak from Parengarenga Harbour.

Beside the highway at Te Kao, 46km south of Cape Reinga, stands a **Ratana temple** (Map p176; 6576 Far North Rd) known as Nga-Tapuwae-Ote-Mangai (the Sacred Steps of the Mouthpiece). Ratana is a Maori Christian sect with more than 50,000 adherents, formed in 1925 by Tahupotiki Wiremu Ratana, who was known as 'the mouthpiece of God'. This temple is built on land where Ratana once stood. It resembles a mosque, with its two domed towers (Arepa and Omeka, alpha and omega) and the Ratana emblem of the star and crescent moon.

Kauri forests covered this area for over 100,000 years, leaving ancient logs and the much-prized gum (used for making varnish and linoleum) buried beneath. **Gumdiggers Park** (Map p176; ☎ 09-406 7166; www.gumdiggerspark. co.nz; Heath Rd, Waiharara; adult/child $10/5; 🕙 9am-5pm) covers a major gumdigging site – the region's main industry from the 1870s to the 1920s. In 1900, some 7000 gumdiggers (wearing gumboots – the NZ name for Wellingtons) were digging holes all over Northland. Start with the 15-minute video telling the story of the trees, their mysterious destruction and the gum industry. Rope paths head through the bush, leading past reproductions of gumdiggers' huts, ancient kauri stumps and holes left by the diggers. It was a hard life for the workers, who used jute sacks for their tents, bedding and clothing.

It's tacky and overpriced, but **Ancient Kauri Kingdom** (Map p176; ☎ 09-406 7172; www.ancientkauri. co.nz; 229 Far North Rd, Awanui; ⊙ 8.30am-5pm) is still worth a stop. Here 50,000-year-old kauri stumps, dragged up from swamps, are fashioned into furniture, woodcraft products and a fair bit of tourist tat. The large complex includes a cafe, gift shop and workshop. A huge kauri log has an impressive spiral staircase carved into it that takes you to the mezzanine level.

Tours

Bus tours go to Cape Reinga from Kaitaia, Ahipara, Doubtless Bay and the Bay of Islands (see p164). There's no other public transport up here and many car-rental companies prohibit driving on the sands of Ninety Mile Beach or the partly unsealed road north of Waitiki Landing.

Cape Reinga Adventures (☎ 09-409 8445; www. capereingaadventures.co.nz; half-/full-day 4WD trips $75/135) Real action men who offer 4WD tours (including sunset visits to the cape after the crowds have gone), fishing, kayaking, sand-boarding and dune-surfing as day activities or as overnight camping trips ($150 to $220). They also hire kayaks ($60 for 24 hours) and sandboards ($20).

Far North Outback Adventures (☎ 09-408 0927; www.farnorthtours.co.nz) Flexible, day-long tours from Kaitaia/Ahipara for $600 (one to three people) to $650 (four or five people), including morning tea and lunch. You can visit remote areas such as Great Exhibition Bay ($10 per person access fee).

Harrison's Cape Runner (☎ 0800 227 373; www. harrisonscapereingatours.co.nz; 123 North Rd, Kaitaia; adult/child $45/25) Day bus trips that include sand tobogganing and a picnic lunch.

Paradise 4x4 (☎ 0800 494 392; www.paradisenz.co.nz; for 2 $600, per additional person $50) Operates flexible, exclusive 4WD tours from Doubtless Bay up Ninety Mile Beach to Cape Reinga, including Devonshire tea and gourmet lunch with local wine. Hokianga tours also available.

Sand Safaris (☎ 0800 869 090; www.sandsafaris.co.nz; adult/child $55/30) A family-owned operation running coach trips, including a picnic lunch and a guided tour of Gumdiggers Park.

Sleeping & Eating

Unless you're a happy camper you won't find much decent accommodation north of Pukenui. Literally 'Big Stomach', it's also the best place to fill yours; you'll find a cafe, takeaways and grocery store. The only other options are unremarkable eateries at Ancient Kauri Kingdom (left), Houhora Heads and Waitiki Landing.

DOC campsites (Map p176; sites per adult/child $7.50/3.50) There are stunningly positioned sites at Kapowairua, Tapotupotu Bay and Rarawa Beach. Only water and toilet facilities are provided. Bring a cooker, as fires are not allowed, and plenty of repellent to ward off the evil mosquitoes and sandflies. 'Freedom/Leave No Trace' camping is allowed along the Cape Reinga Coastal Walkway.

Ninety Mile Beach Top 10 Holiday Park (Map p176; ☎ 09-406 7298; www.ninetymilebeach.co.nz; 6 Matai St, Waipapakauri; sites per person $16, cabins $80-110; 💻) Rows of tidy units line the sunburnt grass at this well-positioned holiday park, within earshot of Ninety Mile Beach's roaring surf.

Pukenui Lodge Motel (☎ 09-409 8837; www.pukenui lodge.co.nz; cnr SH1 & Wharf Rd, Pukenui; dm/r $25/65, units $115-170; 💻 🖳) This clean, welcoming backpackers occupies a historic villa (1891) filled with mismatched furniture and an ancient TV. It's a more charming prospect than the bog-standard motel units.

North Wind Lodge Backpackers (Map p176; ☎ 09-409 8515; www.northwind.co.nz; 88 Otaipango Rd, Henderson Bay; dm/tw/d/tr $27/58/64/84) Six kilometres down an unsealed road on the peninsula's east side, this unusual turreted house offers a homely environment and plenty of quiet spots on the lawn to sit with a beer and a book.

Getting There & Around

Apart from numerous tours, there's no public transport past Pukenui, which is linked to Kaitaia ($5, 45 minutes) by **Busabout Kaitaia** (☎ 09-408 1092; www.cbec.co.nz).

Far North Rd (SH1F) is sealed as far as Waitiki Landing. The final 7km are currently being sealed, starting from Cape Reinga and heading backwards. This project isn't expected to be completed until 2012; prepare for delays. At the end of the road there's a 1km walk from the car park to the lighthouse.

The other major route is Ninety Mile Beach itself, suited to rugged vehicles. Cars have been known to hit soft sand and be swallowed by the tides – look out for unfortunate vehicles

---

NGATI TARARA

As you're travelling around the north you might notice the preponderance of road names ending in '-ich'. *Haere mai, dobro došli* and welcome (as the sign leading into Kaitaia proclaims) to one of the more peculiar ethnic conjunctions in the country.

From the end of the 19th century, men from the Dalmatian coast of Croatia started arriving in NZ looking for work. Many ended up in Northland's gum fields. Pakeha society wasn't particularly welcoming to the new immigrants, particularly during WWI – they were considered Austrians. Not so in the small Maori communities of the north. Here they found an echo of Dalmatian village life, with its emphasis on extended family and hospitality, not to mention a shared history of injustice at the hands of colonial powers.

The Maori jokingly named them Tarara, as their rapid conversation in Serbo-Croat sounded like 'ta-ra-ra-ra-ra' to Maori ears. Many Croatian men married local *wahine* (women), founding clans that have left several of today's famous Maori with Croatian surnames, like singer Margaret Urlich and former All Black Frano Botica. You'll find large Tarara communities in the Far North, Dargaville and West Auckland.

---

poking through the sands. Check tide times before setting out; avoid it 2½ hours either side of high tide. Watch out for 'quicksand' at Te Paki Stream – keep moving. If you get stuck, your hire-car insurance won't cover you. Enquire at Tuatua Tours (opposite) about 4WD hire.

Fill up with petrol before hitting the Aupouri Peninsula. The petrol station at Waitiki Landing has been known to run out.

KAITAIA
pop 5300

Nobody comes to the Far North to hang out in this provincial town, but it's a handy stop if you're after a supermarket, a post office or an ATM. It's also a jumping-off point for tours to Cape Reinga and Ninety Mile Beach (see p181).

The **Far North i-SITE** (☎ 09-408 0879; www.topofnz.co.nz; Jaycee Park, South Rd; ⊙ 8.30am-5pm) has internet access and information on the region. Nearby, the **Far North Regional Museum** (☎ 09-408 1403; www.farnorthmuseum.co.nz; 6 South Rd; adult/child $4/1; ⊙ 10am-4pm) has an eclectic mix of exhibits focusing on local history, including a massive 1769 anchor.

Just south of Kaitaia, off the road to Ahipara, **Okahu Estate Winery** (Map p176; ☎ 09-408 2066; www.okahuestate.co.nz; cnr Okahu & Awaroa Rds; ⊙ noon-4pm Mon-Fri) offers free tastings.

The friendly owners of **Mainstreet Lodge** (☎ 09-408 1275; www.mainstreetlodge.co.nz; 235 Commerce St; dm $26-30, s $55-70, d $62-75, tr $87-99, q $112-128; 🖳 🛜) know the area inside-out. Maori carvings abound at this groovy old cottage, which has a modern purpose-built wing facing the rear courtyard.

Beachcomber (☎ 09-408 2010; 222 Commerce St; mains $16-32; ⊙ 11am-late Mon-Sat) is easily the best place to eat in town, with a wide range of seafood and meatier fare, all deftly executed, and a well-stocked salad bar.

The airport is 6km north of town, and **Air New Zealand** (☎ 0800 737 000; www.airnz.co.nz) offers daily flights between Kaitaia and Auckland (45 minutes, check website for prices).

Alternatively, **InterCity** (☎ 09-623 1503; www.intercity.co.nz) buses stop at the i-SITE, travelling to Mangonui ($21, 40 minutes) and Kerikeri ($33, 1½ hours). **Busabout Kaitaia** (☎ 09-408 1092; www.cbec.co.nz) has services to Doubtless Bay ($5, one hour), Pukenui ($5, 45 minutes) and Ahipara ($3.50, 15 minutes).

AHIPARA
pop 1200

All good things must come to an end, and Ninety Mile Beach does it at this spunky beach town. A few holiday mansions have snuck in, but mostly it's just the locals keeping it real, rubbing shoulders with visiting surfers. The area is known for its huge sand dunes and massive gum field, where 2000 people once worked. Sand tobogganing and quad-bike rides are popular activities on the dunes above Ahipara and further around the Tauroa Peninsula.

Activities

Ahipara Adventure Centre (☎ 09-409 2055; www.ahiparaadventure.co.nz; 15 Takahe St) hires out sand- and surfboards ($10 per hour), mountain bikes ($25 per hour), kayaks ($25 per hour), blokarts for sand yachting ($60 per hour) and quad bikes ($70 per hour).

Tuatua Tours (☎ 09-409 4875; www.tuatuatours.com; 250 Ahipara Rd; 2hr ride per person $135, 2 people $150) gets great word-of-mouth for its reef- and dune-rider tours and *Ultimate Sand Dune Safaris* (three hours including sand tobogganing, per one/two people $185/200). You can hire a 4WD ($280 per day) to explore Ninety Mile Beach at your own pace without risking the wrath of regular hire companies.

Another option for exploring the beach is on horseback. **Ahipara Treks** (☎ 09-409 4122; ahiparahorsetreks@xtra.co.nz) offers one- to five-hour beach canters ($60 to $150), including some farm and ocean riding (when the surf permits). Surf and ride packages are another option ($180).

Sleeping & Eating

90 Mile Beach Ahipara Holiday Park (☎ 09-409 4864; www.ahiparaholidaypark.co.nz; 168 Takahe St; sites per person $16, dm/r $28/75, cabins $55-90, units $125-145; ▣) There's a large range of accommodation on offer at this holiday park, including cabins, motel units and a worn but perfectly presentable YHA-affiliated backpackers' lodge. The communal hall has an open fire and colourful murals.

our pick **Endless Summer Lodge** (☎ 09-409 4181; www.endlesssummer.co.nz; 245 Foreshore Rd; dm $28, d $68-80; ▣) Across from the beach, this superb kauri villa (1880) has been beautifully restored and converted into the Far North's best hostel. There's no TV, which encourages bonding around the long table on the vine-covered back terrace. Free boogie boards and sandboards are available, and surfboards can be hired ($20). Book ahead or be very sorry.

Beach Abode (☎ 09-409 4070; www.beachabode.co.nz; 11 Korora St; apt $125-185; ☎) Wander through the subtropical garden to the beachfront from your self-contained studio or two-bedroom apartment, or just lie in bed and lose yourself in the view.

Beachfront (☎ 09-409 4007; www.beachfront.net.nz; 14 Kotare St; apt $175-360) Who cares if it's a bit bourgeois for Ahipara? These two upmarket, self-contained apartments have stunning views and there's direct access to the beach. Both sleep up to six people.

Bidz Takeaways (☎ 09-409 4727; Takahe St; meals $5-11; ◷ 8.30am-8pm) You'll need a flip-top head to fit Bidz' seafood burger ($11) into your mouth – it's jam-packed with battered oysters, scallops, mussels and fish. Bidz also has a store attached.

Gumdiggers Cafe (☎ 09-409 2012; 3 Ahipara Rd; meals $6-16; ◷ 8am-7pm Easter-Christmas, 7.30am-10pm Christmas-Easter) Good coffee and tasty treats are the hallmarks of this funky little cafe, owned by the people who run Sand Safaris (p181).

Getting There & Around

Busabout Kaitaia (☎ 09-408 1092; www.cbec.co.nz) runs services from Kaitaia ($3.50, 15 minutes).

HOKIANGA

The Hokianga Harbour stretches out its skinny tentacles to become the fourth-biggest in the country. Its ruggedly beautiful landscape is painted in every shade of green and brown. The water itself is rendered the colour of ginger ale by the bush streams that feed it.

Of all the remote parts of Northland, this is the pocket that feels the most removed from the mainstream. Pretension has no place here. Isolated, predominantly Maori communities nestle around the harbour's many inlets as they have done for centuries. Discovered by legendary explorer Kupe, it's been settled by Ngapuhi since the 14th century. Hippies settled in the late 1960s and their legacy is a thriving little artistic scene.

Many of the roads remain unsealed and in poor repair after decades of neglect from government bodies. Tourism dollars are channelled eastward to the Bay of Islands, leaving this truly fascinating corner of the country remarkably undeveloped, which is the way many of the locals like it.

EASTERN HOKIANGA
Puketi & Omahuta Forests

Inland from the eastern reaches of the harbour, the Puketi and Omahuta Forests form a continuous expanse of native bush. Logging in Puketi was stopped in 1951 to protect not only the remaining kauri but also the endangered kokako bird. Keep an eye out for this rare charmer (grey with a blue wattle) on your wanders.

The forests are reached by several entrances and contain a network of walking tracks varying in length from 15 minutes (the wheelchair-accessible Manginangina kauri walk) to two days (the challenging Waipapa River track). You'll find a **DOC campsite** (☎ 09-407 0300; www.doc.govt.nz; Waiare Rd; sites per adult/child $7/3.50), three-person cabins ($20) and

NGAWHA SPRINGS

Near Kaikohe, these hot springs have been used by Ngapuhi for their curative powers since the 17th century. Hone Heke brought his injured warriors here during the Northland War.

Unlike many of NZ's thermal resorts, there are no hydroslides or big pools for the kids to splash about in. There aren't even any showers. Here it's all about stewing in the murky water in small pools of varying temperatures. Ngawha has two complexes next to each other, the better of which is **Ngawha Springs Pools** (☎ 09-405 2245; adult/child $4/2; ☽ 9am-9pm).

24-bunk hut (exclusive use $60) at Puketi Recreation Area on the forests' eastern fringe. The hut has hot showers, a kitchen and a flush toilet, while the cabins and campsite make do with cold showers.

See the DOC website for other walk options.

Horeke

Tiny Horeke was NZ's second European settlement after Russell. A Wesleyan mission operated here from 1828 to 1855. In 1840, 3000 Ngapuhi gathered here for what was the single biggest signing of the Treaty of Waitangi.

Completed in 1839, **Mangungu Mission House** (☎ 09-401 9640; www.historic.org.nz; Motukiore Rd; adult/child $3/1; ☽ noon-4pm Sat & Sun) is a sweet wooden cottage with relics of the missionaries and Horeke's shipbuilding past. In the grounds you'll see a large stone cross and a simple wooden church. You'll find it 1km down the unsealed road leading along the harbour from Horeke village.

Wairere Boulders Nature Park (☎ 09-401 9935; www.wairereboulders.co.nz; McDonnell Rd; adult/child $10/5; ☽ daylight hr) resembles a Jurassic Zen garden. Paths lead around and over massive basalt rock formations that have been eroded into odd fluted shapes by the acidity of ancient kauri forests. The main loop takes about 40 minutes and follows a burbling Coca-Cola–coloured stream. It's a good path, but wear sensible shoes and expect a few ducks and climbs. An additional hour leads through rainforest to a platform at the end of the boulder valley. The park is sign-

posted from SH1 and Horeke; the last 3km are unsealed.

You'll feel like lord of the manor in **Riverhead Guest House** (☎ 09-401 9610; www.hokianga.co.nz/riverheadguesthouse; Main Rd; s/d/tr $75/95/130), an 1871 kauri villa with old-world furnishings literally looking down on Horeke. The cheaper upstairs rooms share a bathroom, but the harbour views more than compensate.

NORTHERN HOKIANGA
Kohukohu
pop 190

Quick, someone slap a preservation order on Kohukohu before it's too late. There can be few places in NZ where a Victorian village full of interesting kauri buildings has been so completely preserved with nary a modern monstrosity to be seen. During the height of the kauri industry it was a busy town with a sawmill, shipyard, two newspapers and banks. These days it's a very quiet backwater on the north side of Hokianga Harbour, 4km from the car ferry (opposite).

ourpick Tree House (☎ 09-405 5855; www.treehouse.co.nz; 168 West Coast Rd; sites per person $18, dm $30-38, s/d $66/76) is a fantastic place with helpful hosts and brightly painted little cottages set among exotic fruit and nut trees. This quiet retreat is 2km from the ferry terminus (turn sharp left as you come off the ferry). You can sleep in an old school bus ($26 to $40 per person), wander the macadamia orchard or just sink into beanbags in the communal lounge.

Waterline Cafe (☎ 09-405 5552; meals $8-18; ☽ breakfast & lunch daily, dinner Fri & Sat) serves superb food, including interesting pizzas and burgers, from a building jutting over the water. The chairs look like they've been raided from an old school, and newspaper clippings about the town are imbedded in the tables.

We're assured that the cheese-makers are indeed blessed at **Waitawa Farm** (Map p176; ☎ 09-409 5809; www.farmstaynz.co.nz; 164 Pukemiro Rd, Broadwood; s $60, d $70-80), a working dairy and sheep farm offering accommodation and cheese-making courses (four to six people, $250).

There are no regular bus services, but you might be able to arrange to jump off a Crossings Hokianga (p164) bus from Paihia and continue the tour at a later date; call to enquire. Kohukohu is connected to Rawene by a car ferry (opposite).

Mitimiti

The tiny community at Mitimiti, which consists of only 30 families and not even a shop, has the ruggedly beautiful 20km stretch of coast between the Hokianga and Whangape Harbours all to itself. The 40km drive from Kohukohu via Panguru (14km of it unsealed), is quite an experience: prepare to dodge cows, sheep, potholes and kids.

About halfway along, it's worth a short detour to visit **St Mary's Church** (Motuti Rd), where NZ's first Catholic bishop is buried beneath the altar. Jean Baptiste Pompallier arrived in the Hokianga in 1838, celebrating NZ's first Mass at Totara Point. He was interred here in 2002 after an emotional 14-week pilgrimage full of Maori ceremony brought his remains back from France.

Sandtrails Hokianga (☎ 09-409 5035; wwwsand trailshokianga.co.nz; 32 Paparangi Dr) offers an inside perspective on Mitimiti's tight-knit Maori community, with two-hour Sandscapes dune buggy tours, which head 12km along the beach to the giant dunes that form the harbour's north head (adult/child $135/60), or personally tailored tours staying overnight in the guide's house (adult $395).

Mitimiti Beach House (☎ 09-409 5347; www.beach -house.co.nz; 3881 West Coast Rd; s/d/tr/q $100/130/150/180; 🖳) is a self-contained three-bedroom bach, sleeping up to eight ($25 per additional person). It's a comfortable base for exploring the often-deserted beach.

RAWENE

pop 440

Founded shortly after Horeke, Rawene was NZ's third European settlement. There is still a surprising number of historic buildings (including six churches) from a time when the harbour was considerably busier than it is now. There aren't any ATMs or banks, but you can get petrol here.

A heritage trail complete with information boards tours the main sights. **Clendon House** (☎ 09-405 7874; www.historic.org.nz; Clendon Esplanade; adult/child $5/2.50; 🕒 10am-4pm Sat-Mon Nov-Apr, 10am-4pm Mon & Tue May-Oct) was built in the bustling 1860s by James Clendon, a trader, shipowner and magistrate. After his death, his 34-year-old half-Maori widow Jane was left with a brood of kids and a whopping £5000 debt. She managed to clear the debt and her descendants remained in the house until 1972, when it passed to the Historic Places Trust.

Quirky **Outpost Hokianga** (☎ 09-405 7423; 5 Parnell St) stocks local art, crafts, clothing, music, cosmetics and both second-hand and new books. Across the road **Hokianga Art Gallery** (☎ 09-405 7899; hokiangaartgallery@hotmail.com; 2 Parnell St; 🕒 Wed-Sun 10am-3pm) sells interesting contemporary art, also with a local focus.

Sleeping

Rawene Motor Camp (☎ 09-405 7720; www.rawene motorcamp.co.nz; 1 Marmon St; sites per adult/child $14/7, dm $18, cabins $40-80; 🖳 🖳) Sheltered tent sites hide in the bush at this nicely managed caravan park. The cabins are simple, with one converted into a bunkroom for backpackers. Linen is extra.

Postmaster's Lodgings (☎ 09-405 7676; www. thepostmasterslodgings.co.nz; 3 Parnell St; d $100-120, tr $125-145; 🖭) Comfortable high-ceilinged rooms, four-poster beds, rolled-end leather couches and a wraparound veranda are all part of the old-world charm offered in this kauri villa.

Hokianga Blue (☎ 09-405 7675; wicked1s@xtra.co.nz; 49 Parnell St; d/tr $110/135) Offers a studio apartment with harbour views and a kitchenette. It's on the main road leading into town.

Old Lane's Store Homestay (☎ 09-405 7554; 9 Clendon Esplanade; r $120) Right by the harbour, accommodation is offered in a self-contained apartment above the historic store. If you're after a glam cocktail dress, check out the owner's workshop downstairs.

Eating & Drinking

Wardy's (☎ 09-405 7717; 12 Parnell St; 🕒 11am-6.30pm Mon-Fri, 11am-2pm Sat & Sun) At Wardy's you can stock up on (mainly) organic fruit, vegetables and meat.

Boatshed Cafe (☎ 09-405 7728; 8 Clendon Esplanade; mains $6-17; 🕒 8.30am-4pm) You can eat overlooking the water at this excellent cafe, a cute place with heart-warming food and a gift shop.

Masonic Hotel (☎ 09-405 7822; 8 Parnell St) The local pub, with occasional live country-and-western music.

Getting There & Away

The **car ferry** (☎ 09-405 2602; car & driver one way/ return $14/19, passenger $2/4; 🕒 7.30am-7.30pm) heads to northern Hokianga, docking near Kohukohu at least hourly. You can buy your ticket for this 15-minute ride on board. It usually leaves Rawene on the half-hour and the north side on the hour. There are no regular bus services, but Magic Travellers Network (p172) and Crossings Hokianga (p164) have tourist buses.

OPONONI & OMAPERE

pop 500

These tranquil settlements near the south head of Hokianga Harbour more or less run into one another. The water's much clearer here and good for swimming. Views are dominated by the mountainous sand dunes across the water at **North Head**.

The **Hokianga i-SITE** (☎ 09-405 8869; hokianga@ visitnorthland.co.nz; SH12, Opononi; ☼ 9am-5.30pm) has internet access.

Activities

The **Hokianga Kai Iwi Coastal Track** leads south along the coast from the **Arai-Te-Uru Recreation Reserve** (Signal Station Rd), on the South Head of Hokianga Harbour. It's three hours to Kaikai Beach, six hours to Kawerua and 12 hours to the Kerr Rd exit, or you can tramp the entire 15 hours (allow about three days) to Kai Iwi Lakes. Hikers must carry all their own water and food, and cross the major rivers within two hours either side of low tide. It's usually possible to camp on the beach. DOC advises that you check with them before setting out, particularly to discuss the river crossings.

From Cemetery Rd on the eastern outskirts of Opononi, a half-hour climb leads up **Mt Whiria**, a *pa* site with harbour views.

Two kilometres east of Opononi, Waiotemarama Gorge Rd turns south for 6km to the **Waiotemarama Waterfall Loop Walk**, which passes kauri and a picturesque waterfall. From the top of the loop you can detour on the Hauturu Highpoint Track which climbs Mt Hauturu (679m). It's a five-hour walk to the summit and back again. On the road to the walks you'll pass **Labyrinth Woodworks** (☎ 09-405 4581; 647 Waiotemarama Gorge Rd; www.nzanity.co.nz; maze $4; ☼ 9am-5pm), an Aladdin's cave of handmade puzzles and games. Crack the code in the outdoor maze by collecting letters to form a word.

The **Six Foot Track** at the end of Mountain Rd gives access to many Waima Forest walks.

Tours

Hokianga Express (☎ 09-405 8872; adult/child $25/15) leaves from Opononi Jetty and takes you across the harbour to the large golden sand dunes, where you can sandboard down a 30m

slope and skim over the water. Boats leave on the hour, on demand; board provided.

Sandtrails Hokianga (☎ 09-409 5035; www. sandtrailshokianga.co.nz; 32 Paparangi Dr, Mitimiti) collects you from Opononi for a dune buggy tour to Mitimiti (3¾ hours, adult/child $220/105) or a 70-minute Sandsecrets tour (adult/ child $110/55); prices include the Hokianga Express.

Footprints Waipoua (☎ 0800 687 836; www.foot-printswaipoua.co.nz; adult/child $95/35) is a four-hour twilight tour led by Maori guides into Waipoua Kauri Forest (opposite). As an introduction to Maori culture, it's fantastic. Tribal history and stories are shared, and mesmerising *karakia* recited before the giant trees. A (child-friendly) shorter version is offered (90 minutes, adult/child $70/35), as well as guided daytime visits, meeting at the Tane Mahuta car park ($25).

Sleeping & Eating

Each of these neighbouring villages has its own superette and takeaways.

OPONONI

Okopako Lodge Farm Hostel (☎ /fax 09-405 8815; 140 Mountain Rd; sites per adult/child $12/5, dm/s/d $25/42/54) High up in the bush 5km east of Opononi and 1.5km down a gravel road, this simple hostel is quiet and suited to hikers (the Six Foot Track starts here). It was for sale at the time of research, so call ahead.

Opononi Hotel (☎ 09-405 8858; www.opononihotel. com; SH12; s $114, d $114-129, tr $134-150, q $172) The old Opononi pub has reinvented itself into elegant accommodation. The rooms aren't huge, but the white-paint and blond-wood makeover has left them quietly stylish. Try to grab one of the front two – they're a bit bigger and have the best views. Otherwise aim for those facing away from the very cool pub (open 9am till late), which also happens to be the best spot to eat down this end (meals $18 to $26).

Opononi Lighthouse Motel (☎ 09-405 8824; www. lighthousemotel.co.nz; SH12; d/tr/q $140/165/195; ☐) Scrupulously clean, this refurbished motel has very comfortable harbour-side units, plus a great communal barbecue, a spa pool, and a cutesy lighthouse and waterfall in the front garden.

OMAPERE

GlobeTrekkers Lodge (☎ 09-405 8183; www.globe trekkerslodge.com; SH12; dm $26/60, f $76-96; ☐) This home-style lodge is ideally placed to put you in touch with myriad local activities, or you can just relax and unwind in casual style.

Ti Kouka B&B (☎ 09-405 8622; tikouka@xtra.co.nz; 68 Signal Station Rd; r $100) Look forward to nights in red satin (bedding) in this hilltop house with views straight through the heads. The room opens on to a beautiful garden at the bottom of the house.

Hokianga Haven B&B (☎ 09-405 8285; www. hokiangahaven.co.nz; 226 SH12; r $160) This modern house with original Kiwi art on the walls offers spacious accommodation on the harbour's edge and glorious views of the sand dunes. Alternative healing therapies can be arranged.

Copthorne Hotel & Resort (☎ 09-405 8737; www. omapere.co.nz; SH12; d $169-350, tr $204-385; 🛜 🖵) Despite the original grand Victorian villa being violated by aluminium joinery, this waterside complex remains an attractive spot for a summer's drink or bistro meal ($13 to $30). A modern wing has smart units; the more expensive have terraces and water views.

Getting There & Away

There's no regular public transport to Opononi, but Magic Travellers Network (p172) and Crossings Hokianga (p164) are options.

KAURI COAST

Apart from the odd bluff and river, this coast is basically unbroken and undeveloped for the 110km between the Hokianga and Kaipara harbours. The main reason for coming here is to marvel at the kauri forests, one of the great natural highlights of NZ. This is one for the chubby chasers of the tree-hugging fraternity – you'd need 8m arms to get them around some of the big boys here.

HOKIANGA TO DARGAVILLE

Here's where most of the action lies. If you're planning to stay overnight, bring your own food as there are few stores or restaurants between Opononi and Dargaville, and no ATMs. Trampers should check DOC's website for walks in the area (www.doc.govt.nz); see also Hokianga Kai Iwi Coastal Track (opposite).

Waipoua Kauri Forest

The highlight of Northland's west coast, this superb forest sanctuary – proclaimed in 1952

after much public pressure – is the largest remnant of the once-extensive kauri forests of northern NZ. The forest road (SH12) stretches for 18km and passes some huge trees – a kauri can reach 60m in height and have a trunk 5m in diameter.

Control of the forest has recently been returned to Te Roroa, the local *iwi* (tribe), as part of a settlement for Crown breaches of the Treaty of Waitangi. Te Roroa runs the **Waipoua Forest visitor centre** (☎ 09-439 6445; www. teroroa.iwi.nz; 1 Waipoua River Rd; 🕑 9am-6.30pm summer, 9am-4.30pm winter) and camping ground near the south end of the park.

SIGHTS & ACTIVITIES

Near the north end of the park, not far from the road, stands mighty **Tane Mahuta**, named for the Maori forest god. At 51m, with a 13.8m girth and wood mass of 244.5 cubic metres, he's the largest kauri alive. You don't so much look at Tane Mahuta; it's as if you're granted an audience to his hushed presence. He's been holding court here for somewhere between 1200 and 2000 years.

A little further south a short road leads to the Kauri Walks car park. Theft from cars has been a problem and the car park is often guarded ($2 donation suggested). From here, a 20-minute (each way) walk leads to **Te Matua Ngahere** (the Father of the Forest). Even the most ardent tree-hugger wouldn't consider rushing forward to throw their arms around him and call him 'Daddy', even if there wasn't a fence. At 30m he's shorter than Tane Mahuta, but he has the same noble presence, reinforced by his substantial girth – he's the widest living kauri (16.4m). He presides over a clearing surrounded by mature trees that look like matchsticks in comparison.

Close by are the **Four Sisters**, a graceful stand of four tall trees that have fused together at the base. A 40-minute walk leads to **Yakas**, the seventh-largest kauri.

Near the very south end of the park there's a turn-off to a **forest lookout** that offers spectacular views. The 10-minute **Toatoa viewpoint walk** is 1km further on.

SLEEPING & EATING

Waipoua Forest Campground (☎ 09-439 6445; www.tero roa.iwi.nz; 1 Waipoua River Rd; sites per adult/child $14/7, cabin s/tw/tr/q $15/50/60/80, house $175) Situated next to the Waipoua River and the visitor centre, this peaceful camping ground offers hot showers, flush toilets and a kitchen. The cabins are DOC-style – spartan, with unmade swab beds (bring your own linen or hire it).

Waipoua Lodge B&B (☎ 09-439 0422; www.waipoua lodge.co.nz; SH12; r incl breakfast $570-590; 🛜) This fine old villa at the southern edge of the forest has four luxurious, spacious suites, which were originally the stables, the woolshed and the calf-rearing pen! Decadent dinners ($90) are available.

Morrell's Cafe (☎ 09-405 4545; 7235 SH12, Waimamaku; mains $8-14; 🕤 9am-4pm) Perhaps this is where Hokianga's hippies ended up. This bright-yellow cafe and craft shop serves up tasty snacks in a former cheese factory near the north end of the forest.

Trounson Kauri Park

The 450-hectare Trounson Kauri Park has an easy half-hour walk leading from the picnic area by the road. It passes through beautiful forest with streams, some fine kauri stands, a couple of fallen trees and another Four Sisters – two pairs of trees with conjoined trunks. DOC operates a **campsite** (sites per adult/child $10/5) at the edge of the park, which has a communal kitchen and hot showers.

Just 2km from SH12, **Kauri Coast Top 10 Holiday Park** (☎ 09-439 0621; www.kauricoasttop10. co.nz; Trounson Park Rd; sites per person $25, units $70-180; 🖳) is an attractive riverside camping ground with good facilities and a small shop. It also organises night-time **nature walks** (adult/child $20/12), which explain the flora and nocturnal wildlife that thrives here. This is a rare chance to see a kiwi in the wild. Trounson has a predator-eradication program and has become a mainland refuge for threatened native bird species, so you should at least hear a morepork (a native owl) or a brown kiwi.

If you're approaching from the north it's easier to take the second turn-off to the park, near Kaihu, which avoids a rough unsealed road.

Kai Iwi Lakes

These three trout-filled freshwater lakes nestle near the coast, 12km off SH12. The largest, Taharoa, has blue water fringed with sandy patches and pine trees. Lake Waikere is popular with water-skiers, while Lake Kai Iwi is relatively untouched. A half-hour walk leads from the lakes to the coast and it's another two

hours to reach the base of volcanic Maunganui Bluff (460m); the hike up and down it takes five hours.

Camping (☎ 09-439 0986; lakes@kaipara.govt.nz; adult/ child $10/5) is permitted among the pines at the side of Lake Taharoa; cold showers, drinking water and flush toilets are provided.

Baylys Beach

A village of brightly coloured baches and a few new holiday mansions, Baylys Beach is 12km from Dargaville, off SH12. It lies on 100km-long Ripiro Ocean Beach, a surf-pounded stretch of coast that has been the site of many shipwrecks. The beach is a gazetted highway: you can drive along its hard sand at low tide, although it is primarily for 4WDs. Despite being NZ's longest drivable beach, it's less well known and hence less travelled than Ninety Mile Beach. Ask locals about conditions and check your hire-car agreement before venturing onto the sand. Quad bikes can be hired at the holiday park.

It's pretty kooky, but **Skydome Observatory** (☎ 09-439 1856; www.skydome.org.nz; 28 Seaview Rd; stargazing $20-40) is a massive, technologically advanced telescope and it's located on the front lawn of someone's house. Call ahead for bookings.

A midsized camping ground, **Baylys Beach Holiday Park** (☎ 09-439 6349; www.baylysbeach.co.nz; 24 Seaview Rd; sites per adult/child $15/8, cabins $50-110, units $90-180; 🖳) has good management and facilities, and quad bikes for hire ($75 to $95 per hour).

If gin-in-hand sunset-gazing is your thing, **Sunset View Lodge** (☎ 09-439 4342; www.sunsetview lodge.co.nz; Alcemene Lane; r $150-175; 🖳 🐾), a large, modern B&B, fits the bill. The upstairs rooms have terrific sea views and there's a self-service bar with an honesty box in the guest lounge.

At **Sharky's** (☎ 09-439 4549; 1 Seaview Rd; meals $6-17; 🕤 breakfast, lunch & dinner), a handy combination of bottle shop, general store, bar and takeaway, quick snacks and all-day breakfasts are the order of the day.

Brightly decorated with murals and mosaics **Funky Fish** (☎ 09-439 8883; 34 Seaview Rd; lunch $11-16, dinner $18-30; 🕤 11am-late Tue-Sun) is a highly popular restaurant, cafe and bar with a wide-ranging menu, although the fish dishes are the standouts. Bookings are advisable in summer.

A taxi to Baylys Beach from Dargaville should cost around $25.

DARGAVILLE

pop 4500

When a town proclaims itself the 'kumara capital of NZ' (it produces two-thirds of the country's sweet potatoes), you should know not to expect too much. Founded in 1872 by timber merchant Joseph Dargaville, this once-important river port thrived on the export of kauri timber and gum. As the forests were decimated, it declined and today is a quiet backwater servicing the agricultural Northern Wairoa area.

Information

DOC Kauri Coast Area Office (☎ 09-439 3450; 150 Colville Rd; 8am-4.30pm Mon-Fri)

Post office (80 Victoria St)

Visitor information centre (☎ 09-439 8360; www.kauriinfocentre.co.nz; 4 Murdoch St; 9am-6pm;) Operates out of the interesting Woodturners Kauri Gallery & Working Studio. Books accommodation and tours.

Sights & Activities

Perched on top of a hill, the **Dargaville Museum** (☎ 09-439 7555; www.dargavillemuseum.co.nz; adult/child $10/2; 9am-4pm) is more interesting than most. There's a large gumdigging display, plus maritime, Maori and musical-instrument sections and a neat model railway. Outside, the masts of the *Rainbow Warrior* (see the boxed text, p177) are mounted on a lookout near a *pa* site.

In the centre of town, **Taha Awa Riverside Gardens** has cool stuff for the kids, including a playground shaped like a tall ship and a whale jawbone. You'll also find a fernery, and swamp, coastal and scented gardens. The 5km **Historic River Walk** starts its loop here; pick up a brochure from the information centre and follow the yellow signs up to the museum.

If you want to learn more about the district's knobbly purple claim-to-fame, catch Kumara Ernie's show at the **Kumara Box** (☎ 09-439 1813; www.kumarabox.co.nz; 503 Pouto Rd; tours $15, bookings essential) – it's surprisingly entertaining.

Sleeping & Eating

Greenhouse Backpackers (☎ 09-439 6342; greenhouse backpackers@ihug.co.nz; 15 Gordon St; dm/d $23/56;) This converted 1921 schoolhouse has classrooms partitioned into large dorms, cosy units in the back garden and colourful, school-like murals.

McLeans B&B (☎ 09-439 5915; mcleans@igrin.co.nz; 136 Hokianga Rd; s/d $50/90) Guests share a large upstairs lounge in this spacious 1934 house,

decorated with antique plates and lacy bedspreads. The affable hosts provide breakfast, tea-making facilities and yummy biscuits.

Blah, Blah, Blah... (☎ 09-439 6300; 101 Victoria St; breakfast $6-20, lunch $8-28, dinner $20-28; breakfast & lunch daily, dinner Tue-Sat) The number-one eatery in Dargaville (admittedly that's not saying much) has a garden area, hip music, deli-style snacks, a global menu (dukkha, nachos, steak) and cocktails.

Self-caterers should head to **Woolworths** supermarket (129 Victoria St; 7am-9pm). Pop into the **Central Hotel** (☎ 09-439 8034; cnr Victoria & Edward Sts) if you feel like a handle of something cold in a straight-up NZ pub.

Getting There & Away

The main bus stop is in Kapia St. **Main Coachline** (☎ 09-278 8070; www.maincoachline.co.nz) runs six buses per week to and from Auckland ($48, three hours) via Matakohe ($18, 35 minutes). A private operator runs a **Whangarei-to-Dargaville Shuttle** (☎ 021 380 187; trip $10) on weekdays. Magic Travellers Network (p172) is an option if you're coming from Paihia, Rawene or Opononi and continuing on to Matakohe or Auckland.

POUTO POINT

A narrow spit descends south of Dargaville, bordered by the Tasman Sea and Wairoa River, and comes to an abrupt halt at the entrance of Kaipara Harbour, NZ's biggest. It's an incredibly remote headland, punctuated by dozens of petite dune lakes and the lonely **Kaipara Lighthouse** (built from kauri in 1884). Less than 10km separates Kaipara Harbour's north and south heads, but if you were to drive between the two you'd cover 267km.

A 4WD can be put to its proper use on the ocean-hugging 71km stretch of beach from Dargaville to **Pouto Point**. DOC's *Pouto Hidden Treasures* pamphlet has a helpful guide for motorists, with tips for protecting both your car and the fragile ecosystem. The inland road is a similar distance but it's winding and partly unsealed. If you'd rather not risk getting stuck, **Taylor Made Tours** (☎ 09-439 1576; www.taylormade tours.co.nz; tour $95) run guided excursions.

Lighthouse Lodge B&B (☎ 09-439 5150; www.light house-lodge.co.nz; 6577 Pouto Rd; d $350, ste $350-450;) is a contemporary building in a remote spot, with bright, stylish rooms with verandas and sea views. Meals and tours can be arranged on request.

MATAKOHE

pop 400

Matakohe's a sweet village on one of the Kaipara's many inlets. Apart from its rural charms, the reason for visiting is the superb **Kauri Museum** (☎ 09-431 7417; www.kaurimuseum.com; 5 Church Rd; adult/child $15/3; ⌚ 9am-5pm). The giant cross-sections of trees are astounding in themselves, but the entire industry is brought to light through life-sized reproductions of a pioneer sawmill, boarding house, gumdigger's hut and Victorian home – along with photos, artefacts, and fabulous furniture and marquetry. The Gum Room holds a weird and wonderful collection of kauri gum, the amber substance that can be carved, sculpted and polished to a jewel-like quality. The museum shop stocks mementoes crafted from kauri wood and gum.

Facing the museum is the tiny kauri-built **Matakohe Pioneer Church** (1867), which served both Methodists and Anglicans, and acted as the community's hall and school. Nearby, you can wander through a historic **school house** (1878) and **post office/telephone exchange** (1909).

Sleeping & Eating

Matakohe Top 10 Holiday Park (☎ 09-431 6431; www.matakohetop10.co.nz; Church Rd; sites per person $19, cabins $50-87, units $105-145; 💻) With perhaps the cosiest lounge you'll find in a camping ground, this little park has modern amenities, plenty of space and good views of Kaipara Harbour.

Petite Provence (☎ 09-431 7552; www.petiteprovence.co.nz; 703c Tinopai Rd; s/d $110/150) This attractive, French-influenced B&B is a popular weekender for Aucklanders, so it pays to book ahead. Excellent dinners can be arranged for a bargain $45 per person.

Matakohe House (☎ 09-431 7091; www.matakohehouse.co.nz; 24 Church Rd; s/d $135/160; 💻) A short walk from the museum, this B&B occupies a pretty villa with a cafe attached (mains $29 to $32). The simply furnished rooms open out onto a veranda and offer winning touches like complimentary port and chocolates.

Sahara (☎ 09-431 6833; cnr Franklin & Paparoa Valley Rds, Paparoa; brunch $10-15, mains $18-33; ⌚ brunch, lunch & dinner Thu-Sun) Nothing about the cuisine or fit-out screams North African desert, but the incongruity of the name is nothing on the surprise of finding such a stylish restaurant in little Paparoa, 6km east of Matakohe. Housed in a lovingly restored bank building, Sahara offers a small but stellar menu with a focus on local produce.

Getting There & Away

Main Coachline (☎ 09-278 8070; www.maincoachline.co.nz) runs six buses per week to/from Auckland ($40, 2½ hours) and Dargaville ($18, 35 minutes). See p172 for details of the Magic Travellers Network service.

Coromandel Region

Looking a bit like the side view of a hand with its middle finger raised, the Coromandel Peninsula juts defiantly into the Pacific east of Auckland and forms the eastern edge of the Hauraki Gulf. Its dramatic, mountainous spine bisects it into two very distinct parts.

The eastern edge has some of the North Island's best white-sand beaches. When Auckland shuts up shop for Christmas/New Year this is where it heads. Marinas and cafes cater to the chattering set in the wealthier enclaves, while sandy toes and board shorts are the norm elsewhere. The cutesy historic gold-mining towns on the west side escape the worst of the influx, their muddy wetlands and stony bays holding less appeal for the masses. This coast has long been a refuge for alternative lifestylers – although the hippy communes have gradually given way to organic farms and Buddhist retreats.

Down the middle, the mountains are crisscrossed with walking tracks, allowing trampers to lose themselves (hopefully only figuratively) among large tracts of untamed bush where kauri trees once towered and are starting to do so again. At the base of the peninsula the Hauraki Plains were once massive swampy wetlands, rich with bird life. Pockets remain, with Miranda being the premier holiday spot for feathered jetsetters and their admirers.

Although relatively close to Auckland, the Coromandel offers easy access to splendid isolation. Some of the more remote communities in these parts are still accessed by gravel roads, and an aura of rugged individualism hangs like mist over this compact and special region.

COROMANDEL REGION

HIGHLIGHTS

- Travelling remote gravel roads under a crimson canopy of ancient pohutukawa trees in **Far North Coromandel** (p200)
- Staking out your own patch of footprint-free sand at **Opoutere Beach** (p208), **Otama Beach** (p202) or **Opito Beach** (p202)
- Exploring hidden islands, caves and bays by kayak from **Whitianga** (p202), **Hahei** (p205) or **Coromandel Town** (p198)
- Burning your butt in a freshly dug thermal pool in the sands of **Hot Water Beach** (p206)
- Pigging out on smoked mussels in **Coromandel Town** (p200)
- Penetrating the mystical depths of the dense bush of **Coromandel Forest Park** (p197) and **Karangahake Gorge** (p211)

- Telephone code: 07
- www.thecoromandel.com
- www.ew.govt.nz

COROMANDEL REGION

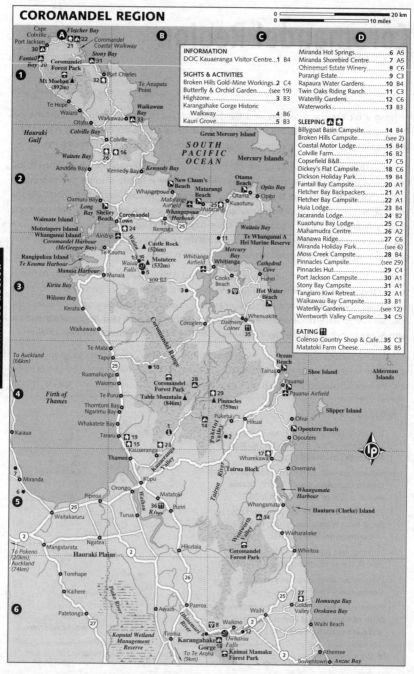

INFORMATION	
DOC Kauaeranga Visitor Centre.....**1** B4	
SIGHTS & ACTIVITIES	
Broken Hills Gold-Mine Workings.**2** C4	
Butterfly & Orchid Garden......(see 19)	
Highzone...................................**3** B3	
Karangahake Gorge Historic	
Walkway...............................**4** B6	
Kauri Grove.............................**5** B3	

Miranda Hot Springs..................**6** A5
Miranda Shorebird Centre..........**7** A5
Ohinemuri Estate Winery............**8** C6
Purangi Estate..........................**9** C3
Rapaura Water Gardens.............**10** B4
Twin Oaks Riding Ranch.............**11** C3
Waterlily Gardens.....................**12** C6
Waterworks..............................**13** B3

SLEEPING	
Billygoat Basin Campsite............**14** B4
Broken Hills Campsite.............(see 2)
Coastal Motor Lodge.................**15** B4
Colville Farm...........................**16** B2
Copsefield B&B........................**17** C5
Dickey's Flat Campsite..............**18** C6
Dickson Holiday Park................**19** B4
Fantail Bay Campsite.................**20** A1
Fletcher Bay Backpackers..........**21** A1
Fletcher Bay Campsite...............**22** A1
Huia Lodge.............................**23** B4
Jacaranda Lodge......................**24** B2
Kuaotunu Bay Lodge.................**25** C2
Mahamudra Centre...................**26** A2
Manawa Ridge.........................**27** C6
Miranda Holiday Park.............(see 6)
Moss Creek Campsite................**28** B4
Pinnacles Campsite..............(see 29)
Pinnacles Hut..........................**29** C4
Port Jackson Campsite...............**30** A1
Stony Bay Campsite..................**31** A1
Tangiaro Kiwi Retreat................**32** A1
Waikawau Bay Campsite............**33** B1
Waterlily Gardens.................(see 12)
Wentworth Valley Campsite........**34** C5

EATING	
Colenso Country Shop & Cafe...**35** C3
Matatoki Farm Cheese..............**36** B5

History

This whole area, including the peninsula, the islands and both sides of the gulf, was known to Maori as Hauraki. Various *iwi* (tribes) held claim to pockets of it, including the Pare Hauraki branch of the Tainui tribes and others descended from Te Arawa and earlier migrations. Polynesian artefacts and evidence of moa-hunting have been found, pointing to around 1000 years of continuous occupation.

The Hauraki *iwi* were some of the first to be exposed to European traders. The region's proximity to Auckland, safe anchorages and ready supply of valuable timber initially lead to a booming economy. Kauri logging was big business on the peninsula. Allied to the timber trade was shipbuilding, which took off in 1832 when a mill was established at Mercury Bay. Things got tougher once the kauri around the coast became scarce and the loggers had to penetrate deeper into the bush for timber. Kauri dams, which used water power to propel the huge logs to the coast, were built. By the 1930s virtually no kauri remained and the industry died.

Gold was first discovered in New Zealand (NZ) near Coromandel Town in 1852. Although this first rush was short-lived, more gold was discovered around Thames in 1867 and later in other places. The peninsula is also rich in semiprecious gemstones, such as quartz, agate, amethyst and jasper. A fossick on any west-coast beach can be rewarding.

Despite successful interactions with Europeans for decades, the Hauraki *iwi* were some of the hardest hit by colonisation. Unscrupulous dealings by settlers and government to gain access to valuable resources resulted in Maori losing most of their lands by the 1880s. Even today there is a much lower Maori presence on the peninsula than in neighbouring districts.

Climate

Being mountainous, the region attracts more rainfall (3000mm or even 4500mm a year) than elsewhere on the east coast.

Getting There & Around

Car is the only option for accessing some of the more remote areas, but be careful to check hire agreements as there are plenty of gravel roads and a few streams to ford. Most of them are in good nick and even a small car can cope unless the weather's been particularly wet.

MAORI NZ: COROMANDEL REGION

Although it has a long and rich Maori history, the Coromandel doesn't offer many opportunities to engage with the culture. Pioneer pursuits such as gold-mining and kauri logging have been given much more attention, although this is starting to change.

Historic *pa* sites are dotted around, with the most accessible being Paku (p207). There are others at Opito Beach (p202), Hahei (p205) and Hot Water Beach (p206).

Daily buses on the Auckland-to-Tauranga route pass through Thames and Waihi, while others loop through Coromandel Town, Whitianga and Tairua.

It's definitely worth considering the beautiful ferry ride from Auckland via Waiheke Island to Coromandel Town (see p200).

MIRANDA

It's a pretty name for a settlement on the swampy Firth of Thames, just an hour's drive from Auckland. The two reasons to come here are splashing around the thermal pools and birdwatching – but doing both at the same time might be considered impolite.

This is one of the most accessible spots for studying waders or shore birds all year round. The vast mud flat is teeming with aquatic worms and crustaceans, which attract thousands of Arctic-nesting shore birds over the winter – 43 species of wader have been spotted here. The two main species are the bar-tailed godwit and the lesser or red knot, but it isn't unusual to see turnstones, sandpipers and the odd vagrant red-necked stint. One godwit tagged here was tracked making an 11,570km nonstop flight from Alaska. Short-haul travellers include the pied oystercatcher and the threatened wrybill from the South Island, and banded dotterels and pied stilts.

The **Miranda Shorebird Centre** (Map p192; ☎ 09-232 2781; www.miranda-shorebird.org.nz; 283 East Coast Rd; ☼ 9am-5pm) has bird-life displays, hires out binoculars and sells useful birdwatching pamphlets ($2). Nearby are a hide and several walks (30 minutes to two hours). The centre offers clean bunk-style accommodation (dorm beds/double rooms $20/60) with a kitchen.

COROMANDEL REGION FACTS

Eat Buckets of bivalves at Whitianga's Scallop Festival (p203)

Drink Boiled water from a mountain campsite

Read *The Penguin History of New Zealand* (2003) by the late Michael King, an Opoutere resident

Listen to Top kiwi bands at the Coromandel Gold New Year's Eve festival (p203)

Watch The birds in the Firth of Thames (p193)

Swim at Any of the peninsula's beautiful east coast beaches

Festival The peninsula-wide Pohutukawa Festival (www.pohutukawafestival.co.nz)

Tackiest tourist attraction Scallop-headed marching band at Whitianga's Scallop Festival (p203)

Go green Witness forest regeneration at Driving Creek Railway (p199)

Miranda Hot Springs (Map p192; ☎ 07-867 3055; Front Miranda Rd; adult/child $13/6; ⏱ 9am-9.30pm), 5km south, has a large thermal swimming pool (reputedly the largest in the Southern Hemisphere), a toasty sauna pool and private spas ($10 extra).

Next door is **Miranda Holiday Park** (Map p192; ☎ 07-867 3205; www.mirandaholidaypark.co.nz; sites per adult/child $21/11, dm $33, units $139-305; 🖥 🛜 🏊), which has excellent sparkling-clean units and facilities, its own hot-spring pool and a flood-lit tennis court.

THAMES
pop 10,000

Thames dates from a time when gold-digging had a much different connotation to what it does today. Dinky 19th-century wooden buildings still dominate the town centre, but grizzly prospectors have been replaced by alternative lifestylers. If you're a vegetarian ecowarrior you'll feel right at home. It's a good base for tramping or canyoning in the nearby Kauaeranga Valley.

Captain Cook arrived here in 1769, naming the Waihou River 'Thames' 'on account of its bearing some resemblance to that river in England'. This area belonged to the Ngati Maru, a tribe of Tainui descent. Their spectacular meeting house, Hotunui (1878), holds pride of place in the Auckland Museum (p98).

After opening Thames to gold-miners in 1867, the Ngati Maru were swamped by 10,000 European settlers within a year. When

the initial boom turned to bust, a dubious system of government advances resulted in Maori debt and forced land sales.

Information

Post office (517 Pollen St) Offers poste restante service.

Thames i-SITE (☎ 07-868 7284; www.thamesinfo. co.nz; 206 Pollen St; ⏱ 8.30am-5pm Mon-Fri, 9am-4pm Sat & Sun) Information and internet access.

Sights

The i-SITE stocks free Historic Places Trust self-tour pamphlets of Thames' significant buildings. The Trust also runs tours of the interesting **School of Mines & Mineral Museum** (☎ 07-868 6227; 101 Cochrane St; adult/child $5/2; ⏱ 11am-3pm Wed-Sun), which has an extensive collection of NZ rocks, minerals and fossils. The oldest section (1868) was part of a Methodist Sunday school, situated on a Maori burial ground.

The **Goldmine Experience** (☎ 07-868 8514; www. goldmine-experience.co.nz; cnr Moanataiari Rd & SH25; adult/child $15/5; ⏱ 10am-4pm Jan-Mar, 10am-1pm Apr-Sep) allows you to walk through a gold-mine tunnel, watch a stamper battery crush rock, learn about the history of the Cornish miners and try your hand at panning for gold ($2 extra).

The **historical museum** (☎ 07-868 8509; cnr Cochrane & Pollen Sts; adult/child $5/2; ⏱ 1-4pm) houses pioneer relics, rocks and old photographs of the town.

Kids (little or large) with a fairy complex will adore the **Butterfly & Orchid Garden** (Map p192; ☎ 07-868 8080; Victoria St; adult/child $9.50/5; ⏱ 10am-4pm), north of town within the Dickson Holiday Park. It's an enclosed jungle full of hundreds of exotic flappers.

Activities

Bird lovers can take advantage of the **Karaka Bird Hide**. Built with compensation funds from the *Rainbow Warrior* bombing, it's reached by a boardwalk through the mangroves just off Brown St. Nearby, young 'uns can ride on the cute-as-a-button 900m **Thames Small Gauge Railway** (☎ 07-868 6803; tickets $2; ⏱ 11am-3pm Sun).

Eyez Open (☎ 07-868 9018; www.eyezopen.co.nz; per day $30, 1- to 4-day tours $110-750) rents out bikes and organises small-group cycling tours of the peninsula (minimum four to six people).

Canyonz (☎ 0800 422 696; www.canyonz.co.nz; trips $235) runs canyoning trips to the Sleeping God Canyon in the Kauaeranga Valley. Expect a vertical descent of over 300m, requiring

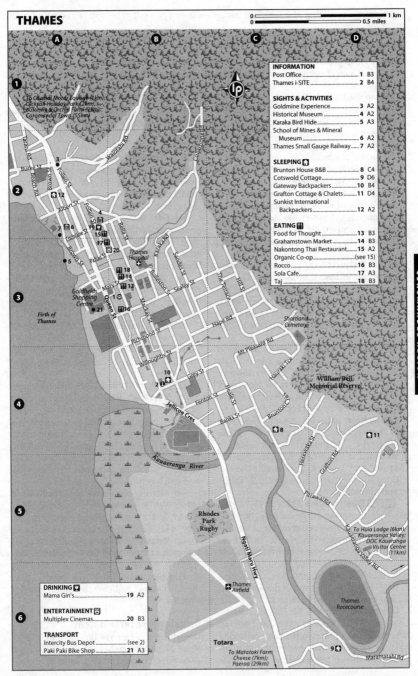

THAMES

INFORMATION		
Post Office	1	B3
Thames i-SITE	2	B4
SIGHTS & ACTIVITIES		
Goldmine Experience	3	A2
Historical Museum	4	A2
Karaka Bird Hide	5	A3
School of Mines & Mineral Museum	6	A2
Thames Small Gauge Railway	7	A2
SLEEPING		
Brunton House B&B	8	C4
Cotswold Cottage	9	D6
Gateway Backpackers	10	B4
Grafton Cottage & Chalets	11	D4
Sunkist International Backpackers	12	A2
EATING		
Food for Thought	13	B3
Grahamstown Market	14	B3
Nakontong Thai Restaurant	15	A2
Organic Co-op	(see 15)	
Rocco	16	B3
Sola Cafe	17	A3
Taj	18	B3
DRINKING		
Mama Gin's	19	A2
ENTERTAINMENT		
Multiplex Cinemas	20	B3
TRANSPORT		
Intercity Bus Depot	(see 2)	
Paki Paki Bike Shop	21	A3

COROMANDEL REGION

abseiling, water-sliding and jumping (minimum four people).

Sleeping

Thames has a good crop of B&B accommodation, but budget operators are more thinly spread.

Dickson Holiday Park (Map p192; ☎ 07-868 7308; www.dicksonpark.co.nz; sites per person $16, dm $25, cabins $55-109, units $99-120; 🖳 🛜 🖳) Tucked away in a valley 3km north of Thames, this aging camping ground has a shop, free bikes, bush walks and roaming ducks.

Gateway Backpackers (☎ 07-868 6339; www.gatewaybackpackers.co.nz; 209 Mackay St; dm $23-26, s $45, d $58-72; 🖳) Generations of Kiwis grew up in state houses just like this, giving it a homely feel. This relaxed hostel has basic rooms, a nice garden and simple facilities. Bathrooms are in short supply but free laundry and bikes are on offer.

Sunkist Backpackers (☎ 07-868 8808; www.sunkistbackpackers.com; 506 Brown St; dm $24-28, r $64; 🖳) This character-filled 1860s heritage building has spacious dorms, spotless bathrooms and a garden. It offers free bikes, 4WD hire ($65 per day) and shuttles to the Kauaeranga Valley ($35 return).

Huia Lodge (Map p192; ☎ 07-868 6557; www.thames-info.co.nz/HuiaLodge; 589 Kauaeranga Valley Rd; s/d/tr $75/110/150) The affable empty-nesters who own this homely farmhouse close to the forest park provide decent rooms, full cooked breakfasts and good advice for walkers.

Coastal Motor Lodge (Map p192; ☎ 07-868 6843; www.stayatcoastal.co.nz; 608 Tararu Rd; units $140-185; 🛜) Motel and chalet-style accommodation is provided at this smart, welcoming place, 2km north of Thames. It overlooks the sea, making it a popular choice, especially in the summer months.

ourpick Brunton House B&B (☎ 07-868 5160; www.bruntonhouse.co.nz; 210 Parawai Rd; r $160-180, tr $195; 🖳 🛜 🖳) Recent renovations of this impressive two-storey kauri villa (1875) have upgraded the kitchen and bathrooms, while staying true to the building's historic credentials (there are no en suites). Guests can relax in the grounds, by the pool, in the designated lounge or on the upstairs terrace.

Cotswold Cottage (☎ 07-868 6306; www.cotswoldcottage.co.nz; 36 Maramarahi Rd; r $165-200) Looking over the river and racecourse, this pretty villa has had a modern makeover with luxuriant linen (225-thread-count sheets) and an out-door spa pool. The comfy rooms all open onto a deck.

Grafton Cottage & Chalets (☎ 07-868 9971; www.graftoncottage.co.nz; 304 Grafton Rd; units $165-210; 🖳 🖳) Perched on a hill, most of these attractive wooden chalets have decks with awesome views and are self-contained. The hospitable hosts provide free internet access and breakfast, as well as use of the pool, spa and three barbecue areas.

Eating

Food for Thought (☎ 07-868 6065; 574 Pollen St; pies $1.80-4; ☽ breakfast & lunch Mon-Sat) You might toy with a panini, cake or coffee, but it is really the award-winning pies that you come here for.

Sola Cafe (☎ 07-868 8781; 720b Pollen St; mains $9-13; ☽ 8am-4pm; Ⓥ) Bright and friendly, this meat-free cafe is first rate. Expect excellent coffee and a range of vegan, dairy-free and gluten-free options that include heavenly salads.

Taj (☎ 07-868 8122; 620 Pollen St; mains $11-16; ☽ lunch Wed-Fri, dinner daily; Ⓥ) A simple curry house perhaps, but Taj does a sublime *saag paneer* and all the other spicy favourites.

Nakontong Thai Restaurant (☎ 07-868 6821; 730 Pollen St; mains $16-21; ☽ lunch Mon-Fri, dinner daily; Ⓥ) Although the bright lighting may not induce romance, the tangy Thai dishes should provide a warm glow.

ourpick Rocco (☎ 07-868 8641; 109 Sealey St; mains $24-25; ☽ lunch daily, dinner Tue-Sun) Housed in one of Thames' gorgeous kauri villas, Rocco serves a lively tapas selection and more substantial mains, making good use of local ingredients (mussels, fish) and high-quality Spanish imports (chorizo, cheese, olives). In clement weather take a seat among the crushed-shell and swirling brick paths outside.

Self-catering options include **Organic Co-op** (☎ 868 8797; 736 Pollen St; ☽ 9am-5pm Mon-Fri, 8.30am-noon Sat; Ⓥ), a good source of planet-friendly vegetables, nuts, bread, eggs and meat. There is also **Matatoki Farm Cheese** (Map p192; ☎ 07-868 1284; cnr SH26 & Wainui Rd; ☽ 8am-4.30pm Mon-Fri, 10am-4pm Sat & Sun), where you can taste and buy cheeses handmade from milk produced by the farm's cows and ewes, including organic varieties.

Drinking & Entertainment

One thing you can say for Thames, it isn't short of historic pubs. Most of them have some rough edges and are clustered around

Pollen St. You won't need us to plot your pub crawl.

Mama Gin's (☎ 07-868 6994; 746 Pollen St; ☺ 7pm-late Wed-Sat) The cutest little bar in the 'Mandel, with art-deco chandeliers, zany wallpaper and regular live music. It's the sort of place where a solo traveller of any gender can chill out over a glass of wine.

Multiplex Cinemas (☎ 07-868 6602; www.cinema thames.co.nz; 708 Pollen St; adult/child $12/8) Screening recent blockbusters in poorly sound-insulated cinemas.

Shopping
Pollen St has a good selection of gift and homeware stores selling local art and craft. On Saturday mornings the **Grahamstown Market** (Pollen St; ☺ 9am-noon Sat) fills the street with organic produce and handicrafts.

Getting There & Around
Thames is the transport hub of the Coromandel. **InterCity** (☎ 09-583 5780; www.inter city.co.nz) and its associates have daily buses to/from Auckland ($28, two hours), Coromandel Town ($16, 72 minutes), Whitianga ($34, 90 minutes), Tairua ($17, 44 minutes), Waihi ($20, 45 minutes), Hamilton ($24, 1¾ hours) and Tauranga ($28, 1¾ hours), stopping outside the i-SITE and Sunkist Backpackers.

Naked Bus (www.nakedbus.com) operates in conjunction with **Tairua Bus Company** (☎ 07-864 7770; www.tairuabus.co.nz) for daily services between Thames and Tairua (from $1, 50 minutes), stopping at Ngatea for connections to Auckland, Tauranga and Rotorua.

Go Kiwi (☎ 0800 446 549; www.go-kiwi.co.nz) has daily shuttles to/from Auckland ($42, two hours), Auckland Airport ($54, 90 minutes), Whitianga ($36, 1¾ hours), Tairua ($26, 70 minutes) and Whangamata ($64, 75 minutes).

Paki Paki Bike Shop (☎ 07-867 9026; www.pakipaki bikeshop.co.nz; Goldfields Shopping Centre) rents out bikes for $25 a day and performs repairs.

COROMANDEL FOREST PARK
More than 30 walks crisscross the Coromandel Forest Park, spread over several major blocks throughout the centre of the peninsula. The most popular hike is the challenging six- to eight-hour return journey up to the **Pinnacles** (759m) in the Kauaeranga Valley behind Thames. Other outstanding tramps include

the **Coromandel Coastal Walkway** from Fletcher Bay to Stony Bay (see p201) and the **Puketui Valley** walk to abandoned gold mines (see p208).

The **Department of Conservation (DOC) Kauaeranga Visitor Centre** (Map p192; ☎ 07-867 9080; Kauaeranga Valley Rd; ☺ 9am-4pm daily Oct-Apr, 9am-3pm Wed-Sun May-Sep) is a flash new complex with interesting displays about the kauri forest and its history. Its staff sell maps ($1 to $2), dispense advice and take bookings for the Pinnacles hut. The centre is 14km off SH25; it's a further 9km along a gravel road to the start of the trails. Enquire at the Thames hostels about shuttles.

The DOC **Pinnacles hut** (Map p192; adult/child $15/7.50) has 80 beds, gas cookers, heaters, toilets and cold showers, and must be pre-booked. There are also three basic **backcountry campsites** (Map p192; adult/child $5/2) in this part of the park: one near the hut and others at Moss Creek and Billygoat Basin. Expect only a toilet and running water. A further eight **conservation campsites** (adult/child $9/2) are accessible from the forest road and, at the time of research, there was talk of building a second hut.

Other campsites in other parts of the park are mentioned later in this chapter.

THAMES TO COROMANDEL TOWN
Narrow SH25 snakes along the coast past pretty little bays and rocky beaches. Sea birds are plentiful, and you can fish, dig for shellfish and fossick for quartz, jasper and even gold-bearing rocks on the beaches. The landscape turns crimson when the pohutukawa (often referred to as the 'NZ Christmas tree') blooms in December. At Wilsons Bay the road heads away from the coast and climbs over several hills and valleys before dropping down to Coromandel Town, 55km from Thames. The view looking towards the island-studded Coromandel Harbour is exquisite.

A handful of stores, motels, B&Bs and camping grounds are scattered around the tiny settlements that front the picturesque bays. At Tapu it's worth turning inland for a mainly sealed 6km drive to the **Rapaura Water Gardens** (Map p192; ☎ 07-868 4821; www.rapaura.com; 586 Tapu-Coroglen Rd; adult/child $12/5; ☺ 9am-5pm), a marriage of water, greenery, sculpture and platitudes. There's also accommodation (cottage/lodge $165/275) and a decent cafe.

COROMANDEL TOWN
pop 1620

Even more crammed with heritage buildings than Thames, Coromandel Town is a thoroughly quaint little place. Its natty cafes, interesting art stores, excellent sleeping options and delicious smoked mussels could keep you here longer than you expected.

Gold was discovered at Driving Creek in 1852. Initially the local Patukirikiri *iwi* kept control of the land and received money from digging licences. After initial financial success the same fate befell them as the Ngati Maru in Thames (see p194). By 1871, debt had forced them to sell all but 778 mountainous acres of their land. Today fewer than 100 people remain who identify as part of this *iwi*.

Information

Coromandel Town i-SITE (☎ 07-866 8598; www.coromandeltown.co.nz; 355 Kapanga Rd; ☼ 9am-5pm Mon-Fri, 9am-4pm Sat & Sun Apr-Oct, 9am-5pm daily Nov-Mar) Has internet access ($6 per hour) and maps of local walks ($1).

Police station (☎ 07-866 1190; 405 Kapanga Rd)

Post office (Kapanga Rd)

Sights

Heritage buffs can tour around 28 historic sites featured in the Historic Places Trust's Coromandel Town pamphlet (free from the i-SITE).

The **Coromandel Goldfield Centre & Stamper Battery** (☎ 07-866 7933; 410 Buffalo Rd; adult/child $10/5; ☼ tours 2pm & 3pm Tue, Thu, Sat & Sun) is an

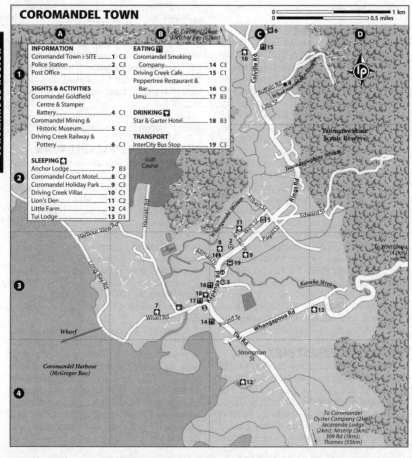

COROMANDEL TOWN

| 0 | 1 km |
| 0 | 0.5 miles |

INFORMATION
Coromandel Town i-SITE 1 C3
Police Station 2 C3
Post Office 3 C3

SIGHTS & ACTIVITIES
Coromandel Goldfield
Centre & Stamper
Battery 4 C1
Coromandel Mining &
Historic Museum 5 C2
Driving Creek Railway &
Pottery 6 C1

SLEEPING
Anchor Lodge 7 B3
Coromandel Court Motel 8 C3
Coromandel Holiday Park 9 C3
Driving Creek Villas 10 C1
Lion's Den 11 C2
Little Farm 12 C4
Tui Lodge 13 D3

EATING
Coromandel Smoking
Company 14 C3
Driving Creek Cafe 15 C1
Peppertree Restaurant &
Bar 16 C3
Umu 17 B3

DRINKING
Star & Garter Hotel 18 B3

TRANSPORT
InterCity Bus Stop 19 C3

1899 rock-crushing plant with informative one-hour tours. You can also try panning for gold ($5). Outside of the tours it's worth stopping for a gander at NZ's largest working water wheel.

The small **Coromandel Mining & Historic Museum** (☎ 07-866 7251; 841 Rings Rd; adult/child $3/50c; 🕙 10am-1pm Sat & Sun Feb–mid-Dec, 10am-4pm daily mid-Dec–late Jan) provides a glimpse of pioneer life.

Activities

The amazing **Driving Creek Railway & Potteries** (☎ 07-866 8703; www.drivingcreekrailway.co.nz; 380 Driving Creek Rd; adult/child $20/11; 🕙 departures 10.15am & 2pm) is 3km north of Coromandel Town. The unique train runs up steep grades, across four trestle bridges, along two spirals and a double switchback, and through two tunnels, finishing at the 'Eye-full Tower'. The hour-long trip passes artworks and regenerating native forest – more than 17,000 natives have been planted, including 9000 kauri. It's worth lingering for the video about the extraordinary guy behind it all, well-known potter Barry Brickell.

Megan from **Mussel Barge** (☎ 07-866 7667; adult/child $50/25) offers fishing trips with a uniquely local flavour and lots of laughs. Her father runs **Argo Tours** (3hr trips $150), exploring native bush and old gold workings in a mini 8WD. If you can muster a posse (up to five people), prices drop as low as $40 per person.

Coromandel Kayak Adventures (☎ 07-866 7466; www.kayakadventures.co.nz) offers paddle-powered tours ranging from half-day ecotours (for 1/2/3/4/5/6 paddlers; $200/200/267/356/425/474) to fishing trips (half-/full day $195/375).

Tri Sail Charters (☎ 0800 024 874; www.trisailcharters.co.nz; half/full day $50/100) will have you and your mates (a minimum of four) exploring the Coromandel Harbour on an 11.2m trimaran (three-hulled yacht).

Sleeping

Coromandel Town is spoilt for accommodation choice, with much better budget options than Thames.

ourpick **Tui Lodge** (☎ 07-866 8237; www.coromandeltuilodge.co.nz; 60 Whangapoua Rd; sites per person $12, dm $25, r $55-75; 🖥) Pleasantly rural, this cheery backpackers has plenty of trees, a sauna ($5), free bikes, fruit (in season) and straight-up rooms. The pricier ones have en suites.

Coromandel Holiday Park (☎ 07-866 8830; www.coromandelholidaypark.co.nz; 636 Rings Rd; sites per person $20, dm $30, cabins $77-137, units $137-177; 🖥 🤶 🛒) Well-kept and welcoming, with nicely painted cabins and manicured lawns, this large park includes the semi-separate Coromandel Town Backpackers. It gets busy in summer, so book ahead.

Lions' Den (☎ 07-866 8157; www.lionsdenhostel.co.nz; 126 Te Tiki St; dm/r $24/55; 🤶) Chill out to the hippy vibe in this magical place. A tranquil garden with fish pond, fairy lights and wisteria vines, and a relaxed collection of comfy rooms (dotted with African and North American bits and bobs) make for a soothing spot to rest your bones. There are no locks on the doors, but we suspect the right spells have been set to protect your materialistic trappings. Hey, who really owns anything anyway?

Anchor Lodge (☎ 07-866 7992; www.anchorlodgecoromandel.co.nz; 448 Wharf Rd; dm $25, d $60-65, units $125-275; 🤶 🛒) Not many places can boast its own goldmine and glowworm cave, but this upmarket backpacker/motel combo has them and a heated swimming pool and spa to boot. The 2nd-floor units look over the nikau palms and agaves to the harbour.

Jacaranda Lodge (Map p192; ☎ 07-866 8002; www.jacarandalodge.co.nz; 3195 Tiki Rd; s $75, d $120-160; 🤶) Jacaranda is a two-storey cottage located among six hectares of bucolic farmland and rose gardens. Some rooms share bathrooms, but expect fluffy towels and personalised soap in mini *kete* (woven flax bags). Kosher facilities available and Hebrew spoken.

Little Farm (☎ 07-866 8427; www.thelittlefarmcoromandel.co.nz; 750 Tiki Rd; r $100-120) Positioned overlooking a private wetland reserve at the rear of a fair dinkum farm, these three comfortable units offer plenty of peace and quiet. The largest has a full kitchen and superb sunset views.

Coromandel Court Motel (☎ 07-866 8402; www.coromandelcourtmotel.co.nz; 365 Kapanga Rd; units $145-215; 🤶) These spick-and-span units are spotless, smart and ideally located, just behind the information centre. The owners clearly love their lot.

Driving Creek Villas (☎ 07-866 7755; www.drivingcreekvillas.com; 21a Colville Rd; villas $275-415; 🤶) This is the posh, grown-up's choice – two spacious, self-contained, modern wooden villas, with plenty of privacy. The interior design is slick (with a Polynesian bent), the appliances first-rate and the bush setting, complete with bubbling creek, sublime.

COROMANDEL REGION

Eating

our pick **Driving Creek Cafe** (☎ 07-866 7066; 180 Driving Creek Rd; mains $8-16; 🕑 9.30am-5pm; 🖥 Ⓥ) A large selection of vegetarian, vegan, gluten-free, organic and fair-trade delights awaits at this funky mud-brick cafe. The food is wonderful – beautifully presented, fresh and healthy. Once sated, the kids can play in the sandpit while the adults check their email ($6 per hour).

Umu (☎ 07-866 8618; 22 Wharf Rd; breakfast $9-16, lunch $9-24, dinner $14-32; 🕑 breakfast, lunch & dinner daily; 🛜) Umu serves up classy cafe fare, including excellent pizza, mouth-watering counter food (tarts and quiches around $7), superb coffee and tummy-taming breakfasts.

Pepper Tree Restaurant & Bar (☎ 07-866 8211; 31 Kapanga Rd; lunch $17-25, dinner $23-33; 🕑 lunch & dinner daily; 🛜) C-Town's most upmarket option, Pepper Tree dishes up generously proportioned French-style cooking with a particular emphasis on fresh seafood. On a summer's evening, the courtyard tables under the shady tree are the place to be.

For a delicious snack or cooking supplies, **Coromandel Smoking Co** (☎ 07-866 8793; 70 Tiki Rd; 🕑 9am-5pm Sun-Thu, 9am-5.30pm Fri & Sat) has a wonderful range of smoked fish and seafood. You can't leave town without trying the extremely addictive smoked mussels.

If you prefer your bivalves au naturel, the roadside **Coromandel Oyster Company** (☎ 07-866 8028; 1611 Tiki Rd; 🕑 7.30am-6.30pm) is the place for newly landed mussels, scallops, cooked crayfish and, of course, oysters.

Drinking

Coromandel doesn't have the same volume of pubs as Thames, but there are still several choices on the main street.

Star & Garter Hotel (☎ 07-866 8503; 5 Kapanga Rd; 🛜) Making the most of the simple kauri interior of an 1873 building, this smart pub has pool tables, decent sounds and a roster of live music and DJs on the weekends. The beer garden is awesome, smartly styled in corrugated iron.

Getting There & Away

By far the nicest way to travel from Auckland is by ferry. Operator **360 Discovery** (☎ 0800 888 006; www.360discovery.co.nz) has five boats weekly to/from Auckland (one way/return $49/79, two hours) via Orapiu on Waiheke Island (one way/return $39/69, 70 minutes). It makes

SENSIBLE CYCLISTS' LEAPFROG

There's no charge for carrying your bike on a 360 Discovery ferry. Touring cyclists can avoid Auckland's traffic fumes and treacherous roads completely by catching the ferry at Gulf Harbour (p145) to Auckland's ferry terminal, and then leapfrogging directly to Coromandel Town.

a great day trip, and there's a guided-tour option (adult/child $136/78) that includes Driving Creek Railway and the Goldfield Centre. The boats dock at Hannafords Wharf, Te Kouma, where free buses shuttle passengers the 10km into town.

InterCity (☎ 09-583 5780; www.intercity.co.nz) and its partners have daily buses to/from Whitianga ($18, 80 minutes), Thames ($16, 72 minutes), Te Aroha ($20, 2¾ hours) and Hamilton ($40, 3¾ hours).

Naked Bus (www.nakedbus.com) operates in conjunction with **Tairua Bus Company** (☎ 07-864 7770; www.tairuabus.co.nz; advance fares from $1) for daily services to Tairua (two hours), via Whitianga (one hour), Hahei (90 minutes) and Hot Water Beach (95 minutes).

Go Kiwi (☎ 0800 446 549; www.go-kiwi.co.nz) runs shuttles from late October to Easter to/from Auckland ($50, 3¾ hours), Auckland Airport ($66, 3¼ hours) and Whitianga ($23, 50 minutes).

FAR NORTH COROMANDEL

Supremely isolated and gobsmackingly beautiful, the rugged tip of the Coromandel Peninsula is well worth the effort required to reach it. The best time to visit is summer, when the metal roads are dry, the pohutukawa are in their crimson glory and camping's an option (there isn't a lot of accommodation up here).

The 1260-hectare **Colville Farm** (Map p192; ☎ 07-866 6820; www.colvillefarmholidays.co.nz; 2140 Colville Rd; sites per person $12, dm/s/d $23/38/62, units $70-158; 🖥) has a range of interesting accommodation, including bare-basics bush lodges and self-contained houses. Guests can try their hands at farm work (including milking) or go on horse treks ($30 to $120, one to five hours).

The nearby **Mahamudra Centre** (Map p192; ☎ 07-866 6851; www.mahamudra.org.nz; sites per person $12, dm $20, s $40-75, tw/d $60/85) is a serene Tibetan Buddhist retreat that has a stupa, meditation hall and regular meditation courses. It offers simple accommodation in a parklike setting.

Another kilometre brings you to the tiny settlement of **Colville** (25km north of Coromandel Town). It's a remote rural community by a muddy bay and a magnet for alternative lifestylers. There's not much here except for **Colville Café** (☎ 07-866 6690; 2312 Colville Rd; mains $5-19; ☺ 11am-4pm Mon-Wed, 8am-4pm Thu-Sun), which has extended hours in summer, and the quaint **Colville General Store** (☎ 07-866 6805; Colville Rd; ☺ 8.30am-5pm), selling just about everything from organic food to petrol (warning: this is your last option for either).

Three kilometres north of Colville the seal stops and the road splits to straddle each side of the peninsula. Following the west coast, ancient pohutukawa spread overhead as you pass turquoise waters and stony beaches. The small DOC-run **Fantail Bay campsite** (Map p192; adult/child $9/2), 23km north of Colville, has running water and a couple of long-drop toilets under the shade of puriri trees. Another 7km brings you to the **Port Jackson campsite** (Map p192; adult/child $9/2), a larger DOC site right on the beach.

There's a spectacular lookout about 4km further on, where a metal dish identifies the various islands on the horizon. Great Barrier Island (p136) is only 20km away, looking every part the extension of the Coromandel Peninsula that it once was.

The road stops at **Fletcher Bay** – a magical land's end. Although it's only 37km from Colville, allow an hour for the drive. There's another DOC **campsite** (Map p192; adult/child $9/2) here, as well as **Fletcher Bay Backpackers** (Map p192; ☎ 07-866 6685; www.fletcherbay.co.nz; dm $25) – a simple affair that has four rooms with four bunks in each. Bring sheets and food.

The **Coromandel Coastal Walkway** is a scenic, three-hour one-way hike between Fletcher Bay and **Stony Bay**. It's a relatively easy walk with great coastal views and an ambling section across farmland. If you're not keen on walking all the way back, **Coromandel Discovery** (☎ 0800 668 175; www.coromandeldiscovery.co.nz; adult/child $95/55) will drive you from Coromandel Town up to Fletcher Bay and pick you up from Stony Bay four hours later.

There's another DOC **campsite** (Map p192; adult/child $9/2) at Stony Bay, where the east-coast road terminates. Heading south you pass a couple of nice beaches peppered with baches (holiday homes) on your way to the slightly larger settlement of **Port Charles**.

Tangiaro Kiwi Retreat (Map p192; ☎ 07-866 6614; www.kiwiretreat.co.nz; 1299 Port Charles Rd; units $225-350; ☞) offers eight brand-new one- or two-bedroom self-contained wooden cottages, each pair sharing a barbecue. There's a bush-fringed spa, an in-house masseuse (per hour $70) and, in summer, a cafe and licensed restaurant.

Another 8km brings you to the turn-off leading back to Colville, or you can continue south to **Waikawau Bay**, where there's a large DOC **campsite** (Map p192; ☎ 07-866 1106; adult/child $9/2, bookings required Dec-Jan) which has internet access (per hour $10) and a summer-only store. The road then winds its way south past **Kennedy Bay** before cutting back to come out near the Driving Creek Railway.

COROMANDEL TOWN TO WHITIANGA

There are two routes from Coromandel Town southeast to Whitianga. The main road is the slightly longer but quicker SH25, which follows the coast, enjoys sea views and has short detours to pristine sandy beaches. The other is the less-travelled but legendary 309 Rd, an unsealed, untamed route through deep bush.

State Highway 25

SH25 starts by climbing sharply to an incredible lookout before heading steeply down with craggy Castle Rock (526m) in the distance. The turn-off at Te Rerenga follows the harbour to Whangapoua. There's not much here but generic holiday homes, but you can walk along the rocky foreshore to the often-deserted **New Chum's Beach** (30 minutes).

Continuing east you soon reach **Kuaotunu**, a more interesting holiday town on a beautiful stretch of white-sand beach, with a cafe-gallery, store and ancient petrol pump. **Black Jack Backpackers** (☎ 07-866 2988; www.black-jack.co.nz; 201 SH25; dm/tw $25/70, d $80-90) has a prime position directly across from the beach. It's a lovely little hostel with smart facilities and bikes and kayaks for hire. The owners sometimes shut up shop in the off-season.

For a touch more luxury, head back along the beach and up the hill to **Kuaotunu Bay Lodge** (Map p192; ☎ 07-866 4396; www.kuaotunubay.co.nz; SH25; s $180-225, d $250-275), an elegant B&B set among manicured gardens, offering a small set of spacious sea-gazing rooms.

Heading off the highway at Kuaotunu takes you (via an unsealed road) to one of Coromandel's best-kept secrets. First the long stretch of **Otama Beach** comes into view – deserted but for a few houses and farms. There's extremely basic camping (think long-drop toilet in a corrugated shack) in a farmer's field at **Otama Beach Camp** (☎ 07-866 2362; www.otamabeachcamp.co.nz; 400 Blackjack Rd; sites per adult/child $10/5, cottage $220-260). Down by the beach they've recently built a self-contained, ecofriendly cottage (sleeping six), with solar power, a composting waste water system and ocean views.

Continue along the road and you'll be in for a shock. Just when you think you're about to fall off the end of the earth, the seal starts again and you reach **Opito** – a hidden-away enclave of 250 flash properties (too smart to be called baches), of which only 16 have permanent residents. It's more than a little weird, but it is a magical beach. You can walk to a Ngati Hei *pa* (fortified village) site at the far end.

One of the 'real' residences houses the delightful folks of **Leighton Lodge** (☎ 07-866 0756; www.leightonlodge.co.nz; 17 Stewart Pl; s/d/tr $125/160/195; 🖳). This smart B&B has an upstairs room with a view-hungry balcony and a self-contained flat downstairs.

309 Road

Starting 3km south of Coromandel Town, the 309 cuts through the ranges for 21km (14km of which is unsealed but well maintained), rejoining SH25 7km south of Whitianga. The **Waterworks** (Map p192; ☎ 07-866 7191; www.thewaterworks.co.nz; 471 309 Rd; adult/child $15/10; 🕙 9am-6pm Nov-Apr, 10am-4pm May-Oct), 5km from SH25, is a wonderfully bizarre park filled with whimsical water-powered amusements made from old kitchen knives, washing machines, bikes and toilets.

Two kilometres later there's a two-minute walk through a pretty patch of bush to the 10m-high **Waiau Falls**. Stop again after another 500m for an easy 10-minute walk through peaceful native bush to an amazing **kauri grove** (Map p192). This stand of 13 600-year-old giants escaped the carnage of the 19th century, giving a majestic reminder of what the peninsula once looked like. The biggest has a 6m circumference.

If you're carless or unwilling to risk the metal road, Coromandel Discovery (p201) has a **309 Road and Coromandel Highlights Tour** (adult/child $150/90), taking the 309 from Coromandel Town, stopping at the Waterworks, kauri grove, Cathedral Cove and Hot Water Beach (or Whitianga's Lost Spring spa if the tides aren't right) before looping back on SH25.

WHITIANGA

pop 3800

If you come to Whitianga you'd better want to get wet. The big attractions are the sandy beaches of Mercury Bay and the diving, boating and kayaking opportunities afforded by the craggy coast and nearby Te Whanganui-A-Hei Marine Reserve. If you've a lust for the luxe, a number of upmarket eateries and accommodation options have sprung up, catering to the boatie set who constantly breeze into the pretty harbour. Most of the restaurants are overpriced and not particularly interesting.

A genuine nautical hero, the legendary Polynesian explorer and seafarer Kupe, is believed to have landed near here in around 950AD. The name Whitianga is a contraction of Te Whitianga a Kupe (the Crossing Place of Kupe). Nearby are two famous and fantastic natural attractions, Cathedral Cove and Hot Water Beach.

Information

Medical Centre (☎ 07-866 5911; 87 Albert St; 🕙 8.30am-5pm Mon-Fri, 9-11am Sat)

Post office (72 Albert St)

Whitianga i-SITE (☎ 07-866 5555; www.whitianga.co.nz; 66 Albert St; 🕙 9am-5pm Mon-Fri, 9am-4pm Sat & Sun, extended in summer) Information and internet access ($9 per hour).

Sights & Activities

Buffalo Beach stretches along Mercury Bay, north of the harbour. A five-minute **passenger ferry ride** (adult/child/bicycle $2/1/50c; 🕙 7.30am-2.15am Christmas-Jan, 7.30am-6.30pm & 7.30-8.30pm & 9.30-11pm Feb-Christmas) will take you across the harbour to **Whitianga Rock Scenic & Historical Reserve**, **Flaxmill Bay**, **Shakespeare's Lookout**, **Captain Cook's Memorial**, **Lonely Bay** and **Cooks Bay**, all within walking distance. Further afield are Cathedral Cove (p205; 15km), Hahei (p205; 13km) and Hot Water Beach (p206; 18km, one hour by bike). On the way to Hahei, **Purangi Estate** (Map p192; ☎ 07-866 3724; www.purangi.co.nz; 501 Purangi Rd; 🕙 9am-5pm) has a cafe and free tastings of fruit wines and liqueurs.

The **Lost Spring** (☎ 07-866 0456; www.thelostspring.co.nz; 121a Cook Dr; hr/day $25/50) is an intriguing

Disney-meets-Rotorua thermal complex, involving a series of hot pools in a lush junglelike setting, complete with an erupting volcano. Yet this is an adult's indulgence (children under 14 not permitted), leaving the grown-ups to marinate themselves in tranquillity, cocktail in hand. There's also a day spa (treatments $20 to $320) and an excellent restaurant.

Mercury Bay Museum (☎ 07-866 0730; 11a The Esplanade; adult/child $5/50c; ☺ 10am-4pm) is small but interesting, focusing on local history – especially Whitianga's most famous visitors, Kupe and Cook.

Dive HQ (☎ 07-867 1580; www.divethecoromandel. co.nz; 7 Blacksmith Lane; trips $120-225) is a PADI five-star accredited dive facility offering a range of shore, kayak and boat dives. Come November, it also organises a **dive festival** (www.divefestival. co.nz).

If you're more interested in catching fish than admiring them, the Whitianga marina is a well-known base for **game-fishing** (particularly marlin and tuna) between January and March. There are numerous charters on offer, starting at around $500 and heading into the thousands. Enquire at the i-SITE or around the marina. See p178, for a guide to sustainable fishing.

Seafari Windsurfing (☎ 07-866 0677; Brophy's Beach), 4km north of Whitianga, hires out sailboards (from $25 per hour) and kayaks (from $15 per hour), and provides windsurfing lessons (from $40 including gear).

Another option for watery fun is a bright-yellow, motorised **Banana Boat** (☎ 07-866 5617; www.whitianga.co.nz/bananaboat; rides $10-30), but these only operate between Boxing Day and the end of January.

Twin Oaks Riding Ranch (Map p192; ☎ 07-866 5388; www.twinoaksridingranch.co.nz; SH25; 2hr trek $50) will take you horse-trekking over farmland and through bush 9km north of Whitianga.

Highzone (Map p192; ☎ 07-866 2113; www.highzone. co.nz; 49 Kaimarama Rd; activities $10-70) offers high adventure on a ropes course, including a trapeze leap and flying fox. It's located 7km south of Whitianga, just off the main road. Call for opening hours.

Tours

There are a baffling number of tours to **Te Whanganui-A-Hei Marine Reserve**, where you'll see amazing rock formations and, if you're lucky, dolphins, fur seals, penguins and orcas.

Some are straight cruises while others offer optional swims and snorkels. Try one of these tour companies:

Cave Cruzer (☎ 0800 427 893; www.cavecruzer.co.nz; 1-2½hr tour $50-75) A rigid-hull inflatable.

Glass Bottom Boat (☎ 07-867 1962; www.glassbottom boatwhitianga.co.nz; 2hr tour adult/child $85/50)

Whitianga Adventures (☎ 0800 806 060; www. whitianga-adventures.co.nz; 1½hr tour adult/child $55/35) Offers a two-hour Sea Cave Adventure in an inflatable (adult/child $65/40) and four-hour trips to the Mercury Islands in a 14m launch (adult/child $125/70).

Windborne (☎ 07-866 4607; www.windborne.co.nz; per person $80) Day sails in a 19m 1928 schooner.

Festivals & Events

In August, the **Scallop Festival** (www.scallopfestival. co.nz) provides a week of sublime food and entertainment. The inaugural 2009/2010 New Year's Eve **Coromandel Gold Festival** (www.coromandel gold.co.nz; Ohuka Farm, Buffalo Beach Rd; tickets $88) got a big thumb's up from punters, showcasing top NZ bands.

Sleeping

Mercury Bay Holiday Park (☎ 07-866 5579; www.mercury bayholidaypark.co.nz; 121 Albert St; sites per adult/child $22/8, cabins & units $100-268; 💻 🛜 🛋) Strangely planted in a suburban neighbourhood, this small camp is comfortable and clean, with playgrounds, trampoline, swimming pool and pool table.

Cat's Pyjamas (☎ 07-866 4663; www.cats-pyjamas. co.nz; 12 Albert St; dm $23, d $55-65; 💻 🛜) Good communal facilities make this place not just the cat's pyjamas but also the bee's knees. It's perfectly positioned between the pubs and the beach.

On the Beach Backpackers Lodge (☎ 07-866 5380; www.coromandelbackpackers.com; 46 Buffalo Beach Rd; dm $24-26, s $49-53, d $66-96; 💻) Brightly painted, beachside and brilliant, this well-run YHA has a large choice of sleeping options, including some with sea views and en suites. It provides free kayaks, boogie boards and spades (for Hot Water Beach).

Cosy Cat Cottage B&B (☎ 07-866 4488; www.cosycat. co.nz; 41 South Hwy; s/d/tr/q $85/105/120/160) Kooky in the extreme, this long-running B&B is crawling with feline images, including a human-sized one in the front garden. Not all rooms have en suites, but they're comfortable enough.

our pick Pipi Dune B&B (☎ 07-869 5375; www. pipidune.co.nz; 5 Pipi Dune; s/d $85/125; 🛜) You'll be

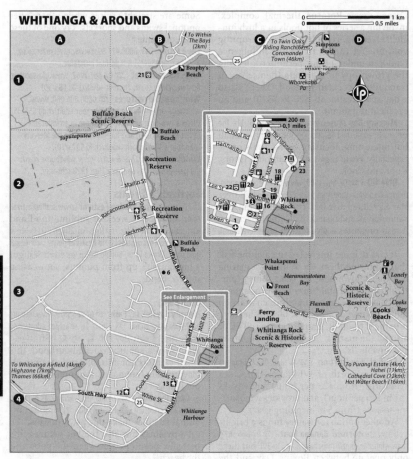

WHITIANGA & AROUND

as snug as a pipi in its shell in this attractive B&B in a quiet cul-de-sac, and you'll have a lot more room to move: pipi shells don't tend to come with guest lounges with kitchenettes, laundries and free wi-fi.

Albert Number 6 (☎ 07-866 0036; www.albertnumber6.co.nz; 6 Albert St; r $95-140; 🖳) Close to the beach and shops, these bright and sunny units are like motel rooms without kitchenettes. The hosts provide a light breakfast.

Within the Bays (☎ 07-866 2848; www.withinthebays.co.nz; 49 Tarapatiki Dr; r $360; 🖳) Modern European design couples with incredible views at this hilltop B&B. It's extremely well set up for guests with restricted mobility – there's even a wheelchair-accessible bush track on the property.

Eating

Tuatua (☎ 07-866 0952; 45 Albert St; tapas $5-14, mains $25-37; 🕑 10am-5pm Mon-Thu, noon-late Fri & Sat) The tapas craze has made it to Whitianga, but with a local flavour – try the Madrid-style Coromandel mussels.

Cog (☎ 07-866 0592; 10 Coghill St; mains $8-18; 🕑 7am-5pm) Get an early start on the sunny terrace of this side-street cafe, where the counter food beckons enticingly and the toasted sandwiches have gourmet aspirations.

Cafe Nina (☎ 07-866 5440; 20 Victoria St; mains $8-18; 🕑 breakfast & lunch) Barbecue for breakfast? Why the hell not. Too cool to be constricted to four walls, the kitchen grills bacon and eggs on an outdoor hotplate while the punters spill out onto tables in the park.

Sangam Indian Cuisine (☎ 07-867 1983; 13/1 Blacksmith Lane; mains $15-22; Ⓨ dinner; Ⓥ) North India comes to Whitianga via this large, up-market restaurant with exotic light fittings. If the kids aren't spice-friendly there's a fish-and-chips lifeline.

our pick **18sixtyfive** (☎ 07-866 0456; 121a Cook Dr; lunch $14-17, dinner $32-35; Ⓨ lunch & dinner) A fitting indulgence after a hot-water soak, the Lost Spring's restaurant offers smart fusion dining in the elegant surrounds of a converted 1865 schoolhouse.

Self-catering foodies should head to **Monk St Market** (☎ 07-866 4500; 1 Monk St; Ⓨ 10am-6pm Mon-Sat) for deli goods, imported chocolate and organic produce.

Entertainment

Mercury Twin Cinemas (☎ 07-867 1001; Lee St) Offers latest-release mainstream and independent films as an alternative to getting wet.

Getting There & Around

InterCity (☎ 0508 353 947; www.intercity.co.nz) has a daily bus to/from Thames ($34, 90 minutes)

via Tairua ($17, 44 minutes), stopping at the i-SITE, Cat's Pyjamas and On the Beach.

Naked Bus (www.nakedbus.com) partners with **Tairua Bus Company** (☎ 07-864 7770; www.tairuabus.co.nz; advance fares from $1) for daily services to Coromandel Town (one hour), Hahei (30 minutes), Hot Water Beach (40 minutes) and Tairua (one hour).

Go Kiwi (☎ 0800 446 549; www.go-kiwi.co.nz) shuttles head to Tairua ($24, one hour), Thames ($36, 1¾ hours) and Auckland ($65, four hours) daily, with services to Waihi ($42, 2¼ hours) and Tauranga ($60, three hours) from December to Easter.

HAHEI

pop 270 (7000 in summer)

A legendary Kiwi beach town, little Hahei balloons to bursting in summer but is nearly abandoned otherwise – apart from the busloads of tourists doing the obligatory stop-off at Cathedral Cove. It's a charming spot, and a great place to unwind for a few days, especially in the quieter months. It takes its name from Hei, the eponymous ancestor of the Ngati Hei people, who arrived in the 14th century on the *Te Arawa* canoe.

Sights & Activities

Beautiful **Cathedral Cove**, with its famous gigantic stone arch and natural waterfall shower, is best enjoyed early or late in the day – avoiding the worst of the hordes. At the car park, a kilometre north of Hahei, the signs suggest that the walk to the cove will take 45 minutes, but anyone who's not on a ventilator will do it in 30. On the way there's rocky **Gemstone Bay** (which has a snorkelling trail where you're likely to see big snapper, crayfish and stingrays) and sandy **Stingray Bay**.

It's a 70-minute walk from Cathedral Cove to **Hahei Beach**. From the southern end of Hahei Beach, it's a 15-minute walk up to **Te Pare**, a *pa* site with splendid coastal views.

Cathedral Cove Sea Kayaking (☎ 07-866 3877; www.seakayaktours.co.nz; 88 Hahei Beach Rd; half/full day $85/145) runs guided kayaking trips around the rock arches, caves and islands in the Cathedral Cove area. The Remote Coast Tour heads the other way when conditions permit, visiting caves, blowholes and a long tunnel.

If that sounds too much like hard work, you can tour the coast in an hour-long jet boat ride with **Hahei Explorer** (☎ 07-866 3910; www.haheiexplorer.co.nz; adult/child $65/40).

Cathedral Cove Dive & Snorkel (☎ 07-866 3955; www.hahei.co.nz/diving; Hahei Beach Rd; dives $69-105) takes daily dive trips and rents out scuba gear ($60), snorkelling gear ($20), bikes ($20) and boogie boards ($20). A Discover Scuba half-day beginners' course costs $160 including all the gear.

Sleeping & Eating

Hahei really does have a 'gone fishing' feel in the off-season. The local store remains open and the eateries take it in turns so that there's usually one option every evening. For more choice, catch the ferry over to Whitianga.

our pick Tatahi Lodge (☎ 07-866 3992; www.tatahilodge.co.nz; Grange Rd; dm/d $30/80, units $140-310; 🖳 🛜) A wonderful place where backpackers are treated with at least as much care and respect as the lush bromeliad-filled garden. The dorm rooms and excellent communal facilities are just as attractive as the pricier self-contained units. Gifts of free fruit in season provide much-needed vitamin replenishment to those hardcore bag-of-rice-a-week types.

Church (☎ 07-866 3533; www.thechurchhahei.co.nz; 87 Hahei Beach Rd; cottages $130-220; 🖳) These beautifully kitted-out, rustic timber cottages have stylish, modern interiors in a photogenic garden setting. Housed in the ultracharming wooden church at the top of the drive is Hahei's swankiest eatery (mains $30 to $37).

Getting There & Around

Tairua Bus Company (☎ 07-864 7770; www.tairuabus.co.nz; advance fares from $1), in association with **Naked Bus** (www.nakedbus.com), has daily services to Coromandel Town (90 minutes) via Whitianga (30 minutes) and Tairua (30 minutes) via Hot Water Beach (10 minutes).

From Boxing Day to Waitangi Day the council runs a bus service from the Cooks Beach side of the Ferry Landing to Hot Water Beach, stopping at Hahei (adult/child $2/1).

HOT WATER BEACH

Justifiably famous, Hot Water Beach is quite extraordinary. For two hours either side of low tide, you can access an area of sand in front of a rocky outcrop at the middle of the beach where hot water oozes up from beneath the surface. Bring a spade, dig a hole and voila, you've got a personal spa pool. Surfers stop off before the main beach to access some decent breaks. The headland between the two beaches still has traces of a Ngati Hei *pa*.

GETTING YOURSELF INTO HOT WATER...

Hot Water Beach has dangerous rips, especially directly in front of the main thermal section. It's one of the four most dangerous beaches in NZ in terms of drowning numbers, although this may be skewed by the huge number of tourists that flock here. Regardless, swimming here is *not* safe, so restrict your activities to burning your bum – unless the beach is patrolled.

Spades ($5) can be hired from the **Hot Water Beach Store** (☎ 07-866 3006; Pye Pl; 🕑 9am-7pm summer, low tide winter), which has a cafe attached. The wonderful **Hot Waves Café** (☎ 07-866 3887; 8 Pye Pl; meals $10-17; 🕑 8.30am-4pm) also hires spades ($5) and serves excellent food in cool surroundings. In summer there are queues out the door.

Near the beach, **Moko** (☎ 07-866 3367; www.moko.co.nz; 24 Pye Pl; 🕑 10am-5pm) is full of beautiful things – art, sculpture, jewellery – with a modern Pasifika/Maori bent.

Bordered by bamboo and gum trees **Hot Water Beach Holiday Park** (☎ 07-866 3116; www.hotwaterbeachholidaypark.com; 790 Hot Water Beach Rd; sites per person/dm $20/35; 🖳) is a smallish, newish camping ground with a modern shower and toilet block and four bunk-room cabins.

Auntie Dawn's Place (☎ 07-866 3707; www.auntiedawn.co.nz; 15 Radar Rd; dm $25, units $120-135) is a comfortable, spacious and homely house with a big garden that includes ancient pohutukawa trees. Backpacker beds are available in garden huts in summer.

A nice hillside pad, **Hot Water Beach B&B** (☎ 07-866 3991; www.hotwaterbedandbreakfast.co.nz; 48 Pye Pl; r $250) has priceless views, a spa bath on the deck and attractive living quarters.

The Hahei bus services also stop here, but only on prebooked requests.

COROGLEN & AROUND

Coroglen is a blink-and-you'll-miss-it village on SH25, south of Whitianga and west of Hot Water Beach. The legendary **Coroglen Tavern** (☎ 07-866 3809; www.coroglentavern.com; 1937 SH25) is the archetypal middle-of-nowhere country pub that attracts big-name Kiwi bands in summer.

Coroglen Farmers Market (☎ 07-866 3315; SH25; 🕑 9am-1pm Sun) sells a bit of everything produced in the local area, from vegetables to compost.

Nearby, the folks at **Rangihau Ranch** (☎ 07-866 3875; www.rangihauranch.co.nz; Rangihau Rd; 1/2hr trek $40/60) will lead you on horseback up a historic packhorse track, through beautiful bush to spectacular views.

Colenso Country Shop & Cafe (Map p192; ☎ 07-866 3725; Whenuakite; mains $7-17; ☒ 10am-5pm) has excellent fair-trade coffee, scones, cakes and light snacks, and a sweet atmosphere.

TAIRUA
pop 1269

Tairua and its twin town Pauanui sit either side of a river estuary that's perfect for windsurfing or for little kids to splash about in. Both have decent surf beaches (Pauanui's is probably a shade better), but that's where the similarity stops. Where Tairua is a functioning residential town (with shops, ATMs and a choice of eateries), Pauanui is an upmarket refugee camp for over-wealthy Aucklanders – the kind who jet in and park their private planes by their grandiose beach houses before knocking out a round of golf. Friendly Tairua knows how to keep it real. Both are ridiculously popular in the summertime.

Information
Tairua Information Centre (☎ 07-864 7575; www.tairua.info; 223 Main Rd; ☒ 9am-5pm Mon-Fri, 9am-4pm Sat & Sun)

Sights & Activities
Forming the north head of the harbour is craggy **Paku**, which around seven million years ago was a volcanic island. More recently it was a Ngati Hei *pa*, before being invaded by Ngati Maru in the 17th century. It's a steep 15-minute walk to the summit from the top of Paku Dr, with the payoff being amazing views over Tairua, Pauanui and the Alderman Islands. Plaques along the way detail Tairua's colonial history, with only one rather dismissive one devoted to its long Maori occupation.

Tairua Dive & Fishinn (☎ 07-864 8054; www.divetairua.co.nz; The Esplanade; ☒ 8am-5pm Wed-Sun, daily summer) hires out kayaks (some with glass bottoms), plus scuba, snorkel and fishing gear. The company also runs fishing charters, dive trips out to the Alderman Islands (dive and full gear $220, trip only $130, snorkelling $95) and PADI courses ($595).

Various operators offer fishing charters and sightseeing trips, including **Waipae Magic** (☎ 07-864 9415; dewy@slingshot.co.nz), **Taranui Charters** (☎ 07-864 8511; www.tairua.info/taranui), **Pauanui Charters** (☎ 07-864 9262; www.pauanuicharters.co.nz) and **Epic Adventures** (☎ 07-864 8193; www.epicadventures.co.nz). For a much cheaper option, the Tairua–Pauanui ferry (p208) offers two-to three-hour evening fishing trips for $25 (minimum four people).

Sleeping
Tairua Beach Villa Backpackers (☎ 07-864 8345; tairuabackpackers@xtra.co.nz; 200 Main Rd; sites per person $22, dm $25-28, s $50-55, d $60-64, tr/q $90/116; ☐) Rooms are homey and casual at this estuary-edge hostel in a converted house, and the dorm scores great views. Guests can help themselves to avocados, feijoas, eggs, fishing rods, kayaks, sailboards and bikes, and windsurfing lessons cost a paltry $20.

Pinnacles Backpackers (☎ 07-864 8448; www.pinnaclesbakpak.co.nz; 305 Main Rd; dm $25-28, d $56; ☐ ☐) A more than life-sized Obelix cartoon welcomes you to this midsized hostel, north of the town centre. A recent renovation has left new carpets and paintwork in its wake and there's a balcony, a free pool table and bikes for hire.

Pacific Harbour Lodge (☎ 07-864 8581; www.pacificharbour.co.nz; 223 Main Rd; chalets $189-259; ☐ ☐) This 'island-style' resort in the town centre has spacious self-contained chalets, with natural wood and Gauguin decor inside and a South Seas garden outside. Discount packages are usually available.

Dell Cote (☎ 07-864 8142; www.dellcote.com; Rewarewa Valley Rd; s/d $210/240) Nontoxic mud bricks and macrocarpa timber give this place an organic feel, and the swooping gardens add a dose of tranquillity. The loft room is particularly lovely.

Eating & Drinking
Out of the Blue Cafe (☎ 07-864 8987; 227 Main Rd; meals $8-18; ☒ 7am-4pm) This popular meeting place serves decent coffee, breakfast, counter snacks and light meals such as salads and sandwiches.

Old Mill Cafe (☎ 07-864 9390; 1 The Esplanade; mains $8-19; ☒ 8.30am-4.30pm Thu-Sun) There's nothing run-of-the-mill about this old dear. Zooshed up with bright pink feature walls and elegant veranda furniture, it serves delights such as buttermilk-and-blueberry pancakes, *croque monsieurs*, New England chowder and perfectly gooey chocolate tarts.

Punters Bar & Grill (☎ 07-864 9370; Main Rd; mains $10-30; ☒ 11am-late Tue-Sun) Punters is primarily a pub, but it also serves decent snacks (such

COROMANDEL REGION

as crunchy panini slices with dips) and giant burgers with a choice of scotch fillet or fish instead of the usual random meat patty.

Manaia Cafe & Bar (☎ 07-864 9050; 228 Main Rd; brunch $12-17, dinner $18-27; ✆ breakfast, lunch & dinner Tue-Sun) With courtyard seating for lazy summer brunches and a burnished copper bar to prop up later in the night, Manaia is a slick addition to the Tairua strip. The dinner menu features bistro faves with some artful twists.

Getting There & Around

InterCity (☎ 0508 353 947; www.intercity.co.nz) has daily buses to/from Thames ($17, 44 minutes) and Whitianga ($17, 44 minutes). **Tairua Bus Company** (☎ 07-864 7770; www.tairuabus. co.nz; advance fares from $1), in conjunction with **Naked Bus** (www.nakedbus.com), has daily services to Thames (50 minutes) and to Coromandel Town (two hours) via Hot Water Beach (25 minutes), Hahei (30 minutes) and Whitianga (one hour).

Go Kiwi (☎ 0800 446 549; www.go-kiwi.co.nz) door-to-door shuttles head to Whitianga ($24, one hour), Thames ($26, 70 minutes) and Auckland ($66, 2¼ hours) daily, with services to Waihi ($30, 1½ hours) and Tauranga ($48, 2¼ hours) from December to Easter.

Tairua and Pauanui are connected by a passenger **ferry** (☎ 027-497 0316; one way/return $3/5; ✆ Sat & Sun Mar-Nov, daily Dec-Feb), which departs every two hours from 9am to 5pm, running more frequently and for longer hours in summer.

AROUND TAIRUA
Puketui Valley

Located 12km south of Tairua is the turn-off to Puketui Valley and the historic **Broken Hills gold-mine workings** (Map p192), which are 8km from the main road along a mainly gravel road. There are short walks up to the sites of stamper batteries, but the best hike is through the 500m-long Collins Drive mine tunnel. After the tunnel, look out for the short 'lookout' side trail which affords panoramic views. It takes about three hours return; remember to take a torch and a jacket with you.

You can stay at the basic DOC **campsite** (Map p192; adult/child $9/2), located in a pretty spot by the river. This is a wilderness area so take care and be properly prepared. Water from the river should be boiled before drinking.

Slipper Island

The privately owned **Slipper Island** (☎ 07-864 7560; www.slipper.co.nz) has campsites (adult/child $20/15) in South Bay and chalet accommodation (self-contained units $250 to $750) in Home Bay. You'll need to call ahead to arrange transfers by charter boat ($65 per person, minimum four), light plane or helicopter.

OPOUTERE

File this one under best-kept secrets. Maybe it's a local conspiracy to keep at bay the hordes of Aucklanders who seasonally invade Pauanui and Whangamata, as this unspoilt long sandy expanse has been kept very quiet. Apart from a cluster of houses there's nothing for miles around. Swimming can be dangerous, especially near Hikinui Islet, which is close to the beach. On the sand spit is the **Wharekawa Wildlife Refuge**, a breeding ground for the endangered NZ dotterel.

One of the guardians of the secret is **Opoutere Coastal Camping** (☎ 07-865 9152; www.opouterebeach.co.nz; 460 Ohui Rd; sites per adult/child $13/8, cabins $75-145) – its motto is 'remote and untouched, just the way we like it'. Numbers are strictly limited, so book ahead for this summer-only camping ground, offering flat, sheltered tent sites and a few cabins.

ourpick Opoutere YHA (☎ 07-865 9072; www.yha. co.nz; 389 Opoutere Rd; sites per person $17, dm $27-30, d $76-106; 🖳 🛜) is a wonderful get-away-from-it-all hostel with plenty of birdsong. Kayaks, hot-water bottles, alarm clocks, stilts and hula hoops can all be borrowed. The largest dorm is housed in what was once Opoutere Native School. You can harvest shellfish from the beach but you'll need to bring other food with you.

A peaceful country-style villa with kind hosts and en-suite rooms, **Copsefield B&B** (Map p192; ☎ 07-865 9555; www.copsefield.co.nz; 1055 SH25; r $140-200) is set in attractive, lush gardens with a spa and a riverside swimming hole. There's a guest lounge with complimentary hot beverages, which you can sip on the jasmine-scented decks.

Go Kiwi (☎ 0800 446 549; www.go-kiwi.co.nz) runs shuttles between Opoutere and Whangamata ($11, 10 minutes); call for dates and times.

WHANGAMATA
pop 3600

While Auckland's socially ambitious flock to Pauanui, the city's young and horny head to Whangamata to surf, get stoned and hook up.

It can be a raucous spot over New Year, when the population swells to over 40,000. A true summer holiday town, in the off-season there may as well be tumbleweeds rolling down the main street.

Information

Bartley Internet & Graphics (☎ 07-865 8832; 706 Port Rd) Internet access.

Whangamata i-SITE (☎ 07-865 8340; www.whanga matainfo.co.nz; 616 Port Rd; 9am-5pm Mon-Fri, 10am-4.30pm, 10am-2pm Sun)

Activities

Besides fishing (game-fishing runs from January to April), snorkelling near Hauturu (Clarke) Island, surfing, kayaking, orienteering and mountain biking, there are excellent walks. The **Wentworth Falls walk** (end of Wentworth Valley Rd) takes two hours one way; it starts 3km south of the town and 4km down a good gravel road. A further 3km south of Wentworth Valley Rd is the turn-off to the **Wharekirauponga walk** (end of Parakiwai Quarry Rd), a sometimes muddy 10km return track (allow four hours) to a mining camp, battery and waterfall that passes unusual hexagonal lava columns and loquacious birdlife.

A local version of Crocodile Dundee, Doug Johansen offers informative one- to 14-day wilderness walks under the name **Kiwi Dundee Adventures** (☎ 07-865 8809; www.kiwidundee. co.nz).

Sleeping

Wentworth Valley campsite (Map p192; ☎ 07-865 7032; adult/child $9/2) More upmarket than most DOC camping grounds, it's accessed from the Wentworth Falls walk, and has toilets, hot showers ($1) and gas barbecues.

Southpacific Accommodation (☎ 07-865 9580; www.thesouthpacific.co.nz; 249 Port Rd; dm $27-29, s $46, d $68-74, units $138-153;) This hard-to-miss, corner-hogging complex consists of a big barn for backpackers and self-contained motel units. Facilities are clean and modern; bikes and kayaks are available for hire.

Gabry's Place (☎ 07-865 6295; livio@xtra.co.nz; 103 Mark St; unit $80) If you feel like you missed out by not having Italian grandparents, come and stay here. The very sweet hosts will fuss around a bit, make sure you're set up with milk and cookies, and then leave you to enjoy this large, scrupulously clean, self-contained unit.

Marine Reserved (☎ 07-865 9096; www.marine reservedapartments.co.nz; cnr Ocean Rd & Lowe St; units $250;) It's a peculiar name but the other strange thing about this excellent townhouse complex is that up to six of you can stay here in considerable comfort for $250. Each has secure ground floor parking, a full modern kitchen and barbecues on the decks. Try for the three-level apartments fronting Ocean Rd – they're larger, and the extra height ensures sea views.

Eating & Drinking

Craig's Traditional Fish & Chips (☎ 07-865 8717; 701 Port Rd; meals $4-10; lunch & dinner Wed-Mon) All you could ask for in a chippie, Craig's cooks up pieces of grilled fresh fish and fat, salted chips. The service is friendly, and there's a TV and a stack of trashy mags to speed up the wait.

Lazy Lizard (☎ 07-865 7340; 427 Port Rd; mains $6-14; 7.30am-3.30pm Tue-Sun) Winning points for bizarre hand-shaped stools, this funky lizard does delicious counter food, cooked breakfasts, bagels and salads. The fair-trade organic coffee is first rate.

Soul Burger (☎ 07-865 8194; 441 Port Rd; burgers $7-11; dinner Thu-Sun winter, daily summer) It's hard to argue with the 'Eat, Love, Live' motto or the audacious burgers of this hip corner joint. Try a Coromandel Ninja (beef, wasabi, pickled ginger, salad) or a Vegan Vibe.

The monster-sized **New World** (☎ 07-865 0400; 300 Aickin St; 7.30am-6.30pm) will take care of your grocery needs.

Getting There & Away

Go Kiwi (☎ 0800 446 549; www.go-kiwi.co.nz) has shuttles to Thames ($64, 70 minutes), Auckland ($82, 2¼ hours) and Hamilton ($70, 3½ hours), with services to Waihi ($25, 35 minutes) and Tauranga ($40, 90 minutes) from December to Easter.

WAIHI

pop 4500

Where most towns have hole-in-the-wall ATMs for people to access their riches, Waihi's main street has a giant open-cast gold mine. They've been dragging gold and silver out of Martha Mine, NZ's richest, since 1878. The town formed quickly and blinged itself up with grand buildings and a show-offy avenue of phoenix palms, now magnificently mature.

After closing down in 1952, open-cast mining restarted in 1988. The mine is still productive, but only just – it takes a tonne of rock to yield 3g to 6g of gold. It's expected to run out soon, and when it does, plans are afoot to convert the town's gaping wound into a major tourist attraction. Watch this space.

Information
Post office (21 Rosemont Rd) Has poste restante service.
Waihi visitor centre (07-863 6715; www.waihi.org. nz; 126 Seddon St; 9am-5pm) Offers internet access.

Sights & Activities
The main drag, Seddon St, has interesting sculptures, information panels about Waihi's golden past and roundabouts that look like squashed daleks. The *Historic Hauraki Gold Towns* pamphlet (free from the visitor centre) outlines walking tours of both Waihi and Paeroa's town centres.

Opposite the visitor centre, the skeleton of a derelict **Cornish Pumphouse** (1904) is the town's main landmark, atmospherically lit at night. From here the **Pit Rim Walkway** has fascinating views into the 250m-deep Martha Mine. If you want to get down into it, the mining company runs 1½-hour **Waihi Gold Mine Tours** (07-863 9015; tours adult/child $25/13; 10am & 12.30pm Mon-Sat).

Goldfields Railway (07-863 8251; www.waihirail. co.nz; 30 Wrigley St; adult/child return $15/8; Fri-Mon Apr-Aug, daily Sep-Mar) runs vintage trains to Waikino, leaving Waihi station daily at 10am, 11.45am and 1.45pm; from Waikino it's 11am, 1pm and 2.30pm. The 7km-long scenic journey takes 25 minutes.

The **Waihi Arts Centre & Museum** (07-863 8386; www.waihimuseum.co.nz; 54 Kenny St; adult/child $5/3; 11am-3pm Thu-Sun) features displays and models of the region's gold-mining history and a gallery. Prepare to squirm before the collection of miners' chopped-off thumbs preserved in glass jars.

Waterlily Gardens (Map p192; 07-863 8267; www.waterlily.co.nz; 441 Pukekauri Rd; adult/child $8.50/free; 10am-4pm Oct-Apr) is 18 acres of ponds, peacocks and pretty things, 7km southwest of Waihi. There's a cafe on-site.

If that sounds a bit too clean and calm, you can hit the slopes on a mutant snowboard/skateboard with **Dirtboard Waihi** (021-244 1646; www.dirtboard.co.nz; per hr $30) or take an on-/off-road dirt bike tour with **Over The Top Adventures** (021-205 7266; www.overthetopadventures.co.nz; 1 Surrey St; tours $90-460). The latter also rents mountain bikes (per day $35 to $45), which will be especially handy when the **Hauraki Rail Trail** is completed. At the time of research the gov-

ernment had announced the decision to fast-track this cycle route from Waihi to Paeroa via the Karangahake Gorge, incorporating it into its proposed National Cycleway.

If you'd rather exercise your wallet than your calf muscles, **Artmarket** (07-863 9010; 65 Seddon St; 10am-5pm) has a first-rate selection of local arts and crafts.

Sleeping & Eating
Westwind B&B (07-863 7208; westwindgarden@xtra. co.nz; 58 Adams St; s/d $50/90) Run by a charming couple who are inveterate travellers themselves, this old-fashioned homestay B&B has two comfortable rooms with a shared bathroom. Expect a good chat over breakfast.

Waterlily Gardens (Map p192; 07-863 8267; www. waterlily.co.nz; 441 Pukekauri Rd; cottages $250) You get the gardens all to yourself after-hours if you're staying in one of the two gorgeous modern cottages. They're beautifully decked out with comfy beds, quality linen, polished concrete floors and interesting art.

Manawa Ridge (Map p192; 07-863 9400; www. manawaridge.co.nz; 267 Ngatitangata Rd; r $650) The views from this castlelike ecoretreat, perched on a 310m ridge 6km northeast of Waihi, take in the entire Bay of Plenty. Made entirely of recycled railway timber, mud brick and lime-plastered straw walls, the rooms marry earthiness with sheer luxury.

Ti-tree Cafe (07-863 8668; 14 Haszard St; brunch $5-17, dinner $17-24; breakfast & lunch daily, dinner Fri & Sat) Housed in a cute little wooden building with punga-shaded outdoor seating, Ti-tree serves fair-trade organic coffee, cooked breakfasts and wood-fired pizza.

Meeting Place Bar & Restaurant (07-863 7474; 22 Haszard St; mains $16-28; lunch Mon-Sat, dinner daily) These grand chambers once belonged to the local council. The cosy bar is more appealing than the cavernous dining room, but servings are massive and the slightly retro fare is surprisingly nice.

Getting There & Away
Waihi is a stop for **InterCity** (0508 353 947; www. intercity.co.nz) buses heading between Auckland ($36, 2¾ hours) and Tauranga ($20, one hour) via Thames ($20, 45 minutes), Paeroa ($20, 19 minutes) and Waihi Beach ($9, 12 minutes).

Naked Bus (0900 625 33 per min $1.80; www.naked bus.com; advance fares from $1) also has daily buses on the Auckland–Tauranga route, with connections to Paihia, Rotorua and Gisborne.

Go Kiwi (☎ 0800 446 549; www.go-kiwi.co.nz) offers seasonal shuttles from December to Easter between Whitianga ($42, 2¼ hours) and Mt Maunganui ($28, 80 minutes), also stopping in Tairua ($30, 1½ hours) Whangamata ($25, 35 minutes) and Tauranga ($25, one hour).

WAIHI BEACH
pop 1800

While Waihi is interesting for a brief visit, it's Waihi Beach where you'll want to linger. The two places are as dissimilar as surfing is from mining, separated by 11km of farmland. The long sandy beach stretches 9km to Bowentown, on the northern limits of Tauranga Harbour, where you'll find sheltered harbour beaches such as beautiful Anzac Bay. There's a very popular 45-minute walk north through bush to pristine Orokawa Bay, which has no road access.

Sunshine Surf Coaching (☎ 07-863 4857; www.sunshinesurfcoaching.co.nz; lesson $80) takes advantage of Waihi Beach's relatively gentle breaks to offer all-age surf instruction.

Down the south end, **Bowentown Beach Holiday Park** (☎ 07-863 5381; www.bowentown.co.nz; 510 Seaforth Rd; sites per adult/child $19/11, cabins $65-145, units $105-218; 🖥) has nabbed a stunning stretch of sand. It's impressively maintained and even has a barbecue area with a water feature.

Hugging the harbour is **Athenree Hot Springs & Holiday Park** (☎ 07-863 5600; www.athenreehotsprings.co.nz; Athenree Rd; sites per adult/child $22/11, cabins $60, units $140-150; 🖥 🛜), with two blissful outdoor thermal pools (adult/child $7/4.50, open 10am to 7.30pm). Entry is free if you stay in the smart accommodation.

The massive, resort-style **Waihi Beach Top 10 Holiday Park** (☎ 07-863 5504; www.waihibeach.com; 15 Beach Rd; sites per adult/child $25/16, cabins $75-175, units $160-250; 🖥 🛜) is pretty damn flash, with a pool, gym, spa, beautiful kitchen and smorgasbord of sleeping options.

Beachfront B&B (☎ 07-863 5393; www.beachfrontbandb.co.nz; 3 Shaw Rd; d/tr $120/160) is true to its name, with absolute beachfront and spectacular sea views. The comfortable downstairs flat has a TV, fridge and direct access to the surf.

Porch (☎ 07-863 1330; 23 Wilson Rd; brunch $12-19, dinner $26-33; breakfast & lunch daily, dinner Tue-Sat) is the town's coolest chow-down spot, serving sophisticated, substantial mains.

Funky, licensed and right by the beach, **Flatwhite** (☎ 07-863 1346; 21 Shaw Rd; brunch $13-20,

dinner $17-30; breakfast, lunch & dinner;) has a lively brunch menu and decent pizzas.

KARANGAHAKE GORGE

The road between Waihi and Paeroa, through the bush-lined ramparts of the Karangahake Gorge, is one of the best short drives in the country. There are interesting walks in the area, taking in old Maori trails, historic mining and rail detritus, and spookily dense bush. In Maori legend the area is said to be protected by a *taniwha*, a supernatural creature. The local *iwi* managed to keep this area closed to miners until 1875, aligning themselves with the militant Te Kooti (see the boxed text, p368).

The very worthwhile 4.5km **Karangahake Gorge Historic Walkway** (Map p192) takes 1½ hours (each way) and starts from the car park, 14km west of Waihi. It follows the disused railway line and the Ohinemuri River to Owharoa Falls and Waikino station, where you can pick up the vintage train to Waihi. **Waikino Station Café** (☎ 07-863 8640; SH2; mains $4-16; 9.30am-3pm daily, dinner Fri) is a perfect lunch stop before heading back.

There are a range of shorter walks and loop tracks leading from the car park; bring a torch as some head through tunnels. A two-hour tramp will bring you to Dickey's Flat, where there's a free DOC **campsite** (Map p192; Dickey's Flat Rd) and a decent swimming hole. River water will need to be boiled for drinking. You'll find DOC information boards about the walks and the area's history at both the station and the main car park.

Across from the car park, **Golden Owl Backpackers** (☎ 07-862 7994; www.goldenowl.co.nz; 3 Moresby St; dm/d $28/60; 🖥 🛜) is a homely, handy tramping base, sleeping only 12. Allow $5 extra for linen in the dorm rooms.

Further up the same road, **Ohinemuri Estate Winery** (Map p192; ☎ 07-862 8874; www.ohinemuri.co.nz; Moresby St; mains $17-28; 10am-5pm daily Oct-Apr, 10am-5pm Fri-Sun May-Sep) has Latvian-influenced architecture and serves excellent lunches. The portions are large and the prices extremely reasonable. You'd be right if you thought it was an unusual site for growing grapes – the winery imports fruit from other regions. Tastings are $5, refundable with purchase. If you imbibe too much, snaffle the chalet-style hut and revel in the charming atmosphere of this secluded place (double/triple/quad $110/125/140).

Nearby **Talisman Cafe** (☎ 07-862 8306; SH2; meals $5-21; ☟ 9am-4pm) is more distinguished by its magical new-age decor and kitschy crafts than its coffee and food, but there's plenty to sustain hungry hikers.

PAEROA
pop 4000

If you find yourself scratching your head in Paeroa, don't worry too much about it. The whole town is an elaborate Kiwi in-joke. It's the birthplace of Lemon & Paeroa (L&P), an icon of Kiwiana that markets itself as 'world famous in NZ'. The fact that the beloved fizzy drink is now owned by global monster Coca-Cola Amatil and produced in Auckland only serves to make the ubiquitous L&P branding on every shopfront even more darkly ironic.

Still, generations of Kiwi kids have pestered their parents to take this route just to catch a glimpse of the giant L&P bottles.

The small **museum** (☎ 07-862 8486; 37 Belmont Rd; adult/child $2/1; ☟ 10.30am-3pm Mon-Fri) has a grand selection of Royal Albert porcelain and other pioneer and Maori artefacts – look in the drawers. If pretty crockery is your thing, Paeroa is known for its antique stores.

L&P Cafe & Bar (☎ 07-862 7773; SH2; mains $11-19; ☟ breakfast & lunch daily, dinner Wed-Sun) has a truck-stop ambience, but is as good a place as any to find out what all the fuss is about. You can order L&P fish and chips or an L&P brekkie, along with the lemony lolly water itself. The cafe shares the space with the **information centre** (☎ 07-862 8636; www.paeroa.org.nz; ☟ 9am-4pm).

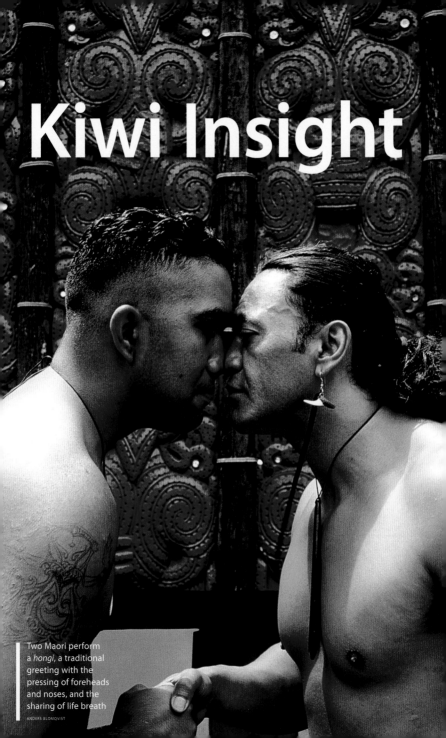

Kiwi Insight

Two Maori perform a *hongi*, a traditional greeting with the pressing of foreheads and noses, and the sharing of life breath

ANDERS BLOMQVIST

Going Bush

NAME	Furhana Ahmad
AGE	48
OCCUPATION	Guide & Owner-Operator, Ruggedy Range Wilderness Experience
RESIDENCE	Stewart Island

'the fantastic night skies I've experienced on Stewart Island are like being in a planetarium'

'It's hard not to fall for New Zealand. There are mountain tops that take your breath away, river systems winding their way to sea level, and lush forests with ferns that date back millions of years. Vast areas of the country have seen little change and you really can wander for hours without seeing anyone else. NZ's lively weather also continually changes the mood of the scenery, and the incredible natural energy makes you feel a bit humble when you look around and see what nature has carved.

'Stewart Island has got extra appeal for me. It's a largely unmodified wilderness with luxuriant primeval forest ringing with native birds. There are tiny orchids you could easily overlook, and unspoiled beaches that are lashed by wild seas. The crystal-clear waters are literally teeming with marine life, and the fantastic night skies I've experienced on Stewart Island are like being in a planetarium.'

AS RELATED TO AUTHOR BRETT ATKINSON

Trampers descend into the lush forests of Te Urewera National Park (p374)

OLIVER STREWE

Dwarfed by the landscape – a lone hiker tackles the Cascade Saddle Route (p633)

GARETH MCCORMACK

THREE GREAT TRAMPS

Heaphy Track (p480) Marvel at the array of different vegetation, from inland forest to the tussock-covered Gouland Downs and desert-island nikau palms beside wild west-coast surf.

Rakiura Track (p676) Complete a day hike from Port William for a tempting taste of Stewart Island's forest and coastal scenery with birdsong and bird life unlike elsewhere in New Zealand.

Rees-Dart Track (p631) Take a side trip along the Dart Glacier for stunning views of Mt Aspiring from the Cascade Saddle. Expect to be wrapped up in magnificent scenery from all points of your compass.

The sun sets over secluded Stewart Island (p672)

DAVID WALL

Crossing the suspension bridge over Kohaihai River at the start of the Heaphy Track (p480)

ROSS BARNETT

Urban Pasifika

NAME	Shimpal Lelisi
AGE	38
OCCUPATION	Actor (*bro'Town, Sione's Wedding*)
RESIDENCE	Auckland

'At its core Polyfest is still about teaching the young people all of the old songs, but it's really exciting to see change.'

'To try Pacific Island food in Auckland, head to the markets at Otara, Avondale or Mangere, or to a festival day put on by the community – Pasifika and Polyfest are always good. Polyfest is in March, and it's the biggest PI cultural festival in the world. It's been going on since the early '70s and it's enormous, with thousands of people coming through. I was in the Niuean group when I was at school, and it was when I first got the buzz for performing. It's amazing now watching the calibre of the performances. The students take it really seriously, and there are new moves every year – it's like *Strictly Ballroom*! Last year they were even doing krumping. At its core Polyfest is still about teaching the young people all of the old songs, but it's really exciting to see change.'

AS RELATED TO AUTHOR BRETT ATKINSON

Feather-clad dancers representing the Cook Islands wait to go on-stage for their Pasifika (p113) performance

PAUL KENNEDY

Polyfest (p113) celebrates Pacific Island culture through the performances of students throughout Auckland

MARTY TAYLOR / HEDGEHOG HOUSE / PHOTONEWZEALAND

ESSENTIAL URBAN PASIFIKA

O'Kai Oceanikart (p126) Specialising in art from across the Pacific, this gallery is the place to see works by well-known artists such as Fatu Feu'u and exciting up-and-comers.

Otara Market (p126) Pick up the best of reggae and hip-hop beats from across the Pacific at Auckland's best market. Be sure to buy a still-warm coconut bun before you leave.

Polyfest (p113) Dive into the Maori and Pacific Island cultural festival for Auckland's youth. Performers incorporate the latest hip-hop moves into traditional songs and dances.

Multicultural Auckland (p94) boasts the largest Polynesian population of any city in the world

HOLGER LEUE

Telling Stories

NAME	Mary Varnham
AGE	Timeless
OCCUPATION	Publisher & History Buff
RESIDENCE	Wellington

'to this day, the town (Akaroa) mantains a strong French character – a reminder that NZ may well have become another French country in the Pacific.'

'The French had New Zealand pegged as their colony, but the British beat them to it. They still managed to settle in Akaroa, however, and to this day the town maintains a strong French character – a reminder that NZ may well have become another French country in the Pacific.

'In the 1870s and '80s Arrowtown was home to many poor Chinese men who lived lonely lives in tiny dwellings, with bitter winters to contend with, trying to eke a living out of gold mining after the main spoils were gone.

'Mercury Bay's Maori tribe – Ngati Hei – lived an idyllic life with a kind climate and bounty from the sea. This came to a brutal end when Ngapuhi chief Hongi Hika exchanged gifts from George VI for muskets, and after returning home rampaged down the North Island's east coast, massacring the Ngati Hei at Hahei. Their *pa* sites can still be seen at the eastern end of the beach.'

AS RELATED TO AUTHOR SARAH BENNETT

The restored gold-mining settlement of Arrowtown (p625) is a half-hour drive from the extreme-sports haven of Queenstown

GLENN VAN DER KNIJFF

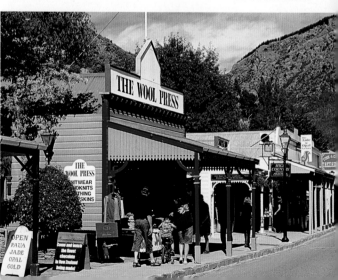

The lives of the early settlers are recreated in the gold-mining towns of Central Otago (p589)
JON DAVISON

NATURAL HISTORY HIGHLIGHTS

Cathedral Cove (p205) With its beautifully sculptured volcanic cliffs and spectacular arch, this is the perfect place to get married, if you have a mind to.

Central Otago (p589) Proof that not all modified landscapes are bad! Home to some of the country's finest pinot noir, Bannockburn has been significantly altered by mining, while the vast artificial lake, Dunstan, is beautiful and dramatic.

French street signs hint at the origins of Akaroa (p542), an easy day trip from Christchurch
PAUL KENNEDY

Wild at Heart

NAME	Paul McGahan
AGE	56
OCCUPATION	NZ Historic Places Trust Manager
RESIDENCE	Kaikoura

WILDLIFE HOTSPOTS

Kaikoura (p449) Kaikoura is wildlife central! Whale-watching is big business here (from boat, plane or helicopter), or you can hang out with dolphins, albatross or sea lions.

Otago Peninsula (p585) Spread your wings not far from Dunedin: encounter an enormous albatross or a wee (but no less impressive) yellow-eyed penguin.

Stewart Island (p672) The place to see NZ's iconic nocturnal kiwi – if you're lucky, they might even be awake during the day!

'Kaikoura is an outstanding place to see marine mammals – sperm, southern right and humpback whales, plus endangered Hector's dolphins, dusky dolphins, killer whales, New Zealand fur seals and leopard seals. You'll also see humpback whales off Arapawa Island in the Marlborough Sounds. The Catlins coast is the place for Hooker's sea lions.

'Kaikoura is also fantastic for sea birds: albatross, shearwaters, even southern crested grebes. Farewell Spit is great for gannets and bar-tailed godwits; Stewart Island for kiwi. The Otago Peninsula near Dunedin has yellow-eyed penguins and albatross. Karori Sanctuary in Wellington has tuatara.

'If travellers want to do some volunteering, there's a Hutton's shearwater translocation project here on the Kaikoura Peninsula, the Codfish Island kakapo project, or the yellow-eyed penguin project in Dunedin. There's some fantastic volunteer work happening on Tiritiri Matangi Island off Auckland, too. Have a look at the DOC website (www.doc.govt.nz) – there are a lot of projects going on.'

AS RELATED TO AUTHOR CHARLES RAWLINGS-WAY

Left Dolphin leaping at Kaikoura (p449)

MICHAEL GEBICKI

Right The ancient tuatara (p69)

DAVID WALL

Waikato & the King Country

If the colour green had a homeland this would be it. Verdant fields give way to rolling hills in the countryside around New Zealand's mightiest river, the Waikato. Visitors from southern England might wonder why they bothered leaving home, especially in quaint towns like Cambridge where every effort has been made to replicate the 'mother country'. It's little wonder that Peter Jackson chose the Waikato as the bucolic Shire in his movie adaptation of *Lord of the Rings*.

But this veneer of conspicuous Englishness only partly disguises another reality. Move over hobbits, this is Tainui country. This powerful coalition of related tribes joined with others to elect a king in the 1850s to resist the loss of their land and sovereignty. Although the fertile Waikato was taken from them by war, they retained control of the limestone crags and forests of what became known as the King Country to within a whisper of the 20th century. The back roads along the coast still contain tiny outposts of Maoridom, echoes of an earlier era.

Today's visitors can experience first-hand the area's genteel/free-wheeling dichotomy. Adrenaline junkies will be drawn to the wild surf of Raglan or rough-and-tumble underground pursuits in the extraordinary Waitomo Caves, while others will warm to the more sedate delights of Te Aroha's Edwardian thermal complex or Hamilton's gardens.

It's the Waikato River that symbolises this best – in places idyllic lakes have been created by harnessing it to hydroelectric projects while elsewhere its *mauri* (life force) flows fast and free.

HIGHLIGHTS

- Seeking subterranean thrills in the **Waitomo Caves** (p242)
- Hanging with the bronzed crowd while hanging-ten at **Raglan** (p230)
- Discovering your own bush-framed black-sand beach on the rugged **west coast** (p246)
- Pigging out on Maori culture at Kawhia **Kai Festival** (p240)
- Soaking up 'the love' in the thermal waters of **Te Aroha** (p239)
- Plotting a pub crawl in surprisingly buzzy **Hamilton** (p228)
- Tramping through an inland island paradise at **Maungatautari** (p235)

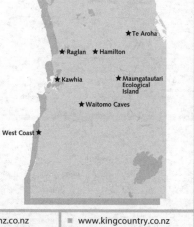

■ Telephone code: 07　　■ www.waikatonz.co.nz　　■ www.kingcountry.co.nz

WAIKATO & THE KING COUNTRY

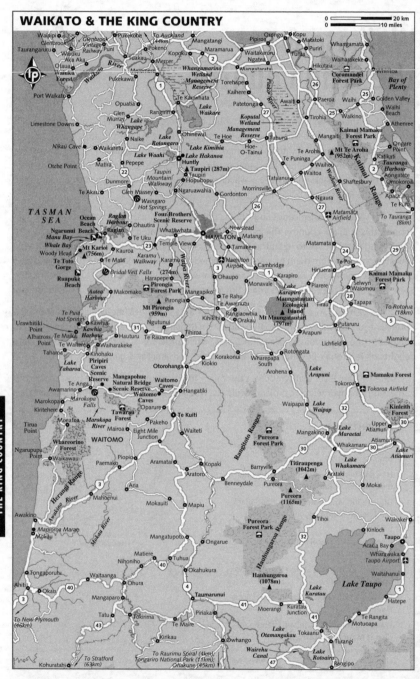

Climate

The southern area around Taumarunui is wetter and colder than the rest of the region, which can suffer summer droughts.

Getting There & Around

Hamilton is the transport hub, with its airport (p229) servicing some international and extensive domestic routes. Buses link the city to everywhere in the North Island. Most inland towns are also well connected on bus routes, but the remote coastal communities (apart from Mokau on SH3) are less well served.

Trains are another option but they are infrequent and surprisingly expensive on short legs. The main trunk-line between Auckland and Wellington stops at Hamilton, Otorohanga, Te Kuiti and Taumarunui.

WAIKATO

History

By the time Europeans started to arrive, this region – stretching as far north as Auckland's Manukau Harbour – had long been the homeland of the Waikato tribes, descended from the Tainui migration (p224). In settling this land they displaced or absorbed tribes from earlier migrations.

Initially European contact was on Maori terms and to the advantage of the local people. Their fertile land, which was already cultivated with kumara and other crops, was well suited to the introduction of new fruits and vegetables. By the 1840s the Waikato economy was booming, with bulk quantities of produce exported to the settlers in Auckland and beyond. Rangiaowhia, near Te Awamutu, became a prosperous farming town – much to the envy of the new arrivals, who coveted the flat fecund Waikato plains.

Relations between the two cultures soured during the 1850s, largely due to the colonists' pressure to purchase Maori land. In response, a confederation of tribes united to elect a king to safeguard their interests, forming what became known as the 'King Movement' (see the boxed text, p225).

In July 1863 Governor Grey sent a huge force to invade the Waikato and exert colonial control. After almost a year of fighting, known as the Waikato War, the Kingites retreated south to what became branded the King

---

WAIKATO & THE KING COUNTRY FACTS

Eat Rotten corn at Kawhia's Kai Festival (p240)

Drink Gut-cleansing soda water in Te Aroha (p239)

Read *Potiki* (1986) by Patricia Grace

Listen to The sacred sounds of Te Awamutu (see the boxed text, p234): Crowded House's 'Mean to Me', Split Enz' 'Kia Kaha', 'Haul Away'

Watch *Black Sheep* (2006) – those Te Kuiti shearers should be very afraid

Swim at Ngarunui Beach near Raglan (p232)

Festival Running of the Sheep, Te Kuiti (p247)

Tackiest tourist attraction The *Big Shearer*, Te Kuiti (p247)

Go green Off-the-grid tepees at Solscape (p232)

Country. Europeans didn't dare to venture there for several decades.

The war resulted in the confiscation of 360,000 hectares of land, much of which was given to colonial soldiers to farm and defend. In 1995 the Waikato tribes received a full Crown apology for the wrongful invasion and confiscation of their lands, as well as a $170 million package, including the return of land that the Crown still held.

NORTH OF HAMILTON

Most people blast along SH1 between Auckland and Hamilton in about 90 minutes, but if you're in the mood to meander, the upper Waikato has some interesting diversions.

Port Waikato

While the name might conjure up images of heavy industry and crusty seadogs, that's far from the reality of this petite village at the mouth of the mighty river. There's little here apart from an old-fashioned collection of baches (holiday homes), a couple of *marae* (meeting house) complexes, a store and a beautiful but treacherous surf beach. Lifeguards are on duty in summer, but only between 10am and 6pm on weekends and school holidays; strong rips render it unsafe for swimming at other times.

Waikatoa Beach Lodge (☎ 09-232 9961; www.sunsetbeach.co.nz; 8 Centreway Rd; dm/s/d from $28/38/64, tw $56-64) spoils visiting beach-bums with smart rooms, decent linen and a welcoming kitchen/lounge area with gas cooking.

MAORI NZ: WAIKATO & THE KING COUNTRY

Despite or perhaps because of its turbulent history (see p223), this area remains one of the strongest pockets of Maori influence in the country. This is the heartland of the Tainui tribes, descended from those who disembarked from the *Tainui waka* (canoe) in Kawhia in the 14th century. Split into four main tribal divisions (Waikato, Hauraki, Ngati Maniapoto and Ngati Raukawa), Tainui are inextricably linked with the Kingitanga (King Movement; opposite), which has its base in Ngaruawahia.

The best opportunities to interact with Maori culture are the Kawhia Kai Festival (p240), and Ngaruawahia's Regatta Day and Koroneihana celebrations (opposite). Interesting *taonga* (treasures) are displayed at museums in Hamilton (opposite) and Te Awamutu (p233). Reminders of the Waikato Land War can be found at Rangiriri (below), Rangiaowhia (p234) and Orakau (p235).

Dozens of *marae* (meeting house) complexes are dotted around the countryside – including Awakino (p248) and Kawhia (p240), where the *Tainui waka* is buried. You won't be able to visit these without permission but you can get decent views from the gates. Some regional tours include an element of Maori culture, including Ruakuri Cave (p243) and Kawhia Harbour Cruises (p240).

To get here, turn off SH1 at Pokeno, 50km south of central Auckland, and head towards Tuakau (which has some decent cafes) until you see the Port Waikato signs. It's a pleasant 35km drive following the ever-widening river with its abundant bird life. Hobbit-hoppers can continue on the coastal road south past Port Waikato for a further 10km, where the limestone bluffs formed Weathertop Hollow – NZ's northernmost *Lord of the Rings* location.

Keep on this road and turn inland on SH22 to reach **Nikau Cave** (☎ 09-233 3199; www.nikaucave.co.nz; 1770 Waikaretu Rd, Waikaretu; adult/child $30/15; ☾ by appointment), where a tour (minimum two people) will take you through tight wet squeezes to glowworms, limestone formations and subterranean streams. There's a cafe here, too.

Rangiriri

As you follow SH1 south you're retracing the route of the colonial army in the spectacular land grab that was the Waikato War. On 20 November 1863, 1500 British troops (some say it was 850 – either way, there was a lot of 'em), backed by gunboats and artillery, attacked the substantial fortifications erected by the Maori king's warriors at Rangiriri. They were repulsed a number of times and lost 49 men, but overnight many of the 500 Maori defenders retreated; the remaining 183 were taken prisoner the next day after the British gained entry to the *pa* (fortified village) by conveniently misunderstanding a flag of truce. It's worth stopping at the **Rangiriri Heritage Centre** (☎ 07-826 3663; www.nzmuseums.

co.nz; 12 Rangiriri Rd; ☾ 8am-4pm) for an interesting short documentary (20 minutes, $2) about the battle, and a thoroughly British cream scone. Across the road the **Maori War & Early Settlers Cemetery** (Rangiriri Rd; admission free; ☾ 24hr) houses the soldiers' graves and a mound covering the mass grave of 36 Maori warriors.

Next to the heritage centre is the historic, elaborately wallpapered **Rangiriri Hotel** (☎ 07-826 3467; Rangiriri St; mains $15-30; ☾ 11am-11pm), a cheery spot for lunch or a beer at sunny outdoor tables.

Ngaruawahia & Around

From Rangiriri the road follows the Waikato River all the way to Hamilton. Along the way is **Huntly** (population 7070), a utilitarian coalmining town with a large power station. The friendly **Huntly i-SITE** (☎ 07-828 6406; SH1; www.huntly.net.nz; ☾ 9am-5pm Mon-Fri, 9am-3pm Sat & Sun) is a good source of information about visiting Taupiri and Ngaruawahia.

The sacred mountain of the Tainui people, **Taupiri** (287m), is a further 8km south on SH1. You'll recognise it by the cemetery on its slopes and the honking of passing car horns – locals saying hi to their loved ones and their mountain as they pass by. In August 2006 tens of thousands gathered here as the much-loved Maori queen, Dame Te Atairangikaahu, was transported upriver by *waka* (canoe) to her final resting place in an unmarked grave among her ancestors at the top of the mountain. Tourists aren't welcome, but those genuinely wishing to pay their respects may enter as long as they follow the correct protocol (no eating, stick to the paths, wash your hands afterwards to remove the *tapu* – see p58).

If you're fit, the **Taupiri Mountain Walkway** (80 minutes return) offers excellent views. It doesn't actually take you on the sacred mountain but treks through part of the **Hakarimata Scenic Reserve**, which has 600-year-old kauri trees. The Huntly i-SITE has maps and information.

A little further south, **Ngaruawahia** (population 4940), 19km north of Hamilton on SH1, is the headquarters of the Maori King movement (see below). The impressive fences of **Turangawaewae Marae** (☎ 07-824 5189; 29 River Rd) maintain the privacy of this important place, but twice a year visitors are welcomed. Ask at the **post office** (☎ 07-824 8661; www.nzpost.co.nz; 3 Jesmond St; ☾ 8am-5pm Mon-Fri, 9am-4pm Sat) for directions. **Regatta Day** is held in mid-March, with *waka* races and all manner of Maori cultural activities. For a week from 15 August the *marae* is open to celebrate **Koroneihana**, the anniversary of the coronation of the current king, Tuheitia. Call ahead to find out about the opening day's flag-raising ceremony and history tours.

HAMILTON
pop 140,700

Landlocked cities in an island nation are never going to have the glamorous appeal of their coastal sisters. Rotorua compensates with boiling mud while Taupo has its lake – but Hamilton and Palmerston North, despite their majestic rivers, are left clutching the short straws.

However, something strange has happened in Hamilton recently. Perhaps it's a sign of the rising fortunes of Waikato farmers that the city's main street has sprouted a sophisticated and vibrant stretch of bars and eateries around Hood and Victoria Sts that – on the weekend at least – leave Auckland's Viaduct Harbour for dead in the boozy fun stakes.

Oddly, the great grey-green greasy Waikato River rolls right through town, but the city's layout ignores its presence almost completely – unless you're driving across a bridge you'll hardly know it's there.

Information

Anglesea Clinic (☎ 07-858 0800; www.anglesea medical.co.nz; cnr Anglesea & Thackeray Sts; ☾ 24hr) For accidents and urgent medical assistance.

Browsers (☎ 07-839 1919; browsers@clear.net.nz; 221 Victoria St; ☾ 9.30am-9.30pm Mon-Fri, 10am-9.30pm Sat & Sun) A jazzy, musty, locally owned secondhand bookshop with a good NZ section, kids' books and fiction.

City Internet (☎ 07-839 0215; 430 Victoria St; ☾ 9am-1am Mon-Thu, 9am-2am Fri & Sat, 9am-midnight Sun)

Department of Conservation (DOC; ☎ 07-858 1000; www.doc.govt.nz; Level 5, 73 Rostrevor St; ☾ 8am-4.30pm Mon-Fri)

Dymocks (☎ 07-957 0440; www.dymocks.co.nz; 49 Bryce St; ☾ 9am-5pm Mon-Sat, 10am-4pm Sun) Specialist books and maps.

Hamilton i-SITE (☎ 07-839 3580; www.visithamilton. co.nz; 5 Garden Pl; ☾ 9am-5.30pm Mon-Fri, 9.30am-3.30pm Sat & Sun)

Post office (36 Bryce St) Currency exchange available.

Waikato Hospital (☎ 07-839 8899; www.waikatodhb. govt.nz; Pembroke St; ☾ 24hr) South of the centre.

Sights

The excellent **Waikato Museum** (☎ 07-838 6606; www.waikatomuseum.co.nz; 1 Grantham St; admission by donation, charge for touring exhibitions; ☾ 10am-4.30pm)

WAIKATO & THE KING COUNTRY

KINGITANGA

The concept of a Maori people is a relatively new one. Until the mid-19th century, NZ was effectively comprised of many independent tribal nations, operating in tandem with the British from 1840.

In 1856, faced with a flood of Brits, the Kingitanga movement formed to unite the tribes to better resist further loss of land and possible cultural annihilation. A gathering of leaders elected Waikato chief Potatau Te Wherowhero as the first Maori king, hoping that his increased *mana* (prestige) could achieve the cohesiveness that the British had under their queen.

Despite the huge losses of the Waikato War (p223) and the eventual opening up of the King Country (p240), the Kingitanga survived – although it has no formal constitutional role. A measure of the strength of the movement was the huge outpouring of grief when Te Arikinui Dame Atairangikaahu, Potatau's great-great-great-granddaughter, died in 2006 after 40 years at the helm. Although it's not a hereditary monarchy (leaders of various tribes vote on a successor), Potatau's line continues to the present day with King Tuheitia Paki.

has five main areas: an art gallery; interactive science galleries; Tainui galleries housing Maori treasures, including the magnificently carved *waka taua* (war canoe) *Te Winika;* a Hamilton history exhibition entitled 'Never a Dull Moment'; and a Waikato River exhibition. The museum also runs a rigorous program of public events.

Stretching over 50 hectares of riverbank southeast of the centre, **Hamilton Gardens** (☎ 07-838 6782; www.hamiltongardens.co.nz; Cobham Dr; admission free; enclosed section ☻ 7.30am-sunset) incorporates a large park, cafe, restaurant and extravagantly themed enclosed gardens. The Paradise Garden Collection has separate Italian Renaissance, Chinese, Japanese, English,

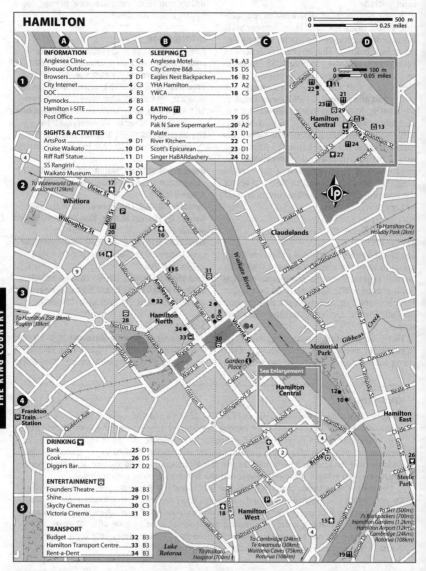

HAMILTON

INFORMATION	
Anglesea Clinic	1 C4
Bivouac Outdoor	2 C3
Browsers	3 D1
City Internet	4 C3
DOC	5 B3
Dymocks	6 B3
Hamilton i-SITE	7 C4
Post Office	8 C3

SIGHTS & ACTIVITIES	
ArtsPost	9 D1
Cruise Waikato	10 D4
Riff Raff Statue	11 D1
SS Rangiriri	12 D4
Waikato Museum	13 D1

SLEEPING	
Anglesea Motel	14 A3
City Centre B&B	15 D5
Eagles Nest Backpackers	16 B2
YHA Hamilton	17 A2
YWCA	18 C5

EATING	
Hydro	19 D5
Pak N Save Supermarket	20 A2
Palate	21 D1
River Kitchen	22 C1
Scott's Epicurean	23 D1
Singer HaBARdashery	24 D2

DRINKING	
Bank	25 D1
Cook	26 D5
Diggers Bar	27 D2

ENTERTAINMENT	
Founders Theatre	28 B3
Shine	29 D1
Skycity Cinemas	30 C3
Victoria Cinema	31 B3

TRANSPORT	
Budget	32 B3
Hamilton Transport Centre	33 B3
Rent-a-Dent	34 B3

WAIKATO & THE KING COUNTRY

American and Indian gardens complete with colonnades, pagodas, dovecotes, raked sand and a mini Taj Mahal. Equally interesting is the Productive Garden Collection with its model family-sized sustainable garden, a fragrant herb garden and the precolonisation Maori Te Parapara garden. Look out for the impressive *Nga Uri O Hinetuparimaunga* (Earth Blanket) sculpture at the main roadside gates.

ArtsPost (☎ 07-838 6928; www.artspost.co.nz; 120 Victoria St; admission free; ☽ 10am-4.30pm), near the museum, is a contemporary gallery and gift shop housed in the grand former post office. It focuses on the best of local art: paintings, glass, prints, textiles and photography. Check out the awesome floorboards.

Hamilton Zoo (☎ 07-838 6720; www.hamiltonzoo. co.nz; 183 Brymer Rd; admission adult/child/family $14/7/42; ☽ 9am-5pm, last entry 3.30pm) houses 500-plus species and takes part in conservation breeding projects. The rotating 'Meet the Keeper' program provides interesting information from the critters' caregivers…and it has NZ's only tapir! The zoo is 8km from the city centre: take Norton Rd off Tristram St, then SH23 west towards Raglan, turn right at Newcastle Rd and then left onto Brymer Rd.

One of Hamilton's more unusual public artworks is a life-size statue of *Rocky Horror Picture Show* writer Richard O'Brien in the guise of **Riff Raff** (Victoria St), the time-warping alien from the planet Transsexual. It looks over a small park on the site of the former Embassy Theatre where O'Brien worked as a hairdresser. The Embassy's 'late-night double-feature picture shows' found a place in the ultimate cult classic – although it's hard to imagine 1960s Hamilton inspired the tale of bisexual alien decadence.

Activities

The strong-flowing Waikato River is well worth investigating. **Cruise Waikato** (☎ 0508 426 458; www.cruise-waikato.co.nz; Memorial Park Jetty; cruises from adult/child $20/10) runs a range of cruises, focussed variously on sightseeing, history or your belly (coffee and muffins, sausage sizzles or picnics).

Another river option is the **City Bridges River Tour** (☎ 07-847 5565; www.canoeandkayak.co.nz; 2hr trip adult/child $50/30), a guided kayak ride through the city. **Wiseway Canoe Adventures** (☎ 021 988 335; www.wisewayadventures.com; 2hr trip adult/child $50/20) runs a similar trip, and offers freedom hire.

Bush-covered riverside walkways run along both sides of the Waikato River and provide the city's green belt. Jogging paths continue to the boardwalk circling **Lake Rotoroa**, west of the centre. **Memorial Park** is closer to town, and has the remains of **SS Rangiriri** – an iron-clad, steam-powered gunboat from the Waikato War – embedded in the riverbank (under restoration at the time of research).

Waterworld (☎ 07-958 5860; www.hamiltonpools. co.nz; Garnett Ave; admission adult/child $5/2.50; ☽ 6am-9pm Mon-Fri, 7am-9pm Sat, 9am-9pm Sun) has indoor and outdoor pools, water slides, a gym, spa and crèche.

Kiwi Balloon Company (☎ 07-843 8538, 021 912 679; www.kiwiballooncompany.co.nz; per person $290) provides the best vehicle for gazing down on the lush countryside. The experience takes about four hours and includes a champagne breakfast and an hour's flying time.

Festivals & Events

In April rev-heads and airheads flock to town for the **Hamilton 400** (www.v8supercar.co.nz) V8 supercar street race, and **Balloons over Waikato** (www.balloonsoverwaikato.co.nz), a hot-air balloon festival.

Sleeping

The road into town from Auckland (Ulster St) is lined with dozens of unremarkable, traffic-noisy midrange motels, adequate enough for short stays.

YWCA (☎ 07-838 2219; www.ywcahamilton.org.nz; cnr Pembroke & Clarence Sts; s/d $25/50) You don't have to be young or female to stay at this four-storey apartment block of a hostel. The rooms are cell-like but they're spotless, cheap and private. Each floor has shared bathroom facilities, a kitchen and TV lounge.

Eagles Nest Backpackers (☎ 07-838 2704; www. eaglesbackpackers.co.nz; 937 Victoria St; dm/s/d $25/50/60; ▣) This 1st-floor eyrie has windowless internal rooms (with skylights) but they're clean and mercifully quiet given the hostel's busy position. The communal lounge is a tad 'nursing-home chic', but there's a decent terrace looking over the street. 'No luxuries', says the lady at the desk.

J's Backpackers (☎ 07-856 8934; www.jsbackpackers .co.nz; 8 Grey St; dm/s/d/tr $28/60/66/82; ▣ ☏) A homely hostel occupying a characterful house near Hamilton Gardens, friendly J's offers good security, a smallish kitchen and bright, tidy rooms with new mattresses. There's also a barbecue out the back.

YHA Hamilton (☎ 07-957 1848; www.yha.co.nz; 140 Ulster St; dm/s $29/49, d $59-69; 🖳 🛜) Freshly painted, super-clean, quality linen, Sky TV, funky lounge, sauna, laundry, supermarket across the street…what's the catch? Well, the hostel occupies a former 'micro hotel', so the rooms and kitchen are tiny. If you're over 6ft tall you might struggle.

Hamilton City Holiday Park (☎ 07-855 8255; www.hamiltoncityholidaypark.co.nz; 14 Ruakura Rd; unpowered/powered sites $30/32, cabins $40-55, tourist flats $70-95; 🖳 🛜) Good simple cabins and well-maintained communal facilities are the rule at this shady park, 2km east of town.

City Centre B&B (☎ 07-838 1671; www.citycentrebnb.co.nz; 3 Anglesea St; s/d/tr $80/99/130; 🖳 🐾) At the quiet riverside end of a central city street (five-minutes walk to the Victoria/Hood St action), this sparkling self-contained apartment opens on to a swimming pool. Self-catering breakfast provided.

Anglesea Motel (☎ 0800 4264 5732, 07834 0010; www.angleseamotel.co.nz; 36 Liverpool St; d/2-bedroom units/3-bedroom units from $135/260/305; 🛜 🐾) A far preferable option to anything on Ulster St's 'motel row', the Anglesea has plenty of space, friendly managers, free wi-fi, pool and squash and tennis courts, and not un-stylish decor. Hard to beat.

Eating

River Kitchen (☎ 07-839 2906; 237 Victoria St; mains $7-16; 🕑 7am-4pm Mon-Fri, 8am-4pm Sat & Sun) Heralded as Waikato's 'Best New Cafe' by *Cafe* magazine, hip River Kitchen does things with simple style: cakes, gourmet breakfasts and fresh seasonal lunches (angle for a slice of the Spanish duck pie), and a barista who knows his beans.

Hydro (☎ 07-859 0020; 33 Jellicoe Dr; mains $8-19; 🕑 9am-3pm Mon & Tue, 8am-3.30pm Wed-Fri, 8am-4pm Sat & Sun; 🛜 🅥) On the east side of the river (you can walk here along the water's edge), Hydro has converted an old block of neighbourhood shops into a fun cafe with tables spilling onto the pavement. Great for brunch and light meals with novel taste combinations.

our pick Singer HaBARdashery (☎ 07-839 1537; 15 Hood St; brunch $11-19, tapas $9-19; 🕑 lunch & dinner) A classy operator on the Hood St strip, Singer is a moody tapas and wine bar occupying the oldest stone building in Hamilton – a former

haberdashery. Expect a dizzying selection of wines and beers, great coffee, satisfying brunches and zingy tapas (try the 'Needle': eye fillet, mussel, scallop, chorizo, and haloumi skewered on a knitting needle).

Scott's Epicurean (☎ 07-839 6680; 181 Victoria St; mains $11-20; 🕑 7am-4pm Mon-Fri, 8.30am-4pm Sat & Sun) This gorgeous joint features swanky leather banquettes, pressed-tin ceilings, great coffee and an interesting and affordable menu: try the sweet orange breakfast couscous or the ever-popular *spaghetti aglio e olio*. Service is friendly, it's fully licensed, and a charming outdoor area beckons in the warmer months.

Palate (☎ 07-834 2921; 170 Victoria St; mains $25-33; 🕑 dinner Tue-Sat) Given this restaurant's deserved status as the best in the central North Island, it's surprisingly reasonably priced. Chef/owner Mat McLean delivers an innovative mod-NZ menu and free tasters between courses.

Self-caterers can swing into **Pak N Save** (☎ 07-839 7870; Mill St; 🕑 8am-10pm).

Drinking

The blocks around Victoria and Hood Sts offer a decent bar hop, with weekend live music and DJs. See also Singer HaBARdashery (left).

Diggers Bar (☎ 07-834 2228; 17b Hood St; 🕑 3pm-late Tue-Sun) This funky good-time bar has a wealth of liquid bread on tap and nightly live music in a huge room out the back. Wednesday night's $25 'pizza, fries and two drinks' is a damn good deal.

Cook (☎ 07-856 6088; 7 Cook St; 🕑 9am-late Mon-Fri, 8.30am-late Sat & Sun) Rambling through a noble, burgundy-coloured timber hall (1874), this buzzy cafe-bar dishes up good pub grub (mains $13 to $24), plus live music, poker, comedy and quiz nights.

Bank (☎ 07-839 4740; cnr Victoria & Hood Sts; 🕑 11am-midnight Sun-Thu, to 3am Fri & Sat) Inside this snappily renovated 1878 heritage building are plenty of beers on tap, a good wine selection and lots of screens to catch the big games.

See also Singer HaBARdashery (left) and Shine (below).

Entertainment

Shine (☎ 07-839 3173; www.shinenightclub.co.nz; 161 Victoria St; 🕑 10pm-3am Sat & Sun) It's a measure of Hamilton's increasing sophistication that its main gay-and-lesbian club is now visible to

lonelyplanet.com

WAIKATO •• Hamilton **229**

Victoria St's passing parade. There's a dance floor at the back and an intimate beer garden in front.

Victoria Cinema (☎ 07-838 3036; www.victoriacinema. co.nz; 690 Victoria St; tickets adult/child $15.50/10; ⏰ 5pm-late) Watch art-house films while sipping on alcoholic beverages.

Skycity Cinemas (☎ 07-835 0088; www.skycity cinemas.co.nz; Level 2, Centreplace Mall, cnr Ward & Anglesea Sts; tickets adult/child $15/9; ⏰ 10am-11pm) A seven-screen mainstream multiplex. Adults pay $10 on Tuesdays.

For live theatre and concerts (anything from Bee Gees tributes to the New Zealand Symphony Orchestra), try **Founders Theatre** (☎ 07-838 6600; www.hamiltontheatres.co.nz; 221 Tristram St; ⏰ box office 9am-5pm Mon-Fri).

Getting There & Away
AIR

Air New Zealand (☎ 0800 737 000; www.airnew zealand.co.nz) has regular direct flights from **Hamilton Airport** (☎ 07-848 9027; www.hamilton airport.co.nz; Airport Rd) to Auckland, Christchurch, Gisborne, Napier, New Plymouth, Palmerston North, Rotorua, Tauranga, Wellington and Whakatane.

Internationally, **Pacific Blue** (☎ 0800 670 000; www.pacificblue.com.au) flies from Hamilton to Sydney and Brisbane.

Sunair Aviation Ltd (☎ 07-575 7799; www.sunair. co.nz) offers direct flights to Gisborne, Napier, New Plymouth, Palmerston North and Whakatane.

BUS

All buses arrive and depart from the **Hamilton Transport Centre** (☎ 07-834 3457; cnr Anglesea & Bryce Sts).

Environment Waikato's **Busit!** (☎ 0800 4287 5463; www.busit.co.nz) has numerous services throughout the region, including Ngaruawahia ($3.70, 25 minutes), Cambridge ($6, 40 minutes), Te Awamutu ($6, 30 minutes) and Raglan ($7.30, one hour).

Dalroy Express (☎ 0508 465 622, 06-759 0197; www. dalroytours.co.nz) operates a daily service between Auckland ($22, two hours) and New Plymouth ($40, four hours), stopping at most towns, including Te Kuiti ($18, 1¾ hours) and Te Awamutu ($12, 20 minutes).

Raglan Shuttle Co (☎ 0800 8873 2 7873, 0212 612 563; www.solscape.co.nz/shuttle.html) links Hamilton with Raglan (one-way $60). Auckland connections are also available.

InterCity (☎ 09-583 5780; www.intercity.co.nz) services numerous destinations including:

Destination	Price	Duration	Frequency
Auckland	$21	2hr	10 daily
Cambridge	$19	25min	5 daily
Matamata	$25	1hr	2 daily
Ngaruawahia	$18	20min	10 daily
Rotorua	$34	1½hr	6 daily
Te Aroha	$10	1hr	2 daily
Te Awamutu	$17	25min	3 daily
Wellington	$75	9hr	4 daily

Naked Bus (☎ 0900 625 33; www.nakedbus.com) services run to the following destinations (among many others). Consider booking in advance for big savings.

Destination	Price	Duration	Frequency
Auckland	$21	2¼hr	3-5 daily
Cambridge	$14	30min	3-4 daily
Matamata	$15	1hr	1 daily
Ngaruawahia	$28	30min	3-5 daily
Rotorua	$24	2hr	2-3 daily
Wellington	$49	10hr	1-3 daily

TRAIN

Hamilton is on the **Overlander** (☎ 0800 872 467; www.tranzscenic.co.nz; daily Oct-Apr, Fri-Sun May-Sep) route between Auckland ($53, 2½ hours) and Wellington ($107, 9½ hours) via Otorohanga ($53, 45 minutes). Trains stop at Hamilton's **Frankton train station** (Queens Ave), 1km west of the city centre; there are no ticket sales here.

Getting Around
TO/FROM THE AIRPORT

Hamilton Airport is 12km south of the city. International departure tax is $25 for those 12 years and over; $10 for kids. The **Super Shuttle** (☎ 0800 748 885, 07-843 7778; www.supershuttle.co.nz; one-way $21) offers a door-to-door service into the city. A taxi costs around $40.

BUS

Hamilton's **Busit!** (☎ 0800 4287 5463; www.busit. co.nz; tickets adult/child $2.90/1.30) network services the city-centre and suburbs daily from around 7am to 7.30pm (later on Friday). All buses pass through Hamilton Transport Centre. Busit! also runs a free **CBD shuttle** (⏰ 7am-6pm Mon-Fri, 9am-1pm Sat), looping around Victoria, Liverpool, Anglesea and Bridge Sts every 10 minutes.

CAR
Budget (☎ 07-838 3585; www.budget.co.nz; 4 Vialou St; ☉ 7.30am-5.30pm Mon-Fri, 9am-noon Sat & Sun)
Rent-a-Dent (☎ 07-839 1049; www.rentadent.co.nz; 383 Anglesea St; ☉ 7.30am-5pm Mon-Fri, 8am-noon Sat)

TAXI
Hamilton Taxis (☎ 07-8477 477)
Red Cabs (☎ 07-839 0500)

RAGLAN
pop 2700
Laid-back Raglan may well be NZ's perfect surfing town. It's small enough to have escaped mass development – perhaps due to a mainstream Kiwi preference for the safer white-sand east-coast beaches – yet it's big enough for a bit of bustle. There are several good eateries and a bar that attracts big-name bands in summer.

The nearby surf spots – Indicators, Whale Bay and Manu Bay – are internationally famous for their point breaks, attracting surfers from around the world. Bruce Brown's classic 1964 wave-chasing film *The Endless Summer* features Manu Bay. Closer to town, the harbour is excellent for kayaking, fishing and swimming. This all serves to attract fit guys and gals from all over the planet; Raglan may also be NZ's best-looking town.

Have a look online at www.raglan.net.nz.

Information
Post office (39 Bow St)
United Video (☎ 07-825 0008; 9a Bow St; ☉ 10am-9pm) Also has internet access.
Visitor Information Centre (☎ 07-825 0556; www.raglan.org.nz; 2 Wainui Rd; ☉ 9.30am-5pm Mon-Fri, 10am-5pm Sat, 10am-4pm Sun) DOC brochures plus information about local accommodation and activities. Reduced hours in winter.
West Coast Health Centre (☎ 07-825 0114; 12 Wallis St; ☉ 9am-5pm Mon-Fri) General medical assistance.

Sights & Activities
A community hub, the **Old School Arts Centre** (☎ 07-825 0023; www.raglanartscentre.co.nz; Stewart St; admission free; ☉ 10am-2pm Mon & Wed, exhibitions vary) has changing exhibitions and workshops, including weaving, carving, yoga and storytelling. The hippie-organic **Raglan Creative Market** (☎ 07-825 8862; www.raglanmarket.com; ☉ 9am-2pm 2nd Sun of the month) happens out the front once a month.

The small, musty **Raglan & District Museum** (☎ 07-825 8416; 13 Wainui Rd; admission by donation; ☉ 1-3.30pm Sat & Sun) explores the stories of local Maori and Pakeha pioneers through artefacts, photos and newspapers.

Te Kopua Recreational Reserve, over the footbridge by the holiday park, is a safe, calm swimming beach popular with families.

The instructors at **Raglan Surf School** (☎ 07-825 7873; www.raglansurfingschool.co.nz; 5b Whaanga Rd, Whale Bay; 3hr lesson incl transport $89) pride themselves on getting 95% of first-timers standing during their first lesson. Experienced wave hounds can rent surfboards (from $15 per hour), boogie boards ($5 per hour) and wet suits ($5 per hour). They're based at Karioi Lodge (p232) in Whale Bay. **Solscape** (☎ 07-825 8268; www.solscape.co.nz; 611 Wainui Rd, Manu Bay; lessons $85) offers 2½-hour lessons, as well as board and wetsuit hire (per half-day $40).

If you'd rather spend more time above the water than in it, **Raglan Kite Surf School** (☎ 07-825 8702, 0212 524 117; lessons per hr $60) runs one-on-one lessons wherever the wind's blowing.

Raglan Harbour is great for kayaking. The gentle Opotoru River is good for learning basic skills, but before too long you'll be wanting to investigate the nooks and crannies of the pancake rocks on the harbour's north edge. Raglan Backpackers (below) has single/double ocean kayaks for hire (per half-day $30/40). Alternatively, see if **Raglan Kayak** (☎ 07-825 8862; www.raglaneco.co.nz) has recovered from the fire that destroyed its premises in April 2010.

Sleeping
It pays to book Raglan accommodation ahead, especially in peak season. See p232 for options at the neighbouring surf beaches.

Raglan Kopua Holiday Park (☎ 07-825 8283; www.raglanholidaypark.co.nz; Marine Pde; sites per adult/child $15/7.50, dm/cabins/units from $23/65/85; ☐ ☎) A nicely maintained facility on the spit of land across the inlet from town (there's a footbridge, or drive the long way around). Not much shade but there's beach swimming and plenty of room to run amuck.

our pick **Raglan Backpackers** (☎ 07-825 0515; www.raglanbackpackers.co.nz; 6 Wi Neera St; dm/s $25/52, d $66-76; ☐) This welcoming, purpose-built hostel has a laid-back holiday-house vibe. It's right on the water's edge, with sea views from some rooms and the rest arranged around a garden courtyard. For small groups there's a

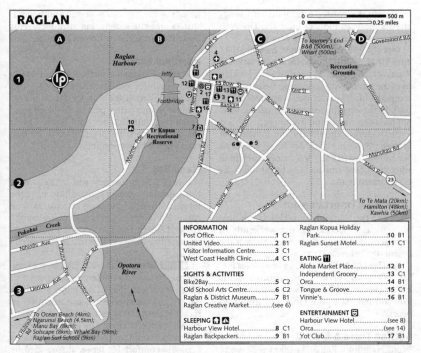

RAGLAN

INFORMATION	
Post Office..............................1	C1
United Video...........................2	B1
Visitor Information Centre........3	C1
West Coast Health Clinic..........4	C1

SIGHTS & ACTIVITIES	
Bike2Bay................................5	C2
Old School Arts Centre.............6	C2
Raglan & District Museum........7	C1
Raglan Creative Market........(see 6)	

SLEEPING	
Harbour View Hotel..................8	C1
Raglan Backpackers..................9	B1

Raglan Kopua Holiday	
Park.....................................10	B1
Raglan Sunset Motel................11	C1

EATING	
Aloha Market Place.................12	B1
Independent Grocery...............13	C1
Orca.....................................14	B1
Tongue & Groove...................15	C1
Vinnie's................................16	B1

ENTERTAINMENT	
Harbour View Hotel.............(see 8)	
Orca..................................(see 14)	
Yot Club...............................17	B1

separate self-contained wing sleeping up to eight. There are kayaks for hire (from $15), or if that's too strenuous you can take a yoga class, swan about in a hammock, strum a guitar or drip in the sauna. Can we stay another night?

Harbour View Hotel (☎ 07-825 8010; harbourview hotel@paradise.net.nz; 14 Bow St; s/d $60/80, f $95-110) If you think that going to bed before the party finishes is for the faint and feeble, then this two-storey 100-year-old pub (licensed until late), with sunny verandas and kauri trimmings, is for you. The rooms are clean although the beds are saggy and you'll be sharing bathrooms.

Raglan Sunset Motel (☎ 07-825 0500; www.raglan sunsetmotel.co.nz; 7 Bankart St; d $140; ☎) A block or so back from the action, this two-storey motel with faux shutters randomly adhered to the facade is barely seven years old. As you'd expect, everything's in good nick. The owners also have self-contained apartments (doubles from $150) and beach houses (four people from $250) available around town.

Journey's End B&B (☎ 07-825 6727; www.raglan ac commodation.co.nz; 49 Lily St; s/d $90/140, exclusive use per 2/4 people $180/240) No, it's not Mt Doom; quite the opposite, in fact. These two attractive en-suite rooms share a central modern lounge with a kitchenette and a deck overlooking the wharf and harbour.

Eating

Aloha Market Place (☎ 07-825 7440; 5 Bow St; sushi $1.50-2, mains $7.50-12; ☼ 11am-5pm) It's takeaway without the grease, Japanese surfer-style. Grab some delicious rolled-to-order sushi, some udon noodles or a *donburi* rice bowl and head for the harbour. Reduced hours in winter.

Vinnie's (☎ 07-825 7273; 7 Wainui Rd; meals $8-23; ☼ 10am-late Tue-Sun; ☎) Run by a long-lost New Yorker, Vinnie's looks like a truck stop from the outside, but inside it's all Hawaiian prints, reggae tunes and surf movies flickering on the walls. On the food front it's burgers, salads, wraps, cheese-steaks, pizzas and its 'famous' meatloaf. Free wi-fi is available, too.

Tongue & Groove (☎ 07-825 0027; 19 Bow St; mains $9-18; ☼ 8.30am-3pm Mon-Thu, 8.30am-8.30pm Fri & Sat, 8.30am-8pm Sun; Ⓥ) There are plenty of street-side seats and retro couches for wine sipping in this funky corner cafe, with surf mags strewn about and lots of local art. The delicious vegetarian roti is a bargain ($14).

Orca (☎ 07-825 6543; 2 Wallis St; breakfast $11-17, mains $17-32; ☾ 9am-late Mon-Fri, 8am-late Sat & Sun) A day started at Orca's window seat, looking over the water, with some eggs Benedict and a superb coffee is a day well launched. Come back in the evening for seafood paella, wine appreciation nights and live music.

Self-caterers should try the **Independent Grocery** (☎ 07-825 6533; 37 Bow St; ☾ 9am-5.30pm Mon-Fri, 10am-5pm Sat & Sun; **V**) for organics, bulk wholefood, fresh fruit and veg, bread and really good peanut butter.

Drinking & Entertainment

Orca and the Harbour View Hotel both host live music, especially on the weekends in summer when the Harbour View attracts the cream of Kiwi rock.

Yot Club (☎ 07-825 8702; 9 Bow St; admission free-$25; ☾ 9pm-late) This raucous, nocturnal bar is where everyone goes to dance, with visiting DJs and bands, a pool table and imported beers.

Getting There & Around

From Hamilton, Raglan is 48km west along SH23. Unsealed back roads connect Raglan to Kawhia, 50km south; they're slow, winding and prone to rockslides, but scenic and certainly off the beaten track. Head back towards Hamilton for 7km and take the Te Mata/Kawhia turn-off and follow the signs; allow at least an hour.

Environment Waikato's **Busit!** (☎ 0800 4287 5463; www.busit.co.nz; adult/child $7.30/3.70) heads between Hamilton and Raglan (one hour) three times daily on weekdays and twice daily on weekends.

Raglan Shuttle Co (☎ 0800 8873 2 7873, 0212 612 563; www.solscape.co.nz/shuttle.html) links Raglan with Hamilton (one-way $60) and Auckland ($100).

Bike2Bay (☎ 07-825 0309; www.bike2bay.com; 24b Stewart St; hire per hr/half-/full day $8/22/33; ☾ 9.30am-5pm) has mountain bikes for hire, and does repairs.

If you need a cab call **Raglan Taxi** (☎ 07-825 0506).

SOUTH OF RAGLAN
Ocean Beach

Just 4km southwest of Raglan, down Riria Kereopa Memorial Dr, this beach at the mouth of the harbour is popular with windsurfers and kite surfers, but strong currents make it extremely treacherous for swimmers.

Ngarunui Beach

Less than a kilometre further south, this is a great beach for grommets learning to surf. On the clifftop is the club for the volunteer lifeguards who patrol part of the black-sand beach from late October until April. This is the only beach with lifeguards and the best ocean beach for swimming.

Manu Bay

Another 2.5km journey will bring you to this legendary surfing spot, said to have the longest left-hand break in the world. The elongated uniform waves are created by the angle at which the Tasman Sea swell meets the coastline (it works best in a southwesterly swell).

our pick **Solscape** (☎ 07-825 8268; www.solscape. co.nz; 611 Wainui Rd; sites per person $15, cabooses dm/d $25/60, tepees s/d/q $50/68/136, cottages d $110-180; ▯ 🛜) has backpacker accommodation in recycled train carriages with a homely communal lounge/kitchen. The ultimate greenie experience could well be chilling out in a surprisingly comfortable tepee, surrounded by native bush, knowing that you're completely 'off the grid' – while not sacrificing hot showers (solar) and decent toilets (composting). Self-contained sea-view cottages, surf lessons (p230) and massage therapy ($65 per hour) complete the bewildering array of services.

Whale Bay

This renowned surfing spot is a kilometre further west from Manu Bay and is usually less crowded, but from the bottom of Calvert St you do have to clamber 600m over the rocks to get here.

Deep in native bush, **Karioi Lodge** (☎ 07-825 7873; www.karioilodge.co.nz; 5b Whaanga Rd; dm/d $27/69; ▯) offers a sauna, a flying fox, mountain bikes, bush and beach walks, sustainable gardening, tree planting and the Raglan Surf School (p230). There are no en suites but the rooms are clean and cosy. These friendly folks also run **Sleeping Lady Lodging** (☎ 07-825 7873; www. sleepinglady.co.nz; 5b Whaanga Rd; lodges $125-240), a collection of luxury self-contained lodges nearby. They range from the Sweet As studio apartment to the Lava Lounge, which has a private spa, ocean views and can sleep up to 12.

Indicators Beach House (☎ 07-825 7889; www.indicators .co.nz; Whaanga Rd, d $150-220, extra person $50; 🖳) is a two-level affair, bookable as one or as two separate self-contained units. Sleeping up to 12, it's roomy and timber-lined, with a huge deck (those views!) and every modern need met. Kids under 12 stay free. You'll want to move in!

Mt Karioi

In legend, **Mt Karioi** (756m), the Sleeping Lady (check out that profile), is the sister to Mt Pirongia (right). At its base the **Te Toto Gorge** is a steep cleft in the mountainside. Starting from the Te Toto Gorge car park south of Whale Bay, a strenuous but scenic track goes up the western slope. It takes 2½ hours to reach a lookout point, followed by an easier hour up to the summit. From the east side, the Wairake Track is a steeper 2½-hour climb to the summit, where it meets the Te Toto Track.

Ruapuke Beach

Whale Bay marks the end of the sealed road, but a gravel road continues to **Ruapuke Beach**, 28km from Raglan, which is dangerous for swimmers but popular with surf-casting fisherfolk. **Ruapuke Beach Motor Camp** (☎ 07-825 6800; unpowered/powered sites $20/24, cabins from $35) is near the beach and has an end-of-the-world feel. The gravel road continues on round Mt Karioi and rejoins the inland road at Te Mata.

Bridal Veil Falls

Just past Te Mata (a short drive south of the main Raglan–Hamilton road) is the turn-off to the 55m Bridal Veil Falls, 4km from the main road. From the car park, it's an easy 10-minute walk through mossy native bush to the top of the falls. It's a magical place, the effect compounded by the dancing rainbows swirling around the khaki-coloured pool far below. A further 10-minute walk leads down to the bottom. Make sure you lock your car, as theft is a problem here.

Back in Te Mata, **Magic Mountain Horse Treks** (☎ 07-825 6892; www.magicmountain.co.nz; 334 Houtchen Rd; rides ½hr $40/65) runs horse treks around the hills, plus a ride to Bridal Veil Falls ($80).

Four Brothers Scenic Reserve

Halfway between Hamilton and Raglan on SH23, the **Karamu Walkway** wanders through this reserve. A 15-minute hike up a gully covered in native bush leads to a hilltop where cows and sheep enjoy panoramic views.

Pirongia Forest Park

The main attraction of this 17,000-hectare park is **Mt Pirongia** (www.mtpirongia.org.nz), its 959m summit clearly visible from much of the Waikato. The mountain is usually climbed from Corcoran Rd (three to five hours, one-way). Interestingly, NZ's tallest known kahikatea tree (66.5m) grows on the mountainside. There's a six-bunk DOC hut near the summit if you need to spend the night. Maps and information are available from DOC in Hamilton (p225).

TE AWAMUTU

pop 9800

Deep into dairy-farming country, Te Awamutu (which means 'The River Cut Short'; the Waikato beyond this point was unsuitable for large canoes) is a real working town with real working people living in it – agrarian integrity by the bucketload! (a sign on the pub door says 'Please Remove Gumboots'). With a blossom-treed main street and a good museum, 'TA' makes a decent overnighter (Finn fans might need longer – see the boxed text, p234).

Information

The **Te Awamutu i-SITE** (☎ 07-871 3259; www.teawa mutuinfo.com; 1 Gorst Ave; ☽ 9am-4.30pm Mon-Fri, 10am-4pm Sat & Sun) has plenty of local information.

Sights

Te Awamutu Museum (☎ 07-872 0085; www.tamuseum. org.nz; 135 Roche St; admission by donation; ☽ 10am-4pm Mon-Fri, 10am-1pm Sat, 1-4pm Sun), 'where history never repeats', has a *True Colours*–painted shrine to local heroes Tim and Neil Finn. There are gold records, original lyrics and Finn memorabilia and oddities such as Neil's form-two exercise book. There's also a fine collection of Maori *taonga* (treasures), including the revered 'Uenuku', and an excellent display on the Waikato War. A great little museum.

The **Rose Garden** (cnr Gorst Ave & Arawata St; admission free; ☽ 24hr) is next to the i-SITE and has 2000 bushes and 51 varieties with fabulously fruity names like Big Daddy, Disco Dancer, Lady Gay and Sexy Rexy. The roses usually bloom from November to April.

Sleeping

Rosetown Motel (☎ 0800 767 386, 07-871 5779; www.rose townmotel.co.nz; 844 Kihikihi Rd; d $99-110, f $155; 🛜 🖵)

The older-style units at Rosetown (plenty of teak veneer and yellow faux-marble) have kitchens, Sky TV and share a spa, making them a solid choice if you're hankering for straight-up small-town sleeps.

Cloverdale House (☎ 07-872 1702; www.cloverdale house.co.nz; 141 Long Rd; d/q $140/200) Indulge your farmer fantasies at this smart new place in the dairy heartland, 8km east of Cambridge Rd. Two double rooms with en suites share a common lounge and kitchen (breakfast ingredients provided).

Eating & Drinking

Indian Aroma (☎ 07-871 5555; 23 Arawata St; mains $13-17; ☺ lunch Mon-Fri, dinner daily; Ⓥ) Brightening up the town with a saffron-yellow glow, this attractive restaurant with orderly glass-topped tables serves all the fragrant favourites.

Redoubt Bar & Eatery (☎ 07-871 4768; cnr Rewi & Alexandra Sts; mains $16-32; ☺ 11am-late) A relaxed little place to eat or drink, with cheap but potent cocktails, old photos on the walls and a decent menu stretching from pasta to curry. Try the chicken bagel.

Entertainment

Regent 3 Cinema (☎ 07-871 6678; www.regent3.itgo. com; Alexandra St; tickets adult/child $15/13; ☺ varies) Built in 1932, this art-deco cinema has five screens and fabulous movie memorabilia in the foyer.

The Redoubt Bar & Eatery (above) has comedy every second Wednesday and live music on Friday nights.

Getting There & Away

Te Awamutu is on SH3, halfway between Hamilton and Otorohanga (29km either way). The regional bus service **Busit!** (☎ 0800 4287 5463; www.busit.co.nz) is the cheapest option for Hamilton (adult/child $6/4, 30 minutes, five daily).

Three daily **InterCity** (☎ 09-583 5780; www.inter city.co.nz) services connect Te Awamutu with Auckland ($43, 2½ hours), Hamilton ($21, 40 minutes) and Otorohanga ($21, 25 minutes).

The **Dalroy Express** (☎ 0508 465 622; www.dalroy tours.co.nz) bus runs daily between Auckland ($28, 2½ hours) and New Plymouth ($39, 3½ hours), leaving from outside the visitor information centre. Stops include Hamilton ($12, 25 minutes) and Otorohanga ($11, 20 minutes).

AROUND TE AWAMUTU
Battle Sites

Before the Waikato invasion, **Rangiaowhia** (5km east of Te Awamutu) was a thriving Maori farming town – with thousands of inhabitants, two churches, a flour mill and a racecourse – exporting wheat, maize, potatoes and fruit to as far afield as Australia. In many ways it was the perfect model of what NZ under the Maori version of the Treaty of Waitangi had desired – two sovereign peoples interacting to mutual advantage.

In February 1864 the settlement was left undefended while King Tawhiao's warriors held fortified positions further north. In a key tactical move, General Cameron outflanked them and took the town, killing women, children and the elderly in the process. This was a turning point in the campaign, demoralising the Maori and drawing the warriors out of their near impregnable *pa* fortifications.

Sadly, all that remains is the cute Anglican **St Paul's Church** (1854) and the Catholic mission's **cemetery**, standing in the midst of rich

---

TE AWAMUTU'S SACRED SOUND

In the opening lines of Crowded House's first single ('Mean to Me'), Neil Finn single-handedly raised his sleepy hometown, Te Awamutu, to international attention. It wasn't the first time it had provided inspiration – Split Enz songs *Haul Away* and *Kia Kaha*, with older brother Tim, include similar references.

Despite NZ's brilliant songwriting brothers being far from the height of their fame, Finn devotees continue to make Te Awamutu pilgrimages – just ask the staff at the i-SITE. They do a brisk trade in Finn T-shirts, Finn stamps and walking-tour brochures of sites from Finn history (their childhood home at 588 Teasdale St, their school, even Neil's piano tutor's house). It's NZ's version of Graceland.

If you're hoping for a close encounter with greatness, it's unlikely: the boys skipped town decades ago.

farming land – confiscated from the Maori and distributed to colonial soldiers.

The war ended further south at **Orakau**, where a roadside obelisk marks the site where 300 Maori led by Rewi Maniapoto repulsed three days of attacks against an unfinished *pa* by 1500 troops, before breaking out and retreating to what is now known as the King Country (losing 70 warriors). Rewi's defiant cry *'Ka whawhai tonu ahau ki a koe, ake, ake, ake'* (We shall fight on forever and ever and ever) is a rallying call for Maori activists to this day. There's a **memorial to Rewi Maniapoto**, who was well respected by both sides, in nearby Kihikihi, 4km south of Te Awamutu on SH3.

Maungatautari

Can a landlocked volcano become an island paradise? Inspired by the success of pest eradication and native species reintroduction in the Hauraki Gulf, a community trust has erected 47km of pest-proof fence around the triple peaks of Maungatautari (797m) to create the impressive **Maungatautari Ecological Island** (☎ 07-823 7455 www.maungatrust.org). This atoll of rainforest dominates the skyline between Te Awamutu and Karapiro and is now home to its first kiwi chicks in 100 years. The shortest route to the peak (an hour and 40 minutes) is from the northern side while the entire north–south walk will take around six hours. Take Maungatautari Rd then Hicks Rd if coming from Karapiro, or Arapuni Rd then Tari Rd from Te Awamutu.

Out In The Styx (☎ 07-872 4505; www.styx.co.nz; 2117 Arapuni Rd, Pukeatua; dm $85, s $130-155, d $260-310), near the south end of the Maungatautari, provides a drop-off service to the northern entrance for guests ($10 per person). The three luxuriously furnished themed rooms (Polynesian, African or Maori) are especially nice, and there's a spa for soothing weary legs. Prices include a four-course dinner and breakfast.

Wharepapa South

A surreal landscape of craggy limestone provides some of the best rock climbing in the North Island. This isn't the best place for wannabe Spidermen (or women) to don their lycra bodysuits for the first time, but if you have the basic skills get ready to let your inner superhero shine.

Bryce's Rockclimbing (☎ 07-872 2533; www.rockclimb.co.nz; 1424 Owairaka Valley Rd; dm/d $25/66) is suited to the serious climber. On site is NZ's largest retail climbing store that sells and hires out a full range of gear and has an indoor bouldering cave (free to those staying out back in the ship-shape accommodation) and a licensed cafe (light meals $4 to $10; open for lunch). A day's instruction for one or two people costs $365.

CAMBRIDGE

pop 15,200

The name says it all. Despite the rambunctious Waikato River looking nothing like the Cam, the good burghers of Cambridge have done all they can to assume an air of English gentility. There are village greens, avenues lined with magnificent exotic trees and an indecent number of faux-Tudor houses. Even the public toilet looks like a Victorian cottage.

Famous for the breeding and training of thoroughbred horses, you can almost smell the wealth along the main street, dotted with fine Edwardian and art-deco buildings. Equine references are rife in public sculpture, and plaques boast of Melbourne Cup winners. It's an altogether pleasant place to work on your 'rah-rah' voice and while away a day or two.

Information

The **Cambridge i-SITE** (☎ 07-823 3456; www.cambridge.co.nz; cnr Victoria & Queen Sts; ☺ 9am-5pm Mon-Fri, 10am-4pm Sat & Sun; 🖳) has free heritage trail and town maps, and internet access.

Sights & Activities

HERITAGE

Whether you're hip to history or tantalised by trees, the **Heritage & Tree Trail** and **Boutique Trail** cover all the sights, including the **Waikato River** and leafy little **Lake Koutu**. Don't miss the impressive vaulted interior of the 1873 **St Andrew's Anglican Church** (☎ 07-827 6751; www.standrewcambridge.wordpress.com; 85 Hamilton Rd; admission free; ☺ services 8am & 9.30am Sun), the oldest building in Cambridge (look for the Gallipoli window).

Apart from its Spanish Mission **town clock**, **Jubilee Gardens** (Victoria St) is a wholehearted tribute to the 'mother country'. A British lion guards the **cenotaph**, with a plaque that reads 'Tell Britain ye who mark this monument faithful to her we fell and rest content'. Outmoded sentiment or awkward grammar – either way, the soldier statue looks confused.

The quirky old **Cambridge Museum** (☎ 07-827 3319; www.cambridgemuseum.org.nz; 24 Victoria St; admission by donation; ✪ 10am-4pm), housed in the former courthouse, has plenty of pioneer relics, a military history room and a scale model of the local Te Totara Pa before it was wiped out.

HORSEY

Cambridge Thoroughbred Lodge (☎ 07-827 8118; www.cambridgethoroughbredlodge.co.nz; tours adult/child $8/5, shows adult/child $12/5; ✪ tours 10am-3pm by arrangement), 6km south of town on SH1, is a top-notch horse stud. Book ahead for hour-long tours, or 'NZ Horse Magic' shows which take place several times a week.

Stud Tours (☎ 07-827 5910, 027 497 5346; www.barrylee.co.nz; tours $120) offers visits to local stud farms by a bloodstock expert. Prices are for up to four people, which makes this a reasonably priced and unique tour. Bookings should be made in advance.

The very verdant **Cambridge Raceway** (☎ 07-827 5506; www.cambridgeraceway.co.nz; Taylor St; admission $5) is the venue for harness and greyhound racing three times a month. Check the website for dates and times.

LAKE KARAPIRO

Eight kilometres southeast of Cambridge, Karapiro is the furthest downstream of a chain of eight hydroelectric power stations on the Waikato River. It's an impressive sight, especially when driving across the top of the 1947 dam. The 21km-long lake is popular for all kinds of aquatic sports, especially rowing.

The **Boatshed Cafe** (☎ 07-827 8286; www.theboatshed.net.nz; 21 Amber Lane; mains $10-17; ✪ 10am-4pm Wed-Fri, 9.30am-5pm Sat & Sun) on the lakeside (take Gorton Rd from SH1) sells mainly homemade food, some of which is gluten- and dairy-free. The rowing boat of Olympian Rob Waddell is part of the decor – he used to practise here. Basic kayaks can be hired for $20/40 per half-/full day or better ones for $25/50. You can paddle to a couple of waterfalls in around an hour.

Camjet (☎ 0800 226 538; www.camjet.co.nz; trips adult/child $65/40) can help adrenaline junkies shake off the Cambridge cobwebs with a 45-minute spin to Karapiro on a jetboat (minimum two people).

CYCLING

Winding east from Cambridge, the 100km **Waikato River Trails** (www.waikatorivertrails.com) track has been ascribed 'Quick Start' status as part of the proposed **New Zealand Cycle Trail** (www.tourism.govt.nz/our-work/new-zealand-cycle-trail-project) project. Much of the track is already open; check the websites for updates.

Sleeping

Lake Karapiro Camping & Pursuits Centre (☎ 07-827 4178; www.lakekarapiro.co.nz; 601 Maungatautari Rd; sites per adult/child $12/9, chalets d/tr/q $60/72/96) Geared for rowing events, this lakeside complex 15 minutes from town is serenely peaceful outside of the big fixtures. The trim wooden chalets have bunk beds, en suites, fridges and communal kitchen facilities.

Cambridge Motor Park (☎ 07-827 5649; www.cambridgemotorpark.co.nz; 32 Scott St; sites $28, cabins s/d from $35/45, units d $95; 🖐) A quiet, well-maintained camping ground with lots of green, green grass. You'll find it over the skinny Victoria Bridge from Cambridge town centre.

Birches (☎ 07-827 6556; www.birches.co.nz; 263 Maungatautari Rd; s/d $80/120; 🐾) There's a pool, spa and tennis court at this picturesque 1930s weatherboard farmhouse, in farmland southeast of Cambridge. Sleep in the main house, or book the self-contained Cherry Tree Cottage. Sheep and daffodils line the driveway.

Lofthouse (☎ 07-827 3693; www.lofthouse.co.nz; 17 Dunning Rd; apt $130) If you're travelling with friends, this self-contained rural retreat is an absolute steal – sleeping four people for the price. Jump in the spa and enjoy the awesome views. It's 3km off SH1, near the top of Karapiro, and 11km from Cambridge.

Cambridge Mews (☎ 07-827 7166; www.cambridgemews.co.nz; 20 Hamilton Rd; units $145-190; 🖐) All the spacious units in this chalet-style motel have double spa baths, decent kitchens and are immaculately maintained. The architect did a great job but the interior decorator less so.

Park House (☎ 07-827 6368; www.parkhouse.co.nz; 70 Queen St; d incl breakfast $160-310; 🐾) Try to avoid the word 'charming' when describing this centrally located 1918 Tudor impostor, full of antiques, brass beds, quilts and period features. The same word applies to the experienced hosts, who serve an ample breakfast (stewed fruits, farm eggs, sausages etc) in the formal dining room.

Houseboat Holidays (☎ 07-827 2195; www.houseboatescape.co.nz; 2 nights $600) Humming 'Proud Mary' is acceptable as Lake Karapiro is technically still a river, but you're more likely to be relaxing than rolling. Load up this smart houseboat (sleeping seven) with kayaks and fishing gear and sail away for a splashy couple of days.

Emanuel's Lake Karapiro Lodge (☎ 07-823 7414; www.emanuels.co.nz; 1829 SH1; d/ste incl breakfast $400/750; ☎) Call it rustic grandeur. This modern house with commanding views of Lake Karapiro has high ceilings, moulded cornices and leadlights. If you think the standard rooms are luxurious, check out the sumptuous Versace Suite (gold bathroom fittings) and mammoth Sir Tristram Suite. It's located 20km from Cambridge, high above the road near the Tauranga turn-off.

Eating

ourpick **Red Cherry** (☎ 07-823 1515; cnr SH1 & Forrest Rd; meals $6-17; ☺ 9am-3pm) With happy staff and a cherry-red espresso machine working overtime, barn-like Red Cherry offers coffee roasted on-site, delicious counter food and impressive cooked breakfasts (perhaps oat hotcakes or a breakfast risotto). It's Cambridge's best cafe by a country mile (it's actually a country 4km out of Cambridge on the way to Hamilton). There are a couple of tables outside, too, if you feel like sniffing the bucolic splendour.

Rata (☎ 07-823 0999; 64c Victoria St; meals $6-20; ☺ 8.30am-4pm) Sit in either the funky old shopfront or the courtyard garden for, as the local media described it, 'robust food – nicely cooked and plenty of it'.

Onyx (☎ 07-827 7740; 70 Alpha St; mains $17-24; ☺ breakfast, lunch & dinner) All-day Onyx occupies a lofty space, with onyx-black furnishings and a warm-toned timber floor. Wood-fired pizzas are the mainstay, plus salads, tortillas, sandwiches, steaks, cakes and good coffee. At night it's almost urbane.

Cafe Oasis (☎ 07-827 8004; 35 Duke St; mains $20-30; ☺ 9am-9pm Mon-Thu, 9am-late Fri & Sat, 10am-9pm Sun; Ⓥ) It's a strange combo – from the name you'd expect felafels but instead you get blaring FM radio and a menu that's half authentic Thai, half classic European. Fusion be damned.

Getting There & Away

Being on SH1, 22km southeast of Hamilton, Cambridge is well connected by bus. Environment Waikato's **Busit!** (☎ 0800 4287 5463; www.busit.co.nz) heads to Hamilton ($6, 40 minutes) three times each weekday.

InterCity (☎ 09-583 5780; www.intercity.co.nz) services numerous destinations including:

Destination	Price	Duration	Frequency
Auckland	$38	2½hr	10 daily
Hamilton	$21	30min	8 daily
Matamata	$20	30min	1 daily
Rotorua	$28	1¼hr	5 daily
Wellington	$75	8½hr	3 daily

Naked Bus (☎ 0900 625 33; www.nakedbus.com) services to the same destinations are as follows. Consider booking in advance for big savings.

Destination	Price	Duration	Frequency
Auckland	$27	2½hr	5 daily
Hamilton	$14	30min	3 daily
Matamata	$12	40min	2 daily
Rotorua	$15	1½hr	2 daily
Wellington	$45	9½hr	1 daily

TIRAU
pop 730

Cambridge's cosy Anglophilia seems even more exaggerated when you reach the next stop on SH1. Tirau has fallen head-over-heels in love with corrugated iron. The **Tirau i-SITE** (☎ 07-883 1202; www.tirauinfo.co.nz; SH1; ☺ 9am-5pm) is inside a giant corrugated dog, while many other buildings have similarly crinkly oversized sculptures (a wedge of cheese, a shepherd, a tulip…).

Just off SH27, 5km north of Tirau, **Oraka Deer Park** (☎ 07-883 1382; www.oraka-deer.co.nz; 71 Bayly Rd; d $100, cottage $200-260; ☎) offers a self-contained cottage (easily sleeping five) or an en-suite room in the house. Kids will love the deer, not to mention the pool, spa and tennis court.

MATAMATA
pop 7800

Not as well-heeled as Cambridge but just as horsey, Matamata was just one of those pleasant country towns you drove through until Peter Jackson's epic film trilogy *Lord of the Rings* put it on the map. During filming Matamata was a great place to live if you were short, chubby-cheeked and Hobbit-like – 300 locals got work as extras (hairy feet weren't a prerequisite).

Most tourists who come to Matamata are dedicated hobbit-botherers: for everyone else there's a great cafe, avenues of mature trees and undulating green hills that are pleasantly

Shire-like. And if your souvenir checklist includes a thoroughbred racehorse, this is the place to come.

Information
The super-helpful **Matamata i-SITE** (☎ 07-888 7260; www.matamatanz.co.nz; 45 Broadway; ☼ 9am-5pm Mon-Fri, 9am-3pm Sat & Sun) has free town maps, all the guff on local attractions and extended summer hours. Hobbiton tours leave from here.

Sights & Activities
Hobbiton Movie Set & Farm Tours (☎ 07-888 6838; www.hobbitontours.com; adult/under 5/5-9yr/10-14yr $58/free/5/29; ☼ tours 9.50am, 10.45am, noon, 1.15pm, 2.30pm, 3.45pm) is the country's top attraction for *LOTR*-ites, and pretty interesting even if you haven't seen the movies. Due to copyright, all of the intricately constructed movie sets around the country had to be destroyed, but Hobbiton's owners successfully negotiated to keep the hobbit holes, albeit without their wonderful exteriors. Still, for the devotee (of which there are many), it's an opportunity to let your imagination fly. Also on offer is a hands-on **Sheep Farm Experience** (adult/child $16/8), explaining all things woolly. Free transfers leave from the Matamata i-SITE. Otherwise, head towards Cambridge and turn right into Puketutu Rd and then left into Buckland Rd, stopping at the Shire's Rest cafe.

Skydive Waikato (☎ 07-888 8763; www.freefall.co.nz; 9000-15,000ft tandem $240-290) and **Dropzone** (☎ 027 494 2537; www.dropzonenz.co.nz; 9000ft tandem $220) both offer thrilling gravity-powered plummets from Matamata Airfield, 10km north of Matamata on SH27.

Firth Tower (☎ 07-888 8369; www.frithtower.co.nz; Tower Rd; admission free; ☼ 10am-4pm) was built by Auckland businessman Josiah Firth after acquiring 56,000 acres from his friend Wiremu Tamihana, chief of Ngati Haua. The 18m concrete tower (1882) was a fashionable status symbol rather than for defensive purposes. It's filled with Maori and pioneer artefacts and around it are 10 other historic buildings (closed Tuesday and Wednesday), including a schoolroom, church and jail. It's 3km east of town.

Opal Hot Springs (☎ 07-888 8198; www.opalhotsprings.co.nz; 257 Okauia Springs Rd; admission adult/child $6/3, 30min private spas $8/4; ☼ 9am-9pm) isn't nearly as glamorous as it sounds but it does have three large thermal pools. Turn off just north of Firth Tower and follow the road for 2km.

Carry on past Opal Pools and then follow the Kaimai Ranges north for 9km to visit the spectacular 150m-high **Wairere Falls**. From the car park it's a 45-minute walk through native bush to the lookout or a steep 90-minute climb to the summit.

Sleeping
Broadway Motel & Miro Court Villas (☎ 07-888 8482; www.broadwaymatamata.co.nz, www.mirocourt.co.nz; 128 Broadway; s $70-135, d $85-155; ☐ ☑) This sprawling motel complex has spread from a well-maintained older-style block to progressively newer and flasher blocks set back from the street. The nicest are the chic apartment-style Miro Court villas. There's a fun kids' play area in the centre.

Southern Belle (☎ 07-888 5518; www.southernbelle.co.nz; 101 Firth St; s & d $120, extra person $40; ☎) Taking over the top floor of a grand old house (a transported vision from Savannah or Baton Rouge), this suite has three elegant bedrooms, a comfortable lounge and a kitchenette (just a microwave for cooking, but there's a barbecue downstairs guests can use).

Eating & Drinking
Redoubt Bar & Eatery (☎ 07-888 8585; 48 Broadway; lunch $10-18, dinner $22-31; ☼ breakfast, lunch & dinner Tue-Sun) The sister establishment of Te Awamutu's Redoubt (p234), Matamata's version is just as good: thin-crust pizzas, chowder, steak sandwiches and live music every Friday. Oh, and plenty of Monteiths!

our pick **Workman's Cafe Bar** (☎ 07-888 5498; 52 Broadway; lunch $15-16, dinner $28-32; ☼ breakfast, lunch & dinner) Truly eccentric (one wall is lined with art-deco mirrors while another holds an impressive collection of busts of African women), this funky eatery has built itself a reputation that extends beyond Matamata. The poached salmon Benedict is quite possibly the best in the country.

Getting There & Away
Matamata is on SH27, 20km north of Tirau.

InterCity (☎ 09-583 5780; www.intercity.co.nz) runs one bus daily to Cambridge ($20, 30 minutes), Hamilton ($25, one hour), Rotorua ($26, one hour) and Tauranga ($21, one hour).

Naked Bus (☎ 0900 625 33; www.nakedbus.com) runs once daily to Auckland ($27, 3½ hours), Cambridge ($12, 30 minutes), Hamilton ($15, one hour) and Tauranga ($12, 45 minutes). Book in advance for fares as low as $1.

TE AROHA
pop 3800

Te Aroha has a great vibe. You could even say that it's got 'the love', which is the literal meaning of the name. Tucked under the elbow of the bush-clad Mt Te Aroha (952m), it's a good base for bushwalking or 'taking the waters' in the town's therapeutic thermal springs.

Information

Te Aroha i-SITE (☎ 07-884 8052; www.tearohanz. co.nz; 102 Whitaker St; ✹ 9.30am-5pm Mon-Fri, 9.30am-4pm Sat & Sun)

Sights & Activities

The town's thermal area is in the quaint Edwardian Hot Springs Domain, a park behind the i-SITE, split into separate facilities for soakers and splashers. The Te Aroha Mineral Spa Bath House (☎ 07-884 8717; www.tearohapools.co.nz; 30min session per couple $30; ✹ 10.30am-10pm) offers relaxing private tubs, massage, beauty therapies and aromatherapy. Near the entrance a drinking fountain allows you to try the warm soda water – an acquired taste but reputedly good for constipation. Also here is the temperamental Mokena Geyser – the world's only known soda geyser – blows its top every 40 minutes or so, shooting water 3m into the air (the most ardent eruptions are between noon and 2pm).

Lower down the domain, the Leisure Pools (☎ 07-884 4498; www.tearohapools.co.nz; admission adult/ child $5/3; ✹ 10am-5.45pm Mon-Fri, to 6.45pm Sat & Sun) have outdoor heated freshwater pools for splashing about in.

Just down the hill, the Te Aroha Museum (☎ 07-884 4427; www.tearoha-museum.com; admission adult/child $3/1; ✹ 11am-4pm Nov-Mar, noon-3pm Apr-Oct) is in the ornate former thermal sanatorium. Displays include quirky souvenir ceramics.

Hiking trails up Mt Te Aroha start at the top of the domain. It takes 45 minutes to climb up to the Bald Spur/Whakapipi Lookout (350m). Then it's another 2.7km (two hours) climbing to the summit.

Sleeping

Te Aroha Holiday Park (☎ 07-884 9567; www.tearoha holidaypark.co.nz; 217 Stanley Rd; sites per person $10, dm $15, cabins $35-45, units $50-90; ☐ ☎ ☎) Wake up to a bird orchestra among the large oaks at this site, equipped with grass tennis court, gym and hot pool, 2km southwest of

town. The owners also speak German and Japanese.

Te Aroha YHA (☎ 07-884 8739; www.yha.co.nz; Miro St; dm/tr $23/56) The Love YHA is a cosy, TV-free, three-bedroom cottage with a homely atmosphere, welcoming management and a well-stocked herb rack. Free mountain bikes are available; a 10km mountain-bike track starts at the back door. Call in advance to make sure they're open (they're closed sometimes in winter).

Te Aroha Motel (☎ 07-884 9417; tearohamotel@ xtra.co.nz; 108 Whitaker St; s/d/tr/q $80/95/115/135; ☎) Welcome to The Love Motel (with a couple of palm trees out the front, this could almost be Vegas!). Inside are old-fashioned but reasonably priced and tidy units with kitchenettes, right in the centre of town. There's free wi-fi, too.

Aroha Mountain Lodge (☎ 07-884 8134; www. arohamountainlodge.co.nz; 5 Boundary St; s/d/ste/cottage $115/125/145/250) Spread over two *aroha*-ly Edwardian villas on the hillside above town, the Mountain Lodge offers affordable luxury (*sooo* much nicer than a regulation motel) and optional breakfasts ($20 per head). The self-contained Gold Miner's Cottage sleeps six.

Eating & Drinking

Behr Burger (☎ 07-884 9451; 176 Whitaker St; burgers $8-12; ✹ 4-9pm Mon-Wed, 11am-9pm Thu-Sun) Awesome gourmet hamburgers are the go at this buzzy main-street nook. 'The Chief' (NZ rump steak, honey-smoked bacon, a free-range egg, cheddar cheese, salad and aioli) will plug any hungry gaps.

Berlusconi on Whitaker (☎ 07-884 9307; 149 Whitaker St; brunch $12-18, mains $22-28; ✹ 5.30pm-late Wed, 10am-late Thu-Sun) We know the Italian PM has fingers in many pies but surely they don't extend to this upmarket wine, tapas and pizza bar in Te Aroha. Mind you, it is suave enough.

Self-caterers should try the Organic Health Shop (☎ 07-884 9696; 9 Lawrence Ave; ✹ 9am-5pm Mon-Fri) for fresh produce, dairy products, cereals and all things gluten-free.

Getting There & Away

Te Aroha is on SH26, 21km south of Paeroa and 55km northeast of Hamilton. Environment Waikato's Busit! (☎ 0800 4287 5463; www.busit.co.nz) has three services on weekdays to Hamilton ($7.80, one hour).

THE KING COUNTRY

Holding good claim to the title of NZ's rural heartland, this is the kind of no-nonsense place that raises cattle and All Blacks. A bastion of independent Maoridom, it was never conquered in the war against the King Movement (see the boxed text, p225). The story goes that King Tawhiao placed his hat on a large map of NZ and declared that all the land it covered would remain under his *mana* (authority), and the region was effectively off limits to Europeans until 1883.

At this stage it was still largely covered by *Te Nehe-nehe-nui* (the big forest) and home to Ngati Maniapoto, descended from the Tainui migration. After allowing railway surveyors to assess the land, Maori control was gradually chipped away. An example is the Waitomo Caves, which were taken by the Crown in 1906 and only returned to its rightful owners in 1989.

The caves are the area's major drawcard. An incredible natural phenomenon in themselves, they've been sexed up even more with a smorgasbord of adrenaline-inducing activities on offer.

For more regional info, see www.sacred peaks.com.

KAWHIA
pop 670

Along with resisting cultural annihilation this fishing village ('Think mafia with a K', says a lady on the street) has avoided large-scale development, retaining its sleepy feel despite its considerable natural attractions. It's basically Raglan (p230) and Hot Water Beach (p206) rolled into one, but without the tourists. There's not much here except for the general store/post office, a couple of takeaways and a petrol station. Even Captain Cook blinked and missed the narrow entrance to the large harbour when he sailed past in 1770.

It was in Kawhia that the *Tainui waka* – one of the ancestral canoes that arrived during the 14th century – made its final landing. The two leaders of the expedition – Hoturoa, the chief/captain, and Rakataura, the *tohunga* (priest) – knew that their new home was destined to be on the west coast, searching until they finally recognised the prophesised place. When they landed, they tied the *waka* to a pohutukawa tree on the shore, naming the tree Tangi te Korowhiti. The unlabelled tree still stands on the shoreline between the wharf and Maketu Marae. At the end of its long, epic voyage, the *waka* was dragged up onto a hill and buried. Sacred stones were placed at either end to mark its resting place.

Famed Ngati Toa warrior chief Te Rauparaha, composer of the famous *haka* 'Ka Mate', was born nearby in the 1760s.

Sights & Activities

Kawhia Museum & Gallery (☎ 07-871 0161; www. kawhiaharbour.co.nz; Kawhia Wharf; admission free; ⌚ 11am-4pm Wed-Sun) is a modest but cute affair near the wharf, and serves as the information centre.

Kayaks can be hired on the incoming tide from Kawhia Beachside S-Cape (below) for $10 per hour. The skipper of **Kawhia Harbour Cruises** (☎ 07-871 0149; cruises 1hr/2hr $25/35) is well placed to provide a cultural and historical commentary as his family has resided in Kawhia since the arrival of the *Tainui waka*. For fishing trips contact **Dove Charters** (☎ 07-871 5854; www.westcoastfishing.co.nz; full day $100).

Four kilometres west of Kawhia is **Ocean Beach** and its high, black-sand dunes. Swimming can be dangerous, but one to two hours either side of low tide you can find the **Te Puia Hot Springs** in the sand – dig a hole for your own natural hot pool.

From the wharf, a track extends along the coast to **Maketu Marae**, which has an impressively carved meeting house, Auaukiterangi. Through the *marae* grounds and behind the wooden fence, two stones (Hani and Puna) mark the burial place of the *Tainui waka* (see left). This *marae* is private property – don't enter without permission from the Maketu Marae Committee (info@kawhia.maori.nz). Unfortunately you can't see a lot from the road.

Festivals & Events

During the annual **Kai Festival** (www.kawhiaharbour. co.nz/maori-kai-festival.html) in early February, over 10,000 people descend to enjoy traditional Maori *kai* (food) and catch up with *whanau* (relations). Once you've filled up on seafood, *rewana* bread and rotten corn you can settle in to watch the bands and rousing *kapa haka* performances.

Sleeping & Eating

Kawhia Beachside S-Cape (☎ 07-871 0727; www.kawhia beachsidescape.co.nz; 225 Pouewe St; sites from $34, cabins dm/s/d from $30/45/55, cottages $130-180) Perfectly positioned on the water's edge at the entrance to Kawhia, this camping ground has comfortable cottages. There's a new laundry and ablutions block, but the backpackers area is rudimentary at best – camping is a better bet.

Kawhia Motel (☎ 07-871 0865, kawhiamotel@xtra. co.nz; cnr Jervois & Tainui Sts; s $99-155, extra person $20) Six perkily painted, well-kept, old-school motel units right next to the shops.

Annie's Cafe & Restaurant (☎ 07-871 0198; 146 Jervois St; meals $5-25; ☺ 9.30am-4pm, closed Mon & Tue in winter) An old-fashioned licensed eatery in the main street, serving espresso, sandwiches and local specialities such as flounder and whitebait. There's also an internet terminal.

Getting There & Away

This remote outpost doesn't have a bus service. Take SH31 from Otorohanga (58km) or explore the scenic but rough unsealed road to Raglan (see p232).

OTOROHANGA
pop 2700

One of several nondescript North Island towns to adopt a gimmick (we're looking at you Tirau, Paeroa, Katikati, Bulls and Hobbiton, sorry, Matamata), Otorohanga (Oto to his mates) has a main street lined with cherished icons of Kiwiana. You'll learn about sheep, gumboots, jandals, No 8 wire, All Blacks, the beloved Buzzy Bee children's toy and – bravely risking fisticuffs with the Australian Country Women's Association – the pavlova (a creamy meringue dessert). Gimmicks aside, the Kiwi House is well worth a visit.

Information

Otorohanga i-SITE (☎ 07-873 8951; www.otorohanga. co.nz; 21 Maniapoto St; ☺ 9am-5pm Mon-Fri, 10am-2pm Sat & Sun) has internet access and local information.

Sights

The **Otorohanga Kiwi House Native Bird Park** (☎ 07-873 7391; www.kiwihouse.org.nz; 20 Alex Telfer Dr; admission adult/child $16/4; ☺ 9am-5pm Sep-May, 9am-4.30pm Jun-Aug) has a nocturnal enclosure where you can see active kiwi energetically digging with their long beaks, searching for food. This is the only place in NZ where you can see a Great Spotted Kiwi, the biggest of the three kiwi species. Other native birds, such as kaka, kea, falcon, morepork and weka, are also on show.

The small **Otorohanga Museum** (☎ 07-873 8849; Kakamutu Rd; admission free; ☺ 1-5pm Sun) covers local history and has a collection of historic buildings, including a church and a lock-up.

As well as the Kiwiana main street, the **Ed Hillary Walkway** running off Maniapoto St has information panels on the All Blacks, Marmite, NZ competing in the America's Cup, and of course, Sir Ed.

Sleeping

Otorohanga Holiday Park (☎ 07-873 7253; www. kiwiholidaypark.co.nz; 20 Huiputea Dr; unpowered/powered sites $30/34, cabins $52-58, units $75-105; ☐ ☎) It's not the most attractive locale, backing on to the train tracks, but the owners are quick with a smile and the park's tidy facilities include a fitness centre and sauna. And if you can't find a bed in Waitomo, Otorohanga is only 16km away.

Eating & Drinking

Thirsty Weta (☎ 07-873 6699; 57 Maniapoto St; meals $7-16; ☺ 10am-1am) The top pick in town, with hearty snacks (of the pizza, pasta and quesadilla variety) and the promise of things kicking off after dinner when the wine-bar vibe takes over and the musos plug in.

Origin Coffee Station (☎ 07-873 8550; 7 Wahanui Cres; coffee $3-5; ☺ 8.30am-4.30pm Mon-Fri) It's a long way from Malawi to the old Otorohanga railway station, but the beans don't seem to mind. The folks at Origin are dead serious about coffee, sourcing, importing and roasting it themselves and then delivering it to your table, strong and perfectly formed, and possibly with a slice of cake.

As there's no supermarket at Waitomo Caves, stock up at Oto's **Woolworths** (☎ 07-873 7378; 123 Maniapoto St; ☺ 7am-10pm) on the Waitomo side of town.

Getting There & Away

InterCity (☎ 09-583 5780; www.intercity.co.nz) buses arrive and depart from outside the i-SITE. There are daily buses to Auckland ($50, 3¼ hours, four daily), Te Awamutu ($21, 20 minutes, three daily), Te Kuiti ($17, 20 minutes, three daily) and Rotorua ($52, 2½ hours, one daily).

Naked Bus (☎ 0900 625 33; www.nakedbus.com) runs around five buses weekly to Waitomo Caves ($12, 20 minutes), Hamilton ($13, 50 minutes) and New Plymouth ($37, 3¼ hours). Book in advance for lower fares.

The **Waitomo Shuttle** (☎ 07-873 8279; waikiwi@ihug.co.nz; one way adult/child $10/5) heads to the caves five times daily, coordinating with bus and train arrivals.

The **Dalroy Express** (☎ 0508 465 622; www.dalroytours.co.nz) bus runs daily between Auckland ($36, three hours) and New Plymouth ($34, 3¼ hours), stopping at Otorohanga. Other stops include Hamilton ($16, 50 minutes) and Te Awamutu ($11, 25 minutes).

Otorohanga is on the **Overlander** (☎ 0800 872 467; www.tranzscenic.co.nz; daily Oct-Apr, Fri-Sun May-Sep) train route between Auckland ($81, 3¼ hours) and Wellington ($107, nine hours) via Hamilton ($53, 50 minutes) and Te Kuiti ($53, 15 minutes).

WAITOMO CAVES

Even if damp, dark tunnels sound like your idea of hell, take a chill pill and head to Waitomo anyway. These limestone caves with accompanying geological formations and glowing bugs are deservedly one of the premier attractions of the North Island.

Your Waitomo experience can be as claustrophobe-friendly as the electrically lit, cathedral-like and extremely beautiful Glow-worm Cave. But if it's adrenaline-pumping, gut-wrenching, soaking-wet, pitch-black, squeezing, plummeting excitement you're after, Waitomo can take care of that, too.

The name Waitomo comes from *wai* (water) and *tomo* (hole or shaft); dotted throughout the countryside are numerous shafts dropping abruptly into underground cave systems and streams. There are more than 300 mapped caves in the Waitomo area. The three main caves – the Glow-worm Cave, Ruakuri and Aranui – have been bewitching visitors for over 100 years.

History

Ruakuri Cave was discovered by Maori 400 to 500 years ago when a hunter travelling in a war party with Kawhia chief Tane Tinorau was attacked by a pack of dogs living in the cave entrance. The dogs were caught and eaten but the name Ruakuri (Den of Dogs) stuck. Shortly after, Tinorau moved his people into the area and the cave became a *wahi tapu*

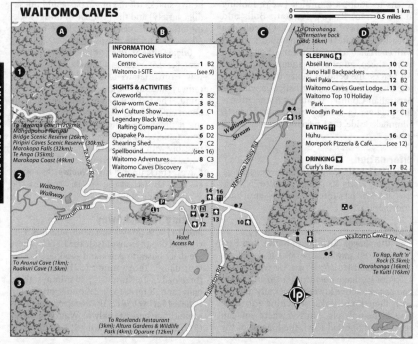

WAITOMO CAVES

INFORMATION
Waitomo Caves Visitor Centre 1 B2
Waitomo i-SITE .... (see 9)

SIGHTS & ACTIVITIES
Caveworld 2 B2
Glow-worm Cave 3 B2
Kiwi Culture Show 4 C1
Legendary Black Water Rafting Company 5 D3
Opapake Pa 6 D2
Shearing Shed 7 C2
Spellbound .... (see 16)
Waitomo Adventures 8 C3
Waitomo Caves Discovery Centre 9 B2

SLEEPING
Abseil Inn 10 C2
Juno Hall Backpackers 11 C3
Kiwi Paka 12 B2
Waitomo Caves Guest Lodge 13 C2
Waitomo Top 10 Holiday Park 14 B2
Woodlyn Park 15 C1

EATING
Huhu 16 C2
Morepork Pizzeria & Café .... (see 12)

DRINKING
Curly's Bar 17 B2

0 .... 1 km
0 .... 0.5 miles

To Otorohanga (alternative back road; 16km)

To Tawarau Forest (20km); Mangapohue Natural Bridge Scenic Reserve (26km); Piripiri Caves Scenic Reserve (30km); Marokopa Falls (32km); Te Anga (35km); Marokopa Coast (49km)

Te Anga Rd

Waitomo Stream

Waitomo Valley Rd

Waitomo Walkway

Tumurumu Rd

Hotel Access Rd

Fullerton Rd

Waitomo Caves Rd

To Aranui Cave (1km); Ruakuri Cave (1.5km)

To Rap, Raft 'n' Rock (5.5km); Otorohanga (16km); Te Kuiti (16km)

To Roselands Restaurant (3km); Altura Gardens & Wildlife Park (4km); Oparure (12km)

(sacred site), used for burials and for storing important *taonga*. By the 20th century the land had passed into the hands of the Holden family, who own it to this day.

The Glow-worm Cave had long been known to local Maori but they had no desire to explore it. That changed in December 1887 when the local chief, another Tane Tinorau, headed into the cave system, taking English surveyor Fred Mace with him. Mace prepared an account of the expedition, a map was made, photographs given to the government, and before long Tane Tinorau was operating tours of the cave. The tours must have made an impression as the government nationalised the land 19 years later – depriving the local *hapu* (subtribe) of a nice little earner. In 1989 this injustice was corrected and the *hapu* now owns and leases back the land, gets a slice of admission charges and provides much of the workforce.

Information

Waitomo i-SITE (☎ 07-878 7640; www.waitomocaves.com; 21 Waitomo Caves Rd; ✆ 8am-8pm Jan & Feb, 8.45am-5pm Mar-Dec; ▯) has internet access and acts as a post office and booking agent.

Sights

WAITOMO CAVES

The big-three caves are all operated by the same company, based at the new **Waitomo Caves Visitor Centre** (☎ 0800 456 922; www.waitomo. com; Waitomo Caves Rd; ✆ 9am-5pm). Various combo deals are available, including the Triple Cave Combo (adult/child $105/44). Try to avoid the large tour groups, most of which arrive between 10.30am and 2.30pm.

The 45-minute guided tour of the **Glow-worm Cave** (Waitomo Caves Rd; tours adult/child $39/18; ✆ tours every 30min 9am-5pm), which is behind the visitor centre, leads past impressive stalactites and stalagmites into a large cavern known as the Cathedral. The acoustics are so good that Dame Kiri Te Kanawa and the Vienna Boys Choir have given concerts here. The highlight comes at the tour's end when you board a boat and swing off onto the river. As your eyes grow accustomed to the dark you'll see a Milky Way of little lights surrounding you – these are the glowworms. You can see them in lots of other places in NZ, but the ones in this cave are something special. Conditions for their growth are just about perfect so there are a remarkable number of them.

Three kilometres west from the Glow-worm Cave is **Aranui Cave** (Tumutumu Rd; tours adult/child $39/18; ✆ 45min tours 10am, 11am, 1pm, 2pm, 3pm). This cave is dry (hence no glowworms) but compensates with an incredible array of limestone formations. Thousands of tiny 'straw' stalactites hang from the ceiling. It's an hour's walk to the caves, otherwise the visitors centre can arrange transport.

Culturally significant **Ruakuri Cave** (☎ 0800 228 464; Tumutumu Rd; tours adult/child $60/24; ✆ 2hr tours 9am, 10am, 11.30am, 12.30pm, 1.30pm, 2.30pm & 3pm) has an impressive 15m-high spiral staircase, removing the need to trample through the Maori burial site (see History, opposite) at the cave entrance (as tourists did for 84 years). Tours lead through 1.6km of the 7.5km system, taking in vast caverns with glowworms, subterranean streams and waterfalls, and intricate limestone structures. For as long as this cave has been open to the public, people have described it as spiritual – some claim it's haunted. It's customary to wash your hands when leaving to remove the *tapu* (see p58). Tours depart from the Legendary Black Water Rafting Company (see below).

Adjoining the i-SITE, this **Waitomo Caves Discovery Centre** (☎ 07-878 7640; www.waitomo -museum.co.nz; 21 Waitomo Caves Rd; admission adult/child $5/3; ✆ 8am-8pm Jan & Feb, 8.45am-5pm Mar-Dec) has excellent exhibits explaining how caves are formed, the flora and fauna that thrive in them and the history of Waitomo's caves and cave exploration.

ALTURA GARDENS & WILDLIFE PARK

At this privately run five-acre **park** (☎ 07-878 5278; www.alturapark.co.nz; 477 Fullerton Rd; adult/child $12/5; ✆ 9am-5pm) you can chat with a cockatoo, outstare a morepork or pat a blue-tongue lizard. There are 85 species of birds and animals here, but it's not a zoo – expect llamas and sheep rather than lions and giraffes. It also runs leisurely **horse treks** (30/60/90min $50/65/80).

Activities

The array of underground adventures available here is overwhelming, with most operators offering various combo experiences. The i-SITE is the best place for info, but booking ahead can often save you a dollar or twenty.

UNDERGROUND

Legendary Black Water Rafting Company (☎ 0800 228 464; 585 Waitomo Caves Rd; www.waitomo) claims to have invented black-water rafting! Its Black Labyrinth tour (three hours, $110, minimum age 12) involves floating in a wetsuit on an inner tube down a river that flows through Ruakuri Cave. The highlight is leaping off a small waterfall and then floating through a long, glowworm-covered passage. The trip ends with showers, soup and bagels in the cafe. The Black Abyss tour (five hours, $215, minimum age 16) is more adventurous and includes a 30m abseil into Ruakuri Cave and more glowworms, tubing and cave climbing.

Spellbound (☎ 0800 773 552, 07-878 7622; www.glowworm.co.nz; 10 Waitomo Caves Rd; tours adult/child $66/24) is a good option if you don't want to get wet and want to avoid the big groups in the main caves. This three-hour tour and raft-ride departs from the pyramid-like booking office in the middle of town (usually 10am, 11am, 2pm and 3pm, varying seasonally) and goes through parts of the glowworm-filled Mangawhitikau cave system, 12km south of Waitomo.

Waitomo Adventures (☎ 0800 924 866, 07-878 7788; www.waitomo.co.nz; 654 Waitomo Caves Rd) offers five different cave adventures, with discounts for various combos and for advance bookings. The Lost World (four-/seven-hour trip $270/395) trip starts with a 100m abseil down into the cave, then – by a combination of walking, climbing, spider-walking, inching along narrow rock ledges, wading and swimming through a river – you take a three-hour journey through a 30m-high cave to get back out, passing glowworms, amazing rock formations, waterfalls and more. The price includes lunch (underground) and dinner. The shorter version skips the wet stuff and the meals.

Haggas Honking Holes (four hours, $215) includes professional abseiling instruction followed by three abseils, rock climbing and travelling along a subterranean river with waterfalls, traversing narrow passageways and huge caverns. Along the way you see glowworms and a variety of cave formations, including stalactites, stalagmites, columns, flowstone (calcite deposited by a thin sheet of flowing water) and cave coral. The adventure's name derives from a local farmer (Haggas) and characters in a Dr Seuss story (honking holers).

TumuTumu Toobing (four hours, $150) is a walking, wading, swimming and tubing trip. St Benedict's Cavern (three hours, $145) includes abseiling and a subterranean flying fox in an attractive cave with straw stalagmites.

Readers recommend **Green Glow Eco-Adventures** (☎ 0800 476 459; www.greenglow.co.nz; 6hr tours per person $100 for 2-4 people, $200 for 1 person), which runs customised, small-group Waitomo tours, putting a caving, rock-climbing, abseiling, photographic or glowworm spin on your day (or all of the above!). It's based in Te Kuiti, 20 minutes from Waitomo. **Caveworld** (☎ 0800 228 396; www.caveworld.co.nz; cnr Waitomo Caves Rd & Hotel Access Rd) runs the Black Magic (2½ hours, $124) black-water rafting trip through glowworm-filled Te Anaroa. You've also got the choice of a day or (glowworm-illuminated) night abseil down a 45m crevice called The Canyon (two hours, night/day $144/175). Various combo discounts apply.

Rap, Raft 'n' Rock (☎ 0800 228 372, 07-873 9149; www.caveraft.com; 95 Waitomo Caves Rd; trips $135) runs five-hour small-group expeditions. It starts with abseil training, followed by a 27m descent into a natural cave, and then floating along a subterranean river on an inner tube with plenty of glowworms. After some caving, a belayed rock climb up a 20m cliff brings you to the surface.

WALKING

The i-SITE has free pamphlets on walks in the area. The walk from the Aranui Cave to the Ruakuri Cave is an excellent short path. From the Glow-worm Cave ticket office, there's a 10-minute walk to a lookout. Also from here, the 5km, three-hour-return **Waitomo Walkway** takes off through farmland, following Waitomo Stream to the **Ruakuri Scenic Reserve**, where a 30-minute return walk passes by a natural limestone tunnel. There are glowworms here at night – drive to the car park and bring a torch to find your way. Near Juno Hall Backpackers a steep 20-minute walk leads through bush then along farmland to the abandoned **Opapake Pa**, where terraces and kumara pits are visible.

The privately run **Dundle Hill Walk** (☎ 0800 924 866, 07-878 7788; www.waitomowalk.com; adult/child $75/35) is a 27km, two-day/one-night loop walk through bush and farmland, including overnight bunk-house accommodation high up in the bush.

OTHER ACTIVITIES

Kiwi Culture Show (☎ 07-878 6666; www.woodlynpark.co.nz; 1177 Waitomo Valley Rd; admission adult/child $25/13;

GLOWWORM MAGIC

Glowworms are the larvae of the fungus gnat, which looks much like a large mosquito without mouth parts. The larva glowworms have luminescent organs that produce a soft, greenish light. Living in a sort of hammock suspended from an overhang, they weave sticky threads that trail down and catch unwary insects attracted by their lights. When an insect flies towards the light it gets stuck in the threads – the glowworm just has to reel it in for a feed.

The larval stage lasts for six to nine months, depending on how much food the glowworm gets. When it has grown to about the size of a matchstick, it goes into a pupa stage, much like a cocoon. The adult fungus gnat emerges about two weeks later.

The adult insect doesn't live very long because it doesn't have a mouth. It emerges, mates, lays eggs and dies, all within about two or three days. The sticky eggs, laid in groups of 40 or 50, hatch in about three weeks to become larval glowworms.

Glowworms thrive in moist, dark caves but they can survive anywhere if they have the requisites of moisture, an overhang to suspend from and insects to eat. Waitomo is famous for its glowworms but you can see them in many other places around NZ, both in caves and outdoors.

When you come upon glowworms, don't touch their hammocks or hanging threads, try not to make loud noises and don't shine a light right on them. All of these things will cause them to dim their lights. It takes them a few hours to become bright again, during which time the grub will go hungry. The glowworms that shine most brightly are the hungriest.

(✪ shows 1.30pm) is a rustic theatre where local blokes put on a one-hour farm show that combines history, broad humour, local critters and audience participation.

At the **Shearing Shed** (☎ 07-878 8371; shearing shed@xtra.co.nz; 718 Waitomo Caves Rd; admission free; ✪ 9am-4pm) big, fluffy, surprisingly sociable Angora rabbits are sheared for an audience (12.45pm daily). It's SPCA-approved and the rabbits really don't seem to mind. The store sells Angora products.

Sleeping

Juno Hall Backpackers (☎ 07-878 7649; www.juno waitomo.co.nz; 600 Waitomo Caves Rd; sites per person $15, dm $27, d with/without bathroom $76/66, tr $95/85, q $120; 📖 🛜 🏋) A slick purpose-built hostel a kilometre from the village with a warm welcome, a warmer wood fire in the woody lounge area, and an outdoor pool and tennis court.

Waitomo Top 10 Holiday Park (☎ 0508 498 666, 07-878 7639; www.waitomopark.co.nz; 12 Waitomo Caves Rd; sites from $20, cabins $65-110, units $130-170; 📖 🛜 🏋) This superb camping ground in the heart of the village has spotless facilities, beaut new cabins and plenty of outdoor action to keep the kids busy (pool, spa, playground and neighbouring rugby pitch…).

Rap, Raft 'n' Rock Backpackers (☎ 0800 228 372, 07-873 9149; www.caveraft.com; 95 Waitomo Caves Rd; dm/d $28/66; 📖 🛜) The homeliest of Waitomo's hostels, this basic bunk-house occupies a farm cottage 7km from the village. The brightly painted walls may burn your retinas after a day spent underground.

Kiwi Paka (☎ 07-878 3395; www.kiwipaka.co.nz; Hotel Access Rd; dm/s/d $29/62/66, chalets tw/d/q $95/110/145; 📖) It's too big to be social but this snazzy, purpose-built, Alpine-style hostel has four-bed dorms, peak-roofed chalets, Morepork restaurant (p246) on-site and super-tidy facilities.

Waitomo Caves Guest Lodge (☎ 07-878 7641; www.waitomocavesguestlodge.co.nz; 7 Waitomo Caves Rd; s $80, d $100-120, extra person $25, all incl breakfast; 🛜) Bags your own cosy little en-suite cabin at this central lodge with a sweet garden setting. The top cabins have valley views. Large continental breakfast and resident dog included.

Abseil Inn (☎ 07-878 7815; www.abseilinn.co.nz; 709 Waitomo Caves Rd; d incl breakfast $135-165; 🛜) A *veeery* steep driveway (abseiling in from a helicopter might be an easier approach) takes you to this delightful B&B with four themed rooms, great breakfasts and witty hosts. The biggest room has a double bath and valley views.

Woodlyn Park (☎ 07-878 6666; www.woodlynpark.co.nz; 1177 Waitomo Valley Rd; d $160-225, extra person $15) Boasting the world's only hobbit motel (set into the ground with round windows and doors), Woodlyn Park's other sleeping options include the cockpit of a combat plane, train carriages and the 'Waitanic' – a converted WWII patrol boat fitted with chandeliers, moulded ceilings and shiny brass portholes.

It's extremely well done and the kids will love you for it.

Eating & Drinking

There isn't a supermarket, ATM or general store in Waitomo: buy provisions in Otorohanga (p241) or Te Kuiti (p248) before you visit.

Morepork Pizzeria & Cafe (☎ 07-878 3395; Kiwi Paka, Hotel Access Rd; breakfast & lunch $7-15, dinner $13-27; ☺ 8am-8pm) At the Kiwi Paka backpackers is this cheery joint, a jack-of-all-trades eatery serving breakfast, lunch and dinner either inside or out on the deck. The 'Caveman' pizza is a winner (the first person to ask for more pork will be shown the door).

our pick **Huhu** (☎ 07-878 6674; 10 Waitomo Caves Rd; lunch $12-19, dinner $23-35; ☺ 10.30am-9pm; ☺ ☑) Easily the best choice, you won't be disappointed if you come here twice a day. Slick and modern with charming service, it has great views from the afternoon-tipple-friendly terrace and sublime contemporary NZ food. Graze from a seasonal tapas-style menu (large or small plates) of Kiwi specialities such as *rewana* bread and beetroot-coloured *urenika* potatoes. Free wi-fi, too. Downstairs the Huhu Store sells designer NZ gifts.

Roselands Restaurant (☎ 07-878 7611; 579 Fullerton Rd; buffet per adult/child $27/14; ☺ 11am-2pm) Set amid genteel gardens 3km from Waitomo and popular with the tour-bus set, Roselands runs a generous lunchtime buffet: fresh fish, stir-fries and great-looking steaks.

Curly's Bar (☎ 07-878 8448; Hotel Access Rd; ☺ 11am-2am; ☐) A decent tavern with lots of beers on tap, good-value pub grub (mains $7 to $18), chunky wooden tables, internet access and occasional live music.

Getting There & Away

Naked Bus (☎ 0900 625 33; www.nakedbus.com) runs around five buses weekly to/from Otorohanga ($12, 20 minutes), Hamilton ($29, one hour) and New Plymouth ($39, three hours). Book in advance for fares as low as $1.

Waitomo Shuttle (☎ 07-873 8279; waikiwi@ihug. co.nz; one way adult/child $10/5) heads to the caves five times daily from Otorohanga (15 minutes away), coordinating with bus and train arrivals.

Waitomo Wanderer (☎ 0508 926 337; www.waitomo tours.co.nz, day tours incl Glow-worm Cave entry $119) operates a daily return services from Rotorua or Taupo, with optional caving and tubing add-ons (packages $188 to $288). Shuttle-only services are $45 each way.

WAITOMO TO AWAKINO

This obscure route, heading west of Waitomo on Te Anga Rd, is the definition of off-the-beaten-track. It's a slow but fascinating alternative to SH3 if Taranaki's your goal. Only 12km of the 111km route remains unsealed, but it's nearly all winding and narrow. Allow around two hours (not including stops) and fill up with petrol.

Walks in the **Tawarau Forest**, 20km west of the caves, are outlined in DOC's *West of Marokopa* pamphlet ($1), including a one-hour track to the Tawarau Falls from the end of Appletree Rd.

The **Mangapohue Natural Bridge Scenic Reserve**, 26km west of Waitomo, is a 5.5-hectare reserve with a giant natural limestone arch. It's a five-minute walk to the arch on a wheelchair-accessible pathway. On the far side, big rocks full of 35-million-year-old oyster fossils jut up from the grass, and at night you'll see glow-worms: allow 15 minutes to loop back to the car park.

About 4km further west is **Piripiri Caves Scenic Reserve**, where a five-minute walk leads to a large cave containing fossils of giant oysters. Bring a torch and be prepared to get muddy after heavy rain. Steps wind down into the gloom…

The impressively tiered **Marokopa Falls** are located 32km west of Waitomo. A short track (15 minutes return) from the road leads to the bottom of the falls.

The falls are near Te Anga, where you can stop for a drink, some pub grub and a game of pool at friendly **Te Anga Tavern** (☎ 07-876 7815; Te Anga Rd; meals $12-13; ☺ noon-1am Tue-Sun), and maybe fire up the jumpin' country jukebox. Just past Te Anga you can turn north to Kawhia (p240), 59km away, or continue southwest to **Marokopa** (population 1560), a small black-sand village on the coast with some scarily big new mansions starting to appear. The whole Te Anga/Marokopa area is riddled with caves.

Marokopa Campground (☎ 07-876 7444; marokopa campground@xtra.co.nz; Rauparaha St; unpowered/powered sites $24/28, dm $18, van d $45) ain't flash but it's in a nice spot, close to the coast. There's a small shop that will cover the catering basics (bread, milk, cheese), as well as a tennis court and tiny library.

The road heads south to Kiritehere where it follows a bubbling stream through idyllic farmland to Moeatoa where it turns right (south) into Mangatoa Rd. Now you're in serious backcountry, heading into the dense **Whareorino Forest**. It would pay not to watch the movie *Deliverance* before tramping in this spectacularly remote tract of native bush. The 16-bunk DOC-run **Leitch's Hut** (www.doc.govt.nz; per adult $5) has a toilet, water and a wood stove; pick up a fact sheet from the DOC office in Hamilton or Te Kuiti.

At Waikawau it's worth taking the 5km detour along the unsealed road to the coast near **Ngarupupu Point**, where a 100m walk through a dank tunnel opens out on an exquisitely isolated stretch of black-sand beach. Think twice about swimming here; if you get caught in a rip you'll be halfway to Melbourne before your friends can reach help (but visit early and the only footprints in the sand will be yours).

The road then continues through another twisty 28km passing lush forest and the occasional farm before joining SH3 east of Awakino (p248).

TE KUITI
pop 4380
Cute little Te Kuiti sits in a valley between picturesque hills. It doesn't so much have a gimmick as an odd claim to fame: welcome to the shearing capital of the world! You won't have any doubt as to the veracity of that statement if you're here for the very sheepish Great New Zealand Muster (see below).

Information
Department of Conservation (DOC; ☎ 07-878 1050; www.doc.govt.nz; 78 Taupiri St; ✆ 8am-4.30pm Mon-Fri)
i-SITE (☎ 07-878 8077; www.waitomo.govt.nz; Rora St; ✆ 9am-5pm Mon-Fri, 10am-4pm Sat & Sun; 💻) Internet access and visitor information.

Festivals & Events
The highlight of the **Great New Zealand Muster** (www.waitomo.govt.nz; ✆ late Mar/early Apr) is the legendary Running of the Sheep. Pamplona's got nothing on the sight of 2000 woolly demons stampeding down Te Kuiti's main street. The festival includes sheep-shearing championships, a parade, Maori cultural performances, live music, barbecues, *hangi* (feast from an oven in the ground) and lots of market stalls.

Sights & Activities
The most prominent landmark in town is the 7m, 7½-tonne **Big Shearer** statue at the south end of the Rora St shopping strip. Diagonally opposite is the magnificently carved **Te Tokanganui-a-noho Marae**. This was guerrilla leader Te Kooti's grateful gift to his hosts, Ngati Maniapoto, who sheltered him before his pardon in 1883 (see p368). You can't enter without permission, but you can get a good view from the gate.

Further down Rora St, **Te Kuititanga-O-Nga-Whakaaro** (the Gathering of Thoughts and Ideas) is a beautiful pavilion of etched-glass, *tukutuku* (woven flax panels) and wooden carvings that celebrates the town's history.

On the northwestern boundary of Te Kuiti, hill-topped **Brook Park** (Te Kumi Rd) has a 40-minute walk leading up the slope to the site of historic Matakiora Pa, constructed in the 17th century.

South of Te Kuiti, the **Central North Island Rail Trail** has been ascribed 'Quick Start' status as part of the proposed **New Zealand Cycle Trail** (www.tourism.govt.nz/our-work/new-zealand-cycle-trail-project) project. Most of the track will be on DOC-administered land; check the website for updates.

Sleeping
Casara Mesa Backpackers (☎ 07-878 6697; casara@xtra.co.nz; Mangarino Rd; dm/tw $25/55, d with/without bathroom $60/55) Feel the stress ease away as you're collected from town and driven five minutes up the hill to this ramshackle, homespun farmstay with a sublime vista from its quiet veranda.

Simply the Best B&B (☎ 07-878 8191; www.simplythebestbnb.co.nz; 129 Gadsby Rd; s/d incl breakfast $50/100) It's hard to argue with the immodest name when the prices are this reasonable and the hosts this charming. Warning: the spectacular views may illicit involuntary choruses of the Tina Turner anthem.

our pick Waitomo Lodge Motel (☎ 07-878 0003; www.waitomo-lodge.co.nz; 62 Te Kumi Rd; d/f from $110/185) If you can't find a bed in Waitomo itself (it happens), then this snappily designed motel at the Waitomo end of Te Kuiti is a brilliant alternative. Twenty spacious, modern rooms clad in plywood feature contemporary art, moody low-voltage lighting, flat-screen TVs and little decks overlooking Mangaokewa Stream in the units at the back. Bosco Cafe (p248) is across the street. Hipness in an un-hip town!

Eating & Drinking

Bosco Cafe (☎ 07-878 3633; 57 Te Kumi Rd; mains $9-20
⊗ breakfast & lunch; Ⓥ) It's not damning it with
faint praise to say that Bosco is the coolest place
in Te Kuiti. This excellent industrial-chic cafe
offers great coffee, tempting food (try the spinach, feta and pine-nut tart) and sweet service.
It comes into its own on a sunny afternoon
when the doors swing open onto Brook Park.

Riverside Lodge (☎ 07-878 8027; 1 Riverside Lane;
lunch $9-23, dinner $18-35; ⊗ lunch & dinner Tue-Sun) On
the riverbank just off King St, this family-
friendly bar and bistro serves excellent shellfish, substantial pub meals or mini pizzas for
a filling snack ($9). There are a couple of pool
tables and the Eagles' 'Lyin' Eyes' on the juke.

Self caterers bound for Waitomo should
stock up at **New World** (☎ 07-878 8072; Te Kumi Rd;
⊗ 8am-8pm).

Getting There & Away

InterCity (☎ 09-583 5780; www.intercity.co.nz) buses
run daily to the following destinations (among
others):

Destination	Price	Duration	Frequency
Auckland	$55	3½hr	4 daily
Mokau	$28	1hr	2 daily
New Plymouth	$28	2½hr	2 daily
Otorohanga	$20	20min	3 daily
Taumarunui	$27	1¼hr	1 daily

Naked Bus (☎ 0900 625 33; www.nakedbus.com) runs
around five buses weekly to Auckland ($33,
four hours), Hamilton ($20, 1½ hours), New
Plymouth ($45, 2¼ hours) and Otorohanga
($13, 40 minutes). Book in advance for lower
fares.

The **Dalroy Express** (☎ 0508 465 622; www.dalroy
tours.co.nz) bus runs daily between Auckland
($38, 3½ hours) and New Plymouth ($28, 2¼
hours), stopping at Te Kuiti. Other stops include Hamilton ($18, 1½ hours), Mokau ($17,
one hour) and Otorohanga ($11, 15 minutes).

Te Kuiti is on the **Overlander** (☎ 0800 872 467;
www.tranzscenic.co.nz; daily Oct-Apr, Fri-Sun May-Sep) train
route between Auckland ($81, 3½ hours) and
Wellington ($107, 8¾ hours) via Hamilton
($53, one hour) and Taumarunui ($53, 50
minutes).

TE KUITI TO MOKAU
☎ 06

From Te Kuiti, SH3 runs southwest to the
coast before following the rugged shoreline

PHONE ZONE

If you've been rabidly punching the 07
area code into your phone for weeks across
Waikato and the King Country, note that the
code changes to 06 from around Awakino
heading south into Taranaki.

to New Plymouth. Along this scenic route
the sheep stations sprout peculiar limestone
formations before giving way to lush native
bush as the highway winds along the course
of the Awakino River.

The river spills into the Tasman at **Awakino**
(population 60), a small settlement where
boats shelter in the estuary while locals find
refuge at the down-to-earth (or down-to-
sea?) **Awakino Hotel** (☎ 06-752 9815; SH3; meals
$5-20; ⊗ 11am-11pm Mon-Wed, 11am-midnight Thu-Sat,
noon-8pm Sun).

A little further south the impressive
Maniaroa Marae dominates the cliff above the
highway. This important complex houses
the anchor stone of the *Tainui waka* which
brought this region's original people from
their Polynesian homeland. Note the palisade
tower and the intimidatingly carved meeting
house, Te Kohaarua. You can get a good view
from outside the fence – don't cross into the
marae unless someone invites you.

Five kilometres further south, as the perfect
cone of Mt Taranaki starts to take shape on
the horizon, is the village of **Mokau** (population
400). It offers a fine stretch of black-sand beach
and good surfing and fishing. From August
to November the Mokau River (the second
longest on the North Island) spawns some
of the best whitebait in the North Island –
and subsequently swarms of fiercely territorial
whitebaiters.

The town's **Tainui Historical Society Museum**
(☎ 06-752 9072; mokaumuseum@vodafone.co.nz; SH3; admission by donation; ⊗ 10am-4pm) has an interesting
collection of old photographs and artefacts
(pianolas, whale bones, dusty photos of the
Queen) from the time when this once-isolated
outpost was a coal and lumber shipping port
for settlements along the river.

Mokau River Cruises (☎ 0800 665 2874, 06-752 9775;
www.mokaurivercruises.co.nz; cruises adult/child $40/15)
operates a three-hour river cruise with commentary onboard the historic *MV Cygnet*.

Just north of Mokau, **Seaview Holiday Park**
(☎ /fax 06-752 9708; SH3; unpowered/powered sites $20/30,

cabins d $50-60, units from $85) is basic but it's right on the beach and the cabins have pastel paint schemes.

On the hill above the village the austere-looking but actually very friendly **Mokau Motel** (☎ 06-752 9725; www.mokaumotels.co.nz; SH3; s/d/tr $80/100/110; ☎) offers fishing advice, no-nonsense self-contained units and three city-standard luxury studios (what a surprise!).

The **River Run Cafe** (☎ 06-752 9859; SH3; meals $5-23; ☼ 7am-7pm) has whitebait on the menu during the season (mid-August till the end of November), as well as everything from burgers, pies and cooked meals to ice cream and homemade cakes.

TAUMARUNUI
pop 5140

Maybe Taumarunui should get a gimmick, as this little town can feel a bit grim. The main reason to stay here is to kayak on the Whanganui River (see p278) or as a cheaper base for skiing in Tongariro National Park.

Information

Department of Conservation (DOC; ☎ 07-895 8201; www.doc.govt.nz; Cherry Grove Domain; ☼ 8am-5pm Mon-Fri) A field office not always open (call in advance).
Taumarunui i-SITE (☎ 07-895 7494; www.visit ruapehu.com; Hakiaha St; ☼ 9am-5pm) Visitor information and internet access. Pick up the *Ruapehu Chosen Pathways* brochure for regional information.

Sights & Activities

The main drag, Hakiaha St, has a few items of interest. At the eastern end is **Hauaroa Whare**, a beautifully carved house. At the western end **Te Rohe Potae** memorialises King Tawhiao's assertion of his *mana* (authority) over the King Country in a sculpture of a top hat on a large rock (see p240). At the end of Marae St, **Ngapuwaiwaha Marae** has interesting carvings and two historic river *waka* visible from the street. Don't enter the complex without permission.

The 3km **Riverbank Walk** along the Whanganui River runs from Cherry Grove Domain, 1km south of town, to Taumarunui Holiday Park (right). **Te Peka Lookout**, across the Ongarue River on the western edge of town, is a good vantage point.

The **Raurimu Spiral**, 30km south, is a unique feat of railway engineering that was completed in 1908 after 10 years' work. Rail buffs can experience the spiral by taking the train (see below) to National Park township (return $106).

Taumarunui Jet Tours (☎ 0800 853 886, 07-896 6055; www.taumarunuijettours.co.nz; Cherry Grove Domain; 30min/1hr tour $60/90) runs high-octane jet-boat trips on the Whanganui River.

For details on the **Forgotten World Highway** between Taumarunui and Stratford, see p264.

For details on Whanganui River canoe and kayak operators, see p278.

Sleeping & Eating

Taumarunui Holiday Park (☎ 07-895 9345; www.taum arunuiholidaypark.co.nz; SH4; sites $27, cabins d $45-55, cottage d $65, extra person $15; ☐) On the banks of the Whanganui River, 3km east of town, this shady camping ground offers safe river swimming and clean facilities.

Twin Rivers Motel (☎ 07-895 8063; www.twin riversinfo.co.nz; 23 Marae St; units $85-185; ☎) Spick and span and constantly being upgraded (civic pride!). Some of the bigger units sleep up to seven.

Flax (☎ 07-895 6611; 1 Hakiaha St; brunch $9-17, dinner $22-34; ☼ 10am-2pm Tue, 9am-2pm & 5pm-late Wed & Thu, 9am-late Fri-Sun) Some locals say this place ain't what it used to be, but it's still the only place in Taumarunui where you can get a haloumi and semidried tomato tart. There are art-hung walls and an inventive modern menu.

Getting There & Away

Taumarunui is on SH4, 81km south of Te Kuiti and 41km north of National Park township.

InterCity (☎ 0508 353 947; www.intercity.co.nz) buses depart daily from the i-SITE, heading to Auckland ($58, 4½ hours, two daily) via Te Kuiti ($27, one hour, two daily), and Palmerston North ($52, 4¾ hours, one daily) via National Park ($21, 30 minutes, one daily).

Taumarunui is on the **Overlander** (☎ 0800 872 467; www.tranzscenic.co.nz; daily Oct-Apr, Fri-Sun May-Sep) train route between Auckland ($81, 4¾ hours) and Wellington ($107, 7½ hours) via Te Kuiti ($53, 1¼ hours) and National Park ($53, 1¼ hours).

OWHANGO
pop 210

A pint-sized village where all the street names start with 'O', Owhango makes a cosy base for walkers, mountain bikers (the 42 Traverse ends here; see p311) and skiers who can't afford to stay closer to the slopes in Tongariro National Park (p84). Take Omaki Rd for a two-hour loop walk through virgin forest in Ohinetonga Scenic Reserve.

Sleeping

Forest Lodge (☎ 07-895 4773; www.forest-lodge.co.nz; 12 Ōmaki Rd; dm/s/d $25/45/65, motel & cottage $95-120; 🖳) An excellent, snug backpackers with comfortable, clean rooms and good communal spaces. For privacy junkies there are separate self-contained motel and cottage units next door. It was up for sale when we visited – we hope the new owners don't drop the ball.

Blue Duck Lodge (☎ 07-895 6276; www.blueduck lodge.co.nz; RD2; dm $35, d $80-185, extra adult/child $37/20) Overlooking the Retaruke River 36km southwest of Owhango (take the Kaitieke turn-off 1km south of town), this ecosavvy place is actually three lodges, offering accommodation from dorms in an old shearers' quarters to a self-contained family cottage sleeping eight. The owners are mad-keen conservationists, restoring native bird habitats and historic buildings (you can volunteer and lend a hand).

Fernleaf B&B (☎ 07-895 4847; www.fernleaffarmstay. co.nz; 58 Tunanui Rd; s $85, d $100-120, all incl breakfast)

This characterful villa on a third-generation cattle-and-sheep farm has two en-suite rooms with garden outlooks, plus a twin and a separate cottage double which share a bathroom. Generous breakfast and dinners ($30 per person by arrangement) are labours of love. It's just off SH4, 7km north of Owhango.

Eating & Drinking

Out Of The Fog Cafe (☎ 07-895 4800; SH4; meals $9-17; ✦ breakfast & lunch Sat & Sun) Transport this uberstylish cafe into any major city and it would get by just fine. The food is delicious and reasonably priced, the coffee is excellent and the electric fire will make you want to linger on cold days. Sadly, it's just open on weekends.

Owhango Hotel (☎ 07-895 4854; SH4; mains $15-24; ✦ 10.30am-late) The country pub doubles as the local store, and dishes up solid fare like lamb shanks and vegetarian pasta.

Getting There & Away

Owhango is 14km south of Taumarunui on SH4. All the **InterCity** (☎ 0508 353 947; www.inter city.co.nz) buses that stop in Taumarunui also stop here.

Taranaki

Halfway between Auckland and Wellington, Taranaki sits out on a limb in more ways than one. Somewhat off the main drag, the region relies upon the fat of the land and the natural riches offshore. Indeed, Taranaki is the Texas of New Zealand, with oil and gas streaming in from the rigs, plumping the region with an enviable affluence and stability. However, it's not only overseas visitors who miss the turn-off to Taranaki; lots of Kiwi travellers do, too.

This is remarkable when you consider what it is that puts the region on the map: the moody and magnetic volcanic cone of Mt Taranaki, standing smack-bang in the middle of Egmont National Park. It demands to be visited.

In the shadow of the mountain are many small towns, mostly sleepy and rural, but friendly to boot. On the eastern boundary of the province you'll find NZ's only republic – Whanga-momona – a bushy little settlement, stranded in paradise.

New Plymouth is the hub of the 'naki (as they call it), home to the fabulous Govett-Brewster Art Gallery and an excellent provincial museum. It also has enough decent espresso joints to keep you wide awake.

Taranaki has a glut of black-sand beaches, and the summer months see the region swell as a wave of surfers and holidaymakers hit the coast. As for the rest of the year, there are plenty of things to see and places to visit – as long as you're as laid-back as the locals.

HIGHLIGHTS

- Walking up or around the massive cone of **Mt Taranaki** (p261)
- Riding the big breaks along **Surf Hwy 45** (p265)
- Getting experimental at New Plymouth's **Govett-Brewster Art Gallery** (p254)
- Taking a seal-spotting trip out to the **Sugar Loaf Islands Marine Park** (p255)
- Wandering through the rhododendron blooms at **Pukeiti Rhododendron Trust** (p260)
- Bouncing from bean to bean in **New Plymouth's cafes** (p259)
- Finding the **Forgotten World Hwy** (p264) and crossing the border into the **Republic of Whangamomona** (p264)

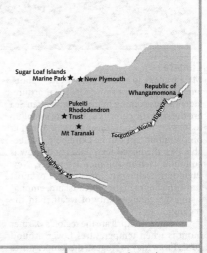

- Telephone code: 06
- www.taranaki.co.nz
- www.newplymouthnz.com

TARANAKI

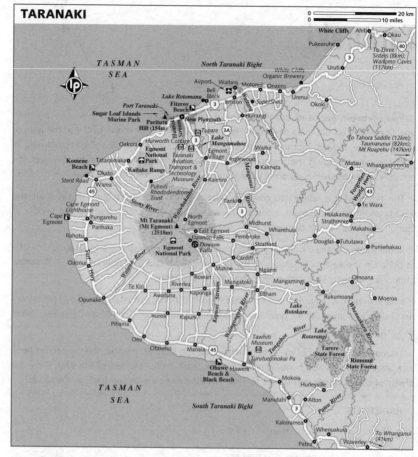

TARANAKI

Climate

Mt Taranaki is one of NZ's wettest spots, and frequently cops snowfalls. The moisture-laden winds coming in from the Tasman Sea are the climatic culprits as they are swept up to freezing heights by the mountain. Weather on the mountain can be extremely change-able (see the boxed text, p262) and snow is common even in summer. Ironically, New Plymouth frequently tops the list of most sunshine hours in the North Island, empha-sising the changeability of weather in the region.

November to April are the region's warmer months when temperatures hover around 20°C. From May to August, the temperatures drop to around 5°C to 14°C.

Getting There & Around

Air New Zealand has domestic flights and onward connections to/from New Plymouth. InterCity and Naked Bus run several bus serv-ices connecting to New Plymouth; Dalroy Express and White Star are smaller companies on local routes.

Getting to Mt Taranaki is easy, as many shuttle services (p263) run between the mountain, New Plymouth and other sur-rounding towns.

NEW PLYMOUTH
pop 45,230

Dominated by Mt Taranaki and surrounded by lush farmland, New Plymouth acts as the west coast's only international deep-water port, handling cargo for much of this part of the North Island. The city has a thriving arts scene and an outdoorsy focus, with good beaches both in and around it and Egmont National Park just a short drive away. The town centre supports a heartening number of locally owned businesses (of little architectural merit), and the obligatory small-town convoy of boy-racers – who get to cruise the longest main street in the country.

History

Local Maori *iwi* (tribes) have long contested Taranaki lands. In the 1820s they fled to the Cook Strait region to escape Waikato tribes, who eventually took hold of the area in 1832. Only a small group remained, at Okoki Pa (New Plymouth), where whalers soon joined the fray. When European settlers arrived in 1841, the coast of Taranaki seemed deserted and there was little opposition to land claims. The New Zealand Company bought extensive tracts from the remaining Maori.

When other members of local tribes returned after years of exile, they fiercely objected to the land sale. Their claims were upheld when Governor FitzRoy ruled that the New Zealand Company was only allowed just over 10 sq km of the 250 sq km it had claimed as its own around New Plymouth. The Crown gradually acquired more land from Maori, and European settlers became increasingly greedy for the fertile land around Waitara.

The settlers forced the government to abandon negotiations with Maori, and war erupted in 1860. While Maori engaged in guerrilla warfare and held the rest of the province, the settlers seized Waitara. Taranaki chiefs had refused to sign the Treaty of Waitangi in 1840 and were brutally treated as rebels. By 1870 over 500 hectares of their land had been confiscated with the remainder acquired through dubious transactions.

In a time of relative peace, economic stability was largely founded on dairy farming. The discovery of natural gas and oil in 1959 and the creation of a natural gas field off the South Taranaki Bight have kept the province economically healthy in recent times.

Orientation

Devon St (East and West) is the city's hub and allegedly the longest main street in the country.

TARANAKI FACTS

Eat Anything at Sugar Juice Café (p266)

Drink A bottle of Mike's Mild Ale from White Cliffs Organic Brewery (p261)

Read *The Captive Wife* by Fiona Kidman, the fictionalised account of Betty Guard's largely satisfactory captivity among Taranaki Maori in the whaling days of the 1830s

Listen to Way, way too much Bryan Adams, Shania Twain and Fleetwood Mac on the local radio stations

Watch *The Last Samurai*, starring Tom Cruise (although Mt Taranaki was the real star)

Swim at Black-sand and surf Oakura Beach (p265)

Festival WOMAD (World of Music Arts and Dance) every March at New Plymouth's Bowl of Brooklands (p257)

Tackiest tourist attraction The 'Welcome to Manaia the Bread Capital' sign on Surf Hwy 45

Go green Environmental Products (p264) – every possum product purchased equals one less varmint chomping beautiful native bush

---

Information

For information about the region, pick up the free guides: *Taranaki: Like No Other, Northern Taranaki* and *South Taranaki*. Online, check out www.newplymouthnz.com and www.windwand.co.nz.

BOOKSHOPS

Benny's Books (☎ 06-759 4350; www.bennysbooks.co.nz; 21 Devon St E; ☒ 8.30am-5.30pm Mon, Wed & Thu, 9am-5.30pm Tue, 8.30am-6pm Fri, 9am-2pm Sat) New releases, kids' books and mags.

INTERNET ACCESS

Internet access is available at the i-SITE and **Cyber Surf** (11b Devon St E; ☒ 8.30am-7pm Mon-Fri, 9.30am-7pm Sat & Sun).

MEDICAL SERVICES

Medicross (☎ 06-759 8915; medicross@xtra.co.nz; 8 Egmont St; ☒ 8am-8pm)

Phoenix Urgent Doctors (☎ 06-759 4295; npdocs@clear.net.nz; 95 Vivian St; ☒ 8.30am-8pm)

Taranaki Base Hospital (☎ 06-753 6139; www.tdhb.org.nz; David St; ☒ 24hr)

MONEY

The major banks have outlets and ATMs here. Visit the post office or **TSB Foreign Exchange** (☎ 06-968 3713; www.tsbbank.co.nz; 87 Devon

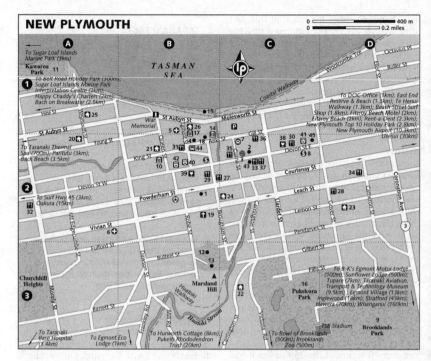

St E; 9am-5pm Mon-Fri, 10am-1pm Sat) for foreign exchange.

POST
Post office (www.nzpost.co.nz; 21 Currie St) Foreign exchange available.

TOURIST INFORMATION
Automobile Association (AA; ☎ 06-759 4010; www.aa.co.nz; 49-55 Powderham St; 8.30am-5pm Mon & Wed-Fri, 9am-5pm Tue)

Department of Conservation (DOC; ☎ 06-759 0350; www.doc.govt.nz; 55a Rimu St; 8am-4.30pm Mon-Fri)

New Plymouth i-SITE (☎ 0800 639 759, 06-759 6060; www.newplymouthnz.com; 1 Ariki St; 9am-6pm Mon, Tue, Thu & Fri, 9am-9pm Wed, 9am-5pm Sat & Sun;) In the Puke Ariki building; internet available.

Sights
PUKE ARIKI
Translating as 'Hill of Chiefs', **Puke Ariki** (☎ 06-759 6060; www.pukeariki.com; 1 Ariki St; admission free; 9am-6pm Mon & Tue, Thu & Fri, 9am-9pm Wed, 9am-5pm Sat & Sun) is home to the i-SITE, a museum, library, a cafe and the fabulous Arborio restaurant (p258). The excellent **museum** has

an extensive collection of Maori artefacts, plus wildlife and colonial exhibits. The regular 'Taranaki Experience' show tells the history of the province while the audience sits in pod-like seats that rumble and glow.

GALLERIES
The **Govett-Brewster Art Gallery** (☎ 06-759 6060; www.govettbrewster.com; 42 Queen St; admission free; 10am-5pm) is arguably the country's best regional art gallery and the crowd-pulling jewel in the town's crown. Presenting contemporary – often experimental – local and international shows, it's most famous for its connection with NZ sculptor, filmmaker and artist Len Lye (1901–80). His work is well represented here, with showings of his 1930s animation as well as sculpture and super-clever kinetic works. The glass-fronted **Café Govett-Brewster** (meals $5-20; 8am-5pm Mon-Fri, 9am-5pm Sat & Sun) is also here.

To see what local artists have to offer, visit the reconstructed warehouse **Real Tart Gallery** (☎ 06-769 5717; www.real.tart.co.nz; 19 Egmont St; admission free; 10am-5pm Mon-Fri, 11am-4pm Sat & Sun). Exhibitions change regularly and most works are for sale.

PARKS

New Plymouth has several picturesque parks, the pick of which is the superb **Pukekura Park** (☎ 06-758 0370; www.pukekura.org.nz; end of Liardet St; ☽ daylight hr). A 10-minute stroll from the city centre, the park has 49 hectares of gardens, playgrounds, bush walks, streams, waterfalls, ponds and display houses (open 8.30am to 4pm). Next to the main lake (full of arm-sized eels and ducklings), the **Tea House** (snacks $3-8; ☽ 10am-5pm) serves up light meals and cream teas. **Row boats** (per 30min $10) make for lazy meanderings across the water on weekends and summer evenings. The technicoloured Festival of Lights (see p257) here draws the summer crowds, as does the classically English cricket oval, with terrace seating cut into the surrounding hills.

Adjoining Pukekura is **Brooklands Park** (☎ 06-759 6060; www.newplymouthnz.com; Brooklands Park Dr; ☽ daylight hr) home to the **Bowl of Brooklands** (www.bowl.co.nz), a world-class outdoor soundshell, hosting festivals like WOMAD (p257) and old-school rockers like Elton John and Fleetwood Mac. The park itself was once the grounds of a settler's home, destroyed by Maori, though the fireplace and chimney survive today. Highlights include a 2000-year-old puriri tree, a 300-variety rhododendron dell and the farmy **Brooklands Zoo** (admission free; ☽ 9am-5pm).

Along the city waterfront is **Puke Ariki Landing** (St Aubyn St), an historic area studded with sculptures, including the wonderfully eccentric **Wind Wand** (www.windwand.co.nz). Designed by Len Lye – the artist who has put this town on the map in modern times – this 45m-high kooky kinetic sculpture is a truly beloved icon of bendy poleness.

HISTORIC SITES

The free *Heritage Trail New Plymouth* brochure available from the i-SITE outlines an interesting self-guided tour of around 31 historic sites.

The humble, artefact-filled **Richmond Cottage** (☎ 06-759 6060; www.pukeariki.com; cnr Ariki & Brougham Sts; admission free; ☽ 11am-3.30pm Sat & Sun) was built in 1854 across St Aubyn St, and was moved to its present site in the early 1960s. We think it still qualifies as one of New Plymouth's oldest buildings!

The austere **St Mary's Church** (☎ 06-758 3111; www.stmarys.org.nz; 37 Vivian St; services 8am, 10am & 5pm Sun), built in 1846, is the oldest stone church in NZ. Its graveyard has the headstones of early settlers and soldiers who died during the Taranaki Land Wars (1860–61 and 1865–69). Impressed by their bravery, the British also buried several Maori chiefs here.

SUGAR LOAF ISLANDS MARINE PARK

These rugged islets, a section of Back Beach on the west side of Paritutu and its waters 1km offshore were made into a **marine park** (http://homepages.ihug.co.nz/~lealand) in 1991. The islands, which are eroded volcanic remnants, are a refuge for sea birds and over 400 NZ fur seals. Most seals come here from June to October but some stay all year round. You can learn more about the marine park at the tiny **Interpretation Centre** (Ocean View Pde; admission

TARANAKI

MAORI NZ: TARANAKI

Ever since Mt Taranaki fled here to escape romantic difficulties (p261), the region has had a turbulent history. The region has seen conflicts between local *iwi* (tribes) and invaders from the Waikato, followed by two wars with the government (see the boxed text, p35) – first in 1860–61, when Waikato *iwi*, traditionally an enemy (p224), came to Taranaki's aid; and then again in 1865–69, when local forces were surprisingly successful under the remarkable general, Titikowaru. Following the wars there were massive land confiscations and an extraordinary passive-resistance campaign at Parihaka (see the boxed text, p266).

To further explore the history of local Maori, visit Puke Ariki (p254) in New Plymouth, and Parihaka if you can. Readers should look out for Dick Scott's *Ask That Mountain* or Maurice Shadbolt's very funny *Monday's Warriors*.

---

free; 9am-5pm daily) on the Lee Breakwater promenade.

You can visit the islands with **Happy Chaddy's Charters** (☎ 06-758 9133; www.windwand.co.nz/chaddies charters; Ocean View Pde; trips adult/child $30/10). Chaddy is quite the character and offers great value for money: expect at least four laughs a minute on this one-hour bob around on the chop. Departs daily from Lee Breakwater, tide and weather permitting. You can also hire kayaks (single/double $15/30 per hour) and bikes ($10 per 30 minutes) here.

See also Canoe & Kayak Taranaki (opposite).

NEW PLYMOUTH OBSERVATORY
Atop Marsland Hill (great views!) is this wee **observatory** (☎ 06-753 2358; http://sites.google.com/site/astronomynp; Marsland Hill, off Robe St; admission $5; 7.30-9.30pm Tue Mar-Oct, 8.30-10pm Tue Nov-Feb). Public nights include a planetarium program and, if the weather is clear, viewing through a 15cm refractor telescope. Also on the hill is the cacophonous 37-bell **Kibby Carillon**, a huge automated glockenspiel-like device which tolls out across the New Plymouth rooftops.

PARITUTU
Above the power station west of town is Paritutu, a steep-sided and craggy **hill** whose name translates appropriately as 'Rising Precipice'. From the summit you can see for miles around: out to the Sugar Loaves, down to the town and back to the mountain beyond. These views have to be earned by a 20-minute scramble to the top. Well worth it.

Activities
SURFING
The black, volcanic-sand beaches of Taranaki are world renowned for surfing and wind-surfing. Close to the eastern edge of town are **Fitzroy Beach** and **East End Beach** (allegedly the cleanest beach in Oceania). There's also decent surf at **Back Beach**, near Paritutu, at the western end of the city. **Oakura** is popular too (p265; reachable by CityLink buses; see p260). In fact there are so many surf beaches along the coast that the road south is now known as Surf Hwy 45 (p265).

Beach Street Surf Shop (☎ 06-758 0400; www.taranaki surf.com; 39 Beach St, Fitzroy; 2hr lesson $75; 9am-6pm) offers lessons, gear hire and tours. **Tarawave Surf School** (☎ 06-752 7474; tarawave@xtra.co.nz; 1½-hr lesson $65) is based further south at Oakura, while **Taranaki Coastal Surf Charters** (☎ 06-751 2483) provides customised guided surf tours.

TRAMPING
The i-SITE stocks the *New Plymouth District Guide to Walkways* leaflet, including coastal, local reserve and park walks. The **Coastal Walkway** (7km) from Lake Rotomanu to Port Taranaki, makes for a scenic orientation of the town. The highly recommended **Te Henui Walkway** (6km), extending from the coast at East End Reserve to the city's southern boundary, is an interesting streamside amble. **Huatoki Walkway** (5km), following Huatoki Stream, makes an attractive walk to the city centre.

OTHER ACTIVITIES
The warm mineral water filling the tanks at **Taranaki Thermal Spa** (☎ 06-759 1666; www.windwand. co.nz/mineralpools; 8 Bonithon Ave; treatments $5-245; 9am-5pm Mon & Tue, 9am-9pm Wed-Fri, noon-9pm Sat, noon-8pm Sun) was discovered during the search for oil around 1910. The private baths are filled on arrival, and there's a suite of massage and beauty therapies available. An absolute tonic.

Just west of town in grassy Kawaroa Park is the **Todd Energy Aquatic Centre** (☎ 06-759 6060; www. newplymouthnz.com; Kawaroa Park; admission adult/child $4/3, waterslide $3.50; ⏰ 6am-8.30pm Mon-Fri, 8.30am-7pm Sat & Sun), which has a waterslide, outdoor pool and indoor pool.

See also Canoe & Kayak Taranaki (below).

Tours

See also Scenic Flights (p262), and Happy Chaddy's Charters (opposite).

Canoe & Kayak Taranaki (☎ 06-769 5506; www. canoeandkayak.co.nz; half-day trips incl hire $70) Paddle out to the Sugar Loaf Islands or over the gentle Waitara River rapids.

Taranaki Adventure Tours (☎ 021 183 9044; www. taranakiadventure.com; tours 1-/2-day $249/949) Comprehensive tours of city, mountain and region involving plenty of exercise.

Taranaki Tours (☎ 0800 886 877, 06-757 9888; www. taranakitours.com; tours half-/full day from $80/120) Offers several themed tours, strong on Maori culture and natural history.

Festivals & Events

Festival of Lights (☎ 06-759 6060; www.festivalof lights.co.nz) Complete with costumed characters roaming the undergrowth, this colourful display lights up Pukekura Park from late December to mid-February.

Taranaki Rhododendron & Garden Festival (☎ 06-759 8412; www.rhodo.co.nz) NZ's oldest and most famous garden festival, held late October/early November each year.

WOMAD (World of Music Arts & Dance; ☎ 06-759 8412; www.womad.co.nz) A diverse array of local and international artists perform at the Bowl of Brooklands each March.

Sleeping

BUDGET

Sunflower Lodge (☎ 0800 422 257, 06-759 0050; www. sunflowerlodge.co.nz; 33 Timandra St; dm/d $25/65; 🖳 🛜) Down a steep driveway a few minutes' drive south of town, Sunflower does its best to transcend its mid-'80s rest-home origins, and (with the exception of some relentlessly floral wallpaper) succeeds. Bonuses like quality mattresses, free local calls and a heavy-duty kitchen and laundry help the cause.

Shoestring Backpackers (☎ 06-758 0404; www. shoestring.co.nz; 48 Lemon St; dm/s/d $28/50/70; 🖳 🛜) Inside a labyrinthine 1920s heritage building with a forest full of timber detailing, this isn't the fanciest option but it's well maintained and brimming with character. The upstairs

rooms are the pick: secluded, quiet and catching the morning sun. Out the back is a deck and barbecue. The co-owned Cottage Mews Motel (p258) is next door.

Egmont Eco Lodge (☎ 06-753 5720; www.yha.co.nz; 12 Clawton St; dm/d from $28/70; 🖳) An immaculate YHA in a glade with chirping birds and a chuckling creek. There are mixed dorms in the main lodge, smaller pinewood cabins down below (sleeping up to four), and a tidy (if small) kitchen. It's a bit of a hike uphill from town, but the prospect of free nightly Egmont cake will put a spring in your step.

Seaspray House (☎ 06-759 8934; www.seasprayhouse. co.nz; 13 Weymouth St; dm/s/d $29/45/70; 🖳) A big old house with gloriously high ceilings, Seaspray has had a recent makeover inside but remains relaxed and affordable, with well-chosen retro and antique furniture. Fresh and arty, it's a rare bunk-free backpackers (just 14 beds!). Closed June and July.

Arcadia Lodge (☎ 0508 272 233, 06-769 9100; www.arca dialodge.net; 52 Young St; dm/d/f incl breakfast $35/85/150; 🖳 🛜) A former rest home tacked onto a big old lemon villa (originally built for the local newspaper editor), Arcadia is a homey B&B with a lovely breakfast room, genteel lounge, spa, barbecue, and a superb timber-ceilinged family room upstairs with sea views.

Belt Road Holiday Park (☎ 0800 804 204, 06-758 0228; www.beltroad.co.nz; 2 Belt Rd; sites $32, cabins $65-120; 🖳 🛜) This pohutukawa-covered holiday park isn't the flashest contender, but it sits atop a bluff overlooking the increasingly interesting Lee Breakwater area, about a 10-minute walk from town. Million-dollar views!

New Plymouth Top 10 Holiday Park (☎ 0800 758 256, 06-758 2566; www.nptop10.co.nz; 29 Princes St, Fitzroy; sites/cabins from $38/75, units $85-110, motels $95-180; 🖳 🛜 🖳) Sequestered in Fitzroy, 3.5km east of town and a seven-minute walk to the beach, the Top 10 feels a bit like a school camp, with a dinky little row of blue-and-yellow units. Life-sized chess set, trampoline, laundry and spacious kitchen make a stay here worthwhile.

MIDRANGE & TOP END

Carrington Motel (☎ 06-757 9431; www.newplymouth motel.co.nz; 61 Carrington St; s/d/f $90/105/165) Sixteen old but tidy units close to Pukekura Park and a 10-minute walk to town. It's very family friendly and great value (especially in winter), but noisy when the hoons careen up

Carrington St. The showers are like a tsunami from the sky.

Cottage Mews Motel (☎ 06-758 0403; www.cottage mews.net.nz; 50 Lemon St; s/d $95/105; ☎) A small, modest motel where you'll feel like family, rather than a guest. The well-kept rooms have interesting layouts, there's a lawn out the front instead of a car park, and you can pop next door to the co-owned Shoestring Backpackers (p257) and remember how travelling was before your career took off.

B-K's Egmont Motor Lodge (☎ 0800 115 033, 06-758 5216; www.egmontmotorlodge.co.nz; 115 Coronation Ave; d $115-170; ☎) Opposite the racecourse, corporate B-K's has ground-floor units and oceans of parking. Rooms are plain but comfortable and clean, and the manager readily shares a few laughs with the cleaners (a good sign). Free internet and DVDs.

Bella Vista (☎ 0800 235 528, 06-769 5932; www.bella vistamotels.co.nz; cnr King & Queen Sts; d $120-160; ☐ ☎) A dependable, vaguely Spanish-looking option right in the centre of town. Basic rooms have toast-making facilities only; fancier rooms have full kitchenettes. Bonuses, such as fair-trade plunger coffee and free bicycles and internet abound.

ourpick Fitzroy Beach Motel (☎ 06-757 2925; www.fitzroybeachmotel.co.nz; 25 Beach St; s/d $120/130, 2br unit $165; ☎) Brand-new when we visited, this old-time motel (just 160m from Fitzroy Beach) has been thoroughly redeemed with a major overhaul and extension. Highlights include quality carpets, double glazing, lovely bathrooms, 32in LCD TVs, and an absence of poky studio-style units (all one- or two-bedroom). Winner!

Waterfront (☎ 06-769 5301; www.waterfront.co.nz; 1 Egmont St; r $190-550; ☐ ☎) Sleek and snazzy, the Waterfront is *the* place to stay, particularly if the boss is paying. The minimalist studios are pretty flash, while the penthouses steal the show with big TVs and little balconies. It's got terrific views from some – but not all – rooms, but certainly from the curvy-fronted bar and restaurant.

Nice Hotel (☎ 06-758 6423; www.nicehotel.co.nz; 71 Brougham St; d/ste from $230/290; ☎) High-class from top to tail, 'nice' is the understatement of the decade. Seven rooms feature luxury furnishings, designer bathrooms and select *objets d'art*: the ground-floor multiroom suite even has a grand piano! The in-house restaurant, Table, is one for the gourmands (mains $35, open for dinner).

Eating
RESTAURANTS

Frederic's (☎ 06-759 1227; 34 Egmont St; plates $7-18; ☺ 2pm-late Mon-Thu, 11am-late Fri-Sun) Freddy's is a fab new gastro-bar with quirky interior design (rusty medieval chandeliers, peacock-feather wallpaper, religious icon paintings), serving generous share-plates. Order some meatballs with bell-pepper sauce, or some green-lipped mussels with coconut cream, chilli and coriander to go with your beer.

Bach on Breakwater (☎ 06-769 6967; Ocean View Pde; brunch $10-20, dinner $24-34; ☺ 9.30am-10pm Wed-Sun; V) Constructed from weighty recycled timbers, this cool cafe-bistro in the emerging Lee Breakwater precinct looks like an old sea-chest washed up after a storm. Expect plenty of seafood and steak, plus Asian- and Middle Eastern–influenced delights (curries, wontons, felafels) and killer coffee. The seafood chowder is a real winter warmer.

ourpick Arborio (☎ 06-759 1241; inside Puke Ariki, 1 Ariki St; brunch $11-13, dinner $16-32; ☺ breakfast, lunch & dinner) Despite looking like a cheese grater, Arborio is the star of New Plymouth's local food show. It's airy, arty and modern, with sea views and faultless service. The Med-influenced menu ranges from an awesome Moroccan lamb pizza to pastas, risottos and barbecued chilli squid with lychee-and-cucumber noodle salad. Cocktails and NZ wines also available.

IndiaToday (☎ 06-758 4444; 40 Devon St E; mains $16-18; ☺ lunch Mon-Fri, dinner daily; V) A sumptuous gold-walled room draped with bolts of silk, IndiaToday wafts with spicy aromas and snaky tabla tunes enticing you in off the street. Dapper waiters, subcontinentally perfect in gold tunics and black pants, serve up classic and creative curries.

Portofino (☎ 06-757 8686; 14 Gill St; mains $19-60; ☺ dinner) This discreet little family-run eatery has been here for years, serving old-fashioned Italian pasta and pizza just like *nonna* used to make. The *rigatoni Portofino* is a knock-out (spinach, fetta, garlic and sun-dried tomatoes).

André L'Escargot (☎ 06-758 4812; 37 Brougham St; mains $30-34; ☺ dinner Mon-Sat, lunch by appointment) If you're looking for the best in town, this is it. Audaciously serving up snails in the 'naki since 1976, we doff our beret to the man who has no doubt raised the bar and kept it there. All classic French fare, indulgent and largely gout-inducing, plus killer cocktails.

TARANAKI

CAFES

Chaos (☎ 06-759 8080; 36 Brougham St; snacks $4-6, meals $6-16; ☻ breakfast & lunch; **V**) Not so much chaotic as endearingly scruffy, Chaos is a dependable spot for a coffee and a zingy breakfast. Ricotta-and-blueberry pancakes, background jazz, smiley staff and boho interior design – hard to beat! Plenty of vegetarian and gluten-free options, too.

Empire (☎ 06-758 1148; 112 Devon St W; lunch $6-10; ☻ 7.30am-4.30pm Mon-Fri, 9am-2pm Sat) A perfectly evolved Kiwi tearoom with pretty china plates nailed to the wall and a sunny courtyard out back. Tasty sandwiches, salads, lasagne and filos, plus delectable cakes and biscuits for afters.

Elixir (☎ 06-769 9020; 117 Devon St E; brunch $7-18, dinner $18-22; ☻ 7.30am-4pm Mon, 7.30am-late Tue-Fri, 9am-late Sat, 9am-3pm Sun) Behind a weird louvered wall facing onto Devon St, Elixir fosters an American-diner vibe, serving up everything from coffee, cake, bagels and eggs on toast, through to more innovative evening fare. Below a wall of rock posters, the coffee machine gets a serious work-out.

Petit Paris (☎ 06-759 0398; 34 Currie St; lunch $8-15; ☻ 7.30am-4pm) Ooh-la-la: lashings of buttery treats! Flying the *tricolore* with pride, Petit Paris is a *boulangerie* and patisserie turning out crispy baguettes and *tart au citron* (lemon tart), or an omelette or *croque monsieur* for lunch.

QUICK EATS

Andre's Pies & Patisserie (☎ 06-758 3062; 44 Leach St; snacks $3-7; ☻ 6am-3.30pm Mon-Fri) Expanding waistlines since 1972, this is an easy pull-over off the main road through town. Dive on in for hefty pies and calorific slabs of cake.

Sandwich Extreme (☎ 06-759 6999; 52 Devon St E; meals $7-13; ☻ 8am-4pm Mon-Fri, 8.30am-3pm Sat) Toasties, sandwiches, baked spuds, coffee, salads, bagels and cakes served fresh and fast by friendly staff.

SELF-CATERING

Fresha (☎ 06-758 8284; cnr Devon & Morley Sts; snacks $7-13; ☻ 9am-6pm Mon-Fri, 9am-5pm Sat; **V**) A drool-worthy emporium for picnic-basket essentials: meats, wines, olive oil, relish, fruit and veg, cheeses, jams and prepackaged meals (try the fish pie). There's an excellent cafe here too.

The gargantuan **Pak N Save** (☎ 06-758 1594; 53 Leach St; ☻ 8am-midnight) supermarket is just east of the town centre.

Drinking

Matinee (☎ 06-759 2088; 69 Devon St W; ☻ 9.30am-late Tue-Sat) A good option (one of the only ones, actually) for those who prefer top shelf to Tui, and electronica to '80s rock. Inside a former theatre, the design is all mirrors, silk drapes and art nouveau wallpaper; the tables outside afford puffing and people-watching. Jazz Fridays; DJs Saturdays.

Powder Room (☎ 06-759 2089; 108 Devon St W; ☻ 4pm-late Tue-Sat) With slabs of shagpile carpet stapled to the wall, this slinky red-white-and-black bar serves super-smooth cocktails and wondrous wines. After sipping a few you might feel like sidling onto the dance floor (frequent DJs) to throw a few decorous shapes.

Crowded House (☎ 06-759 4921; 93 Devon St E; ☻ 10am-late) A sporty hive of boozy activity with pool tables (in good nick), restaurant (fries with everything) and big-screen TVs. No sign of Neil Finn…

Entertainment

Basement Bar (☎ 06-758 8561; Basement, cnr Devon St W & Egmont St; admission free-$10; ☻ varies with gigs) Underneath a regulation Irish pub, the grungy Basement Bar is the best place in town to catch up-and-coming live acts, broadly sheltering under a rock, metal and punk umbrella.

TSB Showplace (☎ 06-759 0021; 92 Devon St W; ☻ box office 9am-5pm Mon-Fri, 10am-1pm Sat) Housed in the old opera house, the three-venue Showplace stages a variety of big performances (*Miss Saigon, Swan Lake*), as does the Bowl of Brooklands (p255), administered by the same people. For bookings go to Ticketek (www.ticketek.co.nz) or Ticket Direct (www.ticketdirect.co.nz).

Top Town Cinema 5 (☎ 06-759 9077; www.skycitycinemas.co.nz; 119 Devon St E; tickets adult/child $12.50/7.50; ☻ 10am-11pm) is a worn cinema complex, the floor a sea of popcorn.

Getting There & Away

You can book tickets for InterCity, Tranz Scenic, Interislander and Bluebridge ferries at the i-SITE inside Puke Ariki.

AIR

Air New Zealand (☎ 0800 737 000, 06-757 3300; www.airnz.co.nz; 12 Devon St E; ☻ 9am-5pm Mon-Wed & Fri, 9.30am-5pm Thu) has daily direct flights to/from Auckland (45 minutes, four daily), Wellington

(50 minutes, four daily) and Christchurch (1½ hours, one daily), with onward connections.

New Plymouth Airport (☎ 06-755 2250) is 11km east of the centre off SH3. **Scott's Airport Shuttle** (☎ 0800-373 001, 06-769 5974; www.npairportshuttle.co.nz; adult from $22) operates a door-to-door shuttle to/from the airport – you can book online.

BUS

The bus centre is on the corner of Egmont and Ariki Sts.

InterCity (☎ 09-583 5780; www.intercity.co.nz) services numerous destinations including:

Destination	Price	Duration	Frequency
Auckland	$52	6¼hr	4 daily
Hamilton	$45	4hr	2 daily
Palmerston North	$29	4hr	1 daily
Wellington	$39	7hr	1 daily
Whanganui	$29	3hr	1 daily

Naked Bus (☎ 0900 625 33; www.nakedbus.com) services run to the following destinations (among many others). Book in advance for big savings.

Destination	Price	Duration	Frequency
Auckland	$29	6¼hr	1 daily
Hamilton	$26	3½hr	1 daily
Palmerston North	$18	3½hr	1 daily
Wellington	$29	6hr	1 daily
Whanganui	$17	2½hr	1 daily

The **Dalroy Express** (☎ 0508 465 622, 06-759 0197; www.dalroytours.co.nz) bus runs daily to/from Auckland ($59, six hours) via Hamilton ($40, four hours), extending south to Hawera ($18, 45 minutes).

White Star (☎ 0800 465 622, 06-759 0197; www.whitestarbus.co.nz) has two buses each Thursday and Friday and one every other day to/from Whanganui ($27, 2½ hours), Palmerston North ($30, 4¼ hours), Wellington ($47, 6¼ hours) and many small towns in between.

Getting Around

CityLink (☎ 06-758 2799; www.taranakibus.info; adult $3-5) services run Monday to Saturday around town, as well as north to Waitara and south to Oakura on weekdays. Buses depart the bus centre on the corner of Egmont and Ariki Sts.

Cycle Inn Bike Hire (☎ 06-758 7418; www.cycleinn.co.nz; 133 Devon St E; per half-/full day $10/15; ☼ 8.30am-5pm Mon-Fri, 9am-3pm Sat, 10.30am-1pm Sun) rents out

bicycles. **Happy Chaddy's Charters** (p256) also rents out bikes.

For cheap car hire, try **Rent-a-Dent** (☎ 06-757 5362; www.newplymouthcarrentals.co.nz; 592 Devon St E), or for a cab call **Energy City Cabs** (☎ 06-757 5580).

For shuttle services to Mt Taranaki, see p263.

AROUND NEW PLYMOUTH

Although Egmont National Park is the pinnacle of the region's attractions, there are plenty of other happy time-wasters around New Plymouth's fringes.

South of Town
PUKEITI RHODODENDRON TRUST

This 4-sq-km **garden** (☎ 06-752 4141; www.pukeiti.org.nz; 2290 Carrington Rd; adult/child $12/free; ☼ 9am-5pm Oct-Mar, 10am-3pm Apr-Sep), located 20km south of New Plymouth, is home to a remarkable collection of rhododendrons and azaleas. The flowers generally bloom between September and November, but it's worth a visit any time of year. The scenic journey there passes between the Pouakai and Kaitake Ranges, both part of Egmont National Park (it's a skinny road – keep your wits about you!). The Gatehouse Café (meals $7 to $18; open 10am to 4pm) is here too.

TUPARE

Tupare (☎ 06-765 7127; www.tupare.info; 487 Mangorei Rd; admission free; ☼ 9am-5pm, tours 11am Mon-Fri) is a Tudor-style house designed by the renowned architect James Chapman-Taylor. It is a picture, but the highlight of this 7km site south of town will likely be the stunning 3.6 hectare garden surrounding it. Bluebells, birdsong – a picnicker's dream.

HURWORTH COTTAGE

This 1856 **cottage** (☎ 06-759 2006; www.historic.org.nz; 906 Carrington Rd; adult/child $5/2; ☼ 11am-3pm Sat & Sun), about 8km south of New Plymouth, was built by four-time NZ prime minister Harry Atkinson. The cottage is the sole survivor of a settlement abandoned at the start of the Taranaki Land Wars, and as such affords interesting insights into the lives of early settlers.

TARANAKI AVIATION, TRANSPORT & TECHNOLOGY MUSEUM & LAKE MANGAMAHOE

Around 9.5km south of New Plymouth is the **Taranaki Aviation, Transport & Technology Museum** (TATATM; ☎ 06-752 2845; www.nzmuseums.co.nz; cnr SH3

& Kent Rd; adult/child $7/2; ⌚ 10.30am-4pm Sat & Sun), which takes you on a trip down memory lane with its ramshackle displays of old planes, trains, automobiles and general household miscellany. Ask to see the stuff made by the amazing bee guy (hexagons ahoy!). The duck-filled Lake Mangamahoe (access from 7am to 8.30pm) is across the highway.

North via SH3

Heading north along the coast from New Plymouth is the scenic SH3. This is the way to Waitomo, and one of the roads to Hamilton. Get the free *Northern Taranaki* brochure from the i-SITEs in Otorohanga (p241) or New Plymouth (p254).

Continuing north on SH3 are various seaward turn-offs to high sand dunes and surf beaches. **Urenui**, 16km past Waitara, is a summer hot spot.

About 5km past Urenui you'll find arguably the highlight of North Taranaki – **White Cliffs Organic Brewery** (☎ 06-752 3676; www.organicbeer.co.nz; Main Rd Nth; tastings free, tours $5; ⌚ 10am-6pm) – home of award-winning beers. The brewery offers tours (book in advance), takeaways, tastings of the legendary Mike's Pale Ale (the pilsener and lager are ace, too), and an Oktoberfest party every (you guessed it) October. A little further on is the turn-off to Pukearuhe and **Whitecliffs**, huge precipices that resemble their Dover namesake. From here the **Whitecliffs Walkway** (⌚ Oct-Jun) leads to the Tongaporutu River via a tunnel from the beach (check the tides – go when it's low). On clear days the five- to seven-hour walk affords superb views of the coastline and the mountains (Taranaki and Ruapehu).

If you're continuing up to Mokau, it's worth stopping at the **Three Sisters**, signposted just south of the Tongaporutu Bridge – you can walk along the coast at low tide. The beach is quietly dramatic, with the two sisters standing somewhat forlornly off the coast (their other sister sadly collapsed in a heap).

MT TARANAKI (EGMONT NATIONAL PARK)

A classic 2518m volcanic cone dominating the landscape, Mt Taranaki is a magnet to all who catch his eye. Geologically, Taranaki is the youngest of three large volcanoes – Kaitake and Pouakai are the others – which stand along the same fault line. With the last eruption over 350 years ago (you can see lava flows covering the top 1400m), experts say that the mountain is overdue for another go. But don't let that put you off – this mountain is an absolute beauty and the highlight of any visit to the region.

History

According to Maori legend, Taranaki belonged to a tribe of volcanoes in the middle of the North Island. However, he was forced to depart rather hurriedly when he was caught with Pihanga, the beautiful volcano near Lake Taupo and the lover of Mt Tongariro. As he fled south (some say in disgrace; others say to keep the peace), Taranaki gouged out a wide scar in the earth (now the Whanganui River) and finally settled in the west in his current position. He remains here in majestic isolation, hiding his face behind a cloud of tears.

It is said that Maori did not heavily settle the area between Taranaki and Pihanga because they feared the reunification of the lovers in a spectacular eruption. Instead, Maori settlements in this district lined the coast between Mokau and Patea, concentrated around Urenui and Waitara. The mountain itself was supremely sacred, both as a burial site for chiefs and as a hideout in times of danger.

It was Captain Cook who named the mountain Egmont, after the Earl he sought to flatter at that particular moment. Egmont National Park was created in 1900, making it NZ's second oldest. Mt Taranaki eventually reclaimed its name, although the name Egmont has stuck like, well, egg. The mountain starred as Mt Fuji in *The Last Samurai* (2003), the production of which caused near-hysteria in the locals, especially when Tom Cruise came to town.

Information

Dawson Falls visitor centre (☎ 027 443 0248; www.doc.govt.nz; Manaia Rd, Kaponga; ⌚ 9am-4pm Thu-Sun Mar-Nov, daily Dec-Feb) On the southeastern side of the mountain, fronted by an awesome totem pole.
Metphone (☎ 0900 999 06) Weather updates.
North Egmont visitor centre (☎ 06-756 0990; North Egmont; www.doc.govt.nz; ⌚ 8am-4.30pm) Current and comprehensive national park info, plus a greasy-spoon cafe (meals $11 to $19).

Activities
TRAMPING
Due to its accessibility, Mt Taranaki ranks as the 'most climbed' mountain in NZ. Nevertheless, tramping on this mountain is dangerous and

should not be undertaken lightly (see the boxed text, below). It's *crucial* to get advice before departing and to leave your intentions with a DOC visitor centre or i-SITE.

Most walks are accessible from North Egmont, Dawson Falls or East Egmont. Check out DOC's pamphlet *Short Walks in Egmont National Park* ($2.50), and the free *Taranaki: A Walker's Guide* booklet for more info.

From North Egmont, the main walk is the scenic **Pouakai Circuit**, a two-day 23km loop through alpine, swamp and tussock areas with awesome mountain views. Short, easy walks from here include the **Ngatoro Loop Track** (one hour), **Veronica Loop** (two hours) and **Connett Loop** (40 minutes return). The **Summit Track** also starts from North Egmont. It's a poled route taking eight to 10 hours (14km) return, and should not be attempted by inexperienced people, especially in icy conditions and snow.

East Egmont has disabled access on **Potaema Track** (30 minutes return) and **East Egmont Lookout** (30 minutes return); a longer walk is the steep **Enchanted Track** (two to three hours return).

At Dawson Falls you can do several short walks including **Wilkies Pools Loop** (one hour return) or the excellent but challenging **Fanthams Peak Return** (five hours return), which is snowed-in during winter. The **Kapuni Loop Track** (1½ hours) runs to the impressive **Dawson Falls** themselves.

The difficult 55km **Around-the-Mountain Circuit** takes three to five days and is for expe-

rienced trampers only. There are a number of huts en route, tickets for which should be purchased in advance (see Sleeping, below).

The **York Loop Track** (three hours), accessible from York Rd north of Stratford, is a fascinating walk following part of a disused railway line.

You can tramp without a guide from February to March when snowfalls are low, but at other times inexperienced climbers can check with DOC for details of local clubs and guides. It costs around $300 per day to hire a guide. Reliable operators include the following:
Adventure Dynamics (☎ 0800 151 589, 06-751 3589; www.adventuredynamics.co.nz)
MacAlpine Guides (☎ 06-765 6234, 027 441 7042; www.macalpineguides.com)
Top Guides (☎ 0800 448 433, 021 838 513; www.topguides.co.nz)

SCENIC FLIGHTS

To get up above the slopes, try the following operators:
Beck Helicopters (☎ 0800 336 644, 06-764 7073; www.heli.co.nz) Scenic mountain flights from $225.
Heliview (☎ 0508 435 484, 06-753 0123; www.heliview.co.nz) Offers a range of sightseeing tours; a 30-minute city-and-mountain flight costs $280.
New Plymouth Aero Club (☎ 06-755 0500; www.airnewplymouth.co.nz) Standard and customised scenic flights from $66.
Precision Helicopters Limited (PHL; ☎ 0800 246 359, 06-752 3291; www.precisionhelicopters.com) A 50-minute mountain flight costs $280.

SKIING

From Stratford take Pembroke Rd up to Stratford Plateau, from where it's a 1.5km walk to the small **Manganui** club ski field (see p85). The Stratford i-SITE has daily weather and snow reports; otherwise you can ring the **snow-phone** (☎ 06-759 1119) or check the webcam at www.skitaranaki.co.nz.

Sleeping

Several DOC huts are scattered about the mountain, accessible by tramping tracks. Most cost $15 per night (Syme and Kahui cost $5); purchase hut tickets in advance from DOC. BYO cooking, eating and sleeping gear, and bookings are not accepted – it's first come, first served. Remember to carry out *all* your rubbish.

Missing Leg (☎ 06-752 2570; missingleg@xtra.co.nz; 1082 Junction Rd, Egmont Village; unpowered/powered sites $15/17, dm/d $25/60; 🖳) This eccentric backpacker

---

DECEPTIVE MOUNTAIN

Mt Taranaki may look like an easy climb, but this scenic mountain has claimed more than 60 lives. The principal hazard is the weather, which can change from summery to white-out conditions unexpectedly and almost in an instant. You may leave New Plymouth in sunshine and find yourself in snowfall up at altitude. There are also precipitous bluffs and steep icy slopes.

There are plenty of short walks, safe for much of the year, but for adventurous trampers January to March is the best time to go. You must take an appropriate map (DOC's detailed *Egmont National Park* map costs $19) and consult a DOC officer for current conditions. You *must* also register your tramping intentions with the DOC visitor centre or i-SITE.

property has a strange lack of natural light – OK for sleeping! Dorm accommodation is up in the loft, plus there's a handful of shabby-chic baches out the back.

Konini Lodge (☎ 06-756 0990; www.doc.govt.nz; Upper Manaia Rd; dm adult/child $20/10) Basic bunkhouse accommodation 100m downhill from the Dawson Falls visitor centre. Dorms feed off a huge communal space.

Eco Inn (☎ 06-752 2765; www.ecoinn.co.nz; 671 Kent Rd; s/tw/d $30/52/60; 🛜) About 6.5km up the road from the turn-off at the Aviation, Transport & Technology Museum (p260), this super ecofriendly place is made from recycled timber and runs on solar, wind and hydropower. There's a spa and pool table, and transport to and from the mountain is available. Good for groups.

Camphouse (☎ 0800 688 272, 06-756 9093; www.mttaranaki.co.nz/retreat/camphouse; North Egmont; dm/d/f $30/70/160) Bunkhouse-style accommodation behind the North Egmont visitor centre in a historic 1850 corrugated-iron building, complete with bullet holes in the walls (from shots fired at settlers by local Maori during the Taranaki Land Wars). Endless horizon views from the porch.

Rahiri Cottage (☎ 06-756-9093; www.mttaranaki.co.nz; Egmont Rd, RD6; d with/without breakfast $160/145) Right on the edge of Egmont National Park on the way to North Egmont, this 1929 clinker-brick cottage was once the park tollgate, and today offers luxury B&B rooms in a bush setting. Upmarket but unpretentious; sleeps five (whole cottage $305).

Anderson's Alpine lodge (☎ 06-765 6620; www.andersonsalpinelodge.co.nz; 922 Pembroke Rd; d incl breakfast $160-190; 🛜) With picture-postcard mountain views, this lovely Swiss-owned lodge is on the Stratford side of the mountain. Inside are three en-suite rooms with lots of timberwork; outside are billions of birds and Lady Hookswood-Smith, a rather obstreperous pig.

Mountain House (☎ 06-765 6100; www.mountainhouse.co.nz; Pembroke Rd; s/d $170/195) This lodge, on the Stratford side of the mountain (15km from the SH3 turn-off and 3km to the Manganui ski area), has recently renovated motel-style rooms and chalets with kitchens. There's a European-style restaurant here too (meals $12 to $42, open for breakfast, lunch and dinner).

Getting There & Away

There are three main entrance roads to Egmont National Park, all of which are well signposted and either pass by or end at a DOC visitor centre. Closest to New Plymouth is North Egmont: turn off SH3 at Egmont Village, 12km south of New Plymouth, and follow the road for 14km. From Stratford, turn off at Pembroke Rd and continue for 15km to East Egmont and the Manganui ski area (p85). From the southeast, Upper Manaia Rd leads up to Dawson Falls, 23km from Stratford.

There are no public buses to the national park but numerous shuttle-bus operators will gladly take you there (one way $30 to $40, return $45 to $50):

Cruise NZ Tours (☎ 0800 688 687; kirkstall@xtra.co.nz) Departs New Plymouth 7.30am for North Egmont; returns 4.30pm. Other pick-ups/drop-offs by arrangement.

Eastern Taranaki Experience (☎ 06-765 7482; www.eastern-taranaki.co.nz) Departs from Stratford; extra charge from New Plymouth.

Kiwi Outdoors (Map p254; ☎ 06-758 4152; www.kiwioutdoorsstores.co.nz; 18 Ariki St, New Plymouth; 🕒 8.30am-5pm Mon-Fri, 9am-2.30pm Sat, 10am-2pm Sun) Pick-up points and times to suit; gear hire available.

Taranaki Tours (☎ 0800 886 877, 06-757 9888; www.taranakitours.com) Pick-up points and times by arrangement.

AROUND MT TARANAKI

There are two principal highways around the mountain, both linking New Plymouth and Hawera. SH3, on the inland side of the mountain, is the road most travelled; the longer coastal route is SH45, aka Surf Hwy 45 (p265).

Inglewood
pop 3090

Handy to the mountain on SH3, the little main-street town of Inglewood (www.inglewood.co.nz) is an adequate stop for supermarket supplies and a noteworthy stop for a steak-and-egg pie at **Nelsons Bakery** (☎ 06-756 7123; 45 Rata St; pies $3-4; 🕒 6am-4.30pm Mon-Fri, 7am-4pm Sat). Inglewood's other shining light is the cute **Fun Ho! National Toy Museum** (☎ 06-756 7030; www.funho.com; 25 Rata St; adult/child $6/free; 🕒 10am-4pm), which shows and sells old-fashioned sand-cast toys of Kiwi yesteryear. It doubles as the local visitor information centre.

On the road into town from New Plymouth, **White Eagle Motel** (☎ 06-756 8252; www.whiteeaglemotel.co.nz; 87b Rata St; s/d from $90/95, extra person $20) is basic but clean and quiet. The two-bedroom units feel bigger than they are.

Inside a fire-engine-red heritage building, jazzy **Macfarlane's Caffe** (☎ 06-756 6665; 1 Kelly St; brunch $9-17, dinner $14-28; ☒ 9am-5pm Sun-Wed, 9am-late Thu-Sat) sells super-sized custard squares and coffee during the day and wild boar sausages at night (among other things). Its venison Taranaki Burger rules.

Funkfish Grill (☎ 06-756 7287; 32 Matai St; mains $24-33; ☒ 4pm-late Tue-Thu, Sat & Sun, 3pm-late Fri) is a hip pizzeria and fish-and-chippery doing eat-in and takeaway meals, and doubles as a bar at night. Try the tempura scallops.

Stratford
pop 5330

Forty kilometres southeast of New Plymouth on SH3, Stratford plays up its namesake of Stratford-upon-Avon, Shakespeare's birthplace, by naming its streets after bardic characters. Stratford also claims NZ's first **glockenspiel** (☒ 10am, 1pm, 3pm & 7pm). Four times daily this clock doth chime out Shakespeare's greatest hits with some fairly wooden performances.

Stratford i-SITE (☎ 0800 765 6708, 06-765 6708; www.stratfordnz.co.nz; Prospero Pl; ☒ 8.30am-5pm Mon-Fri, 10am-3pm Sat & Sun) also houses the **Percy Thomson Gallery** (☎ 06-765 0917; www.percythomsongallery.org.nz; admission free; ☒ 10.30am-4pm Mon-Fri, 10.30am-3pm Sat & Sun), a community gallery displaying eclectic local and touring art shows.

One kilometre south of Stratford on SH3, the **Taranaki Pioneer Village** (☎ 06-765 5399; www.pioneervillage.co.nz; adult/child/family $10/5/20; ☒ 10am-4pm) is a 4-hectare outdoor museum housing 40 historic buildings. It's very bygone-era and more than a little spooky: a visit here will stop you complaining about how hard life is nowadays.

Not far from the Dawson Falls turn-off, 11km from Stratford, is **Environmental Products** (☎ 06-764 6133; www.envirofur.co.nz; 1013 Opunake Rd, Mahoe; ☒ 9am-5pm Mon-Fri, 10am-4pm Sat & Sun), a possum-skin tannery and manufacturer of bags, boots, slippers, hats, rugs and other accessories. Less pesky possums means more native wildlife and vegetation.

Seemingly embalmed in calamine lotion, the pretty-in-pink **Stratford Top Town Holiday Park** (☎ 06-765 6440; www.stratfordtoptownholidaypark.co.nz; 10 Page St; dm from $22, unpowered/powered sites from $28/34, cabins/units from $50/90; ☒) is a trim caravan park offering one-room cabins, motel-style units and backpackers' bunks, plus spa, barbecue and bike hire.

All stone-clad columns, jaunty roof angles, timber louvres and muted cave-colours, flashy **Amity Court Motel** (☎ 06-765 4496; www.amitycourtmotel.co.nz; 35 Broadway N; d/1br/2br $120/140/160; ☒) is the new kid on the Stratford block, upping the town's accommodation standings 100%.

For more accommodation around Stratford, see p262.

Across the street from Stratford i-SITE is the disarmingly retro, trapped-in-a-time-warp tearoom, **Casa Pequena** (☎ 06-765 6680; 280 Broadway; snacks $3-5, meals $12-28; ☒ 6am-4pm Mon-Fri, 7am-1.30pm Sat), serving classics like bangers-and-mash and hot beef-and-gravy sandwiches.

Forgotten World Hwy

The 150km road between Stratford and Taumarunui (SH43) has become known as the Forgotten World Hwy. The drive winds through hilly bush country with 12km of unsealed road, and along the way passes many historic and heritage sites such as Maori *pa*, abandoned coal mines and memorials to those long gone. Allow four hours and plenty of stops, and fill up with petrol at either end as there are no petrol stations along the route itself. A pamphlet is available from i-SITEs or DOC visitor centres in the area.

The town of **Whangamomona** (population 170) is a highlight. This quirky village became an independent republic after disagreements with local councils (see the boxed text, opposite). In the middle of town is the unmissable grand old **Whangamomona Hotel** (☎ 06-762 5823; www.whangamomonahotel.co.nz; 6018 Forgotten World Hwy; meals $12-18; ☒ 11am-late), a pub with accommodation ($110 per person including dinner and breakfast), offering 'real country hospitality'.

In the Tahora Saddle, the highest point on the highway, **Kaieto Café** (☎ 06-762 5858; kaieto cafe@quicksilver.net.nz; SH43; meals $7-20; ☒ lunch) has lunches, panoramic views, a four-bed cabin and a campsite (sites/cabin per person $10/35).

Eastern Taranaki Experience (☎ 06-765 7482; www.eastern-taranaki.co.nz) runs tours through the area (day trips per person from $45; four day/three night trips per person $460, minimum four people).

The **Central Taranaki Tourism Network** (☎ 06-765 7180; cttn@xtra.co.nz) runs several regional day trips, including the Forgotten World Discoveries ($189 per person) and Highway 43 Explorer ($99) excursions.

> **POODLE FOR PRESIDENT!**
>
> Whangamomona is New Zealand's only republic, declared so after a disagreement with government authorities. The story goes that in 1989 the local council sought to adjust the town's boundaries, shifting its jurisdiction from Taranaki council to that of Manawatu-Whanganui. The citizens – independent, flinty folk – were not prepared to take this lying down. For starters it meant they'd have to play for a rival rugby team. And so it was that they dumped both councils and became a republic, complete with democratically elected presidents who have included Billy Gumboot the goat (elected after eating all the opposition's votes) and Tai Poutu the poodle (who stepped down after an assassination attempt). The current overlord is Murt 'Murtle the Turtle' Kennard (who is actually a human).
>
> The town celebrates Republic Day in January every two years, with a military themed extravaganza. Visitors (many railed in from Auckland – passports required) can throw a gumboot, crack a whip, bet on the sheep races, skin a possum and engage in all manner of other forgotten world activities.

SURF HWY 45

Sweeping south from New Plymouth to Hawera, the 105km-long SH45 is known as Surf Hwy 45, and although it does indeed have many good beaches dotted along it, don't expect to see waves crashing ashore the whole way. The drive generally just undulates through farmland – be ready to swerve for random tractors and Holden drivers. Pick up the *Surf Highway 45* brochure at visitor centres.

Oakura
pop 1220

From New Plymouth, first cab off the rank is laid-back Oakura, 15km southwest on SH45. Its broad sweep of beach is hailed by waxheads for its right-hander breaks, but it's also great for families (take sandals – that black sand scorches feet). A surf shop on the main road, **Vertigo** (06-752 7363; vertigosurf@xtra.co.nz; 2hr lessons $75; 9am-5pm Mon-Fri, 10am-4pm Sat) runs surf lessons. See also Tarawave (p256).

SLEEPING & EATING

Wave Haven (06-752 7800; www.thewavehaven.co.nz; cnr Ahu Ahu Rd & SH45; dm/s/d $20/40/60) A surfy backpackers close to the big breaks, this colonial charmer has a coffee machine, a large deck to chill out on, and surfboards and empty wine bottles strewn about the place.

Oakura Beach Holiday Park (06-752 7861; www.oakurabeach.com; 2 Jans Tce; unpowered/powered sites $32/36, cabins $65-120;) A classic beachside park catering best to caravans but with basic cabins and well-placed spots to pitch a tent (absolute beachfront!).

Oakura Beach Motel (06-752 7680; www.oakurabeachmotel.co.nz; 53 Wairau Rd; s/d from $90/100;) A very quiet, seven-unit motel set back from the main road, just three minutes' walk to the beach. It's a '70s number, but the owners keep things ship-shape, and there are 300 DVDs to choose from!

Ahu Ahu Beach Villas (06-752 7370; www.ahu.co.nz; 321 Ahu Ahu Rd; s/d/f from $250/250/350;) Pricey, but pretty amazing. Set on a knoll overlooking the big wide ocean, these luxury, architect-designed villas are superbly eccentric, with huge recycled timbers, bottles cast into walls, lichen-covered roofs and polished-concrete floors with inlaid paua. Even rock stars stay here.

Snickerdoodles (06-752 7227; 1151 SH45; baked goods $4-7; breakfast & lunch Mon-Sat) On the main road this tiny bakery bakes daily. Swing in for a chunky cheese scone, some yummy pumpkin bread or a coffee.

Carriage (06-752 1007; rear of 1145 SH45; brunch $12-15, dinner $14-28; 5pm-late Mon-Thu, 10am-3pm & 5pm-late Fri-Sun) Housed in a very slow moving railway carriage set back from the main street, this is an unusual stop for good-value burgers, steaks, pasta, spring rolls and curries.

Oakura to Opunake

From Oakura, SH45 veers inland, with detours to sundry beaches along the way. On the highway near Okato the 130-year-old **Stony River Hotel** (06-752 4253; www.stonyriverhotel.co.nz; 2502 SH45, Okato; s/d/tr incl breakfast $80/122/183) has simple country-style en suite rooms and a straight-up public bar (mains $10 to $28, open for dinner Wednesday to Saturday).

Just after Warea is **Stent Road**, a legendary shallow reef break, suitable for experienced surfers. Newbies will prefer the gentler waves of **Komene Beach**, which at the mouth of Stony River attracts its fair share of interesting bird life, including black swans.

Another coastward turn-off at **Pungarehu** leads 20km to **Cape Egmont Lighthouse** (☎ 06-278 8599; Bayly Rd; ☼ Sat & Sun by appointment), a photogenic cast-iron lighthouse that was shifted here in 1881. The road to Parihaka (see the boxed text, below) leads inland from this stretch of highway.

Opunake
pop 1500
A summer town and the surfie epicentre of the 'naki, Opunake has a sheltered family beach and plenty of challenging waves further out.

The **Opunake i-SITE** (☎ 0800 111 323, 06-761 8663; opunakei@stdc.govt.nz; Tasman St; ☼ 9am-5pm Mon-Fri, 9.30am-1pm Sat; ☐ ☎) is in the local library and has free internet. **Dreamtime Surf Shop** (☎ 06-761 7570; 102 Tasman St; ☼ 9am-5pm) has internet access and surf-gear hire (surfboards/bodyboards/wetsuits per half-day $30/20/10).

Opunake Motel & Backpackers (☎ 06-761 8330; www.opunakemotel.co.nz; 36 Heaphy Rd; dm $25, cottage & units d $85-100) offers a range of options from old-style motels to a funky dorm lodge on the edge of some sleepy fields (a triumph in genuine retro).

An old bank plastered with hyper-coloured surf murals, **Surf Lodge 45** (☎ 06-761 8345; sl45@xtra. co.nz; cnr Tasman & Napier Sts; s/d/f $25/50/75) is much less exciting inside, with low-key, no-frills backpacker rooms upstairs.

Opunake Beach Holiday Park (☎ 0800 758 009, 06-761 7525; www.opunakebeachnz.co.nz; Beach Rd; sites/cabins/cottages $32/60/85; ☐ ☎) is a mellow spot right on the surf beach. The laugh-a-minute host will direct you to your grassy site, the big camp kitchen or the cavernous amenities block.

ourpick Sugar Juice Café (☎ 06-761 7062; 42 Tasman St; snacks $4-10, mains $25-29; ☼ 9am-4pm Tue & Sun, 9am-10pm Wed-Sat) has the best food on SH45. It is buzzy and brimming with delicious, filling things (try the basil-crusted snapper or cranberry lamb shanks). Terrific coffee, salads, wraps, tarts, cakes and big brekkies too – don't pass it by.

Hawera
pop 11,000
Don't expect much urban virtue from agricultural Hawera, the largest town in South Taranaki. Still, it's a good pit stop for supplies, to stretch your legs, or to bed down for a night. Not quite on the coast, it's 70km south of New Plymouth via SH3 and 90km from Whanganui.

PARIHAKA

From the mid-1860s Parihaka, a small Maori settlement east off Hwy 45 near Pungarehu, became the centre of a peaceful resistance movement, one which involved not only other Taranaki tribes, but Maori from around the country. Its leaders, Te Whiti-o-Rongomai and Tohu Kakahi, were of both Taranaki and Te Ati Awa descent.

After the Land Wars (see the boxed text, p35), confiscation of tribal lands was the central problem faced by Taranaki Maori, and under Te Whiti's leadership a new approach to this issue was developed: resisting European settlement through nonviolent methods.

When the government started surveying confiscated land on the Waimate plain in 1879, unarmed followers of Te Whiti, wearing the movement's iconic white feather in their hair and in good humour, obstructed development by ploughing troughs across roads, erecting random fences and pulling survey pegs. Many were arrested and held without trial on the South Island, but the protests continued and intensified. Finally, in November 1881 the government sent a force of over 1500 troops to Parihaka. Its inhabitants were arrested or driven away, and the village was later demolished. Te Whiti and Tohu were arrested and imprisoned until 1883. In their absence Parihaka was rebuilt and the ploughing campaigns continued into the 1890s. The imprisonment of Parihaka protesters without trial also continued until the late 1890s.

In 2006 the NZ government issued a formal apology and financial compensation to the tribes affected by the invasion and confiscation of Parihaka lands.

Te Whiti's spirit lives on at Parihaka, with annual meetings of his descendants and a public music-and-arts festival held early each year. Parihaka is open to the public on the 18th and 19th of each month. For more information, read Dick Scott's *Ask That Mountain*, Gregory O'Brien and Te Miringa Hohaia's beautiful *Parihaka – The Art of Passive Resistance*, or see www.parihaka.com.

SNELLY!

Opunake isn't just about the surf – it's also the birthplace of iconic middle-distance runner Peter Snell (1938–), who showed his rivals a clean set of heels at the 1960 Rome and 1964 Tokyo Olympics. Old Snelly won the 800m gold in Italy, then followed up with 800m and 1500m golds in Japan. Legend! Check out his funky running statue outside the i-SITE.

INFORMATION

Automobile Association (AA; ☎ 06-278 5095; www.aa.co.nz; 121 Princes St; ⏲ 8.30am-5pm Mon-Fri)

Hawera i-SITE (☎ 06-278 8599; www.stdc.co.nz; 55 High St; ⏲ 8.30am-5.15pm Mon-Fri, 10am-3pm Sat & Sun, reduced hr in winter)

SIGHTS & ACTIVITIES

The austere **Hawera Water Tower** (adult/child/family $2/1/5; ⏲ 10am-2pm) beside the i-SITE is one of the coolest things in Hawera. Grab the key from the i-SITE, ascend, then scan the horizon for signs of life (you can see the coast and Mt Taranaki on a clear day).

Elvis lives! At least he does at the **Elvis Presley Memorial Record Room** (☎ 027 498 2942; www.digitalus.co.nz/elvis; 51 Argyle St; admission by donation; ⏲ by appointment only), which houses a collection of the King's records (over 5000), souvenirs and the man's Cadillac. Maybe.

The excellent **Tawhiti Museum** (☎ 06-278 6837; www.tawhitimuseum.co.nz; 401 Ohangai Rd; adult/child $10/2; ⏲ 10am-4pm Fri-Mon Feb-Apr & Sep-Dec, Sun only Jun-Aug, daily Jan) houses a private collection of remarkable exhibits, models and dioramas. The creepily lifelike human figures were modelled on people around the region, while a large collection of tractors pays homage to the province's rural heritage. It's near the corner of Tawhiti Rd, 4km from town.

Try some white-knuckle white-water sledging with **Kaitiaki Adventures** (☎ 06-752 8242; www.damdrop.com; 3hr trip $100), which involves sliding down a 7m dam on a sledge, then sledging a further 5km on the Waingongoro River (Grade II to III). Also included is a journey past an historic *pa* site, birthplace of the Maori prophet Tohu Kakahi. Kaitiaki also run trips from Rotorua (see p326).

Two kilometres north of Hawera, on Turuturu Rd, are the remains of the pre-European **Turuturumokai Pa**. The name translates to 'stakes for dried heads', which were used to ward off potential attackers. Today, all that's left are a few remains of ramparts and storage pits. The reserve is open to the public daily.

Northeast of Hawera is **Lake Rotorangi**, the longest artificial lake in NZ (46km). There are three access roads: Ball Rd, north of Patea, from which you can visit the dam; Tangahoe Rd (largely unsealed); and Mangamingi Rd, where there's a public domain. Freedom camping is allowed at the Patea Ball Rd, Tangahoe and Eltham (Glen Nui) entrances to the lake, where freshwater access and toilet facilities are available. Ask for a detailed map at the Hawera i-SITE or Automobile Association (left).

SLEEPING & EATING

our pick **Wheatly Downs Farmstay** (☎ 06-278 6523; www.mttaranaki.co.nz; 484 Ararata Rd, unpowered sites $36, dm/s/tw $30/70/70, d with/without bathroom $115/70) Set in a rural idyll, this heritage building is a classic, with its clunky wooden floors and no-nonsense fittings. Host Gary is an affable bloke, showing you his special pigs and letting you milk his cows. To get there, head past Tawhiti Museum and keep going on the Ararata Rd for 5.5km. Pick-ups by arrangement.

Caniwi Lodge (☎ 06-764 7577; www.caniwilodge.co.nz; 505a Aorere Rd, Lake Rotorangi; d cabins/chalets $50/295) On the shores of Lake Rotorangi, this lodge caters for all with its basic cabins and luxury chalets. Back-to-nature activities to enjoy include kayaking, birdwatching or hanging out with the farm animals. From Eltham follow King Edward St (soon Rawhitiroa Rd) for 15km, turning right into Aorere Rd. It's 5km from there.

Hawera Central Motor Lodge (☎ 06-278 8831; www.haweracentralmotorlodge.co.nz; 53 Princes St, Hawera; d $125-165; 🖳) The pick of the town's motels (better positioned and much quieter than any of those along South Rd), the shiny new Hawera Central does things with style: grey-and-eucalypt colour scheme, frameless-glass showers, big flat-screen TVs, good security, DVD players, free movie library… Nice one!

Indian Zaika (☎ 06-278 3198; 91 Princess St, Hawera; mains $16-19; ⏲ lunch Mon-Sat, dinner daily) For a fine lunch or dinner, try this spicy-smelling, black-and-white diner, serving decent curries in upbeat surrounds. Takeaways available.

Whanganui & Palmerston North

The Whanganui and Manawatu districts comprise a sizeable chunk of the North Island's south, running from Tongariro National Park in the north down towards Wellington. This is mellow, pastoral country, draped with rounded green hills, gently bent roads, socially significant cities and magical national parks, rivers and gorges.

The history-rich Whanganui River curls through Whanganui National Park down to Whanganui city. Ripe with outdoor opportunities, the splendiferous Whanganui River Rd mimics the river's bows, while Whanganui itself, a 19th-century river port, has aged gracefully, recently reinventing itself as a centre for New Zealand glass art.

Palmerston North, the Manawatu's main city, is a town of two peoples: tough-talkin' country fast-foodies in hotted-up cars and caffeinated Massey University literati, coexisting with none of Cambridge's 'Town vs Gown' sabre-rattling. During the semester the cafes jump and pubs overflow with students.

Beyond the city the Manawatu blends rural grace with yesterday's pace, cut by the dramatic slice of Manawatu Gorge. A meandering Manawatu drive is the perfect antidote to NZ's tourism juggernaut – you might even squeeze in a little laziness!

HIGHLIGHTS

- Watching a glass-blowing demonstration at one of **Whanganui's glass studios** (p271)
- Blowing out the cobwebs with a jetboat ride on the **Whanganui River** (p279)
- Traversing the rainy **Whanganui River Road** (p280) – it's all about the journey, not how fast you get there
- Tramping the Matemateaonga and Mangapurua Tracks in the **Whanganui National Park** (p279)
- Flexing your All Blacks spirit at Palmerston North's **New Zealand Rugby Museum** (p281)
- Recaffeinating on the hip George St cafe strip in **Palmerston North** (p284)
- Connecting life, art and mind at **Te Manawa** (p281) museum in Palmerston North
- Hiking through the awesome **Manawatu Gorge** (p286)

Whanganui
★ National Park

Whanganui
River ★

★ Whanganui
River Road

★ Whanganui

Palmerston North ★   ★ Manawatu
Gorge

- Telephone code: 06   - www.wanganui.com   - www.manawatunz.co.nz

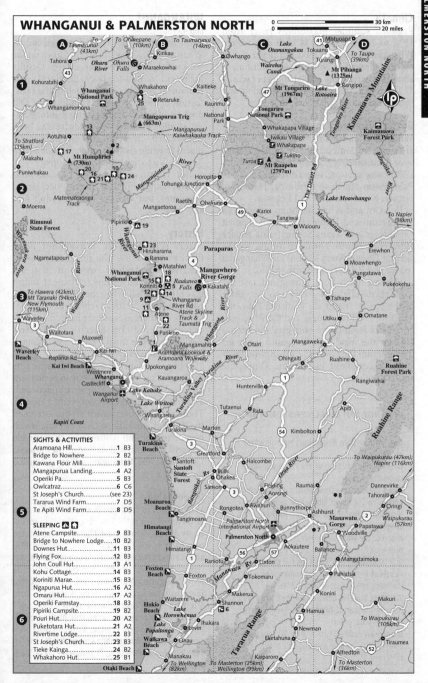

WHANGANUI & PALMERSTON NORTH

0 ———————————— 30 km
0 ———————————— 20 miles

SIGHTS & ACTIVITIES
Aramoana Hill	1 B3
Bridge to Nowhere	2 B2
Kawana Flour Mill	3 B3
Mangapurua Landing	4 A2
Operiki Pa	5 B3
Owlcatraz	6 C6
St Joseph's Church	(see 23)
Tararua Wind Farm	7 D5
Te Apiti Wind Farm	8 D5

SLEEPING
Atene Campsite	9 B3
Bridge to Nowhere Lodge	10 B2
Downes Hut	11 B3
Flying Fox	12 B3
John Coull Hut	13 A1
Kohu Cottage	14 B3
Koriniti Marae	15 B3
Ngapurua Hut	16 A2
Omaru Hut	17 A2
Operiki Farmstay	18 B3
Pipiriki Campsite	19 B2
Pouri Hut	20 A2
Puketotara Hut	21 A2
Rivertime Lodge	22 B3
St Joseph's Church	23 B3
Tieke Kainga	24 B3
Whakahoro Hut	25 B1

Climate

Regional summer maximums range from 19°C to 24°C; 10°C to 14°C during winter. Whanganui winters are mild, but they're chillier on the Palmerston North plains. Sunshine is abundant hereabouts – 2000 hours per year!

The region receives around 60mm of rain through summer and 95mm in winter.

Getting There & Around

Whanganui and Palmerston North airports are serviced domestically by **Air New Zealand** (www.airnewzealand.com). **Sunair Aviation Ltd** (☎ 07-575 7799; www.sunair.co.nz) offers direct flights from Palmerston North to Gisborne, Hamilton, Napier, New Plymouth and Rotorua.

InterCity and White Star buses service both Whanganui and Palmerston North. Tranzit Coachlines and Tranz Scenic trains service Palmerston North. For more details, see the Getting There & Away sections for Whanganui (p276) and Palmerston North (p285).

Heading north from Whanganui, take the scenic State Highway 4 (SH4) to the centre of the North Island via Raukawa Falls, the Mangawhero River Gorge and the Paraparas, an area of *papa* (large blue-grey mudstone) hills, or the winding Whanganui River Rd (p280). From the north, the Whanganui River is road-accessible at Taumarunui, Ohinepane and Whakahoro.

WHANGANUI & PALMERSTON NORTH FACTS

Eat Anything from Whanganui's hip main-street eateries (p275)

Drink A cold handle or six at a Palmerston North student bar (p284)

Read The *Wanganui Chronicle*, NZ's oldest newspaper

Listen to The rockin' album *Back to the Burning Wreck* by Whanganui riff-monsters The Have

Watch The colonial epic *River Queen* (2006), filmed on the Whanganui River

Swim at Palmerston North's Lido Aquatic Centre (p281), whistling Boz Scaggs' *Lido* all the while

Festival Tinted, warped and wonderful glass at the Wanganui Festival of Glass (p274)

Tackiest tourist attraction The kitsch pay-per-view fountain at Virginia Lake Scenic Reserve (p272) in Whanganui

Go Green Paddle a stretch of the Whanganui River (p278) – an awe-inspiring slice of NZ wilderness

---

WHANGANUI

pop 40,700

With rafts of casual Huck Finn sensibility, Whanganui is a raggedy historic town on the banks of the wide Whanganui River. Despite the recent NZ housing boom, local real estate remains relatively cheap, much to the satisfaction of the thriving arts community. Old port buildings are being turned into glass-art studios and the town centre has been rejuvenated – there are few more appealing places to while away a sunny afternoon than beneath Victoria Ave's leafy canopy.

But Whanganui isn't all peaches-and-cream: gang violence makes occasional headlines, but visitors really needn't lose any sleep.

History

Maori settlement at Whanganui dates from around 1100. The first European on the river was Andrew Powers in 1831, but Whanganui's European settlement didn't take off until 1840 when the New Zealand Co could no longer satisfy Wellington's land demands – settlers moved here instead. Initially called Petre, after a director of the New Zealand Co, the town's name was changed to Whanganui in 1844.

When the Maori understood that the gifts the Pakeha had given them were in permanent exchange for their land, they were understandably irate, and seven years of conflict ensued. Thousands of government troops occupied the Rutland Stockade in Queens Park, which dominates the hill. Ultimately, the struggle was settled by arbitration; during the Taranaki Land Wars the Whanganui Maoris assisted the Pakeha.

Orientation

Whanganui is midway between Wellington and New Plymouth. The river slides lugubriously north–south past the city, the centre of which is on the west bank. Somme Pde and Taupo Quay trace the western shoreline; Anzac Pde parallels the east bank and leads to Whanganui National Park in the north. Hanging baskets and deep verandas line Victoria Ave, Whanganui's main street.

Free town maps are available at the i-SITE visitor information centre. You can also pick up maps at the **Automobile Association** (AA; ☎ 06-348 9160; www.aatravel.co.nz; 78 Victoria Ave; ⏰ 8.30am-5pm Mon-Fri).

PALMERSTON NORTH
WHANGANUI &

MAORI NZ: WHANGANUI & PALMERSTON NORTH

A drive up the Whanganui River Road (p280) takes you deep into traditional Maori territory, passing the Maori villages of Atene, Koriniti, Ranana and Hiruharama along the way. Read up on the area's Maori heritage in the History section on p277, and run your eyes over the amazing indigenous exhibits at the Whanganui Regional Museum (below) in Whanganui itself. Also in Whanganui, Putiki Church (below) is emblazoned with superb Maori carvings.

Over in Palmerston North, Te Manawa (p281) museum has a strong Maori focus, while the New Zealand Rugby Museum (p281) pays homage to Maori All Blacks, without whom the team would never have become a world force. Northeast of Palmerston North, Manawatu Gorge (p286) is steeped in Maori lore – well worth the detour.

Information

Major banks and ATMs line Victoria Ave.

Computer Valet (☎ 06-348 5805; 1 Victoria Ave; ☽ 8.30am-5pm Mon-Fri, 10am-12.30pm Sat) Internet access.

Department of Conservation (DOC; ☎ 06-349 2100; www.doc.govt.nz; 74 Ingestre St; ☽ 8.30am-4.30pm Mon-Fri) For tourist information.

Paper Plus (☎ 06-348-0351; www.nzpost.co.nz; Trafalgar Square Shopping Mall, Taupo Quay) Offers postal services.

Post office (☎ 06-345 4103; www.nzpost.co.nz; 226 Victoria Ave; ☽ 8.30am-5pm Mon-Fri, 9am-noon Sat)

Sacred Peaks (www.sacredpeaks.com) For regional information.

Whanganui Hospital (☎ 06-348 1234; www.wdhb. org.nz; 100 Heads Rd; ☽ 24hr)

Whanganui i-SITE (☎ 06-349 0508; www.wanganui. com; 31 Taupo Qy; ☽ 8.30am-5pm Mon-Fri, 9am-3pm Sat & Sun; ▯) Tourist information and internet access.

Whanganui police station (☎ 06-349 0600; www. police.govt.nz; 10 Bell St; ☽ 24hr)

Whitcoulls (☎ 06-345 8747; www.whitcoulls.co.nz; 115 Victoria Ave; ☽ 8.30am-5.30pm Mon-Fri, 9am-4pm Sat, 10am-4pm Sun) A good selection of books.

Sights & Activities
WHANGANUI RIVERBOAT CENTRE

The **Riverboat Centre** (☎ 0800 783 2637, 06-347 1863; www.riverboats.co.nz; 1a Taupo Quay; admission free; ☽ 9am-4pm Mon-Sat, 10am-4pm Sun Sep-Jul) has historical displays, but the crowds come for the *Waimarie*, the last of the Whanganui River's paddle steamers. In 1900 the *Waimarie* was shipped in a box from England then reassembled in Whanganui. After paddling the Whanganui for 50 years, she sank ingloriously at her mooring in 1952. Submerged for 41 years, she was finally raised, restored, then relaunched on the first day of the 21st century. See p273 for details of tours on the coal-fired dreamboat.

Next to the Riverboat Centre on Saturday mornings the **River Traders Market** (☎ 06-343 9795;

www.therivertraders.co.nz; ☽ 9am-1pm Sat) is crammed with local crafts and organic produce.

MUSEUMS, GALLERIES & CHURCHES

The **Whanganui Regional Museum** (☎ 06-349 1110; www.wanganui-museum.org.nz; Watt St, Queens Park; adult/child $10/free; ☽ 10am-4.30pm) is one of NZ's better natural-history museums. Maori exhibits include the carved *Te Mata o Houroa* war canoe and some vicious-looking *mere* (greenstone clubs). The colonial and wildlife installations are first rate, and there's plenty of button-pushing and drawer-opening to keep the kids engaged.

'Historical, Contemporary, Unique' – the elegantly neoclassical **Sarjeant Gallery** (☎ 06-349 0506; www.sarjeant.org.nz; Queens Park; admission free; ☽ 10.30am-4.30pm) covers all the bases with its extensive permanent art exhibition and frequent special exhibits (including glass from the annual Wanganui Festival of Glass; p274).

The pick of Whanganui's many glass studios is the **Chronicle Glass Studio** (☎ 06-347 1921; www.chronicleglass.co.nz; 2 Rutland St; admission free; ☽ 9am-5pm Mon-Fri, 10am-4pm Sat & Sun) where you can watch glass-blowers working, check out the gallery, take a weekend glass-blowing course ($375) or a 'Make a Paperweight' lesson ($100), or just hang out and warm up on a chilly afternoon.

By the river's edge is the **Wanganui Community Arts Centre** (☎ 06-345 1551; www.communityartscentre. org.nz; 19 Taupo Quay; admission free; ☽ 10am-4pm Mon-Sat, 1-4pm Sun), which exhibits mostly local artists and musters up a decidedly South Pacific vibe with glass, ceramics, jewellery, photography and painting.

Across the City Bridge from town and 1km towards the sea is the **Putiki Church**, aka St Paul's Memorial Church. It's nothing out of the ordinary externally but, just like the faithful pew-fillers, it's what's inside that counts.

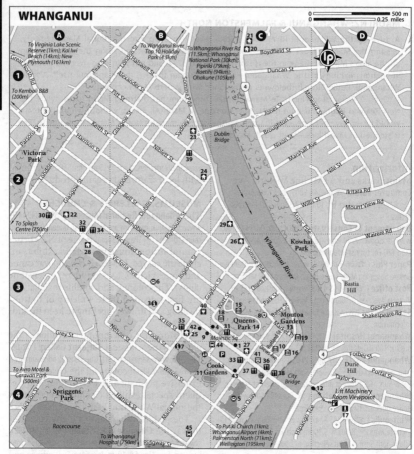

WHANGANUI

The interior is magnificent, completely covered in Maori carvings and *tukutuku* (wall panels). Unless it's a Sunday (service at 9am) the church will probably be closed, but the caretaker (☎ 06-347 8087) might show you through, or you can pick up the key from the i-SITE ($5 plus $20 deposit).

PARKS, LOOKOUTS & BEACHES

Whanganui has a few grassy, stroll-worthy parks, including **Queens Park** (where the museum and gallery are) and **Cooks Gardens**. The i-SITE stocks a couple of free walk and drive brochures directing visitors around the city.

The **Moutoa Gardens** are considered sacred Maori land and were occupied by Maoris for four months in 1995, in an acrimonious land claim that strained local Maori-Pakeha relations. The city council, abandoned by Wellington, fought the claim in the High Court while angry Pakeha counter-demonstrated under the banner of 'One New Zealand'. Police raids exacerbated the situation. When the claim was dismissed by the courts the country expected violence, but the gardens were peacefully relinquished after a moving night-long meeting addressed by Maori leaders.

The **Virginia Lake Scenic Reserve** (Great North Rd; admission free; ☯ winter gardens 9am-5pm, aviary 8.30am-5pm), about 1km north from the top end of Victoria Ave, is a rambling reserve with a lake, colourful winter garden, walk-through aviary and the Higginbottom Fountain – possibly

INFORMATION		
Automobile Association		
(AA)	**1**	C4
Computer Valet	**2**	C4
DOC Office	**3**	B3
Kathmandu	**4**	C3
Paper Plus	**5**	C4
Post Office	**6**	B3
Whanganui i-SITE	**7**	B4
Whanganui Police Station	**8**	C3
Whitcoulls	**9**	B3

SIGHTS & ACTIVITIES		
Chronicle Glass Studio	**10**	C4
Cooks Gardens	**11**	B4
Durie Hill Elevator	**12**	D4
Moutoa Gardens	**13**	C3
Queens Park	**14**	C3
Sarjeant Gallery	**15**	C3
Waimarie Paddle-Steamer		
Tours	(see 19)	
Wanganui Community Arts		
Centre	**16**	C4
War Memorial Tower	**17**	D4

Whanganui Regional		
Museum	**18**	C3
Whanganui Riverboat		
Centre	**19**	C3

SLEEPING		
Acacia Park Motel	**20**	C1
Anndion Lodge	**21**	C1
Aotea Motor Lodge	**22**	A2
Astral Motel	**23**	B2
Braemar House YHA	**24**	B2
Grand Hotel	**25**	B3
Riverview Motel	**26**	C3
Rutland Arms Inn	**27**	C4
Siena Motor Lodge	**28**	A3
Tamara Backpackers Lodge	**29**	C2

EATING		
Ceramic	(see 33)	
Countdown	**30**	A2
Indigo	**31**	C3
New World	**32**	A2
Orange	**33**	C4
Rapido Espresso House	**34**	A2

Red Eye Café	**35**	B3
Stellar	**36**	C4
Thai Villa	**37**	C4
Vega	**38**	C4
Yellow House Cafe	**39**	B2

DRINKING		
Ceramic	(see 33)	
Rosie O'Grady's	(see 25)	
Rutland Arms Inn	(see 27)	
Spirit'd	**40**	B3
Stellar	(see 36)	

ENTERTAINMENT		
Embassy 3 Cinemas	**41**	C4

SHOPPING		
River Traders Market	(see 25)	

TRANSPORT		
Air New Zealand	**42**	B3
Bike Shed	**43**	C4
Tranzit City Link Bus Stop	**44**	C4
Whanganui Travel Centre	**45**	B4

the world's only pay-per-view geyser ($1 per 10-minute eruption).

Across City Bridge from the town centre is the **Durie Hill Elevator** (☎ /fax 06-345 8525; Anzac Pde; one-way $2; ☺ 8am-6pm Mon-Fri, 10am-5pm Sat & Sun), built with grand visions for Durie Hill's residential future. A tunnel burrows 200m into the hillside, from where the elevator rattles 65m to the top. There are two viewpoints at the summit: one on top of the lift machinery room, the other up the 176 steps of the **War Memorial Tower**. Assess the condition of Whanganui's roof-tiles, or scan the horizon for Mt Taranaki, Mt Ruapehu and even the South Island on a clear day.

Kai Iwi Beach is a wild ocean frontier, strewn with black sand and masses of broken driftwood. To get here follow Great North Rd 4km north of town, then turn left onto Rapanui Rd and head seawards for 10km. If the sea is angry, try the **Splash Centre** (☎ 06-349 0113; www.splashcentre.co.nz; Springvale Park, London St; admission adult/child $4.50/3; ☺ 6am-8pm Mon-Fri, 8am-6pm Sat & Sun) for a safe swim.

Tours

See p278 for Whanganui River canoe, kayak and jetboat tours.

Scenic Flights (☎ 06-345 0914; wanganui.aero.club@xtra.co.nz; Whanganui Airport, Airport Rd; 15min-2hr flight from $45) Mile-high panoramas above Whanganui, Moutoa Island, Mt Ruapehu and Whanganui National Park.

Waimarie Paddle-Steamer Tours (☎ 0800 783 2637, 06-347 1863; www.riverboats.co.nz; 1a Taupo Quay; adult/child/family $45/15/105; ☺ tours 2pm daily Nov-May, 1pm Sat & Sun Jun-Oct, closed Aug) Two-hour tour weekdays; three hours with a one-hour stopover at weekends. Also six-hour trips further upriver on the motorised 1904 *Wairua* (adult/child $50/20).

WHANGANUI OR WANGANUI?

Yeah, we know, it's confusing. Is there an 'h' or isn't there? Either way, the pronunciation is identical: 'wan-ga' not (as in the rest of the country) 'fan-ga'.

Everything was originally spelled Wanganui, because in the local dialect *whanga* (harbour) is pronounced 'wan-ga'. However, in 1991 the New Zealand Geographic Board officially adopted the correct Maori spelling (with an 'h') for the Whanganui River and Whanganui National Park. This was a culturally deferential decision: the Pakeha-dominated town and region retained the old spelling, while the river area – Maori territory – adopted the new.

In 2009 the Board assented that the town and region should also adopt the 'h'. This caused much community consternation, opinions on the decision split almost evenly (outspoken Mayor Michael Laws was particularly anti-'h'). Ultimately, NZ Minister for Land Information Maurice Williamson decreed that either spelling was acceptable, and that adopting the querulous 'h' is up to individual businesses or entities. A good old Kiwi compromise! Whanderful...

Whanganui Tours (☎ 06-347 7534; www.whanganui tours.co.nz) Join the mailman on the Whanganui River Road to Pipiriki (weekday/weekend $55/60; departs 7.30am) with lots of social and historical commentary. You can also take the mail van to Pipiriki then canoe back to Whanganui (single/double $80/115, guide $120) or cycle back (one-/two-day trip $80/120, accommodation $55 to $70). There are optional jetboat trips from Pipiriki to the Bridge to Nowhere ($55).

Festivals & Events

NZ Masters Games (☎ 06-349 1815; www.nzmg. com) The country's biggest multisport event, held in early February every odd-numbered year.

Heritage Weekend (☎ 06-349 0511; www.wanganui heritage.org.nz) Riverboats, architectural adoration and markets in mid-March.

Wanganui Festival of Glass (☎ 06-349 0508; www. wanganuiglass.com) Classy glass fest in September.

Wanganui Literary Festival(☎ 06-349 0511; www. writersfest.co.nz) Words, thoughts, and thoughts about words every September.

Cemetery Circuit Motorcycle Race (☎ 06-349 1815; www.cemeterycircuit.co.nz) Pandemonic Boxing Day bike race.

Sleeping

BUDGET

Tamara Backpackers Lodge (☎ 06-347 6300; www.tam aralodge.com; 24 Somme Pde; dm $25, s $45-55, tw $54-64, d $60-64; 🖳) Tamara is a mazelike two-storey heritage house with a wide balcony, kitchen, TV lounge, free bikes and a leafy, hammock-hung back garden. Ask for one of the beaut doubles overlooking the river.

Braemar House YHA (☎ 06-348 2301; www.braemar house.co.nz, www.yha.co.nz; 2 Plymouth St; dm $25, cabin s/d $50/60, guest house incl breakfast s/d $80/100; 🖳 🛜) Riverside Braemar brings together an 1895 Victorian B&B guest house and a rambunctious backpackers. Centrally heated guest-house rooms are floral and fancy; airy dorms and no-frills cabins abut limited tent space out the back.

Avro Motel & Caravan Park (☎ 0800 367 287, 06-345 5279; www.wanganuiaccommodation.co.nz; 36 Alma Rd; unpowered & powered sites from $30, units from $80; 🛜 🛝) Avro's yellow biplane heralds the closest camping to the city centre, 1.5km west. Both powered and unpowered sites have their own freestanding bathrooms, and the camp kitchen is a wee winner. Standard motel units also available.

our pick Anndion Lodge (☎ 0800 343 056, 06-343 3593; www.anndionlodge.co.nz; 143 Anzac Pde; dm/s $35/65, d $85-135, ste $140; 🖳 🛜 🛝) Hell-bent on constantly improving and expanding their business, hosts Ann and Dion (Anndion, get it?) go to enormous lengths to make things homey: stereo systems, big TVs, Playstation, spa, swimming pool, barbecue area, courtesy van etc. It's pricier than your average hostel, but everything's new, clean and thoroughly worth it.

Whanganui River Top 10 Holiday Park (☎ 0800 272 664, 06-343 8402; www.wrivertop10.co.nz; 460 Somme Pde; unpowered & powered sites $38-50, cabins $55-85, units $115-170; 🖳 🛜 🛝) This top-notch Top 10 park sits on the Whanganui's west bank 6km north of Dublin Bridge. Facilities (including pool and jumping pillow) are immaculate and prodigious. Kayak hire also available: the owners shuttle you up river then you paddle back to camp. Self-catering or dining in town is your best bet food-wise.

MIDRANGE & TOP END

Grand Hotel (☎ 0800 843 472, 06-345 0955; www.the grandhotel.co.nz; cnr St Hill & Guyton Sts; s/d $75/95, ste $120-150; 🖳) If you can't face another soulless motel room, rooms at this stately old-school Whanganui survivor have a bit more personality. Singles and doubles are basic but good value; suites are spacious. Rosie O'Grady's Irish pub (opposite) and a restaurant are downstairs.

Kembali B&B (☎ 06-347 1727; www.bnb.co.nz/kem bali.html; 26 Taranaki St, St Johns Hill; s/d incl breakfast from $80/110) Up on leafy St Johns Hill on the way to Taranaki, this home-spun B&B has two private upstairs guest rooms sleeping four, available on an exclusive-use basis. It's a sedate place overlooking some wetlands, all achirp with tuis, pukekos and native whistling frogs.

Astral Motel (☎ 0800 509 063, 06-347 9063; www. astralmotel.co.nz; 46 Somme Pde; s/d/f from $85/95/110; 🛝) Astrally aligned with the terrestrial Dublin Bridge nearby, rooms here are a bit dated but are well serviced and have 24-hour check-in if you're rolling in off the midnight highway.

Acacia Park Motel (☎ 0800 800 225, 06-343 9093; www.acacia-park-motel.co.nz; 140 Anzac Pde; r $95-120) Acacia's dozen jade-coloured bungalows are dotted among mature trees, the boughs home to roosting doves. The retro rooms have seen better days but you get what you pay for.

Riverview Motel (☎ 0800 102 001; 06-345 2888; www. wanganuimotels.co.nz; 14 Somme Pde; d $95-150; 🛜) Take your pick from one of 15 '80s-style kitchenette units in the main block or the five spiffy spa suites out the back. Nothing too flash, but a decent central option.

Siena Motor Lodge (☎ 0800 888 802, 06-345 9009; www.siena.co.nz; 335 Victoria Ave; ste $125-145; 🛜) Aiming for Tuscany but hitting Taranaki, the compact rooms here are five star and spotless. Business travellers enjoy double glazing, a DVD library, heated towel rails, coffee plungers and real coffee.

Rutland Arms Inn (☎ 0800 788 5263, 06-347 7677; www.rutland-arms.co.nz; 48 Ridgway St; ste $130-180; 🛜) Billed as a 'luxury heritage experience', this restored 1849 building has an old-fashioned pub downstairs with colonial-style accommodation above. Rooms have TV, phone, plump pillows and spine-straightening beds. English hunting scenes adorn the bar's beer taps.

Aotea Motor Lodge (☎ 06-345 0303; www.aoteamotorlodge.co.nz; 390 Victoria Ave; d $160-200; 🖳) It gladdens the heart to see a job done well, and the owners of Whanganui's newest motel have done just that. On the upper reaches of Victoria Ave, this flashy, two-storey contemporary motel features roomy suites, lavish linen, dark-timber furniture and plenty of marble and stone –sassy stuff.

Eating

Rapido Espresso House (☎ 06-347 9475; 71 Liverpool St; snacks $3-6; ☽ 7.30am-6pm Mon-Fri, 9am-3pm Sat) If you're hungry, don't expect more than a wedge of cake or some sushi at this raffish, royal blue cafe – what you're here for is the coffee. Organic and fair-trade all the way, the brew here is the best in town.

Red Eye Café (☎ 06-345 5646; 96 Guyton St; meals $5-18; ☽ 7.30am-3.30pm Mon & Tue, to 4pm Wed-Fri, 8am-3pm Sat; Ⓥ) With inexplicable familiarity (maybe it's the friendly staff), this bohemian urban cafe has colourful local art, tasty light snacks (bagels, salads) as well as more substantial meals (curries, organic chicken sandwiches). Good coffee, too.

Yellow House Café (☎ 06-345 0083; cnr Pitt & Dublin Sts; brunch $5-19; dinner $27-34; ☽ 8am-4pm Sun-Wed, to 9pm Thu-Sat; Ⓥ) Local art, funky tunes, outdoor tables, buttermilk pancakes and great omelettes. Dinner veers from lamb to lasagne. Actually, it's more of a taupe colour…

Ceramic (☎ 06-348 4449; 51 Victoria Ave; tapas $6-14, mains $27-29; ☽ 3pm-late Tue-Sat; 🛜) In a split-business arrangement with Orange (right), Ceramic takes over for the dinner shift, serving upmarket cafe food and tapas in a low-lit, rust-coloured interior. Occasional DJs ooze

tunes across the tables to cocktail-sipping seducers.

Orange (☎ 06-348 4449; 51 Victoria Ave; meals $8-22; ☽ 7.30am-5pm Mon-Fri, 9am-5pm Sat & Sun; 🛜) Orange is a babbling espresso bar serving gourmet burgers, big breakfasts, muffins, cakes and sandwiches (try the BLT). The outdoor tables go berserk during summer.

Vega (☎ 06-345 9955; 49 Taupo Quay; mains $10-18; ☽ 9.30am-late Mon-Fri, 9am-late Sat & Sun; 🛜) Vega's riverside building has been a merchant store and a brothel, but today it's 100% class. A packed house testifies to the virtuoso menu, professional service and meticulously constructed wine list. There's plenty of seafood for the *poisson*-impassioned, and vegetarian and children's options too. Open 'til the wee smalls, it's a moody spot for a late-night vino or two, too.

Thai Villa (☎ 06-348 9089; 7 Victoria Ave; lunch from $10, dinner $19-25; ☽ lunch & dinner) There are a few Thai joints along Victoria Ave, but Thai Villa is by far the most authentic. Try the *massaman* beef curry or the *laab* duck washed down with a Singha beer.

ourpick Indigo (☎ 06-348 7459; cnr Majestic Sq & Watt St; lunch $12-19, dinner $18-31; ☽ 10am-4pm Mon & Tue, 10am-late Wed-Fri, 9am-11pm Sat, 9am-4pm Sat) Along with Vega, Indigo dragged Whanganui dining into the new millennium. A decade later and the vibe is still up-to-the-minute snazzy; the lofty interior and outdoor terrace swim with NZ wines, and contemporary meat, pasta and fish dishes are assembled with progressive flair. The lamb pasties are huge.

Stellar (☎ 06-345 7278; 2 Victoria Ave; lunch $15, dinner $20-31; ☽ 10pm-late Mon-Fri, 8.30am-late Sat & Sun; 🛜) Stellar lives up to its name – a cavernous bar-cum-restaurant with a convivial family atmosphere, it's the town's pride and joy. Reclining contentedly on leather couches, locals and tourists alike sip premium lagers and feast on bar morsels, gourmet pizzas and surf 'n' turf fare. Frequent bands, DJs and quiz nights to boot.

Self-caterers can hit the supermarkets:
Countdown (☎ 06-348 9470; cnr Victoria Ave & Glasgow St; ☽ 6am-midnight)
New World (☎ 06-349 0990; 374 Victoria Ave; ☽ 7am-9pm)

Drinking

Rosie O'Grady's (☎ 06-345 0955; cnr St Hill & Guyton Sts; ☽ 11am-late) Siphoning into NZ's insatiable (and, it has to be said, annoying) passion for Irish pubs, Rosie's, in the Grand Hotel, is as good a spot as any to elbow down a few pints of Guinness on a misty river afternoon. Good pub meals too.

Spirit'd (☎ 0800 737 793; 75 Guyton St; ☼ 10am-late) Pool tables, Jack Daniels, Metallica on the jukebox and local young bucks trying to out-strut each other – just like 1989 minus the cigarettes.

See also Rutland Arms Inn (p275), Stellar (p275) and Ceramic (p275).

Entertainment

Embassy 3 Cinemas (☎ 06-345 7958; www.embassy3. co.nz; 34 Victoria Ave; tickets adult/child/concession $12/9/8; ☼ 11am-midnight) Nightly new-release blockbusters selling out faster than you can say 'bored Whanganui teenagers'. All Tuesday tickets are $7.50.

Getting There & Away
AIR

Whanganui Airport (WAG; ☎ 06-345 5593; www.airport.u.nu/WAG) is 4km south of town, across the river towards the sea. **Air New Zealand** (☎ 06-348 3500; www.airnewzealand.co.nz; 133 Victoria Ave; ☼ 9am-5pm Mon-Fri) has direct flights from Whanganui to Auckland (one hour, one to four daily) and Wellington (35 minutes, one daily) with onward connections.

BUS

InterCity (☎ 09-583 5780; www.intercity.co.nz) buses operate from the **Whanganui Travel Centre** (☎ 06-345 7100; www.tranzit.co.nz; 160 Ridgway St; ☼ 8.15am-5.15pm Mon-Fri). Some destinations:

Destination	Price	Duration	Frequency
Auckland	$80	8hr	2-4 daily
New Plymouth	$29	2½hr	1-2 daily
Palmerston North	$20	1½hr	1-3 daily
Taumarunui	$47	2¾hr	1 daily
Wellington	$39	4hr	1-4 daily

Naked Bus (☎ 0900 625 33; www.nakedbus.co.nz) departs from Whanganui i-SITE to most North Island centres, including the following:

Destination	Price	Duration	Frequency
Auckland	$39	9¼hr	1 daily
Hamilton	$27	6½hr	1 daily
New Plymouth	$17	2½hr	1 daily
Palmerston North	$9	1¼hr	1 daily
Wellington	$19	3½hr	1 daily

Also departing the i-SITE, **White Star** (☎ 0800 465 622, 06-349 0508 www.whitestarbus.co.nz) has two

buses each Thursday and Friday and one every other day to/from Wellington ($30, 3½ hours) via Palmerston North ($20, one hour), and New Plymouth ($27, 2½ hours).

Getting Around
BICYCLE

Bike Shed (☎ 06-345 5500; www.bikeshed.co.nz; cnr Ridgway & St Hill Sts; ☼ 8.30am-5.30pm Mon-Fri, 9am-2pm Sat) hires out mountain bikes from $35 per day, including helmet and lock. Ask them for updates on the **Mountain to Sea** Ohakune-to-Whanganui bike track, which has been ascribed 'Quick Start' status as part of the proposed **New Zealand Cycle Trail** (www.tourism. govt.nz/our-work/new-zealand-cycle-trail-project) project.

BUS

Tranzit City Link (☎ 0508 800 800, 06-345 4433; www. horizons.govt.nz; single trip/day pass $2/6) operates four looped local bus routes departing from the Maria Pl bus stop, including routes 5 and 6 past the Whanganui River Top 10 Holiday Park in Aramoho. Buses run from 7am to 6pm Monday to Friday; 10.30am to 5.30pm Saturday.

CAR

The following car-rental companies have pick-up/drop-off at Whanganui Airport:
Avis (☎ 06-358 7528; www.avis.co.nz)
Budget (☎ 06-345 5122; www.budget.co.nz)
Hertz (☎ 06-348 7624; www.hertz.co.nz)

TAXI

Rivercity Cabs (☎ 0800 345 3333, 06-345 3333)
Wanganui Taxis (☎ 06-343 5555)

WHANGANUI NATIONAL PARK

The Whanganui River – the lifeblood of Whanganui National Park – curls 329km from its source on Mt Tongariro (p306) to the Tasman Sea. It's the longest navigable river in NZ, a fact that's been shaping its destiny for centuries (see History, opposite). The river today conveys canoes, kayaks and jetboats, its waters shifting from deep mirror greens in summer to turbulent winter browns.

The native bush here is thick podocarp broad-leaved forest interspersed with ferns. Occasionally you'll see poplar and other introduced trees along the river, remnants of long-vanished settlements. Traces of Maori settlements also crop up here, with old *pa* (fortified village) and *kainga* (village) sites, and Hauhau *niu* (war and peace) poles at the convergence of the Whanganui and Ohura Rivers at Maraekowhai. The Ratakura, Reinga Kokiri and Te Rerehapa Falls, all near Maraekowhai on the Ohura, are where Maori caught small *tuna riki* (freshwater eels).

The impossibly scenic Whanganui River Road, a mostly unsealed river-hugging road from Whanganui to Pipiriki, makes a fabulous alternative to the faster but less magical SH4.

History

In Maori legend the Whanganui River was formed when Mt Taranaki, after brawling with Mt Tongariro over the lovely Mt Pihanga, fled the central North Island for the sea, leaving a long gouge behind him. He turned west at the coast, finally stopping at his current address. Mt Tongariro sent cool water to heal the gouge – thus the Whanganui River was born.

Kupe, the great Polynesian explorer, is believed to have travelled 20km up the Whanganui around AD 800; Maori lived here by 1100. By the time Europeans put down roots in the late 1830s, Maori settlements lined the river valley. Missionaries sailed upstream and their settlements – at Hiruharama, Ranana, Koriniti and Atene – have survived to this day despite a dwindling river population.

Steamers first tackled the river in the mid-1860s, a dangerous time for Pakeha. Aligned with Taranaki Maoris, some river tribes joined the Hauhau Rebellion – a Maori movement seeking to expel settlers.

In 1886 a Whanganui company established the first commercial steamer transport service. Others soon followed, utilising the river between Whanganui and Taumarunui. Supplying river communities and linking the sea with the interior, the steamers' importance grew, particularly after 1903 when the Auckland railway reached Taumarunui from the north.

New Zealand's contemporary tourism leviathan was seeded here. Internationally advertised trips on the 'Rhine of Maoriland' became so popular that by 1905 12,000 tourists a year were making the trip upriver from Whanganui to Pipiriki or downriver from Taumarunui. The engineering feats and skippering ability required on the river became legendary.

From 1918 land upstream of Pipiriki was granted to returning WWI soldiers. Farming here was a major challenge, with many families struggling for years to make the rugged land productive. Only a few endured into the early 1940s.

The completion of the railway from Auckland to Wellington and the improving roads ultimately signed river transport's death warrant; 1959 saw the last commercial riverboat voyage. Today, just one old-fleet vessel cruises the river – the *Waimarie* (p271).

Orientation & Information

Pipiriki and Taumarunui are the main entry and exit points to the river with the most facilities, though you are also able to access the river from Ohinepane and Whakahoro.

For national park information, try the affable Whanganui i-SITE or DOC Office (p271). There's also **Pipiriki DOC** (☎ 06-385 5022; Owairua Rd; www.doc.govt.co.nz; ⏰ 8am-5pm Mon-Fri) and **Taumarunui DOC** (☎ 07-895 8201; Cherry Grove Domain; ⏰ 8am-5pm Mon-Fri), though they're both field centres rather than tourist offices and aren't always staffed. Taumarunui's i-SITE is a safer bet (p249).

Check out www.whanganuiriver.co.nz online; otherwise, a more tangible resource is the NZ Recreational Canoeing Association's *Guide to the Whanganui River* ($10). DOC's *In and Around Whanganui National Park* ($3) covers tramping territory, or the Wanganui Tramping Club (☎ 06-346 5597 www.wanganuitramp ingclub.org.nz) puts out the quarterly *Wanganui Tramper* magazine, full of local info.

Sights

The scenery along the **Whanganui River Road** (Map p269) en route to Pipiriki is camera conducive – stark, wet mountain slopes plunge into lazy jade stretches of the Whanganui River. A French Catholic mission led by Suzanne Aubert established the Daughters of Our Lady of Compassion in Jerusalem in 1892. Around a corner in the road, the picture-perfect **St Joseph's Church** (see p280) stands tall on a spur of land above a deep river bend.

Other sights along the road include the restored 1854 **Kawana Flour Mill** near Matahiwi, **Operiki Pa** and other *pa* sites, and **Aramoana Hill**, from where there's a panoramic view. The Maori villages of **Atene**, **Koriniti**, **Ranana** and **Hiruharama** crop up along the way – ask a local before you go sniffing around. Note that the River Road is unsealed between Matahiwi and 3km south of Pipiriki.

Pipiriki (Map p269) is beside the river at the north end of Whanganui River Road. It's a rainy river town without much going on (no shops or petrol), but was once a humming holiday hot spot serviced by river steamers and paddleboats. Seemingly cursed, the old Pipiriki Hotel, formerly a glamorous resort full of international tourists, burned to the ground twice. Recent attempts to rebuild it have stalled due to funding issues; it's been vandalised and stripped of anything of value, leaving a hollow brick husk riddled with potential. Pipiriki is the end point for canoe trips coming down the river and the launching pad for jetboat rides.

Standing in mute testimony to the optimism of the early settlers is the **Bridge to Nowhere** (Map p269), built in 1936. The walking track from Mangapurua Landing (upstream from Pipiriki, accessible by jetboat) to the lonesome bridge was part of a long-lost 4.5m-wide roadway from Raetihi to the river.

Activities
CANOEING & KAYAKING

The most popular stretch of river for canoeing and kayaking is downstream from Taumarunui to Pipiriki. This has been added to the NZ Great Walks system (p77) and is called the 'Whanganui Journey' (despite the fact that there's more sitting down than walking involved). It's a Grade II river – easy enough for the inexperienced, with enough moiling rapids to keep things interesting. See the free DOC leaflet *Whanganui Journey* for information.

Between 1 October and 30 April you'll need a **Great Walks Hut & Campsite Pass** (adult/child $45/free) for boat trips involving overnight stays between Taumarunui and Pipiriki. The rule applies only to this stretch of the river. The pass is valid for four nights and five days; you can stay overnight in the huts, the camps beside the huts or in other campsites along the river. If you're only doing an overnighter from Taumarunui to Whakahoro the pass costs $10; if you exclude Tieke Kainga *marae* (meeting house complexes) the pass costs $50. If you're just paddling and not sleeping anywhere, there's no charge. Bookings are not required for huts or campsites.

Outside the main season you'll only need a **Backcountry Hut Pass** (adult/child 1 year $90/45, 6 months $60/30), or you can pay on a hut-by-hut basis ($15 to $45 per night). All passes and tickets are available at the Whanganui i-SITE and regional DOC offices; some canoe operators also sell them. During summer, hut wardens and conservation officers patrol the river.

Taumarunui to Pipiriki is a five-day/four-night trip, Ohinepane to Pipiriki is a four-day/three-night trip, and Whakahoro to Pipiriki is a three-day/two-night trip. Taumarunui to Whakahoro is a popular overnight trip, especially for weekenders, or you can do a one-day trip from Taumarunui to Ohinepane or Ohinepane to Whakahoro. From Whakahoro to Pipiriki, 88km downstream, there's no road access so you're wed to the river for a few days; this is the trip everyone clamours to do. Most canoeists stop at Pipiriki.

The season for canoe trips is usually from September to Easter. Up to 5000 people make the river trip each year, mostly between Christmas and the end of January. During winter the river is almost deserted – the winter currents run swift and deep, as cold weather and short days deter potential paddlers.

To hire a two-person Canadian canoe for one/three/five days costs around $80/220/300 including transport. A single-person kayak costs about $50 per day not including transport (around $50 per person). Operators provide you with everything you need, including life jackets and waterproof drums (essential if you go bottom-up).

You can also take guided canoe or kayak trips – prices start at around $300/800 per person for a two-/five-day guided trip.

Operators include the following:

Awa Tours (☎ 06-385 8297; www.wakatours.com; Raetihi)

Blazing Paddles (☎ 0800 252 946, 07-895 5261; www.blazingpaddles.co.nz; Taumarunui)

Bridge to Nowhere Tours (see Jetboating, opposite)

Canoe Safaris (☎ 0800 272 335, 06-385.9237; www.canoesafaris.co.nz; Ohakune)

Taumarunui Canoe Hire (☎ 0800 226 6348, 07-895 7483; www.taumarunuicanoehire.co.nz; Taumarunui)

Wades Landing Outdoors (☎ 0800 226 631, 07-895 5995; www.whanganui.co.nz; Whakahoro)

Whanganui Kayak Hire (☎ 0211 336 938; www.kayakhire.co.nz; Whanganui)

Whanganui River Adventures (see Jetboating, opposite)

Whanganui River Guides (☎ 07-896 6727; www.whanganuiriverguides.co.nz; Taumarunui)

Whanganui Tours (☎ 06-347 7534; www.whanganuitours.co.nz; Whanganui)

Yeti Tours (☎ 0800 322 388, 06-385 8197; www.canoe.co.nz; Ohakune)

Whanganui River canoe companies also operate from National Park Village (p311) and Ohakune (p314).

JETBOATING

Hold onto your hats – jetboat trips give you the chance to see parts of the river that would otherwise take you days to paddle through. Jetboats depart from Pipiriki and Whanganui; four-hour tours start at around $105 per person. The following operators can also provide transport to the river ends of the Matemateaonga and Mangapurua Tracks (see Tramping, below):

Bridge to Nowhere Tours (☎ 0800 480 308, 06-385 4622; www.bridgetonowheretours.co.nz; Pipiriki)

Spirit of the River Jet (☎ 0800 538 8687, 06-342 5572; www.spiritoftheriverjet.co.nz; Whanganui)

Whanganui River Adventures (☎ 0800 862 743, 06-385 3246; www.whanganuiriveradventures.co.nz; Pipiriki)

Whanganui Scenic Experience Jet (☎ 0800 945 335, 06-342 5599; www.whanganuiscenicjet.com; Whanganui)

TRAMPING

The most popular track in Whanganui National Park is the 40-minute walk from **Mangapurua Landing** (Map p269) to the Bridge to Nowhere, 30km upstream from Pipiriki by jetboat.

The Matemateaonga and Mangapurua/ Kaiwhakauka Tracks are brilliant longer tramps (DOC booklets $1). Both are one-way tracks beginning (or ending) at remote spots on the river, so you have to organise jetboat transport to or from the trailheads – ask any jetboat operator (above). To Pipiriki from the Matemateaonga Track is around $50 per person; from the Mangapurua Track it's around $100.

Three to four days from end to end, the 42km **Matemateaonga Track** gets kudos as one of NZ's best walks. Probably due to its remoteness, it doesn't attract the hordes of trampers that amass on NZ's more famous tracks. Penetrating deep into wild bush and hill country, it traces an old Maori track and a disused settlers' dray road between the Whanganui and Taranaki regions. It follows the crest of the Matemateaonga Range along the route of the Whakaihuwaka Rd, started in 1911 to create a more direct link from Stratford to the railway at Raetihi. WWI interrupted planning and the road was never finished.

On a clear day, a 1½-hour side-trip to the top of Mt Humphries (730m) rewards you with sigh-inducing views all the way to Mt Taranaki and the volcanoes of Tongariro. There's a steep section between

the Whanganui River (75m above sea level) and the Puketotara Hut (Map p269; 427m above sea level) but mostly it's easy walking. There are three DOC backcountry huts along the way: Omaru, Pouri and Puketotara (see Map p269); hut tickets cost $15 per person per night.

The **Mangapurua/Kaiwhakauka Track** is a 40km trail between Whakahoro and the Mangapurua Landing, both on the Whanganui River. The track runs along the Mangapurua and Kaiwhakauka Streams (both Whanganui River tributaries). Between these valleys a side track leads to the 663m Mangapurua Trig, the area's highest point, from which cloudless views extend to the Tongariro and Egmont National Park volcanoes. The route passes the Bridge to Nowhere and abandoned farming land cleared by settlers in the 20th century. Unless you're an insane tramping dynamo, walking the track takes 20 hours (three to four days). The Whakahoro Hut (see Map p269) at the Whakahoro end of the track is the only hut, but there's plenty of good camping. There's road access to the track both at the Whakahoro end and from a side track from the end of the Ruatiti Valley–Ohura Rd (from Raetihi).

The DOC booklet *In and Around Whanganui National Park* ($2.50) details a couple of shorter walks branching off the Whanganui River Rd that offers glimpses of wilderness.

The 18km **Atene Skyline Track** begins at Atene on the Whanganui River Rd, 22km north of the SH4 junction. The track takes six to eight hours, showcasing native forest, sandstone bluffs and the **Taumata Trig** (523m), with its broad views as far as Mt Ruapehu, Mt Taranaki and the Tasman Sea. The track ends back on the Whanganui River Rd, 2km downstream from the starting point.

A 1km track cuts through native bush from the Pipiriki DOC field centre to the top of Pukehinau, a hill with great valley vistas.

Sleeping
WHANGANUI NATIONAL PARK

The park has a sprinkling of huts, a lodge and numerous camping grounds (see Map p269). Along the Taumarunui–Pipiriki section are three huts classified as Great Walks Huts during summer and Serviced Huts in the off-season: Whakahoro Hut, John Coull Hut and Tieke Kainga, which has been revived as a *marae*. You can stay at Tieke Kainga, but full *marae* protocol must be observed (see p58). On the lower part of the river, Downes Hut is on the west bank, opposite Atene.

Bridge to Nowhere Lodge (Map p269; ☎ 0800 480 308, 06-385 4622; www.bridgetonowheretours.co.nz; unpowered sites $20, per person self-catering/incl breakfast & dinner $45/125) Across the river from the Tieke Kainga *marae*, this remote lodge lies deep in the national park, 21km upriver from Pipiriki near the Matemateaonga Track. The only way to get here is by jetboat from Pipiriki or on foot. It has a licensed bar, and meals are quality home-cooked affairs. The lodge also runs jetboat tours (p279) and canoe trips (p278).

WHANGANUI RIVER ROAD
Book the following places in advance – no one's going to turn you away, but they appreciate a bit of warning! There's no mobile-phone coverage along the road, and no petrol or shops. There are a couple of takeaway food vans in Pipiriki open during summer. From south to north, accommodation includes the following:

Rivertime Lodge (Map p269; ☎ 06-342 5595; www.rivertimelodge.co.nz; Whanganui River Rd; d self-catering/incl breakfast $110/130) A rural idyll: hills folding down towards the river and the intermittent bleating of sheep. Friendly and farmy, Rivertime is a moss green farmhouse with three bedrooms, a barbecue and no TV!

Flying Fox (Map p269; ☎ 06-342 8160; www.theflyingfox.co.nz; Whanganui River Rd; unpowered sites $20, d $100-200) This place is a superb, eco-attuned getaway on the riverbank across from Koriniti. You can self-cater in the Brewhouse, James K or Glory Cart (self-contained cottages), opt for B&B ($120 per person), or pitch a tent in a secluded bush clearing. Access is by jetboat; otherwise you can park across the river from the accommodation then soar over the river on the flying fox.

Kohu Cottage (Map p269; ☎ 06-342 8178; kohu.cottage @xtra.co.nz; Whanganui River Rd, Koriniti; d $70) A snug little lime green weatherboard cottage (100 years old!) above the road in Koriniti, sleeping three to four bods. There's a basic kitchen and a wood fire for chilly riverside nights.

Koriniti Marae (Map p269; ☎ 06-348 0303, 021 365 176; www.koriniti.com; Koriniti Pa Rd, Koriniti; dm $30) This *marae* on the east bank offers dorm-style beds for prebooked visitors; offer *koha* (a donation) plus the fee. It also runs a 24-hour 'cultural experience' for groups, including a *haka* (war

dance), weaving, storytelling and three meals ($190 per person).

Operiki Farmstay (Map p269; ☎ 06-342 8159; www.whanganuiriver.co.nz; Whanganui River Rd, Operiki; incl breakfast & dinner s/d $55/110) On a steep hillside 1.5km north of Koriniti, this is a cheery in-with-the-family farmhouse. There are scenic walks around the property, and macadamia-nut muffins come hot from the oven.

St Joseph's Church (Map p269; ☎ 06-342 8190; www.compassion.org.nz; Whanganui River Rd, Hiruharama; dm $20) Taking in bedraggled travellers and offering 20 dorm-style beds, the sisters at St Joe's await to issue your deliverance – book ahead for the privilege. Moutoa Island, site of an historic 1864 battle, is just downriver.

There's an informal campsite with toilets and cold water at Pipiriki and another one (even less formal) just north of Atene (see Map p269).

Getting There & Away
From the north, there's road access to the Whanganui River at Taumarunui, Ohinepane and Whakahoro, though the latter is a long, remote drive on mostly unsealed roads. Roads to Whakahoro lead off from Owhango and Raurimu, both on SH4. There isn't any further road access to the river until Pipiriki.

From the south, the Whanganui River Rd veers off SH4 14km north of Whanganui, rejoining it at Raetihi, 91km north of Whanganui. It takes about two hours to drive the 79km between Whanganui and Pipiriki. The full circle from Whanganui through Pipiriki and Raetihi and back along SH4 through the Paraparas and Mangawhero River Gorge takes about four hours. The Whanganui River Rd is unsealed between Matahiwi and Mangeatoroa; petrol is available at Raetihi and Upokongaro but nowhere in between.

Alternatively, take a River Road tour from Whanganui (p274).

PALMERSTON NORTH
pop 80,700

The rich sheep- and dairy-farming Manawatu region embraces the districts of Rangitikei to the north and Horowhenua to the south. The hub of it all, on the banks of the Manawatu River, is Palmerston North, with its moderate high-rise attempts reaching up from the plains. Massey University, NZ's largest, informs the town's cultural and social structures. As a result 'Palmy' has an open-minded, rurally bookish vibe.

None of this impressed a visiting John Cleese who scoffed, 'If you ever do want to kill yourself, but lack the courage, I think a visit to Palmerston North will do the trick.' The city exacted revenge by naming a rubbish dump after him.

Orientation
The grassy expanse of the Square is the centre of city life. One block to the west, George St is the main cafe and restaurant strip. Massey University is 3km south of town.

Free town maps are available at the i-SITE visitor information centre. The **Automobile Association** (AA; ☎ 06-357 7039; www.aatravel.co.nz; 185 Broadway Ave; ☻ 8.30am-5pm Mon-Fri) also stocks maps.

Information
Banks and ATMs proliferate around the Square and Main St.

Bruce McKenzie Booksellers (☎ 06-356 9922; books@bmbooks.co.nz; 37 George St; ☻ 9am-6pm Mon-Thu, to 8pm Fri, to 5pm Sat, 10am-5pm Sun) Palmerston North's only independent bookseller; discount outlet at 16 Coleman Pl.

Department of Conservation (DOC; ☎ 06-350 9700; www.doc.govt.nz; 717 Tremaine Ave; ☻ 8am-4.30pm Mon-Fri) Tourist information 3km north of the Square.

i Café (☎ 06-353 7899; 39 Broadway Ave; ☻ 9am-11pm Sat-Thu, 24hr Fri) Internet access.

Palmerston North City Portal (www.palmy.net.nz)

Palmerston North Hospital (☎ 06-356 9169; www.midcentraldhb.govt.nz; 50 Ruahine St; ☻ 24hr)

Palmerston North i-SITE (☎ 06-350 1922; www.manawatunz.co.nz; the Square; ☻ 9am-5pm Mon-Fri, 10am-4pm Sat & Sun) For tourist information.

Palmerston North police station (☎ 06-351 3600; www.police.govt.nz; 400 Church St; ☻ 24hr)

Post office (☎ 06-356 9495; www.nzpost.co.nz; cnr Main St & the Square; ☻ 8.30am-5.30pm Mon-Fri, 9am-5.30pm Sat)

Radius Medical, The Palms (☎ 06-354 7737; www.radiusmedical.co.nz; 445 Ferguson St; ☻ 8am-7pm Mon-Fri, 9am-6pm Sat & Sun) Doctors by appointment, with a pharmacy next door.

Student City Palmerston North (www.studentcity.co.nz)

Sights & Activities
Taking the English village-green concept to a whole new level, the **Square** is Palmy's heart and soul. Seventeen spacey acres, with a clock tower, duck pond, Maori carvings, statues and trees of all seasonal dispositions.

Locals eat lunch on the manicured lawns in the sunshine.

Te Manawa (☎ 06-355 5000; www.temanawa.co.nz; 326 Main St; museum & gallery admission free, science centre adult/child/family $8/5/20; ☻ 10am-5pm) has merged a museum, art gallery and science centre into one complex. Vast collections (around 55,000 items) join the dots between 'life, art and mind'. The museum has a strong Maori focus, while the gallery's exhibits change frequently. Kids will get a kick out of the hands-on exhibits at the science centre. The New Zealand Rugby Museum will be relocating here as part of a wholesale redevelopment.

Rugby fans holler about the **New Zealand Rugby Museum** (☎ 06-358 6947; www.rugbymuseum.co.nz; 87 Cuba St; admission adult/child $5/2; ☻ 10am-4pm Mon-Sat, 1.30-4pm Sun). This amazing room overflows with rugby paraphernalia, from a 1905 All Blacks jumper to the actual whistle used to start the first game of every Rugby World Cup. After a humiliating exit from the 2007 World Cup in France, NZ is hosting the 2011 event – time to brush up on your *haka*. The museum is planning to relocate to Te Manawa (above) in time for 2011 – look for it there if it's not on Cuba St.

Victoria Esplanade (☻ 8am-6pm Apr-Sep, to 9pm Oct-Mar) is a riverbank park. Mooch around the adventure playground, aviary, conservatory, bike trails, walkways, the **Esplanade Scenic Railway** (☎ 06-357 3049; www.esplanaderail.org.nz; per ride $2; ☻ 1-4pm Sat & Sun) or just chill out on the lawns. The **Dugald MacKenzie Rose Garden**, once voted among the world's top five loveliest gardens, brings tears of pride to local eyes, and there's a permanent **orienteering course** (☎ 06-357 5288; www.rk.orienteering.org.nz; maps $2) here too. Pick up a map from the park cafe or i-SITE.

When the summer plains bake, dive into the **Lido Aquatic Centre** (☎ 06-357 2684; www.lidoaquaticcentre.co.nz; 50 Park Rd; adult/child $3.50/2.50, hydroslide $5; ☻ 6am-8pm Mon-Thu, to 9pm Fri, 8am-8pm Sat & Sun). It's a long way from Lido Beach in Venice, but it has a 50m pool, waterslides, cafe and gym.

Palmy is, as the locals say, 'flat as'. Grab the free *City Heritage Trail* and *City Walkways* booklets from the i-SITE, detailing local pathways. Hire a bike from Crank It Cycles (p286).

Tours
Feilding Saleyard Tours (☎ 06-323 3318; www.feilding.co.nz; 10 Manchester Sq, Feilding; tours $5; ☻ tours 11am Fri) Local farmers instruct you in the gentle art of

selling livestock at this small town north of the city centre.
Farmers market from 9am to 2pm every Friday.

Manawatu Gorge Experience Jet (☎ 0800 945 335,
06-342 5599; www.manawatugorgejet.com; 25min tours
per person $65) Manawatu Gorge jetboat tours, departing
Woodville Ferry Domain on SH3.

Manawatu Wind Farm & Gorge Tour (☎ 0800 626
292, 06-350 1922; www.manawatunz.co.nz; 3hr tours

per person $55; ☿ tours 2pm Mon-Fri) Visits Te Apiti
Windfarm and Manawatu Gorge; bookings/departures at
the i-SITE.

Festivals & Events
Festival of Cultures (☎ 0212 715 862; www.foc.
co.nz) Multicultural food, crafts, dance and music in late
March.

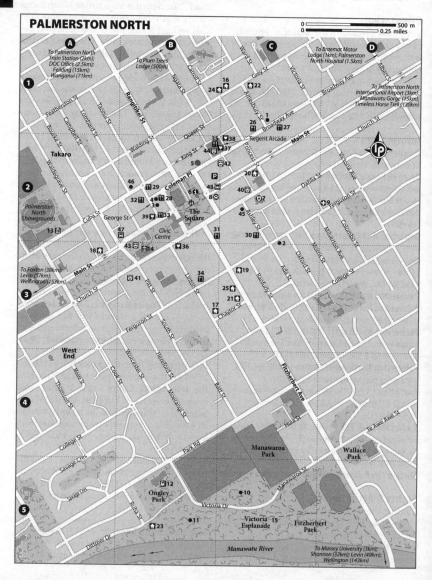

PALMERSTON NORTH

Manawatu Jazz & Blues Festival (☎ 0800 484 253, 06-357 9740; www.manawatunz.co.nz) All things jazzy, bluesy and swingin' in early June, including workshops.

Manawatu Wine & Food Festival (☎ 0800 484 253, 06-357 9740; www.mwff.co.nz) Mid-June weekend fiesta of culinary creations and the best local drops.

Sleeping

BUDGET

Peppertree Backpackers (☎ 06-355 4054; peppertree hostel@clear.net.nz; 121 Grey St; dm/s/d $26/48/62; 🖳) Inexplicably strewn with green-painted boots, this enduring and endearing hostel is the best budget option in town. Mattresses are thick, the kitchen will never run out of spatulas, and the piano and wood fire make things feel downright homey. Doubles off the kitchen are a bit noisy – angle for one at the back.

Grandma's Place (☎ 06-358 6928; www.grandmas -place.com; 146 Grey St; dm/s/d $26/49/66) Ignore the ter- rifying spectre of Grandma on the sign out the front – inside are tidy, old-fashioned rooms with floral wallpaper and macramé rugs. There are plenty of beds and a functional kitchen.

Palmerston North Holiday Park (☎ 06-358 0349; www.holidayparks.co.nz; 133 Dittmer Dr; unpowered & pow- ered sites $30, cabins & units $35-75) About 2km from the Square, off Ruha St, this shady park has a wheezy boot-camp feel to it, but it's quiet and right beside Victoria Esplanade.

Café de Paris Inn (☎ 06-355 2130; www.cafedeparisinn. co.nz; 267 Main St; s/d $60/80) It ain't Montmartre, but this friendly, old-fashioned boozer three minutes' walk from the Square has surprisingly decent pub accommodation upstairs, all rooms with TV and en suite. Parking is limited.

Empire Hotel (☎ 06-357 8002; www.empirehotel.co.nz; cnr Princess & Main Sts; s/d/f $80/90/140) With slicker- than-average, colonial-style pub rooms up- stairs, the Empire is a solid central option. Beyond a tandem bizarrely suspended in the stairwell, rooms have TV and fridge. The pub downstairs gets raucous – steer for a room far from the beer cheer.

Ann Keith's B&B Hotel (☎ 06-358 6928; www.back packersnbnb.co.nz; 123 Grey St; s/d/tw/f from $80/100/110/140) This B&B has five rooms in an old-fangled house, with TV, tea- and coffee-making fa- cilities and electric blankets for cold Palmy nights. Run by the same folks as Grandma's Place; expect similar servings of chintz plus a generous breakfast.

MIDRANGE & TOP END

Fitzherbert Castle Motel (☎ 0800 115 262, 06-358 3888; www.fitzherbertcastle.co.nz; 124 Fitzherbert Ave; d $110-125; 🛜) It looks unapologetically like a Tudor castle from outside, but inside it's more like an intimate hotel. Fourteen immaculate rooms with cork-tiled bathroom floors and quality carpets, plenty of trees, friendly staff and small kitchens in some units. Free wi-fi is available.

Rose City Motel (☎ 06-356 5388; www.rosecitymotel. co.nz; 120 Fitzherbert Ave; units $125-145; 🛜) One for the postmodern aesthetes, Rose City's townhouse- style units are spacey (especially the split-level ones) and shipshape but stylistically rather '80s. Free DVDs, a squash court and a kids' play area are bonuses.

our pick **Plum Trees Lodge** (☎ 06-358 7813; www. plumtreeslodge.co.nz; 97 Russell St; d $135-185; 🖳) In a flat-grid town with more motels than seems plausible, this place comes as sweet relief. Down a leafy driveway on a quiet street, ascend past leadlighting to a secluded lodge. Brilliantly designed using recycled native timbers from demolition sites around Palmerston North, the raked timber ceiling is punctuated with skylights, with the balcony set among swaying boughs. Romantic nights beneath a mosquito net slide lazily into breakfast – a sumptuous hamper of fresh fruit, croissants, jams, eggs, cheese, coffee and juice.

Braemar Motor Lodge (☎ 0800 355 805, 06-355 8053; www.braemarmotorlodge.co.nz; 177 Ruahine St; ste $135-205; 🖵 🛜) It's a bit of a hike into town, but Braemar's studio units have king-size bed, TV, spa, kitchenette, DVD player and stereo, and with 50-plus titles in the DVD library, there should be something up your alley. Units on the street are double-glazed.

Bentleys Motor Inn (☎ 0800 2368 5397, 06-358 7074; www.bentleysmotorinn.co.nz; 67 Linton St; ste $140-300) One of the highest branches on Palmerston North's motel tree, Bentleys' five-star apartments are worth the investment. Inside are new appliances, DVD player, spa, stereo, contemporary furnishings and Sky TV; outside are a full-blown gym, a squash court and a sauna.

Cornwall Motor Lodge (☎ 0800 170 000, 06-354 9010; www.cornwallmotorlodge.co.nz; 101 Fitzherbert Ave; ste $160-240) Cornwall has 27 enormous self-contained apartments on a bleak corner block. But don't let that bother you – rooms have spas, Sky TV, superking-size beds and balconies. Double-glazing culls the Fitzherbert Ave fracas.

Eating

Moxies (☎ 06-355 4238; 67 George St; meals $6-20; 🕑 7am-5pm Mon-Sat, 7.30am-5pm Sun; 🅥) This chipper corner cafe is decked out in primary colours with big windows. Staff members are equally upbeat, the all-day menu is top value (stellar omelettes) and if you've got gluten issues, this is the place for you.

Café Cuba (☎ 06-356 5750; cnr George & Cuba Sts; meals $7-21; 🕑 7am-midnight) Need a sugar shot? Proceed to Café Cuba – the cakes here are for professional chocoholics only. Supreme coffees and traditional cafe fare (risottos, salads, corn fritters) also draw the crowds. Live music Friday nights.

Indian2nite (☎ 06-353 7400; 22 George St; mains $10-20; 🕑 11.30am-2.30pm Wed-Fri, 5pm-late daily; 🅥) A million miles from Bollywood schmaltz, this upmarket place won't break the bank. Behind George St picture windows, northern Indian curries are served by superpolite waiting staff. Try the *dahl makhani*.

Bella's Café (☎ 06-357 8616; 2 The Square; brunch $10-22, dinner $35; 🕑 7.30am-late Tue-Sat) Romantically candlelit Bella's has been around for a while now, its warm red walls continuing to conjure an inviting atmosphere for a mature crowd. Windows fold open in summer revealing an Italian-Pacific menu – pasta rules at lunchtime, dinners are more agricultural (beef, lamb, chicken and salmon).

Aqaba (☎ 06-357 8922; 186 Broadway Ave; meals $13-20; 🕑 7.30am-late Mon-Fri, 9am-late Sat & Sun) Family-friendly cafe classics (pasta, fish and chips, soups, nachos, steaks and pies) served inside a cavernous former Masonic Hall (no secret handshake required). R&B beats are spun as you dine in the Egyptian interiors.

Stage Door Café (☎ 06-359 2233; 96 King St; mains $16-18; 🕑 7.30am-5pm Mon-Fri, 8am-4pm Sat, 9am-4pm Sun) A low-key affair with mellow tunes, spiky green plants, orange plastic chairs and students on the run from the books. Big on coffee, eggs, curries, salads, wraps, muffins and cakes.

ourpick Halikarnas Café (☎ 06-357 5777; 23 Fitzherbert Ave; mains $18-23; 🕑 11am-late) Angling for an *Ali-Baba-and-the-Forty-Thieves* vibe, with magic carpets, brass hookahs and funky trans-Bosphorus beats, Halikarnas plates up generous Turkish delights, from lamb shish kebabs to felafels and kick-arse Turkish coffee. Takeaway kebabs next door.

Aberdeen Steakhouse & Bar (☎ 06-952 5570; 161 Broadway Ave; mains $26-36; 🕑 11am-3pm Tue-Fri, 5pm-late daily) A plush, cow-coloured space studded with photos of prize bulls. Chew into 'The Buster' prime rib, or 'The Contender' Wagyu – the 'granddaddy of marbled steaks'.

For self-caterers:

Countdown (☎ 06-356 6066; cnr Ferguson & Ashley Sts; 🕑 7am-midnight)

Pak N Save (☎ 06-356 4043; 335 Ferguson St; 🕑 8am-midnight)

Drinking

Fish (☎ 06-359 3474; Regent Arcade; admission free; 🕑 4-11pm Wed, to 1am Thu, to 3am Fri & Sat) A progressive, stylish, Pacifically-hewn cocktail bar, the Fish has got its finger firmly on the Palmy pulse. DJs smooth over the week's problems on Friday and Saturday nights as a sexy, urbane crew sips Manhattans and Tamarillo Mules (yes, they kick).

Brewer's Apprentice (☎ 06-358 8888; 324 Church St; admission free; ☽ 11am-late Mon-Fri, 10am-late Sat & Sun) What was once a grungy student pub is now a slick Monteiths-sponsored bar. Business crowds flock for lunch (lunch $10 to $17, dinner $27 to $29), and 20-somethings fill the beer terrace after dark. Live music Friday and Saturday nights.

Mao Bar (☎ 06-354 8410; 64 George St; admission free; ☽ 7am-late) Cool cafe by day, full-scale cocktail bar by night, serving East-meets-West fusion food (lunch $10 to $20, dinner $18 to $32). The interior is aptly bamboo-strewn, with tall screens, red lanterns and dark timbers.

Celtic Inn (☎ 06-357 5571; Regent Arcade; admission free; ☽ 11am-3am Mon-Sat, 4pm-11am Sun) The Celtic expertly offsets the Fish nearby with good old-fashioned pub stuff, labourers, travellers and students bending elbows with a few tasty pints of the black stuff. Friendly staff, live music, red velvet chairs, kids darting around parents' legs – it's all here.

Entertainment

Downtown Cinemas (☎ 06-355 56; www.dtcinemas.co.nz; Downtown Shopping Arcade, Broadway Ave; tickets adult/child $13.50/8.50, Tue all tickets $8.50; ☽ 10am-midnight) The capacious Downtown Cinemas megaplex shows mainstream new-release flicks.

CinemaGold (☎ 06-353 1902; www.cinemagold.co.nz; Downtown Shopping Arcade, Broadway Ave; tickets adult/child $16/11; ☽ 10am-midnight) In the same complex as the Downtown Cinemas, CinemaGold has plush seats and a booze licence to enhance art-house classics and limited-release screenings.

There's a simmering theatre scene in Palmy. Check out what's playing at the following:

Abbey Theatre (☎ 06-355 4165; www.abbeymusical theatre.co.nz; 369 Church St) Quality amateur productions, with a penchant for cheesy musicals.

Centrepoint Theatre (☎ 06-354 5740; www.centre point.co.nz; 280 Church St) Bigger-name professional shows, theatre sports and seasonal plays.

Globe Theatre (☎ 06-351 4409; www.globetheatre. co.nz; cnr Pitt & Main Sts) Large community theatre; home to the Manawatu Theatre Society.

Regent Theatre (☎ 06-350 2100; www.regent. co.nz; 63 Broadway Ave) Divinely detailed theatre hosting big-ticket international acts like the Russian Ballet and the Platters.

Getting There & Away
AIR
Palmerston North International Airport (PMR; ☎ 06-351 4415; www.pnairport.co.nz; Airport Dr) is 4km north of the town centre. **Air New Zealand** (☎ 06-351 8800; www.airnewzealand.co.nz; 382 Church St; ☽ 9am-5pm Mon-Fri) runs daily direct flights to Auckland, Christchurch and Wellington.

Sunair Aviation Ltd (☎ 07-575 7799; www.sun air.co.nz) offers direct flights to Gisborne, Hamilton, Napier, Rotorua, Tauranga and Whakatane.

BUS
InterCity (☎ 09-583 5780; www.intercity.co.nz) buses operate from the **Palmerston North Travel Centre** (☎ 06-355 4955; cnr Main & Pitt Sts; ☽ 8.45am-5pm Mon-Thu, to 7.30pm Fri, to 3.30pm Sat, to 7pm Sun). Destinations include the following:

Destination	Price	Duration	Frequency
Auckland	$81	9hr	2 daily
Napier	$29	2¾hr	2-3 daily
Taupo	$32	4¼hr	3 daily
Wellington	$31	2¼hr	6 daily
Whanganui	$19	1½hr	3 daily

Naked Bus (☎ 0900 625 33; www.nakedbus.co.nz) services also depart the Travel Centre, servicing North Island centres including these:

Destination	Price	Duration	Frequency
Auckland	$36	10¼hr	2-3 daily
Napier	$19	2½hr	1 daily
Taupo	$23	3½hr	1 daily
Wellington	$12	2¼hr	2-3 daily
Whanganui	$11	1¼hr	1 daily

White Star (☎ 0800 465 622, 06-349 0508 www.whitestar bus.co.nz) services also depart the Travel Centre, running two buses each Thursday and Friday and one every other day to/from Wellington ($25, 2¼ hour) and New Plymouth ($30, 4¼ hours) via Whanganui ($20, one hour).

TRAIN
Tranz Scenic (☎ 0800 872 467, 04-495 0775; www. tranzscenic.co.nz) runs long-distance trains between Wellington and Auckland, stopping at the retro-derelict **Palmerston North Train Station** (Mathews Ave), off Tremaine Ave about 2.5km north of the Square. From Palmy to Wellington, take the *Overlander* ($53, 2½ hours, one daily) departing at 5pm (Friday, Saturday and Sunday only May to November); or the *Capital Connection* ($24, two hours, one daily Monday to Friday) departing Palmy at 6.20am. Buy tickets from Tranz Scenic directly (no ticket sales at the station).

Getting Around

TO/FROM THE AIRPORT

There's no public transport between the city and airport, but taxis abound or **Super Shuttle** (☎ 0800 748 885; www.supershuttle.co.nz) can whiz you into town in a minivan ($13; bookings required).

If you're driving into the CBD from the airport, take Ruahine St then turn right onto Main St. If you're heading through to Wellington, Main St becomes SH56 and continues to Wellington via Foxton, or turn left at the Square into Fitzherbert Ave, which leads to SH57 for Wellington via Shannon. It's a two- to three-hour drive either way.

BICYCLE

Crank It Cycles (☎ 06-358 9810; www.crankitcycles.co.nz; 203 Cuba St; ☽ 8am-6pm Mon-Fri, 9am-3pm Sat) hires out mountain bikes from $40 per day, including helmet and lock.

BUS

Tranzit City Link (☎ 0508 800 800, 06-952 2800; www.horizons.govt.nz; ticket $2) runs daytime buses departing from the Main St bus stop on the east side of the Square. Bus 12 goes to Massey University; none go to the airport.

CAR

The following companies have airport offices:
Avis (☎ 06-357 0168, 06-358 7528; www.avis.co.nz)
Budget (☎ 06-356 8565, 06-345 5122; www.budget.co.nz)
Europcar (☎ 06-353 0001; www.europcar.co.nz)
Hertz (☎ 06-357 0921, 06-348 7624; www.hertz.co.nz)
Thrifty (☎ 06-355 4365; www.thrifty.co.nz)

TAXI

A city-to-airport taxi costs around $15.
Gold & Black Taxis (☎ 06-351 2345)
Manawatu Taxis (☎ 06-355 5111)
Taxis Palmerston North (☎ 06-355 5333)

AROUND PALMERSTON NORTH

Just south of 'Student City' in the underrated Horowhenua district, **Shannon** (population 1510) and **Foxton** (population 2000) are sedentary country towns en route to Wellington.

Our fine feathered friends at **Owlcatraz** (Map p269; ☎ 06-362 7872; www.owlcatraz.co.nz; SH57, Shannon; adult/child incl tour $20/7; ☽ 9am-5pm) have obligingly adopted oh-so-droll names like Owlvis Presley and Owl Capone. It's a 30-minute drive south from Palmerston North.

Foxton Beach is one of a string of broad, shallow Tasman Sea beaches along this stretch of coast – brown sand, driftwood and holiday houses proliferate. Other worthy beaches include Himatangi, Hokio and Waikawa.

The town of **Levin** is more sizeable (population 19,550), but suffers from being too close to both Wellington and Palmerston North to warrant the through-traffic making a stop.

Manawatu Gorge & Around

About 15km northeast of Palmerston North, SH2 dips into **Manawatu Gorge** (Map p269). Maori named the gorge Te Apiti (the Narrow Passage), believing the big reddish rock near the centre of the gorge was its guardian spirit. The rock's colour is said to change intensity when a prominent Rangitane tribe member dies or sheds blood. It takes around four hours to walk through the gorge from either end, or you can see it via jetboat (see p282).

On the southwestern edge of the gorge, about 40 minutes drive from Palmerston North, is the **Tararua Wind Farm** (Map p269; ☎ 07-574 4754; www.trustpower.co.nz; Hall Block Rd), allegedly the largest wind farm in the southern hemisphere. From Hall Block Rd there are awesome views of the turbines. Spinning similarly, north of the gorge is **Te Apiti Wind Farm** (Map p269; ☎ 0800 946 463; www.meridianenergy.co.nz; Saddle Rd, Ashhurst). Ask the i-SITE for directions, or take a tour (p282).

Alternatively, flee the city with a visit to **Timeless Horse Treks** (☎ 06-376 6157; www.timelesshorsetreks.co.nz; Gorge Rd, Ballance; 1/2hr rides $35/60). Gentle trail rides take in the Manawatu River and surrounding hills, or saddle up for an overnight all-inclusive trek, taking in the Tararua Wind Farm ($175). Palmerston North pick-up/drop-off costs $40 per person.

Taupo & the Central Plateau

Don't think for a minute that this plateau is some boring old 'elevated flat landmass' as per the dictionary definition. For a start, it ain't flat. In the middle of the plateau, at the heart of Tongariro National Park, are three massive peaks: Tongariro, Ruapehu and Ngauruhoe. Then there's New Zealand's largest lake, Taupo: a vast, water-filled crater – the legacy of a volcanic blast that shook up the world and shattered the island more than 26,500 years ago. This is all part of the Taupo Volcanic Zone, a line of geothermal surfacings that stretches to Whakaari/White Island via Rotorua; and the area is still active, with Mt Ruapehu often having a hissy fit, the last blast occurring in 2007.

And the drama doesn't stop there, for this area now rivals Rotorua for back-to-nature activities and daredevil escapades. Perhaps you fancy fly-fishing in the world-class Tongariro River, hooning up to Huka Falls in a jetboat, or bouncing on a bungy over the Waikato River? Or this could be your chance to skydive. If rambling's your thing, there's always Tongariro Northern Circuit, one of NZ's most achievable Great Walks, or the Tongariro Alpine Crossing, touted as one of the world's top one-dayers. Then again, you could wait until winter, when the mountains are dusted with snow: there's top skiing at Turoa and Whakapapa ski fields.

From river deep to mountain high, and out on the luscious lake, New Zealand's diverse geology takes centre stage here and my-oh-my does it get its shimmy on.

HIGHLIGHTS

- Exploring a fascinating volcanic terrain while tramping the **Tongariro Alpine Crossing** (p308)
- Hurtling to earth from 15,000ft at 200km/h strapped to a complete stranger in the world's skydiving capital, **Taupo** (p291)
- Carving fresh powder at **Turoa Ski Area** or **Whakapapa Ski Area** (p309)
- Biking till your bum burns on the **42 Traverse** (p311)
- Paddling **Lake Taupo** (p292) to check out the modern Maori carvings
- Rediscovering the 'lost valley' of **Orakei Korako** (p300)
- Rocketing up the Waikato River to the base of **Huka Falls** (p298) in a jetboat
- Plunging 47m over the **Waikato River** (p292) on the end of a rubber band

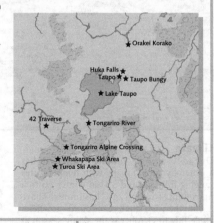

■ Telephone code: 07   ■ www.laketauponz.com   ■ www.visitruapehu.com

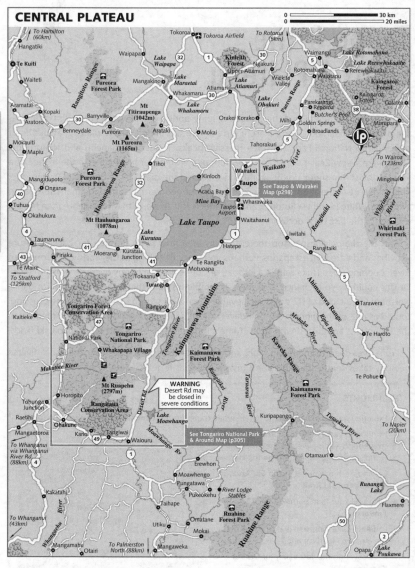

Climate

Due to its altitude, the Central Plateau has a generally cool climate, with temperatures ranging from around 3°C in winter up to a maximum of around 24°C in summer. Above 2500m there is a small year-round snowfield, while July to October is the skiing season at Whakapapa and Turoa, and in some places snow can linger on into spring. On the mountains, storms and freezing temperatures can occur at any time.

Getting There & Around

Air New Zealand (www.airnz.co.nz) has regular flights from Taupo to Auckland and Wellington. The **Tranz Scenic Overlander** (www.tranzscenic.co.nz)

train on the Auckland–Wellington line stops at National Park village, Ohakune and Taihape.

InterCity (www.intercity.co.nz) buses travel to all of the region's major towns, connecting with most major destinations around NZ, while **Naked Bus** (www.nakedbus.com) is useful for Taupo and Turangi. However, there are no direct public buses between the State Hwy 1 (SH1) towns (Taupo and Turangi) and the State Hwy 4 (SH4) towns (National Park and Ohakune). Private shuttle-bus services operate around Tongariro National Park, some picking up from Taupo and Turangi.

LAKE TAUPO REGION

NZ's largest lake, Lake Taupo, sits in the caldera of a volcano that began erupting about 300,000 years ago. The caldera was formed by a collapse during the Oruanui eruption about 26,500 years ago, which threw out 750 cu km of ash and pumice, making Krakatoa (8 cu km) look like a pimple. The surrounding area is still volcanically active and, like Rotorua, has fascinating thermal areas.

Today the 606-sq-km lake and its surrounding waterways are serene enough to attract fishing enthusiasts from all around the world. Well positioned by the lake, both Taupo and Turangi are popular tourist centres. Taupo, in particular, has plenty of activities and facilities to cater for families and independent travellers alike.

TAUPO
pop 21,040

The increasingly exciting town of Taupo now rivals Rotorua as the North Island's adrenaline capital, with an abundance of blood-pumping activities. With a postcard-perfect setting on the northeastern shores of the lake, it boasts shimmering views of the snowy peaks of Tongariro National Park. NZ's longest river, the Waikato, originates from Lake Taupo at the township, before crashing its way through the Huka Falls and Aratiatia Rapids and then settling down for a sedate ramble to the west coast, just south of Auckland.

SH1 passes through the middle of Taupo, making the town easily accessible for travellers and packed with transient traffic for much of the high season.

TAUPO & THE CENTRAL PLATEAU FACTS

Eat Trout, preferably smoked. But you'll have to catch it first!
Drink A mouthful of water from the Waikato River as you bungy over it (p292)
Read *Awesome Forces* by Hamish Campbell and Geoff Hicks – the geological story of NZ in explosive detail
Listen to *Ka mate* – the famous haka, written on the shores of Lake Rotoaira
Watch *The Return of the King,* starring Ngauruhoe (p307) as Mt Doom
Swim at Lake Taupo – truly invigorating
Festival Ohakune's Carrot Festival, celebrating all that is orange and pointy (p316)
Tackiest tourist attraction Shawn the Prawn at Huka Prawn Farm (p299)
Go green Explore Tongariro National Park's alpine flora and geological oddities

History

When Maori chief Tamatea-arikinui first visited this area, his footsteps reverberated – making him think the ground was hollow; he therefore dubbed the area Tapuaeharuru (Resounding Footsteps). The modern name, however, originates from the story of Tia. After Tia discovered the lake and slept beside it draped in his cloak, the area became known as Taupo Nui a Tia (The Great Cloak of Tia).

Europeans settled here in force during the East Coast Land War (1868–72), when it was a strategic military base: Colonel JM Roberts built a redoubt in 1869, and a garrison of mounted police remained until the defeat of Te Kooti (see p368) later that year.

In the 20th century the mass ownership of the motorcar saw Taupo grow from a lakeside village of about 750 people to a large resort town, easily accessible from most points of the North Island. Today the population still grows considerably at peak holiday times, when New Zealanders and international visitors alike flock to the lakeshore.

Information

Automobile Association (AA; Map p290; ☎ 07-378 6000; 3 Tamamutu St)
Cybershed (Map p290; 115 Tongariro St; ◷ 9am-10pm) Offers IT services and internet access and sells British treats to the homesick.

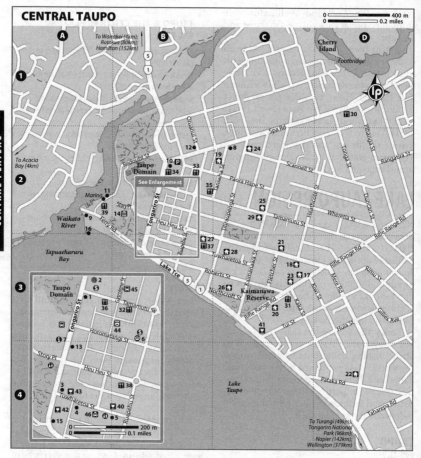

CENTRAL TAUPO

INFORMATION	
Automobile Association	**1** A3
Cybershed	**2** A3
Experience Taupo	**3** A4
Global Gossip	**4** A4
Outdoor Attitude	**5** B4
Post Office	**6** B3
Taupo i-SITE	**7** A3

SIGHTS & ACTIVITIES	
Canoe & Kayak	**8** C2
Chris Jolly Outdoors	**9** A2
Cruise Cat	(see 11)
Greenstone Fishing	**10** B2
Launch Office	**11** A2
Life Cycles	**12** B2
Pointons Ski Shop	**13** A4
Taupo Museum & Art Gallery	**14** B2
Taupo Rod & Tackle	**15** A4
Taupo's Floatplane	**16** A2

SLEEPING	
Beechtree	**17** C3
Bella Vista	**18** C3
Blackcurrent Backpackers	**19** C2
Catelli's of Taupo	**20** C3
Dunrovin Motel	**21** C3
Lake	**22** D4
Lynwood Lodge	**23** C3
Rainbow Lodge	**24** C2
Silver Fern Lodge	**25** C2
Suncourt	**26** C3
Taupo Urban Retreat	**27** B3
Tiki Lodge	**28** C3
YHA Taupo Action Downunder	**29** C2

EATING	
Beaut Bakery	**30** D1
Brantry	**31** C3
Eruption	**32** B3
Fine Fettle	**33** B2
Lotus Thai	**34** B2

Pak N Save	**35** B2
Pimentos	**36** A3
Plateau	**37** B3
Replete	**38** B4
Stir Taupo	**39** A2

DRINKING	
Bond	**40** B4
Finn MacCuhal's	(see 3)
Jolly Good Fellows	**41** C3
Mulligans	**42** A4
Shed	**43** A4

ENTERTAINMENT	
Great Lake Centre	(see 7)
Starlight Cinema Centre	**44** B3

TRANSPORT	
InterCity/Newmans	(see 45)
Taupo Travel Centre	**45** B3
Top Cabs	**46** A4

Experience Taupo (Map p290; ☎ 07-377 0704; www.
experiencetaupo.com; 29 Tongariro St) Books most local
traveller services and has internet access.
Global Gossip (Map p290; 11 Tuwharetoa St) Internet
access.
Post office (46 Horomatangi St) Offers poste restante
service.
Taupo i-SITE (Map p290; ☎ 07-376 0027; www.
laketauponz.com; Tongariro St; ☼ 8.30am-5pm) Handles
bookings for accommodation, transport and activities; has
a free town map as well as Department of Conservation
(DOC) maps and information.

Sights

Taupo's main attraction is the lake and all the
things you can do in, on and around it. The
water is famously chilly, but in several places
(such as **Hot Water Beach**, Map p298, immediately south of the centre) there are thermal
springs just below the surface. You can swim
right at the township, but **Acacia Bay** (Map
p288), 5km west, is a particularly pleasant spot.

The **Taupo Museum & Art Gallery** (Map p290;
☎ 07-376 0414; www.taupomuseum.co.nz; Story Pl;
adult/child $5/free; ☼ 10am-4.30pm) has historical
displays covering the local forestry, nautical and trout-fishing industries, a mock-up
of a 19th-century shop and a moa skeleton.
There are regular visiting art exhibitions, too.
The centrepiece of the collection is a Maori
meeting house, Te Aroha o Rongoheikume,
adorned with elaborate carvings. Situated in
a courtyard, the Ora Garden of Wellbeing is
a re-creation of NZ's gold-medal-winning
entry into the 2004 Chelsea Flower Show.
It's quite small, but features more than 1000
native plants and a steamy lizard scene.

There are 10m-high **Maori carvings**, accessible only by boat, at the lake's Mine Bay
(Map p288; see Fishing & Cruising, p292,
and Water Sports, p292, for boat-charter
operators). They were carved by master
carver Matahi Whakataka-Brightwell in
the late 1970s, and depict Ngatoro-i-rangi,
the visionary Maori navigator who guided
the Tuwharetoa and Te Arawa tribes to the
Taupo area over a thousand years ago. There
are also two smaller Matahi figures here, both
of Celtic design, which depict the south wind
and a mermaid.

Activities

Adrenaline addicts should look out for special deals that combine several activities for a
reduced price.

SKYDIVING

More than 30,000 jumps a year are made from
Taupo, which makes it the skydiving capital
of the world. It's certainly a terrific spot to
do it: all those beautiful places you see from
ground level are patchworked together in a
brilliant blanket of natural colour, the highlights of which are the deep blue lake and the
brilliant white of the snowcapped peaks. The
following operators sit alongside each other
at the airport and offer some of the best rates
in NZ. They offer similar packages, which
can include town pick-ups, video, photos and
T-shirts.
Skydive Taupo (☎ 0800 586 766; www.skydivetaupo.
co.nz; 12,000ft/15,000ft $250/340)
Taupo Tandem Skydiving (☎ 07-377 0428; www.tts.
net.nz; 12,000ft/15,000ft $249/339)

MAORI NZ: CENTRAL PLATEAU

The North Island's central region is home to a group of mountains that feature in several Maori
legends of lust and betrayal, which end with a few mountains fleeing to other parts of the island
(see Mt Taranaki's sad tale, p261).

Long after all that action was over, the chief Ngatoro-i-rangi (see the boxed text, p307), fresh
off the boat from Hawaiki, explored this region and named the mountains that remained. The
most sacred was Tongariro, consisting of at least 12 volcanic cones, seen as the leader of all
the other mountains.

The major *iwi* (tribe) of the region is **Tuwharetoa** (www.tuwharetoa.co.nz), one of the few *iwi* in
NZ that has retained an undisputed *ariki* (high chief). The current *ariki* is Tumu Te Heuheu Tukino
VIII, whose great-great-grandfather, Te Heuheu Tukino IV (a descendent of Ngatoro-i-rangi), gifted
the mountains of Tongariro to NZ in 1887.

To discover the stories of local Maori and their ancestors, visit the meeting house at Taupo
Museum (above), the carved cliff faces at Mine Bay (above), Wairakei Terraces (p299), or take a
Nature-Culture Walk with pureORAwalks (p294).

BUNGY JUMPING

The picturesque **Taupo Bungy** (Map p298; ☎ 07-377 1135; www.taupobungy.co.nz; jump $109; ☽ 8.30am-5pm) site is the most popular on the North Island. It sits on a cliff edge over the mighty Waikato River, with plenty of vantage points if you're too chicken to jump. Nonchickens will be led onto a platform jutting 20m out over a cliff (the world's first cantilever jump, for engineering boffins) and convinced, with masterly skill, to throw themselves off the edge. A heart-stopping 47m hurtle and a few bounces back and it's safely into the boat. You can also opt for a slight dunk in the river, or strap yourself to a friend and leap off together. Alternatively, try the giant swing.

FISHING & CRUISING

Anglers are in the right place because this region is justifiably world famous for trout. Fly-fishing is the only fishing permitted on all rivers flowing into the lake and within a 300m radius of the river mouths. Spin fishing is allowed only on the Waikato River (flowing *out* of the lake) and, on the other side of the lake, on the Tokaanu tailrace, flowing into the lake from the Tokaanu Power Station. A licence is required for lake and river fishing. Make sure you always carry it with you, as there are hefty fines for violations. Licences cost $16/36/85 per day/week/season and are available from the places listed below, as well as via the i-SITE (p289).

There are numerous fishing guides around Taupo and Turangi (see p301); most are happy to negotiate a price depending on the trip ($250 for a half-day is a rough ballpark, and will include equipment and licence).

You can arrange guided trips or get gear and licences for independent trips at **Greenstone Fishing** (Map p290; ☎ 07-378 3714; www.greenstonefishing.co.nz; 147 Tongariro St; gear hire from $10; ☽ 8.30am-5.30pm Mon-Fri, to 4.30pm Sat & Sun) and **Taupo Rod & Tackle** (Map p290; ☎ 07-378 5337; www.tauporodandtackle.co.nz; 7 Tongariro St; gear hire $15-45; ☽ 8.30am-6pm Mon-Sat, 9.30am-5pm Sun).

There are plenty of boat-charter operators offering both lake fishing trips and cruises. Most will take you to the see the Maori carvings at Mine Bay (p291) and take between one and 2½ hours. The 1926 50ft yacht **Barbary** (☎ 07-378 3444; adult/child $40/10; ☽ 10.30am, 2pm & 5pm) is a popular option. For something with a little more zip on calm days, take the **Cruise Cat** (Map p290; ☎ 07-378 0623; www.chrisjolly.co.nz; adult/child $40/16; ☽ 10.30am & 1.30pm), a large, modern launch. Sunday brunch trips ($58) are especially worthwhile.

The best place to book trips – whether fishing or cruising – is through the **launch office** (Lake Taupo Charter Office; Map p290; ☎ 07-378 3444; www.fishcruisetaupo.co.nz; Marina; ☽ 9am-5pm Dec-Mar, 9.30am-3pm Apr-Nov), which books for around 20 boats, catering to individuals or groups.

SWIMMING & BATHING

The **AC Baths** (Map p298; ☎ 07-376 0350; www.taupovenues.co.nz; AC Baths Ave; adult/child $6.50/2.50, slides $4; ☽ 6am-9pm) at the Taupo Events Centre, about 2km east of town, has a big, heated pool with a waterslide, an indoor kids pool, private mineral pools and a sauna. There's also a **climbing wall** (adult/child $13/9; ☽ hours vary).

Twenty minutes' walk from town you'll find the Huka Falls Walkway **hot springs** (Map p298), a pleasant and well-worn spot under a bridge, where you can take a dip for free in natural surrounds.

Taupo Hot Springs Spa (Map p298; ☎ 07-377 6502; www.taupohotsprings.com; SH5; adult/child $15/4; ☽ 8.30am-9.30pm) has a variety of mineral-rich indoor and outdoor thermal pools, freshwater pools and a giant dragon waterslide for the young ones. Adults can enjoy a wide choice of treatments, such as massage and body scrubs. There's a health-food cafe on-site as well as picnic and barbecue facilities.

WATER SPORTS

With the big lake in the middle and the Waikato and Tongariro Rivers at either end (plus the wild Rangitaiki and Wairoa Rivers not far away), there's plenty of opportunity to get wet and wild around Taupo. Kayaking is popular on the lake and rivers, and there are raft trips available on both white-water rapids and gentle river sections. Locals offer rentals and tuition, so there's absolutely no excuse to not get your boat afloat.

Big Sky Parasail (☎ 0800 724 475; www.bigskyparasail.co.nz; Lake Tce; ☽ 8am-6pm summer only) Runs lake parasailing (400ft/800ft $75/85) from the lakefront.

Canoe & Kayak (Map p290; ☎ 07-378 1003; www.canoeandkayak.co.nz; 77 Spa Rd; ☽ 9am-5pm Mon-Sat) Instruction and boat hire (from the lake's edge in high summer), as well as guided tours: two-hour trip on the Waikato River ($45) or a half-day to the Maori carvings ($90).

Chris Jolly Outdoors (Map p290; ☎ 07-378 5596; www.chrisjolly.co.nz; Marina; ☽ 9am-5.30pm) Can sort out all sorts of water sports, including kayak hire (single/double per hour $20/30) and self-drive boats ($70 to $85 per hour). Also organises helicopter tours and books other activities.

Kiwi River Safaris (☎ 07-377 6597; www.krs.co.nz) Two-hour white-water rafting trips on the Rangitaiki ($110), Wairoa ($115) and Tongariro Rivers ($110), including free pick-up from Taupo and lunch. Also runs kayak tours down the Waikato River (adult/child $45/25).

Rapid Sensations/Kayaking Kiwi (Map p298; ☎ 07-378 7902; www.rapids.co.nz, www.kayakingkiwi.com; 413 Huka Falls Rd) Kayak trips to the Maori carvings (4½ hours, $108) and a gentle paddle along the Waikato (two hours, $45). Also runs six-hour white-water rafting trips on the Tongariro River ($135) and shorter trips along a calmer section (2½ hours, $115).

Sailing Centre (Map p298; ☎ 0274 967 350; www.sailingcentre.co.nz; Lake Tce; ☺ 8.30am-8.30pm) Hires out kayaks ($25), canoes ($35), windsurfers ($35), catamarans ($65) and sailboats ($60) in summer. Rates are per hour.

Wilderness Escapes (☎ 07-378 3413; www.wildernessescapes.co.nz) Half-day to multiple-day kayaking trips, including Maori carvings (half-day $85) and a sunset paddle on the lake ($85). Also offers kayak hire ($60 per day). Packages combine kayaking with a helicopter ride, boat cruise or tramp.

CYCLING & MOUNTAIN BIKING

Exploring Taupo on two wheels is fun and easy, with dedicated cycle lanes along Lake Tce and Heu Heu St, and shared paths elsewhere. There are blue bike racks throughout town. Lake Taupo is also the location of two of NZ's biggest annual cycling events: the 160km **Lake Taupo Cycle Challenge** (www.cyclechallenge.org.nz), held on the last Saturday in November, and September's 12-hour **Day-Night Thriller** (www.daynightthriller.co.nz), regularly attracting more than 3000 mountain bikers.

There are good mountain-bike tracks just out of town in the Wairakei and Pureora Forests and along the Waikato River. You can download maps for these from www.biketaupo.org.nz.

Rapid Sensations (above) runs guided three-hour rides in the Wairakei Forest (guided trips $75, bike hire half-/full day $45/55). Rainbow Lodge (p295) and **Life Cycles** (Map p290; ☎ 07-378 6117; 16 Oruanui St; per day $40; ☺ 8.30am-5pm Mon-Fri) also rent bikes. For luxury rough riding, **Heli-Biking** (☎ 07-384 2816; www.kaimanawahelibiking.co.nz; 4hr ride $395) will pick you up in a helicopter and drop you on top of the highest point in the Kaimanawas, allowing you to bike all the way down.

TRAMPING

There are some great walks in and around Taupo, ranging from sedate ambles to more gnarly all-dayers. A good place to start is DOC's leaflet *Lake Taupo – A Guide to Walks and Hikes* ($2.50).

The **Huka Falls Walkway** is an enjoyable, easy walk from Taupo to the falls along the east bank of the Waikato River, crossing a hot stream en route. The falls are about a 1½-hour walk from the centre. To reach the walkway from town, head up Spa Rd, passing the Taupo Bungy site; turn left at County Ave and continue through Spa Thermal Park to the street's end. The path heads off to the left of the end car park, up over a hill and down to the hot springs by the river.

Carrying on from the falls is the **Huka Falls to Aratiatia Rapids Walking Track**. The rapids are 7km away (another two-plus hours). There are good views of the river, Huka Falls and the power station across the river. To just walk this part, drive out to the falls car park and cross the bridge.

Another walk goes to **Mt Tauhara** (Map p298), from the top of which there are magnificent views. Take the Taupo–Napier Hwy (SH5) turn-off, 2km south of Taupo town centre; about 6km along SH5, turn left into Mountain Rd. The start of the track is signposted on the right-hand side. It will take about two hours to the top, walking slowly.

The pleasant **Great Lake Walkway** follows the Taupo lakefront south to Five Mile Bay (8km). It's a flat, easy walk along public-access beaches.

Taupo can also serve as a base from which to walk the Tongariro Alpine Crossing (see p308).

GOLF

Taupo Golf Club (Map p298; ☎ 07-378 6933; www.taupogolf.co.nz; 32 Centennial Dr; 9/18 holes $35/60) Has two good 18-hole courses; one is a park course and the other an inland links.

Wairakei International Golf Course (Map p298; ☎ 07-374 8152; www.wairakeigolfcourse.co.nz; SH1, Wairakei; 18 holes $100-200) 8km north of Taupo; a challenging course set in 150 hectares of beautiful countryside, rated within the top 100 courses worldwide. In late 2009 a 2m-high, 5km-long pest-proof fence was erected, turning the whole course into a native bird sanctuary.

Wairakei Resort (Map p298; ☎ 07-374 8021; www.wairakei.co.nz; SH1, Wairakei; adult/child $12/$8) Nine-hole course set in similarly verdant surroundings 1km up the road from the international course.

HORSE TREKKING

Moehiwa Horse Ventures (Map p298; ☎ 07-378 3727; http://moehiwa.tripod.com; 73 Poihipi Rd; 1-2hr rides $45-80) Treks through pasture, pine forest and riverbeds.

Taupo Horse Treks (Map p298; ☎ 07-378 0356; www.taupohorsetreks.co.nz; Karapiti Rd; per hr $60) Conducts treks through some fine forest with good views over the Craters of the Moon (p299).

SKIING

Taupo is tantalisingly close to the ski fields, being 1¼ hours drive to Whakapapa, and two hours to Turoa (see p309). There's gear hire all around and up the mountain, and also at **Pointons Ski Shop** (Map p290; ☎ 07-377 0087; 57 Tongariro St; ski/snowboard hire $30/40; ☯ 7am-7pm Apr-Sep, 8.30am-5.30pm Mon-Fri, 8.30am-4pm Sat, 10am-3pm Sun Oct-Mar).

OTHER ACTIVITIES

Thrill seekers with petrol-head tendencies should head to the **Taupo Motorsport Park** (off Map p298; ☎ 07-376 5033; www.tauporacetrack.co.nz; Broadlands Rd). This state-of-the-art 3.5km racetrack and drag circuit has staged the A1 Grand Prix. There's often something to watch here, from sidecar races to 'drifters' and, on occasion, the police testing their skills. You can get out on the track in a V8 or Formula Challenge Race Car with **Formula Challenge** (☎ 07-377 0338; www.fcr.co.nz; 1-3 sessions of laps $290-695), or superfast rides with a pro in the driver's seat and driving tuition can be organised through **Track Drive** (☎ 027 288 9037; www.trackdrive.co.nz).

Taupo Quad Adventures (☎ 07-377 6404; www.4x4quads.com; SH1; 1-3hr trips $79-189), 24km north of town opposite the turn-off to Orakei Korako, offers fully guided off-road quad-bike trips.

For a more peaceful activity, **Taupo Gliding Club** (Map p298; ☎ 07-378 5627; www.taupoglidingclub.co.nz; Centennial Dr; flights $120-180) glides daily by appointment (weather permitting) at Centennial Park.

Tours

AERIAL SIGHTSEEING

Air Charter Taupo (☎ 07-378 5467; www.aircharter taupo.co.nz; Taupo Airport; flights $80-250) Scenic flights ranging from 15 minutes to one hour, across Huka Falls, Lake Taupo and Tongariro National Park.

Helipro (☎ 07-377 8805; www.helipro.co.nz; Taupo Airport; flights $95-1695) Specialises in heli-tours, which include alpine and White Island landings, as well as shorter scenic flights over the town, lake and volcanoes (minimum 10 minutes).

Helistar Helicopters (Map p298; ☎ 07-374 8405; www.helistar.co.nz; 415 Huka Falls Rd; flights $99-995) Located about 3km northeast of town, Helistar offers a variety of scenic helicopter flights, from 10 minutes to two hours. Combine a Helistar trip with the Huka Falls Jet in the Huka Star combo (from $193).

Taupo Air Services (☎ 07-378 5325; taupoair@xtra.co.nz; Taupo Airport; flights $90-500) Runs scenic flights, from the 15-minute Local Look to a nearly two-hour trip to White Island.

Taupo's Floatplane (Map p290; ☎ 07-378 7500; www.tauposfloatplane.co.nz; flights $75-590) Located at the entrance to the marina, the floatplane does a variety of trips, including quick flights over the lake and longer ones over Mt Ruapehu or White Island. Packages include the Taupo Trifecta Combo (floatplane trip, followed by a jetboat trip and a walk through Orakei Korako; $385).

OTHER TOURS

Paradise Tours (☎ 07-378 9955; www.paradisetours.co.nz; tours adult/child $99/45) Three-hour tours to the Aratiatia Rapids, Craters of the Moon and Huka Falls. Also offers tours to Tongariro National Park, Orakei Korako, Rotorua, Hawke's Bay and Waitomo Caves.

pureORAwalks (☎ 021-042 2722; www.pureorawalks.com; adult/child $85/62) Four-hour Nature-Culture walks in Pureora Forest Park, Lake Rotopounamu and Whirinaki Forest Park, offering insight into *Maoritanga* (things Maori) – including traditional uses of flora and fauna, local history and legends.

Whirinaki Rainforest Experiences (☎ 07-377 2363; www.rainforest-treks.co.nz) Runs fascinating and educational ecocultural guided walks in the Whirinaki Forest Park (one- to three-day trips $155 to $745). Transport from Taupo, meals and camping necessities are included.

Sleeping

BUDGET

YHA Taupo Action Downunder (Map p290; ☎ 07-378 3311; www.yha.co.nz; 56 Kaimanawa St; campsites/dm/s/tr $16/29/58/97, d $78-88; ☐ 🤝) A good hostel with cosy communal areas and a sun-trap deck with barbecues, a barrel spa pool and an extensive DVD library. The kitchen space is a little limited, but they make up for it with guitar hire.

Taupo DeBretts Spa Resort (Map p298; ☎ 07-378 8559; www.taupodebretts.com; SH5; campsites per adult/child $20/10, cabins $60-115, units $130-190; ☐ 🤝 🐾) More of an upmarket holiday park than a flashy resort, DeBretts offers everything from tent sites to motel-style units, and has kid-friendly features such as a playground and trampoline in well-tended grounds. It's a five-minute drive from downtown, but is well worth the hop for its peaceful location and the indulgent Taupo Hot Springs that shares its home (see p292). At the time of research the neighbouring Terraces Hotel (1889) was being converted into a Hilton, complete with upmarket restaurants.

our pick Blackcurrant Backpackers (Map p290; ☎ 07-378 9292; www.blackcurrentbp.co.nz; 20 Taniwha St; dm $22-25, s/d/tr $50/70/84) Still with that new-paint-and-carpet smell when we visited, this ageing motel has been fitted out with flash en suites and supercomfy beds. The staff rivals the cartoon blackcurrants in the Ribena ads for chirpiness.

Rainbow Lodge (Map p290; ☎ 07-378 5754; www.rainbowlodge.co.nz; 99 Titiraupenga St; dm $23-26, s $45-55, d $52-64, tr/q $78/104; 🖳 🛜) A solid, sociable hostel offering clean rooms, including some with en suite. Bonuses include bike ($20 per day) and fishing-tackle hire, free coffee and a sauna.

Taupo Urban Retreat (Map p290; ☎ 07-378 6124; www.tur.co.nz; 65 Heu Heu St; dm $23-27, d $68; 🖳 🛜) A purpose-built hostel with a publike hub, enjoyed by a younger crowd who fit right in with its carefree style. It's refreshingly modern in design, with a beach-house feel, although it's a busy road on your doorstep instead of the ocean.

Lake Taupo Top 10 Holiday Resort (Map p298; ☎ 07-378 6860; www.taupotop10.co.nz; 28 Centennial Dr; campsites per adult/child $23/13, cabins $99-128, units $149-365; 🖳 🛜 🐾) The slickest of the local camping grounds, this 20-acre park has all the mod cons, including heated swimming pool, tennis courts and an on-site shop. It's about 2.5km from the i-SITE.

All Seasons Holiday Park (Map p298; ☎ 0800 777 272; www.taupoallseasons.co.nz; 16 Rangatira St; campsites per s/d $25/40, dm $37, cabins $60-129, units $95-212) A pleasant holiday park five minutes' walk to town, with well-established trees and hedgerows between sites. Playground, games room, thermal pool and good kitchen facilities.

Also recommended:

Reid's Farm Recreation Reserve (Map p298; Huka Falls Rd; free for max 7 nights in a 14-day period; 🌙 late Oct-early Apr) A beautiful spot for freedom camping beside the Waikato River (summer only). Apart from a handful of portaloos there are no facilities.

Silver Fern Lodge (Map p290; ☎ 07-377 4929; www.silverfernlodge.co.nz; cnr Tamamutu & Kaimanawa Sts; dm $25, r $90-110; 🖳) 'Flash-packers' screams the signage, and what's delivered is a shiny custom-built complex

trimmed in corrugated aluminium, with pleasant, if lifeless, decor. The spruce rooms range from 10-bed dorms to studio units with en suite, and there's a large communal kitchen and lounge.

Tiki Lodge (Map p290; ☎ 07-377 4545; www.tikilodge.co.nz; 104 Tuwharetoa St; dm $26, d $75-85, tr $84-90, q $112-120; 🖳) This slick hostel has great lake and mountain views from the balcony, a spacious kitchen, comfy lounges, lots of Maori artwork and a spa pool out back.

Dunrovin Motel (Map p290; ☎ 07-378 7384; www.dunrovintaupo.co.nz; 140 Heu Heu St; r $90-130; 🖳 🛜) A chirpy old bird, recently given a fresh lick of paint. Functional units remain true to the period (built 1962), and are surrounded by pretty gardens with tui often about.

MIDRANGE

Lynwood Lodge (Map p290; ☎ 07-378 4967; 52 Rifle Range Rd; d/tr/q $110/130/150; 🐾) Taupo's first motel, built in 1952. So what you get is pebble-dash and concrete and rooms as big as a small house, made up like your granny's in residence. It's all shipshape though, and homey, and a real slice of Kiwi hospitality.

Bella Vista (Map p290; ☎ 07-378 9043; www.bellavistamotels.co.nz; 143 Heu Heu St; d $110-145, tr $145-165, q $185; 🛜) One of the growing number of Bella Vista motels nationwide, this one offers personal service by way of dog-loving owners Aaron and Tracey. Rooms are clean and comfortable, if a little bland. The communal barbecue is well located away from the road – good for a sundowner of an evening.

Chelmswood Motel (Map p298; ☎ 07-378 2715; www.chelmswood.co.nz; 250 Lake Tce; r $110-250; 🖳 🐾) This unpretentious Tudor-style manor on the south side of town has simple studios and larger family rooms, most with their own mineral pool. There's a heated outdoor pool, a sauna, and a sandpit for the littlies.

Catelli's of Taupo (Map p290; ☎ 0800 88 44 77; www.catellis.co.nz; 23-27 Rifle Range Rd; r $135-145, ste $160-235; 🛜) The exterior is all hobbitish '80s curves, sloping roofs and nipple-pink trim, but inside these orderly motel units have a fresh, modern feel. In summer it's worth paying the extra $5 for a garden studio with an outside sitting area.

Suncourt (Map p290; ☎ 07-378 8265; www.suncourt.co.nz; 14 Northcroft St; d $135-170, tr $155-190, q $170-220; 🖳 🛜 🐾) This rambling, lake-gazing complex encloses comfortable, well-furnished units with facilities including a spa pool and kids playground. Larger rooms with verandas and full kitchens are ideal for families, though regular conferences can book the place out.

Beechtree (Map p290; ☎ 07-377 0181; www.beech treemotel.co.nz; 56 Rifle Range Rd; d $140-180, tr $170, apt $220-250; 🖳 🛜) The Beechtree, and its sister motel Miro next door, offer classy rooms at a reasonable rate. The neutral-toned decor is fresh and modern, and creates a feeling of light and air, as do the large windows, ground-floor patios and upstairs balconies.

Lake (Map p290; ☎ 07-378 4222; www.thelakeonline. co.nz; 63 Mere Rd; r $150-195) A reminder that 1960s and '70s design wasn't all Austin Powers–style groovaliciousness and bell-bottoms, this unusual boutique motel is crammed with classic furniture from the likes of Saarenin and Mies Van der Rohe. The studio is a tight fit, but the four one-bedroom units all have kitchenettes and dining/living areas.

TOP END

Acacia Cliffs Lodge (off Map p298; ☎ 07-378 1551; http:// acaciacliffslodge.co.nz; 133 Mapara Rd, Acacia Bay; r $650; 🖳 🛜) Pushing the romance switch way past 'rekindle', this luxurious B&B, high in the hills above Acacia Bay, offers four modern suites – three with sumptuous lake views and one that compensates for the lack of them with a curvy bath and a private garden. If you don't want to venture too far from the bedroom, dinners can be arranged.

Huka Lodge (Map p298; ☎ 07-378 5791; www. hukalodge.com; Huka Falls Rd; s/d/tr/cottages from $1095/1460/1905/3060; 🖳 🖳) Welcome to paradise. One of the best hotels in NZ, Huka Lodge basks in accolades and a procession of famous guests, including at least three queens. Surrounded by lush bush and delightful gardens, the main lodge has a homey feel (albeit the home of a wealthy aesthete) and features shared dining and lounge areas, and a library. Individual guest lodges are dotted along the riverside, with views and privacy. Rates include breakfast and a five-course dinner. There are also two entirely self-contained cottages set apart on the grounds.

Eating

Taupo is large enough to offer a good range of options, from burger bars to world-class restaurants.

RESTAURANTS

Lotus Thai (Map p290; ☎ 07-376 9497; 137 Tongariro St; mains $16-21; 🕑 lunch Wed-Fri, dinner Wed-Mon) A warm and inviting restaurant with Siamese trim-

mings throughout, offering standard Thai fare in plentiful portions.

our pick Pimentos (Map p290; ☎ 07-377 4549; 17 Tamamutu St; mains $26-29; 🕑 dinner Wed-Mon) Such a local favourite that you may well need to book to enjoy some of the town's best food in this convivial environment. Its lamb shanks and mash are legendary, but the relatively short menu offers plenty of well-considered experimentation.

Plateau (Map p290; ☎ 07-377 2425; 64 Tuwharetoa St; mains $30-34; 🕑 lunch & dinner) One of a growing number of brewery-branded gastro-pubs, Plateau is a great place for a drink (Monteith's beer being the main poison), but the food is the key. The menu is predominantly modern NZ (think lamb rump and rib-eye), with plenty of fancy fusion twists.

Brantry (Map p290; ☎ 07-378 0484; 45 Rifle Range Rd; mains $32-37; 🕑 dinner) Chef Prue Campbell and sister Felicity continue to run the best and most consistent restaurant in the region at this 1950s town house, a few minutes from the town centre. Dine in intimate, unobtrusive surrounds, inside or out. The menu makes use of some of NZ's finest ingredients, including top-quality cuts of beef and lamb. The set menu (two-/three-courses $40/50) is a gift.

CAFES

Stir Taupo (Map p290; cnr Redoubt St & Ferry Rd; crepes $5-10; 🕑 breakfast & lunch Tue-Sun) Despite operating out of a caravan by the marina, Stir managed to snaffle a 2009 cafe award. The formula's simple: killer coffee and scrumptious sweet and savoury crepes.

Fine Fettle (Map p290; ☎ 07-378 7674; 39 Paora Hape St; mains $6-15; 🕑 breakfast & lunch) An airy cafe on a quieter edge of town, serving wholefood, organic, and GE- and gluten-free options. The healthy, satisfying offerings include quiches and fresh salads, plus juices, smoothies and iced chai.

Replete (Map p290; ☎ 07-378 0606; 45 Heu Heu St; mains $6-16; 🕑 breakfast & lunch) Widely regarded as one of Taupo's best cafes, Replete's counter is packed full of delicatessen delights – running the gamut from sandwiches and salads to sweets. Its pastry selection is particularly commendable. A blackboard menu offers inexpensive and interesting light meals.

Eruption (Map p290; ☎ 027-310 0421; Suncourt Centre, Tamamutu St; mains $7-15; 🕑 breakfast & lunch Mon-Sat) Shelter behind one of the free newspapers while Eruption's espresso machine steams and spurts out black rivers topped with creamy foam. The food selection's limited but tasty.

L'Arté (off Map p298; ☎ 07-378 2962; 255 Mapara Rd, Acacia Bay; mains $10-25; ◷ 9am-4pm Wed-Sun, daily Jan) A 10-minute drive from town will reward you with a fantastically artful cafe in an ebullient sculpture garden with a gallery alongside. Lots of mouth-watering treats are made from scratch here, including the pesto that sits on the must-have antipasto platter. The home baking is a triumph.

SELF-CATERING

Pak N Save (Map p290; Taniwha St; ◷ 8am-9.30pm)
Beaut Bakery (Map p290; 179 Spa Rd; ◷ 5am-3.30pm) Try their award-winning mincemeat-and-gravy pies.

Drinking

Things get lively in the height of summer when the town fills up with travellers. The rest of the year it might pay to take a newspaper to read over your pint.

Bond (Map p290; ☎ 07-377 2434; 40 Tuwharetoa St) Aiming for 007-like sophistication, this is Taupo's most upmarket bar, with European beers, tapas and DJs up late. The drinks cost a pretty Money-Penny, but you may still see a Q at the bar.

Finn MacCuhal's (Map p290; ☎ 07-378 6165; cnr Tongariro & Tuwharetoa Sts) With Irish ephemera nailed to the walls and a backpackers' next door, you can be sure that there will be plenty of craic here; DJs on the weekends.

Jolly Good Fellows (Map p290; ☎ 07-378 0457; 76 Lake Tce) Corr, Guvnor! You ain't seen a pub like this since old Blighty, with lashings of cultural clichés and cheeky humour added to its pub grub, along with Old Speckled Hen, Tetleys and Bulmers cider on tap.

Mulligans (Map p290; ☎ 07-376 9101; 15 Tongariro St) A locals' hang-out, this Irish boozer offers hearty meal-and-drink deals and is a good spot for a quiet Guinness.

Shed (Map p290; ☎ 07-376 5393; 18 Tuwharetoa St) A lively place to sup a beer and catch the big game, sit outside and watch the world go by, or strut your stuff to DJs at the weekends. Food is punter-pleasing pub fare in man-sized portions.

Entertainment

Great Lake Centre (Map p290; ☎ 07-376 0340; Tongariro St) Hosts performances, exhibitions and conventions. Ask at the i-SITE for the current program.

Starlight Cinema Centre (Map p290; ☎ 07-377 1085; Starlight Arcade, off Horomatangi St; adult/child $13/8.50) Screens the latest Hollywood blockbusters.

Getting There & Away
AIR

Taupo Airport (☎ 07-378 7771; www.taupoairport. co.nz; Anzac Memorial Dr) is 8km south of town. **Air New Zealand** (☎ 0800 737 000; www.airnz.co.nz) has daily direct flights to Auckland (45 minutes) and Wellington (one hour), with onward connections.

BUS

The main bus stop is at the **Taupo Travel Centre** (Map p290; ☎ 07-378 9032; 16 Gascoigne St), which operates as a booking office. **InterCity/ Newmans** (☎ 09-583 5780; www.intercity.co.nz) runs several daily buses to Turangi ($25, 44 minutes), Auckland ($57, five hours), Hamilton ($51, three hours), Rotorua ($29, one hour), Tauranga ($47, 2¾ hours), Napier ($35, two hours), Palmerston North ($51, 4¼ hours) and Wellington ($61, six hours).

Budget operator **Naked Bus** (☎ 0900 625 33 per min $1.80; www.nakedbus.com) has daily services to the same destinations (excluding Tauranga), with super-early-bird prices starting from $1. Buses stop outside the i-SITE.

Shuttle services operate year-round between Taupo, Turangi and Tongariro National Park. In winter, services run to Whakapapa Ski Area (1½ hours) and can include package deals for lift tickets and ski hire. See p310 for details.

Getting Around

Taupo's Hotbus (Map p290; ☎ 0508 468 287; www.hotbus. co.nz; 1st stop $15, then per stop $5; ◷ 9am-4pm Oct-Mar, 10am-3pm Apr-Sep) is a hop-on, hop-off bus that does an hourly circuit of all the major attractions in and around Taupo, from the i-SITE.

Taxi services are provided by **Taupo Taxis** (☎ 07-378 5100) and **Top Cabs** (Map p290; ☎ 07-378 9250; Tuwharetoa St). Expect to pay about $23 for a cab to the airport from the centre of town.

AROUND TAUPO
Wairakei Park

Crossing the river at Tongariro St and heading north from town on SH1, you'll arrive at the Wairakei Park area, also known as the Huka Falls Tourist Loop. Take the first right turn after you cross the river and you'll be on Huka Falls Rd, which runs along the river and arches around to meet SH1 further north. Here you can turn left to pass other interesting spots on your way back to town.

HUKA FALLS

Clearly signposted and with a car park and kiosk alongside, these falls mark the spot where NZ's longest river, the Waikato –

which, here, has only just been born from Lake Taupo – is slammed into a narrow chasm, making a dramatic 10m drop into a surging pool. As you cross the footbridge you can see the full force of this torrent that the Maori called Hukanui (Great Body of Spray). On sunny days the water is crystal clear and you can take great photographs

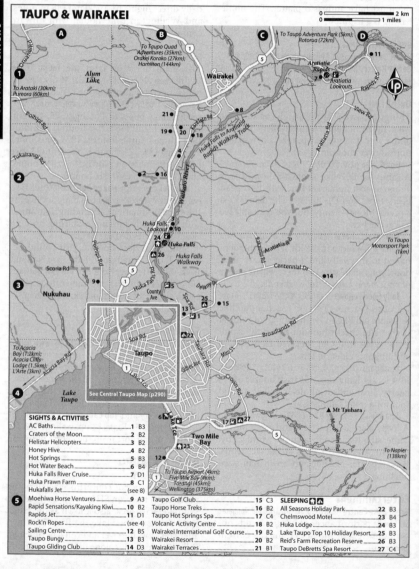

TAUPO & WAIRAKEI

SIGHTS & ACTIVITIES		
AC Baths	1	B3
Craters of the Moon	2	B2
Helistar Helicopters	3	B2
Honey Hive	4	B2
Hot Springs	5	B3
Hot Water Beach	6	B4
Huka Falls River Cruise	7	D1
Huka Prawn Farm	8	C1
Hukafalls Jet	(see 8)	
Moehiwa Horse Ventures	9	A3
Rapid Sensations/Kayaking Kiwi	10	B2
Rapids Jet	11	D1
Rock'n Ropes	(see 4)	
Sailing Centre	12	B5
Taupo Bungy	13	B3
Taupo Gliding Club	14	D3

Taupo Golf Club	15	C3
Taupo Horse Treks	16	B2
Taupo Hot Springs Spa	17	C4
Volcanic Activity Centre	18	B2
Wairakei International Golf Course	19	B2
Wairakei Resort	20	B2
Wairakei Terraces	21	B1

SLEEPING		
All Seasons Holiday Park	22	B3
Chelmswood Motel	23	B4
Huka Lodge	24	B3
Lake Taupo Top 10 Holiday Resort	25	B3
Reid's Farm Recreation Reserve	26	B3
Taupo DeBretts Spa Resort	27	C4

TAUPO & THE CENTRAL PLATEAU

from the lookout on the other side of the footbridge. You can also take a few short walks around the area or pick up the longer Huka Falls Walkway back to town, or the Aratiatia Rapids Walking Track to the rapids (see p293).

ROCK'N ROPES & THE HONEY HIVE
Less than a kilometre beyond the Huka Falls turn-off is the **Honey Hive** (Map p298; ☎ 07-374 8553; www.honeyhivetaupo.com; Karetoto Rd; admission free; ☒ 10am-5pm), which has a glass-enclosed viewing hive, honey tastings and all manner of bee products – edible, medicinal and cosmetic – as well as mead. The cafe serves honey ice cream, too.

Right next door is **Rock'n Ropes** (☎ 07-374 8111; www.rocknropes.co.nz; Karetoto Rd; giant swing $20, adrenaline combo $40, half-day $65), a vertiginous and challenging high-ropes course that includes balancing on teetering 'tree-tops', negotiating a tricky two-wire bridge and scaling ropes. The combo includes the swing, high beam and trapeze.

VOLCANIC ACTIVITY CENTRE
What's the story with all the geothermal activity in this area? The **volcanic activity centre** (Map p298; ☎ 07-374 8375; www.volcanoes.co.nz; Karetoto Rd; adult/child $9.50/5; ☒ 9am-5pm Mon-Fri, 10am-4pm Sat & Sun) has all the answers. This observatory monitors volcanic activity in the volatile Taupo Volcanic Zone, and the visitor centre has some excellent, if text-heavy, displays on NZ's geothermal and volcanic activity, including a working seismograph.

A favourite exhibit with kids is the Earthquake Simulator, a little booth you can sit in to experience an earthquake, complete with teeth-chattering shudders and sudden shakes. You can also configure your own tornado then watch it wreak havoc, or see a simulated geyser above and below ground. A small theatre screens footage of the 1995 Ruapehu eruption and the 2007 breach of the crater lake.

HUKAFALLS JET & PRAWN FARM
Further down the Falls loop road is the launching site for **Hukafalls Jet** (Map p298; ☎ 07-374 8572; www.hukafallsjet.com; trips adult/child $99/59). This 30-minute thrill ride takes you up the river to the spray-filled foot of the Huka Falls and down to the Aratiatia Dam, all the while dodging daringly and doing acrobatic 360-degree turns. Trips run all day (prices include transport from Taupo) and you can bundle it in with a helicopter ride (see p294).

Just next door, the **Huka Prawn Farm** (Map p298; ☎ 07-374 8474; www.hukaprawnpark.co.nz; adult/child $24/14; ☒ 9am-3.30pm, longer hours in summer) is one of the world's only geothermally heated freshwater prawn farms. There's a surprising array of activities here, including prawn 'fishing' and Killer Prawn Golf (balls $1 each, $10 for 20), which allows you to shoot balls over the prawn beds. For a more educational experience, tours leave hourly (11am to 4pm; adult/child $15/10). Best of all, though, is the restaurant where you can try prawns all ways, and nonprawn dishes if you wish (mains $13 to $30).

CRATERS OF THE MOON
This lesser-known geothermal area sprang to life as a result of the hydroelectric tinkering of the 1950s that created the power station. When underground water levels fell and pressure shifted, the **Craters of the Moon** (Map p298; www.cratersofthemoon.co.nz; adult/child $6/2.50; ☒ 8.30am-5.30pm) appeared with new steam vents and bubbling mud pools pocking the landscape. The perimeter loop walk takes about 45 minutes and affords great views down to the lake and mountains beyond. There's a kiosk at the entrance, staffed by volunteers who kindly keep an eye on the car park. Craters of the Moon is signposted on SH1, about 5km north of Taupo.

WAIRAKEI TERRACES
Known to Maori as Waiora and latterly as Geyser Valley, this area was once one of the most active thermal areas in the world, with 22 geysers and 240 mud pools and springs. In 1958 the valley was significantly changed by the geothermal power project and today it's the site of **Wairakei Terraces** (Map p298; ☎ 07-378 0913; www.wairakeiterraces.co.nz; adult/child $18/9; ☒ 9am-5pm), artificially made silica terraces, pools and geysers re-creating, on a smaller scale, the famous Pink and White Terraces, which were destroyed by the Tarawera eruption in 1886. There's also a small meeting house, a re-created Maori village and a carving centre. The **Maori Cultural Experience** (adult/child $85/42.50; ☒ 6pm) here – which includes a traditional challenge, welcome and *hangi* meal – gives an insight into Maori life in the geothermal areas.

ARATIATIA RAPIDS

Two kilometres off SH5, the Aratiatia Rapids were a spectacular part of the Waikato River until the government plonked a hydroelectric dam across the waterway, shutting off the flow. But the spectacle hasn't disappeared completely, with the floodgates opened from 1 October to 31 March at 10am, noon, 2pm and 4pm and from April to September at 10am, noon and 2pm. You can see the water crash through the dam from two good vantage points.

Get another perspective from **Rapids Jet** (Map p298; ☎ 07-374 8066; www.rapidsjet.com; Rapids Rd, off SH5; adult/child $90/50), a jetboat that shoots along the lower part of the rapids. It's a sensational 35-minute ride – some say it rivals the Huka Falls trip. The boat departs from the end of the access road to the Aratiatia lookouts. Go down Rapids Rd and look for the signpost to the National Equestrian Centre.

For a less rapid, more photo-friendly ride, try **Huka Falls River Cruise** (Map p298; ☎ 0800 278 336; www.hukafallscruise.co.nz; Aratiatia Dam; adult/child $35/10; ⏱ departs 12.30 & 2.30pm year-round, plus 10.30am & 4.30pm in summer), a relaxed jaunt (80 minutes) from Aratiatia Dam to Huka Falls.

Five kilometres further north on SH1 is **Taupo Adventure Park** (off Map p298; ☎ 07-374 8495; www.taupoadventurepark.com; activities $3-40; ⏱ 10am-4pm Wed-Sun, school & public holidays), a family-oriented park with minigolf, maze, laser tag, paintball, video games, animal park, quad bikes and go-karts.

Orakei Korako

A bit off the beaten track, **Orakei Korako Cave & Thermal Park** (☎ 07-378 3131; www.orakeikorako.co.nz; adult/child $34/14; ⏱ 8am-5.30pm summer, to 5pm winter) gets fewer visitors than other thermal areas. But, since the destruction of the Pink and White Terraces, it is arguably the best thermal area left in NZ. Although three-quarters of it now lies beneath the dam waters of Lake Ohakuri, the remaining quarter is pretty interesting.

A walking track (allow 1½ hours) that's steep in parts largely follows a boardwalk around the colourful silica terraces for which the park is famous, and passes geysers and **Ruatapu Cave**. This impressive natural cave has a jade-green pool, thought to have been used as a mirror by Maori women who prepared for rituals here (Orakei Korako means 'the place of adorning'). Entry includes a boat ride across Lake Ohakuri.

It's about 25 minutes to Orakei Korako from Taupo. Take SH1 towards Hamilton for 23km, and then travel for 14km from the signposted turn-off. From Rotorua the turn-off is on SH5, via Mihi.

Alternatively, **NZ River Jet** (☎ 07-333 7111; www.riverjet.co.nz; SH5, Mihi; 2½hr ride incl entry to Orakei Korako adult/child $145/75) will zip you there in thrilling fashion from Mihi, 20km upstream on the Waikato River. They also offer the Squeeze – a jetboat ride through Tutukau Gorge to a spot where you can disembark in warm water and edge your way through a crevice to a concealed natural hot spring surrounded by native bush ($130).

Another option is **Riverboat Waireka** (☎ 07-333 8845; www.riverboatwaireka.com), which will transport you from the Mihi bridge to Orakei Korako via a leisurely 3½-hour cruise in a 1908 riverboat.

If it was difficult to resist all that enticing but scalding water at Orakei Korako, but you don't fancy a squeeze, a 30km detour will take you to **Butcher's Pool** (admission free), a bedecked but otherwise purely natural thermal spring in the middle of a farmer's paddock. Alongside is a small parking area and changing sheds. To get there, turn left onto SH5 at Mihi (follow the signs to Rotorua). After 4km look out for Homestead Rd on your right. Follow it to the end, turn left and look for a row of trees lining a gravel driveway off to your right about 300m away (the signpost can be difficult to spot as it's pointing from the other side of the road).

Mangakino & Whakamaru

These neighbouring towns, like their respective lakes (Maraetai and Whakamaru), are by-products of hydroelectric schemes on the Waikato River. Mangakino's population is roughly a fifth of its 1959 peak, when the then 14-year-old town heaved with construction workers, engineers and their families. The power stations are still in operation, but the main drawcards today are activities on or around the lakes.

M-I-A Wakeboarding (☎ 021 864 254; www.m-i-a.co.nz; wakeboard or wakeskate/wakesurf $100/75) tears up the water on Mangakino's Lake Maraetai, offering wakeboarding, wakeskating and wakesurfing as well as canoe tours, mountain-biking trips and backpacker accommodation (dorm/double $23/54).

Free camping is permitted close to the **Bus Stop Café** (☎ 027 203 7110; mains $7-12), where local identity Garry Gradwell dishes out burgers and toasties from the back of an old Bedford bus parked on the Maraetai lakefront.

Eventually Mangakino and Whakamaru will be linked by the **Waikato River Trail** (www.waikatorivertrail.com), a proposed 425km route following the river all the way from Lake Taupo to Port Waikato. A 26km section heading upriver from Whakamaru to Atiamuri has been completed.

Pureora Forest Park

Fringing the western edge of Lake Taupo, the 78,000-hectare Pureora Forest is home to NZ's tallest totara tree. Logging was stopped in this forest in the 1980s after a long campaign by conservationists, and the subsequent regeneration is impressive. There are mountain-bike tracks and hiking routes through the park, including tracks to the summits of Mt Pureora (1165m) and the rock pinnacle of Mt Titiraupenga (1042m). A 12m-high tower, a short walk from the Bismarck Rd car park, provides a canopy-level view of the forest for birdwatchers.

To stay overnight in one of three standard DOC huts (adult/child $5/2.50), you'll need to buy backcountry hut tickets in advance. The three campsites (adult/child $8/2) have self-registration boxes. Hut tickets, maps and information on the park are available from the DOC offices in Turangi (below) and Te Kuiti (p247).

TURANGI
pop 3900

Once a service town for the nearby hydroelectric power station, Turangi's claim to fame nowadays is undoubtedly its fish. It proclaims itself 'Trout Fishing Capital of the World'. The Tongariro River, however, can be enjoyed in many other ways, including white-water rafting and swimming. The township also provides ready access to the ski fields and walking tracks of Tongariro National Park.

Information

The **Turangi i-SITE** (☎ 07-386 8999; www.laketauponz.com; Ngawaka Pl; ☒ 8.30am-5pm) is a good stop for information on Tongariro National Park, Kaimanawa Forest Park, trout fishing, and snow and road conditions. It issues DOC hut tickets (although this may change if hut tickets

become an online-only purchase), ski passes and hunting and fishing licences, and makes bookings for transport, accommodation and activities. It also has internet facilities and a detailed relief model of the national park. The main bus stop is outside.

The Turangi–Taupo **DOC visitors centre** (☎ 07-386 8607; Turanga Pl; ☒ 8am-4.30pm Mon-Fri) is near the junction of SH41 and Ohuanga Rd.

There are plenty of ATMs in the town centre, along with a post office.

Sights & Activities
TROUT FISHING

Ever since trout were introduced into Lake Taupo in 1898 there have been yarns of fish weighing more than a sack of spuds and measuring the length of a surfboard. The truth is that more than 28,000 brown and rainbow trout of legal size are bagged yearly.

February and March are the best months for brown trout, but rainbow fishing is good year-round on the river. This unique fishery is protected by special conditions, including a bag limit of three fish, no use of bait (except flies) and a minimum size of 40cm, depending on where you fish – this is detailed on your licence, which you must carry at all times while fishing. Licences are available from DOC or the i-SITE.

If you're not sure where to start, a fishing guide can give you some local know-how, as well as transport, gear, licence and meals by arrangement.

Brett Cameron (☎ 07-378 8192; www.cpf.net.nz; half-/full day from $280/580) Also offers boat charters (per hour $100, minimum three hours) and quad-bike adventure fishing in National Park (one/two people $750/850). Licences extra.

Ian Jenkins (☎ 07-386 0840; www.tui-lodge.co.nz/guides.php; half-/full day $350/600)

Brent Pirie (☎ 07-377 8054; www.flyfishtaupo.com; half-/full day $350/685)

John Sommervell (☎ 07-386 5931, www.nymphfish.com; half-/full day from $250/500)

Tightline Charters (☎ 07-386 0033; www.tightlinecharters.co.nz; per hr $85)

There are several companies in town that hire and sell gear, and handle bookings for guides and charters.

Barry Greig's Sporting World (☎ 07-386 6911; www.greigsport.co.nz; 59 Town Centre; ☒ 9am-5pm)

Creel Tackle House (☎ 07-386 7929; 183 Taupahi Rd; ☒ 8am-5pm Mon-Fri, 7.30am-3.30pm Sat & Sun)

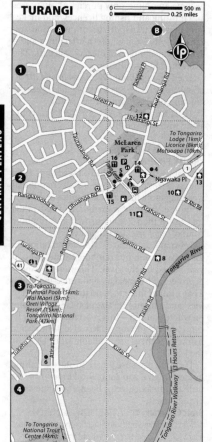

TURANGI

esting stops en route, including an underwater viewing chamber, a hatchery, keeping ponds and a picnic area. The **River Walk visitor centre** (☎ 07-386 8085; www.troutcentre.org.nz; adult/child $2/free; ☷ 10am-3pm), run by volunteers, has polished educational displays, a collection of rods and reels dating back to the 1880s and a theatrette showing a 14-minute film about the river.

TRAMPING

There are several short walks around town, most of which are detailed in DOC's *Lake Taupo – A Guide to Walks and Hikes* ($2.50), along with many others around the district.

A favourite is the **Tongariro River Lookout Track** (one hour loop), a riverside amble affording views of Mt Pihanga. This track joins the **Tongariro River Walkway** (three hours return), which follows the east bank of the river to the Red Hut suspension bridge.

Other good leg-stretchers include **Hinemihi's Track**, near the top of Te Ponanga Saddle, 8km west of Turangi on SH47 (15 minutes return); **Maunganamu Track**, 4km west of Turangi on SH41 (40 minutes return); and **Tauranga-Taupo River Walk** (30 minutes), which starts at Te Rangiita, 12km north of Turangi on SH1.

There is another nice lake stroll at **Lake Rotopounamu** (Greenstone Lake), 11km southwest of Turangi on SH47. A favourite for walkers, swimmers, twitchers and tree huggers alike, it's a 30-minute walk to the lake

Sporting Life (☎ 07-386 8996; www.sportinglife-turangi .co.nz; Town Centre; ☷ 8am-5.30pm) Its website details the latest fishing conditions.

Fishing trips can also be booked via Taupo's launch office (p292).

Ten kilometres east of Turangi at Motuoapa you can hire aluminium dinghies for lake fishing from **Motuoapa Hire Boats** (☎ 07-386 7000; per hr $39). These can be used in the bay only.

TONGARIRO NATIONAL TROUT CENTRE

About 4km south of Turangi on SH1 is the DOC-managed trout hatchery, which is a pleasant stop even if you're not a fish fanatic. The landscaped walkway makes for a short and gentle stroll, and there are several inter-from the car park, and two hours around. Ten Minute Beach and Long Beach are ideal for picnics.

TOKAANU THERMAL POOLS
The **Tokaanu Thermal Pools** (☎ 07-386 8575; Mangaroa St; public pools adult/child $6/4, private pools per 20min $9/5; ◷ 10am-9pm), 5km northwest of Turangi, is an unpretentious facility with hot pools, a trout stream, a picnic area, displays and a shop. A 20-minute stroll along the boardwalk (wheelchair accessible) showcases mud pools and thermal springs.

OTHER ACTIVITIES
The Tongariro River has some superb Grade III rapids for river rafting, as well as Grade I stretches suitable for beginners in the lower reaches during summer. **Tongariro River Rafting** (☎ 07-386 6409; www.trr.co.nz; Atirau Rd; adult/child $109/99) can start you off with a three-hour trip on Grade II Tongariro rapids or take you on a full day's raft fishing (summer only, price on enquiry). The company also hires out mountain bikes (two hours/half-day/full day/42 Traverse, $25/35/45/65) and runs guided and unguided biking trips on the 42 Traverse (see p311), Tongariro River Track, Moerangi Station, Tree Trunk Gorge and Fishers Track (two hours to full day, $70 to $160).

Rafting NZ (☎ 0800 865 226; www.raftingnewzealand.com; 41 Ngawaka Pl) runs the Whitewater Tongariro trip (Grade III) with an optional waterfall jump (four hours, adult/child $119/109), or the Family Fun raft over more relaxed rapids (Grade II, three hours, adult/child $75/65). Groups of four or more can tackle an overnighter (Grade III+, per person $350), rafting to a riverside campsite and then hitting more rapids the following day.

Wai Maori (☎ 07-386 0315; www.waimaori.com; 203 Puanga St, Tokaanu) offers guided white-water kayaking (November to April, per person $129) or trips accompanied only by trout down the gentle Tokaanu Stream to Lake Taupo, passing boiling mud, hot pools and wetlands on the way (90 minutes/half-day/full day $30/40/65).

Rapid Sensations in Taupo also runs white-water trips on the Tongariro River (see p293).

For indoor fun, head to the **Vertical Assault Climbing Wall** (☎ 07-386 8949; 22 Ngawaka Pl; adult/child $15/11) to scale walls that challenge all skill levels.

Sleeping
Parklands Motor Lodge (☎ 07-386 7515; www.parklandsmotorlodge.co.nz; 25 Arahori St; campsites per person $16, r $94-140; ☏ ⚏) On SH1 but set back beyond an epic front lawn, this motor lodge serves campers and motel seekers with its small but functional camping area and splay of well-presented units. There's a swimming pool and play area for the kids, while free-ranging ball sports are definitely on out front.

Extreme Backpackers (☎ 07-386 8949; www.extremebackpackers.co.nz; 22 Ngawaka Pl; dm $23-25, s $43-53, d $56-66; ⚏ ☏) Crafted from pine and corrugated iron, this modern backpackers has the bonus of a climbing wall and cafe. Cheaper dorms have eight bunks and skip the carpet, while pricier doubles have en suites, but all rooms are clean and comfy. A lounge with an open fire, a sunny courtyard with hammocks and a barbecue make this a relaxing budget bet.

Riverstone Backpackers (☎ 07-386 7004; www.riverstonebackpackers.com; 222 Tautahanga Rd; dm $25-30, d $61-84; ⚏) Rob's pad is a cleverly refitted old home reborn as a bijou backpackers. Facilities include sports-gear storage, an enviable kitchen and lounge, and a stylish landscaped yard (with pizza oven) of which any Kiwi homeowner would be proud. This is a true home away from home, although Rob is eager to help you get out of the house and into some local activities.

Sportmans Lodge (☎ 07-386 8150; www.sportmanslodge.co.nz; 15 Taupahi Rd; r $69, cottage $105-120) Backing on to the river, this motel-style spot with a sweet garden is a hidden bargain for trout-fishing folk. All the rooms share the lounge and well-equipped kitchen. The self-contained cottage sleeps three.

Judges Pool Motel (☎ 07-386 7892; www.judgespoolmotel.co.nz; 92 Taupahi Rd; s/d/q $90/100/140) This older motel has tidy, spacious rooms with kitchenettes and new bathrooms, and a fish-cleaning area. All one-bedroom units have outdoor decks for relaxing beers, although the nice new barbecue area is the best place to talk about the one that got away.

ourpick Creel Lodge (☎ 07-386 8081; www.creel.co.nz; 183 Taupahi Rd; s $95-130, d $110-150, tr $130-170, q $150-190; ☏ ⚏) Set in green and peaceful grounds, this heavenly hideaway backs onto a fine stretch of the Tongariro River. All the ground-level suites conveniently have their own kitchens and a balcony overlooking attractive gardens.

Anglers Paradise Motel (☎ 07-386 8980; www.anglers paradise.co.nz; cnr Ohuanga Rd & Raukura St; d $115-160, tr $130-160, q $145-160; 🖳 🔝) Looking like something out of Twin Peaks, this place sits in a 1-hectare leafy pocket where privacy prevails. Rooms are trimmed in dark wood and feature big televisions and superking beds. It's geared up for anglers, with guides happily arranged and a smokehouse on-site. The restaurant has a crackling fireplace.

Oreti Village Resort (☎ 07-386 7070; www.oretivillage. com; Mission House Dr, Pukawa Bay; apt $210-270; 🛜) This enclave of luxury self-contained apartments might give you a hankering for 'village' life – which in Oreti's case entails gazing at blissful lake views from the comfort of a rolled-arm leather couch, before wandering up to the excellent bar and restaurant (below) or down to the beach. Take SH41 for 15km, heading northwest of Turangi, and look for the sign.

Eating

our pick **Oreti** (☎ 07-386 7070; Mission House Dr, Pukawa Bay; mains $29-34; 🕑 lunch Thu-Sun, dinner Tue-Sun) It's hard to imagine a more romantic spot to while away a balmy summer's evening than looking over the lake from Oreti's terrace. It's an added bonus that the food matches up – the modern NZ menu doesn't disappoint. As you pick your way through a heavily laden antipasti lunch platter you might have to remind yourself that you're not actually on the Mediterranean.

Tongariro Lodge (☎ 07-386 7946; Grace Rd; mains $35; 🕑 dinner) Some of the world's most famous blokes (Robert Mitchum, Liam Neeson, Larry Hagman, Jimmy Carter, Timothy Dalton) have come to this luxury riverside fishing lodge, set in 9 hectares of parkland, to relax in wood-panelled anonymity. Not surprisingly, the menu's orientated around man-sized slabs of meat but the real squeals of delight come when a lucky lodger is presented with their day's catch, smoked and served to perfection.

There are also cafe-style options around town:

Grand Central Fry (☎ 07-386 5344; 8 Ohuanga Rd; meals $6-9; 🕑 11am-8.30pm) A local legend serving top fish and chips, plus burgers and anything else fryable.

Thyme for Food (☎ 07-386 0552; Town Centre; meals $6-16; 🕑 breakfast & lunch) A popular tearoom, good for fast and simple fare such as pies, all-day brekkie, burgers and milkshakes.

Licorice (☎ 07-386 5551; SH1, Motuoapa; meals $9-17; 🕑 breakfast & lunch Wed-Sun) It's worth holding off

for this pit stop 8km north of Turangi for excellent coffee, cheap, light meals, and lovely home baking.

Self-caterers should head to the big, centrally located **New World** (☎ 07-386-8780; Ohuanga Rd; 🕑 8am-8pm) supermarket.

Getting There & Away

InterCity/Newmans (☎ 09-583 5780; www.intercity. co.nz) services stop outside the i-SITE. The Auckland–Wellington and Tauranga–Rotorua–Wellington buses that travel along the eastern side of the lake all stop at Turangi (from Taupo $16, 45 minutes).

Naked Bus (☎ 0900 625 33 per min $1.80; www. nakedbus.com; advance fares from $1) uses the same stop for their daily services to Auckland (6½ hours) via Taupo (one hour) and Rotorua (two hours). Going south, buses run to Wellington (5½ hours) via all major stops, including Palmerston North (3 hours).

For Tongariro shuttle services, see p310.

TONGARIRO & AROUND

TONGARIRO NATIONAL PARK

Established in 1887, Tongariro was NZ's first and the world's fourth national park, and is one of NZ's three World Heritage Sites. Originally covering the three mountains of the park (Tongariro, Ngauruhoe and Ruapehu), the name Tongariro comes from *tonga* (south wind) and *riro* (carried away). The three peaks were a gift to NZ from the local *iwi* (tribe), who saw the act as the only way to preserve an area of spiritual significance.

With its towering active volcanoes, Tongariro is one of NZ's most spectacular parks, perhaps best known for its cameo as Mordor in Peter Jackson's *Lord of the Rings* trilogy. In summer it offers excellent short walks and longer tramps, most notably the Tongariro Northern Circuit and the Tongariro Alpine Crossing. In winter it's a busy ski area.

Information

The **DOC visitor centre** (Map p306; ☎ 07-892 3729; www.doc.govt.nz; 🕑 8am-6pm Dec-Mar, to 5pm Apr-Nov) is in Whakapapa (pronounced 'fa-ka-pa-pa') Village, on the northwestern side of the park. It has maps and info on all corners of the park, including walks, huts and current skiing, track and weather conditions. It also

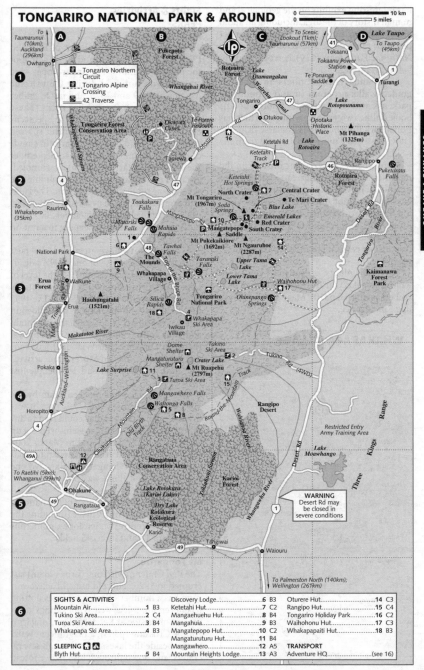

TONGARIRO NATIONAL PARK & AROUND

0 ————— 10 km
0 ————— 5 miles

- - - - Tongariro Northern Circuit
······ Tongariro Alpine Crossing
—·— 42 Traverse

TAUPO & THE CENTRAL PLATEAU

WARNING
Desert Rd may
be closed in
severe conditions

SIGHTS & ACTIVITIES
Mountain Air	1 B3
Tukino Ski Area	2 C4
Turoa Ski Area	3 B4
Whakapapa Ski Area	4 B3

SLEEPING
Blyth Hut	5 B4

Discovery Lodge	6 B3		Oturere Hut	14 C3
Ketetahi Hut	7 C2		Rangipo Hut	15 C4
Mangaehuehu Hut	8 B4		Tongariro Holiday Park	16 C2
Mangahuia	9 B3		Waihohonu Hut	17 C3
Mangatepopo Hut	10 C2		Whakapapaiti Hut	18 B3
Mangaturuturu Hut	11 B4			
Mangawhero	12 A5		**TRANSPORT**	
Mountain Heights Lodge	13 A3		Adventure HQ	(see 16)

has interesting exhibits on the geological and human history of the area, including an audio visual display, and a small shop: the perfect place for rainy days. The detailed *Tongariro National Park* map ($19) is worth buying before tramping.

Each January, DOC offers an excellent guided-walks program in and around the park; ask at DOC centres for information or book online (www.doc.govt.nz). Further national park information is available from the DOC centre in Turangi (p304) and from the i-SITE in Ohakune (p313) .

Many visitors to NZ come unstuck in the mountains. The weather can change more quickly than you expect, and rescues (and fatalities) are not uncommon. When visiting Tongariro National Park, you must be properly equipped and take safety precautions, including leaving your itinerary with a responsible person. For more on track safety, see p77.

There are plenty of transport operators willing to take you to trail heads and pick you up again (see p310). Make sure you book them in advance.

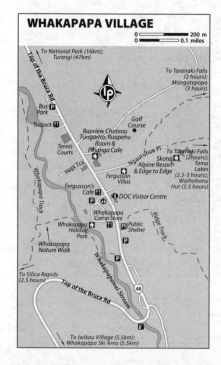

WHAKAPAPA VILLAGE

Sights & Activities
PEAKS
Mt Ruapehu

The long, multipeaked summit of Ruapehu (2797m) is the highest and most active of the park's volcanoes. The upper slopes were sprayed with hot mud during the volcanic hiccups of 1969 and 1975, and in December 1988 the volcano spewed hot rocks. These were just tame precursors to the spectacular 1995 eruptions, when Ruapehu spurted volcanic rock and cloaked the area in clouds of ash and steam. From June to September the following year the mountain rumbled, groaned and thrust ash clouds high into the sky, writing off the 1996 ski season. The latest eruption, accompanied by a small earthquake, came out of the blue in September 2007, seriously injuring a climber sleeping in a hut on the mountain.

Worse events have occurred. In fact, Ruapehu was the cause of one of NZ's deadliest natural disasters. From 1945 the level of Crater Lake rose dramatically as eruptions blocked the overflow. On Christmas Eve 1953 the dam burst and the flood of volcanic mud (known as a lahar) swept down the mountain and took out a railway bridge at Tangiwai (between Ohakune and Waiouru), just moments before a crowded express train arrived. The train was derailed and 153 people lost their lives.

The crater lake was blocked again by the 1995–96 eruption. As the levels rose, it was foreseen that a major lahar could lead to another catastrophe. Alarm systems were set up at the crater lake's edge and in March 2007 they were triggered when a moderate lahar swept down the Whangaehu Valley. No one was injured and there was little damage to infrastructure.

Ruapehu is the centrepiece of the national park, with Whakapapa Village (including the DOC visitor centre) on its slopes, numerous walking tracks and three ski fields.

Mt Tongariro

The Red Crater of Mt Tongariro (1968m) last erupted in 1926. This old but still active volcano has a number of coloured lakes dotting its uneven summit as well as hot springs gushing out of its side at Ketetahi. The Tongariro Alpine Crossing (p308), a magnificent walk, passes beside the lakes, right through several craters, and down through lush native forest.

Mt Ngauruhoe

Much younger than the other two volcanoes, it is estimated that Ngauruhoe (2290m) formed in the last 2500 years. In contrast to the others, which have multiple vents, Ngauruhoe is a conical, single-vent volcano with perfectly symmetrical slopes – the only one of the three that looks like a stereotypical volcano and the reason why it was chosen to star as Mt Doom in *Lord of the Rings*. It can be climbed in summer, but in winter (under snow) this steep climb is only for experienced mountaineers.

TRAMPING

Scattered around the park's tramping tracks are ten huts (Map p305) that can be used for accommodation. Prices vary according to hut and season, but range from $15 to $25 per person. You can camp beside the huts for $5 to $20 per person. The DOC centres and i-SITEs in Turangi, Whakapaka and Ohakune sell hut tickets and Backcountry Hut Passes.

In the summer season – between Labour Weekend (late October) and Queen's Birthday (early June) – a Great Walks Ticket is required for the popular four Tongariro Northern Circuit huts (Mangatepopo, Ketetahi, Oturere and Waihohonu), and must be bought in advance. This pass is also available from DOC centres, i-SITES or online at www.doc.govt.nz; ordinary hut tickets and the Backcountry Hut Pass cannot be used during these months.

Take note that Ketetahi Hut is the most popular in the park. It has bunks for 24 people, but regularly has 50 to 60 people trying to stay there on Saturday nights and at the busiest times of year (summer and school holidays). As bunks are claimed on a first-come, first-served basis, it's advisable to bring camping gear, just in case. Campers can use all of the hut facilities, which can make the kitchen crowded, especially at peak times.

For more information on tramping, hut accommodation and hut passes, see Active New Zealand (p75).

Tongariro Northern Circuit

Classed as one of NZ's Great Walks, the Northern Circuit circumnavigates Ngauruhoe and affords spectacular views all around, particularly of Mt Tongariro. As a circuit, there

---

HOTHEADS TO THE RESCUE

Maori legend tells of the great chief Ngatoro-i-rangi, who climbed Mt Tongariro in search of more land for his tribe. While acclaimed as a warrior, Ngatoro-i-rangi was only an amateur navigator and as night fell he couldn't find his way back down. He called on the fire gods, Te Pupu and Te Hoata, for help. The gods roared underground from Hawaiki to find Ngatoro-i-rangi, but stuck their heads up firstly at Whakaari (White Island), then exploded out at Rotorua before finally bursting forth in the volcanoes of Tongariro to warm the chief.

Because of this divine intervention, Maori revere these sites and once used the pools around them for rituals as well as cooking, dyes and medicine.

---

are several start and finish points, including Whakapapa Village, Ketetahi Rd, Desert Rd and by continuing the Round the Mountain Track. The walk covers the famous Tongariro Alpine Crossing (p308).

Highlights of the circuit include tramping through or past several volcanic craters, including the **South Crater**, **Central Crater** and **Red Crater**; brilliantly colourful volcanic lakes, including the **Emerald Lakes**, **Blue Lake** and the **Upper** and **Lower Tama Lakes**; the cold **Soda Springs**; and various other volcanic formations, including cones, lava flows and glacial valleys.

There are several possibilities for side trips that take from a few hours to overnight. The most popular side trip from the main track is to Ngauruhoe's summit (three hours return), but it is also possible to climb Tongariro from Red Crater (two hours return) or walk to the cold-water Ohinepango Springs from Waihohonu Hut (one hour return).

The safest and most popular time to walk the track is from December to March. The track is served by four well-maintained huts: **Mangatepopo**, **Ketetahi**, **Oturere** and **Waihohonu** (see Map p305). The huts have mattresses, gas cookers in summer, toilets and water. This track is quite difficult in winter, when it is covered in snow, and becomes a tough alpine trek requiring ice axes and crampons. You may need to factor in significant extra walking time, or not attempt it at all.

Estimated walking times in summer:

Route	Time (hr)
Whakapapa Village to Mangatepopo Hut	3–5
Mangatepopo Hut to Emerald Lakes	3½
Emerald Lakes to Oturere Hut	1½
Oturere Hut to Waihohonu Hut	3
Waihohonu Hut to Whakapapa Village	5½

Tongariro Alpine Crossing

Reputedly the best one-day walk in NZ, the Tongariro Alpine Crossing traverses spectacular volcanic geography, from an active crater to steaming vents and beautiful coloured lakes. And the views aren't bad either. The track passes through vegetation zones ranging from alpine scrub and tussock, to places at higher altitudes where there is no vegetation at all, to the lush podocarp forest as you descend from Ketetahi Hut towards the end of the track. It covers the most spectacular features of the Tongariro Northern Circuit between the Mangatepopo and Ketetahi Huts. (Trampers tackling the Northern Circuit complete this section on their second day, with the extra walk along the Ketetahi track.)

Although achievable in one day, the Crossing is exhausting and shouldn't be taken lightly. Weather can change without warning, so make sure you are adequately equipped.

If you're not in top walking condition you may prefer to do the Crossing in two days, throwing in a few side trips to keep it interesting. Worthwhile side trips from the main track include ascents to the summits of Mts Ngauruhoe and Tongariro. Mt Ngauruhoe can be ascended most easily from the Mangatepopo Saddle, reached near the beginning of the track after the first steep climb. The summit of Tongariro is reached by a poled route from Red Crater.

The Mangatepopo Hut, reached via Mangatepopo Rd, is near the start of the track, and the Ketetahi Hut is a couple of hours before the end. Estimated summer walking times:

Route	Time (hr)
Mangatepopo Rd end to Mangatepopo Hut	¼
Mangatepopo Hut to Mangatepopo Saddle	1½
Mangatepopo Saddle to Mt Ngauruhoe summit (side trip)	2 (return)
Red Crater to Tongariro summit (side trip)	1½ (return)
Mangatepopo Saddle to Emerald Lakes	1½–2
Emerald Lakes to Ketetahi Hut	1½
Ketetahi Hut to road end	1½

The Tongariro Alpine Crossing can be reached from Mangatepopo Rd, off SH47, and from Ketetahi Rd, off SH46. Theft from parked vehicles is a problem at both ends: don't leave valuables in the car and keep everything out of sight.

Because of its popularity, there are plenty of shuttle services to both ends of the track. The shuttles need to be booked and you'll need to complete the track in a reasonable time to be assured of your lift home – they won't wait if you dawdle.

Note: this may be one of the world's great walks, but it's not an experience you'll enjoy if you're badly prepared or the weather is awful. In winter, the colourful lakes are hidden under a blanket of snow and much of the effect is lost. If it's blowing a gale, pelting with rain or if you're wearing unsuitable clothing (jeans and flip-flops aren't alpine-appropriate), you're all but guaranteed to have a miserable, not to mention dangerous, time.

Round the Mountain

This off-the-beaten-track hike is known as being a quieter alternative to the busy Northern Circuit, but it's particularly tough, has some potentially tricky river crossings, and is not recommended for beginners or the unprepared. Looping around Mt Ruapehu, the trail takes in a diversity of country, from glacial rivers to tussocky moors to majestic mountain views. You should allow at least four days to complete the hike, with six days a realistic estimate if you're including side trips to the remote Blyth Hut or Tama Lakes.

You can get to the Round the Mountain trail from Whakapapa Village, the junction near Waihohonu Hut, Ohakune Mountain Rd, or Whakapapaiti Hut. Most trampers start at Whakapapa Village and return there to finish the loop.

The track is safest from December to March when there is little or no snow, and less chance of avalanche. At other times of year, navigation and walking is made difficult by snow, and full alpine gear (ice axe, crampons and specialised clothing) is a requirement. To attempt the track you should prepare thoroughly. Take sufficiently detailed maps, check on the latest conditions, and carry clothing for all climes and more-than-adequate food supplies. Be sure to leave your plans and intended return date with a responsible person and check in when you get back.

TAUPO & THE CENTRAL PLATEAU

This track is served by Waihohonu, **Rangipo**, **Mangaehuehu**, **Mangaturuturu** and **Whakapapaiti Huts**, and a side trip can be made to **Blyth Hut** (see Map p305). Estimated summer walking times:

Route	Time (hr)
Whakapapa Village to Waihohonu Hut	5-6
Waihohonu Hut to Rangipo Hut	5
Rangipo Hut to Mangaehuehu Hut	5-6
Mangaehuehu Hut to Mangaturuturu Hut	5
Mangaturuturu Hut to Whakapapaiti Hut	6
Whakapapaiti Hut to Whakapapa Village	2-3
Tama Lakes (side trip)	1½
Blyth Hut (side trip)	1

Other Walks

The DOC and i-SITE visitor centres at Whakapapa, Ohakune and Turangi have maps and information on interesting short and long walks in the park, as well as track and weather conditions.

The walk up to Ruapehu's **Crater Lake** (seven hours return) is a good one, allowing you to see the acidic lake up close, but this walk is strictly off limits when there's volcanic activity. This moderate-to-difficult walk begins at Iwikau Village at the Top of the Bruce Rd. You can cut three hours off it by catching the **chairlift** (adult/child $23/13; ☀ 9am-3.30pm mid-Dec–April) from Whakapapa Ski Area. **Guided walks** (☎ reservations 07-892 3738; adult/child incl lift pass $90/55) to Crater Lake meet daily at 9am at the Vertical store in Iwikau Village. Like most of the walks in Tongariro, you'll need to check conditions before heading out and don't attempt it in winter unless you're a mountaineer.

In addition to those below, several good tracks start from Ohakune Mountain Rd.

A number of fine walks beginning near the Whakapapa visitor centre and from the road leading up to it (see Map p306) are listed in DOC's *Walks in and around Tongariro National Park* ($3), including the following:

Ridge Track A 30-minute return walk that climbs through beech forest to alpine-shrub areas for views of Ruapehu and Ngauruhoe.

Silica Rapids A 2½-hour, 7km loop track to the Silica Rapids, named for the silica mineral deposits formed there by the rapids on Waikare Stream. The track passes interesting alpine features and, in the final 2.5km, passes down Top of the Bruce Rd above Whakapapa Village.

Tama Lakes A 17km track to the Tama Lakes (five to six hours return), on the Tama Saddle between Ruapehu and Ngauruhoe. The upper lake affords fine views of Ngauruhoe and Tongariro (beware of winds on the saddle).

Taranaki Falls A two-hour, 6km loop track to the 20m Taranaki Falls on Wairere Stream.

Whakapapa Nature Walk A 15-minute loop track suitable for wheelchairs, beginning about 200m above the visitor centre and passing through beech forest and gardens typical of the park's vegetation zones.

SKIING

Ruapehu's **Whakapapa Ski Area** (Map p305; ☎ 07-892 3738; www.mtruapehu.com; lift pass per half-day/full day $52/83) and **Turoa Ski Area** (Map p305; ☎ 06-385 8456; website & prices as above) offer similar skiing to suit all levels: around 400 hectares of field each, both taking you up to a maximum altitude of around 2300m. Beginners are well catered for, with gear hire, ski school, good learner areas and some nice easy runs. During the ski season you can tune into SKI FM 93.4, Aerial FM 96.6 or Peak FM 95.8 for updates on the slopes, or ring the **Snowphone** (☎ Turoa 083 222 180, Whakapapa 083 222 182).

You can hire gear in Taupo, National Park, Ohakune, or at Whakapaka at **Edge to Edge** (Map p306; ☎ 0800 800 754; www.edgetoedge.co.nz; Skotel Alpine Resort; 1-day full ski gear $35-43, 1-day snowboard gear $43-50), which also stocks a full range of climbing and alpine gear. The only accommodation at the ski fields is in private lodges, so most skiers stay at Whakapapa Village (see below), National Park village (see p312) or Ohakune (see p315).

The **Tukino Ski Area** (Map p305), on the eastern side of Ruapehu, is only accessible by a 4WD road. See also p84.

Sleeping

There are two basic DOC camping grounds in this area: **Mangahuia** (Map p305; SH47; campsites per person $4), between National Park village and the SH48 turn-off heading to Whakapapa; and **Mangawhero** (Map p305; Ohakune Mountain Rd; campsites per adult/child $4/2), near Ohakune. Both have cold water and pit toilets. See p307 for information on the DOC huts scattered around the park's tramping tracks.

Whakapapa Village has limited accommodation and prices quoted here are for summer; rates are generally much higher during the ski season. National Park village (p312) and Ohakune (p315) offer a greater range of options. National Park has the best selection of budget accommodation while Ohakune is a proper town, with a better array of eateries and shops.

Tongariro Holiday Park (Map p305; ☎ 07-386 8062; www.thp.co.nz; SH47; campsites per person $15-17, cabins $55-80, units $130-140) Located on SH47 halfway between Turangi and National Park (approximately 24km from each), this old Kiwi classic has basic cabins and newer units. Camping is pleasant and the communal facilities are more than adequate. Next door there's a cafe, Adventure HQ (ski hire) and the Tongariro Expeditions' base (below).

Whakapapa Holiday Park (Map p306; ☎ 07-892 3897; www.whakapapa.net.nz; Whakapapa Village; campsites per adult/child $17/10, dm/cabins/units $25/70/99) This well-maintained and popular park in the village has a wide range of accommodation options, including a 32-bed backpackers lodge, campsites perched on the edge of beautiful bushland and self-contained units for couples.

Skotel Alpine Resort (Map p306; ☎ 07-892 3719; www.skotel.co.nz; Whakapapa Village; s/d/tr/cabins $40/55/80/160, r $135-215; 🖳 📶) NZ's highest hotel offers three-bed backpacker rooms, cabins and regular hotel rooms. With timbered decor, the complex has an alpine feel; it also has a few luxuries, including sauna, spa pool, gym, ski shop, games room, licensed restaurant (dinner only; mains $19 to $29) and, most importantly, bar.

Fergusson Villas (Map p306; ☎ 07-892 3809; www.chateau.co.nz; Whakapapa Village; d/q $155/175) These small, self-contained chalets are good for families or small groups, with kitchens and diminutive decks for relaxing on. Booking and check-in is through the Bayview Chateau Tongariro.

Bayview Chateau Tongariro (Map p306; ☎ 07-892 3809; www.chateau.co.nz; Whakapapa Village; d $190-280, ste $350-1000; 🖳 📶) The landmark of the village, the 106-room Chateau harks back to a refined era, with classic European mansion-house grandeur. Opened in 1929, its refurbishments have seen it retain an old-world charm and dramatic snooker-room styling. The hotel boasts a cinema, restaurant, bar and cafe, nine-hole public golf course, tennis court, and, of course, views of mountains out the back and sweeping plateau below.

Eating & Drinking

Fergusson's Cafe (Map p306; mains $5-8; 🕑 breakfast & lunch; 🖳 📶) Across the road from the Chateau, Fergusson's is a casual tearoom with outdoor tables, and proffers pies, sandwiches, cakes and coffee.

Lorenz Bar & Cafe (mains $9-23; 🕑 breakfast & lunch) Up on the edge of the ski field itself, Lorenz offers a similarly unassuming standard of grub.

Tussock (Map p306; mains $14-18; 🕑 3pm-late) At the foot of the village, Tussock has a beer garden, views and occasional live entertainment in winter.

Pihanga Cafe (Map p306; mains $19-25; 🕑 lunch & dinner) One of the Chateau's two in-house dining options, the Pihanga is a consistent performer with good-value meals along the lines of soup, salads and fancier fare such as osso bucco. Next-door, the T-bar is a cosy spot for a winter warmer or a beer outside in the sunshine.

Ruapehu Room (Map p306; mains $34-39; 🕑 dinner) The Chateau's elegant à la carte option.

Whakapapa Camp Store (Map p306) at the Whakapapa Holiday Park sells basic groceries, though you're better off stocking up en route.

Getting There & Around

BUS

There are numerous shuttle services to Whakapapa Village, the Tongariro Alpine Crossing and other key destinations from Taupo, Turangi, National Park and Ohakune. In summer tramping trips are their focus, but in winter most offer ski-field shuttles. Book your bus in advance to avoid unexpected strandings. As well as those listed below, most of the National Park backpackers offer their own shuttles at similar rates (see p315).

Adventure HQ (☎ 07-386 0969; www.adventureheadquarters.co.nz) Runs scheduled Tongariro Alpine Crossing services ($30) from its base at Tongariro Holiday Park. It also sells and hires gear.

Extreme Backpackers (p303) Provides shuttles from Turangi to the Crossing ($35) and Northern Circuit ($40) and, in winter, Whakapapa Ski Area ($40).

Matai Shuttles (p316) Picks up from Ohakune, National Park and Whakapapa for the Crossing (return $35).

Mountain Shuttle (☎ 0800 117 686; mountainman989@hotmail.com) Runs between Turangi and Whakapapa/Tongariro Alpine Crossing daily ($35).

Tongariro Expeditions (☎ 0800 828 763; www.tongariroexpeditions.com) Runs shuttles from Turangi ($35, 40 mins), Taupo ($55, 1¼ hours), National Park village ($35, 30 minutes) and Whakapapa ($35, 15 mins) for the Crossing and the Northern Circuit.

Turangi Coachlines (☎ 07-386 8226; turangicoachlines@xtra.co.nz) Plys the Turangi–Whakapapa route ($40).

CAR & MOTORCYCLE

Tongariro National Park is bounded by roads: SH1 (called the Desert Rd, despite being sandless) to the east, SH4 to the west, SH46 and SH47 across the northern side and SH49 along the south. The main road up into the park is SH48, which leads to Whakapapa Village and continues further up the mountain to the Whakapapa Ski Area. Ohakune Mountain Rd leads up to the Turoa Ski Area from Ohakune. The Desert Rd is regularly closed when the weather is bad – large signs will direct you to other routes. Likewise, the Ohakune Mountain Rd and Top of the Bruce Rd are subject to closures, and access beyond certain points may be restricted to 4WDs or cars with snow chains.

NATIONAL PARK VILLAGE
pop 460

Named for nearby Tongariro National Park, this tiny outpost lies at the junction of SH4 and SH47, 15km from the hub of Whakapapa Village. In ski season the township is packed, but in summer it's sleepy – despite being a great base for activities in and around the park.

There's little to do in National Park itself, its major enticement being its proximity to the ski fields, national park tramps (p307), the 42 Traverse mountain-bike trail (below) and canoe trips on the Whanganui River. Daily shuttles leave from here to the Tongariro Alpine Crossing and Whakapapa Village in summer, and the ski area in winter.

As you'll discover, it's railway country around here. About 20km south on SH4 at Horopito is a monument to the Last Spike, the spike that marked the completion of the Main Trunk Railway Line between Auckland and Wellington in 1908 (the train chugs on through to this day). Five kilometres north from National Park, at Raurimu, is evidence of the engineering masterpiece that is the 'spiral' (p249). Trainspotters will marvel, while non-trainspotters will probably wonder what the hell they're looking at it (there's not much to see).

Information

There's no i-SITE in National Park, so visit www.nationalpark.co.nz for info. For everything else, go to Gasoline Alley on the main road. It's got fuel, postal services, groceries, gear hire, an ATM and slightly dubious convenience food.

Activities
MOUNTAIN BIKING

This area is most famous for the **42 Traverse**, a three- to six-hour, 45km mountain-bike trail through the Tongariro Forest, one of the most popular one-dayers on the North Island. The Traverse follows old logging tracks, making for relatively dependable going, although there are plenty of ups and downs – more downs as long as you start from SH47 and head down to Owhango.

The 50km **Fishers Track** is another revered ride. Starting from National Park, the track itself is mainly downhill – for about 21km – and some lightweights choose to get picked up at the nadir near Owhango. Others, however, continue the loop back to National Park via a fairly gruelling grind.

From National Park, Howard's Lodge provides transport and bike hire, while Plateau and Adventure Lodge offer transport only (see p312).

OTHER ACTIVITIES

For details on **skiing** Whakapapa and Turoa, see p309. Gear hire is available from **Eivins** (☎ 07-892 2843; www.nationalpark.co.nz/eivins; Carroll St), **Roy Turner** (☎ 07-892 2757; www.snowzone.co.nz; Buddo St) and **Ski Biz** (☎ 07-892 2717; www.skibiz. co.nz; 10 Carroll St). Most accommodation in town offers packages for lift passes and ski hire, sparing you the steeper prices further up the mountain.

Mountain Air (Map p305; ☎ 0800 922 812; www. mountainair.co.nz; flights $110-195), on SH47 near the turn-off to Whakapapa, offers three standard **scenic flights**, ranging from 15 to 35 minutes, covering the volcanoes and lakes. They also depart from Turangi ($265, 45 minutes) and Taupo ($295, 65 minutes).

Tongariro Forest Conservation Area can be explored with relatively little effort with **Quad Biking NZ** (☎ 07-378 8349; www.quadbikingnz.co.nz; half-/ full day $195/295).

Adrift Guided Outdoor Adventures (☎ 07-892 2751; www.adriftnz.co.nz) runs guided **canoe trips** on the Whanganui River (half-day to six days, $130 to $950), as well as freedom canoe hire and necessary transfers. They also offer one- to three-day guided tramps in the national park ($125 to $725).

Wade's Landing Outdoors (☎ 07-895 5995; www. whanganui.co.nz) also offers guided canoe trips on the Whanganui River, along with freedom kayak hire and transfers (one to five days, $80 to $180), jetboat rides ($95 to $150) and jetboat/ road transfers to trail heads ($150 to $270).

For those rainy days there's an 8m-high indoor **climbing wall** (☎ 07-892 2870; www.npbc.co.nz;

Finlay St; adult/child $15/10; ☼9am-9pm) at National Park Backpackers. Outdoor climbers with their own gear can find spots near Manataupo Valley and Whakapapa Gorge.

Sleeping

National Park is a town of budget and mid-range accommodation. This makes sense, as you'll probably spend most of your time in the great outdoors. We list summer prices here; be warned they increase somewhat in the ski season when accommodation is tight and bookings are essential.

Discovery Lodge (Map p305; ☎ 07-892 2744; www.discovery.net.nz; campsites per person $14, cabins/d $50/90, units $135-175; ▣) Handy for skiers, this lodge is on SH47, between National Park and the Whakapapa turn-off. The restaurant has excellent views of Ruapehu, plus there's a bar and comfy lounge. Cabins are basic, but large chalets are great getaways for up to four people.

Howard's Lodge (☎ 07-892 2827; www.howardslodge.co.nz; Carroll St; dm $27, s $60-75, d $68-105, tr $84-120, q $140; ▣ ☞) Howard's moved on, but he's left his legacy in this large, freshly decorated lodge with spa, two comfortable lounges with supersized TVs, and spotless, well-equipped kitchens. Dorms are relatively roomy, with only three or four bunks. For outdoor action, there are plenty of skis, snowboards, tramping gear and mountain bikes for hire. Howard's also runs shuttle services around the park. Book InterCity buses and interisland ferries here.

Plateau (☎ 07-892 2993; www.plateaulodge.co.nz; Carroll St; dm $28, d $65-85, tr $93-113, q $141, apt $155-235; ▣ ☞) The sort of schmick backpackers that you don't need to be of college age to enjoy, Plateau has immaculate cosy rooms, some with en suite and TV, and an attractive communal lounge, kitchen and hot tub. The dorms don't get bigger than two sets of bunks and there are two-bedroom apartments (sleeping up to six) available as well.

Adventure Lodge & Motel (☎ 07-892 2991; www.adventurenationalpark.co.nz; Carroll St; lodge dm/s/d/tr/q $30/50/65/90/120, B&B tw/d $130/170, units $130-190; ▣ ☞) This place caters to Tongariro alpine crossers, offering cosy, comfortable accommodation. You can also get dinner as part of a good-value all-inclusive package (two nights, breakfast, lunch, dinner, T-shirt and transport for $165 to $195). For homebodies, there are good facilities including relaxing lounge, spa

pools and a barbecue. The B&B rooms have en suites.

Park Travellers' Lodge (☎ 07-892 2748; www.the-park.co.nz; Millar St; dm $30-35, d $100-130, apt $150-340; ▣ ☞) There's no way you can miss this big flashpackers on the main road. Inside it's smart and comfortable, with a laid-back courtyard surrounded by 200 beds' worth of dorms, doubles and self-contained micro-apartments. Conveniences are modern and hardwearing, while the in-house Spiral cafe does dinner à la blackboard for $11 to $23. The railway-inspired house bar is a highlight (and we're not just saying that because of the beer).

Mountain Heights Lodge (Map p305; ☎ 07-892 2833; www.mountainheights.co.nz; units $110-170, d $140-160) This friendly Swiss-chalet-style lodge on SH4, 2km south of National Park, has good-quality, self-contained motel units that sleep up to six people; and B&B in comfortable en suite rooms with TVs and tea-making facilities. Other meals are offered by arrangement, and mountain bikes are available for hire (per two hours/half-day/full day/42 Traverse $20/30/40/60).

our pick **Tongariro Crossing Lodge** (☎ 07-892 2688; www.tongarirocrossinglodge.com; 37 Carroll St; d $145-164, tr $165-184, q $204; ▣) As pretty as a picture in white weatherboard with baby-blue trim and rambling blooms in summer. Rooms range from a standard double to larger self-contained rooms that include a full kitchen; the lodge also offers B&B with optional dinner (by arrangement).

Eating & Drinking

In the winter season when town is full, all options will be open most of the time. When the ski fields close, however, plan ahead: options dry up, although there's always food to be had somewhere.

Basekamp (☎ 07-892 2872; Carroll St; mains $17-18; ☼ dinner Fri-Sun summer, daily winter) Basekamp does wood-fired pizza, tasty gourmet burgers and other tummy-filling grub for hungry ski folk.

National Park Hotel (☎ 07-892 2805; 61 Carroll St; mains $18-25; ☼ 10am-11pm) The only Kiwi boozer in town, and a good old-fashioned one to boot. Pool tables, mixed grill and chicken Kiev, real live locals having a few quiet ones, and beer by the quart or jug.

Schnapps (☎ 07-892 2788; Finlay St; mains $19-27; ☼ lunch Sat & Sun, dinner daily) This popular pub does excellent pizzas, generous burgers and better-than-average pub fare. Bands pack the place out on wintry Saturday nights.

our pick Station (☎ 07-892 2881; cnr Station & Finlay Sts; mains $24-32; ☺ 10am-11pm) Count your blessings ye who find this little railway station along the line, a lovely old dear lovingly restored and now serving eggy brunch, lunch, coffee and cakes, plus an impressive à la carte evening menu.

Getting There & Away

BUS

InterCity (☎ 09-583 5780; www.intercity.co.nz) buses arrive at, and depart from, outside Ski Haus on Carroll St daily, heading to Auckland ($62, 5½ hours) via Hamilton ($43, 3½ hours), and Palmerston North ($47, four hours) via Whanganui ($37, two hours). Book at Howard's Lodge (opposite).

For local shuttle services, see p310.

TRAIN

The **Tranz Scenic Overlander** (☎ 04-495 0775; www.tranzscenic.co.nz; tickets $49-81) trains on the Auckland–Wellington line stop at National Park (and Ohakune). The service runs in both directions from Friday to Sunday, May to September, and daily October to April. Train tickets are sold from Howard's Lodge, not at the station.

OHAKUNE

pop 1100

Expect to see carrots crop up all over Ohakune, for this is overwhelmingly the country's carrot capital. Not only do they creep into burgers and sneak onto pizzas, they litter the roadside in season. To learn more (and you know you want to), visit during October's annual Carrot Carnival (see the boxed text, p316).

But they needn't mention liver cleansing and eyesight improvement to win us over to the charms of this little town. A pretty retreat in the summer, offering outdoor adventure galore, Ohakune springs to life in winter when the snow drifts down on Turoa Ski Area and the snow bunnies invade (they no doubt love carrots themselves).

There are two ends to the town: the commercial hub strings along the highway, but in winter the northern end around the train station, known as the Junction, is the epicentre of action.

Information

Library (☎ 06-385 8364; Ayr St; ☺ 9am-5pm Mon-Fri) Offers free internet access.

Ruapehu i-SITE (☎ 06-385 8427; 54 Clyde St; ☺ 9am-5pm Mon-Sun) Can make bookings for activities, transport and accommodation; DOC officer on hand from 9am to 3.30pm, Wednesday to Sunday.

Take Note (5 Goldfinch St; ☺ 7am-5pm Mon-Fri, to 4pm Sat) Has a post office.

Activities

SKIING & SNOWBOARDING

Ohakune is all abuzz in winter when the town fills up with skiers, snowboarders, and staff to look after them. Lift passes (half-day/full day $52/83) are available at the ski fields, with equipment available from various places around town, including the following:

Powderhorn Snow Centre (☎ 06-385 9100; www. snowcentre.co.nz; 194 Mangawhero Tce)

Ski Shed (☎ 06-385 9173; www.skished.com; 71 Clyde St)

SLR (☎ 06-385 8018; www.slr.co.nz; 60 Thames St)

TCB (☎ 06-385 8433; www.tcbskiandboard.co.nz; 27 Ayr St)

For more information on skiing and snowboarding, see p84.

TRAMPING

There are several scenic walks near the town, many starting from the Ohakune Mountain Rd, which stretches 17km from Ohakune to the Turoa Ski Area on Mt Ruapehu. The handy DOC brochure *Walks in and around Tongariro National Park* ($3) is a good starting point, available from the i-SITE.

An easy stroll starting near the beginning of Ohakune Mountain Rd is the **Mangawhero Forest Walk** (one hour return, 3km). This takes in native forest and the Mangawhero River. It is well graded and suitable for wheelchairs and pushchairs. Also leaving from Ohakune Mountain Rd are popular and more challenging tracks, including **Waitonga Falls** (1½ hours return, 4km), with magnificent views of Mt Ruapehu and Tongariro's highest waterfall (39m); and **Lake Surprise** (five hours return, 9km).

Tramps in Tongariro National Park (p307), including the Tongariro Alpine Crossing, are easily accessible from Ohakune, and shuttle services are provided by Matai Shuttles (p316). The Round the Mountain track (p308) can be accessed by continuing on the Waitonga Falls track.

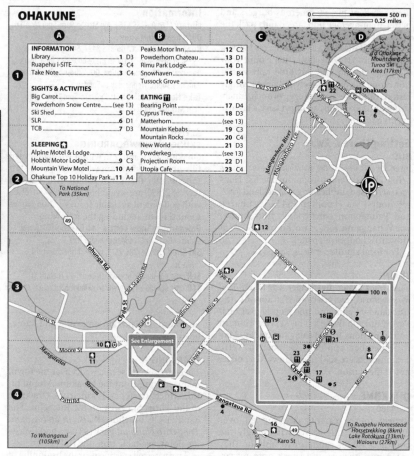

OHAKUNE

INFORMATION
Library	1	D3
Ruapehu i-SITE	2	C4
Take Note	3	C4

SIGHTS & ACTIVITIES
Big Carrot	4	C4
Powderhorn Snow Centre	(see 13)	
Ski Shed	5	D4
SLR	6	D1
TCB	7	D3

SLEEPING
Alpine Motel & Lodge	8	D4
Hobbit Motor Lodge	9	C3
Mountain View Motel	10	A4
Ohakune Top 10 Holiday Park	11	A4

Peaks Motor Inn	12	C2
Powderhorn Chateau	13	D1
Rimu Park Lodge	14	D1
Snowhaven	15	B4
Tussock Grove	16	C4

EATING
Bearing Point	17	D4
Cyprus Tree	18	D3
Matterhorn	(see 13)	
Mountain Kebabs	19	C3
Mountain Rocks	20	C4
New World	21	D3
Powderkeg	(see 13)	
Projection Room	22	D1
Utopia Cafe	23	C4

By the time you read this, the **Old Coach Road** walkway and cycleway should be open. The walk is a community-led restoration of the original coach route from Ohakune to Horopito. Begun in 1886, it was built largely by hand by people who experienced great hardships, living in canvas tents and working in harsh winter conditions. It was gradually upgraded to carry passengers and goods, and used until 1909, when SH49 opened and it fell into disuse. The road has remained largely untouched ever since.

The gently graded walk promises a number of unique engineering features including the historic Hapuawhenua and Toanui viaducts – these are the only two remaining curved viaducts in the southern hemisphere. It passes through ancient forest that survived the Taupo blast, being in the lea of Ruapehu. Giant rimu and totara trees can be seen.

OTHER ACTIVITIES
There are plenty of good **mountain-biking** routes in the area, starting with the 1km descent down the sealed Ohakune Mountain Rd (check those brakes first!). The Old Coach Rd cycleway will eventually form part of a 245km Mountain-to-Sea cycle route, reaching the coast at Whanganui. TCB (p313) is a good source of information and they also rent out bikes (half-day/full day from $30/40).

You can take Whanganui River **kayaking** trips from Ohakune with **Canoe Safaris**

(☎ 06-385 9237; www.canoesafaris.co.nz; guided tours 2-5 days $365-840, freedom hire 2-5 days $140-190), which also runs guided rafting trips on the Mohaka (two to four days, $405 to $895) and the Rangitikei (one to four days, $105 to $765); or **Yeti Tours** (☎ 06-385 8197; www.canoe.co.nz; guided tours 2-6 days $375-795, 2-5 day freedom hire $140-215).

Five minutes out of Ohakune, at Rangataua, **Ruapehu Homestead Horsetrekking** (☎ 06-385 8799; ruapehuhomestead@xtra.co.nz; SH49, Rangataua; 30min-day adult $20-95, child $15-80) runs guided **horse treks** around its paddocks, as well as longer rides along the river and on backcountry trails with views of the mountain.

Sleeping

In summer the Junction is a bit of a ghost town, so stay near SH49. The prices listed here are for summer (October to March); expect to pay up to 50% more in winter and book ahead. Good savings can be made on winter rates by booking midweek.

BUDGET

Ohakune Top 10 Holiday Park (☎ 0800 825 825; www.ohakune.net.nz; 5 Moore St; campsites per adult/child $19/12, s $29-145, d $58-145, tr $75-166, q $97-186; 🖳 🛜) The stream edges this holiday park, which offers spacious communal facilities and several self-catering options. Extras include playground, *pétanque* court, barbecue area and spa bath.

Hobbit Motorlodge (☎ 06-385 8248; www.the-hobbit.co.nz; cnr Goldfinch & Wye Sts; dm $22, units $90-180; 🛜) A leafy and quiet option halfway between the town and the Junction, the Hobbit has a backpacker wing, motel units and fancier suites. The bush-setting hot tub is a real bonus. There's a children's play area, too.

our pick **Rimu Park Lodge** (☎ 06-385 9023; www.rimupark.co.nz; 27 Rimu St; backpackers dm/d $25/60, cabins d/tr/q $60/80/100, carriages $100-120, apt $210-490; 🖳 🛜) This rambling, character-filled complex is close to the Junction and has an option for every budget. Pine Tree Lodge sleeps up to 10 ($180), plus there are cabins, slick self-contained apartments and a 1934 train carriage, popular with families.

Alpine Motel & Lodge (☎ 06-385 8758; www.alpinemotel.co.nz; 7 Miro St; dm $25, d $105-110, tr $115-125, q $130-250; 🖳 🛜) Right in the middle of town, the Alpine offers 40 beds in motor-lodgey rooms and a four-bedroom townhouse next door, great for families or groups. There's also a fairly basic backpackers wing and an in-house restaurant.

Mountain View Motel (☎ 06-385 8675; www.mountain-viewmotel.co.nz; 2 Moore St; d $60-90, tr $90-100, q $110) In this old-style motel the comfortable rooms are clean, quiet and good value, with all other necessary facilities (including spa) on the doorstep.

Peaks Motor Inn (☎ 06-385 9144; www.thepeaks.co.nz; cnr Mangawhero Tce & Shannon St; d $95-109, tr $110-124, q $139; 🖳 🛜) This quadrangular, modern motel offers spacious rooms with good bathrooms. Communal facilities include basic gym, large outdoor spa and sauna.

MIDRANGE & TOP END

Snowhaven (☎ 06-385 9498; www.snowhaven.co.nz; 92 Clyde St; apt/townhouse/r $95/180/190; 🛜) A tasty trio's on offer here: modern studio apartments in a slate-fronted block on the main drag; three self-contained, three-bedroom townhouses by the Junction; or luxury B&B rooms somewhere between the other two. All are top options.

Tussock Grove (☎ 06-385 8771; www.tussockgrove.co.nz; 3 Karo St; r $120-160, tr $175-190, ste $220-250; 🛜) Cooking on holiday? No way, mister. In a town full of motels this boutique hotel fills a gap for those who just want a decent midrange room, perhaps with a mountain view. Facilities include Sky TV, sauna, spa, *pétanque* and tennis courts.

Powderhorn Chateau (☎ 06-385 8888; www.powderhorn.co.nz; cnr Thames St & Mangawhero Tce; ste/apt $198/750; 🖳 🛜 📺) Enjoying a long-standing reputation as the hub of activity during the ski season, the Powderhorn has a Swiss-chalet feel with woody interiors and exposed rafters. The grotto-like indoor pool is a relaxing way to recover from the slopes before enjoying revelry in the popular in-house establishments the Powderkeg and the Matterhorn (p316).

Eating & Drinking

The Junction is active during winter with the après-ski crowd, but little is open in summer. Many hotels open their restaurants during the ski season.

our pick **Utopia Cafe** (☎ 06-385 9120; 47 Clyde St; mains $7-20; ⏱ breakfast & lunch) A funky, upbeat and perennially popular destination for locals and visitors alike, with good reason. Great breakfast staples such as eggs Benedict and brioche with bacon and banana, plus a good vegie selection and fresh homemade counter food.

Mountain Kebabs (☎ 06-385 9047; 29 Clyde St; kebabs $9-12; ☻ lunch & dinner) Any old kebabery can come up with the basic lamb, chicken or felafel varieties – but here camembert, hummus, sprouts and olives are rolled into the mix, too.

Projection Room (☎ 06-385 8664; 4 Thames St; mains $14-30; ☻ 6pm-late Wed-Sun winter) This funky little spot has occasional films and dancing to DJs, as well as a comfort-food menu featuring burgers, curries, noodles and steak.

Powderkeg & Matterhorn (☎ 06-385 8888; cnr Thames St & Mangawhero Tce; bar menu $16-22, à la carte $21-32; ☻ lunch & dinner) The Powderkeg is the party bar of the Powderhorn Chateau, with bands in winter and regular dancing on the tables – once the detritus of the burger and pizza meals have been cleared. Upstairs is the swankier Matterhorn, serving cocktails and sophisticated bar snacks as well as relaxed but chic à la carte dining.

Mountain Rocks (☎ 06-385 8295; cnr Clyde & Goldfinch Sts; mains $20-29; ☻ 8am-late) A log-cabin-like space that feels more like a watering hole than an eatery. However, decent sandwiches, homemade burgers and great cakes are available, as well as substantial evening meals to soak up the alcohol.

Cyprus Tree (☎ 06-385 8857; 19a Goldfinch St; mains $22-30; ☻ lunch Sat & Sun, dinner Thu-Mon) Distinctly Italian food – pizza, pasta and antipasto – served in a chic yet relaxed space. Thursday 'pizza and pint' nights are great value – especially as the 'pizza' stretches to pasta and the 'pint' to house wine.

Bearing Point (☎ 06-385 9006; Clyde St; mains $23-33; ☻ lunch Sat & Sun, dinner Tue-Sun) Hearty après-ski fare is offered at this upmarket establishment run by local identities. Warm your cockles

---

CARROT CRAZY

No matter who you ask in NZ, the name Ohakune means carrots; the town produces two-thirds of the North Island's crop. In 1984 the township saluted the town's biggest vegetable crop by erecting the **Big Carrot** (Rangataua Rd), which quickly became one of NZ's most hugged 'Big Things'. Carrots were first grown in the area during the 1920s by Chinese settlers, who cleared land by hand and explosives! Today the **Carrot Carnival** (www.carrotcarnival.org.nz) is celebrated at the beginning of October with a parade and lots of dressing up in orange.

---

with aged eye fillet, maple-glazed salmon, lamb rump or a seafood curry.

Self-caterers should head for **New World** (☎ 06-385 8587; 14 Goldfinch St; ☻ 7am-7pm), which offers the last chance to stock up before leaving for National Park or Whakapapa.

Getting There & Away

InterCity (☎ 09-583 5780; www.intercity.co.nz) buses stop outside Mountain Kebabs, en route to Auckland ($66, six hours) via Hamilton ($49, four hours), and Palmerston North ($41, three hours) via Whanganui ($31, 1½ hours).

Ohakune is the next stop south of National Park on the Tranz Scenic Overlander route; see p313 for details.

Getting Around

Several operators run services around the area including to and from the ski fields and the national park walks.

Matai Shuttles (☎ 06-385 8724; www.mataishuttles.co.nz) Runs Turoa ski shuttle (return $20) and drop-offs all around the volcanic plateau including the Tongariro Alpine Crossing (return $35). It also run a handy night shuttle around Ohakune's pubs during the ski season ($4).

Snow Express (☎ 06-385 4022; return $20) Offers transport to Turoa.

LAKE ROTOKURA

Rotokura Ecological Reserve is 14km southeast of Ohakune, at Karioi, just off SH49 (*karioi* means 'places to linger'). There are two lakes here: the first is Dry Lake, actually quite wet and perfect for picnicking; the furthest is Rotokura, *tapu* (sacred) to Maori, so eating, fishing and swimming are prohibited. The round-trip walk will take you 45 minutes; longer if you linger to admire the ancient beech trees and waterfowl such as dabchicks and paradise ducks.

WAIOURU

pop 1400

At the junction of SH1 and SH49, 27km east of Ohakune, Waiouru is primarily an army base and a refuelling stop for the 56km-long Desert Rd leading to Turangi. Rangipo Desert isn't a true desert as it receives plenty of rainfall; its stunted scrubby vegetation is due to its high altitude, windswept nature and the Taupo eruption that obliterated the ancient forests, affected the soil quality and caused a mass sterilisation of seeds. The road often closes in winter due to snow.

At the south end of the township in a large, concrete castle is the **National Army Museum** (☎ 0800 369 999; www.armymuseum.co.nz; adult/child $12/7; ☼ 9am-4.30pm), which preserves the history of the NZ army and its various campaigns, from colonial times to the present. Its moving stories are well told through displays of arms, uniforms, memorabilia and other collections.

Once you're done with playing soldier, head 11km south to **Lazy H Horseback Riding & Adventures** (☎ 06-388 1144; www.lazyh.co.nz; 159 Maukuku Rd; 1½hr/half-day/full day/overnight $110/180/250/410), where you can channel your inner cowboy.

TAIHAPE & AROUND
pop 1800

If you have a penchant for gumboots (Wellingtons), a visit to Taihape, 20km south of Waiouru, is a must. The town has the dubious distinction of being the Gumboot Capital of the World, celebrated with – you guessed it – a giant corrugated gumboot on the main street. It is also the access point for **Gravity Canyon** (☎ 06-388 9109; www.gravitycanyon.co.nz; Mokai; 1-/2-/3-activities $110/175/240), 20km southeast, where adrenaline-junkies can take a 1km, 170m-high flying-fox ride at speeds of up to 160km/h; dive from the North Island's highest bridge bungy (80m); or swing on the world's highest tandem swing.

If you didn't give horseback riding a go in Ohakune or Waiouru, giddy-up to **River Lodge Stables** (☎ 06-388 1444; www.rivervalley.co.nz), 28km northeast of Taihape (follow the signs from Taihape's Gretna Hotel). Enjoy views of Mt Ruapehu, the Ruahine Ranges and the Rangitikei River on two-hour ($105), half-day ($165) or day-long ($215) excursions. On summer evenings the two-hour Sunset Ride ends with a glass of champagne. Break in the littlies with a half-hour hand-led Pony Ride.

Rotorua & the Bay of Plenty

Captain Cook christened the Bay of Plenty as he sailed past in 1769, and plentiful it remains to this day, blessed with buckets of sunshine and a long sandy coastline. The Bay stretches from Waihi Beach in the west to Opotiki in the east, with a sprinkling of seaside towns and the happening hub of Tauranga in between. Nearby Mt Maunganui has been popular with Kiwi holidaymakers for generations.

Further east along the pohutukawa-covered coast is Whakatane, the launch pad for tours to New Zealand's most active volcano, Whakaari (White Island). Volcanic activity defines the landscape from here to the Central Plateau, a constant reminder that under this fertile soil lies a molten core, oozing upwards to the surface.

Nowhere is this subterranean sexiness more obvious than in Rotorua, NZ's most famous tourist destination. Here the daily business of life goes on among steaming hot springs, explosive geysers, bubbling mud pools, and the clouds of sulphurous gas responsible for the town's 'unique' eggy smell.

Rotorua and the Bay remain strongholds of Maori tradition and history, so there are plenty of opportunities to explore the rich culture of the indigenous people of NZ: check out a power-packed concert performance, chow down at a *hangi* or discover the meaning and techniques behind Maori arts and crafts.

HIGHLIGHTS

- Watching Rotorua's famous geyser **Pohutu** (p321) blow its top, then tucking into a Maori **hangi** (p323)
- Checking out kaleidoscopic colours and bubbling mud pools at **Wai-O-Tapu** (p337)
- Mountain biking on tracks from humble to hardcore at the **Redwoods – Whakarewarewa Forest** (p325)
- Surfing NZ's first artificial reef at **Mt Maunganui** (p346)
- Flying or boating out to NZ's only active marine volcano, **Whakaari** (White Island; p355)
- Kicking back for a few days in **Whakatane** (p351) – NZ's most underrated seaside town?
- Swimming with dolphins at **Tauranga** (p340) or **Whakatane** (p351)

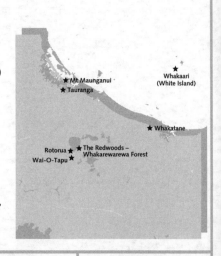

- Telephone code: 07
- www.rotoruanz.com
- www.bayofplenty.co.nz

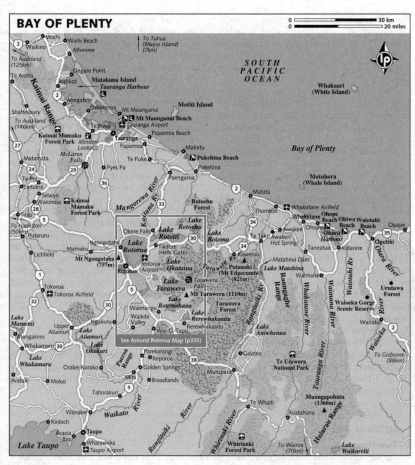

BAY OF PLENTY

(See Around Rotorua Map p335)

Climate

The Bay of Plenty is one of the sunniest regions of NZ, with Whakatane and the Eastern Bay recording the most hours of sunshine (2350 per year on average). In summer, temperatures hover between 20°C and 27°C, while winter sees the mercury fall as low as 5°C, although it's slightly warmer on the coast. Rainfall is heavier inland in places such as Rotorua, which also experiences long dry spells in summer.

Getting There & Around

Air New Zealand has flights from Tauranga and Whakatane to Auckland and Wellington; as well as from Rotorua to Sydney (every Tuesday and Saturday), Auckland, Wellington

and Christchurch. Qantas also links Auckland with Tauranga, Whakatane and Rotorua.

InterCity and Naked Bus services connect Tauranga, Rotorua and Whakatane with most other main cities in NZ. Bay Hopper bus services run between Tauranga, Whakatane and Opotiki. Twin City Express buses link Tauranga and Rotorua.

ROTORUA

pop 70,400

Catch a whiff of Rotorua's sulphur-rich, asthmatic airs and you've already got a taste of NZ's most dynamic thermal area, home to spurting geysers, steaming hot springs and exploding mud pools. The Maori revered this place, naming one of the most spectacular springs Wai-O-Tapu (Sacred Waters). Today 35% of the population is Maori, with their cultural performances and traditional *hangi* as big an attraction as the landscape itself.

Despite the pervasive eggy odour, 'Sulphur City' is one of the most touristed spots on the North Island, with nearly three million visitors annually. Some locals say this steady trade has seduced the town into resting on its laurels, and that socially Rotorua lags behind more progressive towns like Tauranga and Taupo by a long shot. And with more motels than nights in November, the urban fabric of 'RotoVegas' is far from appealing…but still, where else can you see a 30m geothermal geyser!

HISTORY

This area was first settled in the 14th century when the canoe *Te Arawa*, captained by Tamatekapua, arrived from Hawaiki at Maketu in the central Bay of Plenty. Settlers took the tribal name Te Arawa to commemorate the vessel that had brought them here. Tamatekapua's grandson, Ihenga, explored much of the inland forest, naming geographical features as he discovered them. Ihenga unimaginatively dubbed the lake Rotorua (or 'Second Lake') as it was the second lake he came across.

In the next few hundred years, subtribes spread and divided through the area, with conflicts breaking out over limited territory. A flashpoint occurred in 1823 when the Arawa lands were invaded by tribes from the Northland in the so-called Musket Wars (see p31 for more on these conflicts). After heavy losses on both sides, the Northlanders eventually withdrew.

During the Waikato Land War (1863–64) Te Arawa threw in its lot with the government against its traditional Waikato enemies, gaining troop support and preventing East Coast reinforcements getting through to support the Kingitanga movement (see the boxed text, p225).

With peace in the early 1870s, word spread of scenic wonders, miraculous landscapes and watery cures for all manner of diseases. The town boomed. Its main attraction was the fabulous Pink and White Terraces, formed by volcanic silica deposits. Touted at the time as the eighth natural wonder of the world, they were destroyed in the 1886 Mt Tarawera eruption (see p337).

ORIENTATION

Tutanekai St is the central shopping area, part of which is a pedestrian mall. Running parallel is the major through road, Fenton St, which is lined with motels, particularly to the south.

ROTORUA AREA IN...

Two Days

Up with the lark and order breakfast near the lakeside at **Lime Caffeteria** (p332), after which the **Rotorua Museum of Art & History** (p324) will be open. Stroll along the water's edge to **Ohinemutu** (p325) and back to town via steamy **Kuirau Park** (p322). Then head to the **Blue Baths** (p325) for a relaxing soak. In the evening, catch a *hangi* and concert at **Tamaki** (p323) or **Mitai** (p323) Maori villages.

Start the second day with a tour of **Whakarewarewa Thermal Village** (p322) and watch **Pohutu** geyser blow its top. From there, it's a quick hop to **The Redwoods – Whakarewarewa Forest** (p325) for a couple of hours' exploration by mountain bike. Hop across town to ride the gondola, luge and sky swing at **Skyline Skyrides** (p334), but not before catching the falcons at **Wingspan Birds of Prey Trust** (p334).

Four Days

Take the two-day itinerary, then explore further afield starting with **Agroventures** (p336), where you can while away several hours with a farm show, bungy, giant swing and the zany zorb. A compulsory stop en route for nature-lovers is **Rainbow Springs Kiwi Wildlife Park** (p334), where you can take a **Kiwi Encounter** tour. On your last day, head southeast and visit the **Buried Village** (p337), swim in **Lake Tarawera** (p337), or take a long walk on one of the tracks at nearby **Lake Okataina** (p327).

INFORMATION
Bookshops

McLeods Booksellers (Map p322; ☎ 07-348 5388; www.mcleodsbooks.co.nz; 1269 Tutanekai St; ☉ 8.30am-5.30pm Mon-Thu, to 7pm Fri, 9am-4pm Sat, 10am-3pm Sun) Independent bookshop with maps, mags and extensive travel and Maori sections.

Emergency

Ambulance, fire & police (☎ 111)

Internet Access

Cyber World (Map p322; 1174 Haupapa St; ☉ 10am-8pm)

Cybershed (Map p322; 1176 Pukuatua St; ☉ 9.15am-7pm Mon & Fri, to 8.30pm Tue-Thu, 10am-late Sat)

Medical Services

Lakes Care Medical Centre (Map p322; ☎ 07-348 1000; 1165 Tutanekai St; ☉ 8am-11pm) Urgent medical care.

Rotorua Hospital (Map p322; ☎ 07-348 1199; www.lakesdhb.govt.nz; Arawa St; ☉ 24hr)

Money

There's a Travelex at the i-SITE, and most banks offer currency exchange, including Kiwibank at the post office.

Post

Post office (Map p322; www.nzpost.co.nz; 1189 Hinemoa St; ☉ 7.30am-5pm Mon-Fri, 8.30am-2pm Sat)

Tourist Information

Automobile Association (AA; Map p322; ☎ 07-348 3069; www.aatravel.co.nz; 1121 Eruera St; ☉ 8.30am-5pm Mon-Fri) Has maps and other travel information.

Rotorua i-SITE (Map p322; ☎ 0800 768 678, 07-348 5179; www.rotoruanz.com; 1167 Fenton St; ☉ 8am-6pm) The hub for all travel information and bookings including Department of Conservation (DOC) walks. Also has an exchange bureau, cafe, showers and lockers.

Rotorua Sustainable Tourism (www.sustainablenz.com) How to make your Rotorua visit more ecofriendly.

SIGHTS
Geothermal Attractions

Rotorua's main drawcard is **Te Whakarewarewa** (pronounced 'Fa-ka-re-wa-re-wa'), a thermal reserve 3km from the city centre at the south end of Fenton Street. This area's full name is Te Whakarewarewatanga o te Ope Taua a Wahiao, meaning 'The Gathering Together of the War Party of Wahiao', although many people just call it 'Whaka'. Whatever you

---

ROTORUA & THE BAY OF PLENTY

---

prefer, the reserve is as famous for its Maori cultural significance as its steam and bubbling mud. There are more than 500 springs here, varying from cold to boiling cauldrons. The most famous spring is **Pohutu** ('Big Splash' or 'Explosion'), a geyser which erupts up to 20 times a day, spurting hot water up to 30m skyward. You'll know when it's about to blow because the **Prince of Wales' Feathers** geyser will start up shortly before.

There are two main tourist operations here: Te Pui and Whakarewarewa Thermal Village. Pohutu and the Prince of Wales' Feathers geyser are part of **Te Puia** (Map p335; ☎ 0800 837 842, 07-348 9047; www.tepuia.com; Hemo Rd; admission incl tour & daytime cultural performance adult/child $50/25, tour & Te Po evening concert & hangi $99/50, combination $130/65; ☉ 8am-6pm summer, to 5pm winter), the most polished of NZ's Maori cultural attractions. Also here is the National Carving & Weaving School, where you can discover the work and methods of traditional Maori weavers and woodcarvers. More of these arts are displayed at Rotowhio Marae, which has a carved meeting house. Also here are a cafe, two museums, a Kiwi reserve and a gift shop that stocks an excellent range of arts and crafts.

Tours of Te Puia take 90 minutes and depart on the hour from 9am (last tour 4pm in winter, 5pm in summer). Daytime cultural performances (lasting 45 minutes) start at

10.15am, 12.15pm and 3.15pm, while nightly **Te Po Indigenous Experience** *hangi* concerts are held in the evenings at 6.15pm.

Whakarewarewa Thermal Village (☎ 07-349 3463; www.whakarewarewa.com; 17 Tryon St; admission incl tours & concerts adult/child/family $28/12.50/68.50; ⏰ 8.30am-5pm, tours 9am-4pm, concerts 11.15am & 2pm), on the eastern side of Te Whakarewarewa, is a living village, where *tangata whenua* (the locals) still reside, as they and their ancestors have for centuries. It's these local villagers who show you around and tell you the stories of their way of life and the significance of the steamy bubbling pools, silica terraces and the geysers that, although inaccessible from the village, are easily viewed from vantage points (the view of Pohutu is just as good

from here as it is from Te Puia, and is considerably cheaper).

The village shops sell authentic arts and crafts, and you can learn more about Maori traditions such as flax weaving, carving, and *ta moko* (tattooing). Nearby you can eat tasty, buttery sweetcorn pulled straight out of the hot mineral pool – the only genuine geothermal *hangi* in town. There are cultural performances at 11.15am and 2pm, and guided tours at 9.30am, 10.30am, 11.45am, 12.30pm, 1.30pm and 3.30pm.

Want some cheap geothermal thrills? Close to the centre of Rotorua is **Kuirau Park**, a volcanic area that you can wander around for free. Its most recent eruption in late 2003 covered much of the park (including the trees)

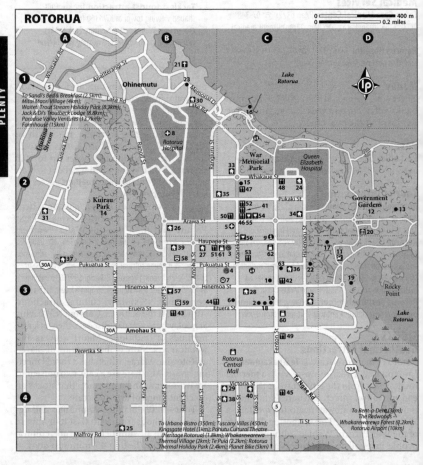

in mud, drawing crowds of spectators hoping for more displays. It has a crater lake, pools of boiling mud and plenty of huffing steam.

Maori Concerts & Hangi

Maori culture is a major drawcard in Rotorua and, although some find it heavily commercialised, it's a great opportunity to learn more about the indigenous culture of NZ. The two big activities are concerts and *hangi* meals, often packaged together in an evening's entertainment that features the famous *hongi*, *haka*, and *poi* dances.

An established favourite is **Tamaki Maori Village** (Map p322; ☎ 07-349 2999; www.maoriculture. co.nz; booking office 1220 Hinemaru St; admission adult/child $100/58; ☒ tours depart 5pm, 6pm & 7pm summer, 5pm & 7pm winter), which does an excellent twilight tour to a *marae* (meeting house) and Maori village 15km south of Rotorua. Buses collect from the Hinemaru St booking office and also from most accommodation, and feature a briefing on *marae* protocol by a Maori 'entertainer' (aka hilarious bus driver). The concert is followed by a meat-heavy *hangi*.

A similar package is offered by **Mitai Maori Village** (Map p335; ☎ 07-343 9132; www.mitai.co.nz;

196 Fairy Springs Rd; concert & hangi adult/child 5-9yr/child 10-15yr/family $99/19/49/259; ☒ 6.30pm). This family-run outfit offers a popular three-hour evening event of concert performance, *hangi* and glowworm bushwalk, which can be combined with a tour of Rainbow Springs Kiwi Wildlife Park (see p334) next door where you can enjoy the coloured nightlights and walk through the open Kiwi enclosure (four hours total, adult/child under 9/child under 15 $116/31.50/63). Pick-ups are available.

Te Puia (p321) puts on three daytime shows (10.15am, 12.15pm & 3.15pm) and one nightly show (6.15pm), while **Whakarewarewa Thermal Village** (opposite) has two daylight shows (11.15am and 2pm; included with admission), great for busy people.

Many of the big hotels offer Maori concerts and *hangi*, making up for what they lack in ambience with convenience. Some of the main venues:

Kingsgate Hotel (Map p335; ☎ 07-348 0199; www. millenniumhotels.co.nz; Fenton St; concert adult/child $30/15, incl hangi $45/22.50; ☒ 6.45pm)
Millennium Hotel (Map p322; ☎ 07-347 1234; www. millenniumrotorua.co.nz; cnr Eruera & Hinemaru Sts; concert adult/child $20/10, incl hangi $65/32.50; ☒ 6.30pm)

HINEMOA & TUTANEKAI

Hinemoa was a young woman of a *hapu* (subtribe) that lived on the western shore of Lake Rotorua, while Tutanekai was a young man of Mokoia Island *hapu*. The pair met and fell in love during a regular tribal meeting. While both were of high birth, Tutanekai was illegitimate and so, while Hinemoa's family thought he was a fine young man, marriage between the two was forbidden.

Home on Mokoia, the lovesick Tutanekai played his flute for his love, the wind carrying the melody across the water. Hinemoa heard his declaration; her people took to tying up the canoes at night to ensure she wouldn't go to him.

Finally, Tutanekai's music won her over. Hinemoa undressed and swam the long distance from the shore to the island. When she arrived on Mokoia, Hinemoa found herself in a quandary. Shedding her clothing in order to swim, she could hardly walk into the island's settlement naked! She hopped into a hot pool to think about her next move.

Eventually a man came to fetch water from a cold spring beside the hot pool. In a deep man's voice, Hinemoa called out, 'Who is it?' The man replied that he was Tutanekai's slave on a water run. Hinemoa grabbed the slave's calabash and smashed it to pieces. More slaves came, but she smashed their calabashes too, until finally Tutanekai came to the pool and demanded that the interloper identify himself – imagine his surprise when it turned out to be Hinemoa! He secreted her into his hut.

Next morning, after a suspiciously long lie-in, a slave reported that someone was in Tutanekai's bed. The two lovers were rumbled, and when Hinemoa's superhuman efforts to reach Tutanekai had been revealed, their union was celebrated.

Descendants of Hinemoa and Tutanekai still live around Rotorua today.

Novotel Rotorua Lakeside (Map p322; ☎ 07-346 3888; www.novotelrotorua.co.nz; 11 Tutanekai St; concerts adult/child $35/15, incl hangi $65/30; ☒ 6.30pm)

Pohutu Cultural Theatre (Heritage Rotorua) (Map p335; ☎ 0800 108 114, 07-348 1189; www.pohututheatre .co.nz; cnr Froude & Tryon St; concerts & hangi adult/child $65/32.50; ☒ 6.30pm)

Lake Rotorua

Lake Rotorua is the largest of the district's 16 lakes and is – underneath all that water – a spent volcano. Sitting in the lake is **Mokoia Island**, which has for centuries been occupied by various subtribes of the area. The lake can be explored by boat with several operators situated at the lakefront.

Mokoia Island Wai Ora Experiences (Map p322; ☎ 0800 665 642; www.mokoiaisland.co.nz; Lakefront, at Volcanic Air Safaris; Ultimate tour adult/child $120/60, Taste tour $75/38) has exclusive rights to take visitors to Mokoia Island, and offers several tours. The 2½- to three-hour Ultimate Island Experience tour (9.30am, 1pm and 3pm) includes hearing famous tales of the island and takes you to the legendary hot pool of Hinemoa (see the boxed text, above). This is followed by an indigenous food tasting. The shorter 1½- to two-hour Taste of Mokoia tour is similar but with less of a walkabout.

The **Lakeland Queen Paddle Steamer** (Map p322; ☎ 0800 572 784; www.lakelandqueen.com; Lakefront) offers one-hour breakfast (adult/child $40/20), and longer lake cruises (lunch $48/24; Saturday-night summer dinner $60/30).

To explore the lake under your own steam, head for **Mana Adventures** (Map p322; ☎ 0800 333 660, 07-348 4186; www.manaadventures.co.nz; Lakefront; ☒ 9am-5pm), which offers (weather permitting) rental of pontoon boats (per hour $95), pedal boats (20 minutes per adult/child $8/5) and kayaks (per hour/half day $25/50). It also runs one-hour lake cruises (per adult/child $55/30) and runs trout-fishing charters (see p327).

Speed things up by jetboating with **Kawarau Jet** (☎ 0800 538 7746; www.nzjetboat.co.nz; Lakefront; 30min $69, 2½hr $120), which tears around the lake.

Rotorua Museum of Art & History

This impressive **museum** (Map p322; ☎ 07-350 1814; www.rotoruamuseum.co.nz; Government Gardens; admission adult/child/family $12/5.50/28; ☒ 9am-5pm Apr-Sep, to 8pm Oct-Mar, tours hourly 10am-4pm plus 5pm Dec-Feb) is housed in a grand mock-Tudor building originally constructed as a spa retreat in 1908. Displays in the former shower rooms offer an insight into the eccentric therapies once practised here, including exposure to radium as a cure for gout, and running an electrical current through baths as a treatment for 'nervous exhaustion'.

A gripping 20-minute film on the history of Rotorua, including the Tarawera eruption, runs every 20 minutes from 9am (not for small kids – the seats vibrate and the eruption noises are authentic!). Also here is a collection of *taonga* (treasures) of Te Arawa, featuring woodcarving, flax weaving and jade. Other exhibits relate the stories of the WWII 28 Maori Battalion, a revered military unit formed of local Arawa people (a movie on the battalion runs every 30 minutes from 9.30am). There's also a cool cafe with picturesque garden views, although the best view in town can be had from the viewing platform on the rooftop.

Government Gardens

The English-style **Government Gardens** (Map p322) surrounding the Rotorua Museum of Art & History are pretty-as-a-picture, with roses aplenty and civilized amenities such as croquet lawns and bowling greens, and steaming thermal pools dotted about. If you fancy some **lawn bowls** (☎ 07-348 0385; 30min/1hr $15/20; ☽ 1-3.30pm Tue & Thu Sep-Apr), reservations are essential. Otherwise there's **Government Gardens Golf** (Map p322; ☎ 07-348 9126; www.governmentgardensgolf.co.nz; Queens Dr; ☽ 7.30am-8pm) – either the nine-hole course (adult/child $20/14), minigolf ($10/8) or the driving range (80 balls $11). As well there's a **baseball batting cage** where you can attempt to drill a few home runs (35 balls $8).

Also within the gardens are the gorgeous Spanish Mission–style **Blue Baths** (Map p322; (☎ 07-350 2119; www.bluebaths.co.nz; admission adult/child/family $11/6/30; ☽ noon-6pm Mon-Fri, 10am-6pm Sat & Sun Apr-Nov, 10am-7pm daily Dec-Mar), which opened in 1933 (and, amazingly, were closed from 1982 to 1999). Today you can visit a small museum (open 10am to 5pm) recalling the building's heyday, with recorded anecdotes and displays in the old changing rooms. If it all makes you feel like taking a dip yourself, the heated pool awaits. Ask about occasional dinner-and-cabaret shows (per person from $125).

Also in the gardens is the Polynesian Spa (see p326).

Ohinemutu

Ohinemutu is a charmingly ramshackle lakeside Maori village that traces the fusing of European and Maori cultures. The historic **St Faith's Anglican Church** (Map p322; ☎ 07-348 2393; cnr Mataiawhea & Korokai Sts; admission by donation; ☽ 8am-6pm, services 9am Sun & 10am Wed) is intricately decorated with Maori carvings, *tukutuku* (woven panels), painted scrollwork and stained-glass windows. One window features an image of Christ wearing a Maori cloak as he appears to walk on the waters of Lake Rotorua.

Opposite the church is **Tama-te-kapua Meeting House**, built in 1905 and named for the captain of the *Arawa* canoe. This sacred meeting house for Te Arawa people is not open to visitors but can be admired from the outside.

ACTIVITIES

Note that several of the following operators have teamed up under the banners of **Rotorua Adventure Combos** (☎ 0800 338 786, 07-357 2236; www.rotoruacombos.com) and **Rotorua Hot Deals** (☎ 0800 768 678; www.rotoruahotdeals.com), delivering a slew of good-value skydiving, white-water rafting, sledging, jetboating and helicopter experiences (plus zorbing, gondola rides, mountain biking...).

See also Argoventures (p336) and Skyline Skyrides (p334).

Mountain Biking

On the edge of town is the **Redwoods – Whakarewarewa Forest** (see p336), home to some of the best **mountain-bike trails** in the country. There are close to 100km of tracks to keep bikers of all skill levels happy for days on end. Note that not all tracks in the forest are designated for bikers, so adhere to the signposts. The Redwoods area of the forest has a **visitor centre** where you can get a trail map and learn more about the area.

At the Waipa Mill car park entrance to the forest, the starting point for the bike trails, you can hire bikes from **Planet Bike** (Map p335; ☎ 07-346 1717; 027 280 2817; www.planetbike.co.nz; Waipa Mill Rd; bikes per 2hr/day $35/55, guided 2hr rides per $65; ☽ 10am-3pm daily Nov-Apr, Sat & Sun only May-Oct). It can also arrange shuttles to get you to the park.

In Rotorua itself you can hire bikes from **Bike Vegas** (Map p322; ☎ 07-347 1151; www.bikevegas.co.nz; 1275 Fenton St; mountain bikes per half/full day from $40/80; ☽ 9am-5.30pm Mon, Tue, Thu & Fri, to 4pm Wed, to 3pm Sat, 10am-2pm Sun) and **Lady Jane's Ice Cream Parlour** (Map p322; ☎ 07-347 9340; 1092 Tutanekai St; bikes per hr/day $10/30; ☽ 10am-late).

Pick up the *Get on Your Bike* Rotorua cycle map and the *Rotorua Mountain Biking*

MAORI NZ: BAY OF PLENTY

The Bay of Plenty's traditional name, Te Rohe o Mataatua, recalls the ancestral *Mataatua* canoe, which arrived here from Hawaiki to make an eventful landfall at Whakatane (see the boxed text, p354). The region's history stretches back further than that, though, with the Polynesian settler Toi setting up what's claimed to be Aotearoa's first settlement in about AD 800.

Major tribal groups in the region are the Ngati Awa (www.ngatiawa.iwi.nz) of the Whakatane area, Whakatohea (www.whakatohea.co.nz) of Opotiki, Ngai Te Rangi (www.ngaiterangi.org.nz) of Tauranga, and Te Arawa (www.tearawa.iwi.nz) of Rotorua. Tribes in this region were involved on both sides of the Land Wars of the late 19th century (see the boxed text, p35), with those fighting against the government suffering considerable land confiscations that have caused legal problems right up to the present day.

There's a significant Maori population in the Bay, and there are many ways for travellers to learn about their culture. Opotiki has Hiona St Stephen's Church (p356) – the death here of government spy Rev Volkner in 1865 inspired the charming eyeball-eating scene in *Utu*. Whakatane has Toi's Pa (p351), perhaps NZ's oldest *pa* site. Rotorua has traditional villages at Te Whakarewarewa (p321) and Ohinemutu (p325), cultural performances and *hangi* meals (p323), and much, *much* more.

---

brochure from the i-SITE (p321) for more info on biking in and around town.

Thermal Pools & Massage

The **Polynesian Spa** (Map p322; ☎ 07-348 1328; www.polynesianspa.co.nz; Government Gardens, off Hinemoa St; main pool adults-only $20, private pools per 30min adult/child $25/4, family pool adult/child/family $13/6/32, spa therapies from $80; 🕓 8am-11pm, spa therapies 9am-8pm) is in the Government Gardens. A bathhouse was opened at these springs in 1882 and people have been swearing by the waters ever since.

There is mineral bathing (36°C to 42°C) in several picturesque pools at the lake's edge, marble-lined terraced pools and a larger, main pool. Also housed in the modern complex are several more commercial activities such as luxury therapies (massage, mud and beauty treatments) as well as a cafe and gift shop.

Beyond the airport, Wai Ora Spa at Hell's Gate (p336) has a full program of massage, mud and spa treatments. If you feel like exploring further, take a dip south of Rotorua at the outdoor Waikite Valley Thermal Pools (p338).

White-water Rafting & Sledging

Thrill seekers can find plenty of white-water action around Rotorua with the chance to take on the Grade V Kaituna River, complete with a startling 7m drop at Okere Falls. Most of these trips take a day, but times are often negotiable. Some companies head further out to the Rangitaiki (Grade III–VI) and Wairoa River (Grade V), raftable only when the dam is opened every second Sunday. Sledging (in case you didn't know) is zooming downriver on a highly manoeuvrable body board.

Most of the following operators can arrange transport.

Kaitiaki Adventures (☎ 0800 338 736, 07-357 2236; www.kaitiaki.co.nz) Offers white-water rafting trips on the Kaituna ($85) and Wairoa ($99), and sledging on the Kaituna ($99) and Wairoa (one guide per person; $299).

Kaituna Cascades (☎ 0800 524 8862, 07-345 4199; www.kaitunacascades.co.nz) Does rafting on the Kaituna ($82), Rangitaiki ($108) and Wairoa ($98).

Raftabout (☎ 0800 723 822, 07-343 9500; www.raftabout.co.nz) Does rafting on the Kaituna ($89), Rangitaiki ($120) and Wairoa ($120), plus raft-sledge combos on the Kaituna ($175).

River Rats (☎ 0800 333 900, 07-345 6543; www.riverrats.co.nz) Takes on the Wairoa ($110), Kaituna ($90) and Rangitaiki ($120), and runs a scenic trip on the Rangitaiki, good for youngsters (adult/child $120/80). Tongariro trips by arrangement.

Wet 'n' Wild (☎ 0800 462 7238, 07-348 3191; www.wetnwildrafting.co.nz) Runs trips on the Kaituna ($95), Wairoa ($99) and the Mokau ($145), as well as easy-going Rangitaiki trips (adult/child $120/80) and longer, helicopter-access trips to remote parts of the Motu and Mohaka (two to five days $550 to $925).

Kayaking

Three companies can get you paddling on the waterways:

Adventure Kayaking (☎ 027-4997 402; www.adventurekayaking.co.nz; hire per day $40, trips per half/full day from $70/110) Takes trips on Lakes Rotorua, Rotoiti, Tarawera and Okataina; also offers freedom hire.

Kaituna Kayaks (☎ 07-362 4486; www.kaitunakayaks.com; half-day trip $149, lessons half/full day

$149/290) Guided tandem trips and kayaking lessons on the Kaituna.

River Rats (☎ 0800 333 900, 07-345 6543; www.river rats.co.nz; hire per half/full day from $25/45, 2/4hr trip $40/95) Freedom hire plus two-hour self-guided trips down the Ohau Channel and four-hour guided paddles to Manupirua Springs Hot Pools on Lake Rotoiti.

Tramping

There are plenty of opportunities to stretch your legs around Rotorua, with day walks a speciality. The booklet *Walks in the Rotorua Lakes area* ($2.50), available from the i-SITE, showcases town walks, including the popular lakefront stroll (20 minutes).

All the following walks are shown on the map on p335.

The area around **Lake Okataina** offers walks of varying distance and difficulty. One of the most popular – albeit not for beginners – is the **Western Okataina Walkway** (seven hours one way), which takes in lake views and a dry crater known as the 'Bullring'. The track runs from Millar Rd at Lake Okareka to Ruato on Lake Rotoiti with public transport past the Ruato end only.

The **Eastern Okataina Walkway** (three hours one way) goes along the eastern shoreline of Lake Okataina to Lake Tarawera and passes the **Soundshell**, a natural amphitheatre that has *pa* (fortified village) remains, and several swimming spots. The **Northern Tarawera Track** (three hours one way) connects to the Eastern Okataina Walkway, creating a two-day walk from either Lake Okataina or Ruato to Lake Tarawera with an overnight camp at either **Humphries Bay** (sites free) or **Tarawera Outlet** (sites per adult/child $7/2). From Tarawera Outlet you can walk on to **Tarawera Falls** (four hours return; see p356). There's a forestry road into Tarawera Outlet from Kawerau – access costs $4, with permits available from the Kawerau visitor centre (p356).

The **Okere Falls** are about 21km northeast of Rotorua on SH33, with an easy **track** (30 minutes return) past the 7m falls (popular for rafting), through native podocarp forest and along the Kaituna River. Along the way is a lookout over the river at **Hinemoa's Steps**.

Just north of Wai-O-Tapu on SH5 (see p337), the **Rainbow Mountain Track** (1½ hours one way) makes for a strenuous walk up to the summit of the peak known to Maori as Maungakakaramea (Mountain of coloured earth). There are spectacular views from the

summit with a panorama that takes in Lake Taupo, Tongariro National Park and the Paeroa Range.

Fishing

There's always good fishing to be had somewhere around the lakes. You can hire guides to fish for trout or go solo, but either way a licence (per day/season $21/105) is essential, available from **O'Keefe's Fishing Specialists** (Map p322; ☎ 07-346 0178; www.okeefesfishing.co.nz; 1113 Eruera St; ☒ 8am-4.30pm Mon-Fri, to 2pm Sat, 8.30am-12.30pm Sun). You can fish Rotorua's lakefront with a licence, though not all lakes can be fished year-round; check with O'Keefe's or the i-SITE (p321).

Some recommended guides:

Clark Gregor (☎ 07-347 1123; www.troutnz.co.nz; per hr $105) Does fly- and boat fishing.

Gordon Randle (☎ 07-349 2555; www.rotoruatrout. co.nz; half-/full-day charters $350/680) Transport, tuition and equipment included, plus cleaning, smoking and vacuum-packing of your catch.

Mana Adventures (p324) Fishing boat hire (per hour from $95), and trout-fishing trips (boat charter with skipper per three hours from $285).

Silver Hilton Trout Fishing (☎ 07-332 3488; www.troutfly.co.nz; boat/river fishing trips from $285/380, charter per day $760) Boat and fly-fishing with gear and lunch supplied.

Trout Man (☎ 021 951 174; www.waiteti.com; 2hr/day trip from $30/120) Learn to fish and share the passion with experienced angler and fishing correspondent Harvey Clark, from a couple of hours to multiday trips.

Other Activities

Another opportunity to get limbered up is at the **Wall Climbing Gym** (Map p322; ☎ 07-350 1400; www.basementcinema.co.nz; basement, 1140 Hinemoa St; admission incl gear adult/child $16/12; ☒ noon-10pm Mon-Fri, 10am-10pm Sat & Sun), which has a three-storey climbing wall with overhangs aplenty.

NZONE (☎ 0800 376 796, 07-345 7520; www.nzone. biz; Rotorua Airport; dives $249-399) offers tandem skydives from 9000ft, 12,000ft or 15,000ft, giving you a bird's-eye view of the lakes and volcanoes. Town pick-ups available.

Several companies will help you saddle up for horse treks on idyllic trails around Rotorua. North of Lake Rotorua at the **Farmhouse** (Map p335; ☎ 07-332 3771; www.thefarm house.co.nz; 55 Sunnex Rd, off Central Rd, Ngongotaha; rides 30min/1hr/2hr $25/40/70), take a shorter trip for beginners or a longer trip for experienced riders. The very safe and professional **Paradise**

Valley Ventures (off Map p335; ☎ 07-348 3300; www.paradisetreks.co.nz; 679 Paradise Valley Rd; rides 1hr/1½hr $65/90) takes treks for novices and experienced riders through a 700-acre farm north of Rotorua. Shorter and longer treks also available.

WALKING TOUR

Start out from **Rotorua Museum of Art & History** (**1**; p324); once a bathhouse for the affluent, it remains the town's most impressive building. Follow the road west through the elegant **Government Gardens** (**2**; p325), which conclude at Princes Gate Arches. Through the arch you'll see the grand **Princes Gate Hotel** (**3**; p331), moved here in the 1920s from Waihi.

Follow Arawa St west to the roundabout then turn right down Fenton St towards the lake. Turn left onto Pukaki St then right onto **Tutaneki St** (**4**; p331), Rotorua's main eat street. Continue north across War Memorial Park to **Lake Rotorua** (**5**; p324) and walk alongside the glittering waters. The road veers away from the water onto Memorial Dr, which in turn takes you to the historic Maori village of Ohinemutu with its intricately carved Tama-te-kapua Meeting House and **St Faith's Anglican Church** (**6**; p325), which combines Christian and Maori traditions.

Double back to Lake Rd and head up the hill to **Kuirau Park** (**7**; p322), with its steamy scenes and whiffs of sulphur. Once you're done exploring, turn left into Pukuatua St, left into Amohia St and right into Haupapa St. Head up this street to the old police station, now the **Pig & Whistle** (**8**; p332) – have you earned yourself a drink yet?

ROTORUA FOR CHILDREN

Rotorua is bound to be a hit with kids. Many of the geothermal areas such as Wai-O-Tapu and Te Puia have pram-able boardwalks, so bring the stroller for when little legs get tired. For legs with energy to burn, go to the **Redwoods – Whakarewarewa Forest** (p336) for

ROTORUA WALKING TOUR

a mini mountain-bike ride or walk in the woods.

To climb up high without dragging your feet, take a gondola ride at **Skyline Skyrides** (p334) and luge the afternoon away. See the sights on land and lake with the biofuelled **Rotorua Duck Tours** (p329), or under your own steam by pedal boat from **Mana Adventures** (p324) at the lakefront. There's a brilliant kids' playground at the lakefront too.

Tree-huggers and animal patters have plenty of choice with a plethora of nature parks (p334) not far out of town. And if all else fails you can threaten to strap troublesome teens into a **zorb** (p336) and roll them down the hill.

TOURS

To make sense of it all, or if time is tight, take a tour – book at the i-SITE or via many hostels and hotels.

Elite Adventures (☎ 07-347 8282; www.eliteadventures.co.nz) Half-day (adult/child from $75/55) and full-day tours (adult/child from $200/110) covering a selection of Rotorua's major cultural and natural attractions.

Geyser Link Tours (☎ 07-343 6764; www.geyserlink.co.nz) Tours of some of the major sights, including Wai-O-Tapu (adult/child $58/29, half-day) and Waimangu Volcanic Valley ($58/29, half-day), or both ($98/49, full day). Transport-only options available.

Indigenous Trails (☎ 07-542 1074; www.itrails.co.nz; day trip $338) Full-day Maori-guided tours around Rotorua, with a bungy jump, river cruise, kiwi-meeting, cultural show and *hangi*.

Mt Tarawera New Zealand (☎ 07-349 3714; www.mt-tarawera.co.nz) Guided half-day 4WD tours to the top of Mt Tarawera (adult/child $133/78) as well as a half-day 4WD/helicopter combo (per person $435) and the full-day Volcanic Eco Tour, which combines the 4WD trip with Wai-O-Tapu and Waimangu (adult/child $255/90). Also available are 4WD/mountain bike ($325) and helicopter/mountain bike ($610) combos.

Pure Cruise New Zealand (☎ 0800 272 456, 027 272 4561; www.purecruise.co.nz) Slow-boat catamaran cruises on Lake Rotoiti on an exclusive charter or nonexclusive basis. Call for prices and sailing times.

Rotorua Duck Tours (☎ 07-345 6522; www.rotoruaducktours.co.nz; adult/child/family $62/35/145; ⏲ tours 11am, 1pm & 3.30pm summer, 11am & 2.15pm winter) Ninety-minute trips in an amphibious, biofuelled vehicle taking in the major sites around town and heading out onto three lakes (Rotorua, Okareka and Tikitapu).

For a bird's-eye tour of the region, opt for a scenic flight. Just as well there are only window seats…there's plenty to see.

Air Discovery (☎ 0800 247 347, 07-575 7584; www.airdiscovery.co.nz; Rotorua Airport; 1½hr/half-day flights $399/599) Volcanic explorations over White Island and the Taupo region (including Mt Ruapehu, Mt Ngarahoe and Mt Tongariro).

Helipro (☎ 0800 435 4776, 07-357 2512; www.helipro.co.nz; 8min-3½hr trips $89-855) Based at Te Puia, Helipro does a variety of helicopter trips including city flights, and Mt Tarawera and White Island landings.

Volcanic Air Safaris (Map p322; ☎ 07-348 9984; www.volcanicair.co.nz; 6min-3¼hr trips $70-845) Float-plane and helicopter flights from the lakefront, including a combined flight and Mokoia Island experience or combined helicopter flight and guided tour of Hell's Gate. The company also runs a 3¼-hour trip exploring White Island and Mt Tarawera.

SLEEPING
Budget

Rotorua has plenty of holiday parks and an ever-changing backpacker scene offering good options close to the action.

Crank Backpackers (Map p322; ☎ 0508 224 466, 07-348 0852; www.crankbackpackers.com; 1140 Hinemoa St; dm $23-25, d with/without bathroom $69/59; 🖳 🛜) A cavernous newcomer determined to compete with the old stagers, Crank occupies an old shopping mall (you might be sleeping in a florist or a delicatessen). Dorms over the street are sunny, and there are sexy co-ed bathrooms, a free gym and a climbing wall and art-house cinema in the basement.

Cactus Jacks Backpackers (Map p322; ☎ 07-348 3121; www.cactusjacksbackpackers.co.nz; 1210 Haupapa St; dm/s/tw/d $24/39/52/57; 🖳) If you're looking for character, pardner, then this Western-themed spot is just your gunfight. Shabby-chic rooms range from Jail (dorms) to Madam Fifi's bordello (two twins). Sociable staff, relaxed lounges, courtyard, and undercover thermal pool make it an ideal spot for weary cowpokes.

our pick Funky Green Voyager (Map p322; ☎ 07-346 1754; www.funkygreenvoyager.com; 4 Union St; dm from $24, d with/without bathroom $65/57; 🖳 🛜) Green on the outside and the inside – due to several cans of paint and a dedicated environmental policy – the Funky GV features laid-back tunes and plenty of sociable chat among a spunky bunch of guests and worldly wise owners, who know what you want when you travel. The best doubles have bathroom; dorms are roomy with quality mattresses.

Rotorua Central Backpackers (Map p322; ☎ 07-349 3285; 1076 Pukuatua St; www.bbh.co.nz; dm $24-27, d $58; 🖳 🛜) This heritage hostel was built in 1936 and retains historic features including dark-wood skirting boards and door frames, deep bathtubs and geothermal radiators. Dorms are no more than six beds (and no bunks), plus there's a spa pool and barbecue, all within strolling distance of the museum.

Treks Rotorua YHA (Map p322; ☎ 0508 487 357; www.yha.co.nz; 1278 Haupapa St; dm $24-29, d $68-84; ☐ ☏) Bright and sparkling-clean, this purpose-built and well-maintained hostel is great for those wanting to get outdoors, with staff eager to assist with trip bookings, and storage for bikes and kayaks. Pricier rooms come with bathroom, and there's a barbecue area and deck for hanging out on. Off-street parking a bonus.

Kiwi Paka (Map p322; ☎ 07-347 0931; www.kiwipaka.co.nz; 60 Tarewa Rd; unpowered & powered sites $21, dm $27, chalets with bathroom d/tr/q $80/100/140, lodge s/d $50/60; ☐ ☏ ☒) One kilometre from town, this hostel is away from the action and feels like a school camp, with acceptable amenities and a range of accommodation from campsites to plain four-bed dorms, lodge rooms and pine-clad chalets. The Twisted Pippie cafe is on-site.

Regent Flashpackers (Map p322; ☎ 07-348 3338; www.regentflashpackers.co.nz; 1181 Pukaki St; dm/d from $25/90; ☐ ☏) Angling for a mature, upmarket backpacker market (is there such a thing?), the very decent Regent does things with style: sturdy bunks, cosy kitchen, quality linen, underfloor heating and fill-your-own mineral pools out the back. A bar was being built when we visited, which should help lower the tone a little.

Base Rotorua (Map p322; ☎ 0800 227 369, 07-348 8636; www.stayatbase.co.nz; 1286 Arawa St; dm/s/d from $27/70/70; ☐ ☏ ☒) Another link in the Base chain, this huge hostel is ever-popular with partying backpackers who love the Lava Bar (cheap meals, toga parties, disco nights etc). Rooms can be tight, with up to 12 beds in some dorms, but extras such as girls-only rooms, a large outdoor heated pool and off-street parking compensate.

Waiteti Trout Stream Holiday Park (Map p335; ☎ 07-357 5255; www.waiteti.com; 14 Okona Cres, Ngongotaha; sites $30, dm from $20, d cabins/motels from $45/80; ☐ ☏) This is a great option for folk who like it rustic and don't mind a short 10-minute drive into town. Set in two acres of garden on the banks of a trout-filled stream, this cute old classic has character-filled motel units, compact cabins, a backpackers'

lodge and relaxed camping. Free kayaks and dinghies.

Rotorua Thermal Holiday Park (Map p335; ☎ 07-346 3140; www.rotoruathermal.co.nz; Old Taupo Rd; unpowered/powered sites $30/34, dm from $21, d cabins/motels from $54/95; ☐ ☏ ☒) This epic holiday park on the edge of town has a real holiday-resort feel, with rows of cabins and tourist flats, a 100-bed lodge, campsites galore and convenience facilities such as a shop and cafe. There's plenty of room to move with lots of open grassy areas, plus hot mineral pools for the soakers.

Rotorua Top 10 Holiday Park (Map p322; ☎ 07-348 1886; www.rotoruatop10.co.nz; 1495 Pukuatua St; unpowered/powered sites $38/40, d cabins/motels $65/95-130, 2br units $150; ☐ ☏ ☒) A small but perfectly formed holiday park with a continual improvement policy that has seen a nice new pool and various other revamps on the agenda. Cabins are in good nick and have small fridges and microwaves. Plenty of shrubbery and picnic tables.

Midrange

Generic motels crowd Fenton St, but better and often more interesting rooms can be found away from the main drag.

Six on Union (Map p322; ☎ 0800 100 062, 07-347 8062; www.sixonunion.co.nz; 6 Union St; d/f from $95/150; ☏ ☒) Hanging baskets ahoy! This modest place is a budget bonanza with pool, spa and small kitchenettes. Rooms are functional and freshly painted, and the swimming-pool area is in good nick. The location is away from traffic noise, but still an easy walk to the city centre.

Ann's Volcanic Rotorua (Map p322; ☎ 0800 768 683, 07-347 1007; www.rotoruamotel.co.nz; 107 Malfroy Rd; d $99-149, 2br ste & house $159-179; ☏) Ann's is a basic and affordable motel that has family charm and an ever-friendly host with loads of advice on things to see and do. Larger rooms feature courtyard spas and facilities for travellers with disabilities, with a house available for big groups. Rooms close to the street are a tad noisy.

Jack & Di's Troutbeck Lodge (Map p335; ☎ 0800 522 526; www.jackanddis.co.nz; 5 Arnold St, Ngongotaha; d/cottage from $99/450; ☏) A lakeside position in a quiet, secluded spot makes this large lodge a good retreat from central Rotorua. Multiple rooms cater for families or groups up to 11, and high-end facilities such as dishwasher, spa and full kitchen make for pleasant stays. Good winter rates; free kayaks.

Ambassador Thermal Motel (Map p322; ☎ 0800 479 581, 07-347 9581; www.ambassrotorua.co.nz; cnr Whakaue & Hinemaru Sts; d/f from \$105/165; 🖥 🖳) Handily located in a quiet corner just a few minutes' walk to town and the lakefront, this mildly kooky motel boasts no fewer than four pools: two indoor mineral pools, an outdoor spa and a large figure-eight swimming pool. Comfortable rooms of various sizes can sleep up to seven, many with full kitchens.

Jack & Di's Lake Road Lodge (Map p322; ☎ 0800 522 526; www.jackanddis.co.nz; 21 Lake Rd; s/d/apt \$99/119/250; 🖥) Lakeside views and a central-but-secluded location make this boutique hotel a persuasive option. The upstairs penthouse is ideal for couples, while downstairs is better for families or groups. A spa pool, lazy lounge areas and full kitchens add to the appeal.

Sandi's Bed & Breakfast (Map p335; ☎ 0800 726 3422, 07-348 0884; www.sandisbedandbreakfast.co.nz; 103 Fairy Springs Rd; d/f incl breakfast \$120/150; 🖥 🖳) A friendly, family B&B run by the well-humoured Sandi who offers helpful tourist advice and a ready smile. The best bets are the two chalets with TV and plenty of room to move. Thoughtful extras including fresh fruit with brekkie and sun deck ensure rave reviews from former guests. Located a couple of kilometres north of town.

Victoria Lodge (Map p322; ☎ 0800 100 039, 07-348 4039; www.victorialodge.co.nz; 10 Victoria St; d/apt \$120/180; 🖥) The friendly Vic is starting to look a bit weary (scuff marks, old carpets, messy gardens), but all the rooms here feel individual, and the studios are particularly attractive with their thermal plunge pools. Fully equipped apartments can squeeze in seven adults, though four would be very comfortable.

Tuscany Villas (Map p335; ☎ 0800 802 050, 07-348 3500; www.tuscanyvillasrotorua.co.nz; 280 Fenton St; d from \$140) With its Italian-inspired architecture, this family-owned hotel is a real eye-catcher from the road. It pitches itself perfectly at both the corporate and leisure traveller, both of whom will appreciate the lavish furnishings, multiple TVs, DVD players and huge, deep spa baths.

Top End

Princes Gate Hotel (Map p322; ☎ 07-348 1179; www. princesgate.co.nz; 1057 Arawa St; d/ste from \$165/275; 🖥 🖥 🖳) A well-loved and warmly welcoming 19th-century dame with 56 different rooms, such as the richly decorated Marvelly suite – perhaps too pink for all but Barbara Cartland. Sink into the bottomless bath, however, and all is forgiven. Other amenities include cascading mineral baths, sauna, restaurant and streetside cafe.

Millennium Hotel (Map p322; ☎ 07-347 1234; www.millenniumrotorua.co.nz; cnr Eruera & Hinemaru Sts; d from \$340; 🖥 🖥 🖳) The slick Maori-inspired lobby sets the scene for this elegant five-storey motel. Lakefront rooms afford excellent views as does the club room, a laid-back lounge available exclusively to guests. The poolside *hangi* is one of the better ones in town (see p323).

EATING

The lake end of Tutanekai St has a strip of good eating places, but there are plenty of others all over town.

Restaurants

Urbano Bistro (Map p335; ☎ 07-349 3770; cnr Fenton & Grey Sts; breakfast & lunch mains \$13-20, dinner \$20-38; 🕙 9am-11pm Mon-Sat, to 3pm Sun) This suburban cafe, with mega-checkerboard floor and striking wallpaper, is a bold move by reputable local restaurateurs. Some of the most delicious fare in town (try the beef, pineapple and capsicum curry), rich and well executed. Fine wines and five-star service.

Indian Star (Map p322; ☎ 07-343 6222; 1118 Tutanekai St; mains \$14-25; 🕙 lunch & dinner; 🅥) Getting rave reviews from readers, this is one of several Indian eateries around town, elevating itself above the competition with immaculate service and marvellous renditions of subcontinental classics. Generous portions and a good vegetarian selection.

Amazing Thai (Map p322; ☎ 07-343 9494; 1246 Fenton St; mains \$15-19; 🕙 lunch & dinner) This large, glass-fronted restaurant dishes up better-than-average, spicy-as-you-like Thai food in generous servings. Obligatory portraits of Thai royals and sundry elephants.

Sabroso (Map p322; ☎ 07-349 0591; 1184 Haupapa St; mains \$15-36; 🕙 5-10pm Thu-Tue) What a surprise! This modest Latin American cantina – adorned with sombreros, guitars, hessian tablecloths and salt-and-pepper shakers made from Corona bottles – serves adventurous south-of-the-border fare to spice up bland Kiwi palates. The black bean chilli is a knock-out (as are the margaritas).

Bistro 1284 (Map p322; ☎ 07-346 1284; 1284 Eruera St; mains \$30-35; 🕙 6pm-late) Definitely one of

RotoVegas' hot dining spots, this intimate place (all chocolate and mushroom colours) serves stylish NZ cuisine with an Asian influence. It's an excellent place to sample great local ingredients, and be sure to leave room for some delectable desserts.

Cafes

Zippy Central Bar & Café (Map p322; ☎ 07-348 8288; 1153 Pukuatua St; snacks $4-10, mains $10-22; ☷ 7am-7pm) A snappy little cafe with a decidedly retro groove (Laminex tables, an ultracool booth…), Zippy zips up all sorts of tasty food from breakfast, sandwiches, snacks to stir-fries and curries. There are plenty of healthy options, which is probably why this place is popular with cyclists and other wholesome types.

Capers Epicurean (Map p322; ☎ 07-348 8818; 1181 Eruera St; breakfast & lunch mains $6-20, dinner $13-28; ☷ 7.30am-late; **V**) This slick, barnlike deli is always busy with diners showing up for cabinets crammed full of delicious gourmet sandwiches, pastries, salads and cakes, and an excellent blackboard menu of brekkies and other tasty hot foods (try the carrot, leek and fetta lasagne). There's also a deli section stocked with olive oils, marinades, relish, jams and chocolates.

Relish (Map p322; ☎ 07-343 9195; 1149 Tutanekai St; breakfast $9-22, lunch & dinner mains $19-33; ☷ 7am-4pm Mon & Tue, to 9pm Wed-Fri, 8am-9pm Sat, to 4pm Sun) A top spot serving all-day breakfast, pizza and the like, with a keen eye on delicate spices, aromatic herbs and wood smoke. A modern and relaxed interior with local artwork on the walls.

Fat Dog Café (Map p322; ☎ 07-347 7586; 1161 Arawa St; breakfast & lunch mains $11-17, dinner $26-30; ☷ breakfast, lunch & dinner; **V**) With paw prints up the walls and silly poems painted on the chairs, this is the town's friskiest and most child-friendly eatery. During the day it dishes up big bowls of brekkie, nachos, salads and sandwiches; in the evening it's candlelit lamb and venison. The only cafe in NZ brave enough to play *Unskinny Bop* by Poison.

ourpick Lime Caffeteria (Map p322; ☎ 07-350 2033; cnr Fenton & Whakaue Sts; mains $13-24; ☷ 7.30am-4.30pm; **V**) Sitting on a quiet, leafy corner near the lake, this refreshing cafe is especially good for alfresco breakfasts and dishes with a welcome twist: try the chicken-and-chorizo salad or prawn-and-salmon risotto in lime sauce. It also offers classy counter snacks,

excellent coffee and outdoor tables. 'This is the best lunch I've had in ages', says one happy punter.

Quick Eats

Weilin's Noodle House (Map p322; ☎ 07-343 9998; 1148 Tutanekai St; mains $11-17; ☷ lunch & dinner Wed-Mon) A neat-and-tidy shop serving trad Chinese dumplings and oodles of noodles in soups and stirfries. Eat in or take away.

Ali Baba's Tunisian Takeaway (Map p322; ☎ 07-348 2983; 1146 Tutanekai St; meals $13-15; ☷ 11.30am-late; **V**) Follow the belly-dancing music (and your nose) into this neat little eatery serving kebabs and Tunisian-inspired pizzas, salads, pastas and rice meals. Eat in or take away.

Self-catering

Countdown (Map p322; ☎ 07-350 3277; 246 Fenton St; ☷ 6am-midnight)

Pak N Save (Map p322; ☎ 07-347 8440; cnr Fenton & Amohau Sts; ☷ 8am-10pm)

DRINKING

There are a few good spots to slake your thirst, with Euro-style pubs well represented.

ourpick Underground Bar (Map p322; ☎ 07-348 3612; www.croucherbrewing.co.nz; basement, 1282 Hinemoa St; ☷ 4-8pm Wed & Thu, to 11pm Fri & Sat, 2-6pm Sun) 'It's all about the beer' at this crafty underground bunker, run by the lads from Croucher Brewing Co, Rotorua's best microbrewers. Sip down a pint of fruity Pale Ale, aromatic Drunken Hop Bitter or malty Pilsener and wonder how you'll manage a sleep-in tomorrow morning.

Pig & Whistle (Map p322; ☎ 07-347 3025; www.pigandwhistle.co.nz; cnr Haupapa & Tutanekai Sts; ☷ 11.30am-late) This excellent microbrewery pub in the former police station offers a conducive atmosphere in which to enjoy its Swine lager (big-screen TV, beer garden, live music Thursday to Saturday), while serving up some of the best simple grub in town (mains $19 to $30). Their menu runs the gamut from spare ribs to a gluten-free vegetarian toastie.

Belgian Bar (Map p322; ☎ 07-348 6190; 1151 Arawa St; ☷ 4pm-late Tue, 11.30am-late Wed-Sun) The best bar in town for lovers of gigs and good beer. Half a dozen Euro-beers on tap and 42 in the bottle make for quality supping while a menu of meatballs, mash and *moules et frites* will allow you to stick around and sup a few more. Regular blues and acoustic acts.

Pheasant Plucker (Map p322; ☎ 07-343 7071; www.
thepheasantplucker.co.nz; 1153 Arawa St; ☽ 4pm-late Mon-
Fri, 3pm-late Sat, 11am-late Sun) Another place for
a proper pint, but this time á l'Anglais. The
Pheasant proffers locally brewed and British
beer, along with bangers 'n' mash and nonstop
carvery with Yorkshire pud (mains $15 to $36).

ENTERTAINMENT

Several local pubs such as the Pig & Whistle and
Chambers regularly host bands. For late-night
action, head to **Bar Barella** (Map p322; ☎ 07-347 6776;
1263 Pukuatua St; admission free-$10; ☽ 11pm-3am Wed, Fri &
Sat), where bands and DJs play metal, hip-hop,
reggae, rock and dub to a nocturnal crowd.

Princes Gate Hotel (Map p322; ☎ 07-348 1179; www.
princesgate.co.nz; 1057 Arawa St; show & meal $85) hosts
regular dinners alongside a 1930s-style cabaret show. Cabaret shows also kick up their
knickers at the Blue Baths (see p325).

Reading Cinema (Map p322; ☎ 07-3490061; www.reading
cinemas.co.nz; 1281 Eruera St; admission adult/child $15/10;
☽ 10.30am-11pm) shows mainstream movies,
while **Basement Cinema** (Map p322; ☎ 07-350 1400;
www.basementcinema.co.nz; basement, 1140 Hinemoa St; adult
$14; ☽ vary) shows art-house and foreign films.

SHOPPING

Being the tourist centre of NZ, Rotorua has an
abundance of souvenirs. Genuine Maori and
other NZ-made arts and crafts will be labelled.
Jade Factory (Map p322; ☎ 07-349 1828; www.jade
factory.com; 1288 Fenton St; ☽ 9am-6pm) Specialises in
high-end, hand-crafted greenstone jewellery and carvings.
Of Hand & Heart (Map p322; ☎ 07-348 9505; 1180
Haupapa St; ☽ 10am-5pm) Gorgeous hand-spun ceramics:
watch the potter at work.
Out of New Zealand (Map p322; ☎ 07-346 2968; 1189
Fenton St; ☽ 9am-6pm) Stocks predominantly NZ-made
craft and gifts including carvings, ceramics and jewellery.
Plenty of affordable, packable souvenirs.

To the south of town, Te Puia and Te
Whakarewarewa (p321) have excellent selections of genuine Maori-made arts.

GETTING THERE & AWAY
Air

Air New Zealand (Map p322; ☎ 07-343 1100; www.
airnewzealand.co.nz; 1103 Hinemoa St; ☽ 9am-5pm Mon-
Fri) offers daily direct flights to Auckland,
Christchurch and Wellington, with onward
connections to other destinations. Air New
Zealand also links Rotorua with Sydney every
Tuesday and Saturday.

Bus

All the major bus companies stop outside
the i-SITE (see p321), from where you can
arrange bookings.

InterCity (☎ 09-583 5780; www.intercity.co.nz) runs
buses to destinations such as the following:

Destination	Price	Duration	Frequency
Auckland	$50	4hr	8 daily
Gisborne	$60	4½hr	1 daily
Hamilton	$35	1½hr	6 daily
Napier	$52	3hr	4 daily
Taupo	$32	1hr	5 daily
Tauranga	$25	1½hr	4 daily
Wellington	$57	8hr	4 daily
Whakatane	$33	1½hr	1 daily

Naked Bus (☎ 0900 625 33; www.nakedbus.com) services run to the same destinations, as listed
below. Substantial fare savings can be made
by booking in advance.

Destination	Price	Duration	Frequency
Auckland	$35	4hr	3 daily
Gisborne	$43	4¾hr	1 daily
Hamilton	$24	1½hr	3 daily
Napier	$29	3hr	1 daily
Taupo	$19	1hr	2 daily
Tauranga	$11	1½-4hr	2-3 daily
Wellington	$39	8hr	1 daily
Whakatane	$21	1½hr	1 daily

Twin City Express (☎ 0800 422 9287; www.bay
bus.co.nz) buses run twice daily Monday to
Friday between Rotorua and Tauranga/Mt
Maunganui via Te Puke ($11, 1½ hours).

GETTING AROUND
To/From the Airport

The airport is about 10km out of town to the
east. **Super Shuttle** (☎ 0800 748 885, 07-345 7790; www.
supershuttle.co.nz) offers a door-to-door airport
service for $20 for the first person and $6 for
each additional passenger. A taxi from the city
centre costs about $25. Cityride (below) runs
a daily airport bus service.

Bus

If you're trying to get around local attractions,
ask about their shuttle services: many offer
courtesy pick-up and drop-off.
Cityride (☎ 0800 422 9287; www.baybus.co.nz) operates
convenient local bus services around town

and Ngongotaha ($2.20), and the airport ($2.50).

Several shuttles run around the town's attractions with pick-ups at most hotels and hostels:

Affordable Adventures (☎ 0508 278 946; www.affordableadventures.co.nz) Runs a small bus wherever you want to go for whatever it costs; good for groups.

Geyser Link Tour Service (☎ 07-343 6764; www.geyserlink.co.nz) Goes to Wai-O-Tapu (return $35) and Paradise Valley Springs (return $25).

Tim's Thermal Shuttle (☎ 027 494 5508) Goes to Wai-O-Tapu (return including entry $50) and the Buried Village on request.

Car

In Rotorua car-rental competition is fierce so there are bargains to be had. Try the following:

Avis (☎ 07-345-6055; www.avis.co.nz; Rotorua Airport; ⏰ 8am-8pm Mon-Fri, 8.30am-3pm Sat, to 4pm Sun)

Budget (Map p322; ☎ 07-348 8127; www.budget.co.nz; 1230 Fenton St; ⏰ 7.30am-5.30pm Mon-Fri, 8am-noon Sat & Sun)

Rent-a-Dent (Map p335; ☎ 0800 736 823, 07-349 3993; www.rotoruacarrentals.co.nz; 316 Te Ngae Rd; ⏰ 8.30am-5.30pm Mon-Fri, 8am-noon Sat)

Taxi

Fast Taxis (☎ 07-348 2444)
Rotorua Taxis (☎ 07-348 1111)

AROUND ROTORUA

NORTH OF ROTORUA
Nature Parks

Surrounding Rotorua are several places devoted to native wildlife.

Rainbow Springs Kiwi Wildlife Park (Map p335; ☎ 0800 724 626, 07-350 0440; www.rainbowsprings.co.nz; 192 Fairy Springs Rd; 24hr pass adult/child/family $26/15/69; ⏰ 8am-10pm) is a must-do for nature-lovers. At the heart of the park are the natural springs, home to wild trout and eels, which you can see from the underwater viewer. There are walkways for wanderings with interpretive displays along the way. Animals abound, both introduced species such as wallabies, emus and rainbow lorikeets, and interesting native birds such as kea, kaka and pukeko.

The highlight of the park is **Kiwi Encounter** (www.kiwiencounter.co.nz; admission adult/child/family $27.50/17.50/75; ⏰ tours hourly 10am-4pm), home to NZ's largest kiwi recovery program – a nationally significant nonprofit conservation project.

It offers visitors a rare peek into the lives of not only these greatly endangered birds, but the people trying to save them from extinction. Be prepared for an emotional roller coaster on the excellent 45-minute tours that have you tiptoeing through the actual incubator and hatchery areas. A combo Kiwi Encounter/ Wildlife Park ticket costs adult/child/family $42/23/110.

Rainbow Springs comes alive at night with colourful illuminations and a chance to walk through the outdoor kiwi enclosure. Also offered are special joint four-hour evening tours with the neighbouring Mitai Maori Village (see p323). Rainbow Springs is 3km north of central Rotorua on SH5 towards Hamilton and Auckland.

In Paradise Valley at the foot of Mt Ngongotaha are two wildlife parks. Eight kilometres from town is **Paradise Valley Springs** (off Map p335; ☎ 07-348 9667; 467 Paradise Valley Rd, www.paradisevalleysprings.co.nz; adult/child $26/13; ⏰ 8am-5pm), a six-hectare park with trout springs, big slippery eels, and various land-dwelling animals such as deer, alpaca, possums and a pride of lions (fed at 2.30pm). There's also a coffee shop and a new elevated treetop walkway.

Wingspan Birds of Prey Trust (off Map p335; ☎ 07-357 4469; www.wingspan.co.nz; 1164 Paradise Valley Rd; adult/child $15/5; ⏰ 9am-3pm) is dedicated to conserving three threatened NZ birds: the falcon, hawk and owl. Learn about the birds in the museum display, then take a sneaky peek into the incubation area before walking through the all-weather aviary. Go in time to see the 2pm flying display.

Mamaku Blue

You may find grapes overrated once you've visited this **blueberry winery** (off Map p335; ☎ 07-332 5840; www.mamakublue.co.nz; Maraeroa Rd, Mamaku; tours $20, museum $2; ⏰ 10am-5pm). There are delicious daily tastings, and also on offer are other blueberry delights such as chocolates, chutneys, jams, sauces, vinegars and liqueurs. Take a tour and find out more, and visit the upstairs museum which has a collection of photos documenting the history of the area.

Mamaku Blue is 20km northwest of Rotorua; take SH5 and turn off onto Maraeroa Rd. It's well signposted.

Skyline Skyrides

Swinging up Mt Ngongotaha is **Skyline Skyrides** (Map p335; ☎ 07-347 0027; www.skylineskyrides.co.nz; Fairy

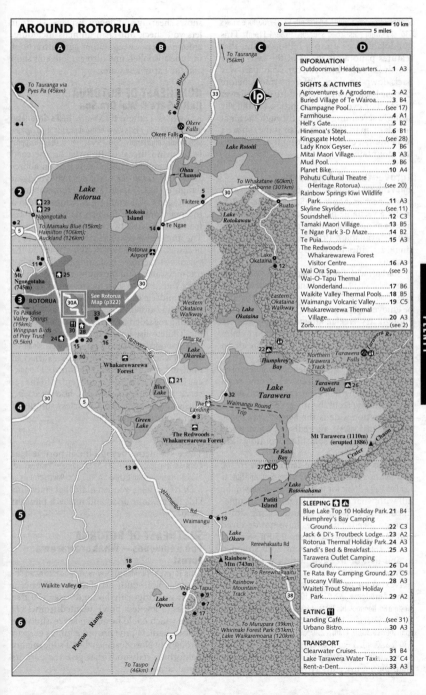

AROUND ROTORUA

0 ——— 10 km
0 ——— 5 miles

ROTORUA & THE BAY OF PLENTY

Springs Rd; gondola adult/child/family $24/12/60, luge 5 rides $30, sky swing adult/child $30/20; ☼ 9am-11pm). This gondola cruises up to a hilltop of fun that features panoramic views of the lake and a speedy luge on which you can scoot part-way back down on three different tracks before coming back up on a chairlift (to do it all over again). For even speedier antics, try the sky swing, a screaming swoosh through the air at speeds of up to 160km/h. Also at the top are a restaurant, a cafe and walking tracks around the mountain.

Agroventures & Agrodome

Agroventures (Map p335; ☎ 0800 949 888, 07-357 4747; www.agroventures.co.nz; Western Rd, Ngongotaha; ☼ 9am-5pm) is a veritable hive of entertaining activities, 9km north of Rotorua on SH5 (courtesy shuttle available). Prices that follow are for single activities but there are lots of deals for combos.

Start off with the 43m **bungy** (www.rotoruabungy.co.nz; adult/child $95/80) and the **Swoop** (www.swoop.co.nz; adult/child $49/35), a 130km/h swing that can be enjoyed alone or with friends. If that's not enough, try **Freefall Xtreme** (www.freefallxtreme.co.nz; 3min per adult/child $85/49) which simulates skydiving by blasting you 5m into the air on a column of wind.

Also here is the **Shweeb** (www.shweeb.co.nz; adult/child $49/35), a monorail velodrome from which you hang in a clear capsule and pedal yourself along recumbently at speeds of up to 60km/h. Alongside is the **Agrojet** (www.agrojet.co.nz; adult/child $49/35), allegedly NZ's fastest jet-boat, speeding and splashing around a 1km manmade course.

Across the road is the **zorb** (☎ 0800 227 474; www.zorb.co.nz; rides from $49; ☼ 9am-5pm Apr-Nov, to 7pm Dec-Mar) – look for the grassy track down the hill with what looks like large, clear, people-filled spheres bouncing and rolling down at some speed. Your eyes have not deceived you! There are two courses: 150m straight, or the 180m zigzag. Do your zorb strapped in and dry, or freestyle with a whole lot of water thrown in.

Next door to Agroventures is the educational **Agrodome** (☎ 07-357 1050; www.agrodome.co.nz; Western Rd, Ngongotaha; 1hr tour adult/child/family $30/15/78, 1hr show $26/13/75, tour & show $50/25/110; ☼ 8.30am-5pm, shows 9.30am, 11am & 2.30pm, tours 10.40am, 12.10pm, 1.30 & 3.40pm). Learn everything you need to know about sheep during a show that parades champion rams, runs a livestock auction, and shows shearing and doggy displays. The tour lets you check out farm animals including, among others, sheep. Other agro-attractions include a woollen mill display, souvenir shop and the Farmview Café.

NORTHEAST OF ROTORUA
Hell's Gate & Wai Ora Spa

Known as Tikitere to Maori, **Hell's Gate** (Map p335; ☎ 07-345 3151; www.hellsgate.co.nz; SH30; admission adult/child/family $30/15/75; ☼ 8.30am-8.30pm) is 16km northeast of Rotorua on the road to Whakatane (SH30). Tikitere is an abbreviation of *Taku tiki i tere nei* (My youngest daughter has floated away), remembering the tragedy of a young girl jumping into a thermal pool. The English name originates from a 1934 visit by George Bernard Shaw. The impressive geothermal reserve covers 10 hectares, with a 2.5km walking track to the various attractions, including the largest hot thermal waterfall in the southern hemisphere. Here you can also see a master woodcarver at work, and learn about flax weaving and other Maori traditions.

Long regarded by Maori as a place of healing, Tikitere also houses the **Wai Ora Spa** (mud bath & spa adult/child/family $105/55/265, massage per 30min/1hr $80/130) where you can relax with a variety of mud and spa treatments. The UltiMUD package (adult/child $235/180) includes entry to the reserve, mud bath, spa and one-hour massage, plus some manuka tea. A courtesy shuttle to/from Rotorua is available.

3-D Maze

Three kilometres beyond the airport, **Te Ngae Park** (Map p335; ☎ 07-345 5275; 3dmaze@wave.co.nz; 1135 Te Ngae Rd; adult/child $7.50/5; ☼ 9am-5pm) is a 3-D, 1.7km-long wooden maze that entertains kids for an hour or so and makes a pleasant picnic spot.

SOUTHEAST OF ROTORUA
The Redwoods – Whakarewarewa Forest

This **forest park** (Map p335; www.redwoods.co.nz; admission free) is 3km southeast of town on Tarawera Rd. It was originally home to over 170 tree species (a few less now), planted from 1899 to see which could be grown successfully for timber. Radiata pine proved a hit (as evident throughout New Zealand), but it's the mighty Californian redwoods that give the park its grandeur today.

Clearly signposted walking tracks range from a half-hour wander through the **Redwood Grove** to an enjoyable whole-day route to the Blue and Green Lakes. Most walks start from the **Redwoods Gift Shop & Visitor Centre** (Map p335; ☎ 07-350 0110; Long Mile Rd; ☼ 8.30am-5.30pm Mon-Fri & 10am-5pm Sat & Sun Oct-Mar, 8.30am-4.30pm Mon-Fri & 10am-4pm Sat & Sun Apr-Sep), where you can get maps and view displays about the forest. There's also a shop featuring a good selection of hand-crafted wooden items and nature-inspired gifts.

Aside from walking, the park is great for picnics, and is acclaimed well beyond the town for its enjoyable and accessible mountain biking (see p325).

Buried Village of Te Wairoa

Fifteen kilometres from Rotorua on the Tarawera Rd, which passes the pretty Blue and Green Lakes, is the **buried village** (Map p335; ☎ 07-362 8287; www.buriedvillage.co.nz; Tarawera Rd; admission adult/child/family $30/8/68; ☼ 9am-5pm Nov-Mar, to 4.30pm Apr-Oct), the site of one of the most dramatic natural events to occur in NZ in the last 150 years – the 1886 eruption of Mt Tarawera. Here you can see the buildings submerged by the eruption, creating an odd time capsule of NZ in the 19th century, with highlights such as the Rotomahana Hotel, a blacksmith's shop and several *whare* (houses).

A small museum tells the stories of the eruption and includes an interesting short film. Of particular interest is the story of the *tohunga* (priest) Tuhoto Ariki who, according to some, was blamed for the destruction. His *whare* has been excavated and reconstructed.

There's a short bush walk through the valley to Te Wairoa Falls, where the Wairoa River drops 30m over a series of rocky outcrops. The end of the track is steep, slippery and unsuitable for young children.

Lake Tarawera

Tarawera means 'Burnt Spear', named by a visiting hunter who left his bird spears in a hut and on returning the following season found both the spears and hut had been burnt. The lake is picturesque and good for swimming, fishing, cruises and nature walks.

A good place to access the lake is at The Landing, about 2km past the buried village. Here you'll find **Clearwater Cruises** (☎ 07-362 8590; www.clearwater.co.nz; The Landing, Lake Tarawera; per hr cruise vessel/self-drive runabout $510/125), which runs scenic cruises for groups and trout-fishing trips aboard a variety of vessels, with self-drive boats available. Also at The Landing is the **Landing Café** (☎ 07-362 8502; mains $26-30; ☼ breakfast & lunch), serving hearty mains like spiced lamb rump, salmon pasta and seafood chowder. Around 2km beyond The Landing is **Lake Tarawera Water Taxi** (☎ 07-362 8080; www.scenictarawera.co.nz; 93 Spencer Rd; lake excursions from $60), which can take you anywhere on the lake, anytime.

There are **DOC campsites** (www.doc.govt.nz) at Hot Water Beach (adult/child $8/4) on Te Rata Bay (boat access only), Tarawera Outlet (adult/child $7/2) and Humphrey's Bay (free). **Blue Lake Top 10 Holiday Park** (☎ 0800 808 292, 07-362 8120; www.bluelaketop10.co.nz; 723 Tarawera Rd; unpowered/powered sites $36/40, cabins $55-229) offers camping next to Blue Lake, 6km before you get to Lake Tarawera. Good facilities, well run and with a handy range of cabins.

SOUTH OF ROTORUA
Waimangu Volcanic Valley

This interesting **thermal area** (Map p335; ☎ 07-366 6137; www.waimangu.com; 587 Waimangu Rd; walking tour adult/child $32.50/10, boat cruise $40/10; ☼ 8.30am-5pm daily, to 6pm Jan) was created during the eruption of Mt Tarawera in 1886, making it young in geological terms. Waimangu (Black Water) refers to the dark, muddy colour of much of the water here.

Taking the easy downhill stroll through the valley you'll pass many spectacular thermal and volcanic features, including Inferno Crater Lake, where overflowing water can reach 80°C, and Frying Pan Lake, the largest hot spring in the world. The walk continues down to Lake Rotomahana (meaning 'Warm Lake'), from where you can either get a lift back up to where you started or take a 45-minute boat trip on the lake, past steaming cliffs and the former site of the Pink and White Terraces.

Waimangu is approximately a 20-minute drive south from Rotorua, 14km along SH5 (towards Taupo) and then 6km from the marked turn-off. Last admission is at 3.45pm (4.45pm in January).

Wai-O-Tapu Thermal Wonderland

Also south of Rotorua, **Wai-O-Tapu** (Map p335; ☎ 07-366 6333; www.waiotapu.co.nz; 201 Loop Rd, off SH5; admission adult/child/family $30/10/75; ☼ 8.30am-5pm), meaning 'Sacred Waters', is one of the most famous of the thermal reserves. It has many interesting features packed into a small area, including the boiling, multi-hued **Champagne Pool**, bubbling **mud pool**, stunning mineral terraces and the **Lady Knox Geyser**, which spouts off (with a little prompting from an organic soap) punctually at 10.15am and gushes up to 20m for about an hour. A fairly commercial attraction, it has a large shopping area and cafe, which makes for a reasonable pit stop.

Wai-O-Tapu is 27km south of Rotorua along SH5 (towards Taupo), and a further 2km from the marked turn-off. Last admission 3.45pm.

Waikite Valley Thermal Pools

Approximately 30km south of Rotorua on SH5 are the open-air **Waikite Valley Thermal Pools** (Map p335; ☎ 07-333 1861; www.hotpools.co.nz; 648 Waikite Valley Rd; public pools adult/child/family $12/6/30, private pools 40min $15; ☉ 10am-9pm). As well as the four main pools there are two more relaxing, smaller pools and four private spas, all ranging from 35°C to 40°C. There's also a cafe and camping on-site (unpowered/powered sites $32/36; pools free for campers).

To get here turn right off SH5 at the signpost opposite the Wai-O-Tapu turn-off, and continue for 6km.

Whirinaki Forest Park

The exceptional feature of this **forest park** (www.doc.govt.nz, www.whirinakirainforest.info) is some of NZ's finest podocarp (conifer) forest, although there is much more to see here, including canyons, waterfalls, lookouts, and many streams and rivers. The Oriuwaka Ecological Area and Arahaki Lagoon are also here.

You can explore the park via a network of tracks varying in length and difficulty. The best source of information is **DOC Rangitaiki visitor centre** (☎ 07-366 1080; SH38) in Murupara. The DOC booklet *Walks in Whirinaki Forest* ($2.50) gives details about walking and camping in the park.

A good short walk is the **Whirinaki Waterfalls Track** (four hours return), which follows the Whirinaki River, while one of the longer walks is the **Whirinaki Track** (two days, 27km), which can be combined with **Te Hoe Track** (four days). There's also a rampaging 16km **mountain-bike track** here.

There are several easily accessible **camping areas** and 10 **backcountry huts** ($5-15) in the park; pay at the DOC office.

Whirinaki Forest Park is 90km southeast of Rotorua, with access off SH38 on the way to Te Urewera National Park; take the turn-off at Te Whaiti to Minginui. The closest town to the park is Murupara, where there are basic amenities.

WESTERN BAY OF PLENTY

The Western Bay of Plenty stretches along the coast from Waihi Beach to Maketu and inland as far as the Kaimai Range. This is where New Zealanders have come on holiday for generations, lapping up salt-licked activities and lashings of sunshine.

TAURANGA

pop 118,200

Tauranga (pronounced Tao-wronger) has been booming since the 1990s and remains one of NZ's fastest-growing cities. The busy port – with its petrol refineries and mountains of coal and lumber – serves the land for miles around, but it's the migrants (many from Auckland) and holidaymakers who have seen the old workhorse reborn as a show pony. Restaurants and bars line the revamped waterfront, fancy hotels rise high, and the once-sleepy suburbs of Mt Maunganui and Papamoa have woken up to new wealth and homogeny.

Tauranga is the place to fulfil all your watery dreams: with marinas chock-a-block with beautiful boats, sandy surf beaches and water sports aplenty, this is about as Riviera as NZ gets.

Information

Automobile Association (Map p339; AA; ☎ 07-927 7760; www.aa.co.nz; cnr Devonport Rd & First Ave; ☉ 8.30am-5pm Mon-Fri, 9am-noon Sat) Maps and driving info.

BA Reader (Map p339; ☎ 07-577 0990; www.bareader. co.nz; 26 Wharf St; ☉ 9.30am-5pm Mon-Fri, 10am-9.30pm Sat, to 4pm Sun) Beachy secondhand reads.

Dymocks (Map p339; ☎ 07-927 7476; www.dymocks. co.nz; 50 Devonport Rd; ☉ 9am-5pm Mon-Fri, to 4pm Sat, 10am-4pm Sun) For books and maps.

Gateway Cyber Cafe (Map p339; ☎ 07-571 1112; 26 Devonport Rd; ☉ 9am-10pm) Internet access.

Paper Plus (Map p339; www.nzpost.co.nz; 17 Grey St; ☉ 8.30am-5.30pm Mon-Fri, 9am-4pm Sat, 10am-3pm Sun) The local NZ Post branch.

ROTORUA & THE BAY OF PLENTY

CENTRAL TAURANGA

INFORMATION	
Automobile Association (AA)	1 D4
B.A Reader	2 D3
Bivouac Outdoor	3 D3
Dymocks	4 D3
Gateway Cyber Café	5 D3
Paper Plus	6 C3
Tauranga i-SITE	7 D2

SIGHTS & ACTIVITIES	
Brain Watkins House	8 C3
Dive HQ	9 C3
Elms Mission Station	10 C1
Monmouth Redoubt	11 D1
Robbins Park	12 D1
Tauranga Art Gallery	13 D1
Te Awanui Waka	14 D2

SLEEPING	
Harbour City Motor Inn	15 C3
Harbourside City	
Backpackers	16 D3
Hotel on Devonport	17 D3
Loft 109 Backpackers	18 D4
Puriri Park Boutique Hotel	19 C2
Roselands Motel	20 C1
Tauranga on the Waterfront	21 D4
Tauranga YHA	22 B3

EATING	
Bravo	23 D3
City Markets	24 D2
Collar & Thai	25 D3
Fresh Fish Market	26 D3
Little India	27 D3
Mediterraneo Café	28 D3
Naked Grape	29 D3
Shima	30 D2
Zeytin	31 D2

DRINKING	
Cornerstone	32 D2
Crown & Badger	33 D2
De Bier Haus	34 D3

ENTERTAINMENT	
Baycity Cinemas	35 D4
Buddha Lounge	36 D2
Colosseum	37 D2
Rialto	(see 25)

TRANSPORT	
Air New Zealand	38 D4
Bay Hopper Bus Stop	39 C3
Bus Terminal	(see 7)
Mt Maunganui Ferry	40 D3

ROTORUA & THE BAY OF PLENTY

Tauranga Hospital (Map p342; ☎ 07-579 8000; www.bopdhb.govt.nz; 375 Cameron Rd; ⏱ 24hr) A couple of kilometres south of town.

Tauranga i-SITE (Map p339; ☎ 07-578 8103; www.bayofplentynz.com; 95 Willow St; ⏱ 8.30am-5.30pm Mon-Fri, 9am-5pm Sat & Sun) Local tourist information, bookings and InterCity bus tickets and DOC maps.

Sights

The **Tauranga Art Gallery** (Map p339; ☎ 07-578 7933; www.artgallery.org.nz; cnr Wharf & Willow Sts; admission by donation; ⏱ 10am-4.30pm) presents historic and contemporary art, and houses a permanent collection along with frequently changing local and visiting exhibitions. The building itself is a former bank, although you'd hardly know it – it's an altogether excellent space

with no obvious compromise (cue: applause!). Touring the ground and mezzanine galleries, with a stop to poke your nose into the video cube, will take an hour or so.

Built in 1847, **Elms Mission Station** (Map p339; ☎ 07-577 9772; www.theelms.org.nz; Mission St; admission house adult/child $5/50c, gardens free; ⏱ house 2-4pm Wed, Sat & Sun, gardens 9am-5pm daily) is the oldest building in the Bay of Plenty. Furnished in period style, it sits among other well-preserved mission buildings in leafy grounds. The spooky **Mission Cemetery** (Map p342) lies not far away at the intersection of Marsh Street and Dive Crescent – good for a little epitaph-reading.

The demure **Brain Watkins House** (Map p339; ☎ 07-578 1835; www.library.tauranga.govt.nz/localhistory; cnr Elizabeth St & Cameron Rd; admission $2; ⏱ 2-4pm Sun) was built in 1881 from kauri (wood) and remains one of Tauranga's best-preserved colonial homes.

Te Awanui Waka (Map p339; The Strand), a replica Maori canoe, is on display in an open-sided building at the top of the Strand. Up the hill, **Monmouth Redoubt** (Map p339; Monmouth St) was a fortified site during the Maori Wars. **Robbins Park** (Map p339; Cliff Rd) is a verdant pocket of roses with excellent views across to Mt Maunganui.

Mills Reef Winery (off Map p342; ☎ 0800 645 577, 07-576 8800; www.millsreef.co.nz; 143 Moffat Rd, Bethlehem; ⊙ tastings 10am-5pm), 7km from the town centre at Bethlehem, has tastings of its award-winning wines (dig the cab sav) and a restaurant (open for lunch and dinner daily; mains $24 to $33).

From **Minden Lookout** (off Map p342), about 10km west of Tauranga towards Katikati, there's a superb view back over the Bay of Plenty. To get there, take SH2 to Te Puna and turn off south on Minden Rd; the lookout is about 4km up the road.

Out near the airport, **Classic Flyers NZ** (Map p342; ☎ 07-572 4000; www.classicflyersnz.com; 8 Jean Batten Dr; admission adult/child $10/5; ⊙ 10am-4pm) is a fascinating aviation museum with on-site cafe.

If you're interested in *marae*, **Huria Marae** (Map p342; ☎ 07-578 7838; www.teara.govt.nz; Te Kaponga St, Judea; admission free; ⊙ varies) is on a nondescript suburban street but has sensational carvings both inside and out. Call to organise permission to visit.

Activities
TRAMPING
The free *Tauranga City Walkways* pamphlet details walks around Tauranga and Mt Maunganui, including the fascinating **Waikareao Estuary Walkway** (9km, two hours), and the popular **Mauao Base Track** (see p346) in Mt Maunganui. History buffs should pick up the free *Historic Tauranga* brochure and stroll around the town's cache of historic sites.

The backdrop to the Western Bay of Plenty is the rugged 70km-long **Kaimai Mamaku Forest Park** (off Map p342), 35km southwest of Tauranga on SH29, with tramps for the intrepid and basic camping (sites free to $5, huts $5 to $10). For more info see DOC's pamphlet *Kaimai Mamaku Forest Park Day Walks* ($1.50).

In the Wairoa River valley, 15km southwest of Tauranga just off SH29, **McLaren Falls Park** (off Map p342; ☎ 07-577 7000; www.tauranga.govt.nz/

mclarenfalls; admission free; ⊙ 8am-5.30pm winter, to 7.30pm summer) is a 190-hectare lakeland park with great trees and picnic areas. There are three basic modern hostels here (dorms $20) and campsites ($5 per person). Also accessible from McLaren Falls is **Marshalls Animal Park** (off Map p342; ☎ 07-543 1099; www.marshallsanimalpark.co.nz; admission adult/child/family $10/5/30; ⊙ 10am-2pm Wed & Thu, to 4.30pm Sat & Sun) which has family fun such as animal petting, a flying fox, playground and pony rides.

SWIMMING WITH DOLPHINS
The waters around Tauranga are particularly blessed with dolphins and even the odd whale in summer. Several operators offer a chance to see or even swim with them.

Butler's Swim With Dolphins (☎ 0508 288 537, 07-578 3197; www.swimwithdolphins.co.nz; full-day trips adult/child $125/100; ⊙ trip leaves Tauranga 9am, Mt Maunganui 9.30am) Even without dolphins, the trips are always entertaining, particularly with Cap'n Butler, a real old salt who protested against nuclear testing at Mururoa Atoll.

Dolphin Seafaris (☎ 0800 326 8747, 07-577 0105; www.nzdolphin.com; half-day trip adult/child $140/90; ⊙ 8am) Eco-attuned trips departing Tauranga and Mt Maunganui.

South Sea Vagabond (☎ 07-579 6376; www.southseasailing.com; trips from adult/child $120/85) Runs trips on an 18m catamaran. Kayaks available for nonswimmers.

FISHING & DIVING
The Bay of Plenty is renowned for its marine life and fishing – especially big game such as marlin and mako sharks, and snapper for your suppertime too. A daylong fishing trip will cost around $70 to $90 per person, with several companies offering 24-hour trips for around $120. The i-SITE can assist with bookings.

Bay Fishing Charters (☎ 0800 229 347; www.bayfishingcharters.co.nz) Small-group half- and full-day fishing charters on the good ship *Resolution*.

Blue Ocean Charters (☎ 0800 224 278; www.blueocean.co.nz) Fishing, diving and sightseeing trips (including one to Tuhua Island) on the TS *Ohorere*, MV *Te Kuia* and MV *Ratahi*.

Dive HQ (Map p339; ☎ 07-578 4050; www.divehqtauranga.co.nz; 213 Cameron Rd; courses from $600, trips from $95) PADI-qualifying courses or trips to local wrecks and reefs, plus gear rental.

Earth2ocean (☎ 07-571 5286; www.earth2ocean.co.nz; courses from $500, trips from $100) Runs an extensive range of diving courses and trips.

Fat Boy Charters (☎ 07-575 5986; fatboycharters@ xtra.co.nz) Runs small-group fishing and diving trips on a 7m runabout.

Tauranga Marine Charters (☎ 07-552 6283; www. taurangamarinecharters.co.nz) Full-day fishing trips and diving trips once a month, on the MV *Manutere*.

KAYAKING

The Wairoa River is great for kayaking, offering something for paddlers at all levels. **Waimarino Adventure Park** (off Map p342; ☎ 07-576 4233; www.waimarino.com; 36 Taniwha Pl, Bethlehem; kayak tours from $55, park day-pass adult/child $39/30), on the banks of the river, offers freedom kayak hire for leisurely paddles along 12km of flat water, runs self-guided tours further up the river, and sea kayaking trips. Its Glowworm Tour ($120 per person) is a magical after-dark journey at McLaren Falls Park where you slip into a secret glowworm-filled wonderland. Waimarino also has an adventure park with a kayak slide, diving board, ropes course, warm pools and wildlife-spotting – a great place to spend a day, especially if there are children in tow.

WHITE-WATER RAFTING & SLEDGING

White-water rafting is popular around Tauranga, particularly on the Wairoa River, although it's definitely a rafting trip for thrill-seekers. The Wairoa's levels are controlled by a dam, so can only be rafted 26 days of the year: advance bookings are essential. You can find a list of rafting operators on p326.

OTHER ACTIVITIES

If you're new to water sports and want to get safely into the action, contact **Elements Watersports** (☎ 0800 486 729; www.elementsonline.co.nz; lessons per hr from $20). It offers tuition in sailing, windsurfing, powerboating and jetskiing, and has gear for hire.

Landlubbers might also consider jumping out of a plane…or maybe they won't. **Tauranga Tandem Skydiving** (Map p342; ☎ 07-576 7990; www.tandem skydive.co.nz; Tauranga Airport; jumps 8000/10,000/12,000ft $245/275/345) with views of White Island, Mount Ruapehu and the East Cape.

Tours

Adventure Bay of Plenty (☎ 0800 238 267; www. adventurebop.co.nz; 2hr/half-day/full-day tours from $85/125/150) Offers an enticing array of adventure tours by boat, kayak, mountain bike and horse. Matakana Island day tours cost $180.

Mount Classic Tours (☎ 07-574 1779; www.mctours. co.nz; 3-6 day tours $1675-3445) Longer tours around the Bay of Plenty including accommodation and most meals.

No.8 Farm Tours (☎ 07-579 3981; www.no8farmtours. co.nz; tours $210) Half-day 4WD tours of a working NZ farm, featuring shearing, milking, sheep dogs, deer and morning tea.

Tauranga Tasting Tours (☎ 07-544 1383; www. tastingtours.co.nz; tours $130) Whips around a local brewery, Mills Reef and Morton Estate wineries, and back to town for cocktails.

Touring Company (☎ 07-577 0057; www.newzealand adventure.co.nz; tours from $140) Half- and full-day local scenic tours and trips further afield to Waitomo, Rotorua and White Island.

Or take to the sky on one of the following aerial escapades – most departing Tauranga Airport (p342) – book through the i-SITE or directly. Minimum passenger numbers apply.

Aerius Helicopters (☎ 0800 864 354; www.aerius. co.nz; flights from $59) Local flights and excursions as far as Waitomo and White Island.

Air Discovery (☎ 0800 247 347, 07-575 7588; www. airdiscovery.co.nz; flights from $299) Offers one- to two-hour fixed-wing flights over White Island and Mt Tarawera.

Gyrate (☎ 07-575 6583; www.gyrate.co.nz; flights from $95) Flights in a gyroplane (the jetski of the sky), from local, scenic flights to learn-to-fly packages.

M*A*S*H Chopper Scenic Flights (☎ 07-572 4077; www.adventureaviation.co.nz; flights 12/20min $110/150) As seen on TV but without Hot Lips Houlihan. City and surrounds.

Festivals & Events

This town is no cultural desert; events on the calendar include the following:

National Jazz Festival (☎ 07-577 7018; www. jazz.org.nz) An Easter extravaganza of big blowers and scoobee-doobee-doobop, with concerts and food galore.

Tauranga Arts Festival (☎ 07-577 7018; www. taurangafestival.co.nz) Kicking off on Labour weekend in October (in odd-numbered years), showcasing dance, comedy, plays and other things arty.

Sleeping
BUDGET

Tauranga Tourist Park (Map p342; ☎ 07-578 3323; www. taurangatouristpark.co.nz; 9 Mayfair St; unpowered/powered sites $24/28, cabins from $50; 🛜) Located on the harbour edge, this is a good option for tenters and campervans with nice grassed sites and a new TV lounge. The amenities are a bit poky, but it's all well maintained, clean and tidy.

ROTORUA & THE BAY OF PLENTY

ROTORUA & THE BAY OF PLENTY

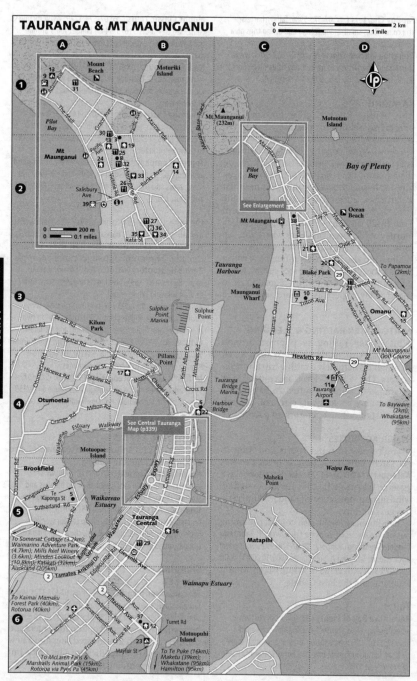

Just the Ducks Nuts Backpackers (Map p342; ☎ 07-576 1366; www.justtheducksnuts.co.nz; 6 Vale St; dm from $24, d with/without bathroom $62/56; 🖳 📶) Just out of the town centre, this is a friendly place with colourful rooms, a fulsome library, TVs and videos strewn about and quirky touches like flowers planted in a bathtub and duck-themed toilets – like a university share-house minus the parties! Free shuttles to/from the bus stop; self-contained flats also available.

Loft 109 Backpackers (Map p339; ☎ 07-579 5638; www.loft109.co.nz; upstairs, 109 Devonport Rd; dm/d/tr $25/58/80; 🖳) This central spot feels like somebody's flat, with an intimate kitchen and lounge, rooftop balconies in upper rooms, and (oddly) a boat built into the roof. It's bright with plenty of skylights and a gas fire for colder days.

Harbourside City Backpackers (Map p339; ☎ 07-579 4066; www.backpacktauranga.co.nz; upstairs, 105 The Strand; dm/d from $28/72; 🖳 📶) Enjoy sea views from this sociable hostel, handy to the Strand's bars. Rooms are smallish but clean, and you'll spend more time on the roof terrace anyway. There's no car park, but down the road is a public car park that's empty at the right time.

Tauranga YHA (Map p339; ☎ 07-578 5064; www.yha.co.nz; 171 Elizabeth St; unpowered sites/dm $36/28, d with/without bathroom $80/72; 🖳 📶) A well-kept, deceptively big YHA with a big grassy backyard and a nearby mangrove swamp boardwalk to explore. Camping spots are spot-on; inviting dorms have individual lockers. There's info available on local coastal-care policies and a noticeboard for all things green.

MIDRANGE
Ambassador Motor Inn (Map p342; ☎ 0800 735 294, 07-578 5665; 9 Fifteenth Ave; www.ambassador-motorinn. co.nz; d/f from $105/165; 📶 📳) On one of the main roads into town, this tidy motor inn has noise-reducing glass for peaceful sleeps and family-friendly facilities including a swimming pool and trampoline. Some rooms have spa baths; all have kitchen facilities. The interiors are a bit '90s (not particularly ambassadorial), but spotlessly clean.

Roselands Motel (Map p339; ☎ 07-578 2294; www.roselands.co.nz; 21 Brown St; d/ste from $115/135; 📶) Tarted up with splashes of orange paint and new linen, this sweet, old-style motel is in a quiet but central location. Expect roomy units (all with kitchens), highchairs for the kids and yoga lessons by arrangement. Don't mess with the resident cat…

Puriri Park Boutique Hotel (Map p339; ☎ 0800 4787 474, 07-577 1480; www.puriri.co.nz; 32 Cameron Rd, ste $130-225; 📳) With large rooms (all with either terrace or balcony), king-sized beds, spas, swimming pool and secure parking, this upmarket motel is popular with wandering business bods. Picasso the turtle surveys proceedings from the lobby.

Harbour City Motor Inn (Map p339; ☎ 07-571 1435; www.taurangaharbourcity.co.nz; 50 Wharf St; d from $150; 📶) In the middle of town with plenty of parking, this newish motor inn has all the mod cons such as a spa bath, TV and business desk in every room. Friendly staff offer sound local advice on your itinerary.

Tauranga on the Waterfront (Map p339; ☎ 0800 109 007, 07-578 7079; www.thetauranga.co.nz; 1 Second Ave; d/ste from $150/195; 🖳) This quiet place, only a short walk to the centre, has some excellent harbour-view suites if you're feeling romantic. Some rooms have deluxe spa baths that will get you back into the mood if the architecture fails you.

ROTORUA & THE BAY OF PLENTY

TOP END

Hotel on Devonport (Map p339; ☎ 07-578 2668; www.hotelondevonport.net.nz; 72 Devonport Rd; d/ste $160/200) City-centre Devonport is top of the town, with bay-view rooms, noise-reducing glass, slick interiors and sassy staff, all of which appeal to business travellers and luxury weekenders.

Sebel Trinty Wharf (Map p342; ☎ 0800 937 373, 07-577 8700; www.mirvachotels.com; 51 Dive Cres; d from $180; ☒ 🖵 📶 🏊) This blocky high-rise is on the water's edge near the harbour bridge. A slick contemporary lobby – all retro white vinyl and trendy plush greys – leads to the in-house restaurant Halo, a key player in the local cuisine scene. Rooms are supersized and luxurious in tones au naturel. Amenities include an underutilised gym and infinity-edge swimming pool.

Eating

Devonport Rd is the place to grab lunch, but places on the Strand excel at dinner and drinks to follow. Tauranga's pubs also do solid meals (see Drinking, right).

Fresh Fish Market (Map p339; ☎ 07-578 1789; 1 Dive Cres; meals from $5; ☒ lunch & dinner) A local legend serving up fresh fish and chips right on the water's edge.

Naked Grape (Map p339; ☎ 07-579 5555; 97 The Strand; breakfast & lunch $7-21, dinner mains $28-32; ☒ 7am-late) With cheery staff, wine-coloured rugs and lilting jazz, this hip Strand wine bar draws the daytime crowds with pastas, pizzas, salads, good coffee and beaut breakfasts. At night it's moodier, with mains like honey-braised lamb and lemon-marinated chicken breast.

Shima (Map p339; ☎ 07-571 1382; 15 Wharf St; mains $10-21; ☒ lunch & dinner Mon-Sat) Shima is a simple, unpretentious sushi and sashimi bar, hung with Japanese fans, umbrellas and lanterns. Bento boxes and set-price menus are great bang for your buck.

Mediterraneo Café (Map p339; ☎ 07-577 0487; 62 Devonport Rd; mains $12-19; ☒ 7am-4pm Mon-Fri; 7.30am-4pm Sat, 8am-4pm Sun) A hot spot, reeling with regulars enjoying terrific coffee and scrumptious all-day breakfasts. Order off the blackboard or from the cabinet stuffed with sandwiches, flans and cakes. Lunchtime crowds can be frantic (but the chicken salad is worth it).

Collar & Thai (Map p339; ☎ 07-577 6655; Goddards Centre, 21 Devonport Rd; mains $16-30; ☒ lunch Mon-Sat, dinner daily) No tie required at this upstairs, upper-end eatery that artfully elaborates on Thai

standards and uses plenty of fresh seafood. This place has good-value lunch specials.

Little India (Map p339; ☎ 07-579 0910; 113 The Strand; mains $17-20; ☒ lunch & dinner; 🇻) Part of a consistent nationwide chain, this flavoursome curry house offers the best value on the Strand, especially for lunch specials. Outdoor tables for a hot night and a hot prawn *jhalfrezee*.

Zeytin (Map p339; ☎ 07-579 0099; 83 The Strand; mains $19-27; ☒ lunch & dinner Tue-Sun) Ask the locals to name their favourite restaurant, and odds-on they'll name Zeytin – a real Turkish delight. Real food, real cheap, with something for everyone along the lines of kebabs, delicious homemade breads, dips and healthy salads, wood-fired pizza and a few exotic surprises.

Bravo (Map p339; ☎ 07-578 4700; Red Sq; mains $23-33; ☒ breakfast, lunch & dinner; 🇻) This trendy, well-regarded restaurant and bar is a pleasant spot for breakfast, flash sandwiches, salads, wood-fired pizza and freshly squeezed juices. There's outside seating on the pedestrianised street and a few good vegetarian options.

Somerset Cottage (off Map p342; ☎ 07-576 6889; 30 Bethlehem Rd, Bethlehem; mains $35; ☒ lunch Wed-Fri, dinner Tue-Sun) The most awarded restaurant in the Bay, Somerset Cottage is a simple-but-elegant venue for that special treat. The food is highly seasonal, made from the best NZ ingredients, impressively executed without being too fussy. Standout dishes include blue cheese soufflé, duck with coconut kumara and the famous liquorice ice cream.

Self caterers should swing by **Pak N Save** (Map p342; ☎ 07-578 7037, 476 Cameron Rd; ☒ 8am-10pm) or the fruit-and-veg **City Markets** (Map p339; ☎ 07-577 0270; cnr Willow & Hamilton Sts; ☒ 9am-5pm Mon-Fri, to noon Sat).

Drinking

De Bier Haus (Map p339; ☎ 07-928 0833; 109 The Strand; ☒ 11am-late) With a pavement packed with happy punters, this hot Haus features Belgian beers and sophisticated environs. The interior's a classic manly hunting lodge with an antler or two in the midst. Kitchen-work is swift and savvy, turning out Euro-offerings such as German sausage, *brezels, moules, frites* and an excellent squid salad (mains $16 to $30).

Crown & Badger (Map p339; ☎ 07-571 3038; cnr The Strand & Wharf St; admission free; ☒ 9am-late) A particularly convincing Brit boozer that does pukka pints of Tennent's and Guinness, and food (mains $13 to $20) along the lines of bangers and mash. Things get lively at the weekends when live bands play.

Cornerstone (Map p339; ☎ 07-928 1120; 55 The Strand; admission free; 🕑 10am-late) A cheerful watering hole attended by on-the-ball staff and a mature crowd (let's say over 25). A solid no-surprises menu offers whopping meals (mains $12 to $35), while sports fans can watch the game on the big telly and groovers can swing a hip (live music Thursday to Sunday).

Entertainment

Colosseum (Map p339; ☎ 07-571 0718; www.colosseumbar.co.nz; 17 Harington St; admission varies; 🕑 7pm-late Thu, 8pm-3am Fri & Sat) Your first choice for big-screen sports (30 screens!) and live music (Katchafire, dub DJs, Hendrix tribute bands etc).

Buddha Lounge (Map p339; ☎ 07-928 1516; www.thebuddhalounge.co.nz; upstairs, 61b The Strand; entry price varies; 🕑 7pm-late Thu, 8pm-3am Fri & Sat) A cocktail lounge and dance venue hosting local and visiting DJs.

There are two cinemas in town: the arthouse **Rialto** (Map p339; ☎ 07-577 0445; www.rialtotauranga.co.nz; Goddards Centre, 21 Devonport Rd; tickets adult/child $15/9; 🕑 vary) and the megaplex **Baycity Cinemas** (Map p339; ☎ 07-577 0800; www.baycitycinemas.co.nz; 45 Elizabeth St; tickets adult/child $15/9; 🕑 10.30am-late).

Getting There & Away

AIR

Air New Zealand (Map p339; ☎ 07-577 7300; www.airnewzealand.co.nz; cnr Devonport Rd & Elizabeth St 🕑 9am-5pm Mon-Fri) has daily direct flights to Auckland, Wellington and Christchurch, with connections to other centres.

BUS

InterCity (☎ 09-583 5780; www.intercity.co.nz) tickets and timetables are available at the i-SITE. It runs buses to destinations including the following:

Destination	Price	Duration	Frequency
Auckland	$45	4¼hr	6 daily
Hamilton	$31	2-3hr	5 daily
Rotorua	$25	1½hr	4 daily
Taupo	$40	3hr	4 daily
Wellington	$96	9hr	3 daily

Naked Bus (☎ 0900 625 33; www.nakedbus.com) offers substantial fare savings when you book in advance. Its services connect Tauranga with a number of destinations including those listed below:

Destination	Price	Duration	Frequency
Auckland	$25	4¼hr	2 daily
Hamilton	$22	2hr	2 daily
Napier	$57	12hr	1 daily
Rotorua	$11	1½hr	3 daily
Taupo	$29	6hr	3 daily
Wellington	$41	12½hr	1 daily
Whakatane	$19	1½hr	1 daily

Bay Hopper (☎ 0800 422 928; www.baybus.co.nz) runs the Twin City Express bus twice daily between Tauranga/Mt Maunganui and Rotorua via Te Puke ($11, 1½ hours). Bay Hopper also runs the a Whakatane–Tauranga Link bus from Monday to Saturday, ($12, two hours), with onward connections to Ohope and Opotiki.

Luxury & Coastline Shuttles (☎ 0800 454 678, 07-574 9600; www.coastlineshuttles.co.nz) runs airport transfers to Auckland ($90), Hamilton ($75) and Rotorua ($90), and runs from Tauranga Airport into Central Tauranga ($15).

CAR

If you're heading to Hamilton on route K, don't forget the toll road costs $1.

Getting Around

Tauranga's bright yellow **Bay Hopper** (☎ 0800 4229 287; www.baybus.co.nz) buses run Monday to Saturday to most locations around the area, including Mt Maunganui ($2.50, 15 minutes) and Papamoa ($3, 30 minutes). There's a central stop on Wharf St; timetables available from the i-SITE. The **Mt Maunganui Ferry** (☎ 07-579 1325; www.kiwicoastcruises.co.nz; one-way adult/child $8/5; 🕑 Dec-Mar) to/from Mt Maunganui departs the Strand; ask the i-SITE for a schedule.

Numerous car-rental agencies have offices in Tauranga, including **Rent-a-Dent** (Map p342; ☎ 0800 736 823, 07-578 1772; www.rentadent.co.nz; 19 Fifteenth Ave) and **Rite Price Rentals** (Map p342; ☎ 0800 250 251; www.ritepricerentals.co.nz; 25 Totara St, Mt Maunganui).

A taxi from the centre of Tauranga to the airport costs around $18. Local taxi companies:

Citicabs (☎ 07-577 0999)
Tauranga Mount Taxis (☎ 07-578 6086)

MT MAUNGANUI

pop 18,600

Named after the hulking 232m hill that punctuates the sandy peninsula occupied by the township, up-tempo Mt Maunganui is often just called 'the Mount', or Mauao, which translates as 'caught by the light of day'. It's considered part of greater Tauranga, but really is an enclave unto itself, with great cafes and restaurants, hip bars and fab beaches. Sun-seekers flock to the Mount in summer, supplied by an increasing number of 10-storey apartment towers studding the spit.

Information

The friendly **Mt Maunganui i-SITE** (Map p342; ☎ 07-575 5099; www.bayofplentynz.com; Salisbury Ave; ⏰ 9am-5pm) will assist you with information and bookings.

Sights & Activities

The Mount lays claim to being NZ's premier surf city (they teach surfing at high school!). Carve up the waves at **Mount Beach**, which has an 100m artificial surf reef not far offshore, or there's sheltered-beach swimming on the western side of the peninsula. To learn to surf, try the following operators:

Backdoor (Map p342; ☎ 07-575 7831; www.backdoor. co.nz; 24 Pacific Ave; 2hr lesson $66)

Hibiscus (☎ 07-575 3792; www.surfschool.co.nz; 2hr/2-day lesson $80/150) Run by experienced surfer Rebecca Taylor.

Mount Surfshop (Map p342; ☎ 07-575 9133; www. mountsurfshop.co.nz; 96 Maunganui Rd; rental per day wetsuit/surfboard $15/40, 2hr lesson $60)

New Zealand Surf School (☎ 021 477 873; www. nzsurfschools.co.nz; 1/2hr lesson $50/80)

To learn more about surfing in the area (and beyond) visit the excellent **Mount Surf Museum** (Map p342; ☎ 07-927 7234; www.mountsurfshop.co.nz; 139 Totara St; admission free; ⏰ 9am-5pm Mon-Sat, 9.30am-5pm Sun). Don't fancy surfing? Learn kiteboarding with **Assault** (☎ 027 245 7540; www.assault.co.nz; 1hr lesson $100), or try rock climbing at the **Rock House** ((Map p342; ☎ 07-572 4920; www.therockhouse. co.nz; 9 Triton Ave; admission adult/child $14/10; ⏰ noon-late Tue-Fri, 10am-6pm Sun).

Mauao itself can be explored via **walking trails**, winding around it and leading up to the summit. The summit walk takes about an hour and gets steep near the top. You can also climb around the rocks on **Moturiki Island**, which adjoins the peninsula. The island and the base of Mauao also make up the **Mauao Base Track** (3½km, 45 minutes), wandering through magical groves of pohutukawa trees that bloom between November and January. **Mauao Tours** (☎ 027 218 1816, 07-575 6961; www.mauao tours.co.nz; tours from 1hr $30) runs guided walking tours around the Mount and Papamoa with a focus on Maori history.

After all that walking you'll have earned a soak at **Mt Maunganui Hot Saltwater Pools** (Map p342; ☎ 07-575 0868; www.tcal.co.nz; 9 Adams Ave; admission adult/child $9.50/7; ⏰ 6am-10pm Mon-Sat, 8am-10pm Sun) at the foot of the Mount. For traditional swimming-pool action plus a wave pool, hydroslide and aqua aerobics, visit **Baywave** (off Map p342; ☎ 07-575 0276; www.tcal.co.nz; cnr Girven & Gloucester Rds; admission adult/child $6.50/4.50; ⏰ 6am-9pm Mon-Fri, 7am-7pm Sat & Sun).

Sleeping

Mt Maunganui is a hugely popular holiday destination with plenty of accommodation – particularly apartment style – with prices higher than Tauranga.

Pacific Coast Lodge & Backpackers (Map p342; ☎ 0800 666 622; www.pacificcoastlodge.co.nz; 432 Maunganui Rd; dm/d from $24/70; 🖥) Not far from the action, this efficiently run, clean hostel is the pick of the bunch for those who want a good night's sleep, with drinkers encouraged to go into town after 10pm. Purpose-built bunkrooms are roomy and spangled with jungle murals.

Mount Backpackers (Map p342; ☎ 07-575 0860; www. mountbackpackers.co.nz; 87 Maunganui Rd; dm/d from $25/70; 🖥 📶) A tight but tidy hostel, bolstered by location – close to the beach and a mere stagger from the restaurants and bars – plus extras like a travel desk, job board, cheap weekly rates and deals on activities including surf lessons.

Beachside Holiday Park (Map p342; ☎ 07-575 4471; www.mountbeachside.co.nz; 1 Adams Ave; sites $30-50; 📶) With three different camping areas all nestled into the base of Mt Maunganui, this community-run park has spectacular camping with all the expected facilities, plus it's handy to the saltwater pools and a strip of good eateries.

Cosy Corner Holiday Park (Map p342; ☎ 07-575 5899; www.cosycorner.co.nz; 40 Ocean Beach Rd; powered sites $40, cabins & flats $75-155; 🖥 📶 📺) This spartan camping ground has a sociable feel, with barbecues, trampolines and a games room. Cabins may prove too cosy for some (and look

ROTORUA & THE BAY OF PLENTY

elsewhere if you're allergic to Laminex), but beach convenience compensates.

Mount Maunganui B&B (Map p342; ☎ 07-575 4013; www.mountbednbreakfast.co.nz; 463 Maunganui Rd; s/d incl cooked breakfast from $60/100) This five-room B&B is on the main road into town and cops some traffic noise, but rooms are presentable (if a little tight). Don't expect too much and you'll be fine.

Westhaven Motel (Map p342; ☎ 07-575 4753; www. westhavenmotel.co.nz; 27a The Mall; d from $100; 🛜) The unmolested 1970s architecture here is soooo *Brady Bunch*, with wooden shelving between kitchen and lounge, and funky mirrors to re-tune your afro. Full kitchens are perfect for self-caterers, plus there are free fishing rods and dinghies. The cheapest hotel in miles.

Mission Belle Motel (Map p342; ☎ 0800 202 434; www.missionbellemotel.co.nz; cnr Victoria Rd & Pacific Ave; d/f $120/180; 🛜) With a distinctly Tex-Mex exterior (like something out of an old Clint Eastwood movie), this family-run motel goes all modern inside, with especially good two-storey family rooms with large bathtubs, plus sheltered barbecue and courtyard areas.

Belle Mer (Map p342; ☎ 0800 100 235, 07-575 0011; www.bellemer.co.nz; 53 Marine Pde; apt $190-450; 🛜 🖥) A classy beachside complex of two- and three-bedroom apartments, some with sea-view balconies and others opening onto private courtyards (though you'll more likely head for the resort-style pool terrace). Rooms are taste-fully decorated in warm tones with soft edges, and have everything you need for longer stays, with proper working kitchens and laundries.

Eating

our pick **Providores Urban Food Store** (Map p342; ☎ 07-572 1300; 19a Pacific Ave; meals $5-18; 🕑 7.30am-5pm; Ⓥ) Surf videos set the mood as your eyes peruse fresh-baked breads, buttery croissants, home-smoked meats and cheeses, organic jams and free-range eggs – perfect ingredients for a bang-up breakfast or a hamper-filling picnic on the beach. Superb!

Slow Fish (Map p342; ☎ 07-574 2949; shop 5, Twin Towers, Marine Pde; meals $6-19; 🕑 7am-4.30pm) There's no slacking about in the kitchen of this award-winning, eco-aware cafe, which promotes the art of savouring fine, locally sourced food. It's so popular you'll have to crowbar yourself in the door or pounce on any available alfresco seat, but it's absolutely worth it for its free-range eggs and ham, Greek salads and divine counter selection.

Gusto (Map p342; ☎ 07-575 5675; 200 Maunganui Rd; breakfast $5-15, lunch $12-16; 🕑 7am-4pm) This friendly spot keeps its menu affordable but interesting, with Kiwi standards such as lamb and kumara (sweet potato) given a refreshing treatment. Cool tunes; sassy staff.

Zambezi (Map p342; ☎ 07-575 4202; 108 Maunganui Rd; breakfast $9-16, lunch $13-18; 🕑 9am-4pm) A cheap-and-cheerful cafe serving burgers, panini and nice simple sandwiches. There's eggy brekkies and coffee of course, plus plenty of healthy options such as juices and salads. Licensed too, if you feel like a Mac's or Monteiths.

Astrolabe (Map p342; ☎ 07-574 8155; 82 Maunganui Rd; brunch $12-20, dinner $22-34; 🕑 10am-1am Mon-Sat, 9am-1am Sun) A clever combo of swish, style and Pacifica-rustica, Astrolabe is probably the Mount's best restaurant, catering largely to a deep-pocketed hip crowd who indulge in gourmet goodies like venison, confit duck and oysters. You can also come in for a bou-tique bevvie in the beer garden and a whack of pool.

Kwang Chow (Map p342; ☎ 07-575 5063; 241 Maunganui Rd; lunch/dinner $13/19; 🕑 lunch & dinner) This all-you-can-eat Chinese place is a local favourite with a bargain bite that maintains tasty flavours rather than resorting to a bland melange. Discount dinners from Monday to Wednesday.

Zeytin Café (Map p342; ☎ 07-574 3040; 118 Maunganui Rd; mains $19-27; 🕑 lunch & dinner Tue-Sun) Readers recommend Greco-Moroccan Zeytin for its slow-cooked tagines, spanakopita and mous-saka, plus live jazz or swing on Thursday nights. Stripy cushions and Arabic lanterns adorn the cavelike interior.

Self-caterers will find **New World** (Map p342; ☎ 07-572 7080; cnr Tweed St & Maunganui Rd; 🕑 7am-9pm) south of town.

Drinking

Latitude 37 (Map p342; ☎ 07-572 3037; 181 Maunganui Rd; 🕑 4pm-1am Mon, noon-1am Tue-Fri, 11.30am-1am Sat & Sun; 🛜) A classy, upmarket bar with stone-faced walls, fold-back windows and flaming torches out the front. A lot of folk come here to eat (brunch $14 to $26, dinner $21 to $42), but it's a beaut spot for a cold Heineken after a day in the surf.

Mount Mellick Hotel (Map p342; ☎ 07-574 0047; 317 Maunganui Rd; meals $9-28; 🕑 11am-1am) A blokey Irish pub with hefty meals, regular jam ses-sions and poker and quiz nights, plus live bands on weekends.

Rosie O'Grady's (Map p342; ☎ 07-575 3135; 2 Rata St; meals from $10; ☯ 7am-1am) Rosie's is slightly less blokey than the Mellick, with NZ boutique beers on tap, open-deck DJ nights, big screens and good-value pub grub.

Entertainment

Once the sun goes down, Mt Maunganui's pubs and bars often host live bands and DJs (see Drinking, p347). Go to the movies at **Cinema 4** (Map p342; ☎ 07-572 3311; www.baycitycinemas.co.nz; 249 Maunganui Rd; admission adult/child $15/9).

Getting There & Away

Mt Maunganui is across the harbour bridge from Tauranga, or accessible from the south via Te Maunga on SH2. See p345 for local Bay Hopper bus details. **InterCity** (☎ 09-583 5780; www.intercity.co.nz) and **Naked Bus** (☎ 0900 625 33; www.nakedbus.com) services also stop at Mt Maunganui, with fares similar to those to/from Tauranga (see p345). All buses depart the i-SITE.

The **Tauranga Ferry** (☎ 07-579 1325 www.kiwicoast cruises.co.nz; tickets one-way adult/child $8/5; ☯ Dec-Mar) to/from Tauranga departs Salisbury Wharf; ask the i-SITE for a schedule (see p346).

AROUND TAURANGA
Papamoa
pop 17,500

Papamoa is a fast-growing suburb near the edge of Mt Maunganui, separated now by just a paddock or two also destined for subdivision. Burgeoning with big new houses on pristine streets, parts of Papamoa have the air of a gated community about them. That said, the beaches beyond the sheltering dunes are truly spectacular, so you can't blame folk for moving in.

For speedsters, **Game On Activities** (☎ 07-572 4033; www.gameonactivities.co.nz; 176 Parton Rd, Papamoa; blokarting 15min $15; ☯ by arrangement) has NZ's first purpose-built course for land-based windsurfing on zippy 'blokarts'.

The huge **Papamoa Beach Top 10 Holiday Resort** (☎ 07-572 0816; www.papamoabeach.co.nz; 535 Papamoa Beach Rd; sites from $36, villas & units $120-210; ☐ ☎) is a spotless, modern park that has been primed and priced-up beyond its caravan-park origins, with an array of accommodation options, including self-contained villas.

With its angular corrugated-iron exterior and tasteful caneware furnishings, **Beach House Motel** (☎ 0800 429 999, 07-572 1424; www. beachhousemotel.co.nz; 224 Papamoa Beach Rd; d from $110; ☐ ☎ ☎) offers an upmarket version of the Kiwi bach holiday, relaxed and close to the beach.

Turkish to Go (☎ 07-542 1404; cnr Beach & Domain Rds; kebabs $8-12; ☯ lunch & dinner) wraps up very big small kebabs and even bigger big ones, with free coffee and apple tea.

Bluebiyou (☎ 07-572 2099; 559 Papamoa Beach Rd; mains $15-35; ☯ 11am-late) is a casual, breezy restaurant riding high on the dunes, serving big brunches and seafood specialities.

Tuhua (Mayor Island)

Commonly known as Mayor Island, this dormant volcano is located 35km north of Tauranga. The island is known for its black, glasslike obsidian rock and diverse bird life including a clutch of kiwi, introduced to the predator-free island in 2006. Walking tracks cut through the now-overgrown crater valley, and the northwest corner is a marine reserve. The area is managed by the Tuhua Trust Board and to land here you need permission from **DOC** (☎ 07-578 7677; taurangainfo@doc.govt.nz) with a $5 landing fee.

There's limited **camping and cabin accommodation** (☎ 07-578 7677; unpowered sites $10, dm from $10) on the island; bring your own food and water (there are no fridges). The landing fee is included in accommodation costs. Several boat-charter companies will take you to the island including Blue Ocean Charters (p340).

Matakana Island

Twenty-four kilometres long and forming, more or less, the seaward side of Tauranga harbour, Matakana Island is laced with secluded white-sand surf beaches on its eastern shore (for the experienced only) and enjoys a laid-back island lifestyle. The best way to explore it is on a **tour** with Adventure Bay of Plenty (see p341). Alternatively you can catch the **vehicle ferry** (☎ 0274 927 251; return passenger/car & passenger $8/50; ☯ departures 7.45am, 9am, 2pm & 4pm) from Omokoroa (between Tauranga and Katikati).

Katikati
pop 3580

'Katikat' to the locals, this small town was the only planned Ulster settlement in the world, and celebrates this history with colourful **murals** spangling the town's buildings – the moniker 'Mural Town' seems to have stuck.

The **Mural Town Information Centre** (☎ 07-549 1658; www.katikati.co.nz; 36 Main Rd; ⊙ 9am-4.30pm Mon-Fri, 9.30am-2pm Sat, 10am-2pm Sun) sells a guide to the various murals for $2.50 (as well as doing other good deeds), but you can also take a small-group **guided tour** (☎ 07-549 0869; per person $4). From the information centre you can also explore the **Haiku Pathway**, rambling along the Uretara River past boulders inscribed with haiku verses.

Katikati Heritage Museum (☎ 07-549 0651; katikati .heritage.museum@xtra.co.nz; cnr SH2 & Wharawhara Rd; admission adult/child $6/4, minigolf adult/child $4/3; ⊙ 8.30am-4.30pm) traces local history with an engaging mix of Maori artefacts and Ulster history, some moa bones and reputedly the largest bottle collection in the southern hemisphere. There's also a carvery serving roast lunches and dinners.

About 7km south of town, the 10-acre **Katikati Bird Gardens** (☎ 07-549 0912; www.bird gardens.co.nz; Walker Rd East; admission adult/child $9/4; ⊙ 10am-4.30pm) is all aflap with native birdlife. There's a cafe and gallery here too.

The monastic-looking **Morton Estate** (☎ 07-552 0795; www.mortonestatewines.co.nz; SH2; ⊙ 9.30am-5pm), one of NZ's bigger wineries, is located on SH2, 8km south of Katikati, and open for tastings and stock-ups. Try the famous chardonnay.

SLEEPING

Wanderlust Backpackers (☎ 07-549 5102; info@ wanderlustbackpackers.com; 5 Main Rd; dm/d $25/50; 🖳) Festooned with more than 80 rugby jumpers and 418 toy fire engines (!), Wanderlust is a pleasantly oddball hostel in a converted 1935 barbershop. The owners can help find you farm work (picking flowers, avocados and kiwifruit), and rope you into a poker game just as easily.

Kaimai View Motel (☎ 07-549 0398; www.kaimai view.co.nz; 78 Main Rd; d from $120; 🛜 🖳) Beyond a funky mural on the streetside wall, this jaunty, modern motel offers neat rooms with CD player, kitchenette and, in larger rooms, spa. Breakfast available on request.

Panorama Country Lodge (☎ 07-549 1882; www. panoramalodge.co.nz; 901 Pacific Coast Hwy; d from $170; 🛜 🖳) Run by jocular Brits, this neat little B&B is set in a diverse orchard 10km north of town, and lives up to its name with sweeping views of the bay. It's a real farm experience, with quail and alpacas wandering the grounds. Luxury rooms have extras beyond

brass beds and DVDs, including slippers and fresh coffee.

Warm Earth Cottage (☎ 07-549 0962; www. warmearthcottage.co.nz; 202 Thompson's Track; d $200) Re-ignite your romance or just simmer in simple pleasures at this rural idyll, 5km south of town then 2km west of SH2. Two pretty cottages sit by the Waitekohe River – they're electricity-less, so indulge in wood-fired outdoor baths and candlelit evenings. There's no kitchen either, so fire up the barbecue (generous barbecue packs $80). A big brunch is included in the price, as is the odd dram of moonshine.

EATING

Rustic Pumpkin (☎ 07-549 1924; 603 SH2; lunch $8-17; ⊙ 8am-4pm; Ⓥ) It's well worth going the extra 5km north of town for this cracker little cafe on the main road, which serves up generous portions of homemade soups, burgers, quiches, sandwiches and cakes. The cinnamon waffles and kumara curry are showstoppers.

Katz Pyjamas (☎ 07-549 1902; cnr SH2 & Beach Rd; meals $12-22; ⊙ 8am-4pm Mon-Fri) Royal blue outside, rude orange inside, this arty main-street cafe serves home-made soups, salads, panini and cakes and the best coffee in town.

Talisman Hotel (☎ 07-549 3218; 7 Main Rd; meals $15-36; ⊙ lunch & dinner) The local pub, with occasional live music and karaoke, and the Landing restaurant serving all-day grub including pizza and steak.

Twickenham Café & Restaurant (☎ 07-549 1383; cnr SH2 & Mulgan St; lunch $13-29, dinner $24-38; ⊙ 9.30am-3.30pm Tue-Sun; dinner from 5.30pm Tue-Sat) In a century-old villa surrounded by elegant gardens, this restaurant is a bit twee but makes amends with admirable Devonshire teas. Lunch and dinner runs along the lines of panini and rib-eye respectively.

Te Puke
pop 6775

Welcome to the 'Kiwifruit Capital of the World', a busy town during the picking season when there's plenty of work around for willing workers (see the boxed text, p350). The **Te Puke visitor information centre** (☎ 07-573 9172; www.tepuke.co.nz; 130 Jellicoe St; ⊙ 8am-5pm Mon-Fri, 9am-noon Sat) is located in the same building as the public library (staff will confirm that 'Puke' rhymes with cookie, not fluke).

For the low-down on all things kiwifruit, swing into **Kiwi360** (☎ 0800 549 4360, 07-573 6340; www.kiwi360.com; 35 Young Rd, off SH2; admission adult/child

lonelyplanet.com

$20/6; 9am-5pm) at the turn-off for Maketu. Sitting among orchards of nashi pears, citrus, avocados and (you guessed it) kiwifruit, this visitor centre peels off a range of attractions including a 35-minute kiwicart orchard ride, kiwifruit viewing tower and a cafe serving up kiwifruit delights.

After something sweeter? About 10km south of Te Puke, **Comvita** (0800 493 782, 07-533 1987; www.comvita.com; 23 Wilson Rd South, Paengaroa; admission free; 8.30am-5pm, talks 10am & 2pm) is home to New Zealand's most famous honey- and bee-derived health-care products. There's an gallery, shop, cafe and educational talks twice daily. Grab a pot of vitamin E cream with bee pollen and manuka honey on the way out.

Not far from Comvita, **Spring Loaded** (0800 867 386, 07-533 1515; www.springloadedfunpark.co.nz; 316 SH33, Paengaroa; adult/child jetboat $95/45, 4WD $75/35, helicopter flights 10min $105; 8.30am-5pm summer, 9am-4.30pm winter) offers various adventures from jet-boat rides on a gorgeous stretch of the Kaituna River, to 'mud bug' 4WD trips, helicopter flights and rafting and sledging trips. There's a cafe and shop on-site.

There aren't many beds in Te Puke town itself, but home- and farmstays dapple the surrounding area: ask the visitor centre for a list. A pretty, private self-contained cottage, **Lazy Daze B&B** (07-573 8188; www.lazydazecottage. co.nz; 144 Boucher Ave; cottage d with/without breakfast $130/120, house $120) sits out the back of Mel and Sharron's property and has a relaxing deck overlooking its own garden. Delicious breakfast provisions are included and there's also a tidy two-bedroom, self-contained house available next door, sleeping six. Call for directions. Right on the main road of

town, the **Beacon** (07-573 7825; beacon.motel@ wave.co.nz; 173 Jellicoe St; s/d $99/120;) is an old-style, mustard-coloured motel. It's a bit noisy, but is passable if you're just passing through. There's a string of cheap burger joints and cafes along Jellicoe St. The lime-coloured **Pizza Place** (07-573 3324; 33 Jellicoe St; mains $9-14; 4.30pm-late) is the pick of them, serving decent discs.

Maketu
pop 1240
Take SH2 through Te Puke and turn left onto Maketu Rd, and you'll find yourself at this historic but rather shabby seaside town.

Maketu played a significant role in NZ's history as the landing site of *Te Arawa* canoe (see p320), which is commemorated with a somewhat underwhelming stone monument on the foreshore. Arguably, though, the town is more famous for **Maketu Pies** (07-533 2358; www.maketupies.co.nz; 6 Little Waihi Rd; pies from $3; 10am-3pm Mon-Fri), baked fresh daily here and employing a good proportion of the population. Very good pies they are, too.

Beach bums should head for **Newdick's Beach**, reached by following Town Point Rd to a small dirt track. It's on private property, so pay the $3-per-car donation at the gate. From here you can walk to Little Waihi, a few kilometres down the coast towards the estuary. Beachside horse treks can be had with **Briars Seaside Ride** (07-533 2582, 0274 062 477; www.briarshorsetrek.co.nz; Town Point Rd, 1½/2/3hr rides $70/90/120).

Maketu Beach Holiday Park (07-533 2165; www. maketubeach.co.nz; 1 Town Point Rd; powered sites $25, d $55-115) is a shabby last-resort resort, with campsites, cabins and motel rooms.

HOT FUZZ

The humble kiwifruit earns NZ over a billion dollars every year, and with the Bay of Plenty in the thick of the action, it's no wonder the locals are fond of this fruit.

The fruit's origins are in China, where it was called the monkey peach because they were considered ripe when the monkeys munched them. As they migrated to NZ, they were renamed the Chinese gooseberry – they were a lot smaller then, but canny Kiwis engineered them to more generous sizes and began exporting them in the 1950s. The fruit was then sexily rebranded the Zespri. Today the Zesprians grow two types of kiwifruit: the common fuzzy-covered green fruit, and the gold fruit with its smooth complexion. To learn more about the kiwifruit, visit Kiwi360 (see p349).

For visitors after a dollar or two, there's always kiwifruit work around the area – most of it during harvest (May and June) and odd jobs at other times. Enquire at Wanderlust backpackers in Katikati (p349), at regional i-SITEs, or check online at www.picknz.co.nz.

EASTERN BAY OF PLENTY

Stretching from Maketu to Opotiki, the Eastern Bay of Plenty's main drawcard is long stretches of sandy beaches with a backdrop of cliffs covered in majestic pohutukawa trees. It's beautiful country, and often overlooked, which is absolutely integral to its charm.

WHAKATANE
pop 17,700

A true pohutukawa paradise, the town of Whakatane (pronounced Fokka-tar-nay) sits in a natural harbour at the mouth of the river of the same name. It's the hub of the Rangitaiki agricultural district, but there's much more to Whakatane than farming – blissful beaches, a sunny main-street vibe and volcanic Whakaari (White Island) for starters. And (despite Nelson's protestations) it's officially the sunniest city in NZ!

Information

Whakatane Hospital (07-306 0999; www.bopdhb.govt.nz; cnr Stewart & Garaway Sts; 24hr) For emergency medical treatment.
Post office (www.nzpost.co.nz; 4 Commerce St) Also has foreign exchange.
Whakatane i-SITE (0800 942 528, 07-308 6058; www.whakatane.com; Quay St; 8am-5pm Mon-Fri, 10am-4pm Sat & Sun;) Free internet access (including 24-hour wi-fi on the terrace outside the building), tour bookings, accommodation and general enquiries for DOC.

Sights

Whakatane Museum & Gallery (07-306 0505; www.whakatanemuseum.org.nz; 11 Boon St; admission by donation; 10am-4.30pm Mon-Fri, 11am-3pm Sat & Sun) is an impressive regional museum with artfully presented displays on early Maori and European settlers. Of particular interest are the *taonga* of local Maori tracing their lineage back to the *Mataatua waka* (see the boxed text, p354), while the art gallery presents a varied program of NZ and international exhibitions.

Beside the roundabout is **Pohaturoa** (cnr The Strand & Commerce St), a large *tapu* (sacred) rock outcrop, where baptism, death, war and *moko* (tattoo) rites were performed. The Treaty of Waitangi was also signed here by Ngati Awa chiefs in 1840 and there's a monument to the Ngati Awa chief Te Hurinui Apanui. Another Maori site is the partially collapsed **Muriwai's Cave** (Te Ano o Muriwa), which once extended 122m into the hillside and sheltered 60 people, including Muriwai, Wairaka's aunt and famous seer. Two exquisitely carved **ceremonial waka** are displayed opposite the cave.

On the clifftops behind the town are two ancient Ngati Awa *pa* sites – **Te Papaka** and **Puketapu** – both of which offer sensational (and very defendable) outlooks over Whakatane. Tumbling down the cliffs, **Wairere Falls** (Te Wairere) occupies a deliciously damp nook, and once powered flax and flour mills and supplied Whakatane's drinking water.

Activities

MARINE MAMMAL–WATCHING, DIVING & FISHING

The sea along the Whakatane coast is alive with marine mammals including dolphins (25,000 of them!), fur seals, orca, pilot and minke whales; as well as bird life such as gannets and little blue penguins. The area is also renowned for diving and big-game fishing. Several operators can get you out among it, including swimming with the dolphins.

Whale & Dolphin Watch (0800 354 7737, 07-308 2001; www.whalesanddolphinwatch.co.nz; 96 The Strand; view adult/child $110/80, swim $150/130; 7.15am, 8.30am & 1pm) runs dolphin-viewing and swimming trips year-round.

Run by White Island Tours (see p355), **Dolphin & Whale Nature Rush** (0800 733 529, 07-308 9588; www.dolphinandwhale.co.nz; 15 The Strand; trips adult/child $80/50; 10am daily Jan-Mar) offers a two-hour trip out to Motuhora (Whale Island), with plenty of critter-spotting in the sea and sky.

Diveworks Charters (0800 308 5896, 07-308 5896; www.whaleislandtours.com; tours per person $85) runs two-hour ecotrips out to Motuhora, plus longer trips where you can swim with dolphins and seals (adult/child $150/125), and fishing and diving trips.

See also Dive White Island (p355).

TRAMPING

The i-SITE sells *Discover the Walks Around Whakatane* ($2), a booklet detailing walks ranging from 30 minutes to half a day. Most walks are part of the **Nga Tapuwae o Toi Track** (Footsteps of Toi; 13 hours, 18km), a large loop that takes in Ohope Beach and several historic sites along the way. A flatter option is the **River Walk** (two to three hours), following the Whakatane River past the

WHAKATANE

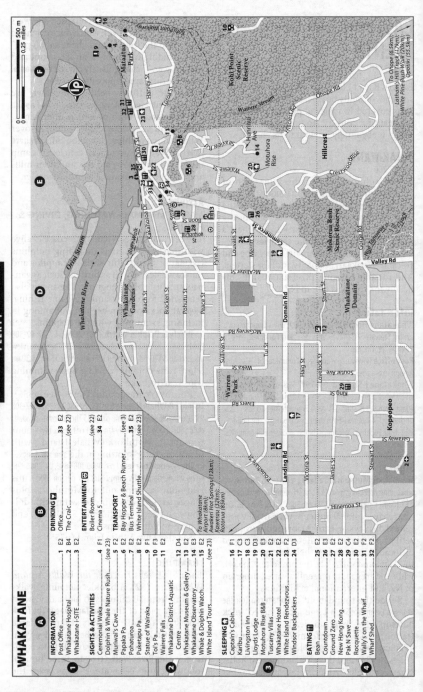

ROTORUA & THE BAY OF PLENTY

Botanical Gardens, Muruwai's Cave and on to Wairaka's statue.

Another popular stroll is **Kohi Point Walkway** (four hours, 5.5km), which extends through the Kohi Point Scenic Reserve, passing lookouts and **Toi's Pa** (Kapua te Rangi), reputedly the oldest *pa* site in NZ. Other walkways include **Latham's Hill Track** (1½ to two hours), starting 17km south of town on SH30, and **White Pine Bush Walk** (30 minutes), accessible by wheelchair and pram and starting 20km south of Whakatane.

OTHER ACTIVITIES

Whakatane District Aquatic Centre (☎ 07-308 4192; www.tlc.net.nz; 28 Short St; admission adult/child $3.60/1.80; ☯ 6am-8pm Mon-Fri, 7am-6pm Sat & Sun) has indoor and outdoor pools, spa pools and a waterslide.

Whakatane Observatory (☎ 07-308 6495; www.skyofplenty.com; Hurinui Ave, Hillcrest; adult/child/family $10/4/15; ☯ dusk Tue & Fri) offers a great chance to star-spot when the sky is clear.

Tours

For boat and helicopter tours out to the explosive Whakaari (White Island), see p355.

Matata Eco Tours (☎ 0800 628 282, 07-322 2102; www.matataecotours.co.nz; tours per person half-/full day $75/135) runs tours of the Tarawera Valley where you can learn about the native flora, fauna, and cultural heritage of the area.

Sleeping

Whakatane Hotel (☎ 07-307 1670; whakatanehotel@ newzealandhotelgroup.co.nz; 79 The Strand; dm/s $20/40, d $50-65) This art-deco classic has basic rooms to suit lively backpackers – those who love to be in the thick of it or those who carry earplugs to muffle weekend band noise.

Windsor Backpackers (☎ 07-308 8040; www.windsor lodge-backpackers.co.nz; 10 Merritt St; dm/s $25/35, d $50-80; 🖳 ☞) Whakatane's best backpackers occupies a converted funeral parlour, so expect a restful sleep. Excellent rooms range from dorms to motel-standard doubles, and the communal kitchen, lounge area and barbecue courtyard are spacious and tidy.

Karibu (☎ 07-307 8276; www.karibubackpackers.co.nz; 13 Landing Rd; sites $28, dm $25-27, s/tw $35/60, 2br units $80-150; 🖳) This converted house a wee walk from town has basic dorms, two-bed units, and a garden out the back with a few tent sites. Barbecues and free bikes available.

Lloyds Lodge (☎ 07-307 8005; www.lloydslodge. co.nz; 10 Domain Rd; dm $27; 🖳) In an old house

plastered with grandma-style floral wallpaper on every available surface, Lloyds is an intimate, friendly option, with just 16 beds and a homey kitchen-dining area. The manager runs a podiatry clinic in the front room if you've stubbed your toe.

Captain's Cabin (☎ 07-308 5719; www.captainscabin. co.nz; 23 Muriwai Dr; r $115) In a serene part of town with breathtaking views of the harbour entrance, this homely self-contained unit is the perfect spot for those hanging round for a few days. A cosy living area cleverly combines bedroom, lounge, kitchen and dining, with a second smaller room and bijou bathroom – all sweetly decorated along nautical lines.

Livingston Inn (☎ 0800 770 777, 07-308 5665; www. livingston.co.nz; 42 Landing Rd; d/f $125/210; ☞) The ranch-style Livingston remains one of the better motels in town, with spacious, well-kept units that are popular with the motor-inn crowd. Large spas in executive suites are a great fringe benefit.

White Island Rendezvous (☎ 0800 242 299; www. whiteisland.co.nz; The Strand; d/f from $130/150, 2br apt per 4 people $260; ☞) An immaculate 26-room complex run by the on-the-ball White Island Tour people. Lots of balcony and deck space for enjoying the sea air, with interiors decked out in timber floors for a beach cottage vibe. Deluxe rooms come with spas and there are facilities for travellers with disabilities.

Tuscany Villas (☎ 0800 801 040, 07-308 2244; www.tuscanyvillas.co.nz; 57 The Strand; d $140-200; ☞) This modern motel may be a long way from Florence, but still offers a few rays of Italian sunshine with interesting architecture, wraparound balcony and attractive floral plantings wherever there is room. Rooms are luxurious and comfy, with spa pools and superking beds.

Motuhora Rise B&B (☎ 07-307 0224; www.motu horarise.com; 2 Motuhora Rise; s/d incl breakfast $200/215; ☞) At the top of the town in both senses (the driveway is steep!), this hilltop spot affords a distant glimpse of Whale Island. You can expect a gourmet cheeseboard on arrival, along with other extras such as a DVD home-theatre suite, outdoor spa pool on decking, and fishing rods and golf clubs.

Eating

Bean (☎ 07-307 0494; 72 The Strand; bagels & soup $5-12; ☯ 8.30am-4pm Mon-Fri, Sat 9.30am-1.30pm) The loungiest spot in town to get good coffee (roasted on the premises). Pull up a chair,

---

WAKA LIKE A MAN

Whakatane's name originated some eight centuries ago, 200 years after the original Maori settlers arrived here. The warrior Toroa and his family sailed into the estuary in a huge ocean-going *waka* (canoe), the *Mataatua*. As the men went ashore to greet local leaders, the tide turned, and the *waka* – with all the women on board – drifted out to sea. Toroa's daughter, Wairaka, cried out *'E! Kia whakatane au i ahau!'* (Let me act as a man!) and, breaking the traditional *tapu* on women steering a *waka*, she took up the paddle and brought the boat safely ashore. A whimsical **statue of Wairaka** stands proudly atop a rock in Whakatane's harbour in commemoration of her brave deed.

---

and get yourself going with a quick fix and a freshly baked biscuit or bagel.

Wally's on the Wharf (☎ 07-307 1100; The Wharf, The Strand; meals $6-18; ◷ 11am-8pm) Wally sure knows a thing or two about fish and chips. Hoki, snapper, flounder, john dory and tarakihi – done in the deep fry, on the grill or in a burger. Whitebait fritters in season, and chips that score well on the crispometer.

New Hong Kong (☎ 07-308 6864; 32 Richardson St; mains $6-23; ◷ lunch Tue-Fri, dinner Tue-Sun) This no-fuss Chinese restaurant does Sino-Kiwi grub such as chop suey, chow mein and, of course, chips. Lunch deals ($6) are a good bet, as is the two-hour $10-dish 'happy hour' from 5.30pm.

Ground Zero (☎ 07-308 8548; 163 The Strand; meals $7-17; ◷ 8am-4.30pm) It's a good sign when the staff can share a laugh with the boss! Ground Zero's chipper vibe is infectious, bolstered by cafe delights like Jamaican chicken burgers, veggie stacks with hummus and garlic aioli, Moroccan wraps, and serious coffee and cakes. Sunny outdoor tables, too.

Wharf Shed (☎ 07-308 5698; The Wharf, The Strand; lunch $11-21, dinner $27-45; ◷ lunch & dinner) An award winner for beef and lamb but famous for its fish dishes, which include locally bagged crayfish, corpulent mussels and fresh Pacific Oysters. Right on the waterside with alfresco dining on balmy evenings.

Rocquette (☎ 07-307 0722; 23 Quay St; lunch $14-30, dinner $18-35; ◷ 10am-late Mon-Sat) A modern waterside restaurant on the ground floor of one of the town's big new apartment blocks, sunny Rocquette serves up refreshing Mediterranean-influenced fare with lots of summery salads, risotto and fish dishes. Laid-back tunes, good coffee and sexy staff to boot.

For self-caterers:

Countdown (☎ 07-306 0014; 105 Commerce St; ◷ 7am-10pm)

Pak N Save (☎ 07-308-0388; King St; ◷ 8am-9pm)

Drinking & Entertainment

There aren't many nocturnal options here – the handsome **Whakatane Hotel** (☎ 07-307 1670; 79 The Strand; ◷ 11am-late) is home to two of them. The Craic is a busy locals' pub of the Irish ilk, good for a pint or two, or a cup of hot chocolate if you're feeling sub-par. Next door, the Boiler Room is a cavernous space with pool tables, Friday-night DJs and live bands on Saturdays.

Across the road is the more upmarket **Office** (☎ 07-307 0123; 82 The Strand; ◷ 10am-late), doing what it does well: beer, big meals with chips and salad all over, and live bands on Friday nights.

Cinema 5 (☎ 07-308 7623; 100 The Strand; admission adult/child $13/8; ◷ 10am-10pm) screens new-release movies.

Getting There & Around

Air New Zealand (☎ 0800 737 000, 07-308 8397; www.airnewzealand.com) has daily flights linking Whakatane to Auckland, with connections to other centres.

Sunair Aviation Ltd (☎ 07-575 7799; www.sunair.co.nz) offers direct flights to Gisborne, Hamilton, Napier, New Plymouth and Palmerston North.

InterCity (☎ 09-583 5780; www.intercity.co.nz) buses stop outside the i-SITE and connect Whakatane with Rotorua ($33, 1½ hours, one daily) and Gisborne ($44, three hours, one daily), with onward connections. Gisborne buses travel via Opotiki.

Naked Bus (☎ 0900 625 33; www.nakedbus.com) services run to the following destinations. Book in advance for big savings.

Destination	Price	Duration	Frequency
Auckland	$54	6½hr	1 daily
Gisborne	$24	3¼hr	1 daily
Hamilton	$37	3hr	1 daily
Rotorua	$24	1½hr	1 daily
Tauranga	$18	1½hr	1 daily
Wellington	$55	10hr	1 daily

Local **Bay Hopper and Beach Runner** (☎ 0800 422 928; www.baybus.co.nz) buses run to Ohope ($3, 30 minutes, four to six daily), Opotiki ($7.50, one hour, one daily Monday and Wednesday) and Tauranga ($12, two hours, one daily Monday to Saturday).

GKM Shuttles (☎ 0800 007 005, 07-308 9906) to/ from the airport cost $20 per adult for the first adult, with discounted prices per additional passenger. Taxi services are available from **Dial a Cab** (☎ 0800 342 522, 07-308 0222).

White Island Shuttle (☎ 0800 733 529; return adult/child $60/35; ☺ Mon-Sat) runs a Rotorua–Whakatane tour shuttle that can be used by nontour people. The shuttle departs Rotorua from pre-arranged pick-up points between 7am and 7.30am, and returns between 4pm and 5pm.

WHAKAARI (WHITE ISLAND)

New Zealand's most active volcano (it last erupted in 2000) lies 49km off the Whakatane coast. The small island was originally formed by three separate volcanic cones of different ages. The two oldest have been eroded, while the younger cone has risen up between them. Mt Gisborne is the highest point on the island at 321m. Geologically, Whakaari is related to Motuhora (Whale Island) and Putauaki (Mt Edgecumbe), as all lie along Taupo Volcanic Zone.

The island is dramatic, with hot water hissing and steaming from vents over most of the crater floor. Temperatures of 600°C to 800°C have been recorded.

The island is privately owned so you can only visit it with a licensed tour operator. Fixed-wing air operators run flyover tours only, while boat and helicopter tours will usually include a walking tour around the island including a visit to the ruins of the sulphur-mining factory – an interesting story in itself.

Numerous helicopter and fixed-wing operators run trips out of Rotorua (see p329) and Tauranga (see p341), while local operators include the following:

Dive White Island (☎ 0800 348 394, 07-307 0714; www.divewhite.co.nz; snorkelling/diving trips per person $180/325) Full-day snorkelling and diving trips with lunch and gear provided.

Vulcan Helicopters (☎ 0800 804 354, 07-308 4188; www.vulcanheli.co.nz; per person from $455) A 2½-hour trip to Whakaari that includes a one-hour guided walk on the volcano.

White Island Tours (Map p352; ☎ 0800 733 529; www.whiteisland.co.nz; 15 The Strand; 6hr tours adult/ child $185/120; ☺ departures btwn 7am-9.15am, plus 12.30pm summer)The only official boat trip to Whakaari, with dolphin-spotting en route and 90-minute tour of the island.

MOTUHORA (WHALE ISLAND)

Nine kilometres off Whakatane is Motuhora, or Whale Island – so-called because of its leviathan shape. This island is yet another volcano along the Taupo Volcanic Zone but is much less active, although there are hot springs along its shore. The summit is 353m high and the island has several historic sites, including an ancient *pa* site, quarry and camp.

Whale Island was originally home to a Maori settlement. In 1829, Maori massacred sailors from the trading vessel *Haweis* while it was anchored at Sulphur Bay. In the 1840s the island passed into European ownership and remains privately owned, although since 1965 it has been a DOC-protected wildlife refuge for sea and shore birds.

The island's protected status means landing is restricted, with tours running only from January to March. Operators include Dolphin & Whale Nature Rush (see p351), Diveworks Charters (see p351) and KG Kayaks (below).

OHOPE
pop 3010

Just 7km over the hill from Whakatane, Ohope has great beaches, perfect for lazing or surfing, and is backed by sleepy **Ohiwa Harbour**. Just beyond the harbour is the small Sandspit Wildlife Refuge. You can explore the harbour with **KG Kayaks** (☎ 07-315 4005; www.kgkayaks.co.nz; tours $70-135, 2hr hire s/d $40/60), which runs a 2½-hour guided tour, plus kayak trips to Whale Island and freedom hire.

If you want to take on the surf, get some lessons from Beaver at **By Salt Surf School** (☎ 07-312 4909, 0211 491 972; beaver@e3.net.nz; 2hr lesson $90), which provides all gear and offers discounts for groups.

There's plenty of accommodation around the town including **Ohope Beach Top 10 Holiday Park** (☎ 0800 264 673, 07-312 4460; www.ohopebeach. co.nz; 367 Harbour Rd; unpowered/powered sites $42/44, cabins $70-130, units $90-195, apts $170-285; ☐ ☺ ▣), a family-friendly caravan park with sports courts, minigolf, pool and apartments peeking over the dunes at the Bay of Plenty. For a quieter, motel-style option, try **Aquarius Motor Lodge** (☎ 07-312 4550; www.aquariusmotorlodge.co.nz; 103 Harbour Rd; d from $75, 1/2br from $110/120; ☺) a basic complex with various options, all with kitchens and just 100m from the beach.

Hungry? The cavernous **Ohope Chartered Club** (☎ 07-312 5008; Bluett Rd; mains $11-16; ☻ dinner) – at which you must sign in as a guest – is the place to meet locals, drink some cheap beers and chow down on pub grub. Upstairs, a quieter dining option is **C'Vue** (☎ 07-312 5808; mains $20-35; ☻ dinner Wed-Sun).

Not far from the holiday park, **Sea Thai** (☎ 07-312 4005; Pier 5, Fisherman's Wharf, Harbour Rd; mains $19-27; ☻ lunch Sat & Sun, dinner Tue-Sun; **(V)**) is a beaut spot overlooking bobbing boats on the harbour. On the highway to Opotiki is **Ohiwa Oyster Farm** (☎ 07-312 4565; Wainui Rd; meals $6-16; ☻ 9am-8pm), perfect for a fish-and-chip (and oyster) picnic.

WHAKATANE TO ROTORUA

Sixteen kilometres from Whakatane to Rotorua along SH30 you'll come to the immaculate **Awakeri Hot Springs** (☎ 07-304 9117; www.awakerisprings.co.nz; SH30; sites $30, d cabins/flats/units $70/80/95), complete with **springs** (admission adult/child $5/3; ☻ 8am-9.30pm), picnic areas and a bed for every budget.

Eighteen kilometres beyond Awakeri is the grim timber town of **Kawerau**, the highlight of which is **Aotearoa Breweries** (☎ 07-323 8370; www.mata.net.nz; 57 Onslow St; ☻ vary), brewing Mata, 'a beer from the edge' (of civilisation?). Call ahead if you want to visit. Kawerau's **visitor centre** (☎ 07-323 7550; www.kawerau.co.nz; Plunkett St bus terminal; ☻ 9am-4pm) has details on local accommodation and sells permits to access walks and camping at Tarawera Outlet and Tarawera Falls (see p327).

Dominating Kawerau is **Putauaki (Mt Edgecumbe)**, a volcanic cone with panoramic views of the entire Bay of Plenty (often closed in summer due to high fire risk). Access permits are $4, available from **Maori Investments** (☎ 07-323 8146) located on the road up. It's closed at the weekends so you need to obtain a permit in advance for weekend tramps.

Close to Kawerau, **Tui Glen Farm** (☎ 07-323 6457; www.tuiglen.net.nz; Kawerau Loop Rd; rides adult/child from $40/30) offers horse treks through bush and farm for beginners and the adventurous. Dorm accommodation also available ($20).

OPOTIKI
pop 9200

The Opotiki area was settled from at least 1150, some 200 years before the larger 14th-century Maori migration. Maori traditions are

well preserved here, with the work of master carvers lining the main street and the occasional facial *moko* passing by. The town acts as a gateway to the East Coast, and has excellent beaches – Ohiwa and Waiotahi – and an engaging museum.

Information

The **Opotiki i-SITE** (☎ 07-315 3031; www.opotikinz.com; cnr St John & Elliott Sts; ☻ 9am-5pm summer, reduced hr in winter) and **DOC** (☎ 07-315 1001; www.doc.govt.nz; ☻ 8am-2.30pm) are in the same building. The i-SITE takes bookings for activities and stocks the indispensable free East Coast booklet *Pacific Coast Highway*. Internet access is available at **Opotiki Internet Café** (97 Church St; ☻ 7am-5pm Mon-Sat, 2-5pm Sun).

The **post office** (www.nzpost.co.nz; 106 Church St) is on the main drag.

Sights & Activities

Pick up the *Historic Opotiki* brochure from the i-SITE for the low-down on the town's heritage buildings.

The excellent **Opotiki Museum** (☎ 07-315 5169; ohas@xtra.co.nz; 123 Church St; admission adult/child/family $5/2.50/10; ☻ 10am-4pm Mon-Fri, to 2pm Sat) offers a chance to learn more about the rich history of the area. Run by volunteers, the museum has interesting heritage displays including Maori *taonga* and militaria, and agricultural items including a horse-drawn wagon. Just down the road is the adjunct **Shalfoon & Francis Museum** (129 Church St), Opotiki's original general store born again, with shelves piled high with old grocery and hardware products – you name it, they had it.

Known by the local Whakatohea tribe to have acted as a government spy, Rev Carl Volkner was murdered in 1865 in the **Hiona St Stephen's Church** (☎ 07-315 8319; 126 Church St; admission free; ☻ services 8am & 9.30am Sun, 10am Thu) on the main street.

Around 8km south of the town centre is **Hukutaia Domain** (☎ 07-315 6167; Woodlands Rd; admission free; ☻ daily), home to one of the finest collections of native plants in NZ. In the centre is Taketakerau, a 23m puriri tree estimated to be more than 2000 years old and a burial place for the distinguished dead of the Upokorere *hapu* (subtribe) of Whakatohea. The remains have been since been reinterred elsewhere.

In the middle of the town's shopping street is **Tangata Whenua Gallery** (☎ 07-315 5558; 106 Church St, ☻ 9am-5pm Mon-Fri, to 2pm Sat & Sun), stocking

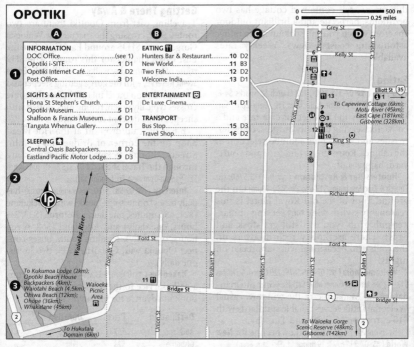

OPOTIKI

INFORMATION
DOC Office.............................(see 1)
Opotiki i-SITE...............................1 D1
Opotiki Internet Café....................2 D2
Post Office...................................3 D1

SIGHTS & ACTIVITIES
Hiona St Stephen's Church............4 D1
Opotiki Museum...........................5 D1
Shalfoon & Francis Museum..........6 D1
Tangata Whenua Gallery...............7 D1

SLEEPING
Central Oasis Backpackers.............8 D2
Eastland Pacific Motor Lodge........9 D3

EATING
Hunters Bar & Restaurant............10 D2
New World.................................11 B3
Two Fish....................................12 D2
Welcome India............................13 D1

ENTERTAINMENT
De Luxe Cinema..........................14 D1

TRANSPORT
Bus Stop....................................15 D3
Travel Shop................................16 D2

Maori- and New Zealand–themed arts and crafts, including *kete* (baskets) and *pounamu* jewellery.

Motu River Jet Boat Tours (☎ 07-325 2735; www.motujet.co.nz; trips per person from $85) has as many as three 1½-hour trips daily on the Motu River.

Wet 'n' Wild (☎ 0800 462 7238, 07-348 3191; www.wetnwildrafting.co.nz; trips from $795) offers two- to four-day rafting and camping adventures on the Motu.

Waioeka River Kayaks (☎ 07-315 5553; www.newzealandsbestspot.co.nz; trips adult/child 1hr $40/30, 2hr $60/40) runs one- and two-hour kayaking trips down the scenic and easy Waioeka River.

Come December, don a cowboy hat for the annual **Opotiki Rodeo** (www.opotikirodeo.co.nz).

Sleeping

Central Oasis Backpackers (☎ 07-315 5165; www.centraloasispackpackers.co.nz; 30 King St; dm/d $20/48;) Inside a late-1800s house, this central backpackers is a snug spot with spacious rooms, a crackling fire and a big front yard to hang out in. The pet rabbit keeps the grass down.

our pick **Opotiki Beach House Backpackers** (☎ 07-315 5117; www.opotikibeachhouse.co.nz; 7 Appleton Rd; dm/d $28/66) A cruisy, shoe-free beachside pad with a sunny, hammock-hung deck, sea views and plenty of opportunities to get in the water with free kayaks and body boards. Beyond the dorms and breezy lounge are attractive doubles and a quirky caravan alongside for those who want a real slice of the Kiwi summer holiday.

Kukumoa Lodge (☎ 07-315 8545; www.kukumoalodge.co.nz; 19a Bairds Rd; d $90-110, f $300;) This imposing farmhouse is five minutes from town on the way to Ohope, and sports a spacious double and a family area sleeping up to six. There's a games room for the kids, a pool and spa, and a large balcony and patio for lounging around in the sunshine.

Eastland Pacific Motor Lodge (☎ 0800 103 003, 07-315 5524; www.eastlandpacific.co.nz; cnr Bridge & St John Sts; d/2br units from $100/140;) Bright, clean Eastland is a well-kept motel with new carpets, spa baths as standard, and a shipshape rose garden in the car park. The two-bedroom units are top value.

Capeview Cottage (☎ 0800 227 384, 07-315 7877; www.capeview.co.nz; 167 Tablelands Rd; d $145;) Set amid chirruping birds and kiwifruit orchards, this serene, self-contained cottage has two bedrooms, barbecue and a brilliant outdoor spa from which you can soak up some rather astonishing coastal views. Weekly rates available.

Eating

Two Fish (☎ 07-315 5548; 102 Church St; snacks $4-8, mains $9-19; ⏱ 8am-4pm Mon-Fri, 9am-2pm Sat) Undoubtedly the best bet for cafe-fare and a coffee fix, serving up hefty burgers, chowder, toasties and salads plus a jumbo selection in the cabinet. Retro-groovy interior and court-yard; happy staff.

Hunters Bar & Restaurant (☎ 07-315 5760; cnr Church & King Sts; mains $12-25; ⏱ 5.30-10pm) On the ground floor of the old Royal Hotel is this reasonably stylish wine bar, serving upmar-ket pub grub (you can still get steak and eggs). There are kooky record covers on the walls and occasional wine-appreciation nights.

Welcome India (☎ 07-315 5879; 120 Church St; mains $13-18; ⏱ lunch & dinner Mon-Sat) Beyond the man-datory Taj Mahal pic in the window, casual Welcome India serves reliable standards with $10 curries on Monday and Tuesday.

Self-caterers should make a beeline for **New World** (☎ 07-315 6723; 19 Bridge St; ⏱ 8am-8pm).

Entertainment

The beguiling old **De Luxe Cinema** (☎ 07-315 6110; 127 Church St; tickets adult/child 8/5; ⏱ varies) shows the occasional movie and brass-band con-cert. Check the window for upcoming events, including the annual **Silent Film Festival** (www.silentfilmfest.org.nz) in September

Getting There & Away

Travelling east from Opotiki there are two routes: SH2, crossing the spectacular Waioeka Gorge, or the SH35 around East Cape (see the East Coast chapter for this route). The SH2 route offers some day walks in the **Waioeka Gorge Scenic Reserve**, with the gorge getting steeper and narrower as you travel inland, before the route crosses typically green, rolling hills, dotted with sheep, on the descent to Gisborne.

Buses pick up/drop off at the Hot Bread Shop on the corner of Bridge and St John Streets, though tickets and bookings are through the **Travel Shop** (☎ 07-315 8881; 104 Church St; ⏱ 9am-5pm Mon-Fri, to noon Sat).

InterCity (☎ 09-583 5780; www.intercity.co.nz) has daily buses connecting Opotiki with Whakatane ($21, 45 minutes, one daily), Rotorua ($33, 2½ hours, one daily) and Auckland ($68, seven hours, one daily). Heading south, buses con-nect Opotiki with Gisborne ($33, two hours, one daily).

Naked Bus (☎ 0900 625 33; www.nakedbus.com) runs a daily service to the following destinations. Book in advance for big savings.

Destination	Price	Duration
Auckland	$57	6hr
Gisborne	$23	2¼hr
Rotorua	$29	2hr
Tauranga	$36	3hr
Wellington	$64	10½hr

The local **Bay Hopper** (☎ 0800 422 928; www.baybus.co.nz) bus runs to Whakatane ($7.50, one hour, one daily Monday and Wednesday).

The East Coast

New Zealand is known for its mix of wildly divergent landscapes, but in this region it's the sociological contours that are most pronounced. From the remote settlements of the East Cape to Havelock North's prosperous, wine-soaked streets, the East Coast displays a spectrum of authentic Kiwi experiences that anyone with a passion for *Maoritanga* (things Maori) will find fascinating.

Maori culture is never more visible than on the East Coast. Exquisitely carved *marae* (meeting house complexes) dot the landscape, and while the locals may not be wearing flax skirts and swinging *poi* (flax balls on strings) like they do for the tourists in Rotorua, you can be assured that *te reo* and *tikanga* (the language and customs) are alive and well.

Intrepid types will have no trouble losing the tourist hordes – along the Pacific Coast Hwy, through the rural back roads, on remote beaches, or in the mystical wilderness of Te Urewera National Park.

When the call of the wild gives way to caffeine withdrawal, a fix will quickly be found in the urban centres of Gisborne and Napier. You'll also find plenty of wine, as the region strains under the weight of grapes. From *kaimoana* (seafood) to berry fruit and beyond, there are riches here for everyone.

HIGHLIGHTS

- Time-warping to the 1930s amid the art-deco delights of **Napier** (p378)
- Avoiding being the designated driver as you embark on a grand wine-tasting tour of **Gisborne** (p369) or **Hawke's Bay** (p388)
- Meeting with Maori culture in the hidden nooks of **East Cape** (p361) and **Te Urewera National Park** (p374)
- Beach-hopping between secluded gems such as **Maraehako Bay** (p363), **Tokomaru Bay** (p364), **Anaura Bay** (p365), **Waimarama** (p386), **Mangakuri** and **Aramoana** (p392)
- Searching for wood nymphs among the magical forest paths of **Eastwoodhill Arboretum** (p368)

- Telephone code: 07 & 06
- www.hawkesbaynz.com
- www.gisbornenz.com

THE EAST COAST

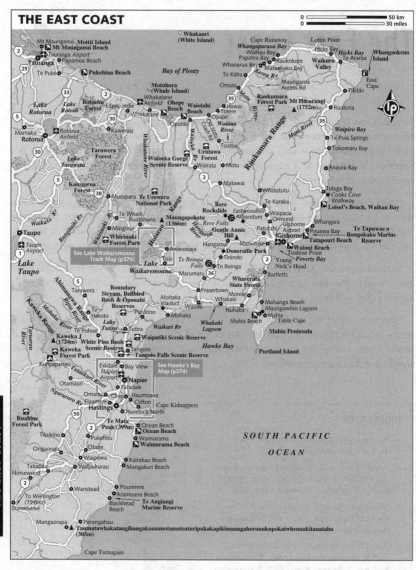

THE EAST COAST

See Lake Waikaremoana Track Map (p376)

See Hawke's Bay Map (p374)

Climate

The East Coast basks in a warm, dry climate. Summer temperatures around Napier and Gisborne nudge 25°C, rarely dipping below 8°C in winter. The Hawke's Bay region also suns itself in mild, dry grape-growing conditions, with an average annual rainfall of 800mm. Heavy downpours sometimes wash out sections of the Pacific Coast Hwy (SH35) around the Cape.

Getting There & Around

The region's only airports are in Gisborne and Napier. Air New Zealand flies to both from Auckland and Wellington, and also to Napier from Christchurch. Sunair Aviation connects Gisborne and Napier to Hamilton, Palmerston North, Rotorua, Tauranga and Whakatane.

Regular bus services ply SH2 and SH5, connecting Gisborne, Wairoa, Napier, Hastings and Waipukurau with all the main centres. Transport is much more limited around East Cape (below) and Te Urewera National Park (p377).

EAST CAPE

The East Cape is quite unlike any other part of NZ. Maori life is at the forefront here, in sleepy villages centred upon the many *marae* that dot the beautiful bays. Housed in close communities, drawing much of their livelihoods off the sea and the land, the *tangata whenua* (local people) of the Cape offer a fascinating insight into what might have been had they not been so vigorously divested of their land in the 19th century.

Everyone seems to know everyone here, with community ties built on rural enterprise and a shared passion for the ocean. The pace is slow and the people are wound down. Horseback commuters, tractors on the beach, fresh fish for tea…its all part of daily life around these parts.

Inland, the wild Raukumara Range forms the Cape's jagged spine. Near the edge of the sea, the Pacific Coast Hwy (SH35) runs from Opotiki to Gisborne, and stupendous views can be had along much of its 323km length. Lonely shores lie strewn with driftwood, while picture-postcard sandy bays lure in modest numbers of visitors. On sunny days the sea is a shimmering turquoise; at other times clouds brood and the surf crashes into the craggy shore in shades of deep green and thick white foam. The summer months see the seaside drive flanked with the crimson blooms of the old, gnarled pohutukawa.

Getting Around

Unless you're behind the wheel, transport around East Cape can be tricky, especially on weekends, but couriers regularly link Opotiki with Gisborne via Hicks Bay.

Coastal View Couriers (☎ 027-249 4200) runs from Tuesday to Friday between Opotiki ($45, three hours, 1.15pm and 2.30pm) and Hicks Bay ($45, three hours, 6.30am). **Polly's Passenger Couriers** (☎ 06-864 4728) continues

---

THE EAST COAST FACTS

Eat Fresh *kaimoana* (seafood) whenever you get the chance

Read Judith Binney's *Encircled Lands: Te Urewera, 1820–1921* (2009) – 680 fresh pages of fascinating Maori history

Listen to Uawa FM (88.5, 99.3 FM) in Tolaga Bay (p365)

Watch *Whale Rider* (2002), then take the tour (p370)

Swim at Anaura Bay (p365)

Festival Art Deco Weekend in Napier and Hastings (p381)

Tackiest tourist attraction The statue of the mystery man at Cook's Plaza on Titirangi, Gisborne (p380)

Go green Millton vineyard (p369) – organic, biodynamic and delicious to boot

---

from here to Gisborne Monday to Friday from Hick's Bay ($40, 3½ hours, 6.30am), and from Gisborne ($40, 3½ hours, 1pm). **Cook's Couriers** (☎ 021-371 364) covers the same route Monday to Friday from Te Araroa ($40, 3½ hours, 7.15am) and from Gisborne (2pm, 1pm Saturday).

An alternative is **Kiwi Experience** (☎ 09-366 9830; www.kiwiexperience.com; per person $395), which runs the four-day 'East As' backpacker bus leaving from Taupo or Rotorua.

PACIFIC COAST HWY

NZ's not short on awesome drives, and SH35 is up with the best of them. You're not going to get anywhere quickly on this route but that's hardly the point. While you can shoot the gap in a solid six hours, lingering along the way will pay rich dividends. If you haven't got time to enjoy the entire coastal road this time around, don't despair. The shorter route between Opotiki and Gisborne (144km) follows SH2 through the bushy Waioeka Gorge before spilling out into picturesque orchards and vineyards.

Before you hit the road, collect the free *Pacific Coast Highway* booklet from the

---

TELEPHONE CODES

The telephone area code from Opotiki east to Hicks Bay, just before East Cape itself, is ☎ 07. The rest of the region is ☎ 06.

THE EAST COAST

MAORI NZ: THE EAST COAST

The main *iwi* (tribes) in the region are Te Whanau-a-Apanui (west side of East Cape), Ngati Porou (east side of East Cape), Ngati Kahungunu (the coast from Hawke's Bay down) and Tuhoe (inland in Te Urewera).

Ngati Porou and Ngati Kahungunu are the country's second- and third-biggest *iwi*. In the late 19th century they produced the great leaders James Carroll (the first Maori cabinet minister) and Apirana Ngata (who was briefly acting Prime Minister). Ngata, whose face adorns the $50 bill, worked tirelessly in parliament to orchestrate a cultural revival within Maoridom. The region's magnificent carved meeting houses are part of his legacy.

There are opportunities to interact with Maori while you're in the region. For accommodation with a distinctly Maori flavour, consider Te Kaha Homestead Lodge (below), Maraehako Bay Retreat (opposite), Mel's Place (p364) and Eastender Backpackers (p364).

For an intimate introduction to *Maoritanga* (things Maori), consider a guided tour. Ask about climbing Mt Hikurangi at the Ngati Porou Visitors Centre (p364), or look out for Motu River AAA Jet Boating (below), Tipuna Tours' Whale Rider tour (p370), Long Island Tours (p387) or Te Hakakino (p387). Te Aute College (p392) welcomes visitors but you'll need to call ahead.

Te Urewera has a long and proud history of resistance to colonisation: start your explorations at Aniwaniwa (p375) and if you have time, visit the unique communities at Ruatahuna and Maungapohatu (p374).

For a more passive brush with the culture, visit Gisborne's Tairawhiti Museum (p368), the Hawke's Bay Museum & Art Gallery (p380), Otatara Pa (p380), and Tikitiki's St Mary's Church (p364). Throughout the text we've listed *marae* that can be admired from the road.

Opotiki or Gisborne i-SITE. Set off with a full petrol tank, and stock up on snacks and groceries – shops and petrol stations are in short supply. Sleeping and eating options are pretty spread out, so we've listed them in the order you'll find them.

Opotiki to Te Kaha

The first leg offers hazy views across to Whakaari (White Island; p355), a chain-smoking active volcano. The desolate beaches at **Torere**, **Hawai** and **Omaio** are steeply shelved and littered with flotsam. Check out the magnificent *whakairo* (carving) on the Torere school gateway. Hawai marks the boundary of the Whanau-a-Apanui tribe whose *rohe* (traditional land) extends to Cape Runaway.

About 42km east of Opotiki the road crosses the broad pebbly expanse of the **Motu River**, the first river in NZ to be designated as a protected wilderness area. Action seekers head here for back-to-nature rafting and jet-boating adventures. **Wet 'n' Wild Rafting** (☎ 0800 462 7238; www.wetnwildrafting.co.nz; 2-5 days $795-925) offers multiday excursions, with the longest taking you 100km down the river. The river is so remote that the two-day tour requires you to be helicoptered in, therefore costing almost as much as the five-day trip. **Motu River AAA Jet Boating** (☎ 027-686 6489; 1hr trip for 2 people $130)

includes an ecological and historical commentary from a Maori perspective (departs near Motu Bridge daily 1 December to 30 April, weather permitting).

Twenty-five kilometres further along, the fishing town of **Te Kaha** once sounded the death knell for passing whales. From the roadside you get a decent view of the sublimely carved Tukaki *marae*. There's a shop here, a modern waterside hotel with an uncertain future (at time of print) and several accommodation options.

The remote **Maungaroa Station** (☎ 07-325 2727; www.maungaroa.co.nz; Maungaroa Access Rd; campsites $10, dm $20) is a Raukumara Range lodge that requires a 45-minute drive up a scenic, gravel road (off Copenhagen Rd) and two river crossings to reach it. Bunk down in the self-contained cottage (sleeps 12 in four bedrooms) or camp outside; dunk yourself in the Kereu River, hug a tree or saddle-up for a horse trek ($35 to $65, one to four hours).

Located on the waterfront, **Te Kaha Homestead Lodge** (☎ 07-325 2194; fax 07-325 2193; SH35; campsites per person $10, dm/s/tw/d $30/40/60/80; ▣) is a friendly hostel that sits among old pohutukawa trees with spa views to White Island. Rooms are basic, but the rambunctious owner organises fishing trips and bursts into choruses of 'Welcome to the Homestead at Te

Kaha' (to the tune of *Hotel California*) given the slightest provocation.

Tui Lodge (☎ 07-325 2922; www.tuilodge.co.nz; Copenhagen Rd, Te Kaha; s/d incl breakfast $125/150; 🖳) is a capacious, modern guest house that sits on groomed three-acre gardens, irresistible to tui and many other birds. Delicious meals are available by arrangement. Horse trekking, fishing and diving trips can be organised for you.

Te Kaha to Cape Runaway

A succession of sleepy bays follows. At **Papatea Bay** stop to admire the gateway of **Hinemahuru marae**, carved with images of WWI Maori Battalion soldiers. Nearby **Christ Church Raukokore** (1894) is an immaculately maintained beacon of belief on a lonely promontory. **Waihau Bay** has an all-in-one petrol station–post office–store–takeaway at its western end, alongside the pub. There's another store-takeaway attached to the holiday park in the centre of the beach. **Cape Runaway**, where kumara was first introduced to NZ, can only be reached on foot. There are few accommodation options in these parts, and what you will find will be small and personal.

Run by the same *hapu* (subtribe) as the retreat next door is **Maraehako Camping Ground** (☎ 07-325 2901; SH35; campsites per adult/child $12/8). Little more is offered than clean toilets (BYO paper), water (needs boiling) and beachfront nirvana. Toddlers will adore splashing about in the clear stream.

Nestled among ancient pohutukawa trees, the waterfront **Maraehako Bay Retreat** (☎ 07-325 2648; www.maraehako.co.nz; SH35; dm/s/d $28/43/63; 🖳) is a hostel that looks like it was cobbled together from flotsam and jetsam washed up in the craggy cove. It's rustic, but unique, for what it lacks in crossed t's and dotted i's it more than makes up for in *manaakitanga* (hospitality). Enjoy a spa under the stars ($5), kayak hire, as well as fishing charters, *marae*

tours, guided walks, horse treks and more, at reasonable prices.

Towards Whanarua Bay, the magical **Waikawa B&B** (☎ 07-325 2070; www.waikawa.net; 7541 SH35; d $100-130; 🖳) sits in a private rocky cove with views of the sunset and White Island. The artful buildings blend weathered timber, corrugated iron and paua inlay to great effect. There are two double B&B rooms, and a two-bedroom self-contained bach ($130 to $200), perfect for two to four people.

There are plenty of beds at **Oceanside Apartments** (☎ 07-325 3699; www.waihaubay.co.nz; 10932 SH35; d $110-130; 🛜), between two nicely kept apartments and a next-door bach. (Add $30 per extra bod beyond the double price.) Meals and picnic lunches are available by arrangement. Bookings can be made for kayak hire and local activities.

Heaven is a tub of homemade macadamia and honey ice cream at **Pacific Coast Macadamias** (☎ 07-325 2960; SH35, Whanarua Bay; snacks $2-9; ⏲ 10am-3pm), accompanied by views along one of the most spectacular parts of the coast. Toasted sandwiches and nutty sweet treats make this a great lunch stop.

Cape Runaway to East Cape

The road heads inland from Whangaparaoa, crossing into Ngati Porou territory before hitting the coast at **Hicks Bay**, a real middle-of-nowhere settlement with a grand beach.

Nearly 10km further is **Te Araroa**, a lone-dog village with a shop, petrol station, take away and beautifully carved *marae*. The geology changes here from igneous outcrops to sandstone cliffs. More than 350 years old, 20m high and 40m wide, Te-Waha-O-Rerekohu, allegedly NZ's largest pohutukawa tree, stands in Te Araroa schoolyard. The progressive **East Cape Manuka Company** (☎ 0508 626 852; www.east capemanuka.co.nz; 4464 Te Araroa Rd; ⏲ 9am-4pm daily Nov-Mar, Mon-Fri Apr-Oct) is also here, selling soaps, oils, creams and honey made from potent East Cape manuka. Stop for coffee and *kai* (food).

FREEDOM TO CAMP

Gisborne District Council (GDC) is one of the few authorities to permit Freedom Camping (extremely cheap informal camping), but only at a handful of designated sites from the end of September to April. You can apply for a permit online (www.gdc.govt.nz/freedom-camping-permit-request) for two, 10 or 28 consecutive nights at a cost of $10, $25 and $60 respectively. Freedom camping is a privilege, so please follow the requirements in the GDC *Freedom Camping* leaflet, available online or at visitor centres. Your own gas cooker, chemical toilet and water supply are obligatory.

THE EAST COAST

From Te Araroa, drive out to see the **East Cape Lighthouse**, the easterly tip of mainland NZ. It's 21km (30 minutes) east of town along a mainly unsealed road, with a 25-minute climb to the lighthouse. Set your alarm and get up there for sunrise.

It's a long way between drinks (or anything else) on this leg. **Mel's Place** (☎ 06-864 4694; www.eastcape.co.nz; 89 Onepoto Beach Rd, Hicks Bay; campsites per person $20, dm $30) is located on an ancestral *pa* (fortified village) site. Mel and Joe manage this hostel with aplomb, sharing with their guests a wealth of local Maori history. As well as a homely dorm there are campsites with wicked bay views (bring your own cooking gear), a supercute double cabin ($125) and smart self-contained caravan by the beach ($75). If you like dogs, you'll get plenty of tail-wags from the family pets.

Brilliant views distract from the barrack ambience at the sprawling **Hicks Bay Motel Lodge** (☎ 06-864 4880; www.hicksbaymotel.co.nz; 5198 SH35; dm $25, d $75-145; ◷ ☯) above Hicks Bay. The old-fashioned rooms are nothing flash, although the restaurant, shop, pool and glowworm grotto offer some compensation.

East Cape to Tokomaru Bay

Heading through farmland south of Te Araroa, the first town you come to is **Tikitiki**. If you've been itching to get on to a *marae*, you'll get a fair idea of what you're missing out on by visiting the extraordinary **St Mary's Church** (1924). It's nothing special from the outside but step inside for a sensory overload. There are woven *tukutuku* (flax panels) on the walls, geometrically patterned stained-glass windows, painted beams and amazing carvings – check out the little guys holding up the pulpit. A stained-glass crucifixion scene behind the pulpit depicts WWI Maori Battalion soldiers in attendance.

Mt Hikurangi (1752m), jutting out of the Raukumara Range, is the highest non-volcanic peak in the North Island and the first spot on the planet to be touched by the sun each day. According to local tradition it was the first piece of land dragged up when Maui snagged the North Island (p54). The Ngati Porou version of the Maui story has his canoe and earthly remains resting here on their sacred mountain. The **Maui Whakairo**, nine massive wooden carvings, has been erected 1000m up on Hikurangi's shoulder to honour their ancestor.

Hikurangi is not a tramp for the inexperienced but hardy walkers can access the mountain by turning off SH35 at Tapuaeroa Valley Rd, 3km north of Ruatoria, and heading towards Pakihiroa Station. From here it's a four-hour tramp to the hut ($15; book at the Ngati Porou Visitors Centre) and then a further two hours to the summit.

A few kilometres off SH35 and 20km south of Tikitiki, **Ruatoria** is the Ngati Porou's biggest town. It's a slow-mo place with a mini-market, petrol station, pub and a couple of cafes. The welcoming **Ngati Porou Visitors Centre** (☎ 06-864 8660; www.ngatiporou.com; 144 Waiomatatini Rd; ◷ 8.30am-5pm Mon-Fri) has authentic local art for sale, but more importantly offers tailored cultural tours, including trips to Hikurangi. Standard options are a 4WD guided tour to Maui Whakairo (four hours), a sunrise tour (departs 4.30am), and guided tours to the summit (eight-hour/overnight). Prices run from $165 to $500 but vary greatly according to numbers. It also runs a pick-up/drop-off service to the mountain (each way $20 to $50), and can arrange *marae* stays, fishing, diving, horse trekking, surfing and kayaking.

About 26km south is **Te Puia Springs**, a blink-and-you'll-miss-it hot-springs village with a handy petrol station–store. The actual thermal pools are in an old shed (with no changing facilities) at the back of the **Te Puia Hot Springs Hotel** (☎ 06-864 6755; 4689 SH35; pools $5). It's an informal set-up; ask at the hotel for access to the small pool of milky water, which reputedly has the highest mineral content of any in the world. Don't splash about as there's a risk of amoebic meningitis. Nearby **Waipiro Bay** is a knockout.

A further 11km south is **Tokomaru Bay**, perhaps the most beautiful spot on the entire route, with its broad beach framed by sweeping cliffs. This romantically crumbling town has weathered hard times since the local freezing works closed in the 1950s. The big attractions here are the famous surf break, Toko Point and the town's great pub. You'll also find a petrol station, a small supermarket and post office, a couple of takeaways and a summer-only cafe.

As far removed from the grim London soap opera as imaginable, the cheery sit-around-the-campfire **Eastender Backpackers** (☎ 06-864 3033; www.eastenderhorsetreks.co.nz; 836 Rangitukia Rd; campsites per person $10, dm $23, d $50-60; ▯) is a farmstay that has clean rooms and snappy communal areas. The beach is dicey for swimming, but there's a safe waterhole nearby. Horse treks (two hours, $85) and bone-carving lessons (from $35) are offered and you might even get to try a *hangi* (Maori feast; $14).

Just a block from the beach, **Footprints in the Sand** (☎ 06-864 5858; www.footprintsinthesand.co.nz; 13 Potae St, Tokomaru Bay; campsites per person $15, dm/d/tr $20/60/80) is a most amenable host that offers a squeaky-clean, comfortable dorm along with a cabin and pleasant camping. Ace alfresco dining area, kayak and bike hire. Look out for continuous improvements.

Up on the hill, **Brian's Place** (☎ 06-864 5870; www.briansplace.co.nz; 21 Potae St, Tokomaru Bay; campsites per person $15, dm/s/d $25/43/60) scores the awards for views and eco-loos. The bunkhouse has tricky loft rooms (stay sober), a couple of rustic tent pitches on the knoll, and desirable cabins.

Experience local hospitality at **Te Puka Tavern** (☎ 06-864 5466; Beach Rd, Tokomaru Bay; meals $5-20; �} 2.30pm-late Tue, 11am-late Wed-Sun), a friendly pub with cracker views and respectable burgers.

Tokomaru Bay to Gisborne

After a bucolic 22km of highway and further 7km to the coast, it's a definite 'wow' moment when isolated **Anaura Bay** springs into view far below. A plaque near the centre of the bay commemorates Captain Cook's arrival in 1769 when he commented on the 'profound peace' in which the people were living and their 'truly astonishing' cultivations. **Anaura Bay Walkway** is a 3.5km ramble through native forest and grassland, starting at the northern end of the bay. There's a basic free Department of Conservation (DOC) campsite here (your own toilet is required).

East Cape's largest community is **Tolaga Bay**, 14km further south. There's an **information centre** (☎ 06-862 6862; 55 Cook St; �}6am-6pm Mon-Fri) in the foyer of the local radio station (Uawa 88.5, 99.3FM). Just off the main street, **Tolaga Bay Cashmere Company** (☎ 06-862 6746; www. cashmere.co.nz; 31 Solander St; �} 10am-4pm Mon-Sat) inhabits the art-deco former council building. You can watch the knitters at work and then purchase one of their delicate, pricey handiworks; the seconds are sold at a discount.

Tolaga is defined by the remarkable **historic wharf** (1929) – the longest in the southern hemisphere at 660m – which is slowly surrendering to the sea (although locals are fundraising to preserve it). Take the time to walk its length. Nearby is **Cooks Cove Walkway** (2½ hours, 5.8km, closed August to October), an easy loop through farmland and native bush to another cove where the captain landed. At the northern end of the beach is the **Tatarahake Cliffs Lookout**, a sharp 10-minute walk to an excellent vantage point.

Te Tapuwae o Rongokako Marine Reserve is a 2450-hectare haven for many species of marine life including fur seals, dolphins and whales – and heaven for snorkellers and divers.

Dive Tatapouri (☎ 06-686 6139; www.divetatapouri. com; SH35, Tatapouri Beach) offers an array of watery activities including dive trips, snorkel hire, a reef ecology tour, shark-cage diving and even stingray feeding.

Campers are catered for best around these parts, although a few B&Bs come and go in the midst. **Anaura Bay Motor Camp** (☎ 06-862 6380; Anaura Bay Rd; unpowered/powered sites adult $12/14, child $6/8) is all about the location – right on the beachfront by the little stream where James Cook once stocked up with water. There's a decent kitchen and perfectly acceptable toilets.

Tolaga Bay Holiday Park (☎ 06-862 6716; www. tolagabayholidaypark.co.nz; 167 Wharf Rd; unpowered/powered sites $12/14, cabins $60-75) There's little here except the dear old wharf, but this is a place where absence becomes substance. The stiff ocean breeze tousles Norfolk Island pines as open lawns bask in the sunshine – who needs anything more?

There's a shabby charm to the 1930s faux-Tudor **Tolaga Inn** (☎ 06-862 6856; hutchroy@xtra.co.nz; 12 Cook St; dm/s/d $25/50/75) with basic but clean rooms. Downstairs is a respectable cafe (meals $8 to $27) with bonzer biscuits and tables in the sunshine.

Freedom Camping (p363) is available at the north end of Tolaga Bay, Waihau Bay and at Pouawa Beach, just off SH35 on the edge of the marine reserve.

GISBORNE
pop 32,700

Gizzy to her friends, Gisborne's a pretty thing and increasingly self-confident. Squeezed between surf beaches and a sea of chardonnay, most Kiwis would describe the lifestyle here as 'not bad' – meaning, of course, bloody brilliant.

It proudly claims to be the first city on earth to see the sun and once it does it hogs it and heads to the beach. Poverty Bay starts here, hooking south to Young Nick's Head.

Perhaps it's the isolated location that's helped Gisborne maintain its small-town charm and interesting main street. Grand Edwardian buildings sit alongside modernist 1950s, five-storey 'skyscrapers' and the odd slice of audacious art deco.

It's a good place to put your feet up for a few days, hit the beaches and sip heavenly wine.

History

The Gisborne region has been settled for over 700 years. A pact between two migratory *waka* (canoe) skippers, Paoa of the *Horouta* and Kiwa of the *Takitimu*, led to the founding of Turanganui a Kiwa (now Gisborne). Kumara flourished in the fertile soil and the settlement blossomed.

In 1769 this was the first part of NZ sighted by Cook's expedition. Eager to replenish supplies and explore the land, they set ashore, much to the amazement of the local people. Setting an unfortunate benchmark for Maori/Pakeha (non-Maori) relations, the crew opened fire when the local men performed their traditional blood-curdling challenge, killing six of them.

The *Endeavour* quickly set sail up the coast without the provisions they were seeking. Cook, perhaps in a fit of petulance, named the area Poverty Bay as 'it did not afford a single item we wanted'. The name stuck, and Cook and crew made a much better impression at their next landfall, Tolaga Bay.

European settlement didn't begin until 1831. Motivated self-starter John Williams Harris established a whaling base on the Turanganui River's west bank and a farm near Manutuke. Whaling boomed and missionaries followed. More Europeans moved to the area but Maori resistance to land sales limited settlement.

In the 1860s battles between settlers and Maori erupted. Beginning in Taranaki, the Hauhau insurrection spread to the East Coast, culminating in the battle of Waerenga a Hika in 1865. The following year the government crushed all opposition and transported survivors, including Te Kooti (p368), to the Chatham Islands.

To discover Gisborne's historical spots on foot, pick up a copy of the trail booklet, *Gisborne: A Historic Walk*, available from the i-SITE (by donation).

Orientation

Known as 'the city of bridges', Gisborne presides over the confluence of the Waimata and Taruheru Rivers, below which the Turanganui River runs to the sea. The main street is Gladstone Rd and Waikanae Beach is immediately south of the town centre. Free town maps are available at Gisborne's i-SITE (below).

Information

The major banks are located along Gladstone Rd.

Ambulance, fire service & police (☎ 111)

DOC (☎ 06-869 0460; www.doc.govt.co.nz; 63 Carnarvon St; ☯ 8am-4.35pm Mon-Fri) Tourist information.

Gisborne Hospital (☎ 06-869 0500; Ormond Rd)

Gisborne i-SITE (☎ 06-868 6139; www.gisbornenz. com; 209 Grey St; ☯ 8.30am-5pm Mon-Fri, 9am-5pm Sat, 10am-4pm Sun) Beside a doozy of a Canadian totem pole, this helpful centre stocks the thorough (and free) *Eastland Region* and *Pacific Coast Hwy* booklets. It also has internet access, toilets and a minigolf course ($3).

Muirs Bookshop (☎ 06-869 0651; www.muirsbook shop.co.nz; 62 Gladstone Rd; ☯ 8.30am-4pm Mon-Fri, 9am-3pm Sat) The best bookshop in Gisborne (and probably the whole East Coast), established in 1905.

Police station (☎ 06-869 0200; Peel St)

Post office (cnr Gladstone Rd & Bright St)

Sights

HISTORIC SITES & MONUMENTS

Gisborne deifies Captain Cook. In a park by the river mouth there's a **statue of Young Nick** (Nicholas Young), Cook's cabin boy, whose eagle eyes were the first to spot NZ (the white cliffs at Young Nick's Head). There's a **Captain Cook statue** here too, erected on a globe etched with his roaming routes.

Across the river at the foot of Titirangi (Kaiti Hill) is the spot where Cook first got NZ dirt on his boots (9 October 1769 according to Cook's journal, but actually the 8th). The **Cook National Historic Reserve** and **Cook monument** is a grim obelisk facing the end of the wharves. This scrappy site is made even more significant by being the landing point of the Horouta *waka*.

Tucked away on the other side of Titirangi is **Te Poho o Rawiri Marae** (☎ 06-868 5364; cnr Ranfurly St & Queens Dr; admission by invitation) with its elaborately carved meeting house. You can get a decent view from the gates but you'll need to call ahead to ask for permission to view the decorated interior.

THE EAST COAST

GISBORNE

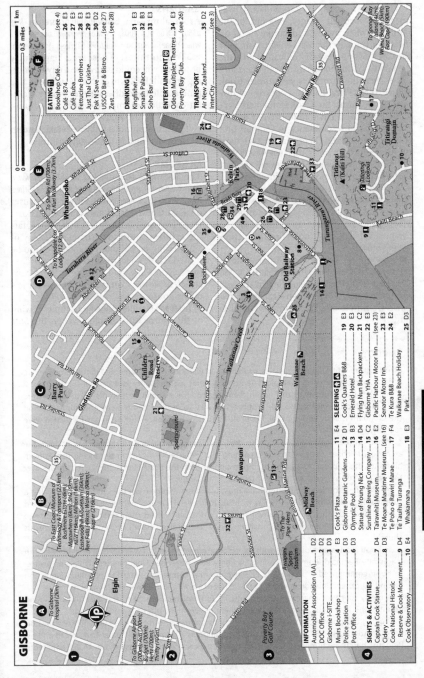

INFORMATION

Automobile Association (AA).....	1 D2
DOC Office.....	2 D2
Gisborne i-SITE.....	3 D3
Muirs Bookshop.....	4 E3
Police Station.....	5 D3
Post Office.....	6 D3

SIGHTS & ACTIVITIES

Captain Cook Statue.....	7 D4
Cidery.....	8 D3
Cook National Historic Reserve & Cook Monument.....	9 D4
Cook Observatory.....	10 E4
Cook's Plaza.....	11 E4
Gisborne Botanic Gardens.....	12 D1
Olympic Pool.....	13 B3
Statue of Young Nick.....	14 D4
Sunshine Brewing Company.....	15 C2
Tairawhiti Museum.....	16 E2
Te Moana Maritime Museum.....	(see 16)
Te Poho o Rawiri Marae.....	17 F4
Te Tauihu Turanga Whakamana.....	18 E3

SLEEPING

Cook's Quarters B&B.....	19 E3
Emerald Hotel.....	20 E3
Flying Nun Backpackers.....	21 C2
Gisborne YHA.....	22 E3
Pacific Harbour Motor Inn.....	(see 23)
Senator Motor Inn.....	23 E3
Te Kura B&B.....	24 E2
Waikanae Beach Holiday Park.....	25 D3

EATING

	(see 4)
Bookshop Café.....	26 E3
Café 1874.....	27 E3
Café Ruba.....	28 E3
Fettucine Brothers.....	29 E3
Just Thai Cuisine.....	30 D2
Pak N Save.....	(see 27)
USSCO Bar & Bistro.....	(see 28)
Zest.....	

DRINKING

Kingfisher.....	31 E3
Smash Palace.....	32 B3
Soho Bar.....	33 E3

ENTERTAINMENT

Odeon Multiplex Theatres.....	34 E3
Poverty Bay Club.....	(see 26)

TRANSPORT

Air New Zealand.....	35 D2
InterCity.....	(see 3)

Titirangi has magical city views. It was once a *pa* (fortified village); look out for the remnants of terracing and kumara pits on the steep track to the top, which starts near the Cook Monument. If you can handle the disdain of sweaty joggers, you can cheat and drive. Near the summit is yet another Cook edifice, **Cook's Plaza**. Due to a cock-up of historic proportions, the Cook statue here isn't garbed in British naval uniform, nor does it bear any facial resemblance to Captain Jim. A plaque proclaims, 'Who was he? We have no idea!' Further on is the **Cook Observatory** (☎ 06-867 7901; public viewing $2; ☼ viewing 8.30pm Tue), the world's easternmost star-gazing facility.

Adding some balance to all the Cook hoopla, **Te Tauihu Turanga Whakamana** (The Canoe Prow; cnr Gladstone Rd & Customhouse Rd) is a large modern Maori sculpture incorporating the images of two men killed during Cook's first interaction with the locals.

Matawhero is 7km west of Gisborne along SH2. The historic **Presbyterian Church** (☎ 868 5573; Church Ln) is the only building in the village to have survived Te Kooti's 1868 raid. It's a sweetly simple affair with lovingly tended gardens.

GARDENS

Arboreal nirvana, **Eastwoodhill Arboretum** (Map p360; ☎ 06-863 9003; www.eastwoodhill.org.nz; 2392 Wharekopae Rd, Ngatapa; adult/child $10/free; ☼ 9am-5pm) is 35km northwest of Gisborne. Staggeringly beautiful, you could easily lose a day wandering around the 25km of themed tracks in this pine-scented paradise. It's the country's largest collection of imported trees and shrubs, but the birds love it just the same.

The less ambitious **Gisborne Botanic Gardens** (Aberdeen Rd) is beside the Taruheru River.

MUSEUMS

The **Tairawhiti Museum** (☎ 06-867 3832; www.tairawhitimuseum.org.nz; 18 Stout St; adult/under 12 $5/free, Mon free; ☼ 10am-4pm Mon-Sat, 1.30-4pm Sun) focuses on East Coast Maori and colonial history. Its gallery is Gisborne's arts hub, with rotating exhibits, and the permanent display of 'Shutterbug Jack's' photographs is not to be missed. There's a tearoom-style cafe overlooking Kelvin Park, and outside is the reconstructed Wyllie Cottage (1872), Gisborne's oldest house.

Te Moana Maritime Museum occupies a wing of the Tairawhiti complex. When the *Star*

TE KOOTI

Maori history is littered with mystics, prophets and warriors – often combined in the same person. A particularly fascinating example is Te Kooti (rhymes with naughty, not booty).

In 1865 he fought with the government against the Hauhau (adherents of the Pai Marire faith, founded by another warrior-prophet) but was accused of being a spy and imprisoned on the Chatham Islands without trial. His protestations of innocence and demands for justice were foolishly ignored.

While on the Chathams, Te Kooti studied the Bible and claimed to receive visions from the archangel Michael. His charismatic preaching and 'miracles' – including producing flames from his hands (his captors claimed he used phosphorus from the head of matches) – helped win over the Pai Marire to his distinctly Maori take on Christianity.

In 1867 Te Kooti led an astounding, almost bloodless escape from the Chathams, hijacking a supply ship and sailing to Poverty Bay with 200 followers. En route he threw a doubter overboard as a sacrifice. Upon their safe arrival Te Kooti's disciples raised their right hands in homage to God rather than bowing submissively; *ringa tu* (upraised hand) became the name of his church.

Te Kooti requested a dialogue with the colonial government but was once again rebuffed, with magistrate Reginald Biggs demanding his immediate surrender. Unimpressed by Pakeha justice, Te Kooti commenced a particularly effective guerrilla campaign – starting by killing Biggs and around 50 others (including women and children, Maori and Pakeha) at Matawhero.

A merry four-year chase ensued. Eventually Te Kooti took refuge in the area known as King Country, the Maori king's vast dominion where government troops feared to tread.

Proving the pointlessness of the government's approach to the whole affair, Te Kooti was officially pardoned in 1883. By this time his reputation as a prophet and healer had spread and his Ringatu Church was firmly established – at the most recent census it boasted over 16,000 adherents.

of Canada foundered on a Gisborne reef in 1912, the ship's bridge and captain's cabin were salvaged, installed in a local home, then later moved here for restoration. Displays on *waka*, whaling and Cook's Poverty Bay visit pale before the sensational vintage surfboard collection.

The **East Coast Museum of Technology & Transport** (SH2, Makaraka; adult/child $5/2; 10am-4.30pm) is an improbable collation of rusty tractors, lawn mowers, engines, spanners, ploughs, ovens, chainsaws, trucks, pumps, harvesters, motorbikes and so on – a shrine to peoples' inventive capacity or their ability to horde junk?

WINERIES

Gisborne is a major wine-producing area, traditionally famous for its chardonnay (producing just under a third of the country's output) but increasingly being noticed for other white varietals, particularly gewürztraminer and pinot gris. Most of the local vineyards offer free tastings, although some will charge a nominal fee which is subsequently deducted from purchases. The *Winery Guide* (free from the i-SITE) has a map and the latest opening hours for most vineyards. The following all have set public tasting hours; many open longer in summer.

Bushmere Estate (06-868 9317; www.bushmere. com; 166 Main Rd, Matawhero; 11am-6pm Fri-Sun). Great chardonnay, gewürztraminer and cafe-style lunches.

KEW (06-862 7722; www.kew.co.nz; 569 Wharekopae Rd, Patutahi; 11am-4pm) Lovely wines across the board from this award-winning winery committed to sustainable winegrowing. Call ahead in winter or for guided tours and antipasto platters.

Matawhero (06-867 6140; www.matawhero.co.nz; Riverpoint Rd, Matawhero; 2-5pm Thu, Fri & Mon, 1-5pm Sat & Sun) Home of a particularly buttery chardy. Enjoy your picnic in a lovely setting, accompanied by a tasting tray ($10, redeemable against purchase).

Millton (06-862 8680; www.millton.co.nz; 119 Papatu Rd, Manutuke; 10am-5pm Mon-Sat) Sustainable, organic and biodynamic to boot. Linger for a picnic in the beautiful gardens.

BREWERIES

Sunshine Brewing Company (Map p367; 06-867 7777; www.gisbornegold.co.nz; 109 Disraeli St; 9am-6pm Mon-Sat), Gisborne's own natural brewery, offers four quality beers including the famous Gisborne Gold and its big brother Green. Free tours and tastings by arrangement.

The **Cidery** (Map p367; 06-868 8300; www.harvest cider.co.nz; 91 Customhouse St; 9am-4.30pm Mon-Fri) is the apple-hued producer of Bulmers Original, Scrumpy, Harvest and pear ciders, with free tastings and factory viewings on offer.

Activities
SURFING & KITEBOARDING

Surfing is mainstream in Gisborne, with the male teenage population looking appropriately shaggy. **Waikanae Beach** is good for learners and young ones; experienced surfers get tubed south of town at the **Pipe**, or east at **Sponge Bay** and **Tuamotu Island**. Further east along SH35, **Wainui** (Map p360) and **Makorori** (Map p360) beaches also have quality breaks.

Surfing with Frank (06-867 0823; www.surfingwith frank.com; 58 Murphy Rd, Wainui Beach) offers lessons ($50 to $75) as well as tours of the best local (and North Island) breaks.

Freestyle NZ (06-868 8840; www.freestylenz. com; 1hr $50, kayak hire per hr $20) offers kitesurfing lessons and gear hire, as well as customised kayak tours and freedom hire.

SWIMMING

Pick your way through the driftwood to swim safely between the flags at Waikanae and Midway beaches; the detritus is cleared in time for summer. If the ocean is chilly, **Olympic Pool** (06-867 6220; Centennial Marine Pde, Midway Beach; adult/child $3.50/2.50; 6am-8pm) is a tepid 50m indoor/outdoor pool with a 98m wormlike waterslide ($3.50) and aquafitness classes ($6.50).

OTHER ACTIVITIES

There are stacks of walks to tackle in the area, starting with a gentle stroll along the river. The i-SITE can provide you with brochures for the **Arts & Crafts Trail** and **Historic Walk**. Winding its way through farmland and forest with commanding views, the **Te Kuri Walkway** (two hours, 5.6km, closed August to October) starts 4km north of town at the end of Shelley Rd.

For free skull-endangering things to do in NZ you can't beat the **Rere Rockslide** (Map p360). This natural phenomenon occurs in a section of the Rere River 50km northwest of Gisborne along the Wharekopae Rd. Grab a tyre tube or boogie board to cushion the worst of the bruises and slide down the 60m-long rocky run into the pool at the bottom. Three kilometres downriver, the **Rere Falls** (Map p360)

THE EAST COAST

send a 30m-wide curtain of water over a 10m drop; you can walk behind it if you don't mind getting wet. Both can be combined with a visit to Eastwoodhill Arboretum (p368).

Further awaken your sense of mortality with a shark-cage dive from **Surfit Charters** (☎ 06-867 2970; www.surfit.co.nz; per person $300). Tamer fishing and snorkelling trips can also be arranged.

Tours

After *Whale Rider* was released, the sleepy Maori village at Whangara, 21km north of Gisborne, was swamped with sightseers – some of whom treated the *marae* and private homes as if they were movie sets. That's why you won't find any signs pointing to this mystical place from SH35. Your best bet for an introduction to Whangara and meaningful insights into Maori culture is to take a tour with **Tipuna Tours** (☎ 06-862 6118; www.tipunatours.com). Tailored, small-group tours are offered, including the **Whale Rider Tour** (two hours, $50 to $70) and trips around the sights of Gisborne and around the Pacific Coast Hwy to Opotiki.

Paradise Leisure Tours (☎ 027 223 9440; grant sue.hughes@ihug.co.nz; tours $25-150) runs a wide range of whole and half-day tours around local hot spots including the wineries, Eastwoodhill Arboretum, Morere Hot Springs and Lake Waikaremoana ($150, nine hours). Book at the i-SITE.

Festivals & Events

On October's Labour weekend, local winemakers and foodies pool talents for the **Gisborne Food & Wine Festival** (☎ 0800 447 267; www.gisbornewine.co.nz/festival; tickets $60), culminating in the main shindig on the Sunday – the price includes buses between the vineyards and tastings. Don't miss Saturday's free street party and the Wine Waiters' Relay.

The huge event on the music calendar is **Rhythm & Vines** (www.rhythmandvines.co.nz; Waiohika Estate; tickets $95-215), a three-day festival leading up to New Year's Eve that attracts big-name local bands and international headliners. You'll be scrambling to find accommodation anywhere near Gisborne at this time.

Sleeping

Gisborne's speciality is midrange motor lodges and unflashy beachside motels, although it tacks on a couple of reasonable budget options and top-enders around the edges.

BUDGET

Flying Nun Backpackers (☎ 06-868 0461; yager@xtra.co.nz; 147 Roebuck Rd; campsites per person $15, dm/d $23/56; 🖳 🛜) It was probably a little more prim and proper when it was a convent, but this grungy old place has plenty of character and tight security.

Gisborne YHA (☎ 06-867 3269; www.yha.co.nz; 32 Harris St; dm/s/d $26/40/62; 🖳 🛜) A short stroll across the river from town, this well-kept hostel fills a rambling mansion with colour and transience. The rooms are large and comfortable, but you'll need to head outside for the bathrooms.

Eastwoodhill Arboretum (Map p360; ☎ 06-863 9003; www.eastwoodhill.org.nz; 2392 Wharekopae Rd, Ngatapa; dm/tw $25/80) The bunks and private rooms are basic and you'll still need to pay the admission on the first day, but once you're here, endless woody delights can fill your days and nights. There's a decent kitchen but bring food as there's nothing for miles around.

Waikanae Beach Holiday Park (☎ 06-867 5634; www.gisborneholidaypark.co.nz; Grey St; unpowered sites $26-28, powered sites $32-35, d $40-62, ste $72-94; 🖳 🛜) Right by the beach and minutes from town, this is a useful spot to pitch a tent. Colourful art doesn't stop the self-contained units from looking like pensioner flats, but along with the 'ranch' cabins they're excellent value.

MIDRANGE & TOP END

Te Kura B&B (☎ 06-863 3497; www.tekura.co.nz; 14 Cheeseman Rd; r $90-140; 🖳 🛜 🖳) Play lord of the manor at this lovely 1920s Arts and Crafts–style riverside home. Two guest rooms (one with clawfoot-bath en suite) share a stately lounge and a bright breakfast room opening on to the river, pool and spa.

Cook's Quarters B&B (☎ 06-863 3708; Cooks-Quarters@hotmail.com; 66 Wainui Rd; d $120) A ship-shape faux-Tudor guest house decked out in a stylish maritime fashion. There are two pleasantly furnished en-suite rooms, comfortable lounge and pretty garden.

Pacific Harbour Motor Inn (☎ 06-867 8847; www.pacific-harbour.co.nz; 24 Reads Quay; r $130, ste $130-190; 🖳 🛜) This apartment-style inn overlooks the harbour, and offers clean and well-kept units with dated decor. Free wi-fi is available.

Senator Motor Inn (☎ 06-868 8877; www.senatormotorinn.co.nz; 2 Childers Rd; s/d/tr/q $140/140/160/180;

⊡ ⊚) Next door to the Pacific Harbour, the Senator offers superior views from its private balconies – the perfect place for sipping your chardonnay. The upstairs rooms have more privacy.

Emerald Hotel (☎ 06-868 8055; www.emeraldhotel. co.nz; cnr Reads Quay & Gladstone Rd; r $130-280; ⊡ ⊚ ⊛) Opened in 2006, the Emerald is all about the swimming pool and patio area, which makes a good fist of looking like a foxy international. Surrounding it are 48 luxury suites running along epic corridors connecting the various wings. There's a gym, day spa, and the Grill Room restaurant (mains $22 to $36).

Knapdale Eco Lodge (☎ 06-862 5444; www.knapdale. co.nz; 114 Snowsill Rd, Waihirere; s/tw incl breakfast $200/300, d incl breakfast $362-418; ⊡ ⊚) Indulge and relax at this tranquil, green idyll complete with lake, farm animals and home-grown produce. The stunning modern lodge is filled with international artwork, its glassy frontage flowing out to an expansive patio area, with brazier, barbecue, and pizza oven. Five-course dinner by arrangement ($85).

Eating

Bookshop Café (☎ 06-867 9742; 62 Gladstone Rd; meals $4-14; ⊙ 8.30am-4pm Mon-Fri, 9am-3pm Sat) Situated above Muirs Bookshop in a heritage building, this place has stripped-brick walls, exposed rafters, lovely leadlights, and a veranda over the street, along with a small but sweet selection of counter food and excellent salads. Fans of Supreme coffee and literature may need to be forcibly removed.

Café Ruba (☎ 06-868 6516; 14 Childers Rd; meals $5-19; ⊙ 7am-3pm Tue-Fri, 8.30am-3pm Sat & Sun; Ⓥ) Urbane Ruba is Gizzy's most stylish daytime stop, offering substantial breakfasts, sandwiches to order (on homemade bread) and adventurous lunches. Finish with strong coffee or an afternoon tipple.

Zest (☎ 06-867 5787; 22 Peel St; meals $7-19; ⊙ 7am-4pm Mon-Sat) Zealously zesty with its lime green frontage, this popular cafe serves good coffee, and a range of sweets, sandwiches, salads and blackboard specials using seasonal and organic produce where possible.

Café 1874 (☎ 06-863 2006; 38 Childers Rd; meals $8-19; ⊙ 7am-3pm) The creaky old grandeur of the Poverty Bay gentleman's club (1874) is reason enough to visit. This cafe within it certainly adds impetus: appealing counter food, all-day brunch, blackboard specials, reasonable prices and a pleasant garden.

Just Thai Cuisine (☎ 06-867 8028; 2 Lowe St; mains $11-17; ⊙ lunch & dinner Mon-Sat, dinner Sun; Ⓥ). A reliable purveyor of traditional Thai classics, housed in a refreshingly simple street-corner room overlooking the Taruheru River. Worthy espresso and fine teas.

Fettuccine Brothers (☎ 06-868 5700; 12 Peel St; mains $24-33; ⊙ dinner Mon-Sat) A highly polished yet relaxed affair with separate bar (live music Wednesday to Friday). The menu runs the gamut from garlic bread and antipasto, through to pasta and mammoth steaks. We give the spaghetti marinara the big thumbs up.

our pick **USSCO Bar & Bistro** (☎ 06-868 3246; 16 Childers Rd; mains $26-39; ⊙ dinner) Housed in the restored Union Steam Ship Company building (hence the name), this place is all class. The talented chef-owner demonstrates silky kitchen skills through a varied and exciting menu featuring the likes of roast duck with coconut sauce, crispy polenta and braised red cabbage. Devilishly good desserts and a drinks list sporting plenty of local wines and NZ beers. Live piano Tuesday to Saturday.

Self-caterers can fill the trolley at **Pak N Save** (☎ 06-868 9029; 274 Gladstone Rd; ⊙ 7am-9pm).

Drinking & Entertainment

Kingfisher (☎ 06-868 8787; 33 Gladstone Rd; ⊙ 11.30am-late Wed-Sun, 3pm-late Tue) This relative newcomer has set up in a grand old banking chamber. Attentive staff, music that's not *too* loud, pool table and proper crispy pizza served from the joint next door.

Soho Bar (☎ 06-868 3888; www.sohobar.co.nz; 2 Crawford St; ⊙ 11am-late Wed-Sun) This hip joint morphs from reputable restaurant to *the* place to boogie late at night. Local and occasional big-name DJs at weekends.

Smash Palace (☎ 06-867 7769; 24 Banks St; 3pm-late Mon-Fri, noon-late Sat, 2pm-late Sun) Get juiced at the junkyard. Iconic drinking den full to the gunwales with ephemera and its very own DC3 crash-landed in the garden bar. Live music most weekends.

Poverty Bay Club (☎ 06-863 2006; 38 Childers Rd; ⊙ enquire at cafe) Look out for the special occasions when this club at Café 1874 (left) is opened up to live bands and DJs. The **Dome Cinema** (www.domecinema.co.nz) shares the club rooms, showing decent films three times a week.

Odeon Multiplex Theatres (☎ 06-867 3339; 79 Gladstone Rd) New-release movies screen throughout the day.

DAME KIRI TE KANAWA

New Zealand's most famous daughter was born in Gisborne in 1944. A true megastar of the operatic world, Te Kanawa has played leading lady in some of the world's most renowned opera houses alongside the top leading men of the age. Along the way she's picked up a Grammy and a knighthood, and sung to an audience of 600 million people at the wedding of Prince Charles and Princess Diana.

In 2005 she pulled out of a concert with Aussie pop crooner John Farnham after watching a video of him performing. No, it wasn't his cheesy soft-rock balladeering that put her off, but rather the footage of women throwing their undies at him on stage. For a high-brow performer whose idea of a risqué show is to slip the odd show tune in among the arias, the risk of a misfired panty hurl was too much too bear.

None too pleased with her withdrawal, the concert promoters took out a lawsuit, which they lost.

Getting There & Around

AIR

Gisborne Airport (☎ 06-868 7951; www.eastland.co.nz/airport; Aerodrome Rd) is 3km west of the city. **Air New Zealand** (☎ 06-868 2700; www.airnewzealand.co.nz; 37 Bright St) flies to/from Auckland (one hour, six daily) and Wellington (70 minutes, four daily), with onward connections. Check the website for fares and special offers.

Sunair Aviation (☎ 0800 786 247; www.sunair.co.nz) offers flights on weekdays to Hamilton ($380, 75 minutes) and Napier ($280, 45 minutes) and onward to New Plymouth, Palmerston North, Rotorua, Tauranga and Whakatane ($280 to $380).

BUS

InterCity (☎ 06-868 6139; www.intercity.co.nz) buses depart daily from the i-SITE for Napier ($44, four hours) via Wairoa ($27, 90 minutes), and Auckland ($81, 9½ hours) via Opotiki ($33, two hours) and Rotorua ($60, 4½ hours).

Organised penny-pinchers can take advantage of limited $1 advance fares on **Naked Bus** (www.nakedbus.com) to Auckland via Opotiki and Rotorua.

For courier services from Gisborne to Opotiki travelling via East Cape's scenic SH35, see p361.

CAR HIRE

The following have counters at the airport:
Avis (☎ 06-868 9084; www.avis.co.nz)
Budget (☎ 06-867 9794; www.budget.co.nz)
Hertz (☎ 06-867 9348; www.hertz.co.nz)
Thrifty (☎ 06-867 4543; www.thrifty.co.nz)

TAXI

A city-to-airport taxi fare costs about $15.
Eastland Taxis (☎ 0800 868 294, 06-867 6767)
Gisborne Taxis (☎ 0800 505 555, 06-867 2222)

GISBORNE TO HAWKE'S BAY

Heading south towards Napier you're confronted with a choice: follow SH2 along the coast or take SH36 inland via Tiniroto. Either way you'll end up in Wairoa.

The coastal route is the better choice, but SH36 is also a pleasant drive. **Doneraille Park**, 49km from Gisborne, is a peaceable bush reserve with a frigid mountain river to jump into. Freedom Camping is permitted (p363). The snow white cascades of **Te Reinga Falls**, 18km further south, are worth a short detour.

South of Gisborne, SH2 runs a few kilometres inland from the coast before entering the Wharerata State Forest. Just out of the woods, 55km from Gisborne, **Morere Hot Springs** (☎ 06-837 8856; www.morerehotsprings.co.nz; SH2; adult/child $6/3; ☼ 10am-5pm, to 9pm summer) burble up from a fault line in the beautiful **Morere Springs Scenic Reserve**. You might want to tackle the bushwalks (20 minutes to two hours) before taking the plunge. The main swimming pool is near the entrance, but a five-minute streamside walk through virgin rainforest leads to the bush setting of Nikau Baths. It's actually ancient seawater that bubbles to the surface here at around 50°C, cooling by 10°C before being pumped into the small stainless-steel baths.

Opposite the springs are the **Morere Tearooms & Camping Ground** (☎ 06-837 8792; SH2; campsites $30, d $60-90). The campsites are located alongside the babbling Tunanui Stream, with basic facilities available, while the cafe makes a respectable toasted sandwich and stocks basic provisions.

Moonlight Lodge (☎ 06-837 8824; www.morere hotsprings.co.nz; SH2, Morere; s/d/tr/q $60/75/95/120) is a peaceful, grassy enclave comprised of a 1917 farmhouse, a cottage, and two cute cabins just off the highway. Graceful trees shelter this

THE EAST COAST

small rural idyll, with a stream, sheep, and Molly, the very sweet dog.

As you continue along SH2 keep an eye out for the unusually brightly painted **Taane-nui-a-Rangi Marae**. You can get a decent view from the road; don't enter unless invited.

SH2 continues south to Nuhaka at the northern end of Hawke Bay. From here it's west to Wairoa or east to the salty Mahia Peninsula. Not far from the Nuhaka roundabout is **Kahungunu Marae** (Ihaka St). From the street you can note the carving at the house's apex of a standing warrior holding a *taiaha* (spear). It's less stylised than most traditional carving, opting for simple realism.

HAWKE'S BAY

Hawke Bay, the name given to the body of water that stretches from the sunburnt Mahia Peninsula to Cape Kidnappers, looks like it's been bitten out of the North Island's eastern flank. Add an apostrophe and an 's' and you've got a region that stretches south and inland to include fertile farmland, surf beaches, mountainous ranges and wild forests.

The southern edge of the bay is a cable-TV lifestyle channel come to life – food, wine and architecture are the shared obsessions. It's smugly comfortable but thoroughly appealing, and is best viewed through a rosé-tinted wineglass. If the weather's putting a dampener on your beach holiday plans, it's a great place to head.

MAHIA PENINSULA

The Mahia Peninsula's eroded hills, sandy beaches and vivid blue sea make it a mini-ringer of the Coromandel, but without the flash tourists and fancy subdivisions, and with the bonus of dramatic Dover-ish cliffs. It's an enduring holiday spot for the locals, who come to fish, dive, surf, birdwatch, and toast their noses. Mahia has several small settlements, a scenic reserve, and the bird-filled Maungawhio Lagoon, all of which you'll need your own transport to explore.

Cappamore Lodge (☎ 06-837 5523; oconnell capamore@clear.net.nz; 435 East Coast Rd; s/d/tr/q $80/120/140/160) is an oddball self-contained Scandinavian-style log house, crafted by Margaret and Bill. It's huge (comfortably sleeping six) with two living areas and great views from the doorstep.

Seashore B&B (☎ 06-837 5525; www.mahianz.com; 182 Newcastle St, Taylors Bay; s/tw/tr $80/140/180; ☐) is indeed right on the seashore. This modern home has friendly hosts, two bright en-suite rooms, a bunkroom sleeping five and guest lounge. Kayaks are available.

On the east coast, **Café Mahia** (☎ 06-837 5094; 476 East Coast Rd; meals $14-20; 10am-4pm Thu-Sun, 10am-4pm daily in summer, dinner Thu & Sat; ☐) sells a surprising array of preserves and doubles as the local post office and bread shop. It also has grandmotherly food, dubious coffee, and lovely deck from which you can drink in the view. Book ahead for dinner.

Sunset Point Sports Bar & Bistro (☎ 06-837 5071; cnr Newcastle & Ratau Sts; mains $20-30; 10am-late) is the (only) place in town to grab a beer and meet the locals. Pool table, darts, (fresh) fish and chips, a quality garden bar and surprisingly tuneful live music most weekends.

WAIROA
pop 5228

Poor little Wairoa is trying really hard to shirk its rough-edged reputation. A new **Wairoa Township River Walkway** takes in sites of interest along the main street, including the old solid kauri **Portland Island Lighthouse** (1877), which once stood off the Mahia Peninsula and now flashes proudly at the entrance to the town centre.

Like many small towns, economic depression seems to have spared heritage buildings from the wrecking ball. As we write there is talk of reopening the restored 1931 **Gaiety Theatre** (252 Marine Pde), so stroll by and take a look. **Wairoa Museum** (☎ 06-838 3108; wairoa museum@xtra.co.nz; 142 Marine Pde; admission by donation; 10am-4pm Mon-Fri, to 1pm Sat) has an Italianate facade from its former life as a bank.

Bird fanciers should explore **Whakamahi Lagoon**, at the river mouth, and **Whakaki Lagoon**, 10km east of town.

The enthusiastic staff at **Wairoa i-SITE** (☎ 06-838 7440; www.wairoadc.govt.nz; cnr SH2 & Queen St; 9am-4.45pm Mon-Fri, 10am-11am & 3.15-4pm Sat & Sun; ☐) have information on the wider area along with maps, internet access ($3 per 15 minutes), fishing licenses and DOC passes.

Sleeping & Eating

our pick Riverside Motor Camp (☎ 06-838 6301; www. riversidemotorcamp.co.nz; 19 Marine Pde; campsites $30, dm/d/tr $20/60/80; ☐) Perky owners and the prettiest facilities block you ever did see make this

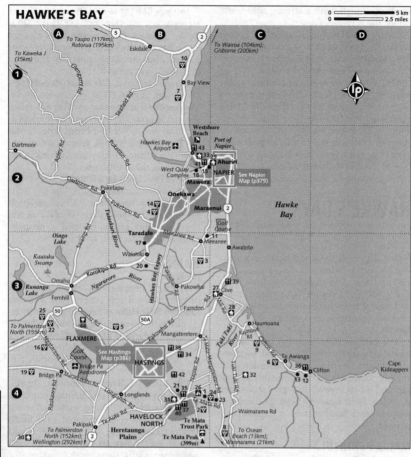

HAWKE'S BAY

place a winner. There's pleasant camping and cute cabins, while the backpacker dorm takes the form of a large room with bunks and TV.

Oslers Bakery & Café (☎ 06-838 8299; 116 Marine Pde; meals $5-15; ☻ 8am-4pm Mon-Fri, to 3pm Sat & Sun) Call in for an award-winning pie ($3 to $4), sweet treats, decent coffee and cooked breakfast (but maybe not all at once).

East End Café (☎ 06-838 6070; 250 Marine Pde; meals $8-18; ☻ 7.30am-4pm Tue-Fri, 8.30am-late Sat, 8.30-4pm Sun) In the same building as the Gaiety Theatre, the East End is a breath of fresh air with its spacious interior, toasted sandwiches ($6), fabulous friands, and a concise blackboard ranging from morning eggs to pizza and seafood chowder. Great coffee and juices, too.

Getting There & Away

All **InterCity** (☎ 06-838 7440; www.intercity.co.nz) buses that travel between Gisborne and Napier pass through Wairoa.

TE UREWERA NATIONAL PARK

Shrouded in mist and mysticism, Te Urewera National Park is the North Island's largest, encompassing 212,673 hectares of virgin forest cut with lakes and rivers. The highlight is Lake Waikaremoana (Sea of Rippling Waters), a deep crucible of water encircled by the Lake Waikaremoana Track, one of NZ's Great Walks. Rugged bluffs drop away to reedy inlets, the lake's mirror surface disturbed only by mountain zephyrs and the occasional waterbird taking to the skies.

The name Te Urewera still has the capacity to make Pakeha New Zealanders feel slightly uneasy – and not just because it translates as 'The Burnt Penis'. There's something primal and untamed about this wild woodland, with its rich history of Maori resistance.

The local Tuhoe people – prosaically known as the 'Children of the Mist' – never signed the Treaty of Waitangi and fought with Rewi Maniapoto at Orakau (p234) during the Waikato Wars. The army of Te Kooti (p368) took refuge here during running battles with government troops. The claimant of Te Kooti's spiritual mantle, Rua Kenana, led a thriving community beneath the sacred mountain Maungapohatu (1366m) from 1905 until his politically inspired 1916 arrest. This effectively erased the last bastion of Maori independence in the country. Maungapohatu never recovered, and only a small settlement remains. Nearby, Ruatahuna's extraordinary Mataatua Marae celebrates Te Kooti's exploits.

Tuhoe remain proud of their identity and traditions, with around 40% still speaking *te reo* (the language) on a regular basis. Te Urewera's immense and remote wilderness of seemingly endless forested ridges and pristine waters is a magical place to learn about their culture.

Information

Te Urewera National Park visitor centre (☎ 06-837 3803; www.doc.govt.nz; SH38; ☻ 8am-4.45pm) at Aniwaniwa is currently limited to one small room in a mouldering building (the future of which was undecided at the time of research).

Get your weather forecasts, accommodation information and hut or camping-ground passes for the Lake Waikaremoana Track here.

Activities
LAKE WAIKAREMOANA TRACK

The 46km track scales the spectacular Panekiri Bluff, with open panoramas interspersed with fern groves and forest. The walk is rated as moderate with the only difficult section being the Panekiri ascent. During summer it can get busy so it pays to book ahead.

Although it's a year-round track, winter rain deters many people and makes conditions much more challenging. At this altitude (580m above sea level), temperatures can drop quickly, even in summer. Walkers should take portable stoves and fuel as there are no cooking facilities en route.

There are five huts (adult/child $25/free) and campsites (per night adult/child $12/free) spaced along the track, all of which must be prebooked through DOC as far ahead as possible, regardless of the season. Book at the Aniwaniwa, Gisborne, Wairoa, Whakatane or Napier DOC offices, i-SITEs or online at www.doc.govt.nz.

If you have a car, it is safest to leave it at the Lake Waikaremoana Motor Camp (p377) or Big Bush Holiday Park (p377) then take a water taxi (p377) to the trail heads.

Propel yourself onto the trail either clockwise from just outside Onepoto in the south or anticlockwise from Hopuruahine Bridge in the north. From Onepoto, all the steep climbing

THE EAST COAST

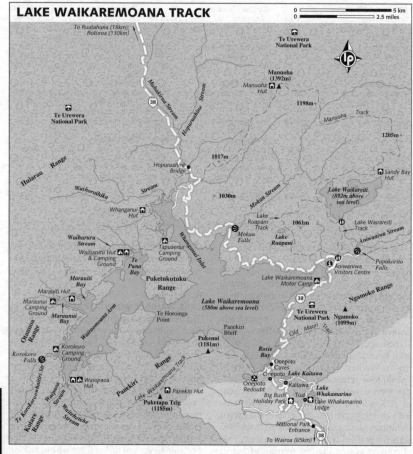

LAKE WAIKAREMOANA TRACK

0 — 5 km
0 — 2.5 miles

To Ruatahuna (18km);
Rotorua (130km)

Te Urewera
National Park

Manuoha
(1392m)
Manuoha
Hut

1198m+

Manuoha Track

1205m+

Te Urewera
National Park

Mahakirua Stream

Hopuruahine Stream

Sandy Bay
Hut

1017m

Hopuruahine
Bridge

Huiarau Range

Waihorotika Stream

Lake Waikareiti
(892m above
sea level)

+1030m

Mokau Stream

Lake Wairareiti
Track

Whanganui
Hut

Lake
Ruapani
Track

1061m

Aniwaniwa Stream

Mokau
Falls

Lake
Ruapani

Papakorito
Falls

Waiharuru
Stream

Tapuaenui
Camping
Ground

Waiharuru Hut
& Camping
Ground

Te
Puna
Bay

Whanganui Inlet

Aniwaniwa
Visitors Centre

Lake Waikaremoana
Motor Camp

Marauiti
Bay

Puketukutuku
Range

Marauiti Hut

Lake Waikaremoana
(580m above sea level)

Ngamoko Range

Marauiti
Camping
Ground

Marauunui
Bay

Te Horoinga
Point

Te Urewera
National Park

Ngamoko
(1099m)

Wairaumoana Arm

Panekiri
Bluff

Old Maori Trail

Otamuna Range

Korokoro
Camping
Ground

Pukenui
(1181m)

Rosie
Bay

Onepoto
Caves

Lake Kaitawa

Korokoro
Falls

Waioaoa
Hut

Panekiri Range

Onepoto

Kaitawa

Onepoto
Redoubt

Lake
Whakamarino

Te Korokoro-o-haatini Str

Panekiri Hut

Lake Waikaremoana Track

Big Bush
Holiday Park

Tual

Lake Whakamarino
Lodge

Waipaoa Stream

Waieheiehe Stream

Kakare Range

Puketapu Trig
(1185m)

National Park
Entrance

To Wairoa (65km)

---

happens in the first few hours. Water on this
section of the track is limited so fill your bottles
before heading off.

Estimated walking times:

Route	Time
Onepoto to Panekiri Hut	5hr
Panekiri Hut to Waiopaoa Hut	3–4hr
Waiopaoa Hut to Marauiti Hut	4½hr
Marauiti Hut to Waiharuru Hut	2hr
Waiharuru Hut to Whanganui Hut	2½hr
Whanganui Hut to Hopuruahine Bridge	2hr

OTHER WALKS

There are dozens of walks within the park's
vast boundaries, some of which are outlined

in DOC's *Lake Waikaremoana Walks* and
Recreation in Northern Te Urewera pamphlets
($2.50).

Three- to five-day adventures for intrepid
and experienced trampers can be had in the
Whakatane River area starting near Ruatahuna.
Be aware that this is serious backcountry and
that there are no transport services.

The **Manuoha–Waikareiti Track** is a tough
three-day walk, starting near Hopuruahine
and heading up to Manuoha Hut, the park's
highest point (1392m). It then follows a ridge
down to Lake Waikareiti via Sandy Bay Hut,
finishing at Aniwaniwa.

Shorter walks and day walks include the
Old Maori Trail (four hours return) from Rosie
Bay to Lake Kaitawa; the **Lake Waikareiti Track**

(two hours return, four hours to Sandy Bay Hut one way) through beech and rimu forest; and the **Lake Ruapani Track** (six hours) including wetland wanderings.

Lake Waikareiti (892m), with its untouched islands, is an enchanting place. A fittingly fabulous way to explore it is in a rowboat (you can pick up a boatshed key from the DOC visitor centre for a small charge). You may also be lured in for a skinny dip.

Walking Legends (☎ 0800 925 569; www.walking legends.com) is an enthusiastic and experienced company running three- to four-day guided walks around Lake Waikaremoana and through Te Urewera (from $1080/880 adult/child all-inclusive).

Sleeping & Eating

DOC has over 30 huts and campsites within the park, most of which are very basic (p375).

Lake Waikaremoana Motor Camp (☎ 06-837 3826; www.lake.co.nz; SH38; campsites per adult/child $12/5, cabins $45, units $78-140) Right on the shore, this place has Swiss-looking chalets, fisherman's cabins and campsites, most with watery views. The on-site shop is full of essentials such as hot pies, chocolate and a swarm of fishing flies. The camp can also hook you up with water taxis and petrol.

Big Bush Holiday Park (☎ 0800 525 392; www.lake waikaremoana.co.nz; SH38; campsites per person $12-15, dm/d $25/80) Located 4km from the Onepoto trail head, Big Bush offers tent sites, trim cabins and acceptable backpacker rooms. Pick-ups, water taxis/scenic charters and storage are available.

Lake Whakamarino Lodge (☎ 06-837 3876; www.lakelodge.co.nz; Esplanade, Tuai; s/d/ste $57/69/100) While the lake's name might provoke sheep jokes, trout is the passion here. Originally workers' housing for the local power station, it's now a comfortable *iwi*-run fishing lodge with home-cooked meals by request.

Getting There & Around

Approximately 95km of State Highway 38 between Wairoa and Rotorua remains unsealed and it'll take around four bone-rattling hours to do the entire journey (Wairoa to Aniwaniwa 61km, Aniwaniwa to Rotorua 139km).

Big Bush Water Taxi (☎ 0800 525 392; www.lakewaikaremoana.co.nz) will ship you to either Onepoto or Hopuruahine trail head ($30 return), with hut-to-hut pack transfers for the less gung-ho. It also runs shuttles to and from Wairoa ($30 one way).

Home Bay Water Taxi & Cruises (☎ 06-837 3826; www.waikaremoana.com) operates from Lake Waikaremoana Motor Camp (left) to either trail head ($35 return) and also offers lake cruises ($30). **Waikaremoana Guided Tours** (☎ 06-837 3729; www.waikaremoanawatertaxi.co.nz) provide a similar service, plus kayak/dinghy hire and guided trips.

WAIROA TO NAPIER

This stretch thrusts through verdant farmland for much of its 117km. Most of it follows a railway line that is currently only used for freight – you'll see what a travesty that is when you pass under the **Mohaka viaduct** (1937), the highest rail viaduct in Australasia (97m).

Occupied by early Maori, **Lake Tutira** has walkways and a bird sanctuary. At Tutira village, just north of the lake, Pohokura Rd leads to the wonderful **Boundary Stream Reserve**, a major conservation area. Three loop tracks start from the road, ranging in length from 40 minutes to three hours. Also along this road you'll find the **Opouahi** and **Bellbird Bush Scenic Reserves**, which all offer rewarding walks.

Off Waipatiki Rd, 34km outside Napier, is the 64-hectare **Waipatiki Scenic Reserve**, echoing with tui and kereru calls while the **White Pine Bush Scenic Reserve**, 29km from Napier on SH2, bristles with kahikatea and nikau palms. **Tangoio Falls Scenic Reserve**, 27km north of Napier, has Te Ana Falls, stands of wheki-ponga (tree ferns) and native orchids. Between White Pine and Tangoio Reserves the **Tangoio Walkway** (three hours return) follows Kareaara Stream.

The highway surfs the coast for the last 25km, with impressive views towards Napier. Hawke's Bay wine country starts in earnest at the mouth of the Esk River. Even the driver should safely be able to stop for a restrained tasting at one of the excellent vineyards just off SH2 (or both if you're spitting).

Esk Valley Estate (Map p374; ☎ 06-872 7430; www.esk valley.co.nz; 745 Main Rd, Bay View; tastings free; ⌚ 10am-5pm) is a lovely spot to bring your picnic and enjoy some great reds. With its relaxed, rustic feel, **Crab Farm Winery** (Map p374; ☎ 06-836 6678; www.crabfarmwinery.co.nz; 511 Main Rd, Bay View; tastings free; ⌚ 10am-5pm Thu-Mon, cafe 12-3pm Thu-Mon, dinner Fri) is a good stop for lunch and a glass of rosé (among others). See p388 for the full rundown on Hawke's Bay wineries.

NAPIER

pop 55,000

You don't have to be particularly cultured to enjoy Napier but you might find its passion for architecture and fine wine surprisingly contagious. Before long you'll be blathering on about the Chicago School, Mayan decorative devices and 'hints of passionfruit on the palate' with the best of them.

The Napier of today is the silver lining of the dark cloud that was NZ's worst natural disaster. Rebuilt after the deadly 1931 earthquake in the popular styles of the time, the city retains a unique concentration of art-deco buildings. Architecture obsessives flock here from all over the world and the town milks it for all it's worth. Don't expect the Chrysler Building – Napier's art deco is resolutely low-rise – but you will find intact 1930s streetscapes, which can provoke a *Great Gatsby* swagger in the least romantic soul.

For the layperson it's a charismatic, sunny, composed city with the air of an affluent English seaside resort about it.

History

The area has been settled since around the 12th century and was known to Maori as Ahuriri. By the time James Cook eyeballed it in October 1769, Ngati Kahungunu was the dominant tribe, controlling the coast to Wellington.

In the 1830s whalers malingered around Ahuriri, establishing a trading base in 1839. By the 1850s the Crown had purchased – by often dubious means – 1.4 million acres of Hawke's Bay land, leaving Ngati Kahungunu with less than 4000 acres. The town of Napier was planned in 1854 and obsequiously named after the British general and colonial administrator Charles Napier.

At 10.46am on 3 February 1931, the city was levelled by a catastrophic earthquake (7.9 on the Richter scale). Fatalities in Napier and nearby Hastings numbered 258. Napier suddenly found itself 40 sq km larger, as the earthquake heaved sections of what was once a lagoon 2m above sea level (Napier Airport was once more 'port', less 'air'). The government claimed the extra land, also taking (without compensation) six former Ngati Kahungunu islands. A fevered rebuilding program ensued, constructing one of the world's most uniformly art-deco cities.

Orientation

Bluff Hill looms at the northern end of town dividing the CBD and Ahuriri, with its cosmopolitan bar and restaurant strip. Murmuring with economic hubbub, Hastings and Emerson Sts are the prime thoroughfares, with Emerson St evolving into a semipedestrian zone.

Free town maps are available at Napier's i-SITE (below). Road maps are available at the **Automobile Association** (AA; ☎ 06-834 2590; www.aatravel.co.nz; 87 Dickens St)

Information

The big banks cluster around the corner of Hastings and Emerson Sts, with ATMs scattered throughout the centre. Internet access is available at the i-SITE and several cafes in the city.

Beattie & Forbes (☎ 06-835 8968; 70 Tennyson St) A good selection of books.

DOC (☎ 06-834 3111; www.doc.govt.nz; 59 Marine Pde; ☼ 9am-4.15pm Mon-Fri) Tourist information.

Napier Health Centre (☎ 06-878 8109; 76 Wellesley Rd; ☼ 24hr)

Napier i-SITE (☎ 06-834 1911; www.visitus.co.nz; 100 Marine Pde; ☼ 9am-5pm; 💻) Tourist information.

Napier police station (☎ 06-831 0700; Station St; ☼ 24hr)

Napier post office (151 Hastings St)

Sights

ARCHITECTURE

The 1931 quake demolished most of Napier's brick buildings. Frantic reconstruction between 1931 and 1933 caught architects in the throes of global art-deco mania. Art deco, along with Spanish Mission and Stripped Classical, was cheap (debts were high), safe (falling stone columns and balconies had killed many during the earthquake) and contemporary (residents wanted to make a fresh start). A cohesive architectural vision grew from the ruins, giving Napier a new *raison d'être*.

The art-deco architectural style first made headlines at the 1925 Paris International Exposition of Modern Decorative and Industrial Arts. The deco is in the detail: zigzags, lightning bolts, sunbursts, fountains, ziggurats, speed lines, streamline shapes and ancient motifs (Mayan, Egyptian and, occasionally, Maori). Soft pastel colours (think *Miami Vice*) are another deco giveaway. Spanish Mission imitates mud-brick adobes,

NAPIER

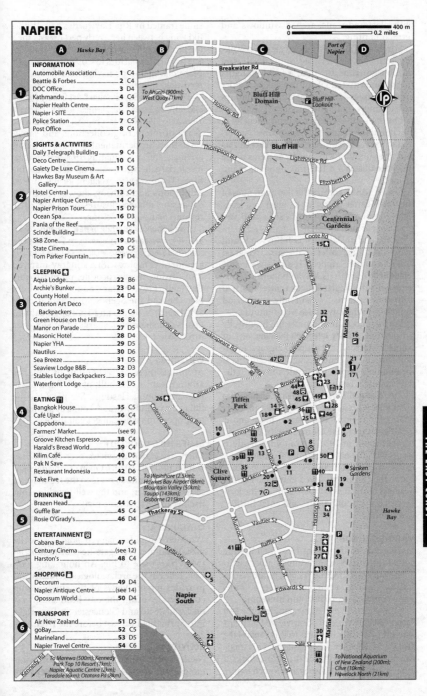

0 _____ 400 m
0 _____ 0.2 miles

INFORMATION
Automobile Association 1 C4
Beattie & Forbes 2 C4
DOC Office 3 D4
Kathmandu 4 C4
Napier Health Centre 5 B6
Napier i-SITE 6 C4
Police Station 7 C5
Post Office 8 C4

SIGHTS & ACTIVITIES
Daily Telegraph Building 9 C4
Deco Centre 10 C4
Gaiety De Luxe Cinema 11 C5
Hawkes Bay Museum & Art
  Gallery 12 D4
Hotel Central 13 C4
Napier Antique Centre 14 C4
Napier Prison Tours 15 D2
Ocean Spa 16 D3
Pania of the Reef 17 D4
Scinde Building 18 C4
Sk8 Zone 19 D5
State Cinema 20 C5
Tom Parker Fountain 21 D4

SLEEPING 🏠
Aqua Lodge 22 B6
Archie's Bunker 23 D4
County Hotel 24 C4
Criterion Art Deco
  Backpackers 25 C4
Green House on the Hill 26 B4
Manor on Parade 27 D5
Masonic Hotel 28 D4
Napier YHA 29 D5
Nautilus 30 D6
Sea Breeze 31 D5
Seaview Lodge B&B 32 D3
Stables Lodge Backpackers 33 D5
Waterfront Lodge 34 D5

EATING 🍴
Bangkok House 35 C5
Café Ujazi 36 C4
Cappadona 37 C4
Farmers' Market .... (see 9)
Groove Kitchen Espresso 38 C4
Harald's Bread World 39 C4
Kilim Café 40 D5
Pak N Save 41 C5
Restaurant Indonesia 42 D6
Take Five 43 D5

DRINKING 🍷
Brazen Head 44 C4
Guffle Bar 45 C4
Rosie O'Grady's 46 D4

ENTERTAINMENT 🎭
Cabana Bar 47 C4
Century Cinema .... (see 12)
Harston's 48 C4

SHOPPING 🛍
Decorum 49 D4
Napier Antique Centre .... (see 14)
Opossum World 50 D4

TRANSPORT
Air New Zealand 51 D5
goBay 52 C5
Marineland 53 D5
Napier Travel Centre 54 C6

THE EAST COAST

with plastered walls, arched windows and terracotta tiling.

For guided and self-guided art-deco walking tours of Napier, see opposite. If you haven't got time for that, a few highlights follow herewith (and if you can, take a wander around Napier at night when many buildings are strikingly highlighted in neon).

On the south side of town on Dickens St you'll find the deluxe Moorish-Spanish spirals and stucco of the former **Gaiety de Luxe Cinema** and fine sunburst window decorations of the old **State Cinema** – a fine mix of Spanish and art deco.

On Dalton St admire the flamingo hues of the **Hotel Central**, all zigzag swagger and leadlight complexity – it's now a strip club and massage parlour.

At the end of Dalton St is Tennyson St and many striking architectural gems. Two great examples of the Stripped Classical style are the **Scinde Building** with its Mayan botanical flourishes and the **Napier Antique Centre** adorned with *koru* patterns – one of only four period buildings in the city to use Maori motifs.

Further along Tennyson is the beautifully proportioned **Daily Telegraph Building**, one of Napier's stars, with its superb zigzags, fountain shapes and central ziggurat aesthetic. If the building is open, nip inside and ogle at the painstakingly restored foyer.

The **National Tobacco Company Building** (Map p374; cnr Bridge & Ossian Sts; ☉ 9am-5pm Mon-Fri) is arguably the region's deco masterpiece and is located a short ride from the city centre in Ahuriri. Built in 1933, it combines art-deco forms with the natural motifs of art nouveau. Roses, raupo (bulrushes) and grapevines frame the elegantly curved entrance. During business hours it's possible to pull on the leaf-shaped brass door handles and enter the first two rooms.

MARINE PARADE

Marine Pde is an elegant tree-lined avenue dotted with motels and restored timber earthquake survivors. Along its length are parks, sunken gardens, a minigolf course, a swimming complex, aquarium and museum.

Near the north end of the parade is the **Tom Parker Fountain** which is best viewed at night when it is lavishly lit. Next to it is **Pania of the Reef** (1954), Napier's iconic statue. This tragi-romantic figure from local folklore looks a little Maori and a lot Disney, her forced toothy smile framed by Rita Hayworth's hair. With a tiki lying between her overly pert breasts she's the perfect embodiment of the dusky maiden. She has her similarities to Copenhagen's *Little Mermaid*, including having been stolen and recovered in 2005.

The **Hawke's Bay Museum & Art Gallery** (☎ 06-835 7781; www.hbmag.co.nz; 9 Herschell St; adult/child/family $10/5/20; ☉ 10am-6pm) is a repository for a wide range of interesting collections and showcases these in permanent displays of Maori artefacts and a fascinating 1931 earthquake memorial gallery (do watch the deeply moving film). There are also excellent locally curated exhibitions and touring shows. Watch for expansion-related closures from late 2010; revamp plans look exciting.

The **National Aquarium of New Zealand** (☎ 06-834 1404; www.nationalaquarium.co.nz; 546 Marine Pde; adult/child $16/8; ☉ 9am-5pm, feedings 10am & 2pm) is a modern complex with a stingray-inspired roof. Inside are a crocodile, piranhas, turtles, eels, kiwi, tuatara and a whole lotta fish. 'Behind the Scenes' tours (adult/child $31/16) leave at 9am and 1pm and qualified divers can swim with sharks (dive $68, gear hire $36).

WINERIES

Although there are a handful of wineries around Napier, the bulk of the Bay's offerings are around Hastings. See p388 for the full winery rundown, and Tours, opposite, for tour operators who can get you there.

BLUFF HILL LOOKOUT

There are expansive views over Hawke Bay from Bluff Hill (102m). Open during daylight hours, the circuitous route to the top makes a pleasant wander, and the well-loved lookout itself is a nice spot for a picnic.

OTATARA PA

Wooden palisades, carved *pou* (memorial posts) and a carved gate help bring this *pa* (Map p374) site to life. An hour-long loop walk takes in the archaeological remains and provides terrific views of the surrounding countryside. From the city head southwest on Taradale Rd and Gloucester St. Turn right into Springfield Rd just before the river.

Activities

Napier's pebbly city beach isn't safe for swimming; locals head north of the city to **Westshore**

(Map p374) or to the surf beaches south of Cape Kidnappers (p391). Otherwise head to **Ocean Spa** (☎ 06-835 8553; 42 Marine Pde; adult/child $8/6; ⊙ 6am-10pm Mon-Sat, 8am-10pm Sun), a spiffy waterfront pool complex that includes a beauty spa, gym and cafe.

To the south of town **Napier Aquatic Centre** (☎ 06-834 4150; www.napieraquatic.co.nz; Maadi Rd, Onekawa; adult/child $4.20/3.10, waterslides unlimited rides $4.20; ⊙ 6am-9pm Mon-Fri, 11am-6pm Sat & Sun) has a 50m pool, waterslides, spas and a kids' pool.

Skaters should head to **Sk8 Zone** (☎ 06-835 6003; Marine Pde; incl skate hire adult/child $11/9; ⊙ 3.30-5.30pm Mon-Fri, 10am-5pm Sat & Sun), where there's an outdoor and indoor skating rink complete with ramps. If you fancy a spin along Marine Pde they also hire rollerblades (adult/child $10/8).

Pandora Kayaks (Map p374; ☎ 06-835 0684; www. pandorakayaks.co.nz; 53 Pandora Rd; kayaks per hr from $14, bikes per day $30; ⊙ daily) hire kayaks, windsurfers, surfboards, small yachts and bikes.

See if you're any closer to challenging Spiderman on the climbing wall at **Kiwi Adventure Co** (Map p374; ☎ 06-834 3500; www.kiwi -adventure.co.nz; 58 West Quay, Ahuriri; adult/child $15/12; ⊙ 3-9pm Tue & Thu, 10am-6pm Sat & Sun). It also organises caving and kayaking trips.

Sixty kilometres north of Napier on SH5 is **Mountain Valley** (☎ 06-834 9756; www.mountainvalley. co.nz; McVicar Rd, Te Pohue), which offers horse trekking, white-water rafting and kayaking ($25 to $150). There's also accommodation on-site.

Hawke's Bay Wine Country Cat (Map p374; ☎ 0800 946 3228; www.hbwinecountrycat.com; West Quay, Ahuriri; cruises $25-65) schmoozes out onto Hawke Bay on a flexible schedule. It also runs the **Hawke's Bay Wine Country Duck** (☎ 0800 946 338; www.hbwine countryduck.com; departs i-SITE; 1hr tour adult/child $40/25; ⊙ tours 10.30am, 1.30pm & 3pm), an amphibious vehicle that heads in and out of the water on a (groan) 'Art Ducko' tour.

Tours

The majority of tours around Napier are focused on architecture, or wineries.

Napier's Art Deco Trust promotes and protects the city's architectural heritage. Its one-hour guided deco walk ($14) departs the i-SITE daily at 10am; the two-hour version ($20) leaves the **Deco Centre** (☎ 06-835 0022; www.artdeconapier.com; 163 Tennyson St; ⊙ 9am-5pm) at 2pm daily. These excellent walks include an introductory spiel, DVD screening and

refreshments. The Deco Centre stocks assorted paraphernalia, including brochures for the excellent self-guided *Art Deco Walk* ($5), *Art Deco Scenic Drive* ($5) and *Marewa Meander* ($3). Marewa is a suburb southwest of Napier's city centre, and deco through-and-through.

Numerous operators offer tours of the deco delights and excursions around the local area:

Absolute de Tours (☎ 06-844 8699; www.absolute detours.co.nz) Runs the 'Deco Tour' of the city, Marewa and Bluff Hill ($38, 75 minutes) in conjunction with the Deco Centre, as well as half-day tours of Napier and Hastings ($60).

Deco Affair Tours (☎ 06-835 4492; www.decoaffair. com; tours $20-90) Trips the light fantastic in a cherry red 1934 Buick hosted by the endearingly eccentric Bertie, clad in full period regalia.

Ferg's Fantastic Tours (☎ 0800 428 687; www. fairwaytours.co.nz; half/full day $65/149) Explores Napier and surrounding areas.

Packard Promenade (☎ 06-835 1455; www.packard promenades.co.nz; tours $130-600) Offers deco and wine tours, in a 1939 Packard Six.

Self-guided bicycle tours are offered by **Takaro Trails** (☎ 06-836 5385; www.takarotrails.co.nz; half- to 5-day tours $55-799) with gear, baggage moving, and back-up supplied. Ask about mountain-bike adventures in Eskdale Mountain Bike Park.

If you fancy going to jail, **Napier Prison Tours** (☎ 06-835 9933; www.napierprison.com; 55 Coote Rd; tours $20) offers fascinating self-guided audio tours (9am to 9pm) and hosted tours (9.30am and 3pm).

For listings of Hawke's Bay winery tours, see p387.

Festivals & Events

In the third week of February, Napier and Hastings co-host the sensational **Art Deco Weekend** (☎ 06-835 0022; www.artdeconapier.com). Dinners, dances, drinks, balls, bands and Gatsby-esque fancy dress fill the week with shenanigans. Bertie, Napier's art-deco ambassador (above), is omnipresent.

In mid-February, Mission Estate (p388) holds the popular open-air **Mission Concert** (☎ 06-845 9350; www.missionconcert.co.nz; tickets $105-205), importing a golden-oldie superstar (Tom Jones, Jimmy Barnes, the Four Tops etc) to belt out some classics.

Not to be outdone, Church Road (p388) hosts **Church Road Jazz** (tickets $45) as part of Harvest Hawke's Bay (p387) in early February.

THE EAST COAST

Sleeping

BUDGET

Aqua Lodge (Map p379; ☎ 06-835 4523; aquaback@inhb.co.nz; 53 Nelson Cres; campsites per person $17, dm $25, d $60-74; 🖥 🛜 🐾) Aqua Lodge sprawls between neighbouring houses on a quiet suburban street, with campsites on the back lawn. It's a fun place – even if 'sex and peeing' are banned from the pool.

Kennedy Park Top 10 Resort (☎ 06-843 9126; www.kennedypark.co.nz; Storkey St, Marewa; campsites per person $19-21, units $107-150; 🖥 🐾) Less a camping ground and more an entire suburb of holidaymakers, this Top 10 park is top dog on the Napier camping scene and winner of the bay's 2009 Sustainable Business Award. It's the closest camping ground to town (2.5km out) and has every facility imaginable, although a larger kitchen would be nice.

our pick Criterion Art Deco Backpackers (Map p379; ☎ 06-835 2059; www.criterionartdeco.co.nz; 48 Emerson St; dm $20, s $40-75, d $55-80, tr/q $78/87 all incl continental breakfast; 🖥 🛜) If it's interesting architecture and a central location you're after, here you have it. The vast communal area showcases the impressive internal features of what is Napier's best Spanish Mission specimen. There are special deals for guests in the bar-restaurant downstairs.

Waterfront Lodge (Map p379; ☎ 06-835 3429; www.napierwaterfront.co.nz; 217 Marine Pde; dm $21-24, s/d $42/62; 🖥 🛜) The affable hosts work hard to create a communal good-time atmosphere at this well-maintained hostel. It's a great choice if you're looking for seasonal work – they actively vet potential employers, weeding out the dodgy ones.

Stables Lodge Backpackers (Map p379; ☎ 06-835 6242; www.stableslodge.co.nz; 370 Hastings St; dm $22-26, d $58; 🖥 🛜) Formerly an actual stables; if you fill one of the small dorm rooms with blokes it'll probably smell that way again by morning. There's a barbecue courtyard, murals, hammocks, a resident cat and free internet.

Archie's Bunker (Map p379; ☎ 06-833 7990; www.archiesbunker.co.nz; 14 Herschell St; dm/s $23/35, d $56-60; 🖥 🛜) One street back from the foreshore, Archie's is a shipshape modern hostel in an old office building. A few of the rooms are windowless, but on the whole this is a well-ventilated, quiet and secure arrangement with friendly owners and bike hire.

Napier YHA (Map p379; ☎ 06-835 7039; www.yha.co.nz; 277 Marine Pde; dm $29-33, s/d $40/68; 🖥 🛜) Napier's friendly YHA is housed in a beach-front earthquake-survivor with a seemingly endless ramble of rooms; try to book one back from the street. There's a fabulous overhanging reading nook and a sunny rear courtyard.

MIDRANGE

Masonic Hotel (Map p379; ☎ 06-835 8689; www.masonic.co.nz; cnr Herschell & Tennyson Sts; s/d/tr $85/105/130) Trading on its deco heritage, the Masonic is right in the heart of town. In fact, it may well *be* the heart of town, with its accommodation, restaurants and pub taking up most of a city block. The old-fashioned rooms have period charm but the worn furnishings certainly don't add to it.

Sea Breeze (Map p379; ☎ 06-835 8067; seabreeze.napier@xtra.co.nz; 281 Marine Pde; s $95, d $110-130) Inside this Victorian seafront villa are three richly coloured themed rooms (Chinese, Indian and Turkish), decorated with a cornucopia of artefacts and exotic flair.

Green House on the Hill (Map p379; ☎ 06-835 4475; www.the-green-house.co.nz; 18b Milton Oaks, Milton Rd; s/d $110/135; 🖥 🛜) This meat-free B&B is up a steep hill and rewards with leafy surrounds and city views. The guest floor has one en suite room and one with its own bathroom. Home-baked goodies and fine herbal teas are likely to make an appearance.

Rocks Motorlodge (Map p374; ☎ 06-835 9626; www.therocksmotel.co.nz; 27 Meeanee Quay, Westshore; units $110-180; 🖥 🛜) Located just 80m from the beach, the Rocks has corrugated stylings and woodcarving that have raised the bar on Westshore's motel row. Interiors are plush with a colour-splash, and some have a spa bath, others a clawfoot. Free internet, free gym, and laundry.

Seaview Lodge B&B (Map p379; ☎ 06-835 0202; cvulodge@xtra.co.nz; 5 Seaview Tce; s $120-130, d $150-170) This grand Victorian villa (1890) is queen of all she surveys – which is most of the town and a fair bit of ocean. The elegant rooms have tasteful period elements and either bathroom or en suite. It's hard to resist a sunset tipple on the veranda, which opens off the swanky guest lounge.

Manor on Parade (Map p379; ☎ 06-834 3885; manoronparade@xtra.co.nz; 283 Marine Pde; d $140-180) Comfortable and friendly, this two-storey wooden villa on the waterfront has proved itself a solid option, having survived the earthquake and in its latter-day incarnation as a B&B.

TOP END

Crown Hotel (Map p374; ☎ 06-833 8300; www.thecrown napier.co.nz; cnr Bridge St & Hardinge Rd, Ahuriri; apt $150-600; 🖳 🛜) The conversion of this 1932 pub into a ritzy apartment-style hotel must have broken a few fishermen's hearts. The new wing may be generically modern but it offers superb ocean views. There's also a gym.

Nautilus (Map p379; ☎ 06-974 6550; www.nautilus napier.co.nz; 387 Marine Pde; studio/ste $175-300; 🖳 🛜) Napier's newest hotel, and a relatively good bit of architecture it is, too. Views from every room, decor with spunk, spa baths, private balconies and an in-house restaurant.

County Hotel (Map p379; ☎ 06-835 7800; www. countyhotel.co.nz; 12 Browning St; r/ste $350/488; 🖳 🛜) There's luxury infused between the masonry at this elegantly restored Edwardian building (a rare brick earthquake survivor). Chambers restaurant breathes refined formality at dinner (mains $30 to $42) while Winston's portrait gazes victoriously over Churchill's Champagne and Snug Bar.

Eating

RESTAURANTS

Provedore (Map p374; ☎ 06-834 0189; 60 West Quay; tapas $6-15, mains $27-35; 🕙 5pm-late Tue-Fri, 10am-late Sat & Sun) A chic little number, from the deco facade in. Partake in some of the best food in Napier, from tapas, to mains, dessert and cheese. With a clutch of good NZ beers and fine wines, Provedore lures the sophisticated barfly, too.

Kilim Café (Map p379; ☎ 06-835 9100; 193 Hastings St; mains $15-19; 🕙 11am-late; Ⓥ) Authentic Turkish cuisine in a rather smart cafe environment, adorned with suitably Ottoman cushions and wall hangings. Kebabs, felafel, hummus, dolmas, pide and meze – all fresh and every one tasty. Eat in or take away.

Bangkok House (Map p379; ☎ 06-835 5335; 205 Dickens St; mains $16-25; 🕙 lunch Tue-Sat, dinner Tue-Sun; Ⓥ) Cheery Thai restaurant with an expansive menu of Siam favourites. Fresh, spicy and good value, too. Deservedly popular with locals.

Restaurant Indonesia (Map p379; ☎ 06-835 8303; 409 Marine Pde; mains $25-29; 🕙 dinner Wed-Sun; Ⓥ) Crammed with Indonesian curios, this intimate space oozes authenticity. Lip-smacking Indo-Dutch *rijsttafel* smorgasbords are the house speciality (14 dishes, $35).

CAFES

our pick **Cappadona** (Map p379; ☎ 06-835 3368; 189 Emerson St; snacks $2-9, mains $9-16; 🕙 7am-5pm) In a town of good cafes, this is a standout, both for its modern, upbeat ambience, and a packed cabinet of downright foxy food. Besides an alluring row of biscuit jars, iced muffins and cakes, there are fresh sandwiches, salads and pastries. The hot menu has brunchy, lunchy dishes.

Westshore Fish Café (Map p374; ☎ 06-834 0227; 112a Charles St; takeaway $4-7, meals $14-26; 🕙 lunch Wed-Sun, dinner Tue-Sun) If you're the type who needs cutlery, proper sit-down meals are served here. Otherwise grab some of the acclaimed fish and chips and contend with the gulls on the beach.

Café Ujazi (Map p379; ☎ 06-835 1490; 28 Tennyson St; snacks $4-9, meals $10-19; 🕙 8am-5pm; Ⓥ) Ujazi folds back its windows and lets the alternative vibe spill out onto the street. The superb coffee, substantial breakfasts and sparkly staff are a great hangover remedy. Try the *rewana* special – a big breakfast on traditional Maori bread.

Hep Set Mooch (Map p374; ☎ 06-833 6332; 58 West Quay; mains $9-17; 🕙 9am-3pm) A good place if you like a marina view, supersize brunch, fresh baking and good coffee. Not so good if you have an aversion to bright yellow and green walls and dubious artwork.

Groove Kitchen Espresso (Map p379; ☎ 06-835 8530; 112 Tennyson St; breakfast & lunch $8-19, dinner $24-27; 🕙 breakfast & lunch Mon-Sun, dinner Fri & Sat) A fitting name for a one of Napier's newer eateries. The sophisticated cafe fare, understated decor and cool tunes give it the X-factor. There's occasional late-night grooving to be had here, too.

Take Five (Map p379; ☎ 06-835 4050; 189 Marine Pde; mains $28-35; 🕙 6pm-late) 'Wine-food-jazz-art-ambience' – that works for us. Live weekend jazz is accompanied by organic, free-range suppers and indulgent desserts.

QUICK EATS & SELF-CATERING

Harald's Bread World (Map p379; ☎ 06-833 6246; 205 Emerson St; lunch $3-7; 🕙 8am-3pm Tue-Fri, to 1pm Sat) A cheap, good stop for lovers of European-style baking, with strong breads, croissants, hefty sandwiches and patisserie.

The weekly **Farmers Market** (Map p379; 49 Tennyson St; 🕙 8.30am-12.30pm Sat) is held behind the Daily Telegraph building and sells an array of local edibles.

Pak N Save (Map p379; ☎ 06-834 3450; 25 Munroe St; 🕙 8am-midnight) is a five-minute walk from the centre of town.

THE EAST COAST

Drinking

If you're looking for late-night action, your best bet is Ahuriri (Map p374), the main feather on Napier's fascinator. This strip of newish restaurant-cum-bars offers a perfunctory array of food (with the exception of the classy Provedore, p383), the focus firmly on emptying the wallets of weekend boozers who flock in, particularly in high summer. Expect barnlike interiors, big screens, nautical themes, open fire, outdoor seating (a highlight) and boring beer options. DJs or live music are a feature, as is the spectacle of the locals breaking out their best dance moves – there's nothing like a bit of '70s twang-rock to bring folk out of their shell. Ahuriri's best is arguably the **Thirsty Whale** (☎ 06-835 8815), followed by **Shed 2** (☎ 06-835 2202) and the **Gintrap** (☎ 06-835 0199). Oh, hang on a minute: that's just about all of them…

Napier town's options for drinking and dancing have a bit more character, and are pretty much centred around Hastings St:

Brazen Head (☎ 06-834 3587; 21 Hastings St) Poker machines compromise the vibe at this Irish bar, but the beer's cold and the outdoor deck is a brazen spot to get through a few.

Guffle Bar (29a Hastings St) Cool tunes, nice drinks and genial pros behind the bar. Ingredients that woo the town's sophisticates through the doors.

Rosie O'Grady's (☎ 06-835 8689; 68 Hastings St) Part of the Masonic megaplex, Rosie's predictable Irishness fills in the gaps between dimly lit corners, pints of Guinness and intermittent live music.

Entertainment

Cabana Bar (☎ 06-835 1102; 11 Shakespeare Rd) This legendary music venue of the '70s, '80s and '90s died in 1997, but thanks to some forward-thinking, toe-tapping folk, it's risen from the grave. Visit its website (www.cabana.net.nz) to see who's on, then get down there and shake your thang.

Harstons (☎ 06-834 1209; 35 Hastings St) The place for live music and DJs. Housed in a former piano showroom which has converted surprisingly well into a music venue (good acoustics, nice dance floor), Harstons brings national and occasionally international artists to town to entertain the late-nighters. A great attempt at big-city sophistication in a city that quite possibly doesn't appreciate it.

Century Cinema (☎ 06-835 7781; www.centurycinema. co.nz; 65 Marine Pde; adult/child tickets $13/9) Part of the Hawke's Bay Museum complex, this cinema screens art-house and international films and hosts plays and classical concerts.

Shopping

If deco devotees survive the Deco Centre (p381) with spare cash, they can go completely bonkers in Napier's numerous antique stores including **Decorum** (☎ 06-835 8951; cnr Tennyson & Herschell Sts) and **Napier Antique Centre** (☎ 06-835 9865; cnr Tennyson St & Cathedral Ln).

Those looking for something warm and woolly should try **Opossum World** (☎ 06-835 7697; 157 Marine Pde; ◷ 9am-5pm) or **Classic Sheepskins** (Map p374; ☎ 06-835 9662; 22 Thames St; ◷ 7.30am-5pm Mon-Fri, 9am-4pm Sat & Sun).

Getting There & Away

AIR

Hawke's Bay Airport (☎ 06-835 3427; www.hawkesbay -airport.co.nz) is 8km north of the city.

Air New Zealand (☎ 06-833 5400; www.airnew zealand.co.nz; cnr Hastings & Station Sts) Daily direct flights to Auckland (55 minutes), Wellington (50 minutes) and Christchurch (1 hour 40 minutes); check website for prices and discount fares.

Sunair Aviation (☎ 0800 786 247; www.sunair.co.nz) Offers direct flights on weekdays to Gisborne ($280, 45 minutes), Hamilton ($380, one hour) and onward to New Plymouth, Palmerston North, Rotorua, Tauranga and Whakatane ($280 to $380).

BUS

InterCity (www.intercity.co.nz) operates from the **Napier Travel Centre** (☎ 06-834 2720; Munroe St; ◷ 8am-5pm Mon-Fri, 8-11.30am & 12.30-1.30pm Sat & Sun). Buses depart daily for Auckland ($89, seven hours) via Taupo ($35, two hours), Gisborne ($44, four hours) via Wairoa ($31, 2½ hours), and Wellington ($37, 5½ hours) via Hastings ($16 to $20, 25 minutes) and Waipukurau ($12 to $27, one hour).

If you're superorganised you can take advantage of $1 advance fares on **Naked Bus** (www.nakedbus.com) on the Auckland–Wellington route via Hastings and Taupo.

Bay Xpress (☎ 0800 422 997; www.bayxpress.co.nz) has a daily service to/from Wellington ($40, five hours) via Waipukurau ($10, one hour).

Getting Around

BUS

goBay (☎ 06-878 9250; www.hbrc.govt.nz) runs the local bus service, covering Napier, Hastings, Havelock North and thereabouts. There are ample services between the main centres

THE EAST COAST

Monday to Friday, including three different routes between Napier and Hastings taking between 30 minutes (express) and 55 minutes (all stops). Buses depart from Dalton St near the corner of Station St (Map p379). On Saturdays there are only five all-stop buses (adult/child $4.50/2.50), between 9am and 5pm; signal the driver and pay on the bus.

BICYCLE
Bikes (including tandems and children's) can be hired from **Marineland** (☎ 06-834 4027; 290 Marine Pde; per hr/half-day/full day $10/20/30; ☻ 8am-5pm).

CAR
The following offices are at Napier Airport:
Avis (☎ 06-835 1828; www.avis.co.nz)
Hertz (☎ 06-835 6169; www.hertz.co.nz)
Rent-a-Dent (☎ 06-834 0688; www.napiercarrentals.co.nz)

TAXI
A city-to-airport taxi ride will cost you around $15.
Napier Taxis (☎ 06-835 7777)
Super Shuttle (☎ 0800 748 885; www.supershuttle.co.nz)

HASTINGS & AROUND
pop 67,443

Positioned at the centre of the Hawke's Bay fruit bowl, Hastings is the commercial hub of the region, 20km south of Napier. Similarly devastated by the 1931 earthquake, its fine collation of art-deco and Spanish Mission buildings also emerged in the aftermath. But apart from the architecture, Hastings itself isn't especially enthralling. It's in the surrounding district that epicurean dreams come true.

A few kilometres of orchards still separate Havelock North from Hastings, although these days it's effectively Hastings' ritziest suburb. SUVs and BMWs cruise the streets as bleached-blonde 50-something women sip lattes in a prosperous village atmosphere. The towering backdrop of Te Mata Peak keeps things in perspective.

Orientation
Hastings' flat grid centres on the railway line, with Heretaunga Sts East and West the main commercial strips on either side of the tracks. SH2 heads northeast to Napier, passing through Clive as it nears the coast. Havelock North is southwest of Hastings.

Information
Hastings i-SITE (Map p386; ☎ 06-873 0080; www.hastings.co.nz; cnr Russell St & Heretaunga St E; ☻ 8.30am-5pm Mon-Fri, 9am-4pm Sat, to 3pm Sun) Internet access, free maps, trail brochures and bookings.
Havelock North visitor information centre (☎ 06-877 9600; www.villageinfo.co.nz; The Roundabout; ☻ 10am-4pm Mon-Fri, to 2pm Sat & Sun)
Hawke's Bay Hospital (☎ 06-878 8109; Omahu Rd)
Police station (Map p386; ☎ 06-873 0500; Railway Rd, Hastings)
Post office (Map p386; cnr Market St & Heretaunga St W, Hastings)

Sights
ARCHITECTURE & ART
While art deco abounds, Spanish Mission has the upper hand here. Cream of the crop is the **Hawke's Bay Opera House** (Map p386; ☎ 06-873 8962; www.hawkesbayoperahouse.co.nz; Hastings St S, Hastings). Although you wouldn't guess from the sturdy Spanish-Mission exterior, its lavish art-nouveau heart betrays it as an earthquake survivor. Built in 1910, it's recently had a multimillion-dollar refit and a modern plaza and foyer added. Tours take place during Art Deco Weekend (p381).

A close second in the glamorous edifice stakes is the **Westerman's Building** (Map p386; cnr Russell & Heretaunga St E, Hastings). Pop into the i-SITE for a closer look at its intricate leadlight shopfront with intact terrazzo floors. The **Spanish Mission Hastings walking tour** (☎ 0800 427 846; $10; ☻ tours 11am-12.15pm Sat) starts here; book at the i-SITE.

The **Hastings City Art Gallery** (Map p386; ☎ 06-871 5095; www.hastingscityartgallery.co.nz; 201 Eastbourne St E, Hastings; admission free; ☻ 10am-4.30pm) presents contemporary New Zealand art in a pleasant, purpose-built space.

TE MATA PEAK
Spiking melodramatically from the Heretaunga Plains, **Te Mata Peak** (Map p374), 16km south of Havelock North, is part of the 98-hectare Te Mata Trust Park. The road to the 399m summit passes sheep trails, rickety fences and vertigo-inducing stone escarpments cowled in a bleak, lunar-meets-Scottish-Highland atmosphere.

The lookout at the top could do with a makeover by the Rotarians, but it's really all about the views which – on a clear day – fall away to Hawke Bay, Mahia Peninsula and distant Mt Ruapehu.

THE EAST COAST

The view of Te Mata is also extraordinary. To local Maori this is the sleeping giant *Te Mata O Rongokako*. From the fields around Havelock North, a little imagination will conjure up the giant, lying on his back with his head to the right.

The park's network of trails offers up walks from 30 minutes to two hours. Our pick is the Peak Trail for views, but all are detailed in the *Te Mata Trust Park* brochure available from local visitor centres.

Activities
FOOD AND WINE
The Hastings area appears to exist solely for the satisfaction of our appetites (for proof, see the *Hawke's Bay Food Trail* brochure, available

from the i-SITE). Beyond a great big bunch of wineries (p388), there is a plethora of boutique food producers:

Arataki Honey (Map p374; ☎ 06-877 7300; www.ara takihoney.co.nz; 66 Arataki Rd, Havelock North; ☉ 9am-5pm) Stock up on buzzy by-products for your toast or your skin. There are kid-conducive hands-on displays outlining the whole sticky cycle from flower to jar.

Filter Room (Map p374; ☎ 06-845 4084; Awatoto Rd; ☉ 10am-5pm) Surrounded by orchards, these folk offer a large range of beers and ciders, all brewed on-site, plus a $12 tasting tray and tummy-filling food.

Hohepa Organic Cheeses (Map p374; ☎ 06-870 0426; www.hohepa.com; 363 Main Rd, Clive; ☉ 9am-5pm Mon-Fri, 9.30am-2.30pm Sat) Part of a Steiner-based community of people with intellectual disabilities, this shop sells local produce, including delicious cheese (made

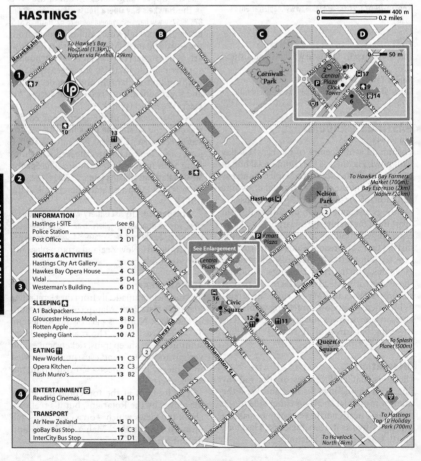

HASTINGS

0 _____ 400 m
0 _____ 0.2 miles

0 ___ 50 m

INFORMATION
Hastings i-SITE .... (see 6)
Police Station 1 D1
Post Office 2 D1

SIGHTS & ACTIVITIES
Hastings City Art Gallery 3 C3
Hawkes Bay Opera House 4 C3
Vidal 5 D4
Westerman's Building 6 D1

SLEEPING
A1 Backpackers 7 A1
Gloucester House Motel 8 B2
Rotten Apple 9 D1
Sleeping Giant 10 A2

EATING
New World 11 C3
Opera Kitchen 12 C3
Rush Munro's 13 B2

ENTERTAINMENT
Reading Cinemas 14 D1

TRANSPORT
Air New Zealand 15 D1
goBay Bus Stop 16 C3
InterCity Bus Stop 17 D1

THE EAST COAST

on-site), biodynamic fruit and vegetables, candles and clothing.

Rush Munro's (Map p386; ☎ 06-878 9634; 704 Heretaunga St W; ice cream $3-8; ☼ noon-5pm Mon-Fri, 11am-5pm Sat & Sun) Rush Munro's is a Hastings icon, serving up locally made ice cream since 1926.

Silky Oak Chocolate Company (Map p374; ☎ 06-845 0908; 1131 Links Rd, Waiohiki; ☼ 9am-5pm Mon-Thu, to 4pm Fri, 10am-4pm Sat & Sun) Watch the chocolatiers at work while deliberating over mouth-watering truffles and chocolate rugby balls. The museum (adult/child $8/5) offers a chocolate-drenched history and the odd ancient Mayan artefact. There's a cafe next door.

Strawberry Patch (Map p374; ☎ 06-877 1350; Havelock Rd; ice creams $3-4; ☼ 9am-5.30pm Mon-Sat, 8.30am-5pm Sun) A berry farm with more to offer than luscious red fruit – fruity ice cream, fresh local produce and espresso.

Telegraph Hill (Map p374; ☎ 06-878 4460; www. telegraphhill.co.nz; 1279 Howard St, Hastings; ☼ 9am-5pm Mon-Fri, 10am-3pm Sat) A small producer of olives, oils and all sorts of Mediterranean-influenced gourmet treats. Four-person picnic baskets ($30) available for on-site indulgence.

Te Mata Cheese Company (Map p374; ☎ 06-875 8282; 393 Te Mata Rd, Havelock North; ☼ 10am-3.30pm) Watch the cheesemakers through the window, have a platter and a glass of vino in the garden, then gather up some picnic supplies to go.

OTHER ACTIVITIES
South of Cape Kidnappers are Ocean Beach and Waimarama, famous for their **surf**. Hastings' massive **Splash Planet** (☎ 06-873 8033; www.splashplanet.co.nz; Grove Rd, Hastings; adult/child $25/18; ☼ 10am-5.30pm Nov-Feb) is the next best thing, with plenty of pools, slides and aquatic excitement.

Early Morning Balloons (☎ 06-879 4229; www.hotair. co.nz; adult/child $325) provides inflated views over grapey Hawke's Bay.

Te Mata is a **paragliding** hotspot, with voluminous updraughts offering exhilarating whooshes through the air. **Airplay Paragliding** (☎ 06-845 1977; www.airplay.co.nz) has tandem paragliding ($140) and full-day beginners' courses ($180).

Tours
Long Island Tours (☎ 0800 875 021; www.longisland toursnz.com) offers customised tours across a wide range of interests including Maori culture, bush walks, kayaking, horse riding and, inevitably, food and wine.

Te Hakakino (☎ 06-879 9302; www.waimaramaori. com; 2½hr tour adult/child $50/25) hosts guided tours of a historic hill fortress revealing history, archaeological remains and cultural insights en route.

See also Absolute de Tours (p381) and the Spanish Mission Hastings walking tour (p385).

WINE TOURS
The majority of tours in this part of the world are focused on wine. Tours are usually by mini-bus, lasting around four hours and starting at $55 per person, with four or five wineries on the agenda. Numerous operators offer various (often customised) tour options:

Bay Tours & Charters (☎ 06-844 0601; www.bay tours.co.nz)
Friendly Kiwi Tours (☎ 021 229 6223; www.friendly kiwi.co.nz)
Grape Escape (☎ 0800 100 489; www.grapeescape. net.nz)
Odyssey NZ (☎ 0508 639 773; www.odysseynz.com)
Prinsy's (☎ 06-845 3703; www.prinsyexperience.co.nz)
Vince's World Of Wine (☎ 06-836 6705; www. vincestours.co.nz)

BIKE TOURS
Costing between $35 and $50 for a full day, a self-guided bicycle tour will temper your viticulture with a little exercise. The following folk will equip you with a bike, map, helmet, water bottle, backpack and mobile phone (in case you get lost/tired/woozy):

Bike About Tours (☎ 06-845 4836; www.bikeabout tours.co.nz)
Bike D'Vine (☎ 06-833 6697; www.bikedevine.com)
On Yer Bike (☎ 06-879 8735; www.onyerbikehb.co.nz)

Festivals & Events
Harvest Hawke's Bay (☎ 0800 442 9463; www.harvest hawkesbay.co.nz; entry $45, bus from Napier, Hastings or Havelock North $20) is the region's premier wine, food and entertainment festival, held in late January at Roy's Hill near Hastings.

Hastings and Napier co-host the Art Deco Weekend (p381) in mid-February. The **Hastings Blossom Festival** (☎ 06-878 9447; www.blossomfestival. co.nz), a petalled spring fling, happens in the second half of September, with parades, arts, crafts and visiting artists.

Sleeping
Much of the superior accommodation lies outside the city's confines. As for Hastings'

THE EAST COAST

HAWKE'S BAY WINERIES

Once upon a time this district was most famous for its orchards. Today it's vines that have top billing, with Hawke's Bay now New Zealand's second-largest wine-producing region. Elaborate modern edifices have sprung up to house restaurants and tasting rooms, but some of the best vineyards still have an authentic horticultural feel. The stony area just to the west of Flaxmere that is ill-suited to fruit trees is fast becoming recognised as its own subappellation, Gimblett Gravels, and has been producing excellent Bordeaux-style reds, syrah and chardonnay.

The following wineries are all open for tastings throughout the summer and most in winter. Tastings are generally free, but there's a small charge at some (refundable on purchase). The *Hawke's Bay Winery Guide* details all the region's wineries and has a useful map, but you might also like to check out the *Classic New Zealand Wine Trail* (www.classicwinetrail.co.nz) – a useful tool for joining the dots throughout the Hawke's Bay, Wairarapa and Marlborough wine regions. See p387 for wine tours.

- **Black Barn Vineyards** (Map p374; ☎ 06-877 7985; www.blackbarn.com; Black Barn Rd; ◷ 10am-5pm) Bistro gallery, Saturday growers market and an amphitheatre.
- **Brookfields** (Map p374; ☎ 06-834 4615; www.brookfieldsvineyards.co.nz; 376 Brookfields Rd; ◷ 11am-4.30pm) Excellent reds and a restaurant among the roses.
- **Church Road** (Map p374; ☎ 06-844 2053; www.churchroad.co.nz; 150 Church Rd; ◷ 10am-5pm). Winery and museum tours (11am and 2pm).
- **C J Pask** (Map p374; ☎ 06-879 7906; www.cjpaskwinery.co.nz; 1133 Omahu Rd; ◷ 10am-5pm Mon-Sat, 11am-4pm Sun) One of the original Hawke's Bay wineries, dedicated to producing great reds.
- **Clearview Estate Winery** (Map p374; ☎ 06-875 0150; www.clearviewestate.co.nz; 194 Clifton Rd, Te Awanga; ◷ 10am-5pm) Award-winning wines and a decent restaurant. Friendly, rustic and ideal for families.
- **Crab Farm** (Map p374; ☎ 06-836 6678; www.crabfarmwinery.co.nz; 511 Main Rd, Bay View; ◷ 10am-5pm Thu-Mon) Decent, reasonably priced wines and a great cafe (p377).
- **Craggy Range** (Map p374; ☎ 06-873 0141; www.craggyrange.com; 253 Waimarama Rd; ◷ 10am-5pm) Definitely one of the flashest wineries – wonderful wines, excellent restaurant (p390) and accommodation.
- **Elephant Hill** (Map p374; ☎ 06-873 0400; www.elephanthill.co.nz; 86 Clifton Rd, Te Awanga; ◷ 11am-5pm) Ubermodern winery and restaurant with sea views (p390).
- **Esk Valley** (Map p374; ☎ 06-872 7430; www.eskvalley.co.nz; 745 Main Rd, Bay View; ◷ 10am-5pm). Excellent Bordeaux-style reds, chardonnay and riesling. See also p377.
- **Mission Estate** (Map p374; ☎ 06-845 9350; www.missionestate.co.nz; 198 Church Rd, Napier; ◷ 9am-5pm Mon-Sat, 10am-4.30pm Sun) NZ's oldest winery with beautiful grounds, and restaurant housed within a restored, historic seminary.
- **Ngatarawa** (Map p374; ☎ 06-879 7603; www.ngatarawa.co.nz; 305 Ngatarawa Rd; ◷ 10am-5pm) An 1890 farmstead with great picnicking opportunities.
- **Sileni Estates** (Map p374; ☎ 06-879 8768; www.sileni.co.nz; 2016 Maraekakaho Rd; ◷ 10am-5pm) Looks like it's been beamed in from space. Tasting room and gourmet food store.
- **Te Awa** (Map p374; ☎ 06-879 7602; www.teawa.com; 2375 SH50; ◷ 10am-4pm) Casually stylish winery with an excellent restaurant (p390) – a must-do lunch where the kids can come too.
- **Te Mata Estate** (Map p374; ☎ 06-877 4399; www.temata.co.nz; 349 Te Mata Rd; ◷ 9am-5pm Mon-Fri, 10am-5pm Sat, 11am-4pm Sun) Producer of the legendary Coleraine red and Elston chardonnay.
- **Trinity Hill** (Map p374; ☎ 06-879 7778; www.trinityhill.com; 2396 SH50; ◷ 10am-5pm) Serious reds and top-ranking chardonnay.
- **Vidal** (Map p386; ☎ 06-872 7440; www.vidal.co.nz; 913 St Aubyn St E, Hastings; ◷ 10am-5pm) One of the Bay's oldest wineries. Quality wines and restaurant.

hostels, you'll have to fight for your bed with hordes of seasonal workers.

BUDGET

Arataki Holiday Park (Map p374; ☎ 06-877 7479; arataki. motel.holiday.park@xtra.co.nz; 139 Arataki Rd, Havelock North; campsites per person $16, caravan from $55, cabins $60, units from $125; 🕭) Judging by its faded minigolf course and museum-piece ovens, this small camping ground has seen plenty of summers. On the upside, it's cheap, pleasantly rural and handy to local attractions.

Sleeping Giant (Map p386; ☎ 06-878 5393; sleeping giant@xtra.co.nz; 109 Davis St; dm/tw $20/50; 🖳 🛜) A comfy backpackers in a suburban street, 10 minutes' walk to town. A posse of tanned, wiry agricultural workers ensures an atmosphere of laid-back sociability, in the fairly close communal confines of lounge and courtyard where the odd barbeque takes place. Off-street parking is available.

Rotten Apple (Map p386; ☎ 06-878 4363; www.rotten apple.co.nz; 114 Heretaunga St, Hastings; dm $22-26, s/d $40/70; 🖳) The central city option and a fairly nondescript affair save for a fresh lick of paint, pleasant TV lounge and a bit of balcony here and there. The Apple is home to a bunch of fruit-pickers; keen weekly rates encourage them to settle in. There's even handy free evening parking.

A1 Backpackers (Map p386; ☎ 06-873 4285; a1back packers@xtra.co.nz; 122 Stortford St, Hastings; dm/s/d $23/33/56; 🖳) Proving that Hawke's Bay hostels during the fruit-picking season don't need to resemble indentured labour camps, this converted suburban house is cheerful and attractive, with leadlight windows, polished wooden floors and a homely garden.

Hastings Top 10 Holiday Park (☎ 06-878 6692; www. hastingstop10.co.nz; 610 Windsor Ave; campsites $30, units $55-155; 🖳 🛜) Putting the 'park' back into holiday park, within its leafy confines are sycamore hedges, a topiary 'welcome' sign, stream, duck pond, aviary and plenty of serenity.

Clive Chalets (Map p374; ☎ 06-870 0609; 31 Farndon Rd, Clive; s/d $55/65) Chalet is a fancy name for the kind of basic cabins and units usually found in a motor camp. Perhaps it's the miniforest of Christmas-tree pines that gives it alpine delusions. There's a semidetached campsite with lots of long-termers next door (per person $15).

MIDRANGE & TOP END

Gloucester House Motel (Map p386; ☎ 06-876 3741; www.gloucesterhousemotel.co.nz; 404 Avenue Rd; units $135-190; 🖳 🕭) Picket fences and colourful roses welcome you to this spick-and-span motel, five minutes' walk from the centre of town. The 11 units are spotlessly clean and spacious, with kitchen facilities and separate lounge-dining areas. Cool off with a dip in the saltwater pool.

Havelock North Motor Lodge (Map p374; ☎ 06-877 8627; www.havelocknorthmotorlodge.co.nz; 7 Havelock Rd; units $135-190) Smack-bang in the middle of Havelock North, this modern motel is a cut above the rest. Tidy one- and two-bedroom units feature spas, Sky TV and cooking facilities.

ourpick Clive Colonial Cottages (Map p374; ☎ 06-870 1018; m.jstones@xtra.co.nz; 198 School Rd, Clive; d from $150) Two minutes walk from the beach and almost equidistant from Hastings, Napier and Havelock, these four purpose-built character cottages sit around a pretty scented garden on two-acre woodland property. Pleasant communal areas include barbecue, games room and *pétanque* court. Bike hire is also available.

Millar Road (Map p374; ☎ 06-875 1977; www.millar road.co.nz; 83 Millar Rd; d $400-500; 🕭) Set above a young vineyard in the Tuki Tuki Hills, Millar Road is architecturally heaven-sent. Two seriously plush self-contained cottages (separated by a swimming pool and bar) burgeon with NZ-made furniture and local artworks. Each comfortably sleeps two couples in separate en-suite rooms. Stylish, uncomplicated, perfect.

Greenhill Lodge (Map p374; ☎ 06-879 9944; www. greenhill.co.nz; 103 Greenhill Rd; s $690-920, d $980, ste $1240; 🖳 🛜 🕭) Siting proudly on a secluded hilltop, this 1895 Victorian mansion is a well-preserved beauty, offering guests a positively alluring combination of luxury rooms, sumptuous meals, billiard room, barbecue patio, swimming pool, spa, gardens and a gorgeous veranda overlooking the green hills themselves.

Eating

Provincial New Zealand is pretty dependable for high quality coffee, cafe fare and bakeries, and the Hastings area is by no means an exception. However, it is the wineries and artisan food producers we have to thank for the area's culinary highlights, which include some particularly fine Bordeaux-style reds (enjoyed best at numerous winery restaurants), ice cream, lovely cheese, and a perplexing amount

THE EAST COAST

of pickle. See p388 for wineries and p386 for just some of the many visitor-friendly local food producers.

RESTAURANTS

Diva (Map p374; ☎ 06-877 5149; Napier Rd, Havelock North; lunch $15-20, dinner $28-33; ☺ dinner) The most happening place in Havelock, Diva offers good value lunch (from fish and chips to Caesar salad) and a bistro-style menu featuring fresh seafood and seasonal specialities. Designed to within an inch of its life, the interior is divided into flash dining room and groovy bar (snacks from $5), plus lively pavement tables.

our pick Pipi (Map p374; ☎ 06-877 8993; 16 Joll Rd, Havelock North; mains $16-30; ☺ 4-10pm Wed-Sun; Ⓥ) Shockingly pink with candy stripes and mismatched furniture, Pipi cheekily thumbs its nose at small-town conventionality. The food focus is on simple pasta dishes and Roman-style thin-crusted pizza.

Elephant Hill (Map p374; ☎ 06-873 6060; 86 Clifton Rd, Te Awanga; mains $21-34; ☺ 11am-10pm) Modern winery with edgy architecture, and food, wine and service to match the stunning sea views.

Te Awa (Map p374; ☎ 06-879 7602; 2375 SH50; mains $24-35; ☺ lunch) The raw-wood-beamed conservatory looking onto the vines is a wonderful locale for a lazy lunch, as is the pretty garden. The menu is packed with fresh, seasonal flavour (lovely salads), chocolate fondant and cheese, which you'd do well to match up with Te Awa's 'wine flight' ($20).

Terrôir at Craggy Range (Map p374; ☎ 06-873 0143; 253 Waimarama Rd, Havelock North; mains $27-35; ☺ lunch Mon-Sun, dinner Mon-Sat) A surprisingly rustic dining room, housed in the cathedral-like 'wine barrel' of the Craggy complex, provides one of the region's most consistent fine-dining experiences. The views of Te Mata peak from the terrace are almost as impressive as the wine list.

CAFES

Jackson's Bakery & Café (Map p374; ☎ 06-877 5708; 15 Middle Rd, Havelock North; pies $3-6; ☺ 6am-5pm Mon-Fri, to 4pm Sat, 7am-4pm Sun) Baking so good it causes pavement snarl-ups on weekends. Blame it on the pies.

Bay Espresso (Map p374; ☎ 06-876 5682; 141 Karamu Rd; snacks/lunch $4-16; ☺ 7am-4pm Mon-Fri, 8am-4pm Sat & Sun) An easy pit stop on the main road, this enduringly popular cafe serves up house-roasted

organic coffee as well as handsome counter food and reasonable brunch, best enjoyed in the sunny courtyard out back.

our pick Opera Kitchen (Map p386; ☎ 06-870 6020; 312 Eastbourne St E; snacks $5-7, breakfast & lunch $10-22; ☺ breakfast & lunch Mon-Sat) This modern and stylish cafe has an interesting menu including healthy brekkie options, such as strawberries with passionfruit-curd yoghurt. For the less calorie conscious the full breakfast is a real winner, too. Heavenly counter food, great coffee and friendly staff round things out nicely. Eat in or outside in the suntrap courtyard.

SELF-CATERING

Fingers crossed you're here for the weekend so you can visit either the **Hawke's Bay Farmers Market** (Map p374; ☎ 06-974 8931; Hawke's Bay Showgrounds, Kenilworth Rd, Hastings; ☺ 8.30am-12.30pm Sun) or **Black Barn Market** (Map p374; ☎ 06-877 7985; www.blackbarn. com; Black Barn Rd; ☺ 9am-noon Sat Nov-Apr).

Picnickers should head for **Bellatino's** (Map p374; ☎ 06-875 8103; 9 Napier Rd, Havelock North; ☺ 8am-7pm Mon-Fri, to 5.30pm Sat & Sun), which stocks gourmet ingredients from the bay and abroad, along with coffee and cakes to eat in or take away.

Hastings and Havelock North have several supermarkets including **New World** (Map p386; ☎ 06-876 9881; 400 Heretaunga E St; ☺ 7am-10pm).

Drinking

There are not a whole lot of options beyond the winery gates.

Roosters Brewhouse (Map p374; ☎ 06-879 4127; 1470 Omahu Rd; ☺ 10am-7pm Mon-Sat) Roosters produces a range of naturally brewed beers 'made with passion and a great disregard of sensible accounting practices'. Five regular beers plus a seasonal special; tasting room, tours and a sunny courtyard for supping.

Rose & Shamrock (☎ 06-877 2999; cnr Napier Rd & Porter Dr, Havelock North; ☺ 10.30am-late) A carpeted, dark-wood, British-style boozer complete with a few Pommy drops on tap and hearty pub grub ($14 to $26). There's live music on Saturday nights.

Loading Ramp (☎ 06-877 6820; 6 Treachers Lane, Havelock North; ☺ 3pm-late) This lofty timber space pulls a mixed crowd of young 'uns up to high jinks, especially on the weekends when the queue can stretch well down the road. Also offers pub-style meals.

See also Diva (left).

Entertainment

Hawke's Bay Opera House (p385) offers a regular program of music and theatre. There's a ticket office on-site.

Reading Cinemas (Map p386; ☎ 06-873 0345; www. readingcinemas.co.nz; 124 Heretaunga St E; tickets adult/child $14.50/10.50) Big-screen blockbusters.

Getting There & Away

Napier's Hawke's Bay Airport (p384) is a 20-minute drive away. Air New Zealand has an office in central Hastings.

InterCity (www.intercity.co.nz), **Bay Xpress** (www. bayxpress.co.nz) and **Naked Bus** (www.nakedbus.com) buses service Napier (p384).

Getting Around

goBay (☎ 06-878 9250; www.hbrc.govt.nz) runs the local bus service, covering Napier, Hastings, Havelock North and thereabouts. There are ample services between the main centres Monday to Friday, including three different routes between Napier and Hastings taking between 30 minutes (express) and 55 minutes (all stops). Buses depart from the Civic Square bus stop (Map p386). On Saturdays there are only five all-stop buses (adult/child $4.50/2.50), between 9am and 5pm. Services between Hastings and Havelock North run from Monday to Friday (adult/child $3/2, 35 minutes, hourly). Signal the driver and pay on the bus.

Hastings Taxis (☎ 06-878 5055) is the local cab service.

CAPE KIDNAPPERS

From mid-September to late April, Cape Kidnappers (named when local Maori tried to kidnap Cook's Tahitian servant boy) erupts with squawking gannets (p144). These big birds usually nest on remote islands but here they settle for the mainland, completely unfazed by human spectators.

The birds nest up as soon as they arrive, and eggs take about six weeks to hatch with chicks arriving in early November. In March the gannets start their migration; by May they're gone.

Early November to late February is the best time to visit. Take a tour (right) or the **walkway**: it's about five hours return from the Clifton Reserve car park (parking $2), located at the Clifton Motor Camp (right). You'll find interesting cliff formations, rock pools, a shelter-picnic spot, and the birds themselves. The walk is tide dependent. Leave no earlier than three hours after high tide; start back no later than 1½ hours after low tide.

No regular buses go to Clifton, but **Kiwi Shuttle** (☎ 027-459 3669; per person one-way $30) goes on demand, with discounts offered for groups.

Tours

All trips depart according to tide times; the region's i-SITEs and individual operators have schedules.

Gannet Beach Adventures (Map p374; ☎ 0800 426 638; www.gannets.com; adult/child/family $38/23/105) Ride along the beach on a tractor-pulled trailer before wandering out on the Cape for 90 minutes. A great, guided return trip of four hours, departing from Clifton Reserve.

Gannet Safaris (Map p374; ☎ 0800 427 232; www. gannetsafaris.co.nz; Summerlee Station, Clifton; adult/child $60/30) Overland 4WD trips across farmland into the gannet colony. Three-hour tours depart at 9.30am and 1.30pm. Enquire also about small-group Wilderness Safaris (www.kidnapperssafaris.co.nz) heading behind the vermin-proof fence into the conservation zone.

Sleeping & Eating

Clifton Motor Camp (Map p374; ☎ 06-875 0263; fax 06-875 0265; Clifton Rd; campsites $11-25, cabins from $50) is a quaint, end-of-the-world kind of place at the start of the gannet trail. Enjoy absolute beachfront sites or those sheltered by rows of static caravans. The friendly owners engender an old-fashioned Kiwiana vibe throughout the well-kept facilities.

Clifton Bay Café (Map p374; ☎ 06-875 0096; 468 Clifton Rd; meals $9-30; ☻ 10am-4pm) is an airy, civilised place for a meal before or after you run the gannet gauntlet.

CENTRAL HAWKE'S BAY

Grassy farmland stretches south from Hastings, dotted with the grand homesteads of Victorian pastoralists. It's an untouristed area, rich in history and deserted beaches. Waipukurau (aka 'Wai-puk'), the main town, isn't exactly thrilling but it's worth calling in to the extremely helpful **Central Hawke's Bay Information Centre** (☎ 06-858 6488; www.central hawkesbay.co.nz; Railway Esp; ☻ 9am-5pm Mon-Fri, to 1pm Sat) in the old railway station. It can sort you out with the comprehensive *Experience Central Hawke's Bay* brochure and pamphlets outlining heritage trails and DOC reserves and walkways.

Sights

There are no less than six windswept and interesting beaches along the coast here – **Kairakau, Mangakuri, Pourerere, Aramoana, Blackhead** and **Porangahau**. The first five are good for swimming, and between the lot they offer a range of sandy, salty activities including surfing, fishing, and driftwoody, rockpooly adventures. Between Aramoana and Blackhead Beach lies the **Te Angiangi Marine Reserve** – bring your snorkel.

The prestigious **Te Aute College** (☎ 06-856 8016; SH2, Pukehou) schooled many Maori leaders including James Carroll and Apirana Ngata. Call ahead if you want to visit the wonderful carved meeting house and church. Across the road next to a *marae* is little **Christ Church** (1859), the district's oldest.

The **Central Hawke's Bay Settler's Museum** (☎ 06-857 7288; High St, Waipawa; entry by donation; ☺ 10am-4pm) has pioneer artefacts, informative 'homestead' displays and a good specimen of a river *waka*.

Ongaonga is a historic village 16km west of Waipawa with interesting Victorian and Edwardian buildings. Pick up a pamphlet for a self-guided walking tour from the information centre in Waipukurau. The next town east is **Tikokino**, once a timber town but now known for its lovely private gardens, open to visitors during spring and early summer. Again, the information centre can help you with details.

It's a nondescript hill in the middle of nowhere, but the place with the world's longest name is good for a photo op. Believe it or not, **Taumatawhakatangihangakoauauo tamateaturipukakapikimaungahoronukupokai whenuakitanatahu** is the abbreviated form of 'The Brow of a Hill Where Tamatea, the Man with the Big Knees, Who Slid, Climbed, and Swallowed Mountains, Known as Land Eater, Played his Flute to his Brother'. Tamatea Pokaiwhenua (Land Eater) was so famous for his epic North Island travels, people said he consumed the land with his strides. After his brother's demise in the Matanui battle, Tamatea sat on this hill with his flute and played a lament to his fallen sibling. To get there, fuel-up in Waipukurau and drive 40km to the Mangaorapa junction on route 52. Turn left and go 4km towards Porangahau. At the intersection with the signposts, turn right and continue 4.3km to the sign.

Sleeping & Eating

Lochlea Backpacker Farmstay (☎ 06-855 4816; www. lochleafarm.co.nz; 344 Lake Rd, Wanstead; campsites per person $23, dm/s $28/37, d $56-60, cottage $125; ⊠) As far removed from urban stress as possible, this idyllic farm has breezy stands of trees on grazing slopes. Rooms are simple but the communal lounge is cosy. There's a pool, tennis court and endless paddocks to wander.

Gwavas Garden Homestead (☎ 06-856 5810; www. gwavasgarden.co.nz; 5740 SH50, Tikokino; d incl breakfast $265-345) Six kilometres from Tikokino, this grand old 1890 homestead is enjoying a faithful room-by-room renovation with pretty floral wallpaper, period furnishings and divine linens. Enjoy breakfast on the veranda before a spot of lawn tennis or a wander through the internationally renowned 9-hectare 'Cornish' garden – widely considered one of the best private tree collections in the land.

Paper Mulberry Café (☎ 06-856 8688; SH2, Pukehou; meals $8-17; ☺ 7am-4pm Thu-Mon) Directly opposite Te Aute College, this hip cafe hands out fluffy toys instead of table numbers and serves excellent Havana coffee and great home-style food.

ourpick Misty River Café (☎ 06-857 8911; 12 High Street, Waipawa; mains $14-18; ☺ 9am-4pm Wed-Sun) A little bit of continental chic on the functional high street, this darling little cafe makes a lip-smacking waldorf salad as well fresh ham, pasta, nachos and other global favourites. Drop-dead-gorgeous baking. All made from scratch, and to order (enquire about the chicken-salad sandwich).

Oruawharo (☎ 06-855 8274; www.oruawharo.com; 379 Oruawharo Rd; morning and afternoon tea $14, lunch $20) One of the area's rural mansions, Oruawharo (1879) is a grand setting for high tea or lunch served on fine bone china. Call ahead for sittings.

Getting There & Away

Bay Xpress (☎ 0800 422 997; www.bayxpress.co.nz) buses stop at Waipawa and Waipukurau along the route that runs between Wellington ($36, four hours) and Napier ($10, one hour) via Palmerston North ($22, 90 minutes). **InterCity** (www.intercity.co.nz) runs the same Wellington–Napier route but is considerably more expensive. Early birds might be able to take advantage of limited $1 advance fares on **Naked Bus** (www.nakedbus.com).

THE EAST COAST

KAWEKA & RUAHINE RANGES

The remote Kaweka and Ruahine ranges separate Hawke's Bay from the Central Plateau. These forested wildernesses offer some of the North Island's best tramping. See the DOC pamphlets *Kaweka Forest Park & Puketitiri Reserves* and *Eastern Ruahine Forest Park* for details of tracks and huts.

An ancient Maori track, now a road, runs inland from Omahu near Hastings to Taihape, via Otamauri and Kuripapango (where there is a basic but charming DOC campground, $5). The route is scenic but partially unsealed and takes around three hours.

Kaweka J, the highest point of the range (1724m), can be reached by a three-to-five-hour walk from the end of Kaweka Rd; from Napier take Puketitiri Rd then Whittle Rd. The drive is worthwhile in itself; it's partly unsealed and takes three hours return.

Wellington Region

If your New Zealand travels thus far have been all about the great outdoors and sleepy rural towns, this is the city that'll blow the cobwebs away. Art-house cinemas, funky boutiques, hip bars, live-music venues and lashings of restaurants – it's all in 'Windy Welly'.

Wellingtonians lay passionate claim to the crown of 'cultural capital', and the mantle is surely theirs. Suited-up civil servants there are, but the city also supports a significant population of creative types who foster an admirably active and accessible arts scene. It's a proud, tight-knit town, where the citizenry are convinced they're living in the world's best-kept secret.

As the crossing point between the North and South Islands, travellers have long been passing through these parts. Te Papa and Zealandia now have visitors stopping in their tracks, and even a couple of days' pause will reveal its myriad other attractions – a beautiful harbour and walkable shoreline, hillsides clad in pretty weatherboard houses, ample inner-city surprises, and some of the freshest city air on the planet.

Less than an hour away to the north, the Kapiti Coast offers more settled weather and a beachy vibe, with the Kapiti Island nature reserve a highlight. On a different tangent, but still only an hour away over the Rimutaka Range, lies the Wairarapa. Here you'll find farming country dotted with cute towns and famed wineries, and a wild, windswept coastline.

HIGHLIGHTS

- Getting interactive at NZ's finest museum, Wellington's **Te Papa** (p403)
- Scaling the lighthouse steps on wild and remote **Cape Palliser** (p426)
- Sampling the great coffee and quality beer that Wellingtonians demand at the city's slick **bars** (p412) and bohemian **cafes** (p411)
- Exploring **Kapiti Island** (p421) and saying hi to the takahe, one of NZ's rarest birds
- Maintaining a straight line on your bicycle as you tour the picturesque **Martinborough wineries** (p424)
- Riding the ratchety **cable car** (p402) from Lambton Quay to the leafy **Wellington Botanic Gardens** (p401)
- Ripping up the trails at **Makara Peak Mountain Bike Park** (p404)

★ Kapiti Island

★ Wellington   ★ Martinborough

★ Cape Palliser

■ Telephone code: 04	■ www.wellingtonnz.com	■ www.wairarapanz.com

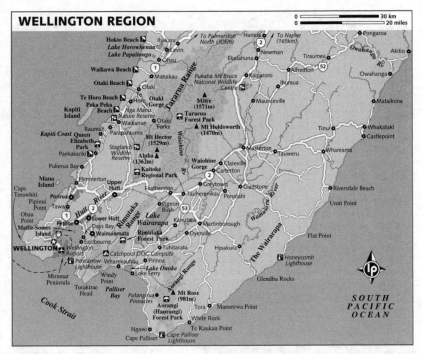

WELLINGTON REGION

Climate

When Wellington's weather turns bad, it can be *truly* foul: lacerating winds and sheets of freezing rain coming in sideways. It ain't called 'Windy Wellington' for nothing…

November to April are the warmer months and the best months to visit, with average maximums hovering around 20°C. From May to August it's colder and wetter – daily temperatures lurk around 12°C.

Getting There & Around

Wellington is a major transport hub, being the North Island port for the interisland ferries. Wellington Airport is serviced by international and domestic airlines.

Easy train and bus connections make commuting into Wellington a viable option – many people travel to work (or to party) in Wellington from the hinterland. Approaching the city from the north, you'll pass through either the Kapiti Coast to the west via State Highway 1 (SH1), or the Wairarapa and heavily populated Hutt Valley to the east via State Highway 2 (SH2).

InterCity (www.intercity.co.nz) is the main North Island bus company, travelling just

about everywhere. Commuter trains run from Wellington to the Kapiti Coast and the Wairarapa; long-distance **Tranz Scenic** (www.tranzscenic.co.nz) trains run from Wellington to Auckland via Palmerston North. See p415 for details on getting to/from Wellington.

WELLINGTON

pop 164,000 (city), 424,000 (region)

A small city with a relatively big reputation, Wellington is most famous for being NZ's capital. It is *infamous* for its weather, particularly the gale-force winds wont to barrel through, wrecking umbrellas and obliterating hairdos. It also lies on a major fault line. And negotiating the inner-city one-way system is like the Krypton Factor on acid.

But don't be deterred. 'Welly' is a brilliant city, as those who spend any more than a couple of days there will attest. For a starter it's lovely to look at, scattered around bushy hillsides encircling a magnificent harbour. There are super lookouts on hilltops, golden sand on the prom, and spectacular craggy shores along the South Coast. Downtown,

GREATER WELLINGTON

WELLINGTON REGION

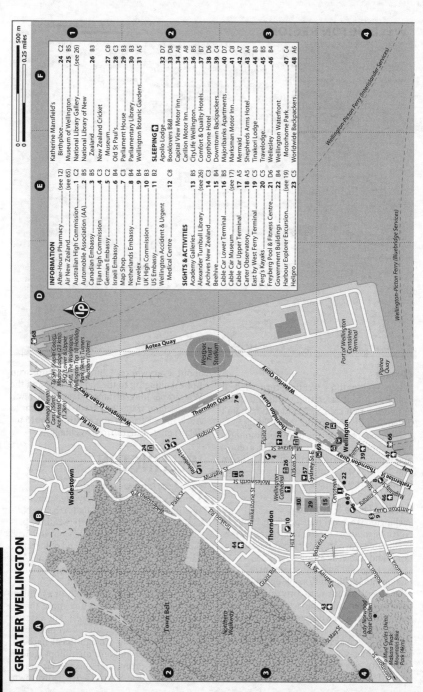

INFORMATION
After-Hours Pharmacy	(see 12)
Air New Zealand	(see 65)
Australian High Commission	1 C2
Automobile Association (AA)	2 B5
Canadian Embassy	3 B5
Fijian High Commission	4 C3
German Embassy	5 C2
Israeli Embassy	6 B4
Map Shop	7 C3
Netherlands Embassy	8 B4
Travelex	9 B4
UK High Commission	10 B3
US Embassy	11 B2
Wellington Accident & Urgent Medical Centre	12 C8

SIGHTS & ACTIVITIES
Academy Galleries	13 B5
Alexander Turnbull Library	(see 26)
Archives New Zealand	14 C3
Beehive	15 B4
Cable Car Lower Terminal	16 B5
Cable Car Museum	(see 17)
Cable Car Upper Terminal	17 A5
Carter Observatory	18 A5
East by West Ferry Terminal	19 C5
Ferg's Kayaks	20 C5
Freyberg Pool & Fitness Centre	21 D6
Government Buildings	22 B4
Harbour Explorer Excursion	(see 19)
Helipro	23 C5

Katherine Mansfield's Birthplace	24 C2
Museum of Wellington	25 B5
National Library Gallery	(see 26)
National Library of New Zealand	26 B3
New Zealand Cricket Museum	27 C8
Old St Paul's	28 C3
Parliament House	29 B3
Parliamentary Library	30 B3
Wellington Botanic Gardens	31 A5

SLEEPING 🛏
Apollo Lodge	32 D7
Booklovers B&B	33 D8
Capital View Motor Inn	34 A8
Carillon Motor Inn	35 A8
CityLife Wellington	36 B5
Comfort & Quality Hotels	37 B7
Copthorne Hotel	38 D6
Downtown Backpackers	39 C4
Majoribanks Apartments	40 D7
Marksman Motor Inn	41 C8
Mermaid	42 A7
Shepherds Arms Hotel	43 A4
Tinakori Lodge	44 B3
Travelodge	45 B5
Wellesley	46 B4
Wellington Waterfront Motorhome Park	47 C4
Worldwide Backpackers	48 A6

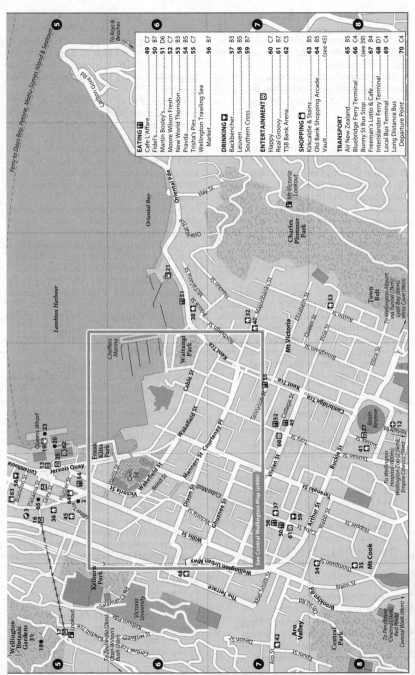

WELLINGTON REGION

the city is compact and vibrant, buoyed by a surprising number of museums, theatres, galleries and shops. A cocktail- and caffeine-fuelled hospitality scene fizzes and pops among the throng.

Brace yourself for a roller coaster of emotions: 'You can't beat Wellington on a good day', they say, but on a bad day this city's a heartbreaker.

HISTORY

Maori legend has it that the explorer Kupe was first to discover Wellington harbour. Wellington's original Maori name was Te Whanganui-a-Tara (great harbour of Tara), named after the son of a chief named Whatonga who had settled on the Hawke's Bay coast. Whatonga sent Tara and his half-brother to explore the southern part of the North Island. When they returned over a year later, their reports were so favourable that Whatonga's followers moved there, founding the Ngati Tara tribe.

The first European settlers arrived in the New Zealand Company's ship *Aurora* on 22 January 1840, not long after Colonel William Wakefield arrived to buy land from the Maori. The idea was to build two cities: one would be a commercial centre by the harbour (Port Nicholson) and the other, further north, would be the agricultural hub.

WELLINGTON REGION FACTS

Eat Yourself silly: Wellington has a gut-busting number of great cafes and restaurants; bring trousers with an elasticised waistband

Drink Aro, Emporio, Fuel, Havana, Immigrant's Son, L'Affare, Mojo, Peoples, Revive and Supreme – that's pretty much every locally roasted coffee bean

Read *Big Weather: Poems of Wellington* (Mallinson Rendel, 2000), billet-doux to a hard-to-love city

Listen to *Happy Ending*, by this author's favourite Welly band, the Phoenix Foundation

Watch 'Golden Days' – the rousing short film screened on rotation at Te Papa

Swim at Oriental Bay: it's not nearly as cold as it looks

Festival Summer City (p406) – brilliant, free fun in the sun (or not…)

Tackiest tourist attraction Cuba St's bucket fountain: tacky, a bit slimy, and often malicious

Go green Check out rare NZ wildlife at Zealandia (p402), Wellington's mainland 'conservation island'

However, Maori denied they had sold the land at Port Nicholson, or Poneke, as they called it, as it was founded on hasty and illegal buying by the New Zealand Company. Land rights struggles ensued – they were to plague the country for years, and still affect it today.

By 1850 Wellington was a thriving settlement of around 5500 people; however, there was very little flat land. Originally the waterfront was along Lambton Quay, but reclamation of parts of the harbour began in 1852. In 1855 an earthquake raised part of Hutt Rd and the area from Te Aro flat to the Basin Reserve, which initiated the first major land reclamation.

In 1865 the seat of government was moved from Auckland to Wellington, due to its central location in the country.

One blustery day back in 1968 the wind blew so hard it pushed the almost-new Wellington–Christchurch ferry *Wahine* onto Barrett Reef at the harbour entrance. The disabled ship dragged its anchors, drifted into the harbour and slowly sank – 51 people perished. The Museum of Wellington (p400) has a moving exhibit commemorating this tragedy.

ORIENTATION

The city congregates in the western corner of Wellington harbour, with the city suburbs clinging to the steep valleys and hills on all sides. Lambton Quay, the city's major business thoroughfare, runs more or less parallel to the seafront (which it once was). The central business district stretches from the train station, at the northern end of Lambton Quay, southeast to Cambridge and Kent Tces.

Parliament clusters around the north end of the city, on the cusp of historic Thorndon where various embassies can be found. The waterfront along Jervois Quay, Cable St and Oriental Pde is an increasingly revitalised area and houses Te Papa museum, Waitangi Park and a man-made beach. The historic sheds of Queens Wharf have been reborn as a museum, galleries, restaurants and a coffee roaster, and joined by a couple of new buildings.

Cuba St (literate, arty types) and Courtenay Pl (young larrikins) are the main nightlife hot spots, while Willis St, Queens Wharf and Lambton Quay are peppered with eating, drinking and shopping opportunities.

The airport is 8km southeast of the city centre.

Maps

Wellington's i-SITE visitor centre has free city maps.

The **Map Shop** (Map p396; ☎ 04-385 1462; www.mapshop.co.nz; 121 Thorndon Quay; 8.30am-5.30pm Mon-Fri, 10am-1pm Sat) carries a range of NZ city and regional maps, plus topographic maps and GPS for trampers.

INFORMATION

Bookshops

Arty Bees Books (Map p400; ☎ 04-384 5339; www.artybees.co.nz; The Oaks, Manners St; 9am-9pm Mon-Thu, to 10pm Fri, 10am-10pm Sat, 11am-9pm Sun) Quality secondhand reads.

Unity Books (Map p400; ☎ 04-499 4245; www.unitybooks.co.nz; 57 Willis St; 9am-6pm Mon-Fri, 10am-5pm Sat, 11am-5pm Sun) A Wellington institution, with an excellent fiction section specialising in NZ literature.

Emergency

Ambulance, fire service & police (☎ 111)

Wellington police station (Map p400; ☎ 04-381 2000; www.police.govt.nz; cnr Victoria & Harris Sts; 24hr)

Internet Access

Internet access rooms are plentiful; expect to pay around $3 per hour.

Cybernomad (Map p400; 43 Courtenay Pl; 9am-11pm Mon-Fri, 10am-11pm Sat & Sun)

Cyber City (Map p400; 97-99 Courtenay Pl; 9am-11pm)

iPlay (Map p400; 1st fl, 49 Manners Mall; 24hr)

Wellington i-SITE (Map p400; www.wellingtonnz.com; Civic Sq, cnr Wakefield & Victoria Sts; 8.30am-5pm Mon-Fri, 9.30am-4.30pm Sat & Sun)

Internet Resources

Feeling Great (www.feelinggreat.co.nz) Events, activities, courses and classes; run by the city council.

Positively Wellington Tourism (www.wellingtonnz.com) Official tourism website for the city.

View Wellington (www.viewwellington.co.nz) Restaurant and bar reviews, activities and special offers.

Word on the Street (www.wordonthestreet.nz) Reader-friendly, entertaining, nonadvertorial site dedicated to the best of the inner city's what, when, where and who.

Wotzon.com (www.wotzon.com) Arts and events listings in Wellington and surrounds.

Media

Capital Times (www.capitaltimes.co.nz) Free weekly newspaper with local news, gossip and gig listings.

Stuff (www.stuff.co.nz) Online news service incorporating Wellington's newspaper, the *Dominion Post*.

Medical Services

Wellington Accident & Urgent Medical Centre (Map p396; ☎ 04-384 4944; 17 Adelaide Rd, Newtown; 8am-11pm) No appointment necessary; also home to the after-hours Pharmacy (open from 8am to 11pm).

Wellington Hospital (off Map p396; ☎ 04-385 5999; www.ccdhb.org.nz; Riddiford St, Newtown; 24hr) One kilometre south of the city centre.

Money

Major banks have branches on Courtenay Pl, Willis St and Lambton Quay. Moneychangers include the following:

City Stop (Map p400; ☎ 04-801 8669; 107 Manners St; 24hr) Convenience store that exchanges travellers cheques.

Travelex (Map p396; ☎ 04-472 8346; www.travelex.com/nz; 120 Lambton Quay; 8.30am-5.30pm Mon-Fri, 9am-4pm Sat) Foreign-exchange office. Also has a branch at the airport.

Post

Post office (Map p400; www.nzpost.co.nz; 2 Manners St) In the centre of town, with post restante.

Tourist Information

Automobile Association (AA; Map p396; ☎ 04-931 9999; www.aa.co.nz; 1st fl, 42-352 Lambton Quay; 8.30am-5pm Mon-Fri, 9am-1pm Sat)

DOC visitor centre (Department of Conservation; Map p400; ☎ 04-384 7770; www.doc.govt.nz; 18 Manners St; 9am-5pm Mon-Fri, 10am-3.30pm Sat) Bookings,

MAORI NZ: WELLINGTON REGION

In legend the mouth of Maui's Fish (see p54), and traditionally known as Te Whanganui-a-Tara, the Wellington area became known to Maori in the mid-19th century as 'Poneke' (a transliteration of Port Nicholas, its European name at the time).

The major *iwi* (tribes) of the region in traditional times were Te Ati Awa and Ngati Toa. Ngati Toa was the *iwi* of Te Rauparaha, who composed the now famous *Ka Mate haka* (see p57). Like most urban areas the city is now home to Maori from many *iwi*, sometimes collectively known as Ngati Poneke.

New Zealand's national museum, Te Papa (p403), presents excellent displays on Maori culture, traditional and modern, as well as a colourful *marae*. History buffs can also see the Treaty of Waitangi at the Archives New Zealand (p401).

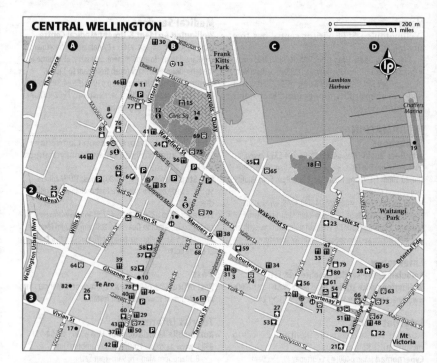

CENTRAL WELLINGTON

passes and information for national and local walks, huts and camping, plus permits for Kapiti Island.

Wellington Airport Information (☎ 04-385 5104; www.wellington-airport.co.nz; Main Terminal; ☒ 24hr) Touch-screen information stations.

Wellington i-SITE (Map p400; ☎ 04-802 4860; www.wellingtonnz.com; Civic Sq, cnr Wakefield & Victoria Sts; ☒ 8.30am-5pm Mon-Fri, 9.30am-4.30pm Sat & Sun; ☐) Staff book almost everything, and cheerfully distribute the *Official Visitor Guide to Wellington*. Internet access and cafe.

Travel Agencies

Air New Zealand (Map p396; ☎ 0800 737 000, 04-474 8950 or 04-388 9900; www.airnewzealand.co.nz; cnr Lambton Quay & Grey St; ☒ 9am-5pm Mon-Fri, 10am-1pm Sat)

STA Travel (Map p400; ☎ 04-385 0561; www.statravel.co.nz; cnr Cuba & Ghuznee Sts; ☒ 9am-5.30pm Mon-Fri, 11am-5pm Sat)

SIGHTS
Museums & Galleries

For an imaginative, interactive experience of Wellington's social and salty maritime history, swing into the **Museum of Wellington**

(Map p396; ☎ 04-472 8904; www.museumofwellington. co.nz; Queens Wharf; admission free; ☒ 10am-5pm). Highlights include a moving documentary about the tragedy of the *Wahine* (see p398), and ancient Maori legends dramatically told using tiny hologram actors and special effects. The building itself is an old Bond Store dating from 1892.

The much-loved **City Gallery** (Map p400; ☎ 04-801 3021; www.citygallery.org.nz; Civic Sq, Wakefield St; admission by donation, charges may apply for major exhibits; ☒ 10am-5pm) reopened late in 2009 after renovations and the addition of a new wing. Expect surprises: the gallery's a little cracker that secures acclaimed contemporary international artists as well as unearthing and supporting those at the forefront of New Zealand's scene. Excellent Nikau Gallery Cafe on-site.

The **New Zealand Film Archive** (Map p400; ☎ 04-384 7647; film info line 04-499 3456; www.filmarchive.org.nz; cnr Taranaki & Ghuznee Sts; admission free, movies $8; ☒ from 9am Mon-Fri, from noon Sat) was established in 1981 to protect New Zealand's moving-image history. Collections date from 1895 and represent every genre of filmmaking. The library has more than 30,000 titles you can watch for free and a big-screen program four nights a week. Combined with a cafe and gallery, it's a great place to while away the hours (or days).

Part of the New Zealand Academy of Fine Arts, **Academy Galleries** (Map p396; ☎ 04-499 8807; www.nzafa.com; 1 Queens Wharf; admission free; ☉ 10am-5pm) features works by New Zealand artists.

The muscular grey concrete of the **National Library of New Zealand** (Map p396; ☎ 04-474 3000; www.natlib.govt.nz; cnr Molesworth & Aitken Sts; admission free; ☉ 9am-5pm Mon-Fri, to 1pm Sat) is a haven to varied collections of national importance. It encompasses the **Alexander Turnbull Library**, which holds historical photographs, drawings, prints, maps and the like. Regular events are held in the **National Library Gallery** (admission free; ☉ 9am-5pm Mon-Fri, to 4.30pm Sat, 1-4.30pm Sun), which has changing exhibits. Watch for renovation-induced disruptions.

One block away, the **Archives New Zealand** (Map p396; ☎ 04-499 5595, www.archives.govt.nz; 10 Mulgrave St; admission free; ☉ 9am-5pm Mon-Fri, to 1pm Sat) is the official guardian of NZ's heritage documents. Inside are gallery displays of significant national treasures, including

the original Treaty of Waitangi (p33), NZ's founding document.

Cricket boffins will be bowled over by the historical memorabilia at the **New Zealand Cricket Museum** (Map p396; ☎ 04-385 6602; www.nzcricket.co.nz; Old Grandstand, Basin Reserve; adult/child $5/2; ☉ 10.30am-3.30pm daily Nov-Apr, Sat & Sun May-Oct). Comprehensive displays cover the history and development of NZ cricket, including the sport's arrival in the colonies and NZ's first test match in 1894. The original 1743 Addington bat is a showstopper.

Gardens & Lookouts

The expansive, hilltop **Wellington Botanic Gardens** (Map p396; ☎ 04-499 1400; www.wellington.govt.nz; admission free; ☉ dawn-dusk; ☐P) can be conveniently visited via a cable-car ride (nice bit of planning, eh?). The hilly 25-hectare gardens boast a tract of original native forest along with varied collections including a beaut rose garden and international plant collections. Add in fountains, a cheerful playground, sculptures, duck pond, cafe, magical city views and much more, and you've got a grand day

WELLINGTON REGION

WELLINGTON REGION IN...

Two Days

To get a feel for the lie of the land, drive up **Mt Victoria** (below), or ride the **cable car** (below) up to the **Wellington Botanic Gardens** (p401). After lunch on cool **Cuba St** (p410), immerse yourself in all things Kiwi at **Te Papa** (opposite) or the **Museum of Wellington** (p400). Drink beer by the jug at **Mighty Mighty** (p412).

The next day, fuel-up with coffee and eggs at **Cafe L'Affare** (p411) then head to **Zealandia** (below) to meet the birds and learn about New Zealand conservation, or take a snoop around the **Beehive** (opposite). For dinner try **Chow** (p410) or **Pravda** (p410), then spend your evenings **bar-hopping** (p412) along Courtenay Pl. Nocturnal entertainment could involve live music, a movie at the gloriously restored **Embassy Theatre** (p415), or a midnight snack at a late-closing cafe – or all three.

Four Days

Shake and bake the two-day itinerary, then decorate with the following: hightail it out of Wellington for some wine-tasting around **Martinborough** (p424), followed by a seal-spotting safari along the wild **Cape Palliser** (p425). The next day, take a picnic to **Paekakariki** (p420), have a swim, and then a wander around **Queen Elizabeth Park** (p420) next door.

---

out. The gardens are also accessible from the Centennial Entrance on Tinakori Rd (Karori bus 3).

One of Wellington's most famous attractions is the little red **cable car** (Map p396; ☎ 04-472 2199; www.wellingtoncablecar.co.nz; one-way adult/child $3/1, return $5/2; ⏱ departs every 10min, 7am-10pm Mon-Fri, 8.30am-10pm Sat, 9am-10pm Sun) that clanks up the steep slope from Lambton Quay to Kelburn. At the top are a cafe, the Wellington Botanic Gardens, an observatory and the small-but-nifty **Cable Car Museum** (Map p396; ☎ 04-475 3578; www.cablecarmuseum.co.nz; admission free; ⏱ 9.30am-5.30pm Nov-Apr, 10am-5pm May-Oct), which tells the cable car's story since it was built in 1902 to open up hilly Kelburn for development. Take the cable car back down the hill, or ramble down through the Botanic Gardens (a 30- to 60-minute walk, depending on your wend).

At the top of the Botanic Gardens, the **Carter Observatory** (Map p396; ☎ 04-910 3140; www.carterobservatory.org; ⏱ 10am-5pm) has re-emerged after a major renovation. New features include a full-dome planetarium in which you can take a simulated trip through the universe; a multimedia display of Polynesian navigation, Maori cosmology, and European explorers; and some of New Zealand's finest telescopes and astronomical artefacts. If your lucky stars are with you, you might be able to safely see our closest star, the Sun, through the Thomas Cooke telescope's solar filter. Check the website for evening stargazing times.

For the best view of the city, harbour and surrounds, venture up to the lookout atop the 196m **Mt Victoria** (Map p396), east of the city centre. You can take bus 20 (Monday to Friday) most of the way up, or if you're feeling energetic sweat it out on the walk. If you've got your own wheels, take Oriental Pde along the waterfront and then scoot up Carlton Gore Rd.

About 3km west of the city is **Otari-Wilton's Bush** (off Map p396; ☎ 04-475 3245; www.wellington.govt.nz; 160 Wilton Rd; admission free; ⏱ dawn-dusk; P), the only botanic gardens in NZ specialising in native flora. Expect to see and hear plenty of birds along the 11km of walking trails. Bus 14 from the city passes the gates.

If you have a car, take a long and winding drive around Wellington's **bays and beaches** (see www.greatharbourway.org.nz) – cruise out of town along Oriental Pde and just keep going, keeping the sea on your left. Along the largely craggy shoreline are pretty inlets, million-dollar houses and the odd cafe. You'll end up at Owhiro Bay, from where you can take Happy Valley Rd back into town. The whole loop is about 30km.

Wildlife

The groundbreaking wildlife sanctuary **Zealandia** (off Map p396; ☎ 04-920 9200; www.visitzealandia.com; Waiapu Rd; adult/child/family $15/7/37; ⏱ 9am-5pm, last entry 4pm; P) is tucked in the hills about 2km west of town (buses 3, 18, 21, 22 and 23 trundle nearby). The fenced mainland 'conservation island' is home to more than 30 native bird species including kiwi, kaka, saddleback and hihi, as well as the most accessible wild population of tuatara. There are more than 30km of attractive walking tracks and a range of guided tours available. A major new exhibition centre showcases New Zealand's natural history and its world-renowned conservation story.

Wellington Zoo (off Map p396; ☎ 04-381 6755; www. wellingtonzoo.com; 200 Daniell St; adult/concession/child $15/10/7.50; ☒ 9.30am-5pm, last entry 4.15pm; ℗) has a commitment to conservation and research. There's a plethora of native and non-native wildlife here, including the residents of the outdoor lion and chimpanzee parks; and the nocturnal kiwi house, which also houses tuatara. Check the website for info on 'close encounters', which allow you to meet the big cats, red pandas and giraffes (for a fee). The zoo is 4km south of the city; catch bus 10 or 23.

Notable Buildings

Three Bowen St buildings comprise NZ's seat of parliamentary power. Office workers buzz around the unmissable modernist **Beehive** (Map p396; Bowen St), which looks exactly like its name. It was designed by British architect Sir Basil Spence and built between 1969 and 1980. Controversy dogged its construction and, love it or loathe it, it's become the architectural symbol of the city.

Adjacent to the Beehive is the austere grey-and-cream **Parliament House** (Map p396; ☎ 04-471 9503; www.parliament.nz; Bowen St; tours free; ☒ tours on the hour 10am-4pm Mon-Fri, to 3pm Sat, 11am-3pm Sun),

completed in 1922. Free, one-hour tours depart from the ground-floor foyer (arrive 15 minutes prior). Next door is the 1899 neo-Gothic **Parliamentary Library** (Map p396) building.

Opposite the Beehive are the gorgeous 1876 **Government Buildings** (Map p396), some of the world's largest wooden buildings. With their chunky corner quoins and slab wooden planking, you have to look twice to realise that they aren't made of stone (knock your knuckles on a wall if you don't believe us).

The last lick of paint was splashed on **Old St Paul's** (Map p396; ☎ 04-473 6722; www.oldsaintpauls. co.nz; 34 Mulgrave St; admission by donation; ☒ 10am-5pm) in 1866, and it still looks good-as-new from the outside. The striking interior is a stellar example of early English Gothic timberwork, with magnificent stained-glass windows and displays on Wellington's early history.

Harbour Ferries

Locals have been jumping on the cross-harbour ferry for a swim at Days Bay for decades. Book a seat on the **East by West Ferry** (Map p396; ☎ 04-499 1282; www.eastbywest.co.nz; Queens Wharf; one-way adult/child $10/5; ☒ 6.25am-7pm Mon-Fri, 10am-5pm Sat & Sun), departing from Queens Wharf 16 times daily on weekdays, and eight times daily on weekends. It's a 30- to 40-minute chug over to **Days Bay**, where there are beaches, a park and a boatshed with canoes and rowboats for hire. A 10-minute walk from Days Bay leads to **Eastbourne**, a beachy township with cafes and other diversions.

East by West ferries also stop at **Matiu-Somes Island** (return fare adult/child $21/11), a wildlife

TREASURES OF TE PAPA

Te Papa (Map p400; ☎ 04-381 7000; www.tepapa.govt.nz; 55 Cable St; admission free; ☒ 10am-6pm Mon-Wed & Fri-Sun, to 9pm Thu; ℗), the 'Museum of New Zealand', is an inspiring, interactive repository of historical and cultural artefacts. 'Te Papa Tongarewa' loosely translates as 'treasure box'. The building dominates the Wellington waterfront and has become a national icon – an innovative celebration of the essence of NZ.

Among Te Papa's treasures is a huge Maori collection; its own *marae;* dedicated hands-on 'discovery centres' for children; natural history and environment exhibitions; Pacific and New Zealand history galleries; and traditional and contemporary art and culture. Exhibitions occupy impressive gallery spaces with a touch of high-tech (eg motion-simulator rides and a house shaking through an earthquake). Big-name, temporary exhibitions incur an admission fee.

You could spend a day exploring Te Papa's six floors but still not see it all. To target your areas of interest head to the information desk on level two. To get your bearings, the one-hour 'Introducing Te Papa' tour ($12) is a good idea; tours leave from the info desk at 10.15am and 2pm daily in winter, more frequently in summer. Two cafes and two gift shops round out the Te Papa experience.

reserve managed by the Department of Conservation (DOC) where you might see weta, tuatara, kakariki and little blue penguins, among other critters. The island is rich in history, having once been a prisoner-of-war camp and quarantine station. Take a picnic lunch, although the eager can camp overnight (adult/child $10/5) or in a DOC house – book online at www.doc.govt.nz or at Wellington's DOC visitor centre (see p399).

On weekends you can also catch the **Harbour Explorer Excursion**, which runs between Queens Wharf and Days Bay via Somes Island, Petone and Seatoun (return fare adult/child $20/10, three daily Saturday and Sunday).

ACTIVITIES
Cycling & Mountain Biking
Wellington's good for cycling, if you don't mind hills. The excellent **Makara Peak Mountain Bike Park** (off Map p396; www.makarapeak.org.nz) in the hills of Karori is 4km west of the city centre. The main entrance is on South Karori Rd – catch bus 3 or 18. Laced through the 200-hectare park are 24km of bike tracks ranging from beginner to expert. **Mud Cycles** (off Map p396; ☎ 04-476 4961; www.mudcycles.co.nz; 338 Karori Rd, Karori; half-/full-day/weekend bike hire $30/45/70; ◷ 9.30am-6pm Mon-Fri) has mountain bikes for hire, is close to the park, and also runs guided tours catering for all levels.

On Yer Bike (Map p400; ☎ 04-384 8480; www.onyer bikeavantiplus.co.nz; 181 Vivian St; half-day/full-day/week bike hire $30/40/150; ◷ 8.30am-5.30pm Mon-Fri, 9am-5pm Sat)

stocks a good range of bicycles for sale and hire, and can help with info on local clubs and trails.

Walking
Wellington will be much enjoyed by walkers. It takes only an hour to amble from one end of the city centre to the other, and there is plenty of good wandering in the immediate surrounds (such as Mt Victoria, Aro Valley and Thorndon), and along one of five walkways around the city fringes (the City to Sea, the Skyline, the Southern, Northern, and Eastern – all accessible by foot or bus). The city council produces excellent 'Explore' walking maps for both inner-city heritage trails and the walkways (available from the i-SITE or at www.feelinggreat.co.nz). See Tours (p406) to connect with a walking guide.

The wild-and-woolly **Red Rocks Coastal Walk** (off Map p396; two to three hours, 8km return), 7km south of the city, follows the tumultuous volcanic coast from Owhiro Bay through Te Kopahou Reserve to Red Rocks and Sinclair Head, where there's a seal colony. Take bus 4 to Owhiro Bay Pde, then it's 1km to the quarry gate where the walk starts.

Other Activities
With all this wind and water, Wellington was made for **sailboarding** and **kiteboarding**, and there are plenty of good launching points within 30 minutes' drive of the city. **Wild Winds** (Map p400; ☎ 04-384 1010; www.wildwinds.co.nz;

KATHERINE MANSFIELD

Often compared to Chekhov and Maupassant, Katherine Mansfield is NZ's most distinguished author, known throughout the world for her short stories.

Born Kathleen Mansfield Beauchamp in 1888, at age 14 she left for Europe, where she spent most of the remainder of her short adult life. She mixed with Europe's most famous writers (DH Lawrence, TS Eliot, Virginia Woolf), and married the literary critic and author John Middleton Murry in 1918. In 1923, aged 34, she died of tuberculosis at Fontainebleau in France. It was not until 1945 that her five books of short stories (In a German Pension, Bliss, The Garden Party, The Dove's Nest and Something Childish) were combined into a single volume, Collected Stories of Katherine Mansfield.

She spent five years of her childhood at 25 Tinakori Rd in Wellington; it's mentioned in her stories Prelude and A Birthday (a fictionalised account of her own birth). The house now opens its doors as **Katherine Mansfield's Birthplace** (Map p396; ☎ 04-473 7268; www.katherinemansfield.com; 25 Tinakori Rd; adult/child $5.50/2; ◷ 10am-4pm Tue-Sun), and is lovingly restored and maintained with a restful heritage garden. The excellent video A Portrait of Katherine Mansfield screens here and the 'Sense of Living' exhibition displays photographs of the period alongside excerpts from her writing. A doll's house has been constructed from details in the short story of the same name. Wilton bus 14 stops nearby.

Chaffers Marina, Oriental Bay; ☯ 10am-6pm Mon-Fri, to 3pm Sat, 11am-3pm Sun) runs two-hour windsurfing lessons for beginners ($110), and three-hour kiteboarding lessons from $195. Prices include equipment but not transport.

At the long-running **Ferg's Kayaks** (Map p396; ☎ 04-449 8898; www.fergskayaks.co.nz; Shed 6, Queens Wharf; ☯ 10am-8pm Mon-Fri, 9am-6pm Sat & Sun) you can punish your tendons with indoor rock climbing (adult/child $15/9), cruise the waterfront on a pair of inline skates ($15 for two hours) or paddle around the harbour in a kayak (from $15 for one hour). There's also bike hire (one hour from $20) and guided kayaking trips.

Gnarly surf rolls in from the ocean at **Lyall Bay** (off Map p396) near the airport (though it's often too choppy or too small), **Palliser Bay** (p425) and the Wainuiomata Coast, southeast of Wellington. The i-SITE can help with fishing and diving charter info.

Freyberg Pool & Fitness Centre (Map p396; ☎ 04-801 4530; www.wellingtonwaterfront.co.nz; 139 Oriental Pde; adult/child $4/2; ☯ 6am-9pm) has a heated indoor lap pool, plus a spa, sauna and gym (casual fitness classes $9.50).

WALKING TOUR

Kick-start your Wellington wander by admiring (or deploring, depending on your aesthetics) the modernist **Beehive** (1; p403), then head east along Bowen St and cross Lambton Quay to the **Government Buildings** (2; p403) – yes indeedy, they're timber, not stone.

Truck south along Lambton Quay, aka the 'Golden Mile', for all its retail revelry. Browse elegant **Kirkcaldie & Stains** (3; p415), the city's only department store. If you haven't done it yet, detour up Cable Car Lane and clank up the hillside on the **cable car** (4; p402), or continue along Lambton Quay and splash some cash at the Edwardian **Old Bank Shopping Arcade** (5; p415). Turn right onto Willis St then left at Mercer St. Civic Sq is straight ahead. Book some theatre tickets at the **Wellington i-SITE** (6; p400), duck into the **City Gallery** (7; p400) or, if you've got the kids in tow, see what's cookin' at **Capital E** (8; right).

From Civic Sq, head south for a cruise up and down **Cuba St** (9): bars, boutiques and coffee shops in the hip heart of the city. Back at Civic Sq take the City to Sea footbridge to the waterfront and stroll past the boatsheds to **Mac's Brewery Bar** (10; p412) for a quick pint of Sassy Red and a bowl of fries. Suitably

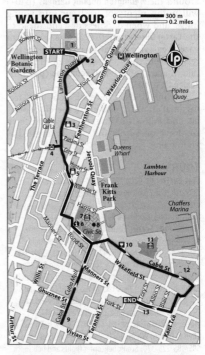

refreshed, it's time to tackle **Te Papa** (11; p403). Once you've reached your museum maximum, pull up a patch of grass at **Waitangi Park** (12) or hurl yourself into the evening fray on **Courtenay Pl** (13).

WELLINGTON FOR CHILDREN

With ankle biters in tow, your best bet is a visit to colourful **Capital E** (Map p400; ☎ 04-913 3720; www.capitale.org.nz; Civic Sq; events free-$12; ☯ 9am-5pm), an educational entertainment complex designed especially for kids. Expect interactive rotating exhibitions, children's theatre and TV, readings, workshops and courses. Call or check the website for the events calendar and prices.

Te Papa (p403) is fantastic for children. The Discovery Centres are loaded with interactive activities, and StoryPlace is designed for children five and under. See the dedicated Kids page on the website for more details. Along the waterfront on either side of Te Papa are **Frank Kitts Park** and **Waitangi Park**, both with playgrounds perfect for expending pent-up energy.

A ride up the **cable car** (p402) and a lap around the **Wellington Botanic Gardens** (p401) will pump plenty of fresh air into young lungs, and when darkness descends head to the **Carter Observatory** (p402) where kids can gaze at galaxies far, far away. On a more terrestrial bent, check out some living dinosaurs (aka tuatara) at the **Wellington Zoo** (p403) or **Zealandia** (p402).

For online ideas, have a look at www.feelinggreat.co.nz, operated by the city council, and follow the Young People link for a rundown on events and courses targeted at young 'uns.

TOURS

Flat Earth (☎ 0800 775 805, 04-977 5805; www.flatearth.co.nz; full-day tours $120-220) An array of themed small-group tours (city highlights, Maori treasures, food, arts and Middle-Earth filming locations).

Hammonds Scenic Tours (☎ 04-472 0869; www.wellingtonsightseeingtours.com; city tour adult/child $55/27.50, Kapiti Coast $95/47.50, Wairarapa $200/100; city tours depart 10am & 2pm, Kapiti 9am & 1.30pm, Martinborough & Wairarapa 8.30am) Runs a 2½-hour city highlights tour, four-hour tour of the Kapiti Coast, and a full-day Wairarapa experience including Cape Palliser. Dedicated Martinborough trip available ($230/115).

Helipro (Map p396; ☎ 04-472 1550; www.helipro.co.nz; Shed 1, Queens Wharf; 10/15/25/35min flights per person $95/185/225/370) Scenic helicopter flights and heli-lunch trips to the Wairarapa, Marlborough Sounds or Wellington's South Coast.

Walk Wellington (☎ 04-802 4860; www.walk.wellington.net.nz; adult/child $20/10; tours 10am daily, plus 5.30pm Mon, Wed & Fri Nov-Mar) Informative two-hour walking tours focusing on the city and waterfront, departing the i-SITE. Book online or just turn up.

Wellington Movie Tours (☎ 027 419 3077; www.movietours.co.nz; tours from adult/child $40/30) Four- to 8½-hour tours for real movie fiends – more props, clips, film sets and *Lord of the Rings (LOTR)* than you can point a lens at. Confirm pick-up locations when booking.

Wellington Rover (☎ 0800 426 211, 04-471 0044; www.wellingtonrover.co.nz; adult/child $40/25; departs i-SITE 9am, 11.30am & 2.30pm) The 2½-hour Explorer Tour with a hop-on/hop-off option visits places that are tricky to reach without a car (Mt Victoria, South Coast beaches, Red Rocks seal colony). Customised tours and half- and full-day *LOTR* trips ($90 and $150) complete with hobbit ears.

Wellington Sights (☎ 0800 775 805, 04-977 5805; www.wellingtonsights.co.nz; 2-3hr tours per adult/child $65/40) Two tours – *LOTR* and Snapshot.

Wild About Wellington (☎ 0274 419 010; www.wildaboutwellington.co.nz; tours from $95) Small-group walking and public-transport tours including City of Style, Sights & Bites, Wild About Chocolate or Boutique Beer Tasting. From a few hours to a full day.

Zest Food Tours (☎ 04-801 9198; www.zestfoodtours.co.nz; tours from $125) Runs 2½- to four-hour small-group city sightseeing tours; longer tours include lunch with matched wines at a top restaurant. Also Wairarapa food and wine tours (from $230).

FESTIVALS & EVENTS

Check at the Wellington i-SITE or visit www.wellingtonnz.com/event for comprehensive festival listings; most tickets can be booked through Ticketek (p414).

January/February

Summer City (☎ 04-499 4444; www.feelinggreat.co.nz) A two-month celebration commencing New Year's Eve; includes countless free outdoor events.

February

Cuba St Carnival (☎ 04-801 9390; www.cubacarnival.org.nz) NZ's largest street carnival, where the locals get uncharacteristically colourful. Biennial (odd years).

New Zealand International Sevens (☎ 04-389 0020; www.nzisevens.co.nz) The world's top seven-a-side rugby teams compete, but it's the crowd that plays up.

February/March

International Jazz Festival (☎ 04-473 0149; www.jazzfestival.co.nz) A week-long shoobedoobop featuring local and international artists. Biennial (odd years).

March

Fringe NZ (☎ 04-382 8015; www.fringe.org.nz) More than three weeks of way-out-there experimental visual arts, music, dance and theatre.

New Zealand International Arts Festival (☎ 04-473 0149; www.nzfestival.nzpost.co.nz) A month-long biennial spectacular (even years) of theatre, dance, music, visual arts and literature. International acts aplenty.

April

New Zealand Comedy Festival (www.comedyfestival.co.nz) Three weeks of hysterics. World-famous-in-New-Zealand comedians, and some truly world famous, too.

June
Matariki (www.tepapa.govt.nz) Celebrating the Maori New Year with a free festival of dance, music and other events at Te Papa.

July/August
International Film Festival (☎ 04-384 3840; www.nzff.co.nz) Two-week indie film fest screening the best of NZ and international cinema.

September
World of WearableArt (WOW; ☎ 0800 4969 746; www.worldofwearableart.com) A two-week run of the spectacular nightly extravaganza of amazing garments. Read more about WOW on p460.

November
Toast Martinborough (☎ 06-306 9183; www.toastmartinborough.co.nz) A day of hedonism around the Martinborough vineyards.

SLEEPING

Wellington accommodation is generally more expensive than in regional areas. Our price listings for the city fall into the following categories: Budget – doubles (with or without bathroom) for under $100; Midrange – doubles (with bathroom) between $101 and $200; Top End – over $201. Accommodation standards are reasonably high, and there are plenty of options right in or within easy walking distance of the city centre. One hassle is the lack of parking; if you have your own wheels, ask about car parking when you book (and be aware you'll probably have to pay for it). Sleeping reviews in this chapter feature a ℗ symbol if on-site parking is available.

Wellington's budget accommodation largely takes the form of multistorey hostel megaliths. There's no 'motel alley' in Wellington, but motels are scattered around the city fringe. Being the hub of government and business, self-contained apartments are popular, and bargains can often be found at the weekends.

During the peak season (December to February), or during major festivals, book your bed well in advance.

Budget
HOSTELS
Downtown Backpackers (Map p396; ☎ 0800 225 725, 04-473 8482; www.downtownbackpackers.co.nz; 1 Bunny St; dm $23, s $62-70, d $60-92; 🖳 🛜) An old charmer at the railway end of town, housed in a grand

art-deco building. Downtown has clean, bright rooms and plenty of character-filled communal areas (be sure to check out the carved fireplace in the bar). Budget meals in the cafe morning and night.

Base Backpackers (Map p400; ☎ 0800 227 369, 04-801 5666; www.basebackpackers.com; 21-23 Cambridge Tce; dm $25-28, d & tr with bathroom from $87; ℗ 🖳 🛜) A slick chain hostel aimed squarely at the young 'uns. Party-perfect location (metres from Courtenay Pl), modern rooms, and the female-only floor will come as a relief to some. Bag yourself a bunkmate at the Basement Bar downstairs. The only gripe: the kitchen and lounge are tiny given the hostel's 200-plus beds. Limited parking $10 per day.

Nomads Capital (Map p400; ☎ 0508 666 237, 04-978 7800; www.nomadscapital.com; 118 Wakefield St; dm $25-31, d with bathroom from $89; 🖳 🛜) Smack-bang in the middle of town Nomads has good security, spick-and-span rooms, an on-site cafe-bar (free modest nightly meals) and discounts for longer stays. Kitchen and lounge spaces are short on elbow room, but heritage features (such as the amazing stairwell) stop you dwelling on the negatives.

Rosemere Backpackers (Map p400; ☎ 04-384 3041; www.backpackerswellington.co.nz; 6 MacDonald Cres; dm/s/tw/d incl breakfast $27/50/62/66; 🖳) A colour-spangled former brothel a short (steep!) walk uphill from the city centre. Free internet and linen, and a couple of tent sites on the tiny lawn out front. Happy vibe.

Wellywood Backpackers (Map p400; ☎ 0508 005 858, 04-381 3899; www.wellywoodbackpackers.co.nz; 58 Tory St; dm $27, s $50, d with/without bathroom $80/70; 🖳 🛜) You'd have to be a zookeeper not to be impressed by this huge zebra-striped building off Courtenay Pl. Rooms are spacious, with weathered retro furniture dotted throughout the place, and unisex bathroom basins in the corridors – very social! Rock music wails over the speakers in communal areas (except the reading room).

Worldwide Backpackers (Map p396; ☎ 0508 888 555, 04-802 5590; www.worldwidenz.co.nz; 291 The Terrace; dm/d incl breakfast $27/66; 🖳) In a 110-year-old house, Worldwide is the most appealing small hostel in town. Clean and homely, with winning features such as free internet, regular barbecues, and nautical reading lamps. It's youthful, down-to-earth and chilled out.

Moana Lodge (off Map p396; ☎ 04-233 2010; www.moana lodge.co.nz; 49 Moana Rd, Plimmerton; dm $29-32, d $60-90; 🖳 🛜) Just off SH1 and only a short train ride or drive from Wellington (25km), this exceptional backpackers right on the beach is immaculate and inviting, with friendly owners superkeen to infuse you with their local knowledge. Kayaks and golf clubs available; occasional boat trips to Mana Island. From Wellington catch the Tranz Metro Paraparaumu train to Plimmerton.

our pick **YHA Wellington City** (Map p400; ☎ 04-801 7280; www.yha.co.nz; cnr Cambridge Tce & Wakefield St; dm $30-33, d with/without bathroom $108/88; ▯ ☎) YHA Welly wins points for the biggest and best communal areas: superior kitchens, cavernous dining areas (group dinner nights are a blast), games room, reading room and dedicated movie room with high-tech projector. Sustainable initiatives (recycling, composting and energy-efficient hot water) impress, and there's a comprehensive booking service at reception.

HOTELS & MOTELS

Cambridge Hotel (Map p400; ☎ 0800 375 021, 04-385 8829; www.cambridgehotel.co.nz; 28 Cambridge Tce; dm $23-25, s/d/tw without bathroom $61/80/85, s/d/tw/tr/f $90/99/109/130/140; ▯ ☎) Top-quality pub accommodation at affordable prices in a heritage hotel. En suite rooms have Sky TV, phone and fridge (try for a room at the back if you're a light sleeper). The backpacker wing has a well-stocked kitchen, flash bathrooms and dorms with no natural light but sky-high ceilings. Cheap bar meals are a plus.

Shepherds Arms Hotel (Map p396; ☎ 0800 393 782, 04-472 1320; www.shepherds.co.nz; 285 Tinakori Rd; s without bathroom $65-85, d with bathroom $99-169; ℗) With wall-to-wall heritage buildings and close to the Botanic Gardens, Thorndon makes a great home base. This well-preserved hotel serves its patrons in fitting style, with a restaurant and bar, and charming rooms upstairs. Shell out a few extra dollars for a larger room.

Carillon Motor Inn (Map p396; ☎ 04-384 8795; www.carillon.co.nz; 33 Thompson St; s/d/tw/tr $80/90/110/139; ℗) Wow, what a relic! Carillon is a rickety old Victorian mansion that's somehow evaded the wrecking ball, developers' ambitions and renovators' brush strokes. Endearing, old-fashioned and chaotic in a *Fawlty Towers* kind of way, it's clean, central and supercheap.

Halswell Lodge (Map p400; ☎ 04-385 0196; www.halswell.co.nz; 21 Kent Tce; hotel r $90, units $135-160; ℗ ☎) Doggone handy to all the central

sights without being too noisy, Tudor-esque Halswell offers a range of options, including small, affordable hotel rooms with TV, fridge and bathroom. The upmarket lodge suites with spa are a better option if you're in the next price bracket; families pile into the two-bedroom motel units.

CAMPING

Campsites are as rare as bad coffee in Wellington. Rosemere Backpackers (see p407) can accommodate a few tents, or head to the Hutt Valley (p419). Motorhomers, however, can now enjoy the brand new and unbelievably convenient **Wellington Waterfront Motorhome Park** (Map p396; ☎ 04-472 3838; www.wwmp.co.nz; 12 Waterloo Quay; powered sites $50; ☎); park during the day (for modest hourly rates) or stay overnight, and make use of the nice new ablution block and power supply.

Midrange
GUEST HOUSES & B&BS

Mermaid (Map p396; ☎ 04-384 4511; www.mermaid.co.nz; 1 Epuni St; s $90-150, d $100-145; ☎) In the ubercool Aro Valley 'hood, Mermaid is a small women-only guest house in a colourfully restored villa. Each room is individually themed with artistic flair (one with private bathroom, three with shared facilities). The lounge, kitchen and deck are homely and laid-back. Great cafe, bakery and deli on your doorstep.

Tinakori Lodge (Map p396; ☎ 0800 939 347, 04-939 3478; www.tinakorilodge.co.nz; 182 Tinakori Rd; s $99-120, d $140-170 all incl breakfast; ℗ ☎) Built in 1868 from native timbers, this lodge is in the thick of historic Thorndon, but a bit too close to the motorway for utter tranquillity. It's still a good option, with its rooms (five with bathroom; four with shared facilities) decorated in refined, motherly style. Free street-parking permits for guests.

Booklovers B&B (Map p396; ☎ 04-384 2714; www.booklovers.co.nz; 123 Pirie St; s/d from $150/180; ℗ ▯ ☎) Booklovers is a gracious B&B run by award-winning author Jane Tolerton (her books are among the thousands shelved around the house). Four guest rooms have TV, CDs and CD/DVD player; three have en suites, one has a private bathroom. Bus 2 runs from the front gate to Courtenay Pl and the train station, and the city's 'green belt' begins right next door. Free wireless internet and limited parking.

HOTELS

Comfort & Quality Hotels (Map p396; ☎ 0800 873 553, 04-385 2156; www.hotelwellington.co.nz; 223 Cuba St; d $100-170; 💻 🐾) Two hotels in one: the sympathetically renovated historic Trekkers building with its smaller, cheaper rooms (Comfort); and the recently built, snazzier high-rise Quality with modern styling and a swimming pool. Both share in-house bar and dining room (meals available, $14 to $28). Two solid options in the heart of Cuba.

Travelodge (Map p396; ☎ 0800 101 100, 04-499 9911; www.travelodge.co.nz; 2-6 Gilmer Tce; d $105-270; 💷 💻 🛜) The zillion-dollar refit is as charmless as a blancmange, but you can't argue with the location and price. An epic 132 smallish rooms, with microwaves, fridges and personal safes. In-house bar and restaurant (mains $25 to $30) will be working pretty hard to win you over with some of Welly's best on your doorstep. Parking $20 per day.

Copthorne Hotel (Map p396; ☎ 0800 782 548, 04-385 0279; www.millenniumhotels.co.nz/copthorneoriental bay; 100 Oriental Pde; d $160-290; 💷 💻 🛜 🐾) A tasteful refurb has this upmarket operation on ritzy Oriental Pde looking as good as gold, from the polished reception, through a seemingly endless maze of corridors, to the fancy bar and dining room. Handsome rooms are spread over two wings: the Bay wing has larger rooms with harbour views, the Roxburgh has smaller rooms, some with harbour views and some without. Parking $20 per day.

MOTELS

Apollo Lodge (Map p396; ☎ 0800 361 645, 04-385 1849; www.apollolodge.co.nz; 49 Majoribanks St; d $125-175; 💷 🛜) Within staggering distance of Courtenay Pl, Apollo Lodge is a loose collation of 35 motel units (one and two bedrooms), ranging from old-school self-contained studios to airy suites.

Victoria Court (Map p400; ☎ 04-472 4297; www.vict oriacourt.co.nz; 201 Victoria St; r $145-200; 💷 🛜) Our top motel choice, right in the city centre, with plenty of parking. The affable owners offer spotless, stylish studios and apartments with spas, cooking facilities, suede couches, slick blond-wood joinery and new TVs. Two disabled-access units; larger units sleep six.

Other options:

Capital View Motor Inn (Map p396; ☎ 0800 438 505, 04-385 0515; www.capitalview.co.nz; 12 Thompson St; d $120-155; 💷 🛜) A dependable option close to Cuba St,

many rooms do indeed enjoy capital views. Undergoing gradual renovation, so ask for options.

Marksman Motor Inn (Map p396; ☎ 0800 627 574, 04-385 2499; www.marksmanmotel.co.nz; 40-44 Sussex St; units $125-275; 💷 🛜) Clean, comfortable studios and apartments across from the Basin Reserve. Can be a tad noisy, but handy for airport runs (or the cricket).

Majoribanks Apartments (Map p396; ☎ 0800 361 645, 04-385 1849; www.apollolodge.co.nz; 38 Majoribanks St; apt for 6 per week $800; 💷 🛜) Run by the Apollo Lodge folk.

Top End

Museum Hotel (Map p400; ☎ 0800 994 335, 04-802 8900; www.museumhotel.co.nz; 90 Cable St; r & apt Mon-Thu $190-325, Fri-Sun $150-325; 💷 💻 🛜 🐾) Sometimes called 'Museum Hotel de Wheels' (to make way for Te Papa, it was rolled here from its original location 120m away), the Museum is a quirky, boutique affair. Eclectic decor (chandeliers, edgy modern art), sassy staff, a decent restaurant and groovy tunes piped into the lobby make a refreshing change from homogenised business hotels. Tasty weekend/weekly rates.

CityLife Wellington (Map p396; ☎ 0800 368 888, 04-922 2800; www.heritagehotels.co.nz; 300 Lambton Quay; d Mon-Thu from $200, Fri-Sun from $169; 💷 💻 🛜) Luxurious serviced apartments in the city centre, ranging from studios to three-bedroom arrangements, some with a harbour glimpse. Features include full kitchen, CD/DVD player, and in-room laundry facilities. Weekend rates are great bang for your buck. The vehicle entrance is from Gilmer Tce, off Boulcott St (parking $15 per day).

Wellesley (Map p396; ☎ 04-474 1308; www.wellesley boutiquehotel.co.nz; 2-8 Maginnity St; d $180-300) A stately central choice with buckets of old-world charm and impeccable service. Formerly a gentlemen's club, the Wellesley retains a refined vibe that makes you want to spark up a cigar. The 13 rooms are decked out with original art, antiques and the odd claw-foot bath. On-site Maginnity's restaurant and bar does everything from high tea to top shelf.

EATING

Wellington is an exciting place to eat. Considering its size, there's a bewildering array of restaurants, cafes and food-focused bars, and keen competition keeps standards high and prices reasonable. Excellent options for contemporary NZ fine dining are nicely complemented by numerous budget eateries, including oodles of noodles.

Restaurants

KK Malaysian Cafe (Map p400; ☎ 04-385 6698; 54 Ghuznee St; mains $8-14; ☿ 11.30am-2.30pm Mon-Sat, 5-9.30pm daily; Ⓥ) Decked out like a dirty protest, tiny KK is one of Wellington's most popular cheap Malaysians in a city obsessed with Southeast Asian cuisine. Satay to die for and *rendang* to put a smile on your face, accompanied by the ubiquitous roti, of course. Unlicensed.

Aunty Mena's (Map p400; ☎ 04-382 8288; 167 Cuba St; meals $9-14; ☿ 5.30-9.30pm Sun & Mon, 11.30am-9.30pm Tue & Wed, to 10pm Thu-Sat; Ⓥ) One of many Cuba St noodle houses, cheap 'n' cheerful Aunty Mena's cranks out yummy veggie/vegan Malaysian and Chinese dishes to a diverse clientele. Easy-clean, over-lit interior. Unlicensed.

Sweet Mother's Kitchen (Map p400; ☎ 04-385 444; 5 Courtenay Pl; mains $10-26; ☿ 8am-late; Ⓥ) Perpetually full, predominantly with young cool cats, Sweet Mother's serves dubious takes on the Deep South, such as burritos, nachos, the po' boys and the New Orleans muffaletta. Key lime pie is about as authentic as it gets, but we don't care. It's cheap, cute, has great cakes and gets good sun.

our pick Scopa (Map p400; ☎ 04-384 6020; cnr Cuba & Ghuznee Sts; mains $14-30; ☿ 9am-late Mon-Sun) Perfect pizza, proper pasta and other authentic Italian treats. Opened in 2006, this modern *cucina* is already a Wellington institution. Slick, friendly service and consistently good food make it deservedly so. Watch the groovy 'Cubans' from a seat in the window. Lunchtime specials; sexy evenings complete with cocktails.

Great India (Map p400; ☎ 04-384 5755; 141 Manners St; mains $15-26; ☿ noon-2pm Mon-Fri, to 3pm Sat & Sun, 5pm-late Mon-Fri; Ⓥ) This is not your average curry house. While a tad more expensive than its competitors, this place consistently earns its moniker. With any luck you'll be served by Rakesh, one of the capital's smoothest maître d's.

Miyabi Sushi (Map p400; ☎ 04-801 9688; Willis St Village, 142 Willis St; mains $15-27; ☿ 11.30am-late Mon-Fri, 5.30pm-late Sat) A steady stream of customers is testament to the satisfying food served at this low-key Japanese cafe hidden away off the main street. The smiling Mr Chuck prepares superfresh sushi, noodles, soups and set meals including teriyaki (chicken, beef or fish) with miso soup, rice and salad – delicious and great value. The *gyoza* (pot-sticker dumplings) are hard to pass up.

Osteria del Toro (Map p400; ☎ 04-381 2299; 60 Tory St; mains $18-28; ☿ 11.30am-late Sun-Fri, 5pm-late Sat) Flamboyantly decorated in a baroque style with influences from all around the Mediterranean. The menu plucks popular classics from the region in a similar fashion. Pastas, pizzas and paella sit happily alongside souvlaki, tagine and tapas. Moreish food in Moorish surrounds; this restaurant, however, doesn't charge like a wounded bull.

Chow (Map p400; ☎ 04-382 8585; level 1, 45 Tory St; meals $18-30; ☿ noon-midnight) Home of the legendary blue cheese and peanut wonton, Chow is a stylish pan-Asian restaurant-cum-bar: a must visit for people who love exciting food, interesting decor, and the odd cocktail. The perfect place to share food and conversation. The hip Motel bar is adjacent.

Flying Burrito Brothers (Map p400; ☎ 04-385 8811; cnr Cuba & Vivian Sts; mains $18-32; ☿ 4.30pm-late) Let it all hang out at this lively Tex-Mex cantina. Quesadillas, tortillas, tacos and tostadas laced with avocado and chilli, plus *bocaditos* (small bites, like tapas) and a kids menu, too. The extensive (and informative) tequila menu and premium margaritas will give you lift-off.

Capitol (Map p400; ☎ 04-384 2855; cnr Kent Tce & Majoribanks St; mains $20-30; ☿ lunch & dinner Mon-Fri, brunch, lunch & dinner Sat & Sun) Simple, seasonal food using premium local ingredients, lovingly prepared with a nod to the classic Italian style. The dining room is elegant and intimate with large windows looking out onto busy Courtenay precinct. No dinner bookings are taken, but it's well worth waiting with an aperitif at the tiny bar.

Le Métropolitain (Map p400; ☎ 04-801 8007; cnr Garrett & Cuba Sts; mains $25-29; ☿ noon-2.30pm & 5-10pm Tue-Sat) Prepare to be transported to the heart of France by your charming hosts. Expect unpretentious bistro fare in a suitably Gallic environment. Classics are well covered and include *moules*, onion soup, *steak frites*, coq au vin and escargot (yum). Cheese or scrumptious tart and a sticky wine for dessert, anyone?

Pravda (Map p396; ☎ 04-499 5570; 107 Customhouse Quay; mains $25-35; ☿ 7.30am-late Mon-Fri, 9am-late Sat) A classy downtown cafe (more chic restaurant by Wellington standards), scoring well with readers and folks that hand out culinary excellence awards. The opulent split-level space (styled in quasi-USSR mode) is a formal backdrop for enjoying well-assembled duck, chicken, fish and NZ lamb mains. Fantastic desserts and coffee.

Martin Bosley's (Map p396; ☎ 04-920 8302; 103 Oriental Pde; mains $28-47; ✆ lunch Mon-Fri, dinner Tue-Sun) Swish fish from one of the country's best chefs, in an elegant restaurant with panoramic harbour views. The degustation menu is an excellent way to sample the skills of the kitchen and is $100 very well spent. For an extra $70, you'll get wines selected to match each delicious dish. Top notch.

Logan-Brown (Map p400; ☎ 04-801 5114; 192 Cuba St; mains $39-48; ✆ noon-2pm Mon-Fri, from 5.30pm nightly) Located in a 1920s banking chamber, Logan-Brown oozes class without being pretentious or overly formal. This is seriously good food brought to you by the 2009 Wellingtonians of the Year, in their award-winning restaurant. Believe the hype, sample the paua ravioli – it's been on the menu forever and a day – and peruse the epic wine list. Bookings recommended.

Cafes

Deluxe (Map p400; ☎ 04-801 5455; 10 Kent Tce; snacks $5-8; ✆ 7am-late Mon-Fri, 8am-late Sat & Sun; **V**) A stalwart of the late-night cafe scene, with off-beat, oft-changing local art adorning the walls. Teeny wee space next to the Embassy Cinema (p415) somehow serves more than 500 coffees a day and mainly vegetarian/vegan counter food and pizza slices to loyal customers.

Lido (Map p400; ☎ 04-499 6666; cnr Victoria & Wakefield Sts; brunch & lunch $5-18, dinner $16-26; ✆ 7.30am-3pm Mon, to late Tue-Fri, 9am-late Sat & Sun) Swing into Lido, at the bottom of a funky old office block, for a wide selection of consistent and reasonably priced Med-inspired food. Pancakes and pasta sit happily alongside, fish, burgers, antipasto and salad. Great coffee and sweet treats, too. Live jazz Saturday and Sunday evenings.

Felix (Map p400; ☎ 04-499 5523; cnr Wakefield & Cuba Sts; brunch $5-22, dinner $10-24; ✆ 7.30am-9pm Mon-Fri, 8.30am-8pm Sat, to 5.30pm Sun) Despite some hard edges in this modern-industrial space, Felix is still a comfortable and attractive cafe that dishes out honest food morning, noon and night. The big windows keep things bright, as do the cheery staff. Great burger and heavenly chips.

Midnight Espresso (Map p400; ☎ 04-384 7014; 178 Cuba St; meals $6-16; ✆ 7.30am-3am Mon-Fri, 8am-3am Sat

& Sun; **V**) The city's original late-night cafe, with food that's hearty, tasty and inexpensive – heavy on the wholesome and vegetarian. Sit in the window with Havana coffee and cake, it's the quintessential Wellington cafe experience.

Cafe L'Affare (Map p396; ☎ 04-385 9748; 27 College St; meals $6-18; ✆ 8am-4pm) Cafe L'Affare is the centre of a small empire, from which its own beans are roasted and distributed. Its Professor Brainstorm–emporium interior is a hive of activity, with speedy baristas, crowded communal tables and a disco ball. At weekends, kids aplenty add to the cacophony, but everyone adds their cheery thanks to snappy service and wicked brekkies of eggie excellence.

Fidel's (Map p396; ☎ 04-801 6868; 234 Cuba St; meals $6-18; ✆ 7.30am-midnight Mon-Fri, 9am-midnight Sat & Sun; **V**) A Cuba St institution for caffeine-craving, upbeat left-wing subversives. Eggs any-which-way, pizza and amazing salads are pumped out of the itsy kitchen, along with Welly's best milkshakes. Revolutionary memorabilia adorn the walls of the funky interior; decent outdoor areas too. A superbusy crew copes with the chaos admirably.

Nikau Gallery Cafe (Map p400; ☎ 04-801 4168; Civic Sq; lunch $11-24; ✆ 7am-4pm Mon-Fri, 8am-4pm Sat; **V**) City Gallery (p400): home to fine contemporary art and its culinary equivalent served up at Nikau. Efficient service, a stylish interior and some of the best cafe fare in town make this an obvious lunch-stop while checking out the abundant artworks. Legendary kedgeree and sunny courtyard.

Quick Eats

Pandoro Panetteria (Map p400; ☎ 04-385 4478; 2 Allen St; items $3-6; ✆ 7am-5pm Mon-Fri, to 4pm Sat & Sun; **V**) A fabulous Italian bakery with smooth coffee, sweet and savoury muffins, stuffed breads, scrolls, cakes and tarts.

Trisha's Pies (Map p396; ☎ 04-801 5515; 32 Cambridge Tce; pies $4-5; ✆ 8am-3.30pm Mon-Fri) Superchunky traditional pies (peppered steak, beef and mushroom) or something different (chicken, apricot and brie). Veggie and fruit options too.

Sushi of Japan (Map p400; ☎ 04-385 0290; 189 Cuba St; meals $5-9; ✆ 8.30am-6pm; **V**) Superfresh, ready-to-run sushi slices that are cheap and tasty.

Crêpes a Go-Go (Map p400; 57 Manners Mall; crepes $5-9; ✆ 9am-9pm; **V**) From a tiny yellow stall in the Manners Mall, a Breton batter-master whips up cheap crêpes with your choice of sweet or savoury fillings.

Burger Fuel (Map p400; ☎ 04-801 9222; 101 Courtenay Pl; burgers $5-12; ☺ 11am-10pm Sun-Thu, to 4am Fri & Sat; Ⓥ) Fast food how it should be. Tasty burgers of all description made with fresh, natural ingredients, beating the pants off Ronald and the Colonel.

Wellington Trawling Sea Market (Map p396; ☎ 04-384 8461; 220 Cuba St; meals $6-14; ☺ lunch-9pm) Locals' favourite fresh-off-the-boat fish and chips, plus oysters, scallops and whitebait in season. Burgers, too.

Phoenician Falafel (Map p400; ☎ 04-385 9997; 10 Kent Tce; meals $8-15; ☺ 11.30am-9.30pm Sun-Wed, to 11pm Thu-Sat; Ⓥ) Authentic falafel, shish and *shawarma* (kebab) served up by cheery Lebanese owners. The best kebabs in town.

Good-value (and very worldly) food courts:

BNZ Centre (Map p400; ☎ 04-499 9300; Willis St; meals $4-10; ☺ 8am-8pm Mon-Fri, 10am-4pm Sat)

Courtenay Central (Map p400; ☎ 04-382 9526; Courtenay Pl; meals $5-10; ☺ 10am-10pm)

Self-Catering

Two excellent produce markets run on Sunday mornings – next to Te Papa (Wakefield St) and on the corner of Victoria and Vivian Sts.

Commonsense Organics (Map p400; ☎ 04-384 3314; 260 Wakefield St; ☺ 9am-7pm Mon-Fri, to 6pm Sat & Sun) Organic produce (wine, fruit, veg, nuts, tea, herbs etc), and food for the intolerant.

New World Metro (Map p400; ☎ 04-417 6580; 70 Willis St; ☺ 7am-11pm Mon-Fri, 8am-11pm Sat, to 10pm Sun); Chaffers (Map p400; ☎ 04-384 8054; 279 Wakefield St; ☺ 7am-midnight); Thorndon (Map p396; ☎ 04-499 9041; Molesworth St; ☺ 7am-11pm)

Moore Wilson Fresh (Map p396; ☎ 04-384 9906; cnr College & Tory Sts; ☺ 7.30am-7pm Mon-Fri, to 6pm Sat, 9am-5pm Sun) An unsurpassed array of (predominantly NZ) produce, baking, mountains of cheese… just endless goodies. Go.

DRINKING

Wellingtonians love a late night, and it's common to see the masses heading into town at a time when normal folk would be boiling the kettle for cocoa. The city's bars and music venues ensure things keep cranking – there are a high number of reputable establishments, with plenty of live music, dance parties, quiz nights and suchlike. You'll also find a raft of great cocktails, fine wines and microbrews, as well as some impressive bar food. Indeed, many places listed below could

easily fit under Eating as well as Drinking (the legendary Matterhorn and Hummingbird, for starters).

Most of the action clusters around two hubs: Courtenay Pl – bustling, brassy, and positively let-your-hair-down; and Cuba St – edgy, groovy and sometimes too cool for school.

our pick Mighty Mighty (Map p400; ☎ 04-384 9085; 104 Cuba St; ☺ 4pm-late Wed-Sat) Possibly the hippest of the capital's drinking establishments and music venues. Inside-a-pinball-machine decor, pink velvet curtains, kitsch gewgaws and Wellington's best barmaid make this an essential port of call for those wanting to experience the best of New Zealand's bar scene. Get dancing.

Matterhorn (Map p400; ☎ 04-384 3359; 106 Cuba St; ☺ 10am-late) Perennially popular bar, with a clientele as interesting as its drinks list. Worthy winner of numerous accolades including New Zealand's best bar and restaurant. Slick and ultracool, with great attention to detail. Occasional live music provided by some of Aotearoa's freshest bands and musicians.

Malthouse (Map p400; ☎ 04-802 5484; 48 Courtenay Pl; ☺ lunch-late Mon-Sat) Beervana. An immense array of beers (both local and international) that would make even the most fervent of hopheads quiver at the knees. New Zealand *does* brew great beer, and this is the place to quaff them. Check out the *Forty Licks*–style toilets in the gents.

Vivo (Map p400; ☎ 04-384 6400; 19 Edward St; ☺ 3pm-late Mon-Fri, 5pm-late Sat) A tomelike list of approximately 700 wines from around the world, with more than 50 available by the glass. Exposed bricks and timber beams give Vivo an earthy cellarlike feel while the fairy lights look like stars set against the dark ceiling. A vinophile's delight with some decent food too.

Southern Cross (Map p396; ☎ 04-384 9085; 35 Abel Smith St; ☺ 9am-late) Welly's most stylish crowd-pleasing pub combines a laid-back restaurant, lively bar, pool table, dance floor and the best garden bar in town. Independent beer on tap and a good bowl of chips.

Mac's Brewery Bar (Map p400; ☎ 04-381 2282; cnr Taranaki & Cable Sts; ☺ 10.30am-late) Occupying a renovated warehouse on a prime waterfront site, this microbrewery does a great job of looking seriously committed to the craft. Author's favourite: Sassy Red, enjoyed in the sun while watching the skateboarders sprain

GAY & LESBIAN WELLINGTON

Wellington is open-minded and sophisticated, so G&L people fit right in almost everywhere they go. The G&L scene is small, but friendly and inclusive, as proven by one of only two gay bars in the city, **Scotty & Mal's** (Map p400; ☎ 04-802 5335; 176 Cuba St; ❤ 5pm-late). This is a stylish, welcoming bar and dance lounge where you can enjoy cocktails, small talk and quiz nights upstairs, or strut your stuff and play some pool in the sultry basement bar (DJ's Friday and Saturday).

Larger newsagents will stock the fortnightly magazine **express** (www.gayexpress.co.nz; $3), featuring the latest news, reviews and events. Useful online resources include www.gaynz.com, which has comprehensive national coverage of all things queer; and the Wellington-specific www.gayline.gen.nz, www.gaywellington.org and www.wellington.lesbian.net.nz. See www.gaystay.co.nz for G&L-hosted accommodation around town. For phone information, or just to talk, contact **Wellington Gay Welfare Group** (☎ 04-473 7878; helpline@gaywellington.org; ❤ 7.30-9.30pm).

See also Gay & Lesbian Travellers, p691.

themselves on the promenade. Excellent fish and chips.

Leuven (Map p396; ☎ 04-499 2939; 135 Featherston St; ❤ 7am-late Mon-Fri, 9am-late Sat & Sun) The menu at this beer cafe is an ode to Belgium's best: mussels come 10 different ways, the *frites* (chips) are cooked to perfection, and the big brewing guns line up at the bar (Hoegaarden, Leffe, Chimay). Popular breakfast specials (waffle, anyone?)

Hummingbird (Map p400; ☎ 04-801 6336; 22 Courtenay Pl; ❤ 9am-late) Popular with the sophisticated set, Hummingbird is usually packed – both inside in the intimate, stylish dining room and bar, and outside on streetside tables. Croony music (with regular live jazz), exciting brunch-to-supper menus, and impressive drinks including fine wines and cocktails.

Backbencher (Map p396; ☎ 04-472 3065; 34 Molesworth St; ❤ 11am-late) You might spot the odd parliamentarian on the turps at the Backbencher, a pub opposite the Beehive where rubbery puppets of NZ pollies are mounted trophy-style on the walls (David Lange is a beauty). Good weekend brunches.

Good Luck (Map p400; ☎ 04-801 9950; basement, 126 Cuba St; ❤ 5pm-late Tue-Sun) Cuba St's Chinese opium den, without the opium. This is a slickly run, sultry basement bar playing fresh hip-hop and electronica. It also brings you the thing no one else could: a middle-of-the-mall alfresco lounge – great for watching the Cuba-cade.

Molly Malone's (Map p400; ☎ 04-384 2896; cnr Courtenay Pl & Taranaki St; ❤ 11am-late) A highly polished Irish bar, complete with Guinness, live music, well-priced pub grub and a bottle store.

Upstairs, the Red Head restaurant has fancier food and a balcony with rare afternoon sun.

The hip, late-night bar scene down Courtenay Place may surprise you with its density and variety. Here are just a few of the many best visited late on a Thursday, Friday or Saturday.

Betty's (Map p400; ☎ 04-803 3766; 32 Blair St) Brassy joint with apothecary theme and wraparound digital screen covering three walls.

Hawthorn Lounge (Map p400; ☎ 04-890 3724; 82 Tory St) Akin to a 1920s gentlemen's club. Play poker, drink cocktails and listen to big-band medleys.

Library (Map p400; ☎ 04-382 8593; 1/53 Courtenay Pl) Velveteen booths, books, booze and beats. Regular live music.

Vespa Lounge (Map p400; ☎ 04-385 2438; 7/21 Allen St) When everyone else is safely tucked up in bed, the Vespa crowd just keeps rolling.

ENTERTAINMENT

Wellington's entertainment scene is a bit like the Tardis: it looks small from the outside, but inside it holds big surprises. Not only does it boast its own vibrant theatres and an inordinate number of local musicians, plenty of high-quality performers visit from around New Zealand and abroad too. Hungry, appreciative crowds help things along.

Event and gig listings can be found in the *Capital Times* – the free weekly rag found all over town. Look out, also, for the *Groove Guide* (www.grooveguide.co.nz), which has a gig guide and pertinent articles.

Live Music & Clubs

Entry to most gigs and club nights can be gained via a door sale. Popular gigs, however, may well sell out, so it pays to buy advance tickets from advertised outlets – often **Real Groovy** (Map p396; ☎ 04-385 2020; www.realgroovy.conz; cnr Cuba & Abel Smith Sts), or **Under the Radar** (www.undertheradar.co.nz). Admission prices vary depending on whom, where and when, but generally range from $5 to $70.

San Francisco Bath House (Map p400; ☎ 04-801 6797; www.sfbh.co.nz; 171 Cuba St; ◷ 5pm-late Wed-Fri, 8pm-late Sat) Wellington's best midsized live-music venue, playing host to the cream of NZ artists, as well as quality acts from abroad (Fleet Foxes, Gomez...). Somewhat de-bauched balcony action, five deep at the bar, but otherwise well run and usually lots of fun.

Bodega (Map p400; ☎ 04-384 8212; www.bodega.co.nz; 101 Ghuznee St; ◷ 4pm-late) A trailblazer of the city's modern live-music scene, and still con-sidered an institution despite its move from a derelict heritage building to a concrete cavern. 'The Bodge' offers a full and varied program of gigs in a pleasant space with a respectable dance floor and filler-up food.

Garden Club (Map p400; ☎ 04-381 2341; www.thegardenclub.co.nz; 13b Dixon St; ◷ 5pm-late Wed-Sat) Three floors of dance-music-fuelled mayhem aimed primarily at a younger crowd. Level one houses the club proper with regular live acts and DJs, while the top floor is home to Welly's other gay bar. In between is a noxious den that pushes NZ's smoking laws to the limit. Well run and definitely fun.

Happy (Map p396; ☎ 04-970 1741; www.myspace.com/happybar; cnr Tory & Vivian Sts) A basement bar that picks up all the cool, stray acts (small and large) that don't seem to fit in anywhere else: spoken word, jazz fusion, acoustic singer-songwriters, electronica, short films and ex-perimental theatre. Open performance nights only.

Sandwiches (Map p400; ☎ 04-385 7698; www.sandwiches.co.nz; 8 Kent Tce; ◷ 4pm-late Tue-Sat) Get yourself a slice of NZ's electronic artists and DJs, regular multiflavoured international acts and the capital's best sound system. Throw shapes in the edgy main room or enjoy cock-tails and pizza in the sultry bar. Great club run by a dedicated team that isn't just in it for the bread.

Theatres

Wellington's accessible performing-arts scene sustains a laudable number of professional and amateur companies. Tickets for many events can be purchased from the **Ticketek box**

offices (☎ 04-384 3840; www.ticketek.co.nz; ◷ 9am-5.30pm Mon-Fri, 10am-2pm Sat) at St James Theatre (Map p400) or the Michael Fowler Centre (Map p400). Discount same-day tickets for some productions are often available at the i-SITE.

BATS (Map p400; ☎ 04-802 4175; www.bats.co.nz; 1 Kent Tce; tickets $15-20; ◷ box office open 2hr before each show) Wildly alternative BATS presents cutting-edge and experimental NZ theatre – varied, cheap, and intimate.

Downstage (Map p400; ☎ 04-801 6946; www.downstage.co.nz; cnr Courtenay Pl & Cambridge Tce; tick-ets $25-45; ◷ box office 9am-5.30pm Mon, to show time Tue-Sat) NZ's most enduring professional theatre company with a strong presence in Wellington (established 1964). Original NZ plays, dance, comedy and musicals in a 250-seat auditorium.

Circa (Map p400; ☎ 04-801 7992; www.circa.co.nz; 1 Taranaki St; tickets adult/stand-by $35/18; ◷ box of-fice 10am-4pm Mon-Sat) Circa's main auditorium seats 240 people, its studio 100. Cheap tickets are available for preview shows (the night before opening night), and there are stand-by tickets available an hour before the show (anything from pantomimes to international comedy).

There are four other significant venues for touring shows and one-off programs:

Michael Fowler Centre (Map p400; ☎ 04-801 4231; www.wellingtonconventioncentre.com; 111 Wakefield St) Home to the New Zealand Symphony Orchestra. The Town Hall next door hosts the occasional concert and special events.

St James Theatre (Map p400; ☎ 04-802 4060; www.stjames.co.nz; 77 Courtenay Pl) A grand old heritage auditorium hosting big productions such as the ballet and opera (www.nzballet.org.nz; www.nzopera.com).

Opera House (Map p400; 111-113 Manners St) Another heritage theatre, with heart-stopping gods, hosting sit-down concerts, touring plays and the odd musical.

TSB Bank Arena (Map p396; www.wellingtonconvention centre.com; Jervois Quay) A hangar-sized venue in which the supersized shows are held.

Cinemas

Movie times are listed in the local newspapers and at www.film.wellington.net.nz. Most cin-emas have a discount day early in the week (Monday or Tuesday).

Real film buffs may want to check out the **Weta Cave** (off Map p396; ☎ 04-380 9361; www.wetanz.com; cnr Camperdown Rd & Weka St, Miramar; admission free; ◷ 11am-6pm Mon-Fri, to 4pm Sat), the minimuseum of the Academy Award–winning company that brought *LOTR*, *King Kong*, and *Narnia* to life.

Embassy Theatre (Map p400; ☎ 04-384 7656; www.deluxe.co.nz; 10 Kent Tce; tickets adult/child $15/9; 🕑 11am-midnight) Wellywood's cinema mothership: built in the 1920s, restored in 2003. Screens mainstream films; bar and cafe on-site.

Paramount (Map p400; ☎ 04-384 4080; www.paramount.co.nz; 25 Courtenay Pl; tickets adult/child $14.50/9; 🕑 noon-midnight) A lovely old complex screening largely art-house, documentary and foreign flicks.

Reading Cinemas (Map p400; ☎ 04-801 4600; www.readingcinemas.co.nz; Courtenay Central, Courtenay Pl; tickets adult/child $16/10.50; 🕑 9.30am-midnight) Mainstream new-release fodder.

Penthouse Cinema (off Map p396; ☎ 04-384 3157; www.penthousecinema.co.nz; 205 Ohiro Rd, Brooklyn; tickets adult/child $15/11; 🕑 9am-11pm) Art-deco charmer screening a smart range of films. Nice cafe too. Well worth the bus ride – take bus 7 or 8 from town.

Empire Cinema (off Map p396; ☎ 04-939 7557; www.empirecinema.co.nz; cnr Parade & Mersey St, Island Bay; tickets adult/child $16/12; 🕑 10am-midnight) A cracker indie cinema screening everything from Hollywood to Harbicht. Take bus 1 from town.

SHOPPING

Lambton Quay is known as the 'Golden Mile' for the array of flash money pits into which to pour your hard-earned dollars. To 'Buy Kiwi Made', head straight to Cuba St to score a good hit rate.

The fanciest department store in town is **Kirkcaldie & Stains** (Map p396; ☎ 04-472 5899; 165-177 Lambton Quay; 🕑 9.30am-5.30pm Mon-Thu, to 7pm Fri, 10am-5pm Sat, to 4pm Sun), NZ's answer to

Bloomingdale's or Harrods, which has been running since 1863. Nearby is the **Old Bank Shopping Arcade** (Map p396; ☎ 04-922 0600; cnr Lambton Quay & Willis St; 🕑 9am-6pm Mon-Thu, to 7pm Fri, 10am-4pm Sat, 11am-3pm Sun), a dear old building home to some lovely boutique shopping (clothing, accessories and gifts).

Wellington is packed with independent designer stores and boutiques. These are a teeny tip of the iceberg:

Aquamerino (Map p400; ☎ 04-384 9290; 97 Willis St) From the sheep's back to the showroom. Hard wearing, stylish woollens of all shapes and sizes.

Hunters & Collectors (Map p400; ☎ 04-384 8948; 134 Cuba St) Off-the-rack and preloved leather (punk, skate and mod), plus shoes and accessories. Best window displays in New Zealand.

Starfish (Map p400; ☎ 04-385 3722; 128 Willis St) The fashionable Wellingtonian's favourite treat. Beautiful clothing, sustainably made.

If you're looking for something uniquely NZ, try the gift shop at Te Papa museum (p403), or these tried-and-true options:

Kura (Map p400; ☎ 04-802 4934; 19 Allen St) Contemporary indigenous art: painting, ceramics, jewellery and sculpture.

Ora Design Gallery (Map p400; ☎ 04-384 4157; 23 Allen St) The latest in Pacific and Maori art: beautiful sculpture, weaving and jewellery.

Vault (Map p396; ☎ 04-471 1404; 2 Plimmer Steps) Jewellery, clothing, bags, ceramics, cosmetics – a beautiful store with beautiful things.

Several outdoor shops gather around Mercer St, the best of which is **Bivouac Outdoor** (Map p400; ☎ 04-473 2587; 39 Mercer St; 🕑 9am-5.30pm Mon-Thu, to 7pm Fri, 10am-5pm Sat, 11am-5pm Sun).

GETTING THERE & AWAY
Air

Wellington is an international gateway to NZ. See p701 for information on international flights. **Wellington Airport** (WLG; ☎ 04-385 5100; www.wellington-airport.co.nz; 🕑 4am-1.30am) has touch-screen information kiosks in the luggage hall. There's also currency exchange, ATMs, car-rental desks, cafes, shops etc. If you're in transit or have an early flight, you can't linger overnight inside the terminal. Departure tax on international flights is adult/child $25/10.

Air New Zealand (Map p396; ☎ 0800 737 000, 04-474 8950 or 04-388 9900; www.airnewzealand.co.nz; cnr Lambton Quay & Grey St; 🕑 9am-5pm Mon-Fri, 10am-1pm Sat) offers flights between Wellington and most domestic centres, including the following:

Destination	Price	Frequency
Auckland	from $49	up to 20 daily
Christchurch	from $49	up to 14 daily
Dunedin	from $120	up to 6 daily
Queenstown	from $116	1 daily
Rotorua	from $95	up to 3 daily
Westport	from $84	2 daily

Jetstar (☎ 0800 800 995; www.jetstar.com) flies between Wellington and Auckland (from $49, three daily), and Christchurch (from $50, one daily).

Soundsair (☎ 0800 505 005, 03-520 3080; www.sounds air.com) flies between Wellington and Picton (from $79, up to eight daily), Nelson (from $90, up to three daily) and Blenheim (from $79, one daily).

Air2there (☎ 0800 777 000; www.air2there.com) flies between Wellington and Blenheim ($99, up to four daily), with other local destinations serviced from Paraparaumu airport, 40 minutes up the coast by car or train.

Boat

On a clear day, sailing into Wellington Harbour or through the Marlborough Sounds is magical. Cook Strait is notoriously rough, but the big ferries handle it well, and sport lounges, cafes, bars, information desks, cinemas but no pool tables. There are two options for crossing the strait between Wellington and Picton (timetables subject to change):

Bluebridge Ferries (Map p396; ☎ 0800 844 844, 04-471 6188; www.bluebridge.co.nz; adult/child $50/25) Crossing takes three hours, 20 minutes. Departs Wellington at 3am, 8am, 1pm and 9pm daily (no 3am or 9pm services Saturday). Departs Picton at 2am, 8am, 2pm & 7pm daily (no 8am service Saturday; no 2am service Sunday). Cars and campervans up to 4m long from $110; campervans under 5.5m from $150; motorbikes $50; bicycles $10.

Interislander (Map p396; ☎ 0800 802 802, 04-498 3302; www.interislander.co.nz; adult/child from $46/23) Crossing takes three hours, 10 minutes. Departs Wellington at 2.25am, 8.25am, 2.05pm and 6.25pm; departs Picton at 6.25am, 10.05am, 1.10pm, 6.05pm and 10.25pm. From November through to April there's an extra 10.25am sailing from Wellington and an extra 2.25pm sailing from Picton. Cars are priced from $101; campervans (up to 5.5m) from $126; motorbikes $46; bicycles $15.

Book ferries at hotels, by phone, online, at travel agents and with operators directly (online is the cheapest option). Bluebridge is based at Waterloo Quay, opposite the Wellington train station. The Interislander terminal is about 2km northeast of the city centre; a shuttle bus ($2) runs to the Interislander from platform 9 at Wellington train station (where long-distance buses also depart) at 7.35am, 9.35am (peak season only), 1.15pm and 5.35pm. It also meets arriving ferries, returning passengers to platform 9. There's also a taxi stand at the terminal.

Car-hire companies allow you to pick-up/drop-off vehicles at ferry terminals. If you arrive outside business hours, arrangements can be made to collect your vehicle from the terminal car park.

Bus

Wellington is a bus-travel hub, with connections north to Auckland and all major towns in between. **InterCity** (☎ 04-385 0520; www.intercity. co.nz) and **Newmans** (☎ 04-385 0521; www.newmans coach.co.nz) buses depart from platform 9 at the train station. Tickets are sold at the Intercity/Newmans ticket window in the train station. Typical fares include Auckland (from $30, 11 hours, three daily), Palmerston North (from $13, 2¼ hours, six daily), Rotorua (from $30, 7½ hours, twice daily). There are good savings when booked online.

White Star Express (☎ 0800 465 622, 04-478 4734; www.whitestarbus.co.nz) departs once daily (twice on Thursday and Friday) from Bunny St, outside the train station, running to Palmerston North ($23, 2¼ hours), Whanganui ($30, four hours) and New Plymouth ($47, 6½ hours). Connect at Palmerston North for services to Masterton, Hastings, Napier and Gisborne. Call for ticket info or visit **Freeman's Lotto & Cafe** (Map p396; 23 Lambton Quay) or the i-SITE.

Bay Xpress (☎ 0800 422 997; www.bayxpress.co.nz) has a daily service connecting Wellington with Palmerston North ($25, 2¼ hours) continuing to Hastings ($40, 4¾ hours) and Napier ($40, five hours).

Naked Bus (☎ 0900 625 33; www.nakedbus.com) runs north from Wellington to all major North Island destinations, including Palmerston North ($1 to $22, 2½ hours, two daily), Napier ($1 to $35, five hours, four times a week), Taupo (from $1 to $43, 6½ hours, one daily) and Auckland (from $1 to $34, 12 hours, one daily), with myriad stops en route. You can buy bus tickets on the ferry to Picton, connecting to the Naked Bus South Island Network. Buses depart from the Bunny St bus stop. Book online or at Wellington i-SITE; get in early for the cheapest fares.

Train

Wellington train station has four **ticket windows** (☎ 04-498 3000, ext 44324; ☼ 6.30am-8pm Mon-Thu, to 1pm Fri & Sat, to 3pm Sun), one selling tickets for Tranz Scenic trains, Interislander ferries and InterCity and Newmans coaches; the other three ticketing local/regional Tranz Metro trains (Johnsonville, Melling, Hutt Valley, Paraparaumu and Wairarapa lines).

Long-haul **Tranz Scenic** (☎ 0800 872 467; www. tranzscenic.co.nz) routes include the *Overlander* between Wellington and Auckland (from $49, 12 hours, one daily) departing Wellington at 7.25am (Friday, Saturday and Sunday only May to September); and the *Capital Connection* between Wellington and Palmerston North ($24, 2¼ hours, one daily Monday to Friday) departing Wellington at 5.17pm.

GETTING AROUND

Metlink (☎ 0800 801 700; www.metlink.org.nz) is the one-stop shop for Wellington's regional bus, train and harbour ferry networks all detailed below.

To/From the Airport

Super Shuttle (☎ 0800 748 885; www.supershuttle.co.nz; 1/2 passengers $15/21; ☼ 24hr) provides a door-to-door minibus service between the city and airport, 8km southeast of the city. It's cheaper if two or more passengers are travelling to the same destination. Shuttles meet all arriving flights.

The **Airport Flyer** (☎ 0800 801 700; www.metlink. co.nz; airport-city per adult/child $8/4.50) bus runs between the airport, Wellington and Lower Hutt (reduced service to Upper Hutt), calling at major stops. Buses run from the city to the airport between 5.50am and 8.50pm; and from the airport, between 6.30am and 9.30pm.

A taxi between the city centre and airport costs around $30.

Bus

Frequent and efficient Go Wellington, Valley Flyer, Newlands Coach Services and Mana Coach Services buses run from 7am to 11.30pm on most suburban routes. Buses depart Wellington train station, or the main bus stop on Courtenay Pl near the Cambridge Tce intersection. Colour-coded route maps and timetables are available at the i-SITE and convenience stores around town. Fares are determined by zones: there are 14 zones, and the cheapest fare is $1 for rides in the city zone, $3 for zones 1 and 2 (maximum fare $15). The Go Wellington Daytripper ticket (zones 1 to 3) costs $6, allowing unlimited bus travel for one day. The Metlink Explorer ticket ($18) gives unlimited travel off-peak and weekends on most services.

After Midnight (☎ 0800 801 700; www.metlink.org.nz) bus services depart the central entertainment strips (Courtenay Pl and Cuba St) between midnight and 4.30am Saturday and Sunday on a number of routes to the outer suburbs. Fares range from $5 to $10, depending on how far away your bed is.

Car

There are a lot of one-way streets in Wellington, the traffic is surprisingly snarly and parking can be a royal (and expensive) pain in the rump. If you've got a car or a caravan, park on the outskirts and walk or take public transport into the city centre.

Aside from the major international rental companies (see p710), Wellington has several operators that will negotiate cheap deals, especially for longer-term rental of two weeks or more, but rates generally aren't as competitive as in Auckland. Rack rates range from around $40 to $85 per day; cars are usually a few years old and in pretty good condition. Operators include the following:

Ace Rental Cars (off Map p396; ☎ 0800 535 500, 04-471 1176; www.acerentalcars.co.nz; 126 Hutt Rd; ☼ 8am-5pm)

Apex Car Rental (Map p400; ☎ 0800 300 110, 04-385 2163; www.apexrentals.co.nz; 186 Victoria St; ☼ 8am-5pm)

Omega Rental Cars (off Map p396; ☎ 0800 667 722, 04-472 8465; www.omegarentals.com; 96 Hutt Rd; ☼ 8am-5pm)

If you plan on exploring both North and South Islands, most companies suggest you leave your car at Wellington and pick up another one in Picton after crossing Cook Strait. This is a common (and more affordable) practice, and car-hire companies make it a painless exercise.

There are often cheap deals on car relocation from Wellington to Auckland (most renters travel in the opposite direction). A few companies offer heavy discounts on this route, with the catch being that you may only have 24 or 48 hours to make the journey.

Turners Auctions (off Map p396; ☎ 04-587 1400; www.turners.co.nz; 120 Hutt Park Rd, Lower Hutt; ☒ 8am-5.30pm Mon-Wed & Fri, to 8pm Thu, 9am-3pm Sat), not far from the Wellington Top 10 Holiday Park (opposite), buys and sells used cars by auction. Also check noticeboards at backpackers for cheap deals.

Taxi
Popular ranks, packed with cabs, can be found on Courtenay Place, at the corner of Dixon and Victoria Sts, on Featherston St, and outside the railway station. Some operators:
Green Cabs (☎ 0508 447 336)
Wellington City Cabs (☎ 0800 388 8000)
Wellington Combined Taxis (☎ 0800 384 444)

Train
Tranz Metro (☎ 0800 801 700; www.tranzmetro.co.nz) operates four train routes running through Wellington's suburbs to regional destinations. Trains run frequently from around 6am to 11pm, departing Wellington train station. The routes: Johnsonville, via Ngaio and Khandallah; Paraparaumu, via Porirua, Plimmerton and Paekakariki; Melling, via Petone; the Hutt Valley via Waterloo to Upper Hutt. A train service also connects with the Wairarapa, calling at Featherston, Carterton and Masterton. Timetables are available from convenience stores, the train station, Wellington i-SITE and online. Standard fares from Wellington to the ends of the five lines range from $4 to $15. A Day Rover ticket ($10) allows unlimited off-peak and weekend travel on all lines except Wairarapa.

HUTT VALLEY
pop 110,000
The Hutt Valley is home to two of Wellington's dormitory cities – imaginatively named Upper Hutt and Lower Hutt – spread out upon the terraces of the Hutt River. Dotted with a

number of town centres and shopping hubs largely functional in form, the main attractions of the Hutt are its forest parks, camping options and the odd museum.

The Hutt Valley begins at the foot of the Tararua Ranges. Upper Hutt lies at the upper end (40km from Wellington city), with Lower Hutt, 15km further downstream, reaching its boundary at Petone, the historic settlement on Wellington Harbour. Visit the **Hutt City i-SITE** (☎ 04-560 4715; www.huttvalleynz.com; 25 Laings Rd, Lower Hutt; ☒ 9am-5pm Mon-Fri, to 4pm Sat & Sun) for the local low-down.

SIGHTS & ACTIVITIES
The shell-strewn Petone foreshore is home to the art-deco **Petone Settlers Museum** (☎ 04-568 8373; www.petonesettlers.org.nz; The Esplanade; admission by donation; ☒ noon-4pm Tue-Fri, 1-5pm Sat & Sun), which recalls local migration and settlement, and presents varying exhibitions. **Jackson Street**, running parallel to the Esplanade a couple of blocks inland, is well worth a wander down for lunching and shopping. A short drive south of the Petone, **Days Bay** and **Eastbourne** make a laid-back afternoon detour via road or ferry (see p403).

Just over the hill from Lower Hutt is Wainuiomata, 14km south of which is Catchpool Valley, the main entrance to **Rimutaka Forest Park** (45 minutes' drive from Wellington). Here there's a creek-side **campsite** (adult/child $10/5) and six sole-occupancy bush huts (sleeping eight to 18) – great bases for short and long walks into the forest and gorgeous Orongorongo River valley. Book at Wellington's DOC visitor centre (see p399) or online (www.doc.govt.nz).

Lower Hutt's **NewDowse** (☎ 04-570 6500; www.newdowse.org.nz; 45 Laings Rd, Lower Hutt; admission free; ☒ 10am-4.30pm Mon-Fri, to 5pm Sat & Sun) is worth visiting for its architecture alone (the pink is positively audacious). It's also a friendly, accessible art museum showcasing NZ art, craft and design. Nice cafe.

The drive from Upper Hutt to Waikanae (on the Kapiti Coast) along the windy, scenic Akatarawa Rd passes the 10-hectare **Staglands Wildlife Reserve** (☎ 04-526 7529; www.staglands.co.nz; Akatarawa Valley; adult/child $16/8; ☒ 10am-5pm) which helps to conserve native NZ birds and animals, such as the blue duck (whio). It's 16km from SH2, 20km from SH1.

Kaitoke Regional Park, 16km north of Upper Hutt on SH2, has a pleasant **campsite** (adult/child

$5/2), swimming, picnicking and walks ranging from 15 minutes to six hours long. *LOTR* fans make the pilgrimage here to size-up the fabled site of Rivendell.

SLEEPING

Harcourt Holiday Park (☎ 04-526 7400; www.har courtholidaypark.co.nz; 45 Akatarawa Rd, Upper Hutt; un-powered/powered sites $30/32, cabins & tourist flats $45-90, motels $110; ☑) Veritably verdant park 35km northeast of Wellington (35-minute drive), just off SH2, set in parkland by the trout-filled Hutt River. Facilities aren't as numerous as the Wellington Top 10 Holiday Park, but the location is more appealing.

Wellington Top 10 Holiday Park (off Map p396; ☎ 0800 488 872, 04-568 5913; www.wellingtontop10. co.nz; 95 Hutt Park Rd, Seaview, Lower Hutt; sites $40, cabins $55-75, units $105-135, motels $120-160; ☑) Utilitarian park 13km northeast of Wellington. Family-friendly facilities include three communal kitchens, games room, jumping pillow and a playground, but its industrial location de-tracts. It's a 15-minute drive from the ferry (follow the signs off SH2 for Petone and Seaview), or take Eastbourne bus 81 or 83.

KAPITI COAST

With wide, people-free beaches, the Kapiti Coast acts as a summer playground and sub-urban extension for Wellingtonians. The re-gion takes its moniker from Kapiti Island, a bird and marine sanctuary 5km offshore from Paraparaumu.

In the Tararua Range, Tararua Forest Park forms a dramatic backdrop along the length of the coastline and has some accessible day walks and longer tramps.

The Kapiti Coast makes an easy day trip from Wellington, but if you're after a few rest-ful days or are heading further north, there's some quality accommodation here. Pick up a copy of the *Kapiti Coast Arts Guide* from the local visitor information centres if you're interested in the region's abundant galleries, artists and studios.

Orientation & Information

The Kapiti Coast stretches 30km along the North Island's west coast from Paekakariki (41km north of Wellington) to Otaki. Most towns are a tale of two settlements: one along the highway (banks, petrol, hamburger joints)

and another by the water (cafes, motels and houses). Paraparaumu is the biggest town here, but still runs at a beachy pace.

The most comprehensive visitor informa-tion centres are at Paraparaumu (p420) and Otaki (p422). Online, check out www.nature coast.co.nz.

Getting There & Around

Getting here from Wellington is a breeze: just track north on SH1. By car, it's about a 45-minute drive to Paraparaumu, and an hour to Otaki, much of it by motorway.

AIR

Plans are underway to upgrade and expand Paraparaumu airport. In the meantime, **Air2there** (☎ 0800 777 000; www.air2there.com) has regular daily flights departing from the cur-rent airstrip, connecting the Kapiti Coast with Blenheim and Nelson.

BUS

InterCity (☎ 04-385 0520; www.intercitycoach.co.nz) has buses between Wellington and Palmerston North ($29 to $36, 2¼ hours, seven daily), stopping at Paekakariki ($20, 40 minutes), Paraparaumu ($22, 45 minutes) and Otaki ($29, 1¼ hours).

The daily services into/out of Wellington run by White Star Express, Naked Bus and Bay Express (see p416) also stop in major Kapiti Coast towns.

From SH1 in Paraparaumu, local buses 260, 261 and 262 run to the beach. Bus 290 heads to Otaki, and 280 and 285 to Waikanae, calling at highway settlements and the beach.

TRAIN

Tranz Metro (☎ 0800 801 700; www.tranzmetro.co.nz) commuter trains between Wellington and the coast are easier and more frequent than buses. Services run from Wellington to Paraparaumu ($10, 55 minutes, generally half-hourly off-peak between 6am and 11pm, with more services at peak times), stopping en route in Paekakariki ($9). Weekday off-peak fares (9am to 3pm) are up to $2.50 cheaper.

Tranz Scenic (☎ 0800 872 467; www.tranzscenic. co.nz) has long-distance *Overlander* trains connecting Wellington and Auckland stop-ping at Paraparaumu, while the weekday-only, peak-hour *Capital Connection* travelling to Wellington in the morning and back to Palmerston North in the evening, stops at

Paraparaumu, Waikanae and Otaki. See p417 for details of these services.

PAEKAKARIKI

pop 1730

Paekakariki is a little seaside village stretched along a black-sand beach, serviced by a train station and passed by the highway. Almost within spitting distance of Wellington (41km to the south), it's an unhurried place to escape for a few days.

Sights & Activities

Queen Elizabeth Park (☎ 04-292 8625; qepranger@ gw.govt.nz; admission free; ☺ 8am-8pm) is a rambling 650-hectare dune-scape park behind the beach, with plenty of opportunities for swimming, walking, cycling and picnicking. There are three entrances: off Wellington Rd in Paekakariki, at MacKays Crossing on SH1, and off the Esplanade in Raumati to the north.

About 5km north of Paekakariki, just off SH1, the **Tramway Museum** (☎ 04-292 8361; www. wellingtontrams.org.nz; Queen Elizabeth Park, MacKay's Crossing; admission adult/child $5/3, with tram ride adult/ child/family $9.50/4/24; ☺ museum 10am-4.30pm daily, trams 11am-4.30pm Sat & Sun, daily 26 Dec-late Jan) has restored wooden trams that ran in Wellington until 1964. A 2km track curls from the museum through Queen Elizabeth Park down to the beach.

Stables on the Park (☎ 06-364 3336; www.stables onthepark.co.nz; Queen Elizabeth Park, MacKay's Crossing; half- /1-/1½hr ride $35/55/75; ☺ daily by arrangement) runs coastal horse riding from its base behind the Tramway Museum. The 1½-hour ride will see you trot along the beach with views of Kapiti Island before heading inland on park tracks. Beginners are welcome.

Sleeping & Eating

Paekakariki Holiday Park (☎ 04-292 8292; www. paekakarikiholidaypark.co.nz; 180 Wellington Rd; sites per adult $13, cabins & flats $65-85) A pleasant, large, leafy park approximately 1.5km north of the township at the southern entrance to Queen Elizabeth Park. Just a hop, skip and a jump from the beach.

Paekakariki Backpackers (☎ 04-902 5967; www. wellingtonbeachbackpackers.co.nz; 11 Wellington Rd; dm $28, d with/without bathroom $76/66; ▢) Atop a steep hill covered with dense gardens, two houses combine to offer an array of rooms, many with sea and sunset views. Ask about the double with flash new en suite – positively

luxurious. Or maybe you'll prefer the yurt in the front yard. Lie in bed looking out to the sunset, and be lured to sleep by the ocean's crashing waves.

our pick Beach Road Deli (☎ 04-902 9029; 5 Beach Rd; snacks $3-8, pizza $9-21; ☺ 7am-8pm Wed-Sun) Bijou deli and pizzeria, packed with home-baked bread and patisserie, cheese, charcuterie and assorted imported goodies. Heaven-sent for the highway traveller, picnic provisioner, or those looking for a sausage to fry and a bun to put it in. Fresh juices and ace coffee.

Finn's (☎ 04-292 8081; www.kapiticoasthotel.co.nz; 2 Beach Rd; mains $15-23; ☺ 10am-3pm Tue-Fri, 9am-3pm Sat & Sun, 6pm-8.30pm Tue-Sun) Opened in 2007, Finn's is the flashy, beige suit of the cutesy railway village, but redeems itself with spacious rooms (doubles $125 to $135), good-value meals, and independent beer on tap. The hush glass keeps the highway at bay.

PARAPARAUMU

pop 6840

Lower-than-low-key Paraparaumu is the principal town on the Kapiti Coast, and a suburban satellite of Wellington. The rough-and-tumble beach is the coast's most developed, sustaining plenty of cafes, motels and takeaway joints. Boat trips to Kapiti Island set sail from here (see opposite).

The correct pronunciation is 'Pah-ra-pah-ra-oo-moo', meaning 'scraps from an oven', which is said to have originated when a Maori war party attacked the settlement and found only scraps of food remaining. It's a bit of a mouthful to pronounce; locals usually just corrupt it into 'Para-par-am'.

Orientation & Information

Coastlands Shoppingtown, the hub of Paraparaumu's highway settlement, is on the left as you head into town from Wellington. Three kilometres west along Kapiti Rd (just past Coastlands) is Paraparaumu Beach; Seaview Rd is the main road here. Sleeping and eating options are most atmospheric (and plentiful) by the beach.

Coastlands has all the services you'll need: banks, ATMs, post office, supermarkets and cinema. The **Paraparaumu visitor information centre** (☎ 04-298 8195; www.naturecoast.co.nz; Coastlands car park, SH1; ☺ 9am-5pm Mon-Fri, 10am-3pm Sat & Sun) is slap-bang in the middle of the Coastlands car park. Pick up the *Nature Coast* brochure while you're here.

Sights & Activities

Paraparaumu Beach, with its beachside park, decent swimming and other watery activities, is the town's raison d'être.

Paraparaumu Beach Golf Club (☎ 04-902 8200; www.paraparaumubeachgolfclub.co.nz; 376 Kapiti Rd; 9/18 holes $55/130; ☀ 7.30am-dusk) is a challenging and beautiful links course that is ranked among NZ's best. It's hosted the NZ Open 12 times and tamed Tiger in 2002. Visitors are welcome: call for tee times, or book online. Clubs, carts and shoes can be hired.

Another kilometre north, just off SH1 in a voluminous hangar, the **Southward Car Museum** (☎ 04-297 1221; www.southward.org.nz; Otaihanga Rd; adult/child $10/3; ☀ 9am-4.30pm) has one of Australasia's largest collections of antique and unusual cars. Check out the DeLorean and the 1950 gangster Cadillac.

Sleeping

Barnacles Seaside Inn (☎ 0800 555 856, 04-902 5856; www.seasideyha.co.nz; 3 Marine Pde; dm/s/f $28/50/90, d $62-80; ☐) Opposite Paraparaumu Beach, Barnacles is a creaky, old-style YHA hostel in a 1920s heritage building. Snug rooms are individually decorated with antique dressers and have sinks and heaters; some have electric blankets and sea views.

Wrights by the Sea (☎ 0508 902 760, 04-902 7600; www.wrightsmotel.co.nz; 387 Kapiti Rd; units $100-150; ☐ ☜) Not quite by the sea, but near enough and even closer to the golf course. A modern motel complex in the conservative style with light, airy rooms, Sky TV and off-road parking. Some with full kitchen.

Eating

Fed Up Fast Foods (☎ 04-902 6686; 40 Marine Pde; meals $5-15; ☀ 10am-9pm Mon-Thu, 9.30am-9.30pm Fri-Sun) A takeaway chippy with the usual battery of fries as well as doner kebabs and fancy burgers. Unfathomably good-value dinner deals, eggy brekkies, espresso and Kapiti ice cream. Clean-as-a-whistle dinette, plus alfresco tables with views to the blue yonder.

Mediterranean Food Warehouse (☎ 0800 334 477, 04-892 0010; Coastlands car park, SH1; meals $13-18; ☀ 9am-9pm) A handy highway pit stop, with excellent wood-fired pizza, luscious cakes, gelato, and a minimarket for picnic supplies. Food so good you'll forget you're in the middle of a car park.

Ambience Café (☎ 04-298 9898; 10 Seaview Rd; lunch $14-18, dinner $20-29; ☀ 8am-4pm Sun-Thu, to late Fri & Sat; **V**) A very 'Wellington' cafe, with both light

and substantial meals made with relish, such as fish cakes, the BLT, and colourful veggie options. Cake cabinet at full capacity, and great coffee (of course).

Soprano Ristorante (☎ 04-298 8892; 7 Seaview Rd; mains $21-28; ☀ 6pm-late Mon-Sat) A welcoming family-run joint with the liveliest evening atmosphere at the beach township. Pizzas, pastas and other Italian classics such as saltimbocca. Sweet treats include the ubiquitous tiramisu and delicious homemade *limoncello* (lemon liqueur). No-nonsense, affordable food and wine in a homely environment – *bella*!

KAPITI ISLAND

Kapiti Island is the coastline's dominant feature, a 10km by 2km slice which since 1897 has been a protected reserve. It's predator-free – many bird species that are now rare or extinct on the mainland still thrive on the island. **Kapiti Island Alive** (☎ 06-362 6606; www.kapitiislandalive.co.nz; walks $20) runs one-hour guided walks and offers homestay accommodation.

The island is open to visitors, limited to around 68 people per day, and it's essential that you book and obtain a permit (adult/child $11/5) at Wellington's DOC visitor centre (p399) – in person, by phone or via email (kapiti.island@doc.govt.nz). During summer it pays to book in advance, especially on weekends. DOC also publishes the detailed *Visiting Kapiti Island* brochure.

Transport is booked separately from the permit (arrange your permit before your boat trip). Two commercial operators are licensed to take visitors to the island, both running to/from Paraparaumu Beach (which can be reached by train, see p419). Departures are between 9am and 9.30am daily, returning between 3pm and 4pm; call in the morning to confirm departure (sailings are weather dependent). All visitors receive an introductory talk; BYO lunch.

Kapiti Marine Charter (☎ 0800 433 779, 04-297 2585; www.kapitimarinecharter.co.nz; adult/child $55/30)

Kapiti Tours (☎ 0800 527 484, 04-237 7965; www.kapititours.co.nz; adult/child $55/30)

WAIKANAE

pop 6930

With a particularly nice stretch of beach, New Zealand's 2008 'Top Town' (and retirees' favourite) is a viable option as your Kapiti Coast rest stop.

About 5km north of Paraparaumu at Waikanae is the turn-off to **Nga Manu Nature Reserve** (☎ 04-293 4131; www.ngamanu.co.nz; 281 Ngarara Rd; adult/child/family $12/4/24; ☼ 10am-5pm), a 15-hectare bird sanctuary dotted with picnic areas, bush walks, aviaries and a nocturnal house with kiwi, owls and tuatara. The eels are fed at 2pm daily, and guided tours run at weekends at 1.30pm (Sunday only in winter). To get here, turn seawards from SH1 onto Te Moana Rd and then right down Ngarara Rd and follow the signs; the sanctuary is 3.5km from the turn-off.

Old but well-maintained **Waikanae Beach Motel** (☎ 0800 486 533, 04-293 6199; www.kapitimotel. co.nz; 95 Te Moana Rd, d $110, f $140; ☐ ☑) has spacious units with full kitchen facilities, about 1km from the beach. All rooms open out onto or overlook the courtyard garden and picturesque golf course beyond. The swimming pool and playground make it an ideal spot for families.

Front Room (☎ 04-905 4142; 42 Tutere St; meals $6-25; ☼ 9am-4pm Mon-Fri, 6-9pm Fri & Sat, 5-9pm Sun) has a stylish, pared-back interior and is home to food a tad more sophisticated that your average cafe. Keep an eye out for the Waikanae crab, a regional speciality. The pleasant garden out back sports a fireplace, welcome on cool evenings.

OTAKI
pop 5650

Unremarkable Otaki is primarily a gateway to the Tararua Range. It has a strong Maori history and presence: the little town has nine *marae* and a Maori college. The historic Rangiatea Church, built under the guidance of Ngati Toa chief Te Rauparaha nearly 150 years ago, tragically burnt to the ground in 1995 but has been rebuilt. This was the original burial site of Te Rauparaha.

Orientation & Information

Most services, including the train station where buses also stop, are on SH1. The main centre of Otaki, with the post office and shops, is 2km seawards on Tasman Rd. Three kilometres further on the same road brings you to Otaki's windswept beach. Note that the telephone area code in Otaki is ☎ 06, not ☎ 04 like most of the rest of the Kapiti Coast.

The **Otaki i-SITE** (☎ 06-364 7620; www.naturecoast. co.nz; Centennial Park, SH1; ☼ 9am-5pm Mon-Fri, 10am-3pm Sat & Sun) is just south of the main roundabout in an 1891 courthouse.

Activities

Two kilometres south of Otaki, scenic Otaki Gorge Rd trucks inland from SH1 and leads 19km (5km unsealed) to **Otaki Forks**, the main western entrance to **Tararua Forest Park**. Otaki Forks has picnic areas, swimming and **campsites** (unpowered sites per adult/child $6/2), plus bush walks from 30 minutes to 3½ hours in the immediate area; longer tracks lead to huts. The i-SITE sells detailed maps and knowledgeable staff proffer information and advice about the walks. Ask at DOC in Wellington (p399) for advice on longer tracks in the park. You can tramp in the Tararua Ranges, but you must bring adequate clothing and equipment, and be well prepared for wild weather.

Sleeping & Eating

Byron's Resort (☎ 0800 800 122, 06-364 8119; www. byronsresort.co.nz; 20 Tasman Rd; unpowered/powered sites $31/35, units & motels $100-150; ☐ ☑) A traditional, family-fuelled resort by the beach. The Scuttlebutt restaurant and garden bar (meals $19 to $27; open Tuesday to Sunday) is a welcome haven after a day spent at the pool, spa, sauna, tennis court and playground.

Red House Café (☎ 06-364 3022; 885 Main Rd, SH1, Te Horo; lunch $10-17, dinner $22-29; ☼ 9am-late Mon-Fri, 8.30pm-late Sat & Sun) One of the best highway pit stops round these parts is this fire-engine red cafe 5km south of Otaki. Inside it's all warm polished wood, all-day breakfasts, excellent baking and an extensive blackboard menu. Bargain two-course roast and pudding special on Sunday.

THE WAIRARAPA

The Wairarapa is the large slab of land east and northeast of Wellington, beyond the craggy Tararua and Rimutaka Ranges. Named after Lake Wairarapa (Shimmering Waters), a shallow 8000-hectare lake, the region has traditionally been a frenzied hotbed of sheep farming. More recently, wineries have sprung up – around Martinborough, most famously – which has turned the region into a decadent weekend retreat. A vigorous foodie culture has evolved alongside the wineries and restored B&B cottages.

See www.wairarapanz.com for regional info, but also check out the **Classic New Zealand Wine Trail** (www.classicwinetrail.co.nz) – a useful tool for joining the dots throughout the Wairarapa and its neighbouring wine regions of Hawke's Bay and Marlborough.

Note that the telephone area code over here is ☎ 06, not ☎ 04 like most of the rest of the Wellington region.

Getting There & Around

From Wellington, **Tranz Metro** (☎ 0800 801 700; www.tranzmetro.co.nz) commuter trains run to Masterton ($15, 1½ hours, five or six daily on weekdays, two daily on weekends), calling at seven stations including Featherston and Carterton. For other Wairarapa towns, connect with the local bus services.

Tranzit Coachlines (☎ 0800 471 227, 06-370 6600; www.tranzit.co.nz; 316 Queen St, Masterton) has a bus between Masterton and Palmerston North (one-way $21, 1¾ hours, one daily), plus local daily services (bus 200) between Martinborough and Masterton ($4) via Featherston, Greytown and Carterton.

Wairarapa Coach Lines (☎ 0800 666 355, 06-308 9352; www.waicoach.co.nz) runs between Masterton and Martinborough ($6, 1¼ hours, three daily) and meets every Featherston train for a run through to Martinborough ($4, 20 minutes, four to five daily).

MARTINBOROUGH

pop 1360

The most popular visitor spot in the Wairarapa, Martinborough is a pretty town with a leafy town square and some charming old buildings, surrounded by a patchwork of pasture and a pinstripe of grapevines. It is famed for its wineries, which draw in visitors to nose the pinot, avail themselves of its excellent eateries, and snooze it off at boutique accommodation. The best time for an overnight visit is midweek, when accommodation is cheaper (although many restaurants shut up shop on Monday and Tuesday).

Orientation & Information

Martinborough is arrowed off the SH2 from both Featherston and Greytown; it's about 20km from either town. Settler and town planner John Martin designed Martinborough's classic grid, a Union Jack street pattern centred upon a leafy square. The **Martinborough i-SITE** (☎ 06-306 5010; www.wairarapanz.com; 18 Kitchener St; ☺ 9am-5pm Mon-Fri, 10am-4pm Sat & Sun) is full of brochures and information.

Sights & Activities

With so many **wineries** scattered around town, there are no points for guessing what is the town's main attraction. This is closely followed by the excellent food that goes with it – Martinborough punches well above its weight when it comes to food cafes and restaurants.

The town's cultural hub is arguably **Circus** (see p425), a stylish art-house cinema where you can watch the cream of contemporary movies as well as eat and drink in the convivial dining room or sunny courtyard.

About 3km from town off Oxford St is **Olivo** (☎ 06-306 9074; www.olivo.co.nz; Hinakura Rd; admission free; ☺ 10am-5pm Mon-Fri), a welcoming olive grove where you can meet the owners, take a tour and tasting, and buy your oil to go.

Patuna Farm Adventures (☎ 06-306 9966; www.patunafarm.co.nz; Ruakokoputuna Rd) offers horse treks (from $40), a challenging pole-to-pole rope course (from $20), and a four-hour self-guided walk through native bush and a limestone chasm (adult/child $15/10). The chasm is open late October until Easter; other activities operate year-round.

Sleeping

A list of local B&Bs, self-contained weekend-away cottages and farmstays can be found on www.wairarapanz.com; the i-SITE can help with bookings. Expect to pay around $160 per night for two people.

ourpick Martinborough Village Camping (☎ 06-306 8946; www.martinboroughcamping.com; cnr Princess & Dublin Sts; unpowered sites $30, cabins s/d $45/60;) An appealing camping ground with grapevine views, just five minutes' walk to town. It has shady trees and the town pool over the back fence, making it a cooling oasis on sticky days. Cabins are basic but great value, freeing up your dollars for the cellar door. Bike hire available for $35 per day.

Kate's Place (☎ 06-306 9935; www.katesplace.co.nz; 7 Cologne St; dm $30, d $80;) An unpretentious home stay–backpackers with a welcoming owner and a laid-back vibe, just a hop and a skip from the Square. The two dorms have solid bunks with extrawide mattresses. Mull over your day's misdemeanours on the front porch.

Claremont (☎ 0800 809 162, 06-306 9162; www.theclaremont.co.nz; 38 Regent St; d $125-160, 4-person apt

WAIRARAPA WINE COUNTRY

Wairarapa's winemakers enjoy an impressive international reputation, but this world-renowned industry was nearly crushed in infancy. The region's first vines were planted in 1883, but the prohibition movement in 1908 soon put a cap on that corker idea. It wasn't until the 1980s that winemaking was revived, after Martinborough's *terroir* was discovered to be similar to Burgundy in France. A few vineyards soon sprang up, but the number has now ballooned to nearly 50 regionwide. Martinborough is the undisputed hub of the action, renowned for its gravels which produce particularly remarkable pinot noir and distinctive whites.

For a good introduction to Wairarapa's wines, visit Martinborough's stylish cinema, **Circus** (☎ 06-306 9442; www.circus.net.nz; 34 Jellicoe St; ☯ screenings 3pm daily; additional screenings peak season), which screens **Vintners' Choice** (www.vintnerschoice.co.nz), a 40-minute documentary with a real-live wine tasting.

The town also plays host to New Zealand's best wine, food and music festival – **Toast Martinborough** (☎ 06-306 9183; www.toastmartinborough.co.nz; tickets $60) held annually on the third Sunday in November. Enjoyable on many levels (standing up and quite possibly lying on the grass), this is a hugely popular event and you'll have to be quick on the draw to get a ticket.

The **Wairarapa Wines Harvest Festival** (☎ 027 477 4717; www.wairarapawines.co.nz; tickets $25-35) celebrates the beginning of the harvest with an extravaganza of wine, food and family fun. It's held at a remote riverbank setting 10 minutes from Carterton on a Saturday in mid-March.

Wairarapa's wineries thrive on visitors; Martinborough's 30-odd are particularly welcoming with well-oiled cellar doors, and noteworthy food served in some gorgeous gardens and courtyards. The *Wairarapa Wine Trail Map* (available from the i-SITE and many other locations) will aid your navigations. Read all about it at www.winesfrommartinborough.com.

You can sample and purchase many wines under one gabled roof at the **Martinborough Wine Centre** (☎ 06-306 9040; www.martinboroughwinecentre.co.nz; 6 Kitchener St; tastings available; ☯ 10am-5pm), which also sells olive oils, books, clothing and art.

Recommended Wineries

Ata Rangi (☎ 06-306 9570; www.atarangi.co.nz; Puruatanga Rd) One of the region's pioneering winemakers. Great drops across the board and cute cellar door.

$275; ▣) A classy accommodation enclave off Jellicoe St, the Claremont has two-storey, self-contained units in great nick, modern studios with spa baths, and sparkling two-bedroom apartments, all at reasonable rates (even cheaper in winter and/or midweek). Attractive gardens, barbecue areas and bike hire.

Peppers Martinborough Hotel (☎ 06-306 9350; www.martinboroughhotel.co.nz; The Square; d incl breakfast $300-385; ▣ ☞) Grand old hotel on the main square that's been magnificently restored, with 16 spacious, luxury rooms, each individually decorated with pizzazz. All open onto either a wide veranda or courtyard garden. Downstairs the Settlers Bar (mains $12 to $20) serves sophisticated pub nosh and local wines by the glass.

Eating & Drinking

Eating and drinking is what Martinborough's all about, with award-winning restaurants and cafes, delicatessens and food shops. Peppers Martinborough Hotel and the no-nonsense pub over the road are the best places to join the locals for a drink.

Café Medici (☎ 06-306 9965; 9 Kitchener St; breakfast & lunch $7-19, dinner $22-30; ☯ 8.30am-4pm Wed-Mon, plus evenings summer) A perennial favourite among townsfolk and regular visitors, this airy cafe has a Florentine/Kiwiana interior and courtyard offering honest home-cooked food. Choose from the tasty counter selection including muffins, pies, quiche and famous scones. The blackboard menu is short but varied with plenty of salad options. Great coffee, too.

Trio Café at Coney Winery (☎ 06-306 8345; Dry River Rd; snacks $10, mains $24-25; ☯ noon-3pm Sat & Sun) Wine and dine in a courtyard featuring gorgeous white roses or in the light and airy tasting room. The great-value food is sophisticated, fresh and delicious, and all made from scratch. The atmosphere is relaxed and fun, a

Coney (☎ 06-306 8345; www.coneywines.co.nz; Dry River Rd) Friendly tastings and lovely restaurant (p424). Winery tours by arrangement.

Margrain (☎ 06-306 9292; www.margrainvineyard.co.nz; cnr Princess St & Huangarua Rd) Pretty winery and site of the Old Winery Cafe, a good pit stop overlooking the vines.

Vynfields (☎ 06-306 9901; www.vynfields.com; 22 Omarere Rd) Five-star, spicy pinot noir and a lush lawn on which to enjoy a platter. Organic/biodynamic wines.

Tours

If you have the time and physical ability, the best and most carbon-friendly way to explore the Wairarapa's wines is by bicycle as the flat landscape makes for puff-free cruising.

From Masterton, **March Hare** (☎ 021 668 970; www.march-hare.co.nz; tours incl all gear & a picnic $65) runs self-guided bike tours of the Opaki winegrowing area.

There are three options in Martinborough:

Christina Estate Vineyard (☎ 06-306 8920; christinaestate@xtra.co.nz; 28 Puruatanga Rd; ☀ 8.30am-6pm) Per hour/day $15/25. Tandems for the coordinated.

Martinborough Village Camping (☎ 06-306 8946; www.martinboroughcamping.com; cnr Princess & Dublin St) Per day $35.

Martinborough Wine Centre (☎ 06-306 9040; www.martinboroughwinecentre.co.nz; 6 Kitchener St) Half-/full day $25/35.

Numerous operators run bus tours around Martinborough and the region:

Dynamic Tours (☎ 04-478 8533; www.dynamictours.co.nz; from $225) Customised wine tours, run from Wellington.

Hammond's Scenic Tours (☎ 04-472 0869; www.wellingtonsightseeingtours.com; full-day tour adult/child $195/97.50) Full-day winery tours including gourmet lunch.

Tranzit Coachlines (☎ 0800 471 227, 06-370 6600; www.tranzit.co.nz; 316 Queen St, Masterton) Two daily tours depart from Wellington or the main Wairarapa towns. The Gourmet Wine Escape ($161) visits Martinborough vineyards and includes tastings and lunch. The Garden Gourmet Escape (adult/child $182/115) takes in two gardens, lunch at the Gladstone Country Inn, and wine tasting.

Zest Food Tours (☎ 04-801 9198; www.zestfoodtours.co.nz; tours incl lunch & wines from $230) Small-group food and wine tours (2½ to five hours) in Greytown and Martinborough.

testament to your host Tim Coney, an affable and knowledgeable character who may sing at random.

Circus (☎ 06-306 9442; www.circus.net.nz; 34 Jellicoe St; mains $18-28, tickets adult/child $14/10; ☀ 2.30pm-late Wed-Mon) A modern microsized movie complex with two comfy studio theatres. The stylish foyer and cafe, opening out on to a rather Zen garden, offer some of the most sociable surroundings in town. Reasonably priced seasonal food includes bar snacks, pizza, mains with plenty of fresh veg, and a short list of sweet delights.

French Bistro (☎ 06-306 8863; 3 Kitchener St; mains $36-40; ☀ 6pm-late Wed-Sun) Wendy Campbell's provincial cooking in this tiny but smart family-run bistro has garnered praise both at home and abroad. Francophiles will delight at her dishes using ingredients from the region and beyond. The decor is eclectic as is the carefully selected wine list offering a variety of mainly local vintages.

CAPE PALLISER

The Wairarapa coast south of Martinborough around Palliser Bay and Cape Palliser is remote and sparsely populated. The bendy road to Cape Palliser is utterly scenic: a big ocean and black-sand beaches on one side; barren hills and sheer cliffs on the other. Look for hints of the South Island, visible on a clear day.

Standing like giant organ pipes in the Putangirua Scenic Reserve are the **Putangirua Pinnacles**, formed by rain washing silt and sand away and exposing the underlying bedrock. Accessible by a track near the car park on Cape Palliser Rd, it's an easy three-hour return walk along a streambed to the pinnacles, or take the 3½-hour loop track past hills and coastal viewpoints. For some more rugged Wairarapa tramping nearby, head to **Aorangi (Haurangi) Forest Park**. For maps and access info contact DOC in Wellington (p399).

Further south is the wind-worn fishing village **Ngawi**. The first things you'll notice here are the rusty bulldozers on the beach, used to drag fishing boats ashore. Next stop is the malodorous **seal colony**, the North Island's largest breeding area. Whatever you do in your quest for a photo, don't get between the seals and the sea. If you block their escape route they're likely to have a go at you!

Get your thighs thumping on the steep, 250-step (or is it 249?) climb to **Cape Palliser Lighthouse**, from where there are yet more amazing coastal views, as far as the South Island if it's not hazy.

On the way there or back, take the short detour to the wind-blown settlement of **Lake Ferry**, overlooking **Lake Onoke**, where there's birdwatching to be enjoyed. This area is also good for exploration – discover the lake edge, the wild and woolly coastline (prime for surfing), and the cliffs behind. You'll also find the **Lake Ferry Hotel** (☎ 06-307 7831; ☺ from 11am) with its retro fitout (check out the formica), which has great views and fish and chips.

Martinborough i-SITE (p423) can help with accommodation options in the Lake Ferry and Cape Palliser area, which include camping grounds and holiday homes for rent.

GREYTOWN
pop 2000
The most popular of several small towns along SH2, Greytown has spruced itself up over recent years and is now full of Wellingtonians on the weekend. It has plenty of accommodation, some decent food, three high-street pubs, and some swanky shopping. Check out www.greytown.co.nz for more information.

Sights
Greytown was the country's first planned inland town: intact Victorian architectural specimens line the main street. The quaint **Cobblestones Village Museum** (☎ 06-304 9687; www.cobblestonesmuseum.org.nz; 169 Main St; adult/child/family $2.50/1/6; ☺ 10am-4pm) is an enclave of period buildings and various historic objects, dotted around pretty grounds inviting a lie-down on a picnic blanket. No picnic? No worries. Visit **Schoc Chocolate** (☎ 06-304 8960; www.chocolatetherapy.com; 177 Main St; ☺ 10am-5pm Mon-Fri, 10.30am-5pm Sat & Sun) in a 1920s cottage that shares the grounds. Sublime flavours, worth every single penny of 10 bucks a tablet. Truffles, rocky road and peanut brittle, too. Free tastings.

About 10km southeast of Carterton is **Stonehenge Aotearoa** (☎ 06-377 1600; www.

stonehenge-aotearoa.com; tours adult $15, child $6-10; ☺ 10am-4pm Wed-Sun, tours 2pm Sat & Sun, public holidays & by appointment). Explore the southern sky – even in daylight – at this full-scale adaptation of the UK Stonehenge, orientated for its location on a grassy knoll overlooking the Wairarapa Plain. The pretour talk and audiovisual presentation are excellent, and the henge itself a pretty surreal sight, day or night, especially when interpreted by one of its tour guides who are consummate storytellers. Self-guided tours are also available for $5.

Sleeping & Eating
Greytown Camping Ground (☎ 06-304 9837; Kuratawhiti St; unpowered/powered sites $30/36) A basic camping option (with equally basic facilities) scenically spread through Greytown Park, 500m from town.

Greytown Hotel (☎ 06-304 9138; www.greytownhotel.co.nz; 33 Main St; s/d $50/80; ☐) A serious contender for 'oldest hotel in New Zealand', the Top Pub (as it's known) is looking great for her age, having just had a major facelift. Upstairs rooms are small and basic but comfortable, with no-frills furnishings and shared bathrooms. Downstairs is a chic new dining room (classic meals $22 to $29), ol' faithful lounge-bar and popular garden-courtyard.

Oak Estate Motor Lodge (☎ 0800 843 625, 06-304 8188; www.oakestate.co.nz; cnr Main St & Hospital Rd; r $125-185) A stand of gracious roadside oaks and pretty gardens shield a smart complex of self-contained units: studios, one- and two-bedroom options.

French Baker (☎ 06-304 8873; 81 Main St; snacks $4-7, mains $13-19; ☺ 7.30am-3pm Mon, Thu & Fri, to 4pm Fri & Sat) Buttery croissants, tempting tarts and authentic breads; artisan baker Moïse Cerson is le real McCoy. Great coffee too and a compact menu of suitably Gallic offerings, such as Roquefort salad and French toast.

Cuckoo Pizza (☎ 06-304 8992; 128 Main St; mains $15-24; ☺ 11am-8.30pm Wed-Sun) Refreshingly unruly pizza joint littered with mismatched retro furniture in an old house on the main street. Try the 'moa' pizza (pepperoni, mushrooms, anchovies, olives and chilli), or pasta specials. Good coffee too.

MASTERTON & AROUND
pop 19,500
Masterton is the Wairarapa's utilitarian hub, an unselfconscious town getting on with its

business. Its main claim to immortality is the 50-year-old sheep-shearing competition, the international Golden Shears (right).

Orientation & Information

State Highway 2 runs through the centre of town. From the south SH2 is named High St, which then becomes Chapel St. Queen St runs parallel to High/Chapel St, one block east. The town's prime attractions are another block east on Dixon St where you will find the **Masterton i-SITE** (☎ 06-370 0900; www.wairarapanz. com; cnr Dixon & Bruce Sts; ☻ 9am-5pm Mon-Fri, 10am-4pm Sat & Sun).

Sights & Activities

Stretch your car-cramped legs in the 32-hectare **Queen Elizabeth Park** (Dixon St; ☻ 24hr), with its aviaries, duck lake, children's playground, minigolf and cricket oval. Opposite the park is **Aratoi Wairarapa Museum of Art & History** (☎ 06-370 0001; www.aratoi.co.nz; cnr Bruce & Dixon Sts; admission by donation; ☻ 10am-4.30pm), documenting the art and cultural heritage of the region, both Maori and Pakeha.

Occupying two historic woolsheds next to Aratoi is **Shear Discovery** (☎ 06-378 8008; www. sheardiscovery.co.nz; Dixon St; adult/child/family $5/2/10; ☻ 10am-4pm), a baaaa-loody marvellous little museum dedicated to NZ's sheep-shearing and wool-production industries.

Castlepoint, on the coast 68km east of Masterton, is an awesome, end-of-the-world place, with a reef, the lofty 162m-high Castle Rock, protected swimming and walking tracks. There's an easy (but sometimes ludicrously windy) 30-minute return walk across the reef to the lighthouse, where 70-plus shell species are fossilised in the cliffs. Another one-hour return walk runs to a huge limestone cave (take a torch), or take the 1½-hour return track from Deliverance Cove to Castle Rock. Keep well away from the lower reef when there are heavy seas. Ask the staff at Masterton i-SITE (above) about accommodation here.

Pukaha Mt Bruce National Wildlife Centre (☎ 06-375 8004; www.mtbruce.org.nz; adult/child/family $15/4/38; ☻ 9am-4.30pm) is not only an important sanctuary for native NZ wildlife (mostly birds), it's also the most readily accessible bush experience off the highway. The visitor centre has various exhibits, while outside there are aviaries, a kiwi house, virgin forest and a scenic one-hour loop track taking in some great views. Slippery eels, tuatara and other creatures also reside here. Take a walk with the ranger (10.30am and 2pm Saturday and Sunday; adult/child $25/12.50) or take the Lookout Lunch Tour (11am Sunday; adult/child $50/25 including lunch). There's a cafe on-site; it's 30km north of Masterton on SH2.

The turn-off to the main eastern entrance of the **Tararua Forest Park** is just south of Masterton on SH2; follow Norfolk Rd about 15km to the gates. Mountain streams dart through virgin forest in this reserve, known as 'Holdsworth'. At the park entrance are swimming holes, picnic areas and **campsites** (unpowered sites adult/child $6/2). Walks include short, easy family tramps, excellent one- or two-day tramps, and longer, challenging tramps for experienced bush-bods (west through to Otaki Forks). The resident caretaker (☎ 06-377 0022) has maps and hut accommodation info. Check weather and track updates before setting off, and be prepared to be baked, battered and buffeted by fickle conditions.

Festivals & Events

For wine and food related events, see p424.
Golden Shears (www.goldenshears.co.nz) Held annually in the first week of March.
Wings over Wairarapa (☎ 06-370 0900; www.wings. org.nz) An exciting three-day air show (biennial; odd years) featuring more than 70 aircraft – from the war birds through to gliders, gyros, jets and batty aerobatics.

Sleeping & Eating

Empire Lodge (☎ 06-377 1902; www.empirelodge. co.nz; 94 Queen St; backpackers dm/s/d $25/30/55, hotel s/d $80/90; ▣) An 1870s budget hotel and backpackers, well worn and badly colour coordinated. Down its long hallways you'll discover a communal kitchen, TV room, and other surprises. Views of the Tararua Range from the rear deck. Cheap sleep in a handy location.

Copthorne Solway Park (☎ 0800 808 228, 06-370 0500; www.solway.co.nz; High St; d $130-345; ▣ ▣) A megabuck refurb has restored this 1970s resort to glory, from its sunken bar and reputable restaurant, to its two swimming pools, tennis court and the driving range which takes up just some of its 24-hectare grounds. Lots of room options, all with classy fit-outs featuring some particularly stylish textiles.

our pick **Ten O'Clock Cookie** (☎ 06-377 4551; 180 Queen St; snacks $3-15; ☻ 7am-4.30pm Mon-Fri,

8am-2.30pm Sat) Loosen that belt and get ready to indulge. Heavenly baking, scrumptious pies, simple sandwiches and cookies of course. Take away or sit down and enjoy your treat with a decent cup of coffee or tea. Relaxed and great value, it's deserving of its many awards.

Lounge Wine Bar (☎ 06-379 6065; 78-81 Main St, Carterton; snacks & meals $5-18; ✷ 3.30pm-late Wed-Sun; **V**) A local hero saves the town of Carterton (indeed, the region) with a steady stream of live music (Friday and Saturday), local wines, independent beers and Spanish food. All this and more lapped up in a groovy 'thrift-shop' interior.

Café Cecille (☎ 06-370 1166; Queen Elizabeth Park; brunch $9-18, dinner $15-30; ✷ 10am-3pm daily, 5-8pm Fri & Sat) In the middle of Queen Elizabeth Park is the century-old Coronation Hall, home to Café Cecille. Its wraparound veranda and simple but wholesome food make it hard to beat on a sunny day. Divine homemade chips.

Gladstone Inn (☎ 06-372 7866; 51 Gladstone Rd, Gladstone; lunch $12-28, dinner $18-30; ✷ 11am-late) Gladstone, 18km south of Masterton, is less a town, more a state of mind. There's very little here except this proud inn, haven of thirsty locals, motorbike enthusiasts, Sunday drivers and lazy-afternoon shandy sippers who hog the tables in the glorious garden bar.

Marlborough & Nelson

For many travellers, Marlborough and Nelson will be their introduction to what South Islanders refer to as the 'Mainland'. Having left windy Wellington, and made a white-knuckled crossing of Cook Strait, folk are often surprised to find the sun shining and the temperature up to 10 degrees warmer.

Good pals, these two neighbouring regions have much in common beyond an amenable climate: both boast renowned coastal holiday spots, particularly the Marlborough Sounds and Abel Tasman National Park. There are two other national parks (Kahurangi and Nelson Lakes) and more mountain ranges than you can poke a stick at.

And so it follows that these two regions have an abundance of luscious produce: summer cherries for a starter, but most famously the grapes that work their way into the wineglasses of the world's finest restaurants. Keep your penknife and picnic set at the ready.

In high season, these regions are popular and deservedly so. Plan ahead and be prepared to jostle for your gelato with Kiwi holidaymakers.

HIGHLIGHTS

- Getting up close to **Kaikoura's wildlife** (p452), including whales, seals, dolphins and albatross
- Nosing your way through the **Marlborough Wine Region** (p446)
- Tramping the **Queen Charlotte Track** (p438) in the Marlborough Sounds
- Getting airborne above **Nelson** (p459) and **Motueka** (p467) for a spot of paragliding or skydiving
- Sea kayaking in postcard-perfect **Abel Tasman National Park** (p474)
- Getting blown away at Blenheim's **Omaka Aviation Heritage Museum** (p442), one of New Zealand's best provincial museums
- Reaching the end of the road around **Farewell Spit** (p479) where there'll be gannets and godwits for company

- Telephone code: 03
- www.destination marlborough.com
- www.nelsonnz.com

MARLBOROUGH & NELSON

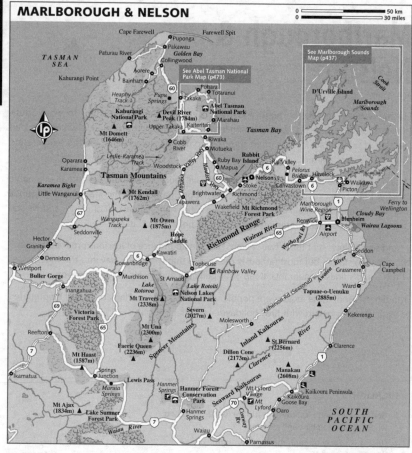

Climate

The forecast is good: Marlborough and Nelson soak up some of NZ's sunniest weather. January and February are the warmest months, with temperatures averaging 22°C; July is the coldest, averaging 12°C. It's wetter and more windswept the closer you get to Farewell Spit and the West Coast.

Getting There & Around

Soundsair (www.soundsair.com) is a local airline connecting Wellington with Blenheim, Nelson and Picton. **Air New Zealand** (www.airnewzealand.com) offers domestic flights.

Interisland Cook Strait ferries pull into Picton, often the starting point for South Island explorations. From here you can connect to almost anywhere in the South Island by bus; InterCity is the major operator, but there are also local shuttles. Tranz Scenic's *TranzCoastal* train takes the scenic route from Picton to Christchurch, via Blenheim and Kaikoura.

Renting a car is easy – there's a slew of car-hire offices in Picton.

Water transport, sea kayaking or walking are the best ways to navigate popular coastal areas, including the Marlborough Sounds and Abel Tasman National Park.

MARLBOROUGH REGION

Picton is the gateway to the South Island and the launching point for Marlborough Sounds' exploration. A cork's pop south of Picton is

---

MARLBOROUGH & NELSON FACTS

Eat Doris' bratwurst at the weekend markets in Nelson (p458) and Motueka (p467)

Drink A remarkable array of New Zealand craft beer at the Free House in Nelson (p463)

Read *Kahurangi Calling* by Gerard Hindmarsh – stories from the backcountry of northwest Nelson

Listen to Regular live music at Golden Bay's Mussel Inn (p479)

Watch The tide roll in, and then watch it roll away again...

Swim at Pelorus Bridge between Nelson and Blenheim (p451). Brrrrr!

Festival Marlborough Wine Festival (p444)

Tackiest tourist attraction The creepy Mickey Mouse and Donald Duck statues standing sentry at the Picton Foreshore playground

Go green Golden Bay (p475) – more sustainable living, untrammelled wilderness and organic food than you can lob a lentil at

---

agrarian Blenheim and the world-famous Marlborough Wine Region, and further south still Kaikoura, made famous by whales.

History

Long before Abel Tasman sheltered on the east coast of D'Urville Island in 1642 (more than 100 years before James Cook blew through in 1770), Maori traders and war parties knew the Marlborough area as Te Tau Ihu o Te Waka a Maui (the prow of Maui's canoe). Cook named Queen Charlotte Sound; his detailed reports made the area the best-known sheltered anchorage in the southern hemisphere. In 1827 French navigator Jules Dumont d'Urville discovered the narrow strait now known as French Pass. His officers named the island just to the north in his honour. In the same year a whaling station was established at Te Awaiti in Tory Channel, which brought about the first permanent European settlement in the district.

PICTON

pop 4000

Half asleep in winter, but hyperactive in summer (with up to eight fully-laden ferry arrivals per day), Picton clusters around a deep gulch at the head of Queen Charlotte Sound. It's the main traveller port for the South Island, and the best place from which to explore the Marlborough Sounds and tackle the Queen

Charlotte Track. To its credit, Picton manages to be touristy and transient but low-key and genuine at the same time.

Information

Creek Pottery (☎ 03-573 6313; 26 High St; ⏰ 9am-5.30pm) Stocks souvenirs and has internet access (per hour $6).

Picton i-SITE (☎ 03-520 3113; www.destinationmarlborough.com; Foreshore; ⏰ 9am-5pm Mon-Fri, to 4pm Sat & Sun) All vital tourist guff including maps and QC Track information. Internet ($6 per hr). Department of Conservation (DOC) counter staffed during summer.

Picton Library (☎ 03-520 7493; 67 High St; ⏰ 8am-5pm Mon-Fri, 10am-1pm Sat) Free wi-fi internet access

Police station (☎ 03-520 3120; picton.police@police.govt.nz; 36 Broadway; ⏰ 8.30am-4.30pm Mon-Fri)

Post office (Mariners Mall, 72 High St)

Sights & Activities

The *Edwin Fox* is purportedly the world's ninth-oldest wooden ship (who counts these things?). Built of teak in Bengal, the 48m, 750-tonne vessel was launched in 1853. During its chequered career it carried troops to the Crimean War, convicts to Australia and immigrants to NZ. The **Edwin Fox Maritime Museum** (☎ 03-573 6868; www.edwinfoxsociety.co.nz; Dunbar Wharf; adult/child $10/4; ⏰ 9am-5pm) has maritime exhibits including the venerable old dear, preserved under cover.

Next door, the **Eco World Aquarium** (☎ 03-573 6030; www.ecoworldnz.co.nz; Dunbar Wharf; adult/child/family $19/9/49; ⏰ 10am-8pm Dec-Feb, 10am-5.30pm Mar-Nov) has hundreds of fish and a veritable menagerie of native critters, including tuatara, gecko and giant weta. Fish-feeding time (11am and 2pm) is a hit with kids. Just before dusk watch the resident blue penguins returning from their fishing trips. There's also an art-house cinema here (p435).

Above the foreshore, the **Picton Museum** (☎ 03-573 8283; pictonmuseum@xtra.co.nz; London Quay; adult/child $4/1; ⏰ 9am-4pm Mar-Nov, to 5pm Dec-Feb) has a collection of whale bones, shells and model ships, and displays on local history and Maori lore.

A free i-SITE map details several walks around town, including an easy 1km track along Picton Harbour's eastern side to Bob's Bay. The **Snout Walkway** (three hours return) continues along the ridge from Bob's Bay offering superb Queen Charlotte Sound views.

Diving opportunities around the Sounds include the wreck of the 577ft *Mikhail*

MARLBOROUGH & NELSON

PICTON

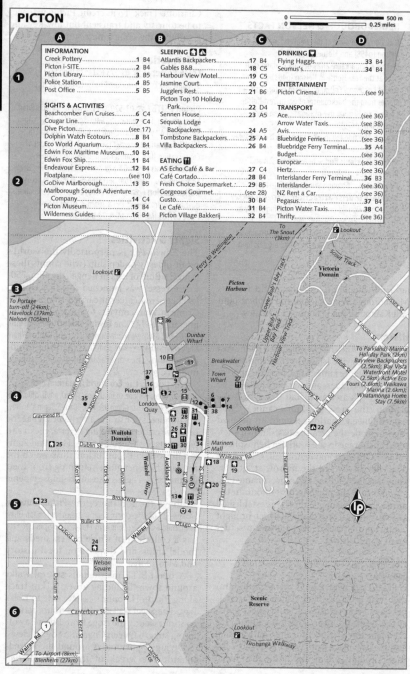

500 m
0.25 miles

INFORMATION
Creek Pottery.............................**1** B4
Picton i-SITE............................**2** B4
Picton Library..........................**3** B5
Police Station...........................**4** B5
Post Office **5** B5

SIGHTS & ACTIVITIES
Beachcomber Fun Cruises.......**6** C4
Cougar Line..............................**7** C4
Dive Picton........................(see 17)
Dolphin Watch Ecotours..........**8** B4
Eco World Aquarium...................**9** B4
Edwin Fox Maritime Museum...**10** B4
Edwin Fox Ship........................**11** B4
Endeavour Express...................**12** B4
Floatplane..........................(see 10)
GoDive Marlborough................**13** B4
Marlborough Sounds Adventure
   Company.............................**14** C4
Picton Museum........................**15** B4
Wilderness Guides...................**16** B4

SLEEPING
Atlantis Backpackers................**17** B4
Gables B&B..............................**18** C5
Harbour View Motel.................**19** C5
Jasmine Court...........................**20** C5
Jugglers Rest............................**21** B6
Picton Top 10 Holiday
   Park.....................................**22** D4
Sennen House...........................**23** A5
Sequoia Lodge
   Backpackers.......................**24** A5
Tombstone Backpackers...........**25** A4
Villa Backpackers.....................**26** B4

EATING
AS Echo Café & Bar **27** C4
Café Cortado............................**28** B4
Fresh Choice Supermarket.......**29** B5
Gorgeous Gourmet..............(see 28)
Gusto..**30** B4
Le Café.....................................**31** B4
Picton Village Bakkerij.............**32** B4

DRINKING
Flying Haggis............................**33** B4
Seumus's..................................**34** B4

ENTERTAINMENT
Picton Cinema.......................(see 9)

TRANSPORT
Ace......................................(see 36)
Arrow Water Taxis................(see 38)
Avis.....................................(see 36)
Bluebridge Ferries................(see 36)
Bluebridge Ferry Terminal.....**35** A4
Budget.................................(see 36)
Europcar..............................(see 36)
Hertz...................................(see 36)
Interislander Ferry Terminal...**36** B3
Interislander........................(see 36)
NZ Rent a Car.......................(see 36)
Pegasus................................**37** B4
Picton Water Taxis...............**38** C4
Thrifty.................................(see 36)

Lermontov, a Russian cruise ship that sank in Port Gore in 1986. Two operators offer dive courses and dive trips (both from around $185, including gear hire):

Dive Picton (☎ 0800 423 483, 03-573 7323; www. scubadive.co.nz; cnr Auckland St & London Quay)

GoDive Marlborough (☎ 0800 463 483, 03-573 9181; www.godive.co.nz; 97 High St)

Floatplane (☎ 021 704 248; www.nz-scenic-flights.co.nz; Picton Ferry Terminal) offers transfers and scenic tours (minimum two people) to Ship Cove (track transfer $125; 20-minute tour $140) and into the outer Sounds (40 minute/one hour $210/325). It also runs Cook Strait crossings from Porirua (near Wellington) to Nelson and the Abel Tasman (from $275).

Tours
There are loads of local tours, most of which focus on the Queen Charlotte Track (on foot, bike or kayak), Motuara Island bird sanctuary and other wildlife in the surrounds. See p436 for the full rundown. For winery tours around Blenheim, see p443.

Sleeping
BUDGET
Atlantis Backpackers (☎ 03-573 7390; www.atlantis hostel.co.nz; cnr Auckland St & London Quay; dm $25-28, tw/d $55/65, units $150, all incl breakfast; 🖳 🛜 🐾) Close to the ferry terminal, the basic rooms at Atlantis are cheap, but dorms are humongous (up to 28 beds). Facilities include an indoor heated pool, pool table and movie room. Basic next-door units sleep four.

Tombstone Backpackers (☎ 0800 573 7116, 03-573 7116; www.tombstonebp.co.nz; 16 Gravesend Pl; dm $25, d with/without bathroom $75/70; 🖳 🛜) Picton cemetery is across the street – a fact these hosts have turned into a marketing masterstroke. Beyond a coffin-lid door is one of the best hostels we've seen, catering to the new breed of 'flashpackers'. Hotel-worthy doubles, immaculate dorms, spa overlooking the harbour, free breakfast, sunny reading room, pool table, DVD library, free ferry pick-up and drop-off…the list goes on.

Villa Backpackers (☎ 03-573 6598; www.thevilla. co.nz; 34 Auckland St; dm $25-29, d with/without bathroom $72/63; 🖳 🛜) A blooming garden beckons you into this 1904 house with a cheery kitchen, log fires, free bikes and a spa. There are indoor and outdoor lounge areas plus in-demand en-suite rooms. Switched-on staff,

fresh flowers and free apple crumble on winter nights make this a real home away from home. The staff will also sort out your Queen Charlotte Track bookings (camping gear hire available), and more.

Sequoia Lodge Backpackers (☎ 0800 222 257, 03-573 8399; www.sequoialodge.co.nz; 3a Nelson Sq; dm $25, d with/without bathroom $78/64, all incl breakfast; 🖳 🛜) A well-managed backpackers in a colourful, high-ceilinged Victorian house. It's a little out of the centre, but a stone's throw from a pub, general store and its namesake conifers. Bonuses include quality linen, jumbo TV, videos, hammocks, barbecues, spa and nightly chocolate pudding!

Parklands Marina Holiday Park (☎ 0800 111 104, 03-573 6343; www.parktostay.co.nz; 10 Beach Rd; unpowered/powered sites $26/28, cabins $45-55, units $70-88; 🖳 🛜 🐾) Large, leafy campground with verdant bush backdrop. Three kilometres out of town, but close to pretty Waikawa Bay. Free Picton pick-up/drop-off.

Bayview Backpackers (☎ 03-573 7668; www.truenz .co.nz/bayviewbackpackers; 318 Waikawa Rd; dm $27, d with/without bathroom $78/64; 🖳) Overlooking Waikawa Bay 4km from town, Bayview feels like your house did in 1987. Or maybe your neighbour's house. Either way, it's a low-key place with friendly owners and sunny porch areas. Free kayaks and bicycles are available too.

Jugglers Rest (☎ 03-573 5570; www.jugglersrest. com; 8 Canterbury St; unpowered sites $36, dm $30, d $64-68; 🖳) Jocular hosts keep all their balls up in the air at this well-run and homely bunk-free backpackers. Peacefully located in the 'burbs, it's a 10-minute walk to the town centre or even quicker on a free bike. Cheery, private gardens are a good place to socialise with fellow travellers or soak in the outdoor bath. Closed from June to October.

Picton Top 10 Holiday Park (☎ 0800 277 444, 03-573 7212; www.pictontop10.co.nz; 70-78 Waikawa Rd; unpowered/powered sites $38/40, cabins $65-85, self-contained units $105-140; 🖳 🛜 🐾) About 500m from town, this is a well-kept park with modern, family-friendly facilities, including playground, covered barbecue area, heated swimming pool and a super recreation room.

MIDRANGE & TOP END
Gables B&B (☎ 03-573 6772; www.thegables.co.nz; 20 Waikawa Rd; s $100, d $130-160, units $155-175, all incl breakfast; 🖳) This historic B&B (once home to Picton's mayor) has three spacious, themed

en-suite rooms in the main house and two more upmarket units with kitchenettes and lounges out the back. Unit prices drop if you organise your own breakfast. Lovely hosts show good humour (ask about the Muffin Club).

Bay Vista Waterfront Motel (☎ 03-573 6733; www.bayvistapicton.co.nz; 303 Waikawa Rd; d $120-165; 🛜) Recently redecorated and neat as a new pin, this motel sits right at the water's edge, with lush lawn and views across Queen Charlotte Sound. All units have kitchen facilities. Located 4km from Picton (courtesy transfer available by request).

Harbour View Motel (☎ 0800 101 133, 03-573 6259; www.harbourviewpicton.co.nz; 30 Waikawa Rd; d $120-170; 🛜) This tastefully decorated motel enjoys an elevated position, affording views of Picton's mast-filled harbour from its self-contained studios with timber decks.

Jasmine Court (☎ 0800 421 999, 03-573 7110; www.jasminecourt.co.nz; 78 Wellington St; d $130-210, f $185-225; 🛜🛜) Top-notch, spacious motel with plush interiors, kitchenette, free DVD player and plunger coffee. Some rooms have a spa; upstairs balconies have harbour views.

Whatamonga Home Stay (☎ 03-573 7192; www.whsl.co.nz; 425 Port Underwood Rd; d incl breakfast $155; 🛜🛜) Follow Waikawa Rd 8km around the eastern side of Picton Harbour (Waikawa Rd becomes Port Underwood Rd), and you'll bump into this classy waterside accommodation. Run by a couple of chirpy Scots, it has two detached, self-contained units with king-sized beds and balconies with magic views. Two other rooms under the main house (also with views) share a bathroom. Free kayaks, dinghies and fishing gear are available.

Sennen House (☎ 03-573 5216; www.sennenhouse.co.nz; 9 Oxford St; d incl gourmet breakfast hamper $269-479; 🛜🛜) Tucked against a steep hillside of regenerating native bush (the odd black-faced sheep in its midst), Sennen House is an exquisitely restored, 1886 weatherboard homestead. Inside are five plush apartments and suites, each with its own entrance and kitchenette facilities, as well as sunny verandas and private lounge/dining areas.

Eating & Drinking

our pick Picton Village Bakkerij (☎ 03-573 7082; 46 Auckland St; items $2-7; ☺ 6am-3.30pm; 🅥) Dutch owners bake trays of European goodies here, including interesting breads, scrumptious pies, super sandwiches, cakes and custardy, tarty treats. Look for the cut-out Amsterdam roofline stapled to the eaves.

Gorgeous Gourmet (☎ 03-573 8388; 3a High St; items $6-14.50; ☺ 7.30am-6pm Mon-Fri, 8am-4pm Sat & Sun; 🅥) Hybrid sandwich shop meets microdeli, with great coffee to boot. Delectable salads, charcuterie, filled rolls, ready meals and artisan cheeses (don't go past the Over the Moon brie).

Seumus's (☎ 03-573 8994; 25 Wellington St; meals $7-24; ☺ noon-1am) An authentically snug drinking den, pouring a reliable Guinness and a good selection of whiskies. Mix it all up with hearty bar food and regular live music, and you've got the recipe for the liveliest joint in town.

Flying Haggis (☎ 03-573 6969; 27 High St; meals $8-24; ☺ noon-late) Proudly displaying a Glaswegian connection, this otherwise nondescript pub rustles up baked potatoes, toasties and fish and chips, which can be washed down with imported Scottish ales. Musos drift in from the hills occasionally and twang their guitars.

AS Echo Café & Bar (☎ 03-573 7498; Shelley Beach; meals $6-30; ☺ 10am-8.30pm daily) The deck of this old trading scow, built in 1905 but now high 'n' dry on concrete stumps, is a quirky place for a drink or home-cooked food, and a good spot to spy the comings and goings in the marina.

Gusto (☎ 03-573 7171; 33 High St; meals $12-19; ☺ 7.30am-2.30pm) This workaday joint, with friendly staff and outdoor tables, injects some class into Picton's cafe scene. Beaut breakfasts (French toast with bacon, maple syrup and berry coulis), fantastic coffee, and locally sourced mains (mussels, lamb and venison).

MAORI NZ: MARLBOROUGH & NELSON

Maori culture on the South Island is often less obvious than in the north, but that doesn't mean it's any less potent. In the Marlborough and Nelson regions, the following operators are keyed into *Maoritanga* (Maori culture):

- **Maori Tours Kaikoura** (p452) Small-group history and cultural tours around Kaikoura
- **Myths & Legends Eco-tours** (p436) Eco-oriented cultural and wildlife cruises on the Marlborough Sounds
- **Shark Nett Gallery** (p441) Contemporary Maori carving gallery

Le Café (☎ 03-573 5588; London Quay; lunch $10-20, dinner $19-28; ⊙ 7.30am-10.30pm) Due credit for longevity and for food that the locals still favour; we found the space a bit tired and the service dicey when we visited. The food, however, tasted made-from-scratch: salami sandwiches, quiche, pasta and mussels, plus sweet tart for afters. Great Havana coffee and occasional live gigs.

Café Cortado (☎ 03-573 5630; cnr High St & London Quay; mains $17-29; ⊙ 8am-late) A pleasant corner cafe with sneaky views of the harbour through the foreshore's pohutukawa and palms. Quite possibly your best bet for a 'sophisticated' meal in a town with limited, decent dining of an evening. The menu focuses on local fish, steak, lamb, pizzas and salads, with bar snacks available too.

Self-caterers can head to **Fresh Choice Supermarket** (☎ 03-573 6463; Mariners Mall, 100 High St; ⊙ 7am-9pm).

Entertainment

Picton Cinema (☎ 03-573 6030; www.pictoncinemas.co.nz; Dunbar Wharf; adult/child $15/9; ⊙ 10am-8pm) Two microtheatres within the Eco World Aquarium complex showing an excellent program of art-house movies. There is a combo-pass available for cinema and aquarium (adult/child $28/15).

Getting There & Away

Make bookings for trains, ferries and buses at Picton i-SITE and Picton Train Station.

AIR

Soundsair (☎ 0800 505 005, 03-520 3080; www.soundsair.com) flies between Picton and Wellington (adult/child $89/77, up to eight daily). There are discounts for online bookings, and a courtesy shuttle bus ($3) to/from the airstrip at Koromiko, 8km south.

BOAT

There are two operators crossing Cook Strait between Picton and Wellington, and although all ferries leave from more or less the same place, each has its own terminal. The main transport hub (and car rental offices) is at the Interislander Terminal, which also has public showers, a cafe and internet facilities. Timetables below are subject to change.

Bluebridge Ferries (☎ 0800 844 844, in Wellington 04-471 6188; www.bluebridge.co.nz; adult/child $50/25)

Crossing takes three hours 20 minutes. Departs Wellington at 3am, 8am, 1pm and 9pm daily (no 3am or 9pm services on Saturdays). Departs Picton at 2am, 8am, 2pm and 7pm daily (no 8am service on Saturdays; no 2am service on Sundays). Cars and campervans up to 4m long from $110; campervans under 5.5m from $150; motorbikes $50; bicycles $10.

Interislander (☎ 0800 802 802, in Wellington 04-498 3302; www.interislander.co.nz; adult/child from $46/23) Crossing takes three hours 10 minutes. Departs Wellington at 2.25am, 8.25am, 2.05pm and 6.25pm. Departs Picton at 6.25am, 10.05am, 1.10pm, 6.05pm and 10.25pm. From November through to April there's an extra 10.25am sailing from Wellington and an extra 2.25pm sailing from Picton. Cars are priced from $101; campervans (up to 5.5m) from $126; motorbikes $46; bicycles $15.

BUS

Buses serving Picton depart the Interislander terminal or nearby i-SITE.

InterCity (☎ 03-365 1113; www.intercitycoach.co.nz; Picton Ferry Terminal) runs services south to Christchurch ($55, 5½ hours, two daily), via Kaikoura ($35, 2½ hours, two daily) with connections to Dunedin, Queenstown and Invercargill. Services also run to/from Nelson ($34, 2¼ hours, three daily), with connections to Motueka and the West Coast; and to/from Blenheim ($15, 30 minutes, five daily). At least one bus daily on each of these routes connects with a Wellington ferry service. Keep an eye on discounted internet fares – at the time of research, Picton to Christchurch was a supercheap $25.

Smaller shuttle buses running from Picton to Christchurch (around $40, door to door) include:

Atomic Shuttles (☎ 03-349 0697; www.atomictravel.co.nz)

Naked Bus (☎ 0900 625 33; www.nakedbus.com)

Southern Link (☎ 0508 458 835, 03-358 8355; www.southernlinkcoaches.co.nz)

TRAIN

Tranz Scenic (☎ 0800 872 467, 04-495 0775; www.tranzscenic.co.nz) runs the *TranzCoastal* service daily each way between Picton and Christchurch via Blenheim and Kaikoura (and 22 tunnels and 175 bridges!), departing Christchurch at 7am, Picton at 1pm. The standard adult one-way Picton–Christchurch fare is $104, but discounted fares can be as low as $39. The service connects with the *Interislander* ferry (included in Wellington to Christchurch fares).

Getting Around

Renting a car in Picton is easy-peasy – as low as $35 per day if you shop around. Most agencies allow drop-offs in Christchurch; if you're planning to drive to the North Island, most companies suggest you leave your car at Picton and pick up another one in Wellington after crossing Cook Strait. Take a punt on a cheaper local operator, or the big-namers at the Interislander terminal:

Ace (☎ 03-573 8939; www.acerentalcars.co.nz)
Apex (☎ 03-573 7009; www.apexrentals.co.nz)
Avis (☎ 03-520 3156; www.avis.co.nz)
Budget (☎ 03-573 6081; www.budget.co.nz)
Europcar (☎ 03-573 8800; www.europcar.com)
Hertz (☎ 03-520 3044; www.hertz.co.nz)
NZ Rent a car (☎ 03-573 7282; www.nzrentacar.co.nz)
Pegasus (☎ 03-577 9066; www.carrentalsblenheim. co.nz)**Thrifty** (☎ 03-573 7387; www.thrifty.co.nz)

Shuttles (and tours) around Picton and wider Marlborough are offered by **Marlborough Sounds Shuttles & Tours** (☎ 03-573 7122). Between Picton and Havelock (via Anakiwa), you can hitch a van ride on **Coleman Post** (☎ 027 255 8882; $15). It departs Picton at 8.15am and Havelock at 10.45am, with other services on request.

See right for details on water taxis servicing the Sounds.

MARLBOROUGH SOUNDS

The Marlborough Sounds are a geographic maze of inlets, headlands, peaks, beaches and watery reaches, formed when the sea flooded into deep valleys after the last ice age. Parts of the Sounds are included in the Marlborough Sounds Maritime Park – a series of small reserves punctuated by private land. To get an idea of how convoluted the sounds are, Pelorus Sound is 42km long but has 379km of shoreline. If you have your own wheels, the wiggly, verdant 35km drive along Queen Charlotte Dr from Picton to Havelock is a great Sounds snapshot (even on a rainy day).

The Queen Charlotte Track is the main lure for trampers, but the two-day Nydia Track (p451) is also worthwhile. Secluded accommodation (boutique and rudimentary) is scattered throughout the Sounds.

Tours

FROM PICTON

The bulk of Marlborough Sounds tours are based in Picton, many at the new Town Wharf.

Active Eco Tours (☎ 03-573 7199; www.sealswimming.com; Essons Valley; full-day seal swim & sightseeing tour incl equipment adult/child $125/95; ◷ 9am-5pm) Get underwater with speedy Sounds seals. Tours leave Picton or Waikawa; free pick-up.
Arrow Water Taxis (☎ 03-573 8229, 027 444 4689; www.arrowwatertaxis.co.nz; Town Wharf)
Beachcomber Fun Cruises (☎ 0800 624 526, 03-573 6175; www.beachcombercruises.co.nz; Town Wharf; mail run $85, cruises $69-85) Two- to four-hour cruises, some with resort lunches. Cruise/walk, cruise/bike, and QC Track options also available.
Cougar Line (☎ 0800 504 090, 03-573 7925; www.cougarlinecruises.co.nz; Town Wharf; cruises adult/child from $68/34) QC Track transport, plus various half- and full-day cruise/walk deals including the rather special (and flexible) ecocruise trip to Motuara Island bird sanctuary.
Dolphin Watch Ecotours (☎ 0800 9453 5433, 03-573 8040; www.naturetours.co.nz; Town Wharf; swimming/ viewing tour $150/100) Half-day 'swim with dolphins' and wildlife tours around Queen Charlotte Sound and Motuara Island bird sanctuary. QC Track cruise/walk options also available.
Endeavour Express (☎ 03-573 5456; www.boatrides.co.nz; Town Wharf; 1- to 4-day cruise/walk options $35-90) Backpacker-friendly company offering cruise/ walk options and QC Track transfers. Mountain bikes and camping gear for hire.
Marlborough Sounds Adventure Company (☎ 0800 283 283, 03-573 6078; www.marlboroughsounds.co.nz; Town Wharf; half- to 3-day tours $75-245) Bike-kayak-walk trips, with options to suit every inclination. The '1-day multi' guided kayak trip followed by QC Track hike ($135) or bike ($155) is a brilliant Sounds sampler. Gear rental (bikes, kayaks, camping gear) also available.
Myths & Legends Eco-tours (☎ 03-573 6901; www.eco-tours.co.nz; half-/full-day cruises $150/200) A Sounds day on the water with a local Maori family – longtime locals, storytellers and environmentalists. There are five different trips to choose from, including birdwatching and visiting Ship Cove.
Picton Water Taxis (☎ 03-573 7853, 027 227 0284; www.pictonwatertaxis.co.nz; Town Wharf; ◷ 24hr)
Sea Kayak Adventure Tours (☎ 0800 262 5492, 03-574 2765; www.nzseakayaking.com; Anakiwa Rd, Anakiwa; half-/1-day guided tours $65/95) Guided and independent kayaking trips around Queen Charlotte and Kenepuru Sounds. Also one-day paddle and walk ($85) or paddle and bike ($120) freedom options. Kayak and mountain-bike hire from $50 per day.
Waterways Boating Safaris (☎ 03-574 1372; www.waterways.co.nz; 745 Kenepuru Rd; half-day $95, full-day $125) It's a boat tour Cap'n, but not as we know it. Buzz around majestic Kenepuru Sound in your own craft, while

MARLBOROUGH SOUNDS

SIGHTS & ACTIVITIES	Camp Bay Campsite..............**8** C5	Nydia Lodge........................**18** A5
Portage Adventure Centre..........(see 19)	Cowshed Bay Campsite..........**9** C2	Portage Resort Hotel............**19** C2
Sea Kayaking Adventure Tours........**1** B6	Davies Bay Campsite............**10** B6	Punga Cove Resort.............**20** C5
Shark Nett Gallery....................**2** A6	DeBretts & Treetops...........(see 19)	Queen Charlotte Wilderness Park..**21** D4
Waterways Boating Safaris............**3** B6	Endeavour Resort................**11** C5	Schoolhouse Bay Campsite......**22** D5
	Furneaux Lodge.................**12** C5	Smiths Farm Holiday Park......**23** B6
SLEEPING	Hopewell........................**13** B5	Te Mahia Bay Resort............**24** C2
Anakiwa Backpackers...............**4** B6	Lochmara Lodge.................**14** C3	Te Mahoerangi..................**25** A5
Anakiwa Lodge....................(see 4)	Mahana Lodge...................**15** C3	Tirimoana House................**26** B6
Bay of Many Coves Campsite........**5** D2	Mistletoe Bay Eco Village.......**16** C3	
Bay of Many Coves Resort..........**6** D2	Noeline's Homestay.............(see 15)	**EATING**
Black Rock Campsite................**7** D2	Nydia Bay Campsite.............**17** A5	Kenepuru Store.................(see 19)

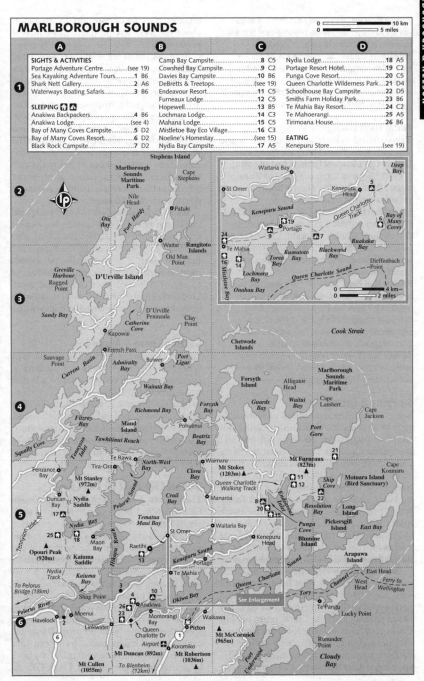

learning about the area's ecology and history. A unique and fun way to see the Sounds. Two people per boat and a maximum of five boats per guide. BYO lunch.

Wilderness Guides (☎ 0800 266 266, 03-520 3095; www.wildernessguidesnz.com; Picton Railway Station, 3 Auckland St; 1- to 4-day trip incl lunch $90-570) Guided and independent kayak/walk or kayak/bike tours on the QC Track or Nydia Track. Bike hire $50 per day.

FROM HAVELOCK

Trips around Pelorus and Kenepuru Sound generally leave from Havelock (see p441).

Captain Clay's Snapper Fishing Charters (☎ 03-574 2911; bluecottage@actrix.co.nz; Havelock Marina; per person $125, min 2 people) Half-day or longer trips. Catch and release or take it home for your tea.

Green Shell Mussel Cruise (☎ 0800 990 800, 03-577 9997; www.greenshellmusselcruise.co.nz; Havelock Marina; adult/child $120/free; ☒ departs 1.30pm) Half-day cruise on a luxury catamaran to mussel in on Kenepuru's aquaculture. Includes a feed of steamed mussels and a glass of wine. Bookings essential.

Pelorus Mail Run (☎ 03-574 1088; www.mail-boat. co.nz; Jetty 1, Havelock Marina; adult/child $120/free; ☒ departs 9.30am Tue, Thu & Fri) Popular full-day boat cruise through the far reaches of Pelorus Sound on a genuine NZ Post delivery run. Bookings essential; BYO lunch. Picton pick-up and drop-off available.

Pelorus Sound Water Taxi (☎ 03-574 2151; www. pelorusbelle.com; Jetty 1a, Havelock Marina) Taxi services and sightseeing trips made to order.

Sleeping & Eating

Some Sounds sleeping options are accessible only by boat and are deliciously isolated, but the most popular are those on (or just off) the Queen Charlotte Track (opposite). Some places close over winter; call ahead to check.

There are over 30 DOC camping grounds throughout the Sounds (many accessible only by boat), providing water and toilet facilities but not much else; cooking facilities are nonexistent.

Picton i-SITE (p431) has a list of local baches for rent, or you could try **Sounds Great Holiday Homes** (☎ 03-574 1221; www.soundsgreat.co.nz).

Queen Charlotte Wilderness Park (☎ 03-579 9025; www.truenz.co.nz/wilderness; Cape Jackson; per person 2 nights/3 days $329 or 3 nights/4 days $429) This private nature reserve allows you to venture on to the Outer Queen Charlotte Track, north of Ship Cove up to Cape Jackson. Inclusive packages includes accommodation in en-suite twins or doubles, meals and Picton transfers. Wildlife-spotting, fishing, kayaking and tramping are

on offer, plus the opportunity to learn more about the local environment and efforts to preserve it.

Hopewell (☎ 03-573 4341; www.hopewell.co.nz; Kenepuru Sound; dm from $30, d with/without bathroom from $120/98, 4-person cottage (for 2 adults) $160; ☒ closed Jun-Aug; ☐ ☎) One of NZ's best-loved backpackers, Hopewell occupies a remote corner of Kenepuru Sound, surrounded by native bush opening onto the sea. Road access is possible, but the long, bumpy drive makes a water taxi from Te Mahia far preferable. Once here, chill out or enjoy the roll-call of facilities: books, games, outdoor spa, mountain bikes, kayaks, fishing equipment, gourmet pizzas and more.

Smiths Farm Holiday Park (☎ 03-574 2806; www. smithsfarm.co.nz; 1419 Queen Charlotte Dr, Linkwater; unpowered/powered sites $32/36, cabins $60-110, motel units $130; ☐ ☎) Just east of the turn-off to Portage, Smiths is a usefully positioned caravan park with lush camping lawns and comfy, well-looked-after cabins and units. Livestock nibbles around the fences; walks extend to a nearby waterfall and glowworm dell.

Getting There & Around

The best way to get around the Sounds is by boat, and fortunately there is a plethora of operators who will oblige either to schedule or on-demand (p436).

Much of the area is accessible by car. The road is sealed to the head of Kenepuru Sound, but beyond that it's nothing but narrow gravel roads with more twists than a hurricane. To drive to Punga Cove from Picton takes two to three hours (45 minutes by boat).

QUEEN CHARLOTTE TRACK

The hugely popular, meandering Queen Charlotte Track offers gorgeous coastal scenery, isolated coves, diverse accommodation and back-to-nature campsites. The coastal forest is lush, and from the ridges you can look down on either side to Queen Charlotte and Kenepuru Sounds. The 71km track connects historic Ship Cove with Anakiwa, passing through privately owned land (40% of the track) and DOC reserves. Access depends on the cooperation of local landowners; respect their property by utilising designated campsites and toilets, and carrying out your rubbish. You can also do your bit for the track by paying the very modest $5 'Track Tribute' fee at the Picton wharf or wherever you see a payment box.

Queen Charlotte is a well-defined track, suitable for people of average fitness. You can do the walk in sections using local water-taxi transport, or walk the whole three- to five-day journey. Sleeping options are only half a day's walk apart; boat operators will transport your pack along the track for you. Though there aren't the hordes that tramp the Abel Tasman, there's some solid summer traffic. You can do part of the trip by sea kayak (see p436).

Mountain biking is a viable alternative for fit, competent off-roaders: it's possible to ride the track in two or three days, guided or self-guided. Note that the section between Ship Cove and Kenepuru Saddle is off-limits to cyclists from December to February. During these months you can still be dropped by boat at the Saddle and ride to Anakiwa.

Ship Cove is the usual (and strongly recommended) starting point – mainly because it's easier to arrange a boat from Picton to Ship Cove than vice versa – but the track can be started from Anakiwa. There's a public phone at Anakiwa but not at Ship Cove. Between Camp Bay and Torea Saddle you'll find the going toughest. About halfway along there's an excellent viewpoint, Eatwell's Lookout, about 20 minutes off the main track.

Estimated walk times:

Track section	Distance	Duration
Ship Cove to Resolution Bay	4.5km	1½-2hr
Resolution Bay to head of Endeavour Inlet	10.5km	2-2¾hr
Endeavour Inlet to Camp Bay/Punga Cove	12km	3-4hr
Camp Bay/Punga Cove to Torea Saddle/Portage	24km	5½-7½hr
Torea Saddle/Portage to Mistletoe Bay	8km	2½-3hr
Mistletoe Bay to Anakiwa	13km	2½-3¾hr

Information

The Picton i-SITE (p431) stocks the *Queen Charlotte Track Visitor Guide* pamphlet and DOC's *Queen Charlotte Track* brochure, and is the best spot for information. Picton's Villa Backpackers is also a hotbed of info, and handles bookings. Check online details at www.qctrack.co.nz.

Tours

Most Picton-based tour companies (see p436) offer Queen Charlotte Track cruises and guided walk/bike/kayak trips.

Sleeping & Eating

Unless you're camping, it pays to book your Queen Charlotte Track accommodation *waaay* in advance, especially in summer. There are six DOC campsites (adult/child $6/1.50) along the track, each with toilets and a water supply but no cooking facilities. There's also a variety of resorts, lodges, backpackers and guest houses.

The following listings are arranged in order heading south from Ship Cove (where camping is not permitted). Your overnight stops will depend on how far you can/want to walk on any given day – do your research and book ahead. Not every accommodation option is covered here.

Schoolhouse Bay campsite (Resolution Bay) Beautifully situated, this is the first DOC campsite off the rank.

Furneaux Lodge (☎ 03-579 8259; www.furneauxlodge.co.nz; Endeavour Inlet; dm $30-40, chalets/studios $195/245; 🖳) One of the Sounds' stalwart resorts, Furneaux's highlights are the historic lodge building and a big flat lawn. Backpackers can choose from the old stone cottage ($10 cheaper) or in fresh, double dorms nearer the water. Fancier options are self-contained two-bedroom chalets (sleeping up to six) and swish waterfront studios. Beer, a bowl of chips or a meal ($16 to $35) are available in the bar/restaurant.

Endeavour Resort (☎ 03-579 8381; www.endeavourresort.co.nz; Endeavour Inlet; dm $30-40, cabins $75-90, motels $100-125) Proudly retro 1950s board-and-batten bach-style accommodation in one of the prettiest parts of the Sounds. It's basic, but classic, clean and tidy. Eight units spread among the gardens, most with toilet-shower and kitchen facilities. Games room and library–video room. Free kayaks and dinghies.

Camp Bay campsite (Punga Cove) On the western side of Endeavour Inlet.

Punga Cove Resort (☎ 03-579 8561; www.punga cove.co.nz; Endeavour Inlet; dm $40, lodge $140-175, chalets $175-425; 🖳 🛒) A fairly rustic resort offering self-contained studios, family and luxury A-frame chalets, most with sweeping sea views. Backpackers get a row of decent cabins and a lounge with balcony views. Ample activities (pool, spa, games, kayak and bike hire) plus a shop, restaurant (meals $26 to $37), and bar (decent beers and $22 pizza).

Mahana Lodge (☎ 03-579 8373; www.mahanahome stead.com; Endeavour Inlet; d $110-150) Ann and John's continuously improving property features a pretty waterside lawn and purpose-built lodge with four en-suite doubles (with another double in a wee bach up the back). Ecofriendly initiatives include bush regeneration and pest trapping, although of greater appeal may be the organic veggies you'll find in your optional breakfast, packed lunch, or three-course dinner ($15 to $45). Free fishing gear and kayaks are available.

Noeline's Homestay (☎ 03-579 8375; Endeavour Inlet; s/tw $30/70) Follow the pink arrows from Camp Bay to this relaxed homestay and be greeted by 70-something Noeline, 'the Universal Grandma', and her home-baked treats. It's a friendly arrangement with beds for five people, cooking facilities and great views.

Bay of Many Coves campsite (Bay of Many Coves) On a saddle above the track.

Bay of Many Coves Resort (☎ 0800 5799 771, 03-579 9771; www.bayofmanycovesresort.co.nz; 1-/2-/3-bedroom apt $500/695/950; 🖳 🐾) Honeymooning? These plush and secluded apartments are appropriately sexy. Each has a private balcony shunting you out towards the water, designer bathrooms and all mod cons. The upmarket cafe and restaurant are staffed by a crew of iron chefs. Arrive by boat or via the steep path leading down from the main track.

Black Rock campsite (Kumutoto Bay) Further along past Bay of Many Coves, above Kumutoto Bay.

Portage Resort Hotel (☎ 03-573 4309; www. portage.co.nz; Kenepuru Sound; dm $40, d $165-365; 🖳 🛜 🐾) This fancy resort is centred upon a smart lodge building with Te Weka restaurant (mains $28 to $35), lounge and view-tastic sundeck overlooking the pool patio and lush grounds. The relaxed Snapper Café (mains $15 to $30) is popular with both guests and locals. The 22-bed backpacker wing is pretty good, with small lounge and cooking facilities; tidy, moderately stylish rooms climb the price ladder from there. The on-site **Kenepuru Store** (☎ 03-573 4445; ☷ 8am-8pm Oct-Apr, to 4.30pm May-Sep) sells newspapers, snacks, select groceries and noteworthy pies which emerge from the bakery out back (along with filled rolls and loaves to go). Underneath the Store is the **Portage Adventure Centre** (☎ 03-573 4111), an outpost of Marlborough Sounds Adventure Company (see p436), offering trips and freedom hire of bikes and boats.

DeBretts (☎ 03-573 4522; www.stayportage.co.nz; s/d $40/80) and **Treetops** (☎ 03-573 4404; www.staytreetops. com; s/d $40/80), run by the same family, offer a combined total of six bedrooms in two homely backpackers high on the hill above Portage Resort.

Cowshed Bay campsite (Cowshed Bay) Not far from the Portage Resort Hotel.

Lochmara Lodge (☎ 03-573 4554; www.lochmara lodge.co.nz; Lochmara Bay; d $90-120, self-contained units/ chalets $180-260; 🖳 🛜) A superb retreat on Lochmara Bay, reached by a side track south of the Queen Charlotte Track or by boat from Picton. Relaxation-inducing facilities include an outdoor spa, hammocks and barbeques. There are en-suite doubles, units and chalets, all set in lush surroundings, and a fully licensed cafe and restaurant serving local, wild and organic produce.

Mistletoe Bay Eco Village (☎ 03-573 4048; www. mistletoebay.co.nz; Mistletoe Bay; unpowered sites adult/child $15/5, dm $25, cabins $120, linen $7.50) On a former DOC reserve and run by a forward-thinking community trust, sweet Mistletoe Bay offers attractive camping, eight irresistible cabins sleeping up to six with communal kitchen, and a cottage with bunks for overflow. Sustainable initiatives include solar power, water conservation, recycling and waste-water treatment. There is also kayak and bike hire.

ourpick **Te Mahia Bay Resort** (☎ 03-573 4089; www.temahia.co.nz; Kenepuru Sound; d $148-245; 🛜) This sweetly low-key resort is north of the track, just off the main road, in a picturesque bay facing Kenepuru Sound. It has roomy, affordable self-contained units in a late-1800s house, pleasant motel units, plus new luxury self-contained apartments. There's also a store selling precooked meals, pizza, coffee and camping supplies (wine!). It also has kayaks for hire.

Davies Bay campsite (Umungata) Also a popular picnic spot, with barbecue facilities nearby.

Anakiwa Backpackers (☎ 03-574 1338; www.anakiwa backpackers.co.nz; 401 Anakiwa Rd; dm $33, d $76-96, unit (sleeps 4) $155; 🖳 🛜) This former schoolhouse (1926) greets you at the southern end of the track – a soothing spot to rest and reflect. There are two doubles (one with en suite, a four-bed dorm and beachy self-contained unit, all freshly decorated. The spirited owners will have you jumping off the jetty for joy (among other available watery activities), but also offer espresso and ice cream (hallelujah) from their little green caravan-cafe (open afternoons). Free kayak hire.

Anakiwa Lodge (☎ 03-574 2115; www.anakiwa.co.nz; 9 Lady Cobham Gr; dm $31, d $77-127; 💻 🛜) This modern YHA backpackers, 70m from the water, has a bush and pasture backdrop. Four-bed dorms and doubles, some with en suite and DVD player. Spa, DVD library, free kayak hire and barbecue area.

Tirimoana House (☎ 03-574 2627; www.tirimoanahouse.com; 257 Anakiwa Rd; d incl breakfast $200-320; 🛜 🐾) Owned by a couple of prolific painters and about 1.5km down the road from the end of the track, this bold B&B is full to the gunwales with fabulous antique furniture. Every room has its own bathroom, sea views and balcony, plus there's a spa-with-a-view and a swimming pool. Gourmet breakfast buffet, and dinner on request.

Getting Around

Numerous boat operators service the track, allowing you to start and finish where you like. Transport costs around $90 return, $50 for a one-way drop-off (depending on where you're going), and usually includes pack transfers so you can walk with a small daypack while your heavy gear awaits you at your chosen accommodation. Bikes and kayaks can also be transported.

A full list of transport operators (many of whom offer walk/bike/kayak combos, scenic cruises and on-demand taxi services) can be found on p436.

HAVELOCK

pop 470

The highlight of tiny Havelock is its industrious harbour, which helps the town maintain the title of 'Greenshell Mussel Capital of the World'. Havelock sits at the confluence of the Pelorus and Kaiuma Rivers, 36km west of Picton, and makes a practical base from which to explore the less visited Pelorus and Kenepuru Sounds.

Located at the YHA, **Havelock Infocentre** (☎ 03-574 2104; www.havelockinfocentre.co.nz; 46 Main Rd; 🕑 8.30am-9pm) books tours and transport, and offers regional advice. The centre doubles as a DOC agent.

Sights & Activities

Shark Nett Gallery (☎ 03-574 2877; admin@sharknett.co.nz; 129 Queen Charlotte Dr; adult/child $12/6.50; 🕑 10am-

4pm) Overlooking the tidal Pelorus estuary, this unique gallery showcases contemporary Maori carving relating to the local Rangitane *iwi* (tribes). Tours provide an educational and evocative insight into how carving is used to record tribal *tikanga* (customs) and *whakapapa* (ancestry). There is also a cafe on-site.

Eighteen kilometres west of Havelock is **Pelorus Bridge Scenic Reserve**, a pretty forest remnant and riverside recreation area. Explore its many tracks, take a dip in the limpid (but chilly) Pelorus River, or indulge in some home-baking at the cafe. Lucky campers can stay overnight in the wonderful **DOC campsite** (☎ 03-571 6019; www.doc.govt.nz; unpowered/powered sites $20/22), managed by the cafe owners.

The **Nydia Track** (27km, 10 hours) starts at Kaiuma Bay and ends at Duncan Bay (or vice versa). Around halfway is beautiful Nydia Bay where there's a **DOC campsite** (adult/child $6/1.50) and DOC's **Nydia Lodge** (Map p437; ☎ 03-520 3002; www.doc.govt.nz; dm $15), an unhosted 50-bed lodge (four-person minimum). You'll need water and road transport to complete the journey; Blue Moon (below) runs a shuttle to Duncan Bay, or make your arrangements at the Havelock Infocentre where you can also pay your camp fees or book the lodge. **Te Mahoerangi** (Map p437; ☎ 03-579 8411; www.nydiatrack.org.nz; dm/d $30/90) offers alternative accommodation at Nydia Bay in a tranquil, ecofocused backpackers. Profits are ploughed back into local environmental protection efforts; ask about volunteering/wwoofing opportunities.

Tours

Look to the water for tours around these parts. Turn to p436 to find them (or book at the Havelock Infocentre).

Sleeping & Eating

Rutherford YHA (☎ 03-574 2104; www.yha.co.nz; 46 Main Rd; unpowered sites $24, dm/d $28/66; 💻 🛜) A well-equipped YHA filling an 1881 schoolhouse once attended by Lord Ernest Rutherford, father of nuclear physics. Rooms are simple and comfy (doubles are nicer than dorms). It might pay to bring the earplugs.

Blue Moon (☎ 03-574 2212; www.bluemoonhavelock.co.nz; 48 Main Rd; dm $25, d $66-86; 💻) This largely unremarkable lodge has homely rooms in the main house (one with en suite), as well as cabins and a bunkhouse in the yard (along with a spa pool). The lounge and kitchen are pleasant and relaxed, as is the sunny barbecue deck.

Havelock Motor Camp (☎ 03-574 2339; www.havelockmotorcamp.co.nz; 24 Inglis St; unpowered/powered sites $26/30, cabins $44; 💻) Near the marina, this well-maintained park offers totally acceptable sites, basic cabins and spick-and-span facilities.

Havelock Garden Motel (☎ 03-574 2387; www.gardenmotels.com; 71 Main Rd; d $99-150) An exemplary family-run motel set in a large, graceful garden complete with dear old trees and a duck-filled creek. The low and long '60s units have been tastefully revamped to offer homely comfort and gas cookers. You may want to stay longer.

our pick **Wakamarinian Café** (☎ 03-574 1180; 70 Main Rd; snacks $2-7; 💛 9.30am-5pm) Heavenly home baking in a cute cottage. Get in early to grab one of the popular pies, or console yourself with proper quiche and a sweet slice – the raspberry and white-chocolate shortcake defies description. Great coffee and excellent value, too, from Beth and Laurie: Havelock's culinary saviours.

Slip Inn (☎ 03-574 2345; Havelock Marina; meals $9-25; 💛 8am-late) Feel appropriately maritime in this surprisingly slick restaurant and bar in the thick of the marina. Its signature dishes are the mussels, as well as beer-battered blue cod, pizza, pasta specials and home-made dessert. Good for a cruise-by beer-stop, too.

Getting There & Away

InterCity (☎ 03-365 1113; www.intercitycoach.co.nz) runs daily from Picton to Havelock via Blenheim ($21, one hour, three daily), and from Havelock to Nelson ($22, 1¼ hours, three daily). **Atomic Shuttles** (☎ 03-349 0697; www.atomictravel.co.nz) plies the same run. To get between Havelock and Picton via the scenic Queen Charlotte Drive, look up Coleman Post (see p436).

BLENHEIM
pop 26,500

Blenheim (pronounced 'Blenum') is a dead-flat, agricultural town 29km south of Picton on the Wairau Plain between the Wither Hills and the Richmond Ranges. The town offers little to enthral or distract except for the brilliant Aviation Heritage Centre and the world-famous wineries just over its back fence.

Information

Automobile Association (AA; ☎ 03-578 3399; www.aa.co.nz; 23 Maxwell Rd; 💛 8.30am-5pm Mon-Fri, from 9am Tue)

Blenheim i-SITE (☎ 03-577 8080; www.destinationmarlborough.com; Railway Station, Sinclair St; 💛 8.30am-5pm Mon-Fri, 9am-3pm Sat & Sun) Information on Marlborough and beyond. Wine trail maps and bookings for everything under the sun.

Blenheim police station (☎ 03-578 5279; 8 Main St; 💛 24hr)

Paperplus (☎ 03-578 3904; The Forum, Market Pl; 💛 8.30am-5.30pm Mon-Fri, 10am-4pm Sat & Sun) Books and magazines.

Post office (cnr Scott & Main Sts)

Travel Stop Cyber Centre (☎ 03-579 1902; Shop 17, 1 Market St; 💛 10am-9pm Mon-Sat, to 4pm Sun) Internet access.

Wairau Hospital (☎ 03-520 9999; www.nmdhb.govt.nz; Hospital Rd; 💛 24hr)

Sights & Activities

Blenheim's 'big attraction' has always been its wineries, but the **Omaka Aviation Heritage Centre** (Map p444; ☎ 03-579 1305; www.omaka.org.nz; Aerodrome Rd; adult/child/family $20/8/48; 💛 10am-4pm) has blown the wine out of the water. Aided by the creative geniuses that brought us *Lord of the Rings* (Peter Jackson, Wingnut Films and Weta Workshop), this amazing collection of original and replica Great War aircraft is brought to life with a series of dioramas depicting dramatic wartime scenes such as the death of Manfred von Richthofen, the Red Baron. Remarkable memorabilia and photographic displays deepen the experience. It's powerful stuff, and we predict eyes on stalks one minute, misty eyes the next. There is a cafe and shop on-site.

On your way back into town, check out the **Marlborough Museum** (☎ 03-578 1712; www.marlboroughmuseum.org.nz; 26 Arthur Baker Pl off New Renwick Rd; admission adult/child $10/5; 💛 10am-4pm), passionately celebrating the region's history. Besides a replica township, vintage mechanicals and well-presented artefact displays, there's the recently opened 'Wine Exhibition' for those looking to cap-off their vineyard experiences.

Conspicuously blue opposite Seymour Sq, the **Millennium Art Gallery** (☎ 03-579 2001; marlpublicart@xtra.co.nz; 13 Seymour Sq; admission by donation; 💛 10.30am-4.30pm Mon-Fri, 1-4pm Sat & Sun) is a contemporary gallery presenting changing exhibitions by local and national artists.

For grand views across the Wairau Valley and out to Cloudy Bay, take a walk or bike ride in the 1100-hectare **Wither Hills Farm Park** (Map p444), which could take from 30 minutes to all day, depending on the route. The two main entrances are at the top of Redwood St and the Taylor Pass Rd; pick up a map from the i-SITE or check the information panels at the gates. Ask about fire bans in high summer. Hire bikes from the Spokesman (see p448).

High Country Horse Treks (☎ 03-577 9424; www.high-horse.co.nz; 961 Taylor Pass Rd; 1/4hr rides $50/150) runs equine exploration from its base 11km southwest of town (call for directions).

Tours
WINE TOURS
Wine tours are generally conducted in a minibus, last between three and seven hours, take in four to seven wineries, and range in price from $45 to $90 (with a few grand tours up to $200 for the day). A winery lunch is usually on the cards. Numerous operators offer various (often customised) tour options:

Bubbly Grape Wine Tours (☎ 0800 228 2253; www.bubblygrape.co.nz)

Highlight Wine Tours (☎ 03-577-9046; www.highlight-tours.co.nz)

Marlborough Wine Tours (☎ 03-578 9515; www.marlboroughwinetours.co.nz)

Na Clachan Wine Tours (☎ 03-578 8881; www.naclachan.co.nz)

Sounds Connection (☎ 0800 742 866, 03-573 8843; www.soundsconnection.co.nz)

Your other option is to get around the grapes by bike. Bike hire is available all over town, or

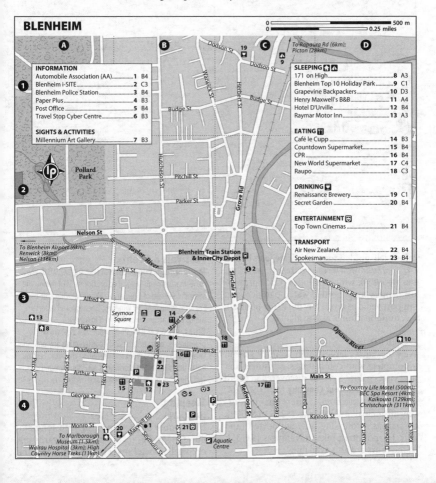

MARLBOROUGH & NELSON

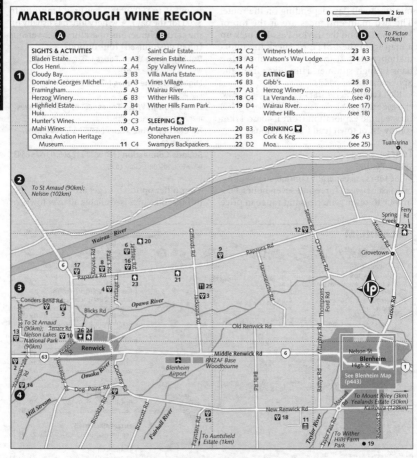

MARLBOROUGH WINE REGION

0 .... 2 km
0 .... 1 mile

SIGHTS & ACTIVITIES		
Bladen Estate	1	A3
Clos Henri	2	A4
Cloudy Bay	3	B3
Domaine Georges Michel	4	A3
Framingham	5	A3
Herzog Winery	6	A3
Highfield Estate	7	B4
Huia	8	A3
Hunter's Wines	9	C3
Mahi Wines	10	A3
Omaka Aviation Heritage Museum	11	C4

Saint Clair Estate	12	C2
Seresin Estate	13	A3
Spy Valley Wines	14	A4
Villa Maria Estate	15	B4
Vines Village	16	B3
Wairau River	17	A3
Wither Hills	18	C4
Wither Hills Farm Park	19	D4
SLEEPING		
Antares Homestay	20	B3
Stonehaven	21	B3
Swampys Backpackers	22	D2

Vintners Hotel	23	B3
Watson's Way Lodge	24	A3
EATING		
Gibb's	25	B3
Herzog Winery	(see 6)
La Veranda	(see 4)
Wairau River	(see 17)
Wither Hills	(see 18)
DRINKING		
Cork & Keg	26	A3
Moa	(see 25)

To Picton (10km)

To St Arnaud (90km); Nelson (102km)

Wairau River

To St Arnaud (90km); Nelson Lakes National Park (90km)

Conders Bend Rd

Blicks Rd

Opawa River

Rapaura Rd

Boyces Rd

Jeffries Rd

Cliffords Rd

Jacksons Rd

Rapaura Rd

Old Renwick Rd

Renwick

Middle Renwick Rd

Omaka River

Godfrey Rd

Dog Point Rd

Mill Stream

Brookby Rd

Brancott Rd

Fairhall River

Paynters Rd

New Renwick Rd

To Auntsfield Estate (1km)

Blenheim Airport

RNZAF Base Woodbourne

Balls Rd

Murphys Rd

Batys Rd

Thompsons Ford Rd

O'Dwyers Rd

Hammericks Rd

Grovetown

Selmes Rd

Murrays Rd

Spring Creek

Ferry Rd

Tuamarina

Grove Rd

Nelson St
Blenheim
High St

See Blenheim Map (p443)

Taylor Pass Rd

Maxwell Rd

Taylor River

To Wither Hills Farm Park

To Mount Riley (3km); Yealands Estate (30km); Kaikoura (128km)

take a self-guided tour with **Wine Tours by Bike** (☎ 03-577 6954; www.winetoursbybike.co.nz; half-/full-day bike hire $40/55), which includes pick-up/drop-off, winery map, bottled water, panniers and support vehicle (if you buy too many bottles!). Accommodation is also available.

OTHER TOURS

New Zealand's largest high-country station – complete with cob cottages, a historic inn, and vistas galore – can be discovered in depth with **Molesworth Tour Company** (☎ 03-577 9897; www.molesworthtours.co.nz). It offers one- to four-day all-inclusive 4WD trips ($235 to $1500), as well as a four-day fully supported (and catered mountain bike) adventures ($1135). Wine tours are also available.

Festivals & Events

Marlborough Wine Festival (☎ 03-577 9299; www.wine-marlborough-festival.co.nz; tickets $50) During the second weekend of February at Montana's Brancott Estate. Features wine from 50 wineries, fine food and entertainment. Book accommodation well in advance.

Blues, Brews & BBQs (☎ 0800 224 224; www.bluesbrews.co.nz; tickets $28) Counteracting any potential wine-wankery, the weekend preceding the Wine Festival hosts this beer fest at Blenheim's A&P showgrounds, featuring live blues, food, booze and bogans.

Sleeping
IN TOWN

Blenheim's budget beds fill with long-stay guests working in the area's vineyards and orchards; hostel owners help find seasonal work and offer reasonable weekly rates. There are masses of midrange motels, with rich pickings on Middle Renwick Rd west of the town centre, and a handful on SH1 towards Christchurch.

Grapevine Backpackers (☎ 03-578 6062; www.the grapevine.co.nz; 29 Park Tce; sites $17, dm $24, d $52-66, tr $78; 🖳 🛜) Inside an old maternity home just out of the centre, Grapevine is a worker-focused hostel with a brilliant sunset deck by Opawa River. There are free canoes, and bike hire is $15 per day. Avoid the three-tier bunks if vertigo is an issue.

Blenheim Top 10 Holiday Park (☎ 0800 268 666, 03-578 3667; www.blenheimtop10.co.nz; 78 Grove Rd; unpowered sites $32-36, powered sites $36-40, cabins $65-85, units & motels $90-140; 🖳 🛜 🐾) About five minutes north of town, this clean holiday park has easy-park motorhome pads and campsites spread out along Opawa River, as well as a spa, playground and the usual cabin/unit suspects. Bike hire costs $30 per day.

Henry Maxwell's B&B (☎ 0800 436 796, 03-578 8086; www.henrymaxwells.co.nz; 28 Henry St; s $80, d $120-140, all incl breakfast; 🖳 🛜) Five minutes' walk from the middle of town, this surprisingly quiet, grand old home has five homely, spacious rooms with their own bathrooms. Guests may avail themselves of their own lounge and kitchen, in-room coffee-making facilities, complimentary port, and the helpful assistance of owners Diana and Graham. There's also a full fry-up for breakfast.

Country Life Motel (☎ 03-578 7069; countrylifemotel@ clear.net.nz; Main Rd South; d $85; 🐾) It may be on SH1 on the edge of town, but as the sweeping drive, neat lawn and blooming rose garden suggest, this cheap-as-chips hotel has its merits. Shell out $20 more than you would at the backpackers and you'll get a respectable old motel unit with fridge, microwave and toaster. And there's a swimming pool.

Raymar Motor Inn (☎ 03-578 5104; raymar@slingshot. co.nz; 164 High St; d $95, extra person $20; 🛜) A recent spruce-up hasn't completely redeemed this old-timer: tacky laminex and patterned glass remain. Still, it's clean enough, central and cheap. Kitchen facilities are communal.

171 on High (☎ 0800 587 856, 03-579 5098; www.171onhighmotel.co.nz; cnr High & Percy Sts; d $125-185; 🖳 🛜) A welcoming option close to town, these tasteful splash-o-purple studios and apartments are bright and breezy in the daytime, warm and shimmery in the evening. A wide complement of facilities includes full

kitchen, Sky TV and guest laundry; staff are well-known for 'extra mile' service.

Hotel D'Urville (☎ 03-577 9945; www.durville.com; 52 Queen St; d $185-300; 🖳 🛜) Injecting some chutzpah into Blenheim's old Public Trust buildings, the 11 dazzling rooms in this boutique hotel are lavishly decorated and individually themed. Downstairs is a classy lounge bar and high-end restaurant (dinner only, mains around $38), while outside the new deck bar traps great afternoon sun.

BEC Spa Resort (☎ 03-579 4446; www.becspa.co.nz; 81 Cobb Cottage Rd; d incl breakfast $325-525; 🖳 🛜 🐾) On a knoll in the golden Wither Hills, this boutique resort basks in beautiful views and the glory of its superstylish architecture. The sophisticated owners have smattered their five en-suite, slick suites and shared living area with fabulous art, but the place manages to retain a *laissez faire* air. It's not hard to kick back in a place like this…lap-pool, spa, steamroom and on-site therapy centre. Who knew Blenheim did bliss?

WINE REGION ACCOMMODATION

The following accommodation options are beyond Blenheim and around the vines.

Swampys Backpackers (Map p444; ☎ 03-570 2180; www.swampys.co.nz; 2 Ferry Rd, Spring Creek; dm/d $25/60; 🖳) A lively hub for travellers and long-termers alike, divided between the new wing and the old grungy. There's a pub and superette nearby, plus funky lounges, two kitchens, tidy bathrooms and a chilled-out courtyard. Bike hire is also available.

Watson's Way Lodge (Map p444; ☎ 03-572 8228; www.watsonswaybackpackers.co.nz; 56 High St; dm $28, d $58-68; 🌜 closed Aug; 🖳) This traveller-focused, purpose-built hostel has three- and four-bed dorms and spick-and-span doubles (some with en suite), in a lodge set in leafy gardens dotted with fruit trees and hammocks. There are bikes for hire (special guest rate $25 per day), an outdoor claw-foot bath, and local information aplenty.

our pick Vintners Hotel (Map p444; ☎ 03-572 5094; www.mvh.co.nz; 190 Rapaura Rd; d $150-260; 🛜 🐾) One of the best among the vines: 16 architecturally designed suites boasting picture windows both sides making the most of vine and valley views, while inside the rooms are truly stylish boasting wet-room bathrooms and abstract art. The stylish reception building has a bar and acclaimed restaurant opening out on to a cherry-tree garden. On-to-it managers are

MARLBOROUGH WINERIES

Marlborough is NZ's vinous colossus producing around three quarters of the country's wine. At last count, there were 23,810 hectares of vines planted – that's approximately 34,000 rugby pitches! Sunny days and cool nights create the perfect microclimate for cool-climate grapes: world-famous sauvignon blanc, top-notch pinot noir, and notable gewürztraminer, riesling, pinot gris and bubbly. Spending a day or two drifting between tasting rooms and dining among the vines is a quintessential South Island experience. See p445 for sleeping options in wine country.

The majority of Marlborough's nearly 200 wineries lie within the Wairau Valley around Blenheim and Renwick with others blanketing the cooler Awatere Valley or creeping up the southern-side valleys of the Wairau. Of the 40 or so that are open to the public, those below (see Map p444) are well worth a look, providing a range of quality cellar-door experiences. For wine tours, see p443.

A Taste of the Tastings

Most tastings are free. Summer hours are given, with some wineries scaling back operations in winter. Also pick up a copy of *The Marlborough Wine Trail* map from Blenheim i-SITE, available online at www.wine-marlborough.co.nz.

- **Auntsfield Estate** (☎ 03-578 0622; www.auntsfield.co.nz; 270 Paynters Rd; ☽ 11am-5pm) Quality handcrafted wines from this historic and picturesque vineyard at the foot of the Wither Hills. Tours Tuesday to Saturday ($10).

- **Bladen Estate** (☎ 03-572 9417; www.bladen.co.nz; Conders Bend Rd; ☽ 11am-5pm) Bijou family winery that's big on charm. Award-winning cellar door.

- **Clos Henri** (☎ 03-572 7923; www.closhenri.com; 639 SH63; ☽ 10am-4pm Mon-Fri) French winemaking meets Marlborough terroir with *très bien* results. Beautifully restored local country church houses the cellar door.

- **Cloudy Bay** (☎ 03-520 9147; www.cloudybay.co.nz; Jacksons Rd; ☽ 10am-5pm) Understated exterior belies the classy interior of this blue-ribbon winery and cellar door. Globally coveted sauvignon blanc, bubbly and pinot noir.

- **Domaine Georges Michel** (☎ 03-572 7230; www.georgesmichel.co.nz; 56 Vintage La; ☽ 10.30am-4.30pm) A slice of France in the heart of Marlborough. Nicely balanced pinot noir, and *La Veranda* – one of our favourite places for lunch (see opposite).

- **Framingham** (☎ 03-572 8884; www.framingham.co.nz; 19 Conders Bend Rd; ☽ 10.30am-4.30pm) Consistent, quality wines including exceptional rieslings.

- **Herzog Winery** (☎ 03-572 8770; www.herzog.co.nz; 81 Jeffries Rd; ☽ 9am-5pm Mon-Fri, 11am-4pm Sat & Sun) Boutique family-owned winery and acclaimed restaurant (see opposite). Try the full-bodied montepulciano, a rare grape in these parts.

- **Highfield Estate** (☎ 03-572 9244; www.highfield.co.nz; Brookby Rd; ☽ 10am-5pm) Impressive views over the Wairau Valley from the tower atop this rosy Tuscan-style winery. The fizz is the biz. The restaurant is open from 11.30am to 4.30pm.

- **Huia** (☎ 03-572 8326; www.huia.net.nz; Boyces Rd; ☽ 10.30am-5pm) Sustainable, small-scale winegrowing and the cutest yellow tasting room in town. Delectable dry-style gewürztraminer.

- **Hunter's Wines** (☎ 03-572 8489; www.hunters.co.nz; 603 Rapaura Rd; ☽ 9am-5pm) Home of viticultural legend Jane Hunter. The garden cafe is open for lunch from 11am to 3pm, and for dinner from 6pm to 9pm, Wednesday to Saturday).

- **Mahi Wines** (☎ 03-572 8859; www.mahiwine.co.nz; 9 Terrace Rd; ☽ 10am-4.30pm) Knowledgeable and friendly staff who are rightly proud of Mahi's stable of fine wines, with a strong focus on single-vineyard varieties.

■ **Mount Riley** (☎ 03-577 9900; www.mountriley.co.nz; 10 Malthouse Rd, Riverlands; ⊙ 10am-4.30pm) Family owned and operated winery producing decent, reasonably priced wines. The striking concrete sarcophagus within the vines houses the cellar door.

■ **Saint Clair Estate** (☎ 03-570 5280; www.saintclair.co.nz; cnr Rapaura & Selmes Rds; ⊙ 9am-5pm) Prepare to be blown away by the Pioneer Block range of sauvignon blanc; some of the finest in NZ. Cafe open from 9am to 5pm.

■ **Seresin Estate** (☎ 03-572 9408; www.seresin.co.nz; 85 Bedford Rd; ⊙ 10am-4.30pm) Organic and biodynamic wines and olive oils from cinematographer Michael Seresin. Shedlike cellar door (tasting $5) and groovy sculptures dotted about.

■ **Spy Valley Wines** (☎ 03-572 9830; www.spyvalleywine.co.nz; Waihopai Valley Rd; ⊙ 10am-4pm) Stylish, edgy architecture at this espionage-themed winery with great wines across the board. Memorable merchandise.

■ **Villa Maria Estate** (☎ 03-520 8470; www.villamaria.co.nz; cnr New Renwick & Paynters Rds; ⊙ 10am-5pm) One of NZ's winemaking giants with awards aplenty. Its black-label pinot noir range is oenophilic nirvana.

■ **Vines Village** (☎ 03-572 8444; www.thevinesvillage.co.nz; 193 Rapaura Rd; ⊙ 9am-5pm) Site of the Bouldevines cellar door (www.bouldevineswine.co.nz) and much more: Prenzel Distillery Company, olive oils, acres of quilts and a reliable cafe serving affordable homemade fare.

■ **Wairau River** (☎ 03-572 9800; www.wairauriverwines.co.nz; 11 Rapaura Rd; ⊙ 10am-5pm) Carbon-neutral family estate with some of Marlborough's oldest vines. Relaxing gardens and a satisfying lunch menu (see below).

■ **Wither Hills** (☎ 03-578 4036; www.witherhills.co.nz; 211 New Renwick Rd; ⊙ 10am-4.30pm) One of the region's flagship wineries and an architectural gem. Premium wines and an excellent lunch (see below).

■ **Yealands Estate** (☎ 03-575 7618; www.yealands.com; cnr Seaview & Reserve Rd, Seddon; ⊙ 10am-4.30pm) Clean, green winemaking on a grand scale, with over 1000 hectares planted. Tours of the space-age winery by arrangement.

All graped out? Cleanse your palate with Marlborough's delicious craft ales (p449).

Best Wining & Dining

With wine there must be food. This is our pick of the bunch for dining among the vines. Opening hours are for summer, when bookings are recommended.

■ **La Veranda** (platters $16; ⊙ 10am-5pm) Keenly priced platters of quality charcuterie, fromages and French desserts – the sort of lunch you *should* be eating at a vineyard. Eat outside or in Domaine George Michel's elegant restaurant.

■ **Wairau River** (mains $17-23; ⊙ noon-3pm) Mudbrick bistro with wide veranda and beautiful gardens with plenty of shade. Order a double-baked blue-cheese soufflé, or the sticky pork and peanut salad. Relaxing and thoroughly enjoyable.

■ **Wither Hills** (mains $17-24, platters $28-45; ⊙ 11am-4pm) Simple, well executed food in a stylish space. Pull up a beanbag on the Hockneyesque lawns and enjoy a platter or Café de Paris steak before climbing the ziggurat for impressive views across the Wairau.

■ **Gibb's** (☎ 03-572 8048; 258 Jacksons Rd; mains $37-40; ⊙ 6.30pm-late) It's not a winery but rather a restaurant nestled among the vineyards. Fresh and sophisticated seasonal food, with a Euro-bent and stellar wine list. Intimate evening dining in a slightly demure environment.

■ **Herzog Winery** (mains $82-129, 5-course degustation menu with/without wine $191/125; ⊙ 6.30-9.30pm mid-Oct–mid-May) Refined dining in Herzog's opulent dining room. Beautifully prepared food and a remarkable wine list. Less extravagant bistro lunches (⊙ noon-3pm) also available.

keen to connect you with the best experiences the region has to offer.

Antares Homestay (Map p444; ☎ 03-572 9951; 106 Jeffries Rd; s/d incl breakfast $175/195, d unit $230, extra person $35; 🖳 🛜 🕮) A four-acre property with juicy lemons, two en-suite rooms in a wing off the main house, plus a self-contained loft unit (sleeping up to five) above the garage. Bikes are available.

Stonehaven (Map p444; ☎ 03-572 9730; www. stonehavenhomestay.co.nz; 414 Rapaura Rd; d incl breakfast $185-280; 🖳 🛜 🕮) A stellar stone-and-timber B&B nestled among the picturesque vines with three commodious guest rooms. Beds are piled high with pillows, proper continental breakfast is served in the summerhouse, dinner is offered by request with rare wines from the cellar, and bike hire is available on-site.

Eating & Drinking

Dining and drinking can be pretty hit and miss in Blenny, and some of the best food will be found yonder at the wineries and breweries (see p446 and opposite).

Café le Cupp (☎ 03-577 7311; 30 Market St; snacks $2-5, meals $6-18; 🕑 8am-3.30pm Mon-Fri, 9am-1pm Sat) The best tearoom in town by a country mile. Ogle your way along the counter (egg sandwiches, mince savouries, luscious lamingtons, carrot cake) or get yourself a brekkie such as the full fry-up, French toast or muesli. We note the presence of the ginger gem… there is a God.

CPR (☎ 03-579 5030; 18 Wynen St; 🕑 7am-4pm Mon-Fri, 8.30am-1pm Sat) Get a fix of Blenheim's own-roast coffee. Muffins if you're lucky, but it's really all about the beans.

Raupo (☎ 03-577 8822; 2 Symons St; lunch $12-18, dinner $22-28; 🕑 7am-late) An airy, high-ceilinged timber-and-stone building alongside the Opawa River. During the day there's a satisfying cafe menu (brekkies, burgers, mussels, lamb shanks) and sweet treats, seguing into slightly more sophisticated fare of an evening. Sheltered outdoor seating, and soft-jazz grooves on the stereo.

Secret Garden (☎ 03-579 5025; 30 Maxwell Rd; 🕑 9am-late; meals $16-23) A leafy oasis in a somewhat dull townscape, this sophisticated restaurant and garden bar spoils its guests with bacon butties and local coffee for breakfast before pressing on towards wild-game pies, craft beer, single malts and cigars later on. Smart service.

See also Hotel D'Urville (p444). For self-catering, hit the supermarkets:

Countdown Supermarket (☎ 03-579 2946; 51 Arthur St; 🕑 7am-midnight)

New World Supermarket (☎ 03-520 9030; 1 Freswick St; 🕑 7am-10pm)

Entertainment

Top Town Cinemas (☎ 03-577 8273; www.toptown cinemas.co.nz; 4 Kinross St; adult/child/concession from $11/8/10; 🕑 10am-midnight) Major Hollywood releases in the main cinemas, with more off-the-wall stuff screening in the 'Lounge'. All tickets are $8 on Tuesdays.

Getting There & Around

AIR

Blenheim Airport is 6km west of town on Middle Renwick Rd. **Air New Zealand** (☎ 0800 747 000, 03-577 2200; www.airnewzealand.co.nz; 29 Queen St; 🕑 9am-5pm Mon-Fri) has direct flights to/from Wellington (from $75, 12 daily), Auckland ($109, five daily) and Christchurch ($89, three daily) with onward connections.

BICYCLE

Spokesman (☎ 03-578 0433; www.bikemarlborough. co.nz; 61 Queen St; hire per half-/full day incl helmet $25/40; 🕑 8am-5.30pm Mon-Fri, 10am-1pm Sat) rents bikes; longer hire and delivery by arrangement.

BUS

InterCity (☎ 03-365 1113; www.intercitycoach.co.nz) buses run daily from the Blenheim i-SITE to Picton ($15, 30 minutes, five daily) continuing through to Nelson ($31, 1¾ hours, three daily). Buses also head down south to Christchurch ($54, five hours, two daily) via Kaikoura ($33, 1¾ hours). A couple of shuttle buses also make the stop at Blenheim on the Nelson–Picton–Christchurch run (see p435).

Ritchies Transport (☎ 03-578 5467; www.ritchies. co.nz) buses traverse the Blenheim–Picton line ($10, 25 minutes, three daily Monday to Friday during school term), departing from Blenheim Railway Station.

Naked Bus (☎ 0900 625 33; www.nakedbus.com) runs from Blenheim to many South Island destinations, including Kaikoura ($20, two hours, two daily), Nelson (from $13, 1¾ hours, one to two daily) and Motueka ($27, 3¾ hours, one daily). Buses depart the i-SITE. Book online or at the i-SITE; cheaper fares for advance bookings.

REAL BEER

It's not all about the wine…Marlborough produces some quality craft beers too. Quaff some at the following establishments dedicated to the world's oldest beverage, a fine antidote to all that sauvignon blanc:

- **Cork & Keg** (☎ 03-572 9328; Inkerman St, Renwick; ☺ noon-late) English-style country boozer with a pleasant beer patio and pub grub. Moa, West Coast and Benger Gold Cider on tap.

- **Moa** (☎ 03-572 5146; www.moabeer.co.nz; Jacksons Rd; ☺ noon-late summer, noon-late Fri-Sun winter) Winemaker's son Josh Scott brews an excellent range of bottle-fermented beers and thirst-quenching ciders at his tasting room-cum-bar in the thick of Marlborough's wineries. Nice garden overlooking the vines. Pricey platters.

- **Renaissance** (Map p443; ☎ 03-579 3400; www.renaissancebrewing.co.nz; 1 Dodson St; ☺ 11am-late Tue-Fri, 10am-late Sat & Sun) Sample quality Renaissance ales at the Dodson Street Bistro & Ale House, next door to the brewery. The malty Stonecutter Scotch Ale is fulsome and delicious. A selection of other craft beers, including Emerson's, 666 and 8-Wired, as well as some decent food too.

TAXI

Call for bookings or for a post wine-touring ride back to your hotel with **Marlborough Taxis** (☎ 03-577 5511).

TRAIN

Tranz Scenic (☎ 0800 872 467, 04-495 0775; www.tranzscenic.co.nz) runs the *TranzCoastal* service, stopping daily at Blenheim en route to Picton ($27, 27 minutes, departing 11.46am) heading north, and Christchurch ($95, five hours, departing 1.33pm) via Kaikoura ($48, two hours) heading south. There are often decent discounts on the fares listed here.

KAIKOURA
pop 3850

Take SH1 132km southeast from Blenheim (or 183km north from Christchurch) and you'll wind around the panoramic coast to Kaikoura, a picture-perfect peninsula town backed by the snowcapped peaks of the Seaward Kaikoura Range. There are few places in the world with such awesome mountains so close to the sea, and such a proliferation of wildlife so close at hand: whales, dolphins, NZ fur seals, penguins, shearwaters, petrels and wandering albatross all stop by or make this area home.

Marine animals are abundant here due to ocean-current and continental-shelf conditions: the seabed gradually slopes away from the land to a depth of about 90m, then plunges to more than 800m – warm and cold water converges. When the southerly current hits the continental shelf it creates an upwelling, bringing nutrients up from the ocean floor into the feeding zone.

Until the 1980s, no one wanted to know about Kaikoura: it was a sleepy crayfishing town ('Kai' meaning food, 'koura' meaning crayfish) with grim prospects. These days it's a tourist mecca, with quality accommodation and many other enticements including eye-popping wildlife tours.

History

In Maori legend, Kaikoura Peninsula (Taumanu o Te Waka a Maui) was the seat where the demigod Maui sat when he fished the North Island up from the depths of the sea. The area was heavily settled before Europeans arrived – at least 14 Maori *pa* (fortified village) sites have been identified, and excavations show that the area was a moa-hunter settlement about 800 to 1000 years ago. The largest moa egg ever found (240mm long, 178mm in diameter) was unearthed in 1857 at a burial site near the present-day Fyffe House.

In 1828 Kaikoura's beachfront was the scene of a tremendous battle. A Ngati Toa war party, led by chief Te Rauparaha, bore down on Kaikoura, killing or capturing several hundred of the Ngai Tahu tribe.

James Cook sailed past the peninsula in 1770, but didn't land. His journal states that 57 Maori in four double-hulled canoes came towards the *Endeavour,* but 'would not be prevail'd upon to put along side'. Europeans established a whaling station here in 1842, and the town remained a whaling centre until 1922. Sheep farming and agriculture also flourished. After whaling ended, the sea and fertile farmland continued to sustain the community.

Information

Global Gossip (☎ 03-319 7970; 19 West End; ⏰ 9am-9pm) Internet access.

Kaikoura i-SITE (☎ 03-319 5641; www.kaikoura.co.nz; West End; ⏰ 9am-5pm Mon-Fri, to 4pm Sat & Sun, extended hr in summer) Helpful staff make tour, accommodation and transport bookings, and help with DOC-related matters.

Paperplus/post office (☎ 03-319 6808; 41 West End; ⏰ 8.30am-5.30pm Mon-Fri, to 7pm Sat, to 4pm Sun) A decent bookshop with post office counter.

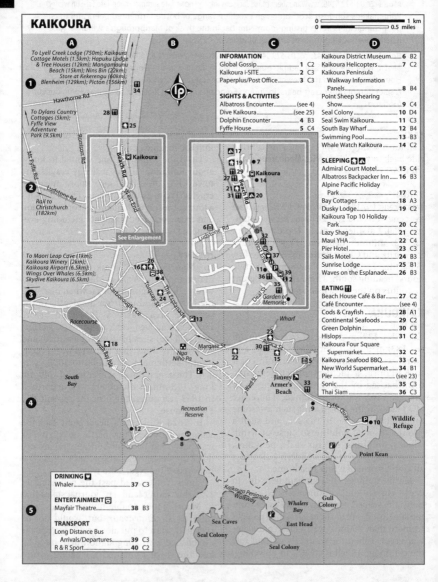

KAIKOURA

0 ——————— 1 km
0 ——————— 0.5 miles

INFORMATION
Global Gossip 1 C2
Kaikoura i-SITE 2 C3
Paperplus/Post Office 3 C3

SIGHTS & ACTIVITIES
Albatross Encounter .... (see 4)
Dive Kaikoura .... (see 25)
Dolphin Encounter 4 B3
Fyffe House 5 C4

Kaikoura District Museum 6 B2
Kaikoura Helicopters 7 C2
Kaikoura Peninsula
  Walkway Information
  Panels 8 B4
Point Sheep Shearing
  Show 9 C4
Seal Colony 10 D4
Seal Swim Kaikoura 11 C3
South Bay Wharf 12 B4
Swimming Pool 13 B3
Whale Watch Kaikoura 14 C2

SLEEPING 🏠🏕
Admiral Court Motel 15 C4
Albatross Backpacker Inn 16 B3
Alpine Pacific Holiday
  Park 17 C2
Bay Cottages 18 A3
Dusky Lodge 19 C2
Kaikoura Top 10 Holiday
  Park 20 C2
Lazy Shag 21 C2
Maui YHA 22 C4
Pier Hotel 23 C3
Sails Motel 24 B3
Sunrise Lodge 25 B1
Waves on the Esplanade 26 B3

EATING 🍴
Beach House Café & Bar 27 C2
Café Encounter .... (see 4)
Cods & Crayfish 28 A1
Continental Seafoods 29 C2
Green Dolphin 30 C3
Hislops 31 C2
Kaikoura Four Square
  Supermarket 32 C2
Kaikoura Seafood BBQ 33 C4
New World Supermarket 34 B1
Pier .... (see 23)
Sonic 35 C3
Thai Siam 36 C3

DRINKING 🍷
Whaler 37 C3

ENTERTAINMENT 🎭
Mayfair Theatre 38 B3

TRANSPORT
Long Distance Bus
  Arrivals/Departures 39 C3
R & R Sport 40 C2

To Lyell Creek Lodge (750m); Kaikoura Cottage Motels (1.5km); Hapuku Lodge & Tree Houses (12km); Mangamaunu Beach (15km); Nins Bin (22km); Store at Kekerengu (60km); Blenheim (129km); Picton (156km)

Hawthorne Rd

To Dylans Country Cottages (5km); Fyffe View Adventure Park (9.5km)

Mt Fyffe Rd

Ramson Rd

Beach Rd

West End

Ludstone Rd

Rail to Christchurch (182km)

Kaikoura

See Enlargement

To Maori Leap Cave (1km); Kaikoura Winery (2km); Kaikoura Airport (6.5km); Wings Over Whales (6.5km); Skydive Kaikoura (6.5km)

Scarborough Tce

Torquay St

The Esplanade

Racecourse

South Bay Pde

South Bay

Nga Niho Pa

Margate St

Wharf

Adca St

West End

Deal St

Garden of Memories

Recreation Reserve

Jimmy Armer's Beach

Fyffe Quay

Wildlife Refuge

Point Kean

Kaikoura Peninsula Walkway

Sea Caves

Seal Colony

Whalers Bay

East Head

Gull Colony

Seal Colony

Sights

Kaikoura's oldest surviving building is **Fyffe House** (☎ 03-319 5835; www.fyffehouse.co.nz; 62 Avoca St; adult/child/family $7/2/15; ☉ 10am-6pm daily Nov-Apr, to 4pm Thu-Mon May-Oct). Built by Scotsman George Fyffe, cousin of Kaikoura's first European settler, Robert Fyffe, it started life as a small cottage in 1842 (with whale vertebrae for foundations) and was completed in 1860. There's plenty to see inside and out, including the original brick oven, historical displays and gardens.

Kaikoura District Museum (☎ 03-319 7440; kk.museum@xtra.co.nz; 14 Ludstone Rd; adult/child $3/50c; ☉ 12.30-4.30pm Mon-Fri, 2-4pm Sat & Sun, extended summer hr) includes the old town jail (1910), historical photos, Maori and colonial artefacts, and an exhibit on the region's whaling era (check out the sperm-whale jaw).

The 30-minute **Point Sheep Shearing Show** (☎ 03-319 5422; www.pointsheepshearing.co.nz; Fyffe Quay; adult/child $10/5; ☉ shows 1.30pm & 4pm) at the Point B&B is fun and educationally ovine. You can also feed a ram, and lambs between September and February. Classic NZ!

Near the Point Kean car park is the smelly **seal colony**. The seals laze around in the grass and on the rocks, wondering why everyone is looking at them. Give the seals a wide berth (10m), and never get between them and the sea – they will attack if they feel cornered and can move surprisingly fast.

If you haven't yet exceeded your annual wine intake around Blenheim, sip a few local drops at **Kaikoura Winery** (☎ 03-319 7966; www. kaikourawinery.co.nz; tasting $5, tour & tasting $15; ☉ 10am-5.30pm, tours 11am, 2pm, 4pm), 2km south of town off SH1. The building and views more than make up for the unremarkable wines (our pick is the bubbly).

Not far from the winery is **Maori Leap Cave** (☎ 03-319 5023; mary.and.scott@xtra.co.nz; SH1; 40min tours adult/child $12/5; ☉ tours on the hour 10.30am-3.30pm), a sea-formed limestone cave discovered in 1958. Tours depart the Caves Restaurant, 3km south of town. Book at the restaurant or i-SITE.

Activities

The **Kaikoura Peninsula Walkway** is a must-do if humanly possible. Starting from the town, this three- to four-hour loop heads out to Point Kean, along the cliffs to South Bay, then back to town over the isthmus. En route you'll see fur seals, and red-billed seagull and shearwater (aka mutton bird) colonies.

Lookouts and interesting interpretive panels abound. Collect a map at the i-SITE or follow your nose.

There's a safe swimming **beach** in front of the Esplanade, and a **pool** (adult/child $3/1.50; ☉ 10am-5pm Nov-Mar) if you have a salt aversion.

The whole coastline, with its rocky formations and abundant marine life, offers fabulous snorkelling and diving. **Dive Kaikoura** (☎ 0800 348 352, 03-319 6622; www.divekaikoura.co.nz; Yarmouth St; half-day $250) runs small-group trips and diver training.

Mangamaunu Beach, 15km north of Kaikoura, has wicked surf (a 500m point break when it's working). **Board Silly Surf Adventures** (☎ 0800 787 352, 03-319 6464; boardsilly@clear.net.nz; 3hr lesson adult/child $80/65) can teach you to surf, or if you already can, it'll hire you a wetsuit and board ($40). R&R Sport (p455) also hires out boards and wetties.

A bit further north is the Clarence River, the bouncy Grade II rapids of which can be rafted with **Clarence River Rafting** (☎ 03-319 6993; www.clarenceriverrafting.co.nz; 5hr trip $30/50) offers. Longer trips are available.

Farmy **Fyffe View Ranch Adventure Park** (☎ 03-319 5069; www.kaikourahorsetrekking.co.nz; Chapmans Rd off Postmans Rd; ½hr/1hr treks $30/50; ☉ 10.30am-2pm) offers horse treks including a sunset trek (with/without supper $95/75). Bone-shaking mountain kart luge, farm-animal feeding and woodshed archery are also available.

Based at Kaikoura Airport, **Skydive Kaikoura** (☎ 0800 843 759; www.skydivekaikoura. co.nz; 9000/11,000/13,000ft $259/319/359), otherwise known as Sarah and Henk, will bring you down to earth in its own personal style. Handicam ($129) and photo packages ($39) are available.

If you're here in winter, you can **ski** yourself silly at nearby Mt Lyford (p87). When there's snow on the slopes, shuttle buses run from Kaikoura to the mountain; enquire at the i-SITE.

Tours

Tours are big business in Kaikoura. It's all about marine mammals: don't miss the chance to see whales (sperm, pilot, killer, humpback and southern right), dolphins (Hector's, bottlenose and dusky) and NZ fur seals up close. During summer, book whale- and dolphin-watching tours a few weeks ahead, and give yourself some leeway to allow for lousy weather.

WHALE-WATCHING

A whale-watch tour is an unforgettable experience, either by boat, plane or helicopter. Aerial options are shorter and pricier, but allow you to see the whole whale, as opposed to just a tail, flipper or spout from a boat.

Kaikoura Helicopters (☎ 03-319 6609; www.world ofwhales.co.nz; Railway Station; 15-60min flight from $100-455) Reliable whale-spotting flights (standard tour 30 minutes $195 for three or more people), plus jaunts around the peninsula, Mt Fyffe, and peaks beyond.

Whale Watch Kaikoura (☎ 0800 655 121, 03-319 6767; www.whalewatch.co.nz; Whaleway Station (ha-ha); 3hr tour adult/child $145/60) With knowledgeable guides and fascinating 'world of whales' onboard animation, Kaikoura's biggest operator heads out (with admirable frequency) in boats equipped with hydrophones (underwater microphones) to pick up whale soundings. It'll refund 80% of your fare if no whales are sighted (success rate: 98%). Sailings may be cancelled if the weather turns to custard, so if this trip is a must for you, allow a few days flexibility.

Wings over Whales (☎ 0800 226 629, 03-319 6580; www.whales.co.nz; 30min flight adult/child $165/75) Light-plane flights departing from Kaikoura Airport 7km south of town. Spotting success rate: 95%.

DOLPHIN & SEAL SPOTTING

Dolphin Encounter (☎ 0800 733 365, 03-319 6777; www.dolphin.co.nz; 96 The Esplanade; swim adult/child $165/150, observation $80/40; ☼ tours 8.30am & 12.30pm year-round, plus 5.30am in summer) Here's your chance to rub shoulders with pods of dusky dolphins on three-hour tours; wet suits, masks and snorkels are provided. Limited numbers, so book in advance.

Kaikoura Kayaks (☎ 0800 452 456, 03-319 7118; www.kaikourakayaks.co.nz; 19 Killarney St; seal tours adult/child $85/70; ☼ tours 8.30am, 12.30pm & 4.30pm Nov-Apr, 9am & 1pm May-Oct) Guided sea-kayak tours to view fur seals and explore the peninsula's coastline. Kayaking lessons, freedom hire and kayak fishing also available.

Seal Swim Kaikoura (☎ 0800 732 579, 03-319 6182; www.sealswimkaikoura.co.nz; shore-based tour adult/child $70/60, boat-based tour $90/70; ☼ tour Oct-May) Two-hour guided snorkelling tours.

Top Spot Seal Swim (☎ 03-319 5540; shore-based tour adult $70) Two-hour guided snorkelling tours.

BIRDWATCHING

Bird-nerds fly at the opportunity for a close encounter with pelagic species: albatross, shearwaters, shags, mollymawks and petrels.

Albatross Encounter (☎ 0800 733 365, 03-319 6777; www.oceanwings.co.nz; 96 The Esplanade; adult/child $110/55; ☼ tours 9am & 1pm year-round, plus 6am in summer) is run by the same folks as Dolphin Encounter.

FISHING TRIPS

Fish Kaikoura (☎ 0800 768 020, 03-319 6277; www.fishkaikoura.co.nz; ½hr trip $55/75) Short-and-sweet fishing (sea perch and blue cod) and crayfishing trips, launching from Kaikoura Beach. Ask about longer trips. No fish: no charge!

Kaikoura Fishing Charters (☎ 03-319 6888; www.kaikourafishing.co.nz; ¾hr trip $100/110) Dangle a line from the good ship *Takapu*, then take your filleted, bagged catch home to eat. Trips depart from South Bay Wharf.

WALKING TOURS

Kaikoura Coast Track (☎ 03-319 2715; www.kaikouratrack.co.nz; package $185) A three-day, 40km, self-guided walk through private farmland and along the photogenic Amuri Coast, 50km south of Kaikoura. The price includes three nights' farm-cottage accommodation and pack transport; BYO sleeping bag and food (some supplies and meals available). A two-day mountain-bike option costs $85.

Kaikoura Wilderness Walks (☎ 0800 945 337, 03-319 6966; www.kaikourawilderness.co.nz; 1-/2-night package $995/1395) offers more creature comforts than the Coast Track walk with the bonus of expert guides. Two-day/one-night, or three-day/two-night trips (graded easy to moderate) through forests and alpine landscapes, with secluded lodgings. Prices include Kaikoura pick-up/drop-off, meals and pack transfers.

OTHER TOURS

Kaikoura Mountain Safaris (☎ 021 869 643; www.kaikouramountainsafaris.co.nz; half-day tour adult/child $100/55, 1-day tour adult/child $175/125) Journey into the backcountry in a 4WD or Unimog – three different tours (two to three daily) taking in alpine vistas, remote farms and the Clarence River valley.

Maori Tours Kaikoura (☎ 0800 866 267, 03-319 5567; www.maoritours.co.nz; 3½hr tour adult/child $115/65; ☼ tours 9am & 1.30pm) Unique and fascinating half-day, small-group tours laced with Maori hospitality and local lore. Visit ancient sites, hear legends and understand indigenous use of trees and plants. Advance bookings required.

Festivals & Events

Seafest (☎ 0800 4732 337, 03 319 5641; www.seafest.co.nz; tickets $30; ☼ early Oct) If you take your seafood seriously, time your visit with Kaikoura's annual fish fiesta on the first Saturday in October (and book your ticket and bed well in advance). Seafest showcases the region's piscatorial prowess: stallholders sell seafood and wine, and there are live bands, family entertainment, and a big Friday-night bash to kick things off.

Sleeping

Book ahead in summer, and during Seafest.

BUDGET

Dusky Lodge (☎ 03-319 5959; www.duskylodge.com; 67 Beach Rd; dm $24-26, d $58-80; 🖳 🛜 🕮) What a whopper! Easily Kaikoura's biggest hostel, the Dusky is an industrious, social place with facilities to cope (including three lounge areas and three kitchens). The crowning glory is the outdoor deck with heated pool, spa and mountain views. Live it up in 'luxury doubles' with en suite and flat-screen TV. There is also a restaurant on-site.

Lazy Shag (☎ 03-319 6662; lazy-shag@hotmail.com; 37 Beach Rd; dm/s/d $25/50/65; 🖳 🛜) The name refers to a local bird species, not the behaviour of guests (but don't rule it out…). This smart lodge occupies a prime spot, with cafes left and right and a party-prone deck taking in mountain views. All rooms have bathroom; there's a separate TV lounge and pleasant back yard.

Sunrise Lodge (☎ 03-319 7444; sunrisehostel@xtra. co.nz; 74 Beach Rd; dm/tr $28/74, tw $60-65; 🖳 🛜) Run by an enthusiastic couple of corporate escapees, this comfortable, sociable lodge continues to garner great feedback from travellers. All rooms are bright and comfortable, and the three-share rooms are bunk-free. Bonuses include free bikes, Friday pub nights, and free nightly sunset tours in a minivan – the perfect introduction to Kaikoura.

Albatross Backpacker Inn (☎ 0800 222 247, 03-319 6090; www.albatross-kaikoura.co.nz; 1 Torquay St; dm/s/d $28/48/65, 6-bed unit $150; 🖳 🛜) This high-quality backpackers in two sweet heritage buildings (one a former post office) is clean, tidy, close to the beach but sheltered from the breeze. As well as a laid-back lounge and separate one for televiewers, there are decks and verandas to chill out on. Homely rooms sport colourful, youthful linen.

Maui YHA (☎ 0800 278 299, 03-319 5931; www.yha. co.nz; 270 The Esplanade; dm $32, d $76-106; 🖳 🛜) This YHA takes the award (as it often does) for location: waterfront, with unimpeded views across the bay to the pine-lined esplanade and mighty peaks beyond. Many rooms enjoy similar views, as does the big-window dining room which you'll find in the same state as

the rest of this purpose-built (1962) hostel: tidy, but slightly crummy in the corners. Half-/full-day bike hire $20/30.

Kaikoura Top 10 Holiday Park (☎ 0800 363 638, 03-319 5362; www.kaikouratop10.co.nz; 34 Beach Rd; unpowered/powered sites $35/38, cabins $55-85, units/motels $95-180; 🖳 🛜 🕮) Invisible behind a massive hedge, this busy, well-maintained campground offers family-friendly facilities (heated pool, spa, trampoline) and cabins and units of the usual Top 10 standard.

Alpine Pacific Holiday Park (☎ 0800 692 322, 03-319 6275; www.alpine-pacific.co.nz; 69 Beach Rd; unpowered/powered sites $38/40, cabins $70, units/motels $120-160; 🖳 🛜 🕮) A quiet little creekside park with mountain outlook, proudly trimmed lawns, a nice pool and barbecue pavilion. Good quality facilities include a spotless kitchen (BYO utensils), and cabins and units slightly more stylish than average. Reduced rates in winter.

MIDRANGE

Pier Hotel (☎ 03-319 5037; www.thepierhotel.co.nz; 1 Avoca St; s/d incl continental breakfast from $75/115; 🛜) A classic heritage hotel with views from sunrise to sunset, the Pier is being gradually restored to glory. The bar and restaurant are now well-known, but its upstairs lodgings – even with their worn fittings and the odd creaky door – have yet to receive their full appreciation.

Bay Cottages (☎ 03-319 5506; www.baycottages.co.nz; 29 South Bay Pde; cottages/motels $90/120) Here's a great value option on South Bay, a few kilometres south of town: five tourist cottages with kitchenette and bathroom sleeping up to four, and two slick motel rooms with stainless-steel benches, low-voltage lighting and flat-screen TVs. The friendly owner may even take you crayfishing in good weather.

Sails Motel (☎ 03-319 6145; www.sailsmotel.co.nz; 134 The Esplanade; d $95-110, apt $120-140) There are no sea (or sails) views at this motel, so the cherubic owners have to impress with quality. Their four secluded, tastefully appointed units are down a driveway in a garden setting (private outdoor areas abound). The apartment sleeps four.

Kaikoura Cottage Motels (☎ 0800 526 882, 03-319 5599; www.kaikouracottagemotels.co.nz; cnr Old Beach & Mill Rds; d $95-140; 🛜) This enclave of eight modern tourist flats is looking mighty fine, surrounded by attractive native plantings now in full flourish. Oriented for mountain views, the self-contained units sleep four between an open plan studio-style living room and one private bedroom. Soothing sand-and-sky colour scheme and quality chattels.

Admiral Court Motel (☎ 0800 555 525, 03-319 5525; www.kaikouramotel.co.nz; 16 Avoca St; d/q from $115/180; 🖥 📶) Away from the town traffic, this solid outfit offers clean, good-value self-contained units (studios and two-bedrooms) with Sky TV. Generally nondescript decor with the odd artful touch hinting at personality and pride.

Dylans Country Cottages (☎ 03-319 5473; www. dylanscottages.co.nz; 268 Postmans Rd; cottages incl breakfast $150) On the grounds of the delightful 'Lavendyl' lavender farm, northwest of town, these two self-contained cottages make for an aromatic escape from seaside fray. One has a private outdoor bath and a shower emerging from a tree; the other an indoor spa and handkerchief lawn. Homemade bread, preserves and free-range eggs for breakfast. Sweet, stylish, and romantic. Closed from May to August.

TOP END
Waves on the Esplanade (☎ 0800 319 589, 03-319 5890; www.kaikouraapartments.co.nz; 78 The Esplanade; apt $190-325; 📶) Can't do without the comforts of home? Here you go: luxury two-bedroom apartments with Sky TV, DVD player, two bathrooms, laundry facilities and full kitchen. Oh, and superb ocean views from the balcony. Rates are for up to four people.

Hapuku Lodge & Tree Houses (☎ 0800 524 5672, 03-319 6559; SH1 at Hapuku Rd; www.hapukulodge.com; d $390-850; 🖥 📶 🐾) Twelve kilometres north of Kaikoura, this fabulous place is perfect for

an indulgent escape. Warm contemporary decor and designer furniture anoint the well-appointed lodge suites, self-contained apartments and gorgeous 'tree houses' (built in a manuka grove at treetop level to snare sea views over the dunes). New additions include an in-house bar and restaurant (guest-only), and swimming pool, spa and sauna. Divine!

Eating & Drinking
Café Encounter (☎ 03-319 6064; 96 The Esplanade; snacks $4-22; ⏰ 7am-5pm; Ⓥ) Housed in the Dolphin Encounter complex (p452), this cafe is more than just somewhere to wait for your trip. Good counter food, and coffee plus cakes, crepes, bagels, toasties and daily specials, such as hot smoked salmon on focaccia. Sea and esplanade views from the sunny patio.

Beach House Café & Bar (☎ 03-319 6030; 39 Beach Rd; mains $8-20; ⏰ 9am-4pm) Serving the best brunch and coffee in town, this chipper roadside cafe garners more than its fair share of the passing trade. Sit on the front terrace or back deck and reconstitute with green eggs and ham, fish and chips or seafood chowder. Good counter food, too.

Whaler (☎ 03-319 3333; 49-51 West End; ⏰ 3pm-late; mains $14-38) A lively leviathan of a pub with good people-watching from the front seats, pool tables, big screens and a spartan deck upstairs. Monteith's and Murphy's on tap and a Neil Young soundtrack.

Store at Kekerengu (☎ 03-575 8600; SH1, Kekerengu; mains $16-42; ⏰ 7.30am-7pm) A good place for a pit stop, being halfway between Blenheim and Kaikoura. Your best bet is the counter food or coffee and cake, rather than the overpriced à

CRAY CRAZY

Among all of Kaikoura's munificent marine life, the one species you just can't avoid is the crayfish. The cray's delicate white flesh dominates restaurant menus and takeaway blackboards. Unfortunately (some say unnecessarily), it's pricey – at a restaurant, you'll shell out (pardon the pun) around $50 for half a cray or nigh on $100 for the whole beast. At fishmongers you'll pay export price, around $85 per kg. You can also buy fresh, cooked or uncooked crays from **Cods & Crayfish** (☎ 03-319 7899; 81 Beach Rd; ⏰ 8am-6pm) and iconic **Nins Bin** (☎ 03-319 6454; SH1; ⏰ 8am-6pm), a surf-side caravan 23km north of town. Upwards of $35 should get you a decent specimen.

Fish-and-chip takeaways usually offer a half-cray with salad and chips for a similar price. Try **Continental Seafoods** (☎ 03-319 5509; 47 Beach Rd; ⏰ 7am-9pm), or the alfresco **Kaikoura Seafood BBQ** (☎ 027 376 3619; Fyffe Quay; ⏰ 10.30am-dark), a roadside stall near the seal colony – the fish or scallop sandwiches (white bread of course) are worthy, affordable alternatives if crayfish doesn't float your boat. Alternatively, take a fishing tour (p452), or buddy-up with a local who might take you crayfishing and share the spoils.

la carte menu. Enjoy it by the fire in the rustic interior, or out on the wide sun decks, with magical sea-peeks.

our pick **Pier Hotel** (☎ 03-319 5037; 1 Avoca St; lunch $14-22, dinner $25-36; ☺ noon-3pm & 5pm-late) Wide views of bay and mountains beyond make this the grandest dining room in town. A cheerful crew serves up generous portions of honest food, such as fresh local fish, venison medallions and crayfish for those with fat wallets. The enticing public bar has reasonably priced beer and bar snacks, historical photos, and a garden bar. What more could you want?

Thai Siam (☎ 03-319 6992; 54 West End; mains $17-28; ☺ noon-2.30pm, 5pm-10pm) Cheerful, vaulted space on the main drag serving a typically expansive Thai menu of over 45 mains including a good selection of Asian salads. The $10 lunch special is a bargain.

Sonic (☎ 03-319 6414; West End; ☺ 3pm-late Mon-Fri, noon-late Sat & Sun; mains $20-31) A casual bar-eatery on West End's southern end, with a pool table, oceans of Mac's beer and occasional live music. Grab a sundowner on the covered deck or terrace and look out to sea through the grand Norfolk pines on the esplanade.

Hislops (☎ 03-319 6971; 33 Beach Rd; lunch $9-21, dinner $20-36; ☺ 9am-9pm, closed Tue & Wed in winter; **V**) This snappy, feel-good cafe maintains its reputation for fresh, wholesome food. Start the morning with fruit salad and toasted muesli, then come back at night for organic meats plus great seafood, veg and vegan choices. The caramelised-pumpkin and blue-cheese salad is delicious.

Green Dolphin (☎ 03-319 6666; 12 Avoca St; mains $29-38; ☺ 5pm-late) Quality Kaikoura fish Asian style, and the omnipresent bovine, ovine and lobstery treats, all made with care and a fondness for good local produce. On busy nights, book ahead or nurse a cocktail or aperitif in the pleasant bar or garden. Those with foresight should plump for a table with a view by the floor-to-ceiling windows.

Self-catering options:

Kaikoura Four Square Supermarket (☎ 03-319 5332; 31-33 West End; ☺ 8am-7pm)

New World Supermarket (☎ 03-319 5723; 124 Beach Rd; ☺ 8am-8pm)

Entertainment

Mayfair Theatre (☎ 03-319 5859; 80 The Esplanade; adult/child $10/6; ☺ 6.30pm-10pm Thu-Sat, daily in summer)

Resembling a pink liquorice allsort, this seafront picture house screens almost-recent releases.

Getting There & Away
BUS

InterCity (☎ 03-365 1113; www.intercity.co.nz) buses run between Kaikoura and Nelson ($64, 3½ hours, one daily), Picton ($35, 2¼ hours, two daily) and Christchurch ($31, 2¾ hours, two daily). Buses belch into the car park next to the i-SITE (tickets and info inside).

Naked Bus (☎ 0900 625 33; www.nakedbus.com) also runs to/from Kaikoura to most South Island destinations, departing from the i-SITE. Book online or at the i-SITE; cheaper fares for advance bookings.

TRAIN

Tranz Scenic (☎ 0800 872 467, 04-495 0775; www.tranz scenic.co.nz) runs the *TranzCoastal* service, stopping at Kaikoura on its daily run between Picton ($58, two hours 20 minutes) and Christchurch ($60, three hours). The northbound train departs Kaikoura at 9.54am; the southbound at 3.28pm. Discount fares (as low as Picton/Christchurch $28/29) are often available online.

Getting Around

Hire bicycles from **R&R Sport** (☎ 03-319 5028; 14 West End; 1hr/half-/full-day hire $10/20/30; ☺ 9am-7pm Mon-Sat, to 5.30pm in winter, 10am-4pm Sun). Maui YHA (p453) also hires bikes.

There's no public transport to Kaikoura Airport, but **Kaikoura Shuttles** (☎ 03-319 6166; www.kaikourashuttles.co.nz) will shunt you there cheaply.

NELSON REGION

The Nelson region, centred upon Tasman Bay but stretching north to Golden Bay and Farewell Spit, and south to Nelson Lakes, is a popular travel destination for both international visitors and locals. It's not hard to see why. Not only does it boast three national parks (Kahurangi, Nelson Lakes and Abel Tasman), but it can also satisfy nearly every other whim, from food, wine and craft beer, to arts and festivals, ecotourism and adventure sports, to that most precious of pastimes for which the region is well known: lazing about in the sunshine.

NELSON

pop 43,500

Dishing up a winning combination of great weather, beautiful surroundings, popular arts events, and a high number of charming wooden houses, Nelson is hailed as one of New Zealand's most 'liveable' cities. While Nelsonians are generally stereotyped as colourful, arty types wont to attend yoga classes and grow their own vegetables, they are in fact a much more diverse group likely to include sun-seeking retirees, heritage fanatics, wealthy entrepreneurs, outdoor enthusiasts, and various takes on the common- or garden-variety family. There are also the itinerant – large numbers of people like you and me, just passing through, who get suckered in by this energetic town and its proximity to some very sunny fun.

Information

BOOKSHOPS

Litter Arty (Map p458; ☎ 03-546 8009; litterarty@tasman.net; 91 Hardy St; ⏲ 10am-5.30pm Mon-Fri, 9.30-2.30pm Sat) Quirky secondhand book exchange.

Page & Blackmore Booksellers (Map p458; ☎ 03-548 9992; www.pageandblackmore.co.nz; 254 Trafalgar St; ⏲ 9am-5.30pm Mon-Fri, to 4pm Sat, 10am-4pm Sun) Independent bookseller.

EMERGENCY

Ambulance, fire service & police (☎ 111)

Nelson police station (Map p458; ☎ 03-546 3840; cnr St John & Harley Sts; ⏲ 24hr)

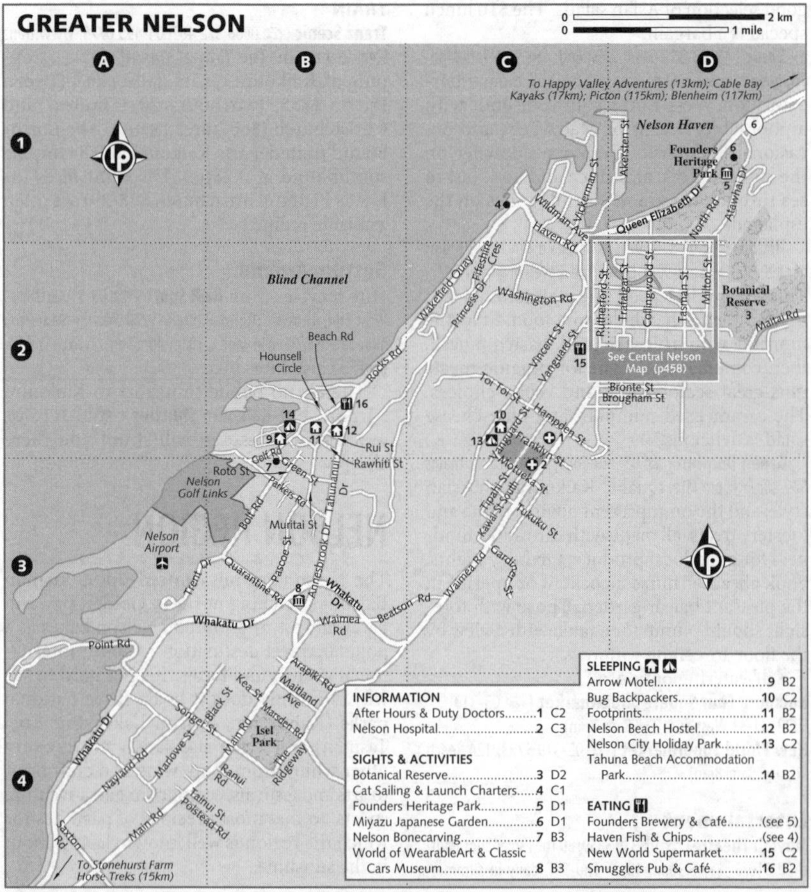
GREATER NELSON
0 2 km
0 1 mile
A
B
C
D
1
2
3
4
To Happy Valley Adventures (13km); Cable Bay Kayaks (17km); Picton (115km); Blenheim (117km)
Nelson Haven
Founders Heritage Park
Blind Channel
Botanical Reserve
See Central Nelson Map (p458)
Nelson Golf Links
Nelson Airport
Isel Park
To Stonehurst Farm Horse Treks (15km)
Queen Elizabeth Dr
Wakefield Quay
Rocks Rd
Washington Rd
Beach Rd
Hounsell Circle
Rui St
Rawhiti St
Golf Rd
Green St
Roto St
Parkers Rd
Muritai St
Tahunanui Dr
Annesbrook Dr
Quarantine Rd
Trent Dr
Whakatu Dr
Waimea Rd
Beatson Rd
Point Rd
Songer St
Black St
Kea St
Main Rd
Nayland Rd
Marlowe St
Saxton Rd
Bronte St
Brougham St
Hampden St
Franklyn St
Motueka St
Tukuku St
Vanguard St
Vincent St
Tipahi St
Kawai St South
Cardiff St
Tor Tor St
Rutherford St
Trafalgar St
Collingwood St
Tasman St
Milton St
Maitai Rd
North Rd
Atawhai Dr
Akersten St
Vickerman St
Wildman Ave
Haven Rd
Princess Dr
Fifeshire Cres
Arapiki Rd
Maitland Ave
Marsden Rd
The Ridgeway
Ranui Rd
Tainui St
Polstead Rd
Pascoe St
Bolt Rd
INFORMATION
After Hours & Duty Doctors......1 C2
Nelson Hospital......2 C3
SIGHTS & ACTIVITIES
Botanical Reserve......3 D2
Cat Sailing & Launch Charters......4 C1
Founders Heritage Park......5 D1
Miyazu Japanese Garden......6 D1
Nelson Bonecarving......7 B3
World of WearableArt & Classic Cars Museum......8 B3
SLEEPING
Arrow Motel......9 B2
Bug Backpackers......10 C2
Footprints......11 B2
Nelson Beach Hostel......12 B2
Nelson City Holiday Park......13 C2
Tahuna Beach Accommodation Park......14 B2
EATING
Founders Brewery & Café......(see 5)
Haven Fish & Chips......(see 4)
New World Supermarket......15 C2
Smugglers Pub & Café......16 B2

INTERNET ACCESS
Aurora (Map p458; 161 Trafalgar St; ☾ 9am-late)
Boots Off Traveller Centre (Map p458; 53 Bridge St;
☾ 9.30am-late)

INTERNET RESOURCES
Backpack Nelson (www.backpacknelson.com) Information for the budget-bound.
Eat Drink Nelson (www.eatdrinknelson.co.nz)
Culinary guide to restaurants, cafes, wines and gourmet produce.
Nelson NZ (www.nelsonnz.com) Official Nelson tourism website.
Nelson Wines (www.wineart.co.nz) Local wineries and galleries.

MEDICAL SERVICES
After Hours & Duty Doctors (Map p456; ☎ 03-546 8881; 96 Waimea Rd; ☾ 8am-10pm) After-hours attention and general practitioners.
Nelson Hospital (Map p456; ☎ 03-546 1800; www.nmdhb.govt.nz; Waimea Rd; ☾ 24hr) Emergency doctor and dentist; entry off Tipahi St.

MONEY
Banks and ATMs pepper Trafalgar St.

POST
Post office (Map p458; 209 Hardy St)

TOURIST INFORMATION
Automobile Association (AA; Map p458; ☎ 03-548 8339; www.aa.co.nz; 45 Halifax St; ☾ 8.30am-5pm Mon-Fri, from 9am Tue)
Nelson i-SITE (Map p458; ☎ 03-548 2304; www.nelsonnz.com; cnr Trafalgar & Halifax Sts; ☾ 8.30am-5pm Mon-Fri, 9am-5pm Sat & Sun) Pick up a copy of the *Nelson/Tasman Region Visitor Guide*. The DOC information desk has the low-down on national parks and walks (including Abel Tasman and Heaphy tracks).

Sights
HISTORIC BUILDINGS
The enduring symbol of Nelson is the art-deco **Christ Church Cathedral** (Map p458; ☎ 03-548 1008; www.nelsoncathedral.org; Trafalgar Sq; admission free; ☾ 8am-7pm summer, to 5pm winter), lording over the city from the top of Trafalgar St. Work began in 1925 but was delayed, and arguments raged in the 1950s over whether the design should adhere to original plans or embrace modern trends. The architectural hybrid was finally completed in 1965 and consecrated in 1972, 47 years after the foundation stone hit the dirt.

Just west of the cathedral, **South Street** (Map p458) contains a row of improbably quaint workers' cottages, built between 1863 and 1867: those in the know say it's the oldest fully intact street in NZ. Some cottages are available as accommodation (see p462).

MUSEUMS & GALLERIES
The **Nelson Provincial Museum** (Map p458; ☎ 03-548 9588; www.nelsonmuseum.co.nz; cnr Hardy & Trafalgar Sts; admission by donation; ☾ 9am-5pm Mon-Fri, 10am-4.30pm Sat & Sun) is one of Nelson's showpieces. The modern space is filled with cultural heritage and natural history exhibits with a regional bias, and there's a great rooftop garden. Charges may apply for major exhibits.

Adjacent to Queen's Gardens, the **Suter** (Map p458; ☎ 03-548 4699; www.thesuter.org.nz; 208 Bridge St; adult/child/concession $3/50c/$1; ☾ 10.30am-4.30pm) is Nelson's bastion of high art, with changing exhibitions, musical and theatrical performances, films, a craft shop and cafe.

Nelson has an inordinate number of commercial galleries, all of which are listed in the *Art & Crafts Nelson City* brochure (with walking trail map) available from the i-SITE. Our favourites:

Flamedaisy Glass Design (Map p458; ☎ 03-548 4475; www.flamedaisy.com; 324 Trafalgar Sq; ☾ 10am-5pm Mon-Fri, to 4pm Sat) Boutique glass-blowing studio.
Jens Hansen (Map p458; ☎ 03-548 0640; www.jenshansen.com; 320 Trafalgar Sq; ☾ 9am-5pm Mon-Fri, to 2pm Sat) Gold and silversmith workshop producing contemporary jewellery (including the accursed ring for the *Lord of the Rings* movies).
Refinery Artspace (Map p458; ☎ 03-548 1721; www.refineryartspace.org; 31 Halifax St; ☾ 9am-5pm Mon-Fri, 10am-2pm Sat) Frequently changing local exhibitions, retail art and workshops.
South St Gallery (Map p458; ☎ 03-548 8117; www.nelsonpottery.co.nz; 10 Nile St W; ☾ 8am-4.30pm Mon-Fri, 10am-4pm Sat & Sun) An extensive collection of kooky, classy and colourful pottery.

While you're in these parts, don't miss Höglund (p466) and the Cool Store Gallery (p466) not far from Nelson city.

PARKS & MARKETS
Founders Heritage Park (Map p456; ☎ 03-548 2649; www.founderspark.co.nz; 87 Atawhai Dr; adult/child/family $7/5/15, under 12yr free; ☾ 10am-4.30pm), near the waterfront 1km from the city centre, houses a replica historic village with a bakery, chocolatier, museums, and more importantly

Founders Brewery & Café (Map p456; ☎ 03-548 4638; www.foundersbrewery.co.nz; meals $13-16, tastings $5, tours & tastings $7; ☽ 10am-8pm, to 4.30pm in winter), NZ's first certified organic brewery. Take a tour, or sip the finished product over a cafe lunch: Tall Blonde, Red Head, Long Black, Generation Ale and Fair Maiden brews. If you're only visiting the brewery there's no admission charge to the park. Also on-site is a weekly **farmers market** (admission free; ☽ 3-6pm Fri).

Walking tracks in Nelson's **Botanical Reserve** (Map p456; Milton St; admission free; ☽ 24hr) ascend Botanical Hill, where a spire proclaims it NZ's geographical centre. NZ's first-ever rugby match was played at the foot of the hill on 14 May 1870: Nelson Rugby Club trounced the lily-livered pansies from Nelson College 2-0.

Just down the road from Founders Park is serene **Miyazu Japanese Garden** (Map p456; Atawhai Dr; admission free; ☽ 24hr), full of sculptures, lanterns and ducks on placid ponds. Sit for a while and ponder something profound.

Don't miss **Nelson Market** (Map p458; ☎ 03-546 6454; Montgomery Sq; ☽ 8am-1pm Sat), a frenzy of fresh produce, food stalls, fashion, local arts, crafts and buskers. **Monty's Sunday Market** (☽ 9am-1pm Sun) is a flea market on the same site.

Activities

Nelson offers boundless opportunities to embrace the great outdoors (something to do with the sunshine?). The clear blue skies are particularly welcome: this is a real NZ hot

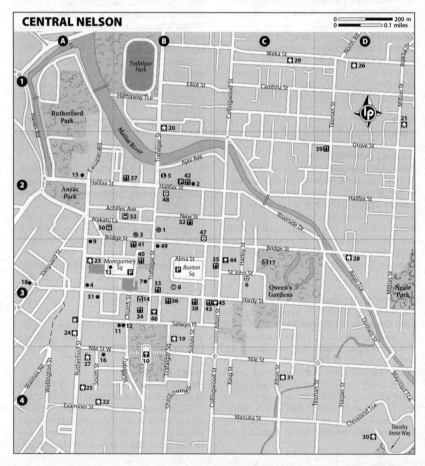

CENTRAL NELSON

spot for paragliding, kiteboarding and hang gliding. Most operators are some way out of town, but will pick-up or drop-off in Nelson.

Tandem paragliding costs around $180, while introductory courses are around $250. Operators include the following:

Adventure Paragliding & Kiteboarding (☎ 0800 212 359, 03-540 2183; www.skyout.co.nz)

Cumulus Paragliding (☎ 03-929 5515; www.cumulus-tandems.co.nz)

Nelson Paragliding (☎ 0508 359 669, 03-544 1182; www.nelsonparagliding.co.nz)

Vertical Limits (Map p458; ☎ 03-545 7511; www.verticallimits.co.nz; 34 Vanguard St; ◷ noon-9pm Mon-Fri, to 4pm Sat & Sun)

An introduction to kiteboarding will cost you around $170:

Adventure Paragliding & Kiteboarding (see above)

Kitescool (☎ 021 354 837; www.kitescool.co.nz)

Kite Surf Nelson (☎ 0800 548 363; www.kitesurf nelson.co.nz)

Hang gliding is arranged through one of two operators: **Nelson Hang Gliding Adventures** (☎ 03-548 9151; www.flynelson.co.nz; flight $165) and **Hang Gliding New Zealand** (☎ 0800 212 359, 03-540 2183; www.hanggliding.co.nz; flight $180).

Rock climbing on the limestone cliffs around Golden Bay and Takaka is popular with the wiry bods. Vertical Limits (above) runs half-/full-day rock-climbing trips ($65/130), plus an indoor climbing wall in Nelson ($16 per day including equipment). Tandem paragliding is also available.

Strap yourself onto a 'skywire' and soar through the air at **Happy Valley Adventures** (off Map p456; ☎ 03-545 0304; www.happyvalleyadventures.co.nz; 194 Cable Bay Rd), a 15-minute drive north-east along SH6. The 1.65km-long Skywire (a chairlift/flying-fox hybrid) dangles you up to 150m above the native forest; rides cost $85/55 per adult/child. Quad-bike tours start at $80/20 per driver/passenger for one-hour forest rides, and 2½-hour horse treks cost $95.

Four kilometres down the road from Happy Valley Adventures is **Cable Bay Kayaks** (off Map p456; ☎ 0508 222 532, 03-545 0332; www.cablebaykayaks.co.nz; Cable Bay Rd), offering guided sea-kayaking trips (half-/full-day from $85/135) exploring the local coastline and marine life.

Cat Sailing & Launch Charters (Map p456; ☎ 03-547 6666; www.sailingcharters.co.nz; from $70) runs reasonably priced half-day, full-day and overnight sailing trips. Options include harbour cruises, fishing trips, the 'Wednesday night races' and Abel Tasman overnighters. **Sail Nelson** (☎ 03-546 7275; www.sailnelson.co.nz) offers charters (around $100 per hour) and official Yachting NZ 'learn-to-sail' courses (two days, $500).

Back on solid ground, **Stonehurst Farm Horse Treks** (off Map p456; ☎ 0800 487 357, 03-542 4121; www.stonehurstfarm.co.nz; RD 1, Richmond; 1hr/half-day rides $65/145), 22km south of town, offers kids' pony rides, one-hour farm rides, 2½-hour sunset and 'musterers', and a half-day riverside ride.

Hit the hillside mountain-bike trails with **Biking Nelson** (☎ 021 861 725; www.bikingnelson.co.nz),

THE WONDROUS WORLD OF WEARABLEART

Nelson exudes creativity: it's hardly surprising that NZ's most inspiring fashion show was born here. It began humbly in 1987 when creator Suzie Moncrieff held a local off-beat fashion show. The concept was to create a piece of art that could be worn and modelled. The idea caught on, and the World of WearableArt Awards Show became an annual event. Wood, papier mâché, paua shell, earplugs, soft-drink cans, ping-pong balls, foodstuffs and more have been used to create garments; 'Bizarre Bra' entries are showstoppers.

The awards show has been transplanted to Wellington (p407), but you can ogle entries at Nelson's **World of WearableArt & Classic Cars Museum** (WOW; Map p456; ☎ 03-547 4573; www. wowcars.co.nz; 1 Cadillac Way; adult/child $20/8; ☒ 10am-5pm). High-tech galleries include a carousel mimicking a catwalk, and glow-in-the-dark room.

More car than bra? Under the same roof are 50 mint-condition classic cars and motorbikes. Exhibits change, but may include a 1959 pink Cadillac, a yellow 1950 Bullet Nose Studebaker convertible and a BMW bubble car. You can view another 70 jalopies in *The Classic Collection* next door ($8 extra). Cafe and art gallery on-site.

which runs three-hour guided rides including equipment for $99, and hire half-/full day $40/60.

Artisic types will love Stephan's bonecarving courses at **Nelson Bonecarving** (Map p456; ☎ 03-546 4275; www.carvingbone.co.nz; 87 Green St, Tahunanui; day course $79). He'll supply all materials, tools, instruction, encouragement and cups of tea (plus free pick-up/drop-off in town if needed); you supply inspiration and talent and you'll emerge with your very own bone carving.

Tours

Avocado Adventures (☎ 03-548 2311; www.avocado adventures.co.nz) Personalised small-group adventures around the region.

Bay Tours (☎ 0800 229 868, 03-548 6486; www. baytoursnelson.co.nz; half-/full-day tours from $78/130) Nelson city, region, wine, food and art tours. The full-day scenic tour includes a visit to Kaiteriteri and a cruise in Abel Tasman National Park.

JJ's Quality Tours (☎ 0800 229 868, 03-548 6486; www.jjstours.co.nz; tours from $78) Scenic, wine-focused and craft tours, plus a half-day brewery trail visiting four boutique breweries.

New Zealand Nature Tours (☎ 0800 326 868, 03-539 4477; www.newzealandnaturetours.com; tours from $123) Wine, scenic and nature tours around Nelson, Marlborough, Golden Bay and the West Coast.

Simply Wild (☎ 03-548 8500; www.simplywild.co.nz) A swathe of half- to five-day active wilderness adventures: walking, mountain biking, sailing, caving, rafting and canoeing around Nelson's national parks. Prices on application.

Tasman Helicopters (☎ 03-528 8075; www.tasman helicopters.co.nz; tours from $150) A host of chopper flights and tours, including D'Urville Island, trout fishing, lunch tours and flights over Farewell Spit, and Kahurangi and Abel Tasman National Parks.

Festivals & Events

Nelson Jazz & Blues Festival (☎ 03-547 7211; www. nelsonjazzfest.co.nz) Sixty scoobedoobop events over eight days in January. Local and international acts in halls and on street corners, regionwide.

Nelson Summer Festival (☎ 03-546 0200; www. nelsonfestivals.co.nz) One-month family-focused frenzy, from mid-January to mid-February. Buskers, outdoor cinema, theatre and concerts.

Marchfest (☎ 03-548 3887; www.marchfest.com) A celebration of beer, wine, music and more beer. Just one day in April, but see www.deadgoodbeerevents.com for Nelson's quarterly beer fetes.

Nelson Arts Festival (☎ 03-546 0212; www.nelson festivals.co.nz) Over 10 days in October; events include a street carnival, exhibitions, cabaret, writers, theatre and music.

Sleeping
BUDGET

our pick **Accents on the Park** (Map p458; ☎ 0800 888 335, 03-548 4335; www.accentsonthepark.com; 335 Trafalgar Sq; sites $30, dm $20-28, d with/without bathroom $92/60; 🖳 🛜) Prepare to be dazzled. This perfectly positioned hostel has a hotel feel with its professional staff, balconies, on-site cafe-bar (with Mother's home cooking and movie nights with free popcorn), soundproofed rooms, quality linen, superclean bathrooms and bikes for hire. Bravo! (Book early.)

Bug Backpackers (Map p456; ☎ 03-539 4227; www. thebug.co.nz; 226 Vanguard St; dm $23-26, d $62-70; 🖳 🛜) A fresh, excellent hostel about 15 minutes' walk to town, occupying a converted villa and brand-new building next door. The Bug emits joie de vivre, with an unashamedly bold colour scheme and swarm of cutesy VW Beetle paraphernalia. Quality beds, nice kitchens, girls' dorm, and a homely backyard. Free bikes and pick-up/drop-offs.

Paradiso Backpackers (Map p458; ☎ 0800 269 667, 03-546 6703; www.backpackernelson.co.nz; 42 Weka St; unpowered sites $36, dm/s/d $25/64; 🖵 🛜 🐾) Club Med for the impoverished, Paradiso is a sprawling place that lures a backpacker-body-beautiful crowd to its poolside terrace. There are two kitchens, a high-rotation hammock, volleyball court and sauna. Book in advance to cut yourself a slice of the action.

Trampers Rest (Map p458; ☎ /fax 03-545 7477; 31 Alton St; dm/s/d $26/42/62; 🖵 🛜) With just a few beds (no bunks), much-loved Trampers is hard to beat for a homely environment. The enthusiastic owner is a keen tramper and cyclist, and provides comprehensive local information and free bikes. There's a small kitchen, book exchange, piano, and Bruce Springsteen on the stereo.

Green Monkey (Map p458; ☎ 03-545 7421; www.the greenmonkey.co.nz; 129 Milton St; dm/d $26/62; 🖵 🛜) Small, homely, comfortable option (carpeted; good linen), run by a friendly English couple. There are just two dorms, and two doubles with TV. Sit and chat among the fruit trees or toast yourself by the log fire. Free bikes and evening cake.

Tasman Bay Backpackers (Map p458; ☎ 0800 222 572, 03-548 7950; www.tasmanbaybackpackers.co.nz; 10 Weka St; unpowered sites $36, dm $27-27, d $64-85; 🖵 🛜) Typical of Nelson's breed of quality backpackers, this well-designed hostel has airy communal spaces, hypercoloured rooms, a sunny outdoor deck and a well-used hammock. Good freebies: bikes, breakfast during winter, and chocolate pudding year-round.

Nelson YHA (Map p458; ☎ 03-545 9988; www.yha.co.nz; 59 Rutherford St; dm/s/d from $31/63/84, d with bathroom $104; 🖵 🛜) A spotless, purpose-built, central hostel with high-quality facilities including a soundproof TV room (free videos and DVDs), two well-organised kitchens, and sunny outdoor terrace. Tour and activity bookings are a given, but some extra-mile care and attention is quite likely too.

Tahuna Beach Accommodation Park (Map p456; ☎ 0800 500 501, 03-548 5159; www.tahunabeach.co.nz; 70 Beach Rd; powered & unpowered sites $34, cabins/units $50-110; 🖵 🛜) A few minutes' walk from the beach, 5km from the city, this huge park is home to thousands in high summer and you'll find it hellish or bloody brilliant depending on your mood. Supermarket, minigolf and playgrounds in situ.

Nelson City Holiday Park (Map p456; ☎ 0800 778 898, 03-548 1445; www.nelsonholidaypark.co.nz; 230 Vanguard St; powered & unpowered sites $36, cabins/units $60-120; 🖵) The closest option to town: convenient, well-maintained, clean, but cramped (although the motel units are pretty good). Limited campsites by the creek out back.

Other backpacker options:

Footprints (Map p456; ☎ 03-546 5441; www.foot prints.co.nz; 31 Beach Rd; dm/s/d/apt from $25/32/68/130; 🖵 🛜) Ask for a room with a window in this well-run, multi-option place in a breezeblock former druid hall near Tahunanui beach.

Nelson Beach Hostel (Map p456; ☎ 03-548 6817; www.nelsonbeachhostel.co.nz; 25 Muritai St; dm/d $26/60; 🖵 🛜) Chilled-out place close to Tahunanui Beach, 4km from town. Free bikes are available, plus there's a pub across the road.

Palace Backpackers (Map p458; ☎ 03-548 4691; www.thepalace.co.nz; 114 Rutherford St; dm/d incl breakfast $25/60; 🖵 🛜) A big, old grungy place with plenty of character and appealing balconies.

MIDRANGE & TOP END

Te Maunga (Map p458; ☎ 03-548 8605; temaungahouse@ xtra.co.nz; 15 Dorothy Annie Way; s $80, d $90-120; 🛜) Aptly named ('the mountain'), this is a grand old family home on a knoll with exceptional views. Two doubles and a single, with their own bathrooms, are filled with characterful furniture and made up with good linens. Your buttery breakfast can be walked off up and down *that* hill. It's only a five-minute climb (15 minutes in all, from town), but only the leggy ones will revel in it. Closed from May to September.

Lynton Lodge (Map p458; ☎ 03-548 7112; www. holidayguide.co.nz/Nelson/LyntonLodge.aspx; 25 Examiner St; apt $95-130) On the hill near the Cathedral with city views, unashamedly dated Lynton Lodge offers self-contained apartments and a guest-house vibe – try for one of the balcony units. Affable host, grassy garden and super-close to town.

Sussex House (Map p458; ☎ 03-548 9972; www.sussex .co.nz; 238 Bridge St; s $110-150, d $150-180; 🖵 🛜) In a historic riverside home, the Sussex has five appealing en-suite B&B rooms, all named after famous composers (Strauss, Beethoven, Mozart et al). Wraparound balcony, views, gardens and French-speaking hosts.

Cedar Grove (Map p458; ☎ 0800 233 274, 03-545 1133; www.cedargrove.co.nz; cnr Trafalgar & Grove Sts; studios $130-180, d $170-220; ☐) A big old cedar landmarks this smart, modern block of spacious apartments just three minutes' walk to town. Its range of studios and doubles are plush and elegant, with cooking facilities and all the business trimmings (phone, fax, internet jack).

Palazzo Motor Lodge (Map p458; ☎ 0800 472 5293, 03-545 8171; www.palazzomotorlodge.co.nz; 159 Rutherford St; studios $130-225, apt $225-290; ☐ ⎈) Hosts with the most offer a cheerful welcome at this popular modern Italian-style motor lodge. The stylish studios and one- and two-room apartments feature enviable kitchens (with quality glassware/crockery, decent cooking utensils and dishwasher) and luxurious textiles. The odd bit of dubious art is easily forgiven. There are spa bath units, and breakfast is available.

Arrow Motel (Map p456; ☎ 03-546 4030; www.arrow motel.co.nz; 24 Golf Rd; d $145-160, q $205-225, 6-bed r $240-300; ☐ ⎈ ⎈) There are one- to three-bedroom options at this tidy motel within walking distance of Tahunanui beach, owner-operated by cheery, enviro-committed folk. All units are self-contained; some have balcony views of the campground and estuary behind. There is also a small pool.

South Street Cottages (Map p458; ☎ 03-540 2769; www.cottageaccommodation.co.nz; 1, 3 & 12 South St; d $215, apt $240) Stay on NZ's oldest preserved street in one of three endearing, two-bedroom self-contained cottages built in the 1860s. Each has all the comforts of home, including kitchen, laundry, log fire and courtyard garden; breakfast provisions supplied. There is a two-night minimum stay. The owners also have a modern two-bedroom apartment on the same street.

Eating
RESTAURANTS
Stefano's (Map p458; ☎ 03-546 7530; 91 Trafalgar St; pizzas $9-25; ☯ 9am-10pm; V) Located upstairs in the State Cinema complex, Stefano's wouldn't win any awards for its decor. This Italian-run joint, however, does get top marks for traditional pizza – thin, crispy and delicious. Escape the movie-time madness and smell of popcorn on one of two balcony tables.

When in Rome (Map p458; ☎ 03-548 1586; 278 Hardy St; mains $10-19; ☯ noon-2pm Mon-Sat, 5pm-late daily) With its swanky Roman-chic fit-out, you might expect to pay Euro prices here. Fear not, the food at this new Italian joint is reasonably priced and darn tasty too. Ample portions of proper pasta, interesting salads and thin, crispy pizzas: *bellissimo*.

Indian Café (Map p458; ☎ 03-548 4089; 94 Collingwood St; mains $12-23; ☯ noon-2pm Mon-Fri, 5pm-late daily) This open-plan, saffron-coloured Edwardian villa houses an Indian restaurant that keeps the *bhaji* raised with impressive interpretations of Anglo-Indian standards, such as chicken tandoori, rogan josh and beef madras. Share the mixed platter to start, then mop up your mains with one of 10 different breads.

Smugglers Pub & Café (Map p456; ☎ 03-546 4084; 8 Muritai St; mains $15-34; ☯ 11am-late) This maritime-themed pub was shipshape when last we boarded, with friendly staff dishing out hearty meals to hungry landlubbers. A dependable family option serving pub grub favourites such as roast-of-the-day, burgers and fish and chips. Good patio area.

Lambretta's (Map p458; ☎ 03-545 8555; 204 Hardy St; mains $16-28; ☯ 7.30am-10pm Mon-Sat, to 5pm in winter, 8.30am-3pm Sun) Feeding what seems like half of Nelson, Lambretta's is a continually busy diner-style joint with ample seating inside and out. Family friendly, the big-eatin' offerings include breakfast, lunch and dinner (pizza, pasta, salad) and hearty counter food along the lines of humongous muffins, pies, filled croissants and sandwiches. Good coffee, too.

Hopgood's (Map p458; ☎ 03-545 7191; 284 Trafalgar St; lunch $14-20, dinner $33-36; ☯ 11am-2pm Thu & Fri, 5.30-late Mon-Sat) Tongue-and-groove-lined Hopgood's is perfect for a romantic dinner or holiday treat. The food is decadent and skilfully prepared but unfussy, allowing quality local ingredients to shine. The Asian crispy duck followed by pork belly with watercress and apple purée was a knockout. Desirable, predominantly Kiwi wine list.

CAFES
Swedish Bakery & Café (Map p458; ☎ 03-546 8685; 54 Bridge St; snacks $2-7; ☯ 8.30am-4pm Mon-Fri, 9am-1.30pm Sat) Delicious breads, croissants, pastries and cakes from the resident Scandinavian baker. Lovely fresh filled rolls such as meatball and beetroot relish, or smoked-salmon bagels. Take your goodies away or eat in the bijou cafe.

Morrison St Café (Map p458; ☎ 03-548 8110; 244 Hardy St; meals $12-19; ☯ 7.30am-4pm Mon-Fri, 8.30am-3pm Sat, 9am-3pm Sun) Part cafe, part gallery, Morrison St is a polished operator, with a menu that sticks out of the cafe crowd. Enjoy raspberry and cinnamon butter pancakes for brekkie, then sneak back for a zingy Burmese chicken salad or an afternoon pick-me-up of coffee and cake.

DeVille (Map p458; ☎ 03-545 6911; 22 New St; meals $15-25; ⏰ 9am-4pm Mon-Sat) Indoor-outdoor DeVille is a cool place, with a pebble-covered courtyard dotted with couches, mirror mosaics and established greenery. Feast on bagels, veggie burgers, nachos and thumpin' breakfasts away from hustle and bustle.

QUICK EATS
Penguino Ice Cream Café (Map p458; ☎ 03-545 6450; Montgomery Sq; items $2-9; ⏰ 11am-5pm) Queuing for Penguino's superb gelato and sorbet, made daily on the premises, is a Nelson ritual. The boysenberry sorbet is a medal winner.

Tozzetti Panetteria (Map p458; ☎ 03-546 8484; 41 Halifax St; items $4-7; ⏰ 7am-4pm Mon-Fri, to noon Sat; Ⓥ) You'll smell fresh bread baking before you see Tozzetti, a pocket-sized bakery serving beautiful breads, sandwiches and sweet treats.

Falafel Gourmet (Map p458; ☎ 03-545 6220; 195 Hardy St; meals $9-22; ⏰ 10am-6pm Mon-Thu, to 8pm Fri, to 4pm Sat) A cranking Middle-Eastern joint dishing out the best kebabs in town, full of salad.

Haven Fish & Chips (Map p456; ☎ 03-548 7969; 268 Wakefield Quay; fish & chips $7-8; ⏰ 11.30-1.30pm & 4.30pm-7.30pm Tue-Sun) Pick your own fillet, then eat your meal by the waterfront. What could be better?

SELF-CATERING
Mediterranean Foods (Map p458; ☎ 03-546 7964; 23 Halifax St; ⏰ 9am-5.30pm Mon-Fri, to 2pm Sat) A terrific deli with great charcuterie, cheese, dried pasta et al, as well as sit-down coffee and sandwiches.

New World Supermarket (Map p456; ☎ 03-548 9111; cnr Vanguard & Gloucester Sts; ⏰ 9am-9pm)

Organic Greengrocer (Map p458; ☎ 03-548 3650; cnr Tasman & Grove Sts; ⏰ 9am-6pm Mon-Fri, to 3pm Sat; Ⓥ) Stocks foods for the sensitive, plus produce, organic tipples and natural bodycare.

Drinking
our pick **Free House** (Map p458; ☎ 03-548 9391; 95 Collingwood St; ⏰ 4pm-late Mon-Fri, noon-late Sat, to 6pm Sun) Come rejoice at this church of ales. Tastefully converted from its original, more reverent purpose, it's now home to an excellent, oft-changing selection of NZ craft beers. You can imbibe inside or out and even bring

a takeaway curry from the Indian Café opposite. Hallelujah.

Sprig & Fern (Map p458; ☎ 03-548 1154; 280 Hardy St; ⏰ 2pm-late Mon-Fri, 10am-late Sat & Sun) Equally hopheaded, the Sprig & Fern brewery in Richmond supplies an extensive range of beers to S&F pubs springing up around the region. Nearly 20 brews on tap, from lager through to doppelbock and berry cider. No pokies, no TV, just decent beer, food, occasional live music and a pleasant outdoor area.

Vic (Map p458; ☎ 03-548 7631; 281 Trafalgar St; ⏰ 11am-late) A commendable example of a Mac's Brewbar, with trademark, quirky Kiwiana fit-out including a striped, knitted stag's head. Quaff a few handles of ale, maybe grab a bite to eat (mains $13 to $30) and tap a toe to regular live music (Tuesday to Saturday). Good afternoon sun and people-watching from streetside seating.

Entertainment
Phat Club (Map p458; ☎ 03-548 3311; www.phatclub.co.nz; 137 Bridge St; admission from $5; ⏰ 10pm-late Wed-Sat) DJs spin techno, dub, drum 'n' bass, breaks and hip-hop, while big-name international and national bands frequently grace the stage. Ambassadors of the local dance-music scene for almost a decade.

State Cinema 6 (Map p458; ☎ 03-548 8123; www.statecinema6.co.nz; 91 Trafalgar St; adult/child $14.50/9; ⏰ 10am-midnight) is the place to see mainstream, new-release flicks.

The theatre at the Suter (p457) often hosts drama, music and dance.

Getting There & Away
AIR
Air New Zealand (Map p458; ☎ 0800 737 000, 03-546 3100; www.airnewzealand.co.nz; cnr Trafalgar & Bridge Sts; ⏰ 9am-5pm Mon-Fri) has direct flights to/from Wellington (from $79, up to 12 daily), Auckland (from $99, up to 10 daily) and Christchurch (from $79, up to six daily).

Soundsair (☎ 0800 505 005, 03-520 3080; www.soundsair.com) flies daily between Nelson and Wellington (from $90, up to three daily).

Air2there (☎ 0800 777 000; www.air2there.com) flies between Nelson and Paraparaumu on the Kapiti Coast ($135, one daily), and onward to Wellington ($45, Fridays).

BUS
Book Abel Tasman Coachlines, InterCity and Interisland ferries at the **Nelson SBL Travel Centre**

(Map p458; ☎ 03-548 1539; www.nelsoncoaches.co.nz; 27 Bridge St).

Abel Tasman Coachlines (☎ 03-548 0285; www.abeltasmantravel.co.nz; departs SLB Travel Centre, Bridge St) operates services to Motueka ($12, one hour, four daily), Takaka ($32, two hours, two daily), Kaiteriteri ($20, two hours, four daily) and Marahau ($20, two hours, four daily). In summer buses also run to Totaranui ($20) and the Heaphy Track ($52).

Atomic Shuttles (☎ 03-349 0697; www.atomictravel.co.nz) runs from Picton to Nelson ($24, 2¼ hours, twice daily) continuing from Nelson to West Coast centres like Greymouth ($40, 5¾ hours, one daily) and Fox Glacier ($65, 9½ hours, one daily). Services depart Nelson i-SITE.

Naked Bus (☎ 0900 625 33; www.nakedbus.com) South Island destinations ex-Nelson include Blenheim (from $14, 1¾ hours, up to two daily), Motueka ($11, one hour, one daily) and Westport ($34, 3¾ hours, one daily). Buses depart the i-SITE. Book online or at the i-SITE; cheaper fares for advance bookings.

InterCity (☎ 03-548 1538; www.intercity.co.nz; departs SLB Travel Centre, Bridge St) runs from Nelson:

Destination	Price	Duration	Frequency
Christchurch	$71	7hr	1 daily
Greymouth	$80	6hr	1 daily
Kaikoura	$64	3½hr	1 daily
Picton	$34	2hr	1-3 daily
Westport	$59	3¾hr	1 daily

See p475 for services to/from Abel Tasman National Park and p478 for services around Golden Bay including the Heaphy Track. Note that many operators run reduced timetables from May to September.

Getting Around
TO/FROM THE AIRPORT
A taxi to the airport costs about $21, or **Super Shuttle** (☎ 0800 748 885, 03-522 5100; www.supershuttle.co.nz; 1/2 passengers $15/18; ☉ 24hr) offers door-to-door service to/from Nelson Airport, 6km southwest of town. It's cheaper if two or more passengers are travelling to the same destination.

BICYCLE
Hire a bike from **Stewarts Avanti Plus Nelson** (Map p458; ☎ 03-548 1666; www.avantiplusnelson.co.nz; 114 Hardy St; hire per day $35-95, per week from $140;

☉ 8am-5.30pm Mon-Fri, 9am-4pm Sat). City and mountain bikes, plus touring bikes, repairs and equipment.

BUS
Nelson Suburban Bus Lines (SBL; ☎ 03-548 3290; www.nelsoncoaches.co.nz; 27 Bridge St; adult $3.80; departs SLB Travel Centre, Bridge St) operates local services from Nelson to Richmond via Tahunanui and Stoke until about 6pm weekdays, 4.30pm on weekends. It also runs the **Late Late Bus** (tickets $3; ☉ hourly 10pm-3am Fri & Sat) from Nelson to Richmond via Tahunanui, departing the Westpac Bank on Trafalgar St.

Departing Wakatu Sq, **The Bus** (Map p458; ☎ 03-548 3290; www.nelsoncoaches.co.nz; tickets adult $2) runs roughly hourly from 7am to 5pm on four routes to outlying areas (including Tahunanui).

TAXI
Nelson City Taxis (☎ 0800 108 855, 03-548 8225)
Sun City Taxis (☎ 0800 422 666, 03-548 2666)

NELSON LAKES NATIONAL PARK
Pristine Nelson Lakes National Park surrounds two mirrorlike glacial lakes – Rotoiti and Rotoroa – fringed by beech forest with a backdrop of forested mountains. There's an unexpected hint of Fiordland about the place, minus the crowds – an unusual sense that you're well off the tourist trail.

Part of the park, east of Lake Rotoiti, is classed as a 'mainland island' where an aggressive conservation scheme aims to eradicate introduced pests (possums, stoats), and regenerate native flora and fauna. There's excellent tramping, including short walks, lake scenery and also winter skiing at Rainbow ski field (p87). The park is flush with bird life, and is famous for brown-trout fishing.

Orientation & Information
To get here take SH6 south from Nelson towards Murchison, or SH65 southwest from Blenheim; the journey will take about 1¼ hours either way. The park itself is accessible from both Lake Rotoiti and Lake Rotoroa. The main town is diminutive St Arnaud near Lake Rotoiti. Lake Rotoroa, 11km off the highway, sees far fewer visitors (mainly trampers, sandflies and fisherfolk), although there is some accommodation down this way.

The **DOC visitors centre** (☎ 03-521 1806; www. doc.govt.nz; View Rd, St Arnaud; ⏰ 8am-5pm, to 6pm peak summer) proffers park information (weather, activities, hut tickets) plus displays on park ecology and Maori history. See also www.st arnaud.co.nz.

Activities

There are many spectacular walks allowing you to appreciate this rugged landscape, but before you tackle them, stop by the DOC visitor centre for maps, track/weather updates and to leave intentions.

The five-hour **Mt Robert Circuit Track** starts south of St Arnaud and circumnavigates the mountain, with options for a side trip along Robert Ridge. Alternatively, the **St Arnaud Range Track** (five hours return), on the east side of the lake, climbs steadily to the ridgeline via Parachute Rocks. Both tracks are strenuous, but reward with jaw-dropping views of glaciated valleys, arête peaks and Lake Rotoiti. Only attempt these walks in fine weather. At other times they are both pointless (no views) *and* dangerous.

Short walks at Rotoiti, most starting from the car park at Kerr Bay, include the **Bellbird Walk** (15 minutes), **Honeydew Walk** (45 minutes), **Peninsula Nature Walk** (1½ hours), **Black Hill Walk** (1½ hours) and **Loop Track** (1½ hours).

Walks around Lake Rotoroa include the **Nature Walk** (25 minutes), **Porika Lookout Track** (one to three hours return) at the northern end of the lake, and **Braeburn Walk** (two hours return) on the western side.

The 80km five- to seven-day **Travers–Sabine Circuit** from St Arnaud is a tramp for the hardy and experienced, with backcountry skills essential.

Sleeping & Eating

DOC campsite (☎ 03-521 1806; unpowered/powered sites Oct-May $20/24, Jun-Sep $14/16) Located on the shores of Lake Rotoiti at Kerr Bay, this inviting site has toilets, hot showers (summer only) and a kitchen. Three kilometres from St Arnaud, West Bay campsite has the bare necessities and is open in summer only. Bookings are essential over the Christmas and Easter holidays.

Travers-Sabine Lodge (☎ 03-521 1887; www.nelson lakes.co.nz; Main Rd, St Arnaud; dm/d $26/59; 🖳 🤶) This modern lodge is a great base for outdoor adventure, being a short walk to Lake Rotoiti, inexpensive, clean and comfortable.

It also has particularly cheerful technicolour linen in the dorms, doubles and a family room. The owners are experienced adventurers themselves, so tips come as standard; tramping equipment and snowshoes available for hire.

Nelson Lakes Motels (☎ 03-521 1887; www.nelson lakes.co.nz; Main Rd, St Arnaud; d $110-129; 🖳 🤶) Next to the Travers-Sabine Lodge and run by the same people, these log cabins and newer board-and-batten units offer all the creature comforts, including kitchenettes and Sky TV. Bigger units sleep up to six.

Alpine Lodge (☎ 03-521 1869; www.alpinelodge.co.nz; Main Rd, St Arnaud; d $145-180; 🖳 🤶) This lodge tries its darnedest to create an alpine mood. There's a range of accommodation, the pick of which are the split-level doubles with mezzanine bedroom, spa and pine timberwork aplenty. A fairly spartan budget chalet (dorm/ double $25/65) is clean and warm, and heading for renovations. The in-house restaurant is a snug, family affair, serving crowd-pleasing meals (mixed grill, nachos, $17 to $33) and a children's menu.

Part of the same complex, **Alpine Lodge Café** (☎ 03-521 1288; Main Rd, St Arnaud; meals $9-27; ⏰ 8am-5pm Wed-Mon) is a toasty spot decked out in retro-Kiwiana. Youthful, on-to-it crew serve up a short, snappy menu, wholesome counter food and Supreme Coffee. Cool tunes on the stereo.

St Arnaud Alpine Village Store (☎ 03-521 1854; Main Rd, St Arnaud; ⏰ 7.30am-8.30pm) The settlement's only general store sells groceries, petrol, good beer and possum-wool socks. Mountain-bike hire per half-/full-day is $20/40. It also has sandwiches, pies and milkshakes, and from 4.30pm to 8.30pm the owners crank up the fish-and-chip shop ($4 to $9).

Tophouse Historic Hotel (☎ 03-521 1848; www.top house.co.nz; Tophouse Rd; s/d $75/135, chalets d $135) Nine kilometres from St Arnaud off the Blenheim road, the hilltop Tophouse was built in 1887. Rich in history, this rare cob highway inn has big open fires and a preloved interior. It has comfy beds with good linen, home cooking (cake and coffee, venison pies, a $45 four-course dinner – bookings are essential) and cheerful hospitality. Reopened after 40 years, 'New Zealand's smallest bar' serves good local beer with a little elbow room; the garden bar has fantastic St Arnaud Range views. Out in the back paddock are four chalets sleeping up to five.

Getting There & Around

Nelson Lakes Shuttles (☎ 03-521 1900, 021 490 095; www.nelsonlakesshuttles.co.nz) provides on-demand transport from St Arnaud to the Mt Robert car park (all prices per person are $10), Lake Rotoroa ($25), Murchison ($30) and further afield, including Nelson ($30), Picton ($35) and the Heaphy Track ($60). Minimum numbers apply, depending on destination; check the website for up-to-the-minute movements.

Rotoiti Water Taxis (☎ 03-521 1894, 021 702 278; www.rotoitiwatertaxis.co.nz) runs to/from Kerr Bay and West Bay to Lakehead Jetty ($75, up to four people) and Coldwater Jetty ($90, up to four people). Kayaks, canoes and rowboats can also be hired from $40 per half-day; fishing trips and scenic lake cruises by arrangement.

NELSON TO MOTUEKA

From Richmond, south of Nelson, SH60 heads northwest to Motueka. This stretch of Tasman Bay teems with local holidaymakers: there's plenty of accommodation, art-and-craft activity, vineyards, fruit stalls and swimming to draw you off the highway. The area is also flap-happy with bird life, particularly Arctic migrant waders.

Sights & Activities
WINERIES

The Nelson region has a significant winemaking industry, and although it can't challenge Marlborough's marketing juggernaut, there are enough quality wineries here to keep the average vinophile busy – 23 at last count; the *Nelson Wine Guide* pamphlet (www.wineart.co.nz) lists them. Chardonnay, pinot noir and aromatic varietals are favoured. See p460 for local wine tours, or tackle the vineyards via a loop from Nelson to Motueka along coastal SH60 and back through the inland Moutere Hwy. Wineries are open for tastings and sales; several have cafes and restaurants.

A few of our fave local wineries:

Neudorf (☎ 03-543 2643; www.neudorf.co.nz; 138 Neudorf Rd, Upper Moutere; ☽ 11am-5pm) Moss-covered barnlike complex; gorgeous pinot noir and some of the country's finest chardonnay.

Seifried (☎ 03-544 5599; www.seifried.co.nz; cnr SH60 & Redwood Rd; ☽ 10am-5pm) One of the region's biggest wineries, at the turn-off to Rabbit Island, and home to a pleasant garden restaurant.

Waimea (☎ 03-544 4963; www.waimeaestates.co.nz; SH60, Richmond; ☽ 11am-5pm) Jazzy cafe and tables by the vines.

Woollaston (☎ 03-543 2817; www.woollaston.co.nz; SH60, Richmond; ☽ 11am-5pm) Multilevel winery set into the hillside with tussock roof, gallery and picturesque surrounds. Enjoy a platter on the lawn.

OTHER SIGHTS & ACTIVITIES

There are loads of craft outlets along these routes too; for details pick up the *Nelson's Creative Pathways* or *Nelson Art Guide* brochures from the Nelson i-SITE and around.

View and/or buy vitreous masterpieces at **Höglund Glass Art** (☎ 03-544 6500; www.hoglundartglass. com; 52 Landsdowne Rd, Appleby; ☽ 10am-5pm), a five-minute drive west of Richmond. The furnace operates between Christmas and Easter: come watch Ola the master and his trainees, who blow most days during this time.

Just up the road (SH60) is the turn-off to **Rabbit Island**, a recreation reserve boasting unspoilt swimming beaches and pine forests. We didn't see any rabbits when we visited, but plenty of walkers, boaters, swimmers and sunbathers. The bridge to the island closes at sunset; overnight stays are not allowed.

Further along, the picturesque Waimea Inlet and twin villages of **Mapua** and **Ruby Bay** sit at the mouth of the Waimea River, one of NZ's biggest estuaries and a haven for bird life. Clustered around Mapua's town wharf are chi-chi shops and art galleries, the best of which is the **Cool Store Gallery** (☎ 03-540 3778; www.coolstoregallery.co.nz; 7 Aranui Rd, Mapua; ☽ 11am-5pm). Packed with high-quality local art, it's brilliant for browsers, while those with dough may find it impossible to leave empty-handed. With the kids in tow, nip into **Touch the Sea** (☎ 03-540 3557; www.seatouchaquarium. co.nz; 8 Aranui Rd, Mapua; adult/child/family $8.50/5/19; ☽ 10am-5.30pm), a small aquarium where you're allowed to touch anything you can reach in the tank.

Sleeping & Eating

Consult staff at Nelson or Motueka i-SITEs for a host of out-of-the-way homestays, cottages and B&Bs in the area.

Mapua Leisure Park (☎ 03-540 2666; www.mapua leisurepark.co.nz; 33 Toru St, Mapua; unpowered/powered sites $32/34, cabins $70-85, motels $115-135; ▯ ⧉ ▣) This is 'NZ's only clothes-optional leisure park' but you don't *have* to nude-up, and the buff option is only available from February to March. It's a bit ragged around the edges, but the location and swimming are sweet, and there are tennis and volleyball courts, kayak hire, pool, sauna, spa and a waterfront cafe.

Clayridge House (☎ 03-540 2548; www.clayridge. co.nz; 77 Pinehill Rd, Ruby Bay; B&B s/d $180/250, cottages $180-200, extra person $25; 🖥) On a property high above Ruby Bay with sea views across Tasman Bay to Nelson, surrounded by orchards and vineyards, this is the perfect place to unwind. There's a choice of B&B guest rooms or modern two-bedroom, self-contained cottages (two-night minimum stay for the cottages).

Golden Bear Brewing Company (☎ 03-540 3210; 12 Aranui Rd; snacks $3-16; ⏰ noon-10pm Thu-Sat, to 8pm Sun) New brewery by the wharf with tuns of stainless steel out back. Eight quality beers on tap – brewed using only South Island ingredients – and authentic Mexican food (burritos, quesadillas and huevos rancheros) to stop you from getting a sore head. Takeaway beers and tours available.

Jester House (☎ 03-526 6742; SH60, Tasman; meals $13-20; ⏰ 9am-5pm) A perennially popular highway stop, as much for its tame eels (which you can feed) as for the peaceful sculpture gardens that encourage you to linger over lunch. A short, simple menu puts a few twists into the staples (wild pork burger, lavender shortbread), and there's Mussel Inn beers and local wine. It's 8km to Mapua or Motueka.

Smokehouse (☎ 03-540 2280; www.smokehouse. co.nz; Mapua Wharf; mains $26-33; ⏰ 9am-9pm) Hamish the white heron surveys proceedings at this water's-edge eatery, which serves fresh, wood-smoked fish and a bevy of seafood dishes in salty surroundings. Its shop next door has excellent fish and chips as well as smoked fish and pâté to go.

MOTUEKA
pop 6900

Motueka (pronounced Mott-oo-ecka, meaning 'Island of Wekas') has morphed from something quite ordinary into a place that the locals are proud to call home. A bustling town servicing a large urban and pretty rural area, visitors will find it a handy pit stop en route to Golden Bay and the Abel Tasman and Kahurangi National Parks. Closer to home, however, are all vital amenities, ample accommodation, cafes, roadside fruit stalls, and a clean and beautiful river offering swimming and fishing.

Information

Cyberworld (☎ 03-528 8090; www.abeltasmaninform ation.co.nz; 178 High St; ⏰ 9am-9pm) Internet access and associated services, plus local info and bookings.

Motueka i-SITE (☎ 03-528 6543; www.motuekaisite. co.nz; 20 Wallace St; ⏰ 8.30am-5pm Mon-Fri, 9am-4pm Sat & Sun) An excellent centre with helpful staff, able to making bookings from Kaitaia to Bluff and offer local national park expertise and necessaries.

Motueka police station (☎ 03-528 1220; 68 High St; ⏰ 24hr)

Take Note/post office (☎ 03-528 6600; 207 High St; ⏰ 8am-5.30pm Mon-Fri, 9am-4pm Sat, 10am-4pm Sun) Bookshop moonlighting as a post office.

Sights & Activities

To get a grip on the town, visit the i-SITE and collect the *Motueka Art Walk* pamphlet, detailing sculpture, mural and occasional peculiarities around town. This will take you past the **Motueka District Museum** (☎ 03-528 7660; savepast@ihug.co.nz; 140 High St; admission by donation; ⏰ 10am-4pm Mon-Sat, closed Mon in winter). It has displays recreating the region's colonial past, plus a cafe.

On Sunday the car park behind the i-SITE fills up with trestle tables for the **Motueka Sunday Market** (☎ 03-540 2709; Wallace St; ⏰ 8am-1pm Sun): produce, jewellery, buskers, arts, crafts and Doris' divine bratwurst.

Ten minutes' walk from the town centre is one of New Zealand's best small airstrips, offering pleasurable spectating (coffee cart on-site in summer). Visitors have three eye-popping/pant-wetting options for getting airborne (accessed off College St). **Skydive Abel Tasman** (☎ 0800 422 899, 03-528 4091; www.skydive. co.nz; jumps 12,000ft/13,000ft $279/299) offers tandem skydiving. Move over Taupo: we've jumped both and think Mot takes the cake (presumably so do the many sports jumpers who favour this drop zone, some of whom you may see rocketing in). DVDs and photos cost extra; free pick-up/drop-off from Motueka and Nelson.

Rather soar than plummet? **Tasman Sky Adventures** (☎ 0800 114 386, 027 229 9693; www.skyad ventures.co.nz) offers a rare opportunity to fly in a microlight. Keep your eyes open and blow your mind on its 30-minute scenic flight above Abel Tasman National Park ($155). Wow. And there's tandem hang gliding for the eager (15/30 minutes, 2500ft/5280ft $185/275).

Next stop is one for the courageous: aerobatics in an open cockpit Pitt-Special with

MARLBOROUGH & NELSON

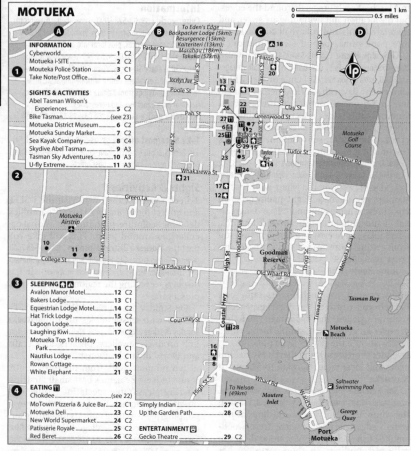

MOTUEKA

0 _____ 1 km
0 _____ 0.5 miles

To Eden's Edge
Backpacker Lodge (5km);
Resurgence (15km);
Kaiteriteri (13km);
Marahau (18km);
Takaka (57km)

Motueka
Golf
Course

Harbour Rd

Motueka
Airstrip

Goodman
Reserve

Tasman Bay

Motueka
Beach

Saltwater
Swimming Pool

To Nelson
(49km)

Moutere
Inlet

George
Quay

Port
Motueka

U-fly Extreme (☎ 0800 360 180, 03-528 8290; www.uflyex
treme.co.nz; 20min $285). No experience necessary,
just a strong stomach. Weaklings can take a
scenic flight in the Cessna (minimum two
people half-/one hour $135/265).

Energetic but more sane folk can hire bikes
from **Bike Tasman** (☎ 0508 254 464, 021 958 890;
www.biketasman.co.nz; 195 High St; half-/full day $40/60).
Guided tours available (from $79).

Sleeping
BUDGET
Lagoon Lodge (☎ 03-528 8652; www.happyapple
backpackers.co.nz; 500 High St; sites per person $14, dm/s/d
$27/40/60; 🖳 🛜) Formerly the Happy Apple;
new owners have made many improvements
to this hostel, freshly paint-licked and swad-

dled in new soft furnishings. Rooms are divided between the house (nice doubles) and
dorm wing. The action's all in the quiet yard
out back where there's an expansive lawn
(camping allowed), gardens, lounging areas
and spa pool.

ourpick Eden's Edge Backpacker Lodge (☎ 03-528
4242; www.edensedge.co.nz; 137 Lodder Ln, Riwaka; sites $15,
dm $30, d with/without bathroom $80/70, tr with/without
bathroom $105/100; 🖳 🛜 🛜) Surrounded by or-
chards just five minutes' drive to Motueka, this
new lodge comes pretty darn close to backpacker heaven. Well-designed facilities include
a spotless kitchen, inviting communal areas
and ample deck space. Dreamy 10m rainwater
pool, and all within walking distance of beer,
ice cream, coffee and fresh bread.

Motueka Top 10 Holiday Park (☎ 0800 668 835, 03-528 7189; www.motuekatop10.co.nz; 10 Fearon St; unpowered & powered sites $40, cabins $50-60, units/motels $105-150; 💻 🛜 🐾) A busy park at the northern end of town, with all the bells and whistles including cabin and motel options. Grassy camp-sites are peppered with shady native trees, and the central amenities block is fresh out of the box. Prices take a tumble either side of December and January. Local wine tours by arrangement.

Other hostels:

Bakers Lodge (☎ 03-528 0102; www.bakerslodge. co.nz; 4 Poole St; dm $23, d with/without bathroom $75/65, f with/without bathroom $125/115; 💻 🛜) A roomy YHA just off the main street. Ceilings are tall, facilities are in reasonable shape, and there are plenty of common areas, including two kitchens and barbecue terrace. Legendary evening muffins.

Hat Trick Lodge (☎ 03-528 5353; www.hattricklodge. co.nz; 25 Wallace St; dm $25, d with/without bathroom $70/62; 💻 🛜) A purpose-built lodge with little personality. It is, however, clean and tidy with a pleasant kitchen-dining area and two 2nd-storey deck areas.

Laughing Kiwi (☎ 03-528 9229; www.laughingkiwi. co.nz; 310 High St; dm $24-26, d with/without bathroom $66/60; 💻 🛜) A two-block combo of rambling old house and a modern, purpose-built bunkhouse. The new section is a better bet, with airy kitchen and sundeck. Free spa.

White Elephant (☎ 03-528 6208; www.white elephant.co.nz; 55 Whakarewa St; dm $24, d with/without bathroom $74/70; 💻 🛜) Dorms in a high-ceilinged colonial villa have a creaky charm, but our pick is the en-suite cabins in the garden.

MIDRANGE & TOP END

Numerous midrange B&Bs and holiday homes are secreted in the surrounds – ask the i-SITE for suggestions.

Equestrian Lodge Motel (☎ 0800 668 782, 03-528 9369; www.equestrianlodge.co.nz; Avalon Ct, off Tudor St; d $110-135, q $160-195; 💻 🛜 🐾) No horses, no lodge, but no matter. This is a lovely option: quiet, close to town, with expansive lawns, rose gardens and shady corners. Family-friendly amenities include several trampo-lines and a heated pool (and spa). Rooms are clean but do need a spruce-up (in progress, thankfully).

Nautilus Lodge (☎ 0800 628 845, 03-528 4658; www.nautiluslodge.co.nz; 67 High St; d $110-220; 💻 🛜) Probably the best motel north of Christchurch, with 12 high-class units dressed in adobe. Rooms feature subtle wall colours, European slatted beds, beautiful bathrooms, flat-screen TVs and plush linen. Good off-season rates; spas and kitchenettes in bigger units.

Avalon Manor Motel (☎ 0800 282 566, 03-528 8320; www.avalonmotels.co.nz; 314 High St; d $125-225; 💻 🛜) Prominent L-shaped motel on the highway heading into town from Nelson. Massive four-star rooms have a contemporary vibe, with cooking facilities, Sky TV, free videos and DVDs. Sumptuous studios have king-size beds and huge flat-screen TVs. There's also a garden and guest barbecue.

Also recommended:

Resurgence (☎ 03-528 4664; www.resurgence.co.nz; Riwaka Valley Rd, Riwaka; lodge $545-645, chalets $445-595; 💻 🛜 🐾) Choose a luxurious en-suite lodge room or self-contained chalet at this magical 50-acre bushland retreat 15 minutes' drive north of Motueka, and half an hour's walk from the picturesque source of the Riwaka River. Lodge rates include cocktails and a four-course dinner as well as breakfast, or you can fire up the barbecue if you're staying in one of the chalets. Chalet rates are for B&B; lodge dinner extra ($90).

Rowan Cottage (☎ 03-528 6492; www.rowancottage. net; 27 Fearon St; d incl breakfast $110-150) Chomp into an organic breakfast in one of two private rooms – choose the studio with outdoor deck and spa. Cheaper sans breakfast.

Eating & Drinking

Red Beret (☎ 03-528 0087; 145 High St; meals $9-19; ⏰ 8am-5pm; 🅥) Slick and chic family-run af-fair that's raised the bar of Mot's cafe scene. Tasty and generous à la carte menu – egg brekkies, steak sandwiches, BLE(egg)T – plus salads galore and the best counter food in town.

MoTown Pizzeria & Juice Bar (☎ 03-528 6060; 107 High St; meals $9-21; ⏰ 11am-late; 🅥) Retro-styled MoTown is a fun place to chew the fat with your friends over decent pizza and fresh juice. Eat up in the little mezzanine lounge or down in the diner with its formica tables and '60s musical motifs. Cutesy named pizzas (the Diana Ross, Smokey Robinson) boast tradi-tional and sensible gourmet toppings.

Simply Indian (☎ 03-528 6364; 130 High St; mains $15-21; ⏰ 11am-2pm & 5.30-9pm Mon-Sat, 5.30-9pm Sun; 🅥) As the name suggests: no-nonsense curry in a no-frills setting. The food, however, is consistently good and relatively cheap. Expect the usual suspects such as tikka, tandoori, ma-dras and vindaloo, and the ubiquitous naan prepared eight different ways. Takeaways are available.

Up the Garden Path (☎ 03-528 9588; 473 High St; meals $15-30; ☻ 9am-5pm Mon-Sun; Ⓥ) Perfect for lunch or a peppy coffee, this licensed cafe-gallery kicks back in an 1890s house amid idyllic gardens. Unleash the kids in the play-room and linger over your cheese platter, seafood chowder, laksa, pasta or lemon tart. Vegetarian, gluten- and dairy-free options, too.

Chokdee (☎ 03-528 0318; 109 High St; mains $16-26; ☻ 11am-2pm & 5.30-late; Ⓥ) is Siamese for 'good luck', but you shouldn't need it at this reliable and homely Thai restaurant. Plenty of spicy and fragrant offerings including tom yum soup, technicolour curries and oodles of noodles and rice dishes. The $9 lunch specials are great value. Takeaways are available.

For fast food and self-catering:

Motueka Deli (☎ 03-528 0385; 195 High St; ☻ 9am-5.30pm Mon-Fri, to 1pm Sat & Sun) Fancy picnic supplies (prosciutto, imported cheese) and delicious local ice cream.

New World Supermarket (☎ 03-528 6245; 271 High St; ☻ 8am-8.30pm)

Patisserie Royale (☎ 03-528 7200; 152-154 High St; ☻ 6am-4.30pm) Delightful sweet treats, sandwiches, quiche and pies.

Entertainment

Gecko Theatre (☎ 03-528 4272; www.geckotheatre. co.nz; 23b Wallace St; adult/child $12/9; ☻ 5pm-midnight) When the weather closes in, pull up an easy chair at this wee, independent theatre for interesting art-house flicks. Cheap tickets ($9) are available on Mondays and Tuesdays.

Getting There & Away

All services depart Motueka i-SITE. See p475 for transport to/from the Abel Tasman Coast Track.

Abel Tasman Coachlines (☎ 03-528 8850; www. abeltasmantravel.co.nz) runs between Motueka and Nelson ($12, one hour, up to five daily), Marahau ($10, 30 minutes, three or four daily), Kaiteriteri ($10, 25 minutes, three or four daily) and Takaka ($23, one hour, two daily). In summer these services connect with Golden Bay Coachline services to the Heaphy, Abel Tasman and other Golden Bay destinations; from May to September all buses run less frequently.

Golden Bay Coachlines (☎ 03-525 8352; www.golden baycoachlines.co.nz) run from Motueka to Takaka ($23, one hour, two daily) and Collingwood

($42, 1½ hours, one daily). In summer services run from Takaka around once daily to Wainui carpark ($16) and Totaranui ($20) with Heaphy Track drops on request (from Motueka, $51).

Naked Bus (☎ 0900 625 33; www.nakedbus.com) runs from Motueka to Nelson ($11, one hour, one daily). Book online or at the i-SITE; cheaper fares for advance bookings.

MOTUEKA TO ABEL TASMAN
Kaiteriteri

Known simply as 'Kaiteri', this seaside hamlet 13km from Motueka is the most popular resort town in the area. On a sunny summer's day, its gorgeous, golden, safe-swimming beach feels more like Noumea than NZ, with more towels than sand. Despite a real-estate boom riding the Kiwi quintessence right out of town, Kaiteri remains a fun place to holiday with the kids, and a buzzy gateway to Abel Tasman National Park (various trips depart Kaiteriteri beach, though Marahau is the main base). Kaiteri now also boasts an all-comers mountain bike park – you'll bump into bike hire all over the show, or get the good oil from Abel Tasman Mountain Biking (see opposite).

SLEEPING & EATING

Kaiteri Lodge (☎ 03-527 8281; www.kaiterilodge.co.nz; Inlet Rd; dm $20-35, d $80-160, f $120-200; 🖳) Modern, purpose-built lodge with small, simple rooms – mainly en-suite doubles. A nautical navy-and-white colour scheme has been splashed throughout; communal facilities (kitchen, laundry, barbecue, bike hire) are excellent.

Kaiteriteri Beach Motor Camp (☎ 03-527 8010; www.kaiteriteribeach.co.nz; Sandy Bay Rd; unpowered & powered sites $30, cabins $43-75; 🖳 🛜) A gargantuan 430-site park in pole position across from the beach. It's hugely popular (make your summer bookings in winter), but it's large enough to cope, and there's an on-site general store. Showers cost a paltry 50c.

Torlesse Coastal Motels (☎ 03-527 8063; www.torlesse motels.co.nz; Kotare Pl, Little Kaiteriteri Beach; d $120-190, q & f $195-280; 🛜) Just 200m from Little Kaiteriteri Beach (around the corner from the main beach) is this congregation of roomy hillside units with kitchens and laundries. The two-bedroom units have lofty ceilings; most have water views.

Bellbird Lodge (☎ 03-527 8555; www.bellbirdlodge. com; Sandy Bay Rd; d incl breakfast $275-325; 🖳 🛜) An upmarket B&B 1.5km up the hill from Kaiteri

Beach, offering bush and sea views, extensive gardens, fluffy towels, spectacular breakfasts (croissants, French toast, poached pears etc) and gracious hosts. Dinner by arrangement in winter, when local restaurant hours are irregular.

Shoreline (☎ 03-527 8507; cnr Inlet & Sandy Bay Rds; meals $14-28, dinner $17-30; ☺ 8am-9pm) A spiffy, modern cafe-bar-restaurant right on the beach. Punters chill on the sunny deck, lingering over panini, pizzas, pasta or fresh fish, but you can also just pop in for coffee and a jumbo muffin. Erratic winter hours; takeaway booth out the back.

Beached Whale (☎ 03-527 8114; Inlet Rd; dinner $20-32; ☺ 4pm-late) Adjacent to Kaiteri Lodge, Beached Whale is a casual, family-friendly affair serving palatable mains (wood-fired pizzas, steaks, fish and chips), with the lodge owner strumming a guitar most evenings. Closed May to September.

GETTING THERE & AWAY
Kaiteriteri is serviced by Abel Tasman Coachlines (see opposite).

Marahau
Further along the coast from Kaiteriteri and 18km north of Motueka, Marahau is the main gateway to the Abel Tasman National Park. From here you can book water taxis, hire kayaks, swim with seals or wander off on foot into the park. Marahau itself doesn't really feel like a town – more like a loose affiliation of houses and businesses.

Abel Tasman Mountain Biking (☎ 0800 808 018, 03-527 8176; www.abeltasmanmountainbiking.co.nz; Abel Tasman Centre, Franklin St, Marahau; half- to 2-day tours $84-339) offers two-wheeled options for experiencing the Abel Tasman area, Kaiteriteri MTB Park, and Canaan Downs/Rameka Track (p475).

If you're in an equine state of mind, **Marahau Horse Treks** (☎ 03 527-8425; clydesdaleadventures@yahoo.com; Harvey Rd) and **Pegasus Park** (☎ 0800 200 888; www.pegasuspark.co.nz; Sandy Bay Rd), both on Sandy Bay Rd, offer chance to belt along the beach on a horse, your hair streaming out behind you (children's pony rides $30 to $35, two-hour rides $80 to $85).

SLEEPING & EATING
Barn (☎ 03-527 8043; Harvey Rd; unpowered sites $15, dm $25-27, d $60-70; 🖳 ☎) Architecturally chaotic, this rustic, tranquil place surrounded by eucalypts offers no-frills microcabins, and bunks and attic doubles in the main house. The star of the communal facilities is the fab new social deck (shade sails, beanbags, outdoor baths), but there are also the necessaries including a separate kitchen for the cabins/campers, tour bookings and secure parking.

Old MacDonald's Farm (☎ 03-527 8288; www.oldmacs.co.nz; Harvey Rd; unpowered/powered sites $28/40, dm $25, cabins/units $80-140; 🖳 ☎) Hang out with your farmyard friends (including llamas) at this rambling 100-acre property offering backpacker huts, cabins, campsites and self-contained units. There are swimming holes in the river, and bushwalks nearby. Ee-aye-ee-aye-oh.

Marahau Beach Camp (☎ 0800 808 018, 03-527 8176; www.abeltasmancentre.co.nz; Franklin St; unpowered & powered sites $30, dm/d/cabins $20/45/70; 🖳 ☎) An established camping ground on Marahau Beach with beds from backpacker dorms to serviceable cabins. Marahau Sea Kayaks (p474), Marahau Water Taxis (p475) and Abel Tasman Mountain Biking (left) operate from the Abel Tasman Centre out the front; Hooked on Marahau (p472) and the camp shop (groceries, beer and wine) are also situated here.

Ocean View Chalets (☎ 03-527 8232; www.accommodationabeltasman.co.nz; Marahau Beach Rd; d $118-165, q $235-255; ☎) Well-priced cypress-lined chalets, 300m from the Abel Tasman Track with views across Tasman Bay to Fisherman Island. Positioned on a leafy hillside for maximum privacy, the chalets are self-contained, some with wheelchair access. Breakfast and packed lunches available.

Abel Tasman Marahau Lodge (☎ 03-527 8250; www.abeltasmanmarahaulodge.co.nz; Marahau Beach Rd; d $130-240; 🖳 ☎) Enjoy halcyon days in this arc of 12 lovely studios and self-contained units with pitched ceilings, fan, TV, phone and microwave. There's also a fully equipped communal kitchen for self-caterers, plus spa and sauna. Cuckoos, tui and bellbirds squawk 'n' warble in the bushy surrounds.

Park Café (☎ 03-527 8270; Harvey Rd; snacks $4-8, meals $9-18; ☺ 8am-10pm mid-Sep–May; Ⓥ) Pretty much on the start of the Abel Tasman Coast Track, this breezy, licensed cafe is perfectly placed for fuelling up or restoring the waistline. High-calorie options include egg breakfast, fat cake, toasted sandwiches, nachos and pizza. Fine views and decent drinks make this a good spot for your sundowner.

Hooked on Marahau (☎ 03-527 8576; Franklin St; meals $13-33; ☺ 6pm-late Oct-May, 8am-late Dec-Apr) This place has the natives hooked – dinner reservations are prudent. The art-bedecked interior (local stuff) opens onto an outdoor terrace with meal-distracting views. Lunch lurks around sandwiches and salads, while the dinner menu hauls up fresh fish of the day, green-lipped mussels and NZ lamb.

GETTING THERE & AWAY

Marahau is serviced by Abel Tasman Coachlines (see p470).

ABEL TASMAN NATIONAL PARK

The accessible, coastal Abel Tasman National Park is NZ's most visited. The park blankets the northern end of a range of marble and limestone hills extending from Kahurangi National Park; its interior is honeycombed with caves and potholes. There are various tracks in the park, including an inland route, although the Coast Track is what everyone is here for.

Abel Tasman Coast Track

This 51km, three- to five-day track is one of the most scenic in the country, passing through native bush overlooking golden beaches lapped by gleaming azure water. Numerous bays, small and large, are like a travel brochure come to life. Visitors can walk into the park, catch water taxis to beaches and resorts along the track, or kayak along the coast.

It's hard to believe, but the Coast Track was once little known beyond the Nelson/Tasman region, but the trail has now been well and truly 'discovered'. In summer hundreds of trampers tackle the track at the same time (far more than can be accommodated in the huts – bring your tent). Track accommodation works on a booking system: huts and campsites must be prebooked year-round. There's no charge for day walks – if you're after a taster, the 2½-hour stretch from Torrent Bay to Bark Bay is as photogenic a stretch as any.

Between Bark Bay and Awaroa Head is an area classified as the **Tonga Island Marine Reserve** – home to a seal colony and visiting dolphins. Tonga Island itself is a small island offshore from Onetahuti Beach.

For a full description of the route, see Lonely Planet's *Tramping in New Zealand* or DOC's *Abel Tasman Coast Track* brochure.

INFORMATION

The track operates on a **Great Walks Pass** (sites/ huts per person Oct-Apr $12/30, May-Sep $12/8) system. Children are free but booking is still required. The **Great Walks Helpdesk** (☎ 03-546 8210; great walksbooking@doc.govt.nz) offers information and can make bookings. You can also book online (www.doc.govt.nz) or in person at the Nelson, Motueka and Takaka i-SITES, where staff can offer suggestions to tailor the track to your needs and organise transport at each end. Fees apply to all bookings other than those made online. Try to book your trip well ahead of time, especially if you're planning on staying in huts between December and March.

WALKING THE TRACK

The Abel Tasman area has crazy tides (up to 6m difference between low and high tide), which has an impact on walking. Two sections of the main track are tidal, with no high-tide track around them: Awaroa Estuary can only be crossed 1½ hours before and two hours after low tide, and the narrow channel at Onetahuti Beach must be crossed within three hours either side of low tide. The estuaries at Torrent and Bark Bay have tracks around them for use during high tide. Tide tables are posted along the track; regional i-SITES also have them. To be immune from the tides, many visitors kayak the track; see p474. Note that you can't pick up kayaks within the park, only at either end (Kaiteriteri and Marahau in the south; Pohara in the north).

Take additional food so you can stay longer should you have the inclination. Bays around all the huts are beautiful, but definitely bring plenty of sandfly repellent and sunscreen.

Estimated walking times from south to north:

Route	Time
Marahau to Anchorage Hut	4hr
Anchorage Hut to Bark Bay Hut	3hr
Bark Bay Hut to Awaroa Hut	4hr
Awaroa Hut to Totaranui	1½hr

Many walkers finish at Totaranui, the final stop for the boat services and bus pick-up point, but it is possible to keep walking around the headland to Whariwharangi Hut (three hours) and then on to Wainui (1½ hours), where buses service the car park.

ABEL TASMAN NATIONAL PARK

0 ————— 4 km
0 ————— 2 miles

SLEEPING 🏕 🏠
Akersten Bay Campsite	**1**	D5
Anapai Bay Campsite	**2**	C2
Anchorage Campsite	(see 5)	
Anchorage Hut	**3**	D5
Apple Tree Bay Campsite	**4**	D5
Aquapackers	**5**	D5
Awaroa Campsite	**6**	D3
Awaroa Hut	**7**	C3
Bark Bay Campsite	**8**	D4
Bark Bay Hut	**9**	D4
Fernbank	**10**	D5
Medlands Beach Campsite	**11**	D4
Mosquito Bay Campsite (boat access only)	**12**	D4
Mutton Cove Campsite	**13**	C2
Observation Beach Campsite (boat access only)	**14**	D5
Onetahuti Bay Campsite	**15**	D4
Te Pukatea Bay Campsite	**16**	D5
Tinline Bay Campsite	**17**	D5
Tonga Quarry Campsite	**18**	D4
Torrent Bay Campsite	**19**	D5
Torrent Bay Village Campsite	**20**	D5
Totaranui DOC Campsite	**21**	C3
Waiharakeke Bay Campsite	**22**	C3
Watering Cove Campsite	**23**	D5
Whariwharangi Campsite	**24**	C2
Whariwharangi Hut	**25**	C2

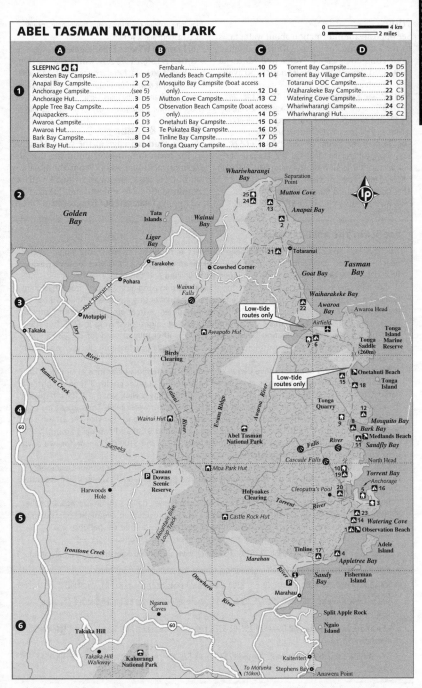

TOURS

See opposite for information about water taxis to the park and for information on flights. Tour companies usually offer free Motueka pick-up/drop-off, with Nelson pick-up available at extra cost:

Abel Tasman Sailing Adventures (☎ 0800 467 245, 03-527 8375; www.sailingadventures.co.nz; Kaiteriteri; full day $75-190, overnight from $270) A range of well-priced catamaran trips, plus private skippered charters.

Abel Tasman Seal Swim (☎ 0800 252 925, 03-527 8383; www.sealswim.com; Aqua Taxi Base, Marahau; 5hr seal swim adult/child $169/130, seal watch $90/70) Tide-scheduled trips to the seal colony.

Abel Tasman Tours & Guided Walks (☎ 03-528 9602; www.abeltasmantours.co.nz; $195) Small-group, day-long walking tours (minimum two people) include packed lunch and water taxis.

Abel Tasman Wilson's Experiences (Map p468; ☎ 0800 221 888, 03-528 2027; www.abeltasman.co.nz; 265 High St, Motueka; half-day cruise $70, cruise & walk $55-70, kayak & walk $89-195) Impressive array of cruises, walks, kayak and combo tours. Luxurious beachfront lodges at Awaroa and Torrent Bay for guided-tour guests.

Sleeping & Eating

At the southern edge of the park, Marahau is the main jumping-off point for the Abel Tasman National Park. From the northern end of the park, the nearest towns with accommodation are Pohara and Takaka. The whopping **Totaranui DOC Campsite** (☎ 03-528 8083;

PADDLING THE ABEL TASMAN

The Abel Tasman Coast Track has long been trampers' territory, but its main attractions – scenic beaches, isolated coves and rock formations – make it an equally seductive spot for sea kayaking. Fortunately, kayaking can easily be combined with walking and camping.

It needn't necessarily be a matter of hiring a kayak then looking after yourself from that point (although it is possible to do that) – a variety of professional outfits are able to float you out on the water, and the possibilities and permutations for guided or freedom trips are vast. You can kayak from half a day up to three days, camping ($12 per night) or staying in DOC huts ($30 per night), baches, even a floating backpackers (p475), either fully catered for or self-catering. You can kayak one day, camp overnight then walk back, or walk further into the park and catch a water taxi back.

Most sea-kayaking operators have plenty of experience, offering similar trips at similar prices. Marahau is the main base, but trips also depart Kaiteriteri. A popular choice if time is tight is a half-day guided kayak trip in the south of the park, followed by a walk along the track between Bark Bay and Torrent Bay. This will cost around $160 including water taxis. Three-day trips usually drop you at the northern end of the park, then you paddle back (or vice versa) and cost around $550 including food. One-day guided trips are around $190 and two-days around $360.

Freedom rentals (double-kayak and equipment hire) are around $100 per person for two days; most companies do not allow solo hires.

Peak season runs from November to Easter, but you can paddle year-round. December to February is the busiest time – it's worth timing your visit earlier or later. In winter you'll see more bird life, and the weather is surprisingly amenable.

Instruction is given to everyone and most tour companies have a minimum age of either eight or 14 depending on the trip. Camping gear is usually provided on overnight trips; if you're disappearing into the park for a few days, most operators provide free car parking.

These are the main players in this competitive market. Shop around.

- **Abel Tasman Kayaks** (☎ 0800 732 529, 03-527 8022; www.abeltasmankayaks.co.nz; Main Rd, Marahau)

- **Golden Bay Kayaks** (p478) Self-guided tours from the park's northern end.

- **Kahu Kayaks** (☎ 0800 300 101, 03-527 8300; www.kahukayaks.co.nz; Sandy Bay Rd, Marahau)

- **Kaiteriteri Kayaks** (☎ 0800 252 925, 03-527 8383; www.seakayak.co.nz; Kaiteriteri Beach & Marahau Beach Rd, Marahau)

- **Marahau Sea Kayaks** (☎ 0800 529 257, 03-527 8176; www.msk.net.nz; Abel Tasman Centre, Franklin St, Marahau)

- **Sea Kayak Company** (Map p468; ☎ 0508 252 925, 03-528 7251; www.seakayaknz.co.nz; 506 High St, Motueka)

www.doc.govt.nz; unpowered sites adult/child $12/6) is also in the north, 32km from Takaka on a narrow, winding road (12km of it unsealed). It's serviced by buses from October to April (right). Sites at Totaranui from December to mid-February are now allocated via ballot. Download a booking form from the DOC website, submit it to Takaka DOC (p476) between specified dates (usually the first week in July) and cross your fingers. There are no powered sites.

Along the Coast Track there are four huts: Anchorage (24 bunks), Bark Bay (34 bunks), Awaroa (26 bunks) and Whariwharangi (20 bunks), plus 19 designated campsites. None of these have cooking facilities – BYO stove. Some of the campsites have fireplaces but, again, you must carry cooking equipment. Hut and camp passes should be purchased before you enter the park (see p472). From Christmas Day to February, huts and campsites fill to the rafters (book with DOC).

Other sleeping options in the park, accessible on foot, by kayak or water taxi, but not by road, include the following:

Aquapackers (☎ 0800 430 744, 027 230 7002; www.aquapackers.co.nz; dm/d incl breakfast$65/180) The *MV Parore* (a former Navy patrol boat) and *Catarac* (a 13m catamaran), moored permanently in Anchorage Bay, provide unusual but buoyant backpacker options. Facilities are basic but decent; prices include bedding and dinner.

Fernbank (☎ 027 369 9555; www.abeltasman accommodation.co.nz; Torrent Bay; d $160, extra adult/child $15/10) Fernbank comprises two classic holiday homes at Torrent Bay; each self-contained house can sleep up to seven and is only a minute from the beach. BYO linen (or pay an extra charge) and food.

Abel Tasman Wilson's Experiences (right) has two lodges on the track but these are largely reserved for those travelling on its tours. That said, it's worth enquiring about availability as staff will fit you in if they can.

Getting There & Away
AIR
If you're time-poor but funds-rich, consider a fly-in option; the following companies fly to Awaroa, and offer scenic flights:

Abel Tasman Air (☎ 0800 304 560, 03-528 8290; www.abeltasmanair.co.nz) Flies to Awaroa from Motueka ($175) or Nelson ($265). Scenic flights available; Heaphy Track connections as well.

Tasman Helicopters (p460) Motueka to Awaroa by helicopter costs from $150, one-way.

BUS
Abel Tasman Coachlines (☎ 03-528 8850; www.abeltas mantravel.co.nz) runs from Nelson to Motueka, then on to the following:

Destination	Price	Duration	Frequency
Kaiteriteri	$10	25min	3 daily
Marahau	$10	30min	3-4 daily
Takaka	$23	1hr	2 daily

Golden Bay Coachlines (☎ 03-525 8352; www.golden baycoachlines.co.nz) runs from November to April from Takaka around once daily to Wainui carpark ($16) and Totaranui ($20).

Getting Around
The beauty of Abel Tasman is that it's easy to get to/from any point on the track by water taxi, either from Kaiteriteri or Marahau. Typical one-way prices from either Marahau or Kaiteriteri: Anchorage and Torrent Bay ($32), Bark Bay ($37), Tonga ($39), Awaroa ($42), Totaranui ($44). Some operators:

Abel Tasman Aqua Taxi (☎ 0800 278 282, 03-527 8083; www.aquataxi.co.nz; Kaiteriteri & Marahau)

Abel Tasman Sea Shuttle (☎ 0800 732 748, 03-527 8688; www.abeltasmanseashuttles.co.nz; Kaiteriteri)

Abel Tasman Wilson's Experiences (Map p468; ☎ 0800 221 888, 03-528 2027; www.abeltasmannz.com; 265 High St, Motueka) Offers an explorer pass (adult/child $135/67.50) for unlimited taxi travel on three days over a five-day period.

Marahau Water Taxis (☎ 0800 808 018, 03-527 8176; www.abeltasmancentre.co.nz; Abel Tasman Centre, Franklin St, Marahau)

GOLDEN BAY

MOTUEKA TO TAKAKA
From Motueka, SH60 takes a stomach-churning meander over Takaka Hill. On the way it passes dramatic lookouts over Tasman Bay and Abel Tasman National Park before swooping down towards Takaka and Collingwood. The best way to tackle this region is with your own wheels.

Takaka Hill (791m) butts-in between Tasman Bay and Golden Bay. Just below the summit (literally) are the **Ngarua Caves** (☎ 03-528 8093; janetdavid@paradise.net.nz; SH60; adult/child $15/5; ⏱ 45min tours hourly 10am-4pm Sep-May, open

Sat & Sun only Jun-Aug), where you can see myriad subterranean delights including moa bones. Access is restricted to tours – you can't go solo spelunking.

Also just before the summit is the turn-off to **Canaan Downs Scenic Reserve** (Map p473), reached at the end of the 11km gravel road. This area starred as Chetwood Forest in the *Lord of the Rings* movies, but **Harwood's Hole** is the most famous feature here. It's one of the largest *tomo* (caves) in the country at 357m deep, 70m wide, with a 176m vertical drop. The cave is a 30-minute walk from the car park. Be careful as you approach the precipice – accidents have occurred. Only *very* experienced cavers should attempt to explore the cave itself. Off-road cyclists quite rightly find Canaan's magical landscape irresistible, and the new **mountain bike loop track** (14km, two hours, intermediate) offers varied terrain, a bit of technical stuff and wonderful views. From here you can link with the Rameka Track; more tracks are currently being planned. Bikes and drop-offs can be negotiated from Takaka (see right) or Marahau (see p471).

Close to the zenith also lies the **Takaka Hill Walkway**, a three-hour loop walk through marble karst rock formations, native forest and private farmland (owned by the Harwoods, of Hole fame), and **Harwood Lookout**, affording fine views down the Takaka River Valley to Takaka and Golden Bay.

TAKAKA
pop 1230

Laid-back to near-horizontal, Takaka is Golden Bay's business centre, and the last 'big' town as you head towards the South Island's northwest extremity, Farewell Spit. The local community of rootsy artists and bearded, dreadlocked types rubs shoulders with hardened farmers and crusty fisherfolk in harmonious equilibrium.

Information

DOC office (☎ 03-525 8026; www.doc.govt.co.nz; 62 Commercial St; ⏰ 8.30am-4pm Mon-Fri) Information on Abel Tasman and Kahurangi National Parks, the Heaphy Track, Farewell Spit and Cobb Valley. Sells hut passes.

Golden Bay i-SITE (☎ 03-525 9136; www.golden baynz.co.nz; Willow St; ⏰ 9am-6pm summer; 10am-5pm Mon-Fri, to 4pm Sat & Sun winter) A friendly little information centre with all necessary information and a booking service.

Unlimited Copies 07 (☎ 03-525 8355; 4 Commercial St; ⏰ 9am-5pm) Internet access ($6 per hour) and associated usefulness.

Sights & Activities

Simply called 'Pupu', **Te Waikoropupu Springs** are the largest freshwater springs in NZ and reputedly the clearest in the world. About 14,000L of water per second surges from underground vents dotted around the Pupu Springs Scenic Reserve, including one with 'dancing sands' propelled upwards by water gushing from the ground. The water looks enticing, but swimming is a no-no. From Takaka, head 4km northwest on SH60, turn inland at Waitapu Bridge and follow Pupu Springs Rd for 3km. From the car park, a walkway (30 minutes return) leads to a slightly scruffy glassed viewing area.

Close by is **Pupu Hydro Walkway**, a two-hour circuit through beech forest, past engineering and gold-mining relics to the restored (and operational) Pupu Hydro Powerhouse, built in 1929. To get here, take the 4km gravel road (signed 'Pupu Walkway') off Pupu Springs Rd.

On the road to Pohara you'll see a signpost to **Labyrinth Rocks Park** (Scotts Rd; admission free; ⏰ dawn-dusk), two wondrous hectares of limestone canyons and native bush making for a fascinating stroll. Down at Clifton you'll find the **Grove** (signposted down Clifton Rd), offering further geological and botanical delights.

An abundance of excellent mountain bike tracks await exploration by beginner and hard-core alike. **Quiet Revolution Cycle Shop** (☎ 03-525 9555; quietrev@hotmail.com; 11 Commercial St; per day $20-40; ⏰ 9am-5pm Mon-Fri, to 12.30pm Sat) hires town and mountain bikes, has local track information and will straighten your wonky spokes. **Escape Adventures** (☎ 03-525 8783; www.escapeadventures.co.nz; behind the Post Shop; per day $35-75; ⏰ 9am-5pm Mon-Sat) will do similar and offers bespoke guided tours and GPS-mapped track info.

Remote Adventures (☎ 0800 150 338, 03-525 6167; www.remoteadventures.co.nz) offers scenic flights around the Bay for as little as $35.

The **Golden Bay Museum** (☎ 03-525 6268; www.virtualbay.co.nz/gbmuseum; Commercial St; admission free; ⏰ 10am-4pm, closed Sun in winter) is a jumble of historical memorabilia. Stand-out exhibits include a diorama depicting Abel Tasman's 1642 Golden Bay landing and some dubious human taxidermy. Sharing the same building is **Golden Bay Gallery** (☎ 03-525 9990; Commercial St;

admission free; 10am-4.30pm, closed Sun in winter), a good example of just one of Golden Bay's many galleries and artist studios. Collect a copy of the *Guide to Artists in Golden Bay* leaflet for more along those lines.

On the Anatoki River 6km south of town, **Bencarri Nature Park & Café** (☎ 03-525 8261; www.bencarri.co.nz; McCallum Rd; adult/child/family $12/6/35, meals $8-16; 10am-5pm, closed April–mid-Sep) is home to farm animals including llamas and a longhorn. The prime attraction, though, is feeding the fat, tame river eels, which can live to be 100, and have apparently been here since 1914.

Fish for salmon next door at the **Anatoki Salmon Farm** (☎ 03-525 7251; www.anatokisalmon.co.nz; McCallum Rd; admission & fishing gear free, salmon price per kg $19; 9am-5pm). The owners will clean and smoke your catch, so you can eat it on the spot. If you're not up for DIY, you can also buy fresh or smoked fish.

Tours
Unsurprisingly, tours revolve around the great outdoors.

Bush & Beyond (☎ 03-528 9054; www.bushandbeyond.co.nz; day/multiday walks from $150/1150) Offers various tramping trips including Mt Arthur or Cobb Valley day walks ($195) through to a guided five-nighter on the Heaphy Track ($1395).

Kahurangi Guided Walks (☎ 03-525 7177; www.kahurangiwalks.co.nz) Specialises in small-group tours including five-day walks along the Heaphy Track or Abel Tasman Coast Track ($1300), and day trips up the Cobb Valley ($140).

Southern Wilderness (☎ 0800 666 044, 03-546 7349; www.southernwilderness.com) Guided four- to five-day tramps on the Heaphy Track ($1495 to $1595) and day walks in Nelson Lakes National Parks ($220).

See p480 for Farewell Spit tours.

Sleeping
Kiwiana (☎ 0800 805 494, 03-525 7676; http://kiwianabackpackers.co.nz; 73 Motupipi St; sites per person $18, dm/s/d $27/42/64;) Beyond the welcoming garden is a cute cottage where rooms are named after classic Kiwiana (the jandal, Buzzy Bee...). There's a free outdoor spa and a converted garage full of treasures: wood-fired stove, pool table, CD player, books, games and bikes for guest use.

Annie's Nirvana Lodge (☎ 03-525 8766; www.nirvanalodge.co.nz; 25 Motupipi St; dm/d $28/66;) It's clean, it's tidy, and it smells good: dorms in

the main house, four doubles at the bottom of the wonderful courtyard garden. We just loved this YHA hostel and its friendly owner. Fluffy the cat sealed the deal – what a charmer. Bike hire is $5 per day.

Golden Bay Motel (☎ 0800 401 212, 03-525 9428; www.goldenbaymotel.co.nz; 132 Commercial St; d $95-135, extra person $20;) It's golden, all right: check out the paint job. Clean, spacious, self-contained units with decent older-style fixtures and decent older-style hosts. The rear patios overlook a lush green lawn with playground.

Anatoki Lodge Motel (☎ 0800 262 333, 03-525 8047; www.anatokimotels.co.nz; 87 Commercial St; d $105-155;) Rhododendrons ahoy at this tidy motel, with studios and one- and two-bedroom units, all with kitchenette, lounge-dining area, and private patio. Solar-heated pool.

Shady Rest (☎ 03-525 9669; www.shadyrest.co.nz; 139 Commercial St; d incl breakfast $130-230;) A short walk along the main road from town, this two-storey dear place has four double rooms (two en suite) freshly dressed in fitting style. Expect wood panelling and heavy drapes galore, with modern bathrooms lending some sparkle. The back garden is great, with streamside seating and a bath in the grotto.

Eating & Drinking
Although Takaka proffers some reasonable hospitality, you may find better options out of town.

Dangerous Kitchen (☎ 03-525 8686; 46a Commercial St; meals $11-28; 10am-10pm Mon-Sat) Dedicated to Frank Zappa ('In the kitchen of danger, you can feel like a stranger'), DK specialises in gourmet pizzas and strong coffee, hefty slabs of cake and bumper burritos. Mellow and laid-back, with sun-trap courtyard out back, and people-watching patio on the main drag.

Brigand Café Bar (☎ 03-525 9636; 90 Commercial St; lunch $14-28, dinner $16-32; 11am-late Mon-Sat) Mainstay of the local entertainment scene; get to the Brigand for Thursday open mic and look out for other gigs. Behind steel gates and a lush garden, Brigand serves sandwiches and chips, chowder and meaty mains in a relaxed, pubby atmosphere.

The **Telegraph Hotel** (☎ 03-525 9445; cnr Commercial & Motupipi Sts; mains $15-26; 11am-late) and the **Junction Hotel** (☎ 03-525 9207; 15 Commercial St; mains $12-23; 11am-late) are old-fashioned pubs if you fancy a quiet lager or pub meal.

Your best bets for quick eats include the **Top Shop** (☎ 03-525 9387; 9 Willow St; items $2-9;

(✆ 6am-6pm Mon-Fri, 7.30am-6pm Sat & Sun), a dairy, tearoom and takeaway at the entrance to town. High-rating pies. Across the road is **Fresh Choice** (☎ 03-525 9383; 13 Willow St; ✆ 8am-8pm) supermarket. In the middle of town, tucked into the Library Carpark is **Paul's Coffee Caravan** – no food, but the best brew in town.

Entertainment

Village Theatre (☎ 03-525 8453; www.villagetheatre.org. nz; 34 Commercial St; adult/child $12/6; ✆ 2-10pm) Catch a flick at Takaka's cinema, screening newish releases.

Getting There & Around

Abel Tasman Coachlines (☎ 03-528 8850; www.abeltas mantravel.co.nz) runs between Takaka and Nelson ($32, 2½ hours, two daily). This company works in with **Golden Bay Coachlines** (☎ 03-525 8352; www.goldenbaycoachlines.co.nz) which connects Takaka with Collingwood ($19, 25 minutes, two daily), the Heaphy Track ($28, one hour, one daily), Totaranui ($20, one hour, one daily) and other stops en route.

Golden Bay Air (☎ 0800 588 885, 03-525 8725; www. goldenbayair.co.nz) flies daily between Wellington and Takaka ($99 to $165) and on-demand between Takaka and Karamea for Heaphy Track trampers (minimum two people, per person $169).

Remote Adventures/Star Line (☎ 0800 150 338, 03-525 6167; www.remoteadventures.co.nz) offers daily flights between Takaka and Nelson (from $90).

If you need a cab, call **Takaka Taxi Service** (☎ 0800 825 252).

POHARA

pop 350

About 10km northeast of Takaka is pint-sized Pohara, a beachside resort with a population that quadruples over summer. It's more 'yuppified' than other parts of Golden Bay, with large modern houses cashing in on sea views, but an agreeable air persists and there's some good accommodation.

The beach is on the way to the northern end of the Abel Tasman Coastal Track; the largely unsealed road into the park passes **Tarakohe Harbour** (Pohara's working port), and **Ligar Bay** which has a lookout and a memorial to Abel Tasman, who anchored here in December 1642.

Rawhiti Cave and its vast, striking entrance is an awesome sight, located between Takaka

and Pohara. Take Packard Rd 2.5km from Motupipi, or contact **Kahurangi Guided Walks** (☎ 03-525 7177; www.kahurangiwalks.co.nz), which runs three-hour tours ($35).

Golden Bay Kayaks (☎ 03-525 9095; www.golden baykayaks.co.nz; Pohara beachfront; half-day guided tours adult/child $75/35, 3-day freedom hire $135) rents out kayaks for hour-long paddles, or can launch you on a three-day exploration of Abel Tasman National Park from Tarakohe Harbour south to Marahau or Kaiteriteri.

Sleeping & Eating

Pohara Beach Top 10 Holiday Park (☎ 0800 764 272, 03-525 9500; www.poharabeach.com; Abel Tasman Dr; unpowered & powered sites $36-42, cabins $58-89, motels/units $108-158; 🖥 🛜) Wow, what a big 'un! On a long grassy strip 'tween the dunes and the main road, the location is primo, but in summer it can feel more like a suburb than the seaside. There's a general store out the front.

Nook (☎ 0800 806 665, 03-525 8501; www.thenook guesthouse.co.nz; Abel Tasman Dr; unpowered sites $30, dm/ tw/d $28/56/70, cottage $120-160) Low-key, nook-sized backpackers with timber floors, and rooms opening out on to homely gardens. A self-contained straw-bale cottage sleeps six, while in the back paddock is a house truck and space for tents. Bikes available; TV banned.

Sans Souci Inn (☎ 03-525 8663; www.sanssouci inn.co.nz; 11 Richmond Rd; s/d/f $80/105/150; ✆ closed Jul–mid-Sep) Meaning 'no worries' in French, that'll be your mantra after staying in one of Sans Souci's seven Mediterranean-flavoured, mud-brick rooms. Guests share a lovely plant-filled, mosaic communal bathroom with composting toilets, as well as an airy lounge and kitchen flowing out on to the semitropical courtyard. Dinner in the on-site restaurant ($30 to $33; bookings essential) is highly recommended; breakfast is by request.

Sandcastle (☎ 0800 433 909, 03-525 9087; www.golden bayaccommodation.co.nz; Haile Lane; d $90-110; 🛜) It sounds like a regal beach fantasy, but it's actually a cluster of bird-bombarded, ecofriendly chalets with a wood-fired sauna, outdoor spa pool, and an emphasis on family frivolities. Look for the sign 600m past the Penguin Café & Bar. Great value.

Penguin Café & Bar (☎ 03-525 6126; 818 Abel Tasman Dr; lunch $12-19, dinner $18-29; ✆ 4-10pm Mon & Tue, 11am-10pm Wed-Sun) A buzzy spot with a large outdoor area, suited to sundowners and thirst-quenchers on sunny days. Open fire and pool table for the odd inclement day. Brunch treats include pizzas, burgers and bar snacks; dinner mains are meatier.

Totally Roasted Café (☎ 03-525 9396; Abel Tasman Dr; meals $10-18; ☼ 8.30am-5pm) A sure bet for primo coffee from its own-roast organic beans, this 'el rancho' style walled garden cafe is also a winner for all-day breakfast. The full fry-up is a cracker, but the home-baked cakes, muffins and pastries aren't bad either.

Getting There & Away

Golden Bay Coachlines (☎ 03-525 8352; www.golden baycoachlines.co.nz) runs from Takaka to Pohara on the way to Totaranui ($10, 15 minutes, one daily).

COLLINGWOOD & AROUND

Far-flung Collingwood (population 250) is the last town in this part of the country, and has a real end-of-the-line, frontier vibe. It's busy in summer, though for most people it's simply a launch pad for the Heaphy Track or trips to Farewell Spit.

The **Collingwood Museum** (☎ 03-524 8131; Tasman St; admission by donation; ☼ 10am-4pm) fills a tiny, unstaffed corridor with a quirky collection of saddlery, Maori artefacts, moa bones, shells and old typewriters, while the next-door **Aorere Centre** houses multimedia presentations, including the works of the wonderful pioneer photographer, Fred Tyree.

No Collingwood visit would be complete without dipping into **Rosy Glow Chocolate House** (☎ 03-524 8348; 54 Beach Rd; chocolates $3-5; ☼ 10am-5pm Sat-Thu). Chocoholics will go nuts for hand-made confection produced with love.

Sleeping

Innlet Backpackers & Cottages (☎ 03-524 8040; www.goldenbayindex.co.nz; Main Rd; unpowered sites $42, dm/d $29/68, cottage/units $70-180; 🖳) A great option 10km from Collingwood on the way to Pakawau. The main house sustains elegant backpacker rooms, and there are various campsites and cabins around the property including a self-contained cottage sleeping six to eight people. The environmentally conscious owners offer kayak and bike hire.

Somerset House (☎ 03-524 8624; www.backpackers collingwood.co.nz; Lower Gibbs Rd; dm/s/d incl breakfast $29/45/70; 🖳 🛜) A small, low-key hostel in a creaky, historic building on the hill with views from the deck. Graft tramping advice from the knowledgeable owners who offer tramper

transport, free bikes, and freshly baked bread for breakfast.

Beachcomber Motel (☎ 0800 270 520, 03-524 8499; www.collingwoodbeachcomber.co.nz; Tasman St; d $100-135; 🖳 🛜) Clean, spacious self-contained units in excellent nick, wedged between the road and the estuary. Good-value family-sized units have nifty mezzanine floors.

Eating & Drinking

Mussel Inn (☎ 03-525 9241; SH60, Onekaka; all-day menu $4-16, dinner $21-26; ☼ 11am-late, closed Jul-Aug) Halfway between Takaka and Collingwood, this earthy tavern-cafe-brewery is a Bay institution. A totem pole with crucified mobile phones heralds the mood: this is no place for urban trappings, just excellent beer, wholesome food (mussels, seasonal scallops, fresh fish and steak), open fires and live music. Try a handle or two of 'Captain Cooker', a brown beer brewed naturally with manuka, or the delicious 'Pale Whale Ale'.

Courthouse Café (☎ 03-525 8472; cnr Gibbs & Tasman Sts; meals $8-28; ☼ 9am-5pm Thu-Mon, plus 6-9pm Fri & Sat) A sophisticated cafe in the 1901 Collingwood courthouse preparing à la carte meals from locally grown organic produce and fresh seafood. Local art; good coffee; interesting wine list. One of the Bay's best dining experiences.

ourpick Naked Possum Café (☎ 03-524 8433; Kaituna River, 10km from Collingwood; meals $10-24; ☼ 10am-6pm Sat-Thu, to 10pm Fri) Relax at this splendid, nouveau-rustic joint after exploring the adjacent Kaituna Track and its goldmining relics and pretty river forks (two hours return). Outdoor fire, ample lawn, great beer and a possum tannery. Wild game a speciality. Book your spot at the popular Friday evening steak barbecue or Sunday roasts.

Getting There & Away

Golden Bay Coachlines (☎ 03-525 8352; www.goldenbaycoachlines.co.nz) runs from Takaka to Collingwood ($19, 25 minutes, two daily).

FAREWELL SPIT & AROUND

Bleak, exposed and unusual, **Farewell Spit** is a wetland of international importance, and a renowned bird sanctuary – the summer home of thousands of migratory waders, notably the godwit (which flies all the way from the Arctic tundra), Caspian terns and Australasian gannets. The 35km beach features colossal, crescent-shaped dunes, from where panoramic views extend across Golden

Bay and a vast low-tide salt marsh. Walkers can explore the first 4km of Spit via a network of tracks, but beyond that point access is via tour only (see below).

The Spit pit stop is **Farewell Spit Visitor Centre** (☎ 03-524 8454; Farewell Spit; ⏲ 9.30am-6.30pm), 24km north of Collingwood, which provides local information and handles Spit tour bookings. It shares its hilltop abode with **Paddlecrab Café** (meals $11-24), a memorable spot for coffee and cake or an honest lunch. How's about those views?

Tours

Two operators run tours of the Spit exploring all the sights, from fossilised shellfish and bird colonies to an old lighthouse. Tours depart daily at low tide (visit websites or ring the visitor centre for schedules) and light refreshments are usually included.

Farewell Spit Eco Tours (☎ 0800 808 257, 03-524 8257; www.farewellspit.com; Tasman St, Collingwood; tours $90-150) Operating for more than 60 years, this outfit runs a range of tours from three to 6½ hours, taking in the Spit, lighthouse, gannets and godwits. Tours depart Collingwood.

Farewell Spit Nature Experience (☎ 0800 250 500, 03-524 8992; www.farewellspittours.com; tours $90-110) Four-hour Spit tours depart Farewell Spit Visitor Centre; six-hour tours depart the Old School Café, Pakawau.

Other Activities

Remote, desolate **Wharariki Beach** is 6km from the turn-off to the visitor centre along an unsealed road, then a 20-minute walk from the car park over farmland (part of the DOC-administered Puponga Farm Park). It's a wild introduction to the West Coast, with mighty dune formations, looming rock islets just offshore and a seal colony at its eastern end (keep an eye out for seals in the stream on the walk here). As inviting as a swim here may seem, there are strong undertows – what the sea wants, the sea shall have…

Befitting a frontier, this is the place to saddle up: **Cape Farewell Horse Treks** (☎ 03-524 8031; www.horsetreksnz.com; 23 McGowan St, Puponga) is en route to Wharariki Beach. Treks in this wind-blown country range from 1½ hours ($50, to Pillar Point) to three hours ($105, to Wharariki Beach), with longer (including overnight) trips by arrangement.

KAHURANGI NATIONAL PARK

Kahurangi, meaning 'Treasured Possession', is the second largest of NZ's national parks and undoubtedly one of the greatest. Its 452,000 hectares are a hotbed of ecological wonderment: 18 native bird species, over 50% of all NZ's plant species, including over 80% of its alpine plant species, a karst landscape and the largest known cave system in the southern hemisphere (explored by local caving groups, but only for the experienced).

Heaphy Track

One of the best-known tracks in NZ, the four-to six-day, 78km Heaphy Track doesn't have the spectacular scenery of the Routeburn or Milford Tracks, but revels in its own distinct beauty. Almost entirely within Kahurangi National Park, track highlights include the mystical Gouland Downs, and the nikau-palm-dotted coast, especially around Heaphy Hut (spend a day or two here at least). At low tide you can cross the Heaphy River mouth; the Crayfish Point section should only be tackled within one hour either side of low tide.

There are seven huts en route, each accommodating around 20 people; all have gas stoves, except Brown and Gouland Downs, which need wood. There are nine campsites along the route, with limited capacity (eight campers maximum at James Mackay Hut, as many as 40 at Heaphy Hut). Huts/campsites cost $15/8 per adult per night from May to September, $25/12 from October to April; all must be prebooked through DOC, or the i-SITE.

INFORMATION

The best spot for detailed Heaphy Track information and bookings is the DOC counter at the Nelson i-SITE (p457). You can also book at the Golden Bay i-SITE in Takaka (p476), online at www.doc.got.nz, or by post, email (greatwalksbookings@doc.govt.nz) or phone (☎ 03-546 8210). See also www.heaphytrack.com.

For a detailed track description, see Lonely Planet's *Tramping in New Zealand*.

WALKING THE TRACK

Most people tramp southwest from the Collingwood end to Karamea. From Brown Hut the track passes through beech forest to Perry Saddle. The country opens up to the swampy Gouland Downs, then closes in with sparse bush all the way to MacKay Hut. The bush becomes more dense towards Heaphy Hut, with beautiful nikau palms growing at lower levels.

The final section is along the coast through nikau forest, and partly along the beach. Unfortunately, sandflies love this beautiful stretch too! The climate here is surprisingly mild, but don't swim in the sea as the undertows and currents are vicious. The lagoon at Heaphy Hut is good for swimming, and the Heaphy River is full of fish.

Kilometre markers crop up along the track – the zero marker is at the track's southern end at Kohaihai River near Karamea. Estimated walking times:

Route	Time
Brown Hut to Perry Saddle Hut	5hr
Perry Saddle Hut to Gouland Downs Hut	2hr
Gouland Downs Hut to Saxon Hut	1½hr
Saxon Hut to James MacKay Hut	3hr
James MacKay Hut to Lewis Hut	3½hr
Lewis Hut to Heaphy Hut	2½hr
Heaphy Hut to Kohaihai River	5hr

Other Kahurangi Tracks

After tackling the Heaphy north to south, you can return to Golden Bay via the more scenic (though harder) **Wangapeka Track**. It's not as well known as the Heaphy, but many consider the Wangapeka a more enjoyable walk. Taking about five days, the track starts 25km south of Karamea at Little Wanganui, running 52km east to Rolling River near Tapawera. There's a chain of huts along the track.

The five to seven day **Leslie-Karamea Track** is a medium-to-hard tramp, connecting the Cobb Valley near Takaka with Little Wanganui, finishing on part of the Wangapeka Track.

See www.doc.govt.nz for detailed information on both tracks, and some excellent full-day and overnight walks around the **Cobb Valley**, **Mount Arthur** and **The Tablelands**.

Tours

See p477 to find operators running day-long and multiday trips in Kahurangi National Park.

Getting There & Away

Abel Tasman Coachlines (☎ 03-528 8850; www.abel tasmantravel.co.nz) will get you as far as Takaka ($23, one hour, two daily). From there you can connect with **Golden Bay Coachlines** (☎ 03-525 8352; www.goldenbaycoachlines.co.nz) which will get you to the Heaphy Track via Collingwood ($28, one hour, one daily).

Heaphy Track Help (☎ 03-525 9576; www.heaphy trackhelp.co.nz) offers car relocations ($200 to $300, depending on the direction and time), food drops, shuttles and advice.

Golden Bay Air (☎ 0800 588 885, 03-525 8725; www. goldenbayair.co.nz) flies on demand between Takaka and Karamea (minimum two people, per person $169). **Remote Adventures** (☎ 0800 150 338, 03-525 6167; www.remoteadventures.co.nz) also offers Karamea pick-ups by air (price on application).

Wadsworths Motors (☎ 03-522 4248; Main Rd, Tapawera) services the eastern ends of the Wangapeka Track, on demand. Price on application.

For transport details at the Karamea end of proceedings see p491.

The West Coast

THE WEST COAST

What a difference a mountain range makes. Hemmed in by the wild Tasman Sea and the peaks of the Southern Alps, the West Coast (aka Westland) is like nowhere else in New Zealand.

Opposite ends of the coast have a remote end-of-the-road feel. In the north the surf-battered coast highway leads to sleepy Karamea, the preferred getaway for alternative lifestylers drawn by its isolation and surprisingly mild climate. The southern end of spectacular State Hwy 6 continues to Haast, an entrée to the excitement and awe of the surrounding wilderness.

With less than 1% of NZ's population scattered amid almost 9% of the country's area, West Coast locals have adapted to become a rugged and individual breed. They may not be too concerned with what's happening in the country's cities, but in the West Coast's heritage pubs you'll be guaranteed a warm welcome that's tinged with a laconic sense of humour. Just don't be too surprised if 'closing time' is viewed as a recommendation, not a directive.

The coast's sublime scenery can be almost too popular, and during summer a phalanx of campervans and tourist buses tick off the 'Must See' Punakaiki Rocks and Franz Josef and Fox Glaciers. The thing is, they are truly 'Must See', and even if you're sharing your glacial gaze, it's not too hard to return to the heartland of the West Coast in laid-back coastal hamlets such as Okarito, Granity and Jackson Bay.

HIGHLIGHTS

- Crafting your own unique keepsake at **Barrytown Knifemaking** (p493)
- Kayaking through the bird-adorned channels of the **Okarito Lagoon** (p506)
- Getting wet 'n' wild on the rivers around **Murchison** (p483)
- Marvelling at nature's beautiful fury at the Pancake Rocks at **Punakaiki** (p492)
- Going underground in the limestone caverns of the **Oparara Basin** (p489)
- Hunting out authentic local greenstone in the craft shops of **Hokitika** (p503)
- Exploring the West Coast's true wilderness on a back-of-beyond river trip around **Haast** (p515)
- Feeling just a tad insignificant compared to the imposing ice flows of the **Franz Josef** (p508) and **Fox Glaciers** (p512)

■ Telephone code: 03   ■ www.west-coast.co.nz   ■ www.westcoast.org.nz

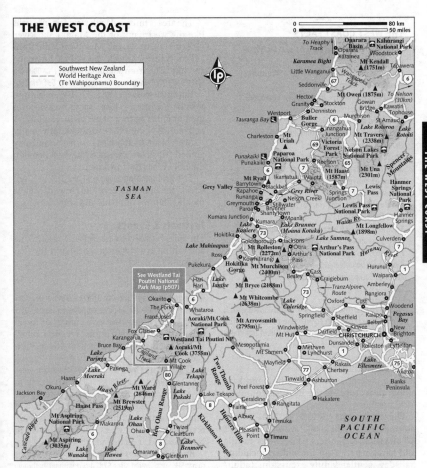

Climate

During summer the coast roads flood with campervans, but May to September can be warm and clear with fewer crowds and cheaper accommodation. At around 5m annually, the West Coast has serious rainfall (Westland = Wetland), but Westland sees as much sunshine as Christchurch. When it's pouring in the east it's just as likely to be fine here.

Getting There & Around

Air New Zealand flies between Westport and Wellington, and Hokitika and Christchurch.

Coaches and shuttles connect to centres like Christchurch, Dunedin, Queenstown and Nelson; major players are Atomic Shuttles, InterCity and Naked Bus.

The *TranzAlpine,* one of the world's great train rides, links Greymouth and Christchurch; see p499.

MURCHISON
pop 850

Up-and-coming Murchison, 125km southwest of Nelson (95km east of Westport) on the Buller Gorge Heritage Hwy/State Hwy 6 (SH6), is the northern gateway to the West Coast. It's an Upper Buller Gorge service town offering lots of summertime ways to get active on the water.

Information

The **Murchison i-SITE** (☎ 03-523 9350; www.murch isonnz.com; 47 Waller St; ☷ 10am-6pm, reduced winter

THE WEST COAST FACTS

Eat A whitebait pizza at Hokitika's Fat Pipi Pizza (p503)

Drink An organic Green Fern lager at Westport's West Coast Brewing Co (p486)

Read Keri Hulme's *The Bone People,* set around peaceful Okarito (p506)

Listen to Karamea's laid-back community radio station on 107.5FM (p490); they'll even let you choose your own tracks

Watch *Bad Blood* (1982), an engrossing portrayal of the Kowhitirangi incident (p504)

Swim at You're joking, right? With water this cold, stick to the spa

Festival Go bush-food crazy at Hokitika's Wild-foods Festival (p502)

Tackiest tourist attraction Pukekura's Bushmans Museum (p505). Just don't tell them you've got friends in Auckland, OK?

Go green Volunteer in the organic vegie garden at Rongo Backpackers in Karamea (p490)

hours) has info on local activities and transport. There are no banks in town; the postal agency is on Fairfax St. The **Commercial Hotel** (cnr Waller & Fairfax Sts) has internet access.

Sights & Activities
Fishing, mountain biking, rafting and kayaking all feature in the area surrounding Murchison.

Ultimate Descents (☎ 0800 748 377, 03-523 9899; www.rivers.co.nz; 51 Fairfax St; half-/full-day rafting $120/220, half-day kayaking $125) offers white-water rafting and kayaking trips on the Buller, including half-day, gentler family excursions (adult/child $105/85). Helirafting trips cost from $450 and you can combine rafting with fishing (two days, $395).

The **New Zealand Kayak School** (☎ 03-523 9611; www.nzkayakschool.com; 22 Grey St; kayaks per day $50, 4-day intro course $795; ☯ Sept-Apr) hires out (to experienced paddlers only) and sells kayaks, and runs professional courses for all levels; price includes transport and accommodation but BYO food.

White Water Action Rafting Tours (☎ 0800 100 582, 03-523 9581; www.whitewateraction.com; Waller St; half-day rafting adult/youth $120/105), behind the i-SITE, runs half-day trips with a riverside lunch. Challenging Grade III and V rapids interspersed with adrenaline-elevating optional 9m cliff jumps.

The area is threaded with **mountain-bike trails** like the west bank of the Matakitaki River (16km return) or the Maruia Saddle Trip (83km return). Check the i-SITE for maps and hire bikes from **Murchison Motels** (☎ 0800 166 500, 03-523 9026; www.murchisonmotels.co.nz; 53 Fairfax St).

Murchison Museum (☎ 03-523 9335; 60 Fairfax St; admission by donation; ☯ 10am-4pm) showcases local memorabilia, with vintage farm equipment and photos of the 1929 earthquake aftermath.

Murchison **trout fishing** is superb. Half-day guided trips cost around $350 (two people); the i-SITE has the lowdown.

Try **gold panning** (equipment hire $10) in Lyell Creek, the Buller River or the Howard Valley; the i-SITE hires out pans and shovels.

Festivals & Events
The **Buller Festival** (www.bullerfestival.co.nz) kayaking and rafting extravaganza is held over the first weekend in March.

Sleeping
Riverview Holiday Park (☎ 03-523 9591; riverview.hp@xtra.co.nz; Riverside Tce; unpowered/powered sites $24/26, d $44) Located near the river north of town, this park has motel rooms, recently refurbished cabins and the excellent River View Café (opposite).

our pick **Lazy Cow** (☎ 03-523 9451; lazycow@xnet.co.nz; 37 Waller St; dm/d $28/66; ☐ ☏) It's easy to be a lazy cow here – so comfy it feels like home. Free muffins are an easy up-sell and there are small and homely surrounds with, according to the owners, the best shower in New Zealand. You be the judge.

Hu-Ha Bikepackers (☎ 03-548 2707; smidgley@ihug.co.nz; SH6; unpowered sites $28, dm/d without bathroom $23/60, d with bathroom $70) This laid-back, cyclist-friendly farm 45km north of Murchison has dorms and doubles (including some new en suite options), and plenty of farm animals, including the biggest and most relaxed pig you'll ever meet. The house sits above the road, 10km north of Kawatiri Junction. Cash only.

Commercial Hotel (☎ 03-523 9848; thecommercial hotel@xtra.co.nz; cnr Waller & Fairfax Sts; s/d without bathroom $40/75; ☐) Excellent value with comfortable rooms and art-deco touches. All rooms have shared facilities.

River Song (☎ 03-523 9011; www.riversong.co.nz; 30 Fairfax St; d from $95) Two minutes' walk from town, these newish self-contained cottages have big decks and gardens. Postkayaking massages are available.

Murchison Lodge (☎ 03-523 9196; www.murchison lodge.co.nz; 15 Grey St; s $125-185, d $150-210, all incl breakfast) Surrounded by native trees, this B&B overlooks the Buller River. Nice interior design touches add to the comfortable feel. The friendly hosts are around to spin yarns of kayak adventures had just steps from the front door.

Murchison Motels (☎ 0800 166 500, 03-523 9026; www.murchisonmotels.co.nz; 53 Fairfax St; d $130-170) Tucked behind Rivers Cafe, with snazzy one- and two-bedroom units. There's also an eight-bed cottage, and mountain bikes for hire (half-/full day $15/30).

Triple Tui (☎ 03-548 4481; www.tripletui.co.nz; 3360 Dry Weather Rd; d $130-180 (min 3 nights); ☺ Sept-May) What happens, when two busy Aucklanders decide to follow their dream and leave the big smoke? How about two luxury log cabins set in 50 beautiful acres in the Tadmore Valley, 35 minutes north of Murchison? Both private cabins include solar water heating and electricity from Triple Tui's own mini hydro-electricity plant. Once you've explored nearby walking trails, fire up the gas barbecue and open a bottle of wine. Bookings essential.

Eating & Drinking

Commercial Hotel (☎ 03-523 9696; cnr Waller & Fairfax Sts; lunch $10-17, dinner $19-27; ☺ 8am-9pm; 🖳) Set yourself up for rafting with a good breakfast, and celebrate a big day on the river with a few beers and a robust pub meal.

River View Café (☎ 03-523 9591; Riverview Holiday Park; pizza $14-21; ☺ 10am-8pm Oct-Apr; 🖳) This open-air cafe is the cat's meow when the weather is fine. Sit back and enjoy the riverside location, have a gourmet pizza and a bottle of Murchison Moonlight Ale as kayakers drift by.

Rivers Cafe (☎ 03-523 9009; 51 Fairfax St; mains $18-30; ☺ 9am-9pm Oct-Mar, 10am-2pm Thu-Mon Apr-Sep) has everything from chicken kebabs and falafel to rib-eye steaks and roast dinners. Make a hard decision between an organic coffee or a frothy pint of Monteith's beer.

Getting There & Away

Buses passing through Murchison from the West Coast to Picton include **Atomic Shuttles** (☎ 03-349 0697; www.atomictravel.co.nz) and **InterCity** (☎ 03-365 1113; www.intercity.co.nz), and **Naked Bus** (www.nakedbus.com) heads both north and south from here. Atomic stops at the i-SITE, InterCity & Naked Bus at Beechwoods Café on Waller St.

BULLER GORGE

The road from Murchison to the coast was shaken up by the 1929 and 1968 earthquakes but still snakes through Buller Gorge. The gorge is a base for white-water rafting and kayaking; see opposite.

About 14km west of Murchison is the **Buller Gorge Swingbridge** (☎ 0800 285 537; www.bullergorge. co.nz; SH6; bridge crossing adult/child $5/2; ☺ 8am-7pm Oct-Apr, 9am-5.30pm May-Sep), NZ's longest (110m). Across the bridge are some excellent short walks, one to the White Creek Faultline, epicentre of the 1929 earthquake. Coming back, ride the 160m **Comet Line flying fox** (seated ride adult/child $30/15, 'Supaman' style ride $45, Tandem $30/15). **Goldrush Jet** (adult/child $75/50) runs 40-minute jetboat trips, departing under the bridge.

Further west the road forks at Inangahua Junction. Continue to the coast through Lower Buller Gorge on SH6, or head south to Greymouth via Reefton on SH69. SH6 is longer but more interesting.

There's a **DOC camping ground** (adult/child $6/1.50) on SH6 at Lyell, Upper Buller Gorge, 10km northeast of Inangahua Junction.

Buller Gorge is dark and foreboding; primeval ferns and cabbage trees cling to steep cliffs; toi toi (tall native grass) flanks the road between gorge and river. The road at Hawks Crag negotiates an overhang just high enough to fit a bus under, and was hacked out of the road by hand.

Buller Adventure Tours (☎ 0800 697 286, 03-789 7286; www.adventuretours.co.nz; SH6), located 4km from the coast, has white-water rafting on the Grade III to IV 'Earthquake Slip' rapids (adult/youth $120/105); 1¾-hour jetboat rides (adult/youth $79/65); two-hour riverbank horse treks (adult/youth $80/75); and 1¾-hour quad-bike rides ($140).

Berlins (☎ 0800 526 405, 03-789 0295; www.xtreme adventures.co.nz; SH6; dm $25-30, d $62) is a stylish cafe-meets-backpackers on the site of the old Berlins Hotel. A recent re-fit has spruced the place up a bit too. You'll also find a restaurant (mains $14 to $17.50; open 9.30am till late) that doubles as a damn fine pub. Berlins is a well-positioned stop for cyclists en route to the West Coast. Don't miss the pics on the wall of the Buller River flowing at dangerously high levels.

WESTPORT
pop 4850
The port of Westport made its fortune in coal mining, though the main mine is at Stockton,

MAORI NZ: THE WEST COAST

For Maori, the river valleys and mountains of the West Coast were the traditional source of *pounamu* (greenstone), and the lustrous jade still dominates the craft shops and galleries of Greymouth and Hokitika. In Hokitika, visit the Mana Pounamu exhibit at the West Coast Historical Museum (p500) to polish your knowledge of the precious rock before admiring the classy carving done by Aden Hoglund at Jagosi Jade (p504). If you're lucky enough to be staying at Awatuna Homestead (p502) near Hokitika, owner Hemi recounts stories of the early migration of Pacific peoples to NZ.

38km north. The town itself is of little interest, but is a good base for active adventures in the Buller Gorge and Charleston ranges. Otherwise head north to relaxed Karamea (for the Heaphy Track), or continue south to the Punakaiki Rocks. Fans of Animal Planet should check out the seal colony (see p488) west of town.

Orientation

The town sprawls where the east bank of the Buller River meets the Tasman Sea. Palmerston St is the main drag, while Brougham St goes northeast to Karamea. Free town and regional maps are available at the i-SITE.

Information

The major banks are along Palmerston St.
Buller Hospital (☎ 03-788 9030; Cobden St)
Department of Conservation office (DOC; ☎ 03-788 8008; 72 Russell St; ☺ 8am-noon & 1-4.30pm Mon-Fri) Tickets for the Wangapeka Track and general tramping info.
Habitat Sports (204 Palmerston St) Internet access $6 per hour.
Police station (☎ 03-788 8310; 13 Wakefield St)
Post office (cnr Brougham & Palmerston Sts)
Take Note (☎ 03-789 8731; 106 Palmerston St) Bookshop.
Westport i-SITE (☎ 03-789 6658; www.westport. org.nz; 1 Brougham St; ☺ 9am-6pm Nov-Mar, to 4pm Apr-Oct) Provides information on local tracks, walkways, tours, accommodation, transport, and DOC hut tickets for the Heaphy Track.

Sights

The **Coaltown Museum** (☎ 03-789 8204; Queen St; www.geocities.com/coaltownnz; adult/child $12/5; ☺ 9am-

4.30pm) includes an interactive walk through a faux mine. Rusty mining artefacts sit beside a brewery, photographic displays and a huge operational steam dredge.

The **West Coast Brewing Co** (☎ 03-789 6201; www. westcoastbrewing.com; 10 Lyndhurst St; ☺ 8.30am-5.30pm Mon-Fri, 11am-5.30pm Sat) crafts seven different beers, including the organic Green Fern lager and the Good Bastards dark ale. Tastings are available and highly recommended – these folks know their beer.

Activities

From Charleston, south of Westport, **Norwest Adventures** (☎ 0800 116 686, 03-788 8168; www.caveraft ing.com) runs cave-rafting trips (Underworld Rafting, $145, four hours) into the glowworm-filled Nile River Caves. If you want the glow without the flow (no rafting), it's $90 per person. Both options start with a rainforest railway ride, available separately (adult/child $20/15, 1½ hours). The Adventure Caving trip ($295, five hours) includes a 30m abseil into Te Tahi *tomo* (hole) with rock squeezes, waterfalls, prehistoric fossils and trippy cave formations.

Westport's sparkling new **swimming pool** aka **Solid Energy Centre** (☎ 03-789 8316; Pakington St; adult/child/family $5/2.50/12.50; ☺ 6am-9pm Mon-Thu, to 8pm Fri, 8am-5pm Sat & Sun) is a state-of-the-art facility with swimming pool, squash courts, workout facilities and gymnasium – just in case it happens to rain.

Festivals & Events

The **Buller Gorge Marathon** (www.bullermarathon.org. nz) traverses a scenic riverside route on the second weekend in February. The **Cape Classic Surfing** gets radical at Tauranga Bay on late October's Labour Day weekend.

Sleeping

Bazil's Hostel (☎ 0800 303 741, 03-789 6410; www. bazils.com; 54 Russell St; dm/d/q $25/58/80; ☐ ☎) Mr Fawlty is notably absent at the sprawling Bazil's. Facilities are uniformly good, including excellent kitchens to bring out your inner celebrity chef, and there are beds to suit every budget. If you're travelling in a group of four, ask about the excellent-value mini-apartments ($80). Larger groups from backpacker buses sometimes swing by.

Westport Holiday Park (☎ 03-789 7043; www.west portholidaypark.co.nz; 31-37 Domett St; unpowered/powered sites $32/34, d $90-145; ☐) A-frame 'chalets' stud this bushy glade with decent amenities, a minigolf course for the kiddies and plenty of room to pitch your tent too.

Cosmopolitan Hotel (☎ 03-789 6305; coshotel@ ihug.co.nz; 136 Palmerston St; s$55, d$75) This classic Kiwiana pub offers affordable rooms upstairs from the lively downtown watering hole. The rooms are compact (small) but despite being directly upstairs from a bar – surprisingly quiet.

Westport Motels (☎ 03-789 7575; www.west portmotels.co.nz; 32 The Esplanade; d $85-140; 🖳 🕸) Surrounded by trees, this spot has comfortable beds, outdoor tables, a spa and a swimming pool. Several family units can accommodate bigger broods. Up and down the Esplanade you'll find other midrange motels if this one is full-up.

Chelsea Gateway Motor Lodge (☎ 0800 660 033, 03-789 6835; www.chelseagateway.co.nz; 330 Palmerston St; ste $130-230; 🖳 🛜) The exterior's never going to threaten the Architect of the Year Awards, but there's design salvation with the well-appointed interiors. There are standard suites, two- and three-bedroom family units, and flasher spa units.

Eating & Drinking

Dirty Mary's (☎ 03-789 7959; 198 Palmerston St; mains $7-18; 🕓 8am-late; 🖳) Start your day with fair-trade coffee and a breakfast burrito or bagel. If you sleep in, rest assured there are fine lunches on offer. At night things get raucous with good pizzas and wine and beer.

our pick Yellow House Cafe (☎ 03-789 8765; 243 Palmerston St; lunch $14-17, dinner $25-30; 🕓 midday-late, reduced winter hours; 🖳 🛜 V) This relaxed and sunny spot has warm wooden floors, the best coffee in town, and a tasty organic tinge to the menu. Try the dips and homemade bread with a glass of wine from nearby Marlborough, or have a latte and hitch your laptop to the wi-fi network.

Denniston Dog Saloon (☎ 03-789 5030; 18 Wakefield St; mains $15-30; 🕓 11am-late; 🖳) Lots of wild West Coast wood and Kiwiana antiques give the Denniston Dog a rustic air. Then again, a couple of beers, some tasty scallops and a good steak probably have the same effect. 'The Dog' is both bar and restaurant. After you're watered and fed, take the locals on at pool. Occasional touring bands raise the roof.

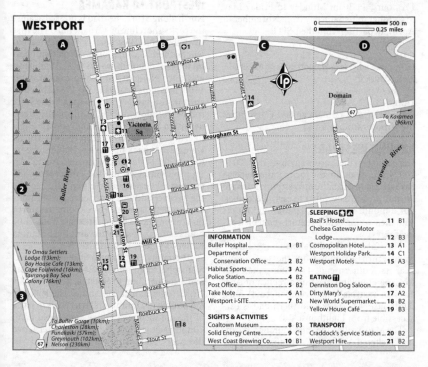

For self-catering, try **New World supermarket** (☎ 03-789 7669; 244 Palmerston St; ☺ 8am-8.30pm).

Getting There & Around

AIR

Air New Zealand (☎ 0800 737 000; www.airnz.co.nz) has two flights per day to/from Wellington (from $129, 50 minutes).

BUS

InterCity (☎ 03-365 1113; www.intercity.co.nz) buses depart from **Craddock's Service Station** (☎ 03-789 7819; 197 Palmerston St) to Nelson ($45, 3½ hours, 3.55pm daily), Greymouth ($25, two hours, 11am daily) and Franz Josef Village ($56, 6½ hours, 11am daily).

Naked Bus (www.nakedbus.com) goes to Nelson ($20, 3½ hours, 3.25pm daily) and Greymouth ($20, 1½ hours, 11am daily), departing from the i-SITE.

East West Coach (☎ 0800 142 622, 03-789 6251) operates a Christchurch service ($55, five hours, 8am daily) departing from Craddock's and returning from Christchurch at 2pm.

Karamea Express (☎ 03-782 6757; info@karamea-express.co.nz) links Westport and Karamea ($30, 1½ hours, 11.30am Monday to Friday May to October, plus Saturday from November to April), departing from the i-SITE.

CAR

Hire some wheels at **Wesport Hire** (☎ 03-789 5038; 294 Palmerston St)

TAXI

Buller Taxis (☎ 03-789 6900) can take you to/from the airport (around $20).

AROUND WESTPORT

Depending on the season, anything from 20 to 200 NZ fur seals dot the rocks at the **Tauranga Bay Seal Colony**, 16km from Westport. Pups are born from late November to early December. For a month afterwards, land-bound mums tend their young before venturing out on feeding forays.

The **Cape Foulwind Walkway** (1½ hours' walk return) extends from the seal colony near its southern end, 4km along the coast to Cape Foulwind, passing a replica of Abel Tasman's astrolabe (a navigational aid) and a lighthouse. The walk's northern end is car-accessible from Lighthouse Rd.

The Maori called the cape Tauranga, meaning 'Sheltered Anchorage'. The first European

here was Abel Tasman in December 1642, naming it Clyppygen Hoek (Rocky Point). When James Cook moored the *Endeavour* here in March 1770, a furious storm made it anything but a 'sheltered anchorage'; hence the cape's modern name.

From the car park it's a five-minute walk to the seal colony lookout. The cliffs are unstable, so stick to the path.

A short stroll from the Cape Foulwind tavern you'll find **Omau Settlers Lodge** (☎ 03-789 5200; www.omausettlerslodge.co.nz; 1054 Cape Rd, Cape Foulwind; s/d incl breakfast $145/155). These contemporary and stylish units offer rest, relaxation and huge buffet breakfasts. A hot tub surrounded by bush maximises the take-it-easy quotient.

One of NZ's best restaurants, the **our pick** **Bay House Cafe** (☎ 03-789 7133; Tauranga Bay, Cape Foulwind; lunch mains $18-22, dinner mains $22-33; ☺ 10.30am-late Mon-Fri, from 9am Sat & Sun) is sophisticated without being stuffy. The chefs use local ingredients like piko piko (fern shoots) and horopito (NZ peppertree) in preparing seafood, West Coast venison and Canterbury lamb. The wine list is easily the best on the West Coast.

WESTPORT TO KARAMEA

North along SH67, the road is pressed against the rocky shoreline by verdant hills. The first town beyond Westport is Waimangaroa, where there's a turn-off to **Denniston**, 9km inland and 600m above sea level. Denniston was once NZ's largest coal producer, with 1500 residents in 1911. By 1981 this had shrunk to eight. The **Denniston Bridle Track** follows sections of the fantastically steep **Denniston Incline**. The incline was an engineering spectacular – empty coal trucks were hauled back up the 45-degree slope by the weight of descending loaded trucks. An information kiosk and the **'Friends of the Hill' museum** (☺ summer weekends only) bring to life the harsh conditions experienced by the miners and their families. Four kilometres north of Waimangaroa is the **Britannia Track** (four hours return), winding towards the Britannia Battery's gold-mining detritus.

At Granity, 30km north of Westport, head 5km uphill to the semi-ghost town of **Millerton**, and a further 3km to **Stockton**, home of NZ's largest operational coal mine. The **Millerton Incline Walk** (20 minutes return) takes in parts of the old incline, a bridge and an old dam. Granity's now a sleepy haven for alternative lifestylers, and just north at Hector you can sometimes see Hector's dolphins, NZ's smallest dolphins.

Further north at Ngakawau, just south of Hector, is the **Charming Creek Walk** (six hours return), an all-weather trail following an old coal line through the Ngakawau River Gorge. Alternatively, pursue the track 10km beyond the return point to **Seddonville**, a small bush town on the Mohikinui River. The short **Chasm Creek Walkway** links Seddonville with SH67.

A good base is the **Charming Creek B&B** (☎ 03-782 8007; www.bullerbeachstay.co.nz; d $75-220; 🖳) in Ngakawau. The rooms are stylish, clean and, well, charming. There's a wood-fire hot tub that overlooks the Tasman Sea – set to be a holiday highlight for every indulger. Budget-minded travellers can bunk down in the beachside caravan for a taste of true Kiwiana style.

Further north, the Seddonville road leads to **Rough and Tumble Bush Lodge** (☎ 03-782 1337; www.roughandtumble.co.nz; s/d $300/450; 🖳). In a gentle bend of the Mohikinui River, this luxury ecolodge is surrounded by walking trails and pristine bush. The beautiful isolation is ambushed each night with gourmet food. Advance bookings are essential and rates include all meals. Worth a splurge.

At the Mohikinui River mouth, 3km off the highway, is the not-so-gentle **Gentle Annie Beach**, and the **Gentle Annie Coastal Enclave** (☎ 03-782 1826; www.gentleannie.co.nz; De Malmanche Rd, Mohikinui; unpowered sites $20, dm $25, cabins $150-180). The surf hammers the coast and the wind shakes the palms at this isolated place that's perfect for quiet contemplation. There's camping, a basic backpacker lodge, and rustic cabins sleeping up to eight. The Cabbage Tree Beach Cottage is a low-key masterpiece of rugged Kiwi architecture.

Between Mohikinui and Little Wanganui the road meanders over **Karamea Bluff**, with rata and matai forests, and expansive views of the Tasman Sea below.

KARAMEA
pop 420

The relaxed town of Karamea is literally the end of the road – the end of SH67 and near the southern ends of the Heaphy and Wangapeka Tracks. Debate rages about continuing the road through to Nelson, but any highway would need to bisect the Kahurangi National Park. Don't hold your breath waiting for a resolution. With a subtropical maritime climate, Karamea is often warmer and drier than the rest of the coast, and is actually further north than Wellington. A take-it-easy mix of locals and chilled-out imports means it's ideal for jumping off the well-trod tourist trail for a few lazy days. When you feel like getting active again, there's good caving, mountain biking and tramping.

Information

The **Karamea visitor information centre** (☎ 03-782 6652; www.karameainfo.co.nz; Market Cross; ⊗ 9am-5pm daily Jan-Apr, to 5pm Mon-Fri, to 1pm Sat May-Dec; 🖳) has the local low-down, internet access, maps and DOC hut tickets. For detailed information on negotiating the Heaphy Track, see www.heaphytrack.com.

Sights

North of Karamea in the **Oparara Basin** are spectacular limestone arches and the unique Honeycomb Hill Caves (ancient home of the moa), the surrounding karst landscape blanketed by primitive rainforest. Moss-laden trees droop over the Oparara River, illuminated by light filtering through a dense forest canopy.

Ten kilometres along the road to the start of the Heaphy Track, turn off at McCallum's Mill Rd and go 15km past the sawmill along a winding gravel (sometimes rough) road to the arches. It's an easy walk (45 minutes return) through old-growth forest to the 200m-long, 37m-high **Oparara Arch**, spanning its namesake river. Its arch-rival is the **Moria Gate Arch** (43m long, 19m high), accessed via a similar track (one hour return). At the time of writing the switched-on Oparara Valley Trust was planning a further series of walking trails. Ask at the visitor information centre about joining a customised tour, including a guided bush walk.

Other quirky calcified features are **Mirror Tarn** (an easy 20 minutes return), a tree-lined tarn full of reflections, and the **Crazy Paving & Box Canyon Caves** (10 minutes return, BYO torch), a cracked-up cave-floor formation and a roomy cave system with fossils on the ceiling. Beyond these, in a protected area of Kahurangi National Park are the superb **Honeycomb Hill Caves & Arch**, only accessible by a prebooked **guided tour** (☎ 03-782 6652; adult/child $75/35); ask at the visitor information centre. These caves contain the bones of nine different moa species and the extinct giant

Haast eagle. Gentle river **kayaking trips** (trips $75; mid-Dec–Apr) are also on offer, but only outside the breeding season of the rare kowhiowhio (blue duck).

Activities

The Karamea River has good swimming, fishing, whitebaiting and kayaking, but ask a local or use common sense before jumping in. **Karamea Outdoor Adventures** (03-782 6181; sylvia.mike@slingshot.co.nz; Bridge St) offers kayaking and mountain-biking trips, including taking on the **K-Road** (bike hire only $35, including transport $55), a purpose-built mountain-bike trail (27km return) along logging roads.

The Little Wanganui, Oparara and Kohaihai Rivers have good swimming holes. Again, ask a local. There are good beaches too but also squadrons of sandflies; lashings of repellent (or wind) will help.

Longer walks around Karamea include the **Fenian Track** (four hours return) leading to **Cavern Creek Caves** and **Adams Flat**, where there's a replica gold-miners hut; a steep tramp for the reasonably fit to the 1084m **Mt Stormy** (eight hours return); and the first leg of the **Wangapeka Track** to Belltown Hut. Shorter walks include the **Lake Hanlon** (30 minutes return), **Big Remu** (45 minutes return), **Flagstaff** (one hour return) and **Zig Zag Track** (one hour return) walks.

If the prospect of walking the entire **Heaphy Track** tires you, just walk as far as the **Heaphy Hut** (five hours, adult/child $25/free), stay overnight, and then head back. Heaphy Track huts must be booked in advance, regardless of season, through DOC or the Karamea visitor information centre. Alternatively, walk as far as **Scotts Beach** (1½ hours return), passing nikau palm groves along the way, or continue to **Crayfish Point**. For detailed information on the Heaphy and Wangapeka Tracks, see p480 and p481.

Helicopter Charter Karamea (03-782 6111; www.adventuresnz.co.nz; 79 Waverley St) will chopper you to anywhere in the area. Options include a one-day helihike ($400 per three persons) where you are dropped off at the Heaphy Hut and walk back to Kohaihai at the southern end of the track.

Sleeping

Wangapeka Backpackers Retreat & Farmstay (03-782 6663; www.wangapeka.co.nz; Atawhai Farm, Wangapeka Valley; campsites per person $10, dm $20, s/d $40/65;) Laid-back and friendly farmstay that's a good place to recharge after completing the Wangapeka Track. Dorms are basic but there's a wood-fired bush bath. Campers are welcome and meals are available. Turn down Wangapeka Rd just north of Little Wanganui and follow the signs. It's a 20km drive south of Karamea.

Karamea Holiday Park (03-782 6758; www.karamea.com; Maori Point Rd; unpowered/powered sites $22/24, cabins $30-40, d $70) Set among native bush, 3km south of Market Cross, this is the ideal place to perfect your whitebaiting skills.

Last Resort (0800 505 042, 03-782 6617; www.lastresort.co.nz; 71 Waverley St; sites $24, dm $30, d $75-150) New owners are doing a great job in resurrecting this iconic Karamea property. Options stretch from tent sites to comfortable motel units. Dissolve into a spa or massage to lose any post-Heaphy aches and pains.

Rongo Backpackers (03-782 6667; www.rongobackpackers.com; Waverley St; unpowered sites per 2 Rongolians $50, dm/d $27/76;) Part neohippie artists' haven and part organic vegie garden, this uberrelaxed hostel even has its own community radio station (107.5 FM or www.karamearadio.com). Popular with long-term guests who often end up working within – either tending the garden or as de facto daytime DJs.

Karamea Farm Baches (03-782 6838; www.karameamotels.com; Bridge Rd; cabins $80-100) Most people would modernise these six 1960s cabins after buying them, but owners Paul and Sanae have kept the retro-Kiwiana ambience here gloriously intact, including riotous carpet last seen at your nana's place. If that sounds like your style – you'll love it.

Karamea River Motels (03-782 6955; www.karameamotels.co.nz; Bridge St; r $120-140) Accommodation at this rural motel ranges from studios to two-bedroom units. The new owners are putting their stamp on the hotel – sprucing it up and freely distributing a friendly vibe.

Karamea Beachfront Farmstay B&B (03-782 676; www.westcoastbeachaccommodation.co.nz; SH67; d incl breakfast $160-180) This friendly farmstay has three comfortable rooms and 2.5km of pristine beachfront 15km south of Karamea. Your host studied cooking in France, so expect the breakfast to be a cut above.

Eating & Drinking

Last Resort (03-782 6617; 71 Waverley St; lunch mains $8-12, dinner mains $22-30; 7am-late) The pleasant ambience of the dining area ushers in the best cuisine in town. Dine at either the all-day cafe, or the flasher evening restaurant with local tastes like Karamea reef and beef ($29.50).

Saracens Café (☎ 03-782 6600; 99 Bridge St; mains $10-15; ✆ 11am-late) The best place in town for a quick bite and a coffee, Saracens morphs into a live-music venue with occasional gigs on summer evenings.

Karamea Village Hotel (☎ 03-782 6800; Waverley St; mains $18-22; ✆ 11am-11pm) Treat yourself to life's simple pleasures. A game of pool or darts with the locals, a pint of Monteith's Original Ale, and a whitebait-fritter sandwich ($12). Sorted.

Just behind Saracens, the **Bush Lounge** (☎ 03-782 6711; ✆ mains $15-20; 6pm-late) aligns a rustic interior with a suitably rustic menu.

Getting There & Away

If you're driving from Westport to Karamea, fill up in Westport as there's no petrol until Karamea, 98km away.

Karamea Express (☎ 03-782 6757; info@karamea-express.co.nz) links Karamea and Westport (adult/child $27/17, 1½ hours, 7.50am Monday to Friday May to October, plus Saturday from November to April), departing from Last Resort.

Karamea Express also services Kohaihai at the southern end of the Heaphy Track, departing Kohaihai at 1pm and 2pm during summer; phone for prices and off-season times. It also services the Wangapeka Track on demand. There are phones at both trailheads to arrange transport out to Karamea.

You can also fly from Karamea to Takaka (around $175 per person) then walk back on the Heaphy Track; contact the visitor information centre for details.

Ask at Rongo Backpackers (opposite) about transport to trailheads (Heaphy $10 per person, Wangapeka $15 per person), and to other destinations in the area including the Oparara Basin ($35 per person).

WESTPORT TO GREYMOUTH

SH6 along the surf-pounded coastline proffers fine Tasman Sea views; so fine that Lonely Planet's *Best of Travel* dubbed the West Coast highway one of the planet's 10 best road trips. Fill up in Westport if you're low on petrol and cash – there's no fuel until Runanga, 92km away, and the next ATM is in Greymouth. The main attractions along this stretch are the geologically fascinating Pancake Rocks at Punakaiki. To break the journey, consider the following.

our pick **Beaconstone** (☎ 027 431 0491; www.beaconstone.co.nz; Birds Ferry Rd; dm/d $25/65; ✆ Oct-Jun) is 17km south of Westport on 52 serene hectares. Solar power, an organic garden and energy-efficient appliances make a bold ecofriendly and sustainable statement. This ubercool establishment is overflowing with character and charm. Beaconstone only has room for 12 guests so booking ahead is recommended.

Jack's Gasthof (☎ 03-789 6501; jack.schubert@xtra.co.nz; SH6; sites $10, d $50; ✆ Oct-May) is 23km south of Westport on the Little Totara River. Laconic Jack swapped Berlin for this gentle spot more than 20 years ago. There are two cruisy doubles, and a pizzeria (mains $16 to $30; open 11am till late) serving pizzas made with organic vegies grown outside the door. Watch out for Jack's huge (and hugely friendly) dog.

For a taste of the region's old mining past, swing into **Mitchell's Gully Gold Mine** (☎ 03-789 6553; www.mitchellsgullygoldmine.co.nz; SH6; adult/child $10/free; ✆ 9am-4pm), 22km south of Westport, with a tumbledown water wheel, old rail tracks and hillside tunnels (BYO torch).

Charleston, 28km south of Westport, boomed during the 1860s gold rush, with 80 hotels, three breweries, and hundreds of thirsty gold-diggers staking claims along the Nile River. Though it was a hot spot in the old days, most will struggle to find reason to hang out here for too long these days. The only pub left is the **Charleston European Tavern** (☎ 03-789 8862; SH6; mains $16-26; ✆ 9am-late), now doing double-duty as a cafe during the day and a boozer at night. It's the base for underground, water-laden trips offered by Norwest Adventures (p486).

Next door, the **Charleston Motel** (☎ 03-789 7599; www.charlestonmotel.co.nz; SH6; d $110) offers comfortable units just off the highway.

Those wanting to sleep under canvas should refer to the **Charleston Motor Camp** (☎ 03-789 6773; www.charlestonmotorcamp.co.nz; SH6; sites per person $10; cabins per person $25) Nothing fancy, but the price is right.

The broken coastline from Fox River to Runanga will remind Californians of Big Sur. Woodpecker Bay, Tiromoana, Punakaiki, Barrytown, Fourteen Mile, Motukiekie, Ten Mile, Nine Mile and Seven Mile are **beaches** sculpted by relentless ocean fury.

THE WEST COAST

Punakaiki & Paparoa National Park

Located midway between Westport and Greymouth is Punakaiki, a small settlement beside the rugged 38,000-hectare Paparoa National Park. For most travellers, it's a quick stop for an ice cream and a squiz at the Pancake Rocks; a shame because there's excellent tramping on offer and some tragically underused charismatic accommodation options.

INFORMATION

The **Paparoa National Park visitor information centre** (☎ 03-731 1895; punakaiki@doc.govt.nz; SH6; ☼ 9am-5pm Oct-Dec, to 6pm Jan-May, to 4.30pm Jun-Sep) has info-laden displays on the park, and details on activities, accommodation and trail conditions. Online see www.punakaiki.co.nz.

SIGHTS

Punakaiki is famous for its fantastic **Pancake Rocks** and **blowholes**. Through a layering-weathering process called stylobedding, the Dolomite Point limestone has formed into what looks like piles of thick pancakes. When the tide is right (tide times are posted at the visitor information centre), the sea surges into caverns and booms menacingly through blowholes. See it on a windy and wild day and be reminded that Mother Nature really is the boss. An easy 15-minute walk loops from the highway out to the rocks and blowholes.

Paparoa National Park is also blessed with sea cliffs, the mountains of the Paparoa Range, rivers, diverse flora and a Westland petrel colony, the world's only nesting site of this rare sea bird.

ACTIVITIES

Tramps in the national park are detailed in the DOC *Paparoa National Park* pamphlet ($1), and include the **Inland Pack Track** (two to three days), a route established by miners in 1867 to dodge difficult coastal terrain. The **Croesus Track** (one to two days), covered by another DOC leaflet (50c), is a tramp over the Paparoa Range from Blackball to Barrytown, passing historic gold-mining areas. Register at the Greymouth or Paparoa visitor information centres before setting out. Some inland walks are susceptible to river flooding; check conditions before you depart.

Shorter options include the **Truman Track** (30 minutes return) and the **Porari River Track** (2½ hours return), which follows a spectacu-lar limestone gorge. The **Fox River Tourist Cave** (three hours return) is open to amateur explorers. BYO torch and wear good walking shoes.

Punakaiki Canoes (☎ 03-731 1870; www.riverkayaking.co.nz; SH6; canoe hire 2hr/full day $35/55) rents canoes and kayaks near the Pororari River bridge. Guided tours start from $70. **Punakaiki Horse Treks** (☎ 03-731 1839; www.pancake-rocks.co.nz; SH6; 2½-hr ride $125; ☼ Oct-May), based at Hydrangea Cottages, conducts four-legged outings alongside the national park.

TOURS

Green Kiwi Tours (☎ 03 731 1843; www.greenkiwitours.co.nz; guided walking tours from $60, caving from $100) runs info-rich excursions throughout the region with an ecofriendly focus. Trips centered around native flora, fauna and local history are on offer as well as caving excursions.

SLEEPING & EATING

Punakaiki Beach Hostel (☎ 03-731 1852; www.punakaikibeachhostel.co.nz; 4 Webb St; tents per person $20, dm/s/d $28/50/70; ☐ ☜) A sandy, beach-bumming hostel with a deep, sea-view veranda and an outdoor spa, just a short stroll from Pancake Rocks and the beach. They were mid-tidy when we came by, so you can expect a fresh feel to the place.

Te Nikau Retreat (☎ 03-731 1111; www.tenikauretreat.co.nz; Hartmount Pl; dm $23, d $60-85, cabins $90; ☐) This unconventional accommodation option is set aesthetically amid the rainforest. Several buildings populate the property, all with their own character. From straightforward dorms in a chilled setting all the way through to cabins that take indoor-outdoor flow to a new level (the kitchen is in an attached greenhouse). There is even a stargazer hut for those who want to sleep under the night sky.

Punakaiki Beach Camp (☎ 03-731 1894; beachcamp@xtra.co.nz; 5 Owen St; unpowered & powered sites $30, d $45) This park is drenched with salty scents and studded with clean, old-style cabins and shipshape amenities.

Rocks Homestay (☎ 03-731 1141; www.therockshomestay.com; 33 Hartmount Pl; s/d incl breakfast from $135/195) Three kilometres north of Punakaiki (100m north of the Truman Track), this house looks over wild scrub to the rolling sea. The breakfasts are tasty, and dinner is available by arrangement. Once you've had your fill of pancakes, the sunny conservatory promotes curling up with a good book.

Hydrangea Cottages (☎ 03-731 1839; www.pancake
-rocks.co.nz; SH6; d $140-295) On a hillside overlook-
ing Pancake Rocks, these five stand-alone and
self-contained cottages are constructed class-
ily from recycled rimu and local river stones.
Punakaiki Horse Treks is based here.

Punakaiki Crafts (☎ 03-731 1813; SH6; coffee & cake
$7; ⏰ 9am-4.30pm, gallery to 7pm) Good coffee, cakes
and slices share an interesting gallery showcasing local artists.

Wild Coast Café (☎ 03-731 1873; SH6; mains $18-26;
⏰ 8am-9pm; 🖳 📶) Beside the visitor information centre is this tourist-swollen cafe, serving
pancake stacks, good pies and ice creams.
Those in need of a dub-dub-dub fix can jump
on the internet here for $3 per hour.

Punakaiki Tavern (☎ 03-731 1188; SH6; mains $19-
31; ⏰ 8.30am-late) Most nights the punters are
a mix of local and international, and the pub
menu with steak, fish and pasta has a similar
slant. When you're done, stick a pin in a map
of the world to show how far you've come.

GETTING THERE & AWAY

InterCity (☎ 03-365 1113; www.intercity.co.nz) links to
Westport ($19) and Greymouth ($25). **Naked
Bus** (www.nakedbus.com) has a similar service along
SH6 to Westport ($22) and Greymouth ($12).
Both companies stop allowing enough time to
check out Pancake Rocks.

The Coast Road

SH6 from Punakaiki to Greymouth is flanked
by white-capped waves and rocky bays on one
side, and the steep, bushy Paparoa Ranges on
the other.

Steve used to design women's lingerie, but
now he runs one of the South Island's most
surprising attractions, **Barrytown Knifemaking**
(☎ 0800 256 433; www.barrytownknifemaking.com; SH6;
classes $120). Put aside a day (9.30am to 3.30pm)
as Steve and wife Robyn steer you through the
process of making your own knife. We're talking the whole shebang here, from hand-forging
the blade to crafting a handle from native
rimu timber. Between the knifemaking, there's
lunch, archery, axe-throwing lessons, and a
stream of entertainingly bad jokes from Steve.
Bookings recommended and transport can
be arranged from Greymouth or Punakaiki.

Barrytown, 16km south of Punakaiki, has
the **All Nations Hotel** (☎ 03-731 1812; allnations@
xtra.co.nz; SH6; unpowered sites $20, dm/d $28/70). Its
coaster-covered walls are opposite the western end of the Croesus Track, handy for

trampers desperate for a beer and a bed (definitely in that order). Also serves pub meals
and attracts backpacker buses.

Ti Kouka House (☎ 03-731 1460; www.tikoukahouse.
co.nz; SH6; d incl breakfast $295) is all rugged sea views,
global antiques and lots of recycled wood,
including history-laden doors and windows.
Three luxury rooms stud this excellent B&B,
which has a luscious backdrop of subtropical
rainforest. Think Santa Fe adobe style meets
West Coast rustic.

For food, try **Darcy's Buffalo Bar & Grill** (☎ 03-
731 1151; SH6, Barrytown; mains $10-22; ⏰ 11am-late), a
spacious cafe perched above the road with lots
of outdoor seating.

Breakers (☎ 03-762 7743; www.breakers.co.nz;
SH6; d incl breakfast $200-330; 📶), 14km north of
Greymouth, is one of the best-kept secrets
on the coast. Breakers sits on a stunning spot
overlooking the sea with fine surfing opportunities at hand for the intrepid. The rooms
are beautifully appointed and the hosts are
friendly.

GREY VALLEY

From Murchison, an alternative to the
SH6 route is to turn off at Inangahua
Junction and travel inland across winding valley roads via Reefton, and over the mountains
into the Grey Valley.

Amid the regenerating forests, small towns
are reminders of futile farming attempts, and
of the gold rush of the 1860s.

Reefton
pop 1000

Reefton is an unconcerned little hamlet in the
heart of superb tramping and trout-fishing
country. As early as 1888, Reefton had its own
electricity supply and street lighting, ahead
of everywhere else in NZ. If you've crossed
Lewis Pass from Christchurch, this is the first
sizeable town you come to.

INFORMATION

The **Reefton i-SITE** (☎ 03-732 8391; www.reefton.co.nz;
67 Broadway; ⏰ 8.30am-6pm Nov-Mar, to 4.30pm Apr-Oct;
🖳) has very helpful staff, and a one-room
recreation of the Quartzopolis Mine (50c).
At the time of writing, plans were afoot to
introduce mine tours in the area.

SIGHTS & ACTIVITIES

Quite a few shops on Broadway date from
the 1870s, and the town feels like a Western

movie backdrop. For more information buy the *Historic Reefton* leaflet ($1).

The community-run **Blacks Point Museum** (Franklin St, Blacks Point; adult/child/family $5/3/15; 9am-noon & 1-4pm Wed-Fri & Sun, 1-4pm Sat Oct-Apr), 2km east of Reefton on the Christchurch road, is inside a former Methodist church and crammed with prospecting paraphernalia. Up the road is the still-functional **Golden Fleece Battery** (adult/child $1/free; 1-4pm Wed & Sun Oct-Apr), used for crushing gold-flecked quartz.

You can also have a chat with the guys at the **Bearded Miner Company** (03-732 8377; Broadway; admission by donation; 11am-4pm). Friendly bearded types will sit you down in a 1860s-style miners hut and give you a cup of billy tea. You might wonder why they haven't formed a ZZ Top tribute band.

If you want to dig a bit deeper check out the **Globe Gold Mine Tours** (027 442 4777; www.reefton gold.co.nz; adult/child $45/28; tours 1.30pm Tue-Sat). This new operation takes in many of the gold-flavoured attractions in town including the Bearded Miners and Blacks Point Museum. The real highlight is the chance to get up close and personal with a working gold mine – hard hat and high-vis vest provided.

Short walks around town include the **Powerhouse Walk** (40 minutes return) and **Reefton Heritage Walk** (30 minutes return). The **Murray Creek Track** (two to seven hours return), from Blacks Point, takes in abandoned coal and gold mines.

There's good tramping in the 182,000-hectare **Victoria Forest Park** (NZ's largest forest park), overgrown by five different species of beech tree. Consider the three-day **Kirwans**, **Lake Christabel** and **Robinson River Tracks** or the two-day **Big River Track** with good **mountain biking** opportunities. Ask at the i-SITE for information and maps.

SLEEPING & EATING

Reefton Motor Camp (03-732 8477; roa.reuben@xtra. co.nz; 1 Ross St; unpowered/powered sites $20/25, d $40) On the Inangahua River at the eastern end of town, this park is encircled by birdsong and stately fir trees.

Old Nurses Home (03-732 8881; reeftonretreat@ hotmail.com; 104 Shiel St; dm/s/d $25/33/54;) In Reefton they're good at transforming stately old buildings into cosy hostels. With colourful duvets and pretty gardens and patios, there's nary a whiff of this place's more buttoned-down institutional past.

Reef Cottage (0800 770 440, 03-732 8440; www. reefcottage.co.nz; 51-55 Broadway; d $100-150) This 1867 cottage, popular with couples and groups of up to eight, was formerly a solicitor's office. There's plenty of heritage timber, warming the mood for the (occasional) West Coast downpour. Adjoining the cottage, the Reef Cottage Café (meals $8 to $20) serves gourmet pies, cakes, quiches, pastas and salads.

Alfresco (03-732 8513; 16 Broadway; mains $12-25; 11am-7pm) With a family bistro atmosphere, Alfresco serves up meat and seafood grills and a half-dozen tasty pizzas. There are gas heaters or tables inside if the alfresco gets too fresco. They also have charming accommodation in the adjacent building – a double room will run you $60 to $120 and you won't be disappointed.

DRINKING

Wilson's (03-732 8800; 32 Broadway; mains $12-20; 11am-11pm) Sleepy Reefton could be the most laid-back place you'll ever visit, but if you do need to slow down, then the two garden bars (count 'em…) at Wilson's will do the trick. Occasional bands raise the excitement level to somewhere under fever pitch.

GETTING THERE & AWAY

East West Coach (0800 142 622, 03-789 6251; east westco@xtra.co.nz) runs daily to Westport ($22, 1¼ hours) and Christchurch ($44, 3¾ hours). **Atomic Shuttles** (03 349 0697; www.atomictravel.co.nz) swings by on its service linking Nelson ($40, six hours) and Franz Josef ($32, 5¾ hours).

State Highway 7 to Greymouth

At Hukarere, 21km south of Reefton, turn east and drive 14km to **Waiuta**, once a burgeoning gold town, now a spectral collection of remnants. The Birthday Reef was unearthed here on King Edward VII's birthday in 1905. By 1906 the Blackwater Mine was booming, and the town's population swelled to 500. In 1951 the mine collapsed and Waiuta was abandoned virtually overnight.

The lonesomely ruinous atmosphere makes Waiuta worth the trip. It's a leafy drive through beech forest, the last 7km on a winding, narrow dirt road. **Waiuta Lodge** (adult/child $15/7.50, plus key deposit $10) is a 30-bunk building with full kitchen facilities. Book and collect the key at the **Reefton i-SITE** (03-732 8391; www. reefton.co.nz; 67 Broadway, Reefton).

BLACKBALL

Northeast of the Grey River, about 25km north of Greymouth, Blackball is a working town established in 1866 to service gold diggers; coal mining kicked in between 1890 and 1964. The National Federation of Labour (a trade union) was conceived here, born from influential strikes in 1908 and 1931.

On the road 1km from Blackball is the trailhead of the **Croesus Track** (DOC leaflet $1), tracking 18km across the Paparoa Range to Barrytown on the West Coast. Do it in a day if you're keen/mad, or stay overnight at DOC's **Ces Clark Hut** (adult $10), halfway along. Book the hut through the Greymouth i-SITE (p496) before you start walking.

The hub of Blackball society is the **Formerly the Blackball Hilton** (☎ 0800 4252 252 255, 03-732 4705; www.blackballhilton.co.nz; 26 Hart St; dm/d $30/110), designated a New Zealand Historic Place. The 'formerly' was added after a certain global hotel chain got antsy. There are B&B doubles and funky dorms. The beer's cold, the pub atmosphere is good value and the kitchen has just been re-fit to ensure the meals are Hilton worthy. Full of character, this establishment alone makes the trip off the main highway well worth the eclectic diversion.

The **Blackball Salami Co** (☎ 03-732 4111; www.blackballsalami.co.nz; 11 Hilton St; ⏲ 8am-4pm Mon-Fri, 9am-3pm Sat) sells low-fat venison and beef salami. If you're planning a barbecue pick up some tasty snarlers as they say in Kiwi-speak – that's sausages for the uninitiated.

LAKE BRUNNER

At Stillwater, detour to Lake Brunner, aka Moana Kotuku (Heron Sea). Locals reckon Lake Brunner and the Arnold River have the world's best **trout fishing** – not an uncommon boast in NZ. Hire a fishing guide in Moana (at the Moana Hotel) or corner a local for advice. Moana is going ahead with lots of flash new holiday homes, but peace and quiet is usually just a boat ride away

Walks include the **Velenski Walk** (20 minutes one-way) from the motor camp through native forest; the **Arnold Dam Walk** (45 minutes return), which crosses a swing bridge over the Arnold River; and the **Rakaitane Track** (45 minutes return) through mixed podocarp forest with glowworms.

Lake Brunner Motor Camp (☎ 03-738 0600; lake.brunner@paradise.net.nz; Ahau St; powered sites $26, s $20) is in dire need of a tidy or perhaps a bulldozer – but it is the best and only budget option in town.

The **Lake Brunner Resort** (☎ 03-738 0083; www.lakebrunnerresort.net.nz; Ahau St; d $145-320) is a step above most places in town with slick facilities, tidy rooms and nice views. The resort's restaurant (mains $15 to $20; open noon till 9pm) does old-school favourites like chicken Kiev. If you're looking for a fishing guide, immerse yourself in the hotel's garden bar and throw out a few lines.

The **Lake Brunner Country Motel** (☎ 03-738 0144; www.lakebrunnermotel.co.nz; 2014 Arnold Valley Rd; tent sites $24, powered sites $35, cabins $52-119) has cabins, cottages and campervan sites ringed by native bush. It's a quiet and peaceful location, made more relaxing with a spa and the regular chorus of birdsong. It's 2km west of Moana; on your right if you're coming from Greymouth.

The **Station House Cafe** (☎ 03-738 0158; 40 Koe St; lunch $12-18, dinner $20-28; ⏲ noon-10pm, from 10am in summer) is on a hillside opposite the Moana Railway Station, where the *TranzAlpine* train pulls in. Aimed at the train-folk but no matter how you got here – it's the best food in town.

GREYMOUTH

pop 10,000

Welcome to the 'Big Smoke' of Westland. Crouched at the mouth of the Grey River (early European settlers had a lot of stuff to name, OK?), the West Coast's largest town has a proud gold-mining history, and a legacy of occasional river floods, now somewhat alleviated by a flood wall.

On the main road and rail route through Arthur's Pass and across the Southern Alps from Christchurch, Greymouth sees its fair share of travellers taking advantage of outstanding budget accommodation. Once you've enjoyed the tasty Monteith's Brewery tour, outdoor adventures including rafting, kayaking, canyoning and quad-biking can fill another couple of days. Motorcyclists and motorcycling enthusiasts rock in over Labour Weekend for October's Downtown Street Racing.

Orientation

The town centre is on the Grey River's south bank, 1km from the river mouth, and around the intersection of Mackay and Tainui Sts.

Free town and regional maps are available at the i-SITE and the **Automobile Association** (AA; ☎ 03-768 4300; www.aatravel.co.nz; 84 Tainui St).

Information

Major banks huddle around Mackay and Tainui Sts. There's internet access at the i-SITE and at the library.

DP:One Cafe (108 Mawhera Quay) Internet access.

Greymouth Hospital (☎ 03-768 0499; High St)

Greymouth i-SITE (☎ 0800 473 966, 03-768 5101; www.greydistrict.co.nz; cnr Herbert & Mackay Sts; ☉ 8.30am-7pm Mon-Fri, 9am-6pm Sat, 10am-5pm Sun Nov-Apr, reduced hours May-Oct; ☐) Very helpful crew and DOC information.

Paper Plus (☎ 03-768 5175; 62 Mackay St) Bookshop.

Police station (☎ 03-768 1600; 45-47 Guinness St)

Post office (Tainui St)

Sights

History House Museum (☎ 03-768 4028; www.history -house.co.nz; Gresson St; adult/child $5/2; ☉ 10am-4pm Mon-Fri) documents Greymouth's gold-prospecting history.

The **Left Bank Art Gallery** (☎ 03-768 0038; www. leftbankart.co.nz; 1 Tainui St; ☉ 10am-2pm winter, to 4pm summer) houses contemporary NZ jade carvings. Prints, paintings and photographs also get an airing.

Jade Country Greymouth (☎ 03-768 0700; 1 Guinness St; admission free; ☉ 8.30am-8pm Oct-Apr, to 5pm May-Sep) has original jade jewellery costing from $30 to thousands of dollars. There's a walk-through Jade Trail display on the precious *pounamu*, and the Jade Boulder Café (mains $10 to $21; open 8.30am till 4pm) serves organic coffee, whitebait and other 'wild food' that's more difficult to catch.

Not happy with your photos? **Stewart Nimmo Gallery** (☎ 03-768 6499; www.stewartnimmo.co.nz; cnr Mackay & Tainui Sts; admission free) is the place to stock up on some pro shots of the stellar West Coast scenery.

Activities

The **Point Elizabeth Walkway** (three hours return) heads north of Greymouth into the Rapahoe Range Scenic Reserve. The **Floodwall Walk** from Cobden Bridge towards Blaketown is shorter (30 minutes return).

Wild West Adventure Co (☎ 0800 147 483, 03-768 6649; www.nzholidayheaven.com; 8 Whall St) runs rafting excursions (priced from $160 to $845), a three-hour river cruise ($145) aboard a 'Jungle Boat' and a 5½-hour 'Dragons

Cave' blackwater rafting expedition ($160). Inflatable kayak trips start at $225.

On Yer Bike (☎ 0800 669 372, 03-762 7438; www. onyerbike.co.nz; SH6, Coal Creek; 2hr ride adult/child $140/120), 5km north of Greymouth, gets down 'n' dirty on quad-bikes and rugged go-karts. Take a two-hour 'Bush 'n' Bog' ride or jump into the amphibious 8WD 'Argo' (one-hour trips $70).

The **surf** at Cobden Beach and Seven Mile Beach in Rapahoe is consistent, but too dangerous for swimming.

Tours

Kea Heritage Tours (☎ 0800 532 868; www.keatours. co.nz; day tours $70-275) Well-informed guides visit West Coast locations like Blackball, Punakaiki and the glaciers. The four-day Te Ara Pounamu tour ($1595) from Greymouth to Queenstown follows the greenstone trading route traditionally used by Maori.

Monteith's Brewing Co (☎ 03-768 4149; www.mont eiths.co.nz; cnr Turumaha & Herbert Sts; admission $15; ☉ tours 11.30am, 2pm, 4pm, 6pm) Finish this excellent 1¼-hour-long tour in the bar by working your way through Monteith's eight brews. Bookings recommended, especially for the 6pm tour ($25) which kicks on for a barbecue at one of three downtown eateries.

Sleeping

BUDGET

Neptunes International Backpackers (☎ 0800 003 768, 03-768 4425; www.neptunesbackpackers.co.nz; 43 Gresson St; dm/d $18/45; ☐ ☎) This two-storey hostel has a prime location in the heart of town. A nautical theme permeates everything, and you won't find any bunks here. This worn-in property is getting dangerously close to worn-out, but the price is right.

Noah's Ark Backpackers (☎ 0800 662 472, 03-768 4868; www.noahsarkbackpackers.co.nz; 16 Chapel St; unpowered sites $34, dm/s/d $22/43/54; ☐ ☎) Originally a monastery, Noah's now has eccentric animal-themed rooms and a sunset-worthy balcony. In true Ark style, the camping price is for two people. Mountain bikes and fishing rods are provided free of charge.

South Beach Motel & Motorpark (☎ 0800 101 222, 03-762 6768; www.southbeach.co.nz; 318 Main South Rd; unpowered/powered sites $25/30, d $45-135; ☐) This low-rise motel and cabin complex propositions with a pastel-hued Miami accent, but the well-established nikau palms bring it firmly back to good old Enzed. Use of a spa and the internet are both gratis. Campervans and tents also welcome.

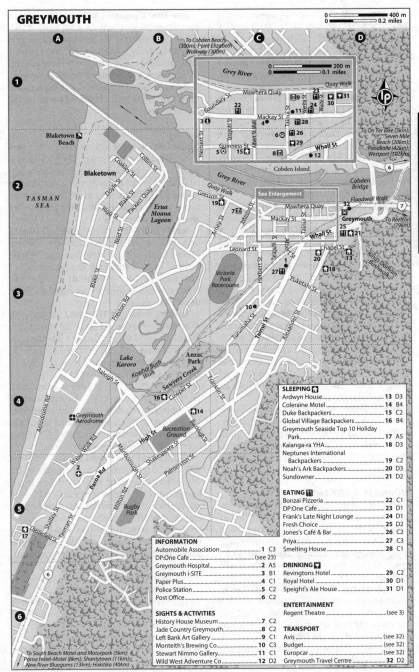

THE WEST COAST

GREYMOUTH

To Cobden Beach (300m); Point Elizabeth Walkway (300m)

Grey River

Quay Walk

Mawhera Quay

Boundary St

Herbert St

Tarapuhi St

Albert St Mall

Guinness St

Mackay St

Tainui St

Werita St

Walle St

Whall St

Cobden Island

Blaketown

Blaketown
Beach

Grey River

Quay Walk

See Enlargement

Cobden
Bridge

Floodwall Walk

Coakley St

Collins St

Doyle St

Blake St

Rigg St

Reid St

Packers Quay

Gresson St

Arney St

Johnston St

Mawhera Quay

Mackay St

Tainui St

Greymouth

Cobden
Island

Kings Domain
Bushwalk

To On Yer Bike (5km);
Seven Mile
Beach (20km);
Punakaiki (42km);
Westport (102km)

To Reefton
(79km)

**TASMAN
SEA**

Erua
Moana
Lagoon

Preston Rd

Blake St

Leonard St

Herbert St

Tarapuhi St

Albert St

Whall St

Chapel St

Puketahi St

Victoria
Park
Racecourse

Turumaha St

Tainui St

Alexander St

Lake
Karoro

Kowhai Bush
Walk

Anzac
Park

Sawyers Creek

Raleigh St

Cowper St

Franklin St

Aerodrome Rd

Water Walk Rd

Paroa Rd

Greymouth
Aerodrome

High St

Marlborough St

Buckland St

Recreation
Ground

Shakespeare St

Palmerston St

Rugby
Park

Milton Rd

Shelley St

Chesterfield St

Tasman St

To South Beach Motel and Motorpark (5km);
Paroa Hotel-Motel (8km); Shantytown (11km);
New River Bluegums (13km); Hokitika (40km)

INFORMATION
Automobile Association **1** C3
DP:One Cafe .... (see 23)
Greymouth Hospital **2** A5
Greymouth i-SITE **3** B1
Paper Plus **4** C1
Police Station **5** C2
Post Office **6** C2

SIGHTS & ACTIVITIES
History House Museum **7** C2
Jade Country Greymouth **8** C2
Left Bank Art Gallery **9** C1
Monteith's Brewing Co. **10** C1
Stewart Nimmo Gallery **11** C1
Wild West Adventure Co **12** D2

SLEEPING
Ardwyn House **13** D3
Coleraine Motel **14** B4
Duke Backpackers **15** C2
Global Village Backpackers **16** B4
Greymouth Seaside Top 10 Holiday
  Park **17** A5
Kaianga-ra YHA **18** D3
Neptunes International
  Backpackers **19** C2
Noah's Ark Backpackers **20** D3
Sundowner **21** D2

EATING
Bonzai Pizzeria **22** C1
DP:One Cafe **23** D1
Frank's Late Night Lounge **24** D1
Fresh Choice **25** C2
Jones's Café & Bar **26** C2
Priya **27** C3
Smelting House **28** C1

DRINKING
Revingtons Hotel **29** C2
Royal Hotel **30** D1
Speight's Ale House **31** D1

ENTERTAINMENT
Regent Theatre .... (see 3)

TRANSPORT
Avis .... (see 32)
Budget .... (see 32)
Europcar .... (see 32)
Greymouth Travel Centre **32** D2

Kaianga-ra YHA (☎ 03-768 4951; www.yha.co.nz; 15 Alexander St; dm $27, s/d $60/68; 🖳 🛜) Built in 1938 as a Marist Brothers' residence, this hostel is big, clean, functional and well behaved – everything you'd expect from YHA. Shatter the monastic ambience by playing guitar on the veranda.

Duke Backpackers (☎ 03-768 9470; www.duke.co.nz; 27 Guinness St; dm $27, s $45, d $64-75; 🖳 🛜) This purple palace has spared no expense when it comes to paint. Duke's is a lively place with an in-house bar, ample social areas and some cool free extras like soup, half-hour internet when you book in and a free second beer at the bar. It's loud, raucous, and popular with groups – love it or hate it.

our pick **Global Village Backpackers** (☎ 03-768 7272; www.globalvillagebackpackers.co.nz; 42-54 Cowper St; sites/dm/s/d/tr/q $30/25/60/60/90/108; 🖳 🛜) A collage of African and Asian art is infused with a passionate travellers' vibe here. Free kayaks – the Lake Karoro wetlands reserve is just metres away – and mountain bikes are on tap, and relaxation comes easy with a spa, sauna and riverside barbecue.

Greymouth Seaside Top 10 Holiday Park (☎ 0800 867 104, 03-768 6618; www.top10greymouth.co.nz; 2 Chesterfield St; unpowered/powered sites $36/40, d $55-115; 🖳) This well-appointed beachside park is 2.5km south of town. Cabins sleep six and the good-value self-contained units sleep up to eight. Kid-friendly distractions include an adventure playground.

Ardwyn House (☎ 03-768 6107; ardwynhouse@hotmail.com; 48 Chapel St; s/d without bathroom incl breakfast $55/90) This old-fashioned B&B nestles amid steep gardens on a quiet dead-end street. Mary, the well-travelled host, cooks a splendid breakfast.

MIDRANGE & TOP END

Sundowner (☎ 0800 080 859, 03-768 4666; www.sundowner.co.nz; 14 Smith St; d $105-115; 🖳 🛜) Just a short walk from the train station, the Sundowner impresses with a versatile range of options, from cheaper family units to newer studios. Brightly coloured duvets will brighten your day.

Coleraine Motel (☎ 0800 270 027, 03-768 077; www.colerainemotel.co.nz; 61 High St; d $139-200; 🖳 🛜) Rattan furniture, spa baths and king-size beds add up to the best accommodation in town. We're talking about the luxury units, but the cheaper one- and two-bedroom studios are not far behind.

New River Bluegums (☎ 03-762 6678; www.bluegumsnz.com; 985 Main South Rd; d incl breakfast $165; 🖳 🛜) Stay either in the cosy upstairs room in the rustic family home, or settle into a private self-contained cabin. Either way there's a farm to be explored, sheep to be shorn (in season), and huge cooked breakfasts to look forward to. Work off that extra rasher of bacon on the tennis court.

Eating

DP:One Cafe (☎ 03-768 4005; 108 Mawhera Quay; meals $6-15; 🕒 8am-5pm, closed Sunday; 🖳 🛜) This bohemian room plugs the grungy cred of a big-city cafe into the artsy vibe of a ramshackle garage sale. The menu features healthy pies, focaccias, salads and cakes, plus good coffee and wicked smoothies.

Jones's Café & Bar (☎ 03-768 6468; 37 Tainui St; lunch $8-15, dinner $19-30; 🕒 11.30am-2pm, 5.50-9pm) Jones's bills itself as a blues bar, but the vibe is more yawn than Stevie Ray Vaughan. It's extremely popular with locals and the trad meat and fish dishes are as dependable as the 12-bar blues.

Smelting House (☎ 03-768 0012; 102 Mackay St; mains $10-16; 🕒 8am-5pm) This is the sort of cafe that entices you to settle in for a lengthy stay. Heaps of mags – check, great coffee – check, tasty bagels, sandwiches and breakfast choices galore – check. Check it out.

Priya (☎ 03-768 7377; 84 Tainui St; mains $13-16; 🕒 noon-12.30pm & 5-10pm; V) An explosion of subcontinental Indian spices on temperate West Coast tastebuds, this seasoned performer is heavily patronised. There's chilled Kingfisher beer and a healthy range of vego delights.

our pick **Frank's Late Night Lounge** (☎ 03-768 9075; 115 Mackay St; mains $13-20; 🕒 5pm-late Thu-Sat; V) Effortlessly cool and retro late-night lounge-bar-cafe. A mirror ball hovers blithely above rescued 1950s furniture while Sinatra and Dean Martin bubble away as the soundtrack. An eclectic list of teas and NZ's best boutique beers partner a small global menu with surprises like Tibetan *momos* (dumplings) and Moroccan fish. Occasional live gigs complete the picture.

Bonzai Pizzeria (☎ 03-768 4170; 31 Mackay St; mains $15-25; 🕒 8am-late Mon-Sat, from 3pm Sun) The name's (kind of) Japanese; the decor is pure 1970s NZ, and the Italian-tinged pizzas, pasta and soup all come reader-recommended. Be sure to save room for one of the awesome homemade cakes.

Self-caterers should check out **Fresh Choice** (☎ 03-768 7545; 174b Mawhera Quay; ☉ 7am-9pm) supermarket.

Drinking

Speight's Ale House (☎ 03-768 0667; 130 Mawhera Quay; mains $20-30; ☉ 11am-late) In a 1909 waterfront building, Dunedin's finest beer has crossed the Southern Alps to take on Monteith's. With Greymouth's best wine list and tasty farm-style meals on offer, it's easy to see why locals have adopted Speight's as their *other* favourite beer.

Royal Hotel (☎ 03-768 4022; 128 Mawhera Quay; ☉ 11am-late) The Royal is an old-fashioned pub with affable Brit owners who welcome all comers with gusto. Grab a beer, get chatting, or watch the football (soccer) on Sky TV.

Revingtons Hotel (☎ 03-768 7055; 46 Tainui St; ☉ 8.30am-late) Alternate between a Monteith's in Revy's Sports Bar, or a Guinness or Kilkenny next door in Danny Doolan's. Steaks and venison pie tick the box marked 'Pub Grub' (mains $12 to $25).

Entertainment

Regent Theatre (☎ 03-768 0920; www.regentgreymouth.co.nz; cnr Herbert & Mackay Sts; adult/child $12/6) has movies and occasional live performances.

Getting There & Around

The **Greymouth Travel Centre** (☎ 03-768 7080; www.westcoasttravel.co.nz; railway station, 164 Mackay St; ☉ 9am-5pm Mon-Fri, 10am-3pm Sat & Sun; 🖳 🛜) books all forms of transport, including buses, trains and interisland ferries, and has luggage-storage facilities. This is also the bus depot and offers wi-fi access.

BUS

InterCity (☎ 03-365 1113; www.intercity.co.nz) has daily 1.30pm buses north to Westport ($25, two hours) and Nelson ($60, six hours), and south to Franz Josef ($42, 3½ hours) and Fox Glaciers ($45, 4¼ hours). Prices vary depending on season and availability.

Naked Bus (www.nakedbus.com) runs north to Nelson and south to Queenstown stopping at Hokitika, Franz Josef and Fox Glaciers, Haast and Wanaka.

Atomic Shuttles (☎ 03-349 0697; www.atomictravel.co.nz) runs daily to Queenstown ($70, 10½ hours, departs at 7.30am), with daily services to Fox Glacier ($35, 4¼ hours, departing 3.15pm), Picton ($60, 7½ hours, departing 1.15pm), and Hokitika ($15, one hour, departing 2pm).

CAR

Greymouth Travel Centre has the following branches of the major hire companies:
Avis (☎ 03-768 0902; www.avis.com)
Budget (☎ 03-768 4343; www.budget.co.nz)
Europcar (☎ 03-768 9980; www.europcar.co.nz)

A local company is **Alpine West** (☎ 0800 257 736, 03-736 4002; www.alpinerentals.co.nz; 11 Shelley St).

TAXI

Try **Greymouth Taxis** (☎ 03-768 7078). To the airport is around $20.

THE TRANZALPINE

The **TranzAlpine** (☎ 0800 872 467, 03-768 7080; www.tranzscenic.co.nz; adult/child $118/70, rates vary seasonally) is one of the world's great train journeys. Traversing the Southern Alps between Christchurch and Greymouth, and from the Pacific Ocean to the Tasman Sea, the *TranzAlpine* tracks through a sequence of unbelievable landscapes. Leaving Christchurch at 8.15am, it speeds across the flat, alluvial Canterbury Plains to the Alps' foothills. Here it enters a labyrinth of gorges and hills called the Staircase, a climb made possible by three large viaducts and a plethora of tunnels.

The train emerges into the broad Waimakariri and Bealey Valleys and (on a good day) the vistas are stupendous. The beech-forested river valley gives way to the snowcapped peaks of Arthur's Pass National Park. At Arthur's Pass itself (a small alpine village), the train enters the longest tunnel, the 8.5km 'Otira', burrowing under the mountains to the West Coast.

The western side is just as stunning, with the Otira, Taramakau and Grey River valleys, patches of podocarp forest, and the trout-filled Lake Brunner (Moana Kotuku), fringed with cabbage trees. The train rolls into Greymouth at 12.45pm, heading back to Christchurch an hour later, arriving at 6.05pm.

This awesome journey is diminished only when the weather's bad, but if it's raining on one coast, it's probably fine on the other.

THE WEST COAST

THE COAST TO COAST

Kiwis really are a mad bunch – take, for instance, the **Coast to Coast** (www.coasttocoast.co.nz), which has grown to become the most coveted one-day multisport race in the country. This annual race starts in Kumara on the West Coast and ends in Christchurch. Intrepid racers start in the wee hours of the morning with a gentle 3km run, followed by a 55km cycle that will wake you up quicker than a 6am espresso. Next it's a 33km mountain run over Goat Pass – you know any pass named after a goat isn't going to be flat. From there all there is to do is ride your bike another 15km, paddle your kayak 67km and get back on the bike for the final 70km.

After all this the strong, the brave and the uberfit will arrive in Christchurch to much fanfare. The course is 243km long and the top competitors will dust it off in just under 11 hours – with mortals taking almost twice that. The race is held annually in mid-February and is good fun to go and watch – if you're not up for racing.

AROUND GREYMOUTH

From Greymouth to Hokitika SH6 crawls along the wild West Coast beside surging waves and tortured driftwood.

Providing context for West Coast history, **Shantytown** (☎ 03-762 6634; www.shantytown.co.nz; Rutherglen Rd, Paroa; adult/child $25/10; ☒ 8.30am-5pm), 8km south of Greymouth and 3km inland from SH6, recreates an 1860s gold-mining town, complete with post office, pub and Rosie's House of Ill Repute. There's gold panning ($5 extra for adults), trains to ride, and a sawmill.

Popular with locals and highway explorers, the **Paroa Hotel-Motel** (☎ 0800 762 6860, 03-762 6860; www.paroa.co.nz; 508 Main South Rd; d $125-140; ☒) is located opposite the Shantytown turn-off and has spacious, garden-fronted units. Its restaurant, **Ham's** (mains $16-23; ☒ 7am-8pm), plates meaty schnitzels amid a blokey display of rugby jerseys.

Heading east across Arthur's Pass on SH73, 39km from Greymouth, the tiny settlement of **Jacksons** is nestled beside the Taramakau River. Campervan travellers and tenters can stay at **Jacksons Retreat** (☎ 03-738 0474; www.jacksonscampervanretreat.co.nz; unpowered/powered sites $20/39), with superb facilities set in 15 acres. The owners run scenic jetboat trips on the Taramakau River (adult/child from $110/55) and just up the road the historic **Jackson's Tavern** (☎ 03-738 0457; ☒ 11am-11pm) is perfect for a pie and a pint.

HOKITIKA

pop 3100

Visit Hokitika's wide and quiet streets in the off season, and you might be excused for thinking you've stumbled into a true Wild West town. Across summer though, there's no room for rogue tumbleweeds in the expansive thoroughfares, and 'Hoki' gets as busy with visitors as when the town was a thriving port during the 1860s gold rush. Only now, green (stone), and not gold, is the colour of choice.

Orientation

The town forms a grid at the mouth of the Hokitika River around Weld and Tancred Sts. Free town maps are available at the **Westland i-SITE** (☎ 03-755 6166; hkkvin@xtra.co.nz; 7 Tancred St).

Information

Look for banks on Weld and Revell Sts.
Bookworms 102 Books (26b Weld St.; ☒ 9am-5pm) Buys/sells/exchanges books.
DOC office (☎ 03-756 9100; 10 Sewell St; ☒ 8am-4.45pm Mon-Fri)
Hokitika Travel Centre (☎ 03-755 5251; 64 Tancred St; ☒ 8.30am-5pm Mon-Fri) Books scenic flights and transport. Based inside the National Kiwi Centre.
Photo Corner (☎ 03-755 7768; 15 Weld St) Internet access including wi-fi.
Police station (☎ 03-756 8310; 50 Sewell St)
Post office (Revell St)
Take Note (☎ 03-755 8167; cnr Weld & Revell Sts) Maps, mags and West Coast books.
Westland i-SITE (☎ 03-755 6166; www.hokitika.org; 7 Tancred St; ☒ 10am-6pm Mon-Fri, to 4pm Sat & Sun)
Westland Medical Centre (☎ 03-755 8180; 54a Sewell St; ☒ 8.30am-10pm)

Sights

Hoki's premier attractions are its arts-and-crafts shops; see p503.

The **West Coast Historical Museum** (☎ 03-755 6898; enquiries@hokitikamuseum.co.nz; Tancred St.; adult/child $5/1; ☒ 8am-6pm) has old photos, Maori artefacts, river and pub-life displays, and the southern hemisphere's biggest Meccano set (a gold dredge replica). The Mana Pounamu exhibition is the ideal primer before you hit the shops looking for greenstone treasures.

Pick up the free *Hokitika Heritage Walk* leaflet from the i-SITE and wander the **Gibson Quay Heritage Waterfront**, imagining when the wharves were choked with old-time sailing ships.

The rather tired **National Kiwi Centre** (☎ 03-755 5251; natkiwi@xtra.co.nz; 60 Tancred St; adult/child/family $14/8/36; ⏱ 9am-5pm Mon-Fri) has seen better days, but at least you'll see a kiwi – peer into the dimly lit enclosure and see what's rummaging about. There are also turtles, tuatara, and 150-year-old eels that get fed every day at 10am, noon and 3pm.

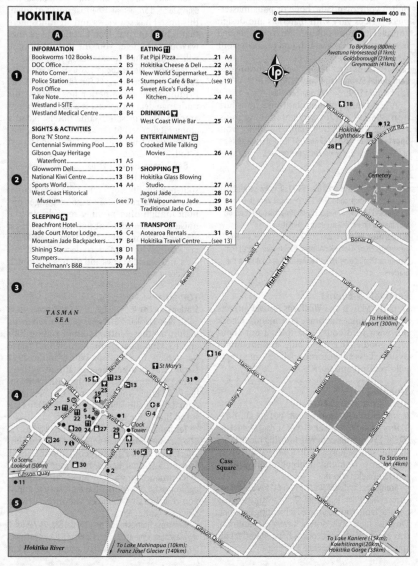

HOKITIKA

INFORMATION	
Bookworms 102 Books	**1** B4
DOC Office	**2** B5
Photo Corner	**3** A4
Police Station	**4** B4
Post Office	**5** A4
Take Note	**6** A4
Westland i-SITE	**7** A4
Westland Medical Centre	**8** B4

SIGHTS & ACTIVITIES	
Bonz 'N' Stonz	**9** A4
Centennial Swimming Pool	**10** B5
Gibson Quay Heritage Waterfront	**11** A5
Glowworm Dell	**12** D1
National Kiwi Centre	**13** B4
Sports World	**14** A4
West Coast Historical Museum	(see 7)

SLEEPING	
Beachfront Hotel	**15** A4
Jade Court Motor Lodge	**16** C4
Mountain Jade Backpackers	**17** B4
Shining Star	**18** D1
Stumpers	**19** A4
Teichelmann's B&B	**20** A4

EATING	
Fat Pipi Pizza	**21** A4
Hokitika Cheese & Deli	**22** A4
New World Supermarket	**23** B4
Stumpers Cafe & Bar	(see 19)
Sweet Alice's Fudge Kitchen	**24** A4

DRINKING	
West Coast Wine Bar	**25** A4

ENTERTAINMENT	
Crooked Mile Talking Movies	**26** A4

SHOPPING	
Hokitika Glass Blowing Studio	**27** A4
Jagosi Jade	**28** D2
Te Waipounamu Jade	**29** B4
Traditional Jade Co	**30** A5

TRANSPORT	
Aotearoa Rentals	**31** B4
Hokitika Travel Centre	(see 13)

0 —— 400 m
0 —— 0.2 miles

To Birdsong (800m);
Awatuna Homestead (11km);
Goldsborough (21km);
Greymouth (41km)

TASMAN SEA

St Mary's

Clock Tower

Cass Square

Hokitika River

To Scenic Lookout (500m)
Gibson Quay

To Lake Mahinapua (10km);
Franz Josef Glacier (140km)

To Hokitika Airport (300m)

To Stations Inn (4km)

To Lake Kaniere (15km);
Kowhitirangi (20km);
Hokitika Gorge (33km)

Hokitika Lighthouse

Cemetery

Just north of town, a short stroll from SH6 leads to a **glowworm dell**. Evening darkness maximises the show.

Activities

Dabble in jade carving with Steve Gwaliasi at **Bonz 'N' Stonz** (☎ 0800 214 949, 03-755 6504; www.bonz-n-stonz.co.nz; 16 Hamilton St; full-day workshop $80-150; ☾ 8.30am-5pm Mon-Sat). Design, carve and polish your own jade, bone or paua masterpiece. Prices vary with materials and design complexity, and bookings are recommended in summer – allow four hours to create your wearable art.

If it rains, get really wet in the heated **Centennial Swimming Pool** (☎ 03-755 8119; 53 Weld St; adult/child $4/2; ☾ 9am-5pm Sep-May).

A good range of mountain-bike trails lurk nearby amid old forestry and mining trails. Hire bikes and get trail maps and advice from **Sports World** (☎ 03-755 8662; 33 Tancred St; bike hire per hr $25; ☾ 8am-5pm Mon-Fri, 9am-1pm Sat).

Tours

Scenic Waterways (☎ 03-755 7239; www.paddleboatcruises.com; adult/child $30/15; ☾ tours 2pm Dec-Apr, on demand May-Nov) Runs 1½-hour paddleboat tours on Mahinapua Creek, 10km south of Hokitika.

Wilderness Wings (☎ 0800 755 8118; www.wildernesswings.co.nz; Hokitika Airport; flights from $320) Has four-hour flights over Hokitika, Aoraki (Mt Cook) and the glaciers.

Festivals & Events

In early March the **Wildfoods Festival** attracts 20,000 curious and brave gourmands. Check out www.wildfoods.co.nz to find out about tasty goodies like huhu bugs and mountain oysters. Less adventurous palates can sample wild venison and pork.

Sleeping

BUDGET & MIDRANGE

Mountain Jade Backpackers (☎ 0800 838 301, 03-755 8007; mtjade@minidata.co.nz; 41 Weld St; dm $21, d $41-44; ☐ ☎) What this concrete housing block lacks in atmosphere it makes up for in value. Cheap sleeps are to be found in this ultracentral mass-market backpackers.

Stumpers (☎ 0800 788 673, 03-755 6154; www.stumpers.co.nz; 2 Weld St; dm $25, d 50-80; ☐ ☎) Stumpers has comfortable rooms above its bustling cafe-bar. Doubles have TVs, dorms have a maximum of three beds, and most rooms have shared facilities. En suite doubles are $10 extra.

Shining Star (☎ 03-755 8921; www.shiningstar.co.nz; 11 Richards Dr; unpowered/powered sites $25/32, d $85-160; ☐ ☎) Sprawling and versatile beachside spot with everything from camping to classy new seafront units. Kids will love the menagerie, including ducks and alpacas straight from Dr Doolittle's appointment book. Mum and Dad might prefer the spa and sauna.

Birdsong (☎ 03-755 9179; www.birdsong.co.nz; SH6; dm/s $28/55, d $70-88; ☐ ☎) Just north of town, this hostel has sea views and an atmosphere that is hard to rival. Don't let the out-of-the-way location deter you; the art-filled house will seduce you into extending your stay.

Jade Court Motor Lodge (☎ 0800 755 885, 03-755 8855; www.jadecourt.co.nz; 85 Fitzherbert St; d $95-140) Priding itself on superior hospitality, this midrange déjà vu special is a slight standout among a sea of same-same hotels. Nearby along Fitzherbert St are several other motels, so you won't have to look far if Jade Court is full.

Beachfront Hotel (☎ 03-755 8344; www.beachfronthotel.co.nz; 111 Revell St; d $125-300; ☎) This split-personality hotel raises the bar in Hoki. The original rooms are a good budget option; though offer nothing remarkable (the noise from the adjacent pub can be an issue at times). The rooms in the Ocean View Wing are another story. Modern decor, flat-screen TVs and seaside views add up to a top-notch choice.

TOP END

Stations Inn (☎ 0508 782 846, 03-755 5499; www.stations.co.nz; Blue Spur Rd; d $170-250) King-sized beds feature in these cottages amid rolling hills and rocking alpacas. Brand-new units have flat-screen TVs and spa baths, and a short stroll away is a heritage restaurant with an award-winning relationship with venison, beef and lamb (mains $26 to $35; open from 6pm daily). Follow Hampden St and Hau Hau Rd to Blue Spur Rd.

Teichelmann's B&B (☎ 0800 743 742, 03-755 8232; www.teichelmanns.co.nz; 20 Hamilton St; d $195-240) Once home to surgeon, mountaineer and professional beard-cultivator Ebenezer Teichelmann, now a luxurious B&B with amicable hosts. All rooms have en suites, and if you're a bit shy consider the more private Teichy's Cottage.

Awatuna Homestead (☎ 0800 006 888, 03-755 6834; www.awatunahomestead.co.nz; 9 Stafford Rd, Awatuna; d incl breakfast $280-360) Set down a quiet road 11km north of Hokitika, the family-run Awatuna Homestead has three lovely guest rooms and a self-contained apartment. Dinner is available by prior arrangement, and in the evening owners Hemi and Pauline recount cultural stories of the discovery of NZ by the early Pacific explorers.

Eating & Drinking

Sweet Alice's Fudge Kitchen (☎ 03-755 5359; 27 Tancred St; per slice $6; ☻ 10am-4pm Mon-Fri, to 2pm Sat & Sun) Treat yourself with a slice of Alice's handmade, all-natural fudge. Your biggest decision of the day could be which flavour to choose. Go for the uberclassic mint-chocolate or spice it up with 'boozy fruit and nut'.

Hokitika Cheese & Deli (☎ 03-755 5432; 84 Revell St; mains $7-16; ☻ 8am-4pm) This airy and open cafe and cheesery is a fine place to start the day. Brunch and light meals are the main forte with fresh coffee and aged cheese at the ready. The chicken and mushroom pies alone are worth a visit.

Stumpers Cafe & Bar (☎ 03-755 6154; 2 Weld St; mains $12-28; ☻ 7am-late) Eating at Hokitika's pubs is pretty uninspiring, but Stumpers is the best of them with a cafe-style atmosphere and a (slightly) more imaginative kitchen dishing up colourful food from blue cod to green-lipped mussels.

ourpick Fat Pipi Pizza (☎ 03-755 6263; 83a Revell St; pizza $19-24; ☻ 5pm-late Thu-Sun; **V**) Vegetarians, carnivores and everyone in between will be salivating for the pizza made with love right before your eyes. If you're in town during whitebait season (September to mid-November) try the Fat Pipi whitebait pizza. Plan to take away – there's no seating to be found here.

West Coast Wine Bar (☎ 03-755 5417; 108 Revell St; ☻ 11am-4pm Mon-Sat, till late Fri) No, you're not seeing things. Upping the posh factor to unseen West Coast heights – they also have cheese platters and marinated olives to nibble on. Don't be scared; they also have beer, if all that sounds too decadent.

If you are self-catering, check out **New World** (☎ 03-755 8390; 116 Revell St; ☻ 8am-7pm Mon-Sat, 9am-6pm Sun) supermarket.

Entertainment

Crooked Mile Talking Movies (☎ 03-755 5309; www.crookedmile.co.nz; 36 Revell St; tickets adult/child $11/6) Vintage building, plus old couches, plus organic chocolate and house bar, plus art-house films, equals – perfect night out.

Shopping

Most of Hokitika's crafty shops are on Tancred St, where things of stone and wood (and glass, gold, bone and shell) are worked into shape. Staff love to talk *pounamu*, and in some studios you can watch carvers in action. Be aware that some shops sell jade imported from Europe and Asia, as local greenstone can often be difficult and expensive to discover in the NZ wilderness.

Traditional Jade Co (☎ 03-755 5233; 2 Tancred St) This family-run studio distils the jade hype into something meaningful. Watch talented artists carving classic Maori greenstone designs.

Te Waipounamu Jade (☎ 03-755 8304; 19 Sewell St) Te Waipounamu is scrupulously authentic, selling only NZ *pounamu* handcrafted into both traditional and contemporary designs – all with an aesthetic flavour.

WHITEBAIT FEVER

Author of *The Bone People* Keri Hulme once opined, 'I'm not particularly serious about anything except whitebaiting'. Okarito's most famous resident recluse may have been commenting on behalf of the entire West Coast, because from September to mid-November, the region's rivers and marine estuaries are crowded with fisherfolk of all ages keen to net a few precious kilos of immature-stage inanga (river smelt). Catches in recent years have been lower than normal, and in 2007 prices for the wee beasties reached $150 per kilogram. With some whitebaiters securing up to 15kg on a good day, it can be a lucrative business. Little wonder it's a practice enjoyed by a wide range of keen Coasters, all with their own distinct financial goals. Teenagers save up for a shiny mobile phone while Mum might be eyeing a new digital TV receiver. The experienced old-timers are usually just happy to make enough for beer money and pay for their riverside crib (cottage) or caravan for a few more weeks.

Try a whitebait fritter wrapped in fresh white bread, or head to Hokitika's Fat Pipi Pizza (above) for its tasty whitebait pizza.

Jagosi Jade (☎ 03-755 6243; 246 Sewell St; ☺ 8.30am-4pm Mon-Fri) Carver Aden Hoglund produces traditional and modern Maori designs from jade sourced from around the South Island.

Hokitika Glass Blowing Studio (☎ 03-755 7775; 28 Tancred St; ☺ 9am-4pm Mon-Fri) Specialising in glass art and covering a continuum from garish to glorious. Wear a T-shirt if you've come to watch the glass-blowers; it can get a tad toasty.

Getting There & Around

AIR

Hokitika Airport is on Airport Dr (off Tudor St), 1.5km east of the centre of town. **Air New Zealand** (☎ 0800 737 000, 09-357 3000; www.airnz.co.nz) has four flights daily (from $65 one-way) to/from Christchurch.

BUS

InterCity (☎ 03-365 1113; www.intercity.co.nz) buses depart from outside the **National Kiwi Centre** (03-755 5251; 60 Tancred St) daily for Greymouth ($14, 45 minutes, departing 12.30pm), Nelson ($65, seven hours, departing 12.30pm) and Fox Glacier ($39, 3½ hours, departing 2.55pm).

Atomic Shuttles (☎ 03-349 0697; www.atomictravel. co.nz) departs i-SITE to Fox Glacier ($35, 3½ hours, departing 8am and 3.15pm), Greymouth ($15, one hour, departing 11.30am and 4.50pm) and Queenstown ($70, 10 hours, departing 8am).

Naked Bus (www.nakedbus.com) heads north to Greymouth, and south to Queenstown stopping at Franz Josef and Fox Glaciers, Haast and Wanaka.

CAR

Car-hire branches at Hokitika Airport:
Avis (☎ 03-768 0902; www.avis.com)
Budget (☎ 03-768 4343; www.budget.co.nz)
Hertz (☎ 03-768 0196; www.hertz.co.nz)

A local company good for day rentals is **Aotearoa Rentals** (☎ 03-755 5222; hokitikacc@xtra. co.nz; Hokitika Car Court, 65 Fitzherbert St).

TAXI

Try **Hokitika Taxis** (☎ 03-755 5075).

AROUND HOKITIKA

A 33km farmland drive or cycle gets you to **Hokitika Gorge**, a ravishing ravine with turquoise waters. Glacial flour (suspended rock particles) imbues the milky hues. Cross the swing bridge for a couple of short forest walks. To get here, head up Stafford St past the dairy factory and follow the signs.

Kowhitirangi, en route to the gorge, was the scene of a massive 12-day manhunt involving the NZ army in 1941. Unhinged farmer Stanley Graham shot dead four Hokitika policemen, disappeared into the bush then returned to murder three others, eventually being killed himself. A grim roadside monument lines up the farmstead site through a stone gun shaft. The 1982 film *Bad Blood* re-enacts the awful incident.

A gravel forest road (lousy for big vehicles) circumnavigates **Lake Kaniere**, passing **Dorothy Falls**, **Kahikatea Forest** and **Canoe Cove**. The Westland i-SITE and DOC in Hokitika have info on other local walks, including the **Lake Kaniere Walkway** (four hours one-way), along the lake's western shore, and the **Mahinapua Walkway** (2½ hours one-way), through the reserve on Lake Mahinapua's northeast side to a wildlife-engorged swamp.

There are **DOC camping grounds** (adult/child $6/1.50) at **Goldsborough**, 17km from Hoki on the 1876 'gold trail'; **Hans Bay**, 19km from Hokitika on Lake Kaniere's eastern shore; and 10km south of Hokitika at **Lake Mahinapua**.

HOKITIKA TO WESTLAND TAI POUTINI NATIONAL PARK

From Hokitika it's 140km south to Franz Josef Glacier. Most travellers fast forward without stopping, but there are some interesting historical highlights, and tramping, kayaking, and birdwatching opportunities along the way. **InterCity** (☎ 03-365 1113; www.intercity. co.nz) and **Atomic Shuttles** (☎ 03-349 0697; www. atomictravel.co.nz) are transport options offering stops along SH6.

Ross

Ross is a town of glories lost, 30km south of Hokitika. It's where the unearthing of NZ's largest gold nugget, the 2.772kg 'Honourable Roddy', caused a kerfuffle in 1907. The **Ross visitor information centre** (☎ 03-755 4077; www.ross. org.nz; 4 Aylmer St; ☺ 9am-5pm Dec-Feb, to 3pm Mar-Nov) features a scale model of the town in its shiny years ($2).

Opposite is the **Miner's Cottage Museum** (admission free; ☺ 9am-5pm), in an 1885 cottage containing two old pianolas and a replica Roddy. The recreated **Ross Gaol** next door will make you glad you're not staying there for the night.

The **Water Race Walk** (one hour return) starts near the museum, passing old gold-diggings, caves, tunnels and a cemetery. Try **gold panning** at the visitor information centre ($10), or hire a pan ($10) and head to Jones Creek to look for Roddy's great, great grandnuggets.

The **Empire Hotel** (☎ 03-755 4005; basilcybil@xtra.co.nz; 19 Aylmer St; unpowered/powered sites $15/20, s $40, d $60-75) has a row of basic cabins and backpacker dorms, with authentic old-timer pub rooms upstairs. Tent and campervan travellers are also welcome to kip down in the adjacent yard. The bar is one of the West Coast's hidden gems – imported directly from a bygone era, it reeks of authenticity and unsaid cool. Classic Kiwiana, and well up in the running for the South Island's best watering hole.

The rustic **Roddy Nugget Cafe & Bar** (☎ 03-755 4245; 5 Moorhouse St; meals $6-15; ☷ 7am-11pm) is a country cafe serving homemade meals, including some stellar blueberry pancakes. Occasionally the bar, and on fine days the outdoor beer garden, threatens to recreate the energy of the town's glory days.

Ross to Okarito

South of Ross the bush closes in and mist and rain often cling to the verdant surroundings.

About 16km south of Ross, the **Old Church** (☎ 03-755 4000; SH6; unpowered sites $12.50, dm/d $20/50) stands remotely on the Kakapotahi River. Bikes, kayaks and fishing are on offer but BYO food as there's no nearby shop.

PUKEKURA

Just north of Lake Ianthe, carved out of the dense bush, is this tiny place, population two.

The tour buses descend on the **Bushmans Centre** (☎ 03-755 4144; www.pukekura.co.nz; SH6; admission free; ☷ 9am-6pm), an overly rustic cafe-shop with a pathological distrust of possums, animal rights activists and Aucklanders. Inside is a souvenir shop and the **Bushmans Museum** (adult $4), laying on blokey bush humour with a 20-minute video on local industry, anti-possum displays and some giant eels. The cafe offers snacks like possum jerky, possum pie and possum pâté. Outside in a paddock are chamois and thar that look happier than the caged possums inside.

Across the road is the Puke Pub and the **Wild Foods Restaurant** (☎ 03-755 4008; mains $10-15; ☷ noon-late), specialising in 'road kill' dishes like 'wheel-tread possum' and 'headlight delight'. (Motto: 'You kill 'em, we'll grill 'em').

Pukekura Lodge (☎ 03-755 4008; SH6; unpowered & powered sites $15, dm $15, d $40) has four rustic rooms right next door. There's a **DOC camping ground** (adult/child $6/1.50) beside Lake Ianthe, 6km south of Pukekura.

HARI HARI

About 22km south of Lake Ianthe, Hari Hari made headlines in 1931 when swashbuckling Australian aviator Guy Menzies completed the first solo trans-Tasman flight from Sydney. Menzies crash-landed the *Southern Cross Junior* into the La Fontaine swamp. Menzies' flight took 11¾ hours, 2½ hours faster than fellow Australian Charles Kingsford Smith in 1928. At the southern end of town is a replica of his trusty biplane. Internet access is available at the Pioneer Cottage Craft Store at the north end of town.

The **Hari Hari Coastal Walk** (aka Doughboy Walk or Coastal Pack Track; 2¾ hours return) is a well-trodden low-tide loop passing the Poerua and Wanganui Rivers. The walk starts 20km from SH6, the last 8km unsealed; follow Wanganui Flats Rd then La Fontaine Dr. There's tidal info at the trailhead, or ask at the Ross visitor information centre.

Flaxbush Motels (☎ 03-753 3116; flaxbush123@xtra.co.nz; SH6; d $50-150; ☐) This decidedly bohemian establishment has gone through something of a reinvention the past few years. Amenities have been spruced up and new facilities added. Cabins and units cover a wide range of budgets. The owners are certainly animal lovers, with peacocks wandering the grounds and a pet possum that has its own room – in the house.

The **Hari Hari Motor Inn** (☎ 03-753 3026; hhmi@paradise.net; SH6; unpowered/powered sites $19/22, dm/d $18.50/100) has serviceable doubles but doesn't have a shared kitchen for campers. The bistro (mains $11 to $29; open noon till late) is Hari Hari's only evening eatery, with tasty pizzas, steak and roasts and cold pints of beer.

WHATAROA & THE KOTUKU SANCTUARY

Near Whataroa, 35km south of Hari Hari, is NZ's only nesting site for the kotuku (white heron), roosting here between November and February. The herons then fly off individually to reconsider the single life over winter.

White Heron Sanctuary Tours (☎ 0800 523 456, 03-753 4120; www.whiteherontours.co.nz; SH6, Whataroa; adult/child $110/45; ☷ 4 tours daily late Oct-Mar) has the only DOC concession to see the herons, with

2½-hour 'jetboat ecotours' (the jetboat doesn't bug the birds). Year-round a scenic rainforest tour without the herons is available for the same price.

Next door is the **Sanctuary Tours Motel** (☎ 0800 523 456, 03-753 4120; www.whiteherontours.co.nz; SH6, Whataroa; cabins $55-65, d $95-125), with basic cabins with shared facilities ($8 extra for bedlinen), and enthusiastically painted motel units.

Okarito

Another 15km south of Whataroa is the Forks and the turn-off to peaceful Okarito, 13km further on the coast. Keri Hulme's Booker Prize–winning bestseller, *The Bone People*, is set in this unpeopled region. The reclusive author is one of a few score permanent residents in this peaceful coastal hamlet. Okarito has no shops, so stock up on food and supplies at New World in Hokitika.

From the southern end of the Strand, there are a couple of coastal walks to **Three Mile Lagoon** (three hours return; low tide only) and to **Okarito Trig** (1½ hours return). Expect Southern Alps and Okarito Lagoon views.

Okarito Nature Tours (☎ 0800 524 666, 03-753 4014; www.okarito.co.nz; kayak rental per half-/full day $50/60) hires out kayaks for paddles into peaceful **Okarito Lagoon**, a fish-laden buffet for waterbirds. The lagoon is NZ's largest unmodified wetland, an intricate ecosystem of shallow water and tidal flats surrounded by rainforest. Guided tours are available (from $75), and overnight rentals ($80) allow the experienced to check out deserted North Beach or Lake Windemere.

Also explore the lagoon with **Okarito Boat Tours** (☎ 03-753 4223; www.okaritoboattours.co.nz), morning and evening sightseeing tours starting at $45. Bookings are recommended for the nature tour, which departs in the mornings for better wildlife-viewing potential (two hours, $75).

Okarito Kiwi Tours (☎ 03-753 4330; www.okarito kiwitours.co.nz; $60) run nightly expeditions (two to three hours). Numbers are limited to eight kiwi fans per night, so booking is recommended during summer. The company will also pick you up from Franz Josef, and it boasts a 90% success rate in spying the iconic birds.

Okarito Campground (off Russell St; adult/child $7.50/ free) is a breezy patch of community-managed greenery complete with barbecues, toilets, hot showers ($1) and a public telephone. Drop

your cash in the honesty box and you're sweet as.

An old 1892 school building is now the DOC-run **Okarito Hostel** (☎ 03-752 0796; westland npvc@doc.govt.nz. The Strand;d $60). This charming heritage building was once the smallest youth hostel in NZ. You can't book individual beds; you can only hire out the whole building. There's room for 12 and it's only $10 a night for extras beyond two people, so get a gang together and go for it.

The **Okarito Beach House & Royal Hostel** (☎ 03-753 4080; www.okaritobeachhouse.com; The Strand; dm $25, d $60-90) has a variety of accommodation options – all filled with charm. The weathered, self-contained 'Hutel' ($90) is worth every cent. The Summit Lodge has commanding views and the best dining-room table you've ever seen. This property is popular with groups, so be sure to book your bed well in advance.

WESTLAND TAI POUTINI NATIONAL PARK

Literally the biggest highlights of the Westland Tai Poutini National Park are the Franz Josef and Fox Glaciers. Nowhere else at this latitude do glaciers come so close to the ocean.

The glaciers' staggering development is largely due to the West Coast's endless rain. Snow falling in the glaciers' broad accumulation zones fuses into clear ice at 20m depth then surges down valleys. The glaciers are particularly steep, so the ice travels a long way before it finally melts.

The rate of descent is mind-blowing: wreckage of a plane that crashed into Franz Josef in 1943, 3.5km from the terminal face, made it down to the bottom 6½ years later – a speed of 1.5m per day. Big Franz usually advances about 1m per day, but sometimes ramps it up to 5m per day, over 10 times faster than the Swiss Alps' glaciers.

Some say Franz Josef is the superior ice experience, and while it's visually more impressive, the walk to Fox is shorter, more interesting and gets you closer to the ice (80m versus 200m).

Beyond the glaciers, the park's lower reaches harbour deserted Tasman Sea beaches, rising up through colour-splashed podocarp forests to NZ's highest peaks. Virtually unique in the world, diverse ecosystems huddle next to each other in interdependent ecological sequence. Seals frolic in the surf as deer sneak through the forests. The resident endangered

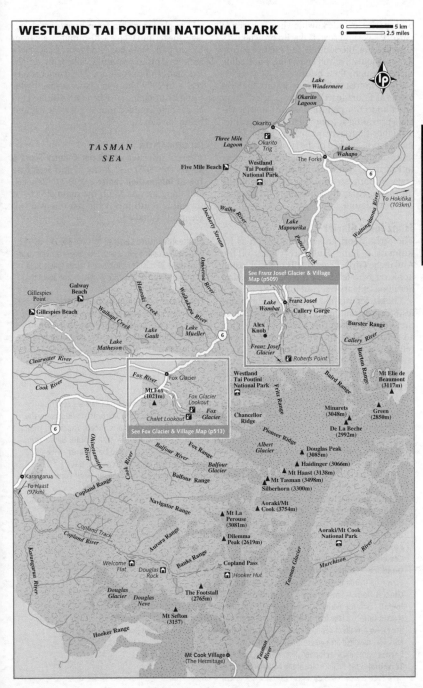

WESTLAND TAI POUTINI NATIONAL PARK

0 ————————— 5 km
0 ————————— 2.5 miles

THE WEST COAST

Lake Windermere

Okarito Lagoon

Okarito

Three Mile Lagoon

Okarito Trig

Lake Wahapo

The Forks

TASMAN SEA

Westland Tai Poutini National Park

Five Mile Beach

To Hokitika (103km)

Waitangitaona River

Waiho River

Docherty Stream

Ohinerima River

Lake Mapourika

Peters Creek

Gillespies Point

Galway Beach

Gillespies Beach

Hauraki Creek

Waikakapo River

Waikapi Creek

Lake Gault

Lake Mueller

Clearwater River

Lake Matheson

Cook River

See Franz Josef Glacier & Village Map (p509)

Lake Wombat

Franz Josef

Callery Gorge

Alex Knob

Franz Josef Glacier

Roberts Point

Burster Range

Callery River

Mt Elie de Beaumont (3117m)

Burton Range

Baird Range

Fox River

Fox Glacier

Mt Fox (1021m)

Fox Glacier Lookout

Chalet Lookout

Fox Glacier

Westland Tai Poutini National Park

Fritz Range

Chancellor Ridge

Pioneer Ridge

Minarets (3048m)

De La Beche (2992m)

Green (2850m)

Balfour River

Fox Range

Cook River

Ohinemataki River

Karangarua

To Haast (97km)

Balfour Glacier

Balfour Range

Navigator Range

Copland Range

Aurora Range

Albert Glacier

Douglas Peak (3085m)

Haidinger (3066m)

Mt Haast (3138m)

Mt Tasman (3498m)

Silberhorn (3300m)

Aoraki/Mt Cook (3754m)

Mt La Perouse (3081m)

Dilemma Peak (2619m)

Aoraki/Mt Cook National Park

Tasman Glacier

Murchison River

Copland Track

Copland River

Karangarua River

Welcome Flat

Douglas Rock

Ranks Range

Copland Pass

Hooker Hut

Douglas Glacier

Douglas Neve

The Footstall (2765m)

Mt Sefton (3157m)

Hooker Range

Tasman River

Mt Cook Village (The Hermitage)

THE WEST COAST

bird species include kowhiowhio, kakariki (a parrot), kaka and rowi (Okarito brown kiwi), as well as kea, the South Island's native parrot. Kea are inquisitive and endearing, but feeding them threatens their health.

Heavy tourist traffic often swamps the twin towns of Franz Josef and Fox Glacier, 23km apart and both picture-postcard tourist villages providing accommodation and facilities at higher-than-average prices. Franz is the more action-packed of the two, but Fox has a more subdued alpine charm. From December to February, visitor numbers can get a little crazy in both, so consider travelling in the off season (May to September) for cheaper accommodation.

Franz Josef Glacier

The early Maori knew Franz Joseph as Ka Roimata o Hine Hukatere (Tears of the Avalanche Girl). Legend tells of a girl losing her lover who fell from the local peaks, and her flood of tears freezing into the glacier.

The glacier was first explored by Europeans in 1865, Austrian Julius Haast naming it after the Austrian emperor. The glacier started advancing again in 1985 after a period of retreat (see the boxed text, below).

The glacier is 5km from Franz Joseph village, the terminal face a 40-minute walk from the car park. Both Fox and Franz glacier faces are roped off to prevent people being caught in icefalls and river surges. The danger is very real – in 2009 two tourists were killed after being hit by falling ice when they ventured too close. Take a guided tour to get close without being too close.

INFORMATION

There's internet at **Glacier Country Tours & Kayaks** (☎ 03-752 0230; 20 Cron St) and **Scott Base Tourist Information Centre** (☎ 03-752 0288; SH6), and there's an ATM on the main street – if travelling south this is the last one you will see until Wanaka.

Alpine Adventure Centre (☎ 0800 800 793, 03-752 0793; www.scenic-flights.co.nz; SH6) Books activities and screens the 20-minute *Flowing West* movie (adult/child $12/6) on a giant screen. Nice visuals, shame about the 1980s soundtrack.
Franz Josef visitor information centre (☎ 03-752 0796; www.glaciercountry.co.nz, www.doc.govt.nz; SH6; ☼ 8.30am-6pm Dec-Feb, to 5pm Mar-Nov) Also the regional DOC office; has an excellent display, weather information and tramping-condition updates.

GLACIERS FOR DUMMIES

During the last ice age (15,000 to 20,000 years ago) the Franz Josef and Fox Glaciers reached the sea; in the ensuing thaw they may have crawled back further than their current positions. In the 14th century a mini ice age descended and for centuries the glaciers advanced, reaching their greatest extent around 1750. The terminal moraines from this time are still visible. Since then the West Coast's twin glaciers have both ebbed and advanced on a cyclic basis, and since 1985 it's estimated the Franz Josef glacier has actually advanced by up to 70 cm per day.

If you get rained in during your time in glacier country, here are a few glacier-geek conversation starters for the pub.

Ablation zone – where the glacier melts.
Accumulation zone – where the snow collects.
Bergschrund – a large *crevasse* in the ice near the glacier's starting point.
Blue ice – as the accumulation zone (*névé*) snow is compressed by subsequent snowfalls, it becomes *firn* and then *blue ice.*
Crevasse – a crack in the glacial ice formed as it crosses obstacles while descending.
Dead ice – isolated chunks of ice left behind when a glacier retreats.
Firn – partly compressed snow en route to becoming *blue ice.*
Glacial flour – finely ground rock particles in the milky rivers flowing off glaciers.
Icefall – when a glacier descends so steeply that the upper ice breaks into a jumble of ice blocks.
Kettle lake – a lake formed by the melt of an area of isolated *dead ice.*
Moraine – walls of debris formed at the glacier's sides (lateral moraine) or end (terminal moraine).
Névé – snowfield area where *firn* is formed.
Seracs – ice pinnacles formed, like *crevasses,* by the glacier rolling over obstacles.
Terminal – the final ice face at the bottom of the glacier.

Medical centre (☎ 03-752 0700; SH6; ☽ 8.30am-5pm Mon-Fri, doctor 9am-noon Mon-Thu, summer only)
Postal agency (cnr Condon St & SH6) At the Mobil station.

ACTIVITIES
Independent Walks

Several glacier viewpoints are accessed from the glacier car park, including **Sentinel Rock** (20 minutes return) and the **Ka Roimata o Hine Hukatere Walk** (1½ hours return), leading you to the terminal face.

Other longer walks include the **Douglas Walk** (one hour return), off the Glacier Access Rd, which passes moraine from the 1750 advance and Peter's Pool, a small 'kettle lake'. The **Terrace Track** (30 minutes return) is an easy amble over bushy terraces behind the village with Waiho River views. The rough **Callery-Waiho Walk** (four hours return) heads off from the village to the Douglas Swing Bridge, optionally extending to Roberts Point. The **Alex Knob Track** (eight hours return) runs from the Glacier Access Rd to the 1303m peak of Alex Knob. Look forward to three glacier lookouts and views to the coast (cloud cover permitting).

Check out the glacier in the morning or evening, before the cloud cover sets in or after it lifts. Expect fewer tour buses as well.

Guided Walks & Helihikes

Small group walks with experienced guides (boots, jackets and equipment supplied) are

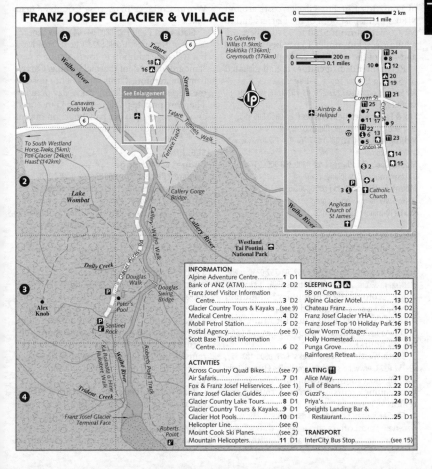

FRANZ JOSEF GLACIER & VILLAGE

offered by **Franz Josef Glacier Guides** (☎ 0800 484 337, 03-752 0763; www.franzjosefglacier.com). Half-/full-day walks are $105/160 per adult (slightly cheaper for children). Full-day trips have around six hours on the ice, half-day trips up to two hours. Full-day ice-climbing trips ($250 including training) and three-hour heli-hikes with two hours on the ice ($390) are also available. Helihikes take you further up the glacier to explore blue-ice caves, seracs and pristine ice formations.

Aerial Sightseeing

Forget sandflies and mozzies. The buzzing you're hearing is more likely to be helicopters and planes cruising past the glaciers and Aoraki (Mt Cook). Most flights also include a snow landing. A 20-minute flight to the head of Franz Josef or Fox Glacier costs around $180. Flights past both of the glaciers and to Mt Cook cost from $280 to $340. These are adult prices; kids under 15 pay between 60% and 70% of the adult price. Shop around.

Recommended operators are all situated on SH6 in Franz Josef Village:

Air Safaris (☎ 0800 723 274, 03-752 0716; www.air safaris.co.nz)

Fox & Franz Josef Heliservices (☎ 0800 800 793, 03-752 0793; www.scenic-flights.co.nz)

Helicopter Line (☎ 0800 807 767, 03-752 0767; www. helicopter.co.nz)

Mount Cook Ski Planes (☎ 0800 368 000, 03-752 0714; www.mtcookskiplanes.com)

Mountain Helicopters (☎ 0800 369 432, 03-752 0046; www.mountainhelicopters.co.nz) Also runs shorter 10-minute flights ($105).

Other Activities

Take a guided kayak trip on Lake Mapourika (7km north of Franz) with **Glacier Country Tours & Kayaks** (☎ 0800 423 262, 03-752 0230; www.glacierkayaks.com; 20 Cron St; 3hr tours $90). Trips include ecological commentary, mountain views and a serene channel detour. The family deal ($220) is good value for Mum, Dad and two kids. You can also hire kayaks ($60 for 2½ hours).

South Westland Horse Treks (☎ 0800 187 357, 03-752 0223; www.horsetreknz.com; Waiho Flats Rd; treks $60-240), 5km south of town, runs one- to six-hour equine excursions across farmland and remote beaches.

Glacier Valley Eco-Tours (☎ 0800 999 739; www.glaciervalley.co.nz) offers three-hour walks ($65) that are leisurely and packed with local

knowledge. Similar walks are offered down at Fox Glacier.

Faster-paced (and certainly noisier) are the four-wheeled outings from **Across Country Quad Bikes** (☎ 0800 234 288, 03-752 0123; www.across countryquadbikes.co.nz Air Safaris Bldg, SH6). Rockin' and rollin' rainforest quad-bike trips (two hours, adult/child $150/75) are joined by off-road adventures on 8WD Argo amphibious vehicles (one hour, $60). Heliquad adventures (2½ hours, $395) traverse the mountains and coastline by air before taking on a remote West Coast beach.

Join **Glacier Country Lake Tours** (☎ 0800 525 386, 03-752 0244; www.laketours.co.nz; 64 Cron St) on placid Lake Mapourika. Fishing and ecotour excursions (1½ hours, $98) are both available.

Hire bikes from Chateau Franz, Glow Worm Cottages or Across Country Quad Bikes.

Glacier Hot Pools (☎ 0800 044 044; www.glacierhot pools.co.nz; Cron St; adult/child $22.50/16; ☽ noon-10pm) is a welcome addition to town, setting a new standard for outdoor thermal bathing. Carved from the rainforest, this series of hot pools is the perfect après-hike or rainy-day activity. There are private pools ($40 per 45 minutes) and massages ($80 per half-hour) on offer if you want to really indulge.

SLEEPING
Budget & Midrange

Rainforest Retreat (☎ 0800 873 346, 03-752 0220; www. rainforestretreat.co.nz; 46 Cron St; unpowered/powered sites $22/30, dm $21-27, d $99-209; ☐ ☎) Campsites and dorms share first-rate facilities (including sauna and spa), and there are also en suite cottages and elevated self-contained 'tree houses' ($259 to $329) that sleep up to seven. The Monsoon Bar – motto: 'It rains, we pour' – is a social option on rainy days.

Chateau Franz (☎ 0800 728 372, 03-752 0738; www. chateaufranz.co.nz; 8 Cron St; dm $23-26, d $53-95; ☐ ☎) When the weather outside is frightful, this is a decent option to hide away for the night. Nice extras like a spa pool, free soup, popcorn and DVDs aplenty are a nice touch. The ramshackle feel of the place, with mismatched everything, will either appeal or annoy – take your pick.

Glow Worm Cottages (☎ 0800 151 027, 03-752 0172; www.glowwormcottages.co.nz; 27 Cron St; dm from $24, d $55-110; ☐ ☎) After a day of adventure, relax at this quiet haven trimmed by native ferns. Be back by 6pm and there's free vegie soup on offer. If the rain settles in, chill out in the spa or with a good DVD.

Franz Josef Glacier YHA (☎ 03-752 0754; www.yha. co.nz; 2-4 Cron St; dm $28-30, s $55, d $75-96; 🖳 🛜) A high-standard, colourful place with over 100 beds (linen provided) in 36 heated rooms. There are three family rooms, a Kiwi sauna (keep your bathers on please) and the rainforest at the back door. The needs of travellers with disabilities are well catered for.

Franz Josef Top 10 Holiday Park (☎ 0800 467 897, 03-752 0735; www.mountainview.co.nz; SH6; unpowered/ powered sites $42, d $55-300; 🖳 🛜) This recently tidied up campground has a sleeping option for every budget. Plenty of tent sites pepper the property, while slightly posher units will suit the alfresco-sleeping disinclined.

Alpine Glacier Motel (☎ 0800 757 111, 03-752 0226; www.alpineglaciermotel.com; 14 Cron St; d $150) Standard motel offerings for the dorm-weary traveller in a U-shaped configuration. Two units have spas, and king-sized units have cooking facilities.

Top End
58 on Cron (☎ 0800 662 766, 03-752 0627; www.58oncron. co.nz; 58 Cron St; d $170-225; 🛜) No prizes for the name, but with trendy, dark-chocolate decor and flash furniture, this new bush-side spot is one of FJ's classier motels.

Punga Grove (☎ 0800 437 269, 03-752 0001; www.punga grove.co.nz; 40 Cron St; d $190-250) Priding itself on top-notch service, Punga is a quality motel on the rainforest verge. Split-level self-contained family units mix it up with spacious studios. Splurge on a luxury rainforest studio with leather couches.

Glenfern Villas (☎ 0800 453 633, 03-752 0054; www. glenfern.co.nz; SH6; d $205-260) A handy 3km out of the tourist hubbub, these self-contained designer villas sit amid nikau palms and have private decks and gardens. Pour yourself a glass of wine and toast your holiday and the nearby alpine peaks.

Holly Homestead (☎ 03-752 0299; www.holly homestead.co.nz; SH6; d $260-420) Guests are welcomed with fresh home baking at this luxury wisteria-draped 1920s B&B. Five gorgeous rooms all have en suites, and a new guest suite features a private deck just made for early evening wine-tasting. Kids under 12 will have to sleep in the car.

EATING & DRINKING
Full of Beans (☎ 03-752 0139; SH6; mains $5-17; 🕑 7.30am-late) This cruisy cafe offers superlative

coffee – the best in town – and tasty home-made cakes from go to whoa. Good-value lunch offerings include burgers, Thai curry and chicken pies that are a particular favourite among locals.

Speights Landing Bar & Restaurant (☎ 03-752 0229; SH6; mains $10-30; 🕑 7.30am-late) From early to late, under the market umbrellas at this cosy pub-cafe is the place to be. Burgers, soups, pasta and wraps give you plenty of opportunity to overhear other travellers going gaga over the glaciers.

Guzzi's (☎ 03-752 0085; 18 Cron St; pizza $12-24; 🕑 noon-late; V) Choose your own toppings – including plenty of vegie options – at this bright yellow and purple pizza and takeaway shack with a matching cute-as-a-button delivery van. Plan to take away; Guzzi's is sans seats.

Alice May (☎ 03-752 0740; cnr Cowan & Cron Sts; mains $12-30; 🕑 4pm-late) At this rustic Nordic-style lodge transplanted from somewhere near the Arctic Circle there's no smorgasbord on offer, but plenty of meaty meals like pork ribs and venison stew. Park yourself on a rustic barstool for happy hour (4pm to 7pm).

Priya's (☎ 03-752 0060; 70 Cron St; mains $14-20; 🕑 lunch 11.30am-2.30pm, dinner 5pm-late) If you're in dire need of a curry fix this is your best option in town. The atmosphere leaves much to be desired – harsh overhead fluorescent lights and a minibar with all the ambience of a takeaway-shop waiting area. The food on the other hand is full of flavour. Mouth- (and eye-) watering curries are the house speciality and they don't disappoint.

GETTING THERE & AROUND
InterCity (☎ 03-365 1113; www.intercity.co.nz) has daily buses south to Fox Glacier ($11, 40 minutes, departing 8am and 5.05pm) and Queenstown ($62, eight hours, departing 8am); and north to Nelson ($84, 10 hours, departing 9.15am). Book at the YHA or Scott Base Tourist Information Centre; buses depart from the YHA.

Atomic Shuttles (☎ 03-349 0697; www.atomictravel. co.nz) has daily services south to Queenstown ($50, 7¼ hours, departing 10.15am) via Fox Glacier ($15, 30 minutes), and north to Greymouth ($30, 2½ hours, departing 2.40pm), leaving from the Alpine Adventure Centre.

Glacier Valley Eco Tours (☎ 03-752 0699; www.glacier valley.co.nz) runs shuttles to the glacier car park (return trip $12.50).

Naked Bus (www.nakedbus.com) runs north to Hokitika and Greymouth, and south to Queenstown stopping at Fox Glacier, Haast and Wanaka.

Fox Glacier

Sir William Fox was NZ's prime minister, and anything but a shy and retiring type, when he named the river of ice in 1872. Even if you've already been to Franz Josef Glacier, it's still worth checking out Fox. Take a walk around beautiful Lake Matheson, and dive into Fox's array of glacier-related attractions: glacier walks, flights and travellers wearing thermals.

INFORMATION

There are no banks or ATMs in town; the BP petrol station is the last fuel stop until Haast, 120km south. Get online at the Internet Outpost, beside the Helicopter Line office.

DOC South Westland Area Office (☎ 03-751 0807; SH6; ☺ 9am-noon & 1-4.30pm Mon-Fri) No longer a general visitor information centre, but has the usual DOC information and weather/track updates.

Fox Glacier Guiding (☎ 0800 111 600, 03-751 0825; www.foxguides.co.nz; SH6) Books most activities and transport; includes postal services and a money exchange.

Fox Glacier Health Centre (☎ 03-751 0836, after hours 027 464 1193; SH6) The nurse here can patch you up on weekday mornings from 9am to noon and most afternoons, and there's a doctor from 2pm to 5pm on Thursdays.

ACTIVITIES

Independent Walks

It's 1.5km from Fox Village to the glacier turn-off, a further 2km to the car park. The terminal face is 30 to 40 minutes' walk from there, finishing 80m from the ice.

Short walks around the glacier include the **Moraine Walk** (over a major 18th-century advance) and **Minnehaha Walk**. The **River Walk** extends to the **Chalet Lookout Track** (1½ hours return) leading to a glacier lookout.

About 6km down Cook Flat Rd is the turn-off to **Lake Matheson**. It's an hour's walk around the lake, and at the far end (on a clear day) are improbably photogenic views of Mt Tasman and Mt Cook reflected in the water. Visit during the early morning or when the sun is low in the late afternoon.

Follow Cook Flat Rd for its full 21km (unsealed for the final 12km) to the remote black

sand and rimu forest of **Gillespies Beach**, from where there's a dune track to **Galway Beach** (3½ hours return). The **Mt Fox Walk** (1021m above sea level; eight hours return), off the highway 3km south of town, makes for a challenging hike, only recommended for well-equipped trampers.

Glacier Walks & Helihikes

Guided walks (equipment provided) are organised by **Fox Glacier Guiding** (☎ 0800 111 600, 03-751 0825; www.foxguides.co.nz; SH6). Half-day walks cost $95/75 per adult/child; full-day walks are $145 (over-13s only). If you're fit, consider the full-day stroll, which takes you further up the glacier; BYO lunch.

Helihikes cost $395 per person, while a day-long introductory ice-climbing course costs $235 per adult. From October to April, there are also easy-going two-hour interpretive walks to the glacier (adult/child $49/35). Longer guided helitrek adventures are also available.

Skydiving & Aerial Sightseeing

With Fox Glacier's backdrop of Southern Alps, rainforest and ocean, it's hard to imagine a better place to jump out of a plane. **Skydive Glacier Country** (☎ 0800 751 0080, 03-751 0080; www.skydiving.co.nz; Fox Glacier Airfield, SH6, Fox Glacier Village) is a professional outfit that challenges Isaac Newton with thrilling leaps from 12,000ft ($295) or 9000ft ($245). Digitise your terror with a DVD/photograph package ($180/35). Smile as you scream.

Aerial sightseeing costs at Fox parallel those at Franz Josef. The recommended operators are all on SH6 in Fox Glacier Village:

Fox & Franz Josef Heliservices (☎ 0800 800 793, 03-751 0866; www.scenic-flights.co.nz)

Helicopter Line (☎ 0800 807 767, 03-751 0767; www.helicopter.co.nz)

Mount Cook Ski Planes (☎ 0800 368 000, 03-752 0714; www.mtcookskiplanes.com; SH6, Franz Josef Village)

Mountain Helicopters (☎ 03-751 0045; www.mountainhelicopters.co.nz)

Southern Lakes Helicopters (☎ 0800 800 732, 03-751 0803; www.heli-flights.co.nz)

SLEEPING

Ivory Towers (☎ 03-751 0838; www.ivorytowerslodge.co.nz; Sullivan Rd; sites $18, dm/s $28/55, d $70-85, f $95 🖳 ☜) This top-notch hostel is tidy, laid-back and colourful, draped in greenery and endowed with good facilities. The friendly staff is accommodating and the tidy facilities will entice you to extend your stay.

Fox Glacier Holiday Park (☎ 0800 154 366, 03-751 0821; www.foxglacierholidaypark.co.nz; Kerrs Rd; unpowered/powered sites $34/38, cabins $62, d $95-194; 🖳 🛜) This park has a range of different sleeping options to suit all budgets. Recent renovations have improved what was already a good choice. New showers, a playground for the kiddies and barbecue facilities are a welcome addition.

our pick **Lake Matheson Motels** (☎ 0800 452 2437, 03-751 0830; www.lakematheson.co.nz; Cook Flat Rd; d $135-190) This unassuming property has been finished off with a real sense of care. From the outside it looks pretty ordinary, but inside the rooms come into their own. The owners have continued to pour profits back into the facilities. You'll find ultratidy rooms with up-market amenities that contradict the midrange price.

Heartland Hotel Fox Glacier (☎ 03-751 0839; cnr SH6 & Cook Flat Rd; d $140-180; 🖳 🛜) This freshly re-booted hotel was in fact the first building in Fox Glacier. Decaying exteriors have been spruced up to complement the tidy interior. Some of the older rooms are still on the to-do

list – be sure to have a look before you shell out.

Rainforest Motel (☎ 0800 724 636, 03-751 0140; www.rainforestmotel.co.nz; Cook Flat Rd; d $145-150) Rustic log cabins on the outside with coolly neutral decor on the inside; now with the added attraction of Sky TV for those rainy West Coast days.

Fox Glacier Lodge (☎ 03-751 0888; www.foxglacier lodge.co.nz; Sullivan Rd; d $180-230) Beautiful timber adorns the exterior and interior of this attractive property. It has that mountain chalet vibe that'll look great in your slide show. Top-notch facilities and a home-away-from-home feel seal the deal.

Reflection Lodge (☎ 03-751 0707; www.reflection lodge.co.nz; Cook Flat Rd; d $190-210; 🖳) Funky '60s ski-lodge style with flash new bathrooms. Blur your eyes a little – well, maybe a bit more – and you could almost be in an old James Bond movie. The West Coast's friendliest little dog brings you back to supercomfy reality.

Westhaven (☎ 03-751 0084; www.thewesthaven. co.nz; SH6; d $195-215; 🖳) These architecturally precise suites are a classy combo of corrugated steel and local stone amid burnt red and ivory

THE WEST COAST

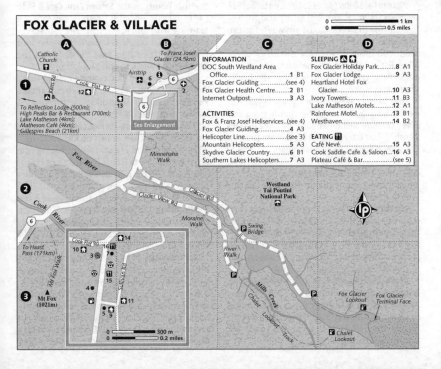

FOX GLACIER & VILLAGE

INFORMATION	
DOC South Westland Area Office	1 B1
Fox Glacier Guiding	(see 4)
Fox Glacier Health Centre	2 B1
Internet Outpost	3 A3

ACTIVITIES	
Fox & Franz Josef Heliservices	(see 4)
Fox Glacier Guiding	4 A3
Helicopter Line	(see 3)
Mountain Helicopters	5 A3
Skydive Glacier Country	6 B1
Southern Lakes Helicopters	7 A3

SLEEPING 🏠🏘	
Fox Glacier Holiday Park	8 A1
Fox Glacier Lodge	9 A3
Heartland Hotel Fox Glacier	10 A3
Ivory Towers	11 B3
Lake Matheson Motels	12 A1
Rainforest Motel	13 B1
Westhaven	14 B2

EATING 🍴	
Café Nevé	15 A3
Cook Saddle Cafe & Saloon	16 A3
Plateau Café & Bar	(see 5)

walls. The deluxe king rooms have spas and there are comfy chairs for relaxing outside.

EATING & DRINKING

our pick **Matheson Café** (☎ 03-751 0878; Lake Matheson Rd; mains $10-17; 7.30am-late) Near the shores of Lake Matheson, this cafe does everything right: slick interior design, inspiring mountain views, strong coffee and upmarket Kiwi fare. Get your sketchpad out and while away the afternoon.

High Peaks Bar & Restaurant (☎ 03-751 0131; Cooks Flat Rd; bar meals $14-24, restaurant mains $27-34; 6pm-late) Angled towards Mt Cook, High Peaks combines eating and drinking. Forget the calories, this is enjoyment food: steaks, pastas, fish and chips, roasts, chunky soups and stews. Have another Monteith's and wait for the clouds to part.

Café Nevé (☎ 03-751 0110; SH6; mains $15-30; 8am-late) Smart choices on the menu include pizza and award-winning ways with beef and lamb, and there's home-baked cookies and cakes available throughout the day. If you're going for a wander grab one of the takeaway focaccia sandwiches.

Plateau Café & Bar (☎ 03-751 0058; cnr Sullivan Rd & SH6; mains $18-30; 10am-late) Buzzy and sophisticated (for the West Coast anyway), Plateau combines snappy service with an eclectic menu, boutique Kiwi beers and an excellent wine list. Chill out on the wisteria-covered deck, or if the sky is grey, enjoy the lovely warm atmosphere inside.

Cook Saddle Cafe & Saloon (☎ 03-751 0700; SH6; meals $18-30; 8am-late) The menu trots out every cowboy cliché – anyone for Lone Ranger Lamb? – but later at night it's a more than an OK corral for locals and travellers.

GETTING THERE & AROUND

Most buses stop outside the Fox Glacier Guiding building.

InterCity (☎ 03-365 1113; www.intercity.co.nz) runs daily buses north to Franz Josef ($11, 40 minutes, departing 8.30am and 3.25pm), the morning bus continuing to Nelson ($85, 11 hours). Daily southbound services run to Queenstown ($58, 7½ hours, departing 8.45am).

Atomic Shuttles (☎ 03-349 0697; www.atomictravel. co.nz) runs daily to Franz Josef ($15, 30 minutes, departing 9am and 1.55pm), continuing to Greymouth ($35, 3¼ hours). Southbound buses run daily to Queenstown ($45, 6½ hours, departing 11am).

Fox Glacier Shuttle (☎ 0800 369 287) will drive you to Lake Matheson or Fox Glacier and allow you enough time for a stroll ($12 return, minimum two people).

Naked Bus (www.nakedbus.com) runs north to Franz Josef Glacier, Hokitika and Greymouth, and south to Queenstown, stopping at Haast and Wanaka.

SOUTH TO HAAST

About 26km south of Fox Glacier, along SH6, the **Copland Valley** is the western end of the **Copland Track**. Treat yourself to one of the best pay-offs of any walk in Aotearoa. Six to seven hours tramping will get you to the **Welcome Flat DOC Hut** (per night $15), where thermal springs bubble just metres from the hut door. Backcountry Hut Passes don't apply here, but you can buy tickets at any West Coast DOC office or visitor information centre.

Popular with Haast–Fox cyclists and Copland Track trampers, the **Pine Grove Motel** (☎ 03-751 0898; SH6; unpowered & powered sites $20, d $50-90) is 8km south of the trailhead. Units are affordable and in reasonable shape.

Like some sort of gigantic edible aquarium, the fish ponds at the **Salmon Farm Café & Shop** (☎ 03-751 0837; SH6; meals $10-32; 8am-4pm) are teaming with lunch, err, fish. The cafe serves salmon-filled omelettes, platters, pastas and fresh pâté. It's $1 to feed the fish, but the plump little buggers don't look hungry.

There's a basic **DOC camping ground** (adult/ child $6/1.50) 70km south of Fox Glacier at **Lake Paringa**, a tranquil trout-filled lake surrounded by swaying forest boughs.

The historic **Haast–Paringa Cattle Track** hoofs off from SH6 (just south of Lake Paringa, 43km northeast of Haast) and emerges on the coast by the Waita River, just north of Haast. The track's first leg to **Blowfly Hut** (four hours return) is an easy-going half-day hike. The full walk takes three days, stopping at **Maori Saddle Hut** and **Coppermine Creek Hut**. The track can get muddy – check conditions and pay hut fees ($5 per night) at the DOC Haast visitor information centre (opposite).

Lake Moeraki, 31km north of Haast, is another rippling fishing lake. An easy 40-minute walk from here brings you to **Monro Beach**, a west-facing gravel beach copping the full Tasman Sea force. There's a breeding colony of Fiordland crested penguins here (July to December) and fur seals. **Wilderness Lodge Lake Moeraki** (☎ 03-750 0881; www.wildernesslodge.co.nz;

SH6; d incl breakfast & dinner $780-980) is a spectacular oasis of ecofriendly accommodation in a vibrant wilderness setting. The rooms are plush, the included meals are bordering on decadent and the activities on offer are top notch. Pricy, yes, but the quality of services is worth every cent.

About 5km south of Lake Moeraki is the much-photographed **Knights Point** (named after a surveyor's dog) where the Haast road was eventually opened in 1965. Deep waters just offshore and uninterrupted Antarctic swells make this a favoured eatery for seals, birds and sometimes whales.

Ship Creek, 15km north of Haast, has a lookout platform and two interesting interpretive walks: the **Dune Lake Walk** (30 minutes return) and the **Kahikatea Swamp Forest Walk** (20 minutes return).

HAAST REGION
The Haast region is a major nature refuge, with enormous stands of rainforest thriving alongside extensive wetlands. The area's kahikatea and flame red rimu forests, swamps, sand dunes, seal and penguin colonies, bird life and sweeping beaches ensured its inclusion in the Southwest New Zealand (Te Wahipounamu) World Heritage Area. Birding buffs might see fantails, bellbirds, kereru (NZ pigeons), falcons, kaka, kiwi and morepork.

Haast
pop 300
Some 120km south of Fox Glacier, Haast crouches around the mouth of the wide Haast River in three distinct pockets: Haast Junction, Haast Village and Haast Beach. After the jaw-dropping scenery of the glaciers or Haast Pass, the area is a functional service hub, but local operators are waiting on your call to transport you deeper into some of NZ's most spectacular wilderness areas.

Haast is also big on whitebaiting; see the boxed text, p503.

INFORMATION
The **DOC Haast Visitor Information Centre** (☎ 03-750 0809; www.doc.govt.nz; cnr SH6 & Jackson Bay Rd; 9am-6pm Nov-Mar, to 4.30pm Apr-Oct) has wall-to-wall regional information and every half-hour it screens the all-too-brief Haast landscape film *Edge of Wilderness* (adult/child $3/free).

TOURS
Take a hair-tousling 2½-hour 'sea to mountain' ecojetboat trip on the wild Waiatoto River with **Waiatoto River Safaris** (☎ 03-750 0780; www.riversafaris.co.nz; Jackson Bay Rd; adult/child $199/129; trips 10am, 1pm & 4pm), departing from the Waiatoto River Bridge 30km south of Haast. **Haast River Safari** (☎ 0800 865 382, 03-750 0101; www.haastriver.co.nz; adult/child $132/55; cruises 9am & 2pm), based in the Red Barn between Haast Village and the visitor information centre, runs more leisurely 90-minute covered-jetboat cruises on the Haast River.

Round About Haast (☎ 03-750 0890; www.roundabouthaast.co.nz; tours $65-135) runs local boat and minibus tours. Out on Jackson Bay you'll see seals, dolphins and (seasonally) penguins, while the bus takes you to beaches, estuaries and forests, with walks and local folklore thrown in.

SLEEPING
Wilderness Accommodation (☎ 03-750 0029; www.wildernessaccommodation.co.nz; Marks Rd; dm/s $24/40, d $65-90;) Your best budget option in town is everything a hostel should be. It's cheap, the facilities are clean, the dorm rooms are spacious and the staff friendly. The large leafy glassed-in courtyard is a fine place to catch up on your journal when the 'Wet Coast' weather doesn't play ball.

Haast Beach Holiday Park (☎ 0800 843 226, 03-750 0860; haastpark@xtra.co.nz; Jackson Bay Rd; unpowered & powered sites $28, dm $25, d $45-110) Close to the beach about 15km south of Haast, this caravan park has old but functional facilities. The Hapuka Estuary Walk (p516) is across the road.

Haast Lodge (☎ 0800 500 703, 03-750 0703; www.haastlodge.com; Marks Rd; sites $30, dm/d $25/60;) There's a bit much beige and shiny lino going on, but the functional rooms here are spotlessly clean and the whole shebang is very well managed.

Aspiring Court Motel (☎ 0800 500 703, 03-750 0777; www.aspiringcourtmotel.com; Marks Rd; d $79-140;) Just as clean and well-run as the associated Haast Lodge – these comfortable motel units are just next door.

Heartland World Heritage Hotel (☎ 0800 696 963, 03-750 0828; www.world-heritage-hotel.com; SH6; d $184-260;) This sprawling hotel is staking its claim as the most comfy place to stay in town. The Frontier Café is open for lunch (mains $12 to $22) and dinner (mains $18 to $32), and the bar has big live-sport-friendly TVs and pool tables. Live bands occasionally rouse the friendly and laid-back locals.

ourpick Collyer House (☎ 03-750 0022; www.collyer house.co.nz; Jackson Bay Rd; s/d incl cooked breakfast $250) This gem of a place has thick bathrobes, quality linen, beach views and an owner as passionate about photography as she is about ensuring her guests have a fantastic stay. This all adds up to make Collyer House an indulgent and aesthetic choice. Follow the signs off SH6 for 12km down Jackson Bay Rd.

EATING & DRINKING

Fantail Café (☎ 03-750 0055; Marks Rd; breakfast & lunch $10-15, dinner $15-27; ☺ 8am-9pm) With cafe fodder like toasted sandwiches, and fish and chips the speciality – what you see is what you get. Nothing fancy, but the grub is good and the views, especially from the table out front, is awesome.

Hard Antler (☎ 03-750 0034; Marks Rd; dinner $18-27; ☺ dining 11am-9pm) Raucous as hell on a Friday night, and all the better for it. An expanding array of deer antlers, pool tables and darts, and robust pub grub (lamb, steak and pork) make this an unpretentious spot.

GETTING THERE & AWAY

InterCity (☎ 03-365 1113; www.intercity.co.nz) and **Atomic Shuttles** (☎ 03-322 8883; www.atomictravel. co.nz) buses stop at the visitor informa- tion centre on their Fox to Wanaka runs. **TrackNET** (☎ 0800 483 262, 03-249 7777; www.tracknet. net) also swings through linking Queenstown and Greymouth.

Naked Bus (www.nakedbus.com) runs north to the glaciers, Hokitika and Greymouth, and south to Queenstown, stopping at Wanaka.

Haast to Jackson Bay & Cascade River

From Haast Junction a side road heads to Jackson Bay, with numerous wilderness walks along the way.

Near Okuru is the **Hapuka Estuary Walk** (20 minutes return), an information-packed boardwalk loop winding its way through a sleepy whitebait sanctuary.

The road continues west from Arawhata Bridge to the isolated fishing hamlet of **Jackson**

Bay. Southern Alps views from here are unfor- gettable, and there are colonies of Fiordland crested penguins near the road. Migrants ar- rived here in 1875 under a doomed assisted- immigration scheme, their farming fantasies mercilessly shattered by never-ending rain and the lack of a wharf, not built until 1938. Today fishing boats bob on the bay, gathering lobster, tuna, tarakihi and gurnard.

Dining at the **Craypot** (☎ 03-750 0035; meals $7-20; ☺ noon-5pm Sep-Easter, to 8pm in summer), is more than a classic Kiwi dining experience – it's verging upon essential. So fresh it was swimming yesterday fish and chips, whitebait sandwiches and mixed grills are served up in an absolute waterfront location. The rustic old caravan with views of snowy peaks is pretty hard to beat.

Walks at Jackson Bay include the **Smooth- water Bay Track** (three hours return) and the **Wharekai Te Kau Walk** (40 minutes return) to Ocean Beach, a tiny bay that hosts pounding waves and some interesting rock formations.

HAAST PASS

Turning inland from Haast towards Wanaka (145km, 2½ hours), SH6 snakes alongside the Haast River, climbing up to Haast Pass and Mt Aspiring National Park. As you move inland the vegetation thins away until you reach the 563m pass – snow country covered in tussock and scrub. There are some stunning waterfalls en route (especially if it's been raining), tum- bling down just minutes from the highway: **Fantail** and **Thunder Creek** falls are worth a look. There's also the **Bridle Track** (1½ hours one- way) between the pass and Davis Flat. See the DOC booklet *Haast Pass/Tioripatea Highway: Walking Opportunities* ($1).

The Haast Pass road (Tioripatea, meaning 'Clear Path' in Maori) opened in 1965; before then Maori walked this route bringing West Coast greenstone to the Makarora River in Otago. The pass (and river and township) take their European name from geologist Julius Haast, who passed through in 1863.

There are food and fuel stops at Makarora and Lake Hawea. If you're driving north, check your fuel gauge: Haast petrol station is the last one before Fox Glacier, 120km north.

Christchurch & Canterbury

The good people of Canterbury are probably only half-joking when they say it would be good if the South Island was a separate country, but when you consider the region surrounding them you can understand their parochial pride and confidence.

Christchurch is undoubtedly one of New Zealand's most liveable cities, combining an easy-going provincial charm with the emerging energy and verve of a metropolis. Modern bars and restaurants complement Gothic architecture, and locals know how lucky they are to blend all the attractions of a city with the relaxed ambience of a small town.

To the east, the volcanically uplifted hills of Banks Peninsula conceal a wealth of hidden bays and isolated beaches, forming a backdrop for kayaking and wildlife cruises with an eventual sunset return to the Francophile attractions of Akaroa. To the north are the up-and-coming vineyards of the Waipara Valley and the take-it-easy spa town of Hanmer Springs. Westwards the preferred weekend backyard of active Cantabrians builds quickly from the well-ordered farms of the Canterbury Plains to the rough-and-tumble wilderness of the Southern Alps.

On February 22, 2011 Christchurch was struck by a 6.3 earthquake, the second within six months, causing multiple fatalities and extensive damage to buildings in the CBD, including Christchurch Cathedral.

CHRISTCHURCH & CANTERBURY

HIGHLIGHTS

- Exploring the history of **Christchurch** (p519) by tram, river punt or two legs
- Marvelling at the views of the Mackenzie Country from atop **Mt John** (p562)
- Discovering funky restaurants and friendly locals in raffish **Lyttelton** (p540)
- Taking a soothing soak at Lake Tekapo's **Alpine Springs & Spa** (p563)
- Negotiating the outer reaches of **Banks Peninsula** (p542) by bike, kayak and boat
- Tramping in the shadow of NZ's highest peak in **Aoraki/Mt Cook National Park** (p566)
- Being surprised by the size of the Canterbury Plains on a balloon flight from **Methven** (p554)

- Telephone code: 03
- www.christchurchnz.com
- www.mtcooknz.com

CHRISTCHURCH & CANTERBURY

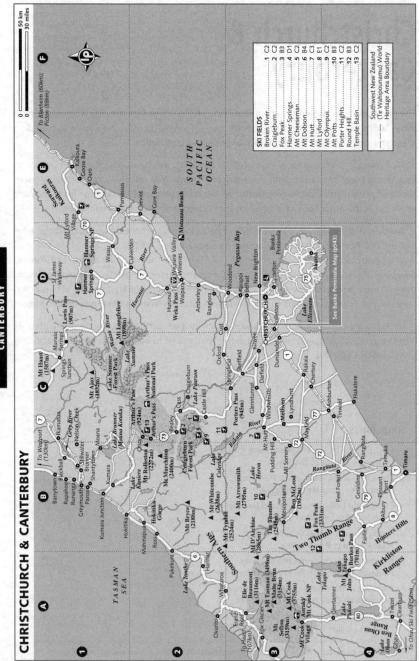

SKI FIELDS

Broken River..................................1	C2
Craigieburn....................................2	C2
Fox Peak...3	B3
Hanner Springs.............................4	D1
Mt Cheeseman..............................5	C2
Mt Dobson.....................................6	B4
Mt Hutt..7	C3
Mt Lyford......................................8	E1
Mt Olympus...................................9	C2
Mt Potts.......................................10	B3
Porter Heights.............................11	C2
Round Hill....................................12	B3
Temple Basin...............................13	C2

Southwest New Zealand
(Te Wahipounamu) World
Heritage Area Boundary

Climate
Canterbury is one of NZ's driest regions. Moisture-laden westerlies from the Tasman Sea hit the Southern Alps and dump their rainfall on the West Coast before reaching the eastern South Island. The result? Canterbury has an annual rainfall of only 750mm, compared with a soaking 5000mm on the West Coast.

Getting There & Around
Christchurch has an international airport serviced by several domestic airlines flying to key destinations around NZ.

Bus and shuttle operators scurry along the east coast, connecting Canterbury's coastal (and near-coastal) settlements with northern destinations such as Picton and Nelson, and southern towns like Dunedin. Operators connect Christchurch to Arthur's Pass, the West Coast and Mt Cook.

Rail options for east-coast and coast-to-coast travel are provided by Tranz Scenic; its *TranzAlpine* service connects Christchurch and Greymouth, and its *TranzCoastal* trains chug north to Picton, with connections to the North Island. For information on getting to and from Christchurch, see p539.

CHRISTCHURCH

pop 344,100
Traditionally the most English of the NZ cities, Christchurch is now embracing the increasingly multicultural nature of urban NZ society. Change is coming through more diverse immigration, and a cosmopolitan tinge is being added to the city's earlier conservatism. There's still plenty to remind visitors of Christchurch's English past though, with a grand Anglican cathedral rising from a stately square, punts gliding down the sleepy Avon River, and trams rattling contentedly along Worcester St. But scratch the surface a little, and a more dynamic Christchurch is reflected in the restored laneways and squares around Lichfield St, High St's hip cafe scene, and locals' immense pride in their beautifully maintained Arts Centre.

HISTORY
Though it still has the Gothic architecture and wooden villas bequeathed by its founders, Christchurch has strayed from the original urban vision. The settlement of Christchurch in 1850 was an ordered Church of England enterprise, and the fertile farming land was deliberately placed in the hands of the gentry. Christchurch was meant to be a model of class-structured England in the South Pacific, not just another scruffy colonial outpost. Churches were built rather than pubs, and wool made the elite of Christchurch wealthy. In 1862, Christchurch was incorporated as a very English city, but its character slowly changed as other migrants arrived; new industries followed, and the city forged its own aesthetic and cultural notions. Like Auckland and Wellington, the city's economic and sporting rivals in the north, Christchurch is becoming a more multicultural society, and increasing immigration is alerting parochial Cantabrians to the wider world around them.

ORIENTATION
Cathedral Sq is the centre of town and is punctuated by the spire of ChristChurch Cathedral. The western inner city is dominated by the Botanic Gardens.

Christchurch is compact and easy to walk around, but slightly complicated by the river twisting through the centre and constantly crossing your path.

Colombo St runs north–south through Cathedral Sq and is the main shopping strip. Southeast the up-and-coming area around Lichfield St and High St has interesting boutiques, galleries, cafes and restaurants. Oxford Tce also features good eating and drinking near the Avon River.

Maps
Christchurch's i-SITE distributes free tourist maps, and maps and road atlases.

Map World (Map p522; ☎ 03-374 5399; www.mapworld.co.nz; cnr Manchester & Gloucester Sts) has NZ city and regional maps, guidebooks, and trampers' topographic maps.

INFORMATION
Bookshops
Arts Centre Bookshop (Map p522; ☎ 03-365 5277; www.booksnz.com; Arts Centre, 2 Worcester St) Excellent NZ-oriented titles.
Scorpio Books (Map p522; ☎ 03-379 2882; 79 Hereford St) Travel, history and Maori culture.
Smith's Bookshop (Map p522; ☎ 03-379 7976; 133 Manchester St) Secondhand book nirvana.
Whitcoulls (Map p522; ☎ 03-379 4580; 111 Cashel St)

CHRISTCHURCH & CANTERBURY FACTS

Eat Amid the up-and-coming restaurant scene in Lyttelton (p541)

Drink A beer from one of Canterbury's microbreweries, such as Brew Moon (p547), Three Boys or the Wigram Brewing Company

Read *The World's Your Lobster* by Lyttelton local and well-known newspaper-columnist Joe Bennett

Listen to The occasional negative comment when you tell Christchurch folk you actually quite like Auckland

Watch The mighty Canterbury Crusaders Super 14 Rugby team at Christchurch's Holy Grail pub (p537)

Swim at Akaroa, with the dolphins (p545), or soak at Hanmer Springs Thermal Reserve (p548)

Festival Free street performances at Christchurch's World Buskers Festival (p531)

Tackiest tourist attraction Christchurch's floral clock (p528)

Go green At the ecofriendly Onuku Farm Hostel (p546)

Emergency

Ambulance, fire service & police (☎ 111)

Police station (Map p522; ☎ 03-363 7400; cnr Hereford St & Cambridge Tce) There is also a police kiosk in Cathedral Sq.

Internet Access

The going rate in Christchurch is around $3 an hour. Most accommodation also offers internet services, including wi-fi.

dub dub dub (Map p522; 140 Gloucester St; 📶)

E Blah Blah (Map p522; 77 Cathedral Sq; 📶) Also offers mobile-phone rentals, wi-fi, and luggage storage.

high://NET (Map p522; 230 High St; 📶)

Internet Resources

Christchurch & Canterbury (www.christchurchnz.com) Official tourism website for the city and region.

Christchurch.org.nz (www.christchurch.org.nz) Operated by the Christchurch City Council.

Local Eye (www.localeye.info) Online regional portal.

Laundry

Central City Laundrette (Map p522; ☎ 03-379 6622; 247 Armagh St; wash & dry per load $10; 🕐 7.30am-5.30pm Mon-Fri & 9am-4pm Sat)

Media

Cityscape (www.cityscape-christchurch.co.nz) Entertainment and events magazine available in inner-city cafes and retailers.

Indulge (www.brownbear.co.nz) Eating, drinking and shopping.

Press (www.stuff.co.nz) Christchurch's newspaper, published Monday to Saturday.

Medical Services

24 Hour Surgery (Bealey Ave Medical Centre; Map p522; ☎ 03-365 7777; cnr Bealey Ave & Colombo St; 🕐 24hr) North of town; no appointment necessary.

After-hours pharmacy (Map p522; ☎ 03-366 4439; 931 Colombo St; 🕐 6-11pm Mon-Fri, 9am-11pm Sat & Sun, plus public holidays) Beside the 24 Hour Surgery.

Christchurch Hospital (Map p522; ☎ 03-364 0640, emergency dept 03-364 0270; 2 Riccarton Ave)

Money

The intersection of Hereford and Colombo Sts is home to major banks.

Travelex i-SITE (Map p522; Cathedral Sq); United Travel (Map p522; cnr Colombo & Armagh Sts)

Post

Post office (Map p522; 736 Colombo St)

Tourist Information

Adventure Centre (Map p522; ☎ 0800 847 486, 03-366 0302; www.adventures.net.nz; 69 Cathedral Sq; 🕐 9am-8pm Mon-Fri, 10am-6pm Sat & Sun) One-stop adventure booking centre with branch at 94 Worcester St (Map p522; 🕐 9am-6pm).

Airport information desks (☎ 03-353 7774) Open to meet all incoming flights for booking transport and accommodation.

Automobile Association (AA; Map p522; ☎ 03-964 3650; Unit 19/293 Durham St N; 8.30am-5pm Mon-Fri)

Christchurch i-SITE (Map p522; ☎ 03-379 9629; www.christchurchnz.com; Cathedral Sq; 🕐 8.30am-5pm, later in summer) Transport, activities and accommodation.

Department of Conservation (DOC; Map p522; ☎ 03-371 3700; www.doc.govt.nz; Level 4, Torrens House, 195 Hereford St; 🕐 8.30am-5pm Mon-Fri) Has information on South Island national parks and walkways.

SIGHTS
Cathedral Square

Cathedral Sq is where locals and tourists meet, giving the city's flat centrepiece a lively bustle. Featured here is the 18m-high *Metal Chalice* **sculpture**, created by Neil Dawson to acknowledge the new millennium.

ChristChurch Cathedral (Map p522; ☎ 03-366 0046; www.christchurchcathedral.co.nz; Cathedral Sq; admission free; 🕐 8.30am-7pm Oct-Mar, 9am-5pm Apr-Sep) was consecrated in 1881 and has an impressive rose window, wooden-ribbed ceiling and tile work

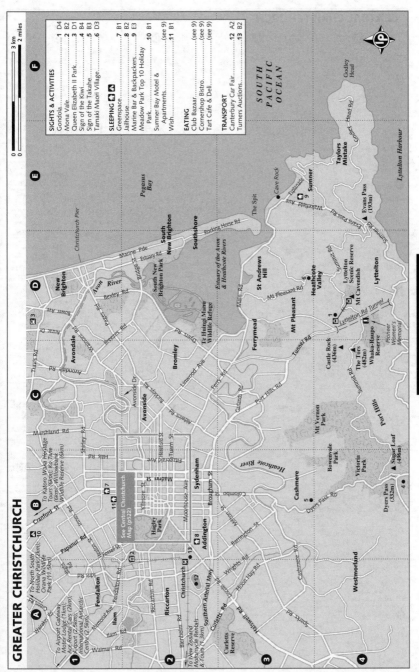

GREATER CHRISTCHURCH

CHRISTCHURCH & CANTERBURY

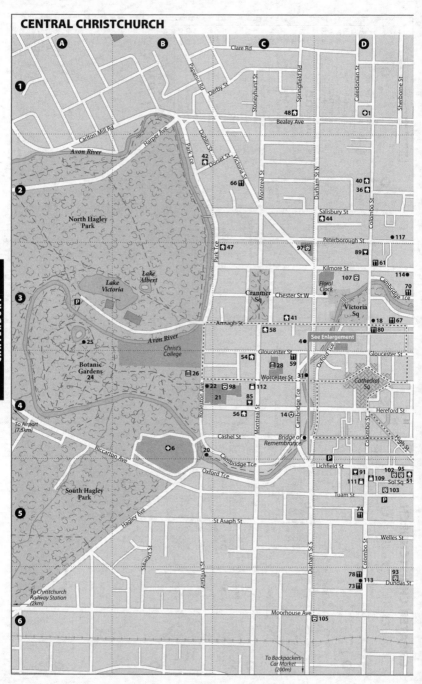

CENTRAL CHRISTCHURCH

CHRISTCHURCH & CANTERBURY

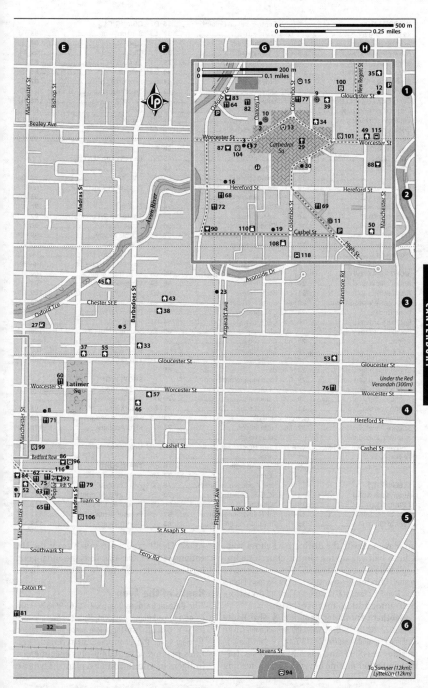

emblazoned with the distinctive Fylfot Cross. Climb halfway up the Gothic church's 63m-high **spire** (adult/child/family $5/2/10, tokens at the visitor centre). Guided 45-minute tours (☼ tours 11am & 2pm Mon-Fri, 11am Sat & 11.30am Sun) are by donation. Self-guided audio tours cost $10.

Southern Encounter Aquarium & Kiwi House (Map p522; ☎ 03-359 0581; www.southernencounter.co.nz; Cathedral Sq; adult/child/family $17/7/41; ☼ 9am-5pm), is beside the i-SITE and has eels, seahorses, turtles and other marine life with specific feeding times. Don't expect too much from the **kiwi enclosure** (☼ 10.30am-4.30pm), as the endangered birds are hypersensitive to sound and light.

Banks of the Avon
The **Botanic Gardens** (Map p522; ☎ 03-941 8999; www.ccc.govt.nz/parks/botanicgardens; Rolleston Ave; admission free; ☼ grounds 7am-1hr before sunset, conservatories 10.15am-4pm; ℗) comprise 30 riverside hectares planted with 10,000-plus specimens of indigenous and introduced plants. There are

conservatories and thematic gardens to explore, lawns to sprawl on, and a cafe at the **Botanic Gardens visitors centre** (Map p522; ☎ 03-941 8999; Rolleston Ave; ☷ 9am-4pm Mon-Fri, 10.15am-4pm Sat & Sun). Get the kids active in the playground adjacent to the cafe. **Guided walks** (adult/child $5/free; ☷ walks 1.30pm Sep-Apr) depart daily from the Canterbury Museum (right), or you can ride around the gardens in the electric **'Caterpillar'** train. Hop-on, hop-off **tickets** (www.gardentour.co.nz; adult/concession $15/6; ☷ 10am-4pm) are valid for two days and include a commentary.

Mona Vale (Map p521; ☎ 03-348 9660; www.monavale.co.nz; 63 Fendalton Rd; admission free; ☷ 9.30am-5pm Oct-Apr, to 4pm May-Sep; ℗) is a charming Elizabethan-style homestead on 5.5 hectares of landscaped gardens, ponds and fountains. Dine in the cafe inside the riverside homestead, wander the gorgeous grounds, or take a half-hour Avon River **punt** (per person $20; ☷ Oct-Apr). Tasty picnic hampers (per couple $27 to $65) need to be ordered by noon the day prior. Mona Vale is just northwest of Hagley Park by bus 9.

Arts Centre

The former Canterbury College site (later Canterbury University), with its enclave of Gothic Revival buildings, is now the excellent **Arts Centre** (Map p522; www.artscentre.org.nz; 2 Worcester St; admission free; ℗), where arts and craft outlets share the premises with cinemas, a live theatre, restaurants and cafes. Visit the workshop and gallery of **Te Toi Mana** (☎ 03-366 4943; toimanamaori@xtra.co.nz) for traditional and contemporary Maori carving and design. **Visually Maori** (☎ 03-379 7855; visually.maori@xtra.co.nz) also showcases interesting Maori art.

There's a good **market** (☷ 10am-4pm Sat & Sun) selling craft and gourmet food items, often with live entertainment and plenty of cheap food stalls.

The **Arts Centre visitors centre** (Map p522; ☎ 03-363 2836; 2 Worcester St; ☷ 9.30am-5pm) is inside the clock tower on Worcester St. The helpful staff can provide information on free **guided tours** (☷ 10.30am-3.30pm) of the complex, including the **Rutherford's Den** (www.rutherfordsden.org.nz; ☷ 10am-5pm) exhibit celebrating the life and work of Ernest Rutherford, the NZ physicist who first split the atom in 1917.

Tramway

Trams were introduced to Christchurch streets in 1905 but were discontinued as a means of transport 50 years later. Restored **trams** (☎ 03-366 7830; www.tram.co.nz; adult/child $15/5; ☷ 9am-9pm Nov-Mar, to 6pm Apr-Oct) now operate a 2.5km inner-city loop that takes in local attractions and shopping areas. Tickets are valid for 48 hours and can be bought from the driver. Expect the odd live jazz band to join you in summer and look forward to travelling through the glass atrium at Cathedral Junction. One tram is fitted out as a **restaurant** (☎ 03-366 7511; dinner packages $73-125; ☷ 7.30pm-late Sep-May, from 7pm Jun-Aug).

At the time of writing, plans were progressing to extend the existing line to incorporate High St and Cashel St in time for the 2011 Rugby World Cup.

You can get combo tickets (adult/child/family $35/12/80) for the tram and gondola (p527) – purchase from the tram or gondola staff. If you're planning on punting on the Avon (left) similar combo tickets including the tram (adult/child $30/15) are also available. A triple pass for tram, gondola and punting (adult/child/family $50/20/120) incorporates three of Christchurch's iconic attractions.

Canterbury Museum

The absorbing **Canterbury Museum** (Map p522; ☎ 03-366 5000; www.canterburymuseum.com; Rolleston Ave; donation $2; ☷ 9am-5pm Apr-Sep, to 5.30pm Oct-Mar) has a wonderful collection of items of significance to NZ. Highlights include the Maori gallery, with some stunning *pounamu* (greenstone) pieces on display; the coracle in the Antarctic Hall used by a group shipwrecked on Disappointment Island in 1907; and a wide array of stuffed bird life from the Pacific and beyond. Don't miss the statuesque Emperor penguin. Guided tours (donations appreciated) run from 3.30pm to 4.30pm on Tuesday and Thursday. Kids will enjoy the interactive displays at Discovery (admission $2).

Christchurch Art Gallery

Set in an eye-catching metal-and-glass construction built in 2003, the city's **art gallery** (Map p522; ☎ 03-941 7300; www.christchurchartgallery.org.nz; cnr Worcester & Montreal Sts; admission free; ☷ 10am-5pm Thu-Tue, to 9pm Wed) has an engrossing permanent collection divided into historical, 20th-century and contemporary galleries, plus temporary exhibitions featuring NZ artists. **Guided tours** (free; ☷ tours 11am Mon-Sun, plus 2pm Sat & Sun & 7.15pm Wed) provide an excellent overview, or you can hire an audio guide ($5) for a self-guided tour. Ask at i-SITE (p520) for the *Cultural Precinct* brochure detailing other nearby galleries.

International Antarctic Centre

The **International Antarctic Centre** (off Map p521; ☎ 0508 736 4846, 03-353 7798; www.iceberg.co.nz; 38 Orchard Rd; adult/child/family $55/36/145, audio guide $6; ☼ 9am-7pm Oct-Mar, to 5.30pm Apr-Sep; Ⓟ) is part of a huge complex built for the administration of the NZ, US and Italian Antarctic programs. See penguins and learn about the icy continent via historical, geological and zoological exhibits, including videos of life on Scott Base. There's also an aquarium of creatures gathered under the ice in McMurdo Sound, and an 'Antarctic Storm' chamber where you get a firsthand taste of minus 18°C wind chill (check at reception for 'storm' forecasts). Admission includes unlimited rides on the **Hägglund**, an all-terrain vehicle that negotiates an outdoor adventure course. An optional extra is the **Penguin Backstage Pass** (adult/child $20/15) taking visitors behind the scenes of the Penguin Encounter. Transport options include the City Flyer airport bus (p539) – it's just a short walk from the main terminal – or the Penguin Express shuttle departing Cathedral Sq on the hour from 9am (adult/child return $6/3).

Science Alive!

Inside the city's old train station, **Science Alive!** (Map p522; ☎ 03-365 5199; www.sciencealive.co.nz; 392 Moorhouse Ave; adult/child/family $14/10/45; ☼ 10am-5pm; Ⓟ) is crammed with ever-changing interactive exhibits, from optical illusions to things that children can push, pull and climb. Kids will love the climbing wall and NZ's highest vertical slide. If the sprogs get bored with reality, movie make-believe (p537) is right next door.

Wildlife Reserves

Orana Wildlife Park (off Map p521; ☎ 03-359 7109; www.oranawildlifepark.co.nz; McLeans Island Rd; adult/child/family $24/8/56; ☼ 10am-5pm; Ⓟ) has an excellent walk-through native bird aviary, a nocturnal kiwi house and a reptile exhibit featuring the wrinkly tuatara. Most of the grounds are devoted to Africana, including lions, rhinos, giraffes, zebras, lemurs, oryx and cheetahs, and Asia is well represented with an array of Sumatran tigers. Guided walks start from the native bird feed at 10.45am and around the African lion enclosure at 2.30pm. Check the website – under 'Exciting Encounters' – for other regular walks and daily feeding times. The Orana Wildlife Park shuttle departs Cathedral Sq at 10am and 1pm daily.

MAORI NZ: CHRISTCHURCH & CANTERBURY

Only 5% of NZ's Maori live on the South Island: the south was settled a few hundred years later than the north, with significant numbers coming south only after land became scarcer on the North Island. Before that, Maori mostly travelled to the south in search of moa, fish and, of course, West Coast *pounamu* (greenstone).

The major *iwi* (tribe) of the South Island is Ngai Tahu (www.ngaitahu.iwi.nz), ironically now one of the country's wealthiest, because it is so much richer in land (per person) than the North Island tribes. In Christchurch, as in other cities, there are urban Maori of many other *iwi* as well.

Ko Tane (☎ 03-359 6226; www.kotane.co.nz; 60 Hussey Rd; dancing-tour-dinner package adult/child $110/54; ☼ packages 5.30pm & 6.30pm Oct-May, 6.30pm Jun-Sep) at Willowbank Wildlife Reserve (opposite) features traditional dancing, a wildlife tour and buffet dinner. Forego the wildlife tour and/or dinner for a cheaper night out – the performance only is $48/24 per adult/child. Another option is to incorporate a paddle in a traditional *waka* (Maori canoe) with Katoro Waka Heritage Tours (opposite), also based at Willowbank.

The Chronicles of Uitara performance at the **Tamaki Maori Village** (Map p521; ☎ 03-366 7333; www.christchurchinfo.co.nz; adult/child under 5yr/child 5-15yr $126/free/73) brings to life early interaction between Maori and European settlers. The evening is set in a recreated Maori village, and concludes with a traditional *hangi* (Maori feast).

More contemporary is the bone carving done by the 'Bone Dude', John Fraser, who trains visitors to do their own carving at his studio (p528), and the work at the Te Toi Mana gallery (p525) at the Arts Centre.

As well as at Christchurch's Canterbury Museum (p525), you'll unearth Maori artefacts at museums in Akaroa (p543) and Okains Bay (Maori & Colonial Museum; p544).

CHRISTCHURCH IN...

Two Days

After breakfast at one of **High Street's cafes** (p535), jump on the **tramway** (p525) and do a full loop to get your bearings. Disembark at the **Arts Centre** (p525) to explore the historic area's galleries, and recharge with lunch at **Dux de Lux** (p536). Walk off your meal in the pretty **Botanic Gardens** (p524), and head to the **Antigua Boatsheds** (below) for a late-afternoon **Avon punt** (below). End the day eating and bar-hopping around the interesting nooks and crannies of **Poplar Street** and **SOL Square** (p536).

On day two, check out the **Canterbury Museum** (p525) and the **Christchurch Art Gallery** (p525), before heading out of town to ride the **gondola** (below) and do some mountaintop walking. In the evening, jump on a bus to the excellent restaurants at **Lyttelton** (p540) or **Sumner** (p534).

Four Days

Follow the two-day itinerary, then head to **Akaroa** (p542) to explore its wildlife-rich harbour, and the peninsula's beautiful outer bays. On day four it's time for **shopping** (p538) in funky High St, before chilling at the **International Antarctic Centre** (opposite) or paddling a Maori canoe and enjoying a traditional Maori feast at **Willowbank Wildlife Reserve** (below).

Willowbank Wildlife Reserve (off Map p521; ☎ 03-359 6226; www.willowbank.co.nz; 60 Hussey Rd; adult/child under 5yr/child 5-15yr/family $25/free/10/65; ⏲ 9.30am-dusk; Ⓟ), about 6km north of the city, is another good animal reserve focusing on native NZ animals and hands-on enclosures with alpacas, wallabies and deer. Tours are held several times a day, and Willowbank's escorted after-dark tours are a good opportunity to see NZ's national bird, the kiwi. Evening Maori performances also take place here (see opposite). Another area of Willowbank is **Katoro Waka Heritage Tours** (off Map p521; ☎ 0800 528 676; www.katoro.co.nz; adult/child from $70/35), blending Maori folklore with a paddle in a traditional *waka* (war canoe) and a visit to a *pa* (Maori village).

Gondola

The **gondola** (Map p521; ☎ 03-384 0700; www.gondola.co.nz; 10 Bridle Path Rd; return adult/child/family $24/10/59; ⏲ 10am-9pm; Ⓟ) whisks you from the Heathcote Valley terminal to the cafe-restaurant complex on Mt Cavendish (500m) in 10 minutes. Expect great views over Lyttelton Harbour and towards the Southern Alps. Paths lead to the Crater Rim Walkway, or you can gondola up and cycle down (see right). Lyttelton bus 28 travels here. Secure a combo deal (adult/child/family $35/12/80) if you're planning on also riding the tram (see p525).

ACTIVITIES

Christchurch's most popular activities are gentler than the adrenaline-fuelled pursuits of Queenstown and Wanaka. Christchurch is better suited to punting down the Avon River, cycling through the easy terrain of Hagley Park, or negotiating the walking trails at Lyttelton Harbour. The city's best swimming is at Sumner and New Brighton beaches, and there is good skiing at nearby Mt Hutt (p86).

Boating

Dating from 1882, the photogenic green-and-white **Antigua Boatsheds** (Map p522; ☎ 03-366 5885; www.boatsheds.co.nz; 2 Cambridge Tce; kayaks per hr from $10, rowboats/paddleboats per 30min/hr $20/30; ⏲ 9am-5pm) rents out various self-propelled vessels for independent Avon River exploration. There's also an excellent **cafe** (mains $10-20; ⏲ 7am-5pm), which is a great spot for brunch or lunch. The boatsheds are the starting point for **Punting on the Avon** (☎ 03-366 0337; www.punting.co.nz; 30min trip adult/child $20/10; ⏲ 9am-6pm Oct-Apr, 10am-4pm May-Sep), where someone else does all the work during a half-hour return trip in a flat-bottomed boat. There is another departure point for punting from the landing stage at the Worcester St bridge. A combination ticket (adult/child $30/15) is available that includes the Tramway (p525).

Cycling

City Cycle Hire (☎ 0800 424 534, 03-377 5952; www.cyclehire-tours.co.nz; half/full day $25/35) will deliver bikes to where you're staying. Mountain bikes (half/full day $30/45) will get you nicely off road. It also offers day trips (adult/child $95/50) on the Little River Rail Trail (p528) and you can pedal downhill from the gondola

THE SLOW ROAD TO LITTLE RIVER

The Little River Rail Trail will eventually traverse 45km from the Christchurch suburb of Hornby to the Banks Peninsula hamlet of Little River. At the time of writing, all sections excluding a 14km stretch were open. See www.littleriverrailtrail.co.nz for the latest information. Join the trail 20km from Little River at Motukarara for the best of the ride. Ask at the Christchurch i-SITE (p520) about bike rental and public transport options. Rail trail day trips including transport can be booked with City Cycle Hire (p527) and Natural High (below). Natural High can also rent out bikes and offer advice for multiday self-guided cycling trips incorporating the Little River Rail Trail.

terminal (p527) on a mountain bike ($50). Price includes the gondola ride up the mountain. Bookings are essential.

Natural High (☎ 0800 444 144; 03-982 2966; www.naturalhigh.co.nz) rents touring and mountain bikes (per day/week from $40/154), and can advise on guided and self-guided bicycle touring through Canterbury and the South Island.

See p530 for details of two-wheeled guided city tours.

Walking

The i-SITE has information on Christchurch walks. Within the city are the **Riverside Walk** and various historical strolls, while further afield is the excellent clifftop walk to **Taylors Mistake** (2½ hours).

For great views of the city, take the walkway from the **Sign of the Takahe** (Map p521) on Dyers Pass Rd. The various 'Sign of the…' places in this area were originally roadhouses built during the Depression as rest stops. Now they vary from the impressive tearooms at the Sign of the Takahe to a simple shelter at the Sign of the Bellbird, and are referred to primarily as landmarks. This walk leads up to the **Sign of the Kiwi** (Map p521) through Victoria Park and then along Summit Rd to Scotts Reserve, with several lookout points along the way.

You can walk to Lyttelton on the **Bridle Path** (1½ hours), which starts at Heathcote Valley (take bus 28). The **Godley Head Walkway** (two hours return) begins at Taylors Mistake, crossing and recrossing Summit Rd, and offers beautiful views on a clear day.

The **Crater Rim Walkway** (nine hours) around Lyttelton Harbour goes some 20km from Evans Pass to the Ahuriri Scenic Reserve. From the gondola terminal on Mt Cavendish, walk to **Cavendish Bluff Lookout** (30 minutes return) or the **Pioneer Women's Memorial** (one hour return).

Other Activities

Queen Elizabeth II Park (Map p521; ☎ 03-941 6849; www.qeiipark.org.nz; Travis Rd, New Brighton; pool adult/child $5/3; 6am-9pm Mon-Fri, 7am-8pm Sat & Sun) has indoor pools (including a wave pool), waterslides, a gym and squash courts. Take bus 43. Closer to town is the **Centennial Leisure Centre** (Map p522; ☎ 03-941 7080; www.centennial.org.nz; 181 Armagh St; adult/child $5/3; 6am-9pm Mon-Fri, 7am-7pm Sat & Sun), with a heated indoor pool.

The closest **beaches** to the city are Waimairi, North Beach, New Brighton and South Brighton; buses 5, 49 and 60 head here. Sumner (see p534), to the city's southeast, is also popular with good restaurants (take bus 3), while further east at Taylors Mistake are some good **surfing** breaks.

Several **skiing** areas lie within a two-hour drive of Christchurch (see p86). Other active options accessible from Christchurch include cruising on Lyttelton Harbour (p541), rafting on the Rangitata River (p561), tandem skydiving, tandem paragliding, hot-air ballooning, jetboating the Waimakariri River and horse trekking. Inquire at i-SITE (p520).

Creative types should book a session with the **Bone Dude** (Map p522; ☎ 03-379 7530; www.thebonedude.co.nz; 229B Fitzgerald Ave; from $60; 9am-noon & 1-4pm Mon-Fri, Sat 10am-1pm). Allow three hours to craft your own bone carving in a creative and supportive environment. Owner John Fraser of Ngati Rangitihi ancestry provides a range of traditional Maori templates, or you can work on your own design. Sessions are limited to 12 carvers, so booking is highly recommended. It's a 15-minute walk from the city, or catch bus 70.

WALKING TOUR

Start your day in **High Street** (**1**; p538) with a leisurely breakfast at C1 Espresso (p536) before checking out nearby boutiques and galleries. Detour down Poplar St to explore the interesting shops of the **Lichfield Lanes** (**2**; p536) precinct, and make a note of which bars to return to after dark. Return to High St and continue to the intersection

WALKING TOUR

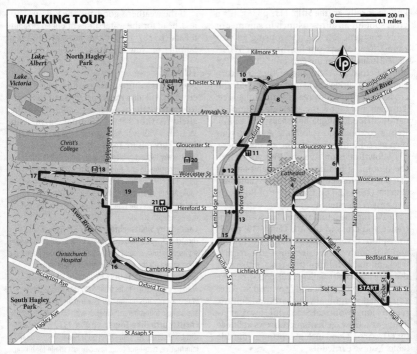

WALK FACTS

Start High St
Finish Dux de Lux
Distance About 5km
Duration Three hours to one day, depending on stops

of Manchester St and Lichfield St. Turn left into Lichfield St and then left again into His Lordship's Lane to explore the quirky design stores around **SOL Sq (3**; p536). Return to High St and follow the pedestrian mall to Colombo St. At the time of writing the tramway was being extended along High St, so maybe watch out for passing trams. Follow Colombo St to **Cathedral Sq (4**; p520). If you've got time, climb the spire of ChristChurch Cathedral (p520). From Cathedral Sq walk along Worcester St with the cathedral on your left. Turn left into the expansive glass atrium of **Cathedral Junction (5)**. Take care because it's also a regular thoroughfare for the **Christchurch Tramway (6**; p525). Cross Gloucester St and walk up pretty **New Regent Street (7)**, full of pastel-coloured Spanish Mission architecture.

Follow the tramline left down Armagh St, and then turn right up Colombo St. To your left is the greenery of **Victoria Square (8)**. In Victoria Sq admire the statues of Queen Victoria and the English explorer Captain James Cook. You are in NZ's most English city, after all.

Head left down the path opposite Oxford Tce and cross the bridge over the gentle **Avon River (9**; p524) to smell the time at the **Floral Clock (10)**. Return to the statue of James Cook and turn right to follow the banks of the river. At Armagh St turn right and cross the Armagh St Bridge. Turn left before the Belgian Beer Café (look for the Stella Artois sign) and, keeping the river on your left, follow the meandering path. Turn left at the Gloucester St bridge and turn right into Oxford Tce for a coffee or lunch stop at **Caffe Roma (11**; p536).

Carry on along Oxford Tce to the Worcester St Bridge where you can arrange to go **punting on the Avon (12**; p527). Back on dry land, follow Oxford Tce to reach the bars and restaurants known locally as **'the Strip' (13**; p536). It's a great spot for an alfresco lunch in summer or more energetic late-night carousing all year round. Keep an eye out for the Water Wheel on **Mill Island (14)** on the corner of Oxford Tce and Hereford St. At the end of 'the Strip' turn right at the **Bridge of Remembrance (15)** and cross Durham St S to reach Cambridge Tce. Turn left and follow the riverside path to the candy-striped **Antigua Boatsheds (16**; p527). Rent a rowboat to explore the Avon at your own pace. Punting can also be arranged here.

Follow Rolleston Ave and lose yourself in the blooming beauty of the **Botanic Gardens (17**; p524) before continuing to the **Canterbury Museum (18**; p525) on the corner of Rolleston Ave and Worcester St.

Leave the museum at the Hereford St entrance and cross to the **Arts Centre (19**; p525) to explore diverse galleries and workshops and – if you've timed it right – the regular weekend market. From the Arts Centre visit the **Christchurch Art Gallery (20**; p525) on the corner of Worcester St and Montreal St. After you've had your fill of visual arts and culture, return along Montreal St to while away a few hours with the excellent microbrews at **Dux de Lux (21**; p536). Good luck in scoring an outside table. You've earned it.

CHRISTCHURCH FOR CHILDREN

There's no shortage of kid-friendly sights and activities in Christchurch. If family fun is a priority, consider planning your travels around NZ's biggest children's festival, **KidsFest** (www.kidsfest.org.nz). It's held every July and is chock-full of shows, workshops and parties. The annual **World Buskers Festival** (opposite) in late January is also bound to be a hit.

For picnics and open-air frolicking, visit the **Botanic Gardens** (p524); there's a playground beside the cafe, and the kids will love riding on the Caterpillar train. Extend your nature-based experience with a **wildlife reserve** (p526), or take a ride on the **gondola** (p527), before burning off excess energy in a rowboat or paddleboat from the **Antigua Boatsheds** (p527). At the engrossing **International Antarctic Centre** (p526), kids will love the storm chamber, the Hägglund Ride, and (of course) the penguins. Educational and attention-getting factors are also high at the Discovery centre at **Canterbury Museum** (p525), and **Science Alive!** (p526); at the latter you can try your hand at minigolf on a glow-in-the-dark course.

If the weather's good and the kids are restless, head for the waterslides of **Queen Elizabeth II Park** (p528), or hit the **beaches** (p528) at Sumner or New Brighton.

TOURS

Numerous companies conduct tours of the city and will also transport you out to nearby towns (Lyttelton, Akaroa) and sites further afield (Arthur's Pass, Hanmer Springs, the Waipara Valley). Ask at the i-SITE (p520).

Canterbury Leisure Tours (☎ 0800 484 485, 03-384 0999; www.leisuretours.co.nz; tours from $100) Offers touring options in and around Christchurch, with everything from three-hour city tours to full-day Akaroa, Mt Cook, Arthur's Pass and Kaikoura outings (day tours are fine if you're short on time, but these places really deserve more in-depth visits).

Canterbury Sightseeing (☎ 027 321 0116; www. christchurchsightseeing.co.nz; tours from $260) Offer themed sightseeing tours around the region with a focus on food and wine, especially the vineyards of the Waipara Valley.

Canterbury Wine Tours (☎ 0800 081 155; www. waiparavalley.co.nz; tours from $75) Experience three Waipara vineyards on the half-day trip, or make a day of it and sample four different wineries with lunch ($119).

Christchurch Bike Tours (☎ 0800 733 257; www. chchbiketours.co.nz; tours from $35) Pedal around on fun, informative, two-hour tours in a city just made for biking. Tours depart from i-SITE, and bookings are recommended. Foodies should ask about the special 'Farmers Market' ($45) and 'Gourmet Christchurch' ($110) tours.

Christchurch Personal Guiding Service (Map p522; ☎ 03-379 9629; tours $15; ⏰ tours 10am & 1pm Oct-Apr, 1pm May-Sep) Nonprofit organisation offering informative, two-hour city walks. Get tickets from the i-SITE or the red-and-black kiosk in Cathedral Sq.

Christchurch Sightseeing Tours (☎ 0508 669 660, 03-366 9660; www.christchurchtours.co.nz; tours $40-46) Offers comprehensive half-day city tours year-round, a 3½-hour circuit of private gardens in spring and summer, and twice-weekly tours of heritage homes.

Hassle Free Tours (☎ 0800 427 753, 03-385-5755; www.hasslefree.co.nz; tours from $215) Options include a 4WD alpine safari, jetboating on the Waimakariri River, and visiting the location of Edoras from the Lord of the Rings trilogy. The scenery is stunning, but don't expect to see anything from the original set.

Ghost Walk (☎ 03-963 0870; tour $20; ⏰ tours 9pm Wed-Fri Oct-Mar, 8pm Wed-Fri Apr-Sep) Dr Aloysius Mort (actually an actor from the Court Theatre) leads spooky night-time strolls through the Gothic cloisters of the Arts Centre. Book at the i-SITE or the Court Theatre (p537).

Unlimited NZ (☎ 03-960 9119; www.unlimitednz. co.nz; adult/child $315/210) Day trips incorporating the

TranzAlpine train (p499) and tramping around Arthur's Pass.

FESTIVALS & EVENTS

Check at the i-SITE or www.bethere.co.nz for a comprehensive listing. Some notable regular events:

January
World Buskers Festival (☎ 03-377 2365; www.world buskersfestival.com) National and international talent entertain passers-by on the city's streets for 10 days in late January. Don't forget to put money in the hat.

January-March
Garden City SummerTimes (☎ 03-941 8999; www. summertimes.co.nz) Say g'day to summer at a huge array of outdoor events. Sweet as.

February-March
Festival of Flowers (☎ 03-365 5403; www. festivalofflowers.co.nz) Christchurch's gardens bloom with the ChristChurch Cathedral Carpet of Flowers and the Wearable Flowers Parade. From mid-February to mid-March.

March
Ellerslie Flower Show (☎ 03-379 4581; www. ellerslieflowershow.co.nz) Hagley Park comes alive in mid-March with NZ's biggest flower show.

July
Christchurch Arts Festival (☎ 03-365 2223; www. artsfestival.co.nz) Biennial midwinter arts event (held in odd-numbered years).

November
NZ Cup and Show Week (☎ 03-379 9629; www. nzcupandshow.co.nz) Includes the NZ Cup horse race, fashion shows, fireworks and the centrepiece A&P Show (Agricultural & Pastoral Show; www.theshow.co.nz) where the country comes to town. Also includes Southern Amp (www.southernamp.co.nz), the South Island's biggest outdoor music festival.

SLEEPING

Christchurch has many hostels, most of them within a 10-minute shuffle of Cathedral Sq. Several budget stalwarts are found around Latimer Sq, with a few smaller options to the east. There are also several well-established hostels near the Botanic Gardens.

Motels are clustered around Bealey Ave and Papanui Rd, north of the centre, and Riccarton Rd, west of town beyond Hagley Park. A number of top-end hotels are around Cathedral Sq.

Consider also staying in either Lyttelton (p540) or Sumner (p534). Both are pleasant waterfront 'burbs easily reached by public transport and with lots of good eating.

Budget
CAMPING
North South Holiday Park (off Map p521; ☎ 0800 567 765, 03-359 5993; www.northsouth.co.nz; cnr John's & Sawyers Arms Rds, SH1; unpowered/powered sites $30/32, cabins & units $52-117; ℗ ⬚ ⬚ ⬚) This place is just five minutes from the airport, and a good first night after picking up your campervan. Facilities include a pool, sauna and playground and newer motel units. Airport transfers are available.

Meadow Park Top 10 Holiday Park (Map p521; ☎ 0800 396 323, 03-352 9176; www.christchurchtop10. co.nz; 39 Meadow St; sites $37-46, cabins & chalets $64-126, motel units $136-176; ℗ ⬚ ⬚ ⬚) Wall-to-wall campervans here, while other accommodation ranges from cabins to motel units. Also well equipped for leisure activities, with an indoor pool, and games rooms and playground for the kids.

Closer to the city, Stonehurst (below) offers powered campervan sites.

HOSTELS
Stonehurst (Map p522; ☎ 0508 786 633, 03-379 4620; www.stonehurst.co.nz; 241 Gloucester St; campervan sites $35, dm $21, s from $50, d $55-65; ℗ ⬚ ⬚ ⬚) Versatility plus, with three buildings covering half a city block. There's everything from campervan sites to dorms and three-bedroom tourist flats (see p533). Decide in advance what you're after (eg don't get a poolside bunk room if you want some quiet times) and book ahead at peak times. The city centre is a short walk away.

Foley Towers (Map p522; ☎ 03-366 9720; foley .towers@backpack.co.nz; 208 Kilmore St; dm $23-26, d with/ without bathroom $64/58; ℗ ⬚ ⬚) Sheltered by well-established trees, Foley Towers provides well-maintained rooms encircling quiet inner courtyards and a friendly welcome in dorms warmed by underfloor heating.

Old Countryhouse (Map p522; ☎ 03-381 5504; www. oldcountryhousenz.com; 437 Gloucester St; dm $24-31, d $56-78; ℗ ⬚ ⬚) Well loved for its easygoing ambience, the Countryhouse features two separate villas with handmade wooden furniture, a reading lounge, and a lovely garden filled with native ferns. It's slightly further out than other hostels, but still only 1km east of Latimer Sq; bus 21 stops opposite.

Vagabond Backpackers (Map p522; ☎ 03-379 9677; vagabondbackpackers@hotmail.com; 232 Worcester St; dm/s/d $25/39/58; P 🖳 🛜) Small, friendly place reminiscent of a big share-house. There's an appealing garden, rustic but comfy facilities, and frisbees and barbecues reinforce that you're definitely in NZ.

Coachman Backpackers (Map p522; ☎ 0800 692 622, 03-377 0908; www.coachmanbackpackers.co.nz; 144 Gloucester St; dm/d from $25/66; 🖳 🛜) Centrally located in a heritage building with stained glass, timber panelling and a grand staircase. Most of the light-filled rooms come with a private bathroom.

Frauenreisehaus (Map p522; ☎ 03-366 2585; www.womanshostel.co.nz; 272 Barbadoes St; dm/s/tw $26/43/66; P 🖳) Sorry guys, this welcoming hostel is for women only. It offers free bikes and laundry, a huge selection of books and DVDs, two well-equipped kitchens and a garden full of fresh herbs. Reconfirm before you arrive.

our pick Jailhouse (Map p521; ☎ 0800 524 546, 03-982 7777; www.jail.co.nz; 338 Lincoln Rd; dm/s/d $26/49/70; P 🖳 🛜) Housed in an old prison that was built in 1874 and only decommissioned in 1999, the Jailhouse is one of NZ's most unique hostels. Twins and doubles are a bit on the small side (remember, it was a prison), but it's still an exceptionally well-run and friendly spot. The city is a pleasant 25-minute walk through Hagley Park, but the upside is that the Jailhouse is quieter than some central hostels.

Dorset House (Map p522; ☎ 03-366 8268; www.dorset house.co.nz; 1 Dorset St; dm/s/d $27/55/74; P 🖳 🛜) This 145-year-old wooden villa has a large regal lounge with log fire, pool table, DVDs, and beds instead of bunks. It's a short stroll to Hagley Park. From November to April it also rents out a couple of nearby self-contained flats (double/quad $89/142) sleeping up to four.

Chester Street Backpackers (Map p522; ☎ 03-377 1897; www.chesterst.co.nz; 148 Chester St E; dm/tw/d $27/58/60; P 🖳 🛜) This relaxed wooden villa is painted in bright colours and has a huge library in the sunny front room and the world-renowned 'Car-be-cue' in the boot of an old Ford Anglia. Chester St's friendly cat is a regular guest at barbecues. It's popular so try and book ahead. Across the road is the cosy self-contained Entwhistle Cottage (opposite).

Base Christchurch (Map p522; ☎ 0800 227 369, 03-982 2225; www.stayatbase.com; 56 Cathedral Sq; dm $27.50-31; 🖳 🛜) Slick and busy hostel pitching itself to young travellers out for social good times. It's right on Cathedral Sq with loads of modern facilities, including plusher women-only 'Sanctuary' dorms.

Central City YHA (Map p522; ☎ 03-379 9535; www.yha.co.nz; yha.christchurch@yha.co.nz; 273 Manchester St; dm $30, d with/without bathroom $95/80; 🖳 🛜) Comfortable bunks and beds; huge, spotless lounges and kitchens; a pool table; and helpful staff characterise this well-equipped, efficiently run hostel.

Also recommended:

Around the World Backpackers (Map p522; ☎ 03-365 4363; www.aroundtheworld.co.nz; 314 Barbadoes St; dm/d $22/50; P 🖳) Owned by a friendly family, Around the World gets rave recommendations for its 'Kiwiana' decor and sunny back garden.

Charlie B's (Map p522; ☎ 03-379 8429; www.charliebs.co.nz; 268 Madras St; dm $24.50-$27.50, s $55, d $60-65; 🖳 🛜) This spacious, centrally located option has a grassy lawn made for relaxation.

Thomas's Hotel (Map p522; ☎ 03-379 9536; www.gaanz.com; 36 Hereford St; dm $25-28, d $65-130; P 🖳 🛜) Well-run budget spot near the Arts Centre with a huge array of different rooms; a good option for groups.

New Excelsior Backpackers (Map p522; ☎ 0800 666 237, 03-366 7570; www.newexcelsior.co.nz; cnr Manchester & High Sts; dm $27-30; d with/without bathroom $75/63; 🖳 🛜) Well placed for the restaurants, nightlife and shopping around nearby High and Lichfield Sts.

Midrange
GUEST HOUSES AND B&BS

Greenspace (Map p521; ☎ 03-377 8832; www.greenspace.co.nz; 5/48 Trafalgar St, St Albans; d with/without breakfast $140/110; P 🖳) This ecofriendly and sunny bed and breakfast – the hosts actually live up the road – oozes privacy with its secluded garden location beside a stream and a stand of native bush. The decor includes retro Kiwiana touches, and there's a well-chosen selection of Kiwi music to ease you in and out of every day. It's an easy 20-minute walk to town, or catch bus 14 or 16.

our pick Wish (Map p521; ☎ 03-356 2455; www.wishnz.com; 38 Edgeware Rd, St Albans; s/d incl breakfast $110/140; P 🖳) The rooms and beds at the stylish and modern Wish are supercomfy, but it could be the locally sourced, sustainable and organic breakfasts that you recommend to other travellers. Contemporary NZ art dots the walls, and the huge native-timber kitchen table is just made for catching up for an end-of-day glass of wine. Central Christchurch is a 15-minute walk away, or bus 14 or 16 stops virtually outside.

Entwhistle Cottage (Map p522; ☎ 03-377 2001; www.chesterst.co.nz; 147 Chester St E; d $125; P) This colonial-style self-contained cottage is aligned to Chester Street Backpackers (opposite). Built in 1870, it's now charmingly modern with a sunny courtyard that could hinder your opportunity to look around Christchurch. There are two bedrooms, with additional guests costing $15. A two-night minimum applies. A port-a-cot, highchair and loads of toys makes it a good option for families.

Orari B&B (Map p522; ☎ 03-365 6569; www.orari.net.nz; 42 Gloucester St; d incl breakfast $190-230; P ☎) Orari is a late-19th-century home that has been stylishly updated with light-filled, pastel-toned rooms, inviting guest areas, and a lovely front garden. Art connoisseurs take note: it's right across the road from Christchurch Art Gallery. Wine connoisseurs can look forward to complimentary wine. Newly built self-contained three-bedroom apartments are equally comfortable (from $300 per night).

On Armagh St are several character-filled homes offering guest-house accommodation: **Windsor Hotel** (Map p522; ☎ 0800 366 1503, 03-366 1503; www.windsorhotel.co.nz; 52 Armagh St; s/d/tr/q incl breakfast $98/140/180/200; P ☎) Trimmed with stately red bricks, this heritage abode has 40 simple, sunny and very comfortable rooms. All facilities are shared (fluffy bathrobes provided). Say hi to the friendly dog usually monopolising the front porch.

Croydon House (Map p522; ☎ 03-366 5111; www.croydon.co.nz; 63 Armagh St; s $110-140, d $140-180, all incl breakfast; P) Flower-filled window boxes decorate this B&B in a charming 1920s building. Rooms have shared facilities or private bathroom. The shared garden is a lovely spot after a busy day, and there is a special toy-filled room for families.

HOTELS & APARTMENTS
Hotel SO (Map p522; ☎ 0508 165 165, 03-968 5050; www.hotelso.co.nz; 165 Cashel St; s $69, d $89-135; P ☎) The sleek Hotel SO has (very) compact rooms that are an ode to whip-smart, ergonomic design. Look forward to flat-screen TVs, flash bathrooms, and iPod docks in hip surroundings. The hotel is close to Christchurch's nightlife precinct, so expect some after-dark noise at the weekend. Note that not all rooms have windows.

Living Space (Map p522; ☎ 0508 454 846, 03-964 5212; www.livingspace.net; 96 Lichfield St; d $80-120; ☎) Pitched somewhere between handy central digs for nightlife-loving visitors and compact studios for longer-term visitors, Living Space has minikitchens, high-speed internet and Sky TV. There's also an industrial-strength shared kitchen and DVD theatres. Rates are cheaper at weekends and longer-stay discounts are available.

Hotel off the Square (Map p522; ☎ 0800 633 843, 03-374 9980; www.offthesquare.com; 115 Worcester St; d $140-180, apt $280; ☎) This boutique hotel provides a stylish antidote to clinical business hotels. No two rooms are alike, and the place radiates warmth, with vibrant colours and lots of original art and plants. Loft-style apartments provide a self-contained option.

MOTELS
Stonehurst (Map p522; ☎ 0508 786 633, 03-379 4620; www.stonehurst.co.nz; 241 Gloucester St; motel d $110-210, q $260, apt per week $805-1400; P ☎) The place to go for great deals on a variety of motel rooms (from studios to two-bedroom units) and fully self-contained tourist flats sleeping up to six (good for groups and not much more expensive than a hostel). Stonehurst is central, modern and superbly equipped, and there's also backpacker accommodation (see p531).

Airport Gateway Motor Lodge (off Map p521; ☎ 0800 242 8392, 03-358 7093; www.airportgateway.co.nz; 45 Roydvale Ave; d/q from $125/165; P ☎) Handy for those early flights, this lodge has a variety of rooms with good facilities; airport pick-ups at no extra charge.

Colombo in the City (Map p522; ☎ 0800 265 662, 03-366 8775; www.motelcolombo.co.nz; 863 Colombo St; d $140-155, apt $165-240; P ☎) has attractive units that are luxuriously equipped (Sky TV, CD players, double glazing, spa baths). Next door, **CentrePoint on Colombo** (Map p522; ☎ 0800 859 000, 03-377 0859; www.centrepointoncolombo.co.nz; 859 Colombo St; d $145-165, apt $175-290; P ☎) is a lookalike with all the same supercomfortable facilities, and the bonus of friendly Kiwi-Japanese management. Cathedral Sq is just 500m away and both motels are near good ethnic restaurants.

Also recommended is the **Focus Motel** (Map p522; ☎ 03-943 0800; www.focusmotel.com; 344 Durham St N; d $140-350; P ☎), a sleek, centrally located new opening with big-screen TVs and supermodern decor.

SEASIDE AT SUMNER

Just 12km southeast of Christchurch by bus 3, the beachy suburb of Sumner is a relaxing place to stay. Commute to central Christchurch for sightseeing and return to Sumner for good restaurants and a cinema at night.

Marine Bar & Backpackers (Map p521; ☎ 03-326 6609; www.themarine.co.nz; 26 Nayland St; dm/s/d $25/35/55, s/d with bathroom $45/65, all incl breakfast; P ⬚ 🛜) A welcoming, social place with top-notch facilities. Some doubles open onto a large upstairs balcony. Downstairs is a bar with pool tables and a sunny outdoor area.

Sumner Bay Motel and Apartments (Map p521; ☎ 0800 496 949, 03-326 5969; www.sumnermotel. co.nz; 26 Marriner St; d $155-205; P 🛜) Studios and one- and two-bedroom units all have balcony or courtyard, quality furnishings and Sky TV and DVD players. Bikes and surfboards can be rented.

Cornershop Bistro (Map p521; ☎ 03-326 6720; 32 Nayland St; brunch $10-17, dinner mains $22-27; 🕑 9.30am-late Wed-Fri, from 8.30am Sat & Sun) Superior French-style bistro that never forgets it's in a relaxed beachside suburb. Spend longer than you planned to lingering over brunch.

Tart Café & Deli (Map p521; ☎ 03-326 7111; 26 Marriner St; brunch $10-15; 🕑 7.30am-5pm Mon-Fri, 8.30am-6pm Sat & Sun) Bright and airy Cape Cod–style decor combines with superior cafe fare including bagels, eggs lots of ways, and just maybe the South Island's biggest and best sausage rolls.

Club Bazaar (Map p521; ☎ 03-326 6155; 15 Wakefield St; pizza $11-30; 🕑 3pm-late, from noon Sun, closed Tue) Surf-themed pizza 'n' pasta bar with tables made from retro longboards. And yes, it does have Hawaiian pizza.

Top End

Hambledon (Map p522; ☎ 03-379 0723; www.hambledon. co.nz; 103 Bealey Ave; ste $250-295, apt $380; P ⬚ 🛜) This sumptuous antique-furnished heritage mansion has elegantly old-fashioned en-suite rooms (some with four-poster beds) that will take your mind off modern-day worries. Complimentary beer and wine may also help achieve that aim. The larger Camellia Apartment is wonderfully self-contained with a private garden, a sunny kitchen, and lots of interesting books.

George (Map p522; ☎ 0800 100 220, 03-379 4560; www.thegeorge.com; 50 Park Tce; r from $350-620; P ⬚ 🛜) The George has 53 handsomely decorated rooms and suites on the fringe of Christchurch's sweeping Hagley Park. Discreet staff attend to every whim, there are two excellent restaurants, and ritzy features including plasma TVs, luxury toiletries and glossy magazines.

EATING

The variety of Christchurch's dining options has increased in recent years. There's a good array of ethnic eateries along Colombo St north of Cathedral Sq from Kilmore to Salisbury Sts, and High St and the nearby Lichfield Lanes feature good cafes. Along 'the Strip' on the eastern side of Oxford Tce between Hereford and Cashel Sts, restaurants with outdoor tables are a good place to tuck into various shared tapas platters, steak and seafood.

Restaurants

Tatsumi Kitchen & Pub (Map p522; ☎ 03-366 1038; Chancery Lane, 100 Gloucester St; small plates $8-13, mains $14-18; 🕑 11.30am-2.30pm & 6pm-late Thu-Tue) Grab a table, or prop yourself at the bar with a handle of draught Asahi beer and choose from an almost-too-big selection of Japanese snacks and small plates. The sushi and sashimi is supremely fresh, and there's a tad more innovation – soft shell crabs or fish carpaccio anyone? – than your usual Japanese eatery. Lunch specials ($15) are particularly good value.

Mum's (Map p522; ☎ 03-365 2211; cnr Colombo & Gloucester Sts; mains $10-20; 🕑 11am-11pm) Nononsense food just like Mum used to make. That's if you grew up in Seoul or Tokyo anyway. More than a few Japanese and Korean language students regularly co-opt Mum's as their tasty home-away-from-home, and the sushi, sashimi and bowls of *ramen* noodles remain authentic.

ourpick **Bodhi Tree** (Map p522; ☎ 03-377 6808; 808 Colombo St; dishes $11-19; 🕑 6-10pm Tue-Sun; V) Christchurch's only Burmese restaurant is also one of the city's best eateries. Don't come expecting bold flavours from neighbouring Thailand, but look forward to subtle food crafted from exceptionally fresh ingredients.

Standout dishes include the *le pet thoke* (pickled tea leaf salad) and the *ciandi thoke* (grilled eggplant). Meat and seafood also feature. Dishes are entrée-sized so drum up a group and sample lots of different flavours. Bookings are essential.

Memphis Belle (Map p522; ☎ 03-389 4590; 391 Worcester St, Linwood; pizza $15-24; ❤ 5-9.30pm Tue-Thu & Sun, to 11pm Fri & Sat) The shortish trek from central Christchurch is definitely worth it for the city's best pizza. Look forward to retro furniture and thin-crust savoury marvels that put to shame the international chains. Cash only and bookings are recommended.

Bicycle Thief (Map p522; ☎ 03-379 2264; 21 Latimer Sq; mains $15-30; ❤ 8am-late Mon-Fri, from 5pm Sat) Tom Waits on the stereo, a corner spot overlooking leafy Latimer Sq, and an excellent wine and beer list. What more could you want? How about great thin-crust pizzas and lovingly prepared rustic Italian cuisine? Cafe, bar or restaurant? You choose.

Nobanno (Map p522; ☎ 03-943 1616; cnr Armagh & Colombo Sts; mains $17-24; ❤ 11.30am-2.30pm & 5pm-late) NZ's only Bangladeshi restaurant dishes up subcontinental flavours that are slightly more subtle and subdued than the sometimes overt spiciness of Indian cuisine. The seafood – including prawn and fish curries – is especially good.

Indochine (Map p522; ☎ 03-365 7323; 209 Cambridge Tce; mains $20-32; ❤ 5pm-late Mon-Sat) Indochine's menu travels seamlessly from China to Thailand, and it's usual for the mains to also feature a brave pan-Asian fusion focus. The successful experimentation continues on the cocktail list, which includes the mighty Indochine Mojito, blending vanilla-infused rum and palm sugar.

Chinwag (Map p522; ☎ 03-365 7363; 161 High St; mains $20-34; ❤ 5pm-late) Designer Thai food comes to Christchurch with subtle spins on the traditional Thai cookbook. Start the night with a heady Wild Thang cocktail and graduate to zingy, zesty dishes including green curry with prawns and baby corn. Bookings recommended. There is another branch dubbed Chinwag II (☎ 03-366 4544) at 131 Victoria St, with the same opening hours.

Liquidity (Map p522; ☎ 03-365 6088; 128 Oxford Tce; mains $26-35; ❤ 10am-late) Liquidity's eclectic and stylish decor mixing chandeliers and warm timber tones combines with a diverse and proudly local menu. Free-range chicken with Israeli couscous and prime Canterbury lamb are a cut above other players on 'the Strip'. Later at night good cocktails and plenty of European beer on tap fuels Liquidity's eventual metamorphosis into a bar. Eclectic beats kick off most nights from 10pm. The morning after it's a good riverside option for brunch ($13 to $20).

Cafes

Christchurch does cafes very, very well, and is undoubtedly a challenger to funky Wellington as the country's caffeine capital.

Avon Café & Bakery (Map p522; ☎ 03-366 0836; cnr Gloucester St & Cambridge Tce; snacks $6-10; ❤ 8am-4pm) Life is really quite simple. Sometimes all you need is a takeaway coffee beside the banks of the Avon River.

our pick Lunes (Map p522; ☎ 03-379 7221; 126 Lichfield St; coffee & cake $6-10; ❤ 8am-5pm) Just maybe the perfect Christchurch cafe: Lunes mixes cool jazz, a professorial approach to making coffee, and perfect midafternoon treats like baked New York cheesecake. Only open for six weeks when we dropped by, and already easily our favourite caffeine haunt in town.

Lotus Heart (Map p522; ☎ 03-379 0324; 595 Colombo St; mains $6-14; ❤ 8am-4pm Mon-Fri; Ⓥ) This organic, vegetarian eatery does curries, freshly squeezed juices and filled pita pockets. There's another more central branch above the i-SITE in Cathedral Sq with longer opening hours, which operates as a more spacious restaurant with tasty veg pizzas and casseroles (mains $8 to $16).

dose (Map p522; ☎ 03-374 9907; 90 Hereford St; mains $7-16; ❤ 7am-4pm Mon-Fri, 8am-3pm Sat) Cunningly mismatched furniture, bold local art, and high art-deco ceilings add up to a top place for wickedly strong coffee, superlative bagels, and quite probably Christchurch's best eggs Benedict.

NG Café (Map p522; ☎ 03-366 8683; 212 Madras St; snacks $8-12; ❤ 9am-4pm Mon-Fri, from 10am Sat) A former warehouse now incorporates an open-plan gallery and clothing boutique. Old meets new with a combination of iconic Kiwi snacks such as Anzac biscuits and relaxing world music beats. Soups and sandwiches tick the box marked 'comfort food'.

Under the Red Verandah (off Map p522; ☎ 03-381 1109; Cnr Tancred & Worcester Sts; breakfast $8-18, lunch $14-24; ❤ 7.30am-5pm Tue-Fri, 8.30am-4pm Sat & Sun) This lovely old villa is always packed with regulars, especially on bustling weekend mornings. Weekdays are slightly less busy, but still a good time for lots of organic and gluten-free baking, and mains including grilled haloumi on ciabatta and wonderfully robust oaty pancakes. The on-site deli and gallery space are further reasons to make the flat 30-minute walk from town.

Caffe Roma (Map p522; ☎ 03-379 3879; 176 Oxford Tce; mains $9-19; ☺ 7am-4pm) Often voted Christchurch's best spot for breakfast, a relaxed attitude at Caffe Roma means goodies such as salmon with hash browns are available until 3.30pm every day.

C1 Espresso (Map p522; ☎ 03-379 1917; 150 High St; mains $10-15; ☺ 7am-10pm Mon-Fri, 8.30am-10pm Sat, to 5.30pm Sun) C1 is a versatile spot with a global selection of teas and coffees, lots of local beers, and everything from robust breakfasts to bagels, wraps and burritos. Check out the selection of framed postcards and plan your next escape.

Joe's Garage (Map p522; ☎ 03-366 8317; 194 Hereford St; mains $10-15; ☺ 7am-4pm) The pride of Queenstown comes to Christchurch and brings along good-value breakfasts and lunches.

Quick Eats

Food and coffee stands are set up daily in Cathedral Sq, or there are many ethnic flavours at the eclectic food stalls at the Arts Centre weekend market (p538).

Copenhagen Bakery & Café (Map p522; ☎ 03-379 3935; PricewaterhouseCoopers Centre, 119 Armagh St; pies $4; ☺ 7am-5pm Mon-Fri) A regular winner in the Supreme Pie Awards – try the chicken satay – but also highly regarded by locals for tasty sandwiches and cakes.

Little Saigon (Map p522; ☎ 03-365 5889; 547 Colombo St; snacks $8-10; ☺ 11.30am-3pm & 5-9pm) Cheap and cheerful with all your Vietnamese favourites, including excellent fresh spring rolls.

High to Hereford Food Court (Map p522; 250 High St & 150 Hereford St; mains $10-15; ☺ 11am-5pm) Spotless food court that travels from Greece and India, to Cambodia, China and Italy.

Burgers & Beer Inc (Map p522; ☎ 03-366 3339; 178 High St; burgers $12.50; ☺ 11am-late) Quirkily named gourmet burgers – try the Moroccan-spiced Woolly Sahara Sand Hopper – and lots of Kiwi brews.

Self-Catering

New World Supermarket (Map p522; South City Centre, Colombo St; ☺ 7.30am-9pm).

Pak N Save Supermarket (Map p522; 297 Moorhouse Ave; ☺ 8am-10pm)

DRINKING

Christchurch sees numerous restaurants and cafes packing away their dinner menus later in the evening and distributing cocktail, wine and beer lists. Riverside Oxford Tce ('the Strip') is popular with a younger crowd, but the most interesting spots for late-night shenanigans are in the Lichfield Lanes area around SOL ('South of Lichfield') Sq and Poplar St.

our pick Cartel (Map p522; ☎ 021 576 857; His Lordships Lane, SOL Sq; ☺ 4pm-late) Cartel may look like the end result of a garage sale at your quirky uncle's house, but inside the retro interior is a wine list and cocktails to die for. In cooler months, pull up a bean bag in front of the toasty outdoor fire and look forward to music you thought only you knew about. There's only room for 30 punters, but that doesn't stop Cartel from hosting occasional DJs and live bands.

Dux de Lux (Map p522; ☎ 03-366 6919; cnr Hereford & Montreal Sts; ☺ 10.30am-late) Quality microbrewed beers underpin this Christchurch icon. There's good food too, especially seafood and vegetarian, and live music features at least four nights a week. On weekend afternoons the garden bar is the place to be after exploring the Arts Centre market.

Indochine (Map p522; ☎ 03-365 7323; 209 Cambridge Tce; ☺ 5pm-late Mon-Sat) If you can't score a dinner reservation at this popular eatery, swing by for one of its Asian-inspired cocktails.

Twisted Hop (Map p522; ☎ 03-962 3688; 6 Poplar St; ☺ noon-late) If you think a bar specialising in English-style cask-conditioned beer is old-fashioned, think again. The architectural élan of the Twisted Hop is reinforcing Poplar St as Christchurch's coolest drinking hub. Mix in an excellent wine list, a tasty tapas menu and boutique beers from around NZ, and you've got a spot that could soon become your surrogate local bar.

Cleaners Only (Map p522; SOL Sq; ☺ 5pm-late Wed-Sun) Good luck finding this place – it's tucked away in the corner of SOL Sq – but once inside you'll be in Christchurch's quirkiest bar. Apparently it used to be the lunchroom for cleaners at nearby warehouses, and a gloriously retro ambience is still intact, complete with comfy old sofas from your first student flat.

Thirsty Weta (Map p522; ☎ 03-372 9232; 56 Lichfield St; ☺ 5pm-late Wed-Thu, 4pm-late Fri & Sat) Not so long ago, the NZ beer scene was as dull as dishwater. Now you can try more than 70 Kiwi microbrews at this slim space incongruously located in Christchurch's retail hub. If you're a bit peckish, have a gourmet pie, or order in from the Indian restaurant upstairs.

Le Plonk (Map p522; ☎ 03-377 7724; 211 Manchester St; ☾ 3pm-late Mon-Fri, 4pm-late Sat & Sun) This wine bar offers superior NZ vintages, lush leather lounges and live jazz on Thursdays from 8pm. A high class of bar snacks kicks off around $8.

Holy Grail (Map p522; ☎ 03-365 9816; 88 Worcester St; ☾ 11am-late) In a converted art-deco theatre, the raucous Holy Grail is about as subtle as an All Blacks fan's reaction to a bad refereeing decision. Watch live sport on a huge 10m screen from the indoor grandstand – if you're watching the Canterbury Crusaders rugby team, wearing red and black is recommended, but not mandatory.

Lyme (Map p522; ☎ 03-365 2393; 817 Colombo St; ☾ 4.30pm-late Wed-Sat) Good for a drink before or after diving into the restaurant strip along Colombo St, Lyme was named NZ's best new bar a few years back. The award-winning bartenders still make damn fine cocktails, and on Friday nights it's a good place to meet young professionals celebrating the end of the working week.

Bard on Avon (Map p522; ☎ 03-377 1493; cnr Gloucester St & Oxford Tce; ☾ 11am-late) The Bard has an authentic English ambience and plenty of traveller-friendly events such as the pub quiz (Sunday at 7pm) and live music from Thursday to Saturday. The pub is a few blocks from 'the Strip', and the better for it.

Tap Room (Map p522; ☎ 03-365 0547; 124 Oxford Tce; ☾ 11am-late) An always-busy option on 'the Strip' with Monteith's beers on tap and bands covering tunes you can sing along to.

Foam Bar (Map p522; ☎ 03-365 2926; 30 Bedford Row; ☾ 5pm-late Wed-Sat) Sophisticated back-alley bar, worth seeking out for its chilled-out crowd, art-bedecked walls and DJ-spun tunes. Expect occasional live bands and jam sessions.

ENTERTAINMENT

Christchurch's vigorous bar-club scene is centred on Lichfield St (usually from 10pm Wednesday to Saturday), while many Oxford Tce bars/restaurants transform with DJs and impromptu dance floors. Nightclub admission ranges from free to $15, though big-name DJ events can cost upwards of $40. Live music in pubs, bars and cafes is mostly free. See www.jagg.co.nz for listings. The weekly

Groove Guide lists local gigs, too; pick it up at **Real Groovy Records** (Map p522; ☎ 03-366-7140; 179 Tuam St; ☾ 9am-6pm Mon-Sat, 10am-5pm Sun) just off Sol Sq. Most gigs are also advertised at Real Groovy, and it is often the booking agent for local and international acts.

Christchurch is the hub of the South Island's performing-arts scene, with several excellent theatres. The major ticketing company is **Ticketek** (Map p522; ☎ 03-377 8899; http://premier.ticketek.co.nz), with outlets inside the Town Hall and the Isaac Theatre Royal.

Performing Arts

Town Hall (Map p522; ☎ 03-366 8899; 86 Kilmore St) The riverside town hall and its two main spaces (the 2500-seat Auditorium and the 1000-seat James Hay Theatre) are the main venues for local performing arts such as orchestras, choirs and bands. The venue's acoustics are excellent.

Isaac Theatre Royal (Map p522; ☎ 03-366 6326; www.isaactheatreroyal.co.nz; 145 Gloucester St) Another versatile stalwart of the local scene, with offers including the Royal New Zealand Ballet, the Canterbury Opera and occasional touring plays.

Court Theatre (Map p522; ☎ 0800 333 100, 03-963 0870; www.courttheatre.org.nz; 20 Worcester St) In the Arts Centre, this theatre performs everything from Beckett and Chekhov to popular NZ playwrights such as Roger Hall. The resident Court Jesters troupe stages its long-running improvised comedy show, *Scared Scriptless*, Friday and Saturday nights at 10pm ($15). Also popular is the theatre's regular Ghost Walk (see p530).

Cinemas

Movies are listed in the local newspapers. Adult tickets cost around $16, children $10, and most cinemas are cheaper on Tuesdays. From late July to mid-August, the NZ International Film Festival (www.nzff.telecom.co.nz) comes to town.

Arts Centre Cinemas (Map p522; ☎ 03-366 0167; www.artfilms.co.nz; Arts Centre, Worcester St) Comprises two venues (the Academy and Cloisters) at the Arts Centre.

Metro Gold Cinema (Map p522; ☎ 03-377 5705; 105 Worcester St) Another Arts Centre Cinemas branch, this one near ChristChurch Cathedral.

Other options:

Hoyts Moorhouse (Map p522; ☎ 0508 446 987; www.hoyts.co.nz; 392 Moorhouse Ave) For all the latest Hollywood blockbusters.

Regent on Worcester (Map p522; ☎ 0508 446 987; www.hoyts.co.nz; 94 Worcester St) Shows art-house and mainstream titles.

Rialto (Map p522; ☎ 03-379 9404; www.rialto.co.nz; cnr Moorhouse Ave & Durham St) Art-house central with plenty of foreign flicks and the occasional mini film festival.

Live Music

Dux de Lux (Map p522; ☎ 03-366 6919; www.thedux. co.nz; cnr Hereford & Montreal Sts; ☿ 10.30am-late) Invites ska, reggae, rock, pop and dub artists to cater to crowds at least four nights a week. On a sunny day the outdoor tables are a mass of raised glasses of the Dux's excellent micro-brewed beers.

Southern Blues Bar (Map p522; ☎ 03-365 1654; 198 Madras St; ☿ 7.30am-late) NZ's oldest blues venue is still going strong; gigs kick off nightly around 10.30pm. Expect a friendly crowd of musos, office workers and the confidently unfashionable.

Yellow Cross (Map p522; SOL Sq; ☿ noon-late) An eclectic live-music haven amid the largely manufactured beats of SOL Sq is a good thing. Wood-fired pizzas and Euro brews are the icing on the cake.

Bedford (Map p522; ☎ 03-374 9988; www.thebedford.co.nz; 46 Bedford Row; ☿ vary by event) The brick building dates back to 1903, but now the sprawling Bedford hosts a thoroughly modern mix of up-and-coming international bands and the best of Kiwi acts with a rocky tinge.

Goodbye Blue Monday (Map p522; 03-961 3353; www. goodbyebluemonday.co.nz; Poplar Lane; ☿ 5pm-late Mon-Sat) Tucked away in Poplar Lane, Goodbye Blue Monday's mismatched retro couches are a cool spot for a drink early in the evening, and then the ambience usually morphs to include live bands and DJ beats, often with an indie accent. It's the preferred venue of about-to-be-famous Kiwi bands. It's also the only place, *anywhere*, you'll find Bodgie Beer's organic Pilsner.

Al's Bar (Map p522; www.alsbar.co.nz; 33 Dundas St; ☿ 8pm-late Wed-Sat) Live music is definitely the hero at Al's Bar, with the cosy brick-lined space and excellent sound system drawing a diverse mix of local and international acts.

Nightclubs

Double Happy (Map p522; ☎ 03-374 6463; 182 Cashel St; ☿ 8pm-late Wed-Sun) The city's best bar-club hybrid with great cocktails, Euro beers on tap and an ever-changing diet of dub, house and soul. Perfect for chilled late-night/early-morning denizens.

Base (Map p522; ☎ 03-377 7149; www.thebase.co.nz; 92 Struthers Lane; ☿ from 9pm Thu-Sat) Down a slightly seedy side alley a few doors along from SOL Sq. Specialises in electro, house and trance. Admission is cheaper until midnight.

Ministry/Propaganda (Map p522; ☎ 03-379 2910; www.ministry.co.nz; 90 Lichfield St) Two venues in one big space combining an intimate lounge bar and an always-pumping club. House and drum and bass is the usual recipe, but the occasional metal night with live bands ambushes things.

Sport

AMI Stadium (Map p522; tickets ☎ 03-377 8899, http:// premier.ticketek.co.nz; www.amistadium.co.nz; 30 Stevens St) This stadium hosts cricket internationals, but it's best known as Canterbury's rugby heartland. Watch the Crusaders in Super 14 action from February to May. The stadium got a whizzbang makeover for the 2011 Rugby World Cup.

Casino

Christchurch Casino (Map p522; ☎ 03-365 9999; www. christchurchcasino.co.nz; 30 Victoria St; ☿ 24hr)

SHOPPING

Colombo St, High St and the pedestrianised Cashel St are all crammed with credit-card-hungry places. Head to the funky southern end of High St (between Lichfield and St Asaph Sts) for the creative output of young NZ fashion designers, and in nearby Poplar St and His Lordship's Lane, design shops share the laneways with bars and restaurants. For a wider range of arts and crafts, visit the Arts Centre and the shops in the art galleries.

Arts Centre (Map p522; ☎ 03-363 2836; www.artscentre.org.nz; 2 Worcester St) Dozens of craft shops and art galleries selling pottery, jewellery, woollen goods and handmade toys. Visually Maori and Te Toi Mana are your best options for Maori art and design (see p525).

Arts Centre market (Map p522; ☿ 10am-4pm Sat & Sun) Every weekend the Arts Centre is host to a craft and produce market.

REAL Aotearoa (Map p522; ☎ 03-377 5418; www. realaotearoa.co.nz; 101 Cashel St) Eclectic Kiwi design from pottery to glassware.

Untouched World (Map p522; ☎ 03-962 6551; www.untouchedworld.com; 301 Montreal St) At the Arts Centre, Untouched World has quality NZ-made clothing. Clothes may be made of 'mountainsilk' (machine-washable fine merino wool) or 'merinomink' (a blend of merino wool and possum fur).

Ballantynes (Map p522; ☎ 03-379 7400; cnr Colombo & Cashel Sts) Venerable Christchurch department store selling men's and women's fashions, cosmetics, travel goods and speciality NZ gifts.

For camping gear, hiking boots and outdoor equipment, head to **Snowgum** (Map p522; ☎ 03-365 4336; 637 Colombo St) or **Mountain Designs** (Map p522; ☎ 03-377 8522; 654 Colombo St) near the intersection of Colombo and Lichfield Sts.

GETTING THERE & AWAY
Air
Christchurch airport (off Map p521; ☎ 03-358 5029; www.christchurchairport.co.nz) is the South Island's main international gateway. For details of international flights, see p701. The airport has excellent facilities, including currency exchange, ATMs, baggage storage (🕑 8am to 6.30pm), plus travel centres (☎ 03-353 7774) in both the domestic terminal (🕑 7.30am to 8pm) and the international terminal (open for all international flight arrivals). Departure tax on international flights is $25, with children under 12 exempt. Prices listed below are for one-way flights.

Air New Zealand (Map p522; ☎ 0800 737 000, 03-363 0600; www.airnz.co.nz; 549 Colombo St; 🕑 9am-5pm Mon-Fri, 9.30am-1pm Sat) also offers numerous direct domestic flights with connections to other centres. There are direct flights to and from Auckland ($59 to $239, 20 flights per day), Blenheim ($79 to $179, three daily), Dunedin ($59 to $169, eight daily), Hamilton ($109 to $259, three daily), Hokitika ($65 to $135, five daily), Invercargill ($79 to $189, eight daily), Napier ($99 to $229, two daily), Nelson ($89 to $219, eight daily), New Plymouth ($139 to $229, one daily), Palmerston North ($99 to $189, four daily), Queenstown ($59 to $199, five daily), Rotorua ($129 to $259, three daily), Tauranga ($99 to $239, one daily), Wanaka ($169 to $199, one daily) and Wellington ($49 to $1792, 15 daily). Check www.grabaseat.co.nz for last-minute deals.

Jetstar (☎ 0800 800 995; www.jetstar.com) offers direct flights to and from Auckland ($49 to $219, six daily), Queenstown ($59 to $189, one daily) and Wellington ($99 to $169, one daily).

Bus
InterCity (Map p522; ☎ 03-365 1113; www.intercity.co.nz; 123 Worcester St; 🕑 7am-5.15pm Mon-Sat, to 5.30pm Sun) buses depart from Worcester St, between the cathedral and Manchester St. Northbound buses go twice daily to Kaikoura (from $14, 2¾ hours), Blenheim (from $24, five hours) and Picton (from $25, 5½ hours), with connections to Nelson ($71, eight hours). One daily bus also goes southwest to Queenstown direct (from $49, eight hours). There are also services to Wanaka (from $79, seven hours) that involve a change in Tarras. Heading south, two buses run daily along the coast via the towns along SH1 to Dunedin (from $37, six hours), with connections via Gore to Invercargill (from $53, 9¾ hours) and Te Anau (from $59, 10½ hours).

Naked Bus (www.nakedbus.com) heads north to Picton and Nelson, south to Dunedin and southwest to Queenstown. Buses leave from opposite the Holy Grail pub at 88 Worcester St.

Shuttles run to Akaroa, Arthur's Pass, Dunedin, Greymouth, Hanmer Springs, Picton, Queenstown, Twizel, Wanaka, Westport and points in between; see the i-SITE (p520).

Train
Christchurch railway station (Map p521; ☎ 0800 872 467, 03-341 2588; Troup Dr, Addington; 🕑 ticket office 6.30am-3.30pm Mon-Fri, to 3pm Sat & Sun) is serviced by a free shuttle that picks up from various accommodation; ring the i-SITE (p520) to request pick-up.

The *TranzCoastal* runs daily each way between Christchurch and Picton via Kaikoura and Blenheim, departing from Christchurch at 7am and arriving at Picton at 12.13pm; the standard adult one-way fare to Picton is $83, but fares can be discounted to $59.

The *TranzAlpine* has a daily route between Christchurch and Greymouth via Arthur's Pass (see p499); the standard adult one-way fare is $137, but fares can be discounted to $89. Ask about any current specials.

Contact **Tranz Scenic** (☎ 0800 872 467; www.tranzscenic.co.nz).

GETTING AROUND
To/From the Airport
The airport is 12km from the city centre.

Super Shuttle (☎ 0800 748 885; www.supershuttle.co.nz) operates 24 hours and charges $17 for

CHRISTCHURCH & CANTERBURY

one person between the city and the airport, plus $4 for each additional person. A cheaper alternative is the **Seven Dollar Bus** (☺ 8am-5pm; one-way $7), which runs every 20 minutes between the airport and Cathedral Sq.

The airport is serviced by the **City Flyer bus** (☎ 0800 733 287; www.redbus.co.nz; adult/child $7.50/4.50), which runs from Cathedral Sq between 5.30am and 11.30pm Monday to Friday and 7.30am to 11.30pm Saturday and Sunday (from the airport 35 minutes later). Pick up the red City Flyer timetable at the i-SITE (p520).

A taxi between the city centre and airport costs around $40 to $45.

Car & Motorcycle
HIRE
Major car- and campervan-rental companies all have offices in Christchurch, as do numerous smaller local companies. Operators with national networks often want cars to be returned from Christchurch to Auckland because most renters travel in the opposite direction, so special rates may apply on this northbound route. For reliable national rental companies, see p710.

Some smaller-scale companies:

Ace Rental Cars (off Map p521; ☎ 0800 202 029, 03-360 3270; www.acerentalcars.co.nz; 20 Abros Pl)

First Choice (Map p522; ☎ 0800 736 822, 03-365 9261; www.firstchoice.co.nz; 132 Kilmore St)

New Zealand Motorcycle Rentals & Tours (off Map p521; ☎ 03-348 1106; www.nzbike.com; 22 Lowther St) Also does guided motorbike tours.

Omega Rental Cars (Map p522; ☎ 0800 112 121, 03-377 4558; www.omegarentalcars.com; 20 Lichfield St)

Pegasus Rental Cars (Map p522; ☎ 0800 354 506, 03-365 1100; www.rentalcars.co.nz; 127 Peterborough St)

PURCHASE
Many vehicles are offered for sale on noticeboards at hostels, cafes and internet places. Check out **Backpackers Car Market** (Map p522; ☎ 03-377 3177; www.backpackerscarmarket.co.nz; 33 Battersea St; ☺ 9.30am-5pm), or the weekly **Canterbury Car Fair** (Map p521; ☎ 03-338 5525; Wrights Rd entrance; ☺ 9am-noon Sun) held at Addington Raceway. **Turners Auctions** (Map p521; ☎ 03-343 9850; www.turners.co.nz; 1 Detroit Place) buys and sells used cars by auction; vehicles priced under $7000 are auctioned at 6pm on Tuesday and Thursday.

Online see www.trademe.co.nz and www.autotrader.co.nz.

Public Transport
The Christchurch **bus network** (Metro; ☎ 03-366 8855; www.metroinfo.org.nz; ☺ 6.30am-10.30pm Mon-Sat, 9am-9pm Sun) is inexpensive and efficient. Most buses run from The Crossing (Map p522), with its pedestrian entrance on Colombo St opposite Ballantynes. The exchange has an information desk here; alternatively, get timetables from the i-SITE (p520). A cash fare to anywhere in the city costs $2.80, including one free transfer within two hours. Metrocards allow two-hour/full-day travel for $2.10/4.20, but the cards must be loaded up with a minimum of $10.

For information on the following two services, contact **Red Bus** (☎ 0800 733 287; www.redbus.co.nz). The big yellow **Central City Shuttle** (fare free; ☺ 7.30am-10.30pm Mon-Fri, 8am-10.30pm Sat, 10am-8pm Sun) is an inner-city service (as far north as Peterborough St, south to Moorhouse Ave) with about 20 pick-up points. The **After Midnight Express** (fare $6; ☺ midnight-4am Sat & Sun) operates hourly on five suburban routes, most of them departing Oxford Tce.

Taxi
Christchurch's main taxi companies:

Blue Star (☎ 0800 379 979)
First Direct (☎ 0800 505 555)
Gold Band (☎ 0800 379 5795)

AROUND CHRISTCHURCH

LYTTELTON
pop 3100

Southeast of Christchurch are the prominent Port Hills, which slope down to the city's port at Lyttelton Harbour. Christchurch's first European settlers landed here in 1850 to embark on their historic trek over the hills. With attractive heritage architecture and eclectic cafe-bars, it's now a popular weekend getaway and dining destination for in-the-know foodies. Lyttelton is still a working port, and the raffish charm of the old waterfront pubs contrasts with the gentrifying scene just up the hill along London St.

Regular ferries and boat cruises provide access to sheltered islands and across the water to sleepy Diamond Harbour. If you've got your own transport, the harbour road wends a scenic 15-minute route to pretty

Governors Bay with a couple of good spots for lunch.

The **Lyttelton visitor information centre** (☎ 03-328 9093; www.lytteltonharbour.co.nz; 20 Oxford St; ☺ 9am-5pm Sep-May, to 4pm Jun-Aug) has accommodation and transport information.

Sights

Lyttelton is linked to Christchurch via a **road tunnel**, but there's a more scenic (and 10km longer) route along the narrow **Summit Rd**, which has breathtaking city, hill and harbour views, and vistas of the Southern Alps; see the *Lyttelton Port Hills Drive* pamphlet ($1).

Lyttelton Museum (☎ 03-328 8972; Gladstone Quay; admission by donation; ☺ 2-4pm Tue, Thu, Sat & Sun) has interesting maritime exhibits such as wreck-recovered artefacts and ship models, plus Lyttelton memorabilia including a 19th-century pipe organ and an Antarctic gallery (both Scott and Shackleton used the port as a base).

The neogothic **Timeball Station** (☎ 03-328 7311; 2 Reserve Tce; adult/child/family $7/2/15; ☺ 10am-5.30pm), built in 1876, was where (for 58 years) a huge time ball was hoisted on a mast and then dropped at exactly 1pm, Greenwich Mean Time, allowing ships in the harbour to set their clocks and thereby accurately calculate longitude. The time ball is still dropped at 1pm on days when the station is open. Access requires a short, steep climb.

Tours

Black Cat (☎ 0800 436 574, 03-328 9078; www.blackcat.co.nz; 17 Norwich Quay; cruises adult/child $60/25; ☺ tour 1.30pm) operates two-hour Christchurch Wildlife Cruises on Lyttelton Harbour, where you may see rare Hector's dolphins, blue penguins and various seabirds. A free shuttle bus for participants leaves Cathedral Sq in Christchurch at 12.50pm. Black Cat also shuttles across to nearby **Quail Island** (adult/child $20/10; ☺ trips 10.20am & 12.20pm Dec-Mar, 12.20pm Apr & Sep-Nov, no sailings May-Aug), and to pretty Diamond Harbour (adult/child $10/5; 23 times daily).

Enquire at the visitor information centre about other ways to get active on the harbour, including kayaking and sailing.

Sleeping & Eating

A few B&Bs dot the surrounding hills; the visitor information centre can help with bookings.

Dockside Accommodation (☎ 03-325 5707; www.dockside.co.nz; 22 Sumner Rd; apt $80-120; 🖳 🛜) Three

homely self-contained apartments each sleep up to four. They're a short, easy walk from town, or you can stay put and enjoy the harbour views from your private deck. It's the kind of place that feels just like home.

Lyttelton Lounge (☎ 03-328 7114; 17 Oxford St; baked goods $4-6; ☺ 8am-4.30pm Mon-Sat, 9am-4.30pm Sun) Dub reggae, freshly baked muffins and supercharged coffee feature at this atmospheric wood-lined haven. Linger for a while before looking for treasures at the vintage and secondhand shops just down the hill.

Lyttelton Roasting Company (☎ 03-328 8096; 29 London St; mains $6-17; ☺ 7.30am-4.30pm Tue-Fri, from 8am Sat & Sun) The best coffee in town – and maybe in all of Canterbury – is roasted daily at this bohemian spot with incredibly high ceilings and an eclectic breakfast and lunch menu. Try the Armenian yoghurt cake as you linger for the regular Saturday afternoon live music.

our pick **Monster Yakitori** (☎ 03-328 9166; 29 London St; per 2 skewers $7-11; ☺ 5pm-late Wed-Sun) Classic cocktails and boutique Kiwi beers and wines provide the liquid sustenance for an extended bout of grazing and drinking at this quirky anime-themed yakitori bar. All the skewered goodies are grilled as you wait; our favourite is the ebi bacon – prawns wrapped in bacon with plum wasabi. DJs kick in most Saturday nights from 10pm.

Volcano Cafe (☎ 03-328 7077; 42 London St; mains $27-33; ☺ 5pm-late) The vaguely Mexican but exceedingly friendly Volcano is a festive, retro-style cafe serving seafood risotto, enchiladas and good curries and pastas. The attached Lava Bar has a cheaper bar menu.

West round the harbour, the **Governor's Bay Hotel** (☎ 03-329 9433; www.governorsbayhotel.co.nz; Main Rd, Governors Bay; mains $15-30; ☺ 11am-10pm) serves tasty burgers, fish and chips, and more innovative meals of chargrilled tuna or curry prawn laksa. Enjoy a beer on the cool veranda dotted with memoirs of the hotel's 140 years of history. Upstairs there is accommodation in simple but sunny rooms with shared bathrooms (doubles $100).

Across the road, **She Chocolat** (☎ 03-328 9285; www.shechocolat.com; 79 Main Rd, Governors Bay; mains $15-26; ☺ 10am-4pm Wed-Fri, to 5pm Sat & Sun) serves excellent brunches and lunches with an organic and new-age tinge. After kumara (sweet potato) oatcakes, make room for locally made Belgian chocolate and take in the harbour views.

Lyttelton's growing rep as a foodie destination is enhanced by the Saturday **farmers market** (www.lyttelton.net.nz; 10am-1pm Sat) held in the local school on Oxford St. Also check out **Ground** (03-328 7275; www.ground.co.nz; 44a London St; 9.30am-7.30pm Mon-Thu, to 8pm Fri & Sat, 10am-5pm Sun), ground zero for the best of Kiwi food, wine and beer. For a quick bite there's megasandwiches ($6.50) and an excellent brunch menu ($7 to $18). If you're staying the night in Lyttelton, it also does gourmet takeaway meals.

Drinking & Entertainment

Wunderbar (03-328 8818; www.wunderbar.co.nz; 19 London St; 5pm-late Mon-Fri, 1pm-late Sat & Sun) Wunderbar is a top spot to see NZ's more interesting acts, from raucous rock to late-night/early-morning dub. The funky decor alone is worth a trip to Lyttelton. Look for the sign on London St that says 'Sorry, nice people only' and head down the steps. Be nice.

Lava Bar (03-328 7077; 42 London St; 5pm-late) Flowing on from Volcano Cafe (naturally) and open for sociable boozing (and snacking) nightly. Has an outdoor terrace crammed with quirky artistic touches, which may seem only slightly quirky after a few drinks.

Harbour Light (03-328 8615; www.harbourlight. co.nz; 24 London St; admission $15-25) This wonderful old theatre (built in 1916) straddles old and new Lyttelton with regular live gigs showcasing jazz, Celtic and world music. Check the website for what's on; there's normally gigs around three nights a week. On show nights, drinks and food are served.

Getting There & Away

Buses 28 and 35 run from Christchurch to Lyttelton (25 minutes). From Lyttelton by car, you can continue around Lyttelton Harbour on to Akaroa. This winding route is longer and more scenic than the route via SH75 between Christchurch and Akaroa.

AKAROA & BANKS PENINSULA

Banks Peninsula and its hills were formed by two giant volcanic eruptions. Small harbours such as Le Bons, Pigeon and Little Akaloa Bays radiate out from the peninsula's centre, giving it a cogwheel shape. The historic town of Akaroa is a highlight, as is the absurdly beautiful drive along Summit Rd around the edge of the original crater.

Akaroa means 'Long Harbour' in Maori and is the site of the country's first French settlement; descendants of the original French settlers still reside here. Located 83km from Christchurch, it's a charming town that strives to recreate the feel of a French provincial village, down to the names of its streets (rues Lavaud, Balguerie, Jolie) and houses (Langlois-Eteveneaux), plus a few choice eateries. The Gallic pretence can sometimes be a tad forced, but it's still an undeniably picturesque spot, especially if you use it as a base for exploring the incredible landscapes and bays of the surrounding area.

If you're not in a hurry, it's worth spending a few leisurely days in the excellent budget accommodation that dots the outer bays of Banks Peninsula. Most accommodation will arrange pick-up in Akaroa after you arrive from Christchurch.

History

James Cook sighted the peninsula in 1770. Thinking it was an island he named it after the naturalist Sir Joseph Banks. The Ngai Tahu tribe, who occupied the peninsula at the time, were attacked at the fortified Onawe *pa* (Maori village) by the Ngati Toa chief Te Rauparaha in 1831 and their population was dramatically reduced.

In 1838, whaling captain Jean Langlois negotiated the purchase of Banks Peninsula from local Maori and returned to France to form a trading company. With French-government backing, 63 settlers headed for the peninsula in 1840. But only days before they arrived, panicked British officials sent their own warship to raise the flag at Akaroa, claiming British sovereignty under the Treaty of Waitangi. Had the settlers arrived two years earlier, the entire South Island could have become a French colony, and NZ's future may have been quite different.

The French did settle at Akaroa, but in 1849 their land claim was sold to the New Zealand Company, and in 1850 a large group of British settlers arrived. The heavily forested land was cleared and soon farming became the peninsula's main industry.

Information

Akaroa visitor information centre (Map p544; 03-304 8600; www.akaroa.com; 80 Rue Lavaud; 9am-5pm) Information on tours, activities and accommodation, including good farmstays.

CHRISTCHURCH & CANTERBURY

Bank of New Zealand (Map p544; Rue Lavaud) With an ATM; opposite the visitor information centre.
Bon-E-Mail (Map p544; ☎ 03-304 7447; 41 Rue Lavaud; ☻ 9am-8pm; ☎) Internet access including wi-fi. There is also wi-fi at the cafe at Tree Crop Farm (see right).

Sights

The **Akaroa Museum** (Map p544; ☎ 03-304 1013; cnr Rues Lavaud & Balguerie; adult/child/family $4/1/8; ☻ 10.30am-4.30pm Oct-Apr, to 4pm May-Sep) is spread over several historic buildings, including the old courthouse, the tiny Custom House by Daly's Wharf, and one of NZ's oldest houses, Langlois-Eteveneaux. It has modest displays on the peninsula's once-significant Maori population, a courtroom diorama, a 20-minute

audiovisual on peninsular history, and Akaroa community archives.

The quirky **Tree Crop Farm** (off Map p544; ☎ 03-304 7158; www.treecropfarm.com; admission $10; ☻ 10am-5pm in good weather only; ☎) is 1.8km off the main road through Akaroa (take Rue Grehan). This private wilderness garden is perfect for wandering on established tracks, relaxing on sheepskin-covered couches on the ramshackle veranda, or flicking through magazines and playing board games. A drink and snack is included in the admission price (try the berry juice). Rustic and romantic accommodation ($200 to $250) and a spa are also available here.

At Barrys Bay, on the western side of Akaroa Harbour (12km from Akaroa), is the enticing **Barrys Bay Cheese** (Map p543; ☎ 03-304 5809;

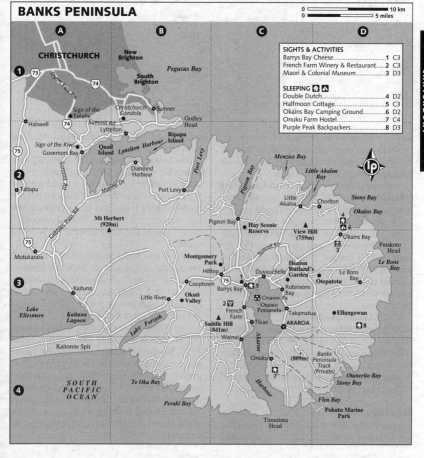

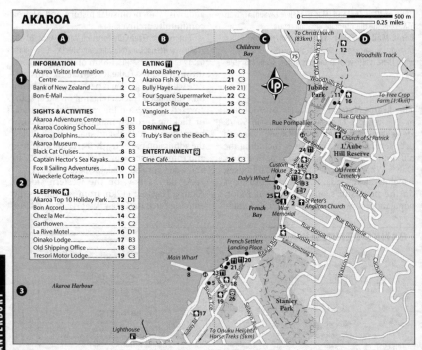

AKAROA

www.barrysbaycheese.co.nz; 9am-5pm), where you can taste and purchase fine cheddar, havarti and gouda. Crackers and chutney are available for a spontaneous seaside snack.

Just west is the turn-off to **French Farm Winery & Restaurant** (Map p543; ☎ 03-304 5784; www.french farm.co.nz; French Farm Valley Rd; platters $25-44, pizza $24-26; 10am-4pm), set in beautiful grounds with a south of France ambience. Sample French Farm's chardonnay and pinot noir ($1 per taste and all crafted from local grapes) or unwind with an antipasto platter or Akaroa salmon cakes. In summer (late October to Easter) wood-fired pizzas are served alfresco from midday.

Maori & Colonial Museum (Map p543; ☎ 03-304 8611; Okains Bay; adult/child $6/2; 10am-5pm) at Okains Bay, northeast of Akaroa, began as a private collection of indigenous and pioneer artefacts but went public 28 years ago. It features a re-production Maori meeting house, a sacred 15th-century god stick and a war canoe.

Activities

See the visitor information centre if you like the sound of jetboating, kayaking or sailing on Akaroa Harbour, touring a working sheep farm or visiting a seal colony.

The **Banks Peninsula Track** (☎ 03-304 7612; www. bankstrack.co.nz; per person $240) is a 35km four-day walk across private farmland and around the dramatic coastline of Banks Peninsula; cost includes transport from Akaroa and hut accommodation. A two-day option ($160) covers the same ground at twice the speed.

The **Akaroa Walk** (☎ 0800 377 378, 03-962 3280; www.tuataratours.co.nz; per person $1486) is a leisurely upmarket 42km stroll across three days from Christchurch to Akaroa with good accommodation and lots of gourmet food. You'll only need to carry a daypack.

The *Akaroa – an Historic Walk* booklet ($9.50) details a walking tour starting at the 1876 **Waeckerle Cottage** (Map p544; Rue Lavaud) and finishing at the old Taylor's Emporium premises near the main wharf. The route takes in the old wooden buildings and churches that give Akaroa its character. Audio guides for self-guided walking tours are available at the visitor information centre ($10 per 90 minutes).

The **Akaroa Adventure Centre** (Map p544; ☎ 03-304 8709; Rue Lavaud; sea kayaks per hr/day $15/55, bikes per hr $15) rents out sea kayaks, bikes, golf clubs, fishing rods and windsurfing gear. For $39 (including bike hire) they'll transport you to the top of the volcanic crater around Banks Peninsula from where you can ride downhill all the way to Akaroa. Ask here about staying at Purple Peak Backpackers (p546).

Captain Hector's Sea Kayaks (Map p544; ☎ 03-304 7866; Beach Rd; www.akaroaseakayaks.co.nz; kayak hire per half/full day $35/60) is another rental company that offers kayaks, canoes and rowboats for self-exploration.

The **Akaroa Cooking School** (Map p544; ☎ 021 166 3737; www.akaroacooking.co.nz; 81 Beach Rd; per person $175) runs popular 'Gourmet in a Day' sessions (10am to 3pm) on Fridays and Saturdays, and occasional specialised seafood and barbecue classes. All sessions end with tucking into your self-prepared feast.

Pohatu Plunge (☎ 03-304 8552; www.pohatu. co.nz) runs evening penguin-viewing tours (per adult/child $66/55). Spying the white-flippered penguin is best between August and January. Sea kayaking (adult/child $75/60) and 4WD nature tours (adult/child $90/50) are also available with the option of staying overnight in a secluded cottage ($60) in the Pohutu Nature Reserve. Book through the visitor information centre.

Surround yourself with the best of the spectacular scenery of Banks Peninsula at **Onuku Heights Horse Treks** (off Map p544; ☎ 03-304 7112; www.onuku-heights.co.nz; 166 Haylocks Rd; from $110; ☿ Nov-May). Onuku Heights is 15 minutes from Akaroa. Follow the signs to Onuku Marae, continue uphill and turn left into Haylocks Rd.

On 2 Wheels (☎ 0800 662 943; www.on2wheels.co.nz; bike trip $80) runs cycling trips featuring 14km of glorious (mostly downhill...) riding, starting at the rim of an ancient volcano, and ending with a beachfront picnic and cold beer. Book at the Akaroa visitor information centre.

Tours

Eastern Bays Scenic Mail Run (☎ 03-304 8600; tour $50; ☿ 9am Mon-Sat) This is a 120km, 4½-hour delivery service to remote parts of the peninsula, and visitors can travel along with the posties to visit isolated communities and bays (beachfront picnic included). The minibus departs the visitor information centre; bookings are essential as there are only eight seats available. See the visitor information centre for other tour options around Banks Peninsula.

To go spy Hector's dolphins and blue penguins, take a harbour cruise.

Akaroa Dolphins (Map p544; ☎ 0800 990 102, 03-304 7866; www.akaroadolphins.co.nz; 65 Beach Rd; adult/child $68/35; ☿ departures 10.15am, 12.45pm & 3.15pm) Two-hour wildlife cruises, plus evening cruises and birdwatching trips by arrangement. Say hi to Murphy, wildlife-spotting dog extraordinaire for us.

Black Cat Cruises (Map p544; ☎ 03-304 7641; www.blackcat.co.nz; Main Wharf; adult/child $65/25; ☿ departures 11am, 1.30pm & 3.40pm, more limited in winter) Two-hour cruises viewing wildlife, caves and cliffs.

Fox II Sailing Adventures (Map p544; ☎ 0800 369 7245; www.akaroafoxsail.co.nz; Daly's Wharf; ☿ departures 10.30am & 1.30pm Dec–mid-May) History, scenery and wildlife on NZ's oldest gaff-rigged ketch.

Festivals & Events

French Fest Akaroa (www.frenchfest.co.nz) is a Gallic-inspired get-together held annually in late September/early October with an emphasis on food, wine, music and art. Don't miss (or stand on) *Le Race D'Escargots*, where sleek, highly trained snails negotiate a compact

---

SWIMMING WITH DOLPHINS

The waters around Akaroa are home to the world's smallest and rarest dolphin, the Hector's dolphin, found only in NZ waters. If viewing the dolphins on a harbour cruise (above) isn't enough, **Black Cat Cruises** (Map p544; ☎ 03-304 7641; www.blackcat.co.nz; Main Wharf; ☿ 5 tours daily 6am-3.30pm Oct-April, 1 tour daily 11.30am May-Sep) can get you swimming alongside the dolphins (assuming it's not the calving season). Trips operate year-round and carry only 10 swimmers per trip, so book ahead. Wet suits and snorkelling gear are provided, plus hot showers back on dry land. Count on a 2½-hour outing including time in and on the water, and a $50 refund if you don't get to swim with the dolphins. Cruises have around a 98% success rate in seeing dolphins, and an 81% success rate in actually swimming with them, so it's pretty good odds. Costs are around $130/110 per adult/child for a cruise and swim, and $70/35 per adult/child for a cruise only.

course. There's also a French Waiter's Race later in the day.

Sleeping

Most Banks Peninsula accommodation is around Akaroa, but the outer bays are also blessed with excellent budget lodgings. Akaroa has some splurge-worthy, romantic B&B accommodation.

Akaroa

Akaroa Top 10 Holiday Park (Map p544; ☎ 0800 727 525, 03-304 7471; www.akaroa-holidaypark.co.nz; 96 Morgans Rd; sites $32-36, cabins & units $65-115; 💻 🛜) On a terraced hillside above town and connected by a pathway to Woodhills Rd, this pleasant park has good harbour views and versatile options for every budget.

Chez la Mer (Map p544; ☎ 03-304 7024; www.chezlamer.co.nz; 50 Rue Lavaud; dm $25, d with/without bathroom $70/60; 💻 🛜) Friendly backpackers with well-kept rooms and a shaded garden, complete with fish ponds, hammocks, barbecue and outdoor seating. Free bikes and fishing rods are available, and it's a TV-free zone.

Bon Accord (Map p544; ☎ 03-304 7782; www.bon-accord.co.nz; 57 Rue Lavaud; dm $27, d $60-70; 💻 🛜) This colourful and quirky backpackers fills a compact 155-year-old house. Relax on the deck or in the two cosy lounges, or dive into the herb-filled garden to release your inner French chef. There's free bikes to get you exploring.

La Rive Motel (Map p544; ☎ 0800 247 651, 03-304 7651; www.larivemotel.co.nz; 1 Rue Lavaud; d $115-165; 💻 🛜) Old-style motel with big rooms and good facilities; well priced considering each unit (studios, two- and three-bedroom options) is fully self-contained. New owners have recently given La Rive a makeover.

Tresori Motor Lodge (Map p544; ☎ 0800 273 747, 03-304 7500; www.tresori.co.nz; cnr Rue Jolie & Church St; d $170-200; 💻 🛜) For designer-conscious lodgings treat yourself to the Tresori, with rich, colourful decor that's anything but bland.

Old Shipping Office (Map p544; ☎ 0800 695 2000; www.akaroavillageinn.co.nz; Church St; d $200) Self-contained apartment in a restored heritage building with an interesting past. Two bedrooms, a spacious shared lounge and a spa make the Old Shipping Office a good option for families or for two couples. No prizes for guessing the building's former incarnation.

Oinako Lodge (Map p544; ☎ 03-304 8787; www.oinako.co.nz; 99 Beach Rd; d incl breakfast $245-285; 💻 🛜) This

glorious timber mansion was built in 1865 for the then British magistrate. Almost 15 decades later, it's now a wonderfully upmarket bed and breakfast with six themed rooms, expansive bay windows with sea and garden views, and gourmet breakfasts you'll definitely want to linger over.

Garthowen (Map p544; ☎ 03-304 7419; www.garthowen.co.nz; 7 Beach Rd; s/d $265-295; 💻 🛜) With two vintage Citroën cars, two friendly Jack Russell terriers and four supercomfortable en-suite rooms, (almost) everything comes in twos at this upscale B&B rebuilt in heritage style using recycled cedar. Breakfast on the deck comes with a side order of the best view in town.

Around Banks Peninsula

Okains Bay Camping Ground (Map p543; ☎ 03-304 8789; 1162 Okains Bay Rd; adult/child $8/5) Pine-tree-peppered ground right by the beach, with kitchen facilities and coin-operated hot showers. Pay your fees at the house at the camping ground's entrance. There's a small general store a few hundred metres down the road.

ourpick Onuku Farm Hostel (Map p543; ☎ 03-304 7066; www.onukufarm.com; Onuku Rd; tent or van sites per person $15, dm/d from $28/66; 🌙 closed Jun-Aug; 💻) An ecominded backpackers (with basic huts, tent sites and a comfy house) on a sheep farm near Onuku, 6km south of Akaroa. From November to March the owners organise swimming-with-dolphins tours ($100) and kayaking trips ($45) for guests, and will pick up from Akaroa. The same family has owned the farm since the 1860s, so you should trust them when they say there's some great walks on the 340-hectare spread.

Purple Peak Backpackers (Map p543; ☎ 03-420 0199; camping by donation, dm/d/tr $25/60/90; 💻) This rustic surf lodge and backpackers has glorious sea views and a rugged out-of-the-way location. Accommodation is simple but clean, and during summer there's the occasional tasty seafood barbecue ($12 per person). Surfboards and gear are available for hire. Free shuttles are provided from Akaroa. See Darin at the Akaroa Adventure Centre (p545).

Halfmoon Cottage (Map p543; ☎ 03-304 5050; www.halfmoon.co.nz; Barrys Bay; dm/s/d $28/48/66; 🌙 often closed Jun-Sep) This marvellous cottage at Barrys Bay (12km from Akaroa) is a blissful place to spend a few days, lazing on the big verandas or in the hammocks dotting the lush gardens. The rooms – mostly doubles – are warmly decorated and there are free bikes and kayaks for guest use.

Double Dutch (Map p543; ☎ 03-304 7229; www.double-dutch.co.nz; 32 Chorlton Rd, Okains Bay; dm/s $28/53, d with/without bathroom $72/66; ⌨) Posh enough to be a B&B, but budget-friendly, this relaxed spot is perched in farmland on a secluded river estuary. There's a general store (and the beach) just a short walk away, but you're best to bring your own ingredients for the flash kitchen.

Eating & Drinking

L'Escargot Rouge (Map p544; ☎ 03-304 8774; 67 Beach Rd; meals $6-14; ⏰ from 8am) Tasty pies ($6), picnic fixings and French-accented breakfasts are the main attractions at the 'Red Snail'. Gourmet 'meals-to-go' ($8 to $14) are perfect for alfresco harbourside dining.

Vangionis (Map p544; ☎ 03-308 7144; Rue Brittan; tapas $8-15, pizza $18-28; ⏰ 11am-late) Thin-crust pizzas, tapas, pasta and Canterbury beers and wines all feature at this Tuscan-style trattoria. Secure an outside table and while away the afternoon or evening. Takeaway pizzas are also available.

Bully Hayes (Map p544; ☎ 03-304 7533; 57 Beach Rd; lunch $13-20, dinner mains $22-30; ⏰ 8am-late) Named after a well-travelled American buccaneer, the menu at this sunny spot kicks off with Akaroa salmon before touching down in New York for gourmet burgers, Italy for pasta, and a leisurely final stop in Spain for tapas. Monteith's beers and a good local wine list make it a worthwhile place to linger.

Truby's Bar on the Beach (Map p544; ☎ 03-308 7144; Rue Jolie; ⏰ 10am-late) An absolute waterfront location teams with rustic outdoor seating to produce Akaroa's best place for a sundowner drink. Toasted ciabatta rolls ($9.50) and good coffee are other distractions earlier in the day.

Get yourself an all-day breakfast at **Akaroa Bakery** (Map p544; ☎ 03-304 7663; 51 Beach Rd; snacks & meals $5-15; ⏰ 7am-4pm), or takeaways from **Akaroa Fish & Chips** (Map p544; ☎ 03-304 7464; 59 Beach Rd; meals $6-10; ⏰ 10am-7pm Sun-Thu, 10.30am-8pm Fri & Sat).

The **Four Square supermarket** (Map p544; Rue Lavaud; ⏰ 9am-6pm Mon-Sat) has a good deli.

Entertainment

Cine Café (Map p544; ☎ 03-304 7678; www.cinecafe.co.nz; cnr Rue Jolie & Selwyn Ave; adult/child $15/13; ⏰ 2-10pm) Part cafe with excellent pastries and soups, and part cinema showing art-house flicks.

Getting There & Away

The **Akaroa Shuttle** (☎ 0800 500 929; return $45) departs from outside the Christchurch i-SITE in Cathedral Sq at 8.30am and 2pm, returning from Akaroa at 10.30am, 3.35pm and 4.30pm. There's an extra departure from Christchurch at 4.30pm on a Friday. Bookings are recommended.

French Connection (☎ 0800 800 575; www.akaroabus.co.nz; return from $20) has a year-round daily departure from the Christchurch i-SITE at 8.45am, returning from Akaroa at 2.30pm and 4.30pm. During summer additional services may operate – ask at the Christchurch i-SITE.

Both companies run scenic tours from Christchurch exploring Banks Peninsula ($110).

NORTH CANTERBURY

From Christchurch, SH1 heads north for 57km through Woodend and Amberley to Waipara. From here SH1 continues northeast to Kaikoura, while SH7 branches due north to Hurunui through flat farming country and reaches Culverden. About 27km from Culverden is the turn-off from SH7 to Hanmer Springs, a thermal resort. The *Alpine Pacific Triangle Touring Guide* outlines things to see and do in this region. See also www.visithurunui.co.nz.

If you're a passionate wine buff or foodie, look for the North Canterbury Food & Wine Trail touring map at the i-SITE in Christchurch (p520). Online see www.foodandwinetrail.co.nz.

The **Brew Moon Garden Café & Brewery** (☎ 03-314 0830; 150 Ashworths Rd, Amberley; mains $15-26; ⏰ 10.30am-late Mon-Fri, 10am-late Sat & Sun) on SH75 in Amberley crafts four different beers; sample them all for $8.80. Our favourite is the gloriously hoppy Hophead IPA. Gourmet pizzas ($20 to $25) and meals including Akaroa salmon and steak sandwiches are also available.

A few kilometres up SH1, the scenic **Waipara Valley** is home to around 20 wineries. See www.waiparawines.co.nz. Sample a pinot noir or riesling and stop for lunch at one of the spectacular vineyard restaurants. **Waipara Springs** (☎ 03-314 6777; www.waiparasprings.co.nz; SH1,

north of Waipara), **Pegasus Bay** (☎ 03-314 6869; www.
pegasusbay.com; Stockgrove Rd, south of Waipara) and the
Mud House (☎ 03-314 6900; www.themudhouse.co.nz;
SH1, south of Waipara) are open daily for wine tasting and sales, and all have restaurant-cafes for
a leisurely lunch.

The annual **Waipara Wine and Food Festival**
(www.waiparawineandfood.co.nz) is held in early
March.

Wine tours are available from several
Christchurch-based companies (p530).

The **Pegasus Bay restaurant** (☎ 03-314 6869;
www.pegasusbay.com; Stockgrove Rd, south of Waipara;
mains $29-36, ☯ noon-4pm) has an old-world
ambience set amid a lovely European-style
garden. The menu takes advantage of superb
local produce and recommends appropriate wines matches. Pegasus Bay is a regular
contender for NZ's Best Winery Restaurant
award.

Near the intersection with SH7 is **Waipara
Sleepers** (☎ 03-314 6003; www.waiparasleepers.co.nz;
12 Glenmark Dr; unpowered/powered sites $20/25, dm $22, s
$35-42, d from $48; 💻 📶), where you can camp,
bunk down in converted train carriages, and
cook your own meals in the 'station house'.
The local pub and general store are located
close by.

HANMER SPRINGS
pop 750

Hanmer Springs, the main thermal resort on
the South Island, is 10km off SH7. It's a pleasantly low-key spot to indulge in pampering
in the hot pools and a flash new spa complex.
There are a couple of good restaurants, and
family-friendly activities include forest walks,
minigolf, horse treks and jetboating.

Information
Bank of New Zealand (☯ 10am-2pm Mon-Fri) At the
i-SITE. Another ATM at the Four Square supermarket.
Hanmer Springs Foodway (43 Amuri Ave; ☯ 10am-
10pm) Internet access.
Hanmer Springs i-SITE (☎ 03-315 0020; www.
visithanmersprings.co.nz, www.visithurunui.co.nz; 42
Amuri Ave; ☯ 10am-5pm) Books transport, accommoda-
tion and activities.
Powerhouse Café (p550) Wi-fi with a purchase.

Sights
THERMAL RESERVE
Visitors have been soaking in the waters of
Hanmer Springs Thermal Pools (☎ 03-315 0020; www.
hanmersprings.co.nz; entry on Jacks Pass Rd; adult/child $18/7;

☯ 10am-9pm) for over 100 years. Local legend
has it that the thermal springs are the fires of
Tamatea that fell from the sky after an erup-
tion of Mt Ngauruhoe on the North Island;
Maoris call the springs Waitapu (Sacred
Waters).

The hot spring water mixes with freshwater to produce pools of varying temperatures. In addition to mineral pools, there
are landscaped rock pools, a freshwater 25m
lap pool, private sauna/steam suites ($24 per
half-hour), a restaurant, and a family activity
area including a waterslide ($6). The adjacent
Hanmer Springs Spa (☎ 0800 873 527, 03-315 0029;
www.hanmerspa.co.nz; ☯ 10am-7pm) has massage
and beauty treatments from $65.

MOLESWORTH STATION
Northeast of Hanmer Springs, Molesworth
Station, at 180,500 hectares, is NZ's largest
farm with the country's largest cattle herd (up
to 10,000). Inquire at the i-SITE about independent visits to Molesworth, which is under
DOC control. Visits are usually only possible
when the Acheron Rd through the station
is open from late December to early April,
weather permitting. The drive from Hanmer
Springs north to Blenheim on this narrow,
unsealed backcountry road takes around six
hours; note that the gates are only open from
7am to 7pm, and overnight camping (adult/
child $6/1.50) is permitted in certain areas (no
open fires allowed). Pick up the Department
of Conservation *Molesworth Station* brochure
from the Hanmer Springs i-SITE or download
it from www.doc.govt.nz.

Trailways Safaris (☎ 03-315 7401; www.molesworth.
co.nz; tours $195-665; ☯ Oct-May) offers 4WD tours
of the station and the remote private land
stretching north to St Arnaud. Day tours include a picnic lunch and there is a five-hour
'no frills' option.

Activities
Hanmer Springs Adventure Centre (☎ 03-315 7233;
www.hanmeradventure.co.nz; 20 Conical Hill Rd; ☯ 9am-
5pm) books activities, and rents mountain
bikes (per hour/day from $19/45), fishing
rods (per day $25) and ski and snowboard
gear. Mountain biking maps ($2) are available
at the i-SITE.

There are two skiing areas nearby. **Hanmer
Springs Ski Field** is the closest, 17km (unsealed)
from town, and **Mt Lyford Ski Field** is 60km
away. They're cheaper than larger resorts (see

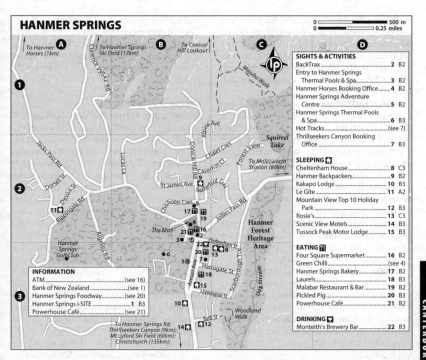

HANMER SPRINGS

CHRISTCHURCH & CANTERBURY

p86). The Hanmer Springs Adventure Centre operates transport.

The *Hanmer Forest Recreation* pamphlet ($2) outlines short walks near town, mostly through picturesque forest. The easy **Woodland Walk** starts from Jollies Pass Rd, 1km from town, and goes through Douglas fir, poplar and redwood stands. It joins the **Majuba Walk** (1½ hours), which leads to Conical Hill Lookout and then back towards town. The i-SITE has details of longer tramps, including those in Lake Sumner Forest Park to the west.

Thrillseekers Canyon (☎ 03-315 7046; www.thrillseekerscanyon.co.nz; SH7) is the adrenaline centre of Hanmer Springs. Bungy off a 35m-high bridge ($145), jetboat the Waiau Gorge (adult/child $110/59) or go white-water rafting (Grade II to III) down the Waiau River (adult/child $145/75). Other activities include quad-biking (adult/child $99/90). Book at the Thrillseekers Canyon centre, next to the bridge where the Hanmer Springs turn-off meets SH7. Another **booking office** (☎ 03-315 7346; 37 Amuri Ave; ⏲ 10am-6pm) is in town.

Hanmer Horses (☎ 0800 873 546; www.hanmerhorses.co.nz; The Mall; 1hr rides adult/child $50/45, 2½hr treks $95)

leave from a forested setting 10 minutes from town on Rogerson Rd. Younger children can be led on a pony for 30 minutes ($20).

BackTrax (☎ 0800 422 258, 03-315 7073; www.backtrax.co.nz; cnr Jacks Pass & Conical Hill Rds; trips from $90) organises guided quad-bike trips up into the hills, and along (and across) the Hanmer River. The region is also popular for mountain biking – the Hanmer Springs Adventure Centre (see opposite) offers trail maps, advice and bike rental, and also does organised rides up over Jacks and Jollies Passes.

Hot Tracks (☎ 021 718 551; www.hottracks.co.nz; 37 Amuri Ave; adult/child from $45/35) takes all-terrain Hagglund vehicles into the forests and hills surrounding Hanmer. If you're feeling a bit gung-ho, then a self-drive option ($180) is also available.

Other activities include kayaking, scenic flights, fishing trips and claybird shooting.

Sleeping

Mountain View Top 10 Holiday Park (☎ 0800 904 545, 03-315 7113; www.mountainviewtop10.co.nz; Bath St; unpowered/powered sites $30/35, cabins & motels $65-140; 🖳 🛜) Family-friendly park a few minutes' walk from the thermal reserve. Kids will love the playground, trampoline and mountain bikes for rent (per hour $10). Take your pick from basic cabins (BYO everything) to two-bedroom motel units with everything supplied. There are two more camping grounds in town if it's full.

Hanmer Backpackers (☎ 03-315 7196; hanmerback packers@xtra.co.nz; 41 Conical Hill Rd; dm/s/d $27/55/58; 🖳 🛜) Centrally located, the township's original backpackers has recently been given a colourful makeover by new owners. Cosy shared social areas, free fruit, coffee and ice cream (!) all add further big ticks.

Le Gîte (☎ 03-315 5111; www.legite.co.nz; 3 Devon St; dm $27, d with/without bathroom $70/60; 🖳 🛜) Charming old converted home a 10-minute walk from the centre. Large rooms (no bunks), relaxing gardens and a lovely lounge area are drawcards; for extra privacy, book a garden 'chalet' with private bathroom.

Kakapo Lodge (☎ 03-315 7472; ww.kakapolodge. co.nz; 14 Amuri Ave; dm $28, d $66-90; 🖳 🛜) The spartan YHA-affiliated Kakapo has a roomy kitchen and lounge, chill-busting underfloor heating, and an outdoor deck. Bunk-free dorms (some with bathroom) are joined by motel-style units ($100) with TV and cooking facilities.

Rosie's (☎ 03-315 7095; roxyrosie@clearnet.nz; 9 Cheltenham St; s $55-90, d $80-130, all incl breakfast) Rosie was originally from Australia, but she's now offering great Kiwi hospitality at this welcoming reader-recommended spot. Rooms offer either en-suite or shared facilities. Look forward to newly decorated bathrooms and a friendly cat.

Scenic View Motels (☎ 03-315 7419; www.hanmer scenicviews.co.nz; 10 Amuri Ave; d $130-200; 🖳 🛜) An attractive timber-and-stone complex with modern, colourful studios and two- and three-bedroom apartments. Mountain views come as standard.

Tussock Peak Motor Lodge (☎ 0800 8877 625, 03-315 5191; www.tussockpeak.co.nz; cnr Amuri Ave & Leamington St; d $145-200; 🛜) Tussock Peak has colourful decor that's an eclectic cut above other motels on Hanmer's main drag. The hardest part is choosing what kind of room: studio, one- or two-bedroom units, spas, courtyards or balconies.

Cheltenham House (☎ 03-315 7545; www.chel tenham.co.nz; 13 Cheltenham St; s $190-220, d $220-260; 🖳 🛜) Centrally located B&B with six snooze-inducing suites, all with bathroom,

and including two in cosy garden cottages. Cooked gourmet breakfasts can be delivered to your room, and there's a billiard table, grand piano and complimentary pre-dinner wine. Avoid the crowds up the road with the private hot tub.

Eating & Drinking

Hanmer Springs Bakery (☎ 03-315 7714; 16 Conical Hill Rd; pies $5; ⏲ 6am-4pm) Grab a takeaway coffee or a gourmet pie at this place that's a taste of old NZ in rapidly modernising Hanmer Springs.

Powerhouse Café (☎ 03-315 5252; 6 Jacks Pass Rd; meals $8.50-16.50; ⏲ 8am-3pm, open late Thu-Sat in summer; 🛜) Recharge your batteries with a huge High Country breakfast, or linger for a more sophisticated lunch of whitebait fritters and Canterbury lamb. An organic fair-trade coffee is a good trade for wi-fi access.

Green Chilli (☎ 03-315 5188; The Mall; mains $14-20; ⏲ 11.30am-2pm Tue-Fri & 4.30pm-9.30pm Tue-Sun) Run by a friendly Thai family, the cosy Green Chilli respects requests for 'spicy please', and also offers good-value lunch specials. Service – usually by the family's kids – can be hit and miss, but that's part of the low-key charm. Takeaways available.

Pickled Pig (☎ 03-315 7441; 47 Amuri Ave; pizza $14-22; ⏲ 11am-9pm) Pizza, pasta and homemade gelato feature at this spot with an Italian accent. There's also a small deli for picnic fixings.

Malabar Restaurant & Bar (☎ 03-315 7745; 5 Conical Hill Rd; mains $28-32; ⏲ lunch 11am-3pm & dinner 5.30pm-late) This elegant eatery presents Asian cuisine from Beijing to Bangalore. Try the Malabar thali showcasing four different curries, or the mustard and star anise flavoured duck. A limited takeaway menu is available ($10 to $15).

Laurels (☎ 03-315 7788; 31 Amuri Ave; mains $30-35; ⏲ 6pm-late) The most common answer to 'So, what's the most romantic place in town?', the Laurels works hard to showcase Waipara Valley wines and local produce including lamb and salmon. On cooler nights, beside the open fire is the place to be, while during summer, the action is alfresco in the delightful bricked courtyard.

Monteith's Brewery Bar (☎ 03-315 5133; 47 Amuri Ave; ⏲ 11.30am-late Mon-Fri, from 9am Sat & Sun) The best (and most central) pub in town features lots of different craft beers and tasty tucker from bar snacks ($10 to $15) to full meals ($20 to $30). Platters ($44 to $52) are good value if you've just met some new friends in the hot pools across the road.

Four Square supermarket (Conical Hill Rd; 8.30am-7pm Mon-Sat, 9am-5.30pm Sun).

Getting There & Away

Hanmer Connection (0800 242 663; www.atsnz.com) runs from Hanmer Springs to Christchurch ($33, two daily).

East West Coach (0800 142 622, 03-789 6251) has a service that runs between Christchurch and Westport via the Lewis Pass and also diverts to Hanmer Springs.

LEWIS PASS HWY

At the northern end of the Southern Alps, the beautiful Lewis Pass Hwy (SH7) wiggles west from the Hanmer Springs turn-off to Lewis Pass, Maruia Springs and Springs Junction. The 907m-high **Lewis Pass** is not as steep or the forest as dense as Arthur's and Haast Passes, with mainly red and silver beech, and kowhai trees growing along river terraces.

The area has some interesting tramps; see the DOC pamphlet *Lake Sumner/Lewis Pass Recreation* ($1). Most tracks pass through beech forest with a backdrop of snowcapped mountains, lakes, and alpine tarns and rivers. The most popular tramps are around **Lake Sumner** in the Lake Sumner Forest Park and the **St James Walkway** (66km; three to five days) in the Lewis Pass National Reserve. Subalpine conditions apply; sign the intentions book at the start of the St James Walkway and at Windy Point for the Lake Sumner area before heading off.

Maruia Springs (03-523 8840; www.maruiasprings. co.nz; SH7; d $179-199, f $259;) is a small thermal resort on the banks of the Maruia River, 69km from the Hanmer turn-off. It has units (accommodation includes admission to the pools), a cafe-bar and a Japanese restaurant. In the **thermal pools** (adult/child/family $18/8/45; 8am-8.30pm) water is pumped into a gender-segregated traditional Japanese bathhouse and outdoor rock pools. It's a magical setting during a winter snowfall, but mind the sandflies in summer. Massages (per 30/50 minutes $45/65) and private spa houses (per person for 45 minutes $25) are available. Check the website for spa and accommodation special deals.

SH7 continues to **Springs Junction**, where the Shenandoah Hwy (SH65) branches north to meet SH6 near Murchison, while SH7 continues west to Reefton and down to Greymouth. Springs Junction has a petrol station and cafe.

CENTRAL CANTERBURY

Two hours west from Christchurch on SH73 is Arthur's Pass National Park. The trans-island crossing from Christchurch to Greymouth over Arthur's Pass is covered by buses and the *TranzAlpine* train (see p499).

Nowhere else in NZ does the coast rise to the mountains so quickly. From Christchurch the road traverses the Canterbury Plains and then escalates rapidly into the Porter Heights and Craigieburn skiing areas before following the Waimakariri and Bealey Rivers and Lakes Pearson and Grasmere to Arthur's Pass. Southwest of Christchurch (reached by SH73 and SH77) is the Mt Hutt ski resort and Methven.

CRAIGIEBURN FOREST PARK

Accessed from SH73, this forest park is 110km northwest of Christchurch and 42km south of Arthur's Pass. The park has many walking tracks, with longer tramps possible in the valleys west of the Craigieburn Range; see the DOC pamphlet *Craigieburn Forest Park: Day Walks* ($1). The surrounding country is also suitable for skiing and rock climbing. Dominating the vegetation is beech, tussock, totara and turpentine scrub, and even a few patches of South Island edelweiss (*Leucogenes grandiceps*).

Craigieburn has a rise of 503m so is one of NZ's best skiing areas. Its wild-country slopes suit the advanced skier; see p87.

Between the entrance to the forest park and the Broken River bridge to the south is **Cave Stream Scenic Reserve**, with a 594m-long cave with a small waterfall at one end. Take all the necessary precautions (two light sources per person etc) if doing the one-hour walk through the pitch-black cave. For details, get the DOC brochure *Cave Stream Scenic Reserve* (50c). The reserve is in the **Castle Hill area** with prominent limestone outcrops loved by rock climbers and boulderers. Scenes from the *Lord of the Rings* trilogy and *Chronicles of Narnia: The Lion, the Witch and the Wardrobe* were filmed in the area.

Sleeping & Eating

Smylie's Accommodation (03-318 4740; www.smylies. co.nz; Main Rd, Springfield; dm/s/d $26/43/58;) Welcoming YHA-associated hostel in the town of Springfield, around 30km southeast of

Craigieburn. Run by a Dutch-Japanese family, there is a popular Japanese bath, a *kotatsu* (foot warmer) and some futon-equipped rooms. A handful of self-contained motel units ($85 to $120) and a three-bedroom cottage ($180) are also available. In winter, packages including ski-equipment rental and ski-field transport are available. Nearby year-round activities include jetboating, rock climbing, mountain biking and horse trekking.

Flock Hill Lodge (☎ 03-318 8196; www.flockhill.co.nz; SH73; dm/d $30/135; 🖥 🛜) High-country sheep station 44km east of Arthur's Pass, adjacent to Lake Pearson and the Craigieburn Forest Park. Backpackers can stay in rustic shearers' quarters, while large groups can opt for two-bedroom motel units or large cottages with kitchenette. After fishing, exploring, horse riding or mountain biking, recharge in the cosy bar-restaurant.

Bealey Hotel (☎ 03-318 9277; www.bealeyhotel. co.nz; s/d without bathroom $60/80, units $140-170; 🖥) Just 12km east of Arthur's Pass, tiny Bealey is famous for a hoax by the local pub owner in 1993. He reckoned he'd seen a real live moa, hence the bogus Big Bird statue standing on a rocky outcrop. There are self-contained motel units and the budget Moa Lodge with eight double rooms. Enjoy expansive alpine views from the Mad Moa restaurant.

Wilderness Lodge (☎ 03-318 9246; www.wilderness lodge.co.nz; SH73; s $490-640, d $780-980, all incl breakfast & dinner; 🖥) Luxurious lodge on a mountain-beech-speckled sheep station (2400 hectares worth), 16km east of Arthur's Pass. Alpine views and the world's longest driveway produce an absolute middle-of-nowhere atmosphere, and standalone studios with private spa baths feel even more remote. Soft adventure including walking, birdwatching and canoeing is on tap.

Original Sheffield Pie Shop (☎ 03-318 3876; Main Rd, Sheffield; pies $4-5; ⏱ 11am-6pm) This roadside bakery in the quiet Canterbury Plains hamlet of Sheffield turns out some of NZ's best pies.

ARTHUR'S PASS
pop 62

Arthur's Pass village is 4km from the pass of the same name and is NZ's highest-altitude settlement. The 924m pass was used by Maoris to reach Westland, but its European discovery was made by Arthur Dobson in 1864, when the Westland gold rush created the need for a crossing over the Southern Alps from

Christchurch. A coach road was completed within a year, but later on the coal and timber trade demanded a railway, duly completed in 1923.

The town is a handy base for tramps, climbs, views and wintertime skiing in Arthur's Pass National Park.

Information

DOC Arthur's Pass visitor information centre (☎ 03-318 9211; www.apinfo.co.nz; arthurspassvc@doc.govt.nz; SH73; ⏱ 8am-5pm) has information on all park tramps, including route guides for longer hut-lined tramps. It doesn't make onward bookings or reservations, but can help with local accommodation and transport information. The centre screens a 17-minute video (adult/child $1/free) on the history of Arthur's Pass and has excellent displays – check out the 1888 Cobb & Co coach.

Purchase detailed topographical maps ($9) and hire mandatory locator beacons ($35) from DOC. DOC also advises on the park's often savagely changeable weather. Check conditions here and fill out an intentions card before venturing out. Sign in again after returning to avoid a search party being organised.

The Arthur's Pass Store has internet access. There is no ATM in Arthur's Pass.

Online see www.arthurspass.com. For specific information on weather conditions in the mountains see www.softrock.co.nz.

Sights & Activities

Near DOC is the small interfaith **chapel**, with wonderful views.

Day tramps offer 360-degree views of snow-capped peaks, many of them over 2000m; the highest is Mt Murchison (2400m). There are huts on the tramping tracks and several areas suitable for camping. Tramping is best in the drier months (January to April). The leaflet *Walks in Arthur's Pass National Park* ($2) details walks to scenic places including **Devils Punchbowl Waterfall** (one hour return), **Temple Basin** (three hours return) and **Avalanche Peak** (six to eight hours return). The pleasant **Dobson Nature Walk** (30 minutes return) is best from November to February when the alpine flowers are blooming. Recommended for fit trampers is the **Bealey Spur Track** (four to six hours return) with expansive views of the Waimakariri River valley and surrounding mountains. Longer tramps with superb alpine backdrops include

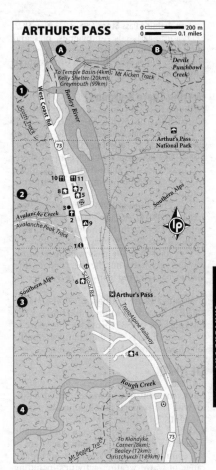

INFORMATION
DOC Arthur's Pass Visitor Information Centre............1 A2

SIGHTS & ACTIVITIES
Chapel..2 A2
Outdoor Education Centre.....................................3 A2

SLEEPING
Arthur's Pass Alpine Motel......................................4 B3
Arthur's Pass Village Motel......................................5 A2
Mountain House Cottages.......................................6 A3
Mountain House YHA Backpackers & Cottages.....7 A2
Mountain House YHA Backpackers & Cottages.....8 A2
Public Shelter...9 A2

EATING
Arthur's Pass Store...10 A2
Wobbly Kea..11 A2

the **Goat Pass Track** (two days), and the longer and more difficult **Harman Pass** and **Harpers Pass Tracks**. These tracks require previous tramping experience as flooding can make the rivers dangerous and the weather is extremely changeable; ask DOC first.

Home in the Hills (☎ 027 451 1550; www.homeinthehills.co.nz) offers short alpine encounters (three to five hours, $100), guided nature walks and birdwatching (two to three hours, $80), and longer personalised mountain and bush experiences.

There's also skiing at Temple Basin; see p86.

Sleeping & Eating

Camp within Arthur's Pass township at the basic **public shelter** (adult/child $6/3), opposite DOC, where there's stream water, a sink, tables and toilets. Camping is free at **Klondyke Corner**, 8km south of Arthur's Pass, and **Kelly Shelter**, 20km to the northwest; both have toilets and the water must be boiled before drinking.

Mountain House YHA Backpackers & Cottages (☎ 03-318 9258; www.trampers.co.nz; SH73; dm $27, s/d/tr/q $73/76/93/116, cottage sleeping up to 10 from $220; ☐ �) has excellent dorms and private rooms on one side of the highway, and older, but still comfortable rooms across the road in what was one of NZ's earliest youth hostels. The owner is a wealth of information on local activities, and also provides transport to trailheads (p554). Self-contained cottages with cosy open fires are also available. Bookings recommended from November to April. You can sometimes camp ($20 per person) near the cottages, but you'll need to phone ahead to check availability first.

In the southern part of town, **Arthur's Pass Alpine Motel** (☎ 03-318 9233; www.apam.co.nz; SH73; d $115-135; ☐ �) has simple but comfortable motel units, some recently refurbished, and with new beds. If you're snowed in there's a good DVD library and Freeview satellite TV.

Centrally located, the **Arthur's Pass Village Motel** (☎ 021 131 0616; www.apmotel.co.nz; SH73; d $145) has two luxury units with cosy leather furniture and warm, natural colours. Booking ahead from November to April is highly recommended.

The **Wobbly Kea** (☎ 03-318 9101; SH73; meals $15-24; ☺ 9am-10.30pm Sun-Thu, to late Fri & Sat) is a friendly cafe-bar serving steaks, pasta and pizza. Takeaway pizza ($26) is also available. Breakfast at the Wobbly Kea ($13 to $19) is also a local tradition.

The **Arthur's Pass Store** (☎ 03-318 9235; SH73; ⌚ 7am-7pm; 🖳) sells sandwiches, pies and good breakfasts. Limited groceries and petrol are very expensive; fill up in Christchurch or Greymouth.

Getting There & Around
Arthur's Pass sees buses travelling between Christchurch ($25 to $36) and Greymouth ($26); both **Atomic Shuttles** (☎ 03-349 0697; www.atomictravel.co.nz) and **West Coast Shuttle** (☎ 027 492 7488, 03-768 0028; www.westcoastshuttle.co.nz) stop here. Bus tickets are sold at the Arthur's Pass Store. In Christchurch, both companies depart from Cathderal Sq.

The *TranzAlpine* train operated by **Tranz Scenic** (☎ 0800 872 467; www.tranzscenic.co.nz) runs between Christchurch and Greymouth via Arthur's Pass. See the boxed text, p499.

The road over the pass was once winding and very steep, but the spectacular Otira viaduct has removed many of the treacherous hairpin bends.

Mountain House Shuttle (☎ 027 419 2354, 03-318 9258), based at Mountain House YHA Backpackers (p553), provides transport to various trailheads. See the Trampers Shuttle tab on www.trampers.co.nz for costs.

METHVEN
pop 1140
Methven is busiest in winter, when it fills up with snow-sports fans heading to nearby Mt Hutt. In summer, Methven town is a laid-back option with quieter (and usually cheaper) accommodation than elsewhere in the country, and a 'what shall I do today?' range of warm-weather activities including ballooning, tramping, fishing and skydiving.

Information
Bank of New Zealand (Main St) With ATM.
Medical centre (☎ 03-302 8105; Main St)
Methven i-SITE (☎ 03-302 8955; www.methveninfo.co.nz, www.amazingspace.co.nz; 160 Main St; ⌚ 8am-6pm daily May-Oct, 9am-5pm Mon-Fri, 11am-4pm Sat & Sun Nov-Apr; 🖳) Books accommodation, skiing packages, transport and activities. Internet available.
PC House (McMillan St; ⌚ 11am-5pm Mon-Tue, to 6pm Wed-Sat) For internet access. There is also paid wi-fi at Cafe 131 (p556).

Activities
Nearby **Mount Hutt** (see p86) offers five months of skiing (June to October, weather permitting), often the longest ski season of any resort in NZ.

For mountain bikes, and ski rental and advice, see **Big Al's Snow Sports** (☎ 03-302 8003; www.bigals.co.nz; cnr Main St & Forest Dr; mountain bikes per hr/day $12/39).

Methven Heliskiing (☎ 03-302 8108; www.methvenheliski.co.nz, www.heliskiing.co.nz; Main St; five-run day trips $525; ⌚ May-Oct) offers trips including guide service, safety equipment and lunch. **Black Diamond Safaris** (☎ 03-302 1884; www.blackdiamondsafaris.co.nz) can take you to uncrowded club ski fields by 4WD. Prices start at $150 for 4WD transport only, while $270 gets you transport, a lift pass, guiding and lunch.

Nearby Pudding Hill is a skydiving centre. **Skydiving NZ** (☎ 03-302 9143; www.skydivingnz.com; Pudding Hill Airfield) offers tandem jumps from 3600m ($369), and the **NZ Skydiving School** (☎ 03-302 9143; www.nzskydivingschool.com) has introductory courses starting at $395.

Aoraki Balloon Safaris (☎ 0800 256 837, 03-302 8172; www.nzballooning.co.nz; flights $385) offers flights that include snowcapped peaks and a champagne breakfast.

The **Mount Hutt Forest** is predominantly mountain beech; it's 14km west of Methven. Adjoining it are the **Awa Awa Rata Reserve** and the **Pudding Hill Scenic Reserve**. There are two access roads: Pudding Hill Rd leads to foot access for Pudding Hill Stream, and McLennan's Bush Rd leads to both reserves. There are many walking trails, including the water-crossing **Pudding Hill Stream Route** (two hours).

There's a good, easy walk through farmland and the impressive **Rakaia Gorge** (three to four hours return), beginning at the car park just south of the bridge on SH77. There are good picnic spots around the bridge. **Rakaia Gorge Alpine Jet** (☎ 03-318 6574; www.rivertours.co.nz; tour $68) and **Rakaia Gorge Scenic Jet** (☎ 03-318 6515; tour $65) both do 40-minute jetboat trips through the gorge.

Terrace Downs (☎ 03-318 6943; www.terracedowns.co.nz; SH72; green fees $140, club hire $45), 30km from Methven near Windwhistle, is a 'high-country resort' with a world-class 18-hole golf course. Take your pick from three restaurants of increasing sophistication, or escape the rigours of life on the road in Terrace Downs' recently opened spa (open 10am to 6pm Wednesday to Sunday).

Ask at the i-SITE about horse riding, mountain biking, fishing, scenic helicopter flights and farm tours.

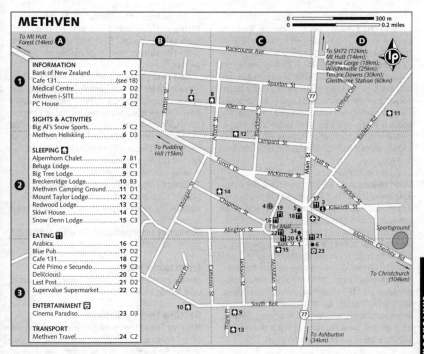

MAP LEGEND: METHVEN

Sleeping

Some accommodation is closed in summer, but the following are open year-round with lower prices often available outside the ski season. During the ski season, it pays to book well ahead, especially for budget accommodation.

our pick Alpernhorn Chalet (☎ 03-302 8779; www.alpenhorn.co.nz; 44 Allen St; dm $25, d $60-85; ☐) This small, inviting home has a conservatory housing an indoor garden and a spa pool. A log fire, free internet and complimentary espresso coffee seal the deal. The bright bedrooms have been recently redecorated, and an in-house reflexologist and massage therapist is on hand if you've come a cropper on the slopes.

Snow Denn Lodge (☎ 03-302 8999; www.methven accommodation.co.nz; cnr McMillan & Bank Sts; dm/d $25/70, d with bathroom $80; ☐ ☎) This YHA-associated lodge has appealing dining/living areas, a large kitchen, and indoor and outdoor spa pools. Prices include breakfast and equipment hire (bikes, golf clubs, fishing gear etc).

Glenthorne Station (☎ 0800 926 868, 03-318 5818; www.glenthorne.co.nz; lodge per person $25-35, holiday house per person $50, chalet per person $160) Beautifully isolated 25,800-hectare sheep station, 60km northwest of Methven on the northern shore of Lake Coleridge. The high-country accommodation ranges from a 15-bed budget lodge (equipped with kitchen, but meals are available from the homestead), to self-contained holiday houses or DB&B (dinner, bed and breakfast) lake-view chalets. There are activities aplenty including 4WD tours, fishing, horse riding and walking.

Methven Camping Ground (☎ 03-302 8005; methven nz@hotmail.com; Barkers Rd; unpowered/powered sites $26/28, cabins $40-55) Small park in a scenic location close to the centre of town. Facilities (including a TV room) are serviceable. Tiny budget cabins are OK, but it's worth spending slightly more at a backpackers.

Big Tree Lodge (☎ 03-302 9575; www.bigtreelodge. co.nz; 25 South Belt; dm $27-29, s/tr 45/90, d $65-110; ☐ ☎) Transformed from a one-time vicarage, this friendly and relaxed lodge has lovely wood-trimmed bathrooms, and a comfy, heritage ambience. Long-term discounts are available.

Redwood Lodge (☎ 03-302 8964; www.snowboardnz. com; 3 Wayne Pl; s $55, d $65-90, tr & q $120; ☐ ☎) Turkish rugs and a bright decor give this family-friendly spot with single, double, triple and quad rooms plenty of charm. En-suite rooms with TV provide privacy and there's a huge shared TV lounge and kitchen.

Beluga Lodge (☎ 03-302 8290; www.beluga.co.nz; 40 Allen St; d incl breakfast $210-250; 🖳) Highly relaxing B&B with king-sized beds, fluffy bathrobes, luscious bathrooms and private decks. Extreme privacy-seekers should consider the garden suite, with its own patio and barbecue. A four-bedroom cottage is also available ($350; minimum three-night stay from June to October).

Also recommended:

Skiwi House (☎ 03-302 8872; www.skiwihouse.co.nz; 30 Chapman St; dm $25, d $58; 🅿 🖳) Smaller backpackers with a family atmosphere and plenty of DVDs if the mountain is closed. Covered storage area for bicycles, and drying and tuning facilities for powderhounds.

Mount Taylor Lodge (☎ 03-302 9699; www.mount taylorlodge.co.nz; 32 Lampard St; s/d incl breakfast $90/180; 🖳) Stylish 11-room lodge with wooden floors.

Breckenridge Lodge (☎ 03-302 8902; www.brecken ridgelodge.com; 49-51 South Belt; s/d/tr/q/f incl breakfast $95/115/140/165/185; 🖳 🛜) Versatile lodge with a wide array of rooms, warm wooden decor, and a lounge bar. A spa pool, sauna and games room provide plenty of distraction before and after hitting the slopes.

Eating & Drinking

Cafe 131 (☎ 03-302 9131; Main St; meals $6-17; ⏱7.30am-late; 🖳 🛜) A warm space with polished timber and leadlight windows. Serves up all-day breakfasts, good-value platters, and soup, pasta, and sandwiches. Beer and wine takes over later in the day. There's also paid wi-fi.

Café Primo e Secundo (☎ 03-302 9309; 38 McMillan St; meals $10-18; ⏱8am-5pm) A treasure trove of retro Kiwiana; the coolest part is that everything is for sale. Sandwiched in and around the souvenir teaspoons and Buzzy Bee bookends are tasty cakes, panini, and legendary bacon and egg sandwiches. You'll also unearth Methven's best coffee.

Blue Pub (☎ 03-302 8046; Main St; mains $10-30; ⏱noon-late) Drink at the bar crafted from a huge slab of native timber, or tuck into surprisingly sophisticated meals like parmesan-crusted blue cod in the quieter restaurant. Challenge the locals to a game of pool or watch rugby on the big screen (most Friday and Saturday nights from March to June).

Arabica (☎ 03-302 8455; 36 McMillan St; mains $15-20; ⏱9am-4pm Tue-Thu & Sat, to late Fri) Coolly

cosmopolitan cafe with an all-day menu featuring brekkie items like corned beef hash with salmon cakes. Beer and wine goes well with the dinner menu available on Friday nights.

Last Post (☎ 03-302 8259; Main St; mains $25-35; ⏱6pm-late Tue-Sat, from 5pm daily in winter) Popular après-ski rendezvous point where the day's downhill escapades are recounted over good cocktails and innovative mains like grilled yellow-fin tuna or crusted Canterbury lamb backstrap. The excellent wine list features the best of the South Island.

Also recommended:

Deli(cious) (☎ 03-302 9239; Bank St; tapas 3 for $25; ⏱11am-3pm Mon & 9am-6pm Tue-Sat) Spanish meatballs and chorizo offer an alternative to another hostel kitchen creation.

Supervalue supermarket (cnr The Mall & MacMillan St; ⏱7am-9pm).

Entertainment

Cinema Paradiso (☎ 03-302 1957; www.cinemaparadiso. co.nz; Main St; adult/child $14/11)

Getting There & Around

Methven Travel (☎ 03-302 8106; www.methventravel. co.nz; 93 Main St; adult/child one-way $36/18; ⏱Mon, Wed, Fri, Sat in summer, up to three times daily in winter) picks up from Christchurch. Cathedral Sq and Christchurch airport departures are available. Other companies offer this service during winter. Ask at the Christchurch i-SITE for details (p520).

Shuttles operate from Methven to Mt Hutt ski field in winter for around $35; enquiries and pick-ups are from Methven i-SITE.

MT SOMERS

Mt Somers is a small settlement just off SH72, the main road between Geraldine and Mt Hutt. The **Mt Somers Subalpine Walkway** (17km, 10 hours) traverses the northern face of Mt Somers, linking the popular picnic spots of Sharplin Falls and Woolshed Creek. Trail highlights include volcanic formations, Maori rock drawings, deep river canyons and botanical diversity. There are two huts on the tramp: **Pinnacles Hut** and **Woolshed Creek Hut** ($10 each). This route is subject to sudden changes in weather and precautions should be taken. Hut tickets and information are available at the **Mt Somers General Store** (☎ 03-303 9831; Pattons Rd). There are other shorter walks in the area.

The **Mt Somers Holiday Park** (☎ 03-303 9719; www.
mountsomers.co.nz; Hoods Rd; sites $26, cabins $54-69) is
small and well-maintained.

At the highway turn-off to Mt Somers is
Stronechrubie (☎ 03-303 9814; www.stronechrubie.co.nz;
SH72; d $110-160), with studios and luxury chalets
scattered across bird-filled gardens. The intimate **restaurant** (mains $29-31; ☼ 6.30pm-late Wed-Sat,
noon-2pm Sun) features excellent Canterbury
lamb and local venison and duck. Consider a
DB&B package (per two people $230 to $280).

SOUTH CANTERBURY

SH1 heading south from Christchurch along
the coast passes through the port city of
Timaru on its way to Dunedin and carries a
lot of traffic. The inland route along SH8 is also
busy, but showcases the stunning landscapes
of the Mackenzie Country. Studded with the
intense blue lakes of Tekapo and Ohau, SH80
veers off at Twizel in the Mackenzie Country
to hug Lake Pukaki all the way to the magnificent heights of Aoraki/Mt Cook National Park.

TIMARU
pop 26,750
The port city of Timaru is a handy stopping-
off point halfway between Christchurch and
Dunedin. Many travellers prefer to kick on
85km further south to the smaller, more
charming Oamaru, but a few good restaurants
and good-value motels means Timaru is worthy of a spot of travellers' R&R. The town's
name comes from the Maori name Te Maru,
meaning the 'Place of Shelter'. No permanent
settlement existed here until 1839 when the
Weller brothers from Sydney set up a whaling
station. The *Caroline*, a sailing ship that picked
up whale oil, gave the picturesque bay its name.

Orientation
SH1 is known by many names as it passes
through Timaru: the Hilton Hwy north of
town, Evans St as it enters town and then
Theodosia St and Craigie Ave as it bypasses
the central business district around Stafford
St. Continuing south, the highway becomes
King St and then SH1 again after emerging
from town. Confused?

Information
The **Timaru i-SITE** (☎ 0800 484 6278, 03-688 6163; www.
southisland.org.nz; 2 George St; ☼ 8.30am-5pm Mon-Fri,

10am-3pm Sat & Sun) is across from the train station (trains in this area only carry freight,
not passengers). The i-SITE has street maps,
information on local walks, and also handles
transport bookings. Internet is available at
the i-SITE and across the road at the Off the
Rail Café (p559).

Sights
South Canterbury Museum (☎ 03-687 7212; www.
timaru.govt.nz; Perth St; admission by donation; ☼ 10am-
4.30pm Tue-Fri, 1.30-4.30pm Sat & Sun) has historical
and natural artefacts of the region. Hanging
from the ceiling is a replica of the aeroplane
designed and flown by local pioneer aviator
and inventor Richard Pearse. Many believe his
mildly successful attempts at manned flight
came before the Wright brothers first flew
in 1903.

At the time of writing, a **Maori Rock Art Centre**
(including tours around the region to see rock
art in situ) was planned near the i-SITE. Ask
for an update.

Aigantighe Art Gallery (☎ 03-688 4424; www.timaru.
govt.nz; 49 Wai-iti Rd; admission free; ☼ 10am-4pm Tue-Fri,
noon-4pm Sat & Sun) is one of the South Island's
largest public galleries, a 900-piece collection
of NZ and European art from the previous
four centuries set up in a 1908 mansion, and
adorned externally by a sculpture garden (always open). The gallery's Gaelic name means
'at home' and is pronounced 'egg-and-tie'.

DB Mainland Brewery (☎ 03-688 2059; Sheffield St;
tours $10; ☼ tours 1pm Mon-Sat) is located 6km north
of town. Enclosed footwear must be worn and
bookings are required.

The **Botanic Gardens** (cnr King & Queen Sts; admission free; ☼ 8am-dusk), established in 1864, have
ponds, a conservatory and a notable collection of roses and native tree ferns. The gardens are south of town; enter from Queen
St. Passionate rose buffs should also visit the
Trevor Griffiths Rose Garden (Caroline Bay; admission free;
☼ open daylight hours) with more than 1000 romantic blooms set around arbours and water
features. The finest display is from December
to February.

Every November Timaru celebrates the
Timaru Festival of Roses (www.festivalofroses.co.nz)
with two weeks of garden tours, exhibitions
and floral workshops.

Activities
One of the few safe, sheltered beaches on
the east coast is Caroline Bay. There's a fun,

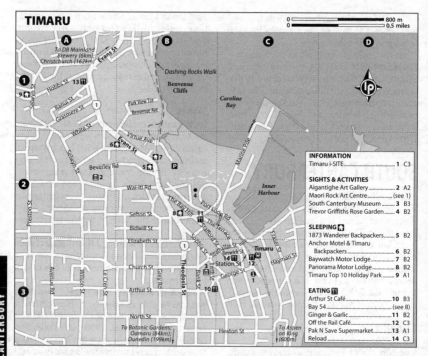

CHRISTCHURCH &
CANTERBURY

crowded **Christmas Carnival** (www.carolinebay.org.
nz) with concerts and events here beginning
26 December and running for about 10 days.
The beachside **park** has a walk-through aviary,
a wading pool, minigolf ($3), kids playground
and a pleasant walkway.

A good one-hour **walk** heads north from
town along Caroline Bay, past the Benvenue
Cliffs and on to the Dashing Rocks and rock
pools at the end of the bay. Ask at the i-SITE
about other walks in the area.

Sleeping
1873 Wanderer Backpackers (☎ 0800 187 392, 03-
688 8795; 1873wandererbackpackers@xtra.co.nz; 24 Evans
St; sites/dm/s/d $16/23/29/58; 🖳) Sprawling spot
with friendly owners offering transfers to/
from the bus station. Rent a mountain bike,
fire up the barbecue and relax in the pretty
garden.

Timaru Top 10 Holiday Park (☎ 0800 242 121, 03-
684 7690; www.timaruholidaypark.co.nz; 154a Selwyn St; un-
powered/powered sites $32/35, cabins & motels d $65-115;
🖳 🛜) Parkland site with excellent amenities
and a golf course next door that's included in
your park tariff.

Panorama Motor Lodge (☎ 03-688 0097; www.
panorama.net.nz; 52 The Bay Hill; d from $120; 🖳 🛜)
Modern, well-appointed units with spa, sauna
and gym. More greenery to soften the concrete
would be nice, but Caroline Bay Park and Bay
Hill's cafes are a short walk away. Family units
are particularly spacious.

Aspen on King (☎ 0800 822 344, 03-688 3034; www.
aspenonking.co.nz; 51 King St; d $145-155; 🖳 🛜) A
three-bedroom apartment features a retro
bathroom complete with a bright red bath
that's straight from the Playboy mansion.
Other newer units are equally spacious and
crisply modern with free broadband internet. It's in a quieter location away from busy
Evans St.

Busy Evans St is wall-to-wall motels, but it's
worth asking for a room at the back if you're a
light sleeper. The best option is **Baywatch Motor
Lodge** (☎ 0800 929 828, 03-688 1886; www.baywatch
timaru.co.nz; 7 Evans St; d $120-140; 🖳 🛜). Its units
offer Hoff-tastic bay views, and double-glazed
windows mask the worst of the road noise
from SH1.

Also recommended is the **Anchor Motel
and Timaru Backpackers** (☎ 03-684 5067; 42 Evans St;

backpackers dm/d $25/60, motels $49-95; 🖳 🛜), a clean and simple property a short walk from the beach at Caroline Bay.

Eating & Drinking

Reload (☎ 03-688 6616; cnr Stafford & Beswick Sts; wraps, salads & juices $5-9; ☯ 8.30am-5.30pm Mon-Fri, to 3.30pm Sat) Self-styled 'health fuel stop' with wraps, salads and smoothies. The not-so-virtuous can recharge on coffee as they read the global array of magazines.

Off the Rail Café (☎ 03-688 3594; Station St; meals $8-17; ☯ 7.30am-5pm Mon-Fri, to 9.30pm Sat; 🖳) This funky licensed cafe is at the train station. Fire up the jukebox crammed with '70s tunes, and sample Kiwi baked goodies and more contemporary globally influenced dishes. It's open late for drinks and occasional live music on Saturday night.

Arthur St Café (☎ 03-688 9449; 8 Arthur St; snacks & meals $10-15; ☯ 7.30am-5.30pm Mon-Thu, to 8pm Fri, 8.30am-3pm Sat) Excellent coffee and cruisy Kiwi dub is always a good way to ease into the day. Timaru's funkiest eatery offers sandwiches, bagels and world-famous (in Timaru) breakfasts.

Bay 54 (☎ 03-688 4367; 56 The Bay Hill; lunch mains $10-18, dinner mains $19-32; ☯ 11am-late) Kiwi craft beers from Monteith's, classy Kiwi pub tucker, and the choice of Caroline Bay views or big-screen sport. Sorted.

Ginger & Garlic (☎ 03-688 3981; 335 Stafford St; mains $25-34; ☯ noon-2pm Mon-Fri & 5-10pm Mon-Sat) Timaru's take on sophisticated food with a subtle Asian spin is showcased at this long-running local favourite. Standouts include calamari and prawn spring rolls, and honey-spice pork on sticky miso rice. The menu also includes dishes with a European and Middle Eastern influence.

Pak N Save supermarket (cnr Ranui & Evans Sts; ☯ 8am-9pm Mon-Fri, to 7pm Sat & Sun).

Getting There & Away

InterCity (☎ 03-365 1113; www.intercity.co.nz) stops outside the train station, with buses to Christchurch ($34, 2½ hours, two daily), Oamaru ($28, one hour, two daily) and Dunedin ($37, three hours, two daily). From Dunedin connect to Queenstown, Te Anau and Invercargill.

Atomic Shuttles (☎ 03-349 0697; www.atomictravel. co.nz) stop in Timaru en route to Christchurch ($25) and Dunedin ($25). Departs Timaru from the i-SITE.

There are no direct buses from Timaru to Lake Tekapo and Mt Cook – you'll need to first get to Geraldine or Fairlie to catch buses to the Mackenzie Country.

INLAND & MACKENZIE COUNTRY

Heading to Queenstown and the southern lakes from Christchurch means a turn off SH1 onto SH79, a scenic route towards the high country and the Aoraki/Mt Cook National Park's eastern foothills. The road passes through Geraldine and Fairlie before joining SH8, which heads over Burkes Pass to the blue intensity of Lake Tekapo.

The expansive high ground from which the scenic peaks of Aoraki/Mt Cook National Park escalate is known as Mackenzie Country after the legendary James 'Jock' MacKenzie, who ran his stolen flocks in this then-uninhabited region in the 1840s. When he was finally caught, other settlers realised the potential of the land and followed in his footsteps. The first people to traverse the Mackenzie were the Maori, trekking from Banks Peninsula to Otago hundreds of years ago.

Online see www.mtcooknz.com and for information on winter activities see www. mackenziewinter.co.nz.

Geraldine
pop 2210

Geraldine has a country-village atmosphere with pretty private gardens and an active craft scene.

The **Geraldine i-SITE** (☎ 03-693 1006; www.go geraldine.co.nz; geraldineinfo@southisland.org.nz; cnr Talbot & Cox Sts; ☯ 8.30am-5pm Mon-Fri, 10am-4pm Sat & Sun) has brochures detailing the gardens and galleries in town, and can book rural B&Bs and farmstays.

Four Peaks Plaza (cnr Talbot & Cox Sts; ☯ 9am-5pm) has a bakery, cafes and the Talbot Forest cheese shop. Also here is **Barker's** (☎ 03-693 9727), a fruit-products emporium selling (and sampling) kiwifruit wines, juices, sauces, smoothies and jams. Every Saturday during summer the town kicks into organic action with a **farmers market** (☯ 9.30am-12.30pm).

The **Vintage Car & Machinery Museum** (☎ 03-693 8005; 178 Talbot St; adult/child $7/free; ☯ 10am-4pm mid-Sep–early Jun) has more than 30 vintage and veteran cars from as far back as 1907. There's also a rare 1929 Spartan biplane.

4x4 New Zealand (☎ 03-693 7254; www.4x4newzealand. co.nz; tour $105-220) operates a range of 4WD tours in the surrounding high country, taking in sheep stations, braided rivers and *Lord of the Rings* film sites. Prices vary according to itinerary and length of tours.

The mind-bending **Medieval Mosaic** (☎ 03-693 9820; www.1066.co.nz; 10 Wilson St; admission free; ☺ 9am-5pm Mon-Fri, 10am-4pm Sat & Sun) is ideal for fans of medieval history, word games and clever-clogs mathematics. If you're feeling chilly, the world's biggest woollen jersey is also on display.

SLEEPING & EATING

Geraldine Holiday Park (☎ 03-693 8147; www.geraldineholidaypark.co.nz; 39 Hislop St; unpowered/powered sites $24/26, cabins & units $45-105; ☐) This holiday park is set amid well-established trees across the road from a grassy oval. Besides budget cabins and self-contained units, there's a TV room and playground.

Rawhiti Backpackers (☎ 03-693 8252; www.rawhitibackpackers.co.nz; 27 Hewlings St; dm/s/d/tr $30/40/68/90; ☐ ☎) Under friendly new ownership, but the standards have been kept up at this old maternity hospital that's now a sunny and spacious hostel with solar electricity and colourfully furnished rooms all with different themes such as 'French' or 'Pacific'. Mountain bikes are available and guests rave about the comfy beds. It's above town off Peel St; grab a map before setting off. If you ask them when you book, they'll usually pick you up from the bus stop.

Scenic Route Motor Lodge (☎ 0800 723 643; www.motelscenicroute.co.nz; 28 Waihi Terrace; d $110-130; ☐ ☎) This spacious motel is built in early-settler style, but the modern studios include double-glazing, Sky TV and the attention of Molly, a friendly feline who definitely thinks she runs the place. You'll find Molly and her human employees Rob and Elaine at the northern end of town.

Cafe Verde (☎ 03-693 9616; 45 Talbot St; mains $8-15; ☺ 9am-4pm) Down the lane beside the old post office is this delightful garden cafe. Grown-ups will appreciate the tasty lunch options such as salmon in filo pastry, while the kids go crazy – with a small, well-behaved 'c' please – in the sweet postage-stamp-sized playground.

Taste (☎ 03-693 8877; 7 Talbot St; mains $20-30; ☺ 5pm-late Tue-Sat) The ritziest place in town sees local farmers enjoying robust Angus steaks, and more delicate palates are catered to with scallops in filo pastry.

Geraldine's best pub meals are available for alfresco dining in the garden bar at the **Village Inn** (☎ 03-693 1004; 41 Talbot St; mains $10-17; ☺ 10am-late).

The eateries at Four Peaks Plaza (p559) are ideal for a quick bite. Newly opened on our last visit were outlets for sushi, bagels and freshly squeezed fruit juices. For a quality sugar rush, visit **Coco** (☎ 03-693 9982; 10 Talbot St; ☺ 10am-5pm Mon-Fri, to 3pm Sat, to 4pm Sun) for handmade choccies, plus designer teas, coffee, hot chocolate and cake.

ENTERTAINMENT

Geraldine Cinema (☎ 03-693 8118; Talbot St; adult/child $10/7) is a quirky local cinema with old sofas.

Peel Forest

Peel Forest, 22km north of Geraldine (signposted off SH72), is among NZ's most important indigenous podocarp (conifer) forests. A road from nearby Mt Peel station leads to **Mesopotamia**, the run of English writer Samuel Butler (author of the satire *Erewhon*) in the 1860s.

Get the *Peel Forest Park: Track Information* brochure ($1) from **Peel Forest Store** (☎ 03-696 3567; ☺ 9am-6pm Mon-Thu, to 7pm Fri & Sat, 10am-5.30pm Sun; ☐), which also stocks petrol, groceries and takeaway food, and has internet access and an on-site cafe-restaurant. The store also manages the pleasant DOC **camping ground** (☎ 03-696 3567, unpowered/powered sites $18/22, cabins $36) beside the Rangitata River, about 3km beyond the store and equipped with basic two- to four-berth cabins, showers, a kitchen, laundry and card phone. Check in at the store and ask about renting a mountain bike ($12/35 per hour/day).

More upmarket is **Peel Forest Lodge** (☎ 03-696 3703; www.peelforestlodge.co.nz; d $350), a self-contained log-cabin-style lodge deep in the forest. Bring your own food along for leisurely barbecues; meals are also available (breakfast/dinner per person $25/50) if you can't/won't cook. The owners don't live on-site so you'll need to book ahead.

Horse trekking (☎ 0800 022 536; 03-696 3703; www.peelforesthorsetrekking.co.nz; 1hr/2hr/half-day/full day $55/110/220/380) in the lush forest is also on offer even if you're not staying at the lodge. Longer multiday treks ($982 to $1673) and accommodation and horse-trekking packages ($550) are available in conjunction with Peel Forest Lodge (see above).

CHRISTCHURCH & CANTERBURY

The magnificent podocarp forest consists of totara, kahikatea and matai. One fine example of totara on the **Big Tree Walk** (30 minutes return) has a circumference of 9m and is over 1000 years old. Local bird life includes the rifleman, kereru (NZ pigeon), bellbird, fantail and grey warbler. There are also trails to waterfalls: **Emily Falls** (1½ hours return), **Rata Falls** (two hours return) and **Acland Falls** (one hour return).

Rangitata Rafts (☎ 0800 251 251, 03-696 3534; www.rafts.co.nz; ☼ Oct-Apr) goes white-water rafting on the Rangitata River, which contains exhilarating Grade V rapids. The company's base is at Mt Peel, 13km past the camping ground, and includes budget **lodge accommodation** (unpowered sites/dm/d $20/20/48). Rafting trips can be joined from either the Rangitata lodge ($185) or from Christchurch ($195 including return transport), and include hot showers and a barbecue. Count on three hours on the river. A less frantic option for families is a Family Fun trip (adult/child $165/120) on the Grade II Lower Rangitata River. Inflatable kayaks are used, and you'll have around two hours on the river followed by a meal at the lodge.

If you can't get enough of NZ's rivers, consider a longer three-day rafting expedition with **Hidden Valleys** (☎ 03-696 3560; www.hiddenvalleys.co.nz; from $1350; ☼ Oct-Mar). One-day to one-week adventure tours around Peel Forest and the Rangitata River are also available.

Fairlie
pop 725
Fairlie is often described as 'the gateway to the Mackenzie'. To the west the landscape changes as the road ascends Burkes Pass to the open spaces of Mackenzie Country.

The **Fairlie visitor information centre** (☎ 03-685 8496; www.fairlie.co.nz; Allandale St; ☼ 10am-4pm) can provide information on nearby **mountain-biking** tracks. There's skiing 29km northwest at **Fox Peak** in the Two Thumb Range. **Mt Dobson**, 26km northwest of Fairlie, is in a 3km-wide basin (see p86). The **Ski Shack** (☎ 03-685 8088; Allandale St) has information and gear rental. Internet is available at **eat** (right).

SLEEPING & EATING
Both Main St pubs offer budget accommodation, or you can try one of the local motels from around $90.

Fairlie Gateway Top 10 Holiday Park (☎ 0800 324 754, 03-685 8375; www.fairlietop10.co.nz; 10 Allandale Rd; unpowered & powered sites $30, cabins & units $50-150; 🖥 ☎) Tranquil, creek-side park that's perfect for families, with a large playground for the kids. Fishing gear is for hire.

Pinewood Motels (☎ 0800 858 599, 03-685 8599; www.pinewoodmotels.co.nz; 25-27 Mt Cook Rd; d from $90; ☎) Comfortable self-contained units, including one that's wheelchair-accessible.

eat (☎ 03-685 6275; 76 Main St; mains $10-18; ☼ 8am-5pm Tue-Sun; 🖥) Family-friendly with a kid's play area, eat also drags in grown-ups with its excellent food – try a hot chicken sandwich ($17.50) – beer, wine, and speedy internet access.

Old Library Café (☎ 03-685 8999; 6 Allandale Rd; dinner mains $20-30; ☼ 11am-late; 🖥) Has elegant touches including an old pressed-metal ceiling, and serves fresh, local food such as roasted Mackenzie lamb or smoked Alpine salmon. There's also a more casual all-day menu featuring pasta, salads and soups.

Lake Tekapo
pop 315
At the southern end of its namesake lake, this town has unobstructed views across turquoise water, and a backdrop of rolling hills and mountains worthy of a Peter Jackson movie. The town has boomed in recent times, with new B&Bs, holiday homes and resort accommodation taking advantage of the epic vistas.

Lake Tekapo is a popular stop on tours of the Southern Alps, with Mt Cook– and Queenstown-bound buses popping in for a quick ice cream or coffee. Rather than rushing on, it's actually worth staying at least a couple of nights to experience the region's glorious night sky from atop nearby Mt John.

For an explanation of why this and other lakes in the region are such a vibrant shade of blue, see the boxed text, p564.

INFORMATION
Lake Tekapo i-SITE (☎ 03-680 6579; www.laketekapountouched.co.nz; Godley Hotel, SH8; ☼ 9am-5pm) handles bookings for activities and transport. Also see www.tekapotourism.co.nz.

There's internet access – including wi-fi – at the Tekapo Helicopters office (p563).

SIGHTS & ACTIVITIES
The diminutive, picturesque **Church of the Good Shepherd** (☼ 9am-5pm) beside the lake was built of stone and oak in 1935 and is a favourite for weddings given its postcard-perfect setting.

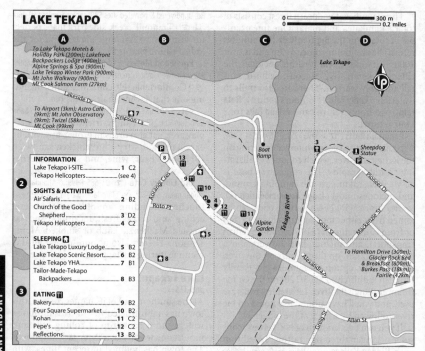

LAKE TEKAPO

To Lake Tekapo Motels &
Holiday Park (200m); Lakefront
Backpackers Lodge (400m);
Alpine Springs & Spa (900m);
Lake Tekapo Winter Park (900m);
Mt John Walkway (900m);
Mt Cook Salmon Farm (27km)

To Airport (3km); Astro Café
(9km); Mt John Observatory
(9km); Twizel (58km);
Mt Cook (99km)

Lake Tekapo

Lakeside Dr

Simpson La

Boat
Ramp

Aorangi Cres

Roto Pl

Alpine
Garden

Tekapo River

Sheepdog
Statue

Pioneer Dr

Mackenzie St

Sealy St

To Hamilton Drive (300m);
Glacier Rock Bed
& Breakfast (800m);
Burkes Pass (18km);
Fairlie (42km)

Alexandra Pl

Greg St

Allan St

INFORMATION
Lake Tekapo i-SITE......................**1** C2
Tekapo Helicopters..................(see 4)

SIGHTS & ACTIVITIES
Air Safaris...................................**2** B2
Church of the Good
  Shepherd.................................**3** D2
Tekapo Helicopters.....................**4** C2

SLEEPING
Lake Tekapo Luxury Lodge...........**5** B2
Lake Tekapo Scenic Resort..........**6** B2
Lake Tekapo YHA.........................**7** B1
Tailor-Made-Tekapo
  Backpackers............................**8** B3

EATING
Bakery..**9** B2
Four Square Supermarket..........**10** B2
Kohan.......................................**11** C2
Pepe's......................................**12** C2
Reflections...............................**13** B2

Nearby is a **statue** of a collie dog, a tribute to the sheepdogs that helped develop the Mackenzie Country. This area is at its scenic best before or after the last bus group leaves, otherwise the place is swarming with quick-stop sightseers, so come early morning or late afternoon. It's also an increasingly popular location for wedding photographic shoots for visiting Asian honeymooners. Try not to walk into their pictures.

Popular walks include the track to the summit of **Mt John** (three hours return) from just beyond the camping ground. From there, continue on to Alexandrina and McGregor Lakes, making it an all-day walk. Other walks are detailed in the brochure *Lake Tekapo Walkway* ($1).

Cruise Tekapo (☎ 027 479 7675; www.cruisetekapo.co.nz; 25/40min cruise $30/45, fishing per hr $80) can get you out and about on Lake Tekapo.

Mountain bikes can be hired (per hour/half-day $10/25) from Lakefront Backpackers Lodge and the Lake Tekapo YHA.

Mackenzie Alpine Horse Trekking (☎ 0800 628 269; www.maht.co.nz; 1/2hr ride $50/80, half-/full day $125/250) organises four-footed high-country explora-tions. Overnight camping trips ($300) are also available.

Thanks to clear skies and its distance from any main towns, Lake Tekapo has top-notch stargazing, and the area is known as one of the finest spots on the planet to explore the heavens. Join a two-hour night-time star-gazing tour operated by **Earth & Sky** (☎ 03-680 6960; www.earthandsky.co.nz; adult/child $80/45) Forty-minute daytime tours (adult/child $30/15) of the University of Canterbury observatory operate on demand from 10am to 4pm from the Astro Café on Mt John; call for start times as these can vary seasonally. On the night tour visitors can use their own cameras to delve into astrophotography with local photo-grapher Fraser Gunn (www.laketekapo.cc).

In winter, Lake Tekapo is a base for **downhill skiing** at Mt Dobson or Round Hill and **cross-country skiing** on the Two Thumb Range.

At the western edge of the lake, the **Lake Tekapo Winter Park** (☎ 0800 353 8283, 03-680 6550; www.winterpark.co.nz; Lakeside Dr; skating adult/child $14/11, snow-tubing adult/child $15/11; ⏰ 10am-10pm) features a year-round skating rink and a winter mini-snow slope for gentle snow-tubing action.

Next door, the **Alpine Springs & Spa** (www.alpine springs.co.nz; hot pools adult/child $16/9; 10am-10pm) is open all year round with hot pools scattered amid quickly growing native trees. Private pools and saunas ($24 per hour) are also available, and spa packages start at $80. 'Skate and Soak' combo deals are available, and there's a good **cafe** (snacks $5-10; 10am-7pm) for coffee and cake, or a snack and something stronger.

TOURS

Air Safaris (03-680 6880; www.airsafaris.co.nz; SH8) Does 50-minute 'Grand Traverse' flights over Mt Cook and its glaciers (adult/child $295/195), taking you up the Tasman Glacier, over the upper part of the Fox and Franz Josef Glaciers, and by Mts Cook, Tasman and Elie de Beaumont. A similar flight goes from Glentanner Park (see p570), but with higher prices (adult/child $340/240).

Tekapo Helicopters (0800 359 835, 03-680 6229; www.tekapohelicopters.co.nz; SH8) Has five options, from a 25-minute flight ($195) to a 70-minute trip taking in Mt Cook and Fox and Franz Josef Glaciers ($500). All flights include icefield landings and views of Mt Cook.

SLEEPING

Lake Tekapo Scenic Resort (0800 118 666, 03-680 6808; www.laketekapo.com; SH8; dm/s $22/50, d $160-190;) Not so much a self-contained resort as a central complex of basic dorms, singles and doubles, and more modern studio and family units. Lacking in character, but undeniably central, and the local pub is just next door.

Tailor-Made-Tekapo Backpackers (03-680 6700; www.tailor-made-backpackers.co.nz; 9-11 Aorangi Cres; dm $25-29, d with/without bathroom $74/62;) This hostel favours beds rather than bunks and is spread over a pair of well-tended houses on a peaceful street away from the main road. The interior is spick and span and there's a barbecue-equipped garden complete with well-established trees, birdsong and a children's playground.

Lakefront Backpackers Lodge (03-680 6227; www.laketekapo-accommodation.co.nz; Lakeside Dr; dm/d $27/80;) An impressive lakeside place owned by the nearby holiday park (about 1km from the township). Relax by the open fire in the comfy lounge area or take in the sensational views from the front deck. Rooms are modern and bathrooms are top-notch. Backpacker buses stop by so it can be a tad social.

Lake Tekapo Motels & Holiday Park (0800 853 853, 03-680 6825; www.laketekapo-accommodation.co.nz;

Lakeside Dr; unpowered/powered sites $30/36, cabins & units $70-150;) Has a pretty and peaceful lakeside locale, plus everything from basic cabins to motel units with full kitchen and Sky TV. Newer chalets come with shared picnic tables, barbecues and spectacular lake vistas.

Lake Tekapo YHA (03-680 6857; www.yha.co.nz; yha.laketekapo@yha.co.nz; 3 Simpson Lane; dm/d $30/78;) Friendly, well-equipped little place with a living room adorned with open fireplaces, a piano and outstanding views across the lake to the mountains beyond.

Glacier Rock Bed and Breakfast (03-680 6669; www.glacierrock.co.nz; 35 Lochinver Ave; d incl breakfast $195-250;) This architecturally designed home doubles as an art gallery. An artist's – or maybe an architect's – eye is evident in the spacious and airy rooms. Breakfast is served in sunny rooms with huge picture windows.

Lake Tekapo Luxury Lodge (0800 525 383, 03-680 6566; www.laketekapolodge.co.nz; 24 Aorangi Cres; d incl breakfast $250-430;) Luxurious hilltop B&B set in an English-manor style home. Three of the four well-appointed rooms have great views from a back deck, and there's also a handy path leading to the village past the owner's quirky corrugated-iron artwork.

Hamilton Drive and the surrounding streets in the eastern part of town have several good B&Bs.

EATING

The dining scene at Lake Tekapo remains rather lacklustre, with most places doing OK business from the passing trade and a cavalcade of bus tours. For lunch, compile a lakeside picnic from the supermarket and the bakery.

our pick Astro Café (Mt John Observatory; coffee & cake $4-8; 9am-6pm) This tiny, glass-walled pavilion atop Mt John has insanely spectacular 360-degree views across the entire Mackenzie Basin. Quite possibly one of the best locations on the planet for a cafe, and the coffee and cake is pretty good, too. On our latest visit they'd branched out into fresh ham-off-the-bone sandwiches. After dark the cafe becomes the location for astrophotography (opposite) with local photographer Fraser Gunn.

Pepe's (03-680 6677; SH8; meals $15-30; 6pm-late) With large booths and walls decorated with skiing paraphernalia, the rustic Pepe's is a cosy little place with good pizza and pasta. Some of the names are a bit naff (Vinnie's Venison or Spag Bol Bada Bing, anyone?), but the dishes are tasty, and later at night it becomes a good spot for a few quiet ones.

Kohan (☎ 03-680 6688; SH8; lunch $10-14, dinner $22-35; ☒ 11am-2pm Mon-Sun & 6-9pm Mon-Sat) The decor's a bit ho-hum, but you should be gazing at the lake and mountains outside anyway. The Japanese food is actually among the South Island's best, and with a salmon farm just up the road, you just know the sashimi is ultra-fresh. Lunch specials are good value.

Reflections (☎ 03-680 6808; SH8; lunch mains $10-17, dinner mains $25-32; ☒ 8am-late) Grab an outdoor table with views to the lake – try and look past the minigolf course – then select from a decent menu that includes roasted venison or baked Mt Cook salmon. Lunchtime offerings are more casual (burgers and salads) and next door is the town's pub for more nocturnal action.

Pick up supplies at the **Four Square supermarket** (SH8; ☒ 7am-9pm) and the nearby **bakery** (☎ 03-680 655; SH8; ☒ 7am-4pm).

GETTING THERE & AWAY
Southbound services to Queenstown and Wanaka, and northbound services to Christchurch, are offered by **Atomic Shuttles** (☎ 03-349 0697; www.atomictravel.co.nz), **InterCity** (☎ 03-365 1113; www.intercity.co.nz) and **Southern Link Coaches** (☎ 0508 458 835; www.southernlinkcoaches.co.nz). One-way fares are around $30.

Cook Connection (☎ 0800 266 526; www.cookconnect.co.nz) operates to Mt Cook (one-way $30, one daily) and for an additional $20 you can carry on from Mt Cook to Twizel. Travel can be over more than one day.

Mt Cook Salmon Farm
Some 15km west of Lake Tekapo along SH8 is the signposted turn-off to the **Mt Cook Salmon Farm** (☎ 03-435 0585; www.mtcooksalmon.com; Canal Rd; adult/child $2/free; ☒ daylight hr). The farm operates in a hydroelectric canal system and is 12km from the turn-off. A scenic drive along the canal has popular fishing spots and enjoys great views of Mt Cook. Stop at the farm to feed the fish, or pick up something smoked or fresh for dinner.

Lake Pukaki
On the southern shore of Lake Pukaki, 45km southwest of Lake Tekapo and 2km northeast of the turn-off to Mt Cook, is the **Lake Pukaki visitor information centre** (☎ 03-435 3280; info@mtcooknz.com; SH8; ☒ 9am-6pm Oct-Apr, 10am-

BLUE CRUSH

The blazing turquoise colour of Lake Pukaki, a characteristic it shares with other regional bodies of water such as Lake Tekapo, is due to 'rock flour' (sediment) in the water. This so-called flour was created when the lake's basin was gouged out by a stony-bottomed glacier moving across the land's surface, with the rock-on-rock action grinding out fine particles that ended up being suspended in the glacial melt water. This sediment gives the water a milky quality and refracts the sunlight beaming down, hence the brilliant colour.

4pm May-Sep), with reams of information on Mackenzie Country. But the highlight here is the sterling **lookout** that on a clear day gives a picture-perfect view of Mt Cook and its surrounding peaks, with the ultrablue lake in the foreground.

Twizel
pop 1015

It wasn't long ago that New Zealanders maligned the town of Twizel, just south of Lake Pukaki. The town was built in 1968 to service construction of the nearby hydroelectric power station, and was due to be abandoned in 1984 when the construction project was completed. Now the town's tenacious residents are having the last laugh as house prices are increasing and new lakeside subdivisions are being built to take advantage of the area's relaxed lakes-and-mountains lifestyle. Mt Cook is just 63km down the road, and Twizel's range of affordable accommodation and a few pleasant eateries make it a good alternative to staying in more expensive Mt Cook Village.

Right in town is the **Twizel i-SITE** (☎ 03-435 3124; www.twizel.com; Twizel Events Centre; ☒ 9am-6pm daily Oct-Apr, 10am-4pm Tue-Sat May-Sep; ☒), which has internet access. In late January, the town hosts the lively Mackenzie Summer Salmon and Wine Festival.

There's an ATM in the main shopping area. Note there's no ATM at Mt Cook. Self-drive travellers should also fill up with petrol in Twizel before heading to Mt Cook.

ACTIVITIES
Nearby Lake Ruataniwha is popular for rowing, boating and windsurfing. Fishing in local

rivers, canals and lakes is also big business and there are a number of guides in the region; ask at the i-SITE.

Discovery Tours (☎ 0800 213 868, 03-435 0114; www.discoverytours.co.nz) is based in Twizel and operates guided, small-group tours around the Mackenzie Country and Aoraki/Mt Cook, including hiking and helibiking, plus a popular two-hour tour (adult/child $75/40) to the site of the Pelennor battlefield in the *Lord of the Rings* movies. You can even get to charge around like a mad thing wearing *LOTR* replica gear. A shorter one-hour *LOTR* tour (adult/child $30/5) is also available.

The wading kaki (black stilt bird) is found only in NZ and is one of the country's rarest birds. A breeding program is now attempting to increase the population and the new Ahuriri Conservation Park is part of this effort. Just south of Twizel, the **Kaki Visitor Hide** (☎ 03-435 3124; adult/child $15/7; ☒ 9.30am & 4.30pm Oct-Apr) gives you a close-up look at these elusive fellows. Bookings are essential for the one-hour tour of the hide; for more info, visit the Twizel i-SITE (you'll need your own transport to get to the hide).

Helicopter Line (☎ 0800 650 652, 03-435 0370; www.helicopter.co.nz; Wairepo Rd) flies over the Mt Cook region from a helipad beside Mackenzie Country Inn. Sightseeing flights last from 25 minutes ($220) to 60 minutes ($525) and include a snow landing.

SLEEPING

High Country Lodge & Backpackers (☎ 03-435 0671; www.highcountrylodge.co.nz; Mackenzie Dr; dm $25, d with/without bathroom $85/75, units $115-150; ☐ ☎) This excellent value place used to be a hostel for construction workers, and new owners have smartened up the decor with colourful curtains and bed linen. A few standalone motel units also see your Kiwi pesos going a long way. They're also YHA-affiliated for additional discounts.

Parklands Alpine Tourists Park (☎ 03-435 0507; www.parklandstwizel.co.nz; 122 Mackenzie Dr; unpowered/powered sites $28/30, dm $25, cabins & cottages d $85-100; ☐ ☎) Offering green, flower-filled grounds and accommodation in a colourfully refurbished maternity hospital. The modern self-contained cottages are particularly good value.

Mountain Chalet Motels (☎ 0800 629 999, 03-435 0785; www.mountainchalets.co.nz; Wairepo Rd; dm/d from $25/105) Recommended place with well-equipped, self-contained A-frame chalets.

The cheapest units are studios, but there are a number of two-bedroom set-ups for larger groups or families. There's also a small, laid-back lodge that's perfect for backpackers.

ourpick Omahau Downs (☎ 03-435 0199; www.omahau.co.nz; SH8; cottages d $115, B&B d $135; ☒ closed Jun-Aug) There's nothing more relaxing than kicking back at this rural homestead 2km north of Twizel. Omahau Downs is run by a laid-back Kiwi–South African couple, and caters to all tastes with two cosy self-contained cottages sleeping up to four, and a B&B lodge with sparkling modern rooms and a view-enhanced deck looking out on the Ben Ohau Range. An essential experience is a moonlit wood-fired outdoor bath ($20). Don't make the mistake of booking for only one night.

Matuka Lodge (☎ 03-435 0144; www.matukalodge.co.nz; Old Station Rd; d incl breakfast $465-535; ☐ ☎) Surrounded by farmland and mountain scenery, this luxury B&B blends modern design with antiques and Oriental rugs sourced on the owners' travels. A library full of well-thumbed Lonely Planet guides is testament to their wanderlust, so look forward to interesting chats over pre-dinner drinks. Also look forward to a breakfast of locally sourced free-range eggs and salmon smoked just up the road at the Twizel Aoraki Smokehouse.

Also recommended:

Colonial Motel (☎ 0800 355 722, 03-435 0100; www.colonialmoteltwizel.co.nz; 38 Mackenzie Dr; d $110-120; ☐ ☎)

Aspen Court Motel (☎ 0800 277 364, 03-435 0274; www.aspencourt.co.nz; 10 Mackenzie Dr; d $130-150; ☐ ☎)

EATING & DRINKING

Poppies Cafe (☎ 03-435 3308; 1 Benmore Pl; breakfast/lunch $9-18, dinner mains $24-32; ☒ 9am-late in summer, restricted hr in winter) The versatile Poppies is a classy addition to the Twizel dining scene. Lunch showcases lighter meals like Thai beef salad, and dinner is a slightly more formal experience with steak *frites* and venison escalope. Excellent pizzas ($17 to $24) occupy a tasty middle ground. Where possible, organic and locally sourced produce is used. You'll find Poppies on the outskirts of town near the Mackenzie Country Inn.

Shawty's Café (☎ 03-435 3155; 4 Market Pl; breakfast & lunch $9-19, dinner mains $20-28; ☒ 8.30am-late) Cool beats and craft microbrews create a mood that's surprisingly sophisticated for Twizel. Big breakfasts and gourmet pizzas ($12 to

$25) are a good way to start and end an active day amid the surrounding alpine vistas.

Jasmine Thai Café (☎ 03-435 3232; 1 Market Pl; lunch $10, dinner mains $10-16; ☺ 11am-2pm & 5-10pm Tue-Sun) Thailand comes to Twizel and the zesty and zingy flavours of your favourite South East Asian beach have travelled well to get this far inland. It's BYO (bring your own), so grab a few cold beers from the Four Square supermarket to ease the authentic heat.

Hunter's Cafe & Bar (☎ 03-435 0303; 2 Market Pl; meals $18-30; ☺ 11am-2.30pm & 5-8.30pm Mon-Thu & Sat, 11am-8.30pm Fri, 11am-2.30pm Sun) An airy space with generous mains of local produce (salmon from nearby Lake Benmore or rib-eye steak), as well as cheaper bar snacks. Later at night it morphs into a pub.

Right next door to Shawty's, its newly opened **Grappa Lounge** (☺ 5pm-late Wed-Fri, 1pm-late Sat & Sun) is a little slice of cosmopolitan cocktail heaven that might have you staying up later than you planned. In summer there's occasional live music and DJs.

GETTING THERE & AWAY
Onward services to Mt Cook, Queenstown and Wanaka, and northbound services to Christchurch, are offered by **Atomic Shuttles** (☎ 03-349 0697; www.atomictravel.co.nz), **InterCity/Newmans** (☎ 03-365 1113; www.intercitycoach.co.nz) and **Southern Link Coaches** (☎ 0508 458 835; www.southernlinkcoaches.co.nz).

Cook Connection (☎ 0800 266 526; www.cookconnect.co.nz) operates to Mt Cook (one-way $22, one daily) and for an additional $28 you can carry on from Mt Cook to Tekapo. Travel can be over more than one day.

Naked Bus (www.nakedbus.com) travel from here to Christchurch and Queenstown/Wanaka.

Lake Ohau & Ohau Forests
Six forests in the Lake Ohau area (Dobson, Hopkins, Huxley, Temple, Ohau and Ahuriri) are administered by DOC. The numerous walks in this vast recreation grove are detailed in the DOC pamphlet *Ohau Conservation Area* ($1); huts and camping areas are also scattered throughout for adventurous trampers.

Lake Ohau Lodge (☎ 03-438 9885; www.ohau.co.nz; Lake Ohau Rd; s $94-165, d $100-190) is idyllically sited on the western shore of the rower-friendly Lake Ohau, 42km west of Twizel. Prices listed are for accommodation only (everything from backpacker-style to upmarket rooms with

deck and mountain views); DB&B packages are good value.

The lodge is the wintertime service centre for the **Ohau Ski Field** (see p86). In the summer it's a quieter retreat.

AORAKI/MT COOK NATIONAL PARK
The spectacular 700-sq-km Aoraki/Mt Cook National Park, along with Fiordland, Aspiring and Westland National Parks incorporates the Southwest New Zealand (Te Wahipounamu) World Heritage Area, which extends from Westland's Cook River down to the Fiordland. Fenced in by the Southern Alps and the Two Thumb, Liebig and Ben Ohau Ranges, more than one-third of the park has a blanket of permanent snow and glacial ice.

Of the 27 NZ mountains over 3050m, 22 are in this park. The highest is the mighty Mt Cook, and at 3755m it's the tallest peak in Australasia. Known to Maori as Aoraki (Cloud Piercer), after an ancestral deity in Maori mythology, the mountain was named after James Cook by Captain Stokes of the survey ship HMS *Acheron*.

The Mt Cook region has always been the focus of climbing in NZ. On 2 March 1882, William Spotswood Green and two Swiss alpinists failed to reach the summit of Cook after an epic 62-hour ascent. But two years later a trio of local climbers – Tom Fyfe, George Graham and Jack Clarke – were spurred into action by the news that two well-known European alpinists were coming to attempt Cook, and set off to climb it before the visitors. On Christmas Day 1884 they ascended the Hooker Glacier and north ridge, a brilliant climb in those days, and stood on the summit.

In 1913, Australian climber Freda du Faur became the first woman to reach the summit. In 1948, Edmund Hillary's party, along with Tenzing Norgay, climbed the south ridge; Hillary went on to become the first to reach the summit of Mt Everest. Since then, most of the daunting face routes have been climbed. Among the region's many great peaks are Sefton, Tasman, Silberhorn, Malte Brun, La Perouse, Hicks, De la Beche, Douglas and the Minarets. Many can be ascended from Westland National Park, and there are climbers' huts on both sides of the divide.

Mt Cook is a wonderful sight – assuming there's no cloud in the way. Most visitors arrive on tour buses, stop at the Hermitage hotel for photos, and then zoom off back down

SH80. Hang around to soak up this awesome peak and the surrounding landscape and try the excellent short walks. On the trails, look for the thar, a goatlike creature and excellent climber; the chamois, smaller and of lighter build than the thar; and red deer. Summertime brings the large mountain buttercup (the Mt Cook lily), and mountain daisies, gentians and edelweiss.

Information

The **DOC Aoraki/Mt Cook visitor information centre** (☎ 03-435 1186; mtcookvc@doc.govt.nz; 1 Larch Grove; ⏰ 8.30am-5pm Oct-Apr, to 4.30pm May-Sep) advises on weather conditions, guided tours and tramping routes, and hires out beacons for trampers ($35). The centre has recently been expanded and includes excellent displays on the flora, fauna and history of the Mt Cook region. Online see www.mtcooknz.com. Most activities can be booked here or at the Activities Desk at the Sir Edmund Hillary Alpine Centre.

The **Alpine Guides shop** (☎ 03-435 1834; www.alpineguides.co.nz; Retail Centre, The Hermitage; ⏰ 8am-5pm) sells travel clothing and accessories, and mountaineering gear, and rents ice axes, crampons, daypacks and sleeping bags.

Internet access – including paid wi-fi – is available at the Old Mountaineer's Café (p571).

Stock up on groceries and petrol at Twizel or Lake Tekapo, and note that Mt Cook has no banking facilities.

Sights

TASMAN GLACIER

Higher up, the **Tasman Glacier** is a predictably spectacular sweep of ice, but further down it's downright ugly. Normally as a glacier retreats it melts back up the mountain, but the Tasman is unusual because its last few kilometres are almost horizontal. In recent decades it has melted from the top down, exposing a jumble of stones, rocks and boulders and forming a lake. In other words, in its 'ablation zone' (where it melts), the Tasman is covered in a solid mass of debris, which slows down its melting rate and makes it unsightly.

Despite this considerable melt, the ice by the site of the old Ball Hut is still estimated to be over 600m thick. In its last major advance

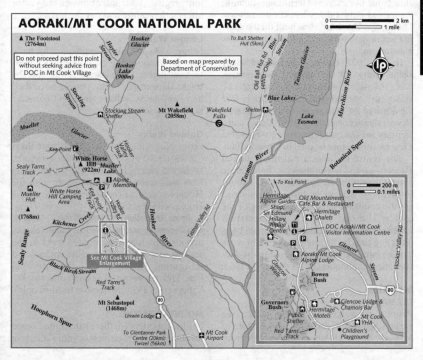

(17,000 years ago), the glacier crept south far enough to carve out Lake Pukaki. A later advance did not reach out to the valley sides, so the Old Ball Hut Rd runs between the outer valley walls and the lateral moraines of this later advance.

Like the Fox and Franz Josef Glaciers on the other side of the divide, the Mt Cook glaciers move fast. The **Alpine Memorial**, near the old Hermitage site on the Hooker Valley Track and commemorating one of the mountain's first climbing disasters, illustrates the glaciers' speed. Three climbers were killed by an avalanche in 1914. Only one of the bodies was recovered at the time, but 12 years later a second one melted out of the bottom of the Hochstetter Icefall, 2000m below where the party was buried.

HERMITAGE

With fantastic views of Mt Cook, this is arguably the most famous hotel in NZ. Originally constructed in 1884, when the trip from Christchurch took several days, the first hotel was destroyed in a flash flood in 1913; you can see the foundations in Hooker Valley, 2km from the current Hermitage. Rebuilt, it survived until 1957, when it burnt down. The present Hermitage was built on the same site and a new wing was added for the new millennium.

In late 2007, the new **Sir Edmund Hillary Alpine Centre** (☎ 0800 686 800; www.hermitage. co.nz; The Hermitage; adult/child/family from $26/13/52; ☺ 8am-late) opened just three weeks before the death of the man regarded as the greatest New Zealander of all time. His recorded commentary for the museum was only recorded a few months before he died in January 2008.

The centre includes a full-dome digital planetarium and screen showing three feature movies as well as the specially made Mount Cook Magic 3D movie, but most poignant are the countless personal memories of the country's beloved 'Sir Ed'. A documentary is screened in the musuem on a continual basis reflecting the charity and development work that Sir Edmund Hillary achieved in the decades after his conquest of Mt Everest in 1953.

Activities
TRAMPING
Various easy walks from the Hermitage area are outlined in the brochure *Walks in Aoraki/ Mt Cook National Park* ($1), available from the visitor information centre. Always be prepared for sudden weather changes.

The trail to **Kea Point** (two hours return from the village) is lined with native plant life and ends at a platform with excellent views of Mt Cook, the Hooker Valley and the ice faces of Mt Sefton and the Footstool. You'll usually share your walk with a few inquisitive kea. The walk to **Sealy Tarns** (three to four hours return) branches off the Kea Point Track and continues up the ridge to **Mueller Hut** (dm $35); a comfortable 30-bunk hut with gas and cooking facilities.

The walk up the **Hooker Valley** (three hours return) crosses a couple of swing bridges to Stocking Stream and the terminus of the Hooker Glacier. After the second swing bridge, Mt Cook totally dominates the valley.

The Tasman Valley walks are popular for their views of the Tasman Glacier. Walks start at the end of the unsealed Tasman Valley Rd, 8km from the village. The **Tasman Glacier View track** (50 minutes return) leads to a viewpoint on the moraine wall, passing the **Blue Lakes** (more green than blue these days) on the way.

If you intend staying at any of the park's huts, register your intentions at the visitor information centre and pay the hut fee.

Longer Walks
Longer walks are only recommended for those with mountaineering experience, as conditions at higher altitudes are severe and the tracks dangerous. Many people have died here, and most walkers shouldn't consider tackling these trails.

Guided Walks
From November to March, **Ultimate Hikes** (☎ 0800 686 800, 03-435 1899; www.ultimatehikes.co.nz; full-day walk adult/child $105/65) offers a day-long 8km walk from the Hermitage through the Hooker Valley to the terminal lake of the Hooker Glacier.

Alpine Recreation (☎ 0800 006 096, 03-680 6736; www.alpinerecreation.com), based in Lake Tekapo, organises high-altitude guided treks in the area, as well as mountaineering courses and ski touring. The challenging three-day Ball Pass Trek between the Tasman and Hooker Valleys costs $650 (November to April only).

MOUNTAINEERING
For the experienced, there's unlimited scope for climbing, but regardless of your skills, take

CHRISTCHURCH & CANTERBURY

TITANIC SCENE ON LAKE TASMAN

When you're only a few kilometres from NZ's highest mountain, the last thing you expect to see is a maze of huge icebergs straight from the planet's polar regions. It's a surreal feeling cruising in an inflatable boat (p570) amid 500-year-old islands of ice on Lake Tasman in the Aoraki/Mt Cook National Park. The ice may be centuries old, but the lake's only been around a few decades. Lake Tasman was first formed around 30 years ago, when huge swathes of ice sheared off the Tasman Glacier's terminal face.

The ice-strewn lake is a dynamic environment and there's always the danger of one of the icebergs breaking up. An icing-sugar-like dusting of snow may have fallen overnight, and even that could be enough to rebalance an iceberg and send it spinning and rotating in the frigid water. With a decent wind the location of the floating islands can change by the hour.

Come back in a few years, and the ongoing impact of climate change will have further increased the size of one of NZ's newest and coldest lakes.

---

every precaution as 200 people have died in climbing accidents in the park. The bleak In Memoriam book in the visitor information centre begins with the first death on Mt Cook in 1907, and since then more than 70 climbers have died on the peak.

Highly changeable weather is typical around here; Mt Cook is only 44km from the coast and weather conditions rolling in from the Tasman Sea can mean sudden storms. Unless you're experienced in such conditions, don't climb anywhere without a guide.

Check with the park rangers before attempting any climb and always heed their advice. Fill out a climbers-intentions card before starting out, so rangers can check on you if you're overdue coming out, and sign out again when you return.

Alpine Guides (☎ 03-435 1834; www.alpineguides.co.nz; Retail Centre, The Hermitage; ☺ Nov-Apr) runs guided climbs and courses, from six-day introductory Mountain Experience courses ($1995) through to six-day ascents of Mt Cook ($4950). It also rents and sells mountaineering and hiking gear from a **shop** (☺ 8am-5pm) adjacent to the Sir Edmund Hillary Centre.

Alpine Recreation (☎ 0800 006 096, 03-680 6736; www.alpinerecreation.com; ☺ Nov-Apr) also has a summertime program of climbing courses (a four-day introduction to climbing costs $1350) and guided ascents of Mt Cook or Mt Tasman ($4000).

SKI TOURING & HELISKIING

Alpine Guides (☎ 03-435 1834; www.alpineguides.co.nz; Retail Centre, The Hermitage; ☺ Jul-Sep) does tailored ski-touring, ski-mountaineering and winter alpine courses. Its specialities are glacier ski-

ing (www.skithetasman.co.nz) and heliskiing (www.wildernessheli.co.nz) on the highest peaks in NZ. Ski the Tasman and Wilderness Heliski are also available ex-Queenstown.

Southern Alps Guiding (☎ 027 342 277, 03-435 1890; www.mtcook.com) has a range of heliskiing and boarding options including Tasman Glacier ($775). Ask at the Old Mountaineers Café (p571).

Alpine Recreation (☎ 0800 006 096, 03-680 6736; www.alpinerecreation.com) has a winter (July to September) program involving two days touring in the high country around Lake Tekapo, wearing skis or snowshoes ($650), and other ways to explore the mountains on two feet.

AERIAL SIGHTSEEING

Mount Cook Ski Planes (☎ 0800 800 702, 03-430 8034; www.mtcookskiplanes.com), based at Mt Cook Airport, offers 40-minute (adult/child $375/275) and 55-minute (adult/child $495/375) flights, both with snow landings. Flightseeing without a landing is a cheaper option; try the 25-minute Mini Tasman trip (adult/child $255/210).

From Glentanner Park, the **Helicopter Line** (☎ 0800 650 651, 03-435 1801; www.helicopter.co.nz) does 20-minute Alpine Vista flights ($210), an exhilarating 30-minute flight over the Ben Ohau Range ($295), and a 45-minute Mountains High flight over the Tasman Glacier and by Mt Cook ($390). All feature snow landings.

Other operators include Air Safaris (see p563) and the Twizel branch of the Helicopter Line (see p565).

OTHER ACTIVITIES

The visitor information centre, the Hermitage, the YHA and Glentanner Park

CHRISTCHURCH & CANTERBURY

570 SOUTH CANTERBURY •• Aoraki/Mt Cook National Park   lonelyplanet.com

provide information and make bookings for activities and tours. Note that most of them are weather-dependent and seasonal.

Glacier Explorers (☎ 0800 686 800, 03-435 1809; www.glacierexplorers.com; adult/child $130/65) heads out on the terminal lake of the Tasman Glacier. It starts with a 20-minute walk to the shore of Lake Tasman, where you board a custom-built MAC boat and get up close and personal with 300-year-old icebergs. See the boxed text, p569. Book at the Activities Desk inside the Sir Edmund Hillary Alpine Centre (p568).

Glacier Sea-kayaking (☎ 03-435 1890; www.mtcook.com; trips $110; ☼ mid-Apr–Oct) has three-hour kayak trips negotiating icebergs across glacial bays in the Hooker Valley.

Glentanner Horse Trekking (☎ 03-435 1855; www.glentanner.co.nz; 1/2/3hr ride $60/80/150; ☼ Nov-Apr) leads guided treks on a high-country sheep station. All levels of experience are welcome.

Tasman Valley 4WD & Argo Tours (☎ 0800 686 800, 03-435 1809; www.mountcooktours.co.nz; adult/child $130/65) offers a three-hour return trip by 4WD and argo (8WD all-terrain vehicle) alongside the morraine walls of the Tasman Glacier. Expect plenty of alpine flora and an interesting commentary along the way. Pre-book online (recommended) or book at the Hermitage hotel activities desk (p568).

Discovery Tours (☎ 0800 213 868; www.discoverytours.co.nz; tour $395; ☼ Oct-May) operates helibiking tours on a high-country station. Afterwards, slow down with a farm tour and meet the local sheep. It also offers guided tours blending sightseeing by van with walking, including a guided wilderness hike to the Ball Ridge (from $130, November to May).

Sleeping

Campers and walkers can use the **public shelter** (☼ 8am-7pm Oct-Apr, to 5pm May-Sep) in the village, which has running water, toilets and coin-operated showers. Accommodation is expensive in Mt Cook Village; consider staying at Twizel (p564) and visiting Mt Cook as a day trip.

White Horse Hill Camping Area (☎ 03-435 1186; Hooker Valley; adult/child $6/3) A basic DOC-run, self-registration camping ground at the starting point for the Hooker Valley Track, 2km from Aoraki/Mt Cook village. There's running water (boil before drinking) and a new amenities block, but no electricity or cooking facilities.

Unwin Lodge (☎ 03-435 1100; www.alpineclub.org.nz; SH80; dm $25; ▣) About 3.5km before the village, this lodge belongs to the New Zealand Alpine Club (NZAC). Members get preference, but beds are usually available for climbing groupies. There are basic bunks, and a big common room with a fireplace, kitchen and excellent views up the Tasman Glacier.

Glentanner Park Centre (☎ 0800 453 682, 03-435 1855; www.glentanner.co.nz; unpowered/powered sites $32/36, dm $25, cabins $80-125) On the northern shore of Lake Pukaki, this is the nearest facility-laden camping ground to the national park and has great views of Mt Cook, 25km to the north. It's well set up with various cabins, a dormitory (open October to April), a restaurant, and books tours and activities.

Mt Cook YHA (☎ 03-435 1820; www.yha.co.nz; mtcook@yha.org.nz; cnr Bowen & Kitchener Dr; dm/d $30/100; ▣ ☜) This excellent hostel has a free sauna, drying room, warming log fires and DVDs. Rooms are clean and spacious, and family rooms and facilities for travellers with disabilities are also available. Try and book a few days in advance. If you're mountain-bound you can store luggage here.

our pick Aoraki/Mt Cook Alpine Lodge (☎ 03-435 1860; www.aorakialpinelodge.co.nz; Bowen Dr; d $159-179, tr/q $164/164, f $200-225; ▣ ☜) With colourful Turkish rugs and underfloor heating, the place ensures a warm welcome. Just a few years old, this cosy lodge with twin, double and family rooms is the best place to stay in the village. Shared facilities include a huge lounge and kitchen area, and the alfresco barbecue with superb mountain views will have you arguing over who's going to grill the steak. Two new, more spacious rooms on the ground floor have simply superb views of Mt Cook.

Hermitage (☎ 0800 686 800, 03-435 1809; www.hermitage.co.co.nz; Terrace Rd; r $160-585; ▣ ☜) A sprawling complex that has long monopolised accommodation in the village and continues to leverage that position with its room rates. Rooms in well-equipped A-frame chalets (double $235) sleep up to four and include a kitchen. Also available are motel units (double from $160) and refurbished rooms (doubles $175 to $585) in various wings of the hotel proper. The higher end rooms are very smart indeed, and include cinematic views of Mt Cook through huge picture windows. Winter (May to September) sees a reduction in accommodation prices.

Eating & Drinking

Glentanner Restaurant (☎ 03-435 1855; SH80, Glentanner; meals $10-20; ☼ 9am-4pm) The decor might resemble a school cafeteria, but there's plenty of robust Kiwi tucker on offer. Steak sandwiches and fish and chips will get you through the longest of exploring days.

our pick **Old Mountaineers Café, Bar & Restaurant** (☎ 03-435 1890; Bowen Dr; mains $20-35; ☼ 11am-late; ▢ ☞) Cosy in winter, with mountain views from outside tables in summer, this place delivers top-notch burgers, pizza, pasta and salad and is a good-value alternative to the eateries at the Hermitage. Linger to study the old black-and-white pics and mountaineering memorabilia. You might still be there for happy hour – actually two hours – when it kicks off at 5pm. Paid wi-fi access is also available.

The Hermitage (p568) has a variety of eating and drinking options. Grab a table outside on the extensive deck of the **cafe** (☼ 9am-5.30pm), or wait for dinner and dine at the **Panorama Restaurant** (dinner mains $25-40; ☼ 6pm-late), an excellent à la carte restaurant with local treats including grilled Mt Cook salmon, Canterbury lamb rack and pan-seared venison. The adjacent Alpine Restaurant offers breakfast ($17 to $38), lunch ($44) and dinner ($63) buffets.

Raise a glass to the outrageous mountain scenery at Sir Ed's Bar at the Sir Edmund Hillary Alpine Centre or the Snowline Lounge. Choose between special beer-appreciation and wine-tasting self-guided tours, and also drink in the outrageous scenery up the valley to Aoraki/Mt Cook's iconic profile (weather and cloud cover permitting, of course). The Hermitage Hotel High Tea is also available in the afternoon ($25 to $55).

A smaller, less formal **Chamois Bar** (☼ 5pm-late daily Oct-Mar, Thu-Sat only Apr-Sep) is upstairs in Glencoe Lodge, 500m from the YHA, where it entertains with a pool table, big-screen TV, and the occasional live gig. It's a good place to catch up over a burger or nachos with the international crew of mountain guides and travellers who call the village home during summer.

Getting There & Away

The village's small airport only serves aerial sightseeing companies. Some of these may be willing to combine transport to, say, the West Coast (ie Franz Josef) with a scenic flight, but flights are heavily dependent on weather.

National bus line **InterCity** (☎ 03-365 1113; www.intercitycoach.co.nz) links Mt Cook to Christchurch ($165, five hours), Queenstown ($145, four hours) and Wanaka (with a change in Tarras, 4¼ hours, $195). Buses stop at the YHA and the Hermitage, both of which handle bookings.

InterCity subsidiary **Great Sights** (☎ 0800 744 487; www.greatsights.co.nz) runs a sightseeing day trip from Christchurch ($199) and from Christchurch to Queenstown ($235) via Mt Cook.

The **Cook Connection** (☎ 0800 266 526, 021 583 211; www.cookconnect.co.nz) has shuttle services to Glentanner (one-way $15), Twizel (one-way $22) and Lake Tekapo (one-way $28). Bus services in these towns link on to major centres such as Christchurch, Queenstown, Wanaka and Dunedin. If you're travelling via Mt Cook from Lake Tekapo to Twizel or vice versa, the all-up cost is $50 and you do the travel over more than one day.

If you're driving here, it's best to fill up at Lake Tekapo or Twizel. There is petrol at Mt Cook, but it's expensive and usually involves summoning an attendant from the Hermitage (for a fee).

Dunedin & Otago

Coastal Otago has attractions both urban and rural, offering travellers a chance to escape the crowds of Queenstown, party down in the South Island's *coolest* city, and get up close and personal with the island's most accessible wildlife.

The heart of Otago is Dunedin, long credited as New Zealand's indie-music heartland and definitive student party town. With a plateful of fabulous restaurants and cafes, it's also a great place to lay off the two-minute noodles and indulge your stomach. From its stately train station (one of many grand old Victorian buildings in town), you can catch the famous Taieri Gorge Railway inland, or continue further on NZ's greatest bike trail, the Otago Central Rail Trail.

Those seeking quiet backcountry NZ will love the tiny towns of inland Otago: historic Clyde, sweet little St Bathans, Disney-cute Naseby – wonderful dots of humanity that don't see a lot of tourist traffic. If you're seeking wildlife, head to the Otago Peninsula, where penguins, albatross, sea lions and seals are easily sighted. Or visit seaside Oamaru, with its active historic district and resident penguin colonies.

Unhurried, and rife with picturesque scenery, Otago is generous to explorers who are after something a little less intense.

HIGHLIGHTS

- Air guitaring to live music or wriggling to DJ sounds in the bars and clubs of **Dunedin** (p582)
- Discovering laid-back charm along the quiet northern shore of **Otago Harbour** (p589)
- Peering at penguins, admiring albatross and staring at sea lions and fur seals on **Otago Peninsula** (p585)
- Cycling through lonely vistas of brown and gold along the **Otago Central Rail Trail** (p592)
- Reliving the days of the gold rush in the cobbled streets of the **Oamaru Historic Precinct** (p597)
- Winding through gorges, alongside canyons and across tall viaducts on the snaking **Taieri Gorge Railway** (p585)
- Exploring NZ's southern heritage in quaint backcountry villages such as **Clyde** (p591)
- Sampling excellent local beers and all-round gastronomic excellence in the cafes and restaurants of **Dunedin** (p580)

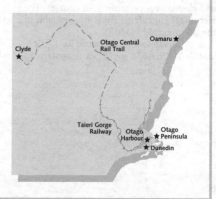

- Telephone code: 03
- www.dunedinnz.com
- www.otago.co.nz

OTAGO

Climate
With the Southern Alps blocking the prevailing wet winds from the Tasman Sea, the east coast of Otago has a relatively dry climate, similar to that of Canterbury to the north. Summer days are generally warm to hot and rainfall is very low. In winter it's a different story: temperatures can drop to well below freezing, as hinted at by the name of NZ's most famous motorcycle rally, the Brass Monkey (as in 'freeze the nuts off a...').

Getting There & Around
Air New Zealand (www.airnewzealand.co.nz) flies from Dunedin to Christchurch, Wellington and Auckland. **Pacific Blue** (www.flypacificblue.co.nz) links Dunedin to Auckland and Brisbane, Australia.

Major bus and shuttle operators include InterCity, Atomic Shuttles, Bottom Bus, Catch-A-Bus, Naked Bus and Wanaka Connexions.

For more information on getting to and from Dunedin, see p584.

DUNEDIN & THE OTAGO PENINSULA

Nestled at the end of Otago Harbour, Dunedin is a surprisingly artsy town, with lots of bars and eateries. If you can unglue yourself from the city's live music and cafe scene, the rugged Otago Peninsula and northern harbour

---

DUNEDIN & OTAGO FACTS

Eat Alfresco from the diverse stalls at the Dunedin Farmers Market (p582)

Drink The fine brews from Dunedin's Emerson's and Green Man breweries (p582)

Read *Owls Do Cry* by Oamaru's Janet Frame

Listen to ...*But I Can Write Songs Okay*, a compilation of 40 years of the Dunedin sound

Watch *Scarfies* (1999), about murderous Dunedin university students

Swim at St Kilda Beach or St Clair Beach (p578)

Festival Victorian Heritage Celebrations (Oamaru; late November; p600)

Tackiest tourist attraction Cromwell's giant fruit salad of apples and stone fruit at the edge of town on the main highway from Queenstown

Go green Tiptoe down to Otago Peninsula beaches in search of yellow-eyed penguins (p587)

---

provide easy day trips (or longer), rich with wildlife and outdoor activities.

DUNEDIN
pop 110,800

Dunedin's compact town centre blends the historic and the contemporary, reflected in its alluring museums, and tempting bars, cafes and restaurants. Weatherboard houses ranging from stately to ramshackle pepper its hilly suburbs, and bluestone Victorian buildings punctuate the centre. The country's oldest university provides loads of student energy to sustain thriving theatre, live-music and after-dark scenes.

Dunedin is an easy city to while away a few days, and more than a few travellers find themselves staying here longer than they expected as they recover from the noise, adrenaline and crowds of Queenstown. The excellent wildlife-viewing opportunities of the Otago Peninsula are also close at hand.

History

The Otakou area's early history was particularly bloody, involving a three-way feud between peninsular tribes that escalated in the early 19th century. This brutal warfare was closely followed by devastating diseases and interracial conflict ushered in via coastal sealing and whaling. The first permanent European settlers, two shiploads of pious, hard-working Scots, arrived at Port Chalmers in 1848, including the nephew of the patron saint of Scots poetry, Robbie Burns. That the city's founders were Scottish is a source of fierce pride today: a statue of Robbie still frowns down upon the city centre, there are a handful of civic haggis 'n' bagpipe occasions every year, and the city even has its own tartan.

Information
BOOKSHOPS

Dunedin is particularly blessed with second-hand bookshops.

Octagon Books (Map p576; 32 Moray Pl; 11am-4pm Mon-Fri, to 2pm Sat) This wonderful-smelling labyrinth of old tomes was voted one of the world's top 10 bookshops. Cash only.

Scribes (Map p576; ☎ 03-477 6874; cnr Great King & St David Sts; 10am-5.30pm Mon-Fri, 11am-4pm Sat & Sun) Dunedin's greatest selection of secondhand books.

University Book Shop (Map p576; ☎ 03-477 6976; www.unibooks.co.nz; 378 Great King St; 8.30am-5.30pm Mon-Fri, 9.30am-3pm Sat, 11am-3pm Sun) An excellent selection of fiction, poetry, Maori/Pacific and NZ titles.

EMERGENCY

Ambulance, fire service & police (☎ 111)

Dunedin Hospital (Map p576; ☎ 03-474 0999; 201 Great King St)

Urgent Doctors & Accident Centre (Map p576; ☎ 03-479 2900; 95 Hanover St; 8am-11.30pm) Deals with emergencies and has a pharmacy open outside normal business hours.

INTERNET ACCESS

Internet access is available at most hostels and accommodation. Wi-fi can be found at the airport and the Otago Museum.

Common Room (Map p576; 18 George St; 8.30am-9pm Mon-Wed, to 5pm Thu-Fri, 9am-1pm Sat) Coffee plus internet.

Net Planet (Map p576; 78 St Andrew St; 10am-late Mon-Sat, noon-late Sun;) Also has LAN and wi-fi.

PC Internet (Map p576; 237 Moray Pl; 10am-8pm;)

POST

Post office (Map p576; 233 Moray Pl)

TOURIST INFORMATION

Automobile Association (Map p576; AA; ☎ 0800 500 222, 03-477 5945; 450 Moray Pl; 8.30am-5pm Mon-Fri) For members' driving queries.

Department of Conservation (Map p576; DOC; ☎ 03-477 0677; www.doc.govt.nz; dunedinvc@doc.govt.nz;

1st fl, 77 Lower Stuart St; 8.30am-5pm Mon-Fri)
Information and maps on regional walking tracks and Great
Walks bookings.

Dunedin i-SITE (Map p576; 03-474 3300; www.
dunedinnz.com; 48 The Octagon; 8.30am-5pm
Mon-Fri, 8.45am-5pm Sat & Sun) Advice and bookings for
accommodation, activities, transport and walking tours.

Sights

Some of the most popular things to do in
Dunedin involve leaving town. See the Otago
Peninsula (p585), the Otago Central Rail Trail
(p592) and Taieri Gorge Railway (p585).

OTAGO MUSEUM

The modern and interactive **Otago Museum**
(Map p576; 03-474 7474; www.otagomuseum.govt.nz;
419 Great King St; admission by donation, guided tour $10;
10am-5pm) explores Otago's cultural and
physical past and present, from geology and
dinosaurs to the modern day. The beautifully designed Tangata Whenua gallery houses
an impressive *waka taua* (war canoe), wonderfully worn old carvings and some lovely
pounamu (greenstone) works. This is one of
the richest repositories of Maori knowledge
on the South Island. If you've already been
out on the peninsula admiring penguins and
albatrosses, the museum's collection of ancient and contemporary wildlife will fascinate.
Join themed guided tours ($10, see website for
times and themes). Children can explore at
the hands-on Discovery World (adult/child/
family $9.50/4.50/24), and there's a smart,
newly expanded cafe with surprisingly good
food. Check the website for always-excellent
temporary exhibitions and special gallery
talks.

DUNEDIN PUBLIC ART GALLERY

Explore NZ's art scene at Dunedin's expansive
and airy **Public Art Gallery** (Map p576; 03-474 4000;
www.dunedin.art.museum; 30 The Octagon; permanent exhibition free; 10am-5pm). Climb the iron staircase
for great city views. Works on permanent
show are mainly contemporary, including a
big NZ collection featuring local kids Ralph
Hotere and Frances Hodgkins, Cantabrian
Colin McCahon, and some old CF Goldie
oils. Rotating exhibits include some European
works and Kiwi masters.

OTHER MUSEUMS & GALLERIES

The eclectic collection at the **Otago Settlers
Museum** (Map p576; 03-477 5052; www.otago.settlers.

museum; 31 Queens Gardens; admission free; 10am-5pm)
gives insights into past residents, whether
Maori or Scots, whalers or farmers. Petrol
heads and trainspotters will love the old Buick
straight eight and 1872-built steam engine;
style hounds will love the original art-deco
bus depot foyer. See p578 for walking tours
covering the city's history.

At the **New Zealand Sports Hall of Fame** (Map
p576; 03-477 7775; www.nzhalloffame.co.nz; Dunedin
Railway Station, Anzac Ave; adult/child $5/2; 10am-4pm)
you can try and match bike-champ Karen
Holliday's average speed of 45.629km/h, or
check out the high-stepping style of iconic All
Black fullback George Nepia. You'll also find
out NZ continually punches above its weight
in the sporting world.

The **Temple Gallery** (Map p576; 03-477 7235; 29
Moray Pl; admission free; 10am-6pm Mon-Fri, to 2pm Sat)
was Dunedin's first synagogue (1863), and
then for 30 years a Masonic temple. The building retains marks of both, and is a fabulous
artspace. The Chills recorded their last album
here, and Dunedin bands still launch new
offerings here. Artists represented are predominantly Otago locals and include Ralph
Hotere, Donna Demente and Anita DeSoto).

OTHER SIGHTS

Follow your chocolate cravings to the massive **Cadbury World** (Map p576; 0800 223 287, 03-467
7967; www.cadburyworld.co.nz; 280 Cumberland St; full tour
adult/child/family $18/12/48, reduced tour adult/child $12/7;
full tour 9am-3.30pm Mon-Fri, reduced tour 9am-3.30pm
Sat & Sun) and don a paper hairnet for the full
75-minute tour of the factory that includes
a spiel on history and production, a look at
their version of a liquid-chocolate waterfall,
and a taste of the end product. The shorter
45-minute weekend tour omits the factory
tour and concentrates on the really yummy
part.

After lots of chocolate, kick on to the
90-minute, interactive tour of **Speight's Brewery**
(Map p576; 03-477 7697; www.speights.co.nz; 200 Rattray
St; adult/child/family $20/8/42; tours 10am, noon, 2pm,
6pm, 7pm Mon-Thu, 10am, noon, 2pm, 4pm, 6pm Fri-Sun),
which has been churning out beer since the
late 1800s. Following the tour you can sample
each of Speight's six different beers.

The world's steepest residential street (or
so says the *Guinness Book of World Records*),
Baldwin St (off Map p576) has a clambering gradient of 1 in 1.286 (19°). From the
city centre, head 2km north up Great King

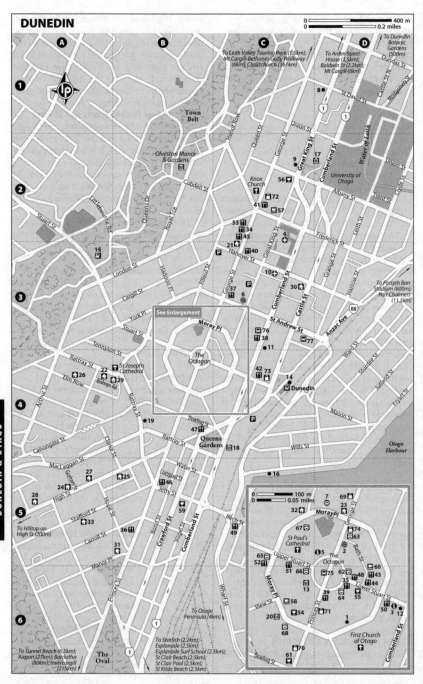

DUNEDIN

0 — 400 m
0 — 0.2 miles

To Leith Valley Touring Park (1.5km);
Mt Cargill-Bethunes Gully Walkway
(6km); Christchurch (361km)

To Arden Street
House (1.5km);
Baldwin St (2.2km);
Mt Cargill (8km)

To Dunedin
Botanic
Gardens
(500m)

Town
Belt

Olveston Manor
& Gardens

Knox
Church

University of
Otago

To Forsyth Barr
Stadium (600m);
Port Chalmers
(11.5km)

Moray Pl

See Enlargement

The
Octagon

Dunedin

Queens
Gardens

Otago
Harbour

St Josephs
Cathedral

bishops rd

To Hilltop on
High St (200m)

To Otago
Peninsula (4km)

To Starfish (2.2km);
Esplanade (2.5km);
Esplanade Surf School (2.5km);
St Clair Beach (2.5km);
St Clair Pool (2.5km);
St Kilda Beach (2.5km)

To Tunnel Beach (6.5km);
Airport (27km); Balclutha
(80km); Invercargill
(215km)

The
Oval

0 — 100 m
0 — 0.05 miles

Moray Pl

St Paul's
Cathedral

The
Octagon

Upper Stuart St

Lower Stuart St

Moray Pl

View St

Princes St

First Church
of Otago

Dowling St

DUNEDIN & OTAGO

St to where the road branches sharp left to Timaru. Get in the right-hand lane and continue straight ahead. This becomes North Rd, and Baldwin St is on the right after 1km. If you've any doubts about your brakes, park at the bottom. Alternatively, grab a Normanby bus at the Octagon ($1.90) and ask the driver to let you know when you're there. The annual 'Gutbuster' race in February sees up to 1000 athletes run to the top of Baldwin St and back. Every July, 10,000 oversized Jaffas (chocolate candies) are rolled down the hill for charity. In November 2009, three particularly dim Dunedin students after taking rides down Baldwin St in a chillie bin (insulated picnic cooler) being towed behind a car. Their only defence was that 'the pubs had shut' and they had nothing to do.

The **Dunedin Botanic Gardens** (off Map p576; cnr Great King St & Opoho Rd; admission free; ☽ dawn-dusk) date from the 1860s and spread across 22 peaceful, grassy and shady hectares. There's also a playground and a cafe.

Dunedin's striking Edwardian **railway station** (Map p576) celebrated its hundredth birthday recently, and claims to be NZ's most-photographed building. There are plenty of reasons to visit even without the mosaic-tile floors and the glorious stained-glass windows. The station houses the NZ Sports Hall of Fame (p575), hosts the Dunedin Farmers Market (p582), and is the departing point for the Taieri Gorge Railway (see p585).

The **Orokonui Ecosanctuary** (Map p586; ☎ 03-482 1755; www.orokonui.org.nz; ☽ 9.30am-4.30pm) occupies a 300-hectare nature reserve on Otago Harbour's north shore. Its mission is to provide a predator-free refuge to repopulate species previously exiled to smaller offshore islands. It's a good chance to see the tuatara, NZ's iconic living dinosaur unchanged for 200 million years. At the time of writing, the ecosanctuary could only be visited on a 90-minute guided walk (tour $38; ☽ 10.30am & 1.30pm), but unguided visits were also planned. Check the Dunedin i-SITE (p574) for an update.

DUNEDIN & OTAGO

Activities

There's more walking and kayaking out on Otago Peninsula (p588).

SWIMMING, SURFING & DIVING

St Clair and St Kilda are both popular swimming beaches (though you need to watch for rips at St Clair). St Clair also has the heated, outdoor, saltwater **St Clair Pool** (off Map p576; ☎ 03-455 6352; Esplanade, St Clair Beach; adult/child $5.50/2.50; ⏰ 6am-7pm Mon-Fri, 7am-7pm Sat & Sun, closed Apr-Oct).

St Clair and St Kilda have consistently good left-hand breaks, and you'll also find good surfing at Blackhead further south, and at Aramoana on Otago Harbour's north shore. **Esplanade Surf School** (off Map p576; ☎ 03-455 7728; www.espsurfschool.co.nz; lessons from $45) is based at St Clair Beach and provides equipment and lessons.

For St Clair, catch bus 8, 9, 28 or 29 ($1.90) from stand 1 at the Octagon. For St Kilda, catch bus 27 ($1.90) also from stand 1 at the Octagon

Back in town, **Moana Pool** (Map p576; ☎ 03-471 9780; 60 Littlebourne Rd; adult/child $5.50/2.50; ⏰ 6am-10pm Mon-Fri, 7am-7pm Sat & Sun) has diving boards, waterslides, wave machines and a spa.

WALKING, TRAMPING & CLIMBING

The **Tunnel Beach Walkway** (Map p576; 45 minutes return; closed August to October) crosses farmland before descending the sea cliffs to Tunnel Beach. Sea stacks, arches and unusual rock shapes have been carved out by the wild Pacific, and a few fossils stud the sandstone cliffs. It impressed civic father John Cargill so much, he had a hand-hewn stone tunnel built to give his family access to secluded beachside picnics. The walk is southwest of central Dunedin. Catch a Corstorphine bus from the Octagon to Stenhope Cres and walk 1.4km along Blackhead Rd to Tunnel Beach Rd, then 400m to the start of the walkway. Strong currents make swimming here dangerous.

Catch a Normanby bus to the start of Norwood St, which leads to Cluny St and the **Mt Cargill-Bethunes Gully Walkway** (Map p576; 3½ hours return). The highlight is the view from Mt Cargill (also accessible by car). From Mt Cargill, a trail continues to the 10-million-year-old lava-formed **Organ Pipes** and, after another half-hour, to Mt Cargill Rd on the other side of the mountain.

The **Otago Tramping and Mountaineering Club** (www.otmc.co.nz) organises weekend day and overnight tramps, often to the Silver Peaks Reserve north of Dunedin. Nonmembers are welcome, but must contact trip leaders beforehand (see website for details).

Traditional rock climbing (nonbolted) is popular at **Long Beach** (off Map p586) and the cliffs at **Mihiwaka** (Map p586), both accessed via Blueskin Rd north of Port Chalmers, and **Lovers Leap** (Map p586; bolted and natural) on the peninsula. Dave Brash, Dunedin's climbing guru, has written *Dunedin Rock* detailing local climbs. Get it from the Dunedin i-SITE or at Bivouac (p584).

OTHER ACTIVITIES

Cycle Surgery (Map p576; ☎ 03-477 7473; www.cyclesurgery.co.nz; 67 Lower Stuart St; per day $35) rents out bikes and has mountain-biking info.

Hare Hill (Map p586; ☎ 0800 437 837, 03-472 8496; www.horseriding-dunedin.co.nz; 207 Aramoana Rd, Deborah Bay) runs horse treks ($75 to $210) including thrilling beach rides and farm treks.

Tours

See the Dunedin i-SITE (p574) for more specialised city tours.

First City Tours (adult/child $20/10; ⏰ buses depart The Octagon 9am, 10.15am, 1pm, 2.15pm & 3.30pm) Hop-on/hop-off double-decker bus tour that loops around the city. Stops include the Otago Museum, Speight's, Botanic Gardens and Baldwin St.

Walk Dunedin (☎ 03-477 5052; 1/2hr walk $12/20; ⏰ 1hr walk 7pm year-round & 9.30am Oct-Apr, 2hr walk 11am year-round) History-themed strolls around the city, organised by the Otago Settlers Museum. Meet at the i-SITE.

For viewing nearby wildlife, see p588.

Sleeping

Most accommodation is within easy walking distance of the city centre, though some spots offer a challenging uphill stroll back from town. Most motels are at the northern end of George St.

BUDGET

Dunedin Holiday Park (Map p586; ☎ 0800 945 455, 03-455 4690; www.dunedinholidaypark.co.nz; 41 Victoria Rd; campsites per adult/child $16/8, powered sites $34, cabins $44-79, units $89-110; 🖥 🛜) Over the sand dunes from St Kilda Beach, this huge complex has a kids playground, barbecue area, a zillion campsites and a variety of well-equipped cabins, flats and motel units.

Arden Street House (off Map p576; ☎ 03-473 8860; www.ardenstreethouse.co.nz; 36 Arden St; dm/s/d $20/40/80, s/d incl breakfast from $55/85; ☐) North of the city up Northeast Valley, this pair of homes atop a (steep) hill share an organic garden and a very welcoming host. With a recurring leopard theme, crazy artworks and a porthole in the bathroom, the B&B is a pretty amazing space. Readers have raved about the fabulous shared dinners ($10 to $25) with neighbours, artists, wwoofers and guests. Head up North Rd toward Baldwin St, then turn right up Glendining St.

Chalet Backpackers (Map p576; ☎ 0800 242 538, 03-479 2075; www.chaletbackpackers.co.nz; 296 High St; dm/s/d $24/39/56; ☐ 🛜) Up a fairly steep hill, with a correspondingly fabulous view, this rambling old building quickly makes guests feel at home. The kitchen is big and sunny and festooned with flowers, and the dining room has one huge long table to help you meet your neighbours. There's also a compact garden, pool table, piano and rumours of a ghost.

Stafford Gables YHA (Map p576; ☎ 0800 600 100, 03-474 1919; www.yha.co.nz; yha.dunedin@yha.org.nz; 71 Stafford St; dm/s/d from $25/55/72; ☐ 🛜) Sprawling and mazelike, this century-old former hospital has a comfortable air. Rooms are fairly big and each one is unique, many with their own small balconies (ask for Room 38). The shared kitchen is truly spacious, and a dungeonlike cellar keeps the sports hounds from imposing their TV habits on everyone else. Upstairs is a sunny rooftop garden.

Elm Lodge (Map p576; ☎ 03-474 1872; www.elmlodge.co.nz; 74 Elm Row; dm/s/d $26/40/60; ☐ 🛜) Two sweet old houses with harbour and peninsula views, Elm Lodge is a popular choice for travellers looking to relax a while. Rooms are quaint but comfortable, and the back garden is just made for barbecues and a few cold beers. Elm Lodge is a fairly steep walk into (or particularly *out from*) town.

Central Backpackers (Map p576; ☎ 0800 423 6872; www.centralbackpackers.co.nz; 243 Moray Pl; dm/tw/d $27/58/64; ☐ 🛜) Located in the heart of town, this recently renovated hostel has inviting common TV lounge and kitchen areas, and a welcoming host in Gizmo the cat. Dorm rooms sleep two to 10 on bunks, and private rooms are spacious.

Leith Valley Touring Park (off Map p576; ☎ 0800 555 331, 03-467 9936; www.leithvalleytouringpark.co.nz; 103 Malvern St; powered sites $32, cabins $50, units d $79-99; ☐) A short drive from central Dunedin, this camping ground is surrounded by native bush studded with walks, glowworm caves, and a wee creek. Self-contained modern motel units are spacious, and tourist flats are smaller but have a more earthy feel (linen required). Catch the Garden Village bus from the Octagon.

our pick **Hogwartz** (Map p576; ☎ 03-474 1487; www.hogwartz.co.nz; 277 Rattray St; dm $27-28, s/d/tr $40/64/90; ☐ 🛜) The Catholic bishop's residence since the 1870s, this beautiful old building has now been converted into a wonderfully complicated warren of comfortable rooms. The five-bed dorm, the bishop's old formal dining room, would almost certainly be the grandest dorm room you have ever stayed in. There's a short, steep walk up a winding path through lush bush from Rattray St.

Also recommended:

Manor House Backpackers (Map p576; ☎ 0800 477 0484, 03-477 0484; www.manorhousebackpackers.co.nz; 28 Manor Pl; dm $22-24, d $60; ☐) Two stately old villas surrounded by gardens and trees.

On Top Backpackers (Map p576; ☎ 0800 668 672, 03-477 6121; www.ontopbackpackers.co.nz; cnr Filleul St & Moray Pl; dm $25-26, s $50, d w/without bathroom $78/60; ☐ 🛜) Modern, well-located hostel atop a pool hall and bar, with large sundeck and shared barbecue area.

MIDRANGE

Living Space (Map p576; ☎ 03-951 5000; www.livingspace.net; 192 Castle St; d $89-149; ☐ 🛜) Living Space combines kitchenettes in funky colours, whip-smart ergonomic design and a central location. There's an on-site laundry and huge shared kitchen, conversation-friendly lounges and a private DVD cinema. Some rooms are pretty compact, but they're all you need, and represent good value. Substantial discounts kick in for longer-stay guests, and it's popular with overseas students.

Hilltop on High St (Map p576; ☎ 03-477 1053; www.hilltoponhighst.co.nz; 433 High St; d $120-170; ☐ 🛜) A wonderful four-bedroom villa atop a steep hill, this place is really great value for money. The fabulous shared lounge has leather armchairs and a nice little library, the kitchen sings out to cater a large meal, and the individually decorated rooms all have a touch of luxury about them. The views are stupendous.

Grandview Bed & Breakfast (Map p576; ☎ 0800 749 472, 03-474 9472; www.grandview.co.nz; 360 High St; d incl breakfast $125-195; ☐ 🛜) Bold colours, exposed brick walls and snazzy art-deco bathrooms are the highlights at this family-owned B&B on the slopes above town. There's more harbour

DUNEDIN & OTAGO

views from the barbecue and deck, and lots of sunny shared spaces. The larger rooms have private spa baths.

TOP END
315 Euro (Map p576; ☎ 0800 387 638, 03-477 9929; www.eurodunedin.co.nz; 315 George St; d $150-250; 🛜) This sleek new opening is in the absolute heart of George St's daytime retail strip and after-dark eating and drinking hub. Choose from modern studio apartments or larger one-bedroom apartments with full kitchens. Decor is modern and luxurious, and soundproofing and double-glazed windows keeps George St's irresistible buzz at bay.

Dunedin Palms Motel (Map p576; ☎ 0800 782 938, 03-477 8293; www.dunedinpalmsmotel.co.nz; 185-195 High St; d $170-210; 🖥 🛜) A short stroll from the Speight's Ale House, the art-deco-style Palms has smartly decorated studios and one- and two-bedroom units arrayed around a central courtyard. You're handily just out of the CBD, but don't have to endure a long walk uphill. More expensive units feature spa baths.

Brothers Boutique Hotel (Map p576; ☎ 0800 477 004, 03-477 0043; www.brothershotel.co.nz; 295 Rattray St; d incl breakfast $170-320; 🖥 🛜) Rooms in this distinctive old 1920s Christian Brothers residence have been refurbished beyond any monk's dreams, while still retaining many unique features. The chapel room ($285) includes the original arched stained-glass windows of its past life. There are great views from the rooftop units.

Fletcher Lodge (Map p576; ☎ 03-477 5552; www.fletcherlodge.co.nz; 276 High St; d $325-450, ste $595-650, all incl breakfast; 🖥 🛜) Originally home to one of NZ's wealthy industrialist families, this gorgeous redbrick manor is just minutes from the city, but the secluded gardens feel wonderfully remote. Rooms are elegantly trimmed with antique furniture, and the ornate plaster ceilings reinforce why the building is listed with the Historic Places Trust.

Eating
Whether you're looking for cheap 'n' cheerful with plastic menus, organic/vegan/herbal omelettes, or fine white linen tablecloths, Dunedin's got it.

RESTAURANTS
Izakaya Yuki (Map p576; ☎ 03-477 9539; 29 Bath St; dishes $5-12; 🕑 noon-2pm Mon-Sat & 5pm-late Mon-Sun; 🔽) Cute and cosy, with a huge array of small

dishes on which to graze, Yuki is a lovely spot for supper or a relaxed, drawn-out Japanese meal. Make a night of it with sake or draught Asahi beer, and multiple plates of *yakitori* (grilled skewers), *gyoza* (dumplings), or sushi and sashimi. The wall-to-wall sumo wrestling videos will ensure you don't eat *too* much.

Minami (Map p576; ☎ 03-477 9596; 126-132 Lower Stuart St; meals $8-20; 🕑 noon-2pm & 5pm-late Mon-Sun) Popular for its simplicity and its prices, Minami is almost always packed with local fans of Japanese food. One half specialises in noodle dishes, while the other side is (slightly) more formal.

Saigon Van (Map p576; ☎ 03-474 1445; 66 St Andrew St; mains $10-15; 🕑 11.30am-2pm Tue-Sun & 5-10pm Mon-Sun; 🔽) The elegant decor looks high-end Asian, but the Vietnamese food is definitely budget-friendly. Try the combination spring rolls ($9 for six) and a bottle of Vietnamese beer to recreate lazy nights in Saigon. The bean-sprout-laden *pho* (noodle soup) and salads are also good.

Anarkali (Map p576; ☎ 03-477 1120; 365 George St; meals $11-18; 🕑 11.30am-2pm Mon-Fri & 5-10pm Mon-Sun; 🔽) Even the most difficult-to-please fans of Indian food rave about Anarkali. Get the sampler dinner to try a bit of everything.

Reef Seafood (Map p576; ☎ 03-471 7185; 333 George St; mains $23-35; 🕑 11.30am-2pm & 5.30pm-late Mon-Sat, from 6pm Sun) Generous plates of oysters, scallops, surf and turf, and crayfish (lobster) lure burly Otago farmers into town for their monthly slap-up meal. Lunch specials are just $10.

Palms Restaurant (Map p576; ☎ 03-477 6534; 18 Queens Garden; dinner $28-35; 🕑 noon-2pm & 6pm-late Mon-Sat; 🔽) Hidden away at the bottom of Dowling St, Palms has long been a landmark Dunedin eatery. Food is innovative and usually locally sourced, and daily lunch specials ($10) are excellent value. How does garlic risotto with grilled halloumi cheese or steamed clams and chorizo sound?

Scotia (Map p576; ☎ 03-477 7704; 199 Upper Stuart St; mains $30-32; 🕑 3pm-late) Now relocated from the Dunedin Railway Station to a cosy heritage town house, Scotia toasts all things Scottish with a wall-full of single malt whisky and hearty fare such as smoked salmon and char-grilled venison. The two Scottish Robbies – Burns and Coltrane – look down approvingly on a menu that also includes haggis, and duck and whisky pâté.

ourpick **Plato** (Map p576; ☎ 03-477 4235; 2 Birch St; dinner mains $30-35, brunch mains $15-23; ⏲ 6pm-late Mon-Sat & 11am-late Sun) A regular winner in *Cuisine* magazine's Best of NZ's gongs, Plato has a retro-themed location near the harbour and a strong beer and wine list. Try standouts like Goan fish curry or slow-braised pork belly with crispy crackling. Plato's spin on seafood is always excellent, and Sunday brunch is worth the shortish trek from the CBD. Bookings are recommended.

Bell Pepper Blues (Map p576; ☎ 03-474 0973; 474 Princes St; mains $30-39; ⏲ 6pm-late Tue-Sat) One of Dunedin's finer dining options, this restaurant boasts one of the region's best-known chefs and is famous for its venison, freshly baked bread and desserts. There's a $10-per-bottle corkage fee for BYO.

Bacchus Wine Bar & Restaurant (Map p576; ☎ 03-474 824; upstairs, 12 The Octagon; mains $33-38; ⏲ noon-3pm Mon-Fri & 6pm-late Mon-Sat) Bacchus is particularly nice for a meal for two or to celebrate a special occasion. There's a wine list that the god of wine himself would approve of, and more than a few dishes combine local produce with subtle Asian influences. Try the pork belly slow cooked in Asian spices.

CAFES
See p582 for where to get the best coffee in town.

Potpourri (Map p576; ☎ 03-477 9983; 97 Lower Stuart St; snacks $7-10, meals $10-14; ⏲ 9.30am-3pm Mon-Fri; Ⓥ) Funky, homey and very kid-friendly, this small cafe has been fattening up Dunedin's vegetarians and vegans for almost 40 years. Tuck into big, inexpensive portions of quiche, pizza, flatbread melts and spicy samosas. There are lots of organic, free-range and gluten-free options, and takeaways are available.

Tangente (Map p576; ☎ 03-477 0232; 111 Moray Pl; meals $7.50-17; ⏲ 8am-3pm Tue-Sat, 9am-3pm Sun; Ⓥ) A cheerful, welcoming space with mismatched tables, toys for the kids, a funky soundtrack, and the glorious aroma of freshly baked bread. Tangente's food is generally organic, free-range and locally sourced.

Mojo (Map p576; ☎ 03-742 1061; 329 Princes St; mains $8-18; ⏲ 7am-5.30pm Mon-Fri, 8.30am-5.30pm Sat & Sun) Quite possibly Dunedin's sunniest spot for a lazy brunch, the spacious and high-ceilinged Mojo teams yummy counter food, bagels and bircher muesli, with superlative coffee all the way from Wellington. From 11am a more substantial menu – think pizza and steak sandwiches – kicks in, with wine and beer also available.

Governors (Map p576; ☎ 03-477 6871; 438 George St; mains $9-16; ⏲ 7am-9pm Mon-Fri, 8am-9pm Sat & Sun) Popular with students, Governors does a nice line in early morning pancakes and other light meals. If you're feeling a little off the pace after the previous night, a strong coffee and an eggy omelette will be just what the doctor ordered.

Modaks (Map p576; ☎ 03-477 6563; 337-339 George St; meals from $9; ⏲ 8am-7pm; Ⓥ) This funky little cafe and bar, with brick walls, mismatched formica tables, and couches for slouching, is popular with students and those who appreciate chilled-out reggae while they nurse a pot of tea. Sundaes, smoothies and beer make it a great escape from the heat, and grilled home-made focaccia bread with yummy, interesting toppings warm the insides in winter.

Circadian Rhythm Café (Map p576; ☎ 03-474 9994; 72 St Andrew St; curry buffet $9.50; ⏲ 8.30am-9pm Mon-Sat; Ⓥ) Specialising in organic Indian curries, this all-vegan cafe is also known for its cookies and cakes. The superfriendly staff will also try to tweak things to oblige gluten-free requests. Circadian Rhythm is a music venue, with a variety of interesting acts on Friday nights from 5.30pm. Dunedin's Emerson's and Green Man beers are both available, so you don't have to be *too* healthy.

Perc (Map p576; ☎ 03-477 5462; 142 Lower Stuart St; mains $10-18; ⏲ 7am-5pm Mon-Fri, 9am-5pm Sat, 10am-5pm Sun) Always busy, and for good reason, the Perc is a grand place to kick-start your day. The decor's kinda retro and kinda art deco, and there's hearty cafe fare ranging from salmon bagels and panini to warming porridge.

Good Oil (Map p576; ☎ 03-479 9900; 314 George St; mains $10-18; ⏲ 8am-5pm) This sleek little cafe is Dunedin's top spot for coffee and cake. Try the lemon and sour cream cake ($4). If you're still waking up, maybe resurrect the day with innovative brunches such as kumara (sweet potato) hash with hot smoked salmon ($15).

Nova Cafe (Map p576; ☎ 03-479 0808; 29 The Octagon; mains $15; ⏲ 7am-11pm Mon-Fri, from 8.30am Sat & Sun; Ⓥ) Not surprisingly, this extension of the Public Art Gallery has a stylish look about it. Cakes and snacks are famously creative, and Nova is also licensed for beer and wine. Escape into Dunedin's best choice of interesting food, travel and arts magazines.

Starfish (off Map p576; ☎ 03-455 5940; 7/240 Forbury Rd, St Clair; mains $18-30; ⏲ 8.30am-late Tue-Sat, to 4.30pm

---

JUST GIVE ME THE COFFEE & NO ONE WILL GET HURT

Dunedin has some excellent coffee bars to refuel and recharge.

Fix (Map p576; ☎ 03-479 2660; 15 Frederick St; ◷ 7.30am-5pm Mon-Fri, 8.30am-3.30pm Sat, 9.30am-late Sun) Wage slaves queue at the pavement window every morning, while students and others with time on their hands relax in the courtyard. Fix don't serve food, but you can bring along your own food or takeaways.

Mazagran Espresso Bar (Map p576; ☎ 03-477 9959; 36 Moray Pl; ◷ 8am-6pm Mon-Fri, 10am-2pm Sat) The godfather of Dunedin's coffee scene, this compact wood-and-brick coffee house is the source of the magic bean for many of the city's restaurants and cafes.

Strictly Coffee (Map p576; ☎ 03-479 0017; 23 Bath St; ◷ 8am-4pm Mon-Fri) The second of Dunedin's seriously serious coffee bars, Strictly Coffee is a stylish retro coffee bar hidden down grungy Bath St. Different rooms provide varying views and artworks to enjoy while you sip and sup.

Sun-Mon) In a cosy, brick-clad space, Starfish is the best of the growing cafe and restaurant scene at St Clair Beach. Pop out on a weekday to score an outside table to enjoy your pizza and wine. Catch bus 8, 9, 28 or 29 ($1.90) from stand 1 at The Octagon.

QUICK EATS & SELF-CATERING
Inexpensive Asian restaurants are clustered along George St, just before St Andrew St. Most also do takeaways.

Dost (Map p576; ☎ 03-477 2477; 19 Princes St; mains $8-12; ◷ 10am-10pm Mon-Wed, 11am-late Thu-Sat, 11am-9.30pm Sun; V) Life's pretty simple really. Sometimes all you want is a good-value kebab or falafel. Especially if you've just left Dunedin's premier nightlife hub.

Velvet Burger (Map p576; ☎ 03-477 7089; 150 Lower Stuart St; mains $10-18; ◷ 11.30am-late; V) Interesting burgers with interesting names make for interesting times. Best consumed after a few beers, but Velvet Burger is also licensed if the night is young. There's another VB at 375 George St (same hours).

Guilty by Confection (Map p576; ☎ 03-474 0835; 44-46 Lower Stuart St; ◷ 9am-2pm Mon, 10am-5pm Tue-Fri, 9.30am-1.30pm Sat) Handmade chocolates, fudges and sweets.

The thriving **Dunedin Farmers Market** (Map p576; www.otagofarmersmarket.org.nz; ◷ 8am-12.30pm Sat) convenes at the Dunedin Railway Station. It's all local, all eatable (or drinkable), and mostly organic, with everything from Speight's-beer-flavoured ice cream, gourmet sausages, and Russian pancakes filled with blue cod. There's usually live music on offer, and a passionate foodie vibe. Grab felafels or espresso to sustain you while you browse, and stock up on interesting fresh meats and seafood, vegies and cheeses for your journey.

Also pick up some locally brewed Green Man organic beer.

Countdown supermarket (Map p576; 309 Cumberland St; ◷ 6am-midnight) Self-catering central.

For coffee supplies head to either Mazagran or Strictly Coffee for freshly roasted beans; see above.

Drinking
Supported by perpetually thirsty students and the city's arty vibe, Dunedin boasts great bars and pubs. Find time to try the local beers – Green Man (organic) and Emerson's (simply magnificent).

The Octagon is the heart of the city's bar scene, with no less than eight different bars at street level (plus two downstairs out of sight). Check www.dunedinmusic.co.nz for news and listings of club nights and bands playing around town.

Albar (Map p576; ☎ 03-479 2468; 135 Lower Stuart St; ◷ 11am-late) This former butchers is now a bohemian little bar attracting just maybe the widest age range in Dunedin. Most punters are drawn by the 50 single malt whiskies, a changing array of interesting tap beers, and a concise menu of cheap-as-chips bar snacks ($4 to $8). Background music stays firmly in the background, making Albar a top spot for conversation.

Mou Very (Map p576; ☎ 03-477 2180; www.mouvery. co.nz; 357 George St; ◷ 11am-late) The tiny Mou Very may well be the world's smallest bar. It's only 1.8m wide, but is still big enough to host regular funk and soul DJ sessions most Fridays from 5pm. There's just six bar stools, so Mou Very's boho regulars usually spill out into an adjacent laneway. By day, it's a handy refuelling spot for your morning or afternoon espresso.

our pick Pequeno (Map p576; ☎ 03-477 7830; www.pequeno.co.nz; alleyway behind 12 Moray Pl; ◔ 5pm-late Mon-Fri, from 7pm Sat) Down the alleyway opposite the Rialto cinema, Pequeno attracts a slightly older, more sophisticated crowd. There are cosy leather couches, a warming fireplace, and an excellent wine selection and interesting tapas menu. Music is generally laid-back and never too loud to intrude on discussions of the latest architectural fashions.

Tonic (Map p576; ☎ 03-471 9194; www.tonicbar.co.nz; 138 Princes St; ◔ 4pm-late Tue-Fri, 6pm-late Sat) Craft beer bar with the best of Kiwi brews, and lots more interesting imports than your average pub. Limited release beers, loads of single malt whiskies and stellar cocktails appeal to an older crowd than Dunedin's student pubs. Antipasto plates and cheese boards mean you've got good reasons to stay for another drink.

12 Below (Map p576; ☎ 03-474 5055; alleyway behind 12 Moray Pl; occasional cover charge $5-10; ◔ 8pm-late Tue-Sat) In the same alleyway as Pequeno, 12 Below is a hip and intimate underground bar. There's mismatched comfy seats and couches, and nooks aplenty for chatting to mates. There's also floor space for those here to listen to live-music acts (a lot of funk and reggae) or to wriggle along with the DJ's choice of hip-hop and drum 'n' bass.

Carousel (Map p576; ☎ 03-477 4141; www.carouselbar.co.nz; upstairs 141 Lower Stuart St; ◔ 4pm-late Tue-Sat) Dark and sophisticated, with great cocktails, loungey music and a late-30s crowd looking pretty pleased with themselves to be seen somewhere so deadly cool.

Captain Cook (Map p576; ☎ 03-474 1935; 354 Great King St; ◔ 11am-late) This grand-daddy of Dunedin student pubs, with a fun garden bar that's packed with the nation's youth over winter, shrinks to a sad pokies venue over the summer months.

Speight's Ale House (Map p576; ☎ 03-477 9480; 200 Rattray St; ◔ 11am-late) Busy even through the off months, the Ale House is a favourite of strapping young lads in their cleanest dirty shirts. A good spot to watch the rugby on TV, and to try the full range of Speight's beers.

Entertainment

NIGHTCLUBS

10 Bar (Map p576; ☎ 03-477 6310; www.10bar.co.nz; 10 The Octagon; ◔ 10pm-late Thu-Sun) Deep downstairs is a complex space filled with loud music, pulsing lights and dancing bogan princesses. A cover charge kicks in at midnight.

Bath Street (Map p576; ☎ 03-477 6750; www.myspace.com/bathst; 1 Bath St; ◔ 9pm-late Tue-Sat) When all the other bars are closed, Bath Street's famously good sound system summons Dunedin's unsleeping dance crowd for drum 'n' bass, house and hip-hop.

di lusso (Map p576; ☎ 03-477 3776; 12 The Octagon; ◔ 6.30pm-late Sun-Thu, 5pm-late Fri & Sat) Grooving to a sexier-than-average house DJ, and darkly cool with crimson walls and a backlit drinks display, di lusso serves seriously good cocktails and offers a submarine perspective through to the toilets.

Pop (Map p576; ☎ 03-474 0842; downstairs, 14 The Octagon; ◔ 8pm-late Tue-Thu, 6pm-late Fri & Sat) Downstairs from di lusso, and possibly even cooler, Pop serves Dunedin's best martinis, and prides itself on seriously good DJs playing funk and house.

CINEMAS

Rates are often cheaper on Tuesdays.

Hoyts Cinema (Map p576; ☎ 03-477 3250; info line 03-477 7019; www.hoyts.co.nz; 33 The Octagon; adult/child $15/8) Blockbuster heaven.

Metro Cinema (Map p576; ☎ 03-471 9635; www.metrocinema.co.nz; Moray Pl; adult/student $13/10) Below the Town Hall; art-house and nostalgic. Backpackers – with student ID – get in for $10.

Rialto Cinemas (Map p576; ☎ 03-474 2200; www.rialto.co.nz; 11 Moray Pl; adult/child $15/9) A mix of blockbusters and art-house flicks with an extensive program of specialised festivals.

THEATRE

Fortune Theatre (Map p576; ☎ 03-477 8323; www.fortunetheatre.co.nz; 231 Upper Stuart St; adult/child $35/15) The world's southernmost professional theatre company has been running dramas, comedies, pantomimes, classics and contemporary NZ productions for almost 40 years. Shows are performed – watched over by the obligatory theatre ghost – in a Gothic-styled old Wesleyan church.

LIVE MUSIC

Sammy's (Map p576; ☎ 03-477 2185; www.sammys.co.nz; 65 Crawford St; ◔ vary by event) Dunedin's premier live-music venue draws an eclectic mix of genres from noisy-as-hell punk to chilled reggae and gritty dubstep. It's also increasingly the venue of choice for visiting Kiwi bands and up-and-coming international acts.

DUNEDIN & OTAGO

Chick's Hotel (Map p586; ☎ 03-472 5074; 2 Mount St, Port Chalmers; ☷ vary by event) Across in Port Chalmers, Chicks is the archetypal rock-and-roll pub, and the venue's 19th-century stone walls now play host to everything from touring alt-country bands from the States to local metal bands. If any of Dunedin's esteemed Flying Nun alumni are performing, chances are it will be here or at Sammy's. Catch bus 13 or 14 from stand 4 outside the Countdown supermarket on Cumberland St.

SPORT
Forsyth Barr Stadium (off Map p576; www.otagostadium. co.nz; Awatea St, North Dunedin) Constructed for the 2011 Rugby World Cup, Dunedin's newest sports venue is 2km from the centre of town. It's the only major stadium in NZ with a fully covered roof and will host the Highlanders Super 14 rugby team from 2012 and the Otago NPC rugby team from 2011. See www.orfu. co.nz and www.highlanders-rugby.co.nz for match schedules.

Shopping
George St is Dunedin's main shopping strip, packed with convenient but largely generic chain stores. Note the following harder-to-find and more interesting spots. Moray Pl – near the Rialto Cinemas – is a funky area.

Disk Den (Map p576; ☎ 03-477 2280; 118 Princes St) Although it mostly carries new and recent-release CDs (and their associated posters, DVDs and other tat), the Den also has a collection of old vinyl, and even some cassette tapes, handy if your rental car happens to date from the Stone Age.

Fern (Map p576; ☎ 03-477 7292; 67 Princes St; ☷ 11.30am-5.30pm Mon, 10am-5.30pm Tue-Fri, 11am-4pm Sat) Specialises in unique clothing, design and jewellery, many from up-coming Dunedin artists and designers.

Stuart St Potters Cooperative (Map p576; ☎ 03-471 8484; 14 Lower Stuart St; ☷ 10am-5pm Mon-Fri, 9am-3pm Sat) Locally designed and made pottery and ceramic art from 12 Dunedin and Otago region craftspeople.

For outdoor equipment and clothing try:
Bivouac (Map p576; ☎ 03-477 3679; 171 George St) Climbing, camping, and tramping gear, and maps and specialist guidebooks.
McKinlays (Map p576; ☎ 03-477 1389; 454 George St; ☷ 9am-5.30pm Mon-Sat) Crafting handmade boots and shoes for 130 years. Customised shoemaking and overseas delivery are both available.

Wild South (Map p576; ☎ 03-477 7856; 78 George St) Fashionable but useful outdoorsy clothes.

Getting There & Away
AIR
There are international flights into Dunedin on **Air New Zealand** (☎ 0800 737 000; www.airnew zealand.co.nz) from Sydney and Melbourne, and flights with **Pacific Blue** (☎ 0800 670 000; www.fly pacificblue.co.nz) to and from Brisbane.

Air New Zealand has domestic flights to and from Auckland (from $109), Christchurch (from $59) and Wellington (from $99). Pacific Blue links Dunedin with Christchurch (from $60) and Auckland (from $100).

BUS
Most buses leave from the Dunedin Railway Station (excluding InterCity, which depart from St Andrew St). Check when you make your booking.

InterCity (Map p576; ☎ 03-471 7143; www.intercity. co.nz; 205 St Andrew St; ☷ ticket office 7.30am-5pm Mon-Fri, 11am-3pm Sat, 11am-5.15pm Sun, tickets by phone 7am-9pm daily) has direct services to Oamaru ($28, one hour 40 minutes), Christchurch ($50, six hours), Queenstown ($45, 4½ hours), Te Anau ($45, 4½ hours) and Invercargill ($43, four hours).

Southern Link (☎ 0508 458 835; www.southernlink coaches.co.nz) connects Dunedin to Christchurch ($40) and Oamaru ($28). **Coastline Tours** (☎ 03-434 7744; www.coastline-tours.co.nz) runs between Dunedin and Oamaru ($30), and will detour to Moeraki, Karitane, Seacliff or the airport if needed. **Naked Bus** (☎ 0900 625 33; www.naked bus.com) connects Dunedin with Christchurch ($18), Queenstown ($29) and Invercargill ($29).

A couple of services connect Dunedin to the Catlins and Southland. The **Bottom Bus** (☎ 03-477 9083; www.bottombus.co.nz) does a circuit from Dunedin through the Catlins to Invercargill, Te Anau, Queenstown and back to Dunedin. **Catlins Coaster** (☎ 03-477 9083; www.catlinscoaster.co.nz) connects Dunedin with Invercargill, returning via the scenic Catlins; see p667.

Other shuttles:
Atomic Shuttles (☎ 03-349 0697; www.atomic travel.co.nz) To and from Christchurch ($35), Oamaru ($20), Invercargill ($35), Queenstown ($40) and Wanaka ($40).
Catch-A-Bus (☎ 03-449-2024; www.catchabus.co.nz) Door-to-door daily between Dunedin and Wanaka ($50),

stopping at Otago Central Rail Trail towns along the way. Bikes cost an additional $10.

Knightrider (☎ 03-342 8055; www.knightrider.co.nz) Night-time service to Christchurch ($56), Oamaru ($36) and Invercargill ($46).

Wanaka Connexions (☎ 03-443 9122; www.time2. co.nz) Shuttles between Dunedin and Wanaka ($45) and Queenstown ($45).

TRAIN

Two interesting train journeys start at Dunedin's **railway station** (Anzac Ave): the Taieri Gorge Railway journey (see the boxed text, below), and the Seasider (www.seasider.co.nz), which journeys along the coast to Palmerston and back (departs 9.30am and returns 1.30pm, one-way/return $48/72). Book via the Taieri Gorge Railway.

Getting Around
TO/FROM THE AIRPORT

Dunedin Airport (off Map p576; ☎ 03-486 2879; www. dnairport.co.nz) is 27km southwest of the city. The cheapest way to reach it is by a door-to-door shuttle (per person from $15). Try **Kiwi Shuttles** (☎ 03-487 9790; www.kiwishuttles.co.nz), **Super Shuttle** (☎ 0800 748 885; www.supershuttle.co.nz) or **Southern Taxis** (☎ 03-476 6300; www.southerntaxis.co.nz).

A standard taxi ride between the city and the airport costs around $80. There is no public bus service to the airport.

BUS

City buses (☎ 0800 474 082; www.orc.govt.nz) leave from stops in the Octagon, while buses to districts around Dunedin depart a block away from stands along Cumberland St near the Countdown supermarket. Buses run regularly during the week, but services are greatly reduced (or nonexistent) on weekends and holidays. View the Dunedin bus timetable at the Dunedin i-SITE, or see www.orc.govt.nz.

For hop-on, hop-off First City Tours, see p578

CAR

The big nationwide car-rental companies all have offices in Dunedin, and you'll find a few inexpensive local outfits here too, such as **Getaway** (☎ 0800 489 761, 03-489 7614; www.geta waycarhire.co.nz) and **Driven Rentals** (☎ 03-456 3600; www.drivengroup.co.nz).

Parking is tight in the central city, and a recent council blitz has installed parking meters across pretty much all of the CBD. The cheapest are on the steepest streets (naturally). Try London St or Cargill St northwest of the centre of town.

TAXI

Dunedin Taxis (☎ 03-477 7777) and **Otago Taxis** (☎ 03-477 3333).

OTAGO PENINSULA

Otago Peninsula has the South Island's most accessible diversity of wildlife. Albatross, penguins, fur seals and sea lions provide a natural background to rugged countryside, wild walks and beaches, and interesting historical sites. Despite the host of tours exploring the peninsula, the area maintains its quiet rural air. Get the *Otago Peninsula* brochure and map from the Dunedin i-SITE and see www .otago-peninsula.co.nz.

Sights
ROYAL ALBATROSS CENTRE

Taiaroa Head, at the peninsula's eastern tip, has the world's only mainland royal albatross colony. The best time to visit is from December to February, when one parent is constantly guarding the young while the other delivers food throughout the day. Sightings are most common in the afternoon when the

---

TAIERI GORGE RAILWAY

With narrow tunnels, deep gorges, winding tracks, rugged canyons and more than a dozen stone and wrought-iron viaduct crossings (up to 50m high), the scenic **Taieri Gorge Railway** (☎ 03-477 4449; www.taieri.co.nz; Dunedin Railway Station, Anzac Ave) consistently rates highly with visitors.

The four-hour return trip aboard 1920s heritage coaches travels to Pukerangi (one-way/return $51/76), 58km away. Some trips carry on to Middlemarch (one-way/return $58/87) or you can opt for a train-coach trip to Queenstown (one-way $115). From Middlemarch, you can also bring your bike along and hit the rail trail; see the boxed text, p592. In summer (October to April), trains depart 2.30pm daily for Pukerangi, plus trips to Middlemarch or Pukerangi some mornings. In winter (May to September) trains depart for Pukerangi at 12.30pm daily.

winds pick up; calm days don't see much bird action.

The only public access is through the **Royal Albatross Centre** (☎ 03-478 0499; www.albatross.org. nz; Taiaroa Head; ☼ 9am-dusk summer, 10am-4pm winter). One-hour tours (adult/child $45/22.50) include viewing from a glassed-in hut overlooking the nesting sites. There's no viewing from mid-September to late November, and from late November to December the birds are nestbound so it's difficult to see that magnificent wingspan. On Tuesdays, the first tour runs at 10.30am.

To make sure you're going to see the birds in the air, ask the staff whether the birds are flying before you pay. You can also sometimes see albatross flying from the car park, particu-

larly from the fine cliff-top lookout out to sea. Time it for the late afternoon when winds are strongest. Pilot Beach, on the harbour side of the car park, often sees blue-eyed penguins, sea lions and fur seals.

Also on the albatross-centre site are the remains of **Fort Taiaroa** and its 1886 Armstrong Disappearing Gun, built along with other gun emplacements on the peninsula when NZ was certain a Russian invasion was imminent. The gun is loaded and aimed underground, then pops up like the world's slowest jack-in-the-box to be fired. Apparently it's still in perfect working order. The Fort Taiaroa tour (adult/child $20/10) or the Unique Taiaroa Experience (adult/child $50/25) include the guns and the birds. There's also an exhibit

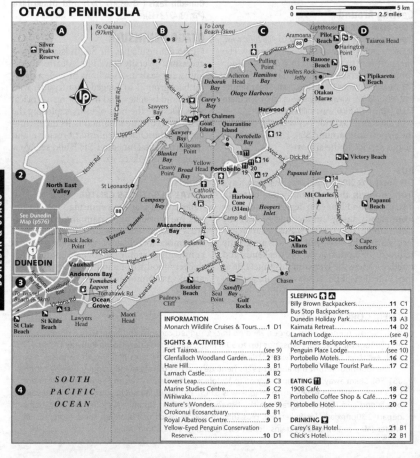

OTAGO PENINSULA

0 ——————— 5 km
0 ——————— 2.5 miles

on peninsular wildlife, and a cafe (mains $10 to $23).

Prices detailed are for December to March; rates are lower in other months.

YELLOW-EYED PENGUIN RESERVES

One of the world's rarest penguins, the hoiho (yellow-eyed penguin) is found along the Otago coast, and several peninsula beaches are good places to watch them come ashore (any time after 4pm).

There are two private operators leading tours to yellow-eye colonies on private land (see following), and other tours (see p588) also visit habitats on private farmland not accessible to the public. The birds also nest at a couple of public beaches, including **Sandfly Bay**, which has a DOC hide. If you go alone, stay on the trails, view penguins *only* from the hide and don't approach these shy creatures; even loud voices can disturb them. The penguins have been badly distressed by tourists using flash photography or traipsing through the nesting grounds. Don't loiter on the beach, as this deters them from coming ashore.

The **Yellow-Eyed Penguin Conservation Reserve** (☎ 03-478 0286; www.penguinplace.co.nz; McGrouther's Farm, Harington Point Rd; tours adult/child $40/12) has replanted the penguins' breeding grounds, built nesting sites, cared for sick and injured birds and trapped predators. Ninety-minute tours include a talk on penguin conservation and close-up viewing from a system of hides. You can see the birds all year round, but summer is best. Between October and March, tours run regularly from 10.15am to 90 minutes before sunset; between April and September they're just from 3.15pm to 4.45pm. The tours are popular, so book ahead. For accommodation at the Penguin Place Lodge, see p588.

Situated just 1km past the albatross colony, and based on a large sheep farm that covers most of the peninsula's tip, **Nature's Wonders** (☎ 0800 246 446, 03-478 1150; www.natureswondersnatu rally.com; Taiaroa Head; tours adult/child $50/45; ☼ tours from 10.15am) runs one-hour tours that take you up close to Stewart Island shags, NZ fur seals, and finally along a private little beach to a yellow-eyed penguin colony, where you can get within metres of the birds without disturbing them. The tour is conducted in 'go-anywhere' Argos vehicles and is an exciting combo of improbable scenery and wildlife adventure. It's worth it for the beautiful vistas alone.

BLUE PENGUINS

Blue penguins can be viewed at Pilot Beach, just below the albatross centre car park. The penguins come ashore just before dusk. Walk down the gravel road to the viewing area near the beach, and remain there until the birds have returned to their burrows. There may be as many as 80 or more in summer, but sometimes none in winter.

SEA LIONS

Sea lions are most easily seen on a tour (see p588), but are regularly present at **Sandfly Bay**, **Allans** and **Victory Beaches**. They are predominantly bachelor males vacationing from Campbell Island or the Auckland Islands. Give them plenty of space, as they can really motor over the first 20 metres.

LARNACH CASTLE

Standing proudly on the peninsula's highest point, **Larnach Castle** (☎ 03-476 1616; www.larnach castle.co.nz; Camp Rd; castle & grounds adult/child $25/10, grounds only $10/3; ☼ 9am-7pm, to 5pm in winter) was an extravagance of the Dunedin merchant, banker and politician William Larnach. Built in 1871 to impress his French-nobility-descended wife (she apparently didn't like it much), the ostentatious, Gothic mansion is filled with exquisite antique furnishings. Larnach committed suicide in Parliament House in 1898, financially ruined, and with his latest wife and favourite son romantically linked.

The **gardens** offer fantastic views of the peninsula and harbour, and the surrounding native rainforest showcases impressive birdsong. There's a cafe in the grand ballroom, and unique accommodation (see p588). Catch the Portobello bus to Company Bay, and then it's a 4km walk uphill.

OTHER SIGHTS

Glenfalloch Woodland Garden (☎ 03-476 1006; www. glenfalloch.co.nz; 430 Portobello Rd; admission by donation; ☼ gardens 9.30am-dusk, cafe-wine bar 11am-3.30pm Mon-Fri, 11am-4.30pm Sat & Sun Sep-Apr) covers 12 hectares with flowers, walking tracks and swaying, mature trees including a 1000-year-old matai. Expect spectacular harbour views. The Portobello bus stops out the front.

The **Marine Studies Centre** (☎ 03-479 5826; www. marine.ac.nz; Hatchery Rd; adult/child/family $12/6/24; ☼ noon-4.30pm) has octopuses, seahorses, crayfish, sharks and a huge pink model squid.

Help with fish-feeding (Wednesday and Saturday 2pm to 3pm), or join a guided tour at 10.30am (adult/child/family $21/11/48 for entry plus tour). The centre showcases the work of the adjacent university-run marine laboratory.

Activities

The peninsula's coastal and farmland walkways offer stunning views and the chance to see wildlife on your own. Pick up a free copy of the detailed *Otago Peninsula Tracks* from the Dunedin i-SITE. A popular walking destination is the beautiful **Sandfly Bay**, reached from Seal Point Rd (moderate; 40 minutes) or Ridge Rd (difficult; 40 minutes). From the end of Sandymount Rd, you can follow a trail to the impressive **chasm** (20 minutes). Most trails are closed during September and October for lambing.

Wild Earth Adventures (☎ 03-489 1951; www.wild earth.co.nz; trips from $95) offers trips in double sea kayaks, with wildlife often sighted en route. Trips run between four hours and a full day, with some starting from Dunedin and some on the peninsula.

Peninsula Bike & Kayak (☎ 03-478 0724; www. bike-kayak.com) rents bikes ($25/35 per hour/ day) and kayaks ($50 for two hours). Guided kayak tours, depart from Portobello and run for two or three hours ($120/170 for one/ two people).

Tours

Back to Nature Tours (☎ 03-479 2009; www.backto naturetours.co.nz; adult/child $89/45)

Citibus (☎ 03-477 5577; www.transportplace.co.nz; adult/child from $90/30) Tours combining albatross and penguin viewing.

Elm Wildlife Tours (☎ 0800 356 563, 03-454 4121; www.elmwildlifetours.co.nz; standard tour $89). Small-group tours of up to six hours. Pick-up and drop-off from Dunedin is included.

Monarch Wildlife Cruises & Tours (Map p586; ☎ 03-477 4276; www.wildlife.co.nz) One-hour boat trips from Wellers Rock (adult/child $45/20), and half- ($85/30) and full-day ($210/105) tours from Dunedin. Include breeding grounds for sea lions, penguins, albatross and seals often inaccessible by land.

Otago Explorer (☎ 0800 322 240, 03-474 3300; www. otagoexplorer.com) Runs 2½-hour tours of Larnach Castle (adult/child $55/27.50) and summertime wildlife tours. Transport from Dunedin included.

Twilight Wildlife Tour (☎ 03-454 4121; www. twilighttours.co.nz; adult $91, student/child $79)

Sleeping

Portobello Village Tourist Park (☎ 03-478 0359; porto bellopark@xtra.co.nz; 27 Hereweka St, Portobello; unpowered/ powered sites per adult $13/15, units d $45-85, tourist flats $90-120) With lots of trees and grass, this is a pleasant place to stake your tent. There's a kids' play area, a modern kitchen and wheelchair-accessible facilities. Backpacker rooms are BYO everything, and self-contained units are smartly decorated.

Penguin Place Lodge (☎ 03-478 0286; McGrouther's Farm, Harington Point Rd; adult/child $25/10) Atop the hill and surrounded by farmland, this lodge has a good shared kitchen, a bright lounge, and basic double and twin rooms. There are views across the farm and harbour, you're close to seals and albatross, and you're next-door neighbours with the penguins. Linen costs $5 extra.

our pick **McFarmers Backpackers** (☎ 03-478 0389; mcfarmers@xtra.co.nz; 774 Portobello Rd; lodge dm/s $27/40, d $55-65, cottage d $90) On a working farm with harbour views, this rustic timber lodge and self-contained cottage are steeped in character and feel instantly like home. Lounge on the window seat or sundeck, barbecue out the back, or get warm in front of the woodburning stove. You'll almost forget you came to visit the nearby albatross and penguins. The cottage is great for families, and there are organic vegies and eggs available. The Portobello bus goes past the gate.

Bus Stop Backpackers (☎ 03-478 0330; www.bus -stop.co.nz; 252 Harington Point Rd; dm $35, cottage d $120-140; 💻) Enjoy harbour views and salty smells from this sweet little house; watch sea lions catching their dinner without even leaving the comfy lounge. Borrow the dinghy and catch your own dinner to be cooked, smoked or barbecued. There's a triple and double in the house, or beds in a 1970s Bedford bus. A new self-contained cottage is also on offer. In season there are also organic vegies.

Portobello Motels (☎ 03-478 0155; www.portobello motels.com; 10 Harington Point Rd, Portobello; d $135-145; 🛜) Sunny, modern, self-contained units just off the main road in Portobello. Studio units have small decks overlooking the bay. One-and two-bedroom units are also available (add $25/15 per extra adult/child), but are viewless.

Larnach Lodge (☎ 03-476 1616; www.larnach castle.co.nz; Camp Rd; stable d $155, lodge d $260-280, all incl breakfast; 💻 🛜) Larnach Castle's back-garden lodge has 12 individually decorated rooms. The Queen Victoria Room has a giant four-poster bed, and in the Goldrush Room guests sleep in an old horse-drawn carriage. Less frivolous are the atmospheric rooms in the 125-year-old Coach House with sloping Tudor ceilings. Dinner available by arrangement.

Kaimata Retreat (☎ 03-456 3443; www.kaimatanz. com; 297 Cape Saunders Rd; s/d $380/450) This luxury ecolodge has three rooms overlooking a gloriously isolated inlet on the eastern edge of Otago Peninsula. Watch sea lions and bird life from the spacious decks, or get even closer with an eco-expedition with local farmer, Dave. Be sure to include a private three-course dinner ($99 per person) from chef Dani, and don't make the mistake of staying just one night.

Eating

1908 Café (☎ 03-478 0801; 7 Harington Point Rd, Portobello; mains $20-34; ☯ 11.30am-10pm) Salmon, venison and steak are joined by fresh fish and blackboard specials, and there's a box of toys for the kids. It's a beautiful old building, cheerfully embellished with local art.

Other dining options near the 1908 Café include the Portobello Hotel, and the Portobello Coffee Shop & Café for excellent burgers ($13.50) and expensive internet. It's a good breakfast ($8 to $14) stop if you're getting an early start from Dunedin. There's takeaways at the Portobello Store, and cafes attached to Larnach Castle, Nature's Wonders, Glenfalloch Woodland Garden and the Royal Albatross Centre.

There are plenty of 'hey-let's-stop-here' places for picnics, so stock up before you leave Dunedin.

Getting There & Around

Up to 10 buses travel each weekday between Dunedin's Cumberland St and Portobello Village ($4), with one or two a day continuing on to Harington Point. Weekend services are more limited. Once on the peninsula, it's tough to get around without your own transport. Most tours will pick you up from your accommodation.

There's a petrol station in Portobello, but opening hours are unpredictable. Fill up in Dunedin before driving out.

OTAGO HARBOUR'S NORTH SHORE

The north shore of Otago Harbour provides a worthy detour from the main tourist track, with one excellent accommodation option. The Orokonui Ecosanctuary (p577) is also worthwhile for nature buffs.

Little **Port Chalmers** (population 3000) is only 15km out of the city (15 minutes' drive, or bus 13 or 14 from stand 4 outside the Countdown supermarket on Cumberland St), but it feels a world away. Somewhere between working class and bohemian, Port Chalmers has a history as a port town but has increasingly attracted Dunedin's arty types. Dunedin's best rock-and-roll pub, **Chick's Hotel** (p583) is an essential after-dark destination, and daytime attractions include a growing range of raffish cafes, design stores and galleries.

The 150-year-old bluestone **Carey's Bay Hotel** (☎ 03-472 8022; 17 MacAndrew Rd, Carey's Bay; mains $15-25; ☯ bar 11.30am-late Mon-Sun, restaurant 11am-3pm Mon-Thu, 11am-9pm Fri-Sun), 1km past the docks, has a bar with views of fishing boats and the harbour. There is a great collection of art from local painter Ralph Hotere, plus other Otago artworks. Meals tend to be focussed on seafood; the salmon fish cakes ($18.50) are good.

On a sheep-and-deer farm 5km down the road from Port Chalmers, **Billy Brown Backpackers** (☎ 03-472 8323; www.billybrowns.co.nz; 423 Aramoana Rd, Hamilton Bay; dm/d $27/66) has magnificent views across the harbour to the peninsula. There's a lovely rustic shared lounge with cosy woodburner, and plenty of retro vinyl to spin.

CENTRAL OTAGO

Rolling hills, grassy paddocks and a succession of tiny, charming little gold-rush towns make this region worth exploring, though most travellers barely pause for breath as they pass through. However it rewards a bit of effort: Naseby and Clyde compete for the title of NZ's cutest towns, and rugged and laconic 'Southern Man' types can be seen propping up the bar in backcountry hotels. There are also fantastic opportunities for those on two wheels, whether speeding down old gold-mining trails or taking it easy on the rail trail (see p592). Online see www.centralotagonz. com.

CROMWELL
pop 2610
Cromwell has a charming little historic precinct near the lake, and courtesy of local farms and orchards, more than a few good

eateries. If you're travelling east to Dunedin or west to Queenstown, it's a good spot to stop for lunch. The nearby Bannockburn region has fine vineyards crafting excellent pinot noir, and also some lovely vineyard restaurants (the boxed text, below).

At the time of writing, the **Cromwell i-SITE** (☎ 03-445 0212; www.centralotagonz.com; 🕑 9am-6pm; 🖳) was in Cromwell's central shopping mall, but it *may* have moved to a new location on the main road from Queenstown in the life of this book.

Grab a copy of *Walk Cromwell,* which covers some cool local mountain-bike and walking trails, including the nearby gold-rush ghost-town of Bendigo. Bikes can be hired from **Cycle Surgery** (☎ 03-445 4100; www.cyclesurgery.co.nz) for $35 per day.

There is internet access at the i-SITE, and laptop users can use the LAN network ($2) at the **public library** (🕑 10am-5pm Mon-Fri, 10am-1pm Sat), also in the Cromwell mall.

Back in 1992, when the Clyde Dam was completed, it flooded the original Cromwell village including the town centre, 280 homes, six farms and 17 orchards. Many historic buildings were disassembled before the flooding and have since been restored as **Old Cromwell Town**. This pedestrianised zone sits beside the lake that swallowed the old town, and as well as featuring interesting historical buildings, there is good eating and interesting galleries. See the cool artworks at **Hullabaloo Art Space** (www.odelle.com) and interesting metalworks at **Stoop Gallery** (www.stoop.co.nz) and don't miss the Grain & Seed Café (opposite). Grab a copy of *Old Cromwell Town Historic Precinct* for a self-guided tour. During summer a **farmers market** kicks off at 8am every Sunday.

Zip around the Kawarau River on a 40-minute jetboat ride with **Goldfields Jet** (☎ 0800 111 038, 03-445 1038; www.goldfieldsjet.co.nz; adult/child $90/49).

The sinuous and hilly roads of Central Otago are perfect for negotiating on two wheels. See **Central Otago Motorcycle Hire** (☎ 03-445 4487; www.comotorcyclehire.co.nz; 271 Bannockburn Rd; motorcycle hire per day from $275) for bike hire – including Harley Davidsons. Much smaller Italian scooters ($90 per day) are perfect for zipping around the area's lakes, orchards and vineyards, and only require a car drivers' licence. The company can also advise on improbably scenic routes around Queenstown, Glenorchy and Wanaka.

Sleeping

Most of Cromwell's motels are huddled near the town's central shopping mall.

Cairnmuir Camping Ground (☎ 03-445 1956; Cairnmuir Rd, Bannockburn; sites adult/child $14/7, cabins adult/child $20/10) Peaceful grassy camping ground beside the lake 10 minutes' drive from Cromwell.

Cromwell Top 10 Holiday Park (☎ 0800 107 275, 03-445 0164; www.cromwellholidaypark.co.nz; 1 Alpha St; unpowered & powered sites $36, cabins d $60-70, units $90-170; 🖳) The size of a small European nation and packed with cabins, self-contained units and rooms of various descriptions, all set in tree-lined grounds.

Quartz Reef Creek (☎ 03-445 0404; www.quartzreefcreek.co.nz; Rapid 349, SH8, Northburn, Cromwell; d incl breakfast $130) This modern B&B enjoys lake views and a quiet location about 3km north of town. Accommodation is in three private studios, and breakfast often includes freshly baked bread and homemade preserves. Ask about the sunny upstairs studio.

SEARCHING FOR THE PERFECT PINOT NOIR

The Bannockburn Valley near Cromwell is home to NZ's finest pinot noir wines, and accounts for over half of Central Otago's total wine production. Vineyards to visit include **Mt Difficulty Wines** (☎ 03-445 3445; www.mtdifficulty.co.nz; Felton Rd, Bannockburn; platters $12-40, mains $25-28; 🕑 cellar door 10.30am-4.30pm, restaurant noon-3pm) and **Carrick Wines** (☎ 03-445 3480; www.carrick.co.nz; Cairnmuir Rd, Bannockburn; platters $12-25, mains $18-25; 🕑 cellar door 11am-4pm, restaurant noon-3pm). Both vineyards also have highly regarded restaurants open for lunch; the alfresco eateries get pretty busy, so it's worthwhile phoning ahead to book. Before you head off to Bannockburn, visit the Cromwell i-SITE and check out the handy display showcasing the area's vineyards.

Vineyard tours can be arranged through **Travel Collective** (☎ 0800 326 228, 03-445 4927; www.travelcollectivegroup.com; 8 Pinot Noir Dr; Cromwell; per person incl lunch $145).

For online information, see www.otagowine.com.

Hills of Gold (☎ 03-445 4487; www.comotorcycle hire.co.nz/accommodation; 271 Bannockburn Rd; d $140) Located 2.7km from Cromwell, and en route to the excellent Bannockburn vineyards, Hills of Gold consists of one modern and comfortable studio flat in a rural location near Lake Dunstan. A big-screen TV, audio system and private garden offer additional touches of luxury. Mountain bikes can be rented, and it's also the home base for Central Otago Motorcycle Hire (p589).

Eating & Drinking

Juice Café (☎ 03-445 2211; SH8; meals from $10; ☺ 8am-5pm) Sitting beside the state highway at the entry to town, this sunny little cafe dishes up delicious salads and world-famous-in-Cromwell fresh fruit smoothies ($6).

Grain & Seed Café (☎ 03-445 1007; Old Cromwell Town; lunch from $10; ☺ 8am-4pm) Set in a beautiful stone building that was once Jolly's Grain Store, this cute cafe serves up big, delicious, inexpensive meals. Grab an outside table beside the lake.

Thai Crom (☎ 03-445 1546; 50 The Mall; dinner mains $15-22; ☺ noon-9pm Mon-Sat, 5-9pm Sun) This Thai eatery is very authentic, with the owner's mother-in-law drifting in and out. Spice levels are carefully adhered to, there's cold Singha beer to cool the palate, and the $10 lunch specials are a tasty way to manage your daily budget.

Brewhouse Bar & Bistro (☎ 03-445 0725; 71 The Mall; mains $15-30; ☺ 11am-late) Cromwell's best spot for a quiet beer also offers robust pub meals big enough to sate the appetite of a 19th-century goldminer. Late 20th-century pop videos and big screen 21st-century sport provide other distractions. A wider than normal range of Speight's finest complements wines from just up the road.

Getting There & Away

Atomic Shuttles (☎ 03-349 0697; www.atomictravel.co.nz), **InterCity** (☎ 03-474 9600; www.intercity.co.nz), **Naked Bus** (☎ 0900 625 33; www.nakedbus.com) and **Wanaka Connexions** (☎ 03-443 9122; www.time2.co.nz) all run from Cromwell to Queenstown and Alexandra for $15 to $20, and to Dunedin for $35 to $40. Some services connect to Christchurch and Invercargill. **Catch-a-Bus** (☎ 03-449 2024; www.catchabus.co.nz) runs a convenient service linking Dunedin and Wanaka, stopping at Middlemarch, Ranfurly, Alexandra and Cromwell. Other stops near the Otago Central Rail Trail (including Naseby) can also be requested.

CLYDE
pop 850

On the banks of the emerald-green Clutha River, the little village of Clyde (www.clyde.co.nz) looks more like a cute 19th-century gold-rush film set than a real town. Despite a recent influx of retirees, Clyde retains a friendly, small-town feel, and even when holidaymakers arrive in numbers over summer, it's a great place to chill out. It's also one end of the Otago Central Rail Trail (p592).

Sights & Activities

Pick up a copy of *Walk Around Historic Clyde* available from the Alexandra i-SITE. **Clyde Historical Museum** (☎ 03-449 2711; Blyth St; adult/child $3/1; ☺ 2-4pm Tue-Sun, closed May-Oct) has random Maori and Victorian exhibits and information about the Clyde Dam.

The **Alexandra-Clyde 150th Anniversary Walk** (three hours one-way) is a riverside trail that's fairly flat with ample resting spots and shade. **Trail Journeys** (☎ 0800 724 587; www.trailjourneys.co.nz; Clyde Railhead; ☺ tours Sep-Apr) rents bikes (from $35 per day) and kayaks (from $40) and offers cycling tours.

Held on Easter Sunday, the **Clyde Wine & Food Festival** (www.promotedunstan.org.nz) showcases the region's bountiful produce and esteemed wines. For the rest of the year, visit **Central Gourmet Galleria** (☎ 03-449 3331; www.centralone.co.nz; 27 Sunderland St; ☺ 9.30am-5pm Mon-Fri, 10am-4pm Sat & Sun) for a stellar collection of award-winning local wines, many of which you won't find anywhere else.

To explore the area's boutique vineyards in a restored retro school bus, contact the **Grape Escape** (☎ 03-449 2696; tours per person $60-80).

Sleeping & Eating

In February and March, Clyde gets very busy and advance booking of accommodation is recommended.

Hartley Arms Backpackers (☎ 03-449 2700; hartley arms@xtra.co.nz; 25 Sunderland St; per person $40) In the old stables behind a beautiful 1869 building that was once the Hartley Arms Hotel, these three cosy rooms look out to a peaceful, private, stone-walled garden and share a small kitchen/lounge. Tables and chairs in the shade of the cherry tree are a fine place to stretch limbs weary from 150km of rail trail.

Dunstan House (☎ 03-449 2295; www.dunstanhouse. co.nz; 29 Sunderland St; d $100-200; 🖳) This restored Victorian-aged, balconeyed inn has lovely guests' bar and lounge areas. Rooms with en suite, individually decorated in period style, are a little pricier, but most have claw-foot tubs. Less expensive (but still flash) rooms are next door in 'Miners Lane'. Dunstan House is only open from September to May.

Bank Café (☎ 03-449 2955; 31 Sunderland St; snacks $8-10; 🕙 9am-4.30pm) Owned by a group of passionate local foodies, everything is made fresh every day at the Bank Café. That includes superlative cakes and slices, and made-to-order ciabatta sandwiches ($8) that are perfect for lunch on the rail trail.

Post Office Café & Bar (☎ 03-449 2488; 2 Blyth St; mains $12-28; 🕙 10am-9pm) Clyde's stately old 1899 post office houses a popular restaurant famous for its garden tables and gourmet versions of substantial favourites such as barbecue steak sandwiches or hotpot. The neighbouring old postmaster's house has lovely rooms (doubles from $95) with antique furnishings such as travelling trunks and bureaus.

Getting There & Away

Although no company has a dedicated stop here, buses travelling between Cromwell and Alexandra pick up and drop off in Clyde on request (it may incur a small surcharge). See p591 for details.

ALEXANDRA

pop 4620

Unless you've come here especially for the Easter Bunny Hunt or September's NZ Merino Shearing Championships, the reason to visit Alexandra is for the nearby mountain biking. Some travellers, entranced by well-shorn sheep and rabbit-free slopes, stay for seasonal fruit-picking work.

The **Alexandra i-SITE** (☎ 03-448 9515; www.central otagonz.com, www.alexandra.co.nz; 22 Centennial Ave;

TWO WHEELS GOOD: OTAGO CENTRAL RAIL TRAIL

Stretching from Dunedin to Clyde, the Central Otago rail branch linked small, inland goldfield towns with the big city from the early 20th century through to the 1990s. After the 150km stretch from Middlemarch to Clyde was permanently closed, the rails were ripped up and the trail resurfaced. The result is a year-round trail that takes bikers, walkers and horseback riders along a historic route containing old rail bridges, viaducts and tunnels. With excellent trailside facilities (toilets, shelters and information), no steep hills, gob-smacking scenery and profound remoteness, the trail attracts well over 10,000 visitors annually. Up to 95% of rail trail riders are Kiwis, so it's an excellent option for overseas visitors to combine meeting New Zealanders with experiencing a beautiful part of the country. March to April is the busiest time, when the trail is packed with urban refugees from Auckland, Wellington, Christchurch and, increasingly, Australia.

The trail can be followed in either direction. One option is to travel from Dunedin on the scenic Taieri Gorge Railway (p585), cycle from Pukerangi to Middlemarch (19km by road) and begin the trail the following day. The entire trail takes approximately four to five days to complete by bike (or a week on foot), but you can obviously choose to do as short or long a stretch as suits your plans. There are also easy detours to towns such as Naseby and St Bathans. See the map on p573 for the route. Many settlements along the route offer accommodation and dining. An evolving highlight of the rail trail is an increasing range of lodgings in restored cottages and rural farmhouses. Check out the two rail trail websites detailed below.

Zeroing the bike computer at Middlemarch, the towns through which you pass, in order of increasing distance away from Dunedin, are: Hyde (27km), Waipiata (49km), Ranfurly (59km, with a possible detour to Naseby), Wedderburn (63km), Oturehua (75km), Ida Valley (90km), Lauder (107km, with a possible detour to St Bathans), Omakau (117km), Chatto Creek (106km), Alexandra (143km), and finally Clyde (151km).

Mountain bikes can be rented in Dunedin, Middlemarch, Alexandra and Clyde. Any of the area's major i-SITEs or other information centres (including Dunedin, Cromwell and Alexandra) can provide detailed information on the trail. See www.otagocentralrailtrail.co.nz and www.otagorailtrail.co.nz to get track information, accommodation options and tour companies. The *Otago Rail Trail Guide Book* – available at information centres in the region, and online at www.otagorailtrail.co.nz – is both an excellent pre-trip planning resource and a great colour souvenir of the experience.

(🕑 9am-6pm; 🖳) has internet access, and a necessary free map of this very spread-out town.

For the essential traveller's combination of internet *and* a laudromat, see **www.wash** (3 Limerick St; wash & dry per load $10; 🕑 8am-8pm; 🖳 🛜).

Sights & Activities

The modern **Alexandra Museum** (☎ 03-448 6230; 22 Centennial Ave; admission by donation; 🕑 9am-6pm) attached to the i-SITE has exhibits on geology, exploration and gold mining. The i-SITE can advise on local tour operators visiting historic gold-mining sites.

Mountain bikers will love the old gold trails weaving through the hills, and of course the **Otago Central Rail Trail** (see the boxed text, opposite). Collect relevant maps from the i-SITE, along with a series of mountain-biking pamphlets for cyclists of all levels. **Altitude Adventures** (☎ 03-448 8917; www.altitudeadventures. co.nz; 88 Centennial Ave) and **Trail Journeys** (☎ 0800 724 587; www.trailjourneys.co.nz; Clyde Railhead) both rent bikes, offer backcountry cycling tours and provide transport to trailheads.

To experience the scenery and history of the region by boat, join a 2½-hour **Clutha River Cruise** (☎ 03-449 3155; www.clutharivercruises.co.nz; cruise $65). Book at the Alexandra i-SITE.

Sleeping

Generic motels line Centennial Ave on the way into town.

Marj's Place (☎ 03-448 7098; www.marjsplace.co.nz; 5 Theyers St; dm $25; 🖳) Two houses have myriad higgledy-piggledy rooms and a nice communal vibe, helped by the peaceful rose garden out back. Modern homestay rooms attached to the main house cost $45 per person. Cash only.

Alexandra Holiday Park (☎ 03-448 8297; www. alexandraholidaypark.com; 44 Manuherikia Rd; sites $30, cabins d $40-60; 🖳 🛜) Sitting beside the road to Ranfurly, with plenty of shade and backing onto the swimmer-friendly Manuherikia River. It's close to where the rail trail enters town. Self-contained units (sleeping up to six) start at $95 for two.

Quail Rock (☎ 03-448 7098; www.quailrock.co.nz; 5 Fairway Dr; d incl breakfast $120-150; 🖳 🛜) Perched high above town, this very comfortable B&B offers equal servings of privacy and mountain views. Homemade preserves give breakfast a unique touch, and dinners are also available. And yes, quail are often seen scratching around the rocks in the garden.

Speargrass Inn (p596) is another interesting option, 13km south towards Roxburgh.

Eating

Monteith's Brewery Bar (☎ 03-448 9189; 26 Centennial Ave; lunch $15-20, dinner $25-30; 🕑 11am-late) Opposite the i-SITE, this craft beer emporium in a stone cottage has a sunny deck, and a wide-ranging menu from cheap-and-cheerful bar snacks to more robust dinners including blue cod, lamb and pork.

Shaky Bridge Café (☎ 03-448 5111; Graveyard Gully Rd; mains $15-30; 🕑 10am-4pm Tue, Wed & Sun, 10am-late Thu-Sat) Over a 110-year-old footbridge near the rail trail, Shaky Bridge is a winery-cafe in a heritage mudbrick building with views of the Manuherikia River. Tuck into locally sourced delicacies such as venison, duck or salmon. Coffee and cake with a side order of vineyard views are perfect anytime.

Red Brick Café (☎ 03-448 9174; Centrepoint car park off Limerick St; mains $15-30; 🕑 10.30am-4pm Mon, 10.30am-late Tue-Sat, 10.30am-2pm Sun; **V**) This funky cafe–wine bar is positioned beside an Alexandra shoppers' car park, the last place you'd expect to find a cafe so stylish or scallops so perfectly seared. Most ingredients (and wines) are locally sourced.

Also recommended:

Courthouse Café (☎ 03-448 7818; 8 Centennial Ave; 🕑 8am-5pm) Providing plenty of evidence of Alex's best coffee.

Foursquare (91 Tarbert St) Self-catering central.

Getting There & Away

See the Cromwell section (p589) for buses that pass along this route. From Alex you can head northwest past Cromwell towards Queenstown, south past Roxburgh and Lawrence towards the east coast or northeast along the Pig Root (see below).

ALEXANDRA TO PALMERSTON

Northeast of Alexandra, an irrigated strip of land tags alongside the highway, with the Dunstan and North Rough Ranges rising impressively on either side. This is the Manuherikia Valley, which tumbles into the Maniototo Plain as State Hwy 85 (SH85). From here to Palmerston and the sea, the scenic, winding road is charmingly known as the Pig Root.

Chatto Creek Tavern (☎ 03-447 3710; www.chatto creektavern.co.nz; SH85; meals $8-28) is a cute stone hotel from the 1880s right beside the rail trail and the highway. Pop in for a whitebait fritter (in season) or steak sandwich, or rest your weary calf muscles in a dorm bed ($20) or double room ($60).

Made up of half a handful of historic buildings, and home to just 50 souls, tiny **Ophir** lies across the Manuherikia River and lays claim to the country's largest range of temperatures (from 35°C above to 22°C below). Take the gravel exit south off SH85 to rattle across the cute, 1870s wooden-planked Dan O'Connell Bridge, a bumpy but scenic crossing. **Black's Hotel** (☎ 03-447 3826; steven.chapman@clear.net.nz; s/d incl breakfast $80/110) has cycle-friendly accommodation.

Back on SH85, Omakau and Lauder are good stops if you're a hungry rail-trailer with a sore bum and a need for a bed. Good-value rooms, excellent food and local company are all on tap at the **Omakau Commercial Hotel** (☎ 03-447 3715; omakaucommercial@xtra.co.nz; 1 Harvey St; s/d $45/80). Accommodation in nearby Lauder includes **Pedal Inn** (☎ 03-447 3460; benandcatherine@farmside.co.nz; SH85, Lauder; d $120), which has two brand-new self-contained units on a working farm, and the cosy **Muddy Creek Cutting** (☎ 03-447 3682; muddycreekcutting@clear.net.nz; per person $60), a charmingly restored 1930s mudbrick farmhouse. Dinners with a local, organic spin are also available ($40 per person).

Take the turn-off north, into the foothills of the imposing Dunstan Range and on to diminutive **St Bathans**, 17km from SH85. This once-thriving gold-mining town of 2000 people is now home to only half-a-dozen permanent residents. **Blue Lake** is an accidental attraction: a large hollow filled with amazingly blue mineral water that's run off abandoned gold workings. Walk around the alien-looking lake's edge to a lookout (one hour return).

The **Vulcan Hotel** (☎ 03-447 3629; www.stbathansnz.co.nz; Main Rd; dm/d $50/100) dates from 1863, has rooms to let, and does pub meals (mains $20 to $25). Considering it has a population of only six people (plus one labrador and a ghost or two), you'll find the bar here pretty busy on a Friday night as thirsty shearers from around the valley descend en masse. The Vulcan also rents some empty houses nearby. Guide (the black lab) will escort you down to a handful of cute cottages (doubles from $100 to $220 per night) including the old gaol. He's also very keen on his battered old rugby ball. Try not to lose it like we almost did.

If you can manage it, get along to the annual Wooden Cup rugby match in September where St Bathans (and helpers) take on the lads from Becks down the road – a near-legendary celebration of small-town rugby. You won't find a room empty for miles around, but might get a campsite at the rugby domain.

Back on SH85, the road swings around to run southeast and passes the historic **Wedderburn Tavern** (☎ 03-444 9548; www.wedderburntavern.co.nz; SH85; dm/d $40/90). Seven kilometres later is the turn-off for Naseby, or it's straight through to Ranfurly.

Naseby
pop 100

Cute as a button, surrounded by forest, and dotted with 19th-century stone buildings, Naseby is the kind of small town where life moves slowly. That the town is pleasantly obsessed with the fairly insignificant world of NZ curling indicates there's not much else going on. It's that lazy small-town vibe, along with good mountain biking and walking trails through the surrounding forest, that makes Naseby an interesting place to stay for a couple of days.

Naseby Information & Crafts (☎ 03-444 9961; Derwent St), in the old post office, has information on local walks and bike trails. For more mountain-biking information and to hire a bike, head to **Kila's Bike Shop** (☎ 03-444 9088; kilas bikeshop@xtra.co.nz; Derwent St; per day $35) near the Black Forest Café. **Naseby Forest Headquarters** (☎ 03-444 9995; Derwent St) is also good for maps of walks through the Black Forest.

All year round, you can shimmy after curling stones at the indoor ice rink at the **Naseby Alpine Park** (☎ 03-444 9878; www.curling.co.nz; Channel Rd; curling per hr $15; ⏰ 10am-5pm). Curling tuition is also available.

From June to August there's ice skating at an adjacent outdoor rink, and a **seasonal ice luge** (☎ 03-444 9270; www.lugenz.co.nz; ⏰ Jul-Aug) runs for a thrilling 360m down a nearby hillside. The luge is open to the public, but booking ahead is essential.

Set in 17 acres of woods, **Larchview Holiday Park** (☎ 03-444 9904; www.larchviewholidaypark.co.nz; Swimming Dam Rd; sites per person $13, cabins $45, self-contained cottages $75; 🖳 🛜) has an alpine feel, a small on-site playground and swimming at a dam nearby. There are also basic timber cabins and cottages.

Mountain View Accommodation (☎ 03-444 9972; www.mountainviewaccommodation.co.nz; 13a Channel Rd; d $95-120) has comfortable lemony flats attached to the owners' house with plush bedding, and the more expensive options have cooking facilities. On the hill across the road, the cottage is a steal at $130 for two ($20 per extra adult). A new self-contained three-bedroom house ($150 for two, plus $25 per extra adult) is a good option for families.

A mudbrick hotel dating from 1863, **Ancient Briton** (☎ 03-444 9990; www.ancientbriton.co.nz; 16 Leven St; s $60, d from $105) has a rambling range of basic-to-comfortable accommodation. Have some traditional pub grub (mains from $17 to $27), or prop yourself up at the bar to admire the trophies of the pub's 'Blue Hats' curling team and get to know the locals.

Fresh baking and good coffee features at the **Black Forest Café** (☎ 03-444 9820; 5 Derwent St; meals from $10; ☯ 9am-5pm), gorgeous inside with its stone walls, bright colours and warm polished wood. The wide-ranging menu features bagels, panini and creamy smoothies using local Central Otago fruit.

The Ancient Briton pub has a courtesy van and will pick up from Ranfurly or the rail trail. If prebooked, **Catch-a-bus** (☎ 03-449 2024; www.catchabus.co.nz) stops in Naseby on its Dunedin–Cromwell route. If you're driving, take the exit off SH85, just north of Ranfurly. From Naseby, you can wind your way northeast through spectacular scenery to **Danseys Pass** and through to Duntroon and the Waitaki Valley (p602).

Ranfurly
pop 840

Ranfurly is trying hard to cash in on its art-deco buildings – much of the town was rebuilt in the architecture of the day after a series of fires in the 1930s – and a few attractive buildings and antique shops line its sleepy main drag. The town holds an annual **Art Deco Festival** (www.ranfurlyartdeco.co.nz) on the last weekend of February.

The **Maniototo visitor information centre** (☎ 03-444 1005; www.maniototo.co.nz; Charlemont St; ☯ 10am-4pm daily Oct-Apr, Mon-Fri May-Sep; ☐) is in the old train station. Grab a copy of *Rural Art Deco – Ranfurly Walk* for a self-guided tour.

The **Old Post Office Backpackers** (☎ 03-444 9588; www.oldpobackpackers.co.nz; 11 Pery St; dm/s/d $25/40/60) is popular with rail-trailers. The art-deco **Ranfurly Lion Hotel** (☎ 03-444 9140; www.ranfurly hotel.co.nz; 10 Charlemont St; s $50, d from $70; ☐) has 16 comfortable rooms, a couple of bars, and does substantial pub meals (dinner from $20 to $27). All you'll need after a long day on two wheels and one bike seat.

Cheery and warm, with an open fire, local art and the Maniototo sports wall of fame, **E-Central Café** (☎ 03-444 8300; 14 Charlemont St; mains $7-15; ☯ breakfast & lunch) is definitely the best lunch option in town. Home-baked panini and giant toasties will find favour. For Ranfurly's best coffee, look for the train-shaped espresso caravan at the northern end of town.

To explore the rugged terrain made famous by local landscape artist Grahame Sydney, contact **Maniototo 4WD Safaris** (☎ 03-444 9703; www.maniototo4wdsafaris.co.nz; per person half-/full day $80/140).

A daily **Catch-a-Bus** (☎ 03-449 2024; www.catch abus.co.nz) shuttle passes through Ranfurly on its way between Wanaka and Dunedin. Rent bikes from **Ranfurly Bike Hire** (☎ 03-444 9245; 20 Charlemont St; per day $35).

Waipiata

About 10km southeast of Ranfurly and right on the rail trail, tiny Waipiata has the **Waipiata Country Hotel** (☎ 03-444 9470; www.waipiatahotel.co.nz; dinner mains $19-22; ☐), good for a cool beer and a comfy bed ($60 per person). There's a sunny CYO ('Cook Your Own') barbecue area, and the restaurant menu includes goodies such as Pig Root Spare Ribs and Bike Faster Pasta.

our pick **Peter's Farm Lodge** (☎ 0800 427 548, 027 686 1692; www.petersfarm.co.nz, peter@otagorailtrail.co.nz; Tregonning Rd; per person $35-45) Set on farmland 4km from Waipiata, this lodge has simple, comfortable rooms in a rustic 19th-century farmhouse. Shared dining tables encourage an end-of-the-day social vibe. Kayaks, fishing rods and gold pans are all available for no extra charge, so it's worth staying a couple of nights. Peter also runs the nearby Tregonnings Cottage ($45 per person), built in 1880, but now with a modern well-equipped kitchen. He'll also pick you up for nix from the Waipiata stop on the rail trail.

Ranfurly to Dunedin

After Ranfurly, SH85 runs 62km to Palmerston, then 55km south to Dunedin or 59km north to Oamaru. Another option is to hop on the southbound SH87 directly to Dunedin, 129km via **Hyde** and Middlemarch.

In Hyde, the **Otago Central Hotel** (☎ 03-444 4800; www.hydehotel.co.nz; dm $50, d $140-200, all incl breakfast) provides boutique accommodation. Linger with the friendly local terrier in the sunny terrace cafe for a second espresso before setting out on two wheels again.

With the Rock and Pillar Range as an impressive backdrop, the small town of **Middlemarch** (pop 200; www.middlemarch. co.nz) is one end of the Taieri Gorge Railway (see p585), and also a start or end-point of the Otago Central Rail Trail (see p592). Rent bikes and gear from **Cycle Surgery** (☎ 03-464 3630; www.cyclesurgery.co.nz; Snow Ave, Middlemarch; per day $35). The company has another branch at the other end of the rail trail in Clyde.

At the famous **Middlemarch Singles Ball** held across Easter in odd-numbered years, southern men from the region gather to woo city gals.

Blind Billy's Holiday Camp (☎ 03-464 3355; www. middlemarch-motels.co.nz; Mold St, Middlemarch; campsites per person $22, dm $22, cabins d $60) has a range of cheap accommodation (including self-contained units for $100 to $110 for two people, $40 for extras), meals and excellent advice for bikers.

On a family-owned farm also just a few hundred metres from the rail trail, **Trail's End** (☎ 03-464 3474; www.trailsend.co.nz; 91 Mason Rd, Middlemarch; d incl breakfast $130) combines secluded luxury cabins with views of the Rock and Pillar Mountain Range, and has the muscle-easing diversion of a spa pool.

Opposite the railway station, **Quench Café & Bar** (☎ 03-464 3070; 29 Snow Ave, Middlemarch; mains $10-30; ☺ 8am-late) is versatility plus, with breakfast goodies such as the Cajun Corn Fritter Stack ($10 – recommended if you're beginning the rail trail), and ice-cold Speight's on tap (*definitely* recommended if you've just finished the trail: you'll have earned it).

ALEXANDRA TO DUNEDIN

Heading south from Alexandra, SH8 winds along rugged, rock-strewn hills above Lake Roxburgh, then follows the Clutha River as it passes lush farms and orchards and cool, shady forestry plantations. En route are a number of small towns, many from gold-rush days.

Only 13km south of Alexandra, **Speargrass Inn** (☎ 03-449 2192; www.speargrassinn.co.nz; SH8; d $140) has three units in attractive gardens behind a charming 1860s building with elegant guest areas. An on-site **restaurant** (mains $15-30;

☺ 10am-5pm Mon, Wed & Thu, 10am-late Fri-Sun) offers cosmopolitan tastes including seared salmon, and mushroom and blue cheese tart.

From here, the road passes through Roxburgh, Lawrence and the **Manuka Gorge Scenic Reserve**, a scenic route through wooded hills and gullies. SH8 joins SH1 in Milton.

Roxburgh

The orchards surrounding Roxburgh provide excellent roadside stalls and equally plentiful seasonal fruit-picking work. **Roxburgh i-SITE** (☎ 03-446 8920; 120 Scotland St; ☺ 9.30am-4pm) has information on mountain biking and water sports.

Villa Rose Backpackers (☎ 03-446 8761; www.villa rose.co.nz; 79 Scotland St; dm $30, units $95) is an old-fashioned villa with spacious dorm rooms and a huge modern kitchen. Newly built heritage-style self-contained units are super-comfortable. The manager can help sort out seasonal fruit-picking work, and provide discounted weekly rates.

For more luxury, **Lake Roxburgh Lodge** (☎ 03-446 8220; www.lakeroxburghlodge.co.nz; Lake Roxburgh Village; studios $120-150, 2-bdrm d $180) has comfortable stylish units. Staff will help you arrange tours, day trips, bike rides and kayaking, or you can just chill in the lakeside lounge.

Stop at Roxburgh's iconic **Jimmy's Pies** (☎ 03-444-8596; 143 Scotland St; pies $3-5; ☺ 7.30am-5pm). Renowned across the South Island since 1960, Jimmy's pastry delights are at their best just out of the oven. Try the apricot and apple flavour – you're in orchard country after all. Heading south, you'll find Jimmy's on your right just as you're leaving town.

Lawrence
pop 480

Lawrence is in a valley surrounded by farmland and forestry plantations. The **visitor information centre** (☎ 03-485 9222; www.lawrence.co.nz; 17 Ross Pl; ☺ 9.30am-4.30pm, closed for lunch) advises on gold-rush sites, walking and mountain-bike trails, and jetboating.

Dating from 1875, **Marama Lodge** (☎ 03-485 9638; www.maramalodge.co.nz; SH8; lodge d incl breakfast $90-120, units $80-90) has a big guest lounge and impressive country-style rooms. Self-contained units are less grand, but very comfortable. Breakfast and dinner options are available.

The two one-bedroom flats and three studio units at **Jafas Motels** (☎ 03-485 9005; www.

jafaslawrence.co.nz; d $120; 🖳 🛜) are comfortable and modern. Rent a mountain bike ($40 per day) to explore the surrounding countryside.

Lemon Tree Café (☎ 03-485 9965; 28 Ross Pl; brunch $7.50-17; 🕒 9am-5pm Oct-May, 10am-4pm Thu-Tue Jun-Sep) is the finest eatery between Dunedin and Gore. This relaxed oasis in rural Otago serves vaguely Mediterranean fare with lots of organic ingredients. If it's a sunny day, sit outside in the garden.

CLUTHA DISTRICT

The mighty Clutha River is NZ's highest-volume river, and is dammed in several places to feed hydroelectric power stations. **Balclutha** is South Otago's largest town but is of little interest to travellers other than as a place to stock up on supplies before setting off into the Catlins (p666). The **Balclutha i-SITE** (☎ 03-418 0388; balclutha@i-SITE.org; 4 Clyde St) has local info and internet access. For more local information, see www.cluthacountry.co.nz.

NORTH OTAGO & WAITAKI

The broad, braided Waitaki River rushes across the northern boundary of Otago, setting the boundary with Canterbury to the north. South of the river on the coast lies Oamaru, a town of penguins and glorious heritage architecture. The Waitaki Valley itself is an alternative route inland, featuring freaky rock formations, Maori rock paintings and ancient fossils. The area is also one of NZ's newest winemaking regions (see p603).

OAMARU
pop 12,000

Nothing moves very fast in Oamaru: tourists saunter, locals languish and penguins waddle. Even oft-celebrated heritage modes of transport – penny farthings and steam trains – reflect an unhurried pace. For travellers, the town focuses mostly on penguins and the historic district, but eccentric gems such as the South Island's yummiest cheese factory, cool galleries and a peculiar live-music venue provide other distractions.

A history of refrigerated-meat shipping made Oamaru prosperous enough in the 19th century to build the imposing limestone buildings that grace the town today. In its 1880s heyday, Oamaru was about the same size as Los Angeles was at the same time. Oamaru also has an affinity with the arts that may well be rooted in its claim to Janet Frame (see the boxed text, p599), but extends to a lively arty and crafty community today.

Information
ATMs line Thames St, Oamaru's main street.
Oamaru i-SITE (☎ 03-434 1656; www.visitoamaru.co.nz; 1 Thames St; 🕒 9am-6pm; 🖳) Mountains of information including details on local walking trips and wildlife. There's internet, bike hire, and an interesting 10-minute DVD on the history of the town. Daily penguin viewing times are also posted outside.
Post office (cnr Coquet & Severn Sts)
Small Bytes Computing (191 Thames St; 🕒 9am-4.30pm; 🖳 🛜) Internet access, including paid wi-fi, is incorporated into the transport booking centre at Lagonda Tearooms.

Sights
HARBOUR-TYNE HISTORIC PRECINCT
Oamaru has some of NZ's best-preserved historic commercial buildings, particularly around the harbour and Tyne St, an area designated the Historic Precinct. They were built from the 19th century, largely using the local limestone (known as Oamaru stone or whitestone) in fashionable classic forms, from Gothic revival to neoclassical Italianate and Venetian palazzo. Pick up the free *Historic Oamaru* pamphlet, and see www.historic oamaru.co.nz. On Thames St, Oamaru's expansive main drag – laid out to accommodate the minimum turning circle of a bullock cart – don't miss the **National Bank** at No 11 and the **Oamaru Opera House** at No 92.

The fascinating area of narrow streets in the historic precinct is now home to bookshops, antique stores, galleries, vintage clothing shops and craft bookbinders. The **Woolstore** (1 Tyne St) has a cafe and souvenirs, and the **Auto Museum** (☎ 03-434 1556; adult/child $6/free; 🕒 10am-4.30pm) is perfect for *Top Gear* fans (the racing cars from the 1930s through '80s are particularly cool). Upstairs, there's a **craft market** (🕒 10am-4pm Sun). Around the corner at the **Photo Shoppe** (☎ 03-434 3372; 🕒 10.30am-1pm, 2-4pm), you can get an old-style photo of yeeself in period dress-ups for $30. Oamaru's best-known artist, Donna Demente is one of the artists running the nearby **Grainstore Gallery** (☎ 027-261 3764; 🕒 noon-4pm Mon-Fri, 10am-4pm Sat & Sun).

DUNEDIN & OTAGO

OAMARU

Also check out the Oamaru limestone being carved at **Ian Andersen's gallery** (www.ianandersensculptor.co.nz; 15 Tyne St) and buy some smaller works to take home. Across the road at **Crucible Gallery** (16 Tyne St) are nice bronzes and custom-made jewellery. Art buffs should seek out the *Oamaru Arts & Crafts* brochure at the Oamaru i-SITE.

At the end of Harbour St, the **NZ Malt Whisky Company** (☎ 03-434 8842; www.nzmaltwhisky.co.nz; 14 Harbour St; ☉ 10am-5pm) uses the upper story of a handsome 130-year-old warehouse to mature barrel-loads of single-malt and blended whisky. Sample whisky and port for $2 per snifter, or there's a guided tour ($15 including four snifters) at 11am and 3pm.

The cafe-bar serves snacks and meals from $6, and you can buy bottles of the good stuff at the shop. It's definitely worth climbing the labyrinthine wooden stairs to the art gallery (free admission) on the upper floors.

On Sundays ride the old **steam train** (www.oamaru-steam.org.nz; adult/child/family one-way $5/2/12, return $8/3/18; 🕙 11am-4pm) from the historic district to the waterfront area. The two steam trains date from 1877 and 1924, although in winter they're occasionally replaced by a diesel.

PENGUINS

In an old limestone quarry near the waterfront, Oamaru's **blue-penguin colony** sees little blue penguins surfing in and wading ashore at the **visitors centre** (☎ 03-433 1195; www.penguins.co.nz; Waterfront Rd; adult/child $22/10; 🕙 9am-sunset). The penguins arrive just before dark (around 5.30pm in midwinter and 9.30pm midsummer) and it takes them about an hour to all come ashore. You'll see the most penguins (up to 150) in November and December; in the cold months from March to August there may be only 30 to 50 birds. Optimum viewing times for each night are posted at the Oamaru i-SITE. Use of camera flashes is prohibited. It can be cool, so dress warmly.

To understand the centre's conservation work, take the 30-minute daytime behind-the-scenes tour (self-guided adult/child $10/4 or guided $17.50/7.50). Forward bookings can be made on www.penguins.co.nz, and packages combining night viewing and the behind-the-scenes tour are also available.

If you head towards the penguin visitors centre around dark, and wait quietly in the car park, you'll see a few penguins waddling across the car park about the time the penguin centre empties out and people head back to their cars and buses. If you want to contribute towards the health of the penguins, pop into the centre and drop some coins in the donation box – their conservation efforts have helped increase the bird population dramatically.

Do not under any circumstances wander around the rocks beside the sea here at night looking for penguins. It's damaging to their environment as well as stuffing up studies on the effect of humans on the little birds.

There are large hides and good trails to the **yellow-eyed penguin colony** at Bushy Beach, where the penguins come ashore in late afternoon to feed their young. Two hours before dark is the best time to see them. Despite their Maori name, *hoiho* (noisy shouter), they're extremely shy; if they see or hear you they'll head back into the water. **Graves Trail**, a 2.5km low-tide walk, starts from the end of Waterfront Rd and follows the rugged coastline around to

OAMARU IN FRAME

One of NZ's best-known novelists, Janet Frame, is intimately linked with Oamaru. The town, disguised in her novels as 'Waimaru', was Frame's home throughout most of her early years. Her writing is often described as 'dense', with early books also somewhat grim, a reflection of her own troubled life. But they are also unique in the construction of their stories and the nature in which the story is told. Later books remain intense, with wordplays, mythological clues and illusions, but are less gloomy.

It was in 1951 that Frame, a (misdiagnosed) sufferer of schizophrenia at Seacliff Lunatic Asylum (p605), found sudden recognition as a writer, happily causing her doctors to rethink her planned lobotomy. Released, with frontal lobe intact, she moved on to gain international recognition in 1957 with her first novel *Owls Do Cry*, in which 'Waimaru' features strongly. Her subsequent literary accomplishments include *Faces in the Water* (1961), *The Edge of the Alphabet* (1962), *Scented Gardens for the Blind* (1963), *A State of Siege* (1967) and *Intensive Care* (1970). Keep an eye out in NZ bookstores and you'll find new or secondhand copies. Or get Jane Campion's film version of *An Angel at my Table*, based on the second volume of Frame's autobiographical trilogy, to watch on DVD.

Many of the settings for these novels can be found in Oamaru. Pick up a free copy of *Janet Frame's Oamaru* from the Oamaru i-SITE and follow the 1½-hour self-guided tour.

Frame received numerous NZ and international awards, and was twice short-listed for the Nobel Prize for literature, most recently in 2003. She died the following year.

Janet Frame's childhood house is also open for viewing (🕙 2-4pm Nov-Apr) at 56 Eden St.

lonelyplanet.com

the yellow-eyed colony at Bushy Beach. Watch out for fur seals, and do not use a flash when photographing the penguins.

FORRESTER GALLERY
Housed in a beautiful, columned 1880s bank building, **Forrester Gallery** (☎ 03-434 1653; www.for restergallery.com; 9 Thames St; admission free; ☺ 10.30am-4.30pm) has an excellent collection of regional art, and hosts diverse temporary exhibits, including contemporary media. This fantastic gallery is a good place to see works by Colin McCahon (p52), renowned for his darkly melancholic style.

OTHER SIGHTS
The **Oamaru public gardens** (main entry on Severn St) were first opened in 1876 and are a lovely place to chill out on a hot day, with endless lawns, waterways, bridges and a children's playground.

In the grand 19th-century library, the **North Otago Museum** (☎ 03-434 1652; www.northotago museum.co.nz; 60 Thames St; admission free; ☺ 10.30am-4.30pm Mon-Fri, 1-4.30pm Sat & Sun) has exhibits on Maori and Pakeha history, writer Janet Frame, architecture and geology.

Activities
Contact Rob at **Vertical Ventures** (☎ 03-434 5010, 021 894 427; www.verticalventures.co.nz) to rent mountain bikes ($45 per day), or join guided mountain-biking trips along forest tracks and coastal roads. To get vertical, join an abseiling or climbing group. Locations include the Elephant Rocks (p602).

Festivals & Events
Oamaru Wine & Food Festival (www.oamaruwine andfoodfest.co.nz) Third Sunday in February; showcase of North Otago's food and wine scene.
Victorian Heritage Celebrations (www.historic oamaru.co.nz) Oamaru livens up for five days in late November with locals wearing Victorian garb, penny-farthing races, and singing, dancing and theatre.

Tours
Living History Players (☎ 0800 548 344; www.living historynz.com; adult/child/family $25/15/75) Professional actors bring to life the 'Secrets of the Old Town' in 50-minute walking tours leaving nightly at 7pm from the i-SITE.
MP3 Self-Guided Tour ($15) MP3 players available at the i-SITE.
Penguins Crossing (☎ 03-477 9083; www.travelhead first.com; adult/child/family $46/23/115) Door-to-door

2½-hour tour taking in the blue and yellow-eyed colonies. Price includes admission to the blue penguin colony. Pick up times vary from 4pm to 7pm throughout the year.
Ralph's Rambles (☺ on demand) Short ($20) and long ($30) tours of Oamaru highlights, and tours of Janet Frame literary sites. Tours range from 45 minutes to three hours ($50). Enquire at the i-SITE.
Victorian Oamaru Passport Tours Guided tours ($10) leave from the i-SITE daily at 10am from November to April.

Sleeping
Empire Hotel (☎ 03-434 3446; www.empirebackpackers oamaru.co.nz; 13 Thames St; dm/s/d $25/35/56; 🖳 🛜) This 150-year-old hotel has been fitted out with cosy but modern backpackers' rooms. The two kitchens are spacious, the communal TV room is warmed by a nice wood burner, and bathrooms are clean and modern. Sitting right on the main street, it's the best-located accommodation in Oamaru.

Red Kettle YHA (☎ 03-434 5008; www.yha.co.nz; cnr Reed & Cross Sts; dm/d $28/60; ☺ closed May-Aug; 🖳 🛜) This red-roofed cottage has colourfully painted inner walls, a well-equipped kitchen, and a cosy lounge. A good old-school vinyl collection will keep you and fellow guests entertained. It's on a quiet side street, a short walk from the town centre.

Oamaru Top 10 Holiday Park (☎ 0800 280 202, 03-434 7666; www.top10.co.nz; Chelmer St; unpowered/powered sites $34/38, cabins d $60, self-contained d $80-150; 🖳 🛜) Grassy and well maintained, with trees out the back and the public gardens next door. Cabins are basic, but units with kitchen and varying levels of self-contained comfort are much nicer.

Anne Mieke Guest House (☎ 03-434 8051; www.theoamarubnb.com; 47 Tees St; s/d incl breakfast $60/85) The decor is a tad chintzy, and the ambience hushed like your Nana's house, but visitors are guaranteed harbour views at this good-value B&B. Look forward to spotless shared bathrooms and a spacious guest lounge.

Criterion Hotel (☎ 03-434 6247; www.criterion.net. nz; 3 Tyne St; s/tw/d without bathroom $80/100/130, d with bathroom $160, all incl breakfast) Period rooms at this 1877 hotel are smallish, but the guest lounge is large, and both are lovingly restored. Also includes home baking and preserves in a homey dining room. Downstairs there's the distraction of one of the South Island's best pubs.

AAA Thames Court Motel (☎ 0800 223 644, 03-434 6963; www.aaathamescourt.co.nz; 252 Thames St; d $105-

130; 🖳 🛜) Good option for families with its comfortable, newly renovated units and a play area for kids. Extra people $15 each. There's also a cheaper self-contained caravan ($70).

Pen-y-bryn Lodge (☎ 03-434 7939; www.penybryn. co.nz; 41 Towey St; s/d incl breakfast $556/888; 🖳) Just past its 120th birthday, this old manor has lavish period rooms and guest areas. Rates include a full breakfast, predinner drinks in the drawing room, and a five-course, gourmet dinner in the fabulous dining room. Retire afterwards to the billiard room and show off on the full-sized billiards table.

Oamaru's motel mile kicks off at the northern end of town as SH1 morphs into Thames St.

Eating

Steam (☎ 03-434 3344; 7 Thames St; ☯ 8.30am-4.30pm Mon-Fri, 10am-4.30pm Sat & Sun). Steam specialises in coffees and fruit juices, and is a good spot to stock up on freshly ground coffee for your own travels.

Whitestone Cheese Factory & Café (☎ 03-434 8098; www.whitestonecheese.co.nz; 3 Torridge St; snacks & mains $5-10; ☯ 9am-5.30pm) The home of tasty, award-winning organic cheeses. Try the creamy Mature Windsor Blue or the ultrarich Mt Domet Double Cream. Buy cheese to take away, or dine here on various cheesy treats after you've tried the range of samples for a gold coin donation. The cheese rolls are an Otago delicacy, and there are also local fruit juices and Central Otago wines.

Roost (☎ 03-434 1165; 30 Thames St; meals $5-15; ☯ 8.30am-4.30pm Mon-Sat, 9am-4pm Sun) Good for the day's first coffee, and the toasted sandwiches ($7 to $12) make it a worthwhile lunch option, too. Grab a seat out the back to soak up the afternoon sun.

ourpick Riverstone Kitchen (☎ 03-431 3505; 1431 SH1; mains $15-30; ☯ 9am-5pm Mon & Wed, 9am-late Thu-Sun, closed Tue Nov-Feb, closed Tue & Wed Mar-Oct; 🅥) This spacious haven 12km north of Oamaru on SH1 blends leather couches and polished concrete for a sophisticated ambience. The menu showcases simply prepared produce and local flavours, with standout options including lamb with smoked eggplant and free-range scrambled eggs with pesto on ciabatta. Beers include the best of the South Island and the North Island, and you can also pick up organic jams and preserves in the cool on-site deli.

Filadelfios (☎ 03-434 8884; 70 Thames St; pizzas $21.50-31.50; ☯ 11.30am-late; 🅥) A brick restaurant-bar that specialises in rather special pizzas and pastas. Read other travellers' notes on the wall while you wait for your meal to arrive. Dips and antipasto are also popular, particularly late at night when it becomes a lively bar.

In the historic precinct, the **Harbour St Bakkeri** (☎ 434 0444; Harbour St; ☯ 8am-4pm Tue-Sun) has beaut gourmet pies and the South Island's best sourdough bread – just perfect with a slab of local Whitestone cheese.

The central **Countdown Supermarket** (cnr Thames & Coquet Sts; ☯ 7am-9pm) is well stocked for self-caterers.

Drinking

Fat Sallys (☎ 03-434 8368; 84 Thames St; closed Mon) Popular with locals, especially early on when they're often tucking into a substantial pub meal. Come along on a Wednesday night for the rollicking pub quiz.

ourpick Criterion Hotel (3 Tyne St) This restored property is the ultimate corner pub in Oamaru's heritage district. The canny owner maintains an ever-changing selection of draught brews and there's also excellent pub food. Don't blame us if you progress to the single malt heaven also on offer. Oamaru's historic district once boasted 13 boozers, and the Criterion is the only one still operating.

Entertainment

Penguin Club (☎ 03-434 1402; www.thepenguinclub. co.nz; Emulsion Lane off Harbour St; admission $10-15) Tucked down a seedy industrial alley off a 19th-century street, the Penguin's bizarre location matches its acts: everything from Flying Nun stalwarts the Clean to punky/grungy/rocky/country locals. Big national acts and up-and-coming international acts sometimes drop by, too. Fridays are open-stage jam night with free admission. If there's something on at Penguin – *anything* – go and see it. It's nominally Members Only, so ask at the Oamaru i-SITE about scoring a guest pass.

Movie World 3 (☎ 03-434 1077; info line 03-434 1070; www.movieworld3.co.nz; 239 Thames St; adult/child $13/8) Cheaper on Tuesdays.

Globe (12 Coquet St; ☯ Fri & Sat) is the town's nightclub. The cafe Filadelfios (left) is another good late-night nightspot with occasional live music.

Getting There & Around

Bookings can be made through i-SITE and at the booking office at the **Lagonda Tearooms** (191

DUNEDIN & OTAGO

Thames St; ⌚ 9am-4.30pm). Buses and shuttles also depart from this location.

The following buses and shuttle buses go to Dunedin (1¾ hours) and Christchurch (3½ hours).

Atomic Shuttles (☎ 03-349 0697; www.atomictravel.co.nz) Dunedin/Christchurch $20/30.

Coastline Tours (☎ 03-434 7744; www.coastline-tours.co.nz) Runs between Dunedin and Oamaru ($30), and will detour to Moeraki, Karitane, Seacliff or Dunedin airport if needed.

InterCity (☎ 03-474 9600; www.intercity.co.nz) Dunedin/Christchurch $28/40.

Knightrider (☎ 0800 317 057; www.knightrider.co.nz) Dunedin/Christchurch $31/41.

Naked Bus (☎ 0900 625 33; www.nakedbus.com) Dunedin/Christchurch $11/$16

Southern Link (☎ 0508 458 835; www.southernlink.co.nz) Dunedin/Christchurch $11/16.

WAITAKI VALLEY

The flat-bottomed pastoral Waitaki Valley is a little-travelled route but includes some unique sights and scenery between the turn-off at SH1 and Omarama. Predominantly farmland, the valley is also an outdoorsy paradise, and a place to shoot ducks, catch trout and salmon, and waterski on the strikingly blue hydro-lakes. This is a possible route to Wanaka and Queenstown if you're heading south, or to Twizel and Mt Cook if you're heading north.

After following SH83 almost to Duntroon, detour left at the signposted turn-off to Danseys Pass. Just on your left, under an impressive limestone overhang on a hill with great views to the mountains, you'll find the Maraewhenua **Maori rock paintings**. The charcoal-and-ochre paintings date back several centuries, tracing everything from pre-European hunting to sailing ships, as well as more contemporary tributes to 1980s Kiwi funk band Supergroove.

Follow the road southish another 4km then turn left towards Ngapara. Two kilometres further on in a peaceful sheep paddock are **Elephant Rocks**. Sculpted by wind, rain and rivers, these huge limestone boulders lie about like giant slumbering animals. The bizarre landscape was utilised as Aslan's Camp in the NZ-filmed *Narnia* blockbuster (2005). If you're feeling adventurous, continue over Danseys Pass to Naseby (p594) from 2km back at the intersection.

Back on SH83 at Duntroon is the **Vanished World Centre** (☎ 03-431 2024; www.vanishedworld.co.nz; 7 Campbell St; adult/family $5/10; ⌚ 10am-4pm Oct-Jun, 11am-3pm Sat & Sun Jul-Sep), with small but interesting displays of 25-million-year-old fossils, including NZ's shark-toothed dolphins and giant penguins. There's also a selection of books on geology, history and talking lions. If you're really into fossils and geology, pick up a copy of the Vanished World Fossil Trail map outlining 20 different locations around North Otago. Just west of Duntroon is the **Takiroa Maori Rock Art Site**, with more drawings dating back many centuries; the fluidity of the shapes is still clear enough to be admired.

Tiny **Kurow** is at the junction of the Waitaki and Hakataramea Rivers. For good coffee and home baking, stop at the **Te Kohurau Restaurant & Café** (☎ 03-436 0603). Pop into the **Kurow Heritage & Information Centre** (☎ 03-436 0950; museum@kurow.co.nz; SH83), which has an interesting local museum. Instead of continuing west from Kurow on SH83, take the 21km scenic detour over the Aviemore dam, around the northern lake shore past walking tracks and scenic campsites ($10), then over the huge Benmore dam earthworks. Rejoin SH83 just west of Otematata.

Omarama

pop 360

At the head of the Waitaki Valley, surrounded by mountain ranges, the Omarama area is at the centre of fabulous landscapes. The bizarre moonscape of the **Clay Cliffs** (admission $5) is the result of two million years of erosion on layers of silt and gravel that were exposed along the active Osler fault line. The cliffs are on private land; the turn-off is 3.5km north of Omarama, then it's another 10km on an unsealed road.

Wrinkly Rams (☎ 03-438 9751; www.thewrinklyrams.co.nz; SH8; adult/child/family $20/10/50; ⌚ 2 or 3 shows daily 10.30am-4.30pm) does 30-minute stage shows of merino sheep being shorn using both modern and traditional methods, along with a sheepdog show. A barbecue lunch is included. Attached is one of the town's better restaurants.

Busy times in town include the Omarama **rodeo** (28 December) and the Omarama **sheepdog trials** (March).

The area's westerlies and warm summer thermals allow for world-class gliding over the hills and spectacular Southern Alps, and a **national gliding meet** is held here in December or January. Two companies will get you aloft from around $285.

Glideomarama.com (☎ 03-438 9555; www.glide omarama.com)
Southern Soaring (☎ 0800 762 746; www.soaring. co.nz)

If your legs are weary after mountain biking or hiking, or you just want to cosy up with your significant other, pop into the **Omarama Hot Tubs** (☎ 03-438 9703; www.hottubsomarama.co.nz; 25 Omamara Ave; ☯ 10am-10pm). The concept, combining private hot tubs (per person $30 to $40), and private 'wellness pods' ($125 for two people) including intimate, personal saunas, is Japanese, but with the surrounding mountain ranges and a pristine night sky, you could only be on the South Island of New Zealand. The chemical-free mountain water is changed daily, and used water is recycled for irrigation.

Omarama Hot Tubs also doubles as the local information office, and can assist with accommodation and transport information.

SLEEPING & EATING
Buscot Station (☎ 03-438 9646; SH8; dm/s/d $21/43/52; 🖳) A slightly chintzy, but very comfortable farmhouse on a huge farm with big, open views. Large doubles in the main house and a large modern dormitory out back are all comfortable. Tony shares his kitchen and lounge, as well as his theories on farming and politics. You'll find the turn-off to Buscot's 10km north of Omarama.

Omarama Top 10 Holiday Park (☎ 03-438 9875; www.omaramatop10.co.nz; SH8; unpowered/powered sites $30/35, cabins d $45-80; 🖳 🛜) Streamside and duckponded, this is a peaceful green space to

camp in. Cabins are compact; larger en suite and self-contained units cost $105 for two.

Heritage Gateway Hotel (☎ 03-438 9850; www. heritagegateway.co.nz; SH8; d $135-165; 🖳 🛜) A large complex of comfortable, modern rooms (all with en suite) and a restaurant-bar on the road towards Queenstown.

Wrinkly Rams (☎ 03-438 9751; SH8; breakfast $10-15, dinner $20-30; ☯ 7am-9pm) Restaurants attached to tourist attractions can be dodgy, but the dinners here (pan-fried cod, tender lamb shanks) are quite delicious. Big glass windows and outside tables give a nice view of the mountains while you eat. Wines from the nearby Waitaki Valley (see the boxed text, below) also feature.

Omarama Hotel (☎ 03-438 9713; cnr SH8 & SH83; meals $15-25) Good pub food and displays of local sheepdog competition winners.

GETTING THERE & AWAY
From Omarama head north up SH8 past beautiful Lake Ohau to Twizel and Mt Cook, or southwest through striking Lindis Pass towards Cromwell and Queenstown. Stop before Lindis Pass to add your own roadside cairn.

Omarama is on the main route from Christchurch, and both **Atomic Shuttles** (☎ 03-349 0697; www.atomictravel.co.nz) and **InterCity** (☎ 03-474 9600; www.intercity.co.nz) swing by.

OAMARU TO DUNEDIN
It's 114km along SH1 from Oamaru to Dunedin and all too easy to blast up at the open-road speed limit without stopping on

DUNEDIN & OTAGO

WAITAKI WINE ON THE WAY UP

The wines of nearby Central Otago already have a robust global reputation, but a few winemaking pioneers in North Otago's Waitaki Valley are also making international wine experts drink up and take notice.

Just 6km east of Kurow on SH83, the **Kurow Winery** (☎ 03-436 0443; www.kurowwinery.co.nz; Duntroon; ☯ cellar door 11am-5pm) only kicked off in 2007, but it already has an excellent reputation for fresh, well-balanced riesling and smoky and spicy pinot noir. When we visited, they were putting the finishing touches to their new tasting room. Drop by for an antipasto platter.

Pinot gris and pinot noir are the stars at **Sublime Wine** (☎ 03-436 0089; www.sublimewine.co.nz; 511 Grants Rd, RD7K, Oamaru), a compact, family-owned vineyard around 2km further east on SH83 past the Kurow Winery. The well-travelled owners also operate the funky **Sublime Bed & Breakfast** (thelodge@sublimewine.co.nz; d incl breakfast $150; 🛜). The rambling old homestead is surrounded by vineyards and mountain valleys, and a twin and double room are decorated with an eclectic combo of old advertising signs, retro furniture and distressed wooden floors. Special Taste of Waitaki three-course dinners ($50 per person including wine) showcasing local produce are available. Ask Steve about his time as a bass player for some of NZ's biggest bands.

the way. There are some really delightful places to stay along here though, and they alone justify spending more time. The narrow, ocean-hugging road travelling south from Oamaru provides a break from SH1, and has some gorgeous coastal views; take Wharfe St out of town (following the signs for Kakanui).

About 5km south of Oamaru, **Old Bones Backpackers** (☎ 03-434 8115; www.oldbones.co.nz; Beach Rd; dm/s/d $30/43/60; 🖳 🛜) is beautifully designed, with rooms off a sunny, central space that encourages a safe, communal feeling. Close enough to the sea to hear the surf at night, this is a place to just relax in front of the huge windows looking over farmland to the sea, or get stuck into your favourite book. One of NZ's best hostels.

Also near the beach, at All Day Bay 16km from Oamaru, is **Coastal Backpackers** (☎ 03-439 5411; www.coastalbackpackers.co.nz; Waianakarua Rd, All Day Bay; dm/d $26/54, self-contained d $85). With a big garden and good swimming at the beach, you may find yourself extending your stay here. Choose from rooms in the main lodge, a compact cabin for two, or the self-contained unit in the main house. When we visited, the friendly Welsh–Kiwi owners were juggling tending their cherry orchard, looking after their baby llamas, and planning the reopening of their rambling garden pub. Not a bad life, really.

Rejoining SH1 again at Waianakarua, backtrack a couple of hundred metres north to the **Olive Grove Lodge and Holiday Park** (☎ 03-439 5830; www.olivebranch.co.nz; SH1, Waianakarua; sites per adult/child $12/6, powered sites $24, dm/d $25/60; 🖳). Surrounded by farm, encircled by the Waianakarua River, and with birdsong and shady trees, this is an extremely popular camping ground for Kiwis around summer. The backpacker rooms are brightly painted, with interesting artworks, and the sunny communal lounge is a treat. Kids will love the adventure playground and highland cattle; parents will love the spa, eco lifestyle, organic vegies and peaceful vibe. En suite rooms (doubles $70, $15 extra for a third person) are good options for families.

Further south on SH1, 30km south of Oamaru, stop to check out the **Moeraki Boulders** (*Te Kaihinaki*), a collection of large spherical boulders on a stunning stretch of beach, scattered about like a giant kid's discarded marbles. Try to time your visit with low tide. There's a perfectly fine restaurant here, but it would be criminal to not dine at Fleur's (right).

Moeraki township is a charming little fishing village that you really should visit before it's overrun by retired folk from Christchurch. It's a nice 1½-hour walk along the beach between the village and the boulders, or head in the other direction towards the Kaiks wildlife trail and a cute old wooden lighthouse – a great spot to see yellow-eyed penguins and fur seals up close. For such a small town, Moeraki has nurtured the creation of more than its fair share of national treasures, from Francis Hodgkins' paintings to Keri Hulme's *The Bone People*…and Fleur Sullivan's cooking.

our pick **Fleur's Place** (☎ 03-439 4480; www.fleurs place.com; Old Jetty, Moeraki; mains $20-35; 🕑 10.30am-late Wed-Sat) has a rumble-tumble look about it, but this stylish timber hut serves up some of the South Island's best food. The speciality is seafood, fresh off the boats that are moored only metres away, and it's equally popular among locals for an evening drink and occasional live music. Head for the upstairs deck and smell the ocean while you tuck into fresh chowder, tender mutton bird, or whatever fish the boats caught last night. From 8am Friday to Tuesday, the adjacent **Fleur's Place Food 2 Go** caravan offers a very affordable taste of the Fleur's experience with seafood chowder ($10), smoked mussels ($8) and *kadoka* (raw fish salad; $8). It's also a handy spot for an alfresco espresso with an outlook of Moeraki's perfect little fishing harbour. Bookings for the restaurant are strongly recommended, but they'll probably squeeze you in if you arrive between the busy lunch and dinner times.

Moeraki Motel (☎ 03-439 4862; www.moeraki beachmotel.co.nz; cnr Beach & Haven Sts; d $95) has self-contained units with balconies, while the **Moeraki Village Holiday Park** (☎ 03-439 4759; www. moerakivillageholidaypark.co.nz; 114 Haven St; campsites $26, powered sites $26, d $45-125; 🖳 🛜) occupies a small field above the road into town and has cabins and motel units.

A growing number of Moeraki locals are also opening their houses as B&B accommodation.

Detouring off SH1 to the coast again towards Karitane, you wind down the scenic coastal road to **Seacliff**.

our pick **Asylum Backpackers** (☎ 03-465 8123; Russell Rd, Seacliff; dm/s/d $25/40/62; 🕑 Nov-May; 🖳), on the grounds of the former Seacliff Lunatic Asylum, is a lovely chilled-out place. The communal lounge, complete with giant palm, has an excellent selection of music, or there's kayaking and fishing ($35), surfing ($15), cycling (free) or horse riding ($55) to be done. The horses occasionally look in the hostel's windows. Many people come here for a day and stay for weeks, those with mechanical skills sometimes pitching in to help with the 50-odd wonderful old classic cars (1920s to '60s), or with restoring the old bluestone building. Cash only.

The rest of the old asylum grounds are now the **Truby King Reserve**, with parklands, overgrown gardens and native forest – perfect a picnic or a stroll. Even though it's a beautiful park, it's a site with a scary, horrible history. Far too many people were essentially imprisoned here, and far too many of them were brutalised by the experience, or by the staff – these were the days when lobotomies and desexing operations were still de rigueur. Almost 30 women, locked in their dorms, were killed in a fire here in 1942. Among Seacliff's most famous residents was one of NZ's greatest novelists, Oamaru's Janet Frame (see p599). If you wander through the gardens you'll find a plaque recording some of her thoughts.

Queenstown & Wanaka

If Queenstown didn't exist, someone would have to invent it. With a cinematic background of mountains and lakes you actually have seen in the movies, and a 'what can we think of next?' array of adventure activities, it's little wonder that the South Island's premier tourist town tops many travellers' Kiwi itineraries. This Disneyland of derring-do will prompt you to scrabble for a hundred synonyms for 'exciting' and 'thrilling' when writing in your travel journal, but lurking in and around the tangle of bungy cords are experiences that will last longer than a shriek-inducing 10 or 20 seconds.

Venture out on the Greenstone and Routeburn Tracks for extended outdoor thrills amid arguably New Zealand's most stunning scenery, or sample world-beating wines in world-beating surroundings in the Gibbston Valley. If you listen really closely, you might even hear the screams of glee across the road at bungy's birthplace, the Kawarau River.

Slow down (slightly) in Wanaka, Queenstown's junior sibling, now offering its own menu of outdoor adventure and a growing restaurant and bar scene. Explore Mt Aspiring National Park to reinforce that you're only a short drive from true NZ wilderness.

Slow down even more in sleepy Glenorchy, a scenic reminder of what Queenstown and Wanaka were before the adventure groupies moved in. Reduce your speed further in Arrowtown to consider the town's gold-mining past over dinner in a quiet bistro. The following day there'll be plenty of opportunities to jump back into the region's cavalcade of fun.

HIGHLIGHTS

- Sampling superb wines amid the dramatic scenery at **Gibbston Valley** (p622)
- Relaxing and dining in **Arrowtown** (p625) after the last of the day-trippers have left
- Doing things you've only dreamed about in **Queenstown** (p611), the adrenaline-rush capital of NZ
- Walking the peaceful **Routeburn Track** (p630)
- Exploring by horseback, kayak and jetboat the upper reaches of Lake Wakatipu from sleepy and stunning **Glenorchy** (p628)
- Watching a flick at **Cinema Paradiso** (p639) in Wanaka, with pizza during intermission
- **Bar-hopping** (p622) and **dining** (p620) in cosmopolitan Queenstown

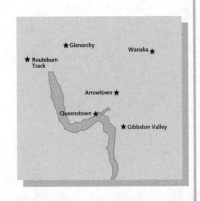

- Telephone code: 03
- www.queenstown-nz.co.nz
- www.queenstown-vacation.com

QUEENSTOWN & WANAKA

QUEENSTOWN & WANAKA

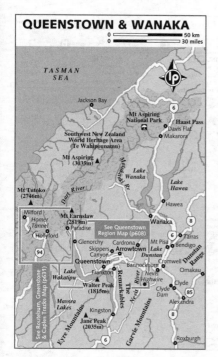

Atomic Shuttles, Naked Bus, Tracknet and Wanaka Connexions.

QUEENSTOWN REGION

Surrounded by the soaring indigo heights of the Remarkables, crowned by Coronet Peak, and framed by the meandering coves of Lake Wakatipu, it's little wonder that Queenstown is a show-off. The town wears its 'Global Adventure Capital' badge proudly, and most visitors take the time to do crazy things they've never done before. But a new Queenstown is also emerging, with a cosmopolitan restaurant and arts scene and excellent vineyards. Go ahead and jump off a bridge or out of a plane, but also make time to slow down and experience Queenstown without the adrenaline. And once you've eased up, look forward to more of the same in historic Arrowtown or beautiful Glenorchy.

QUEENSTOWN
pop 11,000

No-one's ever visited Queenstown and said, 'I'm bored'. Looking like a small town, but displaying the energy of a small city, Queenstown offers a mountain of activities. If your 'Things to Do' list contains bungy jumping, caving, rafting, sledging, jetboating, skiing, skydiving and hang gliding, trained operators are waiting on your call right now.

Maximise bragging rights with your souvenir T-shirt in the town's atmospheric restaurants, laid-back cafes and bustling bars. Be sure to also find a lakeside bench at sunrise or dusk and immerse yourself in one of NZ's most beautiful views. It's a pretty good option for an alfresco afternoon picnic as well.

Confident Queenstown is well used to visitors with international accents, so expect great tourist facilities, but also great big crowds, especially in summer and winter. Autumn (March to May) and spring

Climate
Summer (December to February) has long days with temperatures up to 30°C, but January also sees the region's highest rainfall. This elevated region gets crisp winters (June to August) with daytime temperatures around 5°C to 10°C, dipping to freezing or below at night, and lots of mountaintop snow. Autumn (March to May) is pleasant with relatively warm temperatures (15°C to 20°C), while spring (September to November) is slightly cooler.

Getting There & Around
Air New Zealand links Auckland, Wellington and Christchurch to Queenstown, with connections to Wanaka. Jetstar flies to Auckland and Christchurch from Queenstown. Queenstown's international airport is linked to Australia via Air New Zealand, Jetstar, Qantas and Virgin Blue. Bus and shuttle companies criss-cross Otago from Dunedin to Queenstown and Wanaka. Several divert south to Te Anau and Invercargill, and others migrate north to Christchurch or travel through the Haast Pass and up the West Coast. The major operators include InterCity,

---

MAORI NEW ZEALAND

Kiwi Haka (p624) perform nightly atop the Queenstown gondola. Two Queenstown galleries worth checking out for contemporary Maori art and design are Kapa (p624) and toi o tahuna (p624). For active travellers, Dart River Safaris (p628) is Ngai Tahu owned.

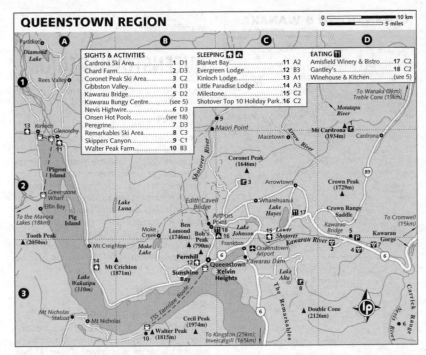

QUEENSTOWN REGION

SIGHTS & ACTIVITIES	
Cardrona Ski Area	1 D1
Chard Farm	2 D3
Coronet Peak Ski Area	3 C2
Gibbston Valley	4 D3
Kawarau Bridge	5 D2
Kawarau Bungy Centre	(see 5)
Nevis Highwire	6 D3
Onsen Hot Pools	(see 18)
Peregrine	7 D3
Remarkables Ski Area	8 C3
Skippers Canyon	9 C1
Walter Peak Farm	10 B3

SLEEPING	
Blanket Bay	11 A2
Evergreen Lodge	12 B3
Kinloch Lodge	13 A1
Little Paradise Lodge	14 A3
Milestone	15 C2
Shotover Top 10 Holiday Park	16 C2

EATING	
Amisfield Winery & Bistro	17 C2
Gantley's	18 C2
Winehouse & Kitchen	(see 5)

(October to November) are slightly quieter, but Queenstown's a year-round destination. The town's restaurants and bars are regularly packed with a mainly young crowd that really know how to enjoy themselves on holiday. If you're a more private soul, drop in to see what all the fuss is about, but then get out and about by exploring the sublime wilderness further up the lake at Glenorchy.

History

The region was deserted when the first Pakeha (white person) arrived in the mid-1850s, although there is evidence of previous Maori settlement. Sheep farmers came first, but after two shearers discovered gold on the banks of the Shotover River in 1862, a deluge of prospectors followed. Within a year Queenstown was a mining town with streets, permanent buildings and a population of several thousand. It was declared 'fit for a queen' by the NZ government, hence Queenstown was born. Lake Wakatipu was the principal means of transport, and at the height of the boom there were four paddle steamers and 30 other craft plying the waters.

By 1900 the gold had petered out and the population was a mere 190. It wasn't until the 1950s that Queenstown became a popular holiday destination. In recent years Queenstown has wrestled with rising water levels in Lake Wakatipu and, in 1999, a third of the town was severely flooded. To thwart a repeat occurrence, there was an initial proposal to permanently lower lake levels. Instead, the town has decided to raise floor levels and put other flood-mitigation measures in place.

Orientation

Queenstown's town centre is compact and pedestrian-friendly, with most tourist facilities situated along Shotover St, Beach St and the Mall. The airport is 8km east of town; see p625.

Information
EMERGENCY

Ambulance, fire service & police (☎ 111)

Queenstown Medical Centre (Map p612; ☎ 03-441 0500; www.qmc.co.nz; 9 Isle St; ⏰ 8.30am-8pm) Emergency care and a pharmacy.

INTERNET ACCESS

Most hostels also offer internet access.
Budget Communications (Map p612; O'Connell's Shopping Centre) Has laptop access and stacks of computers.
Global Gossip (Map p612; 27 Shotover St)
Internet Laundry (Map p612; 1 Shotover St) Surf as you wash.

MONEY

ATMs and banks are scattered throughout town.

POST

Post office (Map p612; 13 Camp St)

TOURIST INFORMATION

Department of Conservation visitor information centre (DOC; Map p612; ☎ 03-442 7935; queenstownvc@doc.govt.nz; 38 Shotover St; ◷ 8.30am-5pm May-Nov, to 6pm Dec-Apr) Backcountry Hut Passes and weather and track updates; on the mezzanine floor above Outdoor Sports.
Info & Track Centre (Map p612; ☎ 03-442 9708; www.infotrack.co.nz; 37 Shotover St) Info on transport to trailheads.
Queenstown i-SITE (Map p612; ☎ 0800 668 888, 03-442 4100; www.queenstown-vacation.com; Clocktower Centre, cnr Shotover & Camp Sts; ◷ 7am-7pm Dec-Apr, to 6pm May-Nov) Also check www.queenstown-nz.co.nz.

TRAVEL AGENCIES

Kiwi Discovery (Map p612; ☎ 0800 505 504, 03-442 7340; www.kiwidiscovery.com; 37 Camp St) Tramping packages, ski transport and equipment hire.
Real Journeys (Map p612; ☎ 0800 656 501, 03-249-7416; www.realjourneys.co.nz; Steamer Wharf, Beach St) Huge range of lake trips and tours.
Station (Map p612; ☎ 03-442 5252; www.thestation.co.nz; cnr Camp & Shotover Sts) Houses AJ Hackett Bungy and Shotover Jet.

Sights

Hop on the **Skyline Gondola** (Map p610; ☎ 03-441 0101; www.skyline.co.nz; Brecon St; adult/child/family return $23/12/59; ◷ 9.30am-6.30pm) for fantastic views of Queenstown, the lake and the mountains. At the top are a cafe, a restaurant with regular Maori cultural shows, and souvenir shops. Walking trails include the **loop track** (30 minutes return) or you can try the Luge (p615). The energetic can forgo the gondola and hike to the top – take the upper, left-hand gravel track from the trailhead on Lomond Cres for an hour's uphill hike.

The **Kiwi Birdlife Park** (Map p612; ☎ 03-442 8059; www.kiwibird.co.nz; Brecon St; adult/child $35/15; ◷ 9am-5pm Oct-Mar, to 6pm Apr-Sep, shows 11am & 3pm) is your best bet to spy a kiwi. There are also 10,000 native plants and scores of birds, including the rare black stilt, kea, morepork and parakeets. Stroll around the sanctuary, watch the conservation show and tiptoe quietly into the darkened kiwi houses. Kids under 15 get in free with a paying adult.

Williams Cottage (Map p612; cnr Marine Pde & Earl St; ◷ 10am-5pm Mon-Sat) is Queenstown's oldest home. An annexe of Arrowtown's Lake District Museum and Gallery (p626), it was built in 1864 and remains close to its original condition, including 1930s wallpaper. The cottage and its 1920s garden are now home to the very cool Vesta shop (p624) and cafe (p621).

Around the corner is the **Church of St Peter** (Map p612; www.stpeters.co.nz; cnr Church & Camp Sts; ◷ services 10am Wed, 10.30am Sun), another oasis of calm. The gift of a faithful parishioner, this pretty wood-beamed building has a beautiful organ and colourful stained glass. Take a look at the cedar-wood lectern, which was carved by Ah Tong, a Chinese immigrant, in the 1870s.

Underwater Observatory (Map p612; ☎ 03-442 6142; Queenstown Bay Jetty; ◷ 9am-5pm) has

QUEENSTOWN & WANAKA

QUEENSTOWN

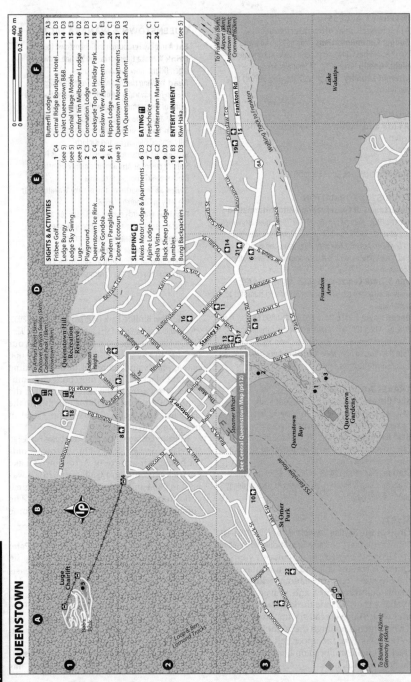

See Central Queenstown Map (p612)

Lake Wakatipu

six giant windows showcasing life under the lake. Brown trout abound, and based on their generous size, look to be impossibly well fed. Keep a keen eye out for freshwater eels and the favourite of the kiddies – the scaup (diving ducks), which dive down and swim right past the windows.

Activities

Purchase ombination tickets for a variety of Queenstown's more heart-stopping activities from **Queenstown Combos** (☎ 0800 423 836, 03-442 7318; www.combos.co.nz).

Some activity operators have an office where you can book directly, but for most head to the Queenstown i-SITE (p609).

BUNGY JUMPING

Queenstown is famous for bungy jumping, and **AJ Hackett Bungy** (Map p612; ☎ 03-442 7100; www.bungy.co.nz; Station, cnr Camp & Shotover Sts) is the activity's best-known representative. Prices for the following include transport out of town and gondola rides where relevant.

The historic 1880 **Kawarau Bridge** (Map p608; per person $175), 23km from Queenstown, became the world's first commercial bungy site in 1988 and allows you to leap 43m. Next door, the **Kawarau Bungy Centre** (Map p608; ☎ 03-442 1177; SH6; ◷ 8am-5.45pm) has a **Secrets of Bungy Tour** which tells the story of bungy and lets the faint-hearted get a feel for the experience – minus the leap.

Atop Queenstown's gondola, the 47m-high **Ledge Bungy** (Map p610; per person $175) is the only place you can bungy after dark.

The gold-standard jump is the truly awe-inspiring/terrifying/crazy (choose one) 134m-high **Nevis Highwire** (Map p608; per person $250), where you jump from a pod suspended over the Nevis River. AJ Hackett's 3Thrillogy (per person $450) combines the Kawarau, Ledge and Nevis jumps.

BUNGY VARIATIONS

Shotover Canyon Swing (off Map p610; ☎ 0800 279 464, 03-442 6990; www.canyonswing.co.nz; per person $199, additional swings $39) is not your average backyard swing. If you can't force yourself to jump, they can release you in a variety of creative ways – backwards, in a chair, upside down; if you can dream it, you can swing it. From there it's a 60m free fall and a wild swing across the canyon at 150km/h. Not for the faint-hearted – it's one of the best buzzes in town.

The new swinger on the block is the **Nevis Arc** (Map p610; ☎ 03-442 4007; www.nevisarc.co.nz), at AJ Hackett's Nevis Highwire Bungy site. Billed as the world's highest swing (120m) here you can fly with a friend in tandem ($300) or go it alone ($170).

Same, same but different is the **Ledge Sky Swing** (Map p610; $120), at AJ Hackett's Ledge

---

QUEENSTOWN IN...

Two Days

Start your day with a breakfast burrito at **Halo** (p622) before heading to Shotover St to book your adrenaline-charged activities for the next day. Spend the rest of the day visiting **Williams Cottage** (p609), **Skyline Gondola** (p609) and **Kiwi Birdlife Park** (p609), before boarding the exciting **Shotover Jet** (p612) or taking a lake cruise on the **TSS Earnslaw** (p617). Wind up with a walk through **Queenstown Gardens** (p615) to capture dramatic views of the Remarkables at dusk. Have a sunset drink at **Pub on Wharf** (p623) or **Monty's** (p623), before dinner at the **Cow** (p621) or **Wai Waterfront Restaurant & Wine Bar** (p621). The evening's still young so head to **Minibar** (p623) or **Bardeaux** (p623). Devote the next day to bungy jumping, skydiving, white-water rafting or perusing the art galleries in Church Lane. Enjoy dinner at **Winnies** (p623), and stay on for the live music or DJs.

Four Days

Follow the two-day itinerary, then head to **Arrowtown** (p625) to wander the enigmatic **Chinese settlement** (p626), browse the local shops and eat a gourmet lunch. The following day drive along the shores of Lake Wakatipu to tiny **Glenorchy** (p628). Have lunch at **Glenorchy Café** (p629) and then strap on your hiking boots and head into **Mt Aspiring National Park** (p633) to do some wonderful short tramps in the vicinity of the **Routeburn Track** (p630). If you'd rather exercise your arms, go kayaking across the lake at **Kinloch** (p629).

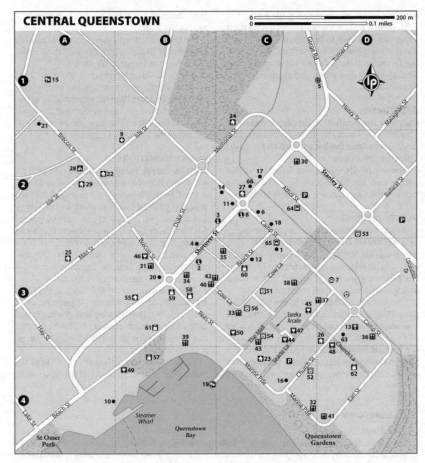

CENTRAL QUEENSTOWN

Bungy site. A shorter swing, but stunning views of Queenstown as you scream your lungs out.

JETBOATING

The Shotover and Kawarau are Queenstown's most popular rivers to hurtle along; the lengthier and more scenic Dart River is less travelled (see p628). Trips depart from Queenstown or go via minibus to the river and awaiting jetboat.

Shotover Jet (☎ 0800 746 868; www.shotoverjet.co.nz; adult/child $109/69) does half-hour trips through the rocky Shotover Canyons, with lots of thrilling 360-degree spins. **Kawarau Jet** (Map p612; ☎ 0800 529 272, 03-442 6142; www.kjet.co.nz; Queenstown

Bay Jetty; adult/child $95/55) does one-hour trips on the Kawarau and Lower Shotover Rivers.

Skippers Canyon Jet (☎ 03-442 9434; www.skip perscanyon.co.nz; adult/child $109/69) incorporates a 30-minute blast in the narrow gorges of Skippers Canyon in its three-hour trips, which cover the region's gold-mining history.

WHITE-WATER RAFTING

The choppy Shotover and calmer Kawarau Rivers are both great for rafting. Trips take four to five hours with two to three hours on the river. There's generally a minimum age of 13 years.

Companies include **Queenstown Rafting** (☎ 0800 723 8464, 03-442 9792; www.rafting.co.nz),

Extreme Green Rafting (☎ 03-442 8517; www.nzraft. com) and **Challenge Rafting** (☎ 0800 423 836, 03-442 7318; www.raft.co.nz); prices start at around $175.

Family Adventures (☎ 03-442 8836; www.family adventures.co.nz; adult/child $155/110) offers gentler (Grade I to II) trips on the Shotover suitable for children three years and older that include swimming, snacks and all sorts of family-flavoured frivolity.

RIVER SURFING & WHITE-WATER SLEDGING
Hang onto a body board and 'surf' down the Kawarau River with **Serious Fun** (☎ 0800 737 468, 03-442 5262; www.riversurfing.co.nz) or **River Boarding Co** (☎ 03-442 7797; www.riverboarding.co.nz). Trips take about four hours (1½ hours in the water), cost around $150 and run from September to June.

Frogz Have More Fun (☎ 0800 437 649, 03-441 2318; www.frogz.co.nz) lets you steer purpose-built, buoyant sledges down the challenging full-day descent of the Kawarau River ($370) and

the more mellow half-day roller-coaster of the Roaring Meg ($149).

CANYONING
Canyoning.co.nz (☎ 03-441 3003; www.canyoning.co.nz; per person $155) runs half-day trips in the nearby 12-Mile Delta Canyons incorporating water slides, rock jumps and abseiling – even a zip-line. Canyoning in the remote Routeburn Valley ($195) is possible with Canyoning .co.nz and with **Routeburn Canyoning** (☎ 0800 222 696, 03-441 4386; www.gycanyoning.co.nz; per person $195).

OVERHEARD #1
'My favourite questions from passengers on the jetboat are "Does the boat run on rails?" and "How long did it take to make the canyon out of all that fake rock?"' – Brett Black, Shotover Jet Driver.

ESPRESSO, LATTE OR DECAF?

Got your head around what's on offer in Queenstown yet? The number of ways to explore the great outdoors can be a little overwhelming, so here's a handy ready-reckoner based on your desired thrill level.

■ **Espresso** – Launch yourself into the extreme thrills of the Shotover Canyon Swing (p611) or the Nevis Highwire (p611). Expect to be babbling like an adrenaline-pumped travelling fool for a few hours afterwards.

■ **Latte** – Combine tangible thrills with a more leisurely look at the stupendous scenery around you with a mountain-top departure on a mountain bike or hang glider (below).

■ **Decaf** – Ride a jetboat (p612) through the twisting and turning ravines of the Shotover River (it feels life-threatening, but it's actually very safe), or take a leisurely paddle in a kayak (p629) on the beautiful upper reaches of Lake Wakatipu at Kinloch.

FLYING, GLIDING & SKYDIVING

Tandem Paragliding (Map p610; ☎ 0800 759 688, 03-441 8581; www.paraglide.net.nz; per person $199, if you are on the gondola by 9am $169) takes off from the top of the gondola, while **Flight Park Tandems** (☎ 0800 467 325; www.tandemparagliding.com; from 1140m/1620m $179/205) offers spectacular views from Coronet Peak.

Those wanting to stay tethered can opt for the more relaxed paraflight. Glide 200m above the lake thanks to **Queenstown Paraflights** (Map p612; ☎ 0800 225 520; www.paraflights.co.nz; Queenstown Bay Jetty; solo per adult/child $129/109, tandem $95/75), who pull you airborne by boat. Soar with **Skytrek Hang Gliding** (☎ 0800 759 873; www.skytrek.co.nz; per person $210) from Coronet Peak or the Remarkables.

Extreme Air (☎ 0800 727 245; www.extremeair.co.nz; day/month $295/2200) can train you at its paragliding and hang-gliding school.

The good folk at skydiving outfit **NZONE** (☎ 0800 376 796, 03-442 5867; www.nzone.biz; from $249) will toss you out of a perfectly good airplane – attached to somebody who knows how to open the parachute.

SKIING

The Remarkables (p85) and Coronet Peak ski fields (p85) are the region's key snow-sport centres (see Map p608). Tune into 99.2FM from 6.45am to 9am to hear snow reports.

For serious skiers, check out **Heli Ski Queenstown** (☎ 03-442 7733; www.flynz.co.nz; from $895), **Harris Mountains Heli-Ski** (☎ 03-442 6722; www.heliski.co.nz; from $775) or **Southern Lakes Heliski** (☎ 03-442 6222; www.southernlakesheliski.co.nz; from $675).

Ski equipment hire companies:
Gravity Action (Map p612; ☎ 03-442 5277; 19 Shotover St)

Green Toad (Map p612; ☎ 03-442 5311; 48 Camp St)
Outside Sports (Map p612; ☎ 03-441 0074; Shotover St)
Snowrental (Map p612; ☎ 03-442 4187; 39 Camp St)

MOUNTAIN BIKING

There's excellent mountain biking around Queenstown. **Fat Tyre Adventures** (☎ 0800 328 897; www.fat-tyre.co.nz; from $195) takes small tours off the main trails. Tours cater to different abilities with day tours, multiday tours, heli-biking and singletrack riding. Bike hire and trail snacks are included.

If you're not keen on strenuous uphill pedalling, chat to the folks at **Vertigo** (Map p612; ☎ 0800 837 8446, 03-442 8378; www.vertigobikes.co.nz; 4 Brecon St). They run guided downhill rides into Skippers Canyon and from the top of the gondola. Both options are $149, and they have helibiking trips on offer too.

Places to hire bikes:
Outside Sports (Map p612; ☎ 03-441 0074; 36 Shotover St; per half-/full day from $30/50) Has mountain bikes – hard tail and full suspension – road bikes, tandems and kids' bikes.
Queenstown Bike Hire (Map p612; ☎ 03-442 6039; cnr Marine Pde & Church St; per hr from $14)
Vertigo (Map p612; ☎ 0800 837 8446, 03-442 8378; www.vertigobikes.co.nz; 4 Brecon St) Has a laundry list of bikes (per half-/full day from $30/50), including full-on DH bikes.

TRAMPING & CLIMBING

Pick up a free copy of *Queenstown Walks and Trails* from the **DOC visitor information centre** (DOC; Map p612; ☎ 03-442 7935; queenstownvc@doc.govt.nz; 38 Shotover St) for local tramping tracks ranging from easy one-hour strolls to tough eight-hour slogs.

The peaceful **Queenstown Gardens** (Map p610) has a number of walking trails to follow. You can also haul yourself up to **Bob's Peak**, where the gondola lands. It's not a particularly scenic walk but the views at the top are excellent. Another short climb is up 900m **Queenstown Hill** (Map p610; two to three hours return); access is from Belfast Tce.

For a spectacular view, climb 1746m **Ben Lomond** (Map p608; six to eight hours return), accessed from Lomond Cres (Map p610). It's a difficult tramp requiring high-level fitness and shouldn't be underestimated; consult DOC on this and the region's other tramps.

Guided Nature Walks (☎ 03-442 7126; www.nzwalks.com; adult/child from $103/60) offers excellent walks in the area, including a Walk and Wine option and helihikes. **Encounter Guided Day Walks** (☎ 03-442 8200; www.ultimatehikes.co.nz; ☼ Oct-Apr) offers day walks on the Routeburn Track (adult/child $145/85), the Milford Track (adult/child $165/95) and near Mt Cook (adult/child $105/65), as well as multiday tramps.

For climbers, **Climbing Queenstown** (☎ 03-450 2119; www.climbingqueenstown.com) offers a variety of vertigo-inducing experiences. It has rock climbing (from $169), abseiling (adult/child $99/59), Via Ferrata (climbing fixed metal rungs, rails, pegs and cables – all attached to the cliff face; adult/child $159/89) and mountaineering (from $250). All activities are guided by highly professional and qualified guides.

For outdoor gear:
Outside Sports (Map p612; ☎ 03-441-0074; 36 Shotover St) Has the largest selection of retail outdoor gear in town and hires almost everything you might need for the great outdoors.
Small Planet Sports Co (Map p612; ☎ 03-442 6393; 17 Shotover St) New and used outdoor equipment.

HORSE TREKS
Ride through a stunning landscape on a 324-hectare working farm with **Moonlight Stables** (☎ 03-442 1229; www.moonlightcountry.co.nz; adult/child $99/65). **Shotover Stables** (☎ 03-442 7486; www.shotoverstables.net; adult/child $65/40) offers gentle rides with bush trekking and a river crossing.

FISHING
The rivers and lakes around Queenstown are home to brown and rainbow trout. All companies practise catch-and-release. Half-day guided trips start at $120.

Some fishing companies:
Stu's Guiding Service (☎ 03-248 8890; www.borntofish.co.nz) Located in Athol 77km south of Queenstown. Offers guided fly-fishing, lessons and multiday trips. Prices drop for two or more patrons.
Fly Fishing (☎ 03-442 5363; www.wakatipu.co.nz) Helifishing, lake trolling, lure fishing and fly-fishing.
Stu Dever Fishing Charters (☎ 03-442 6371; www.fishing-queenstown.co.nz) Salmon and trout fishing from the 34ft launch *Chinook*. Owner Stu can arrange for your catch to be cooked at a local restaurant.

OTHER ACTIVITIES
Ziptrek Ecotours (Map p610; ☎ 0800 947 8735; www.ziptrek.com; adult/child $119/69), the new kid on the adventure tourism block, is also the talk of the town. Incorporating a series of zip-lines (flying foxes), this harness-clad thrill-ride takes you from treetop to treetop high above Queenstown. Ingenious design and ecofriendly values are a bonus on the adrenaline-fuelled two- or three-hour tour.

Hop on a three-wheeled cart to ride the **Luge** (Map p610; ☎ 03-441 0101; www.skyline.co.nz; Brecon St; 2/3/5 rides incl gondola ride $35/40/45) at the top of the gondola. Nail the 'scenic' run once, and then you're allowed on the advanced track with its banked corners and tunnel.

Frisbee Golf (Map p610; www.discgolf.co.nz) has a marked course in Queenstown Gardens. Tees are indicated by numbered arrows on the ground and targets are either trees or

---

THE ADVENTURE PRESCRIPTION

- Do you like driving in a really fast sports car? Try jetboating.
- Do you like letting go and losing control? Try bungy jumping.
- Do you crave control and want to be in charge? Try mountain biking or rock climbing.
- Do you like roller-coaster rides and aren't bothered by having messed-up hair? Try rafting or river boarding.
- Do you own jeans and aren't afraid of chafing? Try horseback riding.
- Have you always wanted to be strapped to some stranger and fall out of an airplane? Try tandem skydiving.
- Do you speak Elvish and like short people? Try a *Lord of the Rings* tour.

chain baskets. BYO frisbee. Nearby is the **Queenstown Ice Rink** (Map p610; ☎ 03-441 8000; www.queenstownicerink.co.nz; adult/child incl skate hire $15/12; ☺ 9am-5.30pm Mon-Thu, 9am-9pm Fri, 10.30am-5pm Sat & Sun, closed summer); come for a skate or a game of ice hockey.

The **Central Otago Wine Experience** (Map p612; ☎ 03-409 2226; www.winetastes.com; 14 Beach St; tasting cards $20; ☺ 10am-10pm) has more than 80 wines to try. A $20 tasting card provides samples of around eight to 10 different wines.

You can also golf, minigolf, quad bike, sail, dive and more. See the Queenstown i-SITE or any booking agencies. For a paddle on the lake, rent a kayak at **Queenstown Bike Hire** (Map p612; cnr Marine Pde & Church St).

Slow down by easing into **Hush Spa** (Map p610; ☎ 03-4009 0901; www.hushspa.co.nz; upstairs, Mountaineer Bldg, cnr Beach & Rees Sts; 30/60min massage from $65/120; ☺ 9am-9pm Tue-Fri, to 7pm Sat) for a massage, aroma stone therapy or a deep bath soak. Call the **Mobile Massage Co** (☎ 027 442 6161; www.queenstownmassage.co.nz; ☺ 9am-9pm) for an in-room massage (one hour $110).

Onsen Hot Pools (Map p608; ☎ 03-442 5707; www.onsen.co.nz; 160 Arthurs Point Rd; adult/child $46/10; ☺ 11am-10pm) has private Japanese-style hot tubs with mountain views. Book ahead and one will be warmed up for you.

Walking Tour

From Beach St, start your walk round the harbourfront, watching for the **TSS Earnslaw** (**1**; opposite) chugging into Queenstown Bay. Stop at **Patagonia** (**2**; p621) for coffee, ice cream or hot chocolate, before heading out on the jetty to the **Underwater Observatory** (**3**; p609) to see what lies beneath. Continue along the beach to **Queenstown Gardens** (**4**) to soak up the quiet or try **Frisbee Golf** (**5**; p615). Complete the garden's loop trail and return up Marine Pde to **Williams Cottage** (**6**; p609) for a little history, retail therapy and lunch. Take a right on Church St to see the pretty **Church of St Peter** (**7**; p609), and then zigzag through the lanes to the Mall to explore some local **boutiques** (**8**; p624). Next, visit the **Central Otago Wine Experience** (**9**; above), as much to appreciate the local pinot as to steel your nerves for your visit to the **Station** (**10**; p609) to book your bungy jump for the next day. Head to Brecon St and visit the **Kiwi Birdlife Park** (**11**; p609) to spy the elusive, long-beaked balls of feathers and then hop on the **Skyline Gondola** (**12**; p609) for a peaceful (and steep) ride up Bob's Peak. Admire the quite Remarkable view before negotiating the graceful but exciting corners on

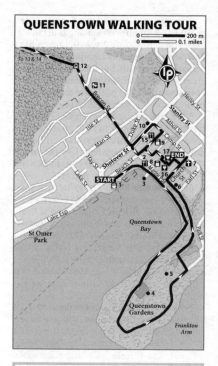

QUEENSTOWN WALKING TOUR

| | 0 | 200 m |
| 0 | 0.1 miles |

WALK FACTS

Start Beach St
Finish Minibar
Distance 3.5km
Duration Three to four hours

the **Luge** (**13**; p615). Brave souls can glide back down with **Tandem Paragliding** (**14**; p614). From the gondola's base, it's a stroll downhill back into town for dinner at **Fishbone Bar & Grill** (**15**), followed by drinks in Eureka Arcade at **Bardeaux** (**16**; p623) or **Minibar** (**17**; p623). You're on your own now.

Queenstown for Children

While Queenstown is brimming with activities, many of them have age restrictions that may exclude the youngest in your group. Nevertheless, you shouldn't have any trouble keeping the youngsters busy.

For a high that will make sugar rushes seem passé, take wilder kids on the Shotover Jet (p612). For older kids, consider a tamer variation on the classic bungy jump with the Ledge Sky Swing (p611) or go tandem with them on

Queenstown Paraflights (p614). At Kawarau Bungy Centre (p611) kids can watch people plunging off the bridge, experience a virtual jump and explore the bungy museum. For tiny tots who don't want to miss out on the fun, **Zoom** (Map p612; ☎ 0800 124 224; Brecon St Hill; child $10; ☼ 11am-5pm Wed-Sun) is a bungy trampoline that safely bounces them 8m into the air.

The Skyline Gondola (p609) offers a slow-moving activity from dizzying heights. At the top of the hill lies a wonderfully curvy Luge (p615) suitable for ages three and up.

Kids who are aspiring Dr Doolittles will love the Kiwi Birdlife Park (p609). Its conservation shows are especially geared to the younger crowd. Queenstown Gardens (p615) is a great place to let your children stretch their legs, and has a good beachside playground near the entrance on Marine Pde. Also in the park, Queenstown Ice Rink (opposite) is great for a rainy day, in winter.

Several places in town hire out child-sized mountain bikes (p614). Queenstown Bike Hire (opposite) hires out pogo sticks ($5 per day), foot scooters ($5 per day) and baby buggies ($15 per day), plus toboggans ($10 per day) in winter. Rookies (p624) hires out snowsuits for children aged one to 14 years, while most ski-hire shops (p614) have gear for tykes.

Consider also lake cruises on the *TSS Earnslaw* (right) and 4WD tours of narrow, snaking Skippers Canyon (right). Family rafting trips are run by Family Adventures (p613), in summer.

For more ideas and information check out Kidz Go! (www.kidzgo.co.nz).

Tours

AERIAL SIGHTSEEING

For a bird's-eye view, join a flightseeing tour.

Air Fiordland (☎ 0800 103 404, 03-442 3404; www.airfiordland.com; from $325) Flights around Milford Sound, Queenstown and surrounding area. Includes wine tasting.

Jag Air (☎ 03-442 3177; www.jagair.co.nz; per person $220) To see the sights upside down, take a 15-minute aerobatic flight.

Milford Sound Scenic Flights (☎ 03-442 3065; www.milfordflights.co.nz; adult/child from $325/195) Takes you south to Milford, does a fly-by and brings you back.

Over the Top Helicopters (☎ 03-442 2233; www.flynz.co.nz; from $225) Heaps of flight options taking in the best of the best views in Queenstown and beyond.

Sunrise Balloons (☎ 0800 468 247, 03-442 0781; www.ballooningnz.com; adult/child $375/245) Cruise the lake and mountain breezes in a hot-air balloon.

4WD TOURS

Nomad Safaris (☎ 03-442 6699; www.nomadsafaris. co.nz; adult/child $149/75) Runs four-hour tours with a *Lord of the Rings* flavour. Visit filming locations used for the iconic trilogy. If you're 'Bored of the Rings', Nomad has trips on offer that simply take in stunning scenery and hard-to-get-to backcountry vistas. It'll even let you drive ($260), or you can ride a quad-bike ($220).

Off Road Adventures (☎ 03-442 7858; www.offroad. co.nz; adult/child $140/70) Does similar tours, with a *Lord of the Rings* tour taking in filming locations. Also offers dirt-bike ($229) and quad-bike ($190) tours.

Skippers Canyon Heritage Tours (☎ 03-442 5949; www.queenstown-heritage.co.nz; adult/child $150/75) Skippers Canyon is reached by a narrow, winding road built by gold panners in the 1800s. This scenic but hair-raising 4WD route runs from Arthurs Point towards Coronet Peak and then above the Shotover River, passing gold-rush sights. Join a four-hour tour brimming with gold-mining stories and including a picnic. Specialist wine tours are also available.

LAKE CRUISES

The stately, steam-powered *TSS Earnslaw* (Map p612) will celebrate its centenary of continuous service in 2012. The elegant lady of the lake continues to churn across Lake Wakatipu at 13 knots. Once the lake's major means of transport, it originally carried more than 800 passengers. Climb aboard for the standard 1½-hour Lake Wakatipu tour (adult/child $48/20) or take a 3½-hour excursion to the high-country **Walter Peak Farm** (Map p608; adult/child $68/20) for sheep-shearing demonstrations and sheep-dog performances. Other tours include barbecue lunches, dinner or horse trekking. Book through **Real Journeys** (Map p612; ☎ 0800 656 503; www.realjourneys.co.nz; Steamer Wharf, Beach St).

MILFORD SOUND

Day trips via Te Anau to Milford Sound (p653) take 12 to 13 hours and cost around

---

OVERHEARD #2

'The water doesn't taste too salty for the ocean.' – Remark from an unnamed tourist after swimming in Lake Wakatipu.

QUEENSTOWN ON A BUDGET

A visit to Queenstown doesn't have to break the budget. Play **Frisbee golf** (p615) in the Queenstown Gardens, or hire a bike or **kayak** (p616) at the lakefront. Catch the bus to Arrowtown to the quirky boutique cinema **Dorothy Browns** (p627), or spy on the diving ducks at the **Underwater Observatory** (p609). Head to the **Mediterranean Market** (p622) for supplies for a lakeside picnic, or peruse the stalls at Queenstown's Saturday morning **arts & crafts market** (p624).

$225/115 per adult/child, including a two-hour cruise on the sound. Bus-cruise-flight options are also available, as is pick-up from the Routeburn Track finish line. Operators:

Great Sights (☎ 0800 744 487; www.greatsights.co.nz)

Kiwi Discovery (Map p612; ☎ 03-442 7340; www.kiwidiscovery.com)

Real Journeys (Map p612; ☎ 0800 656 503, 03-442 7500; www.realjourneys.co.nz; Steamer Wharf, Beach St)

The **BBQ Bus** (☎ 03-442 1045; www.milford.net.nz; adult/child $174/98) takes smaller groups (up to 22 people) and you can look forward to sausages and marinated beef kebabs with herbivore options available too.

To save on travel time and cost, consider visiting Milford from Te Anau (p644).

WINERY TOURS

A guided tour of the region's vineyards means being able to enjoy a drink without having to get behind the wheel.

Appellation Central Wine Tours (☎ 03-442 0246; www.appellationcentral.co.nz; from $155) Runs tasty tours, including an all-day excursion ($195) that also dips into local cheeses. See the boxed text, p622.

Queenstown Wine Trail (☎ 03-442 3799; www.queenstownwinetrail.co.nz; adult from $118) Offers informative, unhurried tours; choose from a five-hour tour with tastings at four wineries or a shorter tour ($136) with lunch included.

OTHER TOURS

Hop on a **Double-Decker Bus Tour** (Map p612; ☎ 03-441 4421; $48; ⌚ tours depart Queenstown 9.30am & 1.30pm) to historic Arrowtown (p625), taking in Gibbston Valley Wines (see the boxed text, p622) and Lake Hayes. You'll have 50 minutes to look around Arrowtown. Tours depart from in front of O'Connell's Shopping Centre.

Festivals & Events

Gibbston Harvest Festival (www.gibbstonharvestfestival.com; Gibbston) Wine buffs should time their visit to coincide with this annual festival – food, wine and good times all on offer.

Queenstown Winter Festival (www.winterfestival.co.nz) This festival in late June/early July provides wacky ski and snowboard activities, live music, a Mardi Gras party, fireworks and plenty of frigid frivolity.

Sleeping

Queenstown has endless places to stay, but many visitors seeking accommodation. Midrange travellers won't find much choice; consider a top-end place or go for one of the excellent budget options and spend up on activities. Places book out and prices rocket during the peak summer (December to February) and ski (June to September) seasons; book well in advance at these times. Rooms with guaranteed lake views often have a surcharge.

The **Queenstown Accommodation Centre** (Map p612; ☎ 03-442 7518; www.qac.co.nz; cnr Camp & Shotover Sts) has a range of holiday homes and apartments on its books (and its website), with prices ranging from around $200 to $500 per week. There is often a minimum-stay period.

BUDGET

Bumbles (Map p610; ☎ 03-442 6298, 0800 286 2537; www.bumblesbackpackers.co.nz; cnr Lake Esplanade & Brunswick St; sites/dm/d $15/28/60; 💻 📶) This popular hostel has recently upped its game with some tidy renovations. Being just down the lake from the heart of town makes for a prime location and one of the best views going. The compact common facilities make for a community living feel, and the modern amenities travellers have come to expect make this hotel a wise choice.

Butterfli Lodge (Map p610; ☎ 03-442 6367; www.butterfli.co.nz; 62 Thompson St; dm/d $24/58; 💻) This smaller hostel sits in a quiet hillside suburb. Commandeer the barbecue on the deck and take in beaut views as you turn your steaks and sausages. Rooms don't have a huge amount of character, but are modern and well maintained.

Nomads (Map p612; ☎ 03-441 3922; www.nomadshostels.com; 5 Church St; dm $25-34, tw/d $110/130; 💻 📶) Blessed with stunning exterior architecture and a prime location, this brand-new hostel is on a fast-track to being the one to beat. Inside, the facilities are top-notch, with en suites aplenty, massive kitchens and other bonuses such as an on-site internet cafe and travel agency. The only downside is the size of the establishment – it's massive.

YHA Queenstown Lakefront (Map p610; ☎ 03-442 8413; www.yha.co.nz; 88-90 Lake Esplanade; dm/d from $26/74; ☒ ☎) This friendly alpine lodge has staff well versed in Queenstown's myriad activities. Rooms are basic but clean; some rooms and the dining area have lake and mountain views. It's somewhat rambling but facilities are good, with a well-equipped kitchen and loads of board games, DVDs and books. Queenstown's nightlife is a 10- to 15-minute lakeside stroll away.

Black Sheep Lodge (Map p610; ☎ 03-442 7289; www.blacksheepbackpackers.co.nz; 13 Frankton Rd; dm/d $27/70; ☒ ☎) This place keeps younger social types happy with a spa, a pool table and a truckload of DVDs. Rooms are basic, but it's a friendly affair and provides plenty of R&R before your next Queenstown outdoor adventure. Kick off a big night in the on-site bar.

Shotover Top 10 Holiday Park (Map p608; ☎ 03-442 9306; www.shotoverholidaypark.co.nz; 70 Arthurs Pt Rd; sites $35, d $60-140; ☒ ☎) High above the Shotover River, this family-friendly park is 10 minutes' drive from the hustle and bustle of Queenstown. Fall out of your campervan straight onto the famous Shotover Jet (p612).

Creeksyde Top 10 Holiday Park (Map p610; ☎ 0800 786 222, 03-442 9447; www.camp.co.nz; 54 Robins Rd; sites $45, d $60-165; ☒ ☎) In a garden setting, this pretty spot has accommodation ranging from basic tent sites to self-contained motel units. An ecofriendly green tinge is added with a disciplined approach to recycling and a commitment to increase planting of native trees.

Also recommended:

Bungi Backpackers (Map p610; ☎ 03-442 8725; www.bungibackpackers.co.nz; 15 Sydney St; dm $23-26, d $53; ☒ ☎) Relaxed hostel with hammocks and a grassy volleyball court. A spa pool and complimentary veggie soup add a touch of home-away-from-home comfort.

Southern Laughter (Map p612; ☎ 03-442 8828; www.southernlaughter.co.nz; 4 Isle St; dm $25-28, tw $56, d $58-68; ☒ ☎) Funky hostel with various kitchens scattered throughout the sprawling complex. Check out the retro B&W pics of old Queenstown before strolling into town to see new Queenstown.

Alpine Lodge (Map p610; ☎ 03-442 7220; www.alpinelodgebackpackers.co.nz; 13 Gorge Rd; dm $26, d $62; ☒ ☎) Friendly, smaller hostel with international staff who've experienced every adventure activity on offer around town.

Hippo Lodge (Map p610; ☎ 03-442 5785; www.hippolodge.co.nz; 4 Anderson Heights; dm $28, s/d from $40/65; ☒ ☎) Well-maintained, relaxed hostel with good views and a correspondingly high number of stairs. Pitch a tent for $18 per person.

Last Resort (Map p612; ☎ 03-442 4320; www.tlrqtn.com; 6 Memorial St; dm $30; ☒ ☎) Super-central, smaller hostel with a tiny brick-and-timber bridge crossing a bubbling brook in the backyard; just a minute from where most transport will drop you off.

MIDRANGE

Queenstown Lakeview Holiday Park (Map p612; ☎ 0800 482 735, 03-442 7252; www.holidaypark.net.nz; Brecon St; sites $36, d $120-160; ☒ ☎) A short stroll from the gondola, this park has a big open field to camp in and great facilities. A few larger trees would soften the slightly spartan ambience for campers, but there are also flasher motel units and lodges.

Colonial Village Motels (Map p610; ☎ 03-442 7629; www.colonialvillage.co.nz; 136 Frankton Rd; s/d $115/120) Older-style motel units with gorgeous lake views have been spruced up with classy bed linen and minikitchens. Expect a bit of daytime road noise, but after dark it is considerably quieter.

Lomond Lodge (Map p612; ☎ 03-442 8235; www.lomondlodge.com; 33 Man St; d $130-160; ☒ ☎) The decor is a bit old-fashioned, but the owners have plenty of ideas to make the most of your stay in Queenstown. Share your own ideas with fellow travellers in the communal kitchen and at the garden barbecue. Larger family apartments ($250 for up to four people) are also available.

Milestone (Map p608; ☎ 03-441 4460; www.themilestone.co.nz; Ladies Mile, RD1; s/d $140/185) This welcoming B&B is 10 minutes' drive from Queenstown, but with ponds, waterfalls and 300 roses set on 4 acres, it feels wonderfully remote. The charming house is filled with antiques, and for $75 per person the friendly Turnbull family will prepare you dinner, complete with local wines. A self-contained cottage is also available at the same good-value rate.

Queenstown Motel Apartments (Map p610; ☎ 0800 661 668, 03-442 6095; www.qma.co.nz; 62 Frankton Rd; d $145) This well-run spot combines newer units with spa bathrooms, trendy decor and private minigardens, and older 1970s-style units that represent good value for larger groups of budget travellers.

Also recommended:

Little Paradise Lodge (Map p608; ☎ 03-442 6196; www.littleparadise.co.nz; Glenorchy-Queenstown Rd; s $45, d $120-140; ☒) Wonderfully eclectic, this slice of arty paradise is the singular vision of the Swiss owner.

Each rustic room features wooden floors, quirky artwork and handmade furniture. Outside, the fun continues with a natural swimming pool and well-crafted walkways along a nearby hillside. Breakfast and boat hire both go for $15. The lodge is on the Queenstown-Glenorchy bus route; see p630 for bus info.

Comfort Inn Melbourne Lodge (Map p610; ☎ 03-442 8431; www.mmlodge.co.nz; 35 Melbourne St; s/d from $75/115) Choose from cheaper rooms with shared bathrooms in Melbourne House or splash out a little more for an en-suite room at Melbourne Lodge next door.

Bella Vista (Map p610; ☎ 03-442 4468; www.bellavista motels.co.nz; 36 Robins Rd; d $150; ☎) Identical to the rest of Bella Vista's Kiwi empire – like all its siblings, clean and good value.

TOP END

Coronation Lodge (Map p610; ☎ 0800 420 777, 03-442 0860; www.coronationlodge.co.nz; 10 Coronation Dr; d $170; ▫ ☎) Right beside the Queenstown Gardens, this recently opened lodge has plush bed linen, cosy wooden floors, Turkish rugs and Sky TV. In a town that's somewhat lacking in good midrange accommodation, Coronation Lodge is highly recommended. Two larger rooms have kitchenettes.

Alexis Motor Lodge & Apartments (Map p610; ☎ 03-409 0052; www.alexisqueenstown.co.nz; 69 Frankton Rd; d $170; ▫ ☎) With energetic family owners, this modern hillside motel with self-contained units is an easy 10-minute walk to town along the lakefront. Molly the dog is always a dependable walking partner, and Louis the cat sometimes comes along too. Ask for an end unit with snap-happy views.

ourpick **Chalet Queenstown B&B** (Map p610; ☎ 0800 222 457, 03-442 7117; www.chalet.co.nz; 1 Dublin St; d $195; ☎) This recently renovated B&B has become the new standard for boutique accommodation in Queenstown. Perfectly appointed rooms sparkle with modern amenities like flat-screen TVs, art that stops you in your tracks and bed linen that will leave you laid up. Be sure to book well ahead so you can secure one of the rooms with a lake view – easily one of the best vistas in town.

Central Ridge Boutique Hotel (Map p610; ☎ 03-442 8832; www.centralridge.co.nz; 4 Sydney St; d incl breakfast $245-455) Visitors rave about the breakfasts, but there's plenty more to be effusive about, such as pre-dinner canapés with Central Otago wines, underfloor heating and spacious, modern bathrooms. With only 14 rooms here, you're guaranteed a winning way with personal service.

Earnslaw View Apartments (Map p610; ☎ 0800 226 652, 03-442 7629; www.earnslawviewapartments.co.nz; 21 Earnslaw Tce; d from $285; ▫ ☎) Thoroughly modern self-contained accommodation for the thoroughly modern self-contained family ($435 for up to six people). The stunning lake and mountain views have been around for much longer.

Dairy (Map p612; ☎ 0800 333 393, 03-442 5164; www. thedairy.co.nz; 10 Isle St; s/d incl breakfast $450/480; ▫ ☎) Once a corner store, the Dairy's now a luxury guest house with 13 rooms packed with classy touches like designer bed linen, silk cushions and luxurious mohair rugs. Rates also include freshly baked afternoon tea. From June to September three-night packages are great value for skiers (double $825 to $945).

Evergreen Lodge (Map p608; ☎ 03-442 6636; www. evergreenlodge.co.nz; 28 Evergreen Pl, Sunshine Bay; d $795; ▫ ☎) Handcrafted wooden furniture from a local Queenstown artisan combines with 21st-century accoutrements like DVD players and wireless internet in the four pristine rooms at this modern lodge. Add in a supremely private location with unfettered views of the Remarkables, complimentary beer and wine, and a sauna and gym, and you've got a very relaxing escape from Queenstown's international hoi polloi.

Eichardt's Private Hotel (Map p612; ☎ 03-441 0450; www.eichardtshotel.co.nz; cnr Marine Pde & Searle Lane; d $1425-1645) Originally opened in the 1860s, this reopened and restored boutique hotel enjoys an absolute lakefront location. Each of the five giant suites has a fireplace, lake views and a blend of antique and modern decor. King-sized beds, heated floors and lake-sized bath tubs provide the ideal welcome after a tough day cruising the vineyards of Central Otago.

Eating

Queenstown's town centre is peppered with busy eateries. Many target the tourist dollar, but dig a little deeper and you'll discover local favourites covering a surprising range of international cuisines. At the more popular places, it's wise to make a reservation for weekend dining.

RESTAURANTS

@Thai (Map p612; ☎ 03-442 3683; 3rd fl, 8 Church St; mains $15-25; ☺ noon-10pm) The title of best Thai in town is a hard-fought battle here in QT – and the winner is @Thai. Find the semi-hidden set of stairs and head on up for a great meal.

The pad Thai is worth writing home about and the *hor-mok* seafood red curry will blow your mind.

Winnies (Map p612; ☎ 03-442 8635; 1st fl, 7 The Mall; pizza $15-25; ☽ noon-late; ☎) Winnies' cool and sassy international team serve up a global array of pizzas with a Thai, Mexican or Moroccan accent. Occasional live music and DJs keep the energy levels up long after you've finished your last slice. Part-bar and part-restaurant, Winnies always seems busy – guess why.

our pick **Cow** (Map p612; ☎ 03-442 8588; Cow Lane; mains $18-30; ☽ noon-midnight) Tucked into a hidden corner of Cow Lane, this is a classic QT eatery. Housed in a former cow shed (hence the name of the restaurant and the street), the Cow hasn't changed its menu since 1976 – and is damn proud of it. Amazing pizzas, simple pasta and stellar garlic bread will leave you satisfied. The atmosphere is cramped with low-slung ceilings, a roaring fire, thick wooden tables and rustic candlelight.

Solero Vino (Map p612; ☎ 03-442 6082; 25 Beach St; mains $19-35; ☽ 11am-late) This tiny French restaurant is hard to find but impossible to forget. Exquisite food is presented in a simple and elegant style. Traditional fare such as escargot and salmon are cooked to perfection. If you're lucky, the soup of the day will be the gazpacho and you'll be in gastronomic nirvana.

Bella Cucina (Map p612; ☎ 03-442 6762; 6 Brecon St; mains $22-29; ☽ 6pm-late) A top-shelf Italian eatery has been long overdue in Queenstown – as of 2008 that role has been taken by this beautiful kitchen. Fresh pasta and risotto are highlights while the pizza is good for sharing. Beautiful, simple food done just right.

Gantley's (Map p608; ☎ 03-442 8999; Arthurs Point Rd; mains $30-40; ☽ 6.30pm-late) An atmospheric dining experience in a historic 1863 stone-and-timber house at Arthurs Point. The contemporary NZ cuisine and highly regarded (and award-collecting) wine list are worth the journey. Reservations are essential; a courtesy bus is run to and from town for à la carte diners.

Botswana Butchery (Map p612; ☎ 03-442 6994; Marine Pde; mains $30-50; ☽ noon-late) This stylish and new face on the local culinary scene is a breath of fresh air. Opulent and aesthetic interior design makes way for a wine list that rivals anywhere in town. The meals are a divine combination of seasonal vegetables augmenting prime cuts of beef, lamb, poultry and seafood. There is an emphasis upon taste in all avenues – whether that is the design of the interior, the creative plating or the elegant flavours that permeate the memorable meals.

Wai Waterfront Restaurant & Wine Bar (Map p612; ☎ 03-442 5969; Steamer Wharf, Beach St; mains $35-50; ☽ 11am-10pm) Small and intimate, Wai (meaning 'water' in Maori) is white-linen classy with lake and mountain views. It's known for lamb and seafood, and the Oyster Bar does the world's favourite bivalve in 17 different ways. The seven-course degustation menu ($115 without wine and $175 with wine) is a splurge-worthy opportunity for a great culinary adventure. Think about it seriously. It's actually less than you'll spend on another round of outdoor adventure activities, and will last a lot longer.

CAFES & QUICK EATS

Joe's Garage (Map p612; ☎ 03-442 5282; Searle Lane; mains $6-20; ☽ 7am-3pm) Joe's is the perennial favourite among locals looking for their morning coffee rescue. The hipster environment flies dangerously close to *too cool for school* but pulls back on the throttle before it's too late. Great coffee and fantastic brunchy food is all found at this locals' hang-out.

our pick **Patagonia** (Map p612; ☎ 03-442 9066; 50 Beach St; coffee & chocolate $5-7; ☽ 10am-10pm; ☎) Delicious hot chocolate, homemade choccies, and Queenstown's best ice cream. What more do you want? How about a lakefront location and free wi-fi? Patagonia's open until 10pm, so it's your best bet for a late-night coffee.

Vesta (Map p612; ☎ 03-442 5687; cnr Marine Pde & Earl St; mains $6-10; ☽ 10am-5pm Mon-Sat) Sometimes it's a good thing when you can't work out exactly what something is. In the case of Vesta, just examine the evidence: a gloriously overgrown 1920s-style garden, a gallery and gift shop specialising in NZ design, and a compact wee cafe serving coffee and cake just made for mid-afternoon recharging. To confuse things, Vesta is housed in Williams Cottage (p609), Queenstown's oldest home, and now an interesting museum.

Kappa Sushi Cafe (Map p612; ☎ 03-441 1423; Level 1, 36a The Mall; sushi $6-10, mains $13-29; ☽ noon-2.30pm Mon-Fri, 6pm-late Mon-Sat) Queenstown's best Japanese eatery is also its most casual. Scarily fresh tuna and salmon feature in good-value bento boxes for lunch. Later at night linger longer with excellent tempura and Japanese beer and sake. In summer watch the passing parade in the Mall from the upstairs deck.

Vudu Cafe (Map p612; ☎ 03-442 5357; 23 Beach St; breakfast $6-15, lunch & dinner $8-25; 🕑 8am-late; 🖳) This local favourite has been sorting out caffeine fixes for ages. Food-wise it boxes above its weight with great eggs, soup and a veggie lasagne that'll put you off meat forever. The funky surrounds, with local art on the walls, complete the scene.

Habebes (Map p612; ☎ 03-442 9861; btwn Beach & Shotover Sts; meals $7-12; 🕑 10am-5pm; 🕑) Super-healthy and decadently delicious. Salads and wraps are the go here – a recent relocation means they've expanded to have two tables – so dash and dine at the beach.

Fergburger (Map p612; ☎ 03-441 1232; 42 Shotover St; burgers $9-15; 🕑 9am-5am) Less of a burger joint and more of a rite of passage for every Queenstown visitor, Ferg serves up the best burgers in town till way past your bedtime. All tastes are catered for including vegetarians, fish lovers and, of course, carnivores. The burgers are huge and the atmosphere festive – this could very well be the best burger stop in all of Aotearoa.

Halo (Map p612; ☎ 03-441 1411; Camp St; mains $12-16; 🕑 7am-10pm) A stylish and sunny place that effortlessly blurs the line between breakfast, lunch and dinner. The breakfast burrito will set you up for a day's adventuring. Come back at night for a Caribbean jerk chicken burger and a glass of local wine. It's beside St James Church.

SELF-CATERING

Mediterranean Market (Map p610; ☎ 03-442 4161; cnr Gorge & Robins Rds; 🕑 8am-6.30pm Mon-Sat, 10am-6pm Sun) This is the place to fill up a basket for a lakeside picnic. There are fresh pastas, sauces, Asian cuisine, good local produce and a fantastic deli and bakery. Have coffee and cake at the attached cafe while you make up your mind.

Around the corner, the well-stocked **Freshchoice** (Map p610; 64 Gorge Rd; 🕑 7am-midnight) is Queenstown's big supermarket. In town, the **Alpine Supermarket** (Map p612; cnr Stanley & Shotover Sts; 🕑 8am-9pm Mon-Fri, 9am-9pm Sat & Sun) has most staples, and next door there's a handy bottle store.

Drinking

Drinking is almost a competitive sport in Queenstown, and there's a good range of options for after-dark carousing. Gone are

---

RIVER WATER OR PINOT NOIR? YOU CHOOSE

More gung-ho visitors to Queenstown might be happiest dangling off a giant rubber band, but as they're submerged in the icy Kawarau River, they'll be missing out on some of Central Otago's most interesting vineyards just up the road. A glass of the area's outstanding pinot noir, or a mouthful of river water? Mmm…tough choice.

On a spectacular river terrace near the Kawarau Bridge, AJ Hackett's original bungy partner Henry van Asch has set up the **Winehouse & Kitchen** (Map p608; ☎ 03-442 7310; www.winehouse.co.nz; mains $15-30; 🕑 10am-5pm). A beautifully restored wooden villa includes a garden cafe and the opportunity to try van Asch's Freefall and Rock Ferry wines, as well as his own van Asch label.

Almost opposite, a winding and scenic road leads to beautiful **Chard Farm** (Map p608; ☎ 03-442 6110; www.chardfarm.co.nz; 🕑 11am-5pm), and a further 700m along is **Gibbston Valley** (Map p608; ☎ 03-442 6910; www.gvwines.co.nz), the area's largest wine producer. Try its pinot noir and take a tour of the impressive wine cave. There are also a 'cheesery' and a restaurant.

A further 4km along SH6, **Peregrine** (Map p608; ☎ 03-442 4000; www.peregrinewines.co.nz; 🕑 10am-5pm) produces excellent sauvignon blanc, pinot noir and pinot gris, and hosts occasional outdoor concerts during summer, sometimes featuring international names.

Further west near the shores of Lake Hayes, the **Amisfield Winery & Bistro** (Map p608; ☎ 03-442 0556; www.amisfield.co.nz; small plates $16.50; 🕑 11.30am-8pm Tue-Sun) is a regular winner of *Cuisine* magazine's Best NZ Winery Restaurant gong. The highly regarded eatery serves tapas-sized plates perfect for sharing with a few friends on the sunny deck, and Amisfield's pinot noir has been awarded internationally.

Ask at the Queenstown i-SITE for maps and information about touring the Gibbston Valley. Alternatively, visit www.gibbstonvalley.co.nz for more info about this compact wine-growing area with its own unique microclimate. You could also join a wine tour (p618) to keep safe.

QUEENSTOWN & WANAKA

the days of the all-night party; bars now shut promptly at 4am.

Bardeaux (Map p612; ☎ 03-442 8284; Eureka Arcade, 11 The Mall; ☺ 6pm-4am) Down a narrow alleyway, this small, low-key wine bar is all class. Under a low ceiling await plush leather armchairs and a fireplace made from Central Otago's iconic schist rock. No beanies, rugby jerseys or work boots allowed.

Monty's (Map p612; ☎ 03-441 1081; Church St; ☺ 11am-late) On warm summer days the patio at Monty's is prime real estate. Same goes for the fire inside when the snow flies. With Monteith's beer on tap, this is a great place for a quiet drink with a predominantly local crowd. Most nights the band cranks up and gets the crowd tapping their feet as they down a few.

Pub on Wharf (Map p612; ☎ 03-441 2155; Steamer Wharf; ☺ 10.30am-late) The newest pub in town is also one if its most stylish. Ubercool interior design is shoved to the fore with handsome woodwork, lighting fit for a hipster hideaway and animal heads on the wall to remind you you're still in NZ. Mac's beer on tap, scrummy nibbles and a decent wine list make this a great place to settle in for the evening.

Surreal (Map p612; ☎ 03-441 8492; 7 Rees St; ☺ 11am-late) With funky music, low lighting and red-velvet booths, this is a private spot for a quiet drink – until later in the evening when things kick off and the dance floor comes to life. Happy hour from 10pm.

Winnies (Map p612; ☎ 03-442 8635; 1st fl, 7 The Mall; ☺ noon-late; ☺) A deservedly popular place with a laid-back ambience, retractable roof, pool table and patio. Daily happy hour from 9pm brings the crowds and the atmosphere keeps 'em around.

Minibar (Map p612; ☎ 03-441 3212; Eureka Arcade, 11 The Mall; ☺ 4pm-4am) Beer, beer and more beer. More than 100 local and international beers are poured in this compact space. A cool name for a cool bar, oozing with style.

Buffalo Club (Map p612; ☎ 03-442 4144; 8 Brecon St; ☺ 3pm-late) Lit by candles and an enormous campfire in the middle of the room, this is a popular after-work hang-out. Pool tables and sports on the big-screen TV make it a low-key spot to kick off the night. Happy hour from 5pm.

Barmuda (Map p612; ☎ 03-442 7300; Searle Lane; ☺ 3pm-3am) A huge open fire makes Barmuda's

atmospheric courtyard the place to be in cooler weather. In summer live jazz on Friday and Saturday nights is sometimes on the cards.

Barup (Map p612; ☎ 03-442 7067; cnr Searle Lane & Eureka Arcade; ☺ 5pm-4am) Take the stairs up (no surprises there…) to this intimate cocktail bar, which is removed from the ground-level hustle and bustle downstairs around Eureka Lane.

Entertainment

Pick up the *Source* (www.thesourceonline .com), a free weekly flyer with a gig guide and events listings. Live music and clubbing are a nightly affair and most Queenstown venues stay open until the wee hours. Most DJ and live-music gigs are free, though you will encounter inexpensive cover charges in some nightclubs.

LIVE MUSIC

Dux de Lux (Map p612; ☎ 03-442 9688; 14 Church St) Lots of live bands and DJs with everything from reggae to drum 'n' bass.

Buffalo Club (Map p612; ☎ 03-442 4144; 8 Brecon St) DJs spin nightly with a top-forty flavour and a raucous atmosphere.

Monty's (Map p612; ☎ 03-441 1081; Church St) On Wednesday to Saturday nights a live cover band will be strumming out the hits and the singalongs.

Pig & Whistle (Map p612; ☎ 03-442 9055; 41 Ballarat St) Covers bands playing songs you can unashamedly sing along to.

NIGHTCLUBS

Surreal (Map p612; ☎ 03-441 8492; 7 Rees St) DJs with house, retro, open-mic and the odd break beat thrown in.

Subculture (Map p612; ☎ 03-442 7685; downstairs 12-14 Church St) Skilful locals and out-of-towners toy with turntables to make drum 'n' bass, hip-hop, dub and reggae noises that get the crowds moving.

Debajo (Map p612; ☎ 03-442 6099; Cow Lane) The perennial end-of-night boogie spot – house and big-beat gets the dance floor heaving till closing time.

Tardis Bar (Map p612; ☎ 03-441 8397; Skyline Arcade, 20 Cow Lane) A good dance bar with regular DJs playing hip-hop, dancehall and dub. Like Dr Who's phone booth, it's surprisingly roomy inside.

Revolver Bar (Map p612; ☎ 03-441 8911; 53 Shotover St) Occasionally hosts gigs from well-known NZ bands and solo artists.

HAKA
Kiwi Haka (Map p610; ☎ 03-441 0101; www.skyline.co.nz; Brecon St; adult/child incl gondola $53/27; ☼ from 5.30pm) To witness traditional Maori dancing and singing, come watch this group at the top of the gondola. There are multiple 30-minute shows nightly, but bookings are essential.

CINEMA
Reading Cinemas (Map p612; ☎ 03-442 9990; www.readingcinemas.co.nz; 11 The Mall; adult/child $15.50/10.50) Mainly Hollywood blockbusters, but occasional art-house and Kiwi flicks too.

Shopping
Queenstown is a good place to shop for souvenirs and gifts. Start exploring and you're likely to discover some unusual goods. Lots of shops specialise in outdoor and adventure gear; prices are competitive and there's a good range. Begin your shopping along the Mall, Shotover St and Beach St. Also try the area around Church Lane joining Church St and Earl St for an expanding array of galleries, or follow your nose to **Central Otago Wine Experience** (Map p612; ☎ 03-409 2226; www.winetastes.com; 14 Beach St; ☼ 10am-10pm) to understand what makes the local wines special.

CLOTHING
Detour (Map p612; ☎ 03-442 7918; O'Connell's Mall) The place to go for fashion-forward urban hipsters and style bunnies looking for the latest cool threads.

rookies (Map p612; ☎ 03-442 8153; 49 Beach St) If you forgot the kids' snowsuits, rent or buy clothes from rookies to keep them cosy. Designer kids clobber for warmer seasons is also available.

OUTDOOR GEAR
Outside Sports (Map p612; ☎ 03-441 0074; 32 Shotover St) Long-standing outdoor outfitters with plenty of gear to get you ready for camping, hiking, skiing or climbing.

Kathmandu (Map p612; ☎ 03-409 0880; 88 Beach St) A well-known and good-value chain with

regular sales making things even cheaper. Join its 'Summit Club' for extra discounts.

DESIGN, MUSIC & ART
Vesta (Map p612; ☎ 03-442 5687; cnr Marine Pde & Earl St) In the historic surroundings of Williams Cottage, this shop has contemporary housewares, jewellery, gift cards, baby clothes, perfumes and accessories. Most of it is designed and made in NZ.

Kapa (Map p612; ☎ 03-442 4401; 29 Rees St) Has an array of quirky and eclectic NZ design infused with a healthy dose of contemporary Maori culture.

Koha (Map p612; ☎ 03-442 8887; 18 Beach St) Meaning 'gift' in Maori, Koha sells authentic and unique gifts. Everything for sale here is from NZ including jewellery, beauty products and designer clothing.

toi o tahuna (Map p612; ☎ 03-409 0787; Church Lane) Exclusively NZ art, with around half the work from contemporary Maori artists. Ask gallery owner Mark Moran for the free 'Galleries & Artist Studios in the Wakatipu' guide – proof that Queenstown's definitely about more than leaping off bridges wearing a giant rubber band.

Arts & crafts market (Map p612; www.marketplace.net.nz; ☼ 9am-4.30pm Nov-Apr, 10am-3.30pm May-Oct) On Saturdays visit this creative market at Earnslaw Park on the lakefront beside Steamer Wharf.

Getting There & Away
AIR
Air New Zealand (Map p612; ☎ 0800 737 000, 03-441 1900; www.airnz.co.nz; 8 Church St) has direct daily flights between Queenstown and Auckland (from $139), Wellington (from $149) and Christchurch (from $89) with connections

---

OVERHEARD #3

'On the road to Kingston there are several signs warning of Road Slumps. It's good fun to tell the passengers that these are some seldom-seen native animal. The truth is, it's nothing more than a pothole.' – unnamed Queenstown tour guide

to Wanaka. **Jetstar** (☎ 0800 800 995; www.jetstar. com) has direct daily flights to Auckland (from $139) and Christchurch (from $100).

BUS

Book seats for **InterCity** (☎ 03-442 4100; www.inter city.co.nz) trips in the i-SITE. It offers daily bus services from Queenstown to Christchurch ($50), Te Anau ($30), Milford Sound ($80), Dunedin ($40) and Invercargill ($45), plus a daily West Coast service to the glaciers ($60) via Wanaka ($17) and Haast Township ($36). Buses leave from the Athol St bus terminal (Map p612). Note that some buses may be branded Newmans.

Naked Bus (www.nakedbus.com) travels to the West Coast, Te Anau, Christchurch, Dunedin and Invercargill.

The **Bottom Bus** (www.bottombus.co.nz) does a loop service around the south of the South Island (see p667). Book at the **Info & Track Centre** (Map p612; ☎ 03-442 9708; 37 Shotover St).

Shuttles charge around $20 to $25 to Wanaka, $40 to Dunedin, $30 to Te Anau and $50 to Christchurch. Book at i-SITE.
Atomic Shuttles (☎ 03-349 0697; www.atomictravel. co.nz) Travels to Wanaka, Christchurch, Dunedin, Greymouth and Invercargill.
Catch-a-Bus (☎ 03-479 9960) Heads to Dunedin.
Wanaka Connexions (☎ 03-443 9122; www.time2. co.nz) Offers regular services to Wanaka.

TRAMPERS' & SKIERS' TRANSPORT
Backpacker Express at the **Info & Track Centre** (Map p612; ☎ 03-442 9708; www.infotrack.co.nz; 37 Shotover St) arranges transport to and from the Routeburn, Greenstone, Caples and Rees-Dart Tracks, all via Glenorchy. The service costs $40 (Queenstown to trailhead), and lots of other transport options are available. **Kiwi Discovery** (Map p612; ☎ 0800 505 504, 03-442 7340; www. kiwidiscovery.com; 37 Camp St) can also arrange transport to the tracks.

Bus services between Queenstown and Milford Sound via Te Anau can be used for track transport. See p650 for information on the tramper-servicing company TrackNet.

For the ski slopes, if you pre-buy your lift ticket to the Remarkables, you are able to catch the ski shuttle for free from the Station (Map p612) – the shuttle to Coronet Peak will cost you $10. The bus to Cardrona is $38 and Treble Cone is $45. Most companies offer transport and lift deals and special rates for children:

Gravity Action (Map p612; ☎ 03-442 5277; 19 Shotover St)
Info & Track Centre (Map p612; ☎ 03-442 9708; www.infotrack.co.nz; 37 Shotover St) Travels to Cardrona only.
Kiwi Discovery (Map p612; ☎ 0800 505 504, 03-442 7340; www.kiwidiscovery.com; 37 Camp St)
Snowrental (Map p612; ☎ 03-442 4187; 39 Camp St)

Getting Around
TO/FROM THE AIRPORT
Queenstown Airport (Map p608; ☎ 03-450 9031; www. queenstownairport.co.nz; Frankton) is 8km east of town.
Super Shuttle (☎ 0800 748 885; www.supershuttle.co.nz) picks up and drops off in Queenstown (from $15). **Connectabus** (Map p612; ☎ 03-441 4471; www. connectabus.com; cnr Beach & Camp Sts) runs to the airport ($6) hourly from 6.30am to 10.20pm.
Alpine Taxis (☎ 03-442 6666) or **Queenstown Taxis** (☎ 03-442 7788) charge around $25.

PUBLIC TRANSPORT
Connnectabus (☎ 03-441 4471; www.connectabus.com) has three colour-coded routes. Catch the blue route for accommodation in Fernhill ($6) and the red or green routes for accommodation in Frankton ($6). The green route continues on to Lake Hayes ($7) and Arrowtown ($8). A day pass ($19) allows travel on the entire network. Pick up a route map and timetable from the i-SITE. Buses leave from the corner of Beach and Camp Sts.

ARROWTOWN
pop 2400
Beloved by day-trippers from Queenstown, exceedingly quaint Arrowtown sprang up in the 1860s following the discovery of gold in the Arrow River. Today the town retains more than 60 of its original wooden and stone buildings, and has pretty, tree-lined avenues, excellent galleries and an expanding array of fashionable shopping opportunities.

The only gold being flaunted these days is on credit cards and, surrounded by a bonanza of daytime tourists, you might grow wary of the quaint historical ambience. Instead take advantage of improved public transport to the town, and use it as a base for exploring Queenstown and the wider region. That way you can enjoy Arrowtown's history, charm and excellent restaurants after dark when the tour buses have decamped back to Queenstown.

QUEENSTOWN & WANAKA

Sights & Activities

The **Arrowtown visitor information centre** (☎ 03-442 1824; www.arrowtown.com; 49 Buckingham St; ☹ 8.30am-5pm) shares premises with the **Lake District Museum and Gallery** (www.museumqueens town.com; adult/child $7/1; ☹ 8.30am-5pm), which has exhibits on the gold-rush era. Younger travellers will enjoy the Museum Fun Pack ($5), which includes activity sheets, museum treasure hunts, stickers and a few flecks of gold.

Arrowtown has NZ's best example of a gold-era **Chinese settlement** (admission by gold coin donation; ☹ 24hr). Interpretive signs explain the lives of Chinese 'diggers' during and after the gold rush, while restored huts and shops make the story more tangible. Subjected to significant racism, the Chinese often had little choice but to rework old tailings rather than seek new claims. The Chinese settlement is off Buckingham St.

Try your luck **gold panning** on the Arrow River. Rent pans from the visitor information centre ($3) and head to the northern edge of town. This is also a good spot for **walking**. Pick up *Arrowtown Area Walks* (free) from the visitor information centre; you'll find routes and history on walks to **Macetown** (14km, seven hours) and on **Tobins Track** (one hour).

Arrowtown Golf Course (☎ 03-442 1719; www.arrow town.nzgolf.net; green fees $55, club hire $30) is picturesque and challenging. Flasher golfers should head to **Millbrook Golf Course** (☎ 03-441 7010; www. millbrook.co.nz; Malaghans Rd; green fees $165, club hire $55), and in January the **New Zealand Golf Open** (www. nzga.co.nz) is held at the private 'Hills' course of NZ retail magnate Michael Hill. Queenstown and Arrowtown are very busy on weekends. Book ahead.

Sleeping

Arrowtown has accommodation from budget to top end, but during summer rooms fill up fast.

Poplar Lodge (☎ 03-442 1466; www.poplarlodge. co.nz; 4 Merioneth St; dm/s/d $27/60/65; ☺) Budget accommodation options are limited in A-town, but this is your best bet. A converted house, Poplar has a cosy feel and is off the bus-bound tourist trail. A couple of self-contained units ($95 to $120) are also available.

Arrowtown Holiday Park (☎ 03-442 1876; www. arrowtownholidaypark.co.nz; 11 Suffolk St; sites $34, d $60-130) Mountain views come as standard, even if you're paying more for the flash new studio units. Amenities blocks are equally pristine.

Viking Lodge (☎ 03-442 1765; www.vikinglodge.co.nz; 21 Inverness Cres; d $95-150; ☻) These older A-frame units have a comfortable and family-friendly stamp. If the kids still have energy after a day's travelling, wear them out even more in the swimming pool or on the playground.

Shades (☎ 03-442 1613; www.shadesofarrowtown. co.nz; cnr Buckingham & Merioneth Sts; d $100-150) A garden setting gives these bungalow-style cottages a relaxed air. Family units ($175) are good value if you're travelling with the whole clan.

Old Villa Homestay B&B (☎ 03-442 1682; www.arrow townoldvilla.co.nz; 13 Anglesea St; s/d $110/160) Freshly baked bread and homemade preserves welcome visitors to this heritage-style villa with a garden just made for summer barbecues. Two en-suite double rooms come trimmed with fresh sprigs of lavender. One of the rooms has an additional single bed if you've got an extra travelling companion.

Arrowtown Lodge (☎ 03-442 1101; www.arrowtown lodge.co.nz; 7 Anglesea St; d incl breakfast $200; ☐ ☺) From the outside, the guest rooms look like heritage cottages, but inside they're cosy and modern. The family owners are super-friendly and the breakfast is hearty.

Millbrook (☎ 0800 800 604, 03-441 7000; www.mill brook.co.nz; Malaghans Rd; d $435-715; ☐ ☺ ☻) Just outside Arrowtown, this enormous resort is a town unto itself. At the end of the day enjoy a massage in the spa, and take your pick from four restaurants.

Eating

For its size, Arrowtown has a good range of restaurants.

Arrowtown Bakery (☎ 03-442 1587; Buckingham St; gourmet pies $5; ☹ 7am-7pm) Once the Arrowtown Bakery has lured you with yummy aromas, you'll be powerless. We can recommend the smoked fish or satay chicken pies. Don't blame us if you order a second.

Café Mondo (☎ 03-442 0227; Ballarat Arcade, Buckingham St; breakfast $7-15, lunch & dinner $12-25; ☹ 8am-late; ☐) In a courtyard, this place is an excellent spot for a relaxed breakfast. Have coffee and a snack if you're in a hurry, or linger with a wine from a range of local tipples. There's a good kids' menu, too.

Stables (☎ 03-442 1818; 28 Buckingham St; mains $15-32; ☹ 11am-9pm) With courtyard tables adjoining a grassy square, Stables is a good spot to share a tasting platter ($29.50) with your closest travelling companion. Have a local Brewski beer from Wanaka, or a glass of Central Otago wine. Later at night, step inside the 1860s stone building for a more intimate dining experience.

Pesto (☎ 03-442 0885; 18 Buckingham St; mains $17-30; ⏰ 5pm-late) This candlelit restaurant serves Italian food with a contemporary spin. It's Saffron's slightly rowdier, younger, family-friendly sibling, and the culinary expectations are kept high with good pasta and gourmet pizzas.

Bonjour Cafe (☎ 03-409 8946; Ramshaw Lane; mains $18-30; ⏰ 8.30am-late) Authentic French cuisine direct from the continent. Come for breakfast and tuck into one of the 17 different crepe options – you'll struggle to choose, that we guarantee. Come back for dinner to treat yourself to cheese fondue.

Saffron (☎ 03-442 0131; 18 Buckingham St; lunch $12-28, dinner $30-50; ⏰ noon-late) One of the South Island's best restaurants, Saffron has grown-up food including duck cassoulet and a trio of curries featuring pork, duck and king prawns. The ambience is more sophisticated than Pesto's.

Drinking

Blue Door (☎ 03-442 0415; 18 Buckingham St; ⏰ 3pm-late) Hidden away behind a tricky-to-find, yet perfectly appropriate, blue door. The low ceilings, low light and abundant candles make for an intimate quaffing location. Blue Door has a formidable wine list and enough rustic ambience to keep you entertained for the evening.

Tap (☎ 03-442 1860; 51 Buckingham St; ⏰ 11am-late) The Tap dates back to the gold rush. Inside, there are wines, a pool table, pub grub and liquid gold on tap. Sit outside and slow down to Arrowtown's languid pace.

New Orleans Hotel (☎ 03-442 1860; 51 Buckingham St; ⏰ 11am-late) With looks transplanted more from the Wild West than the Deep South, this heritage pub is a good escape from Arrowtown's growing array of expensive designer shops.

Entertainment

Dorothy Browns (☎ 03-442 1964; www.dorothybrowns.com; Ballarat Arcade, Buckingham St; adult/child/student $18/6.50/12) This is what a cinema should be. Ultra-comfortable seating with the option to cuddle with your neighbour. Fine wine and

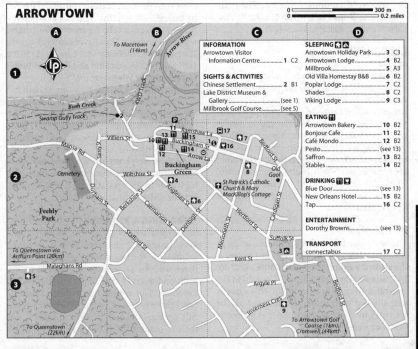

ARROWTOWN

INFORMATION		
Arrowtown Visitor Information Centre	**1**	C2
SIGHTS & ACTIVITIES		
Chinese Settlement	**2**	B1
Lake District Museum & Gallery	(see 1)	
Millbrook Golf Course	(see 5)	
SLEEPING		
Arrowtown Holiday Park	**3**	C3
Arrowtown Lodge	**4**	B2
Millbrook	**5**	A3
Old Villa Homestay B&B	**6**	B2
Poplar Lodge	**7**	C2
Shades	**8**	C2
Viking Lodge	**9**	C3
EATING		
Arrowtown Bakery	**10**	B2
Bonjour Cafe	**11**	B2
Café Mondo	**12**	B2
Pesto	(see 13)	
Saffron	**13**	B2
Stables	**14**	B2
DRINKING		
Blue Door	(see 13)	
New Orleans Hotel	**15**	B2
Tap	**16**	C2
ENTERTAINMENT		
Dorothy Browns	(see 13)	
TRANSPORT		
connectabus	**17**	C2

cheese boards are available to accompany the mostly art-house films on offer. Every screening has an intermission – a perfect opportunity to tuck into a tub of gourmet ice cream.

Getting There & Away

From Queenstown, **connectabus** (☎ 03-441 4471; www.connectabus.com) runs regular services (7.15am to 10pm) on its green route to Arrowtown (adult/child $8/5). If you're planning a day trip to Arrowtown, a day pass (adult/child $19/9.50) is a little cheaper. The bus also stops at Millbrook.

The **Double-Decker Bus Tour** (☎ 03-441 4421; $48) does a three-hour round-trip tour to Arrowtown twice daily. **Arrowtown Scenic Bus** (☎ 03-442 1900; www.arrowtownbus.co.nz) has three services daily (return $25).

AROUND ARROWTOWN

Fourteen kilometres north of Arrowtown lies **Macetown**, a ghost town reached via a rugged, flood-prone road (the original miners' wagon track), which crosses the Arrow River more than 25 times. Don't even think about taking the rental car here – instead four-hour trips are made from Queenstown by 4WD vehicle, with gold panning included. The main operator is **Nomad Safaris** (☎ 03-442 6699; www. nomadsafaris.co.nz; adult/child from $149/75).

GLENORCHY

pop 220

Set in achingly beautiful surroundings, postage-stamp-sized Glenorchy is the perfect low-key antidote to the hype and bustle of Queenstown. An expanding range of adventure operators will get you active on the lake and in nearby mountain valleys by kayak, horse or jetboat, but if you prefer to strike out on two legs, tiny Kinloch just across the lake is the starting point for some of the South Island's finest tramps. Glenorchy lies at the head of Lake Wakatipu, a scenic 40-minute (68km) drive northwest from Queenstown.

Information

The best place for local information, updated weather, track information and hut passes is the **Glenorchy visitor information centre** (☎ 03-409 2049; www.glenorchy-nz.co.nz; Oban St). Located in the general store as you enter town, this place is well stocked with information about all the activities in the area. Its website is an excellent resource.

Also check out the **Destination Glenorchy** (Map p612; ☎ 03-441 3003; 39 Camp St) booking office in Queenstown, and see www.glenorchy.com.

There is a petrol station in Glenorchy, but you'd be wise to fill up with cheaper fuel before you leave Queenstown.

Activities

Almost all organised activities offer shuttles to and from Queenstown for a small surcharge.

TRAMPING & SCENIC DRIVING

The DOC leaflet *Glenorchy Walkway* (free) details an easy waterside walk around the outskirts of town that's pretty but not thrilling. For something more demanding, pick up *Great Wilderness Walks* (free) from the visitor information centre. It's got tramps from two hours to two days, taking in Routeburn Valley, Lake Sylvan, Dart River and Lake Rere. For track snacks or meals, stock up on groceries in Queenstown.

Those with sturdy wheels can explore the superb valleys north of Glenorchy. **Paradise** lies 15km northwest of town, just before the start of the Dart Track. Keep your expectations low: Paradise is just a paddock, but the gravel road there runs through beautiful farmland fringed by majestic mountains. You can also explore the Rees Valley or take the road to Routeburn, which goes via the Dart River Bridge. Near the start of the Routeburn Track in Mt Aspiring National Park is a day hut and the short **Double Barrel** and **Lake Sylvan** tramps.

If you'd rather just be a passenger, you can visit the Rees Valley with **Mountainland Rovers** (☎ 03-441 1323; www.mountainlandrovers.co.nz; 37 Mull St; adult/child from $109/60), which runs 4WD tours into the remote wilderness. It also picks up from Queenstown.

Rural Discovery Tours (☎ 0800 738 687; www.rdtours. co.nz; adult/child $180/90) runs half-day tours of a high country sheep station in a remote valley between Mts Earnslaw and Alfred.

JETBOATING & KAYAKING

Dart River Safaris (☎ 0800 327 8538, 03-442 9992; www. dartriver.co.nz; Mull St; adult/child $199/99) journeys by jetboat into the heart of the spectacular Dart River wilderness, followed by a short nature walk and a 4WD trip down a back road to Paradise. The round trip from Glenorchy takes three hours. A longer 2½-hour jetboat ride up the Dart (adult/child $229/129) ups the excitement level, and you can combine a jetboat ride with a river descent in an inflatable three-seater 'funyak' (adult/child $279/179); from Glenorchy it's seven hours return. For all trips add a couple of hours if you're departing from Queenstown.

Kayak Kinloch (☎ 03-442 4900; www.kayakkinloch. co.nz; adult $40-80, child $35-50) runs excellent guided trips exploring the lake. Trips depart from Queenstown, Glenorchy or Kinloch.

OTHER ACTIVITIES

For horsey types, **Dart Stables** (☎ 0800 474 3464, 03-442 5688; www.dartstables.com; Coll St) offers a two-hour ride ($145ff), a full-day trot ($305) and a 1½-hour Ride of the Rings trip ($165) for Hobbitty types. If you're really keen, consider the overnight two-day trek with a sleepover in Paradise ($595).

High Country Horses (☎ 0508 595 959, 03-442 9915; www.high-country-horses.co.nz) also runs two-hour rides ($105) and full-day rides ($205).

For all horse-riding trips add a couple of hours if starting in Queenstown.

Sleeping & Eating

At the base of the Kinloch Lodge there's a DOC campsite ($7), which has basic lakeside facilities.

Glenorchy Holiday Park (☎ 03-441 0303; www. glenorchy-nz.co.nz; 2 Oban St; unpowered/powered sites $20/25, dm/cabins $20/45) Set up camp in a field surrounded by basic cabins and handy barbecues. Out front is a small shop and the handy Glenorchy Visitor Information Centre.

Glenorchy Hotel (☎ 03-442 9902; www.glenorchynz. com; Mull St; dm $30, d $90-105; 🛜) Attached to a pub, the rooms here are surprisingly comfy. The backpacker unit is bright and basic and a popular base for returning trampers.

our pick **Kinloch Lodge** (Map p608; ☎ 03-442 4900; www.kinlochlodge.co.nz; Kinloch Rd; dm $30-33, d $80-120, r $175-195; 🖳) Across Lake Wakatipu from Glenorchy, this excellent retreat is a great place to unwind or prepare for a tramp. Rooms in the bunkhouse are comfy and colourful, with an outdoor hot tub and an indoor DVD-packed lounge, both just right for putting your feet up after a long tramp. The 19th-century Heritage Rooms are small but plusher. A cafe, a bar and a good restaurant (mains $15 to $31, open 8am to 8pm) are onsite, and if you're eating outside, look forward

to stunning lake views and the attention of maybe the South Island's friendliest dogs. Kinloch is a 26km drive from Glenorchy, or you can organise a five-minute boat ride ($15) across the lake. Kinloch Lodge can also arrange track transfers to various trailheads. Even if you're not a tramping type, it's worth staying at least a night to soak up the relaxed ambience.

Mt Earnslaw Motels (☎ 03-442 6993; mtearnslaw@ xtra.co.nz; Mull St; d $110; 🛜) This cute row of units is older from the outside but redone inside, creating cosy, well-priced rooms with big, comfy recliners, a small kitchen and an enormous bed.

Glenorchy Lodge (☎ 03-442 9968; wakatipu@xtra. co.nz; Mull St; d $120-140; 🛜) Tidy yet tiny rooms live upstairs from this central-as pub. Some rooms have loft-style ceilings and some have en suites – all have great views. Take in the serenity from private balconies before retiring downstairs to Foxy's Café for excellent coffee.

Glenorchy Lake House (☎ 03-442 7084; www. glenorchylakehouse.co.nz; Mull St; d $345-400) Newly opened in late 2007, the three rooms at this luxury lakefront B&B feature Egyptian cotton sheets, flat-screen TVs and luxury toiletries. Good luck tearing yourself away from the inner glories to get active out and about in the Wakatipu area. Once you return, recharge in the spa or with a massage.

Blanket Bay (Map p608; ☎ 03-442 9442; www.blanket bay.com; Glenorchy Rd; r $1450-2750; 🖳 🛜 🍴) An excessively discreet world-class resort that's a home away from home for the rich and famous. This alpine lodge is all native timber and local schist stone, and boasts stunning views. Blanket Bay is multi-award-winning and a firm favourite of the well heeled – whether they are Hollywood A-listers, development demi-gods or regular folk who aren't afraid to spend up large for the stay of their lives.

our pick **Glenorchy Café** (☎ 03-442 9958; Mull St; breakfast & lunch mains $10-15, pizza $20; 🕑 8am-late May-Oct, dinner Nov-Apr) With a reputation extending beyond little old GY, the Glenorchy Café is an institution oozing cool and natural style. The portions are as big as the surrounding peaks, and the coffee has powered many a mountain mission. Perennial favourites like pizza and breakfast stacks keep locals coming back time after time. Sit among the shadow of the peaks in the back garden – you'll struggle to leave.

Getting There & Away

With sweeping vistas and gem-coloured waters, the sealed Glenorchy to Queenstown Rd is wonderfully scenic. Its constant hills are a killer for cyclists. Pick up the *Queenstown to Glenorchy Road* leaflet from the Queenstown i-SITE for points of interest along the way.

Backpacker Express at the **Info & Track Centre** (Map p612; ☎ 03-442 9708; www.infotrack.co.nz; 37 Shotover St) provides transport to Glenorchy from Queenstown (adult/child $20/15). It will also drop you off (and pick you up) from the Routeburn and Greenstone Tracks.

LAKE WAKATIPU REGION

The mountainous region at the northern head of Lake Wakatipu has some gorgeous, remote scenery, best viewed while tramping along the famous Routeburn and lesser-known Greenstone, Caples and Rees-Dart Tracks. For shorter tracks, see the DOC brochure *Lake Wakatipu Walks and Trails* ($1). Glenorchy is a convenient base for all these tramps.

Ultimate Hikes (☎ 03-442 8200; www.ultimatehikes. co.nz) has a three-day guided tramp on the Routeburn ($1100/1240 low/high season); a six-day Grand Traverse ($1525/1725), combining walks on the Routeburn and Greenstone Tracks; and a one-day Routeburn Encounter ($165), which is available from mid-October to April. All prices include return transport, accommodation and all meals.

Track Information

For details of accommodation, transport to and from all trailheads and DOC visitor information centres, see Queenstown (p609) and Te Anau (p644).

DOC staff advise on maps and sell hut and Great Walks passes; before setting out, it's essential that you contact them for up-to-date track conditions. It's also advised that you book your intentions, and but be sure to let DOC know when you return. For more details on all these tracks see Lonely Planet's *Tramping in New Zealand*.

Routeburn Track

Passing through a huge variety of landscapes with fantastic views, the three- to four-day Routeburn Track is one of the most popular

rainforest/subalpine tracks in NZ. Increased pressure on the track has necessitated the introduction of a booking system; reservations are required throughout the main season (October to April), either through DOC visitor information centres, or online via great walksbooking@doc.govt.nz or www.doc.govt. nz. The **Great Walks huts pass** (per night adult/child $45/free) allows you to stay at Routeburn Flats Hut, Routeburn Falls Hut, Mackenzie Hut and Howden Hut; various 'family' passes are also available. A **camping pass** (per night adult/child $15/free) allows you to pitch a tent only at Routeburn Flats and Lake Mackenzie.

Outside the main season, passes are still required; huts cost $15/free per adult/child per night. Camping is $5/free in the off season. Note that the Routeburn Track is often closed by snow in winter and stretches of the track are very exposed and dangerous in bad weather; always check conditions with DOC.

There are car parks at the Divide and Glenorchy ends of the Routeburn, but they're unattended, so don't leave any valuables in your car.

The track can be started from either end. Many people travelling from Queenstown try to reach the Divide in time to catch the bus to Milford and connect with a cruise on the sound. En route, you'll take in breathtaking views from Harris Saddle and the top of nearby Conical Hill, from where you can see waves breaking at Martins Bay. From Key Summit, there are panoramic views of the Hollyford Valley and the Eglinton and Greenstone River Valleys.

Estimated walking times:

Route	Time
Routeburn Shelter to Flats Hut	1½-2½hr
Flats Hut to Falls Hut	1-1½hr
Falls Hut to Mackenzie Hut	4½-6hr
Mackenzie Hut to Howden Hut	3-4hr
Howden Hut to the Divide	1-1½hr

Greenstone & Caples Tracks

Following meandering rivers through lush, peaceful valleys, these two tracks form a loop that many trampers stretch out into a moderate four- or five-day tramp. Basic huts en route are Mid Caples, Upper Caples, McKellar and Greenstone. All are $15/5 per adult/child (11 to 17 years) per night, and Backcountry Hut Passes must be purchased in advance.

ROUTEBURN, GREENSTONE & CAPLES TRACKS

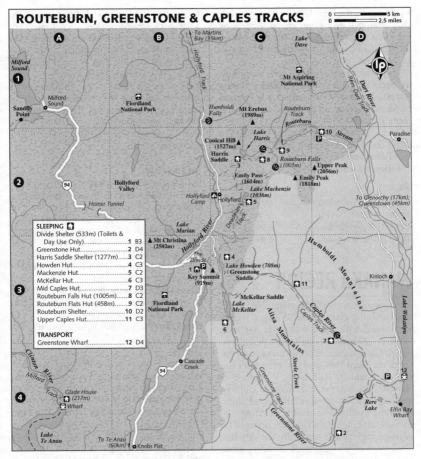

SLEEPING
Divide Shelter (533m) (Toilets & Day Use Only)......................1	B3
Greenstone Hut......................2	D4
Harris Saddle Shelter (1277m)......3	C2
Howden Hut......................4	C3
Mackenzie Hut......................5	C2
McKellar Hut......................6	C3
Mid Caples Hut......................7	D3
Routeburn Falls Hut (1005m)......8	C3
Routeburn Flats Hut (458m)......9	C2
Routeburn Shelter..............10	D2
Upper Caples Hut...............11	C3

TRANSPORT
Greenstone Wharf..............12	D4

You can camp (free) but not on private land; check with DOC for where not to pitch your tent. Both tracks meet up with the Routeburn Track; you can either follow its tail end to the Divide or (if you've prebooked) pursue it back to Glenorchy.

From McKellar Hut you can tramp two or three hours to Howden Hut on the Routeburn Track (you'll need to book this hut from October to April), which is an hour from the Divide.

Access to the Greenstone and Caples Tracks is from Greenstone Wharf; nearby you'll find unattended parking. The road from Kinloch to Greenstone Wharf is unsealed and rough; during the summer season **Backpacker Express** (☎ 03-442 9939) and Kinloch Lodge (p629) usually run a boat across the lake from Glenorchy.

Estimated walking times:

Route	Time
Greenstone Wharf to Mid Caples Hut	3hr
Mid Caples Hut to Upper Caples Hut	2-3hr
Upper Caples Hut to McKellar Hut	5-8hr
McKellar Hut to Greenstone Hut	5-7hr
Greenstone Hut to Greenstone Wharf	4-6hr

Rees-Dart Track

This is a difficult, demanding four- to five-day circular route from the head of Lake Wakatipu, taking you through valleys and over an alpine pass, with the possibility of

QUEENSTOWN & WANAKA

a side trip to the Dart Glacier if you're suitably equipped and experienced. Access by vehicle is possible as far as Muddy Creek on the Rees side, from where it's two hours to 25-Mile Hut.

Park your car at Muddy Creek or arrange transport with Queenstown's **Info & Track Centre** (Map p610; ☎ 03-442 9708; www.infotrack.co.nz; 37 Shotover St). Most people go up the Rees track first and come back down the Dart. The three basic DOC huts (Shelter Rock, Daleys Flat and the Dart) cost $10 per person and Backcountry Hut Passes must be purchased in advance.

Estimated walking times:

Route	Time
Muddy Creek to Shelter Rock Hut	6hr
Shelter Rock Hut to Dart Hut	5-7hr
Dart Hut to Daleys Flat Hut	6-8hr
Daleys Flat Hut to Paradise	6-8hr

WANAKA REGION

With overgrown valleys, unspoiled rivers and tumbling glaciers, the Wanaka region is crowned with the colossal Mt Aspiring (Tititea; 3035m), the highest peak outside the Mt Cook region. Enter this area from the north via Haast Pass, and you encounter the region's beautiful twin lakes, Wanaka and Hawea, two expansive freshwater siblings wedged between awesome hills and cliffs. From the south via Cardrona, stunning valley views and mountain vistas are on tap. The Wanaka region, and especially the activity-filled town of Wanaka itself, is seeing more and more travellers, but it's still a quieter alternative to pumpin' Queenstown. And once you've sampled a few closer-to-Wanaka action activities and told tall stories in the town's pubs and bars, get off the tourist trail by exploring the Mt Aspiring National Park or the forested wilderness around Makarora.

WANAKA
pop 5000

Beautiful scenery, tramping and skiing opportunities, and a huge roster of adrenaline-inducing activities have transformed the lakeside town of Wanaka into a year-round tourist destination. Travellers come here as an alternative to Queenstown, and while some locals worry their home is starting to resemble its hyped-up Central Otago sibling across the Crown Range, Wanaka's lakefront area retains a laid-back, small-town feel. It's definitely not a sleepy hamlet anymore, though, and new restaurants and bars are adding a veneer of sophistication. Note that Wanaka wakes up in a big way for New Year's Eve.

Wanaka is located at the southern end of Lake Wanaka, just over 100km northeast of Queenstown via Cromwell. It's the gateway to Mt Aspiring National Park and to the Treble Cone, Cardrona, Harris Mountains and Pisa Range Ski Areas.

Information

DOC Wanaka visitor information centre (DOC; ☎ 03-443 7660; Ardmore St; ☼ 8am-4.30pm Mon-Fri, 9.30am-4pm Sat & Sun, closed noon-12.30pm) In an A-framed building on the edge of town, this is the place to inquire about tramps, and there's a small museum (admission free) on Wanaka geology, flora and fauna.

Lake Wanaka i-SITE (☎ 03-443 1233; www.lake wanaka.co.nz; ☼ 8.30am-5.30pm, to 7pm in summer) Off Ardmore St, on the waterfront.

Wanaka Medical Centre (☎ 03-443 7811; 21 Russell St; ☼ 9am-5pm Mon-Fri, clinics at 9am & 5pm Sat & Sun) Patches up adventure-sports mishaps.

Wanakaweb (1st fl, 3 Helwick St) Get online here.

Sights

With its emphasis on the stunning outdoors, Wanaka isn't brimming with conventional sights, but you can keep busy on a rainy day.

Puzzling World (☎ 03-443 7489; www.puzzlingworld. com; 188 Main Hwy 84; adult/child $12.50/9; ☼ 8.30am-5.30pm) has a 3-D Great Maze and lots of 'now-you-see-it, now-you-don't' visual tomfoolery to keep kids of all ages bemused, bothered and bewildered. It's en route to Cromwell, 2km from town.

The poignant and interesting **New Zealand Fighter Pilots Museum** (☎ 03-443 7010; www.nzfpm. co.nz; Wanaka Airport; adult/child/family $10/5/25; ☼ 9am-5pm) is dedicated to NZ combat pilots, the aircraft they flew and the sacrifices they made. There is a well-preserved collection of Hawker Hurricanes, de Havilland Vampires and vintage Soviet fighter planes, and at the time of writing plans were under way for a major expansion of the collection and facilities.

More light-hearted is the neighbouring **Wanaka Transport & Toy Museum** (☎ 03-443 8765; www.wanakatransportandtoymuseum.com; SH6; adult/child/family $10/4/20; ☼ 8.30am-5pm), the end result of one man's obsessive collecting. Among the 40,000 items, watch for a Cadillac Coupe de

Ville, a mysteriously acquired MiG jet fighter, and toys that you're guaranteed to remember with a wry smile from rainy childhood afternoons.

Afterwards, toast the past and the future at **Wanaka Beerworks** (☎ 03-443 1865; www.wanaka beerworks.co.nz; SH6; ☒ 9am-4pm, tours 2pm) with this small brewery's three award-winning products: a Vienna lager, a German-style black beer and our favourite, the hops-laden 'Brewski' Bohemian pilsener. Bookings are recommended for brewery tours.

Activities

Wide valleys, alpine meadows, more than 100 glaciers and sheer mountains make **Mt Aspiring National Park** an outdoor enthusiast's paradise. Protected as a national park in 1964, and later included in the Southwest New Zealand (Te Wahipounamu) World Heritage Area, the park now blankets more than 3500 sq km along the Southern Alps, from the Haast River in the north to its border with Fiordland National Park in the south.

TRAMPING

While the southern end of Mt Aspiring National Park is well trafficked by visitors and includes popular tramps such as the Routeburn Track (p630), there are great short walks and more demanding multiday tramps in the Matukituki Valley, close to Wanaka; see the DOC leaflet *Matukituki Valley Tracks* ($1). The dramatic **Rob Roy Valley Track** (three to four hours return) takes in glaciers, waterfalls and a swing bridge, yet is a fairly easy route. The **West Matukituki Valley** track goes on to Aspiring Hut (four to five hours return), a scenic, more difficult walk over mostly grassy flats. For overnight or multiday tramps, continue up the valley to **Liverpool Hut** for great views of Mt Aspiring, or over the very difficult **Cascade Saddle** to link up with the Rees-Dart Track (p631), north of Glenorchy.

Many of these tramps are subject to snow and avalanches and can be treacherous. Register your intentions and seek advice from DOC in Wanaka before heading off. Also purchase hut passes. Tracks are reached from Raspberry Creek at the end of Mt Aspiring Rd, 54km from Wanaka; for shuttle-service details, see p640.

For walks closer to town, pick up the DOC brochure *Wanaka Walks and Trails* ($1). This includes the easy lakeside stroll to **Eely Point** (20 minutes) and on to **Beacon Point** (30 minutes), as well as the **Waterfall Creek Walk** (one hour return) east along the lakeshore.

The fairly gentle climb to the top of **Mt Iron** (549m, 1½ hours return) reveals panoramic views. Fit folks after a view can undertake the taxing, winding 8km tramp up **Mt Roy** (1578m, five to six hours return), starting 6km from Wanaka on the Mt Aspiring Rd. The high track crosses private land and is closed from October to mid-November for lambing. From Mt Roy, continue along the **Skyline Track** (five to six hours) to Cardrona Rd, 10km south of Wanaka. Don't do this in winter; low cloud eliminates views and makes it treacherous.

To the north of Wanaka, the **Minaret Burn Track** (six to seven hours) in the Mt Alta Conservation Area is suitable for walking and mountain biking. You can pick up a map (50c) at DOC.

Many outfits offer guided walking tours around Wanaka, some into Mt Aspiring National Park:

Alpinism & Ski Wanaka (☎ 03-442 6593; www. alpinismski.co.nz; half-/full day $130/195) Day walks and overnight tramps.

Eco Wanaka Adventures (☎ 03-443 2869; www. ecowanaka.co.nz; half-/full day from $105/170) Day, half-day and multiday trips.

Wild Walks (☎ 03-442 4476; www.wildwalks.co.nz; 3 days from $720) Multiday tramps.

JETBOATING & RAFTING

Lakeland Adventures (☎ 03-443 7495; www.lakeland adventures.co.nz; adult/child $95/45), at the i-SITE, offers one-hour jetboat trips across the lake that include an exciting ride in the winding Clutha River. **Pioneer Rafting** (☎ 03-443 1246; www.ecoraft. co.nz; half-day rafts per adult/child $135/75, full-day $185/95) runs ecorafting on the high-volume Clutha, with Grade II to III rapids, gold panning and birdwatching.

CANYONING & KAYAKING

Adventurous souls will love canyoning, a summer activity staged by **Deep Canyon** (☎ 03-443 7922; www.deepcanyon.co.nz; from $225; ☒ mid-Nov–Apr) that involves climbing, swimming and waterfall-abseiling through confined, steep and wild gorges. Transport to the canyon, lunch, instruction and equipment are included. If you're a supremely confident adventure junkie, consider the Leaping Burn trip ($460).

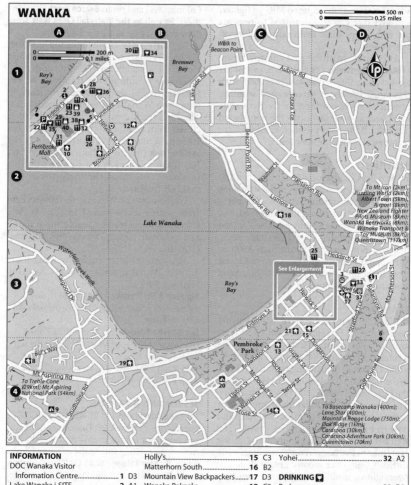

Alpine Kayak Guides (☎ 03-443 9023; www.alpine kayaks.co.nz; half-/full day $149/195; ☺ Nov-May) paddles down the Hawea, Clutha and Matukituki Rivers. Kids can join a more leisurely half-day Grandview trip (two adult and two kids $450), and if you really get a taste for paddling, sign up for a full-day kayaking basics course ($280).

Wanaka Kayaks (☎ 0800 926 925; www.wanaka kayaks.co.nz; ☺ summer only), opposite Subway on the beach, rents kayaks ($10 to $18) and offers guided lake tours (from $60 per person).

Hire kayaks from **Lakeland Adventures** (☎ 03-443 7495; www.lakelandadventures.co.nz), off Ardmore St, on the waterfront, for $15 per hour.

SKYDIVING & PARAGLIDING
Skydive Lake Wanaka (☎ 03-443 7207; www.sky divewanaka.com; adult $295-395) does jumps from 12,000ft and a scary 15,000ft; the latter lets you fall for 60 seconds. Count on another $130 or so for video evidence for the folks back home.

Wanaka Paragliding (☎ 0800 359 754; www.wanaka paragliding.co.nz; adult $180) will take you on tandem flights at 800m from Treble Cone. Count on around 20 minutes soaring on the Central Otago thermals.

ROCK CLIMBING & MOUNTAINEERING
Mt Aspiring National Park is a favourite playground of mountaineering and alpine climbing companies. **Aspiring Guides** (☎ 03-443 9422; www.aspiringguides.com; 5 days from $3350), **Adventure Consultants** (☎ 03-443 8711; www.adventure.co.nz; 5 days from $4100 with a 1:1 guide ratio) and **Alpinism & Ski** (☎ 03-443 6593; www.alpinismski.co.nz; 5 days from $3385) all offer beginners' courses and multiday guided ascents of Mts Aspiring, Tasman and Tutoko.

Excellent rock climbing can be found at **Hospital Flat** – 25km from Wanaka towards Mount Aspiring NP. Those not in the know can climb with **Wanaka Rock Climbing & Abseil Adventures** (☎ 03-443 6411; www.wanakarock.co.nz), which has an introductory rock-climbing course (half-/full day $120/190), a half-day abseiling intro ($120), and bouldering and multipitch climbs for the experienced.

Before you hit the mountains, learn the ropes on the indoor and outdoor climbing walls at **Basecamp Wanaka** (☎ 03-443 1110; www.basecampwanaka.co.nz; 50 Cardrona Valley Rd; adult/child $15/12; ☺ 10am-9pm, to 7pm Sat & Sun). Climbing gear can also be hired.

MOUNTAIN BIKING
Many tracks and trails in the region are open to cyclists. DOC produces *Mountain-Biking Around Wanaka* (50c), describing mountain-bike rides ranging from 2km (the steep Mt Iron track) to 20km (West Matukituki Valley).

For spectacular guided mountain biking, contact **Freeride NZ** (☎ 0800 743 369; www.freeridenz.com), which does full-day trips (from $185), including helibiking options. If you're happiest on two wheels, jump on a three-day ($1050) or eight-day ($2750) expedition.

Rent bikes from **Lakeland Adventures** (☎ 03-443 7495; www.lakelandadventures.co.nz; per hr/full day $10/40).

FISHING
Lakes Wanaka and Hawea (16km away) have excellent trout fishing, and the surrounding rivers are also popular angling spots. Numerous guides are based in Wanaka, including **Hatch** (☎ 03-443 8446; www.hatchfishing.co.nz; 2 adults half-/full day $390/650) and **Riversong** (☎ 03-443 8567; www.wanakaflyfishingguides.co.nz; half-/full day $400/600). Hatch also runs adventure fishing trips incorporating hiking ($650 per day), and for $75 per hour, the expert team at Riversong offer tuition in the dark art of fly-fishing.

Lakeland Adventures (☎ 03-443 7495; www.lakelandadventures.co.nz; up to 3 people $299) offers guided trout fishing on Lake Wanaka.

OTHER ACTIVITIES
For skiers after untouched powder and exclusive views, there are companies offering heliskiing (p87). More easily reached slopes include Treble Cone (p85), Cardrona (p85) and Snow Farm New Zealand (for cross-country skiing; p85).

Wanaka Golf Club (☎ 03-443 7888; www.wanakagolf.co.nz; Ballantyne Rd; green fees $55, club hire from $20) has a view-filled 18-hole course.

Outside Sports (☎ 03-443 7966; www.outsidesports.co.nz; 17 Dunmore St) offers a wide range of outdoor gear – for sale or rent, tramping, skiing, climbing, camping and just about anything else you might need to get into the outdoors.

Tours
AERIAL SIGHTSEEING
The following companies are all based at Wanaka Airport. Book trips through the i-SITE.

Aspiring Air (☎ 0800 100 943, 03-443 7943; www.aspiringair.com) A range of scenic flights, including a

50-minute flight over Mt Aspiring (adult/child $210/120), a Milford Sound fly-past and landing ($375/230) and a sprint around Mt Cook and the glaciers ($395/230).

Classic Flights (☎ 027 220 9277; www.classicflights. co.nz; from $225) Runs sightseeing flights in a vintage Tigermoth. 'Biggles' goggles provided, but BYO flowing silk scarf.

Wanaka Flightseeing (☎ 0800 105 105, 03-443 8787; www.flightseeing.co.nz) Offers similar flights to Aspiring Air at similar prices – it also throws in free admission to the adjacent Fighter Pilots Museum (p632) and discounts on first-thing-in-the-morning flights.

The following offer 20-minute flights around Wanaka for about $175, and 60-minute tours of Mt Aspiring and the glaciers for about $450.

Alpine Helicopters (☎ 03-443 4000; www.alpineheli. co.nz)

Aspiring Helicopters (☎ 03-443 7152; www.aspiring helicopters.co.nz)

Wanaka Helicopters (☎ 03-443 1085; www.heli flights.co.nz)

OTHER TOURS

Book at the i-SITE.

Clean Green Photo Tours (☎ 03-443 7951; www. cleangreen.co.nz; 3hr/half-day/full day $300/400/750) Gives you expert hints and tips as you capture Central Otago's stunning scenery.

Lake Wanaka Cruises (☎ 03-443 1230; www. wanakacruises.co.nz; from $60) Similar tours to Lakeland Adventures aboard a catamaran; with overnight options.

Lakeland Adventures (☎ 03-443 7495; www.lakeland adventures.co.nz) Has 2½-hour trips to Stevensons Island (adult/child $70/40) and a 3½-hour trip with a guided bushwalk on Mou Waho ($90/45). To explore the lake under your own steam, kayaks (from $10 per hour) and aqua bikes ($15 per 20 minutes) are also available.

Ridgeline (☎ 0800 234 000; www.ridgelinenz.com) Runs tours (3½ hours, $195) combining a 4WD farm safari and wine tasting at the beautiful Rippon Vineyard.

Wanaka Sightseeing (☎ 03-443 1855; www.wanaka sightseeing.co.nz; half-/full day $170/299) For any lingering *Lord of the Rings* fans, there are exhaustive tours of filming sights where you can dress up like a hobbit and sometimes hang out with Ian Brodie, author-cum-guru of *The Lord of the Rings: Location Guidebook*.

Festivals & Events

Rippon Festival (www.ripponfestival.co.nz) Music fans should diary this popular festival held every second year in early February at the lakeside Rippon Vineyard. Big-name Kiwi acts headline with a variety of styles represented – dance, reggae, rock and electronica to name a few. If the music doesn't relax you (highly unlikely), the wine certainly will. Rippon's Riesling is great for summer picnics.

Warbirds over Wanaka (☎ 0800 496 920, 03-443 8619; www.warbirdsoverwanaka.com; Wanaka Airport; 3-day adult/child $165/25, 1st day only $45/10, each of last 2 days $70/10) Every second Easter (even-numbered years), Wanaka hosts this huge and incredibly popular international airshow attracting 100,000 people.

Wanaka Fest (www.wanakafest.co.nz) Held mid-October, this festival is a four-day event with the feel of a small-town fair. Street parades, live music and wacky competitions get the locals saying gidday to the warmth of spring.

Sleeping

Like Queenstown, Wanaka is bursting with hostels and luxury accommodation, but good midrange options are harder to find. Across summer, and especially around New Year, prices and demand increase considerably. During winter, the town is hit with an influx of international snowboarders.

BUDGET

our pick **YHA Wanaka Purple Cow** (☎ 03-443 1880; www.yha.co.nz; 94 Brownston St; dm $24-31, d $90-96; 🖳 🛜) Warmed by a wood stove, the lounge at this ever-popular hostel holds commanding lake and mountain views; that's if you can tear yourself away from the regular movie nights. There are four- and six-bed dorms and a small array of nice doubles with en suites. Outdoor patios and bike hire will get you breathing in crisp mountain air.

Fern Lodge (☎ 0800 555 556; www.fernlodge.co.nz; 122 Brownston St; dm $25, d $80-120) Rooms at this sprawling reader-recommended spot run from straightforward doubles to flasher lodge rooms with Sky TV, spa baths and ritzy gas kitchens. The common theme throughout is excellent value for money.

Matterhorn South (☎ 03-443 1119; www.matter hornsouth.co.nz; 56 Brownston St; dm $25-30, s $65, d $65-90, tr & q $110-120; 🖳 🛜) Right at the edge of central Wanaka, this friendly spot has clean, good-value dorms and studios, and a sunny TV and games room. It has a shared country-style kitchen and a private garden to rest up in after a day's outdoor adventuring. The triple and quad en-suite rooms are excellent value.

Wanaka Bakpaka (☎ 03-443 7837; www.wanaka bakpaka.co.nz; 117 Lakeside Rd; dm $26-28, s $50, d $62-76; 🖳 🛜) An energetic brother-and-sister team are steadily upgrading this friendly hostel high above the lake with stunning views. Amenities are top-shelf and the staff is ready to throw down the red carpet for weary travellers. The colourful rooms are good value and the outlook from the lounge will inspire you to (finally) get your diary up to date.

Wanaka Lakeview Holiday Park (☎ 03-443 7883; www.wanakalakeview.kiwiholidayparks.com; 212 Brownston St; sites/cabins $32/46) Grassy sites set amid established pine trees with a kids' playground and lots of space to set up camp. Rooms range from basic cabins to en-suite flats.

Aspiring Campervan Park (☎ 0800 229 8439, 03-443 6603; www.campervanpark.co.nz; Studholme Rd; sites $45; 🖳 🛜) Trimmed grass sites, trees and pretty views add up to a relaxing spot. Great facilities include a barbecue area with gas heaters and a spa and sauna, all at no additional cost. Campervans only, please; no tents.

Altamont Lodge (☎ 03-443 8864; www.altamontlodge.co.nz; 121 Mt Aspiring Rd; d $65; 🖳 🛜) At the quieter end of town, natural wood gives this place a ski-lodge ambience. Tennis courts, a spa pool, and a lounge with a big fire provide plenty of off-piste action. It's often booked by big groups, so reserve ahead.

Also recommended:

Base Backpackers (☎ 03-443 4291; www.stayatbase.com; 73 Brownston St; dm $25-29, d $43; 🖳 🛜) This new hostel is a filing cabinet for backpacker-bus types. The facilities are sparkling and the on-site bar, Mint, is good fun too.

Mountain View Backpackers (☎ 03-443 9050; www.mtnview.co.nz; 7 Russell St; dm/d $25/68) A newly renovated characterful house with a big lawn and warm, comfortable rooms.

Holly's (☎ 03-443 8187; www.hollybackpacker.co.nz; 71 Upton St; dm $26-28, d $64; 🖳 🛜) A family-run low-key hostel that's a good antidote to busier places around town. Showing a bit of wear and tear, but a friendly spot. Bikes are for hire (half-/full day $10/20).

MIDRANGE

Harpers (☎ 03-443 8894; www.harpers.co.nz; 95 McDougall St; s/d incl breakfast $100/140) The garden (with pond and waterfall no less…) is a labour of love at this friendly B&B in a quiet location down a long driveway. Legendary breakfasts are served on a sunny deck with expansive views. You'd be wise to factor a leisurely second cup of breakfast coffee into your day's plans.

Aspiring Lodge (☎ 03-443 7816; www.aspiringlodge.co.nz; cnr Dunmore & Dungarvon Sts; d $135) Older but well-maintained motel units trimmed with

natural wood and with easy access to lakefront bars and restaurants. The following morning the motel's helpful team will have plenty of ideas for local activities.

Brook Vale (☎ 0800 438 333, 03-443 8333; www.brookvale.co.nz; 35 Brownston St; d $135; 🛜 🛋) Self-contained studio and family units with a few classy touches and patios that open onto a grassy lawn complete with a gently flowing creek. You'll also find a barbecue, a spa and a swimming pool for those sunny Central Otago days.

Bay View Motel (☎ 0800 229 843, 03-443 7766; www.bayviewwanaka.co.nz; Studholme Rd; r $135-155; 🖳 🛜) The original units date back 40 years, but the switched-on owners have modernised the interiors nicely with TVs and DVD players to keep up with the sterling views outside.

Riversong (☎ 03-443 8567; www.riversongwanaka.co.nz; 5 Wicklow Tce, Albert Town; d $150-170) On the banks of the Clutha River in the nearby hamlet of Albert Town, Riversong has two rooms in a lovely heritage B&B surrounded by established fruit trees. The well-travelled owners may well have the best nonfiction library in NZ, and if you can tear yourself away from the books, there's excellent trout fishing just metres away. Dinner including wine is available for $55 per person. Riversong is down a no-exit road, so it is very quiet.

TOP END

our pick Mountain Range Lodge (☎ 03-443 7400; www.mountainrange.co.nz; Heritage Park, Cardrona Valley Rd; r incl breakfast $280-390; 🖳 🛜) This stunning lodge is a vision of rustic luxury. Seven rooms named for nearby mountain ranges are home to comfy duvets, fluffy robes, and views that'll distract you from the nearby skiing and tramping options. Cool touches like a complimentary glass of wine – from the lodge's own label no less – and an on-site hot tub complete an already pretty picture.

Wanaka Homestead (☎ 03-443 5022; www.wanakahomestead.co.nz; 1 Homestead Close; d $295, cottages $410-525; 🖳 🛜) Warm wooden interiors, oriental rugs and local artwork punctuate this boutique lodge, which has won awards for its ecofriendly approach to sustainability. Despite the focus on green good deeds, it's still very luxurious, with underfloor heating and an under-the-stars hot tub. Choose from rooms in the main lodge or in self-contained cottages that sleep up to seven.

Eating

Wanaka has a surprising range of places to eat, drink and generally celebrate the fact that you're on holiday.

RESTAURANTS

White House Café & Bar (☎ 03-443 9595; 33 Dunmore St; mains $35-45; ☯ 6.30pm-late; Ⓥ) It looks like a Greek townhouse miraculously airlifted from Santorini, and inside this long-running local favourite you can linger over plates of Mediterranean and Middle Eastern cuisine with lots of vegetarian options. Polished wooden floors and Turkish rugs do nothing to break the delicious spell. In summer, relax under endless Central Otago blue skies seemingly also imported straight from the Med.

Relishes (☎ 03-443 9018; 99 Ardmore St; mains $15-30; ☯ 8am-9pm) A cafe by day, this place whips out the white tablecloths at night and becomes a classy restaurant with a good wine list. Try the antipasto platter ($26) with local salmon, and toast the lakefront setting.

Missy's Kitchen (☎ 03-443 5099; Level 1, 80 Ardmore St; mains $30-35; ☯ 4pm-late) A dramatic upstairs dining room with equally spectacular lake views serves up local beef, lamb and salmon in innovative and award-winning ways. Prolong the experience with a cocktail at the bar. The list of local beers and wine make returning for a second night worthwhile.

Botswana Butchery (☎ 03-443 6745; Post Office Lane; mains $30-45; ☯ 5pm-late) It's a humble name for Wanaka's classiest eatery. In a dining room trimmed with dark wood and leather, Asian-inspired dishes like seven-spiced big eye tuna go head to head with Botswana Butchery's signature aged beef steaks. Definitely food for grown-ups, as is the serious Central Otago–skewed wine list. Just come with a few imbibing partners, as surprisingly few wines are available by the glass. Downstairs in Post Office Lane there's a growing range of bars to explore after dinner. Let us know what you discover.

Lone Star (☎ 03-443 6901; 50 Cardrona Valley Rd; mains $25-33; ☯ 11am-late) The line 'everything's bigger in Texas' seems to fit the food here. Massive plates of grub are the calling card of Lone Star. Tex-Mex flavours and a festive atmosphere keep the mood light – though too many meals here and *you* won't be. Best to tuck into the Fred Flintstone–worthy ribs after going rock climbing at Basecamp Wanaka (p635), which is located in the same building.

CAFES & QUICK EATS

Soulfood Store & Cafe (☎ 03-443 7885; 74 Ardmore St; mains $7-15; ☯ 8am-5pm Mon-Fri, to 3pm Sat & Sun; Ⓥ) Park yourself in a rustic wooden booth and stay healthy with organic soups, pizza, pasta and muffins. Not everything's strictly vegetarian, and breakfast with free-range eggs breaks the spell in a tasty way. The attached organic food store, which has freshly baked bread, is a good spot for a pre-picnic stock-up.

Yohei (☎ 03-443 4222; Spencer House Mall, 23 Dunmore St; snacks $8-12; ☯ 7.30am-6pm; Ⓥ) Tucked away in a shopping arcade, this funky Japanese-inspired eatery does interesting local spins on sushi (how about venison or lamb?), and superlative juices and smoothies. Very cool music too, and a good range of vego options.

Kai Whakapai (☎ 03-443 7795; cnr Helwick & Ardmore Sts; meals $10-30; ☯ 7am-late) A Wanaka institution, Kai (the Maori word for food) is the place to be on a sunny day, with perhaps the best patio in all of Aotearoa. Massive sandwiches, great coffee and exceptionally slow service are all a part of the experience. They have the locally brewed Wanaka Beerworks beer on tap, and some local Central Otago wines as well.

Ardmore St Food Company (☎ 03-443 2230; The Waterfront, 155 Ardmore St; meals $12-18; ☯ 8am-4pm) This cosmopolitan lakefront cafe has everything from muffins the size of Mt Aspiring to quirkily dubbed breakfasts like Green Eggs and Ham (bacon, eggs and pesto if you're wondering…). There's a concise but considered list of local wines and boutique beers, and the attached deli is a good place to pick up gourmet goodies for a lakeside picnic.

Café Gusto (☎ 03-443 6639; 1 Lakeside Rd; mains $15-20; ☯ 8am-5pm) The most common answer to the question 'Who's got the best coffee in town?', Gusto provides robust meals like breakfast burrito with jalapeno peppers, or smoked salmon and scrambled eggs. Both will set you up for the most active of days, and after you've kayaked/mountain biked/rafted/hiked, come back in the afternoon and recount the experience over excellent cakes and Wanaka's best coffee.

Red Star (☎ 03-443 9322; 26 Ardmore St; burgers $9-15; ☯ 11am-late) Burgers are burgers, right? Wrong. Taking the idea that fast food doesn't have to be rubbish (or even that fast) and running with it, Red Star spoils diners with a menu featuring inventive ingredients and 17 different burgers. Everybody is catered for –

even vegetarians, who get a show-stopping three options.

Around the waterfront where Pembroke Mall meets Ardmore St, you'll find a small enclave of cheaper spots for takeaway food. Dubbed 'Curry in a Hurry' by locals, **Sagun** (☎ 03-443 9220; 139 Ardmore St) does good Indian food, and the **Doughbin Bakery** (☎ 03-443 7290; 123 Ardmore St) – motto: 'Baking at sparrow's fart since Adam was a cowboy' – specialises in McGregor's fine pies. With a motto like that, you just know they're going to be fresh.

The **New World supermarket** (Dunmore St; ⏰ 8am-8pm) is well stocked for self-caterers.

Drinking

Barluga (☎ 03-442 5400; Post Office Lane; ⏰ 4pm-late) In the up-and-coming Post Office Lane area, Barluga's leather armchairs and coolly retro wallpaper at first make you think of a refined gentlemen's club. Wicked cocktails and killer back-to-back beats soon break the illusion.

Uno (☎ 03-443 4911; 99 Ardmore St; ⏰ 4pm-late) This slick and contemporary wine bar is the perfect place to watch the sun go down. It's a pretty good spot to head back to after dinner as well.

Red Rock (☎ 03-443 5545; Level 1, 68 Ardmore St; ⏰ 5pm-late) With terracotta-red walls, decks to admire the moon from, and weekend DJs and occasional live gigs from around 10pm, this is a friendly place in which to get cosy in cowhide-covered booths. It's popular in winter with the snowboarder crowd, but in summer the lakefront bars get busier.

Trout (☎ 03-443 2600; 151 Ardmore St; ⏰ 11am-late Wed-Sun, 3pm-late Mon & Tue) The best of the busier beer barns down on the lakefront, this place is more the new Trout than the old trout. It's a slick, designer Kiwi pub with the full range of Monteith's West Coast beers on tap.

Wanaka Ale House (☎ 03-443 2920; 155 Ardmore St; ⏰ 11am-late) Next door to Trout, this place owns the coveted corner office. The rustic ambience morphs into a Southern Man wet dream of exposed beams, mountain views and an ample supply of Monteith's that flows like water.

Entertainment

our pick **Cinema Paradiso** (☎ 03-443 1505; www.paradiso.net.nz; 1 Ardmore St; adult/child $14/9; 🖥) Playing first-run and classic movies, Cinema Paradiso has got to be the coolest movie theatre around. Forget boring, stiff cinema seats, this theatre is filled with vintage couches to snuggle up on. Extra cushions are available to stretch out on the floor and there's even an old Morris Minor to sit in for the true drive-in movie experience. At intermission they throw open the doors and the smell of freshly baked cookies wafts through the theatre and you just can't help yourself. There is a great cafe that can prepare a meal to be ready at the break. Then sit back and watch the second half of the film with a plate of fantastic grub. Now that's dinner and a movie! Try the homemade ice cream and don't forget to arrive early to get a good couch.

Shopping

For its size, Wanaka has a good number of interesting shops.

Originz (☎ 03-443 4488; Pembroke Mall) This gift shop is filled with local crafts, including cards, soaps, clocks, candles, paintings and pottery. You'll find unique, reasonably priced objects, and it's all proudly made in NZ. A good place for unusual gifts that are easy to transport home. It's off Ardmore St.

Gallery Thirty Three (☎ 03-443 4330; 33 Helwick St) Exhibitions of pottery, glass and jewellery. It's pricey, but even if you're not planning to buy, it's an interesting look at what local artists are up to.

Mainly Tramping (☎ 03-443 2888; Dunmore St) This shop is filled with clothes, boots, tents, skis and everything else you need to get out and about.

Outside Sports (☎ 03-443 7966; www.outsidesports.co.nz; Dunmore St) More of the same to rent or buy.

Getting There & Away

AIR

Air New Zealand (☎ 0800 737 000; www.airnz.co.nz) has daily flights between Wanaka and Christchurch (from $99). **Aspiring Air** (☎ 0800 100 943, 03-443 7943; www.aspiringair.com) has daily flights between Queenstown and Wanaka ($155, 20 minutes) in small, twin-engine planes.

BUS

The bus stop for **InterCity** (☎ 03-443 7885; www.intercity.co.nz) is outside the i-SITE on the lakefront. Wanaka receives daily buses from Queenstown ($17), which motor on to Franz Josef ($46) via Haast Pass ($23). For Christchurch ($79) you'll need to change at Tarras.

Naked Bus (www.nakedbus.com) will take you to Queenstown, Christchurch, Cromwell and the West Coast.

Wanaka is well serviced by door-to-door shuttles and buses, nearly all of which can be booked at the i-SITE. **Wanaka Connexions** (☎ 03-443 9122; www.time2.co.nz) and **Atomic Shuttles** (☎ 03-349 0697; www.atomictravel. co.nz) all service Christchurch ($50 to $60) and Queenstown ($20 to $30). Wanaka Connexions and **Catch-a-Bus** (☎ 03-479 9960; www.catchabus.co.nz) head to Dunedin ($50); Atomic Shuttles goes to Fox ($40) and Franz Josef ($45) Glaciers and on to Greymouth ($80). The majority pick up near the i-SITE; inquire when you book.

Getting Around

Alpine Coachlines (☎ 03-443 7966; www.alpinecoach lines.co.nz; Dunmore St) meets and greets flights at Wanaka Airport ($15), and in summer has twice-daily shuttles for trampers ($35) to Mt Aspiring National Park and Raspberry Creek. See it also for winter transport to Treble Cone. **Wanaka Taxis** (☎ 03-443 7999; www.wanakataxis. com) also looks after airport transfers, while **Adventure Rentals** (☎ 03-443 6050; adventurerentals@ xtra.co.nz; 20 Ardmore St) hires cars and 4WDs.

MAKARORA

pop 40

At Makarora you've left the West Coast and entered Otago, but the township still has a West Coast frontier feel. Visit the **DOC visitor information centre** (DOC; ☎ 03-443 8365; www.makarora. co.nz; SH6; ⏰ 8am-4.45pm daily Nov-Apr, 8am-4.45pm Mon-Fri May-Oct) at the Makarora Wilderness Resort for conditions and routes before undertaking any regional tramps.

Activities

TRAMPING

Short tramps in this secluded area include the **Bridal Track** (1½ hours one-way, 5km), from the top of Haast Pass to Davis Flat, and the **Blue Pools Walk** (30 minutes return), where you can see huge rainbow trout.

Longer tramps go through magnificent countryside but shouldn't be undertaken lightly. Alpine conditions, flooding and the possibility of avalanches mean you must be well prepared; consult with DOC before heading off. DOC's *Tramping Guide to the Makarora Region* ($2) is a worthwhile investment.

The three-day **Gillespie Pass** tramp goes via the Young, Siberia and Wilkin Rivers; this is a high pass with avalanche danger. With a jet-

boat ride down the Wilkin to complete it, this rates alongside the Milford Track as one of the great tramps. The **Wilkin Valley Track** heads off from Kerin Forks Hut, at the top of the Wilkin River, and on to Top Forks Hut and the picturesque **Lakes Diana**, **Lucidus** and **Castalia** (one hour, 1½ hours and three to four hours respectively from Top Forks Hut).

Jetboats go to Kerin Forks, and a service goes across the Young River mouth when the Makarora floods; inquire at **Wilkin River Jets** (☎ 0800 538 945, 03-443 8351; www.wilkinriverjets.co.nz; Kerin Forks $75) or at DOC.

OTHER ACTIVITIES

The lush Siberia Valley provides one of NZ's great outdoor adventures. The **Siberia Experience** (☎ 0800 345 666, 03-443 8666; www.siberiaexperience.co.nz; adult $310) is a thrill-seeking extravaganza combining a half-hour scenic small-plane flight, a three-hour bush walk through a remote mountain valley and a half-hour jetboat trip down the Wilkin and Makarora Rivers in Mt Aspiring National Park. To avoid getting lost, keep your eye on the markers as you descend from Siberia Valley. It's also possible to join the trip in Wanaka.

Wilkin River Jets does a superb 50km, one-hour jetboating trip ($95) into Mt Aspiring National Park, following the Makarora and Wilkin Rivers. It's cheaper than Queenstown options, and also offers trips including helicopter rides or tramping.

Southern Alps Air (☎ 0800 345 666, 03-443 4385; www.southernalpsair.co.nz) does trips to Mt Cook and the glaciers (adult/child $395/230) and landings at Milford Sound ($350/210).

Sleeping & Eating

The nearest DOC camping grounds are on SH6 at Cameron Flat, 10km north of Makarora, and at Boundary Creek Reserve, 18km south of Makarora on the shores of Lake Wanaka; both charge $6/3 per adult/child.

Makarora Wilderness Resort (☎ 03-443 8372; www. makarora.co.nz; SH6; powered sites $28, dm $30, d $70-120; 💻 🐾) In scrubby bush are self-contained chalets, basic cabins and backpacker doubles and dorms. They've all got a snug, alpine feel, and you'll find a cafe, outdoor pool, grocery store and petrol station. Campervan travellers are also welcome, and later at night the cafe effortlessly assumes the role of Makarora's pub.

Larrivee Homestay (☎ 03-443 9177; www.larrivee homestay.co.nz; off SH6; d incl breakfast $120 -150) This rustic two-bedroom self-contained cottage sleeping up to four is situated down a side road between DOC and the tourist centre. Surrounded by native bush and with a library full of books, it's a good spot to take the foot off the travel accelerator for a few days.

Getting There & Away

InterCity (☎ 03-442 8238; www.intercity.co.nz) and **Atomic Shuttles** (☎ 03-349 0697; www.atomictravel.co.nz) both travel through Makarora en route to Haast and the West Coast.

HAWEA
pop 1600

The small town of Hawea, 15km north of Wanaka, is mostly a collection of holiday and retiree homes with spectacular lake and mountain views. From **Lake Hawea** look out at the indomitable Corner Peak on the western shore and out to the distant Barrier Range. Separated from Lake Wanaka by a narrow isthmus called the Neck, Lake Hawea is 35km long and 410m deep, and home to trout and landlocked salmon. The lake was raised 20m in 1958 to facilitate the power stations downriver.

Lake Hawea Motor Inn (☎ 0800 429 324, 03-443 1224; www.lakehawea.co.nz; 1 Capell Ave; dm $30, d $140-160) has unbeatable views across the lake and an on-site restaurant.

On the lakeshore is the spacious and relatively peaceful **Lake Hawea Holiday Park** (☎ 03-443 1767; www.haweaholidaypark.co.nz; SH6; sites $28, d $50-100), a favourite of fishing and boating enthusiasts.

CARDRONA

The sealed **Crown Range Road** from Wanaka to Queenstown via Cardrona is much shorter than the route via Cromwell, but it's a narrow, twisting-and-turning mountain road that needs to be tackled with care, especially in poor weather. In winter it is often snow covered, necessitating chaining up the wheels, and is often subject to closure because of snow – you've been warned.

With views of lush valleys, foothills and countless snowy peaks, this is one of the South Island's most scenic drives. The road passes through tall, swaying tussock grass in the **Pisa Conservation Area**, which has a number of short walking trails. There are plenty of **rest stops** to drink in the view; particularly good ones are at the Queenstown end of the road, as you switchback down towards Arrowtown.

The unpretentious-looking **Cardrona Hotel** (☎ 03-443 8153; www.cardronahotel.co.nz; Crown Range Rd; d $135-185) first opened its doors in 1863. Today you'll find lovingly restored, peaceful rooms with snug, country-style furnishings and patios opening onto a garden. You'll also find a deservedly popular pub with a good **restaurant** (mains $15-20; ❤ lunch & dinner), and a garden bar that just might be NZ's best.

The hotel is located near the turn-off for the **Waiorau Snow Farm** (☎ 03-443 7542; www.snow farmnz.com). In winter this is home to fantastic cross-country skiing. Lessons and ski hire are available ($80 for both).

Also situated nearby is **Backcountry Saddle Expeditions** (☎ 03-443 8151; Crown Range Rd; adult/child from $70/50), which runs horse treks through the Cardrona Valley on Appaloosa horses.

Alternatively, the altogether less placid **Cardrona Adventure Park** (☎ 0800 102 122; www.ad venturepark.co.nz; monster trucks from $140, quad-bikes from $75, go-karts from $60; ❤ 10am-5pm) is a rambunctious and noisy collection of monster trucks (including a self-drive option), quad-bikes and off-road go-karts.

Fiordland & Southland

The bottom end of the South Island has some of the country's most spectacular landscape. To the west is Fiordland National Park, with jagged misty peaks, glistening lakes and an air of forbidding remoteness. The park can be accessed via the world-famous Milford Track, one of the various trails that meander through dense forests and allow views of spectacular mountains and glacier-sculpted canyons. Fiordland is also home to Milford and Doubtful Sounds, with forested cliffs soaring almost vertically from the still, deep waters, and relatively easy to access by road, boat or kayak.

In Southland's east, a sharp left turn off the beaten track, the peaceful Catlins are an area of bird-rich native forest, luxuriantly green farmland and rugged, windswept coasts. In addition to the forest birds the area is home to penguins, seals, sea lions, dolphins and the occasional whale. Wonderful accommodation abounds along wild beaches, in the midst of forests and in tiny waterside settlements.

Southland has the kind of New Zealand scenery that travellers dream of and postcards fail to capture. More than once, you're likely to round a corner, stop in your tracks and just say 'oh, wow' before you reach for the camera.

HIGHLIGHTS

- Sea kayaking, dwarfed by the steep cliffs of **Milford Sound** (p653)
- Exploring side roads, forest waterfalls and lonely southern beaches in the peaceful, windswept **Catlins** (p666)
- Walking through forest and mountains on the stunning **Milford Track** (p651) and **Hollyford Track** (p651)
- Overnighting on the vast, remote **Doubtful Sound** (p656)
- Sharing a beach with dolphins, whales, sea lions and penguins at **Porpoise Bay** (p668) in the Catlins
- Admiring the art at Invercargill's **Anderson Park Art Gallery** (p660)
- Diverting from the **Te Anau–Milford Hwy** (p650) to explore forest walks and still mountain lakes

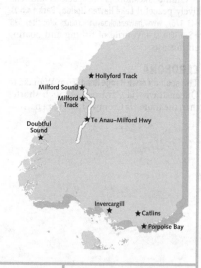

★ Hollyford Track
Milford Sound ★
Milford ★ Track
★ Te Anau–Milford Hwy
Doubtful Sound ★
Invercargill ★
★ Catlins
★ Porpoise Bay

- Telephone code: 03
- www.southland.org.nz
- www.fiordland.org.nz

Climate

Southland has a rather temperamental climate, and downpours can occur frequently in summer. Always prepare well for a cruise on the sounds (where the average annual rainfall is over 6000mm), a bush walk, road trip, or any other type of activity in the great outdoors.

Winter months can yield crisp, sunny days, and it's generally a few degrees cooler here than further north.

Getting There & Around

Air New Zealand connects Invercargill with Christchurch, while Stewart Island Flights connects Invercargill with Oban.

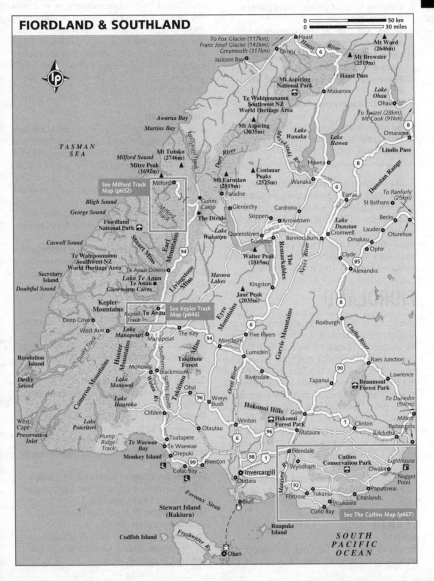

FIORDLAND & SOUTHLAND

FIORDLAND & SOUTHLAND

Major bus operators shuttle to Te Anau and Invercargill from Queenstown or Dunedin, and some ply the Southern Scenic Route and take in Milford Sound. These include InterCity, Topline Tours, Atomic Shuttles, the Bottom Bus and Naked Bus. Companies confining themselves mostly to Southland include TrackNet and Scenic Shuttle.

FIORDLAND

Fiordland is NZ's rawest wilderness area, a jagged, mountainous, forested zone sliced by numerous deeply recessed sounds (which are technically fiords) reaching inland like crooked fingers from the Tasman Sea. Part of the Te Wahipounamu Southwest New Zealand World Heritage Area, it remains formidable and remote. Te Anau and Milford Sound see the bulk of the region's tourists, and small towns hold a small permanent population.

Of the region's wonderful bushwalks, Milford Track may be king, but Kepler and Hollyford are worthy knights, and the Routeburn, Greenstone and Caples Tracks all have one end here too, with the other at Queenstown.

TE ANAU
pop 3000

Peaceful, lakeside Te Anau township is a good base for trekkers and visitors to Milford Sound, and an ideal place to recharge your batteries. There are plenty of activities on offer, and on a sunny day it's also a beautiful place to just chill and step off the travel accelerator for a while.

Lake Te Anau defines the boundary of two very different countrysides. To the east are the relatively flat, pastoral areas of central Southland, while immediately west across the lake lie the rugged forested mountains of Fiordland. NZ's second-largest lake, Te Anau was gouged out by a huge glacier, and has several arms that penetrate into the mountainous forested western shore. The lake's deepest point is 417m, about twice the depth of Loch Ness.

Information

The road along Te Anau's main shopping strip is generally (and confusingly) referred to as 'Town Centre', or sometimes Milford Rd. ATMs are located near Te Anau Outside Sports (p647). Wi-fi is available at the Sandfly Café (p649) and the cafe in the Fiordland Cinema (p649).

Adventure Fiordland (☎ 03-249 8500; Town Centre; ☺ 9am-5pm) An information kiosk that focuses mainly on adventure activities such as kayaking.

Department of Conservation visitor information centre (DOC; ☎ 03-249 0200; www.doc.govt.nz; fiordlandvc@doc.govt.nz; cnr Lakefront Dr & Manapouri Hwy; ☺ 8.30am-6pm) An excellent resource centre for the area with interesting exhibits. Ask to see the DVD about Fiordland's flora and fauna. Includes the Great Walks counter (☎ 03-249 8514; greatwalksbooking@doc. govt.nz; ☺ 8.30am-5pm) for bookings for the Milford, Routeburn and Kepler Tracks, track information and bookings. Computer terminals with NZ-wide DOC information are also available.

Discover NZ information centre (☎ 03-249 7516; Lakefront Dr; ☺ 8am-7.30pm) For more information and activities.

Fiordland i-SITE (☎ 03-249 8900; fiordland-isite@ realjourneys.co.nz; 85 Lakefront Dr; ☺ 8.30am-6pm summer, to 5pm winter) Brochures and info galore along with highway conditions, activities, accommodation and bus bookings.

Gateway Bookshop (64 Town Centre; ☺ 9am-8pm Mon-Thu, to 9pm Fri & Sat, to 7pm Sun) A good place to trade in your post-tramp paperbacks.

Medical Centre (☎ 03-249 7007; Luxmore Dr; ☺ 8am-6pm Mon-Fri, 9am-noon Sat)

Photocentre.com (☎ 03-249 7620; 62 Town Centre; 💻 📶) Internet terminals and gear to print out your digital pics. Includes LAN access.

TE ANAU

0 ——————— 500 m
0 ——————— 0.25 miles

INFORMATION
Adventure Fiordland	(see 35)
ATMs	1 C2
Discover NZ Information Centre	2 B3
DOC Visitor Information Centre	3 C4
Fiordland i-SITE	4 B3
Gateway Bookshop	5 C2
Medical Centre	6 C2
Photocentre.com	7 C2
Post Office	8 C2
Real Journeys	(see 4)
Wash'n'Surf	9 C2

SIGHTS & ACTIVITIES
Bev's Tramping Gear	10 D3
Southern Lakes Helicopters	11 B3
Stardome	12 C2
Te Anau Bike Hire	13 B2
Te Anau Outside Sports	14 C2
Te Anau Wildlife Centre	15 C4
Wings & Water Te Anau	16 B3

SLEEPING
Anchorage Motel	17 C3
Cat's Whiskers B&B	18 C3
Cosy Kiwi	19 C2
Edgewater Motel	20 C3
Keiko's B&B	21 D2
Lakeside Motel	22 C3
Rosies Backpacker Homestay	23 D1
Te Anau Great Lakes Holiday Park	24 C2
Te Anau Lakefront Backpackers	25 C3
Te Anau Lakeview Holiday Park	26 C4
Te Anau Lodge B&B	27 D1
Te Anau Top 10 Holiday Park	28 B2
Te Anau YHA	29 B2

EATING
Fat Duck	30 C2
Fresh Choice Supermarket	(see 37)
Glasshouse	31 C2
La Dolce Vita	32 C2
La Toscana	33 C2
Miles Better Pies	34 B2
Olive Tree Café & Restaurant	35 C2
Redcliff Bar & Restaurant	36 B2
Ruchee	(see 37)
Sandfly Café	37 C2

DRINKING
Moose	38 B2
Ranch Bar & Grill	39 C2

ENTERTAINMENT
Fiordland Cinema	(see 37)

TRANSPORT
InterCity Departure	40 C2
Kepler Water Taxi	41 B2

To Te Anau Glowworm Caves (16km)

Sports Domain

To Bob & Maxines (500m); Te Anau Downs (29km); Milford Sound (120km)

Lions Park

Te Anau Memorial Gardens

Boat Route

To Brod Bay (3km)

Lake Te Anau

To Mossburn (58km); Lumsden (72km); Invercargill (152km)

To Kepler Track (3km); Blue Mountain Cottages (8km); Barnyard Backpackers (9km); Manapouri (20km)

Post office (102 Town Centre) Inside the Paper Plus newsagency.

Real Journeys (☎ 0800 656 501; www.realjourneys. co.nz) Shares a building with the i-SITE and offers a range of Fiordland-focused tours and activities.

Wash'n'Surf (122 Town Centre; per load $8; ☼ 9am-9pm) A combination laundry and internet cafe.

Sights
TE ANAU GLOWWORM CAVES
Once present only in Maori legends, these impressive caves on the lake's western shore were rediscovered in 1948. Accessible only by boat, the 200m-long system of caves is a magical place with sculpted rocks, waterfalls small and large, whirlpools and a glittering glowworm grotto in its inner reaches. Real Journeys (left) runs 2¼-hour guided tours (per adult/child $63/20), reaching the heart of the caves by a walkway and a short underground boat ride.

TE ANAU WILDLIFE CENTRE
The DOC-run **Te Anau Wildlife Centre** (☎ 03-249 0200; Te Anau–Manapouri Rd; admission by donation; ☼ dawn-dusk) hosts native bird species – including the rare flightless takahe – NZ pigeons, tui, kaka, weka and various waterfowl.

Activities
TRAMPING
If you're planning on tramping, pick up information and register your intentions at the DOC office (opposite).

Kepler Track

This 60km circular Great Walk starts less than an hour's walk from Te Anau and heads west into the Kepler Mountains, taking in the lake, rivers, gorges, glacier-carved valleys and beech forest. The walk can be done in four days, or three if you exit at Rainbow Reach. On the first day you reach the tree line, giving panoramic views. The alpine stretch between Luxmore and Iris Burn Huts goes along a high ridge, well above the bush and offers fantastic views when it's clear; in poor weather it can be treacherous. It's recommended that the track be done in the Luxmore–Iris Burn–Moturau direction.

Like any Fiordland track, the weather has a major impact on the walk; you should expect at least one day of rain and be prepared for some wading. The alpine sections require a good level of fitness and may be closed in winter due to bad weather conditions. Other sections are considered moderate with climbs and descents of up to 1000m and unbridged stream crossings.

During the main walking season (October to April), advance bookings must be made by all trampers online at www.booking.doc.govt .nz or at any DOC visitor centre. Over this period, a **Great Walks hut pass** (per night adult/child $45/free) buys accommodation in the track's three well-maintained huts – Luxmore, Iris Burn and Moturau – each with heating and cooking facilities. A **camping pass** (per night adult/child $15/free) permits you to camp at the designated sites at Brod Bay and adjacent to Iris Burn

Hut. Outside this main season, a Backcountry Hut Pass still needs to be prepurchased (per night adult/child $15/free), but no heating or cooking is on offer. Off-season camping is free.

Estimated walking times:

Day	Route	Time
1	Te Anau DOC office to control gates	45min
1	Control gates to Brod Bay	1½hr
1	Brod Bay to Luxmore Hut	3½-4½hr
2	Luxmore Hut to Iris Burn Hut	5-6hr
3	Iris Burn Hut to Moturau Hut	5-6hr
4	Moturau Hut to Rainbow Reach	1½-2hr
4	Rainbow Reach to control gates	2½-3½hr

TrackNet (☎ 0800 483 262; www.tracknet.net) and **Topline Tours** (☎ 03-249 8059; www.toplinetours.co.nz) provide transport to and from the ends of the track for between $5 and $11.

Short Walks

You can set out along the Kepler Track on free day walks. **Kepler Water Taxi** (☎ 03-249 8364; stevsaunders@xtra.co.nz; one way/return $25/40) will scoot you over to Brod Bay from where you can walk to Mt Luxmore (seven to eight hours) or along the southern lakeshore back to Te Anau (two to three hours). Regular shuttles leave Te Anau lakefront at 8.30am and 9.30am during summer. There are also many short walks in the area (see p650).

During summer **Trips'n'Tramps** (☎ 03-249 7081; www.tripsandtramps.com; ☺ Oct-Apr) takes trampers

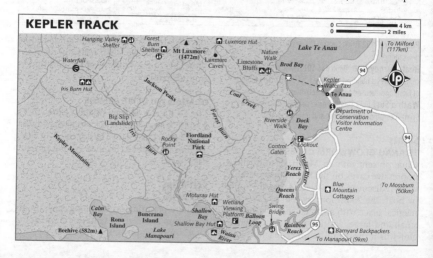

KEPLER TRACK

on small-group, half- to two-day guided hikes on sections of the Routeburn and Kepler and Hollyford Tracks. Some departures incorporate kayaking on Milford Sound. Real Journeys (p645) runs guided day hikes (adult/child $190/123.50, November to mid-April) along an 11km stretch of the Milford Track.

Grab a copy of *Fiordland National Park Day Walks* ($1 from Fiordland i-SITE) for more options.

Equipment
Make sure you're well equipped and have good rain gear before commencing any tracks. **Bev's Tramping Gear** (☎ 03-249 7389; www.bevs-hire .co.nz; 16 Homer St; ◷ 9am-noon & 6.30-8pm, closed Sun morning) Topographical maps for sale and tramping and camping equipment for hire.
Te Anau Outside Sports (☎ 03-249 8195; 38 Town Centre) Equipment for sale or hire.

KAYAKING & JETBOATING
Kayaking in the pristine waterways of the World Heritage Area is unbeatable. **Fiordland Wilderness Experiences** (☎ 0800 200 434; www.fiord landseakayak.co.nz) runs one-day and multiday kayaking explorations of Lake Te Anau and Lake Manapouri. Prices start at $130 per day. See p654 for kayaking trips on Milford Sound and Doubtful Sound.

Luxmore Jet (☎ 0800 253 826, 03-249 6951; www. luxmorejet.com; per adult/child $95/45) does a one-hour ride on the stunningly beautiful Waiau River which links Lakes Te Anau and Manapouri, and includes *Lord of the Rings* locations.

OTHER ACTIVITIES
The i-SITE provides information on guided **trout fishing** (fly, trolling or spinning). River and stream fishing takes place roughly from October to May, while lake fishing occurs year-round. Pick up a licence from DOC.

Te Anau Bike Hire (☎ 03-249 7211; 7 Mokonui St; bike hire per hr/day from $10/25; ◷ from 10am Sep-Apr) hires mountain bikes, kids' bikes and tandems. **High Ride Adventures** (☎ 03-249 8591; www.highride.co.nz; quad-bike trips $145, horse trips $80) offers 3½-hour backcountry trips on quad-bikes and 3½-hour horseback trips along Whitestone River.

Fiordland Astronomy (☎ 0508 COSMOS; www.astro nomyfiordland.co.nz; per person $40; ◷ weather permitting) takes small groups (maximum eight) to view the night sky by binoculars and 30cm telescope on 'Night Sky Safaris'. The newly opened **Stardome** (Events Centre, Luxmore Dr; per person $30) is an interactive digital planetarium that's a good companion activity. Enquire at the Fiordland i-SITE about bookings and times.

Tours
With blue lakes, dark forests and steep snowy mountains visible the moment you get aloft, this is one of the greatest places in NZ to do some aerial sightseeing. **Wings & Water Te Anau** (☎ 03-249 7405; www.wingsandwater.co.nz; Lakefront Dr) has seaplane flights right off Lakefront Dr with a 10-minute zip around the local area (adult/child $95/55) and longer flights over the Kepler Track, and Doubtful and Milford Sounds (from $295). **Air Fiordland** (☎ 0800 107 505; www.airfiordland.co.nz) offers similar deals.

Southern Lakes Helicopters (☎ 03-249 7167; www.southernlakeshelicopters.co.nz; Lakefront Dr) buzzes over Te Anau for 25 minutes ($190) and does longer trips over Doubtful, Dusky and Milford Sounds (from $530) and a chopper/walk/boat option on a part of the Kepler Track ($180).

Sleeping
Although Te Anau has many hostels, cabins, motels and hotels, all the accommodation in town can still be booked out in the middle of the peak season (late December to February). It pays to book early if possible.

BUDGET
Te Anau Lakeview Holiday Park (☎ 03-249 7457; www. teanau.info; 77 Te Anau-Manapouri Rd; sites per person from $15.50, dm $27, s $35, d $60-89, cabins d $68-78, self-contained d $90-130; ☐ ⬤) This huge lakeside complex, 1.5km out of town, combines the Te Anau Lakeview campsite (with tent/van sites and several types of cabins and self-contained motel units sleeping up to seven), West Arm singles accommodation (basic and institutional, but more private than dorms), and Steamers backpackers (characterless rooms but sharing a modern and comfortable communal kitchen and lounge space).

Te Anau Great Lakes Holiday Park (☎ 0800 249 555; www.greatlakes.co.nz; cnr Luxmore Dr & Milford Rd; sites per person $16.50, dm $25, cabins $58-65, units $95-195; ☐ ⬤) A grassy holiday park with a big modern kitchen and a bunch of cabins and units.

Te Anau Lakefront Backpackers (☎ 03-249 7713; www.teanaubackpackers.co.nz; 48-50 Lakefront Dr; tent sites per person $18, dm $26-28, d $72-92; ☐ ⬤) This sprawling collection of buildings has a huge variety of rooms, some sunny and spacious, others pokey and worn. Regardless, the staff are friendly and helpful, there's a nice communal vibe, lots of warm fires in the winter, a shady peaceful garden warbling with tui and a fantastic location right beside the lake. Backpackers are well loved, with lakeview dorms and a virtual encouragement to party, but there's everything through to quieter family options out the back. Bikes are available for hire.

Barnyard Backpackers (Map p646; ☎ 03-249 8006; www.barnyardbackpackers.com; 80 Mt York Rd, off SH95; dm $26-28, d $66; 🖳) On a deer farm 9km south of town towards Manapouri, this charmingly rustic communal building and its collection of log cabins sit on a hillside with a view to the Kepler Mountains. Cabins are comfortable and en-suited, and the communal area is great for playing pool or sitting around the central fireplace. A good home base for the Kepler Track.

Te Anau YHA (☎ 03-249 7847; yha.teanau@yha.co.nz; www.yha.co.nz; 29 Mokonui St; dm/s/d from $28/51/74; 🖳 🛜) The most central of the backpackers in Te Anau. This bright and modern hostel has great facilities and comfortable, colourful rooms. Lounge in the hammock, barbecue in the grassy backyard, or get cosy by the wood fire.

ourpick Bob & Maxines (☎ 03-9313161; bob.anderson@woosh.co.nz; 20 Paton Pl, off Oraka St; dm/tw $30/80; 🖳) Only 2.5km out of town, off the Te Anau–Milford Hwy, but feeling a million miles away, this relaxed hostel gets rave reviews for the big mountain views from the communal lounge. Get toasty beside the woodburner, cook up a storm in the spacious modern kitchen, or just chill out a while. New additions include warming heat pumps and the whole place is wheelchair friendly. Bikes are available to get you back into town.

Rosie's Backpacker Homestay (☎ 03-249 8431; backpack@paradise.net.nz; 23 Tom Plato Dr; dm/d $31/74; 🖳 🛜) You're immediately made to feel part of the family in this small and intimate homestay. It's in the 'burbs a short walk north of the town centre. They're closed June and July.

Te Anau Top 10 Holiday Park (☎ 0800 249 746, 03-249 7462; www.teanautop10.co.nz; 128 Te Anau Tce; sites from $34, cabins $52-68, d $120-170; 🖳 🛜) This classic holiday park near the town and lake has excellent facilities with small but private sites, a playground, sauna, bike hire, barbecue area and modern kitchen. Cabins and units run from basic to fancy.

MIDRANGE & TOP END

If you're here in winter it's always worth asking the motels and B&Bs about a discount on their high-season rates.

Lakeside Motel (☎ 0800 452 537, 03-249 7435; www.lakesideteanau.com; 36 Lakefront Dr; d $130-220; 🖳 🛜) With most units directly facing across the grassy lawns to the lake, this motel has excellent views, particularly from the 1st floor. Inside, there's plenty of light from the large windows and good cooking facilities. It's also wheelchair friendly.

Cosy Kiwi (☎ 0800 249 700, 03-249 7475; www.cosykiwi.com; 186 Milford Rd; s $170-320, d $150-165; 🖳 🛜) The sign says B&B, but this friendly spot is actually more of a smart motel with modern, well-appointed rooms just a short stroll from bustling downtown Te Anau. Breakfast is included in the rates, and host Eleanor usually offers a couple of cooked options. You'll need a good start to the day if you're getting active in the great outdoors.

Te Anau Lodge B&B (☎ 03-249 7477; www.teanaulodge.com; 52 Howden St; s $170-320, d $200-350; 🖳 🛜) The former 1930s-built Sisters of Mercy Convent, relocated to a grand location just north of town, is a positively decadent accommodation option. Sip your drink in a Chesterfield in front of the fire, retire to your spa before collapsing on a king-size bed, then awaken to a fresh, delicious breakfast in the old chapel. Plans are afoot to hold concerts in the spacious lawns.

Cat's Whiskers B&B (☎ 03-249 8112; www.catswhiskers.co.nz; 2 Lakefront Dr; d $175-215; 🖳 🛜) This family home features four large recently redecorated en-suite rooms and great lake views just across the road. There's a sunny alfresco area to relax in at the back of the house, and the family room sleeps four.

Keiko's B&B (☎ 03-249 9248; www.keikos.co.nz; 228 Milford Rd; d $195; 🕑 closed Jun-Aug; 🛜) The private, self-contained cottages here are lovely, and the entirety is surrounded by an explosion of flowers and Japanese-style gardens. A Japanese breakfast in the morning and a bamboo-bordered hot tub in the evening are essential extras.

Blue Mountain Cottages (Map p646; ☎ 03-249 9030; www.bluemountaincottages.co.nz; Hwy 95; cabins $260) These two plush self-contained cabins surrounded by farmland 8km south of town can sleep up to six, so they're a good family option. Home-grown meat and produce is available to guests.

The following is a small selection of the local motels.

Anchorage Motel (☎ 03-249 7256; www.teanaumotel. co.nz; 47 Quintin Dr; d $85-175; 🖥 📶) Good for kids and wheelchair friendly.

Edgewater Motel (☎ 0800 433 439, 03-249 7258; www.edgewater.net.nz; 52 Lakefront Dr; d $140-250; 🖥 📶) Light, comfortable rooms with good cooking facilities. A stand-alone two-bedroom luxury villa is also available ($400).

Eating

RESTAURANTS & CAFES

Olive Tree Café & Restaurant (☎ 03-249 8496; 52 Town Centre; snacks & burgers from $7, mains $21-38; 😋 8am-9.30pm Sep-May, 9am-8pm Jun-Aug) Tucked away at the end of an unremarkable-looking arcade, Olive Tree is warm and funky inside, with excellent outdoor areas to sip coffee in the sun or enjoy a tasty Mediterranean-flavoured meal.

La Toscana (☎ 03-249 7756; 108 Town Centre; pasta $12-20, pizza $12-24; 😋 5.30pm-late) Buzzy, noisy and relaxed, with wooden booths and tables, this is a lively spot for a late-night snack, or a good dinner option. Pizzas and pastas are large and great value, and takeaways and deliveries are available.

Ruchee (☎ 03-249 9298; 5 The Lane; mains $16-22; 😋 5pm-late Mon, noon-3pm & 5pm-late Tue-Sun, closed May-Oct; Ⓥ) It's great to have a subcontinental alternative to Te Anau's plethora of Italian eateries, and this is a pleasant, mellow place for a curry. The cooking isn't going to change your life, but it's not bad for provincial NZ. Takeaways are available.

Glasshouse (Milford Cres; mains $20-33; 😋 9.30am-late) Come along for the ultimate pre-Milford Sound breakfast, and then return for dinner to sample innovative, well-priced variations on lamb, venison and chicken. The minimalist decor is slightly clinical, but the effusive and warm service easily compensates.

Fat Duck (☎ 03-249 8480; 124 Town Centre; dinner mains $22-38; 😋 noon-late Mon-Fri, from 10am Sat & Sun) Friendly service overcomes the slightly bland decor, and the Fat Duck gets top-notch reviews from most travellers. Dishes are tasty, and hearty in proportions, and variations on basics such as crispy duck, pork belly and salmon are imaginative. There's a bar almost as long as Doubtful Sound if you just want a drink before kicking on somewhere else. Closed Monday and Tuesday outside of the peak season.

La Dolce Vita (☎ 03-249 8895; 90 Town Centre; pasta & mains $28-32; 😋 3pm-late) Run by familia Lombardi, this very stylish, ultramodern-looking restaurant stretches beyond simple Italian fare to include Southland cuisine with fresh seafood, local lamb and big steaks. Fresh-made pasta dishes ($22) are also popular.

Redcliff Bar & Restaurant (☎ 03-249 7431; 12 Mokonui St; mains $30-39; 😋 5pm-late) Housed in a replica old settler's cottage, Redcliff specialises in a buzzy, convivial atmosphere and locally sourced produce. Try the wild Fiordland venison or tender herby hare. Wine is affordably priced, but a few more options by the glass wouldn't go amiss. They don't take bookings so kick off your night with a drink in the rustic front bar; it's also *the* place in town for a quiet after-dinner drink. There's occasional live music and a permanent friendly vibe with excellent service.

QUICK EATS & SELF-CATERING

Miles Better Pies (☎ 03-249 9044; cnr Town Centre & Mokonui St; pies $5; 😋 6am-4pm) The classic Kiwi pie has never looked better. Choose from freshly made gourmet venison, Thai curry or apricot pies. There are a few pavement tables, but sitting beside the lake is nicer, and the pies also make a good snack for the road.

Sandfly Café (☎ 03-249 9529; 9 The Lane; breakfast & lunch $6-15; 😋 7am-4.30pm; 🖥 📶) With the best coffee in Te Anau, this is a lovely, chilled-out place to relax. Enjoy the music, the all-day breakfast and the yummy baking including excellent wraps. Sandfly is closed Mondays during winter.

Self-catering provisions can be found at **Fresh Choice Supermarket** (1 The Lane; 😋 7am-8pm).

Drinking & Entertainment

Redcliff Bar & Restaurant (above) has occasional live music and is the most atmospheric option for drinks. More raucous is the **Ranch Bar & Grill** (☎ 03-249 8801; Town Centre; 😋 noon-late), with Happy Hour from 8pm to 9pm and good value Sunday-night roast dinners ($13.50). The cavernous lakefront **Moose** (☎ 03-249 7100; 84 Lakefront Dr) has big-screen sports and a sunny patio. It also does meals and bar snacks.

In between back-to-back showings of the excellent *Ata Whenua* ($10), essentially a 32-minute advertisement for stunning Fiordland scenery, **Fiordland Cinema** (☎ 03-249 8812; www.fiordlandcinema.co.nz; 7 The Lane; $15; 📶)

shows other flicks too. There's also a good bar with lots of South Island wines, beers and wi-fi access.

Getting There & Away

InterCity (☎ 03-249 7559; www.intercity.co.nz) has daily bus services between Te Anau and Queenstown ($38, 2½ hours), Invercargill ($48, 2½ hours) and Dunedin ($45, 4¾ hours). Look online for discounts. Buses depart outside Kiwi Country on Miro St.

Other bus services include:

Bottom Bus (☎ 03-477 9083; http://travelheadfirst. com/bottom-bus/) Hop-on, hop-off bus service linking Te Anau to Queenstown, Invercargill and Milford Sound.

Naked Bus (☎ 0900 625 33; www.nakedbus.com) Connects Te Anau with Queenstown ($29), Invercargill ($24) and Milford Sound ($24).

Scenic Shuttle (☎ 0800 277 483; www.scenicshuttle. co.nz) Via the Southern Scenic Route past Manapouri and Tuatapere to Invercargill ($49).

Topline Tours (☎ 03-249 8059; www.toplinetours. co.nz) Daily door-to-door between Te Anau and Queenstown ($38).

TrackNet (☎ 0800 483 262; www.tracknet.net) Connects Te Anau with Queenstown (adult $43), Milford ($47, 2½ hours), Invercargill ($45) and to and from several tramping tracks.

The following transport options are available for trampers. TrackNet (see above) has daily shuttles to the Kepler, Hollyford and Milford Tracks, and to the western end of the Routeburn, Greenstone and Caples Tracks at the Divide.

The **Kepler Water Taxi** (☎ 03-249 8364; stevsaunders@xtra.co.nz) runs regularly across the lake to Brod Bay (one way $20, 10 minutes) on the Kepler Track in summer. **Wings & Water** (☎ 03-249 7405; www.wingsandwater.co.nz) provides transport to Supper Cove ($315 per person, minimum two passengers) for Dusky Sound trampers.

TE ANAU–MILFORD HWY

If you don't have the opportunity to hike into Fiordland's wilderness, the 119km road from Te Anau to Milford is the most easily accessible taste of its vastness and beauty. Even if you don't do a cruise at the other end, it's still a top road trip for sheer scenic wonder.

Head out from Te Anau early (8am) or later in the morning (11am) to avoid the tour buses heading for midday sound cruises. See p655 for important information about chains and avalanches (in winter) and petrol (always). It's a tricky road, so take care.

The trip takes two to 2½ hours if you drive straight through, but take time to stop and experience the majestic landscape. Pull off the road and explore the many viewpoints and nature walks en route. A few are listed in the following section, but a *Fiordland National Park Day Walks* brochure ($1 from DOC or the i-SITE) will equip you for some self-discovery.

The first part of the road meanders through rolling farmland atop the lateral moraine of the glacier that once gouged out Lake Te Anau. The road passes **Te Anau Downs** (there's accommodation here at Fiordland National Park Lodge, see p653) after 29km and heads towards the entrance of Fiordland National Park, passing patches of beech (red, silver and mountain), alluvial flats and meadows.

Just past the **McKay Creek** campsite (at 51km) are great views over Eglinton Valley with sheer mountains either side and Pyramid Peak (2295m) and Ngatimamoe Peak (2164m) ahead. The boardwalk at **Mirror Lakes** (at 58km) takes you through beech forest and wetlands, and on a calm day the lakes reflect the mountains across the valley. **Knobs Flat** (at 63km) also has accommodation (p653).

At the 77km mark is the area referred to as O Tapara, or more commonly as **Cascade Creek**. O Tapara is the original name of nearby Lake Gunn, and was a stopover historically for Maori parties heading to Anita Bay in search of *pounamu* (greenstone). A walking track (45 minutes) passes through tall red beech forest ringing with bird calls. Side trails lead to quiet lakeside beaches.

At 84km the vegetation changes as you pass across the **Divide**, the lowest east–west pass in the Southern Alps. There's a large roadside shelter here for walkers either finishing or starting the Routeburn, Greenstone or Caples Tracks; it's also used as a terminal for trampers' bus services (above left). A walk from the shelter, initially through beech forest along the start of the Routeburn, then climbing up alpine tussockland to **Key Summit** (two hours return), offers spectacular views of the three valleys that radiate from this point.

From the Divide, the road falls into the beech forest of the **Hollyford Valley** (stop at Pop's View for a great view) and there's a worthwhile detour to **Gunn's Camp & Museum** (p653) 8km along an unsealed road. About 9km further, at the end of that road, is a walk to the high **Humboldt Falls** (30 minutes return) and the start of the Hollyford Track (below).

Back on the main road to Milford, the road climbs to the **Homer Tunnel**, 101km from Te Anau and framed by a spectacular, high-walled, ice-carved amphitheatre. The tunnel is one-way outside avalanche season, with the world's most alpine set of traffic lights to direct traffic. Kea, the delinquent teenagers of the parrot world, hang around the eastern end of the tunnel hoping tourists stopped at the lights will be stupid enough to feed them. (Resist the urge, because what we eat just isn't good for them.) Dark, magnificently rough-hewn and dripping with water, the 1207m-long tunnel emerges at the other end at the head of the spectacular **Cleddau Valley**.

About 10km before Milford, the **Chasm Walk** (20 minutes return and even accessible by wheelchair, though you might appreciate assistance on the steeper parts) is well worth a stop. The forest-cloaked Cleddau River plunges through eroded boulders in a narrow chasm, creating deep falls and a natural rock bridge. From here, watch for glimpses of **Mt Tutoko** (2746m), Fiordland's highest peak, above the beech forest just before Milford.

Hollyford Track

This dramatic track starts in the midst of lowland forest, crossing mountain streams and passing pretty waterfalls as it follows the broad Hollyford River valley all the way to the sea. The Tasman coast makes a satisfying end point, with dolphins, seals and penguins often greeting hikers on their arrival. However, it does mean backtracking another four days back to your start point unless you take one of the sneaky shortcut options.

The 56km track is graded as a moderate hike, but involves some creek crossings and suffers frequent flash floods that can leave trekkers waiting it out en-route for several days until the trail becomes passable. The trickiest part of the route is the ominously named Demon Trail (10km) alongside Lake McKerrow. It's imperative that you check with DOC in Te Anau for the latest track and weather conditions and for detailed maps.

TrackNet (☎ 0800 483 262; www.tracknet.net) has shuttles between the Hollyford Rd turn-off and Te Anau ($47, one hour) and Queenstown ($87, 3¾ hours).

Options for reducing the length of the there-and-back journey include hitching a jetboat

---

TE WAHIPOUNAMU SOUTHWEST NZ WORLD HERITAGE AREA

In the southwest corner of NZ, the combination of four huge national parks make up Te Wahipounamu Southwest New Zealand World Heritage Area. Te Wahipounamu (The Place of Greenstone) covers 2.6 million hectares and is recognised internationally for its cultural significance to the Ngai Tahu, as well as for the area's unique fauna and wildlife. Te Wahipounamu incorporates the following national parks:

- Fiordland National Park (p644)
- Aoraki/Mt Cook National Park (p566)
- Westland Tai Poutini National Park (p506)
- Mt Aspiring National Park (p633)

---

ride south with **Hollyford Track Guided Walks** (☎ 0800 832 226, 03-442 3000; www.hollyfordtrack.com; $110) for the length of Lake McKerrow; book in advance. A more-luxurious, three-day guided walk ($1655) includes fancy accommodation, jetboat trips in both directions along Lake McKerrow and a flight back to Milford Sound from the coastal finish line at Martins Bay.

You can also arrange a flight between Martins Bay and civilisation with **Air Fiordland** (☎ 03-249 6720; www.airfiordland.com; to Milford/Te Anau $580/1160) for up to four people (price is per flight, so you can share the cost). Hollyford Track Guided Walks sometimes has empty seats when it flies from Milford Sound to pick up its walkers at Martins Bay, and can drop you at Martins Bay by plane ($135) or helicopter ($185). Booking these services is essential.

Milford Track

The famous Milford Track is a 53.5km walk often described as one of the finest in the world. The number of walkers is limited in the Great Walks season (late October to late April), and during that period you must follow a one-way, four-day set itinerary. Accommodation is only in huts (camping isn't allowed).

Even in summer, expect *lots* of rain, in the wake of which water will cascade everywhere and small streams will become raging torrents within minutes. Remember to bring wet-weather gear and pack belongings in an extra plastic bag or two.

In the off-season, experienced trampers can walk the track in either direction without bookings (hut tickets must be purchased). At this time there's limited trail transport, the huts aren't staffed, some of the bridges are removed and, in the height of winter, snow and avalanches make it unwise. It's vitally important you first visit DOC (p644) to check avalanche risk, as the geography of the valley makes it impossible to judge for yourself.

BOOKINGS

You can walk the track independently or with a guided tour. For independent bookings, contact DOC in Te Anau (p644) or book online at http://booking.doc.govt.nz/. The track must be booked during the Great Walks season (October to April), and it certainly pays to book as far ahead as possible. Bookings open up to 12 months before the start of the following season. A Great Walks pass (adult/child $135/free) allows you three nights in the huts. During the Great Walks season the track can only be done in one direction (Lake Te Anau to Milford) and

you must begin on the date specified on your DOC permit.

Ultimate Hikes (☎ 0800 659 255, 03-442 8200; www. milfordtrack.co.nz; Dec-Mar adult/child $1900/1700, Apr & Nov adult/child $1740/1540) has five-day guided walks that include everything from packs to snacks to raincoats and stays at much flasher accommodation, ending with a celebratory dinner at their last stay, Mitre Peak Lodge at Milford Sound.

Real Journeys (☎ 0800 656 501; www.realjourneys. co.nz; adult/child $190/123.50; ☺ Nov–mid-Apr) runs guided day hikes along an 11km stretch of the Milford Track.

WALKING THE TRACK

The trail starts at Glade House, at the northern end of Lake Te Anau, accessed by boat from Te Anau Downs or Te Anau. The track follows the flat bottom of the Clinton River Valley up to its head at Lake Mintaro, passing through rainforest and crystal-clear streams. From Mintaro you cross the dramatic **Mackinnon Pass**, which on a clear day gives spectacular views back to yesterday's Clinton Valley and forward to tomorrow's Arthur Valley. (If the pass appears clear when you arrive at Mintaro Hut, make the effort to climb it, as it may not be clear the next day.) From the pass a long, wooden staircase leads you down to Arthur River, following alongside the rapids. The trail then continues down to Quintin and Dumpling Huts and through the valley rainforest to Milford Sound. You can leave your pack at the Quintin public shelter while you make the return walk to the graceful, 630m-high **Sutherland Falls**, NZ's tallest falls. Estimated walking times:

MILFORD TRACK

Day	Route	Time
1	Wharf to Glade House	20min
1	Glade House to Clinton Hut	1-1½hr
2	Clinton Hut to Mintaro Hut	6hr
3	Mintaro Hut to Dumpling Hut	6-7hr
3	Side trip to Sutherland Falls	1½hr return
4	Dumpling Hut to Sandfly Point	5½-6hr

TRANSPORT TO GLADE WHARF

During the Great Walks season, **TrackNet** (☎ 0800 483 262; www.tracknet.net; $22) drives up from Te Anau to Te Anau Downs. TrackNet also offers the option of transport from Queenstown to Te Anau Downs ($65). **Real Journeys** (☎ 0800 656 501; www.realjourneys.co.nz; $65) will then run you by boat from Te Anau Downs to Glade Wharf near the start of the track. Both of these trips can be booked at DOC in Te Anau at the same time as you book your walk. Outside the Great Walks season, talk to TrackNet about transport the whole way to Glade Wharf.

TRANSPORT FROM SANDFLY POINT

There are ferries leaving Sandfly Point at 2pm and 3.15pm for the Milford Sound cruise wharf (adult/child $34/19.50). From there you can bus back to Te Anau with TrackNet ($47, 2½ hours). These can both be booked via DOC at Te Anau.

PACKAGES

Cruise Te Anau (☎ 03-249 7593; www.cruiseteanau.co.nz) does a bus-boat combination trip for around $150.

Sleeping

Along State Highway 94 (SH94) are many basic **DOC camping grounds** (sites $10), the majority of them situated between 45km and 81km from Te Anau. You'll find them in *Conservation Campsites – South Island* (free from DOC in Te Anau), or search www .doc.govt.nz for Te Anau area conservation campsites.

At Te Anau Downs (29km from Te Anau) at the head of the lake where boats depart for Milford Track, **Fiordland National Park Lodge** (☎ 0800 500 805, 03-249 7811; www.teanau-milfordsound. co.nz; SH94; d hotel $65-140, motel $130-160; 💻 🛜) has slightly dated hotel-motel-type units. Views of the lake and mountains are spectacular from the hotel rooms. Motel units have a less spectacular view, but are still comfortable. It's popular with Milford Track walkers, but other travellers are also welcome.

In the grassy Eglinton Valley, 63km from Te Anau, **Knob's Flat** (☎ 03-249 9122; www.knobsflat. co.nz; studio/motel units $115/135) has comfortable units catering to walkers and fisherfolk. TV, mobile phones, email and stress have no place here.

Gunn's Camp (Hollyford Rd; gunnscamp@ruralinzone. net; sites per person $10, d/tw $20/48), also known as Hollyford Camp, is on Hollyford Rd about halfway between SH94 (8km) and the start of the Hollyford Track (9km). The old public-works cabins are very basic (linen hire is $5 per bed), and heating is via a coal/wood-fired stove (fuel provided). A generator supplies limited electricity, turning off at 10.30pm, and there's gas for cooking and for hot showers. There's also a small shop and a small, wonderfully eccentric **museum** (admission adult/child $1/30c, guests free) with pioneering memorabilia.

Milford Sound Lodge (☎ 03-249 8071; www.milford lodge.com; just off SH94; unpowered/powered sites per person $16/20, dm/d $30/80; 💻 🛜) is spectacularly located; nestled in forest, surrounded by towering mountains and alongside the Cleddau River. This simple but comfortable lodge has an unhurried, ends-of-the-earth air. There's no TV, and travellers and trampers relax in the large lounges to discuss their travels. There's a tiny shop-cafe-bar and a free shuttle to Milford Sound, just 1.5km away. Brandnew and very comfortable chalets ($225) enjoy an absolute riverside location, and the entire lodge was undergoing a makeover when we dropped in.

MILFORD SOUND
pop 170

The first sight of Milford Sound is stunning: still, dark waters out of which rise sheer rocky cliffs, and forests clinging to the slopes sometimes relinquish their hold, causing a 'tree avalanche' into the waters. The spectacular, photogenic 1692m-high Mitre Peak rises dead ahead. A cruise on Milford Sound is Fiordland's most accessible experience, complete with seals, dolphins, and an average rainfall of 7m; more than enough to fuel cascading waterfalls and add a shimmering moody mist to the scene.

Milford Sound receives about half a million visitors each year, most of them crammed into the peak months (January and February). Some 14,000 arrive by foot, via the Milford Track which ends at the sound, many more drive from Te Anau, but most arrive via the multitude of buses that pull into the cruise wharf. But don't worry. Out on the water all of this humanity seems tiny compared to nature's vastness.

There's not much else to town apart from the cruise terminal and the car park, though if you take the turn off to Deep Water Basin about 1km out of town, you can explore the small fishing wharf area.

Activities

SEA KAYAKING

One of the best perspectives on Milford Sound is from a kayak at water level dwarfed by the vertically rising cliffs. **Rosco's Milford Sound Sea Kayaks** (☎ 03-249 8500; www.roscosmilfordkayaks.com; $115-169) has tours taking in the sound's most breathtaking sights. Recommended excursions include the 'Morning Glory', a challenging early morning kayak (around five hours in the boat) the full length of the fiord to Anita Bay, and the 'Stirling Sunrise', which includes kayaking under the 151m-high Stirling Falls. For that one, you can probably forego your morning shower. Another option includes a 20-minute paddle to Sandfly Point and a 3½-hour walk on the Milford Track ($89). In Te Anau you'll find Rosco's at Adventure Fiordland (p644).

Fiordland Wilderness Experiences (☎ 0800 200 434, 03-249-7700; www.fiordlandseakayak.co.nz) also runs guided day paddles on the sound; they cost with/without return transport to Te Anau $155/125.

UNDERWATER EXPLORATION

Unique environmental circumstances have allowed the sound to become home to some rarely glimpsed marine life. Heavy rainfall sluicing straight off the rocky slopes washes significant organic matter into the ocean, creating a 5m-deep permanent tannin-stained freshwater layer above the warmer sea water. This dark layer filters out much of the sunlight and, coupled with the sound's calm, protected waters, replicates deep-ocean conditions. The result is that deep-water species thrive not far below the surface. A similar situation exists at Doubtful Sound (p656).

Milford Deep Underwater Observatory (adult/child $29/15; ☼ 9am-3.45pm) is a five-storey mostly submerged building that dangles from a system of interlinked pontoons attached to a rock face. Four storeys below the surface are resident deep-water corals, tube anemones and bottom-dwelling sea perch. The observatory visits are informative, but the accompanying tour groups may dilute the experience. Various operators stop here (charging around $29/15 extra for adults/kids), but not the late-afternoon cruises.

Tawaki Adventures (☎ 0800 829 254; www.tawaki dive.co.nz) takes scuba-dive trips on the sound. Trips include a three-hour boat cruise and two guided dives of a total of 30 minutes

($159); it's an extra $99 for gear hire. If you don't dive you can join the boat trip anyway ($99 plus $45 to hire snorkelling gear).

Tours

MILFORD SOUND CRUISES

Each Milford Sound cruise company claims to be quieter, smaller, bigger, cheaper or in some way preferable to the rest. What really makes a difference is the timing of the cruise; most bus tours aim for 1pm sailings so if you avoid that time of day there'll be less people on the boat (and on the road!). With some companies you get a better price on cruises outside rush hour too. If you're particularly keen on wildlife, ask whether there'll be a nature guide on board. It's wise to book ahead regardless. You generally need to arrive 20 minutes before departure. Most companies offer coach transfers from Te Anau for an additional cost. Day trips from Queenstown make for a very long 13-hour day.

All the cruises visit the mouth of the sound, only 15km from the wharf, poking their prow into the choppy waves of the Tasman Sea. The shorter cruises visit less of the en route 'highlights', which include Bowen Falls, Mitre Peak, Anita Bay and Stirling Falls. You'll have a good chance of seeing dolphins, seals and penguins. All cruises leave from the huge **cruise terminal** (☼ 8am-5.15pm Oct-Apr, 9am-4.15pm May-Sep), a 10-minute walk from the cafe and car park.

Real Journeys (☎ 0800 656 501; www.realjourneys. co.nz) does 1¾-hour scenic cruises (adult $62 to $84, child $15). The company also does 2½-hour nature cruises (adult $68 to $88, child $15) with a nature guide for commentary and Q&A.

Mitre Peak Cruises (☎ 0800 744 633; www.mitrepeak. com) does two-hour tours (adult $64 to $74, child $15) in smallish boats with a maximum capacity of 75. The 4.30pm summer cruise is good because many larger boats are heading back at this time.

Red Boat Cruises (☎ 0800 264 536, 03-441 1137; www. redboats.co.nz) does 1¾-hour trips (adult/child $65/15). The noon cruise is $75, because that's when most passengers will be here. The 2¼-hour wildlife cruise (adult $74 to $90, child $15) is more intimate.

Cruising Milford Sound (☎ 0800 500 121; www. cruizemilford.co.nz) does 1½-hour trips (adult $55 to $70, child $15) on a smallish, comfortable boat with lots of deck space.

OVERNIGHT CRUISES

Real Journeys (☎ 0800 656 501, 03-249 7416; www.real journeys.co.nz) does overnight cruises on two of its boats. You can kayak and take nature tours in tender crafts en route. The cost includes all meals but transport from Te Anau is additional. All depart from the Milford terminal around 4.30pm and return around 9.30am the following day. Cheaper prices apply in April, May, September and October.

The *Milford Wanderer*, modelled on an old trading scow, accommodates 61 passengers in four-bunk cabins (with shared bathrooms) and costs $230/115 per adult/child. The *Milford Mariner* sleeps 60 in more upmarket, en-suite, twin-share cabins ($470/235 per adult/child).

Sleeping & Eating

The excellent Milford Sound Lodge (p653) is just 1.5km back up the road towards Te Anau. A small cafe is attached.

The **Blue Duck Café & Bar** (☎ 03-249 7931; car park; ☺ 8.30am-late; ☐) serves sandwiches and buffet-type meals. At night the attached bar sees a mix of travellers, trampers and locals.

Getting There & Away

BUS

InterCity (☎ 03-249 7559; www.intercity.co.nz) runs daily bus services from Queenstown ($80) and Te Anau ($39). Trampers' buses also operate from Te Anau (p650) and Queenstown (p625) and will pick up at the Milford Sound Lodge. All these buses pass the Divide and the start/end of the Routeburn, Greenstone and Caples Tracks.

Many bus trips include a boat cruise on the sound; most are around $160 from Te Anau (or around $230 from Queenstown).

CAR

It's a magnificent drive from Te Anau to Milford (see p650). Fill up with petrol in Te Anau before setting off. Chains must be carried on avalanche-risk days from May to November (there will be signs on the road) and can be hired from most service stations in Te Anau.

MANAPOURI

pop 210

Manapouri is largely used as a jumping-off point for cruises to the sublime Doubtful Sound (p656), and as a base for walking expeditions.

In 1969, Manapouri was the site of NZ's first major environmental campaign. The original plan for the West Arm power station, built to provide cheap electricity for the aluminium smelter near Invercargill, included raising the level of the lake by 30m. A petition gathered a staggering 265,000 signatures (17% of voting-age New Zealanders at the time) and the issue contributed to the downfall of the government at the following election. The action was successful: the power station was built but the lake's level remains unchanged. It was a success that spawned increasing national environmental action through the '70s and '80s. West Arm power station is NZ's largest producer of electricity: a tunnel dug through the mountain from Lake Manapouri to Doubtful Sound drops a hefty 180m from lake to sound, driving the power station's turbines.

Fiordland Ecology Holidays (☎ 0800 249 660; www.fiordland.gen.nz; 5 Waiau St) has its office on the premises of 45 South, their secondhand/new/rare-books bookshop specialising in local history, exploration and wildlife. Ask about their Doubtful Sound tours for details on their ecology-focused options.

Activities

Adventure Kayak & Cruise (☎ 0800 324 966; www.fiordlandadventure.co.nz), beside the garage in Manapouri, rents kayaks from $50 per person per day for paddles on Lake Manapouri from October to April. They'll only rent to groups of two paddlers or more, and provide VHF radios free-of-charge for safety. See p657 for information on their kayaking trips on Doubtful Sound.

You can rent rowboats from **Manapouri Stores** (☎ 03-249 6619; per day $20). **Fish Fiordland** (☎ 03-249 6855; www.fishfiordland.co.nz; 2hr fishing $195) does scenic trips on Lake Manapouri, guided nature walks, fishing trips, and operates as a water taxi to local walking tracks. **Adventure Manapouri** (☎ 03-249 8070; www.adventuremanapouri.co.nz) is another option for rowboat hire ($20 per day), water taxis and fishing trips.

With some form of water transport (kayak, dinghy or water taxi), you can cross the Waiau River for some easy low-altitude day walks, detailed in the DOC brochure *Fiordland National Park Day Walks* ($1). A walk along the **Circle Track** (three hours return) can be extended to **Hope Arm** (five to six hours return), crossing the uninvitingly named Stinking

Creek. Although Te Anau is the usual access point for the Kepler Track (p646), the trail touches the northern end of Lake Manapouri and part of it can be done as a day walk from Manapouri; access is via the swing bridge at Rainbow Reach, 10km north of town. From Pearl Harbour there's also a walk that doesn't require crossing the river: to **Frasers Beach** (1½ hours return), from where you can gaze across the beautiful lake.

Manapouri is also a staging point for the remote 84km **Dusky Track**, a walk that takes eight days if you tramp between Lakes Manapouri and Hauroko, with an extra two-day detour possible from Loch Maree Hut to Supper Cove on Dusky Sound. With regular tree falls, deep mud, river crossings, delaying floods and 21 three-wire bridges, this is an extremely challenging wilderness walk, suitable only for well-equipped, very experienced trampers. Contact DOC, and read Lonely Planet's *Tramping in New Zealand*, for more details. For transport options from either Te Anau or Tuatapere to the Dusky Track, contact **Lake Hauroko Tours** (☎ 03-226 6681; www.duskytrack.co.nz).

Sleeping

our pick **Freestone Backpackers** (☎ 03-249 6893; free stonebackpackers@vodafone.co.nz; Manapouri–Hillside Rd; dm/cabins $30/60) These clean, comfortable and rustic cabins nestle on a hillside with magnificent views about 3km east of town. Each cabin has a small kitchen, potbelly stove and veranda. Bathrooms and fridges are communal. Dorm beds are also available. More comfortable options include accommodation ($70) with a kitchen and private bathroom, and a deluxe bed and breakfast ($190) with a spa.

Manapouri Lakeview Chalets & Motor Park (☎ 03-249 6624; www.manapourimotels.co.nz; SH95; unpowered/powered sites $30/32, cabins d $52-62, motel units $95-120; 🖥 🛜) This camping ground features eclectic cabins, ranging from mock–Swiss Alpine to mock–shanty town. There's a fabulous fleet of old Morris Minors in various states of repair and a vintage pinball-machine collection to relive your youth. There's also a playground for the kids.

Possum Lodge (☎ 03-249 6623; www.possum lodge.co.nz; 13 Murrell Ave; sites $30, cabins d $42-50; 🌓 Oct-Easter; 🖥 🛜) A charming, shady little campsite only a few trees away from the lakeside, this property has old-school, relatively basic cabins and more modern motel-style units ($95). Best bring some sandfly repellent, too.

Manapouri Lakeview Motor Inn (☎ 03-249 6652; www.manapouri.com; 68 Cathedral Dr; d $85-140; 🖥 🛜) All rooms face the lake and mountains, with the big windows from the budget rooms at the top having the best views. All rooms have en suites and some have cooking facilities, or there's a communal kitchen. Downstairs is a casual restaurant and pub.

Eating & Drinking

Café 23 (☎ 03-249 6988; 23 Waiau St; lunch from $8, meals $25-28; 🌓 7.30am-7.30pm; 🖥) This cafe in a charming old Presbyterian church has great coffees and tasty panini or gourmet sandwiches. If you're heading out on the water, grab your lunch here before you go.

Lakeside Café & Bar (☎ 03-249 6652; 68 Cathedral Dr; lunch $9-16, dinner $18-33; 🌓 11.30am-late; 🖥 🛜) Serves substantial meals with a generous side order of lake views. The public bar attached (open till late) is a large, cheery affair, with crazy silver helicopters providing the wacky ventilation.

Getting There & Away

Scenic Shuttle (☎ 0800 277 483; www.scenicshuttle.co.nz) stops at Manapouri en route from Invercargill to Te Anau. **Topline Tours** (☎ 03-249 8059; www.toplinetours.co.nz; $20) travels between Manapouri and Te Anau daily.

DOUBTFUL SOUND

Massive, magnificent Doubtful Sound is a wilderness area of rugged peaks, dense forest and thundering post-rain waterfalls. It's one of NZ's largest sounds: three times the length and 10 times the area of Milford Sound. Doubtful is also much, *much* less trafficked. If you have the time and the money, it's an essential experience. Fur seals, dolphins, Fiordland crested penguins and seals are all also occasional visitors.

Until relatively recently, only the most intrepid tramper or sailor ever explored Doubtful Sound. Even Captain Cook only observed it from off the coast in 1770, because he was 'doubtful' whether the winds in the sound would be sufficient to blow the ship back out to sea. The sound became more accessible when the road over Wilmot Pass opened in 1959 to facilitate construction of the West Arm power station.

Tours

Doubtful Sound is only accessible by tour. You'll cross Lake Manapouri by boat to the West Arm power station, drive by bus the winding 22km through dense rainforest to Deep Cove (permanent population: one), then head out on Doubtful on another boat. Many tours include the power station. The easiest place to base yourself is Manapouri, although many tours pick up in Te Anau and some in Queenstown.

Real Journeys (☎ 0800 656 502; www.realjourneys. co.nz; Pearl Harbour, Manapouri; day trip adult/child $275/60) has a Wilderness Cruise, beginning with a 45-minute boat ride across Lake Manapouri to West Arm power station, followed by a bus ride over Wilmot Pass to the sound, which you explore on a three-hour cruise. There's pick-up from Te Anau (adult/child $21/10.50) or from Queenstown (adult/child $82/41).

If you'd rather venture underground to admire the engineering marvels of the power station than continue over to the sound, do that on a separate Lake Manapouri cruise (adult/child $65/20, October to April).

From September to May, Real Journeys also runs a Doubtful Sound overnight cruise. The *Fiordland Navigator* sleeps 70 and has twin-share, en-suite cabins (per adult/child $675/348) and quad-share bunkrooms ($365/182.50). Transport to and from Te Anau or Queenstown is available. Prices include meals and kayaking or tender-craft trips.

Fiordland Ecology Holidays (☎ 0800 249 660, 03-249 6600; www.fiordland.gen.nz; 5 Waiau St, Manapouri) has boat tours (maximum 10 guests) of up to a week, led by people with a passion for the area's flora and fauna. The superbly equipped yacht sails into remote parts of the World Heritage Area along Doubtful and Dusky Sounds. Rates start at $745 for an overnight trip.

Adventure Kayak & Cruise (☎ 0800 324 966; www.fiordlandadventure.co.nz; ☽ late Sep-May) does Doubtful Sound day trips; cruise and kayaking is $255 while overnight kayak camping trips on the shores of the sound are $235.

Fiordland Wilderness Experiences (☎ 0800 200 434; www.fiordlandseakayak.co.nz; ☽ Oct-Apr) also does overnight ($380) and up to five-day ($750) guided kayak trips on the sound.

Other cruising options:

Deep Cove Charters (☎ 0800 249 682; www.doubtful -sound.com; overnight per person $380) Intimate overnight cruises with a maximum of 12 passengers. Includes meals, or you can fish for your own dinner.

Fiordland Cruises (☎ 0800 483 262; www.fiordland cruises.co.nz; overnight from $495) Overnight cruise including wildlife viewing and fishing. Maximum 12 passengers. Includes meals and transfers to/from Te Anau.

Fiordland Expeditions (☎ 0508 888 656; www. fiordlandexpeditions.co.nz; overnight cruises adult/child $499/350) Overnight cruise. Ten-passenger maximum. Kayaking, diving, fishing (dinner is whatever they catch that night).

Fiordland Explorer Charters (☎ 0800 434 673; www.doubtfulsoundcruise.com; day cruise adult/child $250/80) Day cruise with maximum of 20 people. Includes power-station tour and three hours on the sound. Free transfers to/from Te Anau.

Sleeping

If you'd like to spend the night on the sound, it generally means joining an overnight cruise

---

THE SOUND OF SILENCE *Brett Atkinson*

Just 90 minutes after leaving Manapouri township in morning sunshine, Doubtful Sound's Deep Cove is shrouded in misty, moody squall. But rain and mist doesn't equate to disappointment, and a chorus of Southern birdsong and the occasional passing raft of yellow-eyed penguins inspires me to keep paddling away.

Technically Doubtful Sound and Milford Sound are both fiords – narrow inlets with steep sides carved by glacial activity – but that's where any similarity ends. The almost-sheer granite cliffs of Milford Sound feel rugged and imposing, but Doubtful Sound is longer, deeper and gentler. The walls are shrouded with more vegetation and escalate upwards more slowly. Negotiating a series of mossy curtains along the banks, I feel like I'm cocooned by nature.

Adorned with a necklace of waterfalls, the spacious natural harbour of Hall Arm provides the opportunity for self-exploration. Amid pristine silence, I dig my paddle purposely into the obsidian-coloured water and catch a glimpse up Hall Arm to Mt Danae. The centuries roll back, and I realise one of New Zealand's most iconic views has been unchanged for millennia.

or kayak/camping trip. The only other option is **Deep Cove Hostel** (☎ 03-218 7655; www.deepcovehostel.co.nz; justinet@woosh.co.nz; per person $25-40; 🖥) with bunks, cooking facilities and dinghies, situated right on Doubtful Sound with a number of bush walks radiating from it. It's predominantly used by school groups, but casual guests are welcome. Booking ahead is essential.

SOUTHERN SCENIC ROUTE

The quiet, unhurried Southern Scenic Route begins in Te Anau and heads south to Tuatapere, Riverton and Invercargill. See www.southernscenicroute.co.nz or pick up *Southern Scenic Route* (free). Public transport is limited, but **Bottom Bus** (☎ 03-477 9083; www.travelheadfirst.com) and **Scenic Shuttle** (☎ 03-477 9083; www.scenicshuttle.co.nz) offer regular shuttles.

From Manapouri the road follows the Waiau River south between the forested Takitimu and Hunter Mountains. Near Clifden is the elegant **Clifden Suspension Bridge**, built in 1899 and one of the longest bridges in the South Island. **Clifden (Waiau) Caves** are signposted on Otautau Rd, 2km from the Clifden Rd corner. These caves offer a scramble through crawl spaces and up ladders. Bring a friend, a spare torch, and lots of caution. Visit Tuatapere visitor information centre (above right) for conditions and a map beforehand.

Just south of the suspension bridge is a turn-off to a walking track through **Dean Forest**, a reserve of ancient totara trees, 23km off the main road. From Clifden you can drive 30km of mostly unsealed road to **Lake Hauroko**, the deepest lake in NZ and surrounded by dark, brooding, steeply forested slopes. The area has many ancient *urupa* (burial sites) so be respectful and keep to trails. The Dusky Track (p656) also ends (or begins) here. **Lake Hauroko Tours** (☎ 03-226 6681; www.duskytrack.co.nz; tours incl lunch $100; ☉ tours Nov-Apr) has day-trip return tours from Tuatapere, connecting with the Scenic Shuttle.

Tuatapere
pop 740

Formerly a timber-milling town, sleepy Tuatapere is now largely a farming centre. Those early woodcutters were very efficient, so only a remnant of a once large tract of native podocarp forest remains. Tuatapere is fondly referred to by Kiwis as NZ's 'sausage

capital'; though it would rather be known as a base for the Hump Ridge Track. Grab some of the real deal from the butcher to cook up. The paua (abalone) flavour is particularly interesting.

Tuatapere visitor information centre (☎ 03-226 6739; www.humpridgetrack.co.nz; 31 Orawia Rd; ☉ 8.30am-5pm, limited hr in winter; 🖥) assists with visits to the Clifden Caves, Hump Ridge hut passes and transport. Adjacent is the **Bushmans Museum** (admission by donation).

For more information on Tuatapere and the Western Southland area, see www.western southland.co.nz.

ACTIVITIES
Hump Ridge Track

The excellent 53km Hump Ridge Track climbs to craggy subalpine heights with views north to Fiordland and south to Stewart Island, and then descends through lush native forests of rimu and beech to the rugged coast. There's bird life aplenty, with the chance to see Hector's dolphins on the lonely windswept coast back to the start point. En route the path crosses a number of towering historic wooden viaducts, including NZ's highest. Beginning and ending at Bluecliffs Beach on Te Waewae Bay, 20km from Tuatapere, the track takes three fairly long days to complete.

Estimated walking times:

Route	Time
Bluecliffs Beach Car Park to Okaka Hut	6-8hr
Okaka Hut to Port Craig Village	7-9hr
Port Craig Village to Bluecliffs Beach Car Park	3-5hr

It's essential to book for this track, which is administered privately rather than by DOC. Contact **Tuatapere Hump Ridge Track** (☎ 03-226 6739; www.humpridgetrack.co.nz). Summer bookings cost from $90 for two nights; winter bookings (May to October) cost $45. There are also guided tour, jetboating and helihiking options.

Jetboating

Jetboat rides cross Lake Hauroko then zoom around up the rugged Wairahurahiri River, the breathtaking ride lasting two or three hours. Operators include **W-Jet** (☎ 0800 376 174; www.wjet.co.nz; adult/child $225/119) and **Humpridge Jet** (☎ 0800 270 556; www.wildernessjet.co.nz; from $150), which also has a jetboat/helicopter option. **Waiau Jet Tours** (☎ 0800 009 993) can take you from Tuatapere Bridge to Clifden Bridge ($50, one hour) or Dean Forest ($100, 3½ hours). See them at Shooters Backpackers & Tuatapere Motel (below).

SLEEPING & EATING

Shooters Backpackers & Tuatapere Motel (☎ 03-226 6250; shooters.backpackers@xtra.co.nz; 73 Main St; unpowered/powered sites $12/30, dm $28, d $60-90, motel s/d $70/110; 🖥) Communal spaces are the highlight here; there's a modern kitchen with a wood stove, a big deck with a barbecue, plus a spa and sauna. Camping is on a stretch of green lawn, and diving and fishing trips can also be arranged.

Waiau Hotel (☎ 03-226 6409; www.waiauhotel.co.nz; 47 Main St; s $35-55, d $70-110; 🖥) Has a number of standard pub-type rooms and en suites. The bistro (lunch $5 to $12, dinner $15 to $24) is renowned for their blue cod, but you can also tuck into world-famous Tuatapere sausages.

For some sausages for the road, see **Tuatapere Butchery** (☎ 03-226 6596; 75 Main St).

Alternatively, head to **Yesteryears Café** (☎ 03-226 6681; 3a Orawia Rd; light meals $8-12; 🕙 from 9am), which boasts a collection of quirky household items from local families. Meals are deliciously home-cooked and the coffee is splendid. Rip into Aunt Daisy's sugar buns and a quintessentially Kiwi milkshake, and buy homemade jams and preserves for future on-the-road breakfasts.

Tuatapere to Riverton

On SH92, around 10km south of Tuatapere, stop at the spectacular lookout at McCracken's Rest. Cast your eye down the arcing sweep of **Te Waewae Bay** – where Hector's dolphins and southern right whales are sometimes seen – to the snowy peaks of Fiordland.

Colac Bay is a popular holiday place and a good surfing spot. Southerlies provide the best swells here, but it's pretty consistent year-round and never crowded. **Dustez Bak Paka's & Camping Ground** (☎ 03-234 8399; www.dustezbakpakas.co.nz; 15 Colac Bay Rd; sites per person $13, dm $27, d $54-58) has basic rooms opening onto a covered courtyard and campsites in a grassy field. Guests can borrow surfboards. Get dinner next door at the Colac Bay Tavern. Down at the beach, the **Pavilion Tavern** (☎ 03-234 8445; 188 Colac Foreshore Rd; 🕙 10am-late) gets visitors from as far as Invercargill hungry for its fresh fish, organic lamb and garden-fresh herbs.

Riverton
pop 1850

Quiet little Riverton, only 38km short of Invercargill, is worth a lunch stop and, if near-Antarctic swimming takes your fancy, the **Riverton Rocks** area and **Taramea Bay** (don't venture past the point) are good for a dip. The town is a common overnight stop between the Catlins and Fiordland.

Riverton visitor information centre (☎ 03-234 8260; www.riverton-aparima.co.nz; 127 Palmerston St; 🕙 10am-5pm) has information about exploring the region's interesting geological heritage. Inside, **Te Hikoi Southern Journey** (☎ 03-234 8260; www.tehikoi.co.nz; adult/child $12/4; 🕙 10am-4pm summer, 11am-3pm winter) tells the story of the area's early Maori and Pakeha history in video and interactive displays. A number of galleries along Palmerston St are also worth a look.

The Riverton visitor information centre can advise on camping, motel and B&B accommodation. **Globe Backpackers** (☎ 03-234 8527; www.theglobe.co.nz; 144 Palmerston St; dm/d $25/65) is well set up for travellers, with basic, comfortable rooms. A couple of attached self-contained motel units cost $100 for two. The bar downstairs does a roaring trade in pizzas (from $10) and other bar snacks.

Beach House (☎ 03-234 8274; 126 Rocks Hwy; snacks from $10, dinner $25-35; 🕙 10am-late; 🖥) is a stylish, comfortable cafe that is famous for its seafood, especially its takeaway chowder ($12). On a sunny day with a warm breeze wafting off Foveaux Strait, the outside tables are a must; the other 90% of the time, retire inside to admire the sea view warm behind the windows. To find the cafe, follow signs along the coast to the lookout.

The chic little **Mrs Clarks Café** (☎ 03-234 8600; 108 Palmerston St; meals $9-16; 🕙 10am-4pm), with lots of reused timbers, chilled-out music and South Island beers and wines, occupies an insanely turquoise building that has been various forms of eatery since 1891. We doubt if its espressos were quite so delicious back then. Don't miss its tasty cheese rolls, amusingly dubbed 'Southland Sushi'.

The **South Coast Environment Centre** (☎ 03-234 8717; www.sces.org.nz; 154 Palmerston St) has a good range of organic fruit, vegies and meats, is the local wwoof agent, and organises the Riverton farmers market (Friday afternoons).

CENTRAL SOUTHLAND

Although it's home to the majority of Southland's permanent population, for travellers the central area of the province serves mostly as a through station. It's a good jumping-off point for the Catlins and Fiordland, and the gateway to Stewart Island.

INVERCARGILL
pop 49,300

Flat and suburban, with endlessly treeless streets, Invercargill won't enthral you if you came here via the Catlins or Fiordland. Nevertheless, most travellers in Southland will find themselves here at some point – perhaps stocking up on supplies and equipment before setting off to the Catlins or Stewart Island. It's worth taking some time to investigate the town's arty bits, some good restaurants, and a great little microbrewery. Forward-thinking local mayor Tim Shadbolt – formerly a 1970s student radical – has put the city on the map with strong support of Invercargill's tertiary education institutions and sporting organisations, and if you're missing an urban buzz just a little, the city's got plenty of options to recharge your socialising skills.

Information

Automobile Association (AA; ☎ 03-218 9033; 47 Gala St; ☺ 8.30am-5pm Mon-Fri)

Comzone.net (45 Dee St; ☺ 10am-10pm; 🖳 📶) Get online. Wi-fi is also available at the Tuatara Café (p663).

DOC office (☎ 03-211 2400; 7th fl, Cue on Don, 33 Don St; ☺ 8.30am-4.30pm Mon-Fri) For info on tracks around Stewart Island and Southland.

Invercargill i-SITE (☎ 03-214 6243; www.invercargill. org.nz; Gala St, Queens Park; ☺ 8am-6pm Oct-Apr, to 5pm May-Sep; 🖳) Handily located in the same building as the Southland Museum & Art Gallery. Bikes can be rented, and it's also a good place to get information on the Catlins and Stewart Island.

Post office (51 Don St)

Sights & Activities
SOUTHLAND MUSEUM & ART GALLERY

This **museum & gallery** (☎ 03-218 9753; www.south landmuseum.com; Gala St, Queens Park; admission by gold-coin donation; ☺ 9am-5pm Mon-Fri, 10am-5pm Sat & Sun) is definitely worth a look after you've visited the adjacent i-SITE. The art gallery hosts visiting exhibitions from contemporary Maori and other local artists as well as occasional international shows.

If you're headed for Stewart Island, check out the museum's interesting 'Beyond the Roaring 40s' exhibition showcasing the natural history of New Zealand's rugged southern islands. Fans of Burt Munro and *The World's Fastest Indian* (2005) movie should race to the small theatrette in the 1st floor sports gallery for a screening of the original 1971 TV documentary *Burt Munro – Offerings to the God of Speed*.

The museum's rock stars are undoubtedly the tuatara, NZ's unique lizardlike reptiles, unchanged for 220 million years and thus proclaimed 'living fossils'. And if the slow-moving 100-years-old-and-counting patriarch Henry is any example, they're not planning to do much for the next 220 million years either.

However, Henry did surprise the reptile world in early 2009 when he finally became a Dad with the sprightly 80-year-old Mildred. You'll find Henry and his mates looking dignified in the tuatara enclosure at the back. Feeding time is 4pm on Fridays, and is your best opportunity to see the tuataras in (slow) motion. Outside opening hours, you can see the tuatara through the viewing windows at the rear of the pyramid.

ANDERSON PARK ART GALLERY

In a 1925 Georgian-style manor, this **gallery** (☎ 03-215 7432; McIvor Rd; admission by donation; ☺ gallery 10.30am-5pm, gardens 8am-dusk) contains works from many NZ artists. There are beautiful, original antique furnishings, block prints, pottery, sculptures, grand landscapes, Greek-mythic Maori village scenes, and portraits. Visit the tearoom to partake of a very civilised (free) cup of tea. Outside, 24 hectares of landscaped gardens are a lovely place to linger, with trees and trails, a children's playground and a *wharepuni* (sleeping house). The gallery is 7km north of the city centre; follow North Rd then turn right into McIvor Rd.

OTHER SIGHTS & ACTIVITIES

Wander around the half-wild, half-tamed **Queens Park**, with its trees, duck ponds, children's playground and Alice's castle.

In town, the **City Gallery** (☎ 03-214 1319; 28 Don St; admission free; ☺ 11am-4pm Tue-Fri, 10am-2pm Sat) showcases talent from NZ's south, including sculpture, photography and paintings (most of which are for sale). If you've been travelling in the South Island, you'll definitely recognise some scenes.

If you're a fan of motorcyclist Burt Munro's speedy achievements, captured in *The World's Fastest Indian* (2005), you can see his **famous motorbike** at E Hayes & Sons (172 Dee St). There are a few other retro two-wheelers on display and film merchandise for sale. Oreti Beach (site of Burt's race against the troupe of insolent young tearaways) is 10km to the southwest and a nice spot for a swim. The helpful folk at the Invercargill i-SITE will happily direct you to other locations relevant to Burt and the film. The Burt Munro Challenge (www.burtmunro challenge.com) is a hugely popular motorbike event held each November.

For a self-guided walk or drive, pick up the *Invercargill Heritage Trail* brochure (free) from the i-SITE. In **Thomson's Bush**, 1km north along Queen's Dr, you can follow a one-hour loop beneath the ancient kahikatea and matai trees that once covered the now-treeless plains of Invercargill.

The **Invercargill Brewery** (☎ 03-214 5070; www. invercargillbrewery.co.nz; 8 Wood St; ⏱ 11am-5.30pm Mon-Thu, to 6.30pm Fri, to 4pm Sat) promotes itself as NZ's southernmost microbrewery, but in reality, its beers are good enough for anywhere in the country. Tastings of the range are free of charge, and if you're a real beer buff, the staff may be able to show you around the brewery (but only if they're not busy). Our favourites are the crisp Biman Pilsner and

INVERCARGILL

0 _____ 800 m
0 _____ 0.5 miles

INFORMATION
Automobile Association (AA)................1 B3
Comzone.net.....................................2 C4
DOC Office..3 D4
Invercargill i-SITE.............................4 B3
Post Office..5 D4
Tuatara Café.............................(see 11)

SIGHTS & ACTIVITIES
City Gallery.......................................6 D4
E Hayes & Sons.................................7 A3
Invercargill Brewery.........................8 C4
Southland Museum & Art Gallery....(see 4)

SLEEPING
Kackling Kea Backpackers................9 B4
Living Space.............................(see 33)
Southern Comfort Backpackers.....10 A3
Tuatara Lodge.................................11 C4
Victoria Railway Hotel....................12 C4

EATING
Buster Crabb..................................13 A2
Countdown.....................................14 B4
Devil Burger....................................15 C4
Duo..16 D4
EuropaNZ.......................................17 D4
Rocks & Shop 5..............................18 C3

Seriously Good Chocolate
  Company......................................19 D3
Sopranos Pizzeria.......................(see 31)
Three Bean Café.............................20 C4
Tuatara Café................................(see 11)
Turkish Kebabs...............................21 C4
Zookeepers Cafe............................22 D4

DRINKING
Kiln..23 C4
Louie's Café....................................24 A3
One Blue Dog.................................25 C4
Saints & Sinners.............................26 D4
Speights Ale House.........................27 C4
Tillermans Music Lounge...........(see 15)
Waxy O'Shea's...............................28 C3

ENTERTAINMENT
Reading Cinemas...........................29 C4
Stadium Southland.........................30 D3

SHOPPING
H&J's Outdoor World..................(see 31)
Southern Adventure......................31 D4

TRANSPORT
Air New Zealand............................32 D4
Cycle Surgery.................................33 C4

the hoppy Stanley Green Pale Ale. Regular seasonal brews are also concocted, including Smokin' Bishop, a German-style *rauchbier* made with smoked malt.

Sleeping

Many places will store luggage for guests heading to Stewart Island. You'll find countless midrange motels along Hwy 1 East (Tay St) and Hwy 6 North (North Rd).

Invercargill Top 10 Holiday Park (☎ 0800 486 873, 03-215 9032; www.invercargilltop10.co.nz; 77 McIvor Rd; sites per person $18, cabins $75, motel units $96-110; 🖳) Near parkland, with trees for shade and surrounded by macrocarpa hedge, this quiet little place 6.5km drive north of town has private sites and good communal facilities. Modern, comfortable studios and self-contained cabins have en suites.

Tuatara Lodge (☎ 03-214 0954; www.tuataralodge. co.nz; 30-32 Dee St; dm $25, d $60-80; 🖳 🛜) Rooms here are fairly basic, but they're clean and comfortable enough. Communal facilities are good too, with cosy TV lounges and a large modern kitchen. Staff are friendly, it's the most central of all the budget accommodation, and downstairs is a nice little traveller-focused cafe-bar. Transport to/from Bluff for Stewart Island stops just outside.

Kackling Kea Backpackers (☎ 03-214 7950; www. kacklingkea.co.nz; 25 Tweed St; dm $26-28, d $62; 🖳) This family-run house south of town is light and spacious, and the relaxed communal areas and rooms have recently been redecorated. Look forward to a huge, well-equipped kitchen and a friendly welcome from the owners' children. A good place to recover after walking the Hump Ridge Track or Stewart Island's Rakiura Track.

Southern Comfort Backpackers (☎ 03-218 3838; 30 Thomson St; dm/d $27/66; 🖳) Mellow, comfortable house with a Zen lounge (hooray, no TV! Watch the fireplace instead), colourful rooms and a modern, well-equipped kitchen. Doubles are spacious, though some prefer the basic playhouse. Lovely gardens provide fresh herbs for cooking. Cash only.

Living Space (☎ 03-211 3800; www.livingspace.net; 15 Tay St; d $89-119; 🖳 🛜) Colourful, modern decor, ergonomically savvy design, and relaxed service are showcased at this transformed 1907 warehouse. The studios – especially, the bathrooms – are not huge, but self-contained kitchenettes, speedy internet access, and lots of Sky channels all come as standard.

Bushy Point Fernbirds (☎ 03-213 1302; www.fern birds.co.nz; 197 Grant Rd, Otatara; s/d incl breakfast $100/120) Two friendly corgis are among the hosts at this very comfortable, eco-aware homestay set on the edge of 4.5 hectares of private forest reserve and wetlands. Some of the trees are over 400 years old and on a clear day you can see across to Stewart Island. Fernbirds is very popular with birding types, so booking ahead is recommended. It's five minutes' drive from central Invercargill, but Ziff's and the Cabbage Tree restaurant (opposite) are both nearby. Rates include a guided walk in the forest reserve.

Victoria Railway Hotel (☎ 0800 777 557, 03-218 1281; www.vrhotel.info; cnr Leven & Esk Sts; d $130-180; 🖳 🛜) For a spot of 19th-century luxury, the plush rooms and swanky guests' areas in this grand old refurbished hotel fit the bill. The guests' dining room is elegant and the opulent house bar is crammed with South Island wines and local beers. This spot is a quietly unique gem underpinned by genuinely personal service.

Eating

Invercargill has a surprisingly diverse restaurant scene, with a few gems worth seeking out.

RESTAURANTS

Rocks & Shop 5 (☎ 03-218 7597; Courtville Pl, 101 Dee St; lunch $13-20, dinner $17-32; 🕙 11am-2pm & 5pm-late Tue-Sat) Tucked away in a shopping arcade, this stylish candlelit bar with a couple of dining areas is a laid-back choice for a tasty meal. Lunch highlights are decent burgers, pasta and salad, and later at night the focus shifts to pork belly, Moroccan chicken and Stewart Island salmon.

Duo (☎ 03-218 8322; 16 Kelvin St; lunch $15, dinner $30; 🕙 10.30am-late) Just off Invercargill's main drag, the elegant Duo has good-value lunch specials (all $15) and a more expensive evening menu. Standout menu items include smoked salmon, herb-and-feta-crusted pork steaks, and oven-baked blue cod. The wine list travels mainly to nearby Central Otago for some hard-to-find boutique tipples.

Buster Crabb (☎ 03-214 4214; 326 Dee St; meals $25-34; 🕙 10.30am-late) Inexplicably named after a British navy frogman who went missing in 1956, Buster Crabb overcomes a silly name to transform a spacious heritage-listed villa into a cosmopolitan dining experience. Local farming types – doing very well thank you –

crowd in for scallops, pork belly, venison and blue cod. A tiny deck is a late afternoon suntrap, and it's one of the only places in town that serves the Invercargill Brewery's excellent Pitch Black stout on tap.

On the main road to the Oreti Beach at Otatara you'll find two restaurants, both specialising in *big* meals, and therefore both local favourites.

Ziff's Café & Bar (☎ 03-213 0501; 143 Dunns Rd, Otatara; mains $18-34; ☼ 10.30am-late) Fun atmosphere and a stylish interior. Transfers from town are $2.

Cabbage Tree (☎ 03-213 1443; 379 Dunns Rd, Otatara; mains $20-40; ☼ 11am-late; **V**) Huge menu, huge dishes, huge wine list, and a free courtesy bus.

CAFES & QUICK EATS

Seriously Good Chocolate Company (☎ 03-218 8060; 147 Spey St; chocolates around $1.20 each; ☼ 8.30am-5pm Mon-Fri) This sunny spot a short walk from central Invercargill specialises in individual homemade chocolates. Order a coffee and then abandon yourself to the difficult task of choosing flavours. The chilli and peanut cluster variations were both good enough for us to return a second day. Like it says on the tin…seriously good.

EuropaNZ (☎ 03-214 6371; 82 Tay St; meals $5-10; ☼ 8am-5pm Mon-Fri, 10am-3pm Sat) Great-value Bavarian-style breakfasts – look forward to an $8 feast of egg, potato and sausage – and Invercargill's best baked cheesecake feature at this German-owned deli-bakery. The daily soup and sourdough special ($5) is almost too affordable. There's a play area for the kids, too.

Tuatara Café (☎ 03-214 0954; 30-32 Dee St; meals $7-20; ☼ 7am-late; 🖥 🛜) The cafe attached to this backpackers' hotel (opposite) is cool in a traveller-focused, dreadlocks-and-Kiwi dub kinda way. Eggs on toast ($7.50) make a hearty good-value start to the day and burgers ($15) are tasty and interesting. Team one with a Biman lager.

Devil Burger (☎ 03-218 9666; 16 Don St; burgers $10-14, wraps $12-14; ☼ 11am-9pm Sun-Wed, to 1am Thu, to 4am Fri & Sat; **V**) Only open a couple of weeks when we dropped by, and already doing great business with tasty gourmet burgers and healthy wraps. Their own beer is on tap, there's loads of vegie options on offer, and even the phone number is a sly in-joke. On weekends, expect crowds of hungry burger fans from upstairs at Tillermans Music Lounge (right).

ourpick Three Bean Café (☎ 03-214 1914; 73 Dee St; meals $10-15; ☼ 7am-5pm Mon-Fri, 8.30am-2pm Sat)

Believe us, we've done the hard yards for the discerning caffeine hound, and hands-down Invercargill's best coffee is at this cosmopolitan main drag cafe. There are switched-on staff that remember you from the day before, and a tasty array of food – kick your day off with a salmon bagel ($11). Leave room for a baked slice of something sweet.

Turkish Kebabs (☎ 03-218 3399; 29 Esk St; kebabs from $11; ☼ 8am-late; **V**) With assorted Turkish paraphernalia, this is an atmospheric spot for a sit-down meal, but it's equally popular for takeaways, with tasty hummusy felafels and the namesake kebabs. For the indecisive diner, there is pretty good Japanese and Indian food a few doors either side.

Zookeepers Cafe (☎ 03-218 3373; 50 Tay St; meals $12-28; ☼ 10am-late Mon-Sat, 11am-late Sun) Easily spotted by the giant corrugated-iron elephant on the ceiling. The zoo-keeping staff are laid-back and friendly, and the meals are good value and tasty. Tuck into a warm balsamic beef salad or sip an Invercargill Brewery beer. Try the Wasp lager, a southern honey-infused spin on a traditional Pilsner.

Sopranos Pizzeria (☎ 03-218 3464; 33 Tay St; pizzas $17-28, pasta $17-24; ☼ 5pm-late Tue-Thu, 11am-late Fri & Sat, 4-9pm Sun) Trying just a little *too* hard to cash in on the mafia shtick, this cafe certainly does good pizzas, and its pasta and gourmet burgers ($21.50) are delicious, too.

SELF-CATERING

Countdown (cnr Doon & Tay Sts; ☼ 8am-midnight)

Drinking & Entertainment

One Blue Dog (☎ 03-214 6970; 34 Esk St; ☼ 9pm-late Thu-Sat) Advertising four Jäger and Red Bulls for 30 bucks when we dropped by, this compact upstairs bar has free pool tables and a raucous devil-may-care, don't-waste-the-weekend atmosphere. DJs and occasional bands kick in later at night. It's definitely not sophisticated, but after four Jägerbombs, will you really care?

ourpick Tillermans Music Lounge (☎ 03-218 9240; 16 Don St; cover charge $5; ☼ 9pm-late) Upstairs from Don St, Tillerman's is an alternative live music/DJ venue, with live music ranging from local thrash bands to visiting rock or reggae talents, and DJs doing mostly dub and house. Decrepit black couches and a battered old dance floor prove its credentials. Free entry Thursdays.

Saints & Sinners (☎ 03-214 3366; 25 Tay St; cover charge varies; ☼ 11am-late) This is the nightclub that ate Invercargill – an intricate collage of bars, pool halls, dance floors and flashing lights. Maybe take a GPS with you. While entrapped, you'll discover Saints & Sinners, the preferred live music venue for touring Kiwi bands, and the equally raucous Players Entertainment Venue.

Louie's Café (☎ 03-214 2913; 142 Dee St; tapas $10, mains $19-28; ☻ 5.30pm-late Sat) This cosy, mellow little cafe-bar specialises in delicious tapas-style snacks, and there's a concise blackboard menu, too. It's a great spot for a late-night wine or an organic beer. Relax fireside, tuck yourself away in various nooks and crannies, or spread out on a comfy padded sofa and enjoy the chilled-out music. There are occasional live gigs.

Kiln (☎ 03-218 2258; 7 Don St) Stylish Monteiths bar with hanging lampshades, underlit bar and Great Aunt Edith's wallpaper. Easily the most civilised drinking option in town and surprisingly good food, too. Try the parmesan -crusted blue cod with a honey- and spice-infused Summer Ale.

Speight's Ale House (☎ 03-214 5333; 38 Dee St) Innumerable TV screens in case someone somewhere takes a wicket or the All Blacks score another try. A good selection of Speight's brews south from Dunedin, and outside tables to watch Invercargill's after dark cavalcade of annoying boy racers in their hotted-up Mazdas. What would Burt Munro think?

Waxy O'Sheas (☎ 03-214 0313; 90 Dee St) Noisy drinking den of the clan O'Bogan. Reputedly the planet's southernmost Irish pub.

Reading Cinemas (☎ 03-211 1555; www.reading cinemas.co.nz; 29 Dee St; adult/child $15/10) shows recent blockbusters. Tuesday nights offer a discount.

Stadium Southland (☎ 03-217 1200; www.stadiumsouth. co.nz; Surrey Park, Isabella St) is home to Invercargill's extremely successful and popular Southern Steel women's netball team (www.southern steel.co.nz; season April to July). You can try out rock climbing here from $5 (7pm Tuesdays and Thursdays) and there's also New Zealand's only indoor velodrome. Come along Tuesday at 5.30pm for the opportunity (per hour $10) to get high on the wall on two wheels. Coaching is provided.

Shopping

Check out **Southern Adventure** (☎ 03-218 3239; 31 Tay St) and **H&J's Outdoor World** (☎ 03-214 2052; 32 Tay St) next door for everything from maps and boots to sleeping bags and dried food.

Getting There & Away

AIR

Flights link Invercargill to Christchurch (from $79, one hour) several times a day via **Air New Zealand** (☎ 0800 737 000; www.airnewzealand.co.nz; 46 Esk St; ☻ 9am-5pm Mon-Fri, to 12.30pm Sat). **Stewart Island Flights** (☎ 03-218 9129; www.stewartislandflights. com) flies to Oban from Invercargill (adult/ child one-way $105/65, return $185/105, 30 minutes) three times a day.

BUS

Buses leave from the Invercargill i-SITE, where you can also book your tickets. **InterCity** (☎ 03-214 6243; www.intercity.co.nz) connects Invercargill with Dunedin ($43, four hours), Te Anau ($48, three hours) and Christchurch ($70, 10 hours). Look online for significant discounts.

Other bus services include:

Atomic Shuttles (☎ 03-214 6243; www.atomictravel. co.nz) Dunedin ($35) and Christchurch ($70).

Knightrider (☎ 0800 317 057; www.knightrider.co.nz) Overnight to Dunedin ($41) and Christchurch ($76).

Naked Bus (☎ 0900 625 33; www.nakedbus.com) Te Anau ($35), Queenstown ($39) and Dunedin ($34). Look online for discounts.

Scenic Shuttle (☎ 0800 277 483; www.scenicshuttle. co.nz) Via the Southern Scenic Route past Tuatapere ($39) to Te Anau ($49).

TrackNet (☎ 0800 483 262; www.tracknet.net) Te Anau ($45) and Queenstown ($45).

Catlins Coaster and Bottom Bus pass through Invercargill; see p667. See opposite for buses to Bluff and p680 for full details on Stewart Island ferries.

Getting Around

Invercargill Airport (☎ 03-218 6920; 106 Airport Ave) is 3km west of central Invercargill. The door-to-door **Airport Shuttle** (☎ 03-214 3434) costs $12 from the city centre to the airport; more for residential pick-up. By taxi it's around $18; try **Blue Star Taxis** (☎ 03-218 6079) or **City Cabs** (☎ 03-214 4444).

Cycle Surgery (☎ 03-218 8055; www.cyclesurgery. co.nz; 21 Tay St; ☻ 8.30am-6pm Mon-Thu, to 7pm Fri, 9.30am-4pm Sat, 10am-3pm Sun) rents mountain bikes for $35 per day.

Invercargill's **Freebie bus** (☎ 03-218 7108; www. icc.govt.nz; ☻ 10am-2.30pm Mon-Sat) is a free bus service around the town centre, departing every 15 minutes. Grab a map of the route from the i-SITE. Other **city buses** (single trip adult/

child $2/1, day pass adult/child $4.50/2.50; 7am-6pm Mon-Fri, 9am-3pm Sat) run to the suburbs; these buses are free from 9am to 2.30pm.

BLUFF
pop 2100

Bluff (www.bluff.co.nz) is Invercargill's port, 27km south of the city. The main reasons to come here are to catch the ferry to Stewart Island, pose for photos beside the **Stirling Point signpost** or buy famous Bluff oysters straight from the wharf. Also at Stirling Point is a huge chain link sculpture by NZ artist Russell Beck. It symbolises the Maori legend where the South Island is the canoe of Maui and Stewart Island is the boat's anchor. At Stirling Point, the chain disappears into the ocean, and a companion sculpture on Stewart Island represents the other end of the anchor chain.

While Bluff isn't the South Island's southernmost point (that claim to fame belongs to Slope Point in the Catlins), and even though Stewart Island and other dots of rock lie even further south, the phrase 'from Cape Reinga to Bluff' is oft-quoted to signify the entire length of NZ. NZ's main highway, SH1, terminates south of Bluff at Stirling Point, so it really does feel like the end of the country.

Kids will enjoy the small **Bluff Maritime Museum** (03-212 7534; 241 Foreshore Rd; adult/child $2/free; 10am-4.30pm Mon-Fri, 1-5pm Sat & Sun) and clambering over a century-old oyster boat, while steam nerds will love the big old 600hp steam engine. Interesting displays on Bluff's history complete the exhibition.

The **Foveaux Walk** (2½ hours return, 6.6km) begins from the signpost around the rugged coast to Ocean Beach. Alternatively, follow that track for 1km and return through rimu and rata forest via the 1.5km **Glory Track**. Drive or walk the 3km to the observation point on top of 265m-high **Bluff Hill** (accessed off Lee St) for a great view of Stewart Island. Pick up *Bluff Walking Tracks* (free) and a Bluff town map from the Invercargill i-SITE.

The **Bluff Oyster & Southland Seafood Festival** (www.bluffoysterfest.co.nz) celebrates Bluff's most famous exports, and is held annually, usually in May. The oysters are in season from late March to late August.

Sleeping & Eating
Bluff Camping Ground (027-626 2018; 11 Gregory St; unpowered/powered sites $25/34, cabins $44) Basic cabins sit on a wide grassy area with sites for vans and tents. The communal facilities are fine, though they cost $6 a pop ($6 for a shower, $6 to use the kitchen, $6 for the laundry). BYO linen.

Foveaux Hotel (03-212 7196; www.foveauxhotel.com; 40 Gore St; s $60-75, d $90-110) This funky art-deco building has a number of clean, spacious rooms and a comfy guests' lounge/bar downstairs (with big comfy red sofas and a big comfy cat). Rooms are good value, and this is a nice spot to relax and catch your breath. Grab fish and chips next door and bring them back for dinner.

Land's End (03-212 7575; www.landsend.net.nz; Stirling Point; s/d incl breakfast $120/165) Opposite the Stirling Point signpost, this prominent house has luxurious if quaint rooms, most with good views of the sea. There's also a restaurant downstairs (lunch from $13, dinner from $27), specialising in fresh seafood and open around 9.30am; closing around 8pm (earlier in winter).

Drunken Sailor Cafe & Bar (03-212 8855; Stirling Point; mains $18-32; 11.30am-4pm Sun-Fri, to late Sat) Up on the hill above the signpost at Stirling Point, this seafood restaurant's huge curve of windows offers magnificent views of the ocean, the islands beyond, and the forested curve of the bluff itself.

Next door to Foveaux Hotel, **Gallery Takeaway** (03-312 7391; 42 Gore St; 11.30am-8pm Sun-Thu, to 9pm Fri & Sat) does arguably the planet's finest fish and chips, and has a small tribute to the sadly lamented Bluff paua-shell house. If fresh oysters aren't in season, try a Blue Cod meal ($13). To buy fresh Bluff oysters, visit **Fowlers Oysters** (03-212 8523; Ocean Beach Rd; 9am-5pm Mar-Aug) on the way into town on the left.

Near the 4 Square supermarket, **Stella's** (03-212 8856; 64 Gore St; 6.30am-2pm) is your best bet for a coffee before braving the ferry crossing to Stewart Island. The seafood chowder and pies are pretty good, too.

Getting There & Away
Stewart Island Experience (0800 000 511, 03-212 7660; www.stewartislandexperience.co.nz) runs a shuttle between Bluff and Invercargill (adult/child $18/9) connecting with the Stewart Island ferry. It also offers secure vehicle storage by the ferry terminal ($5 per day).

INVERCARGILL TO DUNEDIN
Following SH1 across interior farmland is the most direct route between Invercargill

and Dunedin. While the scenery is pretty in a pastoral way, it's certainly not as dramatic as the route via the Catlins. If you have the time, opt for the latter.

Gore

pop 8500

Gore is the proud 'home of country music' in New Zealand, with the annual **Gold Guitar Week** (www.goldguitars.co.nz; ☑ late May/early Jun) ensuring all the town's accommodation is booked out for at least 10 days per year. For the other 355 days, good reasons to stop include a surprisingly cool art gallery, and whisky tasting at the Hokonui Moonshine Museum. Don't leave town without a picture of Gore's Giant Trout; the surrounding region offers excellent trout fishing.

The **Gore i-SITE** (☎ 03-203 9288; www.gorenz.com; 16 Hokonui Dr; ☑ 8.30am-5pm Mon-Fri, 9.30am-4pm Sat & Sun) has information on accommodation, transport, and fishing or bushwalking distractions. The interesting **Hokonui Moonshine Museum** (admission $5; ☑ 9am-4.30pm Mon-Fri, 10am-3.30pm Sat & Sun) and the **Gore Historical Museum** (admission by donation; ☑ hours as above) share the same building, celebrating Gore's proud history of fishing, farming and illegal distilleries. Admission to the Moonshine Museum includes a wee dram of the local product.

Across the car park the **public library** (☑ 9.30am-6pm Mon-Fri, 10.15am-1pm Sat) has internet access.

Across the road, the outstanding **Eastern Southland Gallery** (☎ 03-208 9907; 14 Hokonui Dr; admission by donation; ☑ 10am-4.30pm Mon-Fri, 1-4pm Sat & Sun), in Gore's gorgeous century-old former public library, houses a hefty collection of NZ art including a large Ralph Hotere collection. The amazing John Money Collection combines indigenous folk art from West Africa and Australia with works by iconic New Zealand artist Rita Angus. Nicknamed the 'Goreggenheim', this excellent gallery would be an asset to any city, and is well worth a stop.

Croydon Aircraft Company (☎ 03-208 9755; www.croydonaircraft.com; SH94, Mandeville), 16km down the road to Queenstown, restores vintage aircraft and, for wannabe WWI flying aces, offers flights in a two-seater 1930s Tiger Moth biplane ($85/200 for 10/30 minutes), or other wee aircraft. There's a restaurant attached.

Old Fire Station Backpackers (☎ 03-208 1925; www.thefirestation.co.nz; 19 Hokonui Dr; dm/d $25/60; ☐ ☜) is a small hostel opposite the i-SITE. There's a

good kitchen, laundry and a pleasant patio with a barbecue. Linen costs $2 extra.

There are also plenty of motels in town; the modern **Riverlea Motel** (☎ 03-208 3130; www.riverleamotel.co.nz; 46 Hokonui Dr; s $98-110, d $113-135) is a nice option. Gore i-SITE can hook you up with lots of others, plus local B&Bs or farmstays.

Green Room Café (☎ 03-208 1005; 59 Irk St; mains $8-10; ☑ 7.30am-5pm Mon-Sat; ☐) is a sunlight-dappled cafe with wooden floors, old-fashioned-movie seats and welcoming, relaxed service. The cakes are yummy, coffees are legendary and it is exceptionally child-friendly.

With decor that's faux-Texan and barnlike, **Howl at the Moon** (☎ 03-208 3851; 2 Main St; dinner mains $17-28; ☑ noon-2pm & 6-9pm; ☐) serves up predictably large, but surprisingly tasty, dinners.

THE CATLINS

If you veer off SH1 and head for the coastal route between Invercargill and Dunedin (via SH92), you wind through the enchanting Catlins, a region that combines lush farmland, native forests and rugged bays. With bushwalks, wildlife-spotting opportunities and lonely beaches to explore, the Catlins is well worth a couple of days. You won't find much in the way of facilities but there is plenty of wonderful accommodation.

On a clear summer's day, surrounded by forest greens and ocean blues, there's nothing more beautiful than the Catlins coast, and everyone wants to stay an extra day or two. In the face of a grey, sleety Antarctic southerly, however, travellers tend to leave in droves. This route has many twists, turns and narrow sections; it's similar in distance but slower going than the inland route along SH1.

Flora & Fauna

The Catlins is a wonderful place for independent wildlife-watching. Fur seals and sea lions laze along the coast, while elephant seals breed at Nugget Point (p670). In spring, keep your eyes peeled for southern right whales, which are occasionally spotted offshore. Dolphins are also frequent visitors.

Unlike much of Southland, tall kahikatea, totara and rimu forests still exist in the Catlins. Prolific bird life includes the wonderfully noisy tui, and you'll see more kereru (wood pigeons) here in a day than in a month

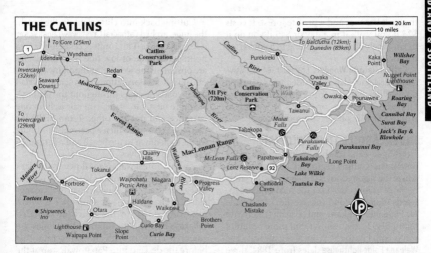

THE CATLINS

in the rest of NZ. There are also many other sea, estuary and forest birds, including the endangered yellow-eyed penguin and the rare mohua (yellowhead).

Information

Contact the main **Catlins information centre** (☎ 03-415 8371; catlinsinfo@cluthadc.govt.nz; 20 Ryley St, Owaka; ◷ 9.30am-1pm & 1.30-4.30pm Mon-Fri, 10am-4pm Sat & Sun; 🖳) in Owaka (p671), or the smaller **Waikawa visitors centre** (☎ 03-246 8464; waikawa museum@hyper.net.nz; Main Rd, Waikawa; ◷ 10am-5pm; 🖳). The Invercargill i-Site (p660) also has lots of Catlins information.

All centres stock the free two-sided *Catlins Highway Guide* map, with comprehensive accommodation phone numbers. Both www .catlins.org.nz and www.catlins-nz.com are well-maintained websites on the region.

The Catlins has no banks and limited options for eating out or grocery shopping (except Owaka). There's an ATM at the 4 Square supermarket in Owaka, and petrol stations (hours can be irregular) in Fortrose, Papatowai and Owaka. Stock up and fill up before you arrive.

Activities

The rugged Catlins coastline is good for surfing. Located in Porpoise Bay near Curio Bay, the **Catlins Surf School** (☎ 03-246 8552; www.catlins -surf.co.nz) runs 90-minute surfing lessons for $50. The occasional group of dolphin spectators is free of charge. You'll usually find local surf guru Nick at his caravan in the Curio Bay

Camping Ground (p669). If you're already confident on the waves, hire a board and wet-suit (very necessary) for three hours ($40).

Explore the idiosyncratic coastline and landscapes on four legs with **Catlins Horse Riding** (☎ 03-415 8368; www.catlinshorseriding.co.nz; 41 Newhaven Rd, RD1 Owaka; 1-/2-/3-hr rides $40/60/80). Full-day rides including lunch are $140.

Tours

Bottom Bus (☎ 03-477 9083; www.bottombus.co.nz) does a regular loop from Queenstown to Dunedin, south through the Catlins to Invercargill, along the Southern Scenic Route to Te Anau, then back to Queenstown. It stops at all main points of interest, and you can always hop off and catch the next bus coming through. There are lots of pass options; the Southlander pass ($425) lets you start anywhere on the loop and includes a Milford Sound cruise.

Catlins Coaster (☎ 03-477 9083; www.catlinscoaster. co.nz), run by Bottom Bus, offers day tours and trips through the Catlins from Dunedin and Invercargill. Ring them or check the website for details. Departures are more limited in winter.

Papatowai-based **Catlins Wildlife Trackers** (☎ 0800 228 5467; www.catlins-ecotours.co.nz) offers ecocentric guided walks and tours (three nights $600, one week $1500) with food, accommodation and transport (from Balclutha if necessary). These conservation gurus have been running tours here since 1990 and also manage **Top Track**, a 26km self-guided walk through beaches and a private forest. It costs $25 if you walk it in a day or $45 if you do it in two, including overnighting in a converted trolley bus.

Catlins Natural Wonders (☎ 0800 304 333; www. catlinsnatural.co.nz) also has guided trips focusing on wildlife. One-day trips cost $130/85 out of Dunedin/Balclutha, or there's an overnight trip ($200/150, plus accommodation).

INVERCARGILL TO PAPATOWAI

Heading east and south from Invercargill, SH92 enters the Catlins region at Fortrose, from where the **Shipwreck Ino** is visible across the sandy harbour at low tide. Take the turn-off here towards Waipapa Point and use the coastal route via Haldane, Waikawa and Niagara (where you rejoin SH92). It's a slower, but more beautiful route, with lots to check out along the way. The **Waipapa Point lighthouse** dates from 1884, three years after a terrible maritime disaster when SS *Tararua* sank and 131 people drowned.

Turn off at Tokanui and drive 13km to **Slope Point**, the South Island's most-southerly point. A 20-minute walk across farmland leads to a stubby beacon and stubbier signpost (photograph compulsory) atop a windswept spur of rock with views up and down the coast. The track is closed in September and October for lambing.

Further east at **Curio Bay**, fossilised Jurassic-age trees are visible for four hours either side of low tide. It's a fun spot to explore among the rock pools down at sea level where the texture of the petrified wood is more easily made out. The lookout is the place to be an hour or so before sunset, when you'll see yellow-eyed penguins waddling ashore. Just before Curio Bay, neighbouring **Porpoise Bay** has excellent accommodation (see Curio Bay sleeping options, opposite) and a gorgeously sandy, windswept beach that's safe for swimming. Blue penguins nest in the dunes and in summer Hector's dolphins come here to rear their young. It's also a good place to learn to surf (p667). Whales are occasional visitors, and fur seals and sea lions are often lounging on the rocks.

A 4km drive past the McLean Falls Holiday Park, the walk to **McLean Falls** (40 minutes return) passes through tree ferns and rimu. Don't stop at the first falls – the real thing is a bit further on. If you're relatively nimble you can clamber up to a cool pool (take care on the climb down).

Cutting back into cliffs right on the beach, the huge, arched **Cathedral Caves** (www.cathedralcaves. co.nz; adult/child $5/1) are only accessible for two hours either side of low tide (tide timetables are posted on the website, at the highway turn-off, at visitor information centres, and myriad other roadside signs throughout the Catlins). If you're happy to wade, you can walk in one entrance and out the other. From SH92 it's 2km to the car park, then a peaceful 15-minute forest walk down to the beach and a further 25 minutes to the caves.

An easy forest walk leads down to the dark peaty waters of **Lake Wilkie** (30 minutes return) and a cool, and educational, boardwalk alongside the lake. A turn-off soon after is worth following down to the beach at secluded **Tahakopa Bay**. In late summer the slopes are smeared crimson with flowering rata. Just before the descent into Papatowai, stop at the Florence Hill lookout with spectacular views of the sweeping arc of **Tautuku Bay**.

Further east is the cute forested village of **Papatowai**, a base for forays into the nearby forests. There's a handful of accommodation, and a general store selling petrol. There's good picnicking here down at the mouth of the Tahakopa River.

Lost Gypsy Gallery (☎ 03-415 8908; SH92, Papatowai; ☽ 11am-5pm, closed Wed) occupies a roadside house bus at Papatowai, and is almost worth a trip to the Catlins on its own. Based on found objects and specialising on self-wound automata and things that go whirrr, this place is guaranteed to make you both laugh and think. A newly opened gallery (admission $5, young children not allowed sorry...) showcases some of artist Blair Sommerville's larger one-off pieces. We especially like the TV that runs on bicycle power. Blair's always up for a good chat, and at the time of writing, future plans included a coffee caravan. Don't miss this place.

Sleeping
SLOPE POINT
Slope Point Backpackers (☎ 03-246 8420; www.slope point.co.nz; Slope Point Rd; powered sites $25, dm $21-26, d $46) Surrounded by trees and farmland, this property has rooms ranging from basic to modern, along with a new well-equipped self-contained unit ($85). There's plenty of grass to park a tent ($11 per person), and the owners' young children are always keen to show visitors what's new on the working farm.

Nadir Outpost (☎ 03-246 8544; www.catlins-slope point.com; 174 Slope Point Rd; d $90) Next door to Slope Point, Nadir offers double rooms inside the owners' house, and a cosy, stand-alone cabin with kitchen facilities. There's a shop selling basic supplies and a forested area to pitch a tent ($12 per person) or park a van ($25 for two people). Meals are also available (breakfast $7 to $14 and dinner $20). Don't make our mistake of calling the owners 'Scottish'. They're actually a very friendly Welsh couple.

CURIO BAY

Curio Bay Camping Ground (☎ 03-246 8897; 601 Curio Bay Rd; unpowered/powered sites $15/25) Very private campsites lost in a sea of tall flax make this a really beautiful spot to camp. The camping ground nestles up to the small outcrop between Curio and Porpoise Bays, within easy walking distance to both. Guided nature walks are available, and it's also where you will usually find Nick from the Catlins Surf School (p667).

Dolphin Lodge (☎ 03-246 8579; dolphin.lodge@ yahoo.co.nz; 529 Curio Bay Rd; dm/d $23/56) There's a focus on surfing here. The rooms are looking slightly tired, but the view from the big lounge and deck towards the Porpoise Bay breakers is just fine. It's $3 more for a duvet in dorm rooms.

Catlins Beach House (☎ 03-246 8340; www.catlins beachhouse.co.nz; 499 Curio Bay Rd; dm $25, d $75-95) This extremely comfortable house has a cosy woodburner for heating, good kitchen and a deck that opens onto a grassy lawn sloping down to the beach. Blue penguins nest hereabouts and can be heard waddling past making cute penguin sounds at night.

Curio Bay Backpackers (☎ 03-246 8897; accommoda tion@curiobay.com; Curio Bay Rd; dm $30, d $70) Right on the sand dunes above the beach, this characterful cottage has a lovely laid-back, communal atmosphere.

Curio Bay Boutique Studios (☎ 03-246 8897; accom modation@curiobay.com; 501 Curio Bay Rd; d $180) With big windows and an even bigger deck, these two plush beachside units are open to awesome sea views. Recline on your giant, rustic, timber-framed bed to feel like a king.

A range of self-contained cottages and houses around Curio Bay can also be rented from **Catlins Surf** (☎ 03-246 8552; www.catlins-surf. co.nz; houses $100-190). One-night rentals are fine, and it's a good option for travelling families or groups of three or four.

WAIKAWA

Penguin Paradise Holiday Lodge (☎ 03-246 8552; www.catlins-surf.co.nz; 1612 Niagara–Waikawa Rd; dm/d/tw $25/50/54) Laid-back backpackers in a heritage cottage in Waikawa village near the estuary. Special combo deals ($65) of one night's accommodation and a 90-minute surf lesson are also available.

Anchorage (☎ 03-205 8006, 03-246 8464; www.anchor age.co.nz; 52 Antrim St; units $90-180) Has a number of roomy units sleeping up to six.

Waikawa Harbourview (☎ 03-246 8866; www.south catlins.co.nz; 14 Larne St; d $110-150) A four-bedroom house that's a good option for families or a group. The newly opened one- and two-bedroom Harakeke and Toi Tois units are also good value.

MCLEAN FALLS

Just off the main road, **McLean Falls Holiday Park** (☎ 03-415 8338; www.catlinsnz.com; SH92; sites per person $20, d $65-195; 🖳 🛜) has a number of Kiwiana-style cabins, newer motel units, and sites for vans and tents. The amenities blocks are spacious and very well maintained. The attached **Whistling Frog Café & Bar** (meals $10-30; ⏱ 8.30am-9pm) does breakfast, lunch and dinner with a surprisingly cosmopolitan spin, and there's a good selection of South Island beer and wine.

PAPATOWAI

Hilltop (☎ 03-415 8028; www.hilltopcatlins.co.nz; 77 Tahakopa Valley Rd; dm $28, d $75-90) High on a hill 1.5km out of town, with native forest at the back door and surrounded by sheep farm, this lovely old renovated pair of houses has the most spectacular view of hills and ocean. The en-suite double makes for a luxurious mini-splurge.

The tour company **Catlins Wildlife Trackers** (☎ 0800 228 5467; www.catlins-ecotours.co.nz) rents two houses in Papatowai: a charmin' old-school crib (two people $70) complete with portaloo, and another larger, modern, very ecofriendly house (two people $145).

Other options in Papatowai:

Kauri Glen (☎ 03-415 8044; 13 Tahakopa Rd; d $50) Wee cabin with sunny deck.

Papatowai Scenic Highway Motel & Store (☎ 03-415 8147; b.bevin@paradise.net.nz; Main Rd; d $90; 🅿) Modern motel units behind the store.

Southern Secrets Motel (☎ 03-415 8777; southern secret@xtra.co.nz; Main Rd; d $99) A simple weatherboard house conceals very comfortable rooms with a quirky nautical theme. The owner's got 900 videos if the weather turns to custard. Also manages Erehwon (double $135), a three-bedroom holiday home that's a good option for families.

Eating

our pick **Niagara Falls Café** (☎ 03-246 8577; Main Rd, Niagara; meals $13-24; ☯ 8am-10pm) Housed in a lovely old schoolhouse, half of which is given over to local arts, this is a warm, friendly spot for a meal. Gaze out the window at the gardens and farm, or tuck into delicious, good-value meals. Home-cooked cakes and muffins, and good coffees, make it a good spot to stop for morning or afternoon play lunch too. The beer and wine list is impressive, and the mighty falls themselves are nearby, only marginally less spectacular than their North American cousins.

You'll also find roadside takeaways in Waikawa and Papatowai. The Papatowai **store** (☯ 9am-6pm Mon-Sat, from 10am Sun) has a limited range of groceries.

PAPATOWAI TO BALCLUTHA

From Papatowai, follow the highway north to **Matai Falls** (a 30-minute return walk) on the Maclennan River, then head southeast on the signposted road to the tiered **Purakaunui Falls** (20 minutes). Both falls are reached via cool, dark forest walks through totara and tree ferns, and both falls are much more impressive after heavy rain.

You can continue along the gravel road from Purakaunui Falls to the 55m-deep **Jack's Blowhole** (☯ closed for lambing Sep & Oct). In the middle of a sheep paddock 200m from the sea but connected by a subterranean cavern, this huge cauldron was named after Chief Tuhawaiki, nicknamed Bloody Jack for his cussin'. It's a fairly brisk 30-minute walk each way.

Owaka is the Catlins' main town (population a hefty 395), with a good information centre, a 4 Square grocery store – including an ATM – and petrol station. An excellent new **museum** (adult/child $5/free; ☯ 9.30am-1pm & 1.30-4.30pm Mon-Fri, 10am-4pm Sat & Sun), attached to the information centre, has displays on local history. An attached theatrette shows interesting videos on the Catlins' deserved reputation as a shipwreck coast. There's accommodation in town, but once you're stocked up and perhaps stopped for a meal (opposite), it's worth venturing off to more remote, more attractive parts of the Catlins.

Pounawea, 4km away, is a beautiful little riverside town with some lovely places to stay (opposite); across the inlet, **Surat Bay** is even quieter and also has accommodation. Sea lions are often seen on the beach between here and **Cannibal Bay**, a 30-minute beach walk away.

Heading north from Owaka, detour off SH92 to **Nugget Point**, stopping for the short walk out to the lighthouse at the end – the last 100m or so, with drops to the ocean on either side, is breathtaking, and the view of wave-thrashed vertical rock formations from the end is great too. A spacious new DOC viewing platform huddles around the lighthouse. Fur seals, sea lions and elephant seals occasionally bask together on the rocks down to your left, a rare and noisy coexistence. Yellow-eyed and blue penguins, shags and sooty shearwaters all breed here. Ten minutes' walk down from a car park is **Roaring Bay**, where a well-placed hide allows you to see yellow-eyed penguins coming ashore (best two hours before sunset). The best viewing is from a newly constructed hide. You should not use a flash when photographing the penguins. If you don't have your own transport, nightly **twilight tours** (☎ 0800 525 278; www.catlins.co.nz; per person $20) are run by the Nugget View & Kaka Point Motels (opposite).

From Nugget Point the road loops back through the little township of **Kaka Point**, which has a sandy, quiet beach, accommodation and a nice spot for a meal. The road continues north from here to Balclutha (p597).

Sleeping

OWAKA & PURAKAUNUI

There are **DOC camping grounds** (campsites $6) at Purakaunui Bay and inland at Tawanui.

Walking distance from Purakaunui Falls, **Falls Backpackers** (☎ 03-415 8724; rmsbkerr@ispnz. co.nz; Purakaunui Falls Rd; dm/d $27/60) is a comfortable old farmhouse with views from some of the windows and the deck of rolling, sheep-dotted hills.

The beautifully renovated **Catlins Backpackers** (☎ 03-454 5635; www.catlinsbackpackers.co.nz; 24 Main Rd; dm/d $30/66; ☐) is a handsome pair of houses sporting warm colours, characterful, comfortable rooms and spacious shared kitchens. This is probably the nicest place to stay in Owaka. Cash only.

Also in Owaka:

Thomas Catlins Lodge & Holiday Park (☎ 03-415 8333; www.thomascatlins.co.nz; cnr Ryley & Clark Sts; unpowered/powered sites per person $10/16, dm $28, d $60-95; 🖳) Old hospital grounds converted to campsites and other accommodation. Unsurprisingly, it's all a bit institutional.

Split Level Backpackers (☎ 03-415 8304; bookings@ thesplitlevel.co.nz; 9 Waikawa Rd; dm $28, d $64-72)

Catlins Area Motel (☎ 03-415 8821; catlinsareamotel @hotmail.com; cnr Ryley & Clark Sts; d $95-110) Modern, spacious self-contained units with individual decks.

POUNAWEA

our pick **Pounawea Motor Camp** (☎ 03-415 8483; www.catlins-nz.com/pounawea-motor-camp/; Park Lane; unpowered/powered sites $22/26, cabins per person $22-60) Sitting right on the estuary (some cabins' decks face right onto the water) and surrounded by native bush ringing with birdsong, this is a gem of a place to park your tent. Others think so too, and in the frenzied post-Christmas season you'll be sharing this beautiful spot with many Kiwi and international holidaymakers.

Kiwi Crib (☎ 03-415 8411; galan@farmside.co.nz; 19 Ocean Grove; d $110) Three-bedroom house up a quiet road surrounded by native bush and just a short walk to the water.

SURAT BAY

Newhaven Holiday Park (☎ 03-415 8834; www.new havenholiday.com; Newhaven Rd; unpowered/powered sites $26/30, cabin d $62, flat d $90-100; 🖳 🛜) Only a few minutes' walk from the beach is this sweet little camping area with modern cabins and facilities and three new self-contained flats. Kayaks and bikes can be rented next door at Surat Bay Lodge.

Surat Bay Lodge (☎ 03-415 8099; www.suratbay. co.nz; Surat Bay Rd; dm/d $28/66; 🖳) Right beside the start of the track down to the beach, and next-door neighbours with the sea lions, this superbly located hostel has cosy, brightly decorated rooms and a friendly vibe. Rent a kayak ($12 to $40) or bike ($30 per day) and get exploring.

NUGGET & KAKA POINTS

Kaka Point Camping Ground (☎ 03-412 8801; kaka point@hotmail.com; 39 Tarata St, Kaka Point; unpowered/pow-ered sites per adult $12/12.50, cabins per adult $22) Cabins here are fairly basic but functional, but there is a lovely grassy, hedged area to pitch tents. There are bushwalks into the surrounding forest and it's a short, though steep, stroll downhill to the beach and town.

Fernlea Backpackers (☎ 03-412 8834, 03-418 0117; Moana St, Kaka Point; dm/d $20/50) Perched atop a hill, and a leafy, zigzag path above the street below, this tiny, basic bungalow is ultrasnug, with lovely sea views and basic facilities.

Nugget View & Kaka Point Motels (☎ 0800 525 278; www.catlins.co.nz; 11 Rata St, Kaka Point; d $85-160) A veritable mini-village of motel options ranging from excellent-value older units through to more modern accommodation with private spa baths and verandas. The friendly owners also operate one- and two-day tours of the Catlins, and twilight tours to view Nugget Point and the penguin colony at Roaring Bay.

Nugget Lodge (☎ 03-412 8783; www.nuggetlodge. co.nz; Nugget Rd, Nugget Point; d $160) Perched above the sea on the road south to the lighthouse, this pair of self-contained units is super-comfortable and has spectacular views up and down the coast. It's worth including their huge breakfast ($12.50 per person) with freshly baked bread and homemade muesli. Wonderfully secluded and a worthwhile splurge. And if you're lucky, you might spy a couple of resident sea lions lolling on the beach below you.

Eating
OWAKA

Things close pretty early in Owaka, so head out for dinner early, or stock up for self-catering at the local 4 Square supermarket. A good eating and drinking option is the cosy **Ryley's Café & Bar** (☎ 03-415 8350; 21 Ryley St; ⊗ 11am-9pm Thu-Mon) at the Catlin's Inn Hotel. It's the locals' favourite, and you can also get meals at the **Lumberjack Bar & Café** (☎ 03-415 8747; 3 Saunders St; mains $15-30; ⊗ 11.30am-9pm Tue-Sun). Park yourself at the wooden bar made from one 6m-long slab of golden-hued timber, and peruse robust options including chicken, steak and venison.

KAKA POINT

Point Café & Bar (☎ 03-412 8800; 58 Esplanade; bar menu $5-15, mains $27-30; ⊗ 11am-late) An interesting beach-themed bar serving up bar meals and more substantial dinners. Prop yourself at the driftwood bar for a cool beer, or grab a window seat for a sea view. Takeaways are also available at the attached store; grab a burger ($5) for the road.

Stewart Island

Travellers who undertake the short jaunt to Stewart Island will be rewarded with a warm welcome from both the local kiwi and the local Kiwis. New Zealand's 'third' island is a good place to spy the country's shy, feathered icon in the wild, and the close-knit community of Stewart Islanders (population 420) are relaxed hosts. If you're staying on the island for just a few days, don't be too surprised if most people quickly know who you are and where you came from – especially if you mix and mingle over a beer at NZ's southernmost pub.

Once you've said g'day to the locals, there's plenty of active adventure on offer including kayaking and setting off on a rewarding tramp in Stewart Island's Rakiura National Park. With a worthwhile injection of effort, relative newcomers to tramping can easily complete one of NZ's Great Walks, and be surprised and entertained with an uninterrupted aria from native birds. And if a multiday tramp still sounds too intense, spying a kiwi in the wild can also be achieved with the straightforward combination of a short boat ride and an even shorter bush and beach walk.

All this exercise is bound to make you hungry, so refuel with the freshest NZ seafood before resurrecting your 'Mainland' journey back on the South Island.

HIGHLIGHTS

- Discovering perfect coves and secluded bays around the **Rakiura Track** (p676)

- Listening to the chorus of birdsong on tiny protected **Ulva Island** (p675)

- Dining on blue cod, mussels and crayfish – all fresh from the southern ocean – in **Oban** (p679)

- Kayaking languidly around the natural harbour of **Paterson Inlet** (p676)

- Heading off in the southern twilight to get up close and personal with a Stewart Island kiwi at **Mason Bay** (p676)

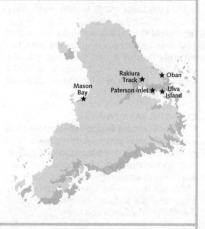

- Telephone code: 03
- www.stewartisland.co.nz

STEWART ISLAND *(vertical sidebar)*

CLIMATE

Stewart Island's changeable weather can bring four seasons in one day. Frequent downpours create a misty, mysterious air and lots of mud, making boots and waterproof clothing mandatory. Nevertheless, the temperature is milder than you'd expect, with winter averaging around 10°C and summer 16.5°C.

HISTORY

Stewart Island's Maori name is Rakiura (Glowing Skies), and catch a glimpse of a spectacular blood-red sunset or the aurora australis and you'll quickly know why. According to myth, NZ was hauled up from the ocean by Maui (p54), who said, 'Let us go out of sight of land, far out in the open sea, and when we have quite lost sight of land, then let the anchor be dropped'. The North Island was the fish that Maui caught, the South Island his canoe and Rakiura was the anchor – Te Punga o te Waka o Maui.

There is evidence that parts of Rakiura were occupied by moa hunters as early as the 13th century. The titi (muttonbird or sooty shearwater) on adjacent islands were an important seasonal food source for the southern Maori.

The first European visitor was Captain Cook, who sailed around the eastern, southern and western coasts in 1770 but couldn't figure out if it was an island or a peninsula. Deciding it was attached to the South Island, he called it South Cape. In 1809 the sealing vessel *Pegasus* circumnavigated Rakiura and named it after its first officer, William Stewart.

In June 1864 Stewart and the adjacent islets were bought from the Maori for £6000. Early industries were sealing, timber-milling, fish-curing and shipbuilding, with a short-lived gold rush towards the end of the 19th century. Today the island's economy is dependent on tourism and fishing, including crayfish (lobster), paua (abalone), salmon, mussels and cod.

FLORA & FAUNA

You don't even have to step off your balcony to experience the island's lush flora and fauna, but the more you explore, the more you'll encounter. Nature has cranked the birdsong up to 11 here; you can't miss the tui, parakeets,

STEWART ISLAND

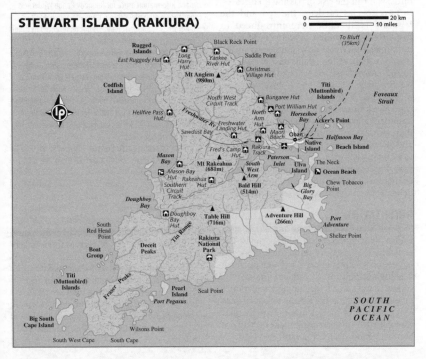

kaka, bellbirds, fernbirds, robins and dotterels that constantly flap overhead and serenade you from gardens. You can also see kiwi and Fiordland crested, yellow-eyed and blue penguins. Ask at the i-SITE about the evening parade of penguins on a small beach near the wharf. Resist the temptation to feed any of the birds; you run the risk of passing on diseases.

Two species of deer, the red and the Virginia (whitetail), were introduced in the early 20th century, as were brush-tailed possums, which are now numerous in the northern half of the island and destructive to the native bush. Stewart Island also has NZ fur seals.

Unlike NZ's North and South Islands, there is no beech forest on Stewart Island. The predominant lowland vegetation is hardwood but there are also lots of tree ferns, ground ferns and several types of orchid. Along the coast there's muttonbird scrub, grass tree, tree daisies, supplejack and leatherwood. Around the shores are clusters of bull kelp, fine red weeds, delicate green thallus and bladder ferns.

ORIENTATION

Stewart Island is 65km long and 40km at its widest point, and only has 20km of roads. The coastline is incised by numerous inlets, the largest of which is known as Paterson Inlet. The highest point is Mt Anglem (980m).

The island's small, easy-going population is primarily settled in the fishing village of **Oban** (Map opposite) in Halfmoon Bay. Regular transport from Invercargill makes getting to Stewart Island straightforward.

INFORMATION

Stop off at the Invercargill i-Site (p660) for a wider range of information than what is available on the ferry from Bluff.

There are no banks on Stewart Island. Credit cards are accepted for most activities but it's wise to bring enough cash for your stay. There's internet access at Justcafé (including wi-fi), the South Sea Hotel, and most accommodation.

Online see www.stewartisland.co.nz.

DOC Rakiura National Park visitor centre (Department of Conservation; Map p675; ☎ 03-219 0009; rakiuravc@doc.govt.nz; Main Rd, Oban; ☉ 8.30am-7.30pm Mon-Fri, 9am-4pm Sat & Sun) The free exhibition is an essential stop to understand Stewart Island's flora and fauna before heading off on your tramp. Backcountry Hut Passes and detailed maps of local tracks are also available.

Post office (Map p675; Elgin Tce, Oban) At Stewart Island Flights.

Ruggedy Range Birds & Forest Booking Office (Map p675; ☎ 0508 484 337, 03-219 1066; www.ruggedyrange.com; cnr Main Rd & Dundee St, Oban; ☉ 7.30am-8pm Mon-Sun Sep-May, 8.30am-5.30pm Mon-Fri, 9.30am-2pm Sat & Sun Jun-Aug) Dedicated booking and information office for Ruggedy Range Wilderness Experience with birdwatching, tramping and water taxis on offer. Note that Ruggedy Range is not represented by other information centres on the island.

Stewart Island Experience (Map p675; ☎ 0800 000 511, 03-212 7660; www.stewartislandexperience.co.nz; 12 Elgin Tce, Oban; ☉ 8am-7pm Mon-Fri, 9am-7pm Sat & Sun summer, 8am-5pm Mon-Fri, 10am-noon Sat & Sun winter) The ferry company is housed in the big red building and books accommodation and activities. Also handles sightseeing tours, and rents scooters, cars, fishing rods, dive gear and golf clubs.

Stewart Island Health Centre (Map p675; ☎ 03-219 1098; Argyle St, Oban; ☉ 10.30am-12.30pm) Has a 24-hour on-call service.

SIGHTS

Rakiura Museum (Map p675; Ayr St, Oban; adult/child $2/50c; ☉ 10am-1.30pm Mon-Sat, noon-2pm Sun) has models of various ferries from over the years, a sobering exhibit on whaling, Maori artefacts and early European settlement.

The wooden **Presbyterian Church Hall** (Map p675; Kamahi Rd, Oban) was relocated to Oban from a whaling base in Paterson Inlet in 1937. At Harrold Bay, 2.5km southwest of town, is a **stone house** (off Map p675) built by Lewis Acker around 1835, one of NZ's oldest stone buildings.

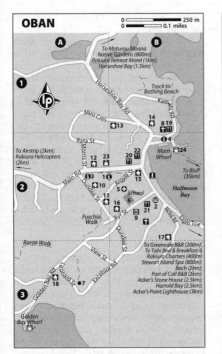

Stop in and learn about the work done at the **Halfmoon Bay Habitat Rehabilitation Project** (Map p675), which is striving to restore the native bird life around Halfmoon Bay.

Ulva Island

Ulva Island (Map p673) is a tiny paradise covering only 250 hectares. An early naturalist, Charles Traill, was honorary postmaster here. He would hoist a flag to signal that mail had arrived and hopefuls would paddle in from surrounding islands. His postal service was replaced by one at Oban in 1921, and in 1922 Ulva Island was declared a bird sanctuary.

With an absence of predators, the air is alive with the song of tui and bellbirds, and you'll also see kaka, weka, kakariki and kereru (NZ pigeon).

Good walking tracks in the island's northwest are detailed in *Ulva: Self-Guided Tour* ($2), available from the Department of Conservation (DOC). Popular routes include **Flagstaff Point Lookout** (20 minutes return) and **Boulder Beach** (1½ hours return). Many paths intersect amid beautiful stands of rimu, miro,

totara and rata. During summer, a ferry (return adult/child $20/10) departs from Golden Bay wharf to Ulva Island at 9am, noon and 4pm, and water taxis can take you to Ulva independently (return $25; p680).

To get the most out of Ulva Island, consider going with a guide from Ruggedy Range Wilderness Experience (p676) or Ulva's Guided Walks (p677).

ACTIVITIES

NZ's third-largest island features unspoilt wilderness and is a haven for a symphony of birdsong. Rakiura National Park protects 85% of the island, making it a mecca for trampers and birdwatchers, and there are countless sandy, isolated coves that are good for swimming if you're brave/mad enough to venture into the cool water.

Tramping

Even if you're not a gung-ho tramper, Stewart Island is great to stretch your legs and immerse yourself in wilderness on a short tramp. For more serious trampers, there are excellent, multiday, DOC-maintained trails. The DOC Rakiura National Park visitor centre (p674) sells Backcountry Hut Passes and has detailed pamphlets on local tramps. Store gear here in small/large lockers for $5/10 per day. Storage bins are $10 per day.

In the north, there's a good network of tracks with huts occupied on a first-come, first-served basis. Each hut has foam mattresses, wood stoves for heating, running water and toilets. You'll need to carry a stove, food, sleeping bags, utensils and first-aid equipment. A tent can be useful over the busy summer holidays and Easter period. The southern part of the island is undeveloped and desolate, and you shouldn't tramp on your own or go off the established tracks.

DAY TRAMPS

There are a number of short tramps, ranging from half an hour to seven hours; the majority are easily accessed from Halfmoon Bay. Pick up *Day Walks* ($1) from DOC Rakiura National Park visitor centre. The walk to **Observation Rock** (Map p675; 30 minutes return) has good views over Paterson Inlet. Continue past the old stone house at Harrold Bay to **Acker's Point Lighthouse** (three hours return), for good views of Foveaux Strait and the chance to see blue penguins and a colony of titi.

MULTIDAY TRAMPS

The 29km, three-day **Rakiura Track** is one of NZ's Great Walks and is a well-defined, easy circuit starting and ending at Oban with copious bird life, beaches and lush bush en route. Huts along this scenic, extensively boardwalked track get quite crowded, particularly those at Port William and North Arm, both of which have room for 30 trampers. There are also camping grounds at Sawdust Bay, Maori Beach and Port William. A rerouting and upgrade of the track was planned to be completed by June 2011, so it's vital to check with DOC for the latest information. Overnight trampers need to buy from DOC either a date-stamped **Great Walks huts pass** (per night adult/child $15/free) or **camping pass** (per night adult/child $5/2.50); there's a limit of two consecutive nights in any one hut.

See the DOC pamphlet *Rakiura Track* ($1) for more info.

Following the northern coast is the **North West Circuit Track**, a 125km trail taking 10 to 12 days that is often plagued with deep, thick mud. It's only suitable for well-equipped and experienced trampers, as is the 56km, four-day **Southern Circuit Track** that branches off it. A **North West Circuit Pass** ($45) gives you a night in each of these tracks' huts. Alternatively, you can buy a 12-month **Backcountry Hut Pass** (adult/child $90/45) to stay in huts on either circuit track, but you'll still have to buy a Great Walks huts pass for use at Port William and North Arm. See the DOC brochure *North West & Southern Circuit Tracks* ($1). Both the Rakiura and North West Circuit Tracks are detailed in Lonely Planet's *Tramping in New Zealand*.

Kiwi-Spotting

The Stewart Island kiwi (*Apteryx australis lawryi*) is a distinct subspecies, with a larger beak and longer legs than its northern cousins. Kiwi are common over much of Stewart Island, particularly foraging around beaches for sand hoppers under washed-up kelp. Unusually, Stewart Island's kiwi are active during the day as well as at night – the birds are forced to forage for longer to attain breeding condition. Many trampers on the North West Circuit Track spot them. For a helping hand with sightings, see Tours (opposite). Because of Stewart Island's often-fickle weather, tours are sometimes cancelled, and you may need to spend a few nights on the island to finally see a kiwi.

Other Activities

Paterson Inlet consists of 100 sq km of sheltered, kayak-friendly waterways, with 20 islands, DOC huts and two navigable rivers. A popular trip is a paddle to **Freshwater Landing** (7km upriver from the inlet) followed by a three- to four-hour walk to Mason Bay to see kiwi in the wild. **Rakiura Kayaks** (☎ 03-219 1160; www.rakiura.co.nz) rents kayaks from $45 a day and also runs half-/full-day guided trips around the inlet ($60/85). You'll find Liz from Rakiura Kayaks at Bunkers Backpackers (p678).

Ruggedy Range Wilderness Experience (Map p675; ☎ 0508 484 337, 03-219 1066; www.ruggedyrange.com; cnr Main Rd & Dundee St, Oban) runs guided walks on Ulva Island and has guided trips from half a day to 3½ days including camping and tramping. Prices range from $100 to $2500.

Stewart Island Experience (Map p675; ☎ 0800 000 511, 03-212 7660; www.stewartislandexperience.co.nz; 12 Elgin Tce, Oban; ☺ 8am-7pm Mon-Fri, 9am-7pm Sat & Sun summer, 8am-5pm Mon-Fri, 10am-noon Sat & Sun winter) rents mountain bikes (half-/full day $25/35) and motor scooters (half-/full day $55/65). The island's **Community Centre** (Map p675; ☎ 03-219 1477; 10 Ayr St, Oban; nonmembers $5) houses a gym, sauna, netball and squash courts, all of which are open to visitors. It's also home to a **library** (☺ 6.30-7.30pm Mon, 2-3pm Wed, 11am-noon Fri & Sat) open to visitors.

Stewart Island Spa (off Map p675; ☎ 03-219 1422; www.stewartislandspa.co.nz; ☺ Dec-Mar) is in a refurbished hilltop cottage. Options include crystal healing, a rainforest bath, and a sauna and massage. Premium organic beauty products are used for all treatments. See Britt at Justcafé (p679).

TOURS

Ulva's Guided Walks (☎ 03-219 1216; www.ulva.co.nz) offers Maori history and conservation included in excellent three- to five-hour tours costing from $95 to $150 (transport included). Options include Ulva Island and Port William, a historic Maori and sealing site.

Coast to Coast (Map p675; ☎ 03-218 9129; www.stewartislandflights.com; Elgin Tce, Oban; adult/child from $185/135) offers adventure-packed days with a flight from Oban and beach landing at Mason Bay, a four-hour tramp and a one-hour boat ride through Paterson Inlet to Golden Bay.

Stewart Island Experience (Map p675; ☎ 0800 000 511, 03-212 7660; www.stewartislandexperience.co.nz; 12 Elgin Tce, Oban; ☺ 8am-7pm Mon-Fri, 9am-7pm Sat & Sun summer, 8am-5pm Mon-Fri, 10am-noon Sat & Sun winter) runs 2½-hour Paterson Inlet cruises (adult/child $80/20, daily at 12.45pm October to April) via

Ulva Island; daily 1½-hour minibus tours of Oban and the surrounding bays (adult/child $42/20); and daily, 45-minute semisubmersible cruises (adult/child $35/120).

To see a kiwi in the wild, **Bravo Adventure Cruises** (☎ 03-219 1144; philldismith@xtra.co.nz) runs twilight tours ($120). In order to protect the kiwi, numbers are limited so make sure you book *well* ahead. Kiwi-spotting is also available with Ruggedy Range.

Ruggedy Range Wilderness Experience (Map p675; ☎ 0508 484 337, 03-219 1066; www.ruggedyrange.com; cnr Main Rd & Dundee St, Oban) takes small groups on guided walks with an ecofriendly, conservation angle. It also specialises in the viewing of pelagic seabirds. Excursions range from a half-day trip to Ulva Island ($100) to a 3½-day wilderness experience ($2500). One- and two-night expeditions to see kiwi in the wild ($425 to $835) are also available.

Charter companies offer various fishing trips and wildlife cruises. Options include the following:

Bravo Adventure Cruises (☎ 03-219 1144; philldismith@xtra.co.nz)

Rakiura Charters (off Map p675; ☎ 0800 725 487, 03-219 1487; www.rakiuracharters.co.nz) Sightseeing and fishing outings on the very comfortable *Rakiura Suzy*. Most popular is the half-day fishing cruise (adult/child $125/80) including a stop at a historic Whalers' Base. Multiday diving, fishing and hunting charters and overnight trips are also available.

Rawhiti Excursions (☎ 03-219 1023; per half-/full day $70/90) Traditional hand fishing with a lunch option of 'catch and cook' your own blue cod.

To see Stewart Island from the air on a scenic flight, see Rakiura Helicopters (p680).

SPOTTING A KIWI: A BRUSH WITH THE GODS

Considered the king of the forest by Maori, the kiwi has been around for 70 million years and is related to the now extinct moa. Brown feathers camouflage the kiwi against its bush surroundings and a nocturnal lifestyle means spying a kiwi in the wild is a challenge. They're a smart wee bird – they even build their burrows a few months before moving in so newly grown vegetation can further increase their privacy.

Stewart Island is one of the few places on earth where you can spot a kiwi in the wild. As big as a barnyard chicken and numbering 20,000, the tokoeka, or Stewart Island brown kiwi, is larger in size and population than other subspecies. They are also the only kiwi active during daylight hours. About two hours after sunrise and an hour before sunset, tokoeka forage for food in grassed areas, particularly on Mason Bay. Watch for white kiwi poo and telltale holes made by their long hunting beaks. When you spot one, keep silent, and stay still and well away. The birds' poor eyesight and single-mindedness in searching for food will often lead them to bump right into you.

STEWART ISLAND

SLEEPING

Despite Oban's surprisingly high number of motels, hostels, holiday homes and B&Bs, finding accommodation can be difficult, even in the low season when many places shut down. It's wise to book ahead. Self-contained holiday homes offer good value, especially for families and groups.

See www.stewartisland.co.nz for the widest range of accommodation options.

Budget

Stewart Island Backpackers (Map p675; ☎ 03-219 1114; www.stewart-island.co.nz/backpackers; cnr Dundee & Ayr Sts, Oban; dm/s/d $25/40/55; ☐) Rooms are basic but brightly painted, and many open onto a courtyard. There are only three beds per dorm, plus a spacious lounge, common kitchen, table tennis table and barbecue keep things nicely social. Tenting is $15 per person.

ourpick Bunkers Backpackers (Map p675; ☎ 03-219 1160; www.bunkersbackpackers.co.nz; 13 Argyle St, Oban; dm/s/d $28/48/76; ☐ ☎) A recently renovated wooden villa houses Stewart Island's newest and friendliest hostel. Shared areas are modern and sunny, and the rooms are spacious and spotless. Owners Liz and Heath can arrange kayaking and seafood barbecues, while friendly canine assistant Pip is always up for a cuddle or a sausage.

Jo & Andy's B&B (Map p675; ☎ 03-219 1230; jariksem@clear.net.nz; cnr Morris St & Main Rd, Oban; s $45-60, d $74; ☐ ☎) An excellent option for budget travellers, this cosy blue home squeezes in twin, double and single rooms. A big breakfast of muesli, fruit and homemade bread prepares you for tramping and dinner is available for $20. After a long tramp, dissolve into the skilful hands of the on-site massage therapist.

Midrange

South Sea Hotel (Map p675; ☎ 03-219 1059; www.stewart-island.co.nz; 26 Elgin Tce, Oban; s $65-100, d $85-110, units $155; ☐ ☎) Built in 1890, this harbourside hotel has floral rooms and a big sunny deck. The downstairs pub often overpowers the ocean sounds on weekends while out the back sunny motel units manage a South Pacific look with high ceilings, kitchenettes and verandas.

Pilgrim Cottage (Map p675; ☎ 03-219 1144; philldismith@xtra.co.nz; 8 Horseshoe Bay Rd, Oban; d $120) This quaint, weatherboard cottage in a leafy oasis near town has wooden furnishings, a potbelly stove and a well-equipped kitchen. Expect lots of bird life.

Rakiura Retreat Motel (off Map p675; ☎ 03-219 1096; www.rakiuraretreat.co.nz; Horseshoe Bay Rd; units $140-160; ☐) Surrounded by native bush, this row of motel units has comfortable and peaceful rooms. It's a pleasant 20-minute walk from town and there's a winding walking track from the motel down to secluded Bragg's Bay. Mountain bikes are complimentary.

Top End

Bay Motel (Map p675; ☎ 03-219 1119; www.baymotel.co.nz; 9 Dundee St, Oban; d $160-200) Modern, comfortable units with lots of light and views over the harbour. Some units have big spa tubs, all rooms have full kitchens and two are wheelchair-accessible. When you've exhausted the island's bustling after-dark scene, Sky TV's on hand for on-tap entertainment.

Te Tahi Bed & Breakfast (off Map p675; ☎ 0800 725 487, 03-219 1487; www.rakiuracharters.co.nz; 14 Kaka Ridge Rd; d $200) A sunny conservatory immersed in verdant bush, ocean views and colourfully decorated bedrooms are the standouts at this friendly B&B just five minutes' walk form the bustling hub of Oban and Halfmoon Bay.

Kaka Retreat (Map p675; ☎ 03-219 1252; www.stewartisland.net; 7 & 9 Miro Cres, Oban; d $320; ☐ ☎) These self-contained studio units have luxury interiors and cosy veranda. With crisply modern decor and flash bathrooms, the newly redecorated superior units are among the island's best. Most mornings you'll be greeted by kaka. Just don't feed them, OK? An older-style family unit ($299) is good value for up to six people.

Greenvale B&B (off Map p675; ☎ 03-219 1357; www.greenvalestewartisland.co.nz; Elgin Tce; s/d $300/375; ☎) Just 50m from the sea, this modern home has stunning views over Foveaux Strait. Both rooms have quality cotton bed linen and contemporary furnishings. It's a five-minute walk to Halfmoon Bay, and a two-second transition to the sunny deck. The owner's family has been resident on Stewart Island for several generations.

Stewart Island Lodge (Map p675; ☎ 03-219 1085; www.stewartislandlodge.co.nz; Nichol Rd, Oban; d incl breakfast $390) This upmarket retreat with six features king-size beds, a shared deck, and a garden teeming with bird life. On a hill at the edge of town, the lodge commands magnificent views. Look forward to complimentary drinks and nibbles at 5pm every night.

It's the little things that make a difference at **Port of Call B&B** (off Map p675; ☎ 03-219 1394;

www.portofcall.co.nz; Leask Bay Rd; s/d incl breakfast $345/385), such as a welcome fruit basket and 20 hectares of surrounding bush. Take in ocean views, get cosy before an open fire or explore an isolated beach. Nearby is a modern self-contained studio unit called the **Bach** (off Map p675; unit $250). You'll find both 1.5km south-west of Oban on the way to Acker's Point. In the heart of Halfmoon Bay, the self-contained **Turner Cottage** (Map p675; Golden Bay Rd; cottage $180) is perfect for romantic island escapees. All three properties have a two-night minimum stay, and guided walks and water taxi trips can also be arranged.

EATING & DRINKING

ourpick Kai Kart (Map p675; ☎ 03-219 1225; Ayr St, Oban; meals $5-20; ☉ 11.30am-2.30pm & 5-9pm, closed Mon-Tue May-Nov) Owned by a mussel farmer, the seafood at this tiny caravan of cuisine is exceptionally fresh. The sweet-as-sweet blue cod could be the best fish you'll ever have, and the mussels with spicy satay sauce aren't far behind. Park yourself in an interior booth, grab an outside table, or eat your goodies on the beach. Don't blame us if you've finished them before you get there.

Justcafé (Map p675; ☎ 03-219 1422; Main Rd, Oban; meals $10-14; ☉ 8am-8pm; 🖳 ⊚) This warm little place has wooden-bench tables and lots of magazines. Fill up on soups, tasty sandwiches and baking. Nurse a good coffee or an even better smoothie or raw juice. There's wi-fi available, and owner Britt also sells wholesale gemstone jewellery and designs made from paua shells.

South Sea Hotel (Map p675; ☎ 03-219 1059; 26 Elgin Tce, Oban; mains $15-30; ☉ 11am-late) With old

---

YOU CAUGHT IT. NOW COOK IT.

You're (literally) surrounded by fishing opportunities on Stewart Island, but if you're not staying in self-contained accommodation, you'll need to explore other avenues to prepare your freshly caught *kai moana* (seafood).

For a small fee, the good people at the Kai Kart (above) will perform kitchen duties on your behalf, and if you're an alfresco kind of chef, fire up the public barbecues (buy charcoal at Ship to Shore, right) in the pleasant **Moturau Moana Native Gardens** on the eastern edge of Halfmoon Bay.

B&W photos, this cafe-style spot does superb fish, and robust seafood chowder. It's listed under 'Starters' but it's a meal in itself. The attached pub is the town's main drinking hole, enlivened by occasional weekend bands and a loads-of-fun pub quiz that kicks off at 6.30pm on Sunday nights. Say hi to Vicky, quiz-mistress extraordinaire. Friday's also a good night to meet the locals, when Happy Hour kicks off at 5.30pm.

Church Hill Cafe, Bar & Restaurant (Map p675; ☎ 03-219 1323; 36 Kamahi Rd, Oban; mains $25-35; ☉ 5.30-9pm) Look beyond the gimmicky 'Stone Grill' menu to local flavours such as blue cod and muttonbird (in season). In summer the sunny, spacious deck and lawn provide hilltop views, and in cooler months you'll need to beat out the friendly cat for a cosy spot by the fire. It's essential to book for dinner, and by 5pm at the latest.

ourpick Perfect Dinner (☎ 027 444 1802; annett_eiselt@web.de; 3-course menu per person $70; ☉ Oct-May) Relocated from Germany to the southern ocean, Annett Eiselt specialises in 'moveable feasts'. That means she's available to provide three-course menus or gourmet platters wherever you desire on the island; at your accommodation, on a beach, or somewhere else with equally terrific views. Produce is always seasonal, and ideally organic and sourced locally. Annett can also recommend on lodge-style accommodation.

Self-caterers can get groceries and beer and wine from Oban's general store. **Ship to Shore** (Map p675; ☎ 03-219 1069; Elgin Tce, Oban; ☉ 7.30am-7pm). Also available are sandwiches and baked goodies ($3 to $6), and staff can prepare a packed lunch if you're going for a day tramp. It's also the kind of friendly place that announces locals' birthdays on a blackboard outside.

The Fishermen's Co-op on the main wharf often sells fresh fish and crayfish.

SHOPPING

Opposite the DOC office, the **Fernery** (Map p675; ☎ 03-219 1216; Main Rd, Oban; ☉ 11am-5pm) sells crafts, paintings and island-themed books, especially titles for kids. Pick up a CD of bird calls, so you'll know your kiwi from your kaka.

Glowing Sky (Map p675; ☎ 03-219 1528; www.glowingsky.co.nz; Elgin Tce, Oban; ☉ 11am-3pm) sells hand-printed T-shirts.

Ruggedy Range Wilderness Experience can set you up with tramping and camping gear at its Birds & Forest Booking Office (p674).

GETTING THERE & AWAY

Air

Rakiura Helicopters (off Map p675; ☎ 03-219 1155; www.rakiurahelicopters.co.nz; 151 Main Rd) is the only helicopter company based on Stewart Island. It's available for transfers from Bluff (per person $250), scenic flights (per person $50 to $560), and charter flights for hunters and trampers.

Stewart Island Flights (Map p675; ☎ 03-218 9129; www.stewartislandflights.co.nz; Elgin Tce, Oban) flies between the island and Invercargill (adult/child one way $105/65, return $185/105). Flights depart three times daily year-round. Phone ahead for occasional discount and standby fares. The bus trip from the island's airstrip to Oban is included in the fare.

Boat

The passenger-only **Stewart Island Experience Ferry** (Map p675; ☎ 0800 000 511, 03-212 7660; www.stewartislandexperience.co.nz; Main Wharf) runs between Bluff and Oban (adult/child $63/31.50) around three times daily. Book a few days ahead in summer. The crossing takes one hour and can be a rough ride. The company also runs a shuttle between Bluff and Invercargill (adult/child $20/10) with pick-up and drop-off in Invercargill at the i-SITE, Tuatara Backpackers and Invercargill Airport. Cars and campervans can be stored in a secure car park at Bluff for an additional cost.

A shuttle also runs between Bluff and Queenstown (adult/child $65/32.50), and Bluff and Te Anau (adult/child $65/32.50) with pick-up and drop-off at the Real Journeys Visitor Centres.

GETTING AROUND

Water taxis offer pick-ups and drop-offs to remote parts of the island – a handy service for trampers. The taxis also service Ulva Island (return $25). Try **Stewart Island Water Taxi & Eco Guiding** (☎ 03-219 1394), **Aihe Eco Charters & Water Taxi** (☎ 03-219 1066; www.aihe.co.nz), **Sea View Water Taxi** (☎ 03-219 1014; www.seaviewwatertaxi.co.nz) or **Rakiura Adventure** (☎ 03-219 1013).

Rent a scooter (per half-/full day $55/65) or a car (per half-/full day $65/105) from Stewart Island Experience (p674).

Directory

CONTENTS

BOOK YOUR STAY ONLINE

For more accommodation reviews and recommendations by Lonely Planet authors,
check out the online booking service at
www.lonelyplanet.com/hotels. You'll find
the true, insider low-down on the best places
to stay. Reviews are thorough and independent. Best of all, you can book online.

ACCOMMODATION

Across New Zealand, you can bed down at
night in guest houses that creak with history,
facility-laden hotels, comfortably uniform
motel units, beautifully situated campsites,
and hostels that range in character from clean-
living and relaxed to tirelessly party-prone.

Accommodation listings in this guidebook
are ordered by budget from cheapest to most
expensive. We generally designate a place as
budget accommodation if it charges up to
$100 per double. Accommodation qualifies as
midrange if it costs roughly $100 to $160 per
double, while we've given the top-end tag to
double rooms costing over $160. Price ranges
generally increase by 20% to 25% in the nation's largest cities (Auckland, Wellington and
Christchurch). Here you can still find budget
accommodation at up to $100 per double, but
midrange stretches from $100 to $200, with
top-end rooms more than $200.

If you're travelling during peak tourist seasons, book your bed well in advance.
Accommodation is most in demand (and
at its priciest) during the summer holidays
from Christmas to late January, at Easter,
and during winter in snowy resort towns like
Queenstown. At other times, weekday rates
may be cheaper than weekend rates (except
in business-style hotels in larger cities, where
the reverse applies), and you'll certainly discover that low-season rates abound. When
they're not run off their feet, accommodation operators often offer walk-in rates that
are significantly below advertised rates – ask
late in the day. Also see the big-name global
accommodation websites (www.wotif.co.nz,
www.lastminute.co.nz, www.hotels.co.nz etc)
for last-minute deals.

Visitor information centres provide reams
of local accommodation information, often in
the form of folders detailing facilities and up-
to-date prices; many can also make bookings
on your behalf. Alternatively, flick through
one of NZ's free, widely available accommodation directories, including the annual *New
Zealand Accommodation Guide* published by
the **Automobile Association** (AA; www.aatravel.co.nz), as
well as the *Holiday Parks & Campgrounds* and
Motels, Motor Lodges & Apartments directories
produced by **Jasons** (www.jasons.com).

B&Bs & Guest Houses

Bed and breakfast (B&B) accommodation in
private homes is a growth industry in NZ, popping up in the middle of cities, in rural hamlets
and on stretches of isolated coastline, with
rooms on offer in everything from suburban

bungalows to stately manors owned by one family for generations.

Guest houses are usually spartan, cheap, 'private' (unlicensed) hotels, mostly low-key places patronised by people who eschew the impersonal atmosphere of many motels. Some guest houses are reasonably fancy and offer self-contained rooms.

Although breakfast is included at genuine B&Bs, it may or may not feature at guest houses. Breakfast may be 'continental' (cereal, toast and tea or coffee), 'hearty continental' (add yoghurt, fruit, home-baked bread or muffins), or a stomach-loading cooked meal including eggs, bacon and sausages. Some B&B hosts, especially in isolated locations or within the smaller towns where restaurants are limited, may cook dinner for guests and advertise dinner, bed and breakfast (DB&B) packages.

Tariffs are typically in the $120 to $180 bracket (per double), though some places charge upwards of $300 per double. Some hosts continue to be cheeky-as-a-kea, charging hefty prices for what is, in essence, a bedroom in their home. Many upmarket B&Bs demand bookings and deposits at least a month in advance, and enforce strict and expensive cancellation policies – ie cancel within a week of your arrival date and you'll forfeit your deposit plus the balance of the room rate. Check conditions before you book.

New Zealand's *Bed and Breakfast Directory* (www.bed-and-breakfast.co.nz) and *Bed & Breakfast Book* (www.bnb.co.nz) are available online, and at bookshops and visitor information centres.

Camping & Campervan Parks

Campers and campervan drivers alike converge upon NZ's hugely popular 'holiday parks', slumbering peacefully in powered and unpowered sites, cheap bunk rooms (dorm rooms), cabins and self-contained units that are often called motels or tourist flats. Well-equipped communal kitchens, dining areas and games and TV rooms often feature. In cities holiday parks are usually a fair way from the action, but in smaller towns they can be impressively central or near lakes, beaches, rivers and forests.

The nightly cost of holiday-park camping is usually between $15 and $18 per adult, with children charged half-price; powered sites are a couple of dollars more. Cabin/unit accommodation normally ranges from $60 to $120 per double. Unless noted otherwise, the prices we've listed for campsites, campervan sites, huts and cabins are for two people.

A fantastic option for campervanners are the 200-plus vehicle-accessible camping grounds run by the **Department of Conservation** (DOC; www.doc.govt.nz), with fees ranging from free (basic toilets and fresh water) to $14 per adult (flush toilets and showers). DOC publishes free brochures with detailed descriptions and instructions to find every campsite (even GPS coordinates). Grab a copy from a DOC office before you hit the road, or visit the website.

DOC also looks after hundreds of backcountry huts, most of which can only be reached on foot. For more info, see Tramping (p79).

Never just assume it's OK to camp somewhere. Always ask a local first. Check at the

---

PRACTICALITIES

- For weights and measures, NZ uses the metric system.

- DVDs and videos viewed in NZ are based on the PAL system – the same system used in Australia, the UK and most of Europe.

- Use a three-pin adaptor (the same as in Australia; different to British three-pin adaptors) to plug yourself into the electricity supply (230V AC, 50Hz).

- For news, leaf through Auckland's *New Zealand Herald,* Wellington's *Dominion Post* or Christchurch's *The Press* newspapers, or check out www.stuff.co.nz.

- Tune in to Radio National for current affairs and Concert FM for classical and jazz (see www.radionz.co.nz for frequencies). Kiwi FM (www.kiwifm.co.nz) plays 100% NZ music; Radio Hauraki (www.hauraki.co.nz) cranks out the classic rock (too much Split Enz is barely enough...).

- Watch one of the national government-owned TV stations (TV One, TV2, TVNZ 6, TVNZ 7, Maori TV and the 100% Maori language Te Reo) or the subscriber-only Sky TV (www.skytv.co.nz).

WWOOFING

If you don't mind getting your hands dirty, an economical way of travelling around NZ involves doing some voluntary work as a member of **Willing Workers on Organic Farms** (WWOOF; ☎ 03-544 9890; www.wwoof.co.nz). Membership of this popular, well-established international organisation (which has representatives in Africa, Asia, North America, Europe and Australia) scores you access to many hundreds of organic and permaculture farms, market gardens and other environmentally sound cottage industries across the country. Down on the farm, in exchange for a hard day's work, owners provide food, accommodation and some hands-on organic farming experience. Contact farm owners a week or two beforehand to arrange your stay, as you would for a hotel or hostel – don't turn up unannounced!

A one-year online membership costs $40 (for one person, or two people travelling together); or $50 for online membership and to have a farm-listing book mailed to you. You should be part of a Working Holiday Scheme (p698) when you visit NZ, as the immigration department considers WWOOFers to be working.

One word of caution: it seems that some hostels have started employing travellers under the name of WWOOFing, without requiring membership or providing any of the benefits (not to mention the lack of an organic farm). It's a vague kind of exploitation, and probably harmless, but it's a definite misnomer.

local i-SITE or DOC office, or with commercial camping grounds. If you are freedom camping, treat the area with respect – see www.camping .org.nz for more info on freedom camping.

Farmstays

Farmstays open the door on the agricultural side of NZ life, with visitors encouraged to get some dirt beneath their fingernails at orchards, and dairy, sheep and cattle farms. Costs can vary widely, with B&B generally ranging from $80 to $120. Some farms have separate cottages where you can fix your own food, while others offer low-cost, shared, backpacker-style accommodation.

Farm Helpers in NZ (FHINZ; www.fhinz.co.nz) produces a booklet ($25) that lists around 190 farms throughout NZ providing lodging in exchange for four to six hours' work per day. **Rural Holidays NZ** (☎ 03-355 6218; www.ruralholidays. co.nz) lists farmstays and homestays throughout the country on its website. See also the WWOOFing boxed text, above.

Hostels

NZ is packed to the rafters with backpacker hostels, ranging from small, homestay-style affairs with a handful of beds to refurbished hotels with scuffed facades and the towering modern structures you'll find in the big cities. Hostel bed prices listed throughout this book are the nonmembership rates.

If you're a Kiwi travelling in your own country, be warned that some hostels only admit overseas travellers, typically inner-city places. If you encounter such discrimination, either try another hostel or insist that you're a genuine traveller and not a bedless neighbour.

HOSTEL ORGANISATIONS

NZ's biggest hostel group is **Budget Backpacker Hostels** (BBH; ☎ 03-379 3014; www.bbh.co.nz), which has around 320 hostels on its books, including homestays and farmstays. Membership costs $45, including a $20 phonecard, and entitles you to stay at member hostels at a cost no greater than the rates advertised in the annual (free) *BBH Backpacker Accommodation* booklet. Nonmembers pay an extra $3 per night, though not all hostel owners charge the difference. Pick up a membership card from any member hostel, or have one mailed to you overseas for $50 (including postage; see the website for details). BBH rates each hostel according to traveller feedback, using a percentage figure that supposedly tells you how good (or at least how popular) each hostel is.

NZ's **Youth Hostels Association** (YHA; ☎ 0800 278 299, 03-379 9970; www.yha.co.nz) has been around for more than 75 years and has hostels in 54 prime NZ locations. The YHA is part of the **Hostelling International** (HI; www.hihostels.com) network. If you're already an HI member in your own country, your membership entitles you to use NZ hostels. If you don't already have a membership card from home, you can buy one at major NZ YHA hostels for $40 for 12 months, or book online and have your card mailed to you overseas for $50. Nightly charges are usually between $20 and $40 per person for members; hostels also take non-YHA members for an extra $3 per night.

YHA hostels provide reliable, basic accommodation for individuals, families and groups in dorms (bunk rooms, usually with four to six beds) and most also have a supply of single, twin and double rooms, sometimes with bathrooms. They have 24-hour access, cooking facilities, a communal area with a TV, laundry facilities and, in larger hostels, travel offices. There's often a maximum-stay period (usually five to seven days). NZ YHA hostels supply all bed linen so you don't need to bring a sleeping bag. The annual *YHA New Zealand Hostel & Discount Guide* booklet details all Kiwi hostels and member discounts (transport, activities etc). Stuff their *Backpacker Map* in your pocket for on-the-road reference.

VIP Backpackers (www.vip.co.nz) run around 70 NZ hostels, mainly in the cities and major tourist spots. VIP is an international organisation with a large network of hostels in nearby Fiji, Australia, southern Africa, Europe and America. For around $52 ($60 including postage) you'll receive a 12-month membership entitling you to a $1 discount on accommodation. You can join online (www.vipbackpackers.com), at VIP hostels or at larger agencies dealing in backpacker travel.

Nomads Backpackers (www.nomadsworld.com) has a handful of franchisees throughout NZ: in Auckland, Paihia, Taupo, Wellington and Rotorua. Membership costs A$35 for 12 months and like VIP offers NZ$1 off the cost of nightly accommodation. You can join at participating hostels, backpacker travel agencies or online.

Base Backpackers (www.stayatbase.com) are a chain with eight hostels around NZ. Expect clean dorms, girls-only areas and party opportunities aplenty.

INDEPENDENT HOSTELS
NZ is an incubator for independent hostels, hatching them across both islands at an impressive rate. Owners try hard to differentiate their properties from their clubby competitors: some promote low-key ambience, lazy gardens, personable management and avoidance of noisy bus groups of backpackers while others bury you in extras such as free breakfasts, free DVDs, spa pools, use of bikes and kayaks, shuttle buses, theme nights and tour bookings. This is usually a successful formula, but with individuality comes risk: if possible, check out your accommodation before handing over the cash to ensure the atmosphere and facilities correspond with your expectations. If travelling with your family, note that a number of hostels designate themselves 'unsuitable for children'.

Independent backpacker establishments typically charge $20 to $30 for a dorm bed, $40 to $50 for a single and $50 to $80 for a twin or double room (usually with shared bathroom facilities). Some also have space for a few tents.

Hotels & Motels
The least expensive form of NZ hotel accommodation is the humble pub. As is often the case elsewhere, some of NZ's old pubs are full of character and local characters, while others are grotty, ramshackle places that are best avoided, especially by women travelling solo. If you're renting a room above a pub towards the end of the week, check whether there's a band cranking out the tunes that night – you could be in for some sleeplessness. In the cheapest pubs, singles/doubles might cost as little as $30/50 (with a shared bathroom down the hall), though $50/70 is more common.

At the other end of the hotel scale are five-star international chains, resort complexes and architecturally splendorous boutique hotels, all of which charge a hefty premium for their mod cons, snappy service and/or historic opulence. We quote 'rack rates' (official advertised rates) for such places throughout this book, but discounts and special deals often mean you won't have to pay these prices.

NZ's towns have a glut of nondescript, low-rise motels and 'motor lodges', charging between $80 and $160 for double rooms. These tend to be squat structures congregating just outside CBDs, or skulking by highways on the edge of towns. Most are modernish (though decor is often mired in the '80s) and have similar facilities (tea- and coffee-making, fridge, TV) – prices vary with standard. Some Kiwis refer to the actual room as a 'motel', rather than the collective complex of rooms – so you might hear, 'Sorry, our motels are full tonight', as opposed to, 'Sorry, our motel is full tonight'.

Rental Accommodation

The basic Kiwi holiday home is called a 'bach' (short for 'bachelor' as they were often used by single men as hunting and fishing hideouts); in Otago and Southland they're known as 'cribs'. These are simple self-contained cottages that can be rented in rural and coastal areas, often in isolated locations. They can be handy for longer stays in a region, although some are only available for one or two nights at a time. Prices are typically $80 to $130 per night, which isn't bad for a whole house or self-contained bungalow.

For more upmarket holiday houses, the current trend is to throw rusticity to the wind and erect luxurious cottages on beautiful nature-surrounded plots. Expect to pay anything from $120 to $400 a double.

Good websites to help you find a bach or holiday house include www.holidayhomes.co.nz and the AA's www.bookabach.co.nz; for swanky self-contained apartments try www.newzealand-apartments.co.nz. If it's a longer stay you're thinking about, check out www.nzflats.co.nz.

ACTIVITIES

See the Active New Zealand chapter (p75) for more info on NZ's outdoor-activity smorgasbord.

Aerial Sightseeing

Small planes and helicopters circle the skies on sightseeing trips (called 'flightseeing' by the locals) all over NZ, operating from local aerodromes. It's a great (but not particularly environmentally friendly) way to absorb the country's contrasting landscapes, soaring mountains and seldom-viewed terrain deep within national parks. Some of the most photo-worthy trips take place over the Bay of Islands (p163), the Bay of Plenty (especially Whakaari Island; p341), Tongariro National Park (from Taupo; p294), Mt Taranaki (p262), Mt Cook (p569), the West Coast glaciers (p510) and Fiordland (from Te Anau; p647).

A far more sedate approach is to jump in a hot-air balloon. A float above Methven (p554) grants you spectacular views of the Southern Alps and contrasting Canterbury Plains, and there are also balloon trips from Queenstown, Auckland, Hamilton, Hastings and Masterton.

Fishing

Thanks to the introduction of trout, salmon, perch and char (among other species), NZ has become one of the world's great recreational fisheries. The central North Island's lakes and rivers are famous for trout fishing, especially around Lake Taupo – the town of Turangi is trout central. South Island rivers and lakes also fare well on the trout index, most notably the Mataura River (Southland) and Lake Brunner and the Arnold River (the West Coast). The rivers of Otago and Southland have some of the best salmon fishing in the world.

In the warm North Island seas, surfcasting and boat fishing can land grey mullet, trevally, mao mao, porae, John Dory, snapper, gurnard, flounder, mackerel, hapuku (groper), tarakihi, moki and kahawai. Ninety Mile Beach (Northland) and the Hauraki Gulf beaches are good for surfcasting. The Bay of Islands, Whangaroa, Tutukaka near Whangarei (all in Northland), Whitianga in the Coromandel and Tuhua (Mayor Island) in the Bay of Plenty are big-time big-game fishing areas.

The South Island's colder waters, especially around the Marlborough Sound, are great for snapper, hake, hapuku, trumpeter, kingfish, butterfish, ling, barracouta and blue cod. Kaikoura Peninsula offers some good surfcasting. Catch and cook your own blue cod off Stewart Island. Kurow, in the Waitaki Valley, North Otago, is good for salmon and trout.

You can hire fishing gear in towns like Taupo and Rotorua and at sports stores in larger towns. If you bring your own rods and tackle they may have to be treated by NZ quarantine officials, especially if they're made with natural materials such as cane or feathers.

A fishing permit is required to fish in inland waters. Sold at sport shops, permits cover particular regions and are valid for a day, month or season. Consult local visitor information centres or DOC offices (p697) for details. Other fishy business is covered at www.fishing.net.nz, a huge website covering recreational fishing in NZ. If you're interested in guided fishing trips, see the **New Zealand Professional Fishing Guides' Association** (www.nzpfga.com) website.

See the boxed text on p178 for some tips on sustainable fishing.

Golf

NZ has more golf courses per capita than any other country, and among over 400 courses there are some magnificently situated fairways and greens. In its 2009 rankings of the world's top 100 courses, *Golf Magazine* gave gongs to two NZ courses: **Cape Kidnappers** (www. capekidnappers.com) in Hawkes Bay (ranked 36th) and **Kauri Cliffs** (www.kauricliffs.com) in the Bay of Islands (ranked 78th). **Paraparaumu Beach** (www. paraparaumubeachgolfclub.co.nz) near Wellington, has made it into such rankings in the past and is regarded as one of the country's best courses.

Other popular courses include Wairakei near Taupo; Clearwater, outside Christchurch; Terrace Downs, in the high country near Methven; and Millbrook, near Queenstown. The Hills course in Arrowtown proclaims itself 'Home to the NZ Golf Open'. The only catch is that you can't play there – it's strictly millionaire members-only.

The average green fee for an 18-hole course usually ranges from $30 to $50, though private resorts can charge a substantial amount more – at Cape Kidnappers you'll pay a hefty $300 to $400 for the privilege; Paraparaumu Beach's green fees are a more manageable $110.

For more information check out www. nzgolf.org.nz.

Sailing

Surrounded by sea, NZ has a habit of producing some of the world's best mariners. There's also a good reason why Auckland is called the 'City of Sails'. If you're keen on yacht racing, try visiting the country's various sailing clubs and ask if you can help crew in local competitions. Otherwise, there are plenty of sailing operators who allow you to just laze around on deck or play a more hands-on role.

The Bay of Islands (and Whangaroa to the north), the southern lakes (Te Anau and Wakatipu) and the cities of Auckland and Nelson are good places to get some wind in your sails.

Go to www.yachtingnz.org.nz for more details.

BUSINESS HOURS

Most shops and businesses open their doors at 9am and close at 5.30pm Monday to Friday, and either 12.30pm or 5pm on Saturday. Late-night shopping (until 9pm) happens in the larger cities on Thursday and/or Friday nights; Sunday trading is the norm in most big towns and cities. Supermarkets are usually open from 8am until at least 7pm, often until 9pm or later in cities. Dairies (corner stores) and superettes (small supermarkets) close later than most shops.

Banks normally open from 9.30am to 4.30pm Monday to Friday (some city branches also open on Saturday mornings). Post offices are open 8.30am to 5pm Monday to Friday, with main branches also open 9.30am to 1pm Saturday; postal desks in newsagencies (Take Note, Paperplus) often open later.

Restaurants typically take orders until at least 9pm, but often serve food until 11pm or later on Friday and Saturday nights; the main restaurant strips in large cities keep longer hours throughout the week. Cafes sometimes open as early as 7am and close around 5pm, though cafe-bar hybrids push the envelope well into the night. Pubs usually serve food from noon to 2pm and from 6pm to 8pm. Pubs and bars generally start pouring drinks at noon and stay open until late, particularly from Thursday to Saturday.

Don't count on many attractions being open on Christmas Day or Good Friday.

CHILDREN

For helpful general tips, see Lonely Planet's *Travel with Children*. All cities and most major towns have centrally located public rooms where mothers (and sometimes fathers) can go to nurse a baby or change a nappy (diaper); check with the local visitor information centre or city council, or ask a local – Kiwis are a friendly bunch!

Practicalities

Many motels and holiday parks have playgrounds, games and DVD players, and occasionally fenced swimming pools and trampolines. Cots, highchairs and baby baths aren't always easy to find at budget and midrange accommodation, but top-end hotels are usually able to supply them and the plushest places have child-minding services. B&Bs are not usually amenable to families – many of these businesses promote themselves as grown-up getaways where peace and quiet are valued above all else. Hostels focusing on the young backpacker demographic don't welcome kids either, but there are plenty of other hostels (including YHA hostels) that do.

There are plenty of so-called family restaurants in NZ, where toddlers' highchairs are provided and kids can choose from their own menu. Pubs often serve kids' meals and most cafes and restaurants (with the exception of upmarket eateries) can handle the idea of child-sized portions.

For specialised childcare, look under 'babysitters' and 'child care centres' in the *Yellow Pages* directory or contact the local council.

Child concessions (and family rates) are often available for accommodation, tours, attraction entry fees, and air, bus and train transport, with discounts of as much as 50% off the adult rate. Do note, however, that the definition of 'child' can vary from under 12 to under 18 years; toddlers (under four years old) usually get free admission and transport.

NZ's medical services and facilities are world-class, with goods like formula and disposable nappies widely available in urban centres. Some smaller car-hire companies struggle with the concept of baby seats – double-check that the company you choose can supply the right size of seat for your child, and that the seat will be properly fitted. Some companies may legally require you to fit the seat yourself.

Sights & Activities

Fabulous kids' playgrounds (with slides, swings, see-saws etc) proliferate across NZ. Some regions produce free information booklets geared towards sights and activities for kids; one example is *Kidz Go!* (www.kidzgo.co.nz), which details child-friendly activities and restaurants in the larger urban centres. Ask at local visitor information centres. Other handy websites for families include www.kidspot.co.nz, with lots of kid-centric info from pregnancy through to school-age, and www.kidsnewzealand.com, which has plenty of activity suggestions. Finally, www.kidsfriendlynz.com has extensive links to various facets of kiddy-culture.

CLIMATE CHARTS

NZ sits smack-bang in the Roaring Forties, which means it gets 'freshened' (some say blasted) by cool, damp winds blowing in from the Tasman Sea and is consistently slapped by the winds howling through Cook Strait.

On the South Island, the Southern Alps act as a barrier for these moisture-laden easterlies, creating a wet climate on the western side

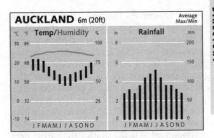

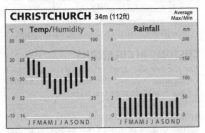

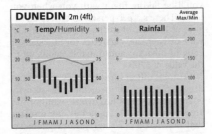

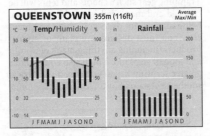

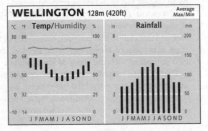

of the mountains (around 7500mm of rain annually!), and a dry climate on the eastern side (about 330mm). After dumping their moisture, the winds continue east, gathering heat and speed as they blow downhill and cross the Canterbury Plains; in summer this katabatic or föhn wind can be hot and fierce.

On the North Island, the western sides of the high volcanoes attract a lot more rain than eastern slopes, but the rain shadow isn't as pronounced as in the south – the barrier here isn't as formidable as the Alps. North Island rainfall averages around 1300mm annually.

See p19 for further seasonal instruction.

CUSTOMS REGULATIONS

For the low-down on what you can and can't bring into NZ, see the **New Zealand Customs Service** (www.customs.govt.nz) website.

When entering NZ you can bring most articles in free of duty provided customs is satisfied they're for personal use and that you'll be taking them with you when you leave. There's a per-person duty-free allowance of 1125mL of spirits or liqueur, 4.5L of wine or beer, 200 cigarettes (or 50 cigars or 250g of tobacco) and dutiable goods up to the value of $700.

Customs officers are obviously fussy about drugs, so declare all medicines. Bio-security is another customs buzzword – authorities are serious about keeping out any diseases that may harm NZ's agricultural industry. Tramping gear such as boots and tents will be checked and may need to be cleaned before being allowed in; ditto golf clubs and bicycles. You must declare any plant or animal products (including anything made of wood), and food of any kind. You'll also come under greater scrutiny if you've arrived via Africa, southeast Asia or South America. Weapons and firearms are either prohibited or require a permit and safety testing.

DANGERS & ANNOYANCES

Although it's no more dangerous than other developed countries, violent crime does happen in NZ, so it's worth taking sensible precautions on the streets at night or if staying in remote areas. Gang culture permeates some parts of the country; give any black-jacketed, insignia-wearing groups a wide berth.

Theft, primarily from cars, is a *major* problem around NZ, and travellers are viewed as easy marks. Avoid leaving valuables in vehicles, no matter where they're parked; the worst places to tempt fate are tourist parking areas and the car parks at trailheads. If the crown jewels simply must be left behind, pack them out of sight in the boot (trunk) of the car – but carry your passport with you, just in case.

Don't underestimate the dangers posed by NZ's unpredictable, ever-changing climate, especially in high-altitude areas; see p77 for information.

NZ has thankfully been spared from the proliferation of venomous creatures found in neighbouring Australia (spiders, snakes, jellyfish etc). Sharks hang out in NZ waters, but are well fed by the abundant marine life and rarely nibble on humans; that said, attacks on humans do occasionally occur. Much greater hazards in the ocean, however, are the rips and undertows that plague some beaches and can quickly drag swimmers out to sea. Take notice of local warnings when swimming, surfing or diving.

The islands' roads are often made hazardous by speeding locals, wide-cornering campervans and traffic-ignorant sheep. Set yourself a reasonable itinerary instead of careening around the country at top speed and keep

---

SANDFLIES Sir Ian McKellen

As an unpaid but enthusiastic proselytiser on behalf of all things Kiwi, including the New Zealand tourist industry, I hesitate to mention the well-kept secret of sandflies. I first met them en masse at the glorious Milford Sound, where visitors (after the most beautiful drive in the world) are met, at least during the summer, by crowds of the little buggers. There are patent unctions that cope, and tobacco repels them too, but I would hope that travellers find them an insignificant pest compared with the glory of their habitat.

Oddly, when actually filming scenes for *Lord of the Rings*, I don't recall being bothered by sandflies at all. Honestly. Had there been, we would have set the orcs on them.

Sir Ian McKellen is a UK-based actor who spent several years in NZ filming and has become something of an unofficial ambassador for NZ tourism.

your eyes on the road no matter how photogenic the scenery may be. If you're cycling, take care – motorists can't always overtake easily on skinny roads.

In the annoyances category, NZ's sandflies are a royal pain (see the boxed text, opposite). Lather yourself with insect repellent in coastal areas.

DISCOUNT CARDS

The **International Student Travel Confederation** (ISTC; www.istc.org) is an international collective of specialist student travel organisations and the body behind the internationally recognised International Student Identity Card (ISIC). The card is issued to full-time students aged 12 years and over and provides red-hot discounts on accommodation, transport and admission to attractions. The ISTC also produces the International Youth Travel Card (IYTC), available to folks between 12 and 26 who are not full-time students, and gives equivalent benefits to the ISIC. A similar ISTC brainchild is the International Teacher Identity Card (ITIC), available to teaching professionals. All three cards (NZ$25 each) are available online at www.isiccard.co.nz, or from student travel companies like **STA Travel** (www.statravel.co.nz).

Another option is the **New Zealand Card** (www.newzealandcard.com), a $35 discount pass that'll score you between 5% and 50% off a range of accommodation, tours, sights and activities.

Senior and disabled travellers who live overseas will find that the cards issued by their respective countries are not always 'officially' recognised in NZ, but that many places still acknowledge such cards and grant concessions where applicable.

EMBASSIES & CONSULATES

Most principal diplomatic representations to NZ are in Wellington, with a few in Auckland. Embassies, consulates and high commissions include the following:

Australia (Map p396; ☎ 04-473 6411; www.australia.org.nz; 72-76 Hobson St, Thorndon, Wellington)
Canada (Map p396; ☎ 04-473 9577; www.newzealand.gc.ca; L11, 125 The Terrace, Wellington)
Fiji (Map p396; ☎ 04-473 5401; www.fiji.org.nz; 31 Pipitea St, Thorndon, Wellington)
France (Map p400; ☎ 04-384 2555; www.ambafrance-nz.org; 34-42 Manners St, Wellington)
Germany (Map p396; ☎ 04-473 6063; www.wellington.diplo.de; 90-92 Hobson St, Thorndon, Wellington)

Ireland (Map p100; ☎ 09-977 2252; www.ireland.co.nz; L7, Citigroup Bldg, 23 Customs St E, Auckland)
Israel (Map p396; ☎ 04-471 0079; L13, Greenock House, 102 Lambton Quay, Wellington)
Japan (Map p400; ☎ 04-473 1540; www.nz.emb-japan.go.jp; L18 & L19, The Majestic Centre, 100 Willis St, Wellington)
Netherlands (Map p396; ☎ 04-471 6390; www.netherlandsembassy.co.nz; L10, Investment House, cnr Featherston & Ballance Sts, Wellington)
UK (Map p396; ☎ 04-924 2888; www.britain.org.nz; 44 Hill St, Thorndon, Wellington)
USA (Map p396; ☎ 04-462 6000; http://wellington.usembassy.gov; 29 Fitzherbert Tce, Thorndon, Wellington)

It's important to know what your national embassy can and can't do to help you if you get into trouble. Generally speaking, embassies won't be much help in emergencies if the fix you're in is self-induced. While in NZ you're bound by NZ laws – your embassy will not be sympathetic if you end up in jail after committing a crime locally, even if such actions are legal in your own country.

In genuine emergencies you might get some assistance, but only if other channels have been exhausted. For example, if you need to get home urgently, a free ticket is exceedingly unlikely – the embassy would expect you to have insurance. If you have all your money and documents stolen, your embassy may assist with getting a new passport, but a loan for onward travel is out of the question.

FESTIVALS & EVENTS

Want to plan your travels around the various food and wine, sporting or arts festivals staged throughout the country? Check out the **Tourism New Zealand** (www.newzealand.com/travel) website – click on Sights, Activities & Events, then Events Calendar. See also www.nzlive.com and www.eventfinder.co.nz.

Details of NZ festivals and events are provided throughout destination chapters in this book. A handful of highlights:

Arts & Cultural Festivals

Te Matatini National Kapa Haka Festival (www.tematatini.org.nz) Maori *haka* competition in February in odd-numbered years; much gesticulation, eye-bulging and tongue extension. Venues vary.
New Zealand International Arts Festival (www.nzfestival.nzpost.co.nz) Month-long biennial spectacular held in February/March every even-numbered year in

DIRECTORY

Wellington. Theatre, dance, music and visual arts; international acts aplenty.

New Zealand International Comedy Festival (www.comedyfestival.co.nz) Three-week laugh-fest in May with venues across Auckland, Wellington and various regional centres.

Matariki (Maori New Year; www.taitokerau.co.nz/matariki.htm) Remembrance, education and tree planting; in June mainly around Auckland and Northland.

New Zealand International Film Festivals (www.enzedff.co.nz) After separate film festivals in Wellington, Auckland, Dunedin and Christchurch, a selection of flicks hits the road for screenings in regional towns from July to November.

World of Wearable Art Award Show (WOW; www.worldofwearableart.com) Bizarre (in the best possible way) two-week Wellington event in September featuring amazing garments.

Food & Wine Festivals

Harvest Hawke's Bay (www.harvesthawkesbay.co.nz) Indulgent wine and food celebration in February, with participating wineries around Napier and Hastings.

Marlborough Wine Festival (www.wine-marlborough-festival.co.nz) Features wine from over 50 Marlborough wineries, fine food and entertainment. Overindulgence aplenty. Held in February.

Wildfoods Festival (www.wildfoods.co.nz) Eat some worms, hare testicles or crabs at Hokitika's comfort-zone-challenging food fest in March.

Auckland Wine & Food Festival (www.aucklandwineandfoodfestival.com) Auckland swills itself silly with the best of Kiwi food and drink in March/April.

Toast Martinborough (www.toastmartinborough.co.nz) Wine-willing Wellingtonians head to Martinborough for a day of indulgence in November.

Music Festivals

Rhythm & Vines (www.rhythmandvines.co.nz) Wine, music and song (all the good things) in sunny Gisborne on New Year's Eve. Top DJs, hip-hop acts, bands and singer-songwriters.

Big Day Out (www.bigdayout.com) Much moshing at this international rock extravaganza in Auckland in January.

Splore (www.splore.net) Cutting-edge outdoor summer festival in February at Tapapakanga Regional Park on the Coromandel Peninsula. Contemporary live music, performance, visual arts and safe swimming!

WOMAD (World of Music Arts & Dance; www.womad.co.nz) Local and international arts performances at the Brooklands Bowl in New Plymouth in March.

National Jazz Festival (www.jazz.org.nz) Every Easter Tauranga hosts the longest-running jazz fest in the southern hemisphere.

Sporting Events

New Zealand International Sevens (NZI Sevens; www.nzisevens.co.nz) The world's top seven-a-side rugby teams crack heads in Wellington in February.

Auckland International Boat Show (www.aucklandinternationalboatshow.com) Auckland harbour blooms with sails and churns with outboard motors in March.

Goldrush Multisport Event (www.goldrush.co.nz) For 376km of kayaking, cycling and running along old gold-mining trails in Central Otago during March.

Rugby World Cup (www.rugbyworldcup.com) NZ hosts the greatest rugby show on Earth in September/October 2011 (go All Blacks!).

New Zealand Cup and Show Week (www.nzcupandshow.co.nz) Have a flutter on the nags or inspect some prize bulls in Christchurch in November.

FOOD

The NZ foodie scene once slavishly reflected Anglo-Saxon stodge, but nowadays the country's restaurants and cafes are adept at throwing together trad staples (lamb, beef, venison, green-lipped mussels) with Asian, European and pan-Pacific flair.

Eateries themselves range from fry-'em-up fish-and-chip shops and pub bistros; to cafes drowned in faux-European, grungy or retro stylings; restaurant-bars with full à la carte service; and fine-dining establishments with linen so crisp you're afraid to prop your elbows on it. For online listings, see www.dineout.co.nz and www.menus.co.nz.

Most large urban centres have at least one dedicated vegetarian cafe or restaurant. See the **New Zealand Vegetarian Society** (www.vegsoc.org.nz) restaurant guide for listings.

On the liquid front, NZ wine is world class (especially sauvignon blanc and pinot noir), and you'll be hard-pressed to find a NZ town of any size without decent espresso. NZ micro-brewed beers have also become mainstream.

Eating recommendations in this book are in budget order, from cheapest to most expensive. Cafes are often the best value, with bang-up meals in casual surrounds for under $20. Some city pubs label themselves 'gastro-pubs', offering classy restaurant-style fare, but most pubs serve standard bistro meals, usually under $20. Midrange restaurants can charge as much as $30 for a main course, but don't be surprised to see mains priced from $35 to $45 at trendy top-end restaurants.

Smoking is banned in all restaurants, pubs and bars. Tipping in restaurants and cafes is not expected.

For more info, see the Food & Drink chapter (p60).

GAY & LESBIAN TRAVELLERS

The G&L tourism industry in NZ isn't as high-profile as in neighbouring Australia, but homosexual communities are prominent in the main cities of Auckland and Wellington, with myriad support organisations across both islands. NZ has relatively progressive laws protecting the rights of gays and lesbians; the legal minimum age for sex between consenting persons is 16. Generally speaking Kiwis are fairly relaxed and accepting about homosexuality, but that's not to say that homophobia doesn't exist.

There are loads of websites dedicated to gay and lesbian travellers. **Gay Tourism New Zealand** (www.gaytourismnewzealand.com) is a good starting point, with links to various sites. Other worthwhile queer websites include www.gaynz.com, www.gaynz.net.nz and www.lesbian.net.nz. For accommodation listings see www.gaystay. co.nz. Queenstown visitors should check out www.gayqueenstown.com.

Check out nationwide magazines like *express* (www.gayexpress.co.nz) every second Wednesday and *Out!* (www.out.co.nz) published every two months for the latest happenings, reviews and listings on the NZ gay scene.

The biggest excuse for a party (food, drink, entertainment) is the free **Big Gay Out** (www. biggayout.co.nz) festival, held every February in Auckland. **Out Takes** (www.outtakes.org.nz) is a G&L film festival staged in Auckland, Wellington and Christchurch in June, while Queenstown stages the annual **Gay Ski Week** (www.gayskiweeknz. com) in August/September.

For more info, see Gay & Lesbian Auckland (p125)and Gay & Lesbian Wellington (p413).

HOLIDAYS
Public Holidays

NZ's main public holidays:
New Year 1 & 2 January
Waitangi Day 6 February
Easter Good Friday & Easter Monday; March/April
Anzac Day 25 April
Queen's Birthday 1st Monday in June
Labour Day 4th Monday in October
Christmas Day 25 December
Boxing Day 26 December

In addition, each NZ province has its own anniversary-day holiday. The dates of these provincial holidays vary – when these holidays fall between Friday and Sunday, they're usually observed the following Monday; if they fall between Tuesday and Thursday, they're held on the preceding Monday – the great Kiwi tradition of the 'long weekend' continues.

Provincial anniversary holidays:
Southland 17 January
Wellington 22 January
Auckland 29 January
Northland 29 January
Nelson 1 February
Otago 23 March
Taranaki 31 March
South Canterbury 25 September
Hawke's Bay 1 November
Marlborough 1 November
Chatham Islands 30 November
Westland 1 December
Canterbury 16 December

School Holidays

The Christmas holiday season, from mid-December to late January, is part of the summer school vacation. It's the time you'll most likely find transport and accommodation booked out, and long, grumpy queues at tourist attractions. There are three shorter school-holiday periods during the year: from mid- to late April, early to mid-July, and mid-September to early October. For exact dates see the **Ministry of Education** (www.minedu.govt.nz) website.

INSURANCE

A watertight travel insurance policy covering theft, loss and medical problems is essential; nothing will ruin your holiday more quickly than an accident or having your duty-free digital camera pilfered. There are plenty of policies to choose from – compare the fine print and shop around.

Some policies specifically exclude designated 'dangerous activities' such as scuba diving, parasailing, bungy jumping, whitewater rafting, motorcycling, skiing, and even bushwalking. If you plan on doing any of these things (a distinct possibility in NZ), make sure the policy you choose covers you fully.

You may prefer a policy that pays doctors or hospitals directly rather than you having to pay on the spot and claim later. If you have to claim later make sure you keep all documentation. Some policies ask you to call back (reverse charges) to a centre in your home country where an immediate assessment of your problem is made. Check that the policy covers ambulances and emergency medical evacuations by air.

It's worth mentioning that under NZ law, you cannot sue for personal injury (other than exemplary damages). Instead, the country's **Accident Compensation Corporation** (ACC; www.acc. co.nz) administers an accident compensation scheme that provides accident insurance for NZ residents and visitors to the country, regardless of fault.

While some people cry foul of this arrangement, others point to the hugely expensive litigation 'industries' in other countries and raise a cheer. This scheme, however, does not cancel out the necessity for your own comprehensive travel insurance policy, as it doesn't cover you for such things as loss of income or treatment in your home country or ongoing illness.

See also p715 for notes on medical insurance. For car insurance information see p712.

Worldwide cover for travellers from over 44 countries is available online at www.lonely planet.com/bookings/insurance.do.

INTERNET ACCESS

Getting online in NZ is easy in all but the most remote locales. If you don't already have one, it's worth setting up a travelling address with one of the many free email services (www.yahoo. com, www.hotmail.com, www.gmail.com etc).

The internet icon (🖳) in accommodation, eating and drinking listings in this book indicates internet access is available (a kiosk or dedicated guest computer); the wi-fi icon (🛜) denotes wireless access.

For a list of useful NZ websites, see p22.

Internet Cafes

Internet cafes in the bigger urban centres or tourist areas are usually brimming with high-speed terminals. Obnoxious teens often swamp the machines in the after-school hours – time your visit any time other than 4pm to 6pm! Facilities are a lot more haphazard in small, out-of-the-way towns, where a so-called internet cafe could turn out to be a single terminal in the corner of a video store.

Most hostels make an effort to hook you up, with internet access sometimes free for guests. Many public libraries have free internet access too, but there can be a limited number of terminals – head for an internet cafe first.

Internet access at cafes ranges anywhere from $4 to $6 per hour – the lowest rates can be found in cities where competition and traveller numbers generate dirt-cheap prices. There's often a minimum period of access, usually 10 or 15 minutes.

Wireless Access & Internet Service Providers

Increasingly, you'll be able to find wi-fi access around the country, from hotel rooms to pub beer gardens to hostel dining rooms. Usually you have to be a guest or customer to access the internet at these locations – you'll be issued with a code, a wink and a secret handshake to enable you to get online. Sometimes it's free; sometimes there's a charge.

The country's main telecommunications company is **Telecom New Zealand** (www.telecom. co.nz), which has wireless hotspots around the country. If you have a wi-fi-enabled device, you can purchase a Telecom wireless prepaid card from participating hotspots. Alternatively, you can purchase a prepaid number from the login page and any wireless hotspot using your credit card. See the website for hotspot listings.

If you've brought your palmtop or notebook computer and want to get connected to a local internet service provider (ISP), there are plenty of options, though some limit their dial-up areas to major cities or particular regions. Major ISPs:

Clearnet (☎ 0508 888 800; www.clearnet.co.nz)

Earthlight (☎ 03-479 0303; www.earthlight.co.nz) Has a page on its website detailing prepaid internet access for travellers to NZ.

Slingshot (☎ 0800 892 000; www.slingshot.co.nz)

Xtra (☎ 0800 003 040; www.xtra.co.nz/products)

Wireless is more common, but if you're planning on manually plugging in, NZ uses British BT431A and RJ-11 jacks, but neither are universal; local electronics shops should be able to help. A lot of midrange accommodation and nearly all top-end hotels have wall sockets, but you'll be hit with expensive call charges. In most cheaper places you'll probably find that phones are hardwired into the wall.

Keep in mind that your PC-card modem may not work in NZ. The safest option is to buy a reputable 'global' modem before you leave home or buy a local PC-card modem once you get to NZ.

LEGAL MATTERS

Marijuana (aka 'New Zealand Green', 'electric puha' or 'dac') is widely indulged in but illegal, and anyone caught carrying this or other illicit drugs will have the book thrown at them. Even if the amount of drugs is small and the fine minimal, a conviction will still be recorded against you, which may affect your visa status.

Always carry your licence when driving; for more info, see p709. Drink-driving is a serious offence and remains a significant problem in NZ despite widespread campaigns and severe penalties. The legal blood alcohol limit is 0.08% for drivers over 20, and 0.03% for those under 20.

If you are arrested, it's your right to consult a lawyer before any formal questioning begins.

MAPS

Top-notch maps are widely available throughout NZ – from detailed street maps and atlases to topographic masterpieces.

The **Automobile Association** (AA; www.aa.co.nz) produces excellent city, town, regional, island and highway maps, available from its local offices; members of affiliated overseas automobile associations can obtain free maps and discounts on presentation of a membership card. The AA also produces a detailed *New Zealand Road Atlas*. Other reliable countrywide atlases, available from visitor information centres and bookshops, are published by Hema, KiwiMaps and Wises.

Land Information New Zealand (www.linz.govt.nz) publishes several exhaustive map series, including street, country and holiday maps, national and forest park maps, and topographical trampers' maps. Scan the larger bookshops, or try the nearest DOC office or visitor information centre for topo maps.

Online, log onto **AA SmartMap** (www.aamaps.co.nz) or the **Yellow Maps** (maps.yellowpages.co.nz) to pinpoint exact addresses in NZ cities and towns.

MONEY

See the Quick Reference section on the inside front cover for a list of exchange rates.

ATMs & Eftpos

Branches of the country's major banks, including the Bank of New Zealand, ANZ, Westpac and ASB, have 24-hour ATMs that accept cards from other banks and provide access to overseas accounts. You won't find ATMs everywhere, but they're widespread across both islands.

Many NZ businesses use electronic funds transfer at point of sale (Eftpos), a convenient service that allows you to use your bank card (credit or debit) to pay directly for services or purchases, and often withdraw cash as well. Eftpos is available practically everywhere, even in places where it's a long way between banks. Just like an ATM, you need to know your personal identification number (PIN) to use it.

Bank Accounts

We've heard mixed reports on how easy it is for nonresidents to open a bank account in NZ. Some sources say it's as simple as flashing a few pieces of ID, providing a temporary postal address (or your permanent address) and then waiting a few days while your request is processed. Other sources say that many banks won't allow visitors to open an account with them unless they're planning to stay in NZ for at least six months, or unless the application is accompanied by some proof of employment. Bank websites are also rather vague on the services offered to short-term visitors. If you think you'll need to open an account, do your homework before you arrive in the country and be prepared to shop around to get the best deal.

Credit & Debit Cards

Perhaps the safest place to keep your NZ travelling money is inside a plastic card! The most flexible option is to carry both a credit and a debit card.

Credit cards (Visa, MasterCard etc) are widely accepted for everything from a hostel bed to a bungy jump. Credit cards are pretty much essential if you want to hire a car. They can also be used for over-the-counter cash advances at banks and from ATMs, depending on the card, but be aware that such transactions incur charges. Charge cards such as Diners Club and Amex are not as widely accepted.

Apart from losing them, the obvious danger with credit cards is maxing out your limit and going home to a steaming pile of debt. A safer option is a debit card with which you can draw money directly from your home bank account using ATMs, banks or Eftpos machines. Any card connected to the international

DIRECTORY

banking network (Cirrus, Maestro, Visa Plus and Eurocard) should work, provided you know your PIN. Fees for using your card at a foreign bank or ATM vary depending on your home bank; ask before you leave. Companies such as Travelex offer debit cards (Travelex calls them Cash Passport cards) with set withdrawal fees and a balance you can top-up from your personal bank account whilst on the road – nice one!

Currency

NZ's currency is the NZ dollar, comprising 100 cents. There are 10c, 20c, 50c, $1 and $2 coins, and $5, $10, $20, $50 and $100 notes. Prices are often still marked in single cents and then rounded to the nearest 10c when you hand over your money.

Unless otherwise noted, all prices quoted in this book are in NZ dollars. For an idea of the costs associated with travelling around the country, see p20.

There are no notable restrictions on importing or exporting travellers cheques. Though not prohibited, cash amounts equal to or in excess of the equivalent of NZ$10,000 (in any currency) must be declared on arrival or departure – you'll need to fill out a Border Cash Report.

Moneychangers

Changing foreign currency or travellers cheques is usually no problem at banks throughout NZ or at licensed moneychangers such as Travelex (formerly Thomas Cook) in the major cities. Moneychangers can be found in all major tourist areas, cities and airports, and conveniently tend to stay open beyond normal business hours during the week (often until 9pm).

Taxes & Refunds

The Goods and Services Tax (GST) is a flat 15% tax on all domestic goods and services. Prices in this book include GST, but look out for any small print announcing that the price is GST-exclusive. There's no GST refund available when you leave NZ.

Tipping

Tipping is completely optional in NZ, and staff do not depend on tips for income – the total at the bottom of a restaurant bill is all you need to pay (note that sometimes there's an additional service charge). That said, it's totally acceptable to reward good service and the tip you leave depends entirely on your satisfaction – between 5% and 10% of the bill is the norm.

Travellers Cheques

The ubiquity of debit- and credit-card access in NZ can make travellers cheques seem rather old-hat. Nevertheless, Amex, Travelex and other international brands of travellers cheques are easily exchanged. You need to present your passport for identification when cashing them. Fees per transaction for changing foreign-currency travellers cheques vary from bank to bank, while Amex or Travelex perform the task commission-free if you use their cheques. Private moneychangers found in the larger cities are sometimes commission free, but shop around for the best rates.

POST

The services offered by **New Zealand Post** (☎ 0800 501 501; www.nzpost.co.nz) are reliable and reasonably inexpensive. Within NZ standard post costs 50c for standard letters and postcards, and $1 for larger letters.

International destinations are divided into two zones: Australia and the South Pacific, and the rest of the world. Standard rates (express services also available):

Item	Aust & South Pacific	Rest of World
Postcard	$1.80	$1.80
Letter	$1.80	$2.30
Large letter	$2.30	$2.80
Oversize letter	$3.50	$5
Approx delivery (work days)	3-10	6-10

International parcel zones are the same as for letters; pricing depends on weight and whether you send the parcel 'economy' (three to five weeks), 'air' (one to two weeks) or 'express' (within a matter of days). To send parcels by 'air' is roughly 20% more expensive; by 'express' at least 50% more. Check out the incredibly precise calculator on the website.

Many NZ post offices are called 'PostShops' these days, as most have been removed from their traditional old buildings and set up in modern shop-style premises, but we still stubbornly refer to them as post offices throughout this guidebook. For standard post office opening hours, see p686. Stamps can usually also be purchased at supermarkets and bookshops.

You can have mail addressed to you care of 'Poste Restante, Main PostShop' in whichever town you require. Mail is usually held for 30 days and you need to provide some form of identification (such as a passport) to collect it.

SHOPPING

NZ isn't one of those countries where it's necessary to buy a T-shirt to help you remember your visit; the spectacular landscapes are mementoes in themselves, to be plucked later from the depths of memory or the innards of your camera. But there are numerous locally crafted items you can purchase for their own unique qualities.

Clothing

The main cities of Auckland (p125), Wellington (p415) and Christchurch (p538) boast fashion-conscious boutiques ablaze with the sartorial flair of young and well-established NZ designers. Check out www.fashionz.co.nz for up-to-date information on the hottest designers and labels and where to find them. Keep an eye out for labels such as Zambesi, Kate Sylvester, Karen Walker, Trelise Cooper, NOM D and Little Brother.

In Auckland, head to places like Newmarket, Ponsonby Rd and High St; Wellington offers retro mix-and-match boutiques on Cuba St and high fashion along Lambton Quay. In Christchurch, pick up new duds on Colombo, High or Cashel Sts, then parade yourself along self-important Oxford Tce. To see just how far New Zealanders are prepared to push the boundaries of fashionable creativity, visit the amazing World of WearableArt & Classic Cars Museum (p460) in Nelson, or attend the namesake festival in Wellington (p407).

From the backs of NZ sheep come sheepskin products such as footwear (including the much-loved ugg boot) and beautiful woollen jumpers (jerseys or sweaters) made from hand-spun, hand-dyed wool. Other knitted knick-knacks include hats, gloves and scarves. Look for garments made from a lovely soft yarn that's a combination of merino wool and possum fur.

Long woollen Swanndri jackets, shirts and pullovers are so ridiculously practical, they're practically the national garment in country areas. Most common are the red-and-black or blue-and-black plaid ones; pick up 'Swannies' in outdoor-gear shops.

Crafts

Fine NZ craft products can be purchased in most sizeable towns. Few (if any) places in the country are devoid of someone who's been inspired to hand-shape items for sale to passing visitors. In Christchurch, the Arts Centre (p525) offers dozens of shops and galleries selling locally designed and crafted jewellery, ceramics, glassware and accessories. The Nelson region (p455) is another very crafty place, heavily populated by galleries and the occasional market. Ditto Devonport (p104), within striking distance of downtown Auckland and replete with galleries; and Arrowtown (p625), an artsy enclave near Queenstown.

Maori Arts

For some brilliant examples of Maori *whakairo rakau* (woodcarving), check out the efforts of artisans at Te Whakarewarewa cultural area (p321) in Rotorua, then browse the town's Maori craft shops; in some cases you may be able to buy directly from the artist. Carvers produce intricate forms like leaping dolphins, as well as highly detailed traditional Maori carvings. You'll pay a premium for high-quality work; avoid buying the poor examples of the craft that line the souvenir shops in Auckland.

Maori bone carvings are undergoing something of a renaissance around NZ. Maori artisans have always made bone carvings in the shape of humans and animals, but nowadays they cater to the tourist industry. Bone fish-hook pendants, carved in traditional Maori and modernised styles, are most common, worn on a leather string around the neck.

Paua

Abalone shell, called paua in NZ, is carved into some beautiful ornaments and jewellery and is often used as an inlay in Maori carvings. Lovers of kitsch and general tackiness will find that it's also incorporated into generic souvenirs, often in delightfully unattractive ways. Shells are used as ashtrays in places where paua is plentiful. Be aware that it's illegal to take natural paua shells out of the country – only processed ornaments can be taken with you.

Pounamu

Maoris consider *pounamu* (greenstone, or jade or nephrite) to be a culturally invaluable raw material. It's found predominantly on the west coast of the South Island – Maoris called the island Te Wahi Pounamu (The Place of Greenstone) or Te Wai Pounamu (The Water of Greenstone).

You're unlikely to come across any *mere* (war clubs) in *pounamu* studios or souvenir shops, but you will find lots of stony green incarnations of Maori motifs. One of the most popular is the *hei tiki,* the name of which literally means 'hanging human form' – in Maori legend, Tiki was the first man created and *hei* is 'to hang'. They are tiny, stylised Maori figures, usually depicted with their tongue stuck out in warlike repose, worn on a leather string or chain around the neck. They've got great *mana* (power), but they also serve as fertility symbols. Other popular motifs are the *taniwha* (monster) and the *marakihau* (sea monster).

The best place to buy *pounamu* is Hokitika (p503), which is strewn with jade workshops and gift shops. Rotorua (p333) also has its fair share of *pounamu* crafts. To see impressive collections both ancient and modern, visit the Otago Museum (p575) in Dunedin, Te Papa museum (p403) in Wellington, Auckland Museum (p98), and Canterbury Museum (p525) in Christchurch.

Traditionally, *pounamu* is bought as a gift for another person, not for yourself. Ask a few questions to ensure you're buying from a local operator who crafts local stone, not an offshore company selling imported (usually Chinese or European) jade.

TELEPHONE

Telecom New Zealand (www.telecom.co.nz) is the country's key domestic player and also has a stake in the local mobile (cell) market. Another mobile network option is **Vodafone** (www.vodafone.co.nz).

Local & International Calls

INFORMATION & TOLL-FREE CALLS

Numbers starting with ☎ 0900 are usually recorded information services, charging upwards of $1 per minute (more from mobiles); these numbers cannot be dialled from payphones.

Toll-free numbers in NZ have the prefix ☎ 0800 or ☎ 0508 and can be called free of charge from anywhere in the country, though they may not be accessible from certain areas or from mobile phones. Telephone numbers beginning with ☎ 0508, ☎ 0800 or ☎ 0900 cannot be dialled from outside NZ.

INTERNATIONAL CALLS

Payphones allow international calls but the cost and international dialling code for calls will vary depending on which provider you're using. International calls from NZ are relatively inexpensive and subject to specials that reduce the rates even more, so it's worth shopping around – consult the *Yellow Pages* for a list of providers.

The toll-free Country Direct service connects callers in NZ with overseas operators to make reverse-charge (collect) or credit-card calls. Country Direct numbers and other details are listed in the front of telephone directories or are available from the NZ international operator. The access number varies, depending on the number of phone companies in the country you call, but is usually ☎ 000-9 (followed by the country code).

To make international calls from NZ you need to dial the international access code (☎ 00), the country code, and the area code (without the initial 0). So for a London number you'd dial ☎ 00-44-20, then the number. Certain operators will have you dial a special code to access their service.

If dialling NZ from overseas, the country code is ☎ 64, followed by the appropriate area code minus the initial zero.

LOCAL CALLS

Local calls from private phones are free! Local calls from payphones cost 50c, though coin-operated payphones are scarce – you'll need a phonecard (see opposite). Both involve unlimited talk time. Calls to mobile phones attract higher rates and are timed.

LONG-DISTANCE CALLS & AREA CODES

NZ uses regional area codes for long-distance calls, which can be made from any payphone.

If you're making a local call (ie to someone else in the same town), you don't need to dial the area code. But if you're dialling within a region (even if it's to a nearby town) you do have to dial the area code, regardless of the fact that the place you're calling has the same code as the place you're dialling from. All the numbers in this book are listed with their relevant area codes.

Mobile Phones

Local mobile phone numbers are preceded by the prefix ☎ 021, ☎ 025 or ☎ 027. Mobile phone coverage is good in cities and towns and most parts of the North Island, but can be patchy away from urban centres on the South Island.

If you want to bring your own phone and use a prepaid service with a local SIM card, **Vodafone** (www.vodafone.co.nz) is a practical option. Any Vodafone shop (found in most major towns) will set you up with a SIM card and phone number (about $35, including $10 worth of calls); top-ups can be purchased at newsagencies, post offices and shops practically anywhere.

Alternatively, if you don't bring your own phone from home, you can rent one from **Vodafone Rental** (www.vodarent.co.nz) priced from $6/25 per day/week, with pick-up and drop-off outlets at NZ's major airports. You can also rent a SIM card for $2.50 per day (minimum charge $10) or $40 per month. You can arrange this in advance via the website. We've also had some positive feedback on **Phone Hire New Zealand** (www.phonehirenz.com), which hires out mobile phones, SIM cards, modems and GPS systems.

Phonecards

NZ has a wide range of phonecards available, which can be bought at hostels, newsagencies and post offices for a fixed dollar value (usually $5, $10, $20 and $50). These can be used with any public or private phone by dialling a toll-free access number and then the PIN number on the card. It's worth shopping around – call rates vary from company to company.

TIME

Being close to the international date line, NZ is one of the first places in the world to start the new day (Pitt Island in the Chatham Islands sees the first sunrise each new year).

NZ is 12 hours ahead of GMT/UTC and two hours ahead of Australian Eastern Standard Time.

In summer, NZ observes daylight-saving time, where clocks are wound forward by one hour on the last Sunday in September; clocks are wound back on the first Sunday of the following April.

So (excluding the duration of daylight saving), when it's noon in NZ it's 10am in Sydney, 8am in Singapore, midnight in London and 5pm the previous day in San Francisco. The Chathams are 45 minutes ahead of NZ's main islands.

TOURIST INFORMATION

Even before the success of recent international marketing campaigns and the country's cult status as a pseudo-Middle-earth, NZ had a highly developed tourism infrastructure that busily generated mountains of brochures and booklets, plus information-packed Internet pages.

Local Tourist Offices

Almost every Kiwi city or town – whether it has any worthwhile attractions or not – seems to have a visitor information centre. The bigger centres stand united within the outstanding **i-SITE** (www.newzealand.com/travel/i-sites) network, which is affiliated with Tourism New Zealand (the official national tourism body), and has trained staff, abundant information on local activities and attractions, and free brochures and maps. Staff also act as travel agents, booking activities, transport and accommodation. Not to be outdone, staff at smaller centres are often overwhelmingly helpful.

Bear in mind that many information centres only promote accommodation and tour operators who are paying members of the local tourist association, while others are ironically hamstrung by the demands of local operators that they be represented equally. In other words, sometimes information centre staff aren't supposed to recommend one activity or accommodation provider over another, a curious situation that exists in highly competitive environments.

There's also a network of **Department Of Conservation** (DOC; www.doc.govt.nz) visitor centres to help you plan your recreation activities and make bookings. Visitor centres usually have displays and info on local lore, and NZ's unique flora and fauna and biodiversity challenges. DOC visitor centres are found in national parks, major regional centres and in each of the major cities. It's important to check local weather conditions at the nearest visitor centre before you set out. Collect the DOC visitor centres brochure from the website or at visitor centres.

In this book, contact details for local visitor information centres or offices are listed under Information headings in relevant city and town sections.

Tourist Offices Abroad

Tourism New Zealand (☎ 04-917 5400; www.newzealand.com) has representatives in various countries around the world. A good place for pretrip research is the official website (emblazoned with the hugely successful 100% Pure New Zealand branding), which has information in several languages (including German and Japanese). Overseas offices:

Australia (☎ 02-8299 4800; L12, 61 York St, Sydney)
UK & Europe (☎ 020-7930 1662; New Zealand House, 80 Haymarket, London, UK)
USA & Canada (☎ 310-395 7480; 501 Santa Monica Blvd, Santa Monica, USA)

TRAVELLERS WITH DISABILITIES

Kiwi accommodation generally caters fairly well for travellers with disabilities, with a significant number of hostels, hotels, motels and B&Bs equipped with wheelchair-accessible rooms. Many tourist attractions similarly provide wheelchair access, with wheelchairs often available at key attractions with advance notice.

Tour operators with accessible vehicles operate from most major centres. Key cities are also serviced by kneeling buses (buses that hydraulically stoop down to kerb level to allow easy access); taxi companies offer wheelchair-accessible vans. Large car-hire firms (Avis, Hertz etc) provide cars with hand controls at no extra charge; advance notice is required. Mobility parking permits are available from branches of **CCS Disability Action** (☎ 0800 227 200, 04-384 5677; www.ccsdisabilityaction.org.nz) in the main centres.

For good general information, see NZ's **disability information website** (www.weka.net.nz). Click on Living with a Disability, then categories including Transport, Holiday Accommodation, and Travel and Tourism. The latter lists NZ tour operators catering specifically to travellers with disabilities.

Travellers with disabilities need not miss out on NZ's great outdoors. If you'd like to tackle a wilderness pathway, pick up a copy of *Accessible Walks* by Anna and Andrew Jameson ($26), which offers first-hand descriptions of more than 100 South Island walks. It's available online at www.accessiblewalks.co.nz. If cold-weather activity is more your thing, see the **Disabled Snowsports New Zealand** (www.disabledsnowsports.org.nz) website.

VISAS

Visa application forms are available from NZ diplomatic missions overseas, travel agents or through **Immigration New Zealand** (☎ 0508 558 855, 09-914 4100; www.immigration.govt.nz). Immigration New Zealand has over a dozen offices overseas; consult the website.

Visitor's Visa

Citizens of Australia don't need a visa to visit NZ and can stay indefinitely (provided they have no criminal convictions). UK citizens don't need a visa either and can stay in the country for up to six months.

Citizens of another 56 countries that have visa-waiver agreements with NZ don't need a visa for stays of up to three months, provided they have an onward ticket, sufficient funds to support their stay (NZ$1000 per month, or NZ$400 per month if accommodation has been prepaid) and a passport valid for three months beyond the date of their planned departure from NZ. Nations in this group include Canada, France, Germany, Ireland, Japan, the Netherlands and the USA.

Citizens of other countries must obtain a visa before entering NZ. Visas come with three months' standard validity and cost NZ$100 if processed in Australia or certain South Pacific countries (eg Samoa, Fiji), or NZ$130 if processed elsewhere in the world.

Visitors' visas can be extended for stays of up to nine months within one 18-month period, or to a maximum of 12 months in the country. Applications are assessed on a case-by-case basis; visitors will need to meet criteria such as proof of ongoing financial self-support. Apply for extensions at any Immigration New Zealand office – see the website for locations.

Work Visa & Working Holiday Scheme

It's illegal for foreign nationals to work in NZ on a visitor's visa, except for Australians who can legally gain work without a visa or permit. If you're visiting NZ to find work, or you already have an employment offer, you'll need to apply for a work visa, which translates into a work permit once you arrive and is valid for up to three years. You can apply for a work permit after you're in NZ, but its validity will be backdated to when you entered the country. The fee for a work visa ranges from NZ$180 to NZ$280 depending on where it's processed and the type of application.

Eligible travellers who are only interested in short-term employment to supplement their travels can take part in one of NZ's working-holiday schemes (WHS). Under these schemes citizens aged 18 to 30 years from 31 countries – including Canada, France, Germany, Ireland, Japan, Malaysia, the Netherlands, Scandinavian countries, the UK and the USA – can apply for a visa. For most nationalities the visa is valid for 12 months. It's only issued to those seeking a genuine working holiday, not permanent work, so you're not supposed to work for one employer for more than three months.

Most WHS-eligible nationals must apply for this visa from within their own country; residents of some countries can apply online. Applicants must have an onward ticket, a passport valid for at least three months from the date they will leave NZ and evidence of at least NZ$4200 in accessible funds. The application fee is NZ$120 regardless of where you apply, and isn't refunded if your application is declined.

The rules vary for different nationalities, so make sure you read up on the specifics of your country's agreement with NZ at www.immigration.govt.nz/migrant/stream/work/workingholiday.

WOMEN TRAVELLERS

NZ is generally a very safe place for women travellers, although the usual sensible precautions apply. It's best to avoid walking alone late at night in any of the major cities and towns, and never hitchhike alone. If you're out on the town, always keep enough money aside for a taxi back to your accommodation. The same applies in rural towns where there may be a lot of unlit, semideserted streets between you and your bed. Lone women should also be wary of staying in basic pub accommodation unless it looks safe and well managed.

Sexual harassment is not a widely reported problem in NZ, but of course it does happen. See www.womentravel.co.nz for more information.

WORK

If you arrive in NZ on a visitor's visa you're not allowed to work for pay. If you're caught breaching this (or any other) visa condition, you could be booted back to where you came from.

If you have been approved for a WHS visa (see opposite), look into the possibilities for temporary employment. There's plenty of casual work around, mainly in agriculture (fruit picking, farming), hospitality or ski resorts. Office-based work can be found in IT, banking, finance and telemarketing. Register with a local office-work agency to get started.

Seasonal fruit picking, pruning and harvesting is prime short-term work for visitors. More than 30,000 hectares of apples, kiwifruit and other fruit and veg are harvested from summer to early autumn. As an optimist once said, 'The pay is bad, but the work is difficult'. Rates are around $10 to $15 an hour for physically taxing toil – turnover of workers is high. You're usually paid by how much you pick (per bin, bucket or kilogram). The picking season is from December to May. Prime picking locations include the Bay of Islands (Kerikeri and Paihia), rural Auckland, Tauranga, Gisborne and Hawke's Bay (Napier and Hastings) on the North Island; Nelson (Tapawera and Golden Bay), Marlborough (around Blenheim) and Central Otago (Alexandra and Roxburgh) on the South Island. Approach prospective employers directly, otherwise local hostels or holiday parks often help travellers to find work. Other agricultural work is available year-round.

Winter work at ski resorts and their service towns includes bartending, waiting, cleaning, ski-tow operation and, if you're properly qualified, ski or snowboard instructing. Check resort websites (p83) for opportunities.

Information

Backpacker publications, hostel managers and other travellers are the best sources of info on local work possibilities.

Kiwi Careers (www.kiwicareers.govt.nz) lists opportunities in various fields (agriculture, creative, health, teaching, volunteer work and recruitment agencies), while **Seek** (www.seek.co.nz) is one of the biggest NZ job-search networks with thousands of jobs listed.

Seasonal Work NZ (www.seasonalwork.co.nz) has a database of thousands of casual jobs, including region-specific 'Harvest Trail' jobs in fruit-picking and agriculture. It gives the contact details of employers looking for workers, rates of pay and nearby accommodation. **Pick NZ** (www.picknz.co.nz) provides a similar service, focusing on seasonal horticultural work.

Base Backpackers (www.stayatbase.com/work) runs an employment service via its website, while the Networking link on **Budget Backpacker Hostels** (BBH; www.bbh.co.nz) lists job vacancies in BBH hostels and a few other possibilities.

Income Tax

There is no escaping it! For the vast majority of travellers, any Kiwi dollars earned in NZ will be subject to income tax, deducted from payments by employers – a process called Pay As You Earn (PAYE). Standard NZ income tax rates are 12.5% for annual salaries up to $17,500, then 21% up to $40,000, 33% up to $75,000, then 39% for higher incomes. A NZ

Accident Compensation Corporation (ACC) scheme levy (1.7%) will also be deducted from your pay packet. At the time of writing, these rates were set to change slightly from April 2011.

If you visit NZ and work for a short time (eg on a working-holiday scheme), you may qualify for a tax refund when you leave. Complete a Refund Application – People Leaving New Zealand (document no IR50) form and submit it with your tax return, along with proof of departure (eg air ticket copies) to the Inland Revenue Department (IRD). For more info see the IRD website, or contact the **Inland Revenue Non-Resident Centre** (☎ 03-467 7020; nonres@ird.govt.nz; Private Bag 1932, Dunedin).

IRD Number

Travellers undertaking paid work in NZ must obtain an IRD number. Download the application form from the **Inland Revenue Department** (www.ird.govt.nz) website – use the search function to find document no IR595. An IRD number normally takes eight to 10 working days to be issued.

Transport

CONTENTS

GETTING THERE & AWAY   701

Entering the Country   701

Air   701
Sea   705
GETTING AROUND   705
Air   705
Bicycle   706
Boat   706
Bus   706
Car & Motorcycle   708
Hitching   713
Local Transport   714
Train   714

New Zealand's peaceably isolated location in
a distant patch of the South Pacific is a major
drawcard, but it also means that unless you
travel from Australia, you have to contend
with a long-haul flight to get there. As NZ is
serviced by good airline and bus networks,
travelling around the country is a much less
taxing endeavour.

Flights, tours and rail tickets can be booked
online at www.lonelyplanet.com/bookings.

GETTING THERE & AWAY

ENTERING THE COUNTRY

Disembarkation in NZ is generally a straightforward affair, with only the usual customs
declarations to endure (see Customs, p688)
and the uncool scramble to get to the luggage
carousel first. Recent global instability has
resulted in increased security in NZ airports,
in both domestic and international terminals, and you may find customs procedures
more time-consuming. One procedure has the
Orwellian title Advance Passenger Screening,
a system whereby documents that used to
be checked after you touched down in NZ
(passport, visa etc) are now checked before
you board your flight – make sure all your
documentation is in order so your check-in
is stress-free.

Passport

There are no restrictions when it comes to
foreign citizens entering NZ. If you have a
current passport and visa (or don't require
one; see p698), you should be fine.

AIR

There's a number of competing airlines servicing NZ and a wide variety of fares to choose
from if you're flying in from Asia, Europe
or North America, though ultimately you'll
still pay a lot for a flight unless you jet in
from Australia. NZ's inordinate popularity
and abundance of year-round activities mean
that almost any time of year airports can be
swarming with inbound tourists – if you want
to fly at a particularly popular time of year
(eg over the Christmas period), book well
in advance.

The high season for flights into NZ is during
summer (December to February), with slightly
less of a premium on fares over the shoulder months (October/November and March/
April). The low season generally tallies with
the winter months (June to August), though
this is still a busy time for airlines ferrying ski
bunnies and powder hounds.

Airports & Airlines

Seven NZ airports handle international
flights, with Auckland receiving most traffic:
Auckland (AKL; ☎ 0800 247 767, 09-275 0789; www.
aucklandairport.co.nz)
Christchurch (CHC; ☎ 03-358 5029; www.christchurch
airport.co.nz)
Dunedin (DUD; ☎ 03-486 2879; www.dnairport.co.nz)

THINGS CHANGE...

The information in this chapter is particularly vulnerable to change. Check directly
with the airline or a travel agent to make
sure you understand how a fare (and ticket
you may buy) works and be aware of the
security requirements for international
travel. Shop carefully. The details given in
this chapter should be regarded as pointers
and are not a substitute for your own careful,
up-to-date research.

TRANSPORT

DEPARTURE TAX

An international departure tax of NZ$25 applies when leaving NZ at all airports except Auckland, payable by anyone aged 12 and over (NZ$10 for children aged two to 11, free for those under two years of age). The tax is not included in the price of airline tickets, but must be paid separately at the airport before you board your flight. Pay via credit card or cash.

Hamilton (HLZ; ☎ 07-848 9027; www.hamiltonairport. co.nz)
Palmerston North (PMR; ☎ 06-351 4415; www. pnairport.co.nz)
Queenstown (ZQN; ☎ 03-450 9031; www.queenstown airport.co.nz)
Wellington (WLG; ☎ 04-385 5100; www.wellingtonair port.co.nz)

AIRLINES FLYING TO & FROM NEW ZEALAND

NZ's own overseas carrier is Air New Zealand, which flies to runways across Europe, North America, eastern Asia and the Pacific. Airlines that connect NZ with international destinations include the following (note that 0800 and 0508 phone numbers mentioned here are for dialling from within NZ only):

Aerolineas Argentinas (airline code AR; ☎ 09-379 3675; www.aerolineas.com.ar)
Air Asia (AK; ☎ 0800 45 25 66; www.airasia.com)
Air New Zealand (NZ; ☎ 0800 737 000, 09-357 3000; www.airnewzealand.co.nz)
Air Pacific (FJ; ☎ 0800 800 178, 09-379 2404; www. airpacific.com)
Air Vanuatu (NF; ☎ 09-373 3435; www.airvanuatu.com)
Cathay Pacific (CX; ☎ 0800 800 454, 09-379 0861; www.cathaypacific.com)
Emirates (EK; ☎ 0508 364 728, 09-968 2208; www. emirates.com)
Garuda Indonesia (GA; ☎ 09-366 1862; www.garuda -indonesia.com)
Jetstar (JQ; ☎ 0800 800 995; www.jetstar.com)
Korean Air (KE; ☎ 09-914 2000; www.koreanair.com)
Malaysia Airlines (MH; ☎ 0800 777 747, 09-379 3743; www.malaysiaairlines.com)
Pacific Blue (DJ; ☎ 0800 670 000; www.flypacificblue. com)
Polynesian Blue (DJ; ☎ 0800 670 000; www.polynesian blue.com)
Qantas (QF; ☎ 0800 808 767, 09-357 8900; www. qantas.com.au)

Royal Brunei Airlines (BI; ☎ 09-977 2209; www. bruneiair.com)
Singapore Airlines (SQ; ☎ 0800 808 909, 09-379 3209; www.singaporeair.com)
Thai Airways International (TG; ☎ 09-256 8518; www.thaiairways.com)
Virgin Blue (DJ; ☎ 0800 670 000; www.virginblue.com)

Tickets

Automated online ticket sales work well if you're doing a simple one-way or return trip on specified dates, but are no substitute for a travel agent with the low-down on special deals, strategies for avoiding layovers and other useful advice.

INTERCONTINENTAL (RTW) TICKETS

If you're flying to NZ from the other side of the world, round-the-world (RTW) tickets can be real bargains. They're generally put together by the three biggest airline alliances, **Star Alliance** (www.staralliance.com), **Oneworld** (www.oneworldalliance. com) and **Skyteam** (www.skyteam.com), and give you a limited period (usually a year) in which to loop the planet. You can go anywhere the participating airlines go, as long as you stay within the prescribed kilometre extents or number of stops and don't backtrack when flying between continents. Backtracking is generally permitted within a single continent, though with certain restrictions; see the websites for details.

An alternative type of RTW ticket is one put together by a travel agent or RTW–specialist websites. These are often more expensive than airline RTW fares but allow you to devise your own itinerary.

Bargain RTW tickets start from around UK£600 ex-UK, US$1500 ex-USA.

CIRCLE PACIFIC TICKETS

A Circle Pacific ticket is similar to a RTW ticket but covers a more limited region, using a combination of airlines to connect Australia, NZ, North America and Asia, with stopover options in the Pacific islands. As with RTW tickets, there are restrictions on how many stopovers you can take.

ONLINE TICKET SITES

For online ticket bookings, including RTW fares, start with the following websites:
Air Brokers (www.airbrokers.com) This US company specialises in cheaper tickets. To fly LA-Tahiti-Auckland-Sydney-Bangkok-Hong Kong-LA costs around US$2200 (excluding taxes).

CLIMATE CHANGE & TRAVEL

Climate change is a serious threat to the ecosystems that humans rely upon, and air travel is the fastest-growing contributor to the problem. Lonely Planet regards travel, overall, as a global benefit, but believes we all have a responsibility to limit our personal impact on global warming.

Flying & Climate Change

Pretty much every form of motor travel generates CO_2 (the main cause of human-induced climate change) but planes are far and away the worst offenders, not just because of the sheer distances they allow us to travel, but because they release greenhouse gases high into the atmosphere. The statistics are frightening: two people taking a return flight between Europe and the US will contribute as much to climate change as an average household's gas and electricity consumption over a whole year.

Carbon Offset Schemes

Climatecare.org and other websites use 'carbon calculators' that allow jetsetters to offset the greenhouse gases they are responsible for with contributions to energy-saving projects and other climate-friendly initiatives in the developing world – including projects in India, Honduras, Kazakhstan and Uganda.

Lonely Planet, together with Rough Guides and other concerned partners in the travel industry, supports the carbon offset scheme run by climatecare.org. Lonely Planet offsets all of its staff and author travel.

For more information check out our website: lonelyplanet.com.

Cheap Flights (www.cheapflights.com) Informative site with specials, destination information and flight searches from the USA.

Cheapest Flights (www.cheapestflights.co.uk) Cheap worldwide flights from the UK; get in early for the bargains.

Expedia (www.expedia.com) Microsoft's travel site; good for USA-related flights.

Flight Centre International (www.flightcentre.com) Respected operator handling direct flights, with sites for NZ, Australia, the UK, the USA, Canada and South Africa.

Flights.com (www.flights.com) International site for flights; cheap fares and an easy-to-search database.

Roundtheworldflights.com (www.roundtheworld flights.com) This excellent site allows you to build your own trip from the UK with up to six stops. A six-stop trip including Asia, Australia, NZ and the USA costs from UK£550 in the NZ winter.

STA Travel (www.statravel.com) Prominent in international student travel (but you don't have to be a student). Linked to worldwide STA sites.

Travel Online (www.travelonline.co.nz) Good place to check worldwide flights from NZ.

Travel.com.au (www.travel.com.au) Good Australian site; look up fares and flights to/from the country.

Travelocity (www.travelocity.com) US site that allows you to search fares (in US dollars) from/to practically anywhere.

Asia

Most Asian countries offer fairly competitive air-fare deals, with Bangkok, Singapore and Hong Kong being the best places to shop around for discount tickets.

Common one-way fares to Auckland cost approximately US$750 from Singapore, US$850 from Kuala Lumpur, Bangkok and Hong Kong, and US$775 from Tokyo. Going the other way, return fares from Auckland to Singapore cost around NZ$1800, and around NZ$2100 to Kuala Lumpur, Bangkok, Hong Kong and Tokyo, depending on the airline.

Hong Kong's travel market can be unpredictable, but excellent bargains are sometimes available. **Phoenix Services** (☎ 2722 7378) is recommended.

STA Travel (Bangkok ☎ 02-236 0262; www.statravel. co.th; Singapore ☎ 6737 7188; www.statravel.com.sg; Tokyo ☎ 03-5391 2922; www.statravel.co.jp) has offices in major Asian cities.

Australia

Air New Zealand and Qantas operate a network of flights linking key NZ cities with most major Australian gateway cities, while quite a few other international airlines include NZ and Australia on their Asia-Pacific routes.

Cohorts Pacific Blue, Virgin Blue and Polynesian Blue offer direct flights between Auckland, Wellington and Christchurch and east-coast capitals, with connections on the domestic Virgin Blue network to many other Australian cities.

Qantas' budget subsidiary, Jetstar, flies between Auckland and Sydney, Cairns and the Gold Coast; and between Christchurch and Sydney, Melbourne, Hobart, Brisbane, Cairns and the Gold Coast.

If you book early, shop around and have the gods smiling upon you, you may pay under AU$180 for a one-way fare on a budget carrier from either Sydney or Melbourne to Auckland, Christchurch or Wellington. More common prices are from AU$200 to AU$250 one-way. You can fly into Auckland and out of Christchurch to save backtracking, but you may not get the cheapest fares with this itinerary.

From key NZ cities, you'll pay between NZ$240 and NZ$280 for a one-way ticket to an Australian east-coast city. There's usually not a significant difference in price between seasons, as this is a popular route year-round. The intense competition, however, inevitably results in some tasty discounting.

For some reasonably priced fares, try an Australian capital-city branch of **STA Travel** (☎ 134 782; www.statravel.com.au). Another good option, also with dozens of offices strewn around the country, is **Flight Centre** (☎ 133 133; www.flightcentre.com.au).

Canada
The air routes flown from Canada are similar to those from mainland USA, with most Toronto and Vancouver flights stopping in a US city such as Los Angeles or Honolulu before continuing to NZ. Air New Zealand has direct flights between Auckland and Vancouver year-round.

The air fares sold by Canadian discount air-ticket sellers (consolidators) tend to be about 10% higher than those sold in the USA. **Travel CUTS** (☎ 866 246 9762; www.travelcuts.com) is Canada's national student travel agency and has offices in all major cities.

Return fares from Vancouver to Auckland cost between C$1800 and C$2100 via the US west coast. From Toronto, fares cost around C$2000. One-way fares from NZ start at around NZ$1800 to Toronto and NZ$1500 to Vancouver.

Continental Europe
Frankfurt and London are the major arrival and departure points for flights to and from

NZ, both with extensive connections to other European cities. From these two launching pads, most flights to NZ travel via one of the Asian capitals. Return air fares from NZ to key European hubs such as Paris and Frankfurt usually cost between NZ$2100 and NZ$2600.

A solid option in the Dutch travel industry is **Holland International** (www.hollandinternational.nl). From Amsterdam, return fares start at around €1400.

In Germany, good travel agencies include the Berlin branch of **STA Travel** (☎ 069-7430 3292; www.statravel.de). Return fares from Frankfurt start at around €1400.

In France, return fares from Paris start from €1200. Recommended companies:
Nouvelles Frontières (☎ 0149 206 400; www. nouvelles-frontieres.fr/nf)
Odysia (☎ 0825 082 525; www.odysia.fr)
Voyageurs du Monde (☎ 0892 235 656; www.vdm. com/vdm)

UK & Ireland
Depending on which airline you travel with from the UK, flights to NZ go via Asia or the USA. If you fly via Asia you can often make stopovers in countries such as India, Thailand, Singapore and Australia; in the other direction, stopover possibilities include New York, Los Angeles, Honolulu and sundry Pacific islands.

Discount air travel is big business in London. Advertisements for many travel agencies appear in the travel pages of the weekend broadsheet newspapers, in *Time Out*, in the *Evening Standard* and in the free magazine *TNT*.

Typical one-way/return fares from London to Auckland start at around £550/750; note that June, July and mid-December fares can go up by as much as 30%. From NZ you can expect to pay between NZ$2500 and NZ$3000 for return fares to London.

Popular agencies in the UK:
Flight Centre (☎ 0800 587 0058; www.flightcentre. co.uk)
STA Travel (☎ 0871 230 0040; www.statravel.co.uk)
Trailfinders (☎ 0845 058 5858; www.trailfinders.co.uk)

USA
Most flights between the North American mainland and NZ are to/from west-coast USA, with the bulk routed through Los Angeles but some going through San Francisco. Some airlines offer flights via various Pacific islands (Hawaii, Tahiti, Cook Islands).

San Francisco is the ticket-consolidator capital of America, although some good deals can be found in Los Angeles, New York and other big cities. **STA Travel** (☎ 800 781 4040; www.statravel.com) has offices all over the USA.

Return tickets to NZ from the US west coast start around US$1100/1350 in the NZ winter/summer; fares from the east coast start at US$1850 in both seasons. Return fares from NZ to the US west coast are around NZ$2200; to New York NZ$2800.

SEA

It's possible (though by no means easy or safe) to make your way between NZ and Australia, and some smaller Pacific islands, by hitching rides or crewing on yachts. Try asking around at harbours, marinas, and yacht and sailing clubs. Popular yachting harbours in NZ include the Bay of Islands and Whangarei (both located in Northland), Auckland and Wellington. March and April are the best months to look for boats heading to Australia. From Fiji, October to November is a peak departure season as cyclones are starting to spin in that neck of the woods.

There are no passenger liners operating to/from NZ and finding a berth on a cargo ship (much less enjoying the experience) is no easy task.

GETTING AROUND

AIR

Those who have limited time to get between NZ's attractions can make the most of a widespread network of intra- and interisland flights.

Airlines in New Zealand

The country's major domestic carrier, Air New Zealand, has an aerial network covering most of the country. Australia-based Jetstar also flies between main urban areas.

Several small-scale regional operators provide essential transport services to the small outlying islands such as Great Barrier Island in the Hauraki Gulf, Stewart Island and the Chathams. Regional operators include the following:

Air Chathams (☎ 0508 247 248, 03-305 0209; www.airchathams.co.nz) Services to the remote Chatham Islands from Wellington, Christchurch and Auckland, and occasionally Napier.

Air Fiordland (☎ 0800 107 505, 03-249 6720; www.airfiordland.com) Services around Milford Sound, Te Anau and Queenstown.

Air New Zealand (☎ 0800 737 000, 09-357 3000; www.airnewzealand.co.nz) Offers flights between 26 domestic destinations.

Air West Coast (☎ 0800 247 937, 03-738 0524; www.airwestcoast.co.nz) Flies between Greymouth and Christchurch and runs charter flights.

Air2there.com (☎ 0800 777 000, 04-904 5130; www.air2there.com) Connects destinations across Cook Strait, including Blenheim, Napier, Nelson and Wellington.

Fly My Sky (☎ 09-256 7025; www.flymysky.co.nz) At least three flights daily from Auckland to Great Barrier Island.

Golden Bay Air (☎ 0800 588 885, 03-525 8725; www.capitalair.co.nz) Flies regularly between Wellington and Takaka in Golden Bay.

Great Barrier Airlines (☎ 0800 900 600, 09-275 9120; www.greatbarrierairlines.co.nz) Plies the skies over Great Barrier Island, Auckland and Whangarei.

Jetstar (☎ 0800 800 995; www.jetstar.com) Joins the dots between key tourism centres: Auckland, Wellington, Christchurch and Queenstown.

Salt Air Xpress (☎ 09-402 8338; www.saltair.co.nz) Flies to Kerikeri from Whangarei and Auckland's North Shore.

Soundsair (☎ 0800 505 005, 03-520 3080; www.soundsair.co.nz) Hops across Cook Strait between Wellington and Picton up to 16 times per day. Also links Wellington with Blenheim and Nelson.

Stewart Island Flights (☎ 03-218 9129; www.stewartislandflights.com) Flies between Invercargill and Stewart Island.

Air Passes

With discounting being the norm these days, and a number of budget airlines now serving the trans-Tasman route as well as the Pacific islands, the value of air passes isn't as red-hot as in the past.

Air New Zealand offers the **South Pacific Airpass** (☎ 1800 262 1234; www.airnewzealand.com), valid for selected journeys within NZ, and between NZ, Australia and a number of Pacific islands. The pass is only available to nonresidents of these countries, and must be issued outside NZ. Passes are issued in conjunction with an international ticket (with any airline) and are valid for the life of that ticket.

The pass involves purchasing coupons for domestic flights (one-way from NZ$99 to NZ$378, depending on distance), or flights to/from major Australian cities or Pacific islands

TRANSPORT

including Fiji, New Caledonia and Tonga, and as far afield as the Cook Islands and Samoa (one-way from NZ$231 to NZ$855).

BICYCLE

Touring cyclists proliferate in NZ, particularly over summer – the roads and trails run thick with fluoro-clad creatures with aerodynamic heads. The country is popular with cyclists because it's clean, green and relatively uncrowded, and has lots of cheap accommodation (including camping) and easily accessible freshwater. The roads are generally in good nick, and the climate generally not too hot or too cold (except on the South Island's rain-soaked West Coast). The many hills make for hard going at times, but there are expansive flats and lows to accompany the highs. As in any country, road traffic is the biggest danger, and you'll hear numerous cyclists' tales about inconsiderate or unsafe behaviour from drivers. Trucks overtaking too close to the cyclist are a particular threat. Take care! Bikes and cycling gear (to rent or buy) are readily available in the main centres, as are bicycle repair shops. A major nationwide project has been in motion since late 2009, expanding and improving NZ's network of bike trails. See the Ministry of Tourism's website for updates (www.tourism.govt.nz).

The choice of itineraries is limited only by your imagination. Cycling some of the coastline will be a highlight, but inland routes have their share of devotees. One increasingly popular expedition is to follow an upgraded path along an old railway line into the former gold-mining heartland of Otago – for details, see the boxed text, p592.

By law all cyclists must wear an approved safety helmet (or risk a fine); it's also vital to have good reflective gear, so that you can be easily seen by cars or trucks overtaking from behind. Cyclists who use public transport will find that major bus lines and trains only take bicycles on a 'space available' basis (meaning bikes may not be allowed on) and charge up to $10. Some of the smaller shuttle bus companies, on the other hand, make sure they have storage space for bikes, which they carry for a surcharge.

If importing your own bike or transporting it by plane within NZ, check with the relevant airline for costs and the degree of dismantling and packing required.

Hire

Rates offered by most outfits for renting road or mountain bikes – not including the discounted fees or freebies offered by accommodation places to their guests – are anywhere from $10 to $20 per hour and $30 to $50 per day.

Purchase

Bicycles can be readily bought in NZ's larger cities, but prices for newer models are high. For a decent hybrid bike or rigid mountain bike you'll pay anywhere from $700 to $1600, though you can get a cheap one for around $400 to $500 – however, then you still need to get panniers, a helmet and other essential touring gear, and the cost quickly climbs. Arguably you're better off buying a used bike (assuming you can't bring your own over), but finding something that's in good enough shape for a long road trip isn't always as easy as it sounds. Other options include the post-Christmas sales and midyear stocktakes, when newish cycles can be heavily discounted.

BOAT

NZ may be an island nation but there's virtually no long-distance water transport around the country. Obvious exceptions include the boat services between Auckland and various islands in the Hauraki Gulf (see p129), the inter-island ferries that chug across Cook Strait between Wellington and Picton (see p416 and p435), and the passenger ferry that negotiates the width of Foveaux Strait between Bluff and the town of Oban on Stewart Island (see p680).

BUS

Bus travel in NZ is relatively easy and well organised, with services transporting you to the far reaches of both islands (including the start/end of various walking tracks), but it can be expensive, tedious and time-consuming. The bus 'terminals' in smaller places usually comprise a parking spot outside a prominent local business.

The dominant bus company is **InterCity** (☎ Auckland 09-583 5780, Wellington 04-385 0520, Christchurch 03-365 1113, Dunedin 03-471 7143; www.intercity.co.nz), which also has an extracomfort travel and sightseeing arm called **Newmans Coach Lines** (☎ 09-623 1504; www.newmanscoach.co.nz). InterCity can drive you to just about anywhere on the North and South Islands, from Invercargill and Milford Sound in the south to Paihia and Kaitaia in the north.

Some smaller regional operators running key routes or covering a lot of ground on the North Island:

Alpine Scenic Tours (☎ 07-378 7412; www.alpine scenictours.co.nz) Has services around Taupo and into Tongariro National Park, plus the ski fields around Mt Ruapehu and Mt Tongariro.

Bay Xpress (☎ 0800 422 997, 06-873 4984; www. bayxpress.co.nz) Connects Wellington with Hastings and Napier via Palmerston North.

Dalroy Express (☎ 0508 465 622, 06-759-0197; www.dalroytours.co.nz) Operates a daily service between Auckland and Hawera via New Plymouth and Hamilton. Also runs from Auckland to Pahia, and from Hamilton to Rotorua and Taupo.

Go Kiwi Shuttles (☎ 07-866 0336; www.go-kiwi. co.nz) Links places like Auckland, Rotorua and Hamilton with various towns across the Coromandel Peninsula.

Magic Travellers Network (☎ 09-358 5600; www. magicbus.co.nz) Has a useful collection of passes available, covering both islands or each individually.

Naked Bus (☎ 0900 625 33; www.nakedbus.com) Low-cost routes across the North (and South) Island, from Auckland to Wellington and most places in between.

Waitomo Wanderer (☎ 0508 926 337, 03-477 9083; www.waitomotours.co.nz) Does a loop from Rotorua to Waitomo.

White Star City to City (☎ 06-759 0197; www.white starbus.co.nz) Shuttles between Wellington, Palmerston North, Wanganui and New Plymouth.

South Island shuttle-bus companies:

Abel Tasman Coachlines (☎ 03-548 0285; www. abeltasmantravel.co.nz) Traverses the tarmac between Nelson, Motueka, Golden Bay, and Kahurangi and Abel Tasman National Parks.

Atomic Shuttles (☎ 03-349 0697; www.atomictravel. co.nz) Has services throughout the South Island, including Christchurch, Dunedin, Invercargill, Picton, Nelson, Greymouth/Hokitika, Te Anau and Queenstown/Wanaka.

Cook Connection (☎ 0800 266 526; www.cook connect.co.nz) Triangulates between Mt Cook, Twizel and Lake Tekapo.

East West Coaches (☎ 0800 142 622, 03-789 6251) Offers a service between Christchurch and Westport, running via the Hanmer Springs turn-off, Maruia Springs and Reefton.

Hanmer Connection (☎ 0800 242 663; www.atsnz. com) Provides services between Hanmer Springs and Christchurch, and three services weekly between Hanmer and Kaikoura.

Knightrider (☎ 03-342 8055; www.knightrider.co.nz) Runs a nocturnal service from Christchurch to Invercargill via Dunedin. David Hasselhoff nowhere to be seen...

Naked Bus (☎ 0900 625 33; www.nakedbus.com) Low-cost routes across the South (and North) Island, from Nelson to Invercargill and most places in between.

Scenic Shuttle (☎ 0800 304 333, 03-477 9083; www. scenicshuttle.co.nz) Drives between Te Anau and Invercargill via Manapouri.

Southern Link Travel (☎ 0508 458 835; www. southernlinkkbus.co.nz) Roams across most of the South Island, taking in Christchurch, Nelson, Picton, Greymouth, Queenstown and Dunedin, among others.

Topline Tours (☎ 03-249 8059; www.toplinetours. co.nz) Connects Te Anau and Queenstown.

Tracknet (☎ 0800 483 262, 03-249 7777; www. tracknet.net) Daily track transport (Milford, Routeburn, Hollyford, Kepler etc) between Queenstown, Te Anau, Milford Sound, Invercargill, Fiordland and the West Coast.

West Coast Shuttle (☎ 03-768 0028; www.westcoast shuttle.co.nz) Daily bus from Greymouth to Christchurch and back.

InterCity Bus Passes

InterCity (☎ Auckland 09-583 5780, Wellington 04-385 0520, Christchurch 03-365 1113, Dunedin 03-471 7143; www. intercity.co.nz) offers bus passes, covering either the whole country, or the North and South Islands separately. If you're covering a lot of ground, passes can be cheaper than paying as you go, but they lock you into using InterCity buses (rather than, say, the convenient shuttle buses that cover much of the country). There's a 15% discount for YHA, BBH and VIP backpacker members; there may be an additional reservation charge ($3 per sector, depending on the agent).

NATIONWIDE PASSES

InterCity's pan-NZ **Travelpass** (☎ 0800 339 966; www.travelpass.co.nz) combines bus travel with a Cook Strait ferry crossing. There are three hop-on/hop-off passes available, each valid for a year. Adult and child prices are the same:

Kia Ora New Zealand ($579; 7-day minimum travel) A one-way trip between Auckland and Christchurch via Rotorua, Wellington, Dunedin, Queenstown and Milford Sound. Available in both directions.

Kiwi Explorer ($623; 9-day minimum travel) A one-way trip between Auckland and Christchurch via Rotorua, Napier, Wellington, the West Coast, Milford Sound and Queenstown. Available in both directions.

Aotearoa Adventurer ($1283; 14-day minimum travel) A monster loop from Auckland to Milford Sound and back, via Northland, Rotorua, Wellington, Christchurch, Queenstown, the West Coast and Napier.

The appropriately named **Flexi-Pass** (☎ 0800 222 146; www.flexipass.co.nz) is valid for one year and allows you to travel pretty much anywhere (and in any direction) on the InterCity network; you can get on and off wherever you like and can change bookings up to two hours before departure without penalty. The pass is purchased in five-hour blocks of travel time, from a minimum of 15 hours ($169) up to a maximum of 60 hours ($605) – the average cost of each block becomes cheaper the more hours you buy. You can top up the pass if you need more time.

NORTH ISLAND PASSES
There are seven InterCity North Island passes:
Thermal Explorer ($39; 1-day minimum travel) Rotorua to Taupo return.
Bay Escape ($106; 1-day minimum travel) Auckland to Paihia and back, via Whangarei.
Eastern Wanderer ($119; 3-day minimum travel) Rotorua to Napier circuit via Whakatane, Gisborne and Taupo.
Maui's Catch ($169; 3-day minimum travel) Auckland to Wellington via Waitomo, Rotorua, Taupo, Napier and Palmerston North. Available in both directions.
Volcanic Explorer ($184; 2-day minimum travel) Auckland to Rotorua loop via Tauranga, Taupo and Waitomo.
Northland Explorer ($205; 3-day minimum travel) Auckland to Paihia return via Whangarei, with a day trip to Cape Reinga.
North Island Discovery ($243; 4-day minimum travel) Auckland to Wellington return via Waitomo, Rotorua, Taupo, Napier, Palmerston North and Hamilton. Available in both directions.

SOUTH ISLAND PASSES
There are 10 InterCity South Island passes:
Kaikoura Discovery ($40; 1-day minimum travel) Christchurch to Kaikoura and back.
West Coast Passport ex-Greymouth ($135; 2-day minimum travel) Greymouth to Queenstown via Franz Josef Glacier, Fox Glacier and Wanaka. Available in both directions.
West Coast Passport ex-Nelson ($155; 2-day minimum travel) Nelson to Queenstown via Greymouth, Franz Josef Glacier, Fox Glacier and Wanaka. Available in both directions.
West Coast Passport ex-Picton ($180; 3-day minimum travel) Picton to Queenstown via Nelson, Greymouth, Franz Josef Glacier, Fox Glacier and Wanaka. Available in both directions.
Southern Trail ($188; 3-day minimum travel) Greymouth to Christchurch via Franz Josef Glacier, Fox Glacier, Wanaka, Queenstown and Tekapo. Available in both directions.

Greenstone Encounter ($189; 2-day minimum travel) Christchurch to Milford Sound via Tekapo, Queenstown and Te Anau. Available in both directions.
Goldminers Trail ($221; 2-day minimum travel) Christchurch to Milford Sound via Dunedin, Queenstown and Te Anau. Available in both directions.
Te Hamo's Adventure ($259; 2-day minimum travel) Christchurch to Milford Sound via Aoraki/Mt Cook, Queenstown and Te Anau. Available in both directions.
Maui's Canoe ($442; 5-day minimum travel) South Island circuit starting/ending in Christchurch via Queenstown, Milford Sound, Fox Glacier, Franz Josef Glacier, Nelson and Kaikoura. Available in both directions.
Alpine Discovery ($539; 5-day minimum travel) South Island circuit starting/ending in Christchurch via Aoraki/Mt Cook, Queenstown, Te Anau, Milford Sound, Fox Glacier, Franz Josef Glacier, Greymouth, Nelson and Kaikoura. Available in both directions.

Seat Classes
There are no allocated economy or luxury classes on NZ buses; smoking is a no-no.

Reservations
Over summer, school holidays and public holidays, book well ahead on more popular routes. At other times you should have few problems accessing your preferred service, but if your long-term travel plans rely on catching a particular bus, book at least a day or two ahead just to be safe.

InterCity fares vary widely depending on availability and how the tickets are booked (online or via an agent). The best prices are generally available online, booked a few weeks in advance.

CAR & MOTORCYCLE
The best way to explore NZ in depth is to have your own transport, which allows you to create your own leisurely, flexible itinerary. Good-value car- and campervan-hire rates are not hard to track down; alternatively, consider buying your own set of wheels.

Automobile Association (AA)
NZ's **Automobile Association** (AA; ☎ 24hr road service 0800 500 222; www.aa.co.nz) provides emergency breakdown services, excellent touring maps and detailed guides to accommodation (from holiday parks to motels and B&Bs).

Members of foreign automobile associations should bring their membership cards – many of these bodies have reciprocal agreements with NZ's AA.

Driving Licence

International visitors to NZ can use their home country's driving licence – if your licence isn't in English, it's a good idea to carry a certified translation with you. Alternatively, use an International Driving Permit (IDP), which will usually be issued on the spot (valid for 12 months) by your home country's automobile association.

Fuel

Fuel is available from service stations with the well-known international brand names. LPG (gas) is not always stocked by rural suppliers; if you're on gas it's safer to have dual fuel capability. Prices vary from place to place, but basically petrol (gasoline) isn't pumped cheaply in NZ, with per-litre costs at the time of research averaging around $1.65. More remote destinations may charge a small fortune to fill your tank and you're better off getting fuel before you reach them – places in this category include Milford Sound (fill up at Te Anau) and Mt Cook (buy fuel at Twizel or Lake Tekapo).

Hire

CAMPERVAN

Check your rear-view mirror on any far-flung NZ road and you'll likely see a shiny white campervan (aka mobile home, motor home, RV) packed with liberated travellers, mountain bikes and portable barbecues cruising along behind you.

Most towns of any size have a camping ground or campervan park with powered sites for around $35 per night. There are also more than 200 vehicle-accessible **Department of Conservation** (DOC; www.doc.govt.nz) campsites, which range in price from free to $14 per adult. DOC publishes free brochures with instructions to find every campsite (even GPS coordinates). Grab a copy from a DOC office before you hit the road, or visit the website.

You should never just assume it's OK to camp somewhere. Always ask a local first or check at the local i-SITE or DOC office. If you are freedom camping, please treat the area with respect – if your van doesn't have toilet facilities, find a public loo. See www.camping.org.nz for more tips on freedom camping.

You can hire campervans from assorted companies, prices varying with time of year, how big you want your home-on-wheels to be, and length of rental. Major operators:

Britz (☎ 0800 831 900, 09-255 3910; www.britz.co.nz)
Kea Campers (☎ 0800 520 052, 09-441 7833; www.keacampers.com)
Maui (☎ 0800 651 080, 09-255 3910; www.maui.co.nz)

A small van for two people typically has a minikitchen and foldout dining table, the latter transforming into a double bed when dinner is done and dusted. Larger 'superior' two-berth vans include shower and toilet. Four- to six-berth campervans are the size of trucks (and similarly sluggish) and, besides the extra space, usually contain a toilet and shower.

BACKPACKER VAN RENTALS

There are several budget players in the campervan industry, offering slick deals and funky, well-kitted-out vehicles to attract young, independent travellers (the kind who would shun the larger, more traditional box-on-wheels). All companies offer living, sleeping and cooking equipment, 24-hour roadside assistance, and maps and travel tips. Rates are competitive (from $35 per day May to September; from $70 per day December to February). Check out the following:

- **Backpacker Sleeper Vans** (☎ 0800 325 939, 03-359 4731; www.sleepervans.co.nz) Low-cost family-run business.

- **Escape Rentals** (☎ 0800 216 171; www.escaperentals.co.nz) 'The freedom to sleep around' – loud, original artwork on van exteriors, pitched squarely at young travellers after something different. DVDs, TVs and outdoor barbecues available for rent.

- **Jucy** (☎ 0800 399 736, 09-374 4360; www.jucy.co.nz) The flashpacker's vehicle of choice.

- **Spaceships** (☎ 0800 772 237, 09-526 2130; www.spaceshipsrentals.co.nz) The customised 'Swiss Army Knife of campervans', with extras including DVD and CD players, roof racks and solar showers.

- **Wicked Campers** (☎ 0800 246 870; www.wicked-campers.co.nz) Spray-painted vans bedecked with everything/everyone from Mr Spock to Sly Stone.

Over summer, rates offered by the main rental firms for two-/four-/six-berth vans start at around $160/290/320 per day, dropping to as low as $50/80/95 in winter for month-long rentals; industry infighting often sees even lower rates.

CAR

Competition between car-rental companies in NZ is torrid – rates tend to be variable and lots of special deals come and go (we've heard of discounted rates as low as $15 per day, so shop around. Car rental is most competitive in Auckland, Christchurch, Wellington and Picton. The main thing to remember when assessing your options is distance – if you want to travel far, you need unlimited kilometres. Some (but not all) companies require drivers to be at least 21 years old – ask around.

Sizeable multinational companies, with offices or agents in most major cities, towns and larger airports:

Avis (☎ 0800 655 111, 09-526-2847; www.avis.co.nz)

Budget (☎ 0800 283 438, 09-529 7784; www.budget.co.nz)

Europcar (☎ 0800 800 115, 03-357 0920; www.europcar.co.nz)

Hertz (☎ 0800 654 321, 03-520 3044; www.hertz.co.nz)

Thrifty (☎ 0800 737 070, 03-359 2720; www.thrifty.co.nz)

Local rental firms and firms with limited locations also dapple the *Yellow Pages* – see the regional chapters in this guide. These are almost always cheaper than the big boys – sometimes half the price – but the cheap rates may come with serious restrictions, vehicles are often older, and with less formality sometimes comes less protective legal structure for renters.

Affordable, independent operators with national networks:

Ace Rental Cars (☎ 0800 502 277, 09-303 3112; www.acerentalcars.co.nz)

Apex Rentals (☎ 0800 939 597, 03-379 6897; www.apexrentals.co.nz)

Ezy Rentals (☎ 0800 399 736, 09-374 4360; www.ezy.co.nz)

Go Rentals (☎ 0800 467 368, 09-525 7321; www.gorentals.co.nz)

NORTH ISLAND ROAD DISTANCES (km)

Distances are approximate only

	Auckland	Cape Reinga	Dargaville	Gisborne	Hamilton	Hicks Bay	Kaitaia	Napier	New Plymouth	Paihia	Palmerston North	Rotorua	Taupo	Tauranga	Thames	Waitomo Caves	Whanganui	Wellington	Whakatane
Cape Reinga	430																		
Dargaville	175	280																	
Gisborne	490	920	675																
Hamilton	125	555	300	390															
Hicks Bay	510	945	690	180	400														
Kaitaia	325	115	170	820	440	800													
Napier	420	860	590	215	300	395	735												
New Plymouth	360	790	530	570	240	580	680	410											
Paihia	225	220	130	720	340	720	120	645	590										
Palmerston North	520	950	690	395	400	570	840	180	230	750									
Rotorua	235	670	405	295	110	285	550	220	300	460	325								
Taupo	280	720	450	330	155	365	600	140	300	505	250	80							
Tauranga	210	635	385	290	110	290	525	300	330	435	400	85	155						
Thames	115	540	280	410	110	400	430	360	340	345	470	170	210	115					
Waitomo Caves	200	620	360	440	75	440	515	300	180	420	340	165	170	150	175				
Whanganui	455	880	615	465	330	645	770	250	160	670	75	310	225	375	430	270			
Wellington	640	1080	805	530	520	730	960	320	350	860	140	450	375	530	590	460	190		
Whakatane	300	740	470	200	190	204	620	300	380	525	410	85	160	95	210	240	380	540	
Whangarei	160	280	55	640	280	650	165	580	515	70	680	390	430	350	265	345	600	790	450

Omega Rental Cars (☎ 0800 525 210, 09-377 5573; www.omegarentalcars.com)
Pegasus Rental Cars (☎ 0800 803 580, 03-548 2852; www.rentalcars.co.nz)

The big firms sometimes offer one-way rentals (eg collect a car in Auckland, leave it in Wellington), but there are a variety of restrictions, and a one-way drop-off fee may apply. However, for rentals of a month or more, fees are often waived between Auckland and Wellington or Christchurch. On the other hand, an operator in Christchurch may need to get a vehicle back to Auckland and will offer an amazing one-way deal (sometimes free!).

Most car-hire firms suggest (or insist) that you don't take their vehicles between islands on the Cook Strait ferries. Instead, you leave your car at either Wellington or Picton terminal and pick up another car once you've crossed the strait. This saves you paying to transport a vehicle on the ferries, and is a pain-free exercise.

The major companies offer a choice of either unlimited kilometres, or 100km (or so) per day free plus so many cents per subsequent kilometre. Daily rates in main cities typically start at around $40 per day for a compact, late-model, Japanese car, and around $75 for medium-sized cars (including GST, unlimited kilometres and insurance). Local firms start at around $30 per day for the smallest option. It's obviously cheaper if you rent for a week or more and there are often low-season and weekend discounts. Credit cards are the usual payment method.

MOTORCYCLE

Born to be wild? NZ has great terrain for motorcycle touring, despite the fickle weather in some regions. If you're tempted to bring your own motorcycle into NZ, be aware that this will entail an expensive shipping exercise, valid registration in the country of origin and a *Carnet de Passages en Douanes* (a customs document that identifies your motor vehicle).

Most of the country's motorcycle-hire shops are in Auckland and Christchurch, where you can hire anything from a little 50cc moped (aka nifty-fifty) for zipping around town, to a throbbing 750cc touring motorcycle and beyond. Recommended operators:

SOUTH ISLAND ROAD DISTANCES (km)

Distances are approximate only

	Aoraki/Mt Cook	Arthur's Pass	Blenheim	Christchurch	Dunedin	Franz Josef Glacier	Greymouth	Hanmer Springs	Hokitika	Invercargill	Kaikoura	Milford Sound	Nelson	Oamaru	Picton	Queenstown	Te Anau	Timaru	Wanaka
Arthur's Pass	410																		
Blenheim	635	420																	
Christchurch	330	150	310																
Dunedin	325	455	665	360															
Franz Josef Glacier	485	230	500	390	560														
Greymouth	510	95	330	250	550	180													
Hanmer Springs	460	265	260	140	490	395	215												
Hokitika	510	100	370	250	550	135	40	255											
Invercargill	440	660	870	570	210	530	710	700	665										
Kaikoura	505	290	130	185	535	540	330	135	390	745									
Milford Sound	540	840	1060	760	410	630	805	890	770	275	930								
Nelson	745	370	115	425	775	470	290	310	335	990	245	1100							
Oamaru	210	340	550	250	115	510	430	375	435	325	420	525	660						
Picton	660	450	30	340	690	530	355	290	400	900	160	1090	120	580					
Queenstown	260	565	785	480	285	355	530	610	490	190	660	290	820	290	815				
Te Anau	420	725	945	640	295	515	690	770	650	160	815	120	980	410	975	170			
Timaru	210	260	465	165	200	490	350	295	360	410	340	605	580	85	495	330	490		
Wanaka	210	510	730	430	280	285	465	555	420	245	600	345	755	230	760	70	230	275	
Westport	610	195	260	340	650	280	100	220	145	810	330	905	230	535	290	630	790	455	565

TRANSPORT

New Zealand Motorcycle Rentals & Tours (☎ 09-634 9118; www.nzbike.com) Yamahas, BMWs, Hondas and Harleys from $120 to $395 per day. Rates vary with size of bike, length of rental and season. Guided tours also available.

Te Waipounamu Motorcycle Tours (☎ 03-372 3537; www.motorcycle-hire.co.nz) Yamahas, Ducatis, Kawasakis, BMWs, Hondas and Suzukis from $115 to $300 per day. Guided tours also available.

Insurance

When it comes to renting a vehicle, know exactly what your liability is in the event of an accident. Rather than risk paying out a large amount of cash if you do have an accident (minor collisions are common in NZ), you can take out your own comprehensive insurance policy, or (the usual option) pay an additional daily amount to the rental company for an 'insurance excess reduction' policy. This brings the amount of excess you must pay in the event of an accident down from around $1500 or $2000 to around $150 or $200. Smaller operators offering cheap rates often have a compulsory insurance excess, taken as a credit-card bond, of around $900.

Most insurance agreements won't cover the cost of damage to glass (including the windscreen) or tyres, and insurance coverage is often invalidated on beaches and certain rough (4WD) unsealed roads – always read the fine print.

For information on the country's no-fault Accident Compensation Corporation scheme, see p692.

Purchase

For longer stays and/or for groups, buying a car then selling it at the end of your travels can be one of the cheapest and best ways to see NZ. You can often pick up a car as cheap as (or cheaper than) a one- or two-month rental, and you should be able to get back most of your money when you sell it. The danger, of course, is that you'll buy a lemon that breaks down every five minutes.

Auckland is the easiest place for travellers to buy a car, followed by Christchurch. An easy option for a cheap car is to scour the noticeboards of backpacker places, where other travellers sell their cars before moving on; you can pick up an old car for just a few hundred dollars. Some backpackers specials are so cheap it may be worth taking the risk that they may expire on you.

Besides, these vehicles often come complete with water containers, tools, road maps and even camping gear.

Car markets and car auctions are also worth investigating – check out information on car markets in the Auckland (p127) and Christchurch (p540) sections. At auctions you can pick up cheap cars from around $1000 to $6000 – **Turners Auctions** (☎ 09-580 9360; www.turners.co.nz) is the country's largest such outfit, with 10 locations.

Make sure any car you buy has a Warrant of Fitness (WoF) and that the registration lasts for a reasonable period. A WoF certificate, proving that the car is roadworthy, is valid for six months but must be less than 28 days old when you buy a car. To transfer registration, both you and the seller are legally required to independently notify **Land Transport New Zealand** (www.landtransport.govt.nz) of the change of ownership within seven days. To do so, fill out a *Notice of Change of Ownership of Motor Vehicle* form (MR 13 or MR 13B), which can be filed at any AA office or post office. Papers are sent to you by mail within 10 days (you'll need an address!). If needed, registration can be purchased for six months ($268) or a year ($388).

Car buyers should also take out third-party insurance, covering the cost of repairs to another vehicle in an accident that is your fault: try the **Automobile Association** (AA; ☎ 0800 500 231; www.aainsurance.co.nz). The no-fault Accident Compensation Corporation scheme (p692) covers personal injury, but make sure you have travel insurance as well (p691).

Car inspections are highly recommended as they'll protect you against any dodgy WoFs (such scams have been reported in the past) and may save you a lot of grief and repair bills later on. Various car-inspection companies will check a car you intend to buy for less than $150; you'll find them at car auctions for on-the-spot inspections, or they will come to you. Try **Vehicle Inspection New Zealand** (VINZ; ☎ 0800 468 469; www.vinz.co.nz). The AA also offers a mobile inspection service – it's slightly cheaper if you bring the car to an AA-approved mechanic. AA checks are thorough, but most garages will inspect a car for less.

Before you buy it's wise to confirm the ownership of the vehicle, and find out if there's anything dodgy about the car in question (eg any outstanding debts on it). A number of companies offer this service, including the AA's **LemonCheck** (☎ 04-233 8590; www.lemoncheck.co.nz). A search costs $25 and is done using the Vehicle Identification Number (VIN; found on a plate near the engine block) or licence-plate number.

BUY-BACK DEALS
One way of getting around the hassles of buying and selling a vehicle privately is to enter into a buy-back arrangement with a car or motorcycle dealer. However, dealers may find ways of knocking down the price when you return the vehicle (even if it was agreed to in writing), often by pointing out expensive repairs that allegedly will be required to gain the WoF certificate needed to transfer the registration. The buy-back amount varies, but may be 50% less than the purchase price – in a strictly financial sense, hiring or buying and selling the vehicle yourself (if you have the time) is usually a much better idea.

Road Hazards
The full spectrum of drivers and driving habits occurs on NZ roads, from the no-fuss motorist who doesn't mind pulling over to let you past, to back-road tailgaters who believe they know a particular stretch of bitumen so well they can go as fast as they like, despite narrow, twisting roads. Traffic is usually pretty light, but it's easy to get stuck behind a slow-moving truck or campervan on uphill climbs – pack plenty of patience. There are also lots of gravel or dirt roads to explore, which require a more cautious driving approach than for sealed roads. And watch out for sheep!

Road Rules
Kiwis drive on the left-hand side of the road and all cars are right-hand drive. A 'give way to the right' rule applies and is interpreted to a rather strange extreme here – if you're turning left and an oncoming vehicle is turning right into the same street, you have to give way to it.

Speed limits on the open road are generally 100km/h; in built-up areas the limit is usually 50km/h. An 'LSZ' (Limited Speed Zone) sign on the open road means that the speed limit is reduced from 100km/h to 50km/h in certain conditions – this applies when conditions are unsafe due to bad weather, limited visibility, pedestrians, cyclists or animals on the road, excessive traffic, or lousy road conditions. Speed cameras and radars are used extensively.

At single-lane bridges (of which there are a surprisingly large number), a smaller red arrow pointing in your direction of travel means that *you* give way, so slow down as you approach and pull a little to the side if you see a car approaching the other end of the bridge.

All new cars in NZ have seat belts back and front and it's the law to wear them – you're risking a fine if you don't. Small children must be belted into an approved safety seat.

Drivers might want to buy a copy of the *New Zealand Road Code*, which will tell you all you need to know about life on the road. Versions applicable to both cars and motorcycles are available at AA offices and bookshops, or you can check the online rundown of road rules on the **Land Transport New Zealand** (www.landtransport.govt.nz/roadcode) website.

HITCHING
Until quite recently it was quite fair and logical to think, 'If there's anywhere in the world where I can still hitch a ride, NZ is it.' However, a few unsavoury incidents in recent years suggest that NZ is no longer immune from the perils of solo hitching (especially for women). Those who decide to hitch should understand that they are taking a small but potentially serious risk. Prospective hitchers will be safer if they travel in pairs and let someone know where they are planning to go. That said, it's not unusual to see hitchhikers by the side of country roads (signalling with a thumbs-up or a downward-pointed finger), although extensive bus networks and cheap car-rental rates mean that hitching a ride isn't as common among travellers as it once was.

People looking for travelling companions for car journeys around the country often leave notices on boards in backpacker accommodation. The website www.carshare.co.nz is an excellent resource for people seeking or offering a lift.

LOCAL TRANSPORT
Bus, Train & Tram
Most of NZ's urban buses have been privatised. Larger cities have fairly extensive bus services but, with a few honourable exceptions, they are mainly daytime, weekday operations; on weekends, particularly on Sunday, bus services can be hard to find or may cease altogether. Negotiating the inner-city area in Auckland is made easier by the Link and City Circuit buses, and in Christchurch by the

Shuttle Bus service and the historic tramway. Most main cities have a late-night bus service roaming central entertainment districts on boozy, end-of-week nights.

The only city with a decent train service is Wellington, which has five suburban routes.

Taxi

The main cities have plenty of taxis and even small towns may have a local service. Taxis cruise the busy areas in Auckland, Wellington and Christchurch, but elsewhere you usually have to either phone for one or find a taxi rank.

TRAIN

With the exception of Wellington's suburban trains, NZ train travel is about the journey, not about getting anywhere in a hurry. **Tranz Scenic** (☎ 0800 872 467, 04-495 0775; www.tranzscenic.co.nz) operates several visually stunning routes: the *Overlander* between Auckland and Wellington; the *TranzCoastal* between Christchurch and Picton; and the *TranzAlpine*, which rattles over the Southern Alps between Christchurch and Greymouth. All routes run in both directions daily. It also operates the weekday *Capital Connection* commuter service between Palmerston North and Wellington.

Reservations can be made through Tranz Scenic directly, or at most train stations (notably *not* at Palmerston North or Hamilton), travel agents and visitor information centres, where you can also pick up booklets detailing timetables. Ask about discount fares – reductions apply for children (50% off standard fares), seniors and students (30% off), and holders of backpackers cards (20% off). Discounts don't apply on the *Overlander* or *Capital Connection* services. See regional chapters for fare and timetable info.

Train Passes

Given NZ's limited rail network, buying a train pass isn't particularly good value.

Tranz Scenic's **Scenic Rail Pass** (www.tranzscenic.co.nz) allows unlimited travel on all of its rail services (with the exception of the *Capital Connection*), with the option of including passage on the Interislander ferry between Wellington and Picton. A pass (with ferry trip) lasting two weeks costs $517/394 per adult/child.

Health Dr David Millar

New Zealand is one of the healthiest countries in the world in which to travel. The risk of diseases such as malaria and typhoid is unheard of, and thanks to NZ's quarantine standards, even some animal diseases such as rabies have yet to be recorded. The absence of poisonous snakes or other dangerous animals makes this a very safe region to get off the beaten track and out into the beautiful countryside.

BEFORE YOU GO

Since most vaccines don't produce immunity until at least two weeks after they're given, visit a physician four to eight weeks before departure. Ask your doctor for an International Certificate of Vaccination (or 'the yellow booklet'), which will list all the vaccinations you've received. This is mandatory for countries that require proof of yellow-fever vaccination upon entry, but it's a good idea to carry it wherever you travel.

Bring medications in their original, clearly labelled containers. A signed and dated letter from your physician describing your medical conditions and medications, including generic names, is also a good idea. If carrying syringes or needles, be sure to have a physician's letter documenting their medical necessity.

INSURANCE

If your current health insurance doesn't cover you for medical expenses incurred overseas, you should think about getting extra insurance – check out www.lonelyplanet.com for more information. Find out in advance if your insurance plan will make payments directly to providers or reimburse you at a later date for overseas health expenditures. (In many countries doctors expect payment in cash.)

RECOMMENDED VACCINATIONS

NZ has no vaccination requirements for any traveller. The World Health Organization recommends that all travellers should be covered for diphtheria, tetanus, measles, mumps, rubella, chickenpox and polio, as well as hepatitis B, regardless of their destination. Planning to travel abroad is an ideal time to ensure that all routine vaccination cover is complete. The consequences of these diseases can be severe and while NZ has high levels of childhood vaccination coverage, outbreaks of these diseases do occur.

INTERNET RESOURCES

You'll find that there's a wealth of travel health advice available on the internet. For further information on health, **Lonely Planet** (www.lonelyplanet.com) is a good place to start. The **World Health Organization** (www.who.int/ith/) publishes an excellent book called *International Travel and Health,* which is revised annually and is available online at no cost. Another good website of general interest is **MD Travel Health** (www.mdtravelhealth.com), which provides complete travel health recommendations for every country and is updated daily.

IN TRANSIT

DEEP VEIN THROMBOSIS (DVT)

Blood clots may form in the legs during plane flights, chiefly because of a prolonged period of immobility. The longer the flight, the greater the risk. The chief symptom of deep vein thrombosis (DVT) is swelling or pain of the foot, ankle or calf, usually – but not always – on just one side. When a blood clot travels to the lungs, it may result in chest pain and difficulty breathing. Travellers with any of these symptoms should seek medical attention immediately.

To prevent the development of DVT on long flights, you should walk about the cabin, perform compressions of the leg muscles (ie flex the leg muscles while sitting), drink plenty of fluids and avoid alcohol and tobacco.

JET LAG & MOTION SICKNESS

Jet lag is common when crossing more than five time zones, resulting in insomnia, fatigue, malaise and/or nausea. To avoid the effects of jet lag, try drinking plenty of nonalcoholic fluids and eating light meals. Upon arrival at your destination, get exposure to natural sunlight and readjust your schedule (for meals, sleep etc) as soon as possible.

Antihistamines such as dimenhydrinate (Dramamine) and meclizine (Antivert, Bonine) are usually the preferred choice for treating motion sickness. Their main side effect is drowsiness. A herbal alternative is ginger, which works like a charm for some people.

IN NEW ZEALAND

AVAILABILITY & COST OF HEALTH CARE

Health insurance is essential for all travellers. While health care in NZ is of a high standard and not overly expensive by international standards, considerable costs can be built up and repatriation can be extremely expensive. See p715 for insurance information.

Health Care in New Zealand

NZ does not have a government-funded system of public hospitals. All travellers are, however, covered for medical care resulting from accidents that occur while in NZ (eg motor-vehicle accidents, adventure-activity accidents) by the Accident Compensation Corporation (ACC). Costs incurred by treatment of a medical illness that occurs while in NZ will only be covered by travel insurance. For more details see www.moh.govt.nz and www.acc.co.nz.

NZ has excellent specialised public health facilities for women and children in the major centres. No specific health concerns exist for women but greater care for children is recommended to avoid environmental hazards such as heat, sunburn, cold and marine hazards.

The 24-hour, free-call **Healthline** (☎ 0800 611 116) offers health advice throughout NZ.

Self-care in New Zealand

In NZ it is possible to find yourself in a remote location where, in the event of a serious accident or illness, there may well be a significant delay in emergency services getting to you. This is usually the result of weather and rugged terrain, particularly on the South Island. Therefore, an increased level of self-reliance and preparation is essential. Consider taking a wilderness first-aid course (such as the one from the Wilderness Medicine Institute). In addition, you should carry a comprehensive first-aid kit that is appropriate for the activities planned. To be really safe, ensure that you

have adequate means of communication – NZ has extensive mobile-phone coverage, but additional radio communication equipment is important for remote areas, and can usually be hired from Department of Conservation visitor centres in popular tramping areas.

Pharmaceutical Supplies

Over-the-counter medications are widely available in NZ through private chemists. These include painkillers, antihistamines for allergies, and skin care products.

Some medications that are available over the counter in other countries are only available by a prescription obtained from a general practitioner. These include the oral contraceptive pill, most medications for asthma and all antibiotics. If you take a medication on a regular basis, bring an adequate supply and ensure you have details of the generic name, as brand names differ between countries. The majority of medications in use outside of the region are available.

INFECTIOUS DISEASES
Amoebic Meningitis

There is a small risk of developing amoebic meningitis as a result of bathing or swimming in geothermal pools in NZ – mostly in regions such as Rotorua and Taupo. In such pools, keeping the head above water to prevent movement of the organism up the nasal passage reduces the risk (which is pretty low to start with). Symptoms usually start three to seven days after swimming in a geothermal pool and early symptoms of this serious disease include headache, fever and vomiting. Urgent medical care is essential to differentiate the disease from other causes of meningitis and for appropriate treatment.

Giardiasis

The giardia parasite is widespread in the waterways of NZ. Drinking untreated water from streams and lakes is not recommended. Using water filters and boiling or treating water with iodine are effective ways of preventing the disease. Symptoms consist of intermittent bad-smelling diarrhoea, abdominal bloating and wind. Effective treatment is available (tinidazole or metronidazole).

Hepatitis C

This disease is a growing problem among intravenous drug users. Blood-transfusion services fully screen all blood before use.

HIV
The country's HIV rates have stabilised after major media campaigns, and levels are similar to other Western countries. Clean needles and syringes are widely available.

Meningococcal Disease
This occurs worldwide and is a risk with prolonged dormitory-style accommodation. A vaccine exists for some types of the disease (meningococcal A, C, Y and W).

Sexually Transmitted Diseases (STDs)
In NZ, STDs (including herpes, gonorrhoea and chlamydia) occur at rates similar to most Western countries. The most common symptoms are pain on passing urine and a discharge. Infection can be present without symptoms, so seek medical screening after any unprotected sex with a new partner. Sexual health clinics are run as part of major hospitals.

TRAVELLER'S DIARRHOEA
If you develop diarrhoea, be sure to drink plenty of fluids, preferably an oral rehydration solution containing lots of salt and sugar. A few loose stools don't require treatment but if you start having more than four or five stools a day, you should start taking an antibiotic (usually a quinolone drug) and an antidiarrhoeal agent (such as loperamide). If diarrhoea is bloody, persists for more than 72 hours and/or is accompanied by fever, shaking chills or severe abdominal pain you should seek medical attention.

ENVIRONMENTAL HAZARDS
Hypothermia
This is a significant risk, especially during the winter months or year-round in the mountains of the North Island and all of the South Island. Mountain ranges and/or strong winds produce a high chill factor which can result in hypothermia, even in moderately cool temperatures. Early signs include the inability to perform fine movements (such as doing up buttons), shivering and a bad case of the 'umbles' (fumbles, mumbles, grumbles, stumbles). The key elements of treatment are changing the environment to one where heat loss is minimised, changing out of any wet clothing, adding dry clothes with wind- and waterproof layers, adding insulation and providing fuel (water and carbohydrate) to allow shivering to build the internal temperature. In severe hypothermia, shivering actually stops; this is a medical emergency requiring rapid evacuation in addition to the above measures.

Spider Bites
NZ has two poisonous spiders, the native katipo (not very poisonous and uncommon to the point of being endangered) and the introduced (thanks, Australia) white-tailed spider (also uncommon). White-tailed spider bites have been known to cause ulcers that are very difficult to heal. Clean the wound thoroughly and seek medical assistance if an ulcer develops.

Surf Beaches & Drowning
NZ has exceptional surf beaches, particularly on the western, southern and eastern coasts. The power of the surf can fluctuate as a result of the varying slope of the seabed at many beaches. Check with local surf life-saving organisations before entering the surf and be aware of your own limitations and expertise.

Ultraviolet Light Exposure
NZ has one of the highest rates of skin cancer in the world, so you should monitor UV exposure closely. UV exposure is greatest between 10am and 4pm – avoid skin exposure during these times. Always use SPF30+ sunscreen, making sure you apply it 30 minutes before exposure and that you reapply regularly to minimise sun damage.

Water
Tap water is universally safe in NZ. Increasing numbers of streams, rivers and lakes, however, are being contaminated by bugs that cause diarrhoea, making water purification when tramping essential. The simplest way of purifying water is to boil it thoroughly. You should also consider purchasing a water filter. It's very important when buying a filter to read the specifications so that you know exactly what it removes from the water and what it doesn't. Simple filtering will not remove all dangerous organisms, so if you cannot boil water it should be treated chemically. Chlorine tablets will kill many pathogens, but not parasites such as giardia or amoebic cysts. Iodine is more effective in purifying water. Follow the directions carefully and remember that too much iodine can be harmful.

HEALTH

Language

New Zealand has two official languages: English and Maori. English is what you'll usually hear, but Maori has been making a comeback. You can use English to speak to anyone in NZ, but there are some occasions when knowing a small amount of Maori is useful, such as when visiting a *marae*, where often only Maori is spoken. Maori is also useful to know since many places in NZ have Maori names.

KIWI ENGLISH

Like the people of other English-speaking countries in the world, New Zealanders have a unique way of speaking the language. The flattening of vowels is the most distinctive feature of Kiwi pronunciation. The NZ treatment of 'fish and chips' – 'fush and chups' – is an endless source of delight for Australians in particular. On the North Island sentences often have 'eh!' attached to the end. In the far south a rolled 'r' is common, a holdover from that region's Scottish heritage – it's especially noticeable in Southland. See the Glossary on p721 for an explanation of some Kiwi English words and expressions.

A Personal Kiwi-Yankee Dictionary by Louis S Leland Jr is an often hilarious book of translations, and explains some of the quirks that distinguish Kiwi and American ways of speaking English.

MAORI

The Maori have a vividly chronicled history, recorded in songs and chants that dramatically recall the migration to NZ from Polynesian Hawaiki as well as other important events. Early missionaries were the first to record the language in a written form, and achieved this with only 15 letters of the English alphabet.

Maori is closely related to other Polynesian languages such as Hawaiian, Tahitian and Cook Islands Maori. In fact, NZ Maori and Hawaiian are quite similar, even though over 7000km separates Honolulu and Auckland.

The Maori language was never dead – it was always used in Maori ceremonies – but over time familiarity with it was definitely on the decline. Fortunately, recent years have seen a revival of interest in it, and this forms an integral part of the renaissance of *Maoritanga* (Maori culture). Many Maori people who had heard the language spoken on the *marae* for years but had not used it in their day-to-day lives, are now studying it and speaking it fluently. Maori is taught in schools throughout NZ, some TV programs and news reports are broadcast in it, and many English place names are being renamed in Maori. Even government departments have been given Maori names: for example the Inland Revenue Department is also known as Te Tari Taake (the last word is actually *take,* which means 'levy', but the department has chosen to stress the long 'a' by spelling it 'aa').

In many places, Maori have come together to provide instruction in their language and culture to young children; the idea is for them to grow up speaking both Maori and English, and to develop a familiarity with Maori tradition. It's a matter of some pride to have fluency in the language. On some *marae* only Maori can be spoken.

PRONUNCIATION

Maori is a fluid, poetic language and surprisingly easy to pronounce once you remember to split each word (some can be amazingly long) into separate syllables.

Most consonants in Maori – **h, k, m, n, p, t** and **w** – are pronounced much the same as in English. The Maori **r** is a flapped sound (not rolled) with the tongue near the front of the mouth. It's closer to the English 'l' in pronunciation.

The **ng** is pronounced as in the English words 'singing' or 'running', and can be used at the beginning of words as well as at the end. To practise, just say 'ing' over and over, then isolate the 'ng' part of it.

The **wh** is generally pronounced as a soft English 'f'. This pronunciation is used in

MAORI GEOGRAPHICAL TERMS

The following words form part of many place names in NZ:

a – of
ana – cave
ara – way, path or road
awa – river or valley
heke – descend
hiku – end; tail
hine – girl; daughter
ika – fish
iti – small
kahurangi – treasured possession; special greenstone
kai – food
kainga – village
kaka – parrot
kare – rippling
kati – shut or close
koura – crayfish
makariri – cold
manga – stream or tributary
manu – bird
maunga – mountain
moana – sea or lake
moko – tattoo
motu – island
mutu – finished; ended; over
nga – the (plural)
noa – ordinary; not *tapu*
nui – big or great
nuku – distance
o – of, place of. . .
one – beach, sand or mud
pa – fortified village
papa – large blue-grey mudstone
pipi – common edible bivalve
pohatu – stone
poto – short

pouri – sad; dark; gloomy
puke – hill
puna – spring; hole; fountain
rangi – sky; heavens
raro – north
rei – cherished possession
roa – long
roto – lake
rua – hole in the ground; two
runga – above
tahuna – beach; sandbank
tane – man
tangata – people
tapu – sacred, forbidden or taboo
tata – close to; dash against; twin islands
tawaha – entrance or opening
tawahi – the other side (of a river or lake)
te – the (singular)
tonga – south
ure – male genitals
uru – west
waha – broken
wahine – woman
wai – water
waingaro – lost; waters that disappear in certain seasons
waka – canoe
wera – burnt or warm; floating
wero – challenge
whaka. . . – to act as . . .
whanau – family
whanga – harbour, bay or inlet
whare – house
whenua – land or country
whiti – east

Knowledge of just a few such words can help you make sense of many Maori place names. For example: Waikaremoana is the Sea *(moana)* of Rippling *(kare)* Waters *(wai)*; Rotorua means the Second *(rua)* Lake *(roto)*; and Taumatawhakatangihangakoauauotamateaturipukakapikimaunga-horonukupokaiwhenuakitanatahu means... well, perhaps you'd better see p392 for that translation. Some easier place names composed of words in this list:

Aramoana – Sea *(moana)* Path *(ara)*
Awaroa – Long *(roa)* River *(awa)*
Kaitangata – Eat *(kai)* People *(tangata)*
Maunganui – Great *(nui)* Mountain *(maunga)*
Opouri – Place of *(o)* Sadness *(pouri)*
Te Araroa – The *(te)* Long *(roa)* Path *(ara)*

Te Puke – The *(te)* Hill *(puke)*
Urewera – Burnt *(wera)* Penis *(ure)*
Waimakariri – Cold *(makariri)* Water *(wai)*
Wainui – Great *(nui)* Waters *(wai)*
Whakatane – To Act *(whaka)* as a Man *(tane)*
Whangarei – Cherished *(rei)* Harbour *(whanga)*

(Note that the adjective comes after the noun in Maori constructions. Thus 'cold water' is *wai makariri* not *makariri wai*.)

many place names in NZ, such as Whakatane, Whangaroa and Whakapapa (all pronounced as if they begin with a soft 'f').
There is some local variation: in the region
around the Whanganui River, for example,
the **wh** is pronounced as in the English
words 'when' and 'why'.

The correct pronunciation of the vowels
is very important. The examples below are
a rough guideline – it helps to listen carefully to someone who speaks the language
well. Each vowel has both a long and a short
sound with long vowels often denoted by a
macron (a line over the letter) or a double
vowel. We have not indicated long/short
vowel forms in this book.

VOWELS
a as in 'large', with no 'r' sound
e as in 'get'
i as in 'marine'
o as in 'pork'
u as the 'oo' in 'moon'

VOWEL COMBINATIONS
ae, ai as the 'y' in 'sky'
ao, au as the 'ow' in 'how'
ea as in 'bear'
ei as in 'vein'
eo as 'eh-oh'
eu as 'eh-oo'
ia as in the name 'Ian'
ie as the 'ye' in 'yet'
io as the 'ye o' in 'ye old'
iu as the 'ue' in 'cue'
oa as in 'roar'
oe as in 'toe'
oi as in 'toil'
ou as the 'ow' in 'how'
ua as the 'ewe' in 'fewer'

Each syllable ends in a vowel and there is
never more than one vowel in a syllable.
There are no silent letters.

There are many Maori phrasebooks,
grammar books and Maori–English dic-
tionaries if you want to take a closer look
at the language. The *Collins Maori Phrase
Book* by Patricia Tauroa is an ideal book
for starting to speak the language, with
sections on every-day conversation and
using the language in a cultural context.
Lonely Planet's *South Pacific Phrasebook*
has a section on the Maori language and
several other Pacific languages that you
may hear spoken around Wellington or
South Auckland.

Other good references include the *English–Maori Maori–English Dictionary* by
Bruce Biggs, and the *Reed Dictionary of
Modern Maori* by PM Ryan, which is one of
the most authoritative.

Learning a few basic greetings will enrich
your travels, especially if you plan to go
onto a *marae*.

GREETINGS & SMALL TALK
Maori greetings are finding increased popularity; don't be surprised if you're greeted
with *Kia ora*.

Haere mai!   Welcome!
Kia ora.   Hello./Good luck./
  Good health.
Tena koe.   Hello. (to one person)
Tena korua.   Hello. (to two people)
Tena koutou.   Hello. (to three or
  more people)
E noho ra.   Goodbye.
  (to person staying)
Haere ra.   Goodbye.
  (to person leaving)

Kei te pehea koe?
  How are you? (to one person)
Kei te pehea korua?
  How are you? (to two people)
Kei te pehea koutou?
  How are you? (to three or more)
Kei te pai.
  Very well, thanks./That's fine.

Glossary

This glossary is a list of abbreviations, 'Kiwi English', Maori, and slang terms and phrases you may come across in New Zealand. Also see the Maori Geographical Terms boxed text (p719) in the Language chapter for Maori words that pop up again and again in NZ place names.

AA – New Zealand's Automobile Association; provides road information and roadside assistance

across the ditch – referring to Australia, across the Tasman Sea

afghan – popular homemade chocolate biscuit (origin of recipe unknown, but unlikely to be Afghanistan)

All Blacks – NZ's revered national rugby union team (the name comes from 'All Backs', which is what the press called the NZ rugby team on an early visit to England); this moniker has started a trend for many national sporting teams to be similarly nicknamed (including the Tall Blacks for the basketball team, the Black Caps for the cricket team and, briefly before being dropped, the Black Cocks for the badminton team!)

ANZAC – Australia and New Zealand Army Corps

Aoraki – Maori name for Mt Cook, meaning 'Cloud Piercer'

Aotearoa – Maori name for NZ, most often translated as 'Land of the Long White Cloud'

ariki – chief

aroha – love

atua – spirits or gods

awa – river

B&B – 'bed and breakfast' accommodation

bach – holiday home, usually a wooden cottage (pronounced 'batch'); see also *crib*

Barrier, the – local name for Great Barrier Island in the Hauraki Gulf

BBH – Budget Backpacker Hostels; a popular hostelry affiliation

Beehive – Parliament House in Wellington, so-called because of its distinctive shape

black-water rafting – rafting or tubing underground in a cave or *tomo*

blokarting – sand sailing

bogan – see *Westie*

boozer – public bar

bro – literally 'brother'; usually meaning mate, as in 'just off to see the *bros*'

BYO – 'bring your own' (usually applies to alcohol at a restaurant or cafe)

BYOW – 'bring your own wine', implying you can't bring beer or any other alcoholic beverages

cervena – farmed deer

chardy – chardonnay

chillie bin – cooler; esky; large insulated box for keeping food and drinks cold

choice/chur – fantastic; great

ciggies – cigarettes

crib – the name for a *bach* in Otago and Southland

cuzzie, cuz – cousin; relative or mate, most often used by Maori to refer to fellow Maori; see also *bro*

cuzzie bro – an emphasised version of both *cuzzie* and *bro*

dairy – small corner store that sells milk, bread, newspapers, ice cream and pretty much everything else

daggy – uncool; from the dags that hang off sheep's bottoms

DB&B – 'dinner, bed and breakfast' accommodation

DOC – Department of Conservation (or *Te Papa Atawhai*); government department that administers national parks and thus all tracks and huts

domain – open grassed area in a town or city, often the focus of recreational activities or civic amenities such as gardens, picnic areas and bowling clubs (and sometimes camping grounds)

Dorkland – derogatory reference to the big city

dropkick – a certain method of kicking a rugby ball; a personal insult

eh – roughly translates as 'don't you agree?' and is commonly added to the end of many *Kiwi* sentences, usually followed by *bro* (as in '*Choice jandals, eh bro?*')

farmstay – accommodation on a *Kiwi* farm where you're encouraged to join in the typical day-to-day activities

football – rugby, either union or league; occasionally soccer

freezing works – slaughterhouse or abattoir for sheep and/or cattle

Godzone – New Zealand (from Richard Seddon who referred to NZ as 'God's own country')

good as gold, good as – very good; no problem

Great Walks – a set of nine popular tramping tracks within NZ

greenstone – jade; *pounamu*

gumboots – rubber boots or Wellingtons; originated from diggers on the gum-fields

haka – any dance, but usually refers to the traditional challenge; war dance

hakari – feast

handle – beer glass with a handle

hangi – oven made by digging a hole and steaming food in baskets over embers in the hole; a feast of Maori food

hapu – subtribe or smaller tribal grouping

hard case – hilarious, unusual or strong-willed character

Hawaiki – Polynesian homeland from where the Maori tribes migrated by canoe (probably Ra'iatea in the Society Islands); also a name for the Afterworld

hei tiki – carved, stylised human figure worn around the neck representing the first human and supposed to bring good luck; also called a *tiki*

hikoi – march, walk, sometimes a protest march or pilgrimage

hoa – friend; usually pronounced 'e hoa'

hokey pokey – delicious variety of vanilla ice cream with butterscotch chips

hoki – type of fish common in fish and chip shops

homestay – accommodation in a family house where you're treated as one of the family

hongi – Maori greeting; the pressing of foreheads and noses, and sharing of life breath

hui – gathering; meeting

Interislander – large ferries crossing Cook Strait between Wellington and Picton

i-SITE – information centre

'Is it what!' – strong affirmation or agreement; 'Yes, isn't it!'

Islander – Pacific Islander; see also *'Nesian, PI* and *Poly*

iwi – large tribal grouping with common lineage back to the original migration from *Hawaiki;* people; tribe

JAFA – Just Another Fucking Aucklander

jandals – a contraction of Japanese sandals; flip-flops; thongs; usually rubber footwear

jersey – jumper, usually woollen; the shirt worn by rugby players

jiff – short measurement of time (as in 'I'll be back in a *jiff'*); see also *two ticks*

judder bars – bumps in the road to make you drive slowly; speed humps

K Rd – Karangahape Rd in Auckland

ka kite (ano) – see you again; goodbye

ka pai – good; excellent

kai – food; almost any word with *kai* in it has a connection with food

kainga – village; pre-European unfortified Maori village

kapa haka – traditional Maori group singing and dancing

karakia – prayer, incantation

kaumatua – highly respected members of a tribe; the people you would ask for permission to enter a *marae*

kauri – native pine

kina – sea urchins, a Maori delicacy

Kiwi – A New Zealander; an adjective to mean anything relating to NZ

kiwi – the flightless, nocturnal brown bird with a long beak that is the national symbol

Kiwiana – the collective term for anything uniquely connected to NZ life and culture, especially from years gone by, and likely to bring on waves of nostalgia in any expat *Kiwi* (examples include *hokey pokey, jandals* and *pavlova*)

kiwifruit – small, succulent fruit with fuzzy brown skin and juicy green flesh; a Chinese gooseberry; never called a *kiwi*

koha – donation

kohanga reo – schools where Maori language and culture are at the forefront of the education process; also called language nest schools

korero – to talk

kumara – Polynesian sweet potato, a Maori staple food

kunekune – type of pig introduced by Chinese gold diggers in the 19th century

Kupe – early Polynesian navigator from *Hawaiki,* credited with the discovery of the islands that are now NZ

L&P – Lemon & Paeroa; lemon-flavoured fizzy drink

laters – 'see you later'

league – rugby league football

lounge bar – more upmarket bar than a public bar; called a 'ladies bar' in some countries

Mainlander – self-referential term for South Islander

mana – spiritual quality of a person or object; prestige; authority of a chief or priest

manaia – traditional carving design; literally means 'bird-headed man'

'Mandel, the – the Coromandel Peninsula

manuhiri – visitor; guest

Maori – indigenous people of NZ

Maoritanga – Maori culture

marae – literally refers to the sacred ground in front of the Maori meeting house, more commonly used to refer to the entire complex of buildings

marakihau – sea monster

Maui – a figure in Maori (Polynesian) mythology

maunga – mountain

mauri – life force/principle

mere – a *patu* made of *greenstone*

metal/metalled road – gravel (unsealed) road

MMP – Mixed Member Proportional; the electoral system used in NZ and Germany; a form of proportional voting

moa – large, extinct flightless bird

moe – sleep

moko – tattoo; usually refers to facial tattoos

Moriori – isolated Polynesian group, inhabitants of the Chatham Islands

motorway – freeway or expressway
marnis – something or someone shameful
munted – damaged, destroyed
munter – see *Westie*

naiad – rigid-hull inflatable boat (used for dolphin swimming, whale watching etc)
'Naki, the – Taranaki
'Nesian – Pacific Islander; see also *Islander, PI* and *Poly*
nga – the (plural); see also *te*
ngai/ngati – literally, 'the people of' or 'the descendants of'; tribe (on the South Island it's pronounced 'kai')
NZ – the universal term for New Zealand; pronounced 'en zed'

OE – Overseas Experience; a working holiday abroad, traditionally to the UK (the young *Kiwi's* near-mandatory 'tour of duty')

pa – fortified Maori village, usually on a hilltop
Pacific Rim – term used to describe modern NZ cuisine; cuisine with an innovative use of local produce, especially seafood, with imported styles
Pakeha – Maori for a white or European person
pakihi – unproductive and often swampy land on the South Island's west coast; pronounced 'par-kee'
papa – large blue-grey mudstones; the word comes from the Maori for Earth Mother
parapenting – paragliding
Pasifika – Pacific Island culture
patch – gang logo worn on clothing
patu – flat war club made of wood, bone or greenstone
paua – abalone; tough shellfish pounded, minced, then made into patties (fritters), which are available in almost every NZ fish-and-chip shop; the beautiful, iridescent *paua* shell is often used in decoration and jewellery
pavlova – meringue cake, usually topped with cream and *kiwifruit;* the quintessential *Kiwi* dessert
PI – Pacific Islander; see also *Islander, Poly* and *'Nesian*
pig islander – derogatory term used by a person from one island for someone from the other island
pillocking – 'surfing' across mud flats on a rubbish-bin lid
pipi – common edible bivalve
piss – urine; urinate; alcohol, as in 'get on the piss'
poi – ball of woven flax
poi dance – women's formation dance that involves singing and manipulating a *poi*
polly – politician
Poly – Pacific Islander; see also *Islander, PI* and *'Nesian*
pou – wooden post, sometimes carved
ponga – the *silver fern;* called a bungy (pronounced 'bungee', with a soft 'g', in parts of the South Island)
pounamu – Maori name for *greenstone*
powhiri – traditional Maori welcome onto a *marae*

quad bikes – four-wheel farm bikes

Rakiura – literally 'Land of Glowing Skies'; Maori name for Stewart Island, which is important in Maori mythology as the anchor of *Maui's* canoe
rap jump – face-down abseil
'rattle your dags' – move quickly; from the dags that hang off sheep's bottoms
raupo – bulrush
Remuera tractor – 4WD, after wealthy suburbanites pointlessly driving them
Rheiny – affectionate term for Rheineck beer
rigger – a refillable half-gallon plastic bottle for holding draught beer
rip – dangerously strong current running away from the shore at a beach
Roaring Forties – the ocean between 40° and 50° south, known for very strong winds
Rotovegas – derogatory term relating to the touristy aspects of Rotorua
rumble – see *scrap*

sav – sauvignon blanc
scrap – a fight
section – small block of land
silver fern – the symbol worn by the *All Blacks* and other national sportsfolk on their jerseys, representative of the underside of a *ponga* leaf; the national netball team is called the Silver Ferns
Steinie – affectionate term for Steinlager beer
superette – grocery store or small supermarket
sweet, sweet as – all-purpose term like *choice;* fantastic, great

taiaha – spear
tall poppy syndrome – NZ tradition of diminishing successful people, as in 'tall poppies get their heads chopped off'
Tamaki Makaurau – Maori name for Auckland
tane – man
tangata – people
tangata whenua – people of the land; local people
taniwha – awe-inspiring water spirit
taonga – something of great value; a treasure
tapu – a strong force in Maori life, with numerous meanings; in its simplest form it means sacred, forbidden, taboo
tatts – tattoos, often of a gang nature; as opposed to *moko*
tauihu – canoe prow
te – the (singular); see also *nga*
Te Kooti – East Coast Maori prophet and rebellion leader
Te Papa – literally 'our place', the national museum in Wellington
Te Papa Atawhai – Maori name for *DOC*
te reo – literally 'the language'; the Maori language

tiki – short for *hei tiki*

tiki tour – scenic tour; roundabout way

toheroa – large clam

tohunga – priest; wizard; general expert

toi toi – tall native grass

tomo – hole; entrance to a cave

tramp – bushwalk; trek; hike

tua tua – type of shellfish

tuatara – prehistoric reptile dating back to the age of dinosaurs

tui – native parson bird

tukutuku – Maori wall panels in *marae* and churches

tuna – eel

two ticks – short measurement of time (as in 'I'll be there in *two ticks*'); see also *jiff*

umu – earth oven

urupa – burial site

varsity – university

wahine – woman

wai – water

waiata – song

Waikikamukau – mythical NZ town, far from anywhere (and pronounced along the lines of 'Why-kick-a-moo-cow')

wairua – spirit

Waitangi – short way of referring to the Treaty of Waitangi

waka – canoe

Warriors – NZ's popular rugby league club, affiliated with Australia's NRL

Watties – the NZ food and canning giant; NZ's answer to Heinz (until Heinz took over the company)

Wellywood – Wellington, because of its thriving film industry

Westie – from West Auckland; rough-edged fellow, probably wearing a black T-shirt, drinking beer and listening to AC/DC; see also *bogan, munter*

whakairo rakau – Maori woodcarving

whakapapa – genealogy

whanau – family

whare – house

wharepuni – sleeping house

whare runanga – meeting house

whare whakairo – carved meeting house

whenua – land

whitebait – tiny translucent fish that is scooped up in nets and eaten whole (head, eyes and all!) or made into patties

wopwops – remote; 'out in the *wopwops*' is out in the middle of nowhere

zorbing – rolling down a hill inside an inflatable plastic ball

The Authors

CHARLES RAWLINGS-WAY
Coordinating Author, Waikato & the King Country, Taranaki, Whanganui & Palmerston North, Rotorua & the Bay of Plenty

English by birth, Australian by chance, All Blacks fan by choice: Charles considers himself a worldly lad, but his early understanding of Aotearoa was less than comprehensive. He realised there was more to NZ when a wandering uncle returned with a faux-jade *tiki* in 1981. He wore it with pride until he saw the NZ cricket team's beige uniforms in 1982... Mt Taranaki's summit, Raglan's breaks and Whanganui's charm have helped him forgive: he's once again smitten with the country's landscapes, locals, and determination to sculpt its own political and indigenous destiny. Roll on Rugby World Cup 2011!

BRETT ATKINSON
Christchurch & Canterbury, Dunedin & Otago, Fiordland & Southland, Stewart Island

Although he's lived in Auckland for four decades, Brett Atkinson never misses a chance to explore the rugged mountains, lakes, and coastline of New Zealand's South Island. On his second extended research trip to the 'Mainland', he kayaked Doubtful Sound, shared the audacious scenery of Banks Peninsula and the Catlins with his family, and unearthed more than a few places to drink NZ's excellent microbrewed beers. Brett has contributed to guidebooks covering four of the planet's continents, and covered more than 40 countries as a freelance travel writer. See www.brett-atkinson.net for his latest work.

SARAH BENNETT
The East Coast, Wellington Region, Marlborough & Nelson

Raised among the cherry trees of Marlborough, Sarah migrated to Wellington at 16 and has lived there ever since, except for various travels and a stint in London working in Lonely Planet's UK office. An arguably flawed guidebook writer due to eternal optimism and irrepressible nationalism ('New Zealand... what's not to like?'), she has done her best to find fault wherever she can, especially in regard to ill-chosen garnish and inadequate beer selection. Sarah's other books are *The Best of Wellington*, *Let's Go Camping* and *The New Zealand Tramper's Handbook*, all of which she co-authored with her husband, Lee Slater.

LONELY PLANET AUTHORS

Why is our travel information the best in the world? It's simple: our authors are passionate, dedicated travellers. They don't take freebies in exchange for positive coverage so you can be sure the advice you're given is impartial. They travel widely to all the popular spots, and off the beaten track. They don't research using just the internet or phone. They discover new places not included in any other guidebook. They personally visit thousands of hotels, restaurants, palaces, trails, galleries, temples and more. They speak with dozens of locals every day to make sure you get the kind of insider knowledge only a local could tell you. They take pride in getting all the details right, and in telling it how it is. Think you can do it? Find out how at **lonelyplanet.com**.

PETER DRAGICEVICH
The Culture, Auckland Region, Northland & the Bay of Islands, Coromandel Region, Taupo & the Central Plateau

After nearly a decade working for off-shore publishing companies, Peter's life has come full circle, returning to West Auckland where he was raised. As managing editor of Auckland-based *Express* newspaper he spent much of the nineties writing about the local arts, club and bar scene. This is the second edition of the New Zealand guide he's worked on and, after co-authoring 17 books for Lonely Planet, it remains his favourite gig.

SCOTT KENNEDY
The West Coast, Queenstown & Wanaka

Scott Kennedy grew up in the mountains of Western Canada and has always been drawn to wild places. When he first set foot in New Zealand a decade ago he knew he'd found the place he was looking for. For the last eight years he's called Queenstown home and jumped at the chance to pass on the inside story to Lonely Planet readers. A passionate fan of the outdoors, Scott is an avid skier, mountain biker, rock climber, tramper, runner and surfer. When Scott isn't travelling the world penning guidebooks for Lonely Planet he works as a freelance writer, photographer and filmmaker – with a focus on adventure of course. Visit Scott's website at www.adventureskope.com.

CONTRIBUTING AUTHORS

Professor James Belich wrote the History chapter (p29). James is one of NZ's pre-eminent historians and the award-winning author of *The New Zealand Wars, Making Peoples* and *Paradise Reforged*. He has also worked in TV – *New Zealand Wars* was screened in NZ in 1998.

Tony Horwitz wrote the Captain James Cook boxed text (p33) in the History chapter. Tony is a Pulitzer-winning reporter and nonfiction author. His fascination with James Cook, and with travel, took him around NZ, Australia and the Pacific while researching *Blue Latitudes* (alternatively titled *Into the Blue*), part biography of Cook and part travelogue.

John Huria (Ngai Tahu, Muaupoko) wrote the Maori Culture chapter (p53). John has an editorial, research and writing background with a focus on Maori culture. He was senior editor for Maori publishing company Huia (NZ) and now runs an editorial and publishing services company, Ahi Text Solutions Ltd (www.ahitextsolutions.co.nz).

Lauraine Jacobs wrote the Food & Drink chapter (p60). Lauraine is an award-winning food writer, and food editor of *Cuisine* magazine. Passionate about NZ's wine and food, she travels the country extensively in her quest to seek out the best culinary experiences.

Josh Kronfeld wrote the Surfing in New Zealand boxed text (p92) in the Active New Zealand chapter. Josh is an ex–All Black flanker, whose passion for surfing NZ's beaches is legendary and who found travelling for rugby a way to surf other great breaks around the world.

Dr David Millar wrote the Health chapter (p715). David is a travel-medicine specialist, diving doctor and lecturer in wilderness medicine.

Gareth Shute wrote the Music section of the Culture chapter (p49). Gareth is the author of four books, including *Hip Hop Music in Aotearoa* and *NZ Rock 1987-2007*. He is also a musician and has toured the UK, Europe and Australia as a member of The Ruby Suns. He now plays in The Conjurors, The Investigations and The Cosbys.

Nandor Tanczos wrote the Environmental Issues in Aotearoa New Zealand boxed text (p68). NZ's first Rastafarian Member of Parliament (NZ Greens Party), and the first to enter parliament in dreadlocks and a hemp suit, he was also the Greens' spokesperson on constitutional issues and the environment from 1999 to 2008.

Vaughan Yarwood wrote the Environment chapter (p67). Vaughan is an Auckland-based writer whose most recent book is *The History Makers: Adventures in New Zealand Biography*. Earlier work includes *The Best of New Zealand, a Collection of Essays on NZ Life and Culture by Prominent Kiwis*, which he edited, and the regional history *Between Coasts: from Kaipara to Kawau*. He has written widely for NZ and international publications and is the former associate editor of *New Zealand Geographic*, for which he continues to write.

Thanks to: Sir Ian McKellen (Sandflies boxed text, p688); Grace Hoet for her contribution to the Maori Culture chapter; and all the New Zealand regional tourism organisations, for their help with pre-research briefings.

Behind the Scenes

THIS BOOK

Lonely Planet founder Tony Wheeler wrote the first edition of Lonely Planet's *New Zealand* way back in 1977, and since then a small army of authors have scoured the roads and trails of Aotearoa putting together ever-better NZ guidebooks. This 15th edition was coordinated by Charles Rawlings-Way, and otherwise researched and written by the all-Kiwi cast of Brett Atkinson, Sarah Bennett, Peter Dragicevich and Scott Kennedy. Contributing authors include an impressive array of specialists: historian Professor James Belich, journo Tony Horwitz, Maori publisher John Huria, food-award judge Lauraine Jacobs, surfer Josh Kronfeld, health expert Dr David Millar, musician/author Gareth Shute, environmental activist Nandor Tanczos, and author Vaughan Yarwood. A diverse group of interesting New Zealanders contributed to our new colour highlights section. This guidebook was commissioned in Lonely Planet's Melbourne office, and produced by the following:

Commissioning Editor Errol Hunt
Coordinating Editors Susan Paterson, Saralinda Turner
Coordinating Cartographer Hunor Csutoros
Coordinating Layout Designer Yvonne Bischofberger
Managing Editors Imogen Bannister, Bruce Evans, Liz Heynes, Laura Stansfeld

Managing Cartographers Ross Butler, David Connolly, Corey Hutchison
Managing Layout Designer Indra Kilfoyle
Assisting Editors Elisa Arduca, Jackey Coyle, Kate Evans, Anne Mulvaney, Alison Ridgway, Elizabeth Swan, Angela Tinson, Simon Williamson
Assisting Cartographers Julie Dodkins, Alex Leung, Peter Shields
Assisting Layout Designers Nicholas Colicchia, Frank Deim
Cover Naomi Parker, lonelyplanetimages.com
Internal Image Research Jane Hart, lonelyplanet images.com
Project Manager Chris Girdler
Language Content Laura Crawford
Thanks to Glenn Beanland, Jessica Boland, Rosie Carnahan, Daniel Corbett, Melanie Dankel, Mark Germanchis, Kiri Gillespie, Michelle Glynn, James Hardy, Geoff Howard, Glenda Hughes, Lisa Knights, Rebecca Lalor, Katie Lynch, John Mazzocchi, Dan Moore, Darren O'Connell, Ainsley Pope, Emma Radcliffe, Kirsten Rawlings, Kate Richter, Averil Robertson, Alice Shearman, Suzannah Shwer, Fiona Siseman, John Taufa, Nick Thorpe, Brian Turnbull, Juan Winata

THANKS
CHARLES RAWLINGS-WAY

Thanks to the many generous, knowledgable and quietly self-assured Kiwis I met on the road, espe-

---

THE LONELY PLANET STORY

Fresh from an epic journey across Europe, Asia and Australia in 1972, Tony and Maureen Wheeler sat at their kitchen table stapling together notes. The first Lonely Planet guidebook, *Across Asia on the Cheap,* was born.

Travellers snapped up the guides. Inspired by their success, the Wheelers began publishing books to Southeast Asia, India and beyond. Demand was prodigious, and the Wheelers expanded the business rapidly to keep up. Over the years, Lonely Planet extended its coverage to every country and into the virtual world via lonelyplanet.com and the Thorn Tree message board.

As Lonely Planet became a globally loved brand, Tony and Maureen received several offers for the company. But it wasn't until 2007 that they found a partner whom they trusted to remain true to the company's principles of travelling widely, treading lightly and giving sustainably. In October of that year, BBC Worldwide acquired a 75% share in the company, pledging to uphold Lonely Planet's commitment to independent travel, trustworthy advice and editorial independence.

Today, Lonely Planet has offices in Melbourne, London and Oakland, with over 500 staff members and 300 authors. Tony and Maureen are still actively involved with Lonely Planet. They're traveling more often than ever, and they're devoting their spare time to charitable projects. And the company is still driven by the philosophy of *Across Asia on the Cheap*: 'All you've got to do is decide to go and the hardest part is over. So go!'

cially the staff at the Palmerston North, Matamata, Waitomo Caves and New Plymouth i-SITEs who flew through my questions with the greatest of ease. Thanks to Errol Hunt for signing me up, and the in-house Lonely Planet staff who schmoozed this book through production. Humongous gratitude to my tireless, witty and professional co-authors – Sarah, Peter, Brett and Scott – who infused this book with local lowdown. Thanks also to Eloise Jones for the buttered date loaf and tea. Most of all, thank you Meg and Ione, my two (very patient) road-trippin' sweethearts.

BRETT ATKINSON

Firstly thanks to my mother and father, and wife Carol, for sharing parts of this research trip with me. Now you know what I really get up to when I disappear for six weeks at a time. Thanks also to the thoroughly professional staff at all the i-SITES, DOC offices, and visitor information centres I tapped for vital facts before, during, and after my research trip. It's always great to work with commissioning editor Errol Hunt, and the rest of a Kiwi-as author team, especially fellow All Blacks supporter and honorary Kiwi, Charles Rawlings-Way.

SARAH BENNETT

First up, thanks to helpful pals Betzy Iannuzzi, Bonita Marshall, Jenny Allan, Reece Miller, Trecia Smith, Maria Grau, Fritz Kuckuck, Tricia and Stewart Macpherson, the Wellington posse, and the Bennett clan. Thanks, too, to the many i-SITE and RTO people who shared their time and insight, especially Tina Narsey, Rebecca Mitchell, Chris Barber, Gaylene Sanderson, Astrid Fisher, Amy Chandler, Rachael Brown, Tracy Johnston, Brent Matthews, Vicky Roebuck, Barbara Hyde, and winery experts Lucy Chambers and Julia Hill. I wish to acknowledge the contribution of all the friendly folks who helped me out on the road, and my fellow authors and editors who supported me through the ether. As ever, my deepest gratitude to Lee – you make every day a flight in a microlight.

PETER DRAGICEVICH

If I were to thank everyone who helped me eat and drink my way around the upper North Island it would be a very long list indeed. Particular thanks must go to Phillippa Steel and Scott Judson, Sally Burgess, Bob Dragicevich, Jack Dragicevich, Shenita and Carlos Palmer, Alison Curtis, Miranda Playfair, Mark and Amy Todd, Adrienne and Ben Preston, Tania Wong, Lesley

Mensah and Tracey Hand. The i-SITE staff in Paihia, Whangarei, Coromandel Town, Tairua, Turangi and Ohakune are among the nicest in the country. And special thanks to the excellent NZ15 team – particularly Scott for accompanying me to Matakana and snapping my On the Road shot – you're all bloody brilliant.

SCOTT KENNEDY

Thanks to my fellow authors Charles, Brett, Peter and Sarah – it's a pleasure to share a title page with this fine lot. Big thanks to our fabulous and fearless editor Errol Hunt who always kept it fun. To all of the fellow travellers I met along the way that offered advice, shared your experiences and helped me out I owe you all a huge thanks. All of the hoteliers, restaurateurs, activity operators and tireless visitor centre staff who answered all my questions – cheers guys. Big thanks to the all-star team – Christian Martin, Alice Hill, Brett Black, Adrian Nankivell, Ned Myopus, Mark Banham, Steve Wilson, 'GC' Mike, Katy Shorthouse, Debbie Nelson, Andy McDonald, Jan & Steve, Di Liddell, Shaun, Becs & Tannin. To mom and dad thanks for all your support over the years and to my wonderful wife Sophie – for everything.

OUR READERS

Many thanks to the travellers who used the last edition and wrote to us with helpful hints, useful advice and interesting anecdotes:

A Elisabeth Nordeng Aanes, John Adam, Nikki Annand, **B** Heike Baars, Selina Barlet, Rebecca Barnshaw, Bridget Beal, Neil Beaumont, Chris Beek, Nicolas Berger, Insa Beuse, Ben Blee, Jason Borthwick, Judy Bounds, Euan Brown, Catherine Bruckner, Anna Bucholz, Wilco Burghout, Lee Burrows, **C** Geoff Caflisch, Sue Cebulko, Laura Claassen, Tiere Clynich, Brendan Connolly, Nicola Coombe, Georgie Curtis, Jonathan Cutler, **D** Matthew Dalton, Stuart & Pamela Davis, Annelies De Bruijne, Jan Dependahl, Jo Drew, Tarne Duffield, Angela Dunlop, Alison Dye, **E** Alec Edwards, Bernadette Ekberg, Rowan Enright, Jo Evans, **F** Robin Falvey, Mutiara Förster, Nick Fowler, **G** Franck Gally, Juliane Gansert, Eleanor Gee, Tanya Genthe, Bob Gilchrist, Katherine Golding, Sharine Gordon, Ed Groves, Peter Gush, Stuart Guy, **H** Steven Hankey, Bernie Healy, Glenda Heywood, Jo Hibbert, Dave Hill, Leah Holloway, Libby Howard-Blood, Barbara Huijgen, **I** Jaki Ilbery, **K** Robert Kennedy, Huia Kirk, Rolf Knütter, **L** Barry Landesman, Steve Lavezzo, Carol Lee, Robert Levy, Ann Lewis, Brian & Lorna Lewis,

SEND US YOUR FEEDBACK

We love to hear from travellers – your comments keep us on our toes and help make our books better. Our well-travelled team reads every word on what you loved or loathed about this book. Although we cannot reply individually to postal submissions, we always guarantee that your feedback goes straight to the appropriate authors, in time for the next edition. Each person who sends us information is thanked in the next edition and the most useful submissions are rewarded with a free book.

To send us your updates – and find out about Lonely Planet events, newsletters and travelnews–visitouraward-winningwebsite: **lonelyplanet.com/contact**.

Note: we may edit, reproduce and incorporate your comments in Lonely Planet products such as guidebooks, websites and digital products, so let us know if you don't want your comments reproduced or your name acknowledged.Foracopyofourprivacypolicy visit lonelyplanet.com/privacy.

Beate Lippold, **M** Michael Macbroom, Jerome Magisson, John Mandeville, Hanna Manski, Jane Manson, Stephen Marais, Lou Mccarthy, Gail Mcconnell, Gillian Mcilroy, Jan Mcverry, Lisa Moeller, Chris Monson, Melanie Morcom, Bruce Morris, Hugh & Eileen Morton, Alastair Moulton, **N** Patrick Näf, Greg Napp, Surasak Netraprajag, Nick Newman, David Nicola, Alexandra Nisbeck, Ronald Noordstrand, Graeme Nye, **O** Andrea O'Connor, Michael Ortiz, Jenny Owen, Maurice Owen, **P** Benoît Panizzon, Natasha Parker-Coughlin, Marie Parton, Lindsay Petrie, Daniela Petroni, Rochelle Pincini, Katerina Poddana, Neville Pulver, Kerrie Purrington, **R** Barbara Rausch, Jim Revell, John Rieley, Christine Rikihana, Valentina Baez Rizzi, Jeffrey Robinson, Louise Rothols, Alba Rull, Jenna Russell, **S** Kane Salanoa, Nathan Sandland-Jones, Miriam Schaefer, Miriam Scherpenzeel, Sybil Schlesinger, Lukas Schomann, Armand Schumer, Jonathan Sims, Frank Sinclair, Ray Sinniger, Maren Skrinjar, Afke Smolders, Raina Reva Snyder, Julie Stapleton, Sue Stone, Mona Strandberg, Anne Street, **T** Sarah Taylor, Steve Taylor, David Taylor, Monique Teggelove, Britta Thiel, Cathelijne Thiel, Petra Joho Thomma, Kay Toon, Steve Tritt, **W** Amanda Watson, Arthur Watts, Kim Whitty, Jackie Whyte, Sven Wiechert, Hanneke Wijkamp, Lynda Willow, Tim Wilson, Carol Wilson, David Wilson-Howarth, **Y** Holly Yelf, Kit Yoon, **Z** Cosetta Zanobetti-Lawlor

ACKNOWLEDGMENTS
Many thanks to the following for the use of their content:

Globe on title page ©Mountain High Maps 1993 Digital Wisdom, Inc.

On the Road: photograph of Scott Kennedy courtesy of Shotover Canyon Swing.

Index

INDEX

INDEX

INDEX

GreenDex

748

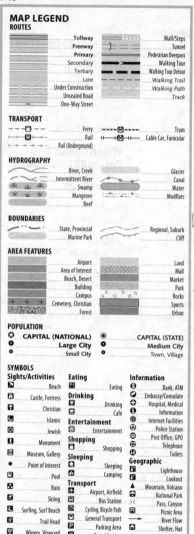

LONELY PLANET OFFICES

Australia (Head Office)
Locked Bag 1, Footscray, Victoria 3011
☎ 03 8379 8000, fax 03 8379 8111
talk2us@lonelyplanet.com.au

USA
150 Linden St, Oakland, CA 94607
☎ 510 250 6400, toll free 800 275 8555
fax 510 893 8572
info@lonelyplanet.com

UK
2nd fl, 186 City Rd,
London EC1V 2NT
☎ 020 7106 2100, fax 020 7106 2101
go@lonelyplanet.co.uk

Published by Lonely Planet Publications Pty Ltd
ABN 36 005 607 983

© Lonely Planet 2010

© photographers as indicated 2010

Cover photograph: Mt Taranaki, Egmont National Park, Harley Betts/ Hedgehog House/Photo New Zealand. Many of the images in this guide are available for licensing from Lonely Planet Images: lonely planetimages.com.